D0301401

First Edition

Corporate Valuation
Theory, Evidence & Practice

ROBERT W. HOLTHAUSEN
The Wharton School, University of Pennsylvania

MARK E. ZMIJEWSKI
The University of Chicago Booth School of Business

Cambridge
BUSINESS PUBLISHERS

To my sons Mike, Matt, and Jeff, and especially to my wife Tina, for her support and encouragement throughout the writing of this book.
— RWH

To my patient and understanding wife Jennifer, my sister Betty, my children Jason, Kimberly, Kate, and Phillip, and my many wonderful grandchildren.
— MEZ

Cambridge Business Publishers, LLC

Corporate Valuation, First Edition, by Robert W. Holthausen and Mark E. Zmijewski.
COPYRIGHT © 2014 by Cambridge Business Publishers, LLC. Published by Cambridge Business Publishers, LLC. Exclusive rights by Cambridge Business Publishers, LLC for manufacture and export.

STANDARD EDITION ISBN: 978-1-61853-036-3

Printed in the United States of America.
10 9 8 7 6 5 4 3 2 1

About the Authors

ROBERT W. HOLTHAUSEN is the Nomura Securities Professor and Ernst and Young Professor of Accounting and Finance at The Wharton School of the University of Pennsylvania. He has been on the faculty there since 1989. He has been Chair of the Accounting Department since 2004. He is also the Chair of the faculty advisory committee for Wharton Research Data Services (WRDS). Prior to 1989, he was on the accounting and finance faculty at the Graduate School of Business of the University of Chicago for 10 years. Dr. Holthausen earned his doctorate at the University of Rochester, where he also earned his M.B.A. Prior to his academic career, Professor Holthausen worked as a C.P.A. for Price Waterhouse and as a financial analyst with Mobil.

His teaching has been concentrated in the areas of investment management and valuation. Currently, his primary teaching responsibility is for the corporate valuation class he developed for Wharton, which he has taught for over 20 years. He has teaching experience at the undergraduate, M.B.A., and Ph.D. levels and has won teaching awards from both the undergraduate and M.B.A. programs at Wharton, including the David J. Hauck award for undergraduate teaching, awarded to one tenured faculty member per year. He has taught in many executive education programs at the Wharton School and is the academic director of Wharton's Mergers and Acquisitions Executive Education program.

Professor Holthausen is widely published in both finance and accounting journals. His research has studied the effects of management compensation and governance structures on firm performance, the effects of information on volume and prices, corporate restructuring and valuation, the effects of large block sales on common stock prices, and numerous other topics. His research has appeared in such journals as *The Accounting Review*, the *Journal of Accounting Research*, the *Journal of Accounting and Economics*, the *Journal of Finance,* and the *Journal of Financial Economics*. He currently serves as one of the editors of the *Journal of Accounting and Economics.*

Professor Holthausen's consulting and company-specific executive education experiences are varied. In the past, he has consulted with over 20 companies on such diverse activities as serving as a compensation consultant, consulting with investment companies on the development of fundamental trading rules used to manage equity portfolios, and performing valuation analysis in a variety of situations.

MARK E. ZMIJEWSKI is the Leon Carroll Marshall Professor of Accounting at The University of Chicago Booth School of Business. He has been a member of Chicago Booth since 1984. Professor Zmijewski earned his doctorate at the State University of New York at Buffalo, where he also earned his B.S. and M.B.A. degrees. Professor Zmijewski's research focuses on the valuation of the firm and its parts, as well as the ways in which various capital market participants use information to value securities. He has published various articles in academic journals such as the *Journal of Accounting Research* and the *Journal of Accounting and Economics*, and won the American Accounting Association's Competitive Manuscript Award (1984). He has been an Associate Editor of *The Accounting Review* and on the Editorial Boards of both the *Journal of Accounting Research* and *The Accounting Review*. In addition to his faculty duties at the University of Chicago, Professor Zmijewski also held the positions of Deputy Dean, Ph.D. Program faculty director, and the Center for Research in Security Prices faculty director. He teaches courses in valuation, mergers and acquisitions, financial analysis, accounting, and entrepreneurship and has won teaching awards for his teaching in both the M.B.A. and Executive M.B.A. programs at Booth.

Professor Zmijewski has consulted with numerous publicly traded and privately owned companies, as well as with entrepreneurs and private equity investors. His consulting focuses on issues related to financial analysis, firm valuation, security valuation, financial distress, and bankruptcy, and other issues in economics, finance, and accounting. Professor Zmijewski is a founder of Chicago Partners, founded in 1994 and subsequently sold to Navigant Consulting, Inc. Within the time he conducted his consulting through Navigant Economics, he was Navigant Economics' Practice Leader, a member of its management committee, and a member of Navigant Consulting Inc.'s corporate Executive Committee. Professor Zmijewski currently conducts his consulting at Charles River Associates.

Preface

Welcome to the first edition of *Corporate Valuation: Theory, Practice & Evidence*. We wrote this book to equip our students and practitioners—many of whom are our former students—with the current knowledge used to value companies, parts of companies, and the securities issued by companies. Our goal is to provide current conceptual and theoretical valuation frameworks and translate those frameworks into practical approaches for valuing companies. We present the research and descriptive data underpinning these frameworks and use detailed examples to demonstrate how to implement them, often using data from real companies.

> **"Corporate Valuation: Theory, Practice & Evidence has been the industry standard on valuation for over a decade despite not being widely available. The corporate valuation course based on this book is one of the few unstated requirements for graduates of The Wharton School that hope to enter into the field of finance. Having hired dozens of Wharton alumni who have learned valuation from this book, I cannot imagine a more thorough guide or a better reference to learn valuation."**

> Ben Frost
> Managing Director
> Morgan Stanley's Mergers and Acquisitions Department

TARGET AUDIENCE

Corporate Valuation: Theory, Practice & Evidence is intended as a college textbook for both graduate and undergraduate courses in valuation. Given the detailed approach, it is also a useful book for practicing professionals. We have been using this material in both valuation-based finance and accounting M.B.A. classes at Chicago Booth and Wharton, as well as in undergraduate finance classes at Wharton, for many years. Although primarily serving as a text in courses that teach valuation, the book can also serve as a background book for case-based courses that include cases on valuation, leveraged buyouts, and mergers and acquisitions. The book can also be used as a "field guide" for those who engage in valuation work. We know that many of our former students refer to our writings in their work involving valuation and security analysis for years after they graduate from our respective institutions.

> **"This textbook has continued to be an invaluable resource for the technical and theoretical elements of corporate valuation. In my opinion, Holthausen and Zmijewski explore the topic in such breadth and depth, it provides students and practitioners with an excellent resource to build a sound valuation framework to apply in practice."**

> Zach Mitschrich
> Analyst
> Blackstone's Restructuring Group

INNOVATIVE, DETAILED, AND PRACTICAL PEDAGOGY

In teaching valuation, we found that students generally lacked the detailed knowledge required to value a company. Although other finance textbooks cover these topics, they do so at a fairly low level of detail and generally do not cover the relevant finance and accounting complexities required to perform valuations. As such, students who use these textbooks typically struggle in the workplace because they either lack the requisite knowledge or fail to understand how to integrate the accounting information with the appropriate finance theory. We integrate the relevant accounting topics with the appropriate finance theory, and demonstrate, using step-by-step examples, how to implement the valuation frameworks we discuss. The book is organized so that instructors can choose not to assign certain chapters or sections of chapters and omit some of these details. In addition, we incorporate relevant empirical evidence and theory from prior studies as well as our own work.

> **"This book contains everything one needs to know before valuing a company. It covers the financial theory of investment analysis, the accounting notions needed to understand, analyze, and forecast financial statements, and many techniques for creating a financial model yielding a rigorous estimate of firm value. It does all that while also providing us with interesting anecdotes and detailed real-world examples. It is excellent both as the main text for a valuation course, and as the primary reference for practitioners on Wall Street."**

> Vincent Glode
> Professor of Finance
> The Wharton School, University of Pennsylvania

Overview of the Structure of the Book

The book consists of six parts. Part I (Chapters 1 through 4) presents an overview of valuation issues and topics, how valuation is used in practice, and discusses the basic tools needed to value a company. These tools include analyzing financial statements, measuring performance, understanding and measuring cash flows, and creating a financial model. Part II (Chapters 5 through 7) discusses the discounted cash flow (DCF) valuation model, including the residual income valuation model. This part of the book rigorously demonstrates the equivalence of the alternative forms of the DCF valuation model and when each of the forms is more appropriate to use. Part III (Chapters 8 through 11) discusses how to measure the various costs of capital used in the different valuation frameworks. Part IV (Chapter 12) discusses how to value and measure the cost of capital for warrants, options, and other equity-linked securities. Part V (Chapters 13 and 14) discusses the conceptual framework and practical application of the market multiple valuation method. Finally, Part VI (Chapters 15 through 17) applies and extends these valuation frameworks to specific settings such as highly leveraged transactions, mergers and acquisitions, and cross-border valuations.

Steps in the Valuation Process

In Chapter 1, we provide a top-level overview of the steps in a valuation process used to value a company. These overview steps include analyzing the competitive landscape, analyzing the company and its potential competitive advantage, creating a financial model, measuring the costs of capital, market multiple valuation, and alternative valuation approaches. In the relevant subsequent chapters, we provide detailed steps for each of these overview steps discussed in

Chapter 1. For example, in Chapter 4, we provide a detailed step-by-step process for developing a financial model. These step-by-step process guides are included in many subsequent chapters. We show an example of this step-by-step process from Exhibit 15.8 for leveraged buyout transactions.

EXHIBIT 15.8	Steps in Assessing the Investment Value of Leveraged and Management Buyout Transactions

1. Establish an initial purchase price for the LBO target (for example, based on recent premiums paid in comparable transactions)
2. Develop the target's initial post-LBO capital structure, including the types and terms for the securities to be issued based on market conditions and the buyer's risk preferences
3. Develop a financial model for the post-LBO operations of the target and incorporate the proposed capital structure
4. Forecast all capital structure items based on the company's capital structure (type of financing, amount of financing, and amount of interest) based on an assumed debt rating, assumed deal terms, and market conditions
5. Assess the target's debt capacity based on the target's post-LBO debt rating and ability to service the debt based on the financial model
6. Iterate steps 1 through 5 until the assumed deal terms and the debt capacity (based on the target's post-LBO debt rating and ability to service the debt) align
7. Measure the internal rate of return (IRR) for each equity investor (as well as debt with option features) based on different exit years and exit valuations
8. Set a new price and iterate steps 1 through 7 until the LBO transaction IRR meets at least the minimum IRR hurdle rate set by the investors
9. Value the firm and equity using the weighted average cost of capital method with relevant exit assumptions to measure the implied market multiples and IRRs to equity investors based on the WACC valuation
10. Use the adjusted present value method and the financial model to determine the overall NPV of the investment and the cost of equity in the transaction, and compare to the IRRs

Real Companies and Detailed Examples Incorporated Throughout

The understanding of valuation and how it plays a role in business decisions is essential to the success of any business and its decision makers. Throughout each chapter we incorporate relevant examples of the use of valuation in industry to engage students and provide an understanding of how the theory is used in practice. Real company data have been integrated throughout each chapter to engage and provide relevance to students as they utilize the concepts in practice. Each chapter contains short illustrations of how the topics in the chapter apply to real companies using the Valuation in Practice notes as well as an opening vignette. In addition, each chapter contains one or more detailed examples demonstrating a step-by-step application of the concepts discussed in the chapter. These detailed examples provide an important bridge from the concepts to practice that students often need to understand how to apply the concepts. Many of these detailed examples use information from real companies and some are created by the authors. For example, we use the Xerox Corporation and Affiliated Computer Services, Inc. merger to demonstrate a step-by-step application of the concepts discussed in Chapter 16 on mergers and acquisitions (Exhibit 16.19 is one of the exhibits detailing a valuation in the context of mergers and acquisitions).

EXHIBIT 16.19   Xerox Corporation—Post-merger Valuation

($ in millions, except per share)	Option Tax Shelter in Initial Valuation	
	Yes	No
Xerox firm value (after using all excess cash to close the transaction)	$16,055.0	
ACS firm value (after using all excess cash to close the transaction)	8,186.9	
Value of synergies	1,485.6	
Post-merger Xerox firm value (including ACS and synergies)	$25,727.4	
Post-merger debt and preferred stock		
Xerox and ACS pro forma combined total debt and liabilities	$11,910.7	
Convertible preferred stock	300.0	
Post-merger total debt and preferred stock	$12,210.7	
Post-merger value of common equity financing (including minority interests)	$13,516.7	
Xerox minority interests	150.0	
Post-merger value of Xerox common equity and options	$13,366.7	$13,366.7
Tax shelter from options	N/A	131.3
Post-merger value of Xerox common equity and options	$13,366.7	$13,498.0
Value of stock options		
ACS stock options assumed in exchange for Xerox equivalent option	$ 298.4	$ 306.5
Xerox stock options	56.6	58.1
Total value of stock options	$ 355.1	$ 364.6
Value of Xerox post-merger common equity	$13,011.7	$13,133.4
Post-merger Xerox shares outstanding		
Xerox shares outstanding	877.5	877.5
ACS shares outstanding × 4.935	481.9	481.9
Total post-merger shares	1,359.4	1,359.4
Value of Xerox post-merger common equity per share	$ 9.572	$ 9.661

Exhibit may contain small rounding errors

The following table lists the real companies discussed in the text by chapter:

Chapter 1	Apple Inc. Altria, Inc. and Kraft Foods Spinoff Daimler-Benz and Chrysler Merger	Facebook Inc. FMC Corporation The Gillette Company
Chapter 2	Bloomberg Cisco Systems, Inc. Dell Inc. Dex Media, Inc. Fort Howard Corporation The Gap, Inc. Hewlett-Packard Company	Main Street Restaurant Group Microsoft Corporation Nike, Inc. Samsonite Corporation The Sherwin-Williams Company Water Pik Technologies, Inc.
Chapter 3	Akamai Technologies, Inc. Alcoa, Inc. Darden Restaurants, Inc.	Facebook Inc. Google Inc. Starbucks Corporation
Chapter 4	Darden Restaurants, Inc. The Estée Lauder Companies Inc. The Gap, Inc.	Integra Life Sciences Holdings Corp. Starbucks Corporation
Chapter 5	Apple Inc. Emerging Communications Inc.	

Chapter 6	Chrysler Corporation Daimler-Benz, AG	Yahoo! Inc.
Chapter 7	Crane Co. HSBC Investment Bank plc	Morgan Stanley Dean Witter Whole Foods Market, Inc.
Chapter 8	America OnLine Aviva plc Dimensional Fund Advisors General Electric Company Hewlett-Packard Development Company, L.P. Honeywell International, Inc.	Ibbotson Associates Laureate Education, Inc. Microsoft Corporation Time Warner, Inc. Vodafone Group plc Wal-Mart Stores, Inc.
Chapter 9	Accenture Limited Alcoa Inc. American Axle & Manufacturing Holdings, Inc.	General Motors Corporation Washington Mutual, Inc.
Chapter 10	Latam Airlines Group, S.A. Noranda, Inc.	Phillip Morris International, Inc. TAM S.A.
Chapter 11	Altria Group, Inc. S.A. AMR Corporation	Coca Cola Hellenic Bottling Company, S.A. Kraft Foods Inc.
Chapter 12	Accenture Limited Alcoa Inc. General Motors Corporation	Intel Corporation International Business Machines Corp. KapStone Paper and Packaging Corp.
Chapter 13	Deutsche Telekom First Data Corporation	Staples, Inc.
Chapter 14	AMR Corporation Bon-Ton Stores, Inc. Acquisition of Carson Stores Coca Cola Company Escalon Medical Corp.	Microsoft Corporation PepsiCo Inc. UAL Corporation (United Airlines) Universal Corporation
Chapter 15	FMC Corporation Met Life vs. RJR Nabisco	RJR Nabisco, Inc.
Chapter 16	Affiliated Computer Services, Inc. (ACS) Cingular Wireless and AT & T Wireless Merger Daimler-Benz and Chrysler Merger LAN Airlines S.A. and TAM S.A. Merger LATAM Airlines Group S.A.	Oracle Corp.'s Acquisition of PeopleSoft, Inc. SIRIUS and XM Satellite Radio Merger Xerox Corporation and ACS Merger
Chapter 17	Caraco Pharmaceutical Laboratories, Ltd. Acquisition by Sun Pharmaceutical Industries Limited Google Inc.	Johnson & Johnson and Synthes, Inc. Merger

Learning Objectives, Vignettes, and Chapter Organizational Charts

At the beginning of every chapter, we present learning objectives for that chapter, a small vignette of a real-world example that applies to the content of the chapter, and an organizational chart of the chapter. Thus, even before reading the introduction to the chapter, the reader has a sense of the content of the chapter, its importance, and how the chapter will be organized, which makes it easier to learn the material that follows.

Example Learning Objectives

After mastering the material in this chapter, you will be able to:

1. Know how financing can affect the value of the firm and its equity (5.1)

2. Measure value using the adjusted present value and weighted average cost of capital valuation models (5.2–5.5)

3. Measure value using the equity free cash flow and dividend valuation models (5.6–5.7)

4. Adjust the implementation of these valuation models for specific circumstances (5.8)

Example Vignette

Emerging Communications' valuation using discounted cash flow valuation models—Emerging Communication Inc. (EmCom) owned various subsidiaries whose businesses provided local telephone service, sold and leased telecommunications equipment, and provided cellular telephone service in the U.S. Virgin Islands. During 1998, EmCom's chairman, CEO, and secretary began a process to acquire EmCom and take the company private. In the first step of the process, the chairman was to secure control of at least 80% of EmCom's shares. In order to accomplish that, a special committee drawn from EmCom's Board of Directors negotiated a $10.25 price per share, and its financial advisor issued a fairness opinion stating that the $10.25 price per share was fair from a financial point of view. EmCom's Board approved the $10.25 bid and EmCom gave notice to its shareholders of a special meeting to vote on the sale. On October 19, 1998, EmCom's shareholders approved the transaction.[1] According to Delaware law—the state in which the company was incorporated—shareholders not wishing to participate in the transaction can exercise their appraisal rights by petitioning the court to assess the fair value of their stock. Some of EmCom's minority shareholders opted to exercise their appraisal rights under Delaware law. The court decided on a share price of $38.05 per share based on a weighted average cost of capital valuation method.

In this chapter, we will explore the intricacies of both the weighted average cost of capital discounted cash flow (DCF) method as well as the adjusted present value DCF method and see how the two methods are related to one another.

Example Chapter Organizational Chart

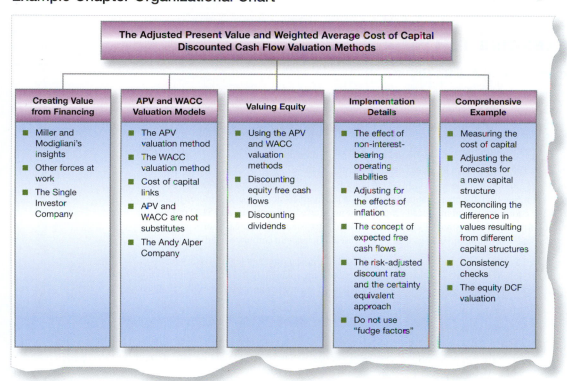

Valuation Keys

Each chapter contains numerous boxed summaries of key concepts and tools called Valuation Keys. The Valuation Keys help focus the reader on the key issue or issues in each section of the chapter.

Valuation Key 13.4

Identifying comparable companies is an important part of any market multiple analysis. We begin by identifying a company's competitors and other companies in the same industry. We then analyze future risk, growth, profitability, investment requirements, and other value drivers from our conceptual framework for the potential comparable companies in order to determine which firms have the best comparability with the firm being valued. It should be obvious that a market multiple valuation means that we need to have a view on the future growth and profitability of the comparable companies—not just the company being valued.

Review Exercises with Solutions Throughout Each Chapter and End-of-Chapter Problems

Conducting a valuation on a real company is challenging to most students. And it is especially challenging for students with less business experience or previous exposure to finance, management, and other valuation-related business courses. To reinforce concepts presented in each section of the chapter, we include review exercises that allow students to apply the topic discussed in each section. The solutions to the review exercises appear at the end of each chapter. In addition, each chapter contains additional end-of-chapter exercises and problems instructors can assign separately.

Example Review Exercise and Solution

REVIEW EXERCISE 16.1

Valuing Synergies—LATAM Airlines Group

Use the following information (taken from the offering memorandum) to measure the value of the synergies for the LAN and TAM merger discussed in Valuation in Practice 16.2. After the completion of the proposed combination, the breakdown of the expected range of annual pre-tax synergies was estimated to be as follows (realized in full in the fourth year after the merger):

- Increased revenues—$225 million to $260 million from the combination of passenger networks and $120 million to $125 million from the combination of cargo services.
- Cost savings—$15 million to $25 million from the consolidation of frequent flyer programs; $100 million to $135 million from the coordination of airport and procurement activities; $20 million to $25 million from the coordination and improved efficiency of maintenance operations; and $120 million to $130 million from the convergence of information technology systems, the increased efficiency of combined sales and distribution processes, and the increased efficiency in corporate overhead costs.

LAN and TAM expected the one-time merger costs—including banking, consulting, and legal advisory fees—to be between $170 million and $200 million. LAN expected a reduction of approximately $150 million in working capital from not having to inventory as many engines and spare parts, which was expected to be fully realized at the end of 2013.

Review Exercise 16.1: Valuing Synergies—LATAM Airlines Group

| Weighted Average Cost of Capital Valuation of Synergies: | | 10.00% | | g= | −10.00% |
| Tax rate = | | 30.0% | | | |

($ in millions)	Low	High	Midpoint
Passenger revenue..............................	$225	$260	$243
Cargo revenue	120	125	123
	$345	$385	$365
Frequent flyer program consolidation	$ 15	$ 25	$ 20
Airport/procurement.............................	100	135	118
Maintenance....................................	20	25	23
Information technology and other	120	130	125
	$255	$315	$285
	$600	$700	$650
Reduced investment in working capital..............	$150	$150	$150
Integration costs and fees	$170	$200	$185
First year synergies	$171	$200	$185

First year synergies midpoint: 28.5%

($ in millions)	2012	2013	2014	2015	2016	CV 2016
Cumulative percentage of synergies achieved		28.5%	50.0%	80.0%	100.0%	
Pre-tax revenue synergies		$103.9	$182.5	$292.0	$365.0	$ 328.5
Pre-tax cost synergies		81.1	142.5	228.0	285.0	256.5
Integration costs and fees	$−185.0					
Less: taxes on synergies and costs		55.5	−55.5	−97.5	−156.0	−195.0	−175.5
Reduced investment in working capital savings		150.0				
After-tax costs, fees, synergies and other	$−129.5	$279.5	$227.5	$364.0	$455.0	$ 409.5
Discount factor for continuing value						5.000
Unlevered free cash flow and CV...................	$−129.5	$279.5	$227.5	$364.0	$455.0	$2,047.5
Discount factor.................................	0.953	0.867	0.788	0.716	0.651	0.651
Present value	$−123.5	$242.3	$179.3	$260.8	$296.3	$1,333.4
Value of synergies............................. $2,188.5						

Exhibit may contain small rounding errors

FLEXIBLE STRUCTURE

The curricula, instructor preferences, and course lengths vary across schools. Accordingly, to the extent possible, we designed many of the chapters in *Corporate Valuation: Theory, Practice & Evidence* so that they can be taught independently of one another. This design provides flexibility and allows instructors to omit certain chapters in a course. Given the nature of the topics covered in the book, however, many of the chapters are interrelated, and certain concepts in a chapter not included in the curriculum would need to be covered by the instructor separately without assigning the entire chapter. We use this approach at Chicago because we have a quarter rather than a semester course schedule. Also, instructors may wish to supplement the course with cases, which might require omitting certain chapters.

Flexibility for Courses of Varying Lengths

Given differing preferences and needs, we provide the following table of possible course designs. In the semester course, faculty members can cover all 17 chapters in the book (Wharton curriculum). In the quarter course, however, covering the entire book is not practicable. For quarter courses, we outline two alternative approaches—one that focuses more on the details underpinning valuation, omitting the transaction and cross-border valuation chapters, and another that covers the valuation topics in less detail and includes the transaction and cross-border valuation chapters (Chicago curriculum). We also present these two versions of the curriculum for the shorter six-week and five-day courses.

Chapter and Topic	15-Week Semester-Course	10-Week Valuation Focused	10-Week Transaction Focused	6-Week Valuation Focused Mini-Course	6-Week Transaction Focused Mini-Course	5-Day Valuation Focused Mini-Course	5-Day Transaction Focused Mini-Course
Chapter 1 Introduction	Week 1	Week 1 Less Detail on Financial Ratios	Week 1	Week 1 Overview of Basic Concepts	Week 1 Overview of Basic Concepts	Day 1 Overview of Basic Concepts	Day 1 Overview of Basic Concepts
Chapter 2 Financial Ratios	Weeks 1 and 2						
Chapter 3 Free Cash Flows	Week 2	Week 2	Week 2 Less Detail on Free Cash Flows				
Chapter 4 Financial Modeling	Week 3	Week 3		Optional	Optional	Optional	Optional
Chapter 5 Discounted Cash Flow Valuation	Weeks 4 and 5	Weeks 3 and 4	Weeks 3 and 4	Weeks 2 and 3	Week 2	Days 2 and 3	Day 2
Chapter 6 Continuing (Terminal) Value	Week 5	Week 4	Week 4 or Optional	Week 3	Optional	Day 3	Optional
Chapter 7 Excess (Residual) Earnings Valuation	Week 6	Week 5	Week 4 or Optional	Week 4	Optional	Day 4	Optional
Chapter 8 Equity Cost of Capital	Week 7	Week 6	Optional	Optional	Optional	Optional	Optional
Chapter 9 Non-Equity Costs of Capital	Week 8	Week 7	Optional	Optional	Optional	Optional	Optional
Chapter 10 Levering and Unlevering	Week 9	Week 8	Week 5	Week 5	Optional	Optional	Optional
Chapter 11 Weighted Average Cost of Capital	Week 10				Optional	Optional	Optional
Chapter 12 Option Pricing Model Applications	Week 11	Week 9	Week 6	Optional	Optional	Optional	Optional
Chapter 13 Market Multiple Valuation I	Week 12	Week 10	Week 7	Week 6	Week 3	Day 5	Day 3 or Optional
Chapter 14 Market Multiple Valuation II							
Chapter 15 Leveraged Buyouts	Week 13	Optional	Week 8	Optional	Week 4	Optional	Day 3 or Optional
Chapter 16 Mergers and Acquisitions	Week 14	Optional	Week 9	Optional	Week 5	Optional	Day 4
Chapter 17 Cross-Border Valuation	Week 15	Optional	Week 10	Optional	Week 6	Optional	Day 5

VALUATION FROM A PRACTICAL PERSPECTIVE

Naturally, it is not possible for a textbook or any other book to discuss the valuation frameworks and applications of those frameworks that apply to every valuation context that might arise. Each company and valuation context will have specific and potentially unique facts and circumstances that require the valuation expert to choose the frameworks and implement them in a way that is appropriate for the specific valuation context. The chapters in this book are meant to provide a guide to understanding the alternative frameworks and ways they can be implemented. Valuation experts must use their informed judgments to choose the specific valuation frameworks to use in a valuation and how to best implement them based on the facts and circumstances for the specific valuation.

SUPPLEMENTS

For Instructors

Solutions Manual Created by the authors and contains solutions to each of the problems at the end of the chapters.

PowerPoint Presentations Created and classroom tested by the authors, the PowerPoint slides outline key elements of each chapter and provide additional examples not used in the textbook. Because most of the examples in the PowerPoint presentations are different from those used in the book, instructors are not just repeating what is in the book.

Spreadsheets We provide author-created Excel spreadsheets for the underlying examples in the PowerPoint presentations. This allows instructors to see exactly how the spreadsheets are created and would also allow instructors to create other examples if they so desired.

For Students

Example, Review Exercise, and Problem Data We provide Excel spreadsheets of "hard-coded" data for chapter examples, review exercises, and end-of-chapter problems. We also provide hard-coded solutions to the chapter examples and review exercises. These hard-coded solutions provide students with the template used as well as the data for the problems, and make it easier to solve the problems, as students do not have to input the raw data into an Excel file.

In some cases, the exhibits in the book have small rounding errors because we do not show enough significant digits in order to avoid the clutter of multiple significant digits. When that occurs, the following phrase appears at the bottom of the exhibit: "Exhibit may contain small rounding errors." The Excel spreadsheets provide more significant digits for students who want to refer to them.

Option Pricing Spreadsheets Chapter 12 includes applications of option pricing theory to plain vanilla options, warrants, employee stock options, convertible debt, and financial distress prediction. We provide several different Excel files that aid with these applications.

ACKNOWLEDGMENTS

We would especially like to thank Jennifer J. Jones, former faculty member at The University of Chicago Booth School of Business, for the countless hours she has contributed to the book by helping us review the chapters, examples, solutions, and galleys. Her devotion to detail and to this project has been incredible, and it is fair to say that the book would not be as good as it is, and we might even still be working on it, without her efforts—and for that, we owe her an enormous amount of gratitude.

We would also like to thank our former students at Chicago and Wharton who have used this material in various forms over the years. They have provided valuable feedback and advice that has shaped the content of this book. In addition, we would like to thank Assistant Professor Vincent Glode at Wharton as well as Hamid Mehran of the New York Federal Reserve Bank and a former visiting faculty member at Wharton, for their insights on the book when teaching the corporate valuation class at Wharton.

This book also benefited from many years of discussions about valuation issues with our colleagues at our respective universities as well as with colleagues at other universities throughout the world.

We would also like to thank The University of Chicago Booth School of Business and The Wharton School for their support during the writing of this book.

We received feedback and suggestions from faculty from around the country during various stages of writing the book. We want to recognize their contribution and thank them for their help.

Ashok Abbott, *West Virginia University*
Jeffrey Allen, *Southern Methodist University*
Peter Brous, *Seattle University*
Tyrone Callahan, *University of Southern California*
Steven Ferraro, *Pepperdine University*
Scott Fine, *Case Western Reserve University*
Susan Fleming, *Cornell University*
Cesare Fracassi, *University of Texas*
Amarjit Gill, *New York Institute of Technology*
Benton Gup, *University of Alabama*
Anurag Gupta, *Case Western University*
Alexander Gurvich, *Pace University*
Jeffrey Hart, *University of Iowa*
Michael Ho, *University of Virgina, Darden School*
Narayanan Jayaraman, *Georgia Institute of Technology*
Rick Johnston, *Purdue University*
Srinivasan Krishnamurthy, *North Carolina State University*
Christiano Manfre, *Loyola Marymount University*
Nathan Mauck, *University of Missouri—Kansas City*
William Maxwell, *Southern Methodist University*
Karl Mergenthaler, *Pace University*
Jamie Pawlukiewicz, *Xavier University*
Peter Pfau, *Pace University*
George Pinteris, *Ohio State University*
Julia Plotts, *University of Southern California*
Richard Shockley, *Indiana University*
Tao Shu, *University of Georgia*
Michel Vetsuypens, *Southern Methodist University*
Joe Wells, *University of Texas—Dallas*
Robert West, *Villanova University*
Jeffrey Zwiebel, *Stanford University*

In addition, we owe particular thanks to George Werthman for believing in this project and for helping us fully develop this book, and we are extremely grateful to Jocelyn Mousel, Liz Haefele, Rich Kolasa, Debbie McQuade, Terry McQuade, and the entire team at Cambridge Business Publishers for their encouragement, enthusiasm, and guidance.

RWH	*MEZ*
Philadelphia, PA	Chicago, IL

Brief Contents

Contents

CHAPTER **3**

**Measuring Free
Cash Flows   80**

CHAPTER **4**

**Creating a Financial
Model   124**

CHAPTER **5**

The Adjusted Present Value and Weighted Average Cost of Capital Discounted Cash Flow Valuation Methods   164

CHAPTER **6**

Measuring Continuing Value Using the Constant-Growth Perpetuity Model   210

CHAPTER **7**

The Excess Earnings Valuation Method   250

CHAPTER **8**

**Estimating the Equity
Cost of Capital   284**

CHAPTER **9**

**Measuring the Cost of
Capital for Debt and
Preferred Securities   336**

CHAPTER **10**

The Effects of Financial Leverage on the Cost of Capital 382

CHAPTER **11**

Measuring the Weighted Average Cost of Capital and Exploring Other Capital Structure Issues 420

CHAPTER **14**

Market Multiple Measurement and Implementation 544

CHAPTER **15**

Leveraged Buyout Transactions 600

CHAPTER **16**

Mergers and Acquisitions   666

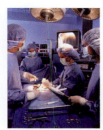

CHAPTER **17**

Valuing Businesses Across Borders   722

After mastering the material in this chapter, you will be able to:

1. Explain the different concepts of value (1.1–1.2)

2. Understand the principles underpinning the valuation methods (1.3)

3. Explain how the different valuation models measure value (1.4–1.6)

4. Describe how managers and investors use valuation models (1.7)

5. Outline the steps in the valuation process (1.8)

Introduction to Valuation

On February 1, 2012, Facebook Inc. filed a registration statement with the U.S. Securities and Exchange Commission to issue publicly traded stock for the first time, called an initial public offering. At what value will Facebook trade in the market?

FACEBOOK INC.

In other words, what is the value of Facebook? As we show in the table below, Facebook increased its revenues from $153 million in 2007 to $3.7 billion in 2011, and it increased its net income from a loss of $138 million in 2007 to a profit of $1.0 billion in 2011. Its free cash flow increased from a negative cash flow of $55 million in 2007 to a positive $470 million in 2011. As of the end of 2011, Facebook held $3.9 billion of cash (or cash-like securities).[1]

($ in millions)	2007	2008	2009	2010	2011
Revenue	$ 153	$ 272	$777	$1,974	$3,711
Operating income.	$–124	$– 55	$262	$1,032	$1,756
Net income.	$–138	$– 56	$229	$ 606	$1,000
Free cash flow	$– 55	$– 88	$ 66	$ 188	$ 470
Cash.	$ 305	$ 297	$633	$1,785	$3,908

After mastering the concepts and tools in this book, you will be able to value a company like Facebook. The chapters in this book lead you through a detailed, step-by-step approach to valuing companies. This book provides the necessary knowledge to adjust and implement the valuation methods to whatever valuation context you are facing.

---

[1] See Facebook's S-1 Registration Statement filed with the Securities and Exchange Commission (SEC) on February 1, 2012, available on February 4, 2012, at http://www.sec.gov/Archives/edgar/data/1326801/000119312512034517/d287954ds1.htm.

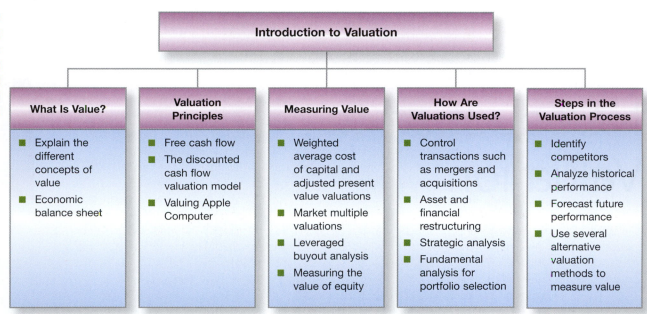

INTRODUCTION

Managers and investors place very big bets and take large risks based on the valuation models discussed in this book. They are willing to make those investments and take those risks because they expect to earn sufficient cash in the future from these investments to create value for their companies or superior returns for their investment portfolios. Managers and investors decide whether or not to make an investment by comparing their assessment of the value—or valuation—of the future cash flows they expect to earn from an investment to the amount they must invest. They will choose investments for which their valuation of the future cash flows is sufficiently greater than the amount they must invest. The valuation models discussed in this book serve as the framework to use to assess whether investments create value.

Since some type of valuation analysis serves as the basis of many decisions managers and investors make every day, all managers and investors benefit from understanding valuation theory and how valuation models work. In this book, we present well-accepted methods or valuation models that managers and investors commonly use to measure value. While managers and investors use these valuation models to measure the value of many different types of investments and as the basis of many different decisions, our focus is on measuring the value of a firm and its common equity. We also discuss ways to value certain securities a firm may issue to raise financial capital. Finally, while we do not discuss project valuation directly, many of the methods presented in this book can be used to assess the value of a company's specific investment projects.

In this chapter, you will gain a general understanding of the primary valuation models used today. Further, you will gain an understanding of the general components of value for a firm. In addition, you will see the various ways that managers and investors use valuation models. For example, the managers of Daimler and Chrysler agreed to merge the two auto manufacturers based in part on the advice of their financial advisors who relied on the models discussed in this book (see Valuation in Practice 1.1). Finally, you will gain an appreciation of the overall valuation process.

1.1 WHAT DO WE MEAN BY "THE VALUE OF A COMPANY"?

LO1 Explain the different concepts of value

We have many terms that are used to describe the value of a company, for example, **fair market value**, **market value**, **fair value**, **intrinsic value**, and **fundamental value** just to name a few. A widely used description of fair market value is the cash equivalent value at which a willing and unrelated buyer would agree to buy and a willing and unrelated seller would agree to sell the company, when neither party is compelled to act, and when both parties have reasonable knowledge of the relevant available information.

Valuation in Practice 1.1

The Daimler-Benz—Chrysler Merger In November 1998, Daimler-Benz, AG (Daimler), which operated in automotive (passenger cars and commercial vehicles), aerospace, and other industry segments, merged with Chrysler Corporation (Chrysler), which operated in the automotive and financial services industry segments. The merger of Daimler and Chrysler resulted in the formation of a new German company, DaimlerChrysler, AG (DaimlerChrysler).

The process started in mid-January 1998, when Mr. Jurgen E. Schrempp, Chairman of Daimler, and Mr. Robert J. Eaton, Chairman and Chief Executive Officer of Chrysler, met and began discussions about a possible merger between the two companies. By late April of that year, they agreed to merge in a **stock-for-stock transaction**. Daimler agreed to an exchange ratio that resulted in a 28%, or more than $7 billion, premium to the Chrysler shareholders.

On the day before they announced the merger, Daimler's market capitalization (or market cap) was over $52.5 billion and Chrysler's market cap was over $26.5 billion, with a combined market cap of over $79 billion. The initial market reaction to the merger announcement was positive. Chrysler's market cap increased by more than $7.5 billion and Daimler's market cap increased by more than $4.5 billion, for a combined increase of more than $12 billion (or 15%).

Mr. Schrempp and Mr. Eaton and their respective boards decided to place their bets, in part, based on the advice of their financial advisors. Credit Suisse First Boston was Chrysler's financial advisor in connection with this merger and the financial advisor for Daimler-Benz was Goldman Sachs. Both financial advisors provided a fairness opinion to their respective clients indicating that the price paid in the merger was fair, and both used the valuation models we discuss in this book as a basis for their conclusions. Of course, we now know that this merger did not work as well as implied by the market's initial reaction to the announcement, as Daimler sold Chrysler in 2007.

Source: See Annex C and Annex D in the DaimlerChrysler AG SEC Form F-4 (Registration Statement). DaimlerChrysler's post-merger financial performance has not yet met pre-merger expectations.

This definition suggests some important characteristics about the valuation context—"arm's length," time-frame constraints, information set, and specific use. For example, a willing and unrelated buyer and seller suggests that the transaction is "arm's length"; that is, it does not include "side payments" or other remuneration beyond the transaction price between the buyer and seller. Neither party being compelled to act suggests a time-frame context—that is, the time frame for the parties to identify and negotiate with each other is such that, whatever it happens to be, it does not affect the price at which a transaction would take place. In addition, this suggests this is not a forced transaction such as might be compelled by a court or a government agency. The definition also indicates the importance of the availability of information—that is, the value is based on an information set that is assumed to contain all relevant and available information. Lastly, part of the relevant information is the specific use of the assets being purchased.

In most valuations, the company is valued as an ongoing business (**ongoing value** or **going-concern value**). There are, however, valuations that presume that the company will not be operated any longer, **liquidation value (forced and orderly)**, or that the company will be broken up into pieces and the pieces will be operated as separate entities, **breakup value**. Liquidation value is used when the company's assets, either collectively or individually, are going to be sold off or liquidated. Forced liquidation suggests a valuation context in which the time frame to sell the company is sufficiently short such that the company will be sold for less than it would have been sold for given more time. Orderly liquidation suggests that the time frame to sell the company does not affect the price at which the company is sold. Breakup value is the value of selling off the different parts of a company—for example, a **conglomerate** selling off all or some of the individual companies it owns.

Of course, there is not just one universal opinion on the value of a company. Different individuals or groups may have differences of opinion regarding the best way to use the company's assets, or they may have different expectations regarding the company's future prospects even if they do agree on the best use of the assets. Naturally, buyers and sellers need not be in exact agreement over the value of a company when they transact. The buyer often believes the value is higher than the price paid for it and the seller often believes the value is lower than the price at which it is sold. In fact, transactions are more likely to occur when the buyer believes a company is worth more than the seller believes it is. Nevertheless, valuation models should approximate the observed market value of the company so long as the inputs used reflect both a specific valuation context and the information and expectations of the buyers and sellers engaged in market transactions.

1.2 THE ECONOMIC BALANCE SHEET: RESOURCES EQUAL CLAIMS ON RESOURCES

The value of the firm and the value of the securities it issues are related in a very fundamental way. A company is a legal entity, that is, nothing but a collection of contracts.[2] One of those contracts must be with the owners of the company (shareholders), because a company cannot own itself. For example, stock certificates and corporate bylaws are the contracts a corporation has with its equity owners. In almost all cases, the equity owners of a company have a **residual interest** in the company's assets; that is, the equity owners get the value that remains after all other contracts are settled. As a result, the value of a company's resources must be equal to the value of the contractual claims on its resources.

$$\text{Value of Resources} = \text{Value of Claims on Resources}$$

$$\text{Value of the Firm} = \text{Value of Non-Equity Claims} + \text{Value of Equity (Residual Interest)}$$

From this relation, it follows that a change in the value created by a company must be equal to the change in the value of the company's securities (we use the Greek letter delta, Δ, to signify the change in value). Said another way, the dollar return on a company's resources must be equal to the dollar return on the claims on its resources.

$$\Delta \text{ Value Firm} = \Delta \text{ Value Non-Equity Claims} + \Delta \text{ Value Equity}$$

$$\$ \text{ Return Firm} = \$ \text{ Return Non-Equity Claims} + \$ \text{ Return Equity}$$

We use several forms of these relations to develop various aspects of the valuation models presented throughout this book. It is sometimes useful to depict this relation in more detail using an **economic balance sheet**.

Example Economic Balance Sheet

Exhibit 1.1 is an example of an economic balance sheet for a hypothetical company. The first thing to note about this exhibit is that the value of the company's resources (or the value of the firm) is equal to the value of the claims on its resources (or the value of its securities). This is a useful relation because information available about the securities that a company issues can be used to assess the company's value and cost of capital.

EXHIBIT 1.1 Economic Balance Sheet for a Hypothetical Company	
HYPOTHETICAL COMPANY **Economic Balance Sheet** **As of 31 December, Year 5**	
Resources (Assets)	**Market Value**
Value of the unlevered (all equity-financed) business operations without excess assets	$ 8,500
Value of the excess assets	500
Value of the unlevered firm	$ 9,000
Value created from financing	1,000
Value of the firm	$10,000
Claims on Resources	**Market Value**
Value of debt	$ 3,000
Value of preferred stock	2,000
Value of equity	5,000
Value of securities issued	$10,000

Resources (Assets). The value of a company's resources has two basic components—the **value of the unlevered firm** and the **value created from financing**. The value of the unlevered firm is what the

---
[2] See Coase (1937) for an important discussion about why firms exist; Coase, R., "The Nature of the Firm," *Economica* 4 (1937), pp. 386–405.

company would be worth if it was entirely financed with common equity but had made all of the same investment decisions. The value created from financing arises in some tax jurisdictions because of the potential tax advantage of debt relative to other forms of financing, such as equity. In many tax jurisdictions, payments to **debtholders** in the form of interest are tax deductible at the corporate level whereas payments or flows to **equityholders** are not tax deductible.

The economic balance sheet does not show the value of all the individual components that make up the value of the unlevered firm, but we are able to break it into two components: the value of the company's business operations on an unlevered basis and the value of its excess assets.

The value of a company's business operations is the value of the company's ongoing businesses, exclusive of any value created from financing and any value in assets that are not needed for the business, such as **excess cash**. The value of the company's business operations is not the sum of the individual values of the assets that the company needs to operate its businesses when considered separately. Rather, it is the value of those assets when valued together as an ongoing business. These assets include monetary assets (such as cash and receivables required for the business), physical assets (such as inventory and property, plant, and equipment), intangible assets (such as intellectual property or a superior R&D capability), and the **value of growth opportunities** (also called the **present value of growth opportunities**). Thus, the value of the business operations includes any expected future value creation resulting from anticipated investments. The latter are not assets already-in-place, but they are part of the value of a company.

The value of the company's **excess assets** includes all resources that are not needed to operate the specific business being valued. Excess assets include assets such as excess cash and marketable securities (sometimes referred to as cash and cash equivalents), land, buildings, equipment, patents, **net pension assets**, and any other asset that is not needed to operate the business. Generally, we value excess assets separately and isolate them from our valuation analysis. Of course, not all cash, land, buildings, equipment, and patents represent excess assets.

Claims on Resources.   In the bottom section of Exhibit 1.1, Claims on Resources, we show that the value of the firm is equal to the sum of the value of a company's securities. We use a simple capital structure in this exhibit: debt, preferred stock, and common equity. The claims on the company's resources consist of all of the securities issued by the company to raise capital. Keep in mind that companies can issue different kinds of debt, preferred and common equity.

All companies have at least one type of claim, called **common equity** (or **equity**). (We use the term *equity* interchangeably with the term *common equity* throughout this book.) The investors who own these securities have a residual interest in the company's resources and almost always control the company. They generally elect the board of directors, which hires and compensates management. Companies can have more than one type of common equity that has different rights, such as different voting rights. Another claim on the resources of the company is any debt that is outstanding. Companies can have different types of debt with varying seniority and differing terms. Debt has seniority over the other claims shown in the economic balance sheet. Many, but not all forms of debt instruments represent a fixed claim on the company's resources.

Companies can also issue another form of security, called **preferred stock**, that typically (but not always) also has a fixed claim on the company's resources. Preferred stock is junior to the company's debt instruments, but it is senior to the common equity. A company can also issue various classes of preferred stock. In most tax jurisdictions, the dividends paid on preferred stock are not generally tax deductible to the corporation; hence, issuing preferred stock is not generally considered to create value from financing. In addition, companies can issue debt and preferred stock that are convertible into common equity at the option of the holder. Companies can also have other types of securities, such as contingent claims like **employee stock options** and **stock warrants**, or other debt-like claims, such as **pension liabilities**.

You might be wondering why the value of the company's non-interest-bearing operating liabilities (such as accounts payable or taxes payable) does not show up in the Claims on Resources section of the economic balance sheet. Operating liabilities result when a company does not have to pay cash for its operating expenses in the same period in which it receives the good or service provided to it. These liabilities are generally classified by accountants as current liabilities (such as accounts payable and other payables). On occasion there are liabilities that the accountant classifies as non-current that also fall under non-interest-bearing operating liabilities. The reason these do not appear in the economic balance sheet is that in the normal process of performing a valuation on a going-concern basis, the non-interest-bearing operating liabilities of the company are implicitly netted against the value of the company's assets in determining the value of the unlevered assets. Since non-interest-bearing operating liabilities are netted out in measuring the resources of the company, none of the claims shown on the economic balance sheet is a non-interest-bearing operating liability. However, since non-interest-bearing operating liabilities have a legal claim on the assets of a company, they do affect the valuation of the company.

Why is it that in the course of a valuation the **non-interest-bearing liabilities** are implicitly netted out against the value of the company's assets in determining the value of the company's unlevered assets? Because financing costs related to non-interest-bearing operating liabilities are embedded in the company's operating expenses, we do not have an easy way to disentangle them. When a company buys a product or service **on account** from a vendor, the vendor charges the company for the product or service plus an implicit financing charge for not paying at the time the good or service is received. Hence, the financing charge is embedded in the cost of the product or service and cannot be separated from the value of the operations. At this point, we don't discuss how this netting takes place in the various types of valuation methods used, but we will return to this topic when we discuss each type of valuation method in subsequent chapters.

Valuation Key 1.1

The economic balance sheet portrays the value of the resources or assets of the firm considered as a whole, as well as the value of the claims the company has issued. The economic balance sheet shows the *market value* of a company's collective resources and the market values of the various claims on its resources (securities issued) at a specific point in time.

The Economic Balance Sheet Does Not Equal the Accounting Balance Sheet

The economic balance sheet is not like the balance sheets companies publish in their **annual reports**, which are **accounting balance sheets** (unless we indicate otherwise, we use the term **balance sheet** to mean the **accounting balance sheet** prepared by a company for its annual report). The economic balance sheet shows the *market value* of a company's collective resources and the market values of the various claims on its resources (securities issued) at a specific point in time. Accountants prepare the accounting balance sheet using specific rules (**Generally Accepted Accounting Principles, GAAP**), which do not, for the most part, purport to measure the market value of a company's resources or claims on its resources. Accountants tend to be conservative in the way they prepare balance sheets and other **financial statements**; they will, more often than not, recognize losses before they are realized but not recognize gains until they are realized. The result is an accounting system that ignores some important assets that add to the company's market value. As a result, the economic balance sheet will generally have a higher value for the company's resources, and therefore a higher value for the claims on its resources, than observed on an accounting balance sheet. Most of this difference in value goes to the **shareholders** of the company. We observe that the ratio of the market value of equity to the **book value** of equity is, on average, greater than one, which is consistent with these differences. But note that not all companies have market-to-book ratios that are greater than one.

REVIEW EXERCISE 1.1

The Market Value Company Economic Balance Sheet

Prepare an economic balance sheet for The Market Value Company as of Year 0 using the following information and the financial statements provided. The company's share price is $12.08 and it has 1,200 shares outstanding. Its debt is trading at a premium, indicating that its market value is equal to 102% of its book value. The company has land valued at $3,000 that is not necessary to operate the business. Based on the amount and type of debt financing, the company creates $3,800 in value from financing.

THE MARKET VALUE COMPANY Income Statement and Balance Sheet Forecasts					
	Year –1	Year 0		Year –1	Year 0
Balance Sheet—Assets			**Balance Sheet—Liabilities & Equity**		
Cash balance	$ 171.4	$ 188.5	Accounts payable.	$ 122.8	$ 135.1
Accounts receivable.	571.2	628.3	Other current operating liabilities	119.9	131.9
Inventory.	286.5	315.2	Total current liabilities.	$ 242.7	$ 267.0
Total current assets	$1,029.1	$1,132.0	Debt	4,800.0	5,200.0
Net property, plant and equipment . . .	7,539.4	8,567.5	Total liabilities	$5,042.7	$5,467.0
Total assets.	$8,568.5	$9,699.5			
			Common stock.	$1,802.4	$1,802.4
			Retained earnings	1,723.3	2,430.0
Income Statement			Total shareholders' equity	$3,525.7	$4,232.4
Revenue	$3,472.0	$3,769.7	Total liabilities and equities.	$8,568.5	$9,699.5
Cost of goods sold.	–1,473.6	–1,621.0			
Gross margin	$1,953.4	$2,148.7			
Selling, general and administrative . . .	–479.8	–527.8			
Operating income.	$1,473.6	$1,621.0			
Interest expense.	–307.0	–384.0			
Income before taxes.	$1,166.6	$1,237.0			
Income tax expense.	–443.3	–470.0			
Net income.	$ 723.3	$ 766.9			

Exhibit may contain small rounding errors

Solution on pages 28–29.

1.3 VALUATION PRINCIPLES

An asset has value to an investor because the investor believes the asset will generate cash flows in the future. The value of an asset depends on the magnitude, timing, and risk of the cash flows the investor expects it to generate. Holding everything else constant, the value of an asset increases if the magnitude of its expected cash flows increases, if its expected cash flows arrive sooner, or if its risk (risk-adjusted discount rate) decreases. As we demonstrate below, the **discounted cash flow (DCF) valuation model** directly results from these valuation principles.

LO2 Understand the principles underpinning the valuation methods

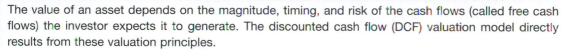

Valuation Key 1.2

The value of an asset depends on the magnitude, timing, and risk of the cash flows (called free cash flows) the investor expects it to generate. The discounted cash flow (DCF) valuation model directly results from these valuation principles.

Introduction to Measuring Free Cash Flows

The DCF model measures the value of an asset as the sum of the expected cash flows the asset generates after adjusting each expected cash flow for its timing and risk. In the context of the valuation of companies, we refer to those cash flows as the **free cash flows** or the **free cash flows of the unlevered firm**. Free cash flows are the cash flows generated by the company after the collection of its revenues, payment of its expenses, and after making its investments, including investments in working capital. They are the cash flows the company would generate if it was entirely financed with equity. We use the word "free" to describe these cash flows not because they were costless to generate, but because the company is "free" (or able) to distribute these flows to its investors without interfering with the execution of its strategy.

Valuation Key 1.3

Free cash flows are the cash flows that could be distributed to all of the company's security holders after it makes all necessary investments, but without consideration of the taxes saved from any interest expense that arises from debt in its capital structure. They are the free cash flows of the company if it were entirely equity financed.

To measure free cash flows, we begin with earnings before interest and taxes, **EBIT**, and deduct income taxes. The income taxes deducted, **TAX**, are the income taxes the company would pay if it had no **interest deductions** (interest expense that is deductible for income tax purposes). The next adjustment is to convert the company's earnings to cash flows. Earnings are not equal to cash flows because earnings include non-cash expenses, non-cash revenues, and other accruals. To convert EBIT to cash flow, we add back any **non-cash expenses or losses (NCEXP)**, for example, depreciation, and subtract any **non-cash revenues or gains (NCREV)**. We also subtract investments, which include any increase in the **required cash balance (Δ RC)**, any increase in **non-cash required operating working capital** (**Δ WCO**, for example, inventory), **capital expenditures**, and any other required investments for the business (**CAPEX**). Non-cash required operating working capital does not include any items related to financing costs (such as interest) or income taxes. We show this calculation in Equation 1.1

$$\text{FCF} = \text{EBIT} - \text{TAX} + \text{NCEXP} - \text{NCREV} - \Delta \text{RC} - \Delta \text{WCO} - \text{CAPEX} \qquad \textbf{(1.1)}$$

This is the most basic calculation of free cash flows. Naturally, as a company's assets, capital structure, economic transactions, and income tax situations become more complex, the calculation of free cash flows becomes more complex as well.

REVIEW EXERCISE 1.2

The Market Value Company Unlevered Free Cash Flow

Use the information in Review Exercise 1.1 to measure the unlevered free cash flow for The Market Value Company for Year 0. The company has $500 in depreciation expense embedded within its cost of goods sold. This is the only depreciation the company records. The company holds no excess cash so the change in cash is its required cash.

Solution on page 29.

The Discounted Cash Flow Valuation Model

The DCF model adjusts expected free cash flows by using **time value of money principles** to discount each expected free cash flow to the date of the valuation, using a risk-adjusted discount rate that reflects the risk of the asset. The DCF model provides a useful framework to convert the sometimes abstract and qualitative strategic concepts (strategic fit, competitive advantage, market power) into quantitative measures that affect value. This framework involves answering three overarching questions: How does the strategic action affect the magnitude of the free cash flows? How does the strategic action affect the timing of the free cash flows? How does the strategic action affect the underlying risk of the cash flows?

Since a company does not have a contractually finite life but can exist forever, the DCF model normally discounts a company's free cash flows to infinity. The DCF model to measure the value of the firm, $V_{F, 0}$, simplified for an all-equity financed company with a constant (risk-adjusted) cost of capital, r_{UA}, which is termed the **unlevered cost of capital**, is:

$$V_{F, 0} = \frac{\text{FCF}_1}{(1 + r_{UA})^1} + \frac{\text{FCF}_2}{(1 + r_{UA})^2} + \dots + \frac{\text{FCF}_\infty}{(1 + r_{UA})^\infty} = \sum_{t=1}^{\infty} \frac{\text{FCF}_t}{(1 + r_{UA})^t}$$

The value of the firm is measured at a particular date, which is as of the end of Period 0 in the above formula. Unless we believe the company will liquidate or otherwise go out of business, the assumption that a company has an infinite life complicates our DCF calculations, for it is not possible to forecast and then discount an infinite series of cash flows unless we make a simplifying assumption about the time series of the expected cash flows. The way we typically solve this problem is to develop detailed forecasts for a company's expected cash flows for some finite period of time, say 10 years. Then, we measure the value of the firm at the end of that finite period. We call the value at the end of the finite period of time the company's **continuing value (CV)**; other terms used for this concept are **terminal value**, **residual value**, and **horizon value**. The way we typically implement the infinite forecast horizon is to construct detailed forecasts for the company for C years and measure the continuing value of the firm, $CV_{F,C}$, as of the end of Year C.

The continuing value represents the value of the company as of the end of Year C. Using a continuing value in our DCF model as of the end of Year C, our DCF model becomes

$$V_{F,0} = \sum_{t=1}^{C} \frac{FCF_t}{(1 + r_{UA})^t} + \frac{CV_{F,C}}{(1 + r_{UA})^C} \qquad (1.2)$$

One way we can measure a company's continuing value is to assume the company's free cash flows grow at a constant rate, g, after the continuing value date. We call this assumption a **constant growth perpetuity** assumption. As long as the growth rate is constant and less than the constant discount rate, r, the infinite series present value calculation summarizes to the constant growth perpetuity formula.

$$CV_{F,C} = FCF_{C+1} \times \frac{1}{(r_{UA} - g)} \qquad (1.3)$$

Substituting the above continuing value into the DCF model we get our widely accepted DCF model with a constant growth perpetuity continuing value:

$$V_{F,0} = \sum_{t=1}^{C} \frac{FCF_t}{(1 + r_{UA})^t} + \frac{FCF_{C+1}}{(r_{UA} - g)} \times \frac{1}{(1 + r_{UA})^C} \qquad (1.4)$$

Illustration of the Discounted Cash Flow Valuation Using Apple Inc.[3]

In this section, we illustrate how to apply the DCF valuation model using Apple Inc. (Apple) while making some simplifying assumptions (for example, we ignore outstanding options, complicated tax issues, etc.). One characteristic of Apple that makes it easier to value is that it has a simple, essentially all-common equity, capital structure. Apple had a market capitalization (measure of firm value) of about $360.5 billion around the end of its 2011 fiscal year (September 2011). To value Apple using a DCF valuation model, we use free cash flow forecasts for 11 years (2012 through 2022), a constant growth rate of 2.5% for free cash flows generated in perpetuity after 2022, and a risk-adjusted discount rate of 12.5%. We construct forecasts that yield Apple's exact market value of $360.5 billion.

Given this information and the simplifying assumptions we made in this illustration, implementing the DCF model is purely a calculation exercise. We discuss the complexities and subtleties of the DCF model, how to develop such forecasts, continuing value growth rates, and risk-adjusted discount rates in the remainder of the book. In Exhibit 1.2, we present two years of summary historical financial statements and free cash flows (2010 and 2011) and selected years of the 11 years of forecasts (2012 through 2022) for Apple. We use the free cash flow forecast for 2022 and constant perpetual growth rate of 2.5% to measure the continuing value of the firm as of the end of 2021.

Apple has excess assets it does not need for its operations totaling $70.7 billion. These excess assets include excess cash ($15.1 billion) and long-term securities ($55.6 billion). We value Apple using the DCF model, excluding the value of its excess assets, and then add the value of its excess assets to the DCF valuation of its operations to measure its total value.

We use Equation 1.4 to measure the value of Apple's operations (excluding the value of Apple's excess assets).

$$V_{Apple, 2011} = \frac{\$20,277}{1.125} + \frac{\$26,129}{1.125^2} + \frac{\$28,548}{1.125^3} + \frac{\$30,579}{1.125^4} + \frac{\$32,361}{1.125^5} + \frac{\$33,925}{1.125^6}$$

$$+ \frac{\$35,305}{1.125^7} + \frac{\$36,668}{1.125^8} + \frac{\$37,431}{1.125^9} + \frac{\$38,816}{1.125^{10}} + \frac{\$39,787}{(.125 - .025)} \times \frac{1}{1.125^{10}} = \$289,716 \text{ million}$$

---

[3] Apple designs, manufactures, and markets personal computers and related software, services, peripherals, and networking solutions worldwide as well as portable digital music players and related accessories and services, including online sale of third-party audio and video products. See Apple's 2011 10-K report available from its website on December 20, 2011, at http://www.apple.com/investor/.

EXHIBIT 1.2   Apple Inc. Historical and Selected Financial Statement and Free Cash Flow Forecasts

APPLE INC.
Income Statement Forecasts
(for the years ended September 30)

($ in millions)	A2010	A2011	F2012	F2015	F2018	F2021	F2022
Revenue	$65,225	$108,249	$121,239	$149,796	$165,438	$178,159	$182,613
Cost of goods sold	−39,541	−64,431	−72,830	−89,985	−99,382	−107,023	−109,699
Gross margin	$25,684	$ 43,818	$ 48,409	$ 59,811	$ 66,057	$ 71,136	$ 72,914
Research and development	−1,782	−2,429	−3,016	−3,727	−4,116	−4,433	−4,543
Selling, general and administrative	−5,517	−7,599	−9,383	−11,593	−12,804	−13,788	−14,133
Operating income	$18,385	$ 33,790	$ 36,009	$ 44,491	$ 49,137	$ 52,915	$ 54,238
Other income and expense	155	415	0	0	0	0	0
Income before taxes	$18,540	$ 34,205	$ 36,009	$ 44,491	$ 49,137	$ 52,915	$ 54,238
Income tax expense	−4,527	−8,283	−9,002	−11,123	−12,284	−13,229	−13,559
Net income	$14,013	$ 25,922	$ 27,007	$ 33,368	$ 36,853	$ 39,686	$ 40,678

APPLE INC.
Balance Sheet Forecasts
(for the years ended September 30)

($ in millions)	A2010	A2011	F2012	F2015	F2018	F2021	F2022
Cash and marketable securities	$25,620	$ 25,952	$ 12,124	$ 14,980	$ 16,544	$ 17,816	$ 18,261
Accounts receivable	5,510	5,369	8,128	10,042	11,091	11,943	12,242
Inventory	1,051	776	1,406	1,738	1,919	2,067	2,118
Other current assets	9,497	12,891	16,045	19,825	21,895	23,578	24,168
Total current assets	$41,678	$ 44,988	$ 37,703	$ 46,584	$ 51,449	$ 55,405	$ 56,790
Property, plant and equipment	$ 7,234	$ 11,768	$ 17,089	$ 37,437	$ 63,480	$ 78,440	$ 82,579
Accumulated depreciation	−2,466	−3,991	−6,135	−17,787	−38,078	−49,962	−53,274
Property, plant and equipment (net)	$ 4,768	$ 7,777	$ 10,953	$ 19,650	$ 25,402	$ 28,478	$ 29,304
Long-term marketable securities	$25,391	$ 55,618	$ 0	$ 0	$ 0	$ 0	$ 0
Intangible assets	1,083	4,432	4,964	6,133	6,773	7,294	7,477
Other assets	2,263	3,556	4,095	5,059	5,587	6,017	6,167
Total assets	$75,183	$116,371	$ 57,715	$ 77,426	$ 89,211	$ 97,194	$ 99,738
Accounts payable	$12,015	$ 14,632	$ 16,754	$ 20,544	$ 22,677	$ 24,420	$ 25,031
Accrued expenses and other	8,707	13,338	15,561	19,227	21,235	22,867	23,439
Total current liabilities	$20,722	$ 27,970	$ 32,316	$ 39,770	$ 43,911	$ 47,288	$ 48,470
Non-current liabilities	6,670	11,786	12,799	15,814	17,465	18,808	19,278
Total liabilities	$27,392	$ 39,756	$ 45,115	$ 55,584	$ 61,377	$ 66,096	$ 67,748
Common stock (and other)	$10,622	$ 13,774	$ 13,774	$ 13,774	$ 13,774	$ 13,774	$ 13,774
Retained earnings	37,169	62,841	−1,174	8,068	14,060	17,324	18,216
Total shareholders equity	$47,791	$ 76,615	$ 12,600	$ 21,842	$ 27,834	$ 31,098	$ 31,990
Total liabilities and equities	$75,183	$116,371	$ 57,715	$ 77,426	$ 89,211	$ 97,194	$ 99,738

APPLE INC.
Free Cash Flow Forecasts
(for the years ended September 30)

($ in millions)	A2010	A2011	F2012	F2015	F2018	F2021	F2022
Earnings before interest and taxes (EBIT)	$18,540	$ 34,205	$ 36,009	$ 44,491	$ 49,137	$ 52,915	$ 54,238
− Income taxes paid on EBIT	−4,527	−8,283	−9,002	−11,123	−12,284	−13,229	−13,559
Earnings before interest and after taxes	$14,013	$ 25,922	$ 27,007	$ 33,368	$ 36,853	$ 39,686	$ 40,678
+ Depreciation expense	1,027	1,814	2,144	4,804	7,762	9,863	10,110
+/− Working capital and other changes	3,555	9,793	−1,723	985	515	549	562
− Change in required cash	−4,302	−4,302	−1,299	−784	−410	−435	−445
Unlevered cash flow from operations	$14,293	$ 33,227	$ 26,129	$ 38,373	$ 44,719	$ 49,663	$ 50,905
− Capital expenditures (net)	−2,779	−7,955	−5,852	−7,794	−9,414	−10,847	−11,118
Unlevered free cash flow	**$11,514**	**$ 25,272**	**$ 20,277**	**$ 30,579**	**$ 35,305**	**$ 38,816**	**$ 39,787**

Exhibit may contain small rounding errors

We constructed the forecasts such that the present value of Apple's discounted free cash flows plus the value of its excess assets is equal to its current market value of $360.5 billion; thus, Apple's current market value is composed of the value of its discounted free cash flows from its operations of $289.7 billion and $70.7 billion in excess assets (cash and long-term securities). Included in the DCF calculation is the value of Apple's continuing value, which we measure using Equation 1.3. Apple's continuing value as of the end of 2021 is equal to $397.9 billion.

$$\text{CV}_{\text{Apple, 2021}} = \frac{\text{FCF}_{2022}}{(r_{\text{UA}} - g)} = \frac{\$39,787}{(0.125 - 0.025)} = 10.0 \times \$39,787 = \$397,870 \text{ million}$$

However, this is the continuing value as of 2021 and not 2011. Once we discount Apple's 2021 continuing value to 2011, the 2011 present value of the continuing value is equal to $122.5 billion ($397.9 \times 1/1.125^{10}$).

While our valuation of Apple is only an illustration of the DCF model, it is clear that developing such a valuation for a company provides a useful way for a manager of a public company to try to understand what expectations the market has for the company's future performance to support its current market value. To the extent the manager has different expectations for the company, the manager can assess whether the company is overvalued or undervalued. In addition, the manager will have some idea of how the company has to evolve in order to meet market expectations. While we do not show the detailed assumptions that we used to construct this model, it is interesting to note that while Apple's revenues grew 66% between 2010 and 2011, we used much more modest growth rates, 12% tapering down to 2.5%, to replicate its market valuation using our DCF model.

REVIEW EXERCISE 1.3

Valuation of Unlevered Free Cash Flows

A company has expected free cash flows of $100.2 million, $114.0 million, and $120.8 million in the next three years. Afterward, the free cash flows will grow in perpetuity by 2% annually. Measure the value of this company as of today using a 12% discount rate.

Solution on page 29.

1.4 MEASURING THE VALUE OF THE FIRM

Now that you have a good sense of general valuation principles and how they relate to the discounted cash flow model, we will discuss two alternative DCF models and other valuation models commonly used to value companies. All of the valuation models discussed in this chapter and the book have applicability in a variety of different contexts. When valuing companies, we are most often interested in the value of the common equity and the value of the firm. The models we discuss in this section are commonly used valuation models for valuing the firm. A subsequent section discusses how we value the common equity. The value of the firm is equal to the combined value of the company's assets, which is equal to the combined value of all of the securities and claims that a company issues. So, if a company issues debt (perhaps of various kinds), preferred stock, and common equity, the value of the firm is the combined value of all these claims.

LO3 Explain how the different valuation models measure value

Different Forms of the Discounted Cash Flow (DCF) Valuation Models

The discounted cash flow (DCF) valuation model is one of the most commonly used valuation methods. In a 1998 survey of large corporations and financial advisors, Bruner et al. (1998) report that 96% of corporations use the DCF valuation method to evaluate investment opportunities and 100% of financial advisors do so.[4] As discussed in the prior section, the value of an investment according to the DCF model is the discounted (or present) value of the expected cash flows of the investment, where the discount rate is the risk-adjusted rate of return, and where the time value of money framework is used to adjust for the

---

[4] See Bruner, R., K. Eades, R. Harris, and R. Higgins, "Best Practices in Estimating the Cost of Capital: Survey and Synthesis," *Financial Practice and Education* (Spring/Summer 1998), pp. 13–28.

passage of time. The inputs for the DCF model are the magnitude and the timing of the expected cash flows and the risk-adjusted discount rate.

There are two DCF methods used to measure the value of the firm: the **adjusted present value method** (**APV**) and the **weighted average cost of capital method** (**WACC**). The latter is sometimes referred to as the **adjusted cost of capital method**. Ignoring excess assets, a company derives its value from two broad sources: the value of the company's operations and the value that results from the way the company chooses to finance itself. Both the APV and WACC methods value the company based on the combined value of the company's operations and the value created from financing. While the two methods take somewhat different paths to measure value, both methods yield the same value if properly implemented. The difference between the two methods is how the methods incorporate the value created from financing. The APV method incorporates the benefit directly, via forecasts of cash flows that are attributable to financing choices. The WACC method incorporates the benefit indirectly, through an adjustment to the discount rate.

You are probably wondering why there are two DCF methods if they yield the same answer. Good question. As it turns out, the APV and WACC methods are not substitutes. Given the information available and the valuation assumptions made, only one of the two methods is appropriate as the starting point for a particular valuation analysis. We will come back to this issue when we discuss the DCF methods in more detail later in the book. The cash flows used to value the firm (the combined value of the debt, preferred equity, and common equity) are the free cash flows of the unlevered firm (free cash flows) irrespective of whether the APV or WACC method is used. The risk-adjusted discount rate used to discount the free cash flows reflects the overall riskiness of the company's operations and, in the case of the WACC method, also incorporates the potential benefit of a company's capital structure.

Instead of performing a going-concern valuation, which is most common, we could assume that a company may liquidate as soon as it is practical to do so or after it operates for some period of time. In a liquidation, one assumes that the assets of the company are sold off in the most advantageous manner in order to pay off all of its liabilities (including any preferred stock), its other contractual obligations, and any costs associated with closing the business (e.g., employee severance packages, costs of plant closings, etc.). To the extent that any cash remains after all of that, the cash is distributed to the equityholders. An orderly liquidation that tries to maximize value usually takes some time to achieve, and the resulting cash flows from the liquidation can be incorporated into a DCF model.

The Discounted Excess Flow Valuation Models

The **discounted excess flow** valuation model has various forms. The most basic form is the **excess cash flow** method. In this method, we discount free cash flows in excess of the required free cash flows that are based on the required rate of return and amount of capital invested. The intuition for this model is quite simple. Suppose a company begins by investing $100,000 in land and the required rate of return for the risk of the land is 10% and that is the only investment the company makes. In this case, the required cash flow that would make this a zero net present value investment is $10,000 ($10,000 = $100,000 × 10%) per year in perpetuity. If the company earns $10,000 per year and distributes that entirely to its claimholders, it has created no value and is simply worth the $100,000 investment. If, however, the company earns more than $10,000 a year, which it distributes entirely to its claimholders, the value created is the discounted value of the distribution above $10,000 per year. The value of the company in this case is simply the $100,000 invested plus the discounted value of the distribution above $10,000 per year.

Another form of this model, called the **excess earnings** or **residual income** valuation model, uses financial accounting information to discount excess accounting earnings. Other forms of the model adjust a company's financial statements in an attempt to refine excess earnings to approximate **excess economic earnings** instead of excess accounting earnings. The excess flow models are algebraically equivalent to the DCF model, and therefore the valuation principles we discussed previously are preserved in the excess flow valuation models.

Market Multiple Valuation Models

Market multiple valuation models are used extensively by investment bankers and other valuation experts. Bruner et al. (1998) report that 100% of financial advisors use market multiple methods based on publicly traded comparable companies as well as comparable transactions in their valuation work. A market multiple represents the value of a firm or its equity scaled by some relevant firm characteristic. The list of market multiples used by managers and investors is long. Some of the more common market multiples for valuing the firm are the market value of the firm to **earnings before interest and taxes (EBIT)**; the market value of the firm to **earnings before interest, taxes, depreciation, and amortization (EBITDA)**; the market value of the firm to sales; and the market value of the firm to total assets or invested capital. Analysts and investment bankers often refer to the market value of the firm as "enterprise value." Thus, it is not uncommon to hear investment bankers refer to multiples such as enterprise value to EBITDA.

To use the **market multiple valuation method** (also called **price multiple**, **comparable company**, or **twin company valuation method**), we first identify a characteristic of the company that we believe should be a primary determinant or driver of the company's value. Then, we identify a set of companies that are comparable to the company we are valuing for which we can observe the same characteristic as well as their values. For each comparable company, we calculate its market multiple by dividing its value by its characteristic (for example, divide the market value of the firm by earnings before interest and taxes, called an EBIT multiple). From the multiples of the comparable companies, we choose the appropriate multiple for the company we are valuing. Then, we multiply that multiple by the characteristic of the company we are valuing to obtain its value.

The market value estimates in these multiples are typically obtained from prices of publicly traded companies or from prices paid in **control transactions** (transactions where there is a change in control, such as a merger or tender offer) or possibly from prices of **initial public offerings (IPOs)**. For example, in considering the value of a company being acquired, a valuation specialist will often base the market multiple on transaction prices of comparable companies that have recently been acquired. Or when valuing a company for an initial public offering, the valuation specialist will often use prices of comparable companies that have recently gone public. Market multiple valuation based on control transactions or IPO transactions is typically referred to as a **comparable transactions analysis** or a **comparable deals analysis**. Irrespective of the source of the values of the comparable companies, valuation by multiples relies on the assumption that the prices used in measuring the multiples are appropriate indicators of value for the underlying companies.

The intuition underpinning market multiple valuation models is the notion of the law of one price. That is, if two assets are identical in terms of the magnitude, timing, and riskiness of their cash flows, they should sell for the same price. On the other hand, if two assets are identical in terms of the timing and riskiness of their cash flows, but the cash flows of one asset are exactly two times as large as the cash flows of the other asset in every period, then that asset should sell for twice as much.

To use the EBIT multiple, we assume that the value of a company is directly proportional to current earnings before deducting interest or taxes (EBIT). If the value of one firm is $10,000 and its EBIT is $1,000, then the market multiple approach assumes that another firm that is *identical in all other relevant respects*, except its EBIT is $2,000, will have a value of $20,000. While market multiple valuation is simple to understand, it is quite difficult to implement. The key issue in implementation is captured in the italicized phrase above, "identical in all other relevant respects."

Assuming that the values that are used in calculating the multiples are based on the valuation principles discussed previously and do not misrepresent market values, a market multiple valuation method preserves those valuation principles. Of course, if the values used to calculate the multiples are based on speculative bubbles, for example, the principles are not likely to be preserved.

Leveraged Buyout Valuation Models

Another typical technique used by investment bankers when measuring the value of a company that is put up for sale is to consider whether that company is a candidate for a **leveraged buyout (LBO)** or **private equity** transaction. An LBO is a form of transaction in which a group of private investors acquires the company using extensive debt financing. The ability of a company to support an LBO transaction depends on such characteristics as the magnitude of the expected cash flows, the stability of those cash flows, the extent to which the company already has debt outstanding, and the current condition of the credit markets. A typical LBO analysis makes assumptions about the cash flows a company can generate, the likely capital structure, and the required rates of return for various capital providers (bank debt, senior subordinated debt, junior subordinated debt, preferred stockholders, and common stockholders). The analysis then measures the maximum price of the buyout that provides those rates of return to the various capital providers. The maximum price the LBO analysis generates is another indication of value, in this case, conditional on a particular transaction. Conditional on this particular form of transaction, the analysis preserves the valuation principles discussed previously regarding the magnitude, timing, and riskiness of the cash flows.

1.5 MEASURING THE VALUE OF THE FIRM'S EQUITY

The most common way to measure the value of the common equity is to first value the firm using any of the methods previously discussed and then to subtract an appropriate value for all of the non-common equity claims, such as debt and preferred stock, warrants and employee stock options, etc. As we discussed previously, operating working capital liabilities such as accounts payable are not included as part of debt because the cost of these liabilities is implicitly netted out in valuing the company's operations. The value of interest-bearing debt, as well as any pension liabilities, environmental liabilities, and potential settlements from lawsuits, must all be subtracted from the value of the firm if they are ignored in the cash flow forecasts. However, items such as accounts payable and taxes payable are not subtracted off since they are generally already factored into the valuation through the cash flow forecasts. The only exception to this is when doing a liquidation analysis. In a liquidation analysis, we basically appraise the individual assets and perhaps some businesses that can be sold. We then subtract the working capital liabilities and the amount of all other debt and preferred stock unless a working capital liability, debt, or preferred stock is transferred to the buyer of any businesses or assets sold.

In many cases, the value of the non-equity claims—subtracted from the value of the firm to measure the value of the common equity—is an estimate of the market value of those securities. For example, if a firm has publicly traded debt, we would subtract the market value of the debt from the value of the firm. In some situations, however, we do not use estimates of market values. Consider a control transaction where a company (the acquirer) is acquiring a firm (the target) and is considering how much to bid for the common equity of the target. Further, assume the debt of the target has a provision that prohibits control transactions if any of the debt is still outstanding. In that situation, the acquirer would have to retire the debt of the target in order to complete the acquisition. If the debt also required that it could only be retired at a premium to its face value prior to its maturity or some other specific date in the future (a **call premium**), then the value that would be subtracted from the value of the firm would not be the market value of the debt, but rather would be the amount that would have to be paid to call the debt and retire it.

Another technique for valuing the common equity is to use a discounted cash flow method that values the common equity directly. This method discounts the free cash flows of the equity by the equity cost of capital. The free cash flows of the equity are equal to the free cash flows of the unlevered firm adjusted for all cash flows to or from non-equity claims, such as payments or receipts from debt and preferred stock investors. There is an analogous discounted excess flow model that values the equity directly as well. Using either a discounted cash flow or discounted excess flow model that values the equity directly is difficult to implement. Hence this technique is often reserved for special situations such as valuing financial institutions. It is seldom used to value manufacturing and service organizations.

There are also market multiple methods that value the common equity directly. So instead of valuing the firm or enterprise value using a market multiple method and then subtracting the value of the non-common equity claims, we value the equity directly using an appropriate equity multiple. For example, a **P/E multiple** or **price-to-earnings ratio**, defined as price per common share divided by earnings available to common equityholders per share, is one such multiple that values the common equity directly. Another is the **market-to-book ratio**, which is calculated as the market value of the equity to the book value of the equity.

1.6 REAL OPTIONS IN VALUATION

The option pricing framework is another potentially useful valuation method in certain situations. Option pricing recognizes that the holder of an asset is not always compelled to act, but instead acts only if it is the holder's best interest to do so. For example, the holder of a **call option** has the right to buy a specific asset at a specified price, called the **exercise price**, for a certain time period. Thus, if the value of the asset is above the exercise price at the time the call option is about to expire, then the holder of the call will be better off exercising the call and buying the asset at the exercise price. Of course, if the value of the asset is below the exercise price of the call, and if the holder of the call wants to purchase the asset, then the holder will buy the asset in the open market and will not exercise the call. Since it is cheaper to buy the asset in the open market than by exercising the call option, the call will not be exercised.

Early work on the potential applications of option pricing methods recognized that the common equity of a levered firm is similar to a call option on the firm, where the exercise price is equal to the amount owed to the debtholders.[5] In other words, the equityholders have the right to buy back the firm from the debtholders by paying off the debtholders, if they choose to do so. If the equityholders do not want the firm back, they simply do not pay off the debtholders. Obviously, if the assets of the company are worth more than the amount owed the debtholders, the equityholders are made better off by paying off the debtholders the amount owed.

More recently, managers and investors have begun to recognize the potential importance and valuation implications of so called **real options**. These are options that are embedded in some investment opportunities that a firm takes on or that arise because of contractual arrangements with other parties. They include options such as the option to delay investing, the option to expand, the option to abandon, the option to invest, and the option to purchase, among others. For example, when a manager invests in a project to build a new product, she might not have to build all of the anticipated capacity requirements at the beginning of the project if the capacity can be built in stages. It is possible that it will be advantageous to delay meeting some of the capacity requirements at the outset if there is a chance that the demand may not be as high as expected. The option to expand capacity allows the manager to analyze the situation and expand later if subsequently needed. It is common that the cost of adding capacity in stages is more expensive than the cost of building all the capacity at once. However, that added cost must be weighed against the cost of having idle capacity if demand for the new product is not as high as expected and some of the capacity is not needed. In some investments, consideration of these options can make the difference between accepting and rejecting an investment. For some companies, especially startups, the options available to them significantly affect their value.

Options can be valued in a variety of ways. The specific method that is most appropriate in a given situation is related to the type and quality of information that is available. Financial options, where there is typically a wealth of relevant data, are often valued using models such as the **Black-Scholes Option Pricing Model** and the **Binomial Option Pricing Model**. These models are also used to measure the value of real options in the context of operating decisions. However, in some cases the required data for those models is not readily available and the effect of real options on value is approximated through a DCF model that explicitly considers the options that are embedded in an investment.

Discounted cash flow techniques and market multiple methods can undervalue a firm relative to its true value if we ignore important options that a firm may possess. A valuation specialist must be aware of the existence of important options in considering the value of a firm or a project and incorporate that option value.

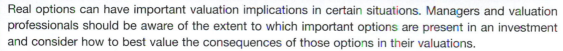

Valuation Key 1.6

Real options can have important valuation implications in certain situations. Managers and valuation professionals should be aware of the extent to which important options are present in an investment and consider how to best value the consequences of those options in their valuations.

---

[5] For a discussion of how options are valued and why equity in a firm with debt is like a call option, see Black and Scholes (1973); Black, F., and M. Scholes, "The Pricing of Options and Corporate Liabilities," *Journal of Political Economy* 91 (May–June 1973), pp. 637–654.

1.7 HOW MANAGERS AND INVESTORS USE VALUATION MODELS

LO4 Describe how managers and investors use valuation models

A valuation analysis is an important input into the decisions managers and investors make about transactions that involve the sale, purchase, investment, or disinvestment of an entire business or a portion of a business. In addition, these same models are used for non-transactional analyses such as making smaller investment decisions or helping set the strategic direction of a company. Managers of large multinational companies, mid-sized companies, and private corporations rely on these models. Even governments rely on valuation models to make decisions. In this section, we discuss the various ways managers, investors, and others rely on valuation analyses to make important decisions, both in transaction analysis and in everyday decision making.

Control Transactions

Control transaction is a term used to describe any transaction that results in a change of control of an entity.[6] A control transaction does not have to involve the sale of the entire company. It could involve the sale of an equity interest so the buyer has sufficient control to make the company's business decisions, or it could involve the sale of only a portion of a company's business. Valuation models are used in these transactions to measure the value of the acquired entity, based on the strategy in place before the transaction as well as the value based on the intended strategy after the transaction. That information is then used to help negotiate a price between the various parties to the transaction.

Mergers and acquisitions (M&As) is a term that defines transactions in which one company acquires or merges with another company. If a company can use another company's assets more effectively, the company may decide to acquire some or all of the assets of that other company (via an **asset purchase**, **acquisition**, or **merger**). Acquisitions can result in the purchase of a subset of a company's assets, of all of the company's assets, or of all a company's common stock. After the transaction, the two companies can remain separate legal entities or they can merge into one legal entity. The valuation conducted in an M&A transaction includes the expected standalone cash flows of the target, plus any expected cost or revenue synergies resulting from the transaction. Thus, the relevant cash flow forecasts used in a DCF model would include additional revenues expected to be generated (revenue synergies) and any anticipated reductions in costs (cost synergies) associated with the transaction. The cash flow forecasts may also embed changes in the strategic direction of the enterprise that a new owner might make.

Certain activist investors, such as Carl Icahn, look for companies that are performing poorly relative to their potential and then take a significant stake in the company. In many cases, that stake is not a controlling interest. Following that, they often attempt to secure one or more seats on the board of directors in order to try to force management to change the company's operations. Since there are inherent uncertainties in being able to get managers to change the operations of the company, investors do not take activist positions like this unless they believe the value-creation opportunities are substantial. These value-creation opportunities are evaluated using the valuation methods we discuss in this book.

Highly leveraged transactions include leveraged buyouts (LBOs) and **management buyouts (MBOs)**, both of which are **change-of-control** transactions, in which control of the entity shifts. LBOs are transactions in which a group of private investors uses extensive debt financing to purchase an entire company or a part of it, such as a division. The company becomes privately held, because its common stock is no longer publicly traded. MBOs are transactions in which the managers of the company comprise part of the group of private investors, which is not uncommon.[7] Valuation models in support of LBOs and MBOs usually embed the benefits of being private, and the cost savings, tax savings, and working capital reductions associated with running the organization more efficiently. The benefits may also include changes in the strategy of the company.

---

[6] See the discussion of the issues and an overview of the early research in this area by Jensen and Ruback (1983); Jensen, M. C., and R. S. Ruback, "The Market for Corporate Control: The Scientific Evidence," *Journal of Financial Economics* 11 (1983), pp. 5–50.

[7] See Jensen (1986) and Kaplan (1989); Jensen, M. C., "Agency Costs of Free Cash Flow, Corporate Finance, and Takeovers," *American Economic Review* 2 (1986), pp. 323–329; Kaplan, S. N., "The Effects of Management Buyouts on Operating Performance and Value," *Journal of Financial Economics* 24 (1989), pp. 217–254.

When companies are bought and sold, it is common for some type of financial advisor, such as an investment bank, to aid in the process. Not only do financial advisors help perform valuations, they play a variety of other roles, such as running an auction process for a company being sold, advising on potential acquirers, helping obtain and evaluate offers, arranging financing, aiding with negotiation tactics, and more.

One of the paramount concerns for a board of directors in any change-of-control transaction, particularly in the United States, is the potential legal liability associated with not using reasonable business judgment and not basing the decision on relevant available information. The business judgment rule, as it is generally applied in courts, protects the board of directors from legal liability (but not from someone filing a lawsuit) if the directors make a decision with adequate information, on an informed basis, and unmotivated by personal incentives that conflict with the incentives of other shareholders. When making business decisions that involve the sale of an entire business, the role of valuation models is to assist the board in deciding whether to accept a bid and to protect the board from legal liability by providing the board with adequate information and demonstrating that it is exercising reasonable business judgment.

In almost all change-of-control transactions, a consultant, typically an investment bank or other valuation specialist, issues an opinion (**fairness opinion**) that indicates whether the price offered in the transaction is fair. While not formally required by U.S. law, since the groundbreaking Van Gorkom ruling, detailed in Valuation in Practice 1.2, almost all change-of-control transactions involving the sale of a publicly traded company will have a fairness opinion. The basis of the valuation expert's judgment on the fairness of the price is based on many of the valuation techniques discussed previously in this chapter.

Valuation in Practice 1.2

The Van Gorkom Case A fairness opinion is essentially a letter from an independent valuation specialist that tells the board of directors that the price of a proposed transaction is fair. The use of "fairness opinions" has its origins in a Delaware Supreme Court ruling in *Smith v. Van Gorkom* in 1985. Smith was a shareholder of Trans Union, and Van Gorkom was the company's chief executive officer. The lawsuit involved the sale of a company, Trans Union, to a private buyer in 1980. Trans Union's stock was trading below $38 during the year before the sale. Mr. Van Gorkom negotiated a price of $55 with a private buyer, and the buyer gave the company's board of directors three days to accept or decline the offer. Mr. Van Gorkom did not consult the board during the short negotiations process.

Mr. Van Gorkom called for a special board meeting, and after a few hours, the board of directors approved the sale of the company and recommended that shareholders accept the offer. The court ruled that the board of directors of Trans Union did not make its decision to sell the company with sufficient information and that the board of directors was not sufficiently informed about the value of the company. In its ruling, the court also noted the lack of a report by an expert consultant, and the board was held liable for not exercising reasonable business judgment in considering this transaction. Since this ruling, the board of directors in virtually any sale of a public company obtains a fairness opinion.

In rendering a fairness opinion, it is common to perform a discounted cash flow valuation, a market multiple valuation based on comparable companies, a market multiple valuation based on comparable transactions, and an analysis of the value that would result from an LBO transaction. An investment banker may also base a fairness opinion, in part, on the process that was used to sell a company and whether there were other bids. In addition, if the company being bought and sold is a public company, it is common to examine the historical trading range of the company's stock price over some recent historical period and to examine the target prices for the company's stock as reported in various analyst reports. The valuation expert generally makes a presentation to the board of directors concerning the valuation, so the board can come to a conclusion as to whether to proceed with the transaction. Between 1994 and 2003, 95% of the deals whose value was at least $10 million had at least one fairness opinion on the target side, and 70% of the same deals had one or more opinions on the acquirer side.[8]

---

[8] See, Kisgen, D., J. Qian, and W. Song, "Are Fairness Opinions Fair? The Case of Mergers and Acquisitions," working paper, Boston College, November 2005.

Asset and Financial Restructuring Activities

Companies undertake a variety of asset and financial restructuring activities to increase the value of the firm and maximize shareholder value. **Asset restructuring activities** involve the sale of assets, businesses, or the stock of subsidiaries. **Financial restructuring activities** involve large changes in a company's capital structure. Management sometimes undertakes these activities proactively and sometimes reactively, such as in response to the threat of a takeover. In a **proactive restructuring** activity designed to maximize shareholder value, management uses valuation models to better understand the economic consequences of a restructuring decision. In **reactive restructuring**, a response to a corporate raider or a threat of a **hostile bid**, management uses valuation models to analyze the economic consequences of the offer as well as the economic consequences of alternative defenses and strategies. In these cases, management will try to demonstrate that its actions will increase the per-share value of the company above the amount of the hostile bid.

Asset Restructuring Activities.

A company can create value if another company can better use some of its assets, if it can use another company's assets better, or if combining the assets of two companies creates value (synergies). If another company can use a company's assets better (best and highest value use), the company should **divest** (sell off) some of those assets (**asset sale** or **divestiture**).[9] Asset restructuring activities can be of various types. One type of restructuring activity is **corporate downsizing**. The goal of corporate downsizing is to reduce the size of, or eliminate, certain businesses or business activities that are not profitable or less profitable than they may potentially be. One way to downsize is by means of **asset sales**, in which a company simply sells some of its assets. For example, a company may sell a manufacturing plant or a patent that it believes a buyer can use more profitably. Another way to downsize is to sell an entire business in a transaction called a **divestiture**. In these transactions, the seller must evaluate the value to potential buyers and attempt to capture as much of the value added by the buyer as possible. The seller must also value the entity being sold as it currently operates it so that it may know whether the bids received will in fact create value for the shareholders relative to continuing to operate the asset or business. In other words, is there a bid for the assets being sold that exceeds the value of those assets if the seller were to continue to operate them? The more potential buyers with whom the seller can negotiate, the more of these benefits the seller can generally capture.

Valuation in Practice 1.3

Gillette's Asset Restructuring Activities The Gillette Company (Gillette) operated in five industry segments—blades and razors, Duracell, oral care, Braun, and personal care. In September 1998, Gillette embarked on an asset restructuring program, which ended up taking Gillette more than two years to complete. The expected restructuring charges reduced pre-tax profits by more than $440 million in 1998. In 2000, Gillette announced still more restructuring and recognized pre-tax charges of $572 million due to the restructuring and the impairment of assets. As a result of these restructuring activities, Gillette closed more than 20 factories, reduced its labor force by more than 15%, and sold its stationery products and other businesses.

Between September 1998 and January 2000, Gillette's stock price decreased from $41 per share to less than $32 per share. Adjusting for dividends, Gillette's stock return was –20% during this period. While –20% does not look very good, it looks even worse when compared to the 42% return on the **S&P 500** during that same period. However, the restructuring positioned Gillette for future growth and profitability. Gillette's net income grew substantially in both 2001 and 2002. While its stock price decreased slightly during this period (–0.4%), this was good relative to the performance of the stock market, as the S&P 500 declined 35.6% during the same period. Although the restructuring process was painful, it allowed Gillette to become a more efficient, competitive, and profitable company. In 2005, the Gillette Company was purchased by Procter & Gamble.

Source: The source for all financial statement information is Gillette's 2002 annual report to shareholders, available at <http://www.gillette.com/investors/shareholderinformation_delivery.asp>; the source for all stock market information is CRSP. See Jatras (2000) for a review of these events; Jatras, T., "Around-the-Globe: Gillette Restructures," Forbes.com, December 18, 2000, 3:18 PM ET, http://www.forbes.com/2000/12/18/1218atg.html. See Gillette's Form 8-K filed with the **U.S. Securities and Exchange Commission (SEC)** on February 18, 1999, and October 19, 2000, for these announcements.

---

[9] Scholarly research shows that, on average, the stock market perceives divestitures as value increasing; see, for example, Klein, L., "The Timing and Substance of Divestiture Announcements: Individual, Simultaneous and Cumulative Effects," *Journal of Finance* (July 1986), pp. 685–696.

Liquidation is an extreme form of asset restructuring in which a company dissolves either a single business or the entire company by selling off all of the assets and paying off any liabilities and any costs of liquidation. If the entire company is liquidated, any remaining cash is distributed to the stockholders. The decision to liquidate is based on a determination that the company is worth more liquidated than operating as a going-concern. Again, management has to value the company as a going-concern and compare that value to the liquidation value of the company. The stock market generally reacts positively to news of asset sales, divestitures, and liquidations.[10] The reason for this is that the assets being sold or divested are generally more valuable to a buyer than to the selling company; and in turn, the selling company captures some of that value. In addition, companies that are liquidated are generally quite unprofitable and the shareholders are better off receiving the liquidation proceeds than having the company continue to operate unprofitably, which dissipates any remaining resources.

Other asset restructuring activities involve a company issuing stock in the public markets for one of its subsidiaries. In **spin-offs**, a company distributes shares of a subsidiary (a separate legal entity) to existing shareholders on a pro-rata basis. The subsidiary then becomes a new standalone company that is publicly traded and operates independently of the parent company. A related restructuring activity is an **equity carve-out**. Equity carve-outs involve the **initial public offering (IPO)** of the stock of a subsidiary. The parent company takes a subsidiary public and retains some of the ownership, but unlike a spin-off, an equity carve-out allows the parent company to retain control over the subsidiary. The average excess stock return to the parent company when it announces transactions of this sort is generally positive.[11] In many cases, the shares of the subsidiary had not been publicly traded, so there is now an active market for the shares of the subsidiary, which provides the potential for using equity and option grants as an incentive for employees. It also provides some financial flexibility to the company. Many spin-offs occur when the subsidiary's business is not part of the parent's core business.

Valuation in Practice 1.4

Altria, Inc. Spins Off Kraft Foods Altria Group, Inc. (Altria), the parent company of Philip Morris, USA, the largest cigarette maker in the United States, also owned 88.9% of the common stock of Kraft Foods, Inc. (Kraft), itself a public company. On March 30, 2007, after legal wrangling that took several years, Altria successfully spun off its shares of Kraft to its (Altria's) shareholders on a pro-rata basis in a tax-free transaction. When Altria announced the spin-off, it stated the following in its press release:

"The separation of Altria and Kraft will benefit both parties and achieve the following benefits:

- Enhance Kraft's ability to make acquisitions, including by using Kraft stock as acquisition currency, to compete more effectively in the food industry;
- Allow management of Altria and Kraft to focus more effectively on their respective business and improve Kraft's ability to recruit and retain management and independent directors.
- Provide greater aggregate debt capacity to both Altria and Kraft; and
- Permit Altria and Kraft to target their respective shareholder bases more effectively and improve capital allocation within the company."

Source: See Altria Group, Inc. press release dated March 30, 2007, "Altria, Group, Inc. to Spin-off Kraft Foods, Inc.," http://www.altria.com/investors/02_00_NewsDetail.asp?reqid=956368.

---

[10] The value of the common stock of selling companies announcing asset sales or divestitures increases approximately 2%, and there is even a greater positive reaction for companies announcing their liquidation. The latter are a peculiar group of companies. For research in this area, see Hite, Owers, and Rogers (1987) and Kose and Ofek (1995); Hite, G. L., J. E. Owers, and R. C. Rogers, "The Market of Interfirm Assets Sales: Partial Sell-Offs and Total Liquidations" *Journal of Financial Economics* 18 (1987), pp. 229–252; Kose, J., and E. Ofek, "Asset Sales and Increase in Focus," *Journal of Financial Economics* 37 (1995), pp. 105–126.

[11] For spin-offs, see the early research by Schipper and Smith, (1983); Schipper, K., and A. Smith, "Effects of Recontracting on Shareholder Wealth: The Case of Voluntary Spin-offs," *Journal of Financial Economics* 12 (1983) pp. 437–467. For research that examines why spin-offs appear to create value for the parent company, see Daley, Mehrota, and Sivakumar (1997); Daley, V., V. Mehrota, and R. Sivakumar, "Corporate Focus and Value Creation: Evidence from Spinoffs, *Journal of Financial Economics* 45 (1997) pp. 257–281. For equity carve-outs, see the early research by Schipper and Smith (1986); Schipper, K., and A. Smith, "Equity Carve-Outs and Seasoned Equity Offerings," *Journal of Financial Economics* 15 (1986), pp. 153–186. For research that investigates the information effects of equity carve-outs, see Slovin, Sushka, and Ferraro (1995); Slovin, M., M. Sushka, and S. Ferraro, "A Comparison of the Information Conveyed by Equity Carveouts, Spinoffs, and Asset Sell-Offs," *Journal of Financial Economics* 37 (1995), pp. 89–104.

Financial Restructuring Activities.   Financial restructuring activities (sometimes referred to as financial engineering) include such actions as issuing debt and repurchasing the company's shares, both of which can increase the company's financial leverage. Financial restructuring can also entail the repayment of debt or an exchange offer where equity is issued for debt, reducing the company's financial leverage. Financial restructuring might lead to the issuance of certain securities that have tax advantages; it might be used as a defensive tactic to thwart a hostile takeover; or it might change who has control of a company.

We often observe a company undertaking financial restructuring activities at the same time it is undergoing asset restructuring activities; the situation that resulted in the need to restructure the company's assets might also result in a need for the company to adjust its capital structure. An asset restructuring can also create an opportunity for a company to change its capital structure. The role of valuation models in financial restructuring is to measure the effects of the restructuring on the value of the firm and to provide a long-term plan for the company's **financial architecture**. Once these valuations are performed, management is in a much better position to make the appropriate value-creation decision.

One type of financial restructuring is a debt recapitalization. The goal of a **debt recapitalization (debt recap)** is to increase the value of the firm by getting better financial terms, such as lower interest rates; more potential tax benefits associated with a more highly leveraged position; and potential benefits from better management incentives associated with higher debt levels. Why might a large amount of debt improve the efficiency of a company's operations? For some firms, a large debt overhang can be an incentive for managers to operate the firm efficiently because it forces them to generate the cash flows necessary to pay off the debt. A debt recap can also be very effective in creating value in situations where investors believe managers have been using the company's cash flows to invest in negative net present value projects.[12] In this case, the company issues a large amount of debt and pays the proceeds out to shareholders in the form of a special dividend or share repurchase at the time the debt is issued. This forces management to stop investing in negative net present value projects, for it paid out the present value of the expected cash flows to shareholders upfront and is now forced to use the cash flows generated by the business to service the debt. Debt recaps can serve as an effective commitment device to stop wasting resources.

Valuation in Practice 1.5

FMC's Debt Recapitalization FMC Corporation (FMC) is a diversified global chemical company operating in three business segments—agricultural products, specialty chemicals, and industrial chemicals. FMC was one of the first companies to undergo a debt recapitalization. In February 1986, FMC's board of directors approved a financial restructuring of the company. The plan did not treat all shareholders in the same way. Management wanted a larger percentage of the company's stock after the debt recapitalization for both itself and its employee benefit plans. Public shareholders were to receive $70 per share and one new share for each old share.

FMC planned on issuing $1.7 billion in debt to finance the debt recapitalization. The company actually issued more debt and paid more to the shareholders to get them to approve the plan, and it reduced $187 million of excess funding in its pension plans as part of the financing. The cash distribution paid by FMC to its shareholders resulted in FMC having a negative net worth (shareholders' equity) of more than $507 million by the end of 1986.

FMC provides us with an example of a successful debt recapitalization. By the end of 1990, FMC had reduced its debt level substantially and had a positive net worth (book value). FMC outperformed the S&P 500 for almost 10 years following its debt recapitalization.

Source: "FMC Corporation Board Approves Recapitalization Plan," *Wall Street Journal* (February 24, 1986); for the company's announcement of this event and the information we discuss in this paragraph, see Rudin (1987); Rudin, B., "Pension Surplus Lightens FMC Debt Load," *Crain's Chicago Business* (October 26, 1987), p. 38. For a discussion of FMC's post-debt recapitalization performance, see "FMC Corp: It Learns That There Can Be Life After Leverage," *Barron's* vol. 70, no. 18 (April 30, 1990), pp. 41–42.

Another type of financial restructuring is a stock repurchase. **Stock repurchases** are a form of dividend because cash is distributed to the shareholders if they sell their stock back to the company. The stock repurchase does not harm shareholders who do not sell their stock as long as the company does not overpay for the stock it repurchases. If the company has more cash and cash flows than profitable

---

[12] See Jensen (1986); Jensen, M. C., "Agency Costs of Free Cash Flow, Corporate Finance, and Takeovers," *American Economic Review* 2 (1986), pp. 323–329.

investment opportunities, that cash may be worth more to the shareholders if the managers distribute it back to shareholders rather than retaining it in the company. An announced stock repurchase plan that buys back the corporation's shares systematically over time can create value for shareholders if the likely alternative is one in which management will reinvest operating cash flows in negative net present value (NPV) projects. Of course, if the managers have great investment opportunities (positive NPV projects), stockholders would rather have management reinvest the cash instead of paying it out. Managers typically value their companies when contemplating a stock repurchase to see how their valuation compares to the company's market valuation. They are more likely to engage in share repurchases when they believe their shares are undervalued. On average, companies that announce leverage-increasing restructuring activities experience positive excess stock returns. Companies that announce leverage-decreasing restructuring activities, on average, experience negative excess stock returns.[13]

Raising Capital

The ability to raise capital is a characteristic of any capitalism-based economy.[14] A company has a variety of different sources it can access to raise capital. Capital can come from both private and public sources, and capital can come in the form of debt, equity, or a security that is a hybrid of the two. For example, a company can raise debt capital from private sources (such as a loan from a bank or consortium of banks), or it can raise private equity capital (such as **preferred** or **common stock** from different types of **private equity** investors). Private equity providers include **venture capitalists**, **angel investors**, **LBO sponsors**, and **mezzanine financing funds**. Of course, companies can also issue debt, preferred stock, or equity in the public markets.

The role of valuation models is important when a company raises long-term capital, particularly with equity instruments or instruments that are part debt and part equity. Similar to their role in financial restructuring activities, valuation models measure the effects of raising capital on the value of the firm and, more importantly, serve as a basis for determining the price of the new capital. Valuations help ensure that a firm does not issue new securities below their fair value, which would harm the company's existing claimholders.

Venture capital funds are a source of private equity (both common and preferred) and sometimes debt. The security issued in about 80% of venture capital investments is convertible preferred stock. Companies typically go to venture capital funds for capital when the company is young. For even younger companies, angel investors are more likely to be the very initial sources of funding. Both angel investors and venture capitalists demand very high expected rates of return, so they are an expensive source of capital. However, since angel investors and venture capitalists generally invest in very risky ventures, it is not surprising that these investors demand high expected rates of return. Venture capital funds are typically short lived, so the venture capitalist who raises the fund usually wants to exit investments the fund makes within five years. Two ways for the venture capital fund to exit an investment are to sell the company to another investor or to have the company issue stock in public markets, called **going public**.

LBO funds are another form of private equity. Many LBO transactions involve public companies or subsidiaries of public companies that are taken private. However, LBO transactions can also involve companies that are already private. As discussed previously, LBO transactions are financed with extensive amounts of debt. The amount of debt in a particular transaction will be a function of the credit markets at the time of the transaction, the magnitude and stability of the company's cash flows, and the quality of the company's assets.

An **initial public offering (IPO)** occurs when a company issues stock in publicly traded markets for the first time. If the company is issuing new shares of stock, the offering is called a **primary offering**, and the company receives the proceeds of the transaction. If the company's initial investors are selling

---

[13] For research on these topics, see Dan and Mikkelson (1984) and Masulis (1980, 1981); Dan, L. Y., and W. H. Mikkelson, "Convertible Debt Issuance, Capital Structure Change and Financing-Related Information: Some New Evidence," *Journal of Financial Economics* vol. 13, no. 2 (1984), pp. 157–186; Masulis, R. W., "The Effects of Capital Structure Change on Security Prices: A Study of Exchange Offers," *Journal of Financial Economics* vol. 8, no. 2 (1980), pp. 139–177; Masulis, R. W., "The Impact of Capital Structure Change on Firm Value: Some Estimates," *Journal of Finance* vol. 38, no. 1 (1983), pp. 107–126; Vermaelen, T., "Common Stock Repurchases and Market Signaling: An Empirical Study," *Journal of Financial Economics* vol. 9, no. 2 (1981), pp. 138–183.

[14] Rajan and Zingales (2003) discuss this issue thoroughly in Rajan, R., and L. Zingales, *Saving Capitalism from the Capitalists: Unleashing the Power of Financial Markets to Create Wealth and Spread Opportunity*, Crown Publications (2003).

some or all of their stock (such as a venture capital fund or management), the offering is called a **secondary offering**, and in this case, the proceeds of the offering go to the selling shareholders. Regardless of whether this is a primary or secondary offering (or a combination of both), shareholders want to make sure that they are receiving fair value for giving up some of their proportionate ownership in the enterprise. In addition to a source of capital, going public provides a source of liquidity for a company's stock. Highly liquid stock can sometimes act like a form of currency for a company, which can be valuable to its investors as well as to employees who have **employee stock options** or hold other equity claims on the company. Valuation models naturally play a role in setting prices any time a company goes public. The **underwriters** shop the issue to various investors to assess the demand for the shares at various prices. The assessed supply and demand determines the final price at which the company issues its shares. Historically, the issue price undervalues the shares by, on average, close to 19%, as measured by the price one day after the issue. Over the longer term, however, IPO stocks do not perform as well as a control group of stocks. We observe these results for both U.S. and non-U.S. IPOs.[15]

Strategic Analysis and Value-Based Management

Companies use a strategic process to continually revise existing strategies and to develop new strategies, strategic plans, and tactics. They execute their strategic plans and tactics to create value. Valuation models use forecasts from alternative strategic plans and other information to measure the effect of different strategies on the value of the firm. Companies can use valuation models to make many decisions beyond strategic decisions, such as deciding whether to invest in certain projects.

Strategic analysis attempts to identify a company's value-maximizing business strategy. The process involves evaluating the businesses that a firm does or can operate and how it can best organize itself to compete in those respective markets. One element of strategic analysis is to perform a valuation analysis of the feasible alternative strategic initiatives to determine which of the alternative business strategies creates the most shareholder value. Managers then look at the valuation implications of the various strategies as well as the risks inherent in each in order to determine the best path for the company to pursue.

Value-based management is one of many terms that describes how a company can operate all aspects of its business and make all management decisions based on the effect its decisions have on shareholder value. While this entails viewing M&A activity, restructurings, and strategic analysis within the framework of shareholder value creation, it also implies using valuation models to capture how all decisions affect value. Value-based management entails providing all levels of management with sufficient information so that they can begin to examine the valuation consequences of their actions and to provide them with incentives to choose the alternatives that increase value. In many organizations, lower-level and mid-level managers are given incentives to focus solely on earnings or earnings-based measures and not on measures that consider the necessary investments, the risk of those investments, and the timing of cash flows associated with such decisions. Value-based management systems attempt to provide managers with incentives to maximize shareholder value.[16] The distinguishing feature of a value-based management process is its more formalized and rigorous analysis of the valuation effects of a multitude of decisions and its direct compensation of management based on the value created.[17] A requirement for a value-based management process is a valuation model that is based on the company's specific inputs and outputs. This requirement provides a distinct role for valuation models.

Contracts Between a Company and Its Investors and Employees

A company begins with a contract between the company and its shareholders and perhaps just between the founders at the outset. A company has contracts with every type of investor from whom it raises capital, which could be another company, some other legal entity, or a single individual. Companies also have contracts with their employees. Many of these contracts, especially the contracts of a privately held company, require a valuation of the company to be conducted from time to time.

---

[15] See Ritter and Welch (2002) for a review of the research on IPOs; Ritter, J. R., and I. Welch, "A Review of IPO Activity, Pricing, and Allocations," *Journal of Finance* vol. LVII, no. 4 (August 2002), pp. 1795–1828.

[16] See Martin and Petty (2000) for a detailed discussion of value-based management; Martin, J. D., and J. W. Petty, *Value Based Management: The Corporate Response to the Shareholder Revolution*, Harvard Business School Press (2000).

[17] While we show and discuss the strategy development as a step-by-step linear process, it is actually a dynamic, continually evolving process.

Privately held companies often have a buy/sell agreement. The buy/sell agreement identifies the conditions under which the equity of the company can be bought or sold and at what price; or it delineates the method used to measure this price. Similarly, privately held companies with an employee stock ownership plan (ESOP) or some type of stock option or incentive compensation plan (based on the value of the firm) must conduct a valuation of the company, usually annually, so employees leaving the company can receive the value of their holdings in the ESOP or the value of their stock options. Even publicly traded companies sometimes provide incentives for division managers with compensation schemes based on the value of the separate divisions, meaning valuations of the separate divisions must be conducted from time to time. Sometimes publicly traded companies create a **special purpose entity (SPE)** in order to isolate certain assets for securitization or self-insurance, to manage risk, or to allocate capital. These SPEs often require a valuation of certain claims or assets of a company.[18]

Regulatory and Legal Uses of Valuation

Governments sometimes sell off government-owned businesses in the process of **privatization**. Governments use valuation models to assess the value of the government-owned businesses to be sold. Regulatory agencies regularly set allowed rates of return in regulated industries based on a company's cost of capital. Sometimes income tax authorities, such as the Internal Revenue Service (IRS) in the United States, base the amount of taxes owed by a taxpayer on the value of assets. This occurs when someone dies and an estate must pay taxes on the value of the decedent's estate at the time of death. Sometimes in an acquisition, a company will be forced to divest of certain assets in order to cure an antitrust issue with an antitrust enforcement agency. In this case, the company will use valuation models to find the cure that maximizes the value of the entity post-transaction.

Courts also rely on valuations when ruling on damages in lawsuits that involve companies. In many of these cases, damages equal the loss in firm value that results from the alleged actions of the defendant. Lawsuits in which damage assessments are likely to rely on a valuation model include those involving patent infringements, theft of trade secrets, business disparagement, breach of contract, appraisal of the value of a merger, and misrepresentation in the purchase of a business or security, among many others.

Identifying Over- and Undervalued Securities

Some investors use valuation models to measure a company's **fundamental value** based on their expectations of the business. They then compare the fundamental value to the price of the company on the stock market in order to identify whether the company is undervalued or overvalued. These investors then take portfolio positions that they hope will yield superior returns. Whether an investor can "beat the market"—that is, earn returns on a portfolio that exceed the returns the market would expect for that portfolio given its risk—depends on how good that individual's valuations are relative to the market's valuations and whether the market subsequently learns information that is consistent with the investor's insights.[19] While we do not discuss portfolio management in this book, the valuation methods we discuss can be used in investment management in order to determine what companies to buy, sell, or sell short. At present, billions of dollars are invested in U.S. investment funds alone that base their portfolio decisions on the valuation models we present in this book.

Some funds that are relatively passive in terms of what securities they hold (such as a fund that holds a broad-based index, like the S&P 500) look for companies in their portfolios that they believe are run inefficiently. They then work with management of these companies, showing them how more value could be created relative to the current operations of these companies. This analysis relies on the valuation models we discuss at length in the book. CalPERS (California Public Employees Retirement System), among others, manages one of the largest public pension funds and has used this technique since the 1980s.

---

[18] See Culp and Niskanen (2003), especially Chapter II-1, for a discussion of SPEs and the use and alleged misuse of SPEs by Enron Corporation; Culp, C., and W. A. Niskanen, editors, *Public Policy Implications of the Enron Failure*, CATO Institute (2003).

[19] See Fama (1994, 1998) for a discussion of the **efficient markets hypothesis**; Fama, G., "Efficient Markets: II," Fiftieth Anniversary Invited Paper, *Journal of Finance*, 46 (December 1991), p. 1575–1617. Fama, G., "Market Efficiency, Long-Term Returns, and Behavioral Finance," *Journal of Financial Economics* 49 (September 1998), pp. 283–306.

1.8 AN OVERVIEW OF THE VALUATION PROCESS

The implementation of any valuation process involves completing a series of specific steps. Some of these steps must be completed in a certain order, while others need not be. The process varies somewhat as a function of the type of company as well as the reason for performing the valuation. Here, we describe one approach to organizing the steps in a valuation. We summarize this overview of the valuation process below and in Exhibit 1.3.

EXHIBIT 1.3   An Overview of the Steps in a Typical Company Valuation
1 Identify the company's direct, indirect, and potential competitors
2 Analyze historical performance, strategy, and sources of competitive advantage
3 Calculate the value of the firm and equity using one of the forms of the discounted cash flow valuation model or excess flow model
• Forecast financial statements and free cash flows
• Measure the business risk of the company and costs of capital
4 Calculate the value of the firm and its common equity using market multiple valuation methods
• Using publicly traded companies
• Using comparable transactions (if applicable)
5 Consider alternative valuation methods such as a leveraged buyout analysis

An early step in any valuation is identifying the company's key competitors, which we designate as being the first step. This step entails identifying the firm's lines of business and then identifying both key competitors and potential competitors for each line of business. Potential competitors include firms that sell similar products in a different geographic area—but could potentially enter the company's geographic area—and companies that might choose to enter a particular line of business. In addition, other firms selling products that the company is thinking of selling are also potential competitors. Finally, firms that sell products that are quite different but have some of the same functionality (e.g., oil and propane gas) may be key competitors as well.

In the second step, when possible, we analyze the past performance of the company and its competitors using historical financials. We also identify the strategy of the company and its competitors in an effort to establish the sources of competitive advantage for each company, and then we determine if the identified sources of competitive advantage are detectable in the historical data. Once the sources of competitive advantage are identified, we determine the extent to which that competitive advantage is sustainable, and—if it is sustainable—for how long.

In the third step, we calculate the value of the firm using one of the forms of the DCF valuation model or excess flow model. For both the DCF and excess flow methods, there are alternative forms of each method, so some thought regarding which is the best alternative is necessary. We often measure the continuing value using the cash flow perpetuity model or, in some valuation contexts, we use a market multiple valuation. Once we analyze the historical performance and sustainability of any identified competitive advantage, we create forecasts of the financial statements and free cash flows and test the reasonableness of those forecasts. These forecasts take economic and industry-specific trends into consideration. To the extent there are important embedded options to consider, the forecasts must consider how to embed those option-like features or how to measure the value of these features separately. As part of this valuation, we also measure the company's business risk and costs of capital. Estimating the company's cost of capital normally relies on data from the company and from relevant comparable companies. Estimating the company's equity cost of capital normally includes implementing a model of how assets are priced, such as the **Capital Asset Pricing Model (CAPM)**, and how the company's financial structure affects its cost of capital. This step includes collecting data on the company being valued and its comparables, choosing an asset pricing model, and implementing the asset pricing model.

Next, in step four, we measure the company's value using a market multiple valuation method. This step involves choosing comparable companies appropriate for both the method and the company being valued, choosing the specific multiples to use, adjusting the financial statements of the companies (if the multiples are based on information in the financial statements), measuring the multiples—both numerator and denominator—for each comparable company, choosing the value or range of values for each multiple, and using the multiples to measure the value of the company and its common equity. If there is potential value in the options available to the company, that option value has to be added to the market multiple valuation, or we have to choose comparable companies with the same options in order to embed that value in the measured multiples.

Finally, we consider whether any other valuation methods are appropriate to use. For example, we might consider the value of the firm in an LBO transaction. In this analysis, we use our projections of cash flows that the company would generate if it did an LBO, determine the most advantageous capital structure possible given credit market conditions and characteristics of the company, and value the company as an LBO transaction based on the required rates of return for its different claimholders. Alternatively, we might consider breaking up or liquidating the company.

SUMMARY AND KEY CONCEPTS

This chapter has provided an overview of the valuation process and the basic valuation models that are commonly used in it, including discounted cash flow, discounted excess flow, market multiples, LBO transaction analysis, and the option pricing framework. In addition, we have discussed the economic balance sheet and the sources of value for a company, including the value of its operations, excess assets, and the value from financing.

In this chapter we have discussed a variety of decision contexts in which valuations are used, both in transactions analysis and with respect to internal decisions within a firm. Further, we have discussed how managers use these valuation methods in their decisions.

This book explores all of the valuation methods discussed in this chapter in detail and gives specific guidance on how to obtain the relevant data necessary in order to implement the models discussed.

ADDITIONAL READING AND REFERENCES

Coase, R., "The Nature of the Firm," *Economica* 4 (1937), pp. 386–405.
Jensen, M. C., "Agency Costs of Free Cash Flow, Corporate Finance, and Takeovers," *American Economic Review* 2 (1986), pp. 323–329.

EXERCISES AND PROBLEMS

P1.1   Review Apple Inc.'s (Apple) financial statements in Exhibit 1.2 and its excess assets and valuation in Section 1.3. Prepare an economic balance sheet for Apple similar to the economic balance sheet in Exhibit 1.1. Discuss potential reasons for the differences between the values on the economic balance sheet and Apple's financial statements.

P1.2   Review Apple Inc.'s (Apple) financial statements and free cash flows in Exhibit 1.2. Explain, with as much detail as possible based on the information in this exhibit, why the expected free cash flow for 2012 of $20,277 decreased relative to Apple's actual free cash flow of $25,272 in 2011.

P1.3   A company has expected free cash flows of $1.45 million, $2.93 million, and $3.2 million in the next three years. Beginning in Year 4, the expected cash flows will grow by 3% in perpetuity. Measure the value of this company as of today using both a 10% and 12% discount rate.

P1.4   A company has expected free cash flows of $1.45 million, $2.93 million, and $3.2 million in the next three years. Beginning in Year 4, the expected cash flows will grow (or decrease) by −5% in perpetuity. Measure the value of this company as of today using a both 10% and 12% discount rate.

P1.5   Compare and discuss the valuations in the previous two problems.

P1.6   A company has expected cash flows of $1.85 million, $2.25 million, and $2.92 million in the next three years. For Years 4 through 10, the free cash flows will grow by 6% annually. Beginning in Year 11, the expected cash flows will grow by 3% in perpetuity. Measure the value of this company as of today using both a 10% and 12% discount rate.

P1.7   Review Exhibit P1.1 for Frits Seegers Inc. and measure the free cash flow for Seegers for Year 0 and six years of forecasts (Year +1 to Year +6) shown. The company does not hold any excess cash, so the change in the cash balance is equal to the change in required cash. The change in Retained Earnings in a year is equal to the company's net income minus the dividends declared by the company in that year. Discuss the major factors that caused the free cash flows to change from year to year.

P1.8   Value Frits Seegers Inc. as of the end of Year 0 using the information in Exhibit P1.1 and a 13% risk-adjusted discount rate.

EXHIBIT P1.1 Frits Seegers, Inc. Financial Statement—Actual and Forecasts

FRITS SEEGERS INC.
Income Statement and Balance Sheet Forecasts
(for the years ended December 31)

	Actual		Forecast					
	Year -1	Year 0	Year 1	Year 2	Year 3	Year 4	Year 5	Year 6
Income Statement								
Revenue	$1,000.0	$1,100.0	$1,650.0	$2,310.0	$3,003.0	$3,303.3	$3,402.4	$3,504.5
Cost of goods sold.	−610.0	−671.0	−1,006.5	−1,409.1	−1,831.8	−2,015.0	−2,075.5	−2,137.7
Gross margin	$ 390.0	$ 429.0	$ 643.5	$ 900.9	$1,171.2	$1,288.3	$1,326.9	$1,366.7
Selling, general & administrative . . .	−120.0	−132.0	−198.0	−277.2	−360.4	−396.4	−408.3	−420.5
Operating income.	$ 270.0	$ 297.0	$ 445.5	$ 623.7	$ 810.8	$ 891.9	$ 918.6	$ 946.2
Interest expense.	−77.0	−96.0	−112.0	−128.0	−136.0	−144.0	−152.0	−160.0
Income before taxes.	$ 193.0	$ 201.0	$ 333.5	$ 495.7	$ 674.8	$ 747.9	$ 766.6	$ 786.2
Income tax expense.	−77.2	−80.4	−133.4	−198.3	−269.9	−299.2	−306.7	−314.5
Net income.	$ 115.8	$ 120.6	$ 200.1	$ 297.4	$ 404.9	$ 448.7	$ 460.0	$ 471.7
Balance Sheet								
Cash balance	$ 50.0	$ 55.0	$ 82.5	$ 115.5	$ 150.2	$ 165.2	$ 170.1	$ 175.2
Accounts receivable.	166.7	183.3	275.0	385.0	500.5	550.6	567.1	584.1
Inventory.	118.6	130.5	195.7	274.0	356.2	391.8	403.6	415.7
Total current assets	$ 335.3	$ 368.8	$ 553.2	$ 774.5	$1,006.8	$1,107.5	$1,140.7	$1,175.0
Land.	1,550.0	1,825.0	2,155.0	2,501.5	2,651.7	2,701.2	2,752.2	2,804.8
Total assets.	$1,885.3	$2,193.8	$2,708.2	$3,276.0	$3,658.5	$3,808.7	$3,893.0	$3,979.8
Accounts payable.	$ 50.8	$ 55.9	$ 83.9	$ 117.4	$ 152.7	$ 167.9	$ 173.0	$ 178.1
Other current operating liabilities . . .	35.0	38.5	57.8	80.9	105.1	115.6	119.1	122.7
Total current liabilities.	$ 85.8	$ 94.4	$ 141.6	$ 198.3	$ 257.8	$ 283.5	$ 292.0	$ 300.8
Debt	1,200.0	1,400.0	1,600.0	1,700.0	1,800.0	1,900.0	2,000.0	2,100.0
Total liabilities.	$1,285.8	$1,494.4	$1,741.6	$1,898.3	$2,057.8	$2,183.5	$2,292.0	$2,400.8
Common stock.	$ 383.6	$ 383.6	$ 450.7	$ 564.5	$ 564.5	$ 564.5	$ 564.5	$ 564.5
Retained earnings	215.8	315.7	515.8	813.3	1,036.3	1,060.7	1,036.5	1,014.5
Total shareholders equity	$ 599.4	$ 699.4	$ 966.6	$1,377.7	$1,600.7	$1,625.2	$1,600.9	$1,579.0
Total liabilities and equities.	$1,885.3	$2,193.8	$2,708.2	$3,276.0	$3,658.5	$3,808.7	$3,893.0	$3,979.8

Exhibit may contain small rounding errors

SOLUTIONS FOR REVIEW EXERCISES

Solution for Review Exercise 1.1: The Market Value Company Economic Balance Sheet

We have sufficient information to value the claims on the company's resources. The company's share price is $12.08 and it has 1,200 shares outstanding or an equity value of $14,496. Its debt is trading at a premium indicating that its market value is equal to 102% of its book value or $5,304. The resulting value of the firm is $19,800. From that amount we subtract the value of the excess asset, land valued at $3,000, and the value created from debt financing, $3,800, to measure the value of the unlevered operations, $13,000.

THE MARKET VALUE COMPANY Economic Balance Sheet	
Economic Balance Sheet—Resources/Assets	
Value of the unlevered business operations without excess assets	$13,000.0
Value of the excess assets	3,000.0
Value of the unlevered firm	$16,000.0
Value created from financing	3,800.0
Value of the firm	$19,800.0
Economic Balance Sheet—Claims on Resources	
Value of debt	$ 5,304.0
Value of equity	14,496.0
Value of securities issued	$19,800.0

Solution for Review Exercise 1.2: The Market Value Company Unlevered Free Cash Flow

We show the calculation of the unlevered free cash flow below. Notice that the unlevered free cash flow is negative. The negative free cash flow occurred not because the company was unprofitable but because the company invested more cash than it generated. Note that the Capital Expenditures equal the change in the Net Property, Plant and Equipment plus the Depreciation Expense for the Year.

THE MARKET VALUE COMPANY Free Cash Flow Forecasts	
Earnings before interest and taxes (EBIT)	$1,621.0
− Income taxes paid on EBIT	−616.0
Earnings before interest and after taxes	$1,005.0
+ Depreciation	500.0
− Change in accounts receivable	−57.1
− Change in inventory	−28.7
+ Change in accounts payable	12.3
+ Change in current other liabilities	12.0
− Change in required cash balance	−17.1
Unlevered cash flow from operations	$1,426.4
− Capital expenditures	1,528.1
Unlevered free cash flow	$ −101.7

Solution for Review Exercise 1.3: Valuation of Unlevered Free Cash Flows

We show the calculation of the value of the unlevered free cash flows below.

Cost of capital		12.0%
Growth rate for free cash flow for continuing value		2.0%

($ in millions)	Year 0	Year 1	Year 2	Year 3	CV_{Firm} Year 3
Unlevered free cash flow for continuing value (CV)					$ 123.22
Discount factor for continuing value					10.000
Unlevered free cash flow and CV		$100.20	$114.00	$120.80	$1,232.16
Discount factor		0.893	0.797	0.712	0.712
Present value		$ 89.46	$ 90.88	$ 85.98	$ 877.03
Value of the firm	$1,143.35				
		FCFg =	13.8%	6.0%	2.0%

Exhibit may contain small rounding errors.

After mastering the material in this chapter, you will be able to:

1. Know how to access information, identify competitors, and use financial statement analysis in valuation (2.1–2.3)

2. Measure the performance of a company using rates of return (2.5–2.7, 2.9, 2.14)

3. Examine a company's asset utilization and working capital management (2.8, 2.10)

4. Analyze a company's fixed assets and financial leverage (2.11–2.13)

5. Assess a company's competitive advantage (2.15)

6. Describe measurement and implementation techniques (2.16)

Financial Statement Analysis

Bloomberg provides various financial ratios as part of its database services. Below, we show a sample of the financial ratios Bloomberg reports for Dell Inc. (Dell) and Hewlett-Packard Company (HP) as reported on August 10, 2011. In this chapter, we

BLOOMBERG

will learn how to measure ratios like these and how we use these ratios in valuation work. Although Dell and HP are direct competitors, some of their financial ratios are not similar. The financial ratios for Dell and HP highlight how a company might not be a good comparable for a particular valuation analysis even though it is a direct competitor. Choosing comparable companies is just one important use of financial statement analysis in valuation work.[1]

	Dell Inc.					Hewlett-Packard Company				
	2006	2007	2008	2009	2010	2006	2007	2008	2009	2010
Profitability Ratios										
Gross margin	18%	17%	19%	18%	18%	24%	24%	24%	24%	24%
Operating margin	8%	5%	6%	5%	4%	7%	9%	9%	10%	10%
Profit margin	6%	4%	5%	4%	3%	7%	7%	7%	7%	7%
Return on assets	16%	11%	11%	9%	5%	8%	9%	8%	7%	7%
Return on common equity	68%	62%	73%	62%	29%	16%	19%	22%	19%	22%
Return on capital	62%	53%	63%	48%	19%	15%	17%	17%	14%	15%
Activity Ratios										
Days to sell inventory	4.2	4.7	6.8	7.4	8.0	38.4	36.5	32.5	29.2	23.9
Days to collect accounts receivable	32.8	36.8	41.2	42.1	51.6	51.3	51.2	54.4	61.3	58.9
Asset turnover	2.4	2.3	2.3	2.3	1.8	1.2	1.2	1.2	1.0	1.1
Debt Factors and Leverage										
Total debt to total assets	3.0	3.0	2.1	7.6	12.1	6.3	9.2	15.8	13.8	17.9
Total debt to common equity	17.0	17.5	15.7	47.1	72.3	13.6	21.2	45.8	39.1	54.7
Total debt to EBITDA	0.1	0.2	0.1	0.5	1.3	0.6	0.7	1.3	1.0	1.3
Assets/Equity	5.7	5.9	7.4	6.2	6.0	2.1	2.3	2.9	2.8	3.1
Net debt to shareholders equity	−207.1	−220.4	−197.7	−165.8	−122.8	−29.4	−8.5	19.5	6.2	27.9
Liquidity Analysis										
Cash ratio	0.6	0.6	0.6	0.6	0.6	0.5	0.3	0.2	0.3	0.2
Quick ratio	0.9	0.9	0.9	0.9	0.9	0.8	0.7	0.6	0.8	0.7
Current ratio	1.1	1.1	1.1	1.1	1.1	1.3	1.2	1.0	1.2	1.1
Inventory to cash–days	37.0	37.0	37.0	37.0	37.0	89.8	87.7	86.8	90.5	82.8
Growth										
Sales growth	13%	3%	6%	0%	−13%	6%	14%	13%	−3%	10%
EBITDA growth	4%	−26%	17%	−4%	−24%	25%	32%	18%	11%	12%
Net income growth	18%	−28%	14%	−16%	−42%	158%	17%	15%	−8%	14%

In this chapter, we explore how to analyze financial statements and how that analysis is used in valuation.

---

[1] Bloomberg L. P. provides a dynamic network of delivering data, news, and analytics through various access platforms; see http://www.bloomberg.com/company/#menu for more information and a description of the company, its products, and its services.

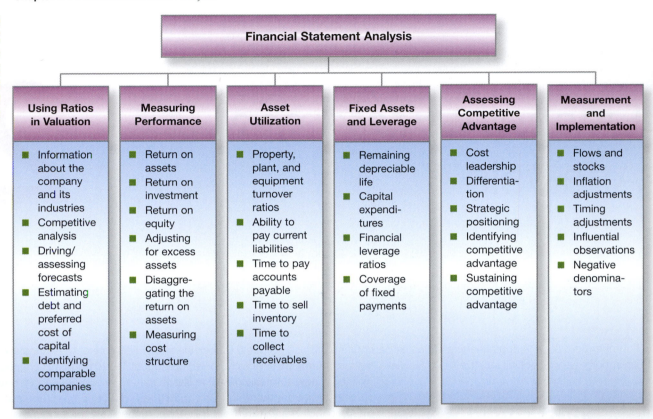

INTRODUCTION

Financial statement relations, or **financial ratios**, are ratios of various financial statement items that attempt to measure certain economic concepts. These economic concepts include such characteristics as a company's operating performance, operating risk, financial risk, growth, efficiency, and asset utilization. We typically use financial ratios to analyze a company relative to its competition and relative to itself over time. We use ratios rather than the numbers in the financial statements directly because we typically need to control for the scale or size of the company before we can make comparisons with other companies or even with the same company over time. For example, instead of comparing operating income as it is reported in the income statement, we compare operating income scaled (divided) by some other financial statement number that reflects the scale of the company, such as the company's sales or assets. Sometimes, we use non-accounting information when calculating financial relations as an alternative way to adjust for scale, such as number of employees, number of stores (or the square feet of retail space), or number of tons of output.

In this chapter, we discuss how to measure and use financial ratios. We begin with a discussion of the ways to use financial ratios when valuing a company. We then focus on accounting-based rates of return, which are a type of financial ratio. It is important to understand that while we use financial ratios as proxies for certain economic concepts, they are, by their nature, accounting-based ratios, not market-based ratios, and therefore are imprecise measures of those economic concepts. However, they are often the best measures available, and we know from scholarly research that these financial ratios contain useful information. We choose the definition and measurement of specific financial ratios to fit the context of our analysis.

We continue our discussion by showing how to decompose accounting-based rates of return into their components and then by discussing ways we can analyze a company's working capital management, fixed assets structure, and capital expenditures. We often use these types of financial ratios as drivers (assumptions) in a financial model used to forecast a company's financial statements and free cash flows. We also discuss how to analyze a company's leverage and financial risk as well as how to use its financial statement information in combination with information not reported directly in its financial statements.

Analyzing the financial statements of a company and its competitors entails the following steps. First, we examine the businesses in which the company operates to identify its potential competitors and potential comparable companies. Second, we analyze all of the companies' financial statements and adjust them for potential distortions due to differences in accounting techniques and estimates, excess assets, the structuring of certain types of transactions (for example, leases), and any other potential distortions. Third, we qualitatively assess whether any of the companies has a potential competitive advantage. We then analyze the companies quantitatively using financial ratios and other performance metrics to determine how the performance amongst the companies has changed over time and the extent to which our assessments of competitive advantage are observable. Finally, we use our analysis to guide our forecasts, choose comparable companies to measure various costs of capital, and choose comparable companies as the basis to estimate market multiples.

2.1 SOURCES OF INFORMATION

Naturally, we need to collect a substantial amount of information in order to analyze a company and its industry. In this section, we discuss the sources of such information. We analyze information on the industry, the company, its actual and potential competitors, other potential comparable companies, and even its suppliers and customers.

LO1 Know how to access information, identify competitors, and use financial statement analysis in valuation

Information About a Company

Many company websites, especially for publicly traded companies, are a very rich source of information (for example, in the investor relations section of the website). Companies often provide access to the company's annual and quarterly reports, earnings announcements, government-filed reports, press releases, conference calls, and information on annual meetings with shareholders (typically transcripts or recordings of important speeches and/or question-and-answer sessions with stockholders). A company's annual and quarterly reports contain, in addition to company financial statements, information about the company's history, operations, operating segments, competition, and more. A company will also issue a press release soon after a significant event occurs. Even privately held companies, which have no public disclosure requirements, often have a substantial amount of information available on their websites.

Even if a company does not have a website (a rarity, to be sure), publicly owned companies have to file financials and other reports with the government. For example, in the United States, publicly traded companies must file annual reports (Form 10-K) and quarterly reports (Form 10-Q) with the U.S. Securities and Exchange Commission (SEC). A company must file its 10-K reports within 90 days of its fiscal year-end and its 10-Q reports within 45 days of each quarter's end. These reports contain extensive information about a company, including some (limited) information on its industries and major customers. Companies must also file a report with the SEC when a significant event occurs for the company (Form 8-K), when it notifies shareholders of a shareholders' meeting (a **proxy statement**), when it proposes to issue certain types of securities (a **registration statement**), and for a variety of other events or circumstances. All of these public filings are available on the SEC's EDGAR website.[2] In addition to filing reports with the SEC, companies often must (or choose to) file reports with government agencies. For example, the Department of Transportation requires airline and commercial trucking companies to file certain reports with it. Banks and other financial institutions also must file with other various government agencies.

In almost all countries, there are filing requirements that companies must meet in order to be listed on an exchange. **Foreign private issuers** (foreign companies listed on U.S. securities exchanges) generally file **Form 20-F** as both a registration statement and an annual report. The Form 20-F report is similar in content to the S-1 registration statement and 10-K annual report filed by U.S. companies.

According to U.S. generally accepted accounting principles (GAAP), companies must report certain (limited) accounting information—for example, revenues, operating assets, and operating incomes—for each of their operating segments.[3] According to U.S. GAAP, an operating segment is a part of a com-

---

[2] The SEC's EDGAR website contains all public filings of U.S. listed companies. It can be found at http://www.sec.gov/edgar.shtml.

[3] See Financial Accounting Standards Board, Statement of Financial Accounting Standards No. 131, "Disclosures About Segments of an Enterprise and Related Information," June 1997.

pany for which separate financial information is made available and evaluated by management, and that accounts for 10% or more of the company's revenues. The information reported should be the same as the information used internally for decision-making. Operating segments are typically of two types: industry segments and geographic segments. U.S. GAAP also requires companies to disclose their major customers, generally defined as customers who purchase 10% or more of the company's good and services. Operating segment information can be useful when valuing a company. However, detailed publicly available information is usually quite limited, and we generally need information not available to the public in order to analyze a segment in detail.

Other sources of information include stock reports and financial analyst reports. Stock reports—such as the *Standard & Poor's Stock Reports* (two-page company summaries)—contain financial and other summary information for publicly traded companies in a quickly accessible and usable form. Analyst reports provide a wealth of information on the companies analysts follow and often include information about important competitors for a given company. Companies often list the analysts who write reports on them on their websites, and these analysts are also listed in certain publications (*Nelson's Directory of Investment Research*).

We typically classify an analyst as either a sell-side analyst, a buy-side analyst, or an independent research analyst. **Sell-side analysts** work for brokerage companies and make recommendations that brokers use to advise clients on sales and purchases of securities. **Buy-side analysts** work for investment management companies and advise portfolio managers on the stocks they might purchase or sell. **Independent research analysts** work for companies that sell analyst reports to investors. Of course, analysts obtain much of their information from the management and financial statements of companies. Although analysts are likely to be more objective than managers are, we know that analysts are, on average, optimistic.[4]

The financial press (newspapers, magazines, periodicals, and news websites), financial websites, stock exchanges, and certain services also provide information on companies. Articles in the financial press sometimes serve to collect and summarize information from a variety of sources (the company, its management, financial analysts, reports filed with the government, etc.). Financial websites such as Hoover's Inc., Google Finance, and Yahoo! Finance provide information about companies and their competitors in much the same way some stock reports do. Many stock exchanges provide information on the companies that have securities that trade on that stock exchange. Some companies—for example, Thomson Reuters, Bloomberg, and Morningstar—provide information on a company as well as conduct analyses using that information.

Large archival databases are another source of individual company information. For example, the Center for Research in Security Prices at the University of Chicago has a comprehensive database of U.S. stock market data. Standard & Poor's Compustat® is a standardized database containing accounting and some market data. Datastream and other databases provide financial statement and stock price information on companies all over the globe. Such databases allow one to investigate a company and its industry in a variety of ways. Wharton's Research Data Services (WRDS) from the Wharton School at the University of Pennsylvania provides convenient access to many databases with a web-based interface.

Information About an Industry

We also have extensive information available on industries. First, companies often disclose information on the industries in which they operate in their 10-K reports and in annual reports to shareholders. Many financial analysts specialize in certain industries and write industry reports as well as individual company reports. Some companies also issue reports containing information on an industry—for example, *Standard & Poor's Industry Surveys*. Industry financial ratios are also made available in some of these publications. Most large industries have an industry or trade association. Such associations often issue industry or trade magazines that contain information on the industry, including various industry statistics. The financial press and financial websites also contain information about industries.

---

[4] Various research studies document the extent to which analysts are optimistic; see, for example, Lin, H., and M. McNichols, "Underwriting Relationships, Analysts' Earnings Forecasts, and Investment Recommendations," *Journal of Accounting and Economics* 25 (1988), pp. 101–127. This article suggests that such optimism sometimes results from a conflict of interest of (at least sell-side) analysts. As it turns out, in the United States, a number of investment banks settled with federal securities regulators on the issue of conflicts of interests faced by their (sell-side) stock analysts. (See http://www.oag.state.ny.us for a variety of press releases and other documents on this topic.)

Privately Held (Owned) Companies

While we have extensive information available on publicly traded companies, we have substantially less information on privately held companies, unless we have the cooperation of the private company (for example, if we are valuing the company because it is considering an initial public offering). Companies like Dun and Bradstreet, Inc. and Robert Morris Associates collect limited information on privately held companies. There are also databases that provide some limited valuation data on private companies sold in change-of-control transactions.

2.2 HOW WE USE FINANCIAL RATIOS IN VALUATION

Scholarly research has shown that financial ratios contain useful information,[5] which provides empirical justification for their widespread use in valuation and other financial analyses. Generally, when we use financial ratios, we typically compare a company to itself over time—a **time-series analysis**—or to other comparable companies—a **cross-sectional analysis**. We often use both types of analyses at the same time—a combined time-series and cross-sectional analysis. While we often use the financial ratios of competitors as "benchmarks" for the company we are analyzing, we often do not have an absolute "benchmark" for what is a "good" or "bad" value.

While we are getting ahead of ourselves a bit, we illustrate this point using the current ratio—the ratio of a company's current assets to its current liabilities. Most companies have more current assets than current liabilities. We typically observe an average current ratio for a broad set of companies in the range of 1.5 to 2. A higher current ratio suggests a more liquid company. But what is a "good" current ratio? Is a good current ratio below the average or above the average? The answer to that question is, "It depends." A low current ratio might suggest potential financial distress; but, if the company has processes in place that allow it to operate efficiently with a low current ratio (for example, very low inventory levels), then a low current ratio might suggest a source of competitive advantage. For example, Dell had a very low current ratio, and its working capital management techniques were seen as a source of competitive advantage. We face the same benchmarking issue for other types of ratios as well.

Competitive Analysis

Conducting a competitive analysis of a company and its industry provides a general understanding of both the company and its industry as well as an assessment of the company's position within the industry. We normally conduct a competitive analysis early in the process of valuing a company unless we are instructed to rely on forecasts provided to us by others, such as management forecasts. Such an analysis can provide insights into the key value drivers of a company's business and help us identify a company's sources of competitive advantage, if any. A competitive analysis often involves analyzing a company's vision, strategy, and strategic objectives.

Measuring the Debt and Preferred Stock Costs of Capital

The debt and preferred stock costs of capital are important inputs in most valuations. We use them when we unlever a company's equity cost of capital or lever its unlevered cost of capital, and when we measure a company's weighted average cost of capital. Since a company's debt and preferred stock are often not publicly traded, we often cannot measure its debt and preferred stock costs of capital directly from market data. In such cases, we typically measure the debt and preferred stock costs of capital using market data from comparable companies, and we determine the comparability of the companies, in part, using financial ratios.

---

[5] A study that examines accounting-based rates of return directly is Amir, E. and I. Kama, "The Market Reaction to ROCE Components: Implications for Valuation and Financial Statement Analysis," Working Paper, Tel Aviv University, November 2004. Also see the work of Ou, J., and S. Penman, "Financial Statement Analysis and the Prediction of Stock Returns," *Journal of Accounting and Economics* 11 (1989), pp. 295–330; Holthausen, R., and D. Larcker, "The Prediction of Stock Returns Using Financial Statement Information," *Journal of Accounting and Economics* 15 (1992), pp. 373–412; and Abarbanell, J., and B. Bushee, "Abnormal Stock Returns to a Fundamental Analysis Strategy," *Accounting Review* 73 (1998), pp. 19–45.

Preparing (Driving) and Assessing the Reasonableness of Financial Forecasts

We use financial ratios to create or "drive" our forecast, and then we use other financial ratios to assess the reasonableness of our financial forecasts. Naturally, we do not use the same financial ratios to both drive and check the reasonableness of the forecasts. As we discuss in Chapter 4, one of the first steps in creating financial forecasts is to identify factors or "**forecast drivers**" to generate the forecasts. A common type of forecast driver is a growth rate, which may be one of the key factors (drivers) in a financial model. We also use financial ratios, such as expense ratios, as forecast drivers. Turnover ratios (the ratio of an item on the income statement to a balance sheet item—for example, revenue to accounts receivable) are another common type of driver. Once we develop our forecasts, we use other financial ratios to help us assess the reasonableness of our forecasts. For example, we compare the rates of return (return on assets and return on equity) in our forecasts to the historic rates of return of the company, its industry, and its close competitors. We might also use liquidity ratios, asset utilization ratios, and asset composition ratios in a similar manner.

Assessing the Degree of Comparability in Market Multiple Valuation

Financial ratios can be useful in a market multiple valuation when assessing the comparability of the company we are valuing to other companies. We use financial ratios to assess the comparability of profitability, rates of return, cost structures, capital expenditure requirements, growth rates, and business risk. Assessing the comparability of these factors is extremely important in a market multiple valuation.

Constraints and Benchmarks in Contracts

Investors often use financial ratios as either constraints or benchmarks in contracts. For example, debt contracts—and to some extent preferred stock contracts—often utilize financial ratios as constraints, called **covenants**, to protect investors' rights. Investors might require a company to maintain a certain amount of liquidity, limit the amount of debt, or limit dividends by using various financial ratios. If a company violates any of these accounting-based covenants, called a **technical default**, the investors typically get additional rights, such as the right to accelerate the maturity of the debt and possibly charge a higher promised return.[6]

Valuation in Practice 2.1

Example Debt Covenant for Dex Media, Inc. Dex Media, Inc. has debt agreements that require it to maintain a certain amount of earnings before interest, taxes, depreciation, and amortization (EBITDA) relative to its interest payments. We call ratios of this type coverage ratios. It describes one such covenant in its registration statement filed with the SEC so that it could issue additional securities as follows:

> "The loan agreement includes certain financial covenants, including an interest coverage ratio based on EBITDA to interest expense with a minimum ratio of 4.75:1 and a debt to EBITDA ratio of 1.75:1 and other covenants limiting Dex's ability to incur additional debt or liens, pay dividends and make investments."

Source: See its S-1 filing (registration statement for issuing securities), filed with the U.S. SEC on May 14, 2004, see p. F-109, available at: http://www.sec.gov/Archives/edgar/data/1284529/000119312504087990/ds1.htm.

Investors use other contract provisions as well to prohibit the company from selling a significant amount of its assets or merging with another company. Investors also use financial ratios as benchmarks (or hurdles). For example, companies might have to meet certain hurdles described in a debt agreement to

---

[6] See Duke, J., and H. Hunt, III., "An Empirical Examination of Debt Covenant Restrictions and Accounting-Related Debt Proxies," *Journal of Accounting and Economics* vol. 1–3 (January 1990), pp. 45–63; and Press, E., and J. Weintrop, "Accounting-Based Constraints in Public and Private Debt Agreements—Their Association with Leverage and Impact on Accounting Choice," *Journal of Accounting and Economics* vol. 1–3 (January 1990), pp. 65–96.

draw cash from a line-of-credit. Some loans, called performance priced debt, determine the yield spread above U.S. Treasuries or LIBOR the borrower is charged based on accounting performance measures. In addition, companies sometimes use accounting-based measures of performance to compensate managers.

> ## Valuation Key 2.1
>
> We use financial ratios in a variety of ways: to perform a competitive analysis of an industry or of a company within an industry, to assess business risk, to measure the debt and preferred stock costs of capital, to drive and assess the reasonableness of financial forecasts, to assess comparability for a market multiple valuation, and to set constraints or benchmarks in contracts.

2.3 IDENTIFYING A COMPANY'S INDUSTRY AND ITS COMPARABLE COMPANIES

To identify a company's comparable companies, we generally begin by identifying a company's existing direct (or "head-to-head") competitors before identifying indirect and potential competitors. For example, if we were valuing Ford Motor Company (Ford), we would first identify what markets Ford serves. As it turns out, Ford competes in the worldwide auto, truck, financing, insurance, and leasing markets. Identifying Ford's competitors in the auto and truck markets is relatively straightforward. Its competitors in the financing, leasing, and insurance business include a much broader group of companies, ranging from other car manufacturers to numerous financial institutions and insurance companies. As discussed earlier, a good starting point for this analysis is Ford's 10-K report.

In its 10-K, Ford provides information on its market share in the U.S. combined car and truck market as well as for its major competitors. For the year ended December 31, 2010, Ford reported that the top six companies in terms of market share in the combined U.S. auto and truck market were General Motors Corp. (GM), Ford, Chrysler Corporation, Toyota Motor Company (Toyota), Honda Motor Company LTD (Honda), and Hyundai-Kia. Ford provided market share data for each individual company as well as the fact that, together, these six companies had over an 85% share of the defined market. Ford also provided information on the non-U.S. market, information on the countries that are most important to it at the current time, and information on emerging markets that it believes will become more important to it over time. *Standard and Poor's Industry Survey* for Autos and Auto Parts identified over 20 different manufacturers of autos.[7]

As of January 2012, Hoovers (www.hoovers.com) listed over 25 competitors for Ford. That list of competitors included other car manufacturers and such major financial institutions as Bank of America, Citigroup, and J.P. Morgan Chase. Therefore, analyzing a company like Ford requires an analysis of the various markets the company serves and of the competitors in each of those markets. We would also identify any of Ford's indirect competitors and any potential new competitors looming on the horizon.

Indirect competitors would be companies that might affect the profitability of the auto industry but that are not directly in that space. Indirect competition may or may not be important for a company. For example, motorcycle manufacturers are indirect competitors for automobile manufacturers, but they do not have a substantive impact on either the profitability of or the demand for automobiles. Reducing the price of motorcycles would probably have a very small impact on the demand for autos. Economists would say that these two industries have a small cross-elasticity of demand.

While indirect competition from motorcycle manufacturers is not very important for analyzing Ford, potential competition could be very important. Potential competitors from China, India, and South Korea could have a significant effect on the worldwide automotive market over time. Great Wall Automobile Co. of China started selling sport-utility vehicles in Russia in early 2005 at prices that were approximately 35% lower than other Asian imports. Chery Automobile, another Chinese automaker, is exporting to Europe and other locations. Both companies have plans to enter the U.S. market. All of these new or potential competitors, though small now, will likely influence the worldwide automotive industry over time. This potential competition would be important to assess in valuing Ford, as the increased competition may affect Ford's future profitability.

---

[7] See *Standard & Poor's Industry Surveys: Autos and Auto Parts*, December 29, 2011, by Efraim Levy.

Once we have identified a company's competitors, we will use those companies to perform a competitive analysis of the industry and determine which companies in the industry, if any, have a competitive advantage. In addition, as we discuss throughout the book, various steps in the valuation process require the identification of comparable companies. The relevant comparable companies used for specific steps in the valuation process are generally a subset of the competitors of a company. For example, when choosing comparable companies for a market multiple analysis, we have to consider which companies are similar to the company we are valuing based on such attributes as risk, profitability, and growth prospects.

2.4 THE GAP, INC.—AN ILLUSTRATION OF THE CALCULATION AND ANALYSIS OF FINANCIAL RATIOS

In this chapter, we use The Gap, Inc. (GAP) to illustrate the calculation and analysis of financial ratios. GAP is a global retailer operating retail and outlet stores that sell apparel, accessories, and personal care products for men, women, and children. We assume for illustrative purposes that GAP's management believes that the market is substantially undervaluing GAP, as GAP's management believes that it can improve GAP's performance in a variety of ways. In Exhibit 2.1, we present GAP's summary historical financial statements A2009 and A2010 (January 2010 and January 2011 fiscal year-ends, respectively) and hypothetical management forecasts (F2011–F2016) of its income statements, balance sheets, and summary free cash flow schedules. We do not show GAP's Statement of Cash Flows (though we show GAP's operating cash flow at the bottom of the schedule), nor do we show its footnotes and other supplemental disclosures. Rather, we discuss relevant footnotes and other disclosures in the chapter as needed. Naturally, a complete financial analysis includes a detailed review of all of a company's footnotes and other disclosures in its financial statements.

Prior to the end of the 2010 fiscal year (end of January 2011), GAP distributed close to one billion dollars in dividends and share repurchases. This was excess cash that GAP management felt it did not need. GAP had a market capitalization (a measure of firm value) of roughly $11 billion at the end of its 2010 fiscal year (after the cash distributions to shareholders had been made). The GAP forecasts assume that management can improve the company's performance. Management believes it can grow revenues above market expectations, reduce GAP's operating expenses to improve GAP's cost structure, manage GAP's working capital better to reduce its investment in working capital, and reduce GAP's capital expenditure requirements without affecting its planned capital maintenance and expansion forecast. Using a cost of capital of 13.5% and a perpetual growth rate of 2.5% after 2016, we can use the valuation framework we discussed in Chapter 1 to value GAP using management's forecasts. We show this valuation in Exhibit 2.2.

If management can attain its forecasts, this illustration indicates that GAP's market value would be $12.8 billion instead of $11 billion, which is a 16% increase in its value. Naturally, management and GAP's investors would all be pleased with such an improvement in GAP's performance. The issue, of course, is whether such an improvement is feasible. As we discuss in Chapter 4, when discussing forecasting models, we can use financial ratios resulting from the forecasts to help assess the reasonableness of the forecasts.

To analyze GAP's historical performance, we use a set of comparison companies. The comparison companies we use are all companies in the Family Clothing Store industry classification (SIC = 5651), which is the primary industry classification for GAP. The number of companies (other than GAP) in that industry, and for which we can measure the financial ratios, varies between 17 and 19 during any one year. We should note that while all of these companies have the same primary industry classification as GAP, they might not all be equally good competitors. This industry code includes such companies as American Eagle Outfitters, Inc. and Abercrombie & Fitch, which are direct competitors of GAP. This industry classification, however, also contains such companies as Casual Male Retail Group, Inc., which does not focus on the same type of shopper as GAP but rather focuses on big and tall men, and Nordstrom, Inc., which sells a broader set of merchandise. The companies also vary in business strategy, size, and other characteristics.

EXHIBIT 2.1	The Gap, Inc.—Financial Statement and Free Cash Flow History for Fiscal Years 2009 and 2010 and Hypothetical Management Forecasts 2011–2016

THE GAP, INC.
Financial Statements and Free Cash Flows

Income Statement ($ in millions)	A2009	A2010	F2011	F2012	F2013	F2014	F2015	F2016
Revenue	$14,197	$14,664	$15,251	$16,013	$16,814	$17,654	$18,096	$18,548
Cost of goods sold	−7,818	−8,127	−8,349	−8,750	−9,188	−9,647	−9,888	−10,136
Gross margin	$ 6,379	$ 6,537	$ 6,902	$ 7,263	$ 7,626	$ 8,007	$ 8,207	$ 8,413
Depreciation and amortization	−655	−648	−674	−708	−743	−780	−800	−820
Operating expenses	−3,909	−3,921	−4,138	−4,329	−4,546	−4,773	−4,892	−5,015
Operating income	$ 1,815	$ 1,968	$ 2,089	$ 2,226	$ 2,337	$ 2,454	$ 2,515	$ 2,578
Interest expense	−6	−6	0	0	0	0	0	0
Interest income	7	20	22	23	24	25	26	27
Income before taxes	$ 1,816	$ 1,982	$ 2,111	$ 2,249	$ 2,361	$ 2,479	$ 2,542	$ 2,605
Income tax expense	−714	−778	−829	−883	−927	−973	−998	−1,023
Net income	$ 1,102	$ 1,204	$ 1,283	$ 1,366	$ 1,434	$ 1,506	$ 1,544	$ 1,583

Balance Sheet ($ in millions)	A2009	A2010	F2011	F2012	F2013	F2014	F2015	F2016
Cash balance	$ 2,573	$ 1,661	$ 1,727	$ 1,814	$ 1,905	$ 2,000	$ 2,050	$ 2,101
Accounts receivable	0	0	0	0	0	0	0	0
Inventory	1,477	1,620	1,664	1,744	1,831	1,923	1,971	2,020
Other current assets	614	645	671	704	740	777	796	816
Total current assets	$ 4,664	$ 3,926	$ 4,062	$ 4,262	$ 4,476	$ 4,699	$ 4,817	$ 4,937
Property, plant, and equipment	$ 7,427	$ 7,573	$ 7,909	$ 8,341	$ 8,879	$ 9,532	$10,332	$11,151
Accumulated depreciation	−4,799	−5,010	−5,684	−6,392	−7,135	−7,915	−8,714	−9,534
Property, plant, and equipment (net)	$ 2,628	$ 2,563	$ 2,225	$ 1,949	$ 1,744	$ 1,617	$ 1,617	$ 1,617
Other assets	$ 693	$ 576	$ 599	$ 629	$ 660	$ 693	$ 711	$ 729
Total assets	$ 7,985	$ 7,065	$ 6,886	$ 6,841	$ 6,880	$ 7,010	$ 7,145	$ 7,283
Accounts payable	$ 1,027	$ 1,049	$ 1,059	$ 1,110	$ 1,165	$ 1,224	$ 1,254	$ 1,286
Accrued expenses	1,104	1,046	1,088	1,142	1,199	1,259	1,291	1,323
Current portion of long-term debt	0	0	0	0	0	0	0	0
Total current liabilities	$ 2,131	$ 2,095	$ 2,147	$ 2,252	$ 2,365	$ 2,483	$ 2,545	$ 2,609
Long-term debt	0	0	0	0	0	0	0	0
Non-current liabilities	963	890	926	972	1,020	1,071	1,098	1,126
Total liabilities	$ 3,094	$ 2,985	$ 3,072	$ 3,224	$ 3,385	$ 3,554	$ 3,643	$ 3,734
Common stock (and other)	$−5,924	$−7,687	$−7,687	$−7,687	$−7,687	$−7,687	$−7,687	$−7,687
Retained earnings	10,815	11,767	11,501	11,304	11,182	11,143	11,189	11,236
Total shareholders equity	$ 4,891	$ 4,080	$ 3,814	$ 3,617	$ 3,495	$ 3,456	$ 3,502	$ 3,549
Total liabilities and equities	$ 7,985	$ 7,065	$ 6,886	$ 6,841	$ 6,880	$ 7,010	$ 7,145	$ 7,283

Free Cash Flows ($ in millions)	A2009	A2010	F2011	F2012	F2013	F2014	F2015	F2016
Earnings before interest and taxes (EBIT)	$ 1,822	$ 1,988	$ 2,111	$ 2,249	$ 2,361	$ 2,479	$ 2,542	$ 2,605
− Income taxes paid on EBIT	−716	−780	−829	−883	−927	−973	−998	−1,023
Earnings before interest and after taxes	$ 1,106	$ 1,208	$ 1,283	$ 1,366	$ 1,434	$ 1,506	$ 1,544	$ 1,583
+ Depreciation expense	655	648	674	708	743	780	800	820
+/− Working capital and other changes	165	−313	−6	8	7	8	4	4
− Change in required cash	0	912	−66	−86	−91	−95	−50	−51
Unlevered cash flow from operations	$ 1,926	$ 2,455	$ 1,884	$ 1,995	$ 2,094	$ 2,199	$ 2,298	$ 2,355
− Capital expenditures (net)	−241	−249	−336	−432	−538	−653	−800	−820
Unlevered free cash flow	$ 1,684	$ 2,205	$ 1,549	$ 1,563	$ 1,556	$ 1,545	$ 1,498	$ 1,536
Cash flow from operations	$ 1,922	$ 1,539	$ 1,951	$ 2,082	$ 2,185	$ 2,294	$ 2,348	$ 2,406

Exhibit may contain small rounding errors

EXHIBIT 2.2	The Gap, Inc.'s Discounted Cash Flow Valuation Using Hypothetical Management Forecasts

THE GAP, INC. Discounted Cash Flow Valuation						
Cost of capital	13.5%					
Growth rate for free cash flow for continuing value	2.5%					
Billions of Dollars	**F2011**	**F2012**	**F2013**	**F2014**	**F2015**	**CV_{Firm} F2015**
Unlevered free cash flow for continuing value (CV)						$ 1,535.5
Discount factor for continuing value						9.091
Unlevered free cash flow and CV..................	$1,548.9	$1,562.9	$1,555.9	$1,545.4	$1,498.1	$13,959.2
Discount factor.................................	0.8811	0.7763	0.6839	0.6026	0.5309	0.5309
Present value	$1,364.6	$1,213.3	$1,064.1	$ 931.2	$ 795.3	$ 7,411.0
Value of the firm	$12,779.6					

Exhibit may contain small rounding errors

Generally, we would conduct a more detailed analysis of these companies before using them as comparable companies. Identifying a specific set of comparable companies for GAP is beyond what we cover in this chapter. We will discuss this issue in detail later in the book when we discuss the use of comparable companies in estimating the cost of capital and conducting a price multiples valuation.

2.5 MEASURING A COMPANY'S PERFORMANCE USING ACCOUNTING RATES OF RETURN

LO2 Measure the performance of a company using rates of return

Accounting rates of return attempt to measure the performance of a company. We can measure a company's accounting rates of return in many ways. All of the alternatives are typically a measure of accounting income divided by a measure of the average level of investment used to generate that income. Some rates of return measure the amount of income generated for each dollar of investment; for example, a company with an annual income of $124 million and an investment of $1,240 million has a 10% rate of return on its investment. The 10% rate of return indicates that the company generates $1 of income each year for each $10 of investment. Conceptually, the higher the rate of return, the better the performance, ignoring the many pitfalls of using financial statement information to measure performance. We can compare a company's current rate of return to its historic rates of return in order to assess the change in its accounting-based performance over time, or we can compare it to the rates of return of competitor companies in order to assess its relative accounting-based performance.

Naturally, it is important to ensure that you use a consistent numerator and denominator when measuring a particular type of rate of return. For example, if the denominator is average assets, then the numerator should be the income generated by those assets; thus, we would measure income before deducting interest expense (on an after-tax basis). If the denominator is average common equity, then the numerator should be income to the common equityholders. Similarly, if we measure income by excluding certain income effects from the numerator such as the effects of discontinued operations or the effects of excess assets, then we should exclude any assets related to the excluded income from the denominator.

We discuss three rate of return measures that attempt to quantify the rate of return related to the company's invested capital: the **return on assets (ROA)**, the **return on investment (ROI)**, and **return on (common) equity (ROE)**. Each of these rates of return attempts to measure the amount of income generated per dollar of invested capital given some specific definition of income and invested capital.

Return on Assets

The numerator in the return on assets (ROA) formula is unlevered income, and the denominator is average total assets for the period over which we are measuring the rate of return. To unlever income, we add back after-tax interest and other effects related to non-equity financing such as preferred dividends; we do this to present what the income would have been had the company been completely financed with equity. The basic formula for computing ROA is

$$\text{ROA} = \frac{\text{Net Income} + (1 - \text{Income Tax Rate for Interest}) \times \text{Interest Expense}}{\text{Average Total Assets}} \qquad (2.1)$$

After reviewing GAP's footnote for income taxes (not shown in the chapter), we assume that GAP's **effective income tax rate** (income tax expense divided by income before taxes) of 39.3% ($0.393 = \$778/\$1,982$) is reasonable to use as the tax rate for interest. However, it should be noted that this is not always an appropriate assumption to make for the income tax rate for interest (we discuss this issue in more detail in the next chapter). GAP has $6 of interest expense and has no preferred dividends. The return on assets for GAP calculated for 2010 is

$$\text{ROA}_{\text{GAP, 2010}} = \frac{\$1,204 + (1 - 0.393) \times \$6}{(\$7,985 + \$7,065)/2} = 0.160$$

In the above formula, we assume that there are no minority interest positions in the company's subsidiaries (as GAP did not report any minority interest). If there were, we would reverse any impact of **minority interest** in the net income of subsidiaries, for the average total assets in the denominator represents the total assets, including any assets attributable to the minority interests. We often measure average total assets—and other financial ratio denominators based on an average—as the beginning-of-year balance plus the end-of-year balance divided by two. This calculation assumes the change in the denominator occurred evenly during the year and that the beginning and ending balances represent the average level of assets during the year. This might not be the case for companies that undertook a major acquisition or divestiture. In that case, we might compute the average from quarterly reports or perhaps from pro forma financials (based on the assumption that the transaction occurred at the beginning of the year).

Return on Investment

The return on investment (ROI) is similar to the return on assets. The major difference between the two formulas is how we measure the denominator. In addition, the numerator is slightly different as well. The denominator for the return on investment is equal to average invested capital instead of average assets as used in the return on assets calculation. One way we can measure invested capital is to add the book value of debt to preferred stock and common equity, or—looking at it from the asset side of the balance sheet—we can subtract operating liabilities (accounts payable, wages payable, income taxes payable, deferred income taxes, etc.) from total assets. Some analysts add non-current net deferred tax liabilities to common equity under the assumption that this is not really a liability and that stockholder's equity was reduced when the deferred tax liability was recorded. They would make the same adjustment in calculating return on equity, discussed next. Since the denominator for the return on investment does not include investments by minority shareholders, we do not adjust the numerator by removing the adjustment to net income for minority interest as we did in the return on assets calculation.

The reason some analysts prefer return on investment to return on assets is that the implicit financing costs of a company's operating liabilities are embedded in the company's operating expenses. (Recall our discussion of this point in Chapter 1.) As a result, it is usually quite difficult to add back the implicit financing costs of these operating liabilities; thus, to have a consistent numerator and denominator, we do not include the value of the operating liabilities in the denominator. The basic formula for the return on investment is

$$\text{ROI} = \frac{\text{Net Income} + (1 - \text{Income Tax Rate for Interest}) \times \text{Interest Expense}}{\text{Average (Book Value of Debt + Preferred Stock + Common Equity)}} \qquad (2.2)$$

Since GAP has no debt and no preferred stock at the beginning or end of the year, the return on investment for GAP for 2010 is simply

$$\text{ROI}_{\text{GAP, 2010}} = \frac{\$1,204 + (1 - 0.393) \times \$6}{(\$4,891 + \$4,080)/2} = 0.269$$

Note that GAP did have a small amount of debt outstanding during the year when it drew down its revolver. If we knew the average debt outstanding over the year, we would include that in the denominator.

Valuation Key 2.2

Rates of return measured using financial statements are popular performance measures. Rates of return measure the amount of income generated per dollar of capital invested, measured in a variety of ways. Alternative types of rates of return measures include return on assets, return on investment, and return on (common) equity.

Sometimes, analysts use the return on long-term capital (long-term debt plus preferred stock plus common equity) as a rate of return measure, called the **return on long-term investment**. Because of the way the denominator is measured, we add back only the portion of interest attributable to long-term debt to our numerator when we measure the numerator for this rate of return.

Return on (Common) Equity

The return on (common) equity (ROE) measures the amount of income to common equity generated per dollar of equity invested (all measured using financial statement information). The basic formula for the return on equity is

$$\text{ROE} = \frac{\text{Net Income} - \text{Preferred Stock Dividends}}{\text{Average Common Equity}} = \frac{\text{Income to Common Equity}}{\text{Average Common Equity}} \qquad (2.3)$$

The return on equity for GAP for 2010 is

$$\text{ROE}_{\text{GAP, 2010}} = \frac{\$1,204 - \$0}{(\$4,891 + \$4,080)/2} = 0.268$$

Since GAP has no debt or preferred stock outstanding at the beginning and end of the year, the ROE and ROI will be very close. The only difference between them, in this case, is caused by the minimal amount of interest expense from debt outstanding at some point during the year, for we did not know the average debt balance for the denominator in the ROI calculation.

The numerator for the return on (common) equity (ROE) is income available to common equityholders, and the denominator is the average common equity. The denominator is the average (common) equity of the company during the period over which we measure the numerator. Again, we typically measure this average by dividing the sum of the beginning and ending balances of the company's (common) equity by two. Since we do not deduct preferred stock dividends when measuring net income, we deduct it from the numerator to represent the income after all payments to non-common equity securities.

Adjusting Financial Ratios for Excess Assets

We can use alternative definitions for the numerator in the rate of return calculations; for example, we can exclude certain types of income from the numerator, such as income from excess assets, income from discontinued operations, one-time expenses from reorganizations, and extraordinary items. Regardless of the definition we use, however, we must make sure that our denominator is consistent with the definition of the numerator. For example, if we exclude income from excess assets in the numerator, we also exclude excess assets from the denominator.

Valuation Key 2.3

Eliminating excess assets from rate of return measures is often very useful in order to gain a true sense of the profitability of a company's operations. That said, there are situations where eliminating the effect of excess assets is not preferred. For example, we would not eliminate excess assets if we wanted to understand the overall profitability of the company from the investors' perspective.

We use the definition that best fits the context of our analysis—that best fits how we plan to use the ratio. No single definition dominates the alternatives in all contexts. For example, if we want to know the overall profitability of a company, we might prefer to include a company's excess assets; however, if we wanted to know the profitability of the company's operations—for example, to compare to comparable companies—we would generally exclude excess assets. The inclusion or exclusion of a company's excess assets can have a substantial effect on its rates of return, and the direction of the effect can be either positive or negative. The direction of the effect depends on the rate of return on the excess assets relative to the rate of return on the company's operations.

We show an example of the potential impact of adjusting for excess assets using Microsoft Corporation in Valuation in Practice 2.2.

Valuation in Practice 2.2

Microsoft's Return on Assets and Return on Equity Excluding Non-Operating Income and Assets Around the mid-2000s, Microsoft Corporation (Microsoft) reported that it had over $60 billion in cash and short-term investments and over $12 billion in equity and other investments. Using Microsoft's reported net income, average total assets, and average common equity, its return on assets is 9.4% and its return on equity is 11.7%. However, this does not reflect Microsoft's rates of return on its operating assets. If we assume that all of the cash, short-term investments, and other investments are non-operating, we would deduct the after-tax income from these non-operating assets ($1.9 billion) from the numerators and the average balance of these non-operating assets from the denominators ($67.8 billion). Using these figures, Microsoft's return on its operating assets is 32.5% and its return on equity is 299%.

($ in millions)	2004 Reported		ROR	Adjustments	2004 Adjusted		ROR
Return on Assets							
Net income....................	$ 8,168	=	9.4%	$ −1,897	$ 6,271	=	32.5%
Average total assets.............	$87,061			$−67,771	$19,290		
Return on Equity							
Net income....................	$ 8,168	=	11.7%	$ −1,897	$ 6,271	=	299.0%
Average common equity	$69,869			$−67,771	$ 2,098		

Alternative Ways to Measure Financial Ratio Inputs

Instead of using a measure of accounting income in the numerator, we can also use various definitions of cash flow to measure rates of return. For example, we could use unlevered cash flow from operations or free cash flow as the numerator in the return on assets or return on investment equations, or we could use operating cash flow (adjusted for preferred stock dividends) or equity free cash flow as the numerator in the return on equity equation.

Cash flow rate of return ratios have become more popular since the standardization of cash flow statements in 1987. Many analysts utilize cash flows from operations for the numerator in equity rate of return measures. One note of caution regarding cash flows from operations is that it does not contain any provision for the replacement of assets, whereas income numbers at least include a depreciation charge. One measure of cash return on assets that captures capital expenditures is free cash flow of the unlevered firm divided by total assets. The limitation of using free cash flow of the unlevered firm in the numerator, however, is that capital expenditures can be "lumpy," that is, large in some years and small in others. However, some type of averaging or normalization of capital expenditures can be used to address this issue.

Limitations of Accounting Rates of Return as Measures of Performance

Accounting rates of return have widely recognized limitations as measures of performance.[8] Accounting rates of return focus on the ratio of a measure of earnings in a single year to a measure of investment

---

[8] See, for example, Solomon, E., and J. Lays, "Measurement of Company Profitability: Some Systematic Errors in the Accounting Rate of Return,", in A. Robichek, ed., *Financial Research and Management Decisions*, Wiley (2003), pp. 152–283; and Fisher, F., and J. McGowan, "On the Misuse of Accounting Rates of Return to Infer Monopoly Profits," *American Economic Review* 73 (1983), pp. 82–97.

calculated using financial statement numbers. We know that the percentage change in the value of an investment is equal to the percentage change in the net present value of the investment, which, as we know, depends on changes in expected future cash flows and risk. Thus, accounting earnings, which generally focus on a single period, cannot reliably measure changes in the value of an investment. In addition, historical cost accounting measures of the value of an investment do not reflect market values. Alternative measures that attempt to address some of these limitations involve some sort of longer-term forecast of expected performance and risk.

Even with these limitations, accounting rates of return are widely used measures of performance. We know that accounting earnings and accounting rates of return as measures of performance have an empirically positive correlation with changes in market value as measured by stock returns.[9]

2.6 DISAGGREGATING THE RETURN ON ASSETS

Disaggregating the rates of return into their various components has two important roles in valuation. First, we disaggregate historical rates of return in order to help us better understand the source and sustainability of a company's competitive advantage or, conversely, why a poorly performing firm is at a competitive disadvantage. Second, once we create the financial forecasts, we disaggregate rates of return based on the financial forecasts in order to assess the reasonableness of those forecasts.

Disaggregating the Return on Assets

The two primary components of a company's return on assets are its unlevered profit margin and its asset utilization. A company's **unlevered profit margin** is equal to unlevered income divided by revenue. A company's **asset utilization** (or **asset turnover**) is equal to the amount of revenue the company generates per dollar of assets. The product of a company's unlevered profit margin and asset utilization ratio is equal to its return on assets (ROA). The basic formulas for unlevered profit margin and asset utilization as well as how to use them to disaggregate the return on assets are as follows:

$$\text{ROA} = \text{Unlevered Profit Margin} \times \text{Asset Utilization}$$

$$\text{ROA} = \frac{\text{Net Income} + (1 - \text{Income Tax Rate}) \times \text{Interest Expense}}{\text{Revenue}} \times \frac{\text{Revenue}}{\text{Average Total Assets}} \quad \textbf{(2.4)}$$

The numerator of the unlevered profit margin formula is identical to the numerator in the return on assets calculation. If there is income attributable to minority issues, the same adjustment must be made to the unlevered profit margin, as discussed with respect to the return on assets calculation. The unlevered profit margin and asset utilization ratios for GAP are

$$\text{ROA}_{\text{GAP, 2010}} = \frac{\$1,204 + (1 - 0.393) \times \$6}{\$14,664} \times \frac{\$14,664}{(\$7,985 + \$7,065)/2} = 0.160$$

$$\text{ROA}_{\text{GAP, 2010}} = 0.082 \times 1.949 = 0.160$$

Valuation Key 2.4

We can disaggregate the return on assets into meaningful components. The components of the return on assets are unlevered profit margin and asset utilization. Decomposing rates of return helps us better understand the source and potential sustainability of a company's return. It will also help us better assess the reasonableness of a set of financial forecasts.

---

[9] For the seminal work on the relation between earnings and stock prices, see Ball, R., and Brown, P., "An Empirical Evaluation of Accounting Income Numbers," *Journal of Accounting Research* (Autumn 1968), pp. 159–178. For research on cash flow and accruals, see Dechow, P., "Accounting Earnings and Cash Flows as Measures of Firm Performance: The Role of Accounting Accruals," *Journal of Accounting and Economics* 18 (1994), pp. 3–42, which shows that current accounting earnings are more informative of a company's valuation than current cash flows, although earnings and cash flows each provide incremental valuation information relative to the other.

From the formula in Equation 2.4, we observe that even with a low profit margin, a company that has a sufficiently high asset utilization can have the same, or even a higher, return on assets as a company with a high profit margin. We also observe that two companies can have the same return on assets even though they have very different profit margins. For example, a company with a 10% return on assets that results from having an 8.6% unlevered profit margin and asset utilization ratio of 1.16 (0.1 = 0.086 × 1.16) has the same return on assets as another company that has a profit margin of 27.4% and an asset utilization ratio of only 0.36 (0.1 = 0.274 × 0.36).

Relation Between the Return on Asset Components

We examine a sample of companies from 2006 through 2010 for different industries. To be included in the sample, a company must have the necessary data available to measure the relevant ratio in at least one year in the Compustat®[10] North American Industrial Annual files, which requires that a company have a publicly traded security on the New York Stock Exchange, American Stock Exchange, or NASDAQ Exchange. In Exhibit 2.3, we show the asset utilization and unlevered profit margin ratios for selected industries with an ROA of approximately 5%.[11]

EXHIBIT 2.3	Return on Assets and Components for Selected Industries in the Compustat® Financial Ratio Sample, 2006–2010

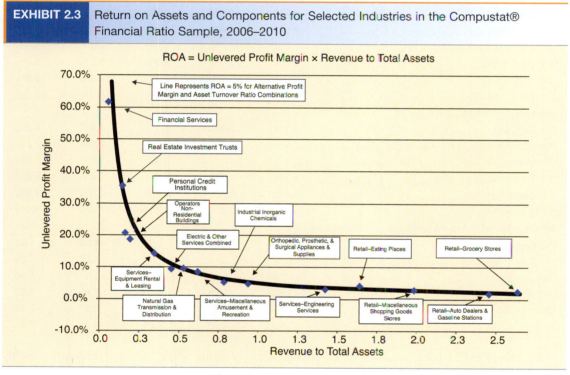

The solid line in the exhibit shows the unlevered profit margin and revenue to total assets combinations that result in a return on assets equal to 5%. For example, a 10% unlevered profit margin and a 0.5 ratio of revenue to total assets results in a 5% return on assets, as does a 2.5% unlevered profit margin and a ratio of revenue to total assets equal to 2.0. The diamonds on the graph show the specific combinations for selected industries. If a diamond is above the solid line, it indicates that the industry's return on assets is somewhat greater than 5%; if it's below the solid line, it indicates that the industry's return on assets is slightly less than 5%. We can quickly observe from this graph that many of the industries have a return on assets that is close to 5 percent, even though they have different—sometimes substantially different—unlevered profit margins. The grocery store industry, for example, is a high-turnover (revenue to total assets of more than 2.5) and low-margin (unlevered profit margin of 2%) business with a return on assets of close to 5%. However, the real estate investment trust business

---

[10] Standard & Poor's Compustat® is a standardized database delivering accounting and market data on over 54,000 securities to clients through a variety of databases and analytical software products. Standard & Poor's Investment Services is a division of McGraw-Hill, Inc.

[11] This type of analysis was first presented in Selling, T., and C. Stickney, "The Effects of Business Environment and Strategy on a Firm's Rate of Return on Assets," *Financial Analysts Journal* (January–February 1989), pp. 43–52.

is a low-volume (revenue to total assets of 0.14) and high-margin (unlevered profit margin of 36%) business that also has a return on assets of about 5%.

How Does GAP Perform Relative to Other Companies in Its Industry?

In Exhibit 2.4, we show the ratios for GAP's return on assets, unlevered profit margin, and revenue to total assets for the fiscal years 2006 through 2010. We also show various percentiles of the distribution of those ratios for other companies in the Family Clothing Store industry classification (SIC = 5651), which is the primary industry classification for GAP. The number of companies (other than GAP) in that industry, and for which we could measure the financial ratios, varies between 17 and 20.

EXHIBIT 2.4	Return on Asset and Related Ratios for The Gap, Inc. and the Distribution of Companies in the Family Clothing Store Industry Classification (SIC = 5651)				
	2006	**2007**	**2008**	**2009**	**2010**
Return on Assets					
The Gap, Inc..	**9.3%**	**10.9%**	**12.6%**	**14.2%**	**16.0%**
10th percentile	2.6%	−1.6%	−15.3%	−2.0%	1.5%
25th percentile	5.0%	1.6%	−5.9%	2.9%	5.4%
50th percentile	12.6%	9.3%	7.8%	5.5%	8.7%
75th percentile	14.8%	15.3%	13.2%	14.2%	15.9%
90th percentile	15.9%	19.1%	18.9%	18.2%	19.1%
Unlevered Profit Margin					
The Gap, Inc..	**5.1%**	**5.6%**	**6.7%**	**7.8%**	**8.2%**
10th percentile	1.0%	−0.8%	−23.7%	−1.0%	2.7%
25th percentile	2.8%	1.1%	−3.1%	2.2%	3.5%
50th percentile	5.1%	3.9%	4.2%	3.6%	5.6%
75th percentile	8.4%	9.4%	6.7%	7.8%	7.2%
90th percentile	10.5%	12.4%	11.5%	14.2%	14.2%
Revenue to Total Assets (Utilization or Turnover)					
The Gap, Inc..	**1.84**	**1.92**	**1.89**	**1.83**	**1.95**
10th percentile	1.17	1.14	1.09	1.03	1.20
25th percentile	1.55	1.50	1.48	1.41	1.38
50th percentile	1.83	1.79	1.73	1.83	1.89
75th percentile	2.37	2.11	2.03	2.07	2.15
90th percentile	3.00	2.73	2.91	2.85	2.81

In 2006, GAP's return on assets is below the 50th percentile of its industry group and steadily increases during this period and by 2010, it is above the 75th percentile. We can examine the two primary components of the return on assets to learn more about what caused the change in GAP's return on assets relative to the other companies. It turns out that GAP's unlevered profit margin also steadily increased during this period, from the 50th percentile to above the 75th percentile, while its asset utilization ratio (revenue to total asset) stayed relatively constant, varying between 1.83 and 1.95. Thus, the increase in GAP's unlevered profit margin is the main reason why its return on assets increased relative to that of the other companies.

REVIEW EXERCISE 2.1

The Gap, Inc. Return on Asset Forecasts for 2011 and Beyond

Use the information in Exhibit 2.1 to calculate GAP's return on assets and its components for one or more of the years in the forecasts (F2011 through F2016). Compare GAP's return on assets and its components in the forecasts to GAP's time-series and to SIC 5651 in Exhibit 2.4.

Solution on page 78.

2.7 MEASURING A COMPANY'S COST STRUCTURE USING EXPENSE RATIOS

A company's **cost structure**—that is, the relation between a company's revenues and its costs—can be one source of its competitive advantage or competitive disadvantage. Understanding a company's cost structure allows us to more thoroughly understand its accounting-based rates of return because it allows us to understand what drives a company's unlevered profit margin. In addition, we use an analysis of a company's cost structure when we identify comparable companies and when we forecast its financial statements and cash flows.

A common way to analyze a company's cost structure is to analyze the **expense ratios** (an expense item divided by operating revenues) of each of its relevant expenses. When comparing the company to itself and to comparable companies, expense ratios related to a company's operations often provide useful insights into understanding its profit margin. Common operating expense ratios include the cost of goods sold ratio and the selling, general, and administrative expense ratio.

Certain expense ratios are usually less informative—for example, the income tax expense ratio (income tax expense to revenues) and the expense ratios for such one-time costs as reorganization costs. We typically analyze those types of expenses in other ways. Since generally accepted accounting principles in the U.S. do not generally require companies to use the same accounting principles for financial statement and income tax purposes, analyzing income tax expenses and measuring income tax rates is complex. We analyze a company's income taxes by computing its income tax rates with both income statement information and its income tax footnote disclosures (which we discuss in Chapter 3).

We show the formulas for the **cost of goods sold expense ratio**; **selling, general, and administrative expense ratio**; and **depreciation and amortization expense ratio** below. We can measure other expense ratios in a similar manner.

$$\text{Cost of Goods Sold Expense Ratio} = \frac{\text{Cost of Goods Sold}}{\text{Revenue}} \tag{2.5}$$

$$\text{Selling, General, and Administrative Expense Ratio} = \frac{\text{Selling, General, and Administrative Expense}}{\text{Revenue}} \tag{2.6}$$

$$\text{Depreciation and Amortization Expense Ratio} = \frac{\text{Depreciation and Amortization}}{\text{Revenue}} \tag{2.7}$$

At first glance, one might think that we want managers to minimize a company's expense ratios because it appears that lower expense ratios lead to higher profit margins, higher rates of return, and, therefore, better performance. This conclusion is not always correct for expenses that affect a company's future performance. Generally accepted accounting principles (GAAP) in the United States and the GAAP of most other countries in the world tend to **expense** an **expenditure** for which the future benefits cannot be reasonably measured, even though the expenditure likely has future benefits. Examples of such expenditures include expenditures on marketing and research and development. A company could minimize its expense ratio for marketing (or research and development) to increase its current-year profitability. That decision, however, could have negative effects on the company's performance in future years and ultimately destroy value. Thus, minimizing expense ratios is not necessarily consistent with maximizing the value of the firm.

Consistency in the numerator and denominator is important when analyzing financial ratios. For example, we typically exclude non-operating revenues when measuring operating expense ratios. Consistency across companies is also important when analyzing financial ratios. Companies sometimes classify costs differently; for example, one company may include depreciation in cost of goods sold, while another company might show it as a separate line item in the income statement. Similarly, companies sometimes use different accounting principles; for example, one company might use the last-in-first-out (LIFO) inventory method, and another company might use the first-in-first-out (FIFO) inventory method. Our goal when measuring financial ratios is to adjust the financial statements for all material inconsistencies over time and across companies if the adjustment affects the qualitative results from the analysis.

The Gap, Inc.'s Expense Ratios

In Exhibit 2.5, we show certain expense ratios for GAP for the fiscal years 2006 through 2010. We also show various percentiles of the distribution of those ratios for other companies in the Family Clothing Store industry classification (SIC = 5651), which is the primary industry classification for GAP.

EXHIBIT 2.5	Expense Ratios for The Gap, Inc. and the Distribution of Companies in the Family Clothing Store Industry Classification (SIC = 5651)				
	2006	**2007**	**2008**	**2009**	**2010**
Cost of Goods Sold to Revenue					
The Gap, Inc..	**60.7%**	**59.8%**	**58.0%**	**55.1%**	**55.4%**
10th percentile	52.0%	50.5%	53.9%	**52.6%**	52.7%
25th percentile	57.6%	**56.4%**	**58.0%**	55.8%	**54.8%**
50th percentile	**60.7%**	60.7%	61.8%	61.5%	61.2%
75th percentile	71.7%	73.5%	74.2%	71.6%	71.0%
90th percentile	82.4%	86.6%	97.0%	88.5%	85.3%
Operating Expenses to Revenue					
The Gap, Inc..	**28.1%**	**27.6%**	**26.8%**	**27.5%**	**26.7%**
10th percentile	16.8%	16.7%	16.7%	16.4%	16.9%
25th percentile	23.8%	23.4%	**23.4%**	**23.2%**	23.0%
50th percentile	**25.8%**	**26.7%**	27.4%	28.1%	**26.7%**
75th percentile	34.0%	31.9%	30.7%	32.3%	31.3%
90th percentile	47.0%	47.5%	40.1%	44.3%	38.3%
Depreciation and Amortization to Revenue					
The Gap, Inc..	**3.8%**	**4.0%**	**4.5%**	**4.6%**	**4.4%**
10th percentile	1.9%	2.0%	2.1%	2.1%	2.0%
25th percentile	2.9%	2.9%	3.3%	3.0%	3.3%
50th percentile	**3.2%**	**3.4%**	3.9%	4.1%	3.8%
75th percentile	4.4%	4.7%	4.6%	5.0%	5.3%
90th percentile	4.8%	5.2%	6.4%	8.2%	6.6%
Advertising Expense to Revenue					
The Gap, Inc..	**3.6%**	**3.0%**	**3.0%**	**3.6%**	**3.5%**
10th percentile	0.5%	0.6%	0.5%	0.5%	0.4%
25th percentile	1.2%	1.0%	0.9%	0.8%	1.0%
50th percentile	1.8%	1.7%	1.7%	1.7%	1.9%
75th percentile	**3.5%**	**3.0%**	**2.8%**	**3.0%**	**3.5%**
90th percentile	6.3%	4.5%	4.3%	4.3%	4.6%

Recall that GAP had an increase in its return on assets over the 2006 to 2010 period and moved from below the 50th percentile to above the 75th percentile relative to other stores in SIC 5651. This improvement was caused by a steady increase in its unlevered profit margin. Using the expense ratios, we should be able to better understand why this happened. Looking at Exhibit 2.5, it appears that most of this change was caused by a steadily declining ratio of cost of goods sold to revenue (from 60.7% to 55.4%) as GAP moved from the 50th percentile to very near the 25th percentile. GAP's operating expense ratio is roughly around the median for all years, as is its depreciation and amortization expense ratio, and its advertising expense ratio is above the 75th percentile in all years. However, there is little systematic movement in the sum of these three expense ratios over time, as the combined ratio for operating expense, depreciation and amortization, and advertising expense to revenue is 35.5% in 2006 and 34.6% in 2010. As we discussed earlier, when making such comparisons, we assume that the companies we are analyzing have consistently prepared income statements.

Valuation Key 2.5

A company's cost structure can be a source of its competitive advantage. We can use expense ratios—the ratio of an expense line item, such as cost of goods sold, to revenue—to analyze a company's cost structure. We also typically use expense ratios as forecast drivers in financial models.

2.8 ANALYZING A COMPANY'S ASSET UTILIZATION USING TURNOVER RATIOS

A company's **asset utilization**—that is, the revenue generated per dollar of investment in a certain type of asset—is another potential source of a company's competitive advantage. Like expense ratios, we often use asset utilization ratios to create and assess the reasonableness of forecasts. A common way to measure a company's asset utilization is to analyze its **asset utilization** or **turnover ratios**, measured by dividing operating revenues by an operating asset item on its balance sheet. We discussed the overall measure of asset utilization, which is revenue divided by average total assets. This ratio measures the dollars of revenue generated per dollar of investment in all types of assets. We can disaggregate this overall measure of asset utilization into various components. Turnover ratios give some sense of whether a company invests more or less in a particular asset, relative to revenues, either over time or relative to competitors.

LO3 Examine a company's asset utilization and working capital management

Common asset utilization measures include measures for cash; accounts receivable; inventory; other current assets; property, plant, and equipment; and other non-current assets. We typically examine a company's current asset turnover ratios in the context of how the company manages its working capital, which we discuss later in the chapter. That analysis is somewhat different from the revenue turnover ratios discussed here. Two common asset utilization ratios unrelated to working capital are revenues to average gross (and net) property, plant, and equipment. The formulas for these ratios are as follows:

$$\text{Gross Property, Plant, and Equipment Turnover Ratio} = \frac{\text{Revenue}}{\text{Average Gross Property, Plant, and Equipment}} \quad (2.8)$$

$$\text{Net Property, Plant, and Equipment Turnover Ratio} = \frac{\text{Revenue}}{\text{Average Net Property, Plant, and Equipment}} \quad (2.9)$$

The calculations for the above turnover ratios for GAP are as follows:

$$\text{Gross Property, Plant, and Equipment Turnover Ratio}_{\text{GAP, 2010}} = \frac{\$14,664}{(\$7,427 + \$7,573)/2} = 1.96$$

$$\text{Net Property, Plant, and Equipment Turnover Ratio}_{\text{GAP, 2010}} = \frac{\$14,664}{(\$2,628 + \$2,563)/2} = 5.65$$

Again, at first glance, we might conclude that we want managers to maximize a company's asset utilization because conceptually, higher asset utilization ratios lead to higher rates of return, and therefore better performance. However, as with expense ratios, this conclusion is only correct if maximizing the asset utilization ratios does not affect the company's future performance in a negative way. For example, cutting inventory levels leads to greater inventory turnover at first, but if customers begin to experience delays in receiving their orders, sales are likely to decline.

In order to calculate the overall asset turnover ratio (sales to total assets) from individual turnover ratios, we actually calculate inverse turnover ratios for each asset in the balance sheet (for example, cash/revenue, accounts receivable/revenue, etc.). To then determine the overall asset utilization measure (revenue to total assets), we compute the inverse of the sum of the individual inverse turnover ratios. We illustrate this with GAP in the next section of the chapter. Of the two property, plant, and equipment turnover ratios, the one that feeds into the overall asset turnover ratio is the net property, plant, and equipment turnover ratio. Thus, we tend to focus our attention on the net turnover ratio.

REVIEW EXERCISE 2.3

The Gap, Inc. Asset Utilization Ratios for 2011 and Beyond

Use the information in Exhibit 2.1 to calculate GAP's asset utilization ratios for one or more of the years in the forecasts (F2011 through F2016). How are GAP's asset utilization ratios in the forecasts changing relative to 2010?

Solution on page 78.

We do not compare the turnover ratios to those of the companies that are in SIC 5651, for the changes in GAP's return on assets were caused primarily by changes in its unlevered profit margins and not in its asset utilization.

Valuation Key 2.6

Asset utilization can be a source of a company's competitive advantage. We can use turnover ratios—the ratio of revenue to an asset line item such as accounts receivable or fixed assets—to analyze a company's asset utilization. We also sometimes use these ratios, or working capital management ratios, as forecast drivers in financial models.

2.9 SUMMARY OF DISAGGREGATING THE GAP, INC.'S RATES OF RETURN

In Exhibit 2.6, we graphically present the process of disaggregating a company's rates of return and illustrate this disaggregation using GAP. For now, we will concentrate on the return on assets, for we have not yet discussed disaggregating the return on equity. In the exhibit, you can clearly see how the return on assets is disaggregated into unlevered profit margin and overall asset utilization (revenue divided by total assets). Below each of these components, we further break them down into their respective expense ratios and turnover ratios.

EXHIBIT 2.6 Disaggregating the Return on Equity and Return on Assets for The Gap, Inc.

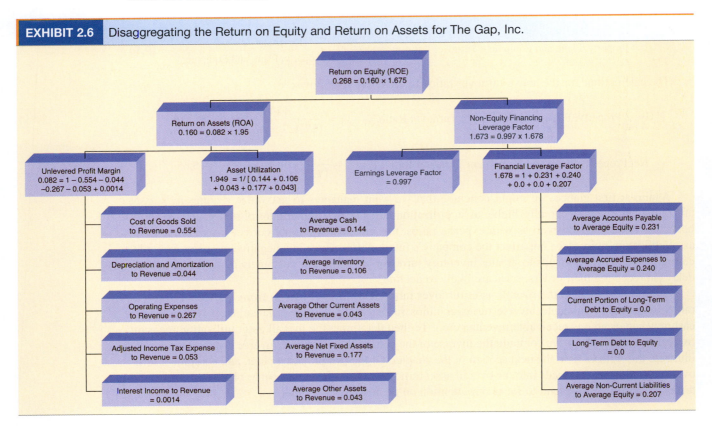

2.10 ANALYZING A COMPANY'S WORKING CAPITAL MANAGEMENT

Working capital is equal to current assets minus current liabilities. Most companies have more current assets than current liabilities; therefore, most companies have positive working capital. U.S. GAAP require companies to disclose current assets and current liabilities on their balance sheets. **Current assets** are cash, cash-like assets, and other assets expected to be used or converted into cash within one year or within the company's normal operating cycle, whichever is longer. Examples include cash, accounts receivable, and inventory. **Current liabilities** are liabilities that mature or are discharged within one year. Examples include accounts payable, wages payable, income taxes payable, short-term bank notes, and the current portion of long-term debt. We define operating working capital as operating current assets minus operating current liabilities, excluding short-term debt, the current portion of long-term debt, and excess cash.

Operating working capital is an investment made by the company so that it can operate its business. All else equal, companies prefer to minimize the amount of operating working capital they carry. It is difficult, however, to minimize working capital, holding everything else constant. For example, a company could reduce its working capital by requiring all customers to pay in cash; such a policy, however, would also likely have the negative effect of decreasing revenues. A company could also reduce working capital by holding less inventory; however, such a policy would also likely lead to reductions in revenues since it would take longer to get products to customers. Last, a company could reduce its working capital by not paying its accounts payable until after the due dates, but again, this action would likely cost the company additional financing charges, or it might result in an inability to purchase the necessary materials to operate the company. In this section of the chapter, we discuss various ways we can analyze working capital.

Ability to Pay Current Liabilities

We often use three ratios to examine the overall working capital management of a company. These ratios are the current ratio, the quick (or acid test) ratio, and the ratio of cash flow to current liabilities. We calculate the **current ratio** as the ratio of a company's current assets to its current liabilities:

$$\text{Current Ratio} = \frac{\text{Current Assets}}{\text{Current Liabilities}} \qquad \textbf{(2.10a)}$$

The current ratio attempts to measure the ability of a company to pay its current liabilities with its current assets. Naturally, going-concern companies must continually replenish their current assets such as receivables and inventory, so current assets cannot be depleted. The **quick or acid test ratio** is the ratio of cash, marketable securities, and accounts receivable to current liabilities. This ratio also attempts to measure the ability of a company to pay its current liabilities with the company's more liquid current assets.

$$\text{Quick or Acid Test Ratio} = \frac{\text{Cash} + \text{Marketable Securities} + \text{Accounts Receivable}}{\text{Current Liabilities}} \qquad \textbf{(2.10b)}$$

The **cash flow to current liabilities ratio** is the ratio of a specific measure of cash flow (cash flow from operations or free cash flows) to current liabilities. This ratio is a measure of the company's ability to pay its current liabilities with its cash flow. The formula for this ratio using operating cash flow is:

$$\text{Operating Cash Flow to Current Liabilities Ratio} = \frac{\text{Operating Cash Flow}}{\text{Current Liabilities}} \qquad \textbf{(2.10c)}$$

As with most financial ratios, we can define the numerator and denominator in various ways as per our earlier discussion. Once again, the choice of numerator and denominator should depend on the context of the analysis, and consistency between the numerator and denominator is important. Sometimes we exclude short-term debt from current liabilities and excess assets from current assets if we want to focus our analysis on operating assets and liabilities. The calculation of GAP's current, quick, and operating cash flow to current liabilities ratios is shown on the next page. Note, we do not provide the cash flow statement for GAP, but we can see its operating cash flow for 2010 in Exhibit 2.1 of $1,539.

$$\text{Current Ratio}_{\text{GAP, 2010}} = \frac{\$3,926}{\$2,095} = 1.87$$

$$\text{Quick or Acid Test Ratio}_{\text{GAP, 2010}} = \frac{\$1,661}{\$2,095} = 0.79$$

$$\text{Operating Cash Flow to Current Liabilities Ratio}_{\text{GAP, 2010}} = \frac{\$1,539}{\$2,095} = 0.73$$

Excess assets can sometimes have a significant effect on these financial ratios because companies often hold excess assets in short-term investments. A company's current and quick ratios would change significantly if it has significant excess (current) assets and we assume that the company distributed those excess assets to its equityholders or used them to pay off its debt. To illustrate the effect of eliminating an excess asset, we assume 50% of GAP's cash is an excess asset; GAP's current ratio would decrease to 1.5 [1.5 = ($3,926 − 0.5 × $1,661)/$2,095] and its quick ratio would decrease to 0.4 (0.4 = 0.5 × $1,661/$2,095). A way to deal with adjustments such as for excess assets is to first adjust the financial statements for the effect of the excess assets and then compute the ratios with the adjusted financials.

Inventories, Accounts Receivable, Accounts Payable, and Trade Cash Cycle Ratios

Inventories, accounts receivable, and accounts payable all involve the production and sales cycle of a company. A company must first purchase materials and services, which it will eventually sell. While a company usually makes these purchases "on credit," the length of the maturity period is typically short. Then, it takes time for the company to produce and sell its inventory, and it takes additional time for the company to collect cash on its credit sales. Thus, companies typically have a **trade cash cycle** or **cash conversion cycle** they must finance—that is, the time from when the company pays its payables until the time it is able to sell its inventory and ultimately collect its receivables.

Before we analyze the trade cash cycle in more detail, let us first analyze each component of the trade cash cycle—days of purchases outstanding, days of inventory held, and the accounts receivable collection period. These measures are variations of the turnover ratios we previously discussed. We can measure these ratios using either the average balance or ending balance. Below, we show the formulas for these ratios using the average balances because they are the most common. We measure the **days of accounts payable outstanding**, the **days sales held in inventory**, and the **accounts receivable collection period** as

$$\text{Days of Accounts Payable Outstanding} = \frac{\text{Average Accounts Payable}}{\text{Purchases}/365} \qquad (2.11)$$

$$\text{Days of Sales Held in Inventory} = \frac{\text{Average Inventory}}{\text{Cost of Goods Sold}/365} \qquad (2.12)$$

$$\text{Accounts Receivable Collection Period} = \frac{\text{Average Gross Accounts Receivable}}{\text{Credit Sales}/365} \qquad (2.13)$$

Once we know these three ratios, we can measure a company's trade cash cycle—that is, the time from when it must pay out cash until the time it collects cash. In other words, a company's trade cycle measures the length of time for which the company must finance its purchases. The greater this number, the larger investment the company has to make in receivables and inventory net of payables. The formula for the trade cash cycle is:

$$\begin{array}{c}\text{Trade Cash}\\\text{Cycle}\end{array} = \begin{array}{c}\text{Accounts}\\\text{Receivable}\\\text{Collection}\\\text{Period}\end{array} + \begin{array}{c}\text{Days of}\\\text{Inventory}\\\text{Held}\end{array} - \begin{array}{c}\text{Days of}\\\text{Payables}\\\text{Outstanding}\end{array} \qquad (2.14)$$

As with all financial ratios, the above measurement of a company's trade cash cycle, while commonly used, is a crude proxy for the underlying economic concept we attempt to measure. For example, it does not include all of the cash a company must pay out to operate its business before it collects cash from receivables, and it does not adjust for the profit margin embedded in accounts receivable. These limitations are in addition to the limitations of using annual averages of the account balances for the financial ratios used in the trade cash cycle formula. That being said, we can still learn something from comparing this measure for a company over time or across companies in cross-section. In 1988, Dell's trade cash cycle was almost 60 days, and as it began to work on improving its working capital management, its trade cash cycle fell steadily. By 1995, its trade cash cycle was negative for the first time, and by the early 2000s, it was almost −60 days. This occurred through a combination of reducing both the days of inventory held and the accounts receivable collection period while simultaneously leaning on suppliers to extend days payables outstanding. While its competitors instituted the same practices, Dell's trade cash cycle was consistently lower.

Some people compute accounts receivable turnover, inventory turnover, and accounts payable turnover ratios instead of the "days" calculations. These turnover ratios are closely related to the above calculations and, in fact, are just the denominator (not divided by 365) over the numerator. Hence, inventory turnover would simply be cost of goods sold divided by average inventory and accounts receivable turnover would simply be credit sales divided by average accounts receivable. You can also simply compute the relevant turnover ratio by dividing 365 by the relevant "days" calculation. These are different from the asset utilization ratios discussed in Section 2.8 because, in that case, every turnover ratio was computed relative to revenues, but here, we try to relate the numerator and the denominator more closely (e.g., inventory and cost of goods sold instead of inventory and revenues).

Analysts also sometimes examine the "quality" of a company's net account receivables by analyzing the ratio of the provision for bad debts to gross accounts receivable (net accounts receivable plus allowance for uncollectible accounts), called the provision for bad debts ratio.

$$\text{Provision for Bad Debts Ratio} = \frac{\text{Allowance for Uncollectible Accounts}}{\text{Gross Accounts Receivable}} \qquad \textbf{(2.15)}$$

Below, we show the calculation of GAP's inventory, accounts receivable, and accounts payable ratios. Since GAP does not have any accounts receivable, its accounts receivable collection period is zero and the provision for bad debts ratio is not relevant.

$$\text{Days of Accounts Payable Outstanding}_{\text{GAP, 2010}} = \frac{(\$1,027 + \$1,049)/2}{(\$8,127 + \$1,620 - \$1,477)/365} = 45.8$$

$$\text{Days of Sales Held in Inventory}_{\text{GAP, 2010}} = \frac{(\$1,477 + \$1,620)/2}{\$8,127/365} = 69.5$$

$$\text{Accounts Receivable Collection Period}_{\text{GAP, 2010}} = 0 \text{ days (no accounts receivable)}$$

$$\text{Trade Cash Cycle}_{\text{GAP, 2010}} = 0 + 69.5 - 45.8 = 23.7 \text{ days}$$

$$\text{Provision for Bad Debts Ratio}_{\text{GAP, 2004}} = \text{Not a Meaningful Figure (no accounts receivable)}$$

Even though GAP accepts credit cards, it has no accounts receivable. According to GAP's 10-K report, GAP recognizes revenue and assumes the cash is in transit when a customer purchases merchandise at the register, even if a customer pays with a credit card. Other companies do not follow this same policy for credit card sales. These companies record a receivable because it takes two to three days for a company to receive payment from third-party credit card sales. For example, Nordstrom, Inc., one of GAP's competitors, changed its accounting treatment of this issue and reclassified its two or three days of outstanding credit card balances from cash (which is how GAP treats them) to accounts receivable. Nordstrom also has its own credit cards, which have a longer accounts receivable collection period. Its accounts receivable balances and allowances for uncollectible accounts for 2010 and 2009 were $2,026 and $2,035, and $85 and $76, respectively. Nordstrom's accounts receivable collection period for 2010, when it had $9,310 of revenues, was 82.8 days:

$$\text{Accounts Receivable Collection Period} = \frac{[(\$2,035 + \$76) + (\$2,026 + \$85)]/2}{\$9,310/365} = 82.8 \text{ days}$$

Nordstrom has a 4% provision for bad debts for its accounts receivable, which we calculate as

$$\text{Provision for Bad Debts Ratio} = \frac{\$85}{\$2,026 + \$85} = 0.04$$

2.11 ANALYZING A COMPANY'S FIXED ASSET STRUCTURE AND CAPITAL EXPENDITURES

LO4 Analyze a company's fixed assets and financial leverage

Naturally, when valuing a company, understanding its capital expenditures (its investments in fixed assets—property, plant, and equipment) is important. We can use both a company's property, plant, and equipment accounts and its depreciation accounts in order to assess the depreciable life of its fixed assets. We can also examine its capital expenditures relative to revenues, depreciation, and earnings. As with most of the financial ratios we have discussed, these financial ratios can be useful in identifying comparable companies and in preparing and assessing the reasonableness of forecasts.

Depreciable Life (Age)

All else equal, companies with older plant and equipment will have higher capital expenditures in the future. The specific ratios to learn about the age of the assets are:

$$\text{Depreciable Life of Gross Plant} = \frac{\text{Average Gross Property, Plant, and Equipment}}{\text{Depreciation}} \quad \text{(2.16)}$$

$$\text{Depreciable Life of Net Plant} = \frac{\text{Average Net Property, Plant, and Equipment}}{\text{Depreciation}} \quad \text{(2.17)}$$

The **depreciable life of the net plant** is useful because it provides a crude indication of the average remaining life of the net plant so long as the company uses estimated useful lives that are close to the economic lives. Consider two companies in the same industry that use the same depreciation policies. If one company has a depreciable life of net plant that is smaller than the other, then it is likely that the two companies have assets of different ages. This has implications for the replacement of those assets. Such analysis can be useful in identifying comparable companies or in forecasting capital expenditures.

Depreciation should include all depreciation—that is, depreciation expense plus additional depreciation taken but capitalized (for example, depreciation included in inventory). Companies sometimes disclose this information in a separate schedule; if not, the cash flow statement can provide information on depreciation in addition to the information provided on the income statement. If possible, we would also prefer to exclude such non-depreciable assets as land from the numerator in the above calculations. We assume that GAP has no amortization of intangible assets. A detailed reading of the footnotes indicates that GAP has a minimal amount of amortization, which we choose to ignore for the purposes of this example. GAP does not disclose the cost of land separately in its 10-K, so we are unable to eliminate it from the calculation as we would like to. The calculations of these ratios for GAP for 2010 are as follows:

$$\text{Depreciable Life of Gross Plant}_{\text{GAP, 2010}} = \frac{(\$7,427 + \$7,573)/2}{\$648} = 11.57$$

$$\text{Depreciable Life of Net Plant}_{\text{GAP, 2010}} = \frac{(\$2,628 + \$2,563)/2}{\$648} = 4.0$$

However, for GAP (and other retailers), this is just a small proportion of its assets, as many retailers have leased significant amounts of assets and do not record many leased assets on their balance sheets. We will provide more discussion about this issue when we discuss leverage in Section 2.13.

Capital Expenditures

We can analyze a company's capital expenditures relative to its revenues and measures of earnings and cash flows. We can also measure a company's capital expenditures relative to its depreciation. The goal of analyzing these ratios is to help us assess, and possibly forecast, a company's capital expenditures. All else equal, companies have larger relative capital expenditures if they are capital intensive, are in need of replacing assets, or are growing. Some example ratios include the following:

$$\text{Capital Expenditures to Revenue} = \frac{\text{Capital Expenditures}}{\text{Revenues}} \tag{2.18}$$

$$\text{Capital Expenditures to EBITDA} = \frac{\text{Capital Expenditures}}{\text{EBITDA}} \tag{2.19}$$

$$\text{Capital Expenditures to Depreciation} = \frac{\text{Capital Expenditures}}{\text{Depreciation}} \tag{2.20}$$

Capital expenditures are often "lumpy"—that is, they are large in some years and small in others, especially for smaller companies. In such situations, we sometimes try to smooth the capital expenditures by using the average over a few years. Again, when we compare companies using these ratios, we either assume that they either have similar policies regarding leasing versus buying plant and equipment, or we make the appropriate adjustments in our calculations for the relevant differences. Below, we show the calculations of these ratios for GAP in 2010, which had $249 of capital expenditures according to its statement of cash flows.

$$\text{Capital Expenditures to Revenue}_{\text{GAP, 2010}} = \frac{\$249}{\$14,664} = 0.017$$

$$\text{Capital Expenditures to EBITDA}_{\text{GAP, 2010}} = \frac{\$249}{\$1,204 + \$6 + \$778 + \$648} = 0.095$$

$$\text{Capital Expenditures to Depreciation}_{\text{GAP, 2010}} = \frac{\$249}{\$648} = 0.384$$

Note that our calculation of EBITDA includes interest income in EBITDA; thus, we are assuming it is part of the company's operations. GAP's capital expenditures to revenue ratio is quite small, but remember that GAP leases most of its stores, so the capital expenditure number does not fully reflect its total investment in fixed assets.

2.12 OTHER TYPES OF FINANCIAL STATEMENT RELATIONS—GROWTH, TRENDS, PER SHARE, PER EMPLOYEE, AND PER UNIT OF CAPACITY AND OUTPUT

Analyzing per share measures and growth rates is a standard part of most financial analyses. Historical growth rates—both annual growth rates and compound annual growth rates—are widely used company characteristics utilized by analysts. Analysts often use historical growth rates as part of the basis for developing forecasts. We also analyze a company using its financial statement information in combination with its non-financial information. For example, we often use a per share measure as an input into the calculation of certain market multiples (for example, the P/E ratio) and to compare a company to itself over time. We also use ratios based on non-financial information in order to analyze a company's historical performance, identify comparable companies, and prepare and assess the reasonableness of forecasts. For example, in the retail industry, analysts often measure such company characteristics as revenue or earnings per square foot of retail space or number of stores.

Employee, Unit of Capacity, and Unit of Output Measures

It is sometimes useful to examine various financial statement items—for example, revenues, assets, cash flows—on a per employee, per unit of capacity, and per unit of output basis. All else equal, we can use such measures as operating income per employee as a proxy for productivity. Similarly, we can use measures based on the unit of capacity as a proxy for capacity utilization.

For GAP, for example, we might measure capacity using the number of square feet of retail space; for paper mills and heavy manufacturing, we might measure capacity using tons of productive capacity; for the airline industry, we might measure capacity using available seat miles. We can use measures based on output to realize the average revenue and cost per unit of output. We might measure revenue per transaction for an online retailer or revenue per check for a restaurant. Naturally, we would analyze these measures by comparing the company we are valuing to its comparable companies currently and over time, just as we do for all other financial ratios.

Since many of the financial statement items are affected by inflation but the denominators are not (number of square feet or number of employees, etc.), we often adjust the numerators in these calculations for inflation in order to restate them in constant dollars (or any other currency) to more readily see real trends. Naturally, we would want to use an inflation index that is relevant to the numerator. A common inflation index is the Consumer Price Index; another general index that could be more appropriate for manufacturers is the Producer Price Index; however, these indices might not be relevant for all industries. Some industries might face a different price level index than that faced by the general economy (for example, the personal computer manufacturer industry, which has faced decreasing prices at times).

Growth Rates and Trend Analyses

We often measure growth rates for free cash flows and for certain items on the income statement, balance sheet, and cash flow statement. Growth rates are often used to drive revenues in forecasting models. We cannot, however, measure a growth rate if the base year is negative. For example, a company that has earnings last year of $10, and this year of $12, has a 20% growth rate ($0.2 = \$12/\$10 - 1$). The same calculation is not meaningful if that company has earnings last year of $-\$10$ and this year of 12; ($\$12/-\$10$) $- 1$ is not a meaningful calculation. We discuss this issue—negative denominators—in more detail later.

Sometimes, we also examine the **index trend** of a characteristic of interest, in which we divide all years by the first year to measure the cumulative growth rate. For example, if a company's operating income during a five-year period is $100, $110, $125, $180, and $220, its index trend for those five years is 1.0, 1.1, 1.25, 1.8, and 2.2. The index trend in the first year is always equal to 1.0 because we are dividing a number by itself. This feature of the index trend is useful because we can easily compare different characteristics of the company to each other (for example, comparing revenue to operating income), or we can compare one characteristic of the company to that of comparable companies. For example, if the index trend of sales goes from 1 to 1.5 over a five-year period and the index trend of operating income goes from 1 to 2 over the same period, it indicates that the company is likely benefiting from economies of scale as it grows. If the operating income trend index moves in lockstep with sales, then the firm is not experiencing any scale economies.

Growth rates for companies tend to vary somewhat every year, as in the example of operating income immediately above. In the first year the growth rate was 10% ($0.1 = \$110/\$100 - 1$), and in the second year, the growth rate was 13.64% ($0.1364 = \$125/\$110 - 1$). Analysts often compute a **compound annual growth rate**, **CAGR**, which indicates what yearly growth rate would have resulted from the observed growth for the period analyzed. Therefore, in our example above, we would be asking what yearly growth in operating income would have resulted from it growing from $100 to $220 in four years. We calculate the compound average growth rate in X, over the period from t to t + n, as

$$\text{CAGR}_{t,\,t+n} = \sqrt[n]{\frac{X_{t+n}}{X_t}} - 1 = \left(\frac{X_{t+n}}{X_t}\right)^{\frac{1}{n}} - 1 \tag{2.21}$$

$$\text{CAGR}_{t,\,t+n} = \sqrt[4]{\frac{\$220}{\$100}} - 1 = \left(\frac{\$220}{\$100}\right)^{\frac{1}{4}} - 1 = 0.218$$

Therefore, if the company's operating income started at $100 and grew 21.8% each year for four years, the operating income would have reached $220.

Per Share Measures

We also measure the per share amount of free cash flows and of various items on an income statement, balance sheet, and cash flow statement. On the income statement, we might analyze revenues, gross margin, operating income, and net income on a per share basis. On the balance sheet, we might analyze the major components of assets as well as their book value on a per share basis. On the cash flow statement, we might analyze cash flow from operations and capital expenditures on a per share basis. Last, we might analyze free cash flow and equity free cash flow on a per share basis. Naturally, rather than analyze all of these per share measures, we choose the per share measures of importance based on the context of the analysis. Normally, these involve parts of the income statement.

To measure a financial statement number on a per share basis, we divide this number by the number of shares outstanding. A company usually reports more than the shares it has outstanding. In addition to the number of shares it has outstanding, it might report the number of shares it is authorized to issue and the number of shares it has issued. The **number of shares outstanding** is equal to the number of shares a company issued net of the number of shares it has repurchased and not reissued, called **treasury shares**.

When available, we typically use one of two U.S. GAAP definitions for the number of shares outstanding in order to measure basic earnings per share and diluted earnings per share. For **basic earnings per share**, we divide net income to common equity by the weighted average shares outstanding. The **weighted average shares outstanding** is the number of shares outstanding during the year weighted by how long the shares were outstanding during the year. For **diluted earnings per share**, we again divide net income to common equity by the weighted average shares outstanding, but we adjust both the numerator and denominator for the dilutive effects of non-equity securities (such as convertible debt, convertible preferred stock, and stock options) that we assume are converted into common equity. For some companies, the difference between the two earnings per share numbers can be substantial because of their reliance on stock options to compensate employees.

2.13 ANALYZING A COMPANY'S FINANCIAL LEVERAGE AND FINANCIAL RISK

We define financial leverage as the use of non-common equity financing. All else equal, the more non-common equity financing a company uses, the more financial leverage it has. We measure a company's financial leverage and financial risk in two ways using financial statement relations. We use financial leverage ratios to measure the degree to which a company is using financial leverage. We use coverage ratios to measure the ability of a company to service, or cover the payments on, its non-equity securities. When using financial statement values to measure the degree to which a company is using financial leverage, we often use the ratio of a specific measure of non-equity securities (for example, debt) to a specific measure of total investment (for example, total assets or total invested capital). To measure a company's ability to service its non-equity securities, we typically use a ratio of a specific measure of income or cash flow to a specific measure of required payments to non-equity security holders.

As we discuss in many parts of this book, we always use market values to measure a company's financial leverage ratio in order to measure its cost of capital or evaluate its capital structure strategy. In this section, we use financial statement numbers to measure financial leverage ratios. We do not recommend using financial leverage ratios based on financial statement numbers to measure a company's cost of capital—for example, to lever and unlever the cost of capital (beta), or to measure the weighted average cost of capital. If that is the case, why are we discussing these ratios that are dependent on financial statement figures? We discuss financial leverage ratios based on financial statement numbers because they are commonly used by analysts and managers, in debt contracts, and by debt rating agencies. Moreover, these leverage ratios are correlated with ratings, yields, and the probability of default. In doing a valuation analysis, we might need to determine if a company is in compliance with its debt covenants, or we might need to estimate its debt rating. As such, we discuss these ratios in this section of the chapter. In Chapter 9, we show how one can use these ratios to estimate a debt rating.

A common way to examine the financial leverage of a company is to examine the ratio of debt and other non-equity financing to total assets (or total invested capital or common equity). For the numerator in our financial leverage ratios, we use such figures as total debt, total debt plus preferred stock, long-term debt, and long-term debt plus preferred stock.

When measuring these financial leverage ratios, analysts sometimes net out cash against non-equity claims, assuming that the cash could be used to redeem the non-equity claims. We show three popular financial leverage ratios here. For companies that have other non-equity securities, we could also assign financial leverage ratios to those securities as well.

$$\text{Total Debt to Total Assets} = \frac{\text{Total Debt}}{\text{Total Assets}} \qquad \textbf{(2.22)}$$

$$\text{Total Liabilities to Total Assets} = \frac{\text{Total Liabilities}}{\text{Total Assets}} \qquad \textbf{(2.23)}$$

$$\text{Total Debt to Common Equity} = \frac{\text{Total Debt}}{\text{Common Equity}} \qquad \textbf{(2.24)}$$

From Exhibit 2.1, as of the end of 2010, GAP has current and non-current liabilities but no debt; however, we can also see that GAP had \$6 million in interest expense in 2010, which means that GAP had a small amount of debt at some point during the year. The debt GAP incurred was associated with drawing on its **line-of-credit**, probably to fund a buildup of inventory during its busy season. For GAP, the calculations of these financial leverage ratios—measured using year-end financial statement data as opposed to market data—are as follows:

$$\text{Total Debt to Total Assets}_{\text{GAP, 2010}} = \frac{\$0}{\$7,065} = 0$$

$$\text{Total Liabilities to Total Assets}_{\text{GAP, 2010}} = \frac{\$2,985}{\$7,065} = 0.423$$

$$\text{Total Debt to Common Equity}_{\text{GAP, 2010}} = \frac{\$0}{\$4,080} = 0$$

Measurement Issues—What Is Debt?

Debt is sometimes difficult to define and measure for two reasons. First, not all liabilities on an accounting balance sheet are debt. Accountants define liabilities as:[12] "A liability has three essential characteristics: (a) it embodies a present duty or responsibility to one or more other entities that entails settlement by probable future transfer or use of assets at a specified or determinable date, on occurrence of a specified event, or on demand, (b) the duty or responsibility obligates a particular entity, leaving it little or no discretion to avoid the future sacrifice, and (c) the transaction or other event obligating the entity has already happened."

While not all liabilities are debt, accountants do not have a specific definition of debt. We use the term **debt** to represent certain types of financing. These include notes, mortgages, bonds (debentures), and other financing instruments that typically have an explicit or implicit interest rate attached to them; thus, from a valuation perspective, we can define debt as an amount contractually owed to another party that has an explicit or implicit interest payment *that we can measure*. This definition excludes such liabilities as deferred income taxes, unearned revenue, and most other operating liabilities (for example, accounts payable, wages payable, accruals, etc.). For other reasons, convertible debt is also not entirely debt, even though accountants classify it as debt under U.S. GAAP. The convertible feature of convertible debt is a claim on equity, and the value of that convertible feature is not debt. Under **International Financial Reporting Standards (IFRS)**, convertible debt is actually split into a debt and equity component on the balance sheet.

The second reason it is difficult to define and measure debt is that companies can use debt that does not appear on the balance sheet, called **off-balance-sheet financing**. An example of off-balance-sheet financing is a non-capitalized operating lease. A company typically rents or leases some of its assets. We know that companies in certain industries, such as the airline, retail, and restaurant industries, lease many of their assets. Since these companies do not own leased assets, the most straightforward way to record lease payments is to record an operating expense for the amount of the lease payment each year; we call such leases **operating leases**, and they are a form of off-balance-sheet financing.

U.S. GAAP, however, requires companies to capitalize the present value of their lease payments on leases with certain characteristics that essentially transfer the ownership of the asset leased; we call these leases **capitalized leases** or **capital leases**.[13] When a company capitalizes the present value of the lease payments on a leased asset, it records an asset (leased asset) and liability (lease liability) equal to the present value of the lease payments. Each period, the company depreciates (expenses) the leased asset and recognizes interest expense on the lease liability. Over the life of the lease, the sum of the expenses of a capitalized lease (depreciation and interest) is equal to the sum of the lease payments. In the early years of a lease, however, a capitalized lease has higher expenses than an operating lease (which reverses in

---

[12] Financial Accounting Standards Board, *Statement of Financial Accounting Concepts No. 6*, "Elements of Financial Statements," December 1985, p. 36.

[13] See *Statement of Financial Accounting Standards No. 13*, "Accounting for Leases," November 1976, p. 7.

later years) even though the cash flow (lease payment) is identical for both the capitalized and operating leases. Some analysts capitalize all leases in analyzing a company's capital structure.

Another type of off-balance-sheet financing is an **unconditional purchase obligation**. These are future obligations to make certain payments in the future for fixed or minimum quantities to be delivered in the future. While U.S. GAAP requires companies to disclose the terms of these unconditional requirements (for the next five years) in the footnotes, they do not require that the company record a liability for these payments because the items being purchased have not yet been received.

In addition, companies sometimes create **special purpose vehicles** or **entities (SPVs or SPEs)** to transfer risks from the balance sheet to another entity. SPVs and SPEs became highly publicized after the failure of the Enron Corporation. Another term for an entity of this type is a "bankruptcy-remote entity." Regardless of what we call them, the key to such entities is that their operations are limited to the acquisition and financing of specific assets. The SPV or SPE is usually a subsidiary company with an asset and liability structure that isolates it from the parent company. Companies use SPVs and SPEs to isolate financial risk. For example, a company can use an SPV or SPE to finance a large project without putting the entire firm at risk.

Companies can use many other types of financial instruments that may be classified as debt but do not have the characteristics of a debt instrument. These include exchangeable debentures, interest rate swaps, recourse obligations on receivables sold, options, financial guarantees, interest rate caps and floors, futures contracts, forward contracts, and so forth. Many financial instruments have debt-like and equity-like characteristics, and it is important to understand both the economics of these transactions and how the accountant records and discloses them to conduct a detailed financial analysis of a company.

Coverage Ratios

Coverage ratios attempt to measure the ability of a company to pay its fixed charges (for example, interest payments). Conceptually, a company with a higher coverage ratio has a greater ability to service its non-equity securities. To measure coverage ratios, we typically use a ratio of a measure of income or cash flow (before the payment of fixed charges) to a measure of fixed charges. A general formula for coverage ratios is

$$\text{Coverage Ratio} = \frac{\text{Earnings Available to Pay Fixed Charges}}{\text{Fixed Charges}}$$

Alternative numerators include earnings before interest and taxes (EBIT), EBIT plus depreciation and amortization (EBITDA), operating cash flow before interest and taxes, and free cash flow before income taxes. Alternative denominators include interest payments and interest payments plus preferred stock dividends (grossed up for income taxes because we use a pre-tax numerator and preferred stock dividends are not tax deductible). Interest includes all interest payments, usually even **capitalized interest**. Typically, companies expense all interest accrued or paid; however, in some cases, when a company borrows money to finance the construction of a long-lived asset, the company will capitalize the interest. In other words, the company will include the interest that accrues during the construction of a building in the value of the asset. Since capitalized interest must be paid like most other interest, we include the capitalized interest in the denominator.

Sometimes companies issue **zero-coupon** or **paid-in-kind** debt, often referred to as PIK debt. In this case, the company does not actually have to pay the interest currently. Instead, the principal amount of the loan just increases by the amount of the unpaid but accrued interest. Depending on the reason we are calculating the coverage ratio, we might decide not to include the interest from the zero-coupon or paid-in-kind debt. For example, if you are analyzing the company's current ability to pay its fixed charges, you might want to exclude the interest on the PIK debt, for that portion of the interest is not a current requirement to be paid; the firm does not default for deferring payment since it is not contractually liable for that payment until later.

A common adjustment to the financial statements when measuring coverage ratios is to capitalize non-capitalized (or operating) leases, which is the same adjustment we discuss in the market multiple and cost of capital chapters later in the book. This adjustment affects both the numerator and the denominator. The numerator increases because we add back rent expense from the operating leases, and it decreases from the depreciation on the capitalized leased asset (assuming depreciation is not backed out of the numerator already, for example, as it is backed out of earnings before interest, taxes, depreciation, and amortization). The denominator increases by the additional interest on the capitalized leases. An alternative treatment is to include both the capitalized lease and operating lease payments in the denominator as a fixed charge and not to subtract out expenses associated with the leases from the numerator.

Valuation in Practice 2.3

Standard and Poor's Uses Financial Ratios in Its Credit Ratings Standard and Poor's (S&P) is a widely known credit rating agency. S&P describes its ratings as an "opinion of the general creditworthiness of an obligor, or the creditworthiness of an obligor with respect to a particular debt security or other financial obligation, based on relevant risk factors." S&P uses letters of the alphabet for its ratings; for example, AAA is the highest rating, followed by AA, A, BBB, and so forth. Here, S&P reports the median of key financial ratios of U.S. industrial corporations.

	20-Year Cumulative Default Rates of Debt Initially Rated in Category						
	AAA	**AA**	**A**	**BBB**	**BB**	**B**	**CCC**
Default rate....................	0.2%	1.4%	3.3%	9.4%	31.8%	54.7%	83.4%

	Key Financial Ratios of U.S. Industrials by Rating Category						
Average of 3-Year Medians	**AAA**	**AA**	**A**	**BBB**	**BB**	**B**	**CCC**
Operating margin (before D&A) (%) ...	22.2%	26.5%	19.8%	17.0%	17.2%	16.2%	10.5%
Return on capital (%)	27.0%	28.4%	21.8%	15.2%	12.4%	8.7%	2.7%
EBIT interest coverage (x)	26.2	16.4	11.2	5.8	3.4	1.4	0.4
EBITDA interest coverage (x)	32.0	19.5	13.5	7.8	4.8	2.3	1.1
Free cash flow to debt (%)..........	155.5%	79.2%	54.5%	35.5%	25.7%	11.5%	2.5%
Free operating cash flow to debt (%)..	129.9%	40.6%	31.2%	16.1%	7.1%	2.2%	−3.6%
Debt to EBITDA (x)	0.4	0.9	1.5	2.2	3.1	5.5	8.6
Debt to debt + equity (%)..........	12.3%	35.2%	36.8%	44.5%	52.5%	73.2%	98.9%
Number of observations............	6	14	111	213	306	354	22

S&P uses these ratios as part of a complex credit rating process, which includes using various financial ratios in conjunction with the company's business risk as guidelines. Not surprisingly, as the rating deteriorates from AAA to CCC, coverage ratios decline, leverage ratios increase, and profitability measures decline. S&P also reports default rates for debt initially rated in specific categories. The default rates are consistent with lower debt rating classes having higher default rates. The default rates reported here are the cumulative default rates over 20 years.

Source: Table 1 in Lugg, D., A. Balasubramanian, N. Pradhan, and V. Vishwanathan, "CreditStats: 2007 Adjusted Key U.S. Industrial and Utility Financial Ratios," September 10, 2008, Standard & Poor's, a division of the McGraw-Hill Companies, reprinted with permission.

Analysts typically do not include required principal repayments in fixed charges because with a sufficiently high coverage ratio, a company can likely refinance itself to repay the principal. If the company's ability to refinance its debt is in doubt, you may want to include required principal payments in the denominator. As with all financial ratios, we should make sure that our numerators and denominators are consistent, regardless of which way we measure them. If we include a fixed charge in the denominator, we should make sure that we do not deduct it from the numerator. Basic formulas for some of the common coverage ratios appear below (it is also common to use income from continuing operations instead of net income in the following formulas). We divide the preferred stock dividend by one minus the income tax rate because preferred stock dividends are not tax deductible.

$$\text{EBIT}/(\text{INT} + \text{PSDiv}) = \frac{\text{Net Income} + \text{Interest} + \text{Income Taxes}}{\text{Interest} + \text{Preferred Stock Dividends}/(1 - \text{Income Tax Rate})} \tag{2.25}$$

$$\text{EBITDA}/(\text{INT} + \text{PSDiv}) = \frac{\text{Net Income} + \text{Interest} + \text{Income Taxes} + \text{Depreciation} + \text{Amortization}}{\text{Interest} + \text{Preferred Stock Dividends}/(1 - \text{Income Tax Rate})} \tag{2.26}$$

GAP does not have any preferred stock or debt financing outstanding at the end of fiscal 2010, but it had a small amount of debt outstanding during the year, resulting in $6 million of interest in 2010. The coverage ratios for GAP for 2010 are

$$\text{EBIT/INT}_{\text{GAP, 2010}} = \frac{\$1{,}204 + \$6 + \$778}{\$6 + \$0/(1 - 0.393)} = 331.3$$

$$\text{EBITDA/INT}_{\text{GAP, 2010}} = \frac{\$1{,}204 + \$6 + \$778 + \$648}{\$6 + \$0/(1 - 0.393)} = 439.3$$

Our calculations of EBIT and EBITDA for GAP above assume that the interest income is from operations and not from excess assets. If they were from excess assets, an alternative treatment that some analysts use is to reduce the EBIT and EBITDA for the interest income, but then to pay down the debt with the excess assets and calculate a revised interest amount.

Making additional adjustments to our calculations for GAP is beyond the scope of this chapter; however, in a more detailed analysis of GAP, we would consider capitalizing GAP's operating leases as well as those of its competitors. GAP uses a significant amount of operating leases. Most of its stores are leased and GAP also leases most of its offices and distribution facilities. GAP's leases are, for the most part, not capitalized on its balance sheet; rather, GAP recognizes the lease payments as rent expense on its income statement. In GAP's case, capitalizing operating leases will increase financial leverage ratios. In addition, capitalizing those leases would affect its coverage ratios, as would the alternative treatment of including the lease payments as a fixed charge in the denominator if not capitalized.

U.S. Securities and Exchange Commission

The SEC requires a company to disclose its coverage ratio (earnings to fixed charges) in registration statements (prospectuses) for both debt and preferred stock issuances. The SEC provides a specific definition of both fixed charges and earnings. The definition of fixed charges includes "(a) interest expensed and capitalized, (b) amortized premiums, discounts and capitalized expenses related to indebtedness, (c) an estimate of the interest within rental expense, and (d) preference security dividend requirements of consolidated subsidiaries," and the definition of earnings is, in essence, earnings from continuing operations adjusted for the fixed charges and income taxes.[14] The SEC requires companies to disclose a coverage ratio of less than 1.0 as a "deficiency."

Valuation Key 2.7

Coverage ratios measure the ability of a company to pay its fixed charges (for example, interest). We measure coverage ratios as the ratio of a measure of income or cash flow to a measure of fixed charges (payments to non-equity security holders).

2.14 DISAGGREGATING THE RETURN ON (COMMON) EQUITY

We can disaggregate the return on equity into three components. The first two components are similar to the components in the return on assets—(levered) profit margin and asset utilization. We measure profit margin using net income to common equity in the numerator, called the **levered profit margin**, for we are disaggregating the return on equity. The third component is a **financial leverage factor** that considers the impact of using non-equity financing—the average of total assets to the average equity. We show the basic formula to disaggregate the return on equity in Equation 2.27.

---

[14] See Regulation S-K, Part 229 — Standard Instructions for Filing Forms Under Securities Act of 1933, Securities Exchange Act of 1934 and Energy Policy and Conservation Act of 1975. You can find the definition of the coverage ratio and related disclosures at http://www.sec.gov/divisions/corpfin/forms/regsk.htm#ratio.

$$\text{ROE} = \qquad \text{Levered Profit Margin} \qquad \times \quad \text{Asset Utilization} \quad \times \text{ Financial Leverage Factor}$$

$$\text{ROE} = \frac{\text{Net Income} - \text{Preferred Stock Dividends}}{\text{Revenue}} \times \frac{\text{Revenue}}{\text{Average Total Assets}} \times \frac{\text{Average Total Assets}}{\text{Average Equity}} \qquad \textbf{(2.27)}$$

The decomposition of the return on equity for GAP using the numbers from 2010 is

$$\text{ROE}_{\text{GAP, 2010}} = \frac{\$1{,}204 - \$0}{\$14{,}664} \times \frac{\$14{,}664}{(\$7{,}985 + \$7{,}065)/2} \times \frac{(\$7{,}985 + \$7{,}065)/2}{(\$4{,}891 + \$4{,}080)/2} = 0.268$$

$$\text{ROE}_{\text{GAP, 2010}} = 0.082 \times 1.95 \times 1.68 = 0.268$$

Return on assets and return on equity are algebraically related to each other. The return on equity is equal to the return on assets multiplied by a non-equity financing leverage factor. The non-equity financing leverage factor has two components. The first component is a **leverage factor for earnings**, and the second is a financial leverage factor that measures the amount of non-equity financing in the balance sheet. We show the relation between the return on assets and return on equity in Equation 2.28.

$$\text{ROE} = \text{ROA} \times \qquad\qquad \text{Non-Equity Financing Leverage Factor}$$

$$\text{ROE} = \text{ROA} \times \Big[\qquad \text{Leverage Factor for Earnings} \qquad \times \text{ Financial Leverage Factor} \Big]$$

$$\text{ROE} = \text{ROA} \times \left[\frac{\text{Income to Common Equity}}{\text{Net Income} + (1 - \text{Income Tax Rate}) \times \text{Interest Expense}} \times \frac{\text{Average Total Assets}}{\text{Average Equity}} \right] \qquad \textbf{(2.28)}$$

The relation between the return on assets and return on equity for GAP is as follows:

$$\text{ROE}_{\text{GAP, 2010}} = 0.160 \times \left[\frac{\$1{,}204 - \$0}{\$1{,}204 + (1 - 0.393) \times \$6} \times \frac{(\$7{,}985 + \$7{,}065)/2}{(\$4{,}891 + \$4{,}080)/2} \right] = 0.268$$

$$\text{ROE}_{\text{GAP, 2010}} = 0.160 \times [0.997 \times 1.68] = 0.268$$

$$\text{ROE}_{\text{GAP, 2010}} = 0.160 \times 1.67 = 0.268$$

In Exhibit 2.6 (which is in Section 2.9), we depict the decomposition of GAP's return on equity, just as we presented the decomposition of the return on assets.

REVIEW EXERCISE 2.5

The Gap, Inc. Return on Equity Forecasts for 2011 and Beyond

Use the information in Exhibit 2.1 to calculate GAP's return on equity for one or more of the years in the forecasts (F2011 through F2016). How is GAP's return on equity in the forecasts changing relative to 2010?

Solution on page 79.

2.15 ASSESSING COMPETITIVE ADVANTAGE

LO5 Assess a company's competitive advantage

As we discussed briefly in Chapter 1, assessing a company's competitive advantage is part of the valuation process. A company's competitive advantage affects the forecasts we use in our valuation. A competitive advantage is any characteristic that allows a company to compete within its industry so that it performs better than its rivals perform and allows a company to earn a return higher than its cost of capital. Michael Porter identified two primary types of competitive advantage: **cost leadership** and **differentiation**.[15] It is

---

[15] See for example, Porter, Michael E., *Competitive Advantage: Creating and Sustaining Superior Performance*, The Free Press (1985).

also possible for a company to have a competitive advantage via government or legal avenues by means of patents, licenses to do business, subsidies, and tariffs.

In order to have a competitive advantage, a company has to have the resources and the capabilities or competencies to achieve that competitive advantage. By understanding those capabilities, management and valuation experts are able to understand the nature of a company's competitive advantage and, more importantly, to make predictions about the sustainability of a company's competitive advantage. In the end, we want to forecast a company's free cash flows. Those free cash flows are affected by a company's competitive advantage, the returns associated with that competitive advantage, how long the competitive advantage is sustainable, and the likelihood the company can create new sources of competitive advantage in the future.

A company generally develops a competitive advantage by being a low-cost provider or by differentiating its product or service from those of its competitors. Differentiation can come in the form of specific attributes of the product, servicing of the product, speed of delivery, or perceived and actual quality (brand differentiation). A company can be a low-cost provider by either using its assets more efficiently than its competitors (effectively delivering more sales per dollar of invested assets) or by keeping costs of production, marketing, and distribution lower. While some companies are considered to be low-cost producers, their product offering is still somewhat differentiated.

Cost Leadership as a Competitive Advantage

Companies that are cost leaders have found some way to provide a product or service to a customer at a lower cost. Consider the case of a commodity product (e.g., oil) where there is no differentiation. In a competitive environment, with no differentiation, all producers will charge the same price. The only way to achieve superior profitability in this case will be to produce and deliver the product to the customer at a lower cost. Companies may be able to achieve lower costs in a variety of ways. Examples include lowering costs by operating with scale-efficient plants, taking advantage of economies of scale (buying power) and scope, using simpler designs that allow for lower costs of production, having technological advantages that lower costs, having a skilled and more efficient workforce, creating low-cost distribution networks, and keeping tight control of overhead, advertising, and research and development (R&D).

Companies that pursue cost leadership strategies must build capabilities and incentives within the organization to achieve that cost advantage. Those capabilities include the design of efficient processes of production or the ability to create technologies for efficient production, tight cost controls on operations, and a reporting system that quickly alerts managers if either the production process or spending gets out of control. In addition, companies pursuing a cost leadership strategy typically create incentives for employees and managers that focus on costs and cost control.

A company pursuing cost leadership as its primary strategy may also attempt to differentiate its products to some degree. So while cost leaders typically have reasonably limited and standardized offerings, they still may engage in differentiation through some mechanism. For example, McDonald's has a limited menu, and the menu is the same every day (except in the case of product introductions). Moreover, its offerings are quite standardized (employees don't ask you how you like your hamburger cooked). That being said, McDonald's still attempts to differentiate itself through branding and innovative product offerings.

Differentiation as a Competitive Advantage

A company pursues a differentiation strategy by offering unique product or service attributes that the customer will value. Thus, pursuing a differentiation strategy entails understanding the product or service attributes that customers value and then supplying those attributes to customers in a unique manner. Differentiation is achieved by emphasizing things such as product quality and design, service quality, branding, and product variety.

A company focused on differentiation typically has capabilities in advertising and branding, product design, engineering skills, R&D, and/or service and distribution networks that focus on maintaining the company's differentiation. An example of a company like this is the BMW Group, which produces BMW automobiles and is considered to be a leader in engineering and design. Another example is Nike, Inc., which advertises, markets, distributes, and sells athletic shoes and apparel and is well known for its focus on branding and promotion.

That said, a company pursuing a differentiation strategy still has to worry about costs. In the end, customers are always trading off quality attributes they desire against the cost of those attributes.

Automobile manufacturers have improved the design and quality of their cars over time while simultaneously finding manufacturing processes that reduce costs.

Strategic Positioning

Achieving competitive advantage is not just about choosing a cost advantage or a differentiation strategy. Indeed, one can envision a whole series of combinations of differentiation and relative cost. Firms with a great degree of differentiation will generally have high relative costs. Firms with no differentiation would want to operate with low costs. However, many combinations of differentiation and relative cost could result in a good competitive position for a company.

As a result, a viable strategy in some industries might be to operate with some degree of differentiation, but to give up some relative cost advantage that would have been feasible with no differentiation. Companies will choose to position themselves with the combination of cost effectiveness and differentiation that is both feasible for them and that creates the greatest long-term competitive advantage relative to their peers.

Achieving and Sustaining Competitive Advantage

We discussed some of the capabilities and competencies that a company must create in order to earn a competitive advantage relative to its competitors. Companies achieve competitive advantage by creating these core competencies. However, because the world is dynamic, sustaining a competitive advantage takes ongoing focus and innovation. Once a company has a competitive advantage, other companies in the industry will attempt to undermine that competitive advantage. They will attempt to replicate a competitive advantage or eliminate it by creating their own distinct competitive advantage. Companies that were once industry leaders for years have seen their brands shrink due to this. For example, Eastman Kodak Co.'s (Kodak) core business in film and developing was slowly eroded by film introduced by Fuji Photo Film Co (Fuji) and by film processing labs that did not rely on Kodak products. Subsequently, Kodak saw new technology, digital cameras, further erode its market position. A second reason why competitive advantage may be temporary is that shocks external to the industry can alter which companies in an industry have a competitive advantage. For example, an increase in gasoline prices could lead auto manufacturers with more fuel-efficient cars to suddenly have a competitive advantage relative to those who have focused their strategy on large SUVs.

In analyzing the sustainability of competitive advantage, we have to ask: what is the source of the competitive advantage; what are the core competencies that the company has created to sustain that competitive advantage; how easy is it for someone to imitate its success; how likely is it that the nature of the competitive advantage will shift due to either external shocks, changes in regulation, new technologies, competitor innovation, or any other source; and how nimbly can the company react to those shifts in competitive advantage?

Identifying the Source of Competitive Advantage

Managers often make statements about their companies' competitive advantage, but that does not mean the sources of competitive advantage are real or create value. While a company may have capabilities, those capabilities may not be unique, or competitors may have compensating capabilities (different capabilities that lead to similar outcomes). If so, the company would not have a competitive advantage. Once you think you have identified a source of competitive advantage and understand the degree of competition in an industry, it is useful to test whether your initial view can be "observed in the data." We can observe a company's competitive advantage in its data in a variety of ways.

One way to identify a company's competitive advantage is by comparing the financial performance of the company to that of its competitors. If we identify a difference in the performance of the company, we then assess whether the difference is due to different accounting technique choices, different classifications of expenses between categories, or something else that would indicate that the differences are not real (the result of accounting differences or short-term effects). If we conclude that the difference in performance is not the result of accounting differences or short-term effects, we then attempt to identify economic explanations for the difference.

What if we think a company has a competitive advantage but fail to see evidence of the competitive advantage in the data? In that case we must decide if (i) no competitive advantage actually exists, (ii) the competitive advantage, while real, is too small to be detected given the general imprecision and level of aggregation in financial statements, or (iii) management somehow obfuscates the effect of the competitive advantage because it does not want its competitors to see direct evidence of its success.

Assessing the Sustainability of Competitive Advantage

If we document a company's competitive advantage from its historical financial statements, then we must assess the sustainability of that competitive advantage. Can a company's competitive advantage last in perpetuity? That is unlikely in a competitive industry. The nature of competition and free markets is that competitors have incentives to work hard to make sure that they are not at a competitive disadvantage by either imitating someone else's competitive advantage or creating competitive advantage for themselves in a different manner. That said, some companies have been able to sustain competitive advantages for long periods.

We do not have a single way to assess the sustainability of a company's competitive advantage. Rather, we formulate questions to ask, collect as much information as reasonably possible, and then use our judgment to answer them. For example, we might ask: Is it a process or a technology that is patented and difficult to imitate in other ways? If so, how long does the patent last, and what is the likelihood that a similar outcome can be achieved through a different process or technology? Is it a long-term contract on an important raw material for production that guarantees a supply at a lower price? If so, what is the length of the contract, and could the competition utilize alternative materials with somewhat different manufacturing techniques to lower its costs? Is it a patent on a blockbuster drug? If so, how long will the patent last? Is the competitive advantage the result of a unique process in manufacturing or some support service such as procurement or distribution? If so, how obvious are the necessary capabilities that support that process, and how difficult would it be to replicate the capabilities required for that process? These questions are of importance to both managers and valuation experts. You may require help in answering some of these questions. For example, unless you are both a technology expert and a valuation expert, you may need someone to advise you on the difficulty of replicating the benefits of a particular technology.

Valuation Key 2.8

Valuing a company involves assessing a company's sources of competitive advantage and the sustainability of its competitive advantage. This analysis leads directly to an overall picture of the future profitability of the company being valued that will then be embedded in the forecasts.

Fort Howard Corporation

Fort Howard Corporation (Fort Howard) is an example of a company whose competitive advantage was its ability to produce a commodity product (tissue paper, toilet paper, etc. for the commercial market) at a lower cost. For years, Fort Howard had a proprietary de-inking technology, which allowed it to use a greater proportion of recycled wastepaper in the production of commercial tissues. At one point, Fort Howard used 100% recycled fiber while major competitors such as Scott Paper, Inc. (Scott Paper) and James River Corporation used 15% and 10% recycled fiber, respectively. At that time, recycled wastepaper was approximately 20% of the cost of non-recycled pulp because most states had passed mandatory recycling laws, and there were relatively few good uses for recycled paper.[16] In fact, Fort Howard created a division that collected recycled paper that gave the company a further cost advantage and allowed it to control the quality of the recycled fiber. Since the end-products were not differentiated in any meaningful way, Fort Howard was able to charge essentially the same prices as its competitors, and consequently enjoyed much higher margins because of its lower cost structure.

How might we have discovered Fort Howard's competitive advantage? Fort Howard continually disclosed in its 10-K that it had a proprietary de-inking technology. For example, it disclosed in one 10-K that, "The de-inking technology employed by the Company allows it to use a broad range of

---

[16] See "Fort Howard Corporation," *Fixed Income Research Report*, February 5, 1991, Credit Research and Trading (Greenwich, CT).

wastepaper grades, which effectively increases both the number of sources and the quantity of waste-paper available for its manufacturing process. The Company believes that its use of wastepaper for substantially all of its fiber requirements gives it a cost advantage over its competitors."[17] Of course, just indicating that it had a proprietary technology did not necessarily imply that the technology was a source of competitive advantage, nor did it quantify it. For example, other companies might have found other ways to achieve the same cost structure as Fort Howard. Analysts also discussed Fort Howard's superior technology and advantageous cost structure. Industry sources indicated the extent to which the tissue manufacturers relied on recycled paper in the manufacturing processes, and those sources corroborated management statements that Fort Howard was the leader in the use of recycled paper.

Where would we expect to observe Fort Howard's competitive advantage in its financial statements? Before we address that, we have to think a little about whether a cost advantage for Fort Howard would lead management to lower sales prices. Since commercial tissue is a commodity product, the sales price is essentially identical across manufacturers, which is determined by industry capacity and demand. Fort Howard's management could have reduced its price in an effort to capture market share or drive out a weakly capitalized competitor. However, since Fort Howard was operating close to its capacity and did not have the resources to expand production facilities aggressively (in fact, it had capital expenditure con-straints in its debt contracts), it had no reason to try to increase market share by cutting prices. By drop-ping prices, it would not capture all the benefits of its competitive advantage since it would have given some of those benefits to its consumers. At the time, Fort Howard had undergone an LBO, was highly levered, had to generate substantial cash flows to service that debt, and was in no position to engage in predatory pricing. Further, it faced competitors that were more strongly capitalized than it was. As such, Fort Howard had no incentive to cut price.

Now that we think there was no incentive to cut price, let us think about where we might observe Fort Howard's competitive advantage in its financial statements. We would expect Fort Howard's ratio of cost of goods sold to sales to be lower than that of other companies in the commercial tissue business. Why? To answer, we believe we identified a source of competitive advantage that allowed Fort Howard to produce products more cheaply than its competitors were able to. We have no indication that Fort Howard's de-inking technology allowed it to produce more products with less production capacity, but there was some indication that Fort Howard's plants were more expensive, as it suggested in one 10-K: "The Company has invested heavily in its manufacturing operations. . . .the Company's annual capital spending program includes significant investments for the ongoing modernization of each of its mills. For example, as new de-inking technologies and converting equipment are developed, the Company adds such technology and equipment at each mill to maintain low cost structures."[18] If these investments are large relative to those of its competitors, Fort Howard's EBIT margin might be reduced by additional depreciation, and we might expect to see its sales to total assets ratio to be somewhat lower than that of its competitors. Finally, there was nothing inherent in its strategy that should have led to increases in selling, general, and administrative expenses (SG&A).

In Exhibit 2.7, we show various ratios for Fort Howard Corporation, Fort James Corporation (Fort James, which had been called James River Corporation up until Year 8 when it merged with Fort How-ard), and Pope and Talbot, Inc. (Pope and Talbot) up to Year 9. We picked these two competitors because they are largely in the commercial tissue market, and Fort Howard's other competitors in the commercial tissue market also had significant operations in the consumer tissue market, which is not considered a commodity product.

We first review the data through Year 7, the last year for which we have data for Fort Howard. By examining the ratio of cost of goods sold to revenue, we can see immediately that Fort Howard has substantially lower cost of goods sold relative to its competitors. It is possible that this is due to some differences in how the three companies classify their costs. An examination of Fort Howard's EBIT to revenue (EBIT profit margin) shows a substantial advantage for Fort Howard. Thus, the advantage in gross margins was not just due to some reclassification of expenses to other parts of the income statement, for the gross margin advantage translates all the way down to EBIT. In addition, this means that higher depreciation charges did not offset the cost advantage of using more recycled fiber. In its last year (Year 7), Fort Howard's EBIT margin is 31.3% relative to 7.8% for Fort James and 2.1% for Pope and Talbot.

---

[17] See Fort Howard Corporation's 10-K for December 31, 1994, p. 7.

[18] See Fort Howard Corporation's 10-K for December 31, 1994, p. 6.

| **EXHIBIT 2.7** | Fort Howard Corporation, Fort James Corporation, and Pope and Talbot, Inc. Preliminary Financial Analysis |

	Year 1	Year 2	Year 3	Year 4	Year 5	Year 6	Year 7	Year 8	Year 9
Cost of Goods Sold to Revenue									
Fort James Corporation	72.5%	71.5%	76.6%	75.3%	74.8%	70.2%	66.7%	63.1%	61.3%
Fort Howard Corporation.	52.7%	52.5%	56.0%	58.6%	60.5%	64.2%	53.3%		
Pope and Talbot, Inc.	84.8%	89.4%	88.6%	83.5%	85.7%	88.8%	86.7%	81.9%	94.9%
EBIT Profit Margin (EBIT to Revenues)									
Fort James Corporation	8.1%	5.3%	1.0%	2.5%	3.1%	7.0%	7.8%	14.6%	15.9%
Fort Howard Corporation.	23.5%	23.8%	23.5%	22.2%	23.3%	22.2%	31.3%		
Pope and Talbot, Inc.	6.1%	−0.2%	0.9%	7.2%	3.4%	−1.4%	2.1%	4.5%	−7.7%
Sales to Total Assets									
Fort James Corporation	0.94	0.80	0.79	0.76	0.79	0.90	0.82	1.02	0.94
Fort Howard Corporation.	0.30	0.32	0.33	0.45	0.77	0.97	0.97		
Pope and Talbot, Inc.	1.59	1.43	1.52	1.52	1.33	1.04	1.02	0.84	1.02
Return on Assets (EBIT to Average Total Assets)									
Fort James Corporation	7.6%	4.3%	0.8%	1.9%	2.4%	6.3%	6.4%	14.8%	15.0%
Fort Howard Corporation.	7.1%	7.6%	7.7%	10.1%	17.8%	21.6%	30.3%		
Pope and Talbot, Inc.	9.6%	−0.3%	1.3%	10.9%	4.4%	−1.5%	2.1%	3.8%	−7.8%

An examination of Fort Howard's sales to total assets indicates that its turnover was much lower than that of its competitors until Year 5, likely due to more extensive investments in de-inking equipment and new capacity. However, by Year 6, Fort Howard's turnover ratio is similar to that of both Fort James and Pope and Talbot. Because of its higher EBIT margin, Fort Howard's EBIT return on assets is greater than that of the other two companies in every year except Year 1, when Fort Howard's asset turnover ratio was very low relative to that of the other two companies. By Year 5, Fort Howard's EBIT return on assets is far above the EBIT return on assets of both Fort James and Pope and Talbot. We focus on the EBIT return on assets, instead of the more typical return on assets, in order to remove the effect of some non-recurring charges that were taken by Fort Howard and some of the other companies, such as the write-off of goodwill.

Suppose that we were valuing Fort Howard in Year 5, and we were interested in determining how long Fort Howard's competitive advantage was likely to persist. To do this, we would need to understand the nature of its competitive advantage, its current position, and the position of its competitors. Fort Howard had undergone a leveraged buyout and was still highly levered in Year 5. Thus, it wasn't clear how much it could afford to spend on maintaining its competitive edge in the use of recycled paper. Moreover, Fort Howard faced well-capitalized competitors who were likely trying to develop improvements in their own processes for the efficient use of recycled paper.

Of course, an understanding of Fort Howard's technology and that of its competitors would allow us to make more informed judgments on the ability of Fort Howard's competitors to substantially improve their processes and reduce Fort Howard's cost advantage. Interestingly, the company relied on trade secret protection for its proprietary de-inking technology as opposed to seeking patent protection. One advantage of not filing a patent was that competitors were not able to observe how Fort Howard had achieved its superior usage of recycled fiber (and neither can we for purposes of analyzing the sustainability of Fort Howard's competitive advantage). Of course, there is always the danger that the trade secret will slip to the competition.

If your analysis determines that the current source of competitive advantage is not sustainable, you must then estimate how long it will take the current advantage to dissipate and whether new sources of competitive advantage can be created by the company. If you believe that Fort Howard will lose its competitive advantage, you will then have to project the level of profitability that it will attain. One approach to the latter issue is to start by examining the level of profitability of other companies in the commercial tissue market. That margin, though much lower than Fort Howard's, is sufficient to keep those companies from exiting the industry, so it is a reasonable prediction of where Fort Howard's margin will wind up once its competitive advantage is eliminated. Interestingly enough, Fort Howard merged with James

River in Year 8, and James River's margins improved immediately, suggesting that Fort Howard's competitive advantage was still largely intact at least through Year 9, the last year of data in the exhibit.

Nike, Inc.

Nike, Inc. (Nike) is famous for its athletic shoes and other athletic apparel. It performs market research and designs, markets, and distributes its athletic shoes; but, it outsources the manufacture and assembly of its shoes to companies in other countries. This is not unusual in the footwear industry. For example, Reebok International, Ltd. (Reebok) and Stride Rite Corporation (Stride Rite) have similar operating practices for the manufacture of their products. Lacrosse Footwear, Inc. (Lacrosse) had traditionally manufactured its products in the United States but was in the process of outsourcing the manufacturing overseas.

Nike spends a relatively large amount on endorsements and advertising relative to companies such as Lacrosse, Reebok, and Stride Rite in an attempt to differentiate its apparel and create a source of competitive advantage. If Nike's endorsements and advertising are a source of competitive advantage, where would we expect to see it in the financial statements? First, if it spends more, we should see that its ratio of advertising to revenue far exceeds that of its competitors. To the extent that advertising allows it to differentiate its products from those of its competitors who spend relatively little, we should expect to see that Nike's gross margin is higher than that of its competitors. If it is not, then one has to wonder whether Nike gets any advantage from its extensive advertising and endorsements. Of course, we should expect Nike's selling, general, and administrative expenses to be higher since advertising is a component of that cost. Whether Nike's advertising and marketing creates any competitive advantage will depend on whether its bottom line profit margin exceeds that of its competitors after extra advertising and marketing costs are taken into consideration.

In Exhibit 2.8, we provide various ratios for Nike and its competitors over an eight-year history. Nike's ratio of advertising to revenue always exceeds 10%, whereas Nike's competitors' is generally less

| EXHIBIT 2.8 | Nike, Inc., Lacrosse Footwear, Inc., Reebok International, Inc., and Stride Rite Corporation Preliminary Financial Analysis |

	Year 1	Year 2	Year 3	Year 4	Year 5	Year 6	Year 7	Year 8
Advertising to Revenue								
Lacrosse Footwear, Inc.	1.7%	1.5%	2.2%	2.3%	2.4%	1.7%	2.1%	2.1%
Nike, Inc.	**10.6%**	**11.8%**	**11.1%**	**10.9%**	**10.5%**	**10.4%**	**10.9%**	**11.2%**
Reebok International, Ltd.	5.8%	4.5%	4.4%	3.7%	3.8%	4.8%	4.2%	4.3%
Stride Rite Corporation.	5.5%	5.5%	6.4%	6.5%	6.1%	5.7%	4.3%	4.8%
Cost of Goods Sold to Revenue								
Lacrosse Footwear, Inc.	69.5%	69.4%	71.0%	71.5%	71.7%	69.6%	70.4%	67.7%
Nike, Inc.	**58.4%**	**61.6%**	**60.3%**	**58.0%**	**58.9%**	**58.4%**	**56.8%**	**55.1%**
Reebok International, Ltd.	60.6%	61.9%	61.9%	60.2%	60.7%	62.1%	61.6%	60.7%
Stride Rite Corporation.	63.7%	61.7%	62.0%	61.5%	61.6%	61.0%	60.7%	59.5%
Selling, General, & Admin Expenses to Revenue								
Lacrosse Footwear, Inc.	19.5%	19.0%	21.7%	25.3%	26.0%	26.8%	27.8%	27.3%
Nike, Inc.	**25.1%**	**27.5%**	**27.6%**	**29.0%**	**28.3%**	**28.5%**	**29.3%**	**30.1%**
Reebok International, Ltd.	30.6%	29.4%	32.4%	33.5%	31.9%	30.5%	30.5%	31.2%
Stride Rite Corporation.	32.9%	30.4%	29.9%	29.1%	29.3%	30.4%	29.9%	31.1%
EBIT Profit Margin (EBIT to Revenues)								
Lacrosse Footwear, Inc.	8.3%	9.0%	4.2%	−0.3%	−0.6%	0.2%	−1.0%	3.5%
Nike, Inc.	**14.8%**	**8.8%**	**9.5%**	**10.7%**	**10.5%**	**10.6%**	**11.6%**	**12.6%**
Reebok International, Ltd.	7.6%	7.6%	4.4%	4.8%	5.8%	6.2%	6.9%	7.2%
Stride Rite Corporation.	1.2%	6.0%	6.4%	7.7%	6.9%	5.9%	6.5%	7.0%
Return on Assets (EBIT to Average Total Assets)								
Lacrosse Footwear, Inc.	12.1%	13.6%	5.6%	−0.4%	−0.8%	0.3%	−1.4%	5.8%
Nike, Inc.	**29.2%**	**15.7%**	**15.7%**	**17.4%**	**17.1%**	**17.2%**	**18.9%**	**21.2%**
Reebok International, Ltd.	15.4%	15.6%	8.0%	8.4%	10.9%	12.3%	12.7%	13.0%
Stride Rite Corporation.	1.5%	8.8%	10.2%	12.9%	10.8%	8.9%	10.1%	11.4%

than 6%. Thus, Nike does spend substantially more than its competitors on advertising. Does that allow Nike to achieve greater gross margins? An examination of the ratio of cost of goods sold to revenue indicates that Nike's cost of goods sold to revenue is lower than that of its competitors, so Nike's gross margins are greater. Interestingly, Nike's ratio of selling, general, and administrative expenses to revenue is not greater than that of its competitors in spite of the fact that this line item includes advertising. Thus, Nike is doing something to curtail non-advertising SG&A costs, and we would want to try to determine how that had been achieved. Some suggest that because the Nike campus (corporate headquarters) is such a great place to work, employees are willing to work for lower wages because of the environment.

Not surprisingly, given the above we see that Nike's EBIT profit margins (operating income after depreciation to revenue) are consistently above the competition, indicating that Nike does have some competitive advantage. Finally, Nike's return on assets consistently exceeds the return on assets of the competition by a wide margin. Thus, Nike's competitive advantage is readily observable in its financial statements. Nike's performance has continued at the same pace relative to its competition through its 2010 fiscal year. While Adidas Group did not file financial statements at the time of the analysis above, it does now, and Nike's return on assets is larger than that of Adidas, which has a relatively similar strategy (Adidas Group now owns Reebok).

2.16 IMPLEMENTATION AND MEASUREMENT ISSUES

The selection of the specific methods we use to measure financial ratios depends on why we are analyzing a company. The inputs, and even the formula, can differ in different contexts. Regardless of the specific purpose of our analysis, we typically face certain measurement issues, which is the topic we discuss in this section of the chapter.

LO6 Describe measurement and implementation techniques

Some Basic Measurement Rules

Below, we list some basic measurement rules to follow when developing financial ratio formulas and measuring financial ratios. We refer to "flow" and "stock" variables in our discussion. A **flow variable** represents items on the income statement or cash flow statement. A **stock variable** is a value at a specific time, a balance, such as the items on the balance sheet.

- Flow divided by a flow—divide the most recent flow by the most recent flow. Some financial ratios that fall under this rule are profit margin (but not rate of return on assets or rate of return on equity), coverage of fixed cost (earnings before interest and taxes to interest), and expense ratios (cost of goods sold to sales).

- Stock divided by a stock—use the ending balances (adjusted for seasonality, see below). Relations that fall under this rule are liquidity ratios (current assets to current liabilities) and financial leverage ratios (total debt to equity).

- Flow divided by a stock or a stock divided by a flow—we generally use the most recent flow and the average stock (seasonally adjusted when appropriate). Relations that fall under this rule are rate of return on assets and rate of return on equity. In certain situations, it may be more appropriate to use ending stock balances. For example, we sometimes do this with working capital management ratios (receivables, inventory, and payables).

Inflation Adjustments

Naturally, inflation adjustments tend to be less important if inflation is low during the period over which you are analyzing a company. These adjustments are also less important for "flow to flow" ratios because flow variables tend to be similarly affected by inflation. However, this is not true when one of the flow variables contains depreciation and amortization expenses, because the underlying asset accounts are typically composed of assets purchased in the more distant past. Inflation adjustments are more important for "flow to stock" or "stock to flow" ratios; this is especially true when either the numerator or denominator of a financial ratio is not measured in dollars. For example, examining a time-series of revenues per square foot of retail space or of revenues per employee is more influenced by inflation, because one of the inputs (square feet or number of employees) is not affected by inflation at all.

One of the difficulties in adjusting financial ratios for inflation is the difficulty of identifying the appropriate adjustment factor or inflation index. For example, a computer manufacturer might be experiencing decreasing costs for some raw materials but increasing costs for others. Thus, in many circumstances, an overall inflation index, like the consumer price index, may not be appropriate. As a result, many analysts do not make inflation adjustments in their analyses unless the company is experiencing very high rates of inflation.

Seasonality

Some businesses are seasonal in nature; for example, many types of retailers depend heavily on their sales in the fourth quarter. The cash position of such companies tends to be highest in January and lowest in October, whereas their inventories and short-term debt balances tend to be highest in October and lowest in January. Consequently, many retailers choose a fiscal year-end near the end of January. Thus, using fiscal year-end balances can result in misleading financial ratios depending on why you are using the ratios. One way to address this issue is to use the average quarterly (or even monthly) balance instead of the ending annual balance. This approach better reflects the average balance of certain balance sheet items over the year.

Quarterly Data

We might be tempted to analyze financial ratios calculated on a quarterly basis—that is, calculate the return on assets, profit margin, turnover ratios, and so forth for each fiscal quarter. This approach does not always work well. Quarter-end balances for both flow and stock variables can be highly seasonal, which can distort the financial ratios. That is why we usually do not use flow data from an individual quarter; rather, we typically construct annual data from the last four quarters—usually called **last twelve months (LTM)** or **trailing twelve months (TTM)**. Of course, if you want to make comparisons between companies in the same industry for particular quarters, the use of quarterly data may be appropriate. In addition, because of the seasonal nature of some businesses as discussed above, we often compute quarterly averages of the stock variables. If there is little seasonality, year-end stock values may be fine.

Different Fiscal Year-ends

When we compare a company's financial ratios over time, we can get misleading results if a company changes its fiscal year-end during our analysis period. Similarly, when we compare a company's financial ratios to the ratios of its comparable companies, we can get misleading results if we are using annual financial statement data and the companies have different fiscal year-ends. Fortunately, we do not observe these issues very frequently. Companies rarely change their fiscal year-ends. In addition, companies in the same industry tend to cluster to a specific fiscal year-end due to industry factors. For example, as we noted earlier, most retail stores in the United States use January 31 as their fiscal year-end as opposed to December 31.

Adjusting the Data for Influential Observations (Outliers)

An **outlier** or **influential observation** is an unusual observation that appears to be outside the distribution of other observations. If the observation is truly an outlier, in that it is not part of the distribution of other observations, then using it can be misleading. Sometimes, an outlier is a data error, and sometimes it occurs because the denominator is close to zero; sometimes, however, it is the result of real economic effects.

What do you do with an outlier? First, identify whether it is a data error; if it is, correct it or exclude it if you cannot correct it. Second, identify potential economic rationales for why you should exclude it from your analysis or how you might adjust it to use in your analysis. For example, a company with a stock price of $10 and earnings per share of $0.01 has a price-to-earnings (P/E) ratio of 1,000. We know that a P/E ratio of 1,000 is likely an outlier. We would analyze this issue by assessing the reason for the company's earnings per share of $0.01; for example, ascertain if it is the result of a one-time or non-recurring effect. If it is, then we know that the P/E of 1,000 is merely an artifact of a non-recurring item and not a representative P/E ratio. In this case, we might consider adjusting the P/E ratio by adjusting the earnings for the non-recurring item or by using another definition of earnings that is not affected by the non-recurring item.

Other ways we might address a potential outlier issue include the following. If we are going to use a measure of central tendency or a range of representative values as benchmarks, we might use statistics that are less influenced by outliers (for example, use the median instead of the mean). We can also exclude a certain number or percentage of the observations from each tail of the distribution, called **trimming the distribution**. We can also set a certain number or percentage of the observations in each tail of the distribution at a "reasonable" value, called, **winsorizing the distribution**.

Negative Denominators

A negative denominator usually results in a misleading financial ratio. For example, a company with negative shareholders' equity of −$100 and an earnings to common of $10 will have a negative return on equity of −10% (−0.1 = $10/−$100), which is misleading and not a meaningful number. Sometimes it is possible to substitute a denominator that does not have a negative value or to invert a ratio to avoid a negative denominator. For example, if we invert a price-to-earnings ratio, the resulting earnings-to-price ratio can never have a negative denominator.

If a company has negative net income, it will have a negative return on equity as long as it has a positive equity balance; however, the same company can have a positive return on assets. The rate of return on assets will be positive as long as the company's unlevered income is positive; however, the rate of return on equity will be negative even when unlevered income is positive so long as the sum of after-tax interest plus preferred stock dividends is greater than unlevered earnings.

The Role of Accounting

The analysis of financial statements obviously relies on financial statement information. As such, expertise in financial statement analysis requires a thorough understanding of the economics of the transactions that parties are engaged in and how the accounting system records those transactions. That is why understanding financial disclosures and generally accepted accounting principles (GAAP) is an important part of any financial analysis. The better you understand accounting principles, the better equipped you will be to analyze a company.

GAAP is continually evolving in the United States and throughout the world. Knowledge of changes in GAAP is important for conducting financial statement analysis. For example, some companies engage in a variety of mechanisms to obtain financing that is not disclosed directly on the balance sheet, called **off-balance-sheet financing**. Standard setting bodies, such as the Financial Accounting Standards Board, respond to these strategies and change accounting principles in an attempt to improve the quality of disclosures. However, the process is never ending, for companies respond to changes in accounting policies with new types of transactions.

Because accounting principles vary from country to country, understanding accounting principles becomes more complicated when using the financial statements of companies in different countries. Apparent differences between two companies from different countries may be driven by differences in accounting principles in the two countries. The good news is that the International Accounting Standards Board (IASB) is in the process of creating a set of accounting standards called the International Financial Reporting Standards (IFRS). Many countries have adopted IFRS, and many other countries have committed to adopt them in the next few years. The bad news is that we still observe significant differences in the properties of accounting numbers across countries even when the standards are identical, due to differences in institutions, regulations, monitoring, enforcement, and legal systems. Thus, the properties of accounting numbers across countries are unlikely to ever be the same, even if the standards being used are identical.[19]

"Quality" of the Financial Disclosures

One dimension of the quality of a financial disclosure is its detail and transparency so that the reader can readily understand the economics underpinning it. Another dimension of the quality of a financial disclosure is how well it represents economic reality. As part of our analysis, we assess the transparency of the company's financial disclosures. We assess if the company chooses income-increasing or income-decreasing accounting policies. Examples of more conservative accounting policy choices include capi-

---

[19] See Ball, R., A. Robin, and J. Wu, "Incentives Versus Standards: Properties of Accounting Income in Four East Asian Countries," *Journal of Accounting and Economics* (December 2003), pp. 235–270, and Holthausen, R., "Testing the Relative Power of Accounting Standards Versus Incentives and Other Institutional Features to Influence the Outcome of Financial Reporting in an International Setting," *Journal of Accounting and Economics* (December 2003), pp. 271–284.

talizing rather than expensing leases, expensing rather than capitalizing operating expenses, and consolidating special-purpose entities. We also examine the difference between a company's accounting earnings and its operating cash flows in order to assess a company's accruals. We even consider the manager's reputation for being either aggressive or conservative, and we consider if the company structured certain transactions to achieve a "beneficial" accounting treatment.

We might also assess how transparent the company's disclosures are. Do they provide detailed discussions in the management discussion and analysis (MD&A) section of the 10-K? What about in conference calls on the business, the competition, or the company's strategy? Do they appear to obfuscate? Some analysts and researchers run linguistic programs on the MD&A and on the Q&A of conference calls in order to assess how forthcoming management is. Are the segment disclosures useful? Do they provide management forecasts? A company that is more forthcoming in these disclosures is generally consistent with higher overall accounting quality. However, we must keep in mind that management cannot disclose all of its strategy and tactical plans because disclosing it to investors also entails disclosing it to competitors. Thus, management has to worry about the tradeoff between informing investors and disclosing proprietary information to competitors.

Valuation Key 2.9

Understanding a company's accounting choices and policies, as well as the thoroughness of its financial disclosures, is an important part of a detailed financial analysis of a company.

SUMMARY AND KEY CONCEPTS

We use financial statement relations (financial ratios) in an attempt to measure certain economic concepts, such as a company's performance, operating risk, financial risk, growth, efficiency, and asset utilization. We analyze a company relative to both itself and other companies over time. To measure financial ratios, we divide a number from a company's financial statements by a number that adjusts the numerator for differences in size or scale. For example, we divide operating income by revenues to calculate a company's operating margin.

We use financial ratios in many ways in valuation—to assess the degree of comparability of potential comparable companies, to measure a company's cost of capital, to drive financial forecasts, to evaluate financial forecasts, and to establish constraints or hurdles in contracts. When measuring a company's financial ratios, we need to address various measurement issues that may arise for a company and for a specific use.

ADDITIONAL READING AND REFERENCES

Ball, R., and P. Brown, "An Empirical Evaluation of Accounting Income Numbers," *Journal of Accounting Research* (Autumn 1968), pp. 159–178.

Beaver, W., P. Kettler, and M. Scholes, "The Association Between Market-Determined and Accounting-Determined Risk Measures," *Accounting Review* (1970), pp. 654–682.

Fisher, F., and J. McGowan, "On the Misuse of Accounting Rates of Return to Infer Monopoly Profits," *American Economic Review* 73 (1983), pp. 82–97.

EXERCISES AND PROBLEMS

P2.1 **Cisco Systems, Inc.**: Review the time-series of various rates of return and rates of return components for Cisco Systems, Inc. in Exhibit P2.1. (Cisco manufactures and sells networking and communications products worldwide. It sells its products and services through its direct sales force, distributors, and retail partners.)

  a. Discuss the change in the return on assets during this period using its components.

  b. Discuss the change in the return on equity during this period using its components.

  c. Why are the unlevered and levered profit margins the same in all years, whereas the leverage ratios (as measured by total assets to common equity) are not equal to each other in any year?

EXHIBIT P2.1	Rates of Return and Components for Cisco Systems, Inc.

CISCO Systems, Inc.	Year 1	Year 2	Year 3	Year 4	Year 5	Year 6	Year 7	Year 8	Year 9	Year 10
Return on assets	30.0%	33.9%	23.1%	18.8%	17.7%	11.2%	–3.0%	5.2%	9.6%	13.7%
Return on equity..............	37.8%	43.5%	29.5%	23.7%	22.3%	14.0%	–3.8%	6.8%	12.6%	18.4%
Unlevered profit margin	21.3%	22.3%	16.3%	16.0%	17.2%	14.1%	–4.5%	10.0%	19.0%	22.5%
Levered profit margin	21.3%	22.3%	16.3%	16.0%	17.2%	14.1%	–4.5%	10.0%	19.0%	22.5%
Revenue to average total assets ..	1.41	1.52	1.42	1.18	1.03	0.80	0.65	0.52	0.50	0.61
Total assets to common equity ...	1.26	1.28	1.28	1.26	1.26	1.25	1.27	1.31	1.32	1.35

P2.2   **The Sherwin-Williams Company**: Review the time-series of various rates of return and rates of return components for the Sherwin-Williams Company in Exhibit P2.2. (Sherwin-Williams manufactures, distributes, and sells coatings and related products in North America and South America. It operates four segments: paint stores, consumer, automotive finishes, and international coatings.)

  a.   Discuss the change in the return on assets in the time-series using its components.
  b.   Discuss the change in the return on equity in the time-series using its components.
  c.   Why does the return on equity increase much more than the return on assets during this time period?
  d.   Why is the return on equity less than the return on assets in Year 6?

EXHIBIT P2.2	Rates of Return and Components for the Sherwin-Williams Company

Sherwin-Williams Company	Year 1	Year 2	Year 3	Year 4	Year 5	Year 6	Year 7	Year 8	Year 9	Year 10
Return on assets	9.9%	9.5%	8.8%	7.8%	8.4%	1.4%	8.1%	9.5%	10.0%	10.6%
Return on equity..............	17.7%	17.5%	17.4%	16.5%	17.8%	1.0%	17.8%	22.0%	23.7%	25.3%
ROE to ROA	1.80	1.84	1.97	2.10	2.11	0.74	2.21	2.31	2.37	2.39
Unlevered profit margin	6.2%	5.9%	6.3%	6.4%	6.8%	1.0%	5.9%	6.5%	6.6%	6.9%
Levered profit margin	6.1%	5.5%	5.3%	5.5%	6.1%	0.3%	5.2%	6.0%	6.1%	6.4%
Revenue to average total assets ..	1.60	1.61	1.39	1.22	1.23	1.34	1.37	1.47	1.52	1.54
Total assets to common equity ...	1.81	1.97	2.35	2.45	2.38	2.46	2.49	2.50	2.54	2.56

P2.3   **Dell Inc.**: Review the time-series of various working capital management ratios for Dell Inc. (formerly Dell Computer Corporation) in Exhibit P2.3. (Dell designs, develops, manufactures, and sells computer systems and services around the world.)

  a.   Discuss the change in Dell's current and quick ratios over the time-series. Is this change "good" or "bad" for Dell? In other words, should Dell try to reverse the trend in its time-series of current and quick ratios?
  b.   Using Dell's component ratios, discuss the change in Dell's trade cash cycle over the time-series.

EXHIBIT P2.3	Working Capital Management Ratios for Dell Inc.

Dell Inc.	Year 1	Year 2	Year 3	Year 4	Year 5	Year 6	Year 7	Year 8	Year 9	Year 10
Current assets to current liabilities	2.1	1.7	1.5	1.7	1.5	1.5	1.1	1.0	1.0	1.2
Quick ratio	1.5	1.4	1.2	1.5	1.3	1.3	0.8	0.8	0.8	1.0
Days of sales held in inventory....	31.4	20.5	9.3	6.6	6.1	5.7	4.9	6.4	7.8	5.4
Accounts receivable collection period	43.6	38.3	35.4	39.7	37.3	31.9	30.2	25.0	27.4	29.9
Accounts payable payment period	38.5	46.8	51.4	52.4	54.1	56.6	67.5	68.9	72.2	74.7
Trade cash cycle..............	36.5	12.0	–6.8	–6.1	–10.8	–19.0	–32.4	–37.5	–37.0	–39.5

P2.4   **Water Pik Technologies, Inc.**: Review the time-series of various working capital management ratios for Water Pik Technologies, Inc. in Exhibit P2.4. (Water Pik designs, manufactures, and sells personal health care products, swimming pool products, and water heating systems.)

  a.   Discuss the change in Water Pik's current and quick ratios over the time-series. Is this change "good" or "bad" for Water Pik? In other words, should Water Pik try to reverse the trend in its time-series of current and quick ratios?

b. Using Water Pik's component ratios, discuss the change in Water Pik's trade cash cycle over the time-series.

EXHIBIT P2.4 Working Capital Management Ratios for Water Pik Technologies, Inc.

Water Pik Technologies, Inc.	Year 1	Year 2	Year 3	Year 4	Year 5	Year 6
Current assets to current liabilities..........	1.8	1.8	2.1	2.3	2.4	2.0
Quick ratio	1.1	1.1	1.4	1.4	1.5	1.1
Days of sales held in inventory.............	55.8	59.2	67.7	69.3	69.6	91.2
Accounts receivable collection period	74.5	74.0	88.2	98.9	98.4	104.6
Accounts payable payment period	55.4	51.3	49.0	43.9	41.3	52.6
Trade cash cycle........................	74.9	81.9	106.9	124.3	126.7	143.3

P2.5 **Samsonite Corporation**: Review the time-series of various financial leverage and coverage ratios for Samsonite Corporation in Exhibit P2.5. (Samsonite designs, develops, manufactures, and sells luggage and travel-related consumer products.)

a. Discuss the change in Samsonite's financial leverage and coverage ratios over the time-series.

b. Using its financial leverage and coverage ratios, discuss what you know about its common equity.

c. Which is larger—interest expense or preferred stock dividends—for each year in the time series? (Assume that an income tax rate of zero was used to measure the financial ratios.)

EXHIBIT P2.5 Financial Leverage and Coverage Ratios for Samsonite Corporation

Samsonite Corporation	Year 1	Year 2	Year 3	Year 4	Year 5	Year 6	Year 7	Year 8	Year 9
Total debt to total assets	0.5	0.5	0.3	0.8	0.8	0.8	0.9	0.7	0.7
Preferred stock to total assets	0.0	0.0	0.0	0.3	0.4	0.4	0.5	0.6	0.3
Total debt to common equity	12.7	10.8	0.9	NMF	NMF	NMF	NMF	NMF	NMF
Preferred stock to common equity.........	0.0	0.0	0.0	NMF	NMF	NMF	NMF	NMF	NMF
EBIT coverage (interest only)	−0.2	0.7	3.6	0.5	1.1	1.2	0.9	1.5	1.7
EBIT coverage (interest + preferred stock dividends).....	−0.2	0.7	3.6	0.4	0.7	0.7	0.5	0.8	1.0

"NMF" = not a meaningful figure

P2.6 Use the financial statements in Exhibit P2.6 to calculate the return on assets, return on equity, and their respective top-level components (unlevered profit margin, asset utilization, earnings leverage factor, and financial leverage factor) for the Jake and Luke Schnall Company for Year 10. In addition, for each of the events described below, recalculate the return on assets, return on equity, and their respective components assuming the event occurred at the end of Year 9. Assume that the company distributes an annual dividend to common shareholders equal to net income minus any dividends distributed to preferred stockholders.

a. The company issues additional debt at its current interest rate to fund capital expenditures and raise the working capital necessary to grow the company by 50 percent in 2010; the new investment will earn an ROA equal to the company's current ROA.

b. Same information as part (a) except the company issues additional preferred stock instead of debt.

c. Same information as part (a) except the company issues additional common stock instead of debt.

d. The company issues additional debt at its current interest rate to repurchase 10 percent of the company's common stock at a price equal to two times its book value.

e. The company refinances all of its existing debt and issues debt in a highly levered transaction. Its new interest rate is 2 percent higher than its previous interest rate. It used the cash proceeds from the debt issuance to repurchase 55 percent of the company's common stock at a price equal to two times its book value.

f. The company issues additional common stock to repurchase all of the existing debt and preferred stock at book value with no taxable gains or losses on the debt.

g. The company sells 20 percent of its business (operating assets and liabilities) at book value with no taxable gain or loss. The sale of the business reduces the company's revenue and all operating expenses by 10 percent. The company uses the cash flow from the sale to redeem debt at book value with no taxable gains or losses on the debt.

h. The company sells 20 percent of its business (operating assets and liabilities) at book value with no taxable gain or loss. The sale of the business reduces the company's revenue and all operating expenses by 10 percent. The company uses the cash flow from the sale to repurchase some of the company's common stock.

EXHIBIT P2.6	Financial Statements for the Jake and Luke Schnall Company

Income Statement ($ in millions)	Rate	Year 10
Operating revenue		$ 5,000
Operating expenses		1,750
Operating income (EBIT)		$ 3,250
Interest expense	7.0%	263
Income before income tax expense (EBT)		$ 2,988
Income tax expense (benefit)	40.0%	1,195
Net income		$ 1,793

Common Equity Balance	Rate	Year 10
Beginning balance		$ 4,875
Net income		1,793
Preferred stock dividends	8.0%	−150
Dividends		−1,643
Ending balance		$ 4,875

Balance Sheet ($ in millions)	Year 9	Year 10
Total current assets	$ 2,500	$ 2,500
Property, plant, and equipment, net	10,000	10,000
Total assets with excess assets	$12,500	$12,500
Total current liabilities	$ 2,000	$ 2,000
Total debt	3,750	3,750
Total liabilities	$ 5,750	$ 5,750
Preferred stock	$ 1,875	$ 1,875
Common stock (equity)	4,875	4,875
Total stockholders' equity	$ 6,750	$ 6,750
Total liabilities and stockholders' equity	$12,500	$12,500

P2.7   Exhibit P2.7 presents certain rates of return, profit margins, and other information on the Nate and Evelyn Z's Furniture Company. Using the information in the exhibit, complete the partial financial statements and calculate the missing financial ratios (shown as "?-#") in Exhibit P2.7. (All financial ratios using balance sheet numbers were calculated using Year 12 ending balances instead of average balances.)

EXHIBIT P2.7	Nate and Evelyn Z's Furniture Company

Income Statement ($ in millions)	Year 12	Financial Ratios	Year 12
Operating revenue	$30,000	Return on assets	17.5%
Operating expenses	?-1	Return on investment	19.4%
Operating income (EBIT)	?-2	Return on equity	?-13
Interest expense	?-3	Unlevered profit margin	14.0%
Income before income tax expense (EBT)	?-4	Total asset utilization (turnover)	?-14
Income tax expense (benefit)	?-5	Levered profit margin (to common)	10.8%
Net income	?-6	Financial leverage factor	2.938

Balance Sheet ($ in millions)	Year 12	Other Information	Year 12
Total assets with excess assets	?-7	Constant income tax rate	30.0%
		Preferred stock dividend rate	9.0%
Total current liabilities	?-8	Change in preferred stock at end of Year 12	$1,000
Total debt	?-9	Preferred stock dividends	$432
Preferred stock	?-10		
Common stock (equity)	?-11		
Total liabilities and stockholders' equity	?-12		

P2.8 You are an analyst and have certain rates of return, profit margins, and other information on the Jeff, Matt, and Mike Associates Company. Using the information in the exhibit, complete the partial financial statements and calculate the missing financial ratios (shown as "?-#") in Exhibit P2.8. The company had no purchases or other additions to Intangible Assets. (All financial ratios using balance sheet numbers are calculated using Year 7 ending balances instead of average balances. The company had no sales or retirements of property, plant, and equipment or intangible assets. Essentially all of the company's property, plant, and equipment is depreciable. All changes in financing occur at the end of the fiscal year.)

EXHIBIT P2.8 Financial Statements for Jeff, Matt and Mike Associates

Income Statement ($ in millions)	Year 7	Other Information	Year 7
Operating revenue	?-1	Income tax rate	30.0%
Cost of goods sold	?-2	Preferred stock dividend rate	9.0%
Selling, general and administrative	?-3	Change in preferred stock	$ 1,000
Depreciation and amortization (All)	?-4	Retained earnings—beginning balance	$ 4,400
		Inventory purchases	$12,400
Operating income (EBIT)	?-5	Capital expenditures (PPEQ)	$15,000
Interest expense	?-6	Beginning of year balance—intangible assets	$ 2,500
		Common dividends	$ 3,014
Income before income tax expense (EBT)	?-7		
Income tax expense (benefit)	?-8		
Net income	?-9		

Balance Sheet ($ in millions)	Year 7	Financial Ratios (Based on Ending Balances)	Year 7
Cash	?-10	Cost of goods sold expense ratio	28.571%
Accounts receivable	?-11	Selling, general and administrative expense ratio	33.333%
Inventory	?-12	Total liabilities to total assets	0.546
Current assets	?-13	EBITDA to interest	8.000
		EBITDA to fixed charges	4.776
Property, plant and equipment—gross (PPEQ)	?-14	Quick (asset test) ratio	1.531
Accumulated depreciation	?-15	Days of inventory held	133.833
		Accounts receivable collection period	32.776
Property, plant and equipment—net	?-16	Trade cash cycle	103.028
Intangible assets	?-17	Provision for bad debts ratio	4.546%
		Depreciable life of gross plant	12.500
Total assets with excess assets	?-18	Depreciable life of net plant	8.500
		PPEQ investment (CAPEX) to revenues	35.714%
Accounts payable	?-19	PPEQ investment (CAPEX) to depreciation	2.500
Accruals	?-20		
Total current liabilities	$ 3,070	Earnings per share (EPS)—basic	$4.375
Total debt	?-21	Shares outstanding for basic EPS	984.0
Total liabilities	?-22		
Preferred stock	?-23		
Common stock—paid-in-capital	?-24		
Retained earnings	?-25		
Shareholders' equity	?-26		
Total liabilities and stockholders' equity	?-27		

P2.9 **Main Street Restaurant Group:** A young analyst was asked to measure the return on assets and return on equity for *the operations* of the Main Street Restaurant Group by using the abbreviated balance sheets and income statements that appear in Exhibit P2.9. (The company operates TGI Friday's and other restaurants.) Based on this information, the analyst calculated the rates of return using the following formulas

$$\text{Return on Assets} = \frac{\text{Net Income} + (1 - \text{Average Tax Rate}) \times \text{Interest Expense}}{\text{Average Total Assets}}$$

$$\text{Return on Equity} = \frac{\text{Net Income}}{\text{Average Common Equity}}$$

a. Comment on the formulas the analyst used to measure the rates of return on the company's operations shown in the exhibit.

b. Using the information in the exhibit, correctly calculate the return on assets and return on equity for the company's operations, for each year for which you have data available.

c. Calculate the components of the correctly calculated return on assets and return on equity for each year for which you have data available.

EXHIBIT P2.9 Abbreviated Balance Sheets and Income Statements for the Main Street Restaurant Group

Main Street Restaurant Group

Balance Sheet (Abbreviated)	Year 1	Year 2	Year 3	Year 4	Year 5	Year 6
Current assets	$ 8.56	$ 13.20	$ 15.82	$ 12.55	$ 9.83	$ 10.04
Plant, property & equip (net)	58.00	63.85	65.23	71.27	68.13	66.45
Other assets	19.96	31.20	31.42	28.58	28.25	26.69
Total assets	$ 86.52	$108.25	$112.47	$112.40	$106.21	$103.18
Total current liabilities	$ 25.22	$ 20.89	$ 23.81	$ 27.58	$ 26.80	$ 29.74
Long term debt	31.51	44.40	47.23	52.00	47.87	42.23
Other liabilities	2.41	2.47	1.22	3.21	2.44	1.92
Total liabilities	$ 59.14	$ 67.76	$ 72.26	$ 82.79	$ 77.11	$ 73.89
Common stock	$ 44.20	$ 53.63	$ 53.66	$ 53.94	$ 54.95	$ 54.95
Retained earnings	−16.82	−13.14	−13.45	−24.33	−25.85	−25.66
Treasury stock	0.00	0.00	0.00	0.00	0.00	0.00
Common equity (total)	$ 27.38	$ 40.49	$ 40.21	$ 29.61	$ 29.10	$ 29.29
Liabilities and shareholders' equity	$ 86.52	$108.25	$112.47	$112.40	$106.21	$103.18
Debt in current liabilities	$ 1.83	$ 2.01	$ 3.01	$ 3.50	$ 3.82	$ 3.85
Average income tax rate	35.0%	35.0%	35.0%	35.0%	35.0%	35.0%
Closing stock price	$ 3.25	$ 3.03	$ 4.94	$ 2.12	$ 2.86	$ 1.60
Common dividends	$ 0.00	$ 0.00	$ 0.00	$ 0.00	$ 0.00	$ 0.00

Main Street Restaurant Group

Income Statement (Abbreviated)	Year 1	Year 2	Year 3	Year 4	Year 5	Year 6
Sales (net)	$141.16	$187.15	$214.26	$229.15	$227.49	$224.75
Cost of goods sold	121.29	161.65	184.86	194.79	200.79	199.75
Gross profit	$ 19.87	$ 25.50	$ 29.40	$ 34.36	$ 26.70	$ 25.00
Selling, general, & admin expenses	9.93	11.15	11.20	12.39	10.08	9.52
Depreciation, depletion, & amortiz.	5.65	8.49	9.68	8.36	8.99	8.87
Operating income	$ 4.29	$ 5.86	$ 8.52	$ 13.61	$ 7.63	$ 6.61
Interest expense	2.60	3.62	3.83	3.90	4.52	3.97
Minority interest in income	0.00	0.00	0.00	0.00	0.00	0.00
Non-operating income (expenses)	−0.49	1.69	−3.45	−7.99	−2.08	−1.69
Pretax income	$ 1.20	$ 3.93	$ 1.24	$ 1.72	$ 1.03	$ 0.95
Income taxes	0.42	1.38	0.43	0.60	0.36	0.33
Income before extraordinary items & discontinued oper.	$ 0.78	$ 2.55	$ 0.81	$ 1.12	$ 0.67	$ 0.62
Extraordinary items and discontinued operations	−0.17	−0.02	0.00	0.00	0.00	0.00
Net income	$ 0.61	$ 2.53	$ 0.81	$ 1.12	$ 0.67	$ 0.62

SOLUTIONS FOR REVIEW EXERCISES

Solution for Review Exercise 2.1: The Gap, Inc. Return on Assets 2011 and Beyond

Return on Assets	A2010	F2011	F2012	F2013	F2014	F2015	F2016
Return on assets	16.0%	18.4%	19.9%	20.9%	21.7%	21.8%	21.9%
Unlevered profit margin	8.2%	8.4%	8.5%	8.5%	8.5%	8.5%	8.5%
Total asset utilization (turnover)	1.95	2.19	2.33	2.45	2.54	2.56	2.57
Return on assets (check)	16.0%	18.4%	19.9%	20.9%	21.7%	21.8%	21.9%

Solution for Review Exercise 2.2: The Gap, Inc. Expense Ratio Forecasts for 2011 and Beyond

Expense Ratios (to Revenue)	A2010	F2011	F2012	F2013	F2014	F2015	F2016
Cost of goods sold	55.4%	54.7%	54.6%	54.6%	54.6%	54.6%	54.6%
Gross margin	44.6%	45.3%	45.4%	45.4%	45.4%	45.4%	45.4%
Depreciation and amortization	4.4%	4.4%	4.4%	4.4%	4.4%	4.4%	4.4%
Operating expense	26.7%	27.1%	27.0%	27.0%	27.0%	27.0%	27.0%
Operating income	13.4%	13.7%	13.9%	13.9%	13.9%	13.9%	13.9%
Interest expense	0.0%	0.0%	0.0%	0.0%	0.0%	0.0%	0.0%
Other income (expense), net	0.1%	0.1%	0.1%	0.1%	0.1%	0.1%	0.1%
Income before income tax expense	13.5%	13.8%	14.0%	14.0%	14.0%	14.0%	14.0%
Income tax expense (benefit)	5.3%	5.4%	5.5%	5.5%	5.5%	5.5%	5.5%
Net income	8.2%	8.4%	8.5%	8.5%	8.5%	8.5%	8.5%

Solution for Review Exercise 2.3: The Gap, Inc. Asset Utilization Ratios for 2011 and Beyond

Asset Utilization (Turnover) Ratios	A2010	F2011	F2012	F2013	F2014	F2015	F2016
Cash—required (total revenues)	6.93	9.00	9.04	9.04	9.04	8.94	8.94
Accounts receivable, gross (total revenues)							
Inventories (total revenues)	9.47	9.29	9.40	9.40	9.40	9.29	9.29
Other current assets (total revenues)	23.29	23.18	23.29	23.29	23.29	23.02	23.02
Total current assets (total revenues)	3.41	3.82	3.85	3.85	3.85	3.80	3.80
Property, plant, and equipment, net (total revenues)	5.65	6.37	7.67	9.10	10.50	11.19	11.47
Other assets (total revenues)	23.11	25.96	26.08	26.08	26.08	25.77	25.77
Total assets w/o excess assets (total revenues)	2.08	2.21	2.34	2.44	2.52	2.53	2.55
Property, plant, and equipment, gross (total revenues)	1.96	1.97	1.97	1.95	1.92	1.82	1.73
Total assets (total revenues)	2.08	2.21	2.34	2.44	2.52	2.53	2.55

Solution for Review Exercise 2.4: The Gap, Inc. Working Capital Management Ratio Forecasts for 2011 and Beyond

Working Capital Management Ratios	A2010	F2011	F2012	F2013	F2014	F2015	F2016
Current ratio (operating liabilities).	1.87	1.89	1.89	1.89	1.89	1.89	1.89
Quick (asset test) ratio	0.79	0.80	0.81	0.81	0.81	0.81	0.81
Cash flow to current liabilities (operating)	0.73	0.91	0.92	0.92	0.92	0.92	0.92
Days of purchases outstanding (payable)	45.81	45.84	44.83	44.77	44.77	45.51	45.51
Days of inventory held	69.55	71.79	71.09	71.03	71.03	71.87	71.87
Accounts receivable collection period							
Trade cash cycle.	23.73	25.95	26.26	26.25	26.25	26.36	26.36

Solution for Review Exercise 2.5: The Gap, Inc. Return on Equity Forecasts for 2011 and Beyond

Return on Equity	A2010	F2011	F2012	F2013	F2014	F2015	F2016
Return on equity.	26.8%	32.5%	36.8%	40.3%	43.3%	44.4%	44.9%
Profit margin (to common)	8.2%	8.4%	8.5%	8.5%	8.5%	8.5%	8.5%
Total asset utilization (turnover)	1.949	2.186	2.333	2.451	2.542	2.557	2.571
Financial leverage factor	1.678	1.767	1.847	1.929	1.998	2.035	2.046
Return on equity (check)	26.8%	32.5%	36.8%	40.3%	43.3%	44.4%	44.9%
Return on assets	16.0%	18.4%	19.9%	20.9%	21.7%	21.8%	21.9%
Leverage factor for earnings	0.997	1.000	1.000	1.000	1.000	1.000	1.000
Financial leverage factor	1.678	1.767	1.847	1.929	1.998	2.035	2.046
Return on equity (check)	26.8%	32.5%	36.8%	40.3%	43.3%	44.4%	44.9%

After mastering the material in this chapter, you will be able to:

1. Measure free cash flows (3.1–3.2)

2. Create a cash flow statement (3.3–3.4)

3. Analyze income tax disclosures (3.5–3.6)

4. Measure the effects of net operating losses on taxes and interest tax shields (3.7)

Measuring Free Cash Flows

Facebook uses free cash flow to manage the company and measure performance:

FACEBOOK

In addition to other financial measures presented in accordance with U.S. generally accepted accounting principles (GAAP), we monitor free cash flow (FCF) as a non-GAAP measure to manage our business, make planning decisions, evaluate our performance, and allocate resources. . . .

We believe that FCF is one of the key financial indicators of our business performance over the long term and provides useful information regarding whether cash provided by operating activities is sufficient to fund the ongoing property and equipment investments required to maintain and grow our business. . . .

. . . We present FCF in this document in the same manner it is shared with our senior management and board of directors. . . .

FCF has limitations as an analytical tool, and you should not consider it in isolation or as a substitute for analysis of other GAAP financial measures, such as net cash provided by operating activities. Some of the limitations of FCF are:

- FCF does not reflect our future contractual commitments; and
- other companies in our industry present similarly titled measures differently than we do, limiting their usefulness as comparative measures.[1]

Facebook does not use exactly the same definition of free cash flows that we use to value companies. In this chapter, you will learn additional details about calculating the free cash flows we use in our valuation work, how to create a cash flow statement, and how to analyze income tax disclosures (including those related to net operating losses).

---

[1] See page 41 of Facebook's S-1 Registration Statement, filed with the Securities and Exchange Commission (SEC) on February 1, 2012, http://www.sec.gov/Archives/edgar/data/1326801/000119312512034517/d287954ds1.htm, February 4, 2012.

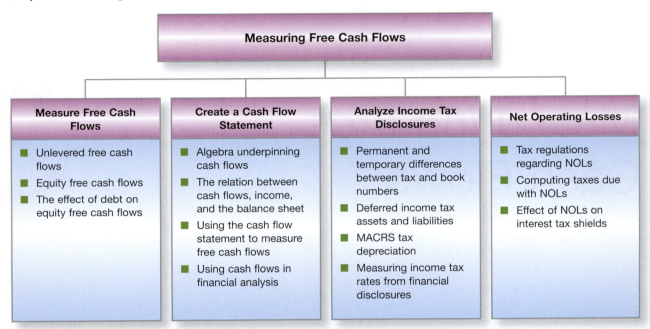

Measuring Free Cash Flows

Measure Free Cash Flows	Create a Cash Flow Statement	Analyze Income Tax Disclosures	Net Operating Losses
■ Unlevered free cash flows ■ Equity free cash flows ■ The effect of debt on equity free cash flows	■ Algebra underpinning cash flows ■ The relation between cash flows, income, and the balance sheet ■ Using the cash flow statement to measure free cash flows ■ Using cash flows in financial analysis	■ Permanent and temporary differences between tax and book numbers ■ Deferred income tax assets and liabilities ■ MACRS tax depreciation ■ Measuring income tax rates from financial disclosures	■ Tax regulations regarding NOLs ■ Computing taxes due with NOLs ■ Effect of NOLs on interest tax shields

INTRODUCTION

What is a cash flow? The term "cash flow" has many definitions, but most are of little help to an analyst interested in valuation. For example, a net change in the cash holdings of a firm can be called the net cash flow, but this cash flow would not be very useful in valuing a company. In valuation analysis, an important characteristic of the cash flow concept is the relevant cash flow to a particular security holder. For example, if we were valuing a long-term simple bond that matures in 20 years, the relevant cash flows are the interest and principal payments.

In valuing a company, the relevant cash flows are the (unlevered or asset) free cash flows that we briefly introduced in Chapter 1. Free cash flows are the cash flows available for distribution to all of a company's security holders. They are the cash flows measured after a company collects its revenues, pays its expenses, and makes all of the investments necessary to implement its business strategy, including investments in working capital. They are the cash flows the company would generate if it was entirely financed with equity, which is why they are called unlevered cash flows. In this chapter, we discuss both the concept of free cash flows and the alternative approaches to measuring them in much more detail. We also discuss another cash flow concept—equity free cash flows. Equity free cash flows are free cash flows adjusted for all cash flows to and from non-equity investors and represent the cash flows that are available for distribution to the common equityholders after the company has made all required investments.

After discussing free cash flows, we turn our attention to the cash flow statement, one of the financial statements filed by companies in their annual and quarterly reports. We can use the cash flow statement as the basis for calculating free cash flows. The operating accrual adjustments used to convert income to operating cash flow in the cash flow statement are useful for calculating free cash flows, for those adjustments are basically the same ones used in the free cash flow calculation. Thus, it is extremely useful to understand, at the very least, the basics of accounting, particularly the cash flow statement, in order to do this work.

In our discussion of the cash flow statement and free cash flow schedule, we begin to introduce financial models, which we then discuss in more detail in Chapter 4. While we do not discuss any financial models directly in this chapter, the flow of information that begins with the income statement and balance sheet into the cash flow statement and ends with the free cash flow schedule is the same flow used in financial modeling.

3.1 INTRODUCTION TO MEASURING FREE CASH FLOWS

LO1 Measure free cash flows

The cash flows that we discount are an important input into any discounted cash flow (DCF) valuation of a company. We call these **free cash flows**. If a company only uses equity financing, then it will have one type of investor and one type of free cash flow, which we call **unlevered free cash flows** or **free cash flows** (**FCF**), for short. If a company uses other types of financing such as debt or preferred stock, we still want to know the free cash flows that are available to all investors. These are the same unlevered free cash flows for the company. When a company uses both non-equity financing and equity financing, we often want to know the free cash flows that are available to its equityholders. A company's **equity free cash flows** (**EFCF**) are equal to the company's unlevered free cash flows adjusted for all after-tax cash flows paid to, or received from, non-equity security holders.

Interest expense is only relevant when measuring the free cash flows to common equityholders. The free cash flows (of the unlevered firm) are not affected by interest expense. Dividends do not affect free cash flows, but they may affect equity free cash flows. Since we measure equity free cash flows by adjusting free cash flows for all after-tax flows to or from non-common equity securities, we deduct preferred stock dividends to calculate equity free cash flow (but we do not deduct common dividends). Similarly, changes in financing do not affect free cash flows. However, changes in debt and preferred financing affect equity free cash flows, but changes in common equity financing do not. Changes in common equity financing and dividends to common equityholders help reconcile equity free cash flows to the change in cash, but they do not affect free cash flows or equity free cash flows.

Measuring (Unlevered) Free Cash Flows (FCF)

As discussed in Chapter 1, to measure free cash flows, we begin with earnings before interest and taxes, **EBIT**, and deduct income taxes. The income taxes deducted (**TAX**) are the income taxes the company would pay if it had no **interest deductions** (interest expense that is deductible for income tax purposes). The result is the company's **unlevered earnings** (**UE**)—the earnings the company would have if it were all-equity financed. The next adjustment we make in our calculation of free cash flows is to convert the company's unlevered earnings into unlevered operating cash flows.

Recall from your basic accounting background that net income is not equal to cash flows, for earnings contain the effect of non-cash expenses, non-cash revenues, and various other accruals. To convert unlevered earnings to an unlevered operating cash flow, we add back any **non-cash expenses or losses** (**NCEXP**) that affect EBIT (for example, depreciation) and subtract any **non-cash revenues or gains** (**NCREV**) that affect EBIT. We then subtract any increases in non-cash operating working capital (Δ**WCO**) (for example, inventory). The non-cash operating working capital adjustment does not include any items related to financing costs (such as interest) or income taxes. We then subtract any increase in the **required cash balance** (Δ**RC**). Here, we have a company's unlevered cash flow from operations (**UCFO**). We then calculate unlevered free cash flow (**FCF**) by subtracting investments—which include capital expenditures (**CAPEX**) measured net of any long-lived assets sold—from the unlevered cash flow from operations. Note, a company can also have decreases in required cash and non-cash operating working capital as well as negative capital expenditures, all of which would increase cash flows. For example, this is possible for a company that engages in restructuring activities or whose businesses are contracting. We summarized this calculation in Chapter 1 with Equation 1.1:

$$FCF = EBIT - TAX + NCEXP - NCREV - \Delta RC - \Delta WCO - CAPEX \qquad (1.1)$$

This is the most basic calculation of free cash flows. Naturally, as a company's assets, capital structure, economic transactions, and income tax situations become more complex, the calculation of free cash flows becomes more complex as well.

Valuation Key 3.1

Free cash flows are the cash flows that could be distributed to all of the company's security holders after making all necessary investments. They do not, however, take into consideration the taxes saved from any interest expense that arises from the debt in a company's capital structure. These are the free cash flows of the company if it were entirely equity financed.

Measuring Equity Free Cash Flows (EFCF)

Equity free cash flows are the cash flows available for distribution to the equityholders after all cash flows are paid to, or received from, non-equity security holders. To measure the equity free cash flows, we begin with a company's unlevered free cash flows. From the unlevered free cash flows, we subtract all of the after-tax cash flows paid to non-equity security holders, and we add all of the after-tax cash flows received from non-equity security holders. For a company with debt, preferred stock, and equity financing, this means we subtract after-tax interest, preferred stock dividends, the repayment or retirement of debt, and the repurchase or retirement of preferred stock; likewise, we add the net cash flows resulting from the issuance of debt or preferred stock. Transactions with common equityholders are not considered in the calculation of equity free cash flows. Note, preferred stock dividends and the repurchase or retirement of preferred stock generally do not have any income tax effect. The repayment or retirement of debt, however, can have income tax effects if the debt is repaid or retired at an amount other than book value.

Subtracting after-tax interest is equivalent to subtracting cash interest paid and then adding back the expected tax shield resulting from the interest expense. We separate after-tax interest into these two components because we will often use the interest tax shields in our valuation of the company. In addition, the interest tax shield is based on the interest expense (INT), which may be quite different from the cash interest paid. **Interest tax shields** are the reductions in income taxes that result from interest expense. The interest tax shield is equal to the amount of tax-deductible interest multiplied by the **marginal tax rate for interest**, T_{INT}. This income tax rate (T_{INT})—applied to interest expense in order to calculate a company's interest tax shield—is equal to the tax rate that measures the savings in corporate taxes, which results from the interest expense being deducted when calculating a company's taxable income.

In a straightforward situation, we can easily calculate a company's interest expense. For example, when a company issues debt at its face (or par) value with interest payments that occur at the end of fiscal periods, interest expense is equal to cash interest paid. To simplify calculations, we assume throughout the book that changes in debt occur at the end of the year, and in turn, interest expense is based on the beginning-of-year debt balance. Note, it is not uncommon to base interest expense on the average debt balance in a year. With our simplifying assumption, interest expense is equal to the interest rate (r_{INT}) multiplied by the book value of the debt outstanding at the beginning of the period (D_{t-1}). To calculate cash interest paid (CINT), we must adjust the interest expense for changes in interest payable and other issues we discuss later (such as **paid-in-kind debt**, which occurs when the interest accrues but is not paid until later).

The interest tax shield (ITS) is equal to the interest expense, not the cash interest paid, multiplied by the tax rate that measures the tax deduction from interest—T_{INT}.

$$ITS = INT \times T_{INT} = r_{INT} \times D_{t-1} \times T_{INT} \tag{3.1a}$$

To calculate equity free cash flows, we then subtract preferred stock dividends paid (PSDiv). In a straightforward situation, this is equal to the dividend rate of the preferred stock (the preferred stock cost of capital)—r_{PS}—multiplied by the amount of preferred stock outstanding at the beginning of the period (PS_{t-1}).

$$PSDiv = r_{PS} \times PS_{t-1} \tag{3.1b}$$

Typically, we do not need to make any income tax adjustment for preferred stock dividends, for they are usually not tax deductible. Finally, we add any changes in the company's debt (ΔD) and preferred stock (ΔPS). We show this calculation in Equation 3.2.

$$EFCF = FCF - CINT + ITS - PSDiv + \Delta D + \Delta PS \tag{3.2}$$

Valuation Key 3.2

The equity free cash flows are available for distribution to the equityholders of the firm after consideration of all required investments and all payments both to and from non-equity security holders—on an after-tax basis.

How Issuing and Repaying Debt Affects Equity Free Cash Flows

For some, it is a little confusing at first to see why issuing and repaying non-equity securities affect equity free cash flows. When a company issues non-equity securities (for example, debt or preferred stock), the company has more cash flow that year than it would have had otherwise. The company can then use the cash flow from the non-equity securities to make new investments, pay dividends, and so forth. The net effect of issuing non-equity securities is more cash flow available to the company's equityholders than they would have had otherwise at the time of issuance. On the face of it, this might seem counterintuitive. How can the equityholders have more cash flow by issuing non-equity securities? If this were the case, the equityholders would continue to issue more and more non-equity securities in order to increase their cash flows, which in turn increases the value of their equity. While it would be nice for money to grow on trees in this way, this is not the effect of issuing non-equity securities.

If a company issues non-equity securities today, it must generally pay the security holders an appropriate annual risk-adjusted rate of return, and it must also repay the amount of capital raised no later than the maturity date of the security. Some non-equity securities—for example, zero-coupon debt—do not pay an annual return to investors, but sometime later, on or before the maturity date, the return is paid. Some non-equity securities—for example, perpetual preferred stock—do not even have a maturity date. In the year a company issues non-equity securities, its equity free cash flow is larger than it would have been otherwise, but for all future years—as the company pays a return to those security holders (interest on debt or dividends on preferred) or repays the capital raised—its equity free cash flows will be smaller. Assuming that the company issues non-equity securities at the appropriate risk-adjusted rate of return, and assuming that the company does not get any other benefits from issuing non-equity securities (such as interest tax shields), the equityholders are no better off than they would have been had they not issued the non-equity security.

For example, assume an investor is making a $100 investment in a company today and expects the company to earn and pay the investor $300 at the end of two years. The investor's expected cash flows are

Year 0	Year 1	Year 2
−$100	$0	+$300

If the investor wants to receive a dividend of $50 at the end of Year 1, the investor can have the company borrow $50 for one year at 10% interest and pay the $50 dividend. This creates a new time-series of expected cash flows to the investor. (The cash flow in Year 2 is $245 = $300 − 1.1 × $50.)

Year 0	Year 1	Year 2
−$100	+$50	+245

The investor was able to shift some of the cash flow from Year 2 to Year 1 by borrowing $50. Naturally, shifting $50 of the expected cash flow from Year 2 to Year 1 did not come without a cost. The investor's expected cash flows in Year 2 decreased by $55 ($55 = 1.1 × $50). Regardless of whether or not it was a good decision, it is clear that borrowing the $50 had a direct positive effect on the expected cash flow in Year 1 and the repayment of the debt and interest had a direct negative effect on the expected cash flow in Year 2. Changing the amount of non-equity financing has a direct effect on equity free cash flows. Of course, there are many reasons why a company might decide to issue non-equity securities. Interest tax shields are one such reason. In addition, if the firm has more investment opportunities than available capital, issuing debt may allow it to take advantage of valuable investment opportunities without issuing equity, which is generally more costly to issue than debt.

3.2 THE BOB ADAMS COMPANY EXAMPLE

A few years ago, the Bob Adams Company financed itself with a significant amount of debt. The company is now in a situation in which it plans to make relatively large capital expenditures for the next three years, and some of the debt it had previously issued is coming due. The company's chief financial officer (CFO) prepared a set of forecasts (Exhibit 3.1) that management will use to assess the company's ability to fund the capital expenditures internally and repay the debt coming due.

The Bob Adams's Unlevered Free Cash Flows

While our focus in this section is on a company's free cash flows, it is important to understand that in order to calculate free cash flows, we need essentially all of the same information used to calculate a company's cash flow statement. That is why it is usually helpful to calculate a company's cash flow statement before calculating the company's free cash flows. For now, we will ignore the cash flow statement and calculate the free cash flows of the Bob Adams Company from the income statement and balance sheet. For the Bob Adams Company, which has an income tax rate of 40% on all income statement items, we can use Equation 1.1 and the information in Exhibit 3.1 to measure its free cash flow for Year 0.

EXHIBIT 3.1	The Bob Adams Company Balance Sheet and Income Statement Forecasts				

THE BOB ADAMS COMPANY **Income Statement and Balance Sheet Forecasts**					
	Actual **Year −1**	**Actual** **Year 0**	**Forecast** **Year 1**	**Forecast** **Year 2**	**Forecast** **Year 3**
Income Statement					
Revenue.	$14,960	$15,708	$16,493	$17,813	$18,882
Operating expenses.	−8,976	−9,425	−9,896	−10,688	−11,329
Depreciation expense.	−1,500	−1,725	−1,976	−2,305	−2,643
Earnings before interest and taxes.	4,484	4,558	4,622	4,820	4,910
Interest expense.	0	−1,200	−1,160	−1,150	−1,120
Income before taxes.	4,484	3,358	3,462	3,670	3,790
Income tax expense.	−1,794	−1,343	−1,385	−1,468	−1,516
Net income.	$ 2,690	$ 2,015	$ 2,077	$ 2,202	$ 2,274
Statement of Retained Earnings					
Beginning-of-year balance.	$ 4,088	$ 6,196	$ 7,847	$ 9,462	$11,117
Net income.	2,690	2,015	2,077	2,202	2,274
Preferred stock dividends	−83	−110	−125	−130	−142
Common equity dividends	−500	−254	−336	−417	−328
End-of-year balance.	$ 6,196	$ 7,847	$ 9,462	$11,117	$12,921
Balance Sheet					
Cash.	$ 1,496	$ 2,152	$ 2,230	$ 2,362	$ 2,469
Net operating working capital	2,992	3,142	3,299	3,563	3,776
Property, plant, and equipment (net)	15,708	16,493	17,813	18,882	19,815
Total assets.	$20,196	$21,787	$23,342	$24,807	$26,061
Debt	$12,000	$11,600	$11,500	$11,200	$10,400
Preferred stock.	1,000	1,140	1,180	1,290	1,540
Common stock.	1,000	1,200	1,200	1,200	1,200
Retained earnings	6,196	7,847	9,462	11,117	12,921
Total shareholders' equity	$ 7,196	$ 9,047	$10,662	$12,317	$14,121
Total liabilities and equities.	$20,196	$21,787	$23,342	$24,807	$26,061

Exhibit may contain small rounding errors

We show the calculation of the company's free cash flows in Exhibit 3.2. To calculate the company's free cash flow for Year 0, we begin with EBIT, $4,558, which we can find on the company's income statement. In this simple example, income taxes on EBIT, TAX, is equal to EBIT multiplied by the income tax rate of 40% (TAX = $1,823 = 0.4 × $4,558). The only non-cash expense or revenue for this company is depreciation, $1,725 (NCEXP = $1,725, NCREV = $0). The company does not present its non-cash current assets and current liabilities separately on its balance sheet. It only reports the company's net operating working capital. We can measure the change in the company's net operating working capital by calculating the change on the balance sheet from Year −1 to Year 0 (ΔNWC = $150 = $3,142 − $2,992). Increases in net working capital indicate that the company is, on net, investing in working capital (for example, its inventory increases more than its accounts payable does, and the net increase is positive). Increases in net working capital indicate an outflow of cash. Assume further that we are told that the company's change in required cash is equal to $75 in Year 0 and that the forecasted change in the cash balance in the balance sheet for Years 1 to 3 represents the change in required cash necessary to operate the business in each future year as projected by the CFO. Using this information, we can calculate the company's unlevered cash flow from operations.

EXHIBIT 3.2   The Bob Adams Company Free Cash Flow Schedule

THE BOB ADAMS COMPANY
Free Cash Flow and Equity Free Cash Flow Forecasts

		Actual Year 0	Forecast Year 1	Forecast Year 2	Forecast Year 3
Earnings before interest and taxes.............	+ EBIT	$4,558	$4,622	$4,820	$4,910
Income taxes paid on EBIT	− TAX	−1,823	−1,849	−1,928	−1,964
Unlevered earnings	**= UE**	**2,735**	**2,773**	**2,892**	**2,946**
Depreciation expense (non-cash expenses)	+ NCEXP	1,725	1,976	2,305	2,643
Non-cash revenues	− NCREV	0	0	0	0
Change in required cash	− ΔRC	−75	−79	−132	−107
Change in net operating working capital	− ΔWCO	−150	−157	−264	−214
Unlevered cash flow from operations	**= UCFO**	**4,235**	**4,513**	**4,801**	**5,268**
Capital expenditures (net of dispositions)	− CAPEX	−2,510	−3,295	−3,374	−3,577
Unlevered free cash flow...................	**= FCF**	**1,725**	**1,218**	**1,427**	**1,691**
Cash interest paid	− CINT	−1,200	−1,160	−1,150	−1,120
Interest tax shield.........................	+ ITS	480	464	460	448
Preferred stock dividends	− PSDIV	−110	−125	−130	−142
Cash flow before changes in financing	**CFBFIN**	**895**	**396**	**607**	**878**
Change in debt financing	+ ΔDFIN	−400	−100	−300	−800
Change in preferred stock financing	+ ΔPSFIN	140	40	110	250
Equity free cash flow	**= EFCF**	**635**	**336**	**417**	**328**
Common equity dividends paid...............	− CDIV	−254	−336	−417	−328
Change in common equity financing	+ ΔCEFIN	200	0	0	0
Change in excess cash	= ΔXC	581	0	0	0
Change in required cash	+ ΔRC	75	79	132	107
Change in cash balance...................	**= ΔC**	**$ 656**	**$ 79**	**$ 132**	**$ 107**

Exhibit may contain small rounding errors

We calculate the company's capital expenditures by using both the income statement and balance sheet. The balance in the company's net property, plant, and equipment account, as listed on the balance sheet, increases if the company makes a capital expenditure and it decreases when the company depreciates these assets. (The balance in this account also changes if a company sells or retires some of its property, plant, and equipment during the year. However, we assume that the company is not selling or retiring any of its property, plant, and equipment.) Bob Adams Company's capital expenditures are equal to the change in its net property, plant, and equipment account on the balance sheet plus the depreciation on the income statement (CAPEX = $2,510 = $16,493 − $15,708 + $1,725). From this information, we can complete the calculation of the free cash flows for the Bob Adams Company, which we show in Exhibit 3.2. The unlevered free cash flows for Year 0 equal $1,725.

Bob Adams's Equity Free Cash Flows

We continue our calculations for Year 0 by calculating the company's equity free cash flows. To calculate a company's equity free cash flows, we begin with its free cash flows, subtract all of the after-tax cash flows paid to non-equity security holders, and add all of the after-tax cash flows received from non-equity security holders. For the Bob Adams Company, which has a debt cost of capital of 10%, we can use Equation 3.2 and the information in Exhibit 3.1 to measure its equity free cash flow for Year 0.

We begin our calculation of the equity free cash flows with the unlevered free cash flow, calculated earlier to be $1,725. From that, we subtract cash interest paid, which is equal to the debt cost of capital of 10% multiplied by the beginning balance of debt (CINT = $1,200 = 0.1 × $12,000), assuming that the company does not have any change in its interest payable. Next, we add back the interest tax shield on the debt, which is equal to interest expense multiplied by the income tax rate for interest (ITS = $480 = 0.4 × 0.1 × $12,000). We then subtract preferred stock dividends, equal to the preferred stock cost of capital of 11%, multiplied by the beginning balance of preferred stock

(PSDIV = $110 = 0.11 × $1,000). The result of the previous calculation is the cash flow the company has before changes in its financing. If this cash flow is negative, it indicates the amount of financing that the company must obtain from some source, or if the cash flow is positive, it indicates the amount of cash available to pay down debt or preferred stock, pay dividends, repurchase stock, or accumulate excess cash.

We calculate equity free cash flows by adding the change in non-equity financing—in this example, the change in debt and preferred stock (ΔDFIN = −$400 = $11,600 − $12,000 and ΔPSFIN = $140 = $1,140 − $1,000)—to the cash flow before changes in financing. From Exhibit 3.2, we see that the company's equity free cash flow is equal to $635. The company can use this to pay dividends, repurchase stock, or keep excess cash. We see in Exhibit 3.1 that the company paid dividends to its equityholders (CDIV = $254). We can also see that the company issued additional equity ($200 = $1,200 − $1,000). As a result, the company increased its excess cash by $581. Looking at the forecasts for Years 1 to 3, we see that the equity free cash flows are projected to be positive for every year, so the company can make its planned capital expenditures, pay down its debt coming due, and even pay some common dividends, all of which is reflected in the forecast.

Reconciling Free Cash Flows to Change in Cash Balance

As a partial check on our calculations, we should always be able to reconcile a company's equity free cash flow to the change in its cash balance. This reconciliation is useful as a check on our free cash flow and equity free cash flow calculations. We begin by adjusting the equity free cash flow for common dividends and changes in equity investments in order to arrive at the change in the company's excess cash. We add the change in required cash to the change in excess cash, which, if we calculated everything correctly, reconciles to the change in the company's cash balance. We show this calculation for the Bob Adams Company at the bottom of Exhibit 3.2.

Generally, once we begin forecasting the company's free cash flows, we no longer assume that the company issues common equity unless it needs to do so. Further, we often assume that the company distributes all of its equity free cash flows to its equityholders; in other words, the company no longer accumulates any excess cash. These are common assumptions we make when valuing a company, which we explain in more detail in the next chapter that focuses on creating financial models. We can see in the forecasts for Bob Adams for Years 1 to 3 that it does not accumulate excess assets.

REVIEW EXERCISE 3.1

Frits Seegers, Inc. Free Cash Flow Schedule

Use the information on Frits Seegers to prepare a free cash flow schedule for Year 0 that includes unlevered free cash flows, equity free cash flows, and a reconciliation to the change in the company's cash balance. Assume that the cash shown is required cash for the business and that the only items that affect retained earnings are net income and dividends. (Note, for more practice, see Problem 1.7 where more years of data for Frits Seegers, Inc. are presented.)

FRITS SEEGERS INC. Income Statement and Balance Sheet				
	Year −1	Year 0	Year −1	Year 0
Balance Sheet—Assets			**Balance Sheet—Liabilities and Equity**	
Cash balance	$ 50.0	$ 55.0	Accounts payable. . . . . $ 50.8	$ 55.9
Accounts receivable.	166.7	183.3	Other current operating liabilities 35.0	38.5
Inventory.	118.6	130.5	Total current liabilities. 85.8	94.4
Total current assets	$ 335.3	$ 368.8	Debt 1,200.0	1,400.0
Land	$1,550.0	$1,825.0	Total liabilities $1,285.8	$1,494.4
Total assets.	$1,885.3	$2,193.8	Common stock. $383.6	$383.6
			Retained earnings 215.8	315.7
			Total shareholders' equity . . . . $ 599.4	$ 699.4
			Total liabilities and equities. $1,885.3	$2,193.8

continued

continued from prior page

Income Statement	Year –1	Year 0
Revenue	$1,000.0	$1,100.0
Cost of goods sold	–610.0	–671.0
Gross margin	$ 390.0	$ 429.0
Selling, general, and administrative	–120.0	–132.0
Operating income	$ 270.0	$ 297.0
Interest expense	–77.0	–96.0
Income before taxes	$ 193.0	$ 201.0
Income tax expense	–77.2	–80.4
Net income	$ 115.8	$ 120.6

Exhibit may contain small rounding errors

Solution on page 119.

3.3 CASH FLOW STATEMENT BASICS

The balance sheet and income statement are two widely used and reasonably well-understood financial statements (although many do not recognize their limitations). The statement of cash flows is not as well understood as the balance sheet and income statement are. The cash flow statement prepared by accountants reconciles the change in the cash balance of the firm with changes in the other items on the balance sheet. Under U.S. accounting principles, the cash flow statement partitions this reconciliation into four parts:

LO2 Create a cash flow statement

> Cash flow from operations
> Net cash flows from Investing activities
> Net cash flows from financing activities
> Foreign currency translation adjustment*
>
> Change in cash and cash equivalents

* The foreign currency translation adjustments are beyond the scope of our discussion in this chapter. For the remainder of this chapter, we assume foreign currency translation adjustments are not relevant to either our discussion or our examples.

In this section, we discuss the algebra underpinning the cash flow statement. We also discuss the relation between the free cash flow schedule and the cash flow statement. What we will quickly learn is that the adjustments that we make to unlevered earnings to convert it to unlevered operating cash flow are mostly the same adjustments that we make to net income to convert it to cash flow from operations. The information on the cash flow statement is also quite useful for calculating the investments made by a company and changes in its financing. We also show how to calculate free cash flows directly from cash flows from operations.

The Algebra Underpinning the Cash Flow Statement

Understanding the algebra that underpins the cash flow statement provides a useful framework for understanding its mechanics. The basic accounting identity or equality equates assets (resources) with liabilities and shareholders' equity (claims on the assets). Even though preparing the cash flow statement is somewhat complex, it is, in reality, merely a restatement of that accounting equality. The cash flow statement reconciles the change in the cash balance on the balance sheet with the changes in all of the other accounts on the balance sheet, and it partitions the changes in a systematic manner (as described earlier).

We present a typical balance sheet and statement of retained earnings on the left side of Exhibit 3.3. We present variable names for each of the accounts on the balance sheet, each of the changes in those accounts (column labeled "change"), and each of the components in the retained earnings statement, but we ignore other components of shareholders' equity (such as comprehensive income adjustments) to simplify our discussion.

EXHIBIT 3.3   Relationships Between Changes in the Balance Sheet Accounts and the Cash Flow Statement

Using this notation, we can present the equation for the accounting identity (eliminating any time subscripts) as

$$TA = TL + SE$$

$$C + COA + PPEQ + NCOA = COL + INT/P + CLTD + LTD + NCOL + PS + CS + RE$$

The above equality still holds if we restate the equation in terms of the changes in the balance sheet accounts. (We use the Greek letter Δ to represent the change in a balance sheet account: $\Delta X = X_t - X_{t-1}$.)

$$\Delta C + \Delta COA + \Delta PPEQ + \Delta NCOA$$

$$= \Delta COL + \Delta INT/P + \Delta CLTD + \Delta LTD + \Delta NCOL + \Delta PS + \Delta CS + \Delta RE$$

If we assume the change in accumulated comprehensive income is zero, then the change in retained earnings increases or decreases each year by the amount of net income net of preferred and common dividends ($\Delta RE = NI - PSDIV - CDIV$). We can substitute this relation into the above equation.

$$\Delta C + \Delta COA + \Delta PPEQ + \Delta NCOA$$

$$= \Delta COL + \Delta INT/P + \Delta CLTD + \Delta LTD + \Delta NCOL + \Delta PS + \Delta CS + NI - PSDIV - CDIV$$

Recall that the cash flow statement reconciles the change in the cash balance with changes in the balances of all of the other balance sheet accounts; thus, we can rearrange the previous equation to approximate a cash flow statement. (The partitioning is actually much more complicated than represented below, so do not take this partitioning as being literally true.)

$$
\begin{aligned}
\Delta C = \\
&+ NI - \Delta COA - \Delta NCOA + \Delta COL + \Delta INT/P + \Delta NCOL && [CFO] \\
&- \Delta PPEQ && [CFI] \\
&+ \Delta CLTD + \Delta LTD + \Delta PS + \Delta CS - PSDIV - CDIV && [CFF]
\end{aligned}
$$

In Exhibit 3.3, we show a more detailed and more accurate mapping of the changes in the balance sheet accounts to the cash flow statement. We typically need to use the income statement (which we do not show in Exhibit 3.3) to identify non-cash expenses (depreciation and amortization) and non-cash revenues (gains on dispositions).

The algebra demonstrates how we can always prepare a cash flow statement given two years of a balance sheet, an income statement, and a statement of retained earnings. However, although it is possible to prepare a cash flow statement with only these financial statements, preparing a precise cash flow statement typically requires more detailed information that explains the changes in the balance sheet accounts. This, in turn, allows us to better classify parts of the change in balance sheet accounts into the four categories of cash flows on the cash flow statement. The footnotes in a 10-K are helpful in preparing a more detailed reconciliation. Not having or using that information can result in a misclassification of part or all of a change in a balance sheet account. Such misclassifications may or may not be important, depending on how they affect our free cash flow calculations.

Using the Cash Flow Statement to Measure Free Cash Flows

It is clear from comparing Exhibits 3.2 and 3.3 that the adjustments we make to unlevered earnings to convert it to unlevered cash flows from operations are very similar to the adjustments we make to net income to convert it to cash flow from operations. Thus, it is of no surprise that we can calculate free cash flows from cash flow from operations. We begin our calculation with cash flow from operations. The primary difference between cash flow from operations on the cash flow statement (prepared according to generally accepted accounting principles—GAAP) and the unlevered cash flow from operations as shown in Exhibit 3.2 is the after-tax cash flow effect of interest deductions and the change in required cash. Thus, we add back after-tax cash interest paid (cash interest paid minus the interest tax shield) to the cash flow from operations and subtract increases in required cash in order to calculate unlevered cash flow from operations. This is the same unlevered cash flow from operations that we calculated in Exhibit 3.2. When we start with cash flows from operations for our free cash flow calculation, we call it the CFO method. If EBIT is the starting point for the free cash flow calculation, we call it the EBIT method. Now that we have the same unlevered cash flow from operations, the remainder of the free cash flow calculation is the same as in Exhibit 3.2. Likewise, the calculation of equity free cash flow and the reconciliation of the equity free cash flow to the change in the cash balance are the same for both the EBIT and CFO methods.

Valuation Key 3.3

The algebra of the accounting system allows us to prepare a statement of cash flows with a comparative balance sheet, income statement, and statement of retained earnings. Once we have prepared a cash flow statement, it makes the calculation of free cash flows relatively straightforward when using either the EBIT method or the CFO method.

The Bob Adams Company Revisited

In Exhibit 3.4, we map changes in the balance sheet accounts to the cash flow statement for Year 0 for the Bob Adams Company. For this company, the only information we need from the income statement is depreciation expense, which we show at the bottom of this exhibit (see Exhibit 3.1 for the income statement). Since the Bob Adams Company has a straightforward balance sheet and income statement, and since it did not have any complex transactions, preparing its cash flow statement is relatively straight-forward. Capital expenditures is the only number on the cash flow statement that is neither directly from the change column on the balance sheet nor from the income statement or statement of retained earnings. For the cash flow statement, the calculation of capital expenditures is generally the same calculation as the one used for the free cash flow statement. An exception to this occurs when a company has non-cash transactions—for example, purchasing a building by borrowing the money from the seller. We would treat that as a dual transaction on the free cash flow statement—showing both the purchase of the building and the issuance of debt—but nothing would be shown on the cash flow statement according to U.S. GAAP.

EXHIBIT 3.4   The Bob Adams Company Statement of Cash Flows for Year 0

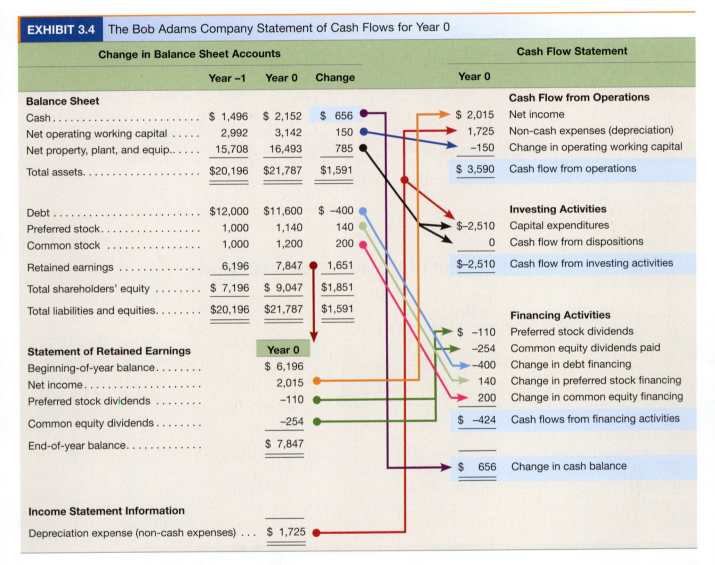

Change in Balance Sheet Accounts				Cash Flow Statement	
	Year –1	Year 0	Change	Year 0	
Balance Sheet				**Cash Flow from Operations**	
Cash	$ 1,496	$ 2,152	$ 656	$ 2,015	Net income
Net operating working capital	2,992	3,142	150	1,725	Non-cash expenses (depreciation)
Net property, plant, and equip.	15,708	16,493	785	–150	Change in operating working capital
Total assets	$20,196	$21,787	$1,591	$ 3,590	Cash flow from operations
Debt	$12,000	$11,600	$ –400	**Investing Activities**	
Preferred stock	1,000	1,140	140	$–2,510	Capital expenditures
Common stock	1,000	1,200	200	0	Cash flow from dispositions
Retained earnings	6,196	7,847	1,651	$–2,510	Cash flow from investing activities
Total shareholders' equity	$ 7,196	$ 9,047	$1,851		
Total liabilities and equities	$20,196	$21,787	$1,591	**Financing Activities**	
				$ –110	Preferred stock dividends
				–254	Common equity dividends paid
Statement of Retained Earnings		Year 0		–400	Change in debt financing
Beginning-of-year balance		$ 6,196		140	Change in preferred stock financing
Net income		2,015		200	Change in common equity financing
Preferred stock dividends		–110		$ –424	Cash flows from financing activities
Common equity dividends		–254			
End-of-year balance		$ 7,847		$ 656	Change in cash balance
Income Statement Information					
Depreciation expense (non-cash expenses)		$ 1,725			

In Exhibit 3.5, we show the cash flow statements for the Bob Adams Company for all years. The cash flow statement for Year 0 is the same cash flow statement that appears in Exhibit 3.4. We prepared the cash flow statements for the remaining years in the same manner. In fact, to do this, we merely copied the formulas in our spreadsheet from the column representing Year 0 to the columns representing Years 1 to 3. Based on the calculations in Exhibit 3.4, we can see that each number in the cash flow statement results from a calculation based on two balance sheets, the income statement and/or the statement of retained earnings. Our relatively simple Bob Adams Company example shows how it is possible to create spreadsheet templates in order to calculate a company's cash flow statement and, therefore, its free cash flows from its income statement, balance sheet, and statement of retained earnings. In a financial model, we typically forecast a company's income statements, balance sheets, and supplemental information (for example, more detailed schedules of income taxes and property, plant, and equipment) before using templates (like those in the Bob Adams example) to calculate the company's cash flow statement and free cash flows.

In Exhibit 3.6, we show the free cash flow calculations for the Bob Adams Company using the cash flow from operations method. We add back after-tax interest to cash flow from operations and subtract the increases in required cash in order to calculate unlevered cash flow from operations, which is the same unlevered cash flow from operations calculated in Exhibit 3.2.

EXHIBIT 3.5   The Bob Adams Company Statement of Cash Flows Year 0 to Year 3

THE BOB ADAMS COMPANY
Cash Flow Statement Forecasts

		Actual Year 0	Forecast Year 1	Forecast Year 2	Forecast Year 3
Cash Flow from Operations					
Net income..........................	+NI	$ 2,015	$ 2,077	$ 2,202	$ 2,274
Depreciation expense (non-cash expenses)	+NCEXP	1,725	1,976	2,305	2,643
Non-cash revenues	−NCREV	0	0	0	0
Change in net operating working capital	−ΔWCO	−150	−157	−264	−214
Cash flow from operations....................	=CFO	$ 3,590	$ 3,896	$ 4,243	$ 4,703
Investing Activities					
Capital expenditures	−INVEST	$−2,510	$−3,295	$−3,374	$−3,577
Cash flow from dispositions..................	+DISP	0	0	0	0
Cash flow from investing activities.............	=CAPEX	$−2,510	$−3,295	$−3,374	$−3,577
Financing Activities					
Common equity dividends paid...............	−CDIV	$ −254	$ −336	$ −417	$ −328
Preferred stock dividends	−PSDIV	−110	−125	−130	−142
Change in debt financing.....................	+DFIN	−400	−100	−300	−800
Change in preferred stock financing	+PSFIN	140	40	110	250
Change in common equity financing	+CEFIN	200	0	0	0
Cash flows from financing activities............	=CFF	$ −424	$ −522	$ −737	$−1,019
Change in cash balance....................	=ΔC	$ 656	$ 79	$ 132	$ 107

Exhibit may contain small rounding errors

EXHIBIT 3.6   The Bob Adams Company Free Cash Flow Measured Using the Cash Flow Statement

THE BOB ADAMS COMPANY
Free Cash Flow Forecasts

		Actual Year 0	Forecast Year 1	Forecast Year 2	Forecast Year 3
Cash flow from operations..................	+ CFO	$3,590	$3,896	$4,243	$4,703
Interest paid in cash.......................	+ CINT	1,200	1,160	1,150	1,120
Interest tax shield.........................	− ITS	−480	−464	−460	−448
Change in required cash	− ΔRC	−75	−79	−132	−107
Unlevered cash flow from operations	**= UCFO**	**$4,235**	**$4,513**	**$4,801**	**$5,268**
Capital expenditures	− CAPEX	−2,510	−3,295	−3,374	−3,577
Unlevered free cash flow................	**= FCF**	**$1,725**	**$1,218**	**$1,427**	**$1,691**

Now that we have the same unlevered cash flow from operations, the remainder of the free cash flow calculation is the same as in Exhibit 3.2. Likewise, the calculation of equity free cash flows and the reconciliation of the equity free cash flows to the change in the cash balance are the same for the cash flow from operations method as they are for the EBIT method, which we presented in Exhibit 3.2. We do not repeat that part of the schedule in the exhibit. While it is useful to understand the cash flow from operations method for its insights into the EBIT method, most practitioners use the EBIT method when they measure free cash flows.

REVIEW EXERCISE 3.2

Frits Seegers, Inc. Cash Flow Statement

Use the information on Frits Seegers in Review Exercise 3.1 to prepare a cash flow statement in order to then calculate the company's unlevered free cash flow using the CFO method. (Note, for more practice, see Problem 1.7 where more years of data for Frits Seegers, Inc. are presented.)

Solution on pages 119–120.

3.4 MEASURING STARBUCKS' FREE CASH FLOW

In this section, we use the reported financial statements of Starbucks Corporation (Starbucks) to measure its free cash flow. Formed in 1985, Starbucks purchases and roasts whole bean coffees in order to sell them along with brewed coffees, related beverages, a variety of complementary food items, and coffee-related accessories and equipment. Starbucks also sells coffee and tea products and licenses its trademark through other channels. We show Starbucks' summarized income statements and balance sheets for Year 11 and Year 12 in Exhibit 3.7. We also show a column of reference numbers. Under "FCF Ref," we list reference numbers to help us prepare Starbucks' free cash flow schedule.

EXHIBIT 3.7   Starbucks' Income Statements and Balance Sheets

Starbucks Corporation Income Statements ($ in thousands)	Year 11	Year 12	FCF Ref #	Starbucks Corporation Balance Sheets ($ in thousands)	Year 11	Year 12	FCF Ref #
Sales	$6,369,300	$7,786,942		Cash and cash equivalents	$ 173,809	$ 312,606	12
				Short-term investments	133,227	141,038	
Cost of goods sold	−2,605,212	−3,178,791		Receivables	190,762	224,271	
Store and other operating expenses	−2,362,935	−2,947,902		Inventories	546,299	636,222	
General and administrative expenses	−357,114	−473,023		Other current assets	165,237	215,651	
Depreciation and amortization	−340,169	−387,211					
Other operating income	76,648	93,937		Total current assets	$1,209,334	$1,529,788	
Operating income	$ 780,518	$ 893,952	1	Land, buildings, and equipment, net	1,842,019	2,287,899	
				Goodwill and other intangible assets	127,883	199,433	
Interest and other income	17,101	23,396	21	Long-term investments	261,564	224,904	
Interest expense	−1,272	−11,105	15	Other non-current assets	72,893	186,917	
Earnings before income taxes	$ 796,347	$ 906,243		Total assets	$3,513,693	$4,428,941	
Provision for income taxes	−301,977	−324,770					
Cumulative effect of accounting change	0	−17,214		Accounts payable	$ 220,975	$ 340,937	
				Short-term debt	277,000	700,000	
Net earnings	$ 494,370	$ 564,259		Current portion of long-term debt	748	762	
				Accrued expenses and other	552,907	661,148	
				Interest payable	318	847	
				Deferred revenue	175,048	231,926	
				Total current liabilities	$1,226,996	$1,935,620	
				Long-term debt	2,870	1,958	
				Other non-current liabilities	193,565	262,857	
				Total liabilities	$1,423,431	$2,200,435	
				Common stock and surplus	$ 130,361	$ 40,149	
				Retained earnings	1,938,987	2,151,084	
				Cumulative comprehensive income (loss)	20,914	37,273	
				Total stockholders' equity	$2,090,262	$2,228,506	
				Total liabilities and stockholders' equity	$3,513,693	$4,428,941	

The line items on Starbucks' balance sheet are the typical line items we observe for most companies. When we calculate free cash flows, we isolate a company's cash flows from operations from its cash flows from its excess assets. For Starbucks, we will assume that all of its cash and cash equivalents are required to operate the company and that all of its investments (short-term investments and long-term investments) are excess assets. These assumptions are, of course, simplistic. First, Starbucks is unlikely to need all of its cash balance ($312 million) to operate the company. In addition, even though some of its Long-Term Investments appear to be investments in government securities and are likely excess assets, at least some of the investments are related to operations and are not excess assets. For example, the company has partial equity interests in various partnerships, especially partnerships outside the United States (Starbucks Coffee Korea Company, Limited, and many others).

With a few exceptions, most of the line items in the income statement are common revenue and expense items that are easily understood. Two of the exceptions, however, are worth noting. The first exception is the line item titled, interest and other income. We assume that all of this income is related to the company's excess assets. The second exception is the line item titled, cumulative effect of accounting change.

While the details of the accounting change are not relevant to our discussion, recall that accounting changes do not affect cash; they only affect accounting accruals. Thus, this is an expense that Starbucks will add back in its calculation of operating cash flows. The word "cumulative" indicates that the amount adjusts the company's accounting accruals for not only Year 12 but for its entire history. Last, accountants show accounting changes, like this one, net of any income tax effects; thus, the provision for income taxes on the income statement is not related to this accounting change.

On the left side of Exhibit 3.8, we show Starbucks' summarized cash flow statements. Starbucks uses a standard form for its cash flow statement, and most of the items are typical items on the cash flow statement. Comparing Starbuck's cash flow statements to its income statements, we can make several observations. First, we see that Starbucks' cash flow from operations is about twice as large as its net earnings. We can explain much (about 70%) of that difference with the add-back for depreciation and amortization. The remaining difference is largely the result of changes in various working capital accounts. Second, we see that Starbucks' operating cash flow was $923 million in Year 11 and $1.13 billion in Year 12 (an increase of more than 22%), while its earnings grew from $494 million to $564 (an increase of about 14%). The higher growth rate for the company's Year 12 operating cash flow resulted from changes in various accruals.

EXHIBIT 3.8   Starbucks' Cash Flow Statements and Free Cash Flow Schedules

Starbucks Corporation Cash Flow Statement ($ in thousands)	Reported Year 11	Reported Year 12	FCF Ref #	Starbucks Corporation Free Cash Flows ($ in thousands)	Reported Year 12	FCF Ref #
				Earnings before interest and taxes (EBIT) . . .	$893,952	1
Net earnings	$ 494,370	$ 564,259		Income taxes paid on EBIT	–320,365	1 × 2
Depreciation and amortization	367,207	412,625	3	**Earnings before interest and after taxes . . . .**	**$573,587**	Sum
Cumulative effect of accounting change	0	17,214	24	Depreciation and amortization	412,625	3
Asset impairment charges	19,464	19,622	4	Asset impairment charges	19,622	4
Adjustments for operating working capital:				Receivables		5
Receivables			5	Inventories	–85,527	6
Inventories	–121,618	–85,527	6	Other current assets		7
Other current assets			7	Accounts payable	104,966	8
Accounts payable	9,717	104,966	8	Accrued expenses and other	145,427	9
Accrued expenses and other	30,216	145,427	9	Deferred revenue	56,547	10
Interest payable	80	529	16	Other, net	–104,029	11
Deferred revenue	53,276	56,547	10	Change in required cash balance	–138,797	12
Other, net	70,204	–104,029	11			
Net cash provided by operating activities	**$ 922,915**	**$ 1,131,633**	25	**Unlevered cash flow from operations . . . . . .**	**$984,421**	Sum
				Capital expenditures, net	–771,230	13
Purchase of investments, net	$ 444,264	$ 21,924	22	Acquisitions, net of cash acquired	–91,734	14
Capital expenditures, net	–643,296	–771,230	13	**Unlevered free cash flow . . . .**	**$121,457**	Sum
Acquisitions, net of cash acquired	–21,583	–91,734	14	Interest expense	–11,105	15
Net cash used by investing activities	**$ –220,615**	**$ –841,040**		Change in interest payable	529	16
				Interest tax shield	3,980	15 × 2
Proceeds from issuance of common stock . . .	$ 163,555	$ 276,617	19	**Cash flow before changes in financing . . . . .**	**$114,861**	Sum
Repurchase of common stock	–1,113,647	–854,045	20	Increase (decrease) in short-term debt	423,000	17
Increase (decrease) in short-term debt	277,000	423,000	17	Increase (decrease) in long-term debt	–898	18
Increase (decrease) in long-term debt	–735	–898	18	**Equity free cash flow . . . .**	**$536,963**	Sum
Net cash used by financing activities	**$ –673,827**	**$ –155,326**		Proceeds from issuance of common stock	276,617	19
				Repurchase of common stock	–854,045	20
Effect of exchange rate changes	$ 283	$ 3,530	23	**Add back effects of excess assets . . . .**		
				Interest and other income, after-tax	15,011	21 × (1.0 – 2)
Increase (decrease) in cash	$ 28,756	$ 138,797		Purchase of investments	21,924	22
				Effect of exchange rate changes	3,530	23
Cash interest paid	$ 1,060	$ 10,576		**Change in excess cash . . . .**	**$ –0**	Sum
Cash income taxes	$ 227,812	$ 274,134		Change in required cash	138,797	12
				Change in cash	**$138,797**	Sum
				Tax rate (assume effective tax rate)	35.84%	2

Measuring Starbucks' Unlevered Free Cash Flow

We show our calculation of Starbucks' free cash flows on the right side of Exhibit 3.8. For now, we focus on the column titled "Reported Year 12," which we calculate using both the cash flow statement reported by Starbucks for that period and some additional information from the income statement. We first measure Starbucks' Year 12 free cash flow using the earnings before interest and taxes (EBIT) method in Exhibit 3.8, and we then measure the same free cash flow using the cash flow from operations (CFO) method in Exhibit 3.9.

Starbucks' Unlevered Cash Flow from Operations.

We begin our EBIT method calculation by identifying (and when necessary, calculating) the company's EBIT from its income statement. We exclude any income statement items that are not related to the company's operations from EBIT. For Starbucks, we exclude the cumulative effect of accounting change because it is unrelated to the company's Year 12 operations; we do the same for interest and other income because we assume it is related to the company's excess assets, which we are not going to treat as ongoing in our forecast. While the interest and other income would be part of the company's free cash flows for this historical period, there is no need to incorporate them in the model that we are going to build to forecast Starbucks. The relevant EBIT for our free cash flow calculations is $894 million, which we get from the income statement in Exhibit 3.7 (FCF 1).

If reported EBIT was Starbucks' taxable income, and if there was no change in taxes payable (which does not appear to change in this case based on the information provided), then we would subtract the taxes that the company would pay (cash amount paid) based on its EBIT. For our Starbucks illustration, we make the simplifying assumption that the company's effective accounting tax rate is the appropriate tax rate to use for EBIT (later in the chapter we discuss why this is likely to be a simplifying assumption). We calculate the effective accounting tax rate using information on the company's income statement. Dividing the provision for income taxes in the income statement ($324.8 million) by earnings before income taxes ($906.2 million), we see that the effective accounting tax rate is equal to 35.8% (0.358 = $324.8/$906.2). We show this at the bottom of the free cash flow statement in Exhibit 3.8. Our calculation of income taxes paid on EBIT, $320.4 million, is equal to EBIT multiplied by the income tax rate (FCF 1 × FCF 2 = 0.358 × $894 = $320.4). We can now calculate EBIT after taxes.

With a few exceptions, we now adjust after-tax EBIT for all of the non-cash revenues, non-cash expenses, and changes in accounting accruals that appear on the cash flow from operations section of Starbucks' cash flow statement in Exhibit 3.8. In addition to all of the company's operating working capital adjustments (FCF 5 through 11), these adjustments include the adjustments for depreciation and amortization (FCF 3) and asset impairment charges (FCF 4). However, we do not adjust for interest payable (FCF 16), for free cash flows exclude all effects of non-equity financing. An alternative way to say this is that since we are adjusting EBIT, we do not consider any item in the operating section of the cash flow that is not related to EBIT (since interest is not part of EBIT, we do not consider changes in interest payable).

In addition, in this section of our free cash flow calculation, we also subtract the change in required cash, for it represents an investment in working capital that is similar to the investment in inventory and other operating current assets (FCF 12, $139 million). We do not adjust after-tax EBIT for the cumulative effect of accounting change (FCF 24) because the EBIT amount (FCF 1) we begin with does not include this amount (whereas net earnings does, which is why this adjustment is in the operating section of the cash flow statement). We added back the asset impairment charges, for they are non-cash expenses, and the company books an expense by writing down the carrying value of some of its assets. The sum of the above items is equal to the company's **unlevered cash flow from operations**—in other words, the cash flow the company generates from its operations before any capital expenditures and before cash flows either to or from its investors. Starbucks' unlevered cash flow from operations is equal to $984 million.

Starbucks' Unlevered Free Cash Flow.

To calculate a company's (unlevered) free cash flow, we reduce the company's unlevered cash flow from operations by the amount of capital expenditures necessary for the company to implement its strategic plan. In general, we identify capital expenditure information from the investing section of the company's cash flow statement. Starbucks has three items in the investing section of its cash flow statement presented in Exhibit 3.8. The first item is the purchase of investments (net of sales). We assume that these investments are excess assets, and therefore we exclude them from our calculation of free cash flows. However, we include the other two items. One of the items—capital expenditures, net (FCF 13, $771 million)—is included in the calculation of free cash flows because it represents investments in the company's operating assets.

The second item—acquisitions, net of cash acquired (FCF 14, $92 million)—represents the net assets acquired by the company through acquisitions and is also included in the calculation of free cash flows. This item understates the amount paid for acquisitions for two reasons. First, it excludes the cash acquired, but it is likely that this is only a relatively small amount. Second, and likely more important, it nets out any debt and other interest-bearing liabilities assumed by the company, and only shows the net amount. Since we are primarily interested in measuring unlevered free cash flows, we want to get the correct amount spent on investments. Hence, we treat the financing of any investments separately from the investing cash flows rather than net them. By netting out the debt and other interest-bearing liabilities assumed in the acquisition, we understate the amount invested in calculating unlevered free cash flows. We would need additional information to measure this more accurately.

A somewhat related issue regarding how accountants prepare cash flow statements (discussed briefly before) is how they exclude what we refer to as dual purchase / financing transactions. For example, the cash flow statement would exclude the purchase of a manufacturing plant financed by means of a mortgage from the seller. However, to measure free cash flows, we treat the transaction as two transactions: the purchase of the manufacturing plant, which we show as a capital expenditure, and the financing of that purchase with a mortgage. A rather common example of such a dual transaction is the capitalization of leases in which the company records an asset and a liability for the amount of the capitalized lease. In this case, neither the increase in the asset nor the increase in the liability appears on the cash flow statement. Fortunately, accounting standards require companies to disclose such non-cash transactions in supplemental disclosures. Starbucks had no such non-cash transactions in Year 12. Starbucks' (**unlevered**) **free cash flow** is equal to its unlevered cash flow from operations ($984 million) less its capital expenditures and acquisition expenditures ($771 million and $92 million), which equals $121 million ($121 = $984 − $771 − $92).

Measuring Starbucks' Equity Free Cash Flow

To calculate a company's equity free cash flow, we deduct all after-tax cash flows to or from non-equity investors from the (unlevered) free cash flow. An intermediate calculation between free cash flow and equity free cash flow is the cash flow before changes in financing (also often referred to as the pre-debt repayment cash flow). To calculate the cash flow before changes in financing, we deduct all after-tax interest and preferred stock dividend cash flows paid to the company's non-equity investors.

Starbucks does not have any preferred stock, but it does have some debt; thus, we calculate Starbucks' cash flow before changes in financing by deducting the after-tax interest paid to debtholders from its free cash flow. Starbucks' interest expense appears on its income statement (FCF 15, $11 million). We adjust interest expense for the change in interest payable (FCF 16 $0.5 million)—which appears on its cash flow statement—to measure the amount of interest it paid in cash. We then add back any interest tax shield from its interest. In this illustration, using a simple calculation to measure its interest tax shield, we multiply the effective tax rate (calculated earlier as 0.358) by the amount of interest expense (FCF 15 × FCF 2, $4 = $11 × 0.358). Starbucks' cash flow before changes in financing is $115 million ($115 = $121 − $11 + $0.5 + $4). This cash flow is relevant to Starbucks as it executes its capital structure strategy. Since this cash flow is positive ($115 million), Starbucks does not need to raise additional capital for this period unless it needs to pay off debt or wants to repurchase common stock or pay dividends.

We calculate Starbucks' equity free cash flow by deducting any change in its non-equity financing from the cash flow before changes in financing. Starbucks increased its short-term debt by $423 million (FCF 17) and decreased its long-term debt by $1 million (FCF 18). Thus, its equity free cash flow is equal to $537 million ($537 = $115 + $423 − $1).

Reconciling Starbucks' Equity Free Cash Flow to Its Change in Cash Balance

The remainder of the free cash flow schedule in Exhibit 3.8 reconciles Starbucks' equity free cash flow to the change in its cash balance. This reconciliation has three parts. The first part adjusts for the cash flows to and from equityholders. For Starbucks, these adjustments include an issuance of stock (FCF 19, $277 million) and a repurchase of stock (FCF 20, −$854 million). You might be wondering why Starbucks issued and repurchased stock in the same year. Most of the issuance of the stock was the exercise of employee stock options or other stock-related compensation. Further, the repurchase of the stock was part of the company's stock repurchase plan. Knowing this, we now see why Starbucks might have issued the short-term debt; it needed extra cash to be able to repurchase shares that were worth over $850 million.

The second part of the reconciliation is for the cash flow resulting from excess assets. Although we do not include it in EBIT, we now include any after-tax interest income—FCF 21 adjusted for taxes, $15 million = $23 × (1 − 0.358)—and any increase or decrease in the amount of excess assets (FCF 22, $22 million), in order to reconcile to the change in cash. If we add these two parts to equity free cash flow, we arrive at the change in the company's excess cash. Next, we add the change in the company's required cash balance (FCF 12) to the change in the company's excess cash to reconcile to the change in the company's total cash balance.

Calculating Starbucks' Free Cash Flow Using the Cash Flow Statement

In Exhibit 3.9, we show the calculation of Starbucks' free cash flow using the cash flow from operations method. Using this method, we begin with a company's cash flow from operations (FCF 25, $1.131 billion). Next, we adjust it for any effects that we do not consider to be part of the company's operations. For Starbucks, this adjustment includes deducting the income from its excess assets (FCF 21 adjusted for income taxes, which we calculate to be $15 million in the prior section). Since the change in the company's required cash balance (FCF 12) is deducted when calculating free cash flows (a deduction not made by accountants when measuring cash flow from operations), we also deduct this as well. The sum of these amounts is equal to the company's adjusted cash flow from operations.

EXHIBIT 3.9	Starbucks' Free Cash Flow Measured Using the Cash Flow Statement		
Starbucks Corporation **Free Cash Flows ($ in thousands)**	**Reported** **Year 12**	**FCF** **Ref #**	
Net cash provided by operating activities	$1,131,633	25	
Remove effects of excess assets on CFO			
Interest and other income, after tax	−15,011	21 × (1.0 − 2)	
Change in required cash balance.	−138,797	12	
Adjusted cash flow from operations	**$ 977,825**	Sum	
Interest expense.	11,105	15	
Change in interest payable.	−529	16	
Interest tax shield	−3,980	15 × 2	
Unlevered cash flow from operations	**$ 984,421**	Sum	
Acquisitions, net of cash acquired.	−91,734	14	
Capital expenditures	−771,230	13	
Unlevered free cash flow	**$ 121,457**	Sum	

We add back after-tax cash interest to measure the company's unlevered cash flow from operations. For Starbucks, this adjustment has three parts—adding back interest (FCF 15), adding back the change in interest payable (FCF 16), and deducting the interest tax shield (FCF 15 × FCF 2). The unlevered cash flow from operations we measure using this method is the same as the unlevered cash flow from operations using the EBIT method. To calculate free cash flow we subtract the amount spent on acquisitions (FCF 14) and capital expenditures (FCF 13). The remaining equity free cash flow and cash reconciliation calculations are the same for both free cash flow calculation methods, so we do not repeat them here.

Using Cash Flows in Financial Analysis and Valuation

Forecasting free cash flows requires an understanding of both the firm in its present state and any likely future changes. We discussed this extensively in Chapter 2 as we sought to analyze the competitiveness of an industry and a company's competitive advantage. One potentially useful financial analysis practice is to use a company's historical financial statements to calculate its historical free cash flows as we did for Starbucks. Analyzing a company's historical free cash flows can help us think about the company's future free cash flows, which we will forecast from our financial model. This allows us to determine what forecasts we want to have in our model.

Since our purpose for analyzing historical cash flows is to understand the past in order to forecast the future, it is useful to partition the cash flow measures into cash flows related to existing and ongoing operations from cash flows related to "one-time" events or circumstances. For example, even though a company may have experienced effects from foreign currency translation on its balance sheet accounts, we would not generally forecast these effects going forward, as they are non-cash in nature. Hence, we will not likely allow for this complexity in our forecasts.

Unlevered operating cash flows and free cash flows provide a useful complement to earnings as we analyze the performance of a company. Neither earnings measures nor cash flow measures reveal the true performance of a firm on its own. Both types of measures can be useful. Earnings measures can provide better information on the long-run earning power of the firm. Cash flow measures can provide information on the consumable resources, and they are less easily manipulated; however, they can match revenues and expenses poorly and not portray future earning power accurately. Cash flows are typically more variable than earnings, usually due to "lumpy" capital expenditures and other investments that earnings generally smooth (capital expenditures are not subtracted in calculating earnings but are smoothed using a depreciation charge against earnings over time).

The ratio of earnings to cash flows from operations indicates the magnitude of accruals in earnings. One can examine this ratio over time to discern if earnings and cash flows are both growing. If not, where are the cash flows going? It is possible they are needed to fund either current asset growth or long-term investments, but it is also a possible sign that accounting manipulations have taken place. Cash flows before changes in financing provide a useful measure to help us understand the flexibility of a company's financing situation. A positive cash flow before changes in financing indicates that the company can either pay down or redeem its non-equity securities, distribute cash to its owners, or accumulate excess cash. A negative cash flow before changes in financing indicates the need for additional financing or that the company will draw down its cash balance.

The degree of correlation between earnings measures and cash flow measures depends on the definition of cash flows. Naive definitions (earnings plus depreciation) are highly correlated with net income, and measures such as operating cash flows are generally less highly correlated. Most studies indicate that operating cash flows, by themselves, do not provide us with a superior ability to predict events—such as bankruptcy—relative to historical cost accounting earnings, nor do they explain much variation in stock returns. However, some recent studies indicate that earnings and cash flows, when used in conjunction with each other, explain stock price movements more accurately than using either alone.[2]

In valuing a company, it is important to understand where various balance sheet accounts flow into the different sections of the statement of cash flows—operating, investing, and financing. While it is very obvious where some balance sheet accounts flow to the cash flow statement—such as accounts receivable and inventory—it is not equally obvious for some balance sheet accounts—such as other assets or other liabilities. It is important for us to understand this mapping, for if we know exactly how the various balance sheet accounts map into the different partitions of the statement of cash flows, we can more accurately estimate the unlevered free cash flows. We are not overly concerned with misclassifying something between operating cash flows and investing cash flows, for both are used in calculating unlevered free cash flows. However, if we misclassify something between the operating and financing sections or between the investing and financing sections, this can lead to serious errors in measuring unlevered free cash flows. Thus, even if we projected the balance sheet and income statement for future years with perfect accuracy, our measured unlevered free cash flows could be forecasted with significant error if we do not know where certain balance sheet accounts map into the statement of cash flows.

We can reconstruct the company's cash flow statement from its income statement, balance sheet, statement of shareholders' equity and supplemental footnote information; we can then use the reconstructed cash flow statements to calculate free cash flows. For most companies, the reconstructed cash flow statements and free cash flow schedules will not be the same as the reported cash flow statement and related free cash flows. This is true for a variety of reasons. However, we can usually learn enough through the reconstruction process to be confident about where the balance sheet accounts map into the statement of cash flows. Once we achieve that, we can be more confident about how the relevant accounts map in the calculation of the free cash flows.

---

[2] See, for example, Dechow, P., "Accounting Earnings and Cash Flows as Measures of Firm Performance: The Role of Accounting Accruals," *Journal of Accounting and Economics* (July 1994), pp. 3–42.

3.5 OVERVIEW OF INCOME TAX ISSUES

LO3 Analyze income tax disclosures

Naturally, measuring marginal income tax rates on different types of income and expenses, such as interest, is a necessary step in most valuation analyses. In this section, we provide an overview of income tax issues that can arise when conducting a valuation. The first issue that arises is that the income before tax in a company's financial statements typically does not represent the taxable income reported to the taxing authority. Thus, the income tax expense (**provision for income taxes**) in the financial statements does not equal the taxes due on the company's tax forms. These differences arise as a result of differences between the accounting rules required by taxing authorities and the accounting principles used to prepare financial statements.

Some differences between a company's tax records and its financial statements are **permanent differences**; that is, the revenues and/or expenses on the tax records are permanently different from the revenues and/or expenses in the financial statements. However, there are also some differences between a company's tax records and its financial statements that are **temporary differences**; that is, the revenues and/or expenses on the tax records are temporarily different from the revenues and/or expenses in the financial statements, but the difference eventually reverses so that the cumulative revenues and expenses are the same in the long run.

Permanent Differences Between Book and Tax Accounting

Permanent differences exist because certain revenues or expenses must be recognized for financial reporting purposes but not for income tax purposes, and vice versa. A U.S. example of a permanent difference is the interest on municipal bonds that is not taxable; that is, the investor in a municipal bond does not have to pay income taxes on the interest earned on those bonds. The accounting records show income for municipal bond interest, but the tax records do not. Other U.S. examples of permanent differences include the following: compensation expense for certain stock options (expense is not tax deductible), dividends received exclusion (a portion of the dividends received from other corporations is not taxable), the write-down of non-tax deductible goodwill due to impairment (expense is not deductible), premiums paid and proceeds received on life insurance policies of key managers (premiums are not tax deductible, and proceeds are not taxable), and fines resulting from the violation of the law (fines are not tax deductible).

For a company with only permanent differences, the provision for income taxes (income tax expense) in the financial statements is equal to the income tax that the company must pay to the taxing authority. The **effective income tax rate** based on the financial statements (provision for income taxes divided by income before taxes), however, will differ from the income tax rate reflected in the company's tax forms. Thus, the effective tax rate in the financial statements does not represent the tax rate used to calculate interest tax shields, nor does it reflect the income tax rate that the company will pay on additional income.

Assume a company has taxable income equal to $100,000, but it also has $10,000 in interest on non-taxable municipal bonds. Assume further that the company faces a 40% marginal and average tax rate on its taxable income. For financial accounting purposes, the company has income before tax equal to $110,000. It is incorrect, however, to calculate the provision for income taxes using the $110,000 and the 40% tax rate, for the $10,000 in municipal bond interest will never be taxed. For income tax purposes, the company has income equal to $100,000 and an income tax liability equal to $40,000 ($40,000 = 0.4 × $100,000). Since the municipal bond interest is a permanent difference, the financial accounting records also reflect the $40,000 income tax liability. The correct calculation and presentation of the company's income taxes is as follows:

	Tax (40%)	Book
Income before municipal bond interest	$100,000	$100,000
Municipal bond interest		10,000
Taxable income or income before taxes	$100,000	$110,000
Income tax payable or expense (provision)	−40,000	−40,000
Net income	$ 60,000	$ 70,000
Effective income tax rate	40.0%	36.4%

A permanent difference in net income—between the income tax records and financial statements—causes the effective tax rate implied in the financial statements to differ from the statutory tax rate. The effective tax rate implied in the financial statements is simply calculated as the provision for income taxes (income tax expense) divided by income before tax. In our example, the effective income tax rate is 36.4% ($40,000/$110,000) rather than 40.0%. This difference is important because the effective tax rate implied in the financial statements does not represent the tax rate used in the calculation of interest tax shields, nor does it reflect the income tax rate that the company pays on its taxable income. The reconciliation is useful because it provides us with information relevant to determining the tax rate the company faces. In this case, the reconciliation would indicate that the company is paying at the 40% tax rate on its taxable income. The reconciliation for the company in our example is as follows:

Reconciliation to the Statutory Rate	
Statutory rate	40.0%
Municipal bond interest*	–3.6%
Effective income tax rate	36.4%

*Calculated as 0.4 × $10,000/$110,000

Temporary Differences Between Book and Tax Accounting

A company's income tax expense shown on the income statement in its annual reports or quarterly reports to shareholders usually does not equal the income taxes on its tax forms that are currently payable to various governments. While some countries have uniformity between book and tax accounting, in the United States and in many other countries, a company's financial statements are not identical to its income tax records (filed with various tax authorities), and the differences are not just permanent differences.

Temporary differences arise when the revenues and/or expenses on the tax records are temporarily different from the revenues and/or expenses in the financial statements. One key to understanding temporary differences is that the differences between the book and tax records eventually reverse themselves so that the cumulative expenses or revenues are the same over the life of the firm. Temporary differences result in the creation of either deferred income tax asset or liability accounts (or both). Deferred income tax asset or liability accounts arise when the values of the assets and liabilities on a company's financial statements (the **book value** of its assets and liabilities) are not the same as the values in its income tax records (specifically, the **tax basis** of the assets and liabilities) because of temporary differences. Permanent differences do not create deferred income taxes. Another thing to note about temporary differences is that when they exist, the financial reporting records will record income tax expense based on the income reported for financial reporting purposes and not on the amount reported on the tax forms.

Deferred tax asset and liability accounts do not represent cash flows. If this is true, why do we care about them when valuing a company? We care about deferred income taxes for two reasons. First, since we typically do not have access to a company's income tax records, we need to understand deferred income taxes in order to measure the company's income tax payable to the tax authorities, which we need in order to forecast free cash flows. While deferred tax asset and liability accounts are not cash flows in themselves, they are items one needs in order to adjust net income to cash flow from operations because the deferred tax accounts help reveal the difference between income tax expense for financial reporting purposes and the amounts payable to the tax authorities. Second, since it is very likely that we do not have the income tax records of a company's comparable companies, we need financial-reporting-based financial forecasts of the company we are valuing—which includes forecasts of deferred income taxes— to conduct a comparative analysis and reasonableness checks with comparable companies.

Conceptually, the balance of a company's net deferred income taxes (that is, the net of the company's deferred tax assets and deferred tax liabilities) is equal to the difference between the book value and tax basis of the company's assets and liabilities, multiplied by the appropriate tax rate. The provision for income taxes reported on the company's income statement is equal to the sum of the income tax on the company's income tax returns and the adjustments for deferred income taxes and other items related to the current period. The deferred tax adjustment to a company's income tax provision is equal to the change in deferred income taxes for deferred tax items that affect the income statement.

More specifically, a deferred tax liability results whenever the book value of an asset is greater than the tax basis of that asset, or when the book value of a liability is less than the tax basis of that liability—

that is, when the cumulative expenses deducted for tax purposes are greater than the cumulative expenses deducted for accounting purposes. A deferred tax asset results whenever the book value of an asset is less than the tax basis of that asset, or when the book value of a liability is greater than the tax basis of that liability—that is, when the cumulative expenses deducted for tax purposes are less than the cumulative expenses deducted for accounting purposes.

Deferred tax assets are not really assets, and deferred tax liabilities are not really non-equity claims for the purposes of valuing a company. Since we calculate the value of the company (or its securities) as the present value of the relevant cash flow series (including estimates of actual taxes to be paid), deferred tax assets and liabilities are an important part of the adjustment of the provision for income taxes on the financial statements in order to measure actual taxes paid, but that is their sole role. When valuing the equity of a company, we subtract the value of the non-common equity claims from the value of the firm. However, we do not include deferred tax liabilities as a non-common equity claim. In other words, it is not appropriate to deduct deferred tax liabilities (or add the value of deferred tax assets) when measuring the value of the common equity by taking the value of the firm less the market value of the non-common equity claims. Further, it is not appropriate to use deferred tax liabilities to measure the capital structure ratios of a company in order to then estimate the company's cost of capital.

Example of a Deferred Tax Liability Resulting from Depreciation

Even though the calculation of deferred income taxes is complex, we demonstrate the basic deferred tax issues with a simple example. In Exhibit 3.10, we show the tax forms of a company with $100,000 in income before it deducts $20,000 of depreciation. The company has a 40.0% income tax rate on taxable income. Since the company has $80,000 in taxable income, it must pay $32,000 in income taxes. The company only has $10,000 of depreciation expense for financial reporting purposes for the current year because it uses a slower rate for depreciation for financial reporting purposes, and thus has income before taxes equal to $90,000 in its financial records.

EXHIBIT 3.10	Income Tax Payable Versus Provision for Income Taxes		
		Tax (40%)	**Book**
Income before depreciation		$100,000	$100,000
Depreciation		−20,000	−10,000
Taxable income or income before taxes		$ 80,000	$ 90,000
Income tax payable or provision		−32,000	??
Net income		$ 48,000	??

What is the company's provision for income taxes (income tax expense) for financial reporting purposes? Some might argue that the provision for income taxes ought to be equal to the amount payable to the taxing authorities ($32,000), for this is what the company must pay. Others might argue that showing a provision for income taxes of $32,000 does not convey useful information because it distorts the implied tax rate in the income statement; it is true that a provision for income taxes equal to $32,000 would imply an effective tax rate of 35.6% ($32,000/$90,000), which is lower than the statutory tax rate of 40.0%. In the United States, GAAP requires companies to include in income tax expense any amount that is deferred to future periods when measuring the provision for income taxes (income tax expense).

To calculate the provision for income taxes using current accounting standards, we need additional information. We need to know the **acquisition cost** (the amount the company originally paid) of the asset and the total amount of depreciation deducted for income tax purposes and expensed for financial reporting purposes. Assume the company originally paid $200,000 for the asset three years ago. During the last three years, the company deducted a total of $90,000 in depreciation on this asset for income tax purposes, which includes $20,000 in depreciation for this year. Thus, the asset has a taxable basis of $110,000 at the end of the year and $130,000 at the beginning of the year. Assume the company uses the straight-line depreciation method and expenses $10,000 in depreciation each year for financial reporting purposes. The net book value of the asset is $170,000 at the end of the year and $180,000 at the beginning of the year, which we show in Exhibit 3.11.

We know that this difference will eventually reverse so that the asset is fully depreciated on both the tax and financial accounting records. In the early years, the tax depreciation will be larger than the book depreciation. In the later years, the book depreciation will be larger than the tax depreciation, and eventually the cumulative tax and book depreciation will be the same. Until the difference completely reverses, however, cumulative taxable income will not equal cumulative income reported in the financial statements.

EXHIBIT 3.11   Tax Basis Versus Book Value

	Tax Basis	Book Value	Difference (Book Value – Tax Basis)
Original amount paid (acquisition cost)	$200,000	$200,000	$ 0
Depreciation deducted or expensed as of the beginning of the year	−70,000	−20,000	50,000
Taxable basis or book value as of the beginning of the year	$130,000	$180,000	$50,000
Depreciation deducted or expensed during the current year	−20,000	−10,000	10,000
Taxable basis or book value as of the end of the year.	$110,000	$170,000	$60,000

The tax basis of the asset at the end of the year is $110,000, and its net book value is $170,000. The difference between the tax basis and book value of $60,000 is the additional depreciation that has been deducted on the tax records relative to what the company expensed on its income statement. The income tax effect of this difference is $24,000 (40.0% × $60,000), which is the balance required in the deferred tax liability account for this asset as of the end of the current year. The appropriate income tax rate for the calculation of deferred income taxes is the rate that the company expects to be paying at the time of the reversal, which may differ from the current income tax rate. In our example, we assume a constant income tax rate for all types of income currently and in future years, so we only use one income tax rate, 40%. The tax basis of the asset at the beginning of the year was $130,000, and its net book value was $180,000. The difference between the tax basis and book value of $50,000 resulted in a deferred tax liability balance of $20,000 (40.0% × $50,000) at the beginning of the year.

Recall that the provision for income taxes reported on the company's income statement is equal to the amount of income tax payable ($32,000 noted earlier) plus the change in its net deferred income taxes for the year ($4,000 = $24,000 − $20,000). Thus, the provision for income taxes is equal to $36,000, of which $32,000 is currently payable and $4,000 is deferred (as shown in Exhibit 3.12). Note that recording deferred income taxes in this way will result in an effective tax rate implied in the income statement that is equal to the statutory tax rate. The effective income tax rate (implied in the company's income statement) is now 40.0% ($36,000/$90,000), which is equal to the statutory tax rate. It is not always the case that the effect of a deferred tax adjustment will result in the effective tax rate (provision for income taxes divided by income before taxes) being equal to the statutory tax rate. Rather, it is usually the case that the deferred income tax adjustment will make the effective tax rate closer to the statutory tax rate.

EXHIBIT 3.12   Income Tax Payable Versus Completed Provision for Income Taxes

	Tax (40%)	Book
Income before depreciation	$100,000	$100,000
Depreciation.	−20,000	−10,000
Taxable income or income before taxes.	$ 80,000	$ 90,000
Provision for income taxes:		
Current	$–32,000	$–32,000
Deferred		−4,000
Provision for income taxes—total	$–32,000	$–36,000
Net income.	$ 48,000	$ 54,000
Effective income tax rate	40.0%	40.0%

The $24,000 in additional deductions recorded on the tax records will reverse in the future because tax depreciation will eventually be lower than book depreciation. By the end of the life of the asset, the cumulative depreciation deducted for tax purposes and expensed for book purposes will be the same. In the future, as the difference reverses, the company will pay higher income taxes than the reported income tax expense in its financial reports; for this reason, accountants classify this timing difference as a liability (something to be paid in the future). Of course, at an aggregate level, the deferred tax liability associated with depreciation (or anything else) might not reverse if the company continues to grow. For example, while the deferred tax liability will eventually disappear for an individual asset, the aggregate deferred tax liability associated with depreciation could continue to grow if the company keeps growing.

Valuation Key 3.4

For most companies, an important difference between income for financial reporting and tax purposes is the use of straight-line depreciation for financial reporting purposes and the use of accelerated depreciation for tax purposes. In many valuations, it will be important to model the effect of the accelerated depreciation deductions on free cash flows. Accelerated depreciation deductions in the United States are based on the Modified Accelerated Cost Recovery System (MACRS).

Overview of the Modified Accelerated Cost Recovery System (MACRS)

Naturally, for income tax purposes, tax-paying companies generally prefer to depreciate a capitalized asset as quickly as possible in order to minimize the present value of the income taxes they pay. In the United States, companies use the MACRS depreciation schedules for tax purposes, which we illustrate in Exhibit 3.13. This same approach—depreciate as quickly as possible—is not necessarily the best depreciation method to use for reporting company performance to investors. In the United States and in some other countries, generally accepted accounting principles allow companies to use different depreciation methods for income tax and financial reporting purposes.

EXHIBIT 3.13	MACRS Depreciation Schedule Using Half-Year Convention					
	Depreciation Period (Half-Year Convention)					
Year	3	5	7	10	15	20
SL*	33.333%	20.000%	14.286%	10.000%	6.667%	5.000%
1	33.330%	20.000%	14.290%	10.000%	5.000%	3.750%
2	44.450%	32.000%	24.490%	18.000%	9.500%	7.219%
3	14.810%	19.200%	17.490%	14.400%	8.550%	6.677%
4	7.410%	11.520%	12.490%	11.520%	7.700%	6.177%
5		11.520%	8.930%	9.220%	6.930%	5.713%
6		5.760%	8.920%	7.370%	6.230%	5.285%
7			8.930%	6.550%	5.900%	4.888%
8			4.460%	6.550%	5.910%	4.522%
9				6.560%	5.900%	4.462%
10				6.550%	5.910%	4.461%
11				3.280%	5.900%	4.462%
12					5.910%	4.461%
13					5.900%	4.462%
14					5.910%	4.461%
15					5.900%	4.462%
16					2.950%	4.461%
17						4.462%
18						4.461%
19						4.462%
20						4.461%
21						2.231%
	100%	100%	100%	100%	100%	100%

* SL = straight line depreciation annual percentage

In the United States, companies are required to use the Modified Accelerated Cost Recovery System (MACRS) depreciation method for most business and investment property placed in service after 1986. MACRS is actually made up of two depreciation systems: the General Depreciation System (GDS) and the Alternative Depreciation System (ADS); however, the ADS system is used in limited situations, and companies use the GDS system for most assets. We use the acronym MACRS when we describe the GDS system. MACRS depreciates a certain percentage of an asset's cost every year. We show these percentages using the "half-year" convention. In other words, regardless of when the asset was purchased, a company depreciates one-half of a full-year of MACRS depreciation in the year acquired. This convention extends the depreciation to one year after the MACRS depreciation period. (Companies can adopt other timing conventions as well, and there are elections available to use straight-line depreciation instead of accelerated methods.)

REVIEW EXERCISE 3.3

Deferred Tax Liabilities and Depreciation

Assume a company originally paid $600,000 for an asset three years ago. The asset has a three-year life and zero salvage value at the end of the three years. For the past two years, the company deducted depreciation on this asset for income tax purposes according to the MACRS depreciation schedule using the half-year convention in Exhibit 3.13. It uses straight-line depreciation for financial reporting purposes. In the past, the company had $400,000 of taxable income and book income before deducting depreciation expense, and it expects to have that same income for the foreseeable future. The company has a 40% income tax rate. Calculate the following for Year 3: the amount of tax the company will pay, the depreciation expense and cumulative depreciation expensed for tax and book purposes, the income tax expense shown on the income statement, the net income shown on the income statement, and the balance in its deferred tax asset and liability accounts. Assume the company records a full year of straight-line depreciation in its accounting records in the year it acquires the asset but must use the half-year convention for its tax records.

Solution on pages 120–121.

Example of a Deferred Tax Asset Arising from a Warranty Liability

As we indicated previously, one of the ways a deferred tax asset arises is if the book value of a liability exceeds the tax basis of a liability. One common way this occurs is when the liability is not recognized at all for tax purposes, but is recognized for financial reporting purposes. Said differently, the deduction for tax purposes only occurs when the company actually incurs the cost. For example, financial reporting rules require companies to estimate warranty liabilities they will incur when they sell a product, whereas the tax rules only allow the deduction when the company pays for warranty work performed.

Consider the following example. If a company in its first year of operations sold products and booked $5,000 in estimated warranty expenses, but only incurred actual warranty costs of $1,000, there would be a difference between book and taxable income of $4,000. If the company had $10,000 of income before warranty expenses, its tax records would show $9,000 of taxable income and $3,600 of taxes due the taxing authority (assuming a 40% tax rate). For financial reporting purposes, the company would show $5,000 of income before tax and a provision for income taxes of $2,000. For financial reporting purposes, at the end of the year, the company would have a $4,000 warranty liability ($4,000 = $5,000 − $1,000) and would record a deferred tax asset of $1,600 ($1,600 = $4,000 × 40%). The increase in the deferred tax asset from $0 to $1,600 indicates that the company's taxes due were $1,600 higher than the provision for income taxes on its financial reports.

3.6 UNDERSTANDING AND ANALYZING INCOME TAX DISCLOSURES

The accounting rules used to prepare financial statements (**generally accepted accounting principles, or GAAP**) require certain disclosures related to the provision for income taxes on the income statement in addition to disclosures related to deferred income taxes on the balance sheet. These disclosures include the following. For the provision for income taxes, companies must disclose the current and deferred portions of the income tax provision (expense). Companies must also disclose a reconciliation between the **statutory income tax rate** (the income tax rate stated by the government as the income tax rate to be paid on income before adjustments) and the effective income tax rate (income tax expense divided by income before taxes). For the balance sheet, the company must show a schedule of the company's deferred tax assets (gross and net of any valuation allowance), deferred tax liabilities, and net operating loss carryforwards. Also, on the balance sheet, the company reports both current and non-current deferred income taxes, so it is possible that a company will report both current and non-current deferred tax assets and liabilities.

We can glean information from these disclosures regarding the tax status of the company. For example, the change in the balance of a deferred tax item divided by the appropriate tax rate indicates the difference between the corresponding expense (or revenue) on the financial statement and the deduction (or revenue) on the tax form.

- If a deferred tax liability increases, this indicates that the related expense on the financial statements is less than the tax deduction on the tax forms in the current year (or the related revenue on the financial statements is greater than the revenue on the tax forms).

- If a deferred tax liability decreases, this indicates that the related expense on the financial statements is greater than the tax deduction on the tax forms in the current year (or the related revenue on the financial statements is less than the revenue on the tax forms).

- If a deferred tax asset increases, this indicates that the related expense on the financial statements is greater than the tax deduction on the tax forms in the current year (or the related revenue on the financial statements is less than the revenue on the tax forms).

- If a deferred tax asset decreases, this indicates that the related expense on the financial statements is less than the tax deduction on the tax forms in the current year (or the related revenue on the financial statements is greater than the revenue on the tax forms).

Analysis of Income Tax Disclosures

Since the discounted cash flow valuation models use free cash flows that reflect expected income tax payments, a financial model must include a forecast of the amount of income tax the company will pay on its taxable income. We can use one of two approaches to develop a financial model that includes such a forecast.

The first approach is to ignore the difference between book and tax income and model only the company's tax records (tax-based financial statements). In this approach, income tax expense in the income statement will reflect expected income tax payments. The potential shortcoming of this approach is that the financial model does not provide forecasts of the income that the company will report to its shareholders, bankers, and other investors. Forecasting the tax records is the more common approach when the company has small differences between book and tax income. This approach is not used when the differences are large, for we may want to model financial statement numbers that are used in contracts (for example, as the basis of debt covenants) and for market multiple valuation methods. Hence, we need reasonable forecasts of the financial statements.

The alternative approach is to forecast financial statements in the financial model and include supplemental schedules to forecast the difference between book and tax financial statements in order for the model to incorporate expected income tax payments. The potential shortcoming of this approach is the potential complexity that it can create in a financial model. This is the more common approach when the company has large differences between book and taxable income. To use this approach, we need certain information. First, we need the company's income tax rate that it pays on its taxable income (tax form). Second, we need to be able to adjust our forecast of (book) income in the financial statements for the items that differ between the income statement and the tax forms. Once we know all of this information, we include forecasts of these items in our financial model, much in the same way we forecast the other items in our financial model. Because of the complexities that this creates in a financial model, we often concentrate on the major differences between financial reporting income and taxable income.

Measuring the Income Tax Rate Used on the Tax Forms

As we discussed earlier, the implied income tax rate used to measure a company's interest tax shields is often not equal to the company's average income tax rate and it is often not equal to the company's statutory income tax rate either. We can develop an initial estimate of a company's tax rate (for taxable income in its recent financial statements) from the reconciliation schedule for the effective and statutory income tax rate. Our goal is to assess the ongoing income tax rate with the information we collect from an analysis of the reconciliation in addition to other relevant information. We begin with the federal statutory rate and adjust it for other items in the reconciliation that we believe are ongoing and not the result of a permanent difference between book financial statements and tax records. This is only a potential starting point in estimating the appropriate income tax rate for interest tax shields.

In Exhibit 3.14, we present an example of this approach to measuring a company's income tax rate using the tax rate reconciliation of two companies—Darden Restaurants, Inc. (Darden) and Alcoa, Inc. (Alcoa). We can see from the exhibit that Darden's effective tax rate is 31.4% in Year 5 and that it has very few reconciliation items. The first item, state income taxes, reflects the impact of state income taxes (adjusted for the benefit of being able to deduct state income taxes on the federal tax form). This is a common reconciliation item for U.S. companies. Another related, and common, reconciliation item that is not relevant to Darden is the reconciliation item for foreign income taxes, which Alcoa reports. The reconciliation for Alcoa indicates that the taxes it pays on foreign income are below the rates it pays on its U.S. income. Other common reconciliation items we might see are for permanent differences between tax and book income, such as various credits or non-taxable interest and dividend income. Darden reports one of these items—income tax credits—separately. In this case, the credits are due to certain tax rules related to the income of restaurant employees. It does not report any of these other items specifically but instead reports a combined category labeled "other."

EXHIBIT 3.14	Tax Rate Reconciliation of Darden Restaurants, Inc. and Alcoa, Inc.					
	Darden Restaurants, Inc.			**Alcoa, Inc.**		
	Year 3	**Year 4**	**Year 5**	**Year 3**	**Year 4**	**Year 5**
U.S. federal statutory rate	35.0%	35.0%	35.0%	35.0%	35.0%	35.0%
State and local taxes, net of federal benefit..........	3.0%	3.2%	2.9%			
Taxes on foreign income				−7.5%	−4.3%	−10.1%
Income tax credits	−4.5%	−5.2%	−5.0%			
Permanent differences on restructuring charges......				0.5%	3.4%	11.8%
Audit and adjustments to prior years' accruals				−3.3%	−0.1%	−2.8%
Minority interests				0.4%	0.4%	5.0%
Statutory tax rate changes.....................				0.1%	0.2%	3.5%
Other.........................	−0.4%	−1.3%	−1.5%	−0.9%	−0.8%	0.8%
Effective tax rate.............................	33.1%	31.7%	31.4%	24.3%	33.8%	43.2%

For Darden, the likely marginal tax rate for computing the interest tax shields in Year 5 is the combined federal and state taxes, 37.9%, as the other items in its reconciliation are unlikely to be affected by changes in its taxable income due to variation in interest expense. Regarding the tax on Darden's overall income, we may or may not use that tax rate in our forecasts, depending on our view of whether or not the income tax credits and the other reconciliation adjustments are ongoing and change with a company's scale. In Darden's case, since the income tax credits of 5% are related to the income of restaurant employees, we would expect them to continue in the future. As such, we would take the magnitude of those credits into consideration in computing Darden's future taxes (multiplying the 5% times Darden's income before tax for financial reporting purposes is a reasonable estimate of the reduction in taxes arising from those credits). Without more information about "other," it is a judgment call as to how to best treat it.

Alcoa has some additional categories. Alcoa has the adjustment for foreign income taxes that we previously mentioned. In addition to audit adjustments, it also has adjustments for restructuring charges, minority interests, and changes in statutory rates. Alcoa does not indicate that it has any state and local tax effects—a rarity, to be sure. The computation of the taxes and interest tax shields for multinational companies is very complicated, and we discuss this in the last chapter of the book when we discuss cross-border acquisitions. As with Darden, the tax rate we use in our forecasts depends on our view of whether or not the reconciliation adjustments are ongoing. If we are not anticipating additional restructuring charges, that adjustment would not be included, and the adjustments for the previous year's taxes are also something we would generally not consider to be ongoing.

Note that sometimes companies do not report percentages for each of these items but instead report dollar values. To convert the dollar values into percentages, one takes each item and divides it by income before taxes. See Problem 3.8 involving Google's effective tax rate reconciliation for an example of such a disclosure.

Identifying the Differences Between Book Financial Statements and Tax Records

We can estimate the differences between a company's book financial statements and the tax records in its most recent financial statements by examining its deferred income tax schedule. Our goal is to develop a model to forecast the differences between the company's books (financial statements) and tax records, using the information collected from an analysis of the deferred income tax schedule and other relevant information. Recall that the balance for a deferred tax item represents the cumulative difference between the company's book value and tax basis of its assets and liabilities, multiplied by the appropriate income tax rate expected to be in effect on the reversal of the difference. We can think of the difference between the book value and tax basis of the assets and liabilities as the cumulative difference in book expenses (or revenues) and tax deductions and revenues. Thus, we can measure the difference in the book value and tax basis (or cumulative difference in book and tax expenses or revenues) by dividing the balance of the deferred tax item by the tax rate. Once we know this difference, we can examine the change in the difference over two years in order to determine the difference in the related expense for the year. We can then adjust the income (before the provision for income taxes on the financial statements) for the difference in expenses during the year in order to estimate taxable income (tax forms).

Valuation Key 3.5

We do not consider deferred tax liabilities to be a non-equity claim for either measuring the value of a company's equity (equal to the value of the firm minus the value of the company's non-equity claims) or measuring the company's cost of capital (deferred tax liabilities have no impact on measuring capital structure ratios).

3.7 NET OPERATING LOSS CARRYFORWARDS

LO4 Measure the effects of net operating losses on taxes and interest tax shields

A net operating loss occurs when a company's expenses are greater than its revenues. In this section, we focus on the income tax concept of a net operating loss. For income tax purposes, a company has a **net operating loss** (**NOL**) for a fiscal year when its taxable revenue (revenue listed on the company's income tax forms) is less than its tax deductible expenses (expenses it deducts on its income tax forms).

Most countries allow companies to carry back an NOL to previous years (for an income tax refund of taxes paid in previous years) and, to the extent that the company had insufficient income in previous years, to carry the NOL forward against future income. The number of years a company can carry back a loss and carry forward losses is generally limited. In the United States, a company can offset an NOL in the current year against the company's taxable income for the previous two years in order to obtain a refund of taxes paid during that period (**net operating loss carryback**), and it can offset future income for up to 20 years (**net operating loss carryforward**). U.S. tax laws allow a company to elect to not carryback a loss and just carry it forward, which might be optimal if the company expected to face a higher tax rate in the future than it faced in the past. In the United States, generally accepted accounting principles require a company to disclose the amount of its NOLs in its income tax disclosures. Countries have many varied income tax rules concerning NOLs. Countries often have minimum income tax calculations such that a company must pay a minimum amount of tax in some circumstances. A company's ability to use its NOLs may also be limited after it is acquired, and NOLs may be reduced to the extent that a company has debt forgiven in bankruptcy.

Since NOLs can reduce future income tax payments and are sometimes large, they can be an important consideration when valuing a company. First, NOLs can reduce a company's future income tax payments and hence increase free cash flows. This results in the company having a lower income tax rate than the statutory income tax rate and even not paying taxes for some time. Second, if a company has NOLs that will offset future income, this has the potential effect of also deferring the benefit of the company's interest tax shields. In addition, if a company continues to have losses and fails to use its NOL within the limited time period, it actually loses some of its interest tax shields rather than just deferring them to future years.

Valuation in Practice 3.1

Net Operating Loss Carryforwards Can Shelter Pre-Tax Income for Many Years—Akamai Technologies, Inc.

Below is a quote from Akamai Technologies, Inc.'s 2005 10-K filing with the U.S. SEC that provides an example of the information disclosed on the magnitude of a company's NOLs:

> As of December 31, 2005, the Company had United States federal NOL carryforwards of approximately $723.8 million and state NOL carryforwards of approximately $368.9 million, which expire at various dates through 2024. The Company also had foreign NOL carryforwards of approximately $8.2 million as of December 31, 2005. The foreign NOL carryforwards have no expiration dates.

Akamai's NOL carryforwards are large relative to its revenue in 2005 of $283.1 million and pre-tax income of $70.4 million. In 2005, Akamai's current income tax was $1.7 million ($0 U.S. federal income tax, $0.1 million U.S. state income tax, and $1.6 million foreign income tax). Thus, given its large NOL carryforwards, Akamai will likely be able to use its NOLs to shelter much of its pre-tax income for several years; however, it will not gain the benefits of any interest tax shields during that period, which is one explanation for its essentially zero net debt capital structure.

Source: Akamai provides services for the delivery of information over the Internet. The information for this Valuation in Practice came from Akamai's 2005 10-K report filed with the U.S. SEC and is available from the company's website, www.akamai.com.

Net Operating Loss Carryforwards Are Common

"Start-up" companies often have NOL carryforwards, as many companies incur operating losses in the early years of operations. Since these companies do not have previous income to which they can carry back the operating losses, these companies have NOL carryforwards. However, NOL carryforwards are more common across all companies than we might imagine. In Exhibit 3.15, we show the percentage of companies in the non-finance industry sector (in the Compustat® database) with NOL carryforwards in each year from 2001 through 2011. This exhibit shows that the proportion of companies with NOL carryforwards has been gradually increasing during this period, with over 40% of publicly listed companies having some NOLs by 2011. To assess the relative magnitude of these NOL carryforwards, we also present the median NOL carryforward to revenues for firms with NOLs. As you can see, the NOLs as a percent of revenues for the median company with NOLs are substantive; the ratio of NOLs to revenues is above 20% for the median firm with NOLs over the entire time period. What this graph does not portray is the tremendous variation in NOLs to revenues across firms, with some firms having NOLs that are more than 1,000 times revenue.

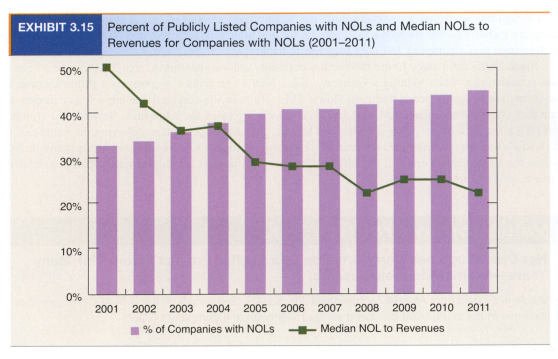

EXHIBIT 3.15   Percent of Publicly Listed Companies with NOLs and Median NOLs to Revenues for Companies with NOLs (2001–2011)

The George Conrades Company (Conrades) Example

Conrades started its business in Year −1. It was moderately successful in its first two years of operations. Mr. Conrades, CEO, believes that if the company makes a substantial investment in branding in Year +1, the company will grow substantially. We show the company's EBIT, interest, and taxable income in Exhibit 3.16 for the last two historical years (Year −1 and Year 0) and for the next four forecasted years (Years +1 to +4).

EXHIBIT 3.16   The George Conrades Company's EBIT, Interest, and Taxable Income

	Actual		Forecast			
Levered Company	**Year −1**	**Year 0**	**Year +1**	**Year +2**	**Year +3**	**Year +4**
Earnings before interest and taxes.......	$8,000	$10,000	$ −8,000	$12,000	$22,000	$25,000
Interest..........................	6,000	6,000	6,000	6,000	6,000	6,000
Taxable income	$2,000	$ 4,000	$−14,000	$ 6,000	$16,000	$19,000

The company has a 40% income tax rate, and we assume that the company's income tax records are identical to its financial accounting records. We also assume that a company can carry back operating losses for two years. Conrades' income taxes were $800 in Year −1 ($800 = 0.4 × $2,000) and $1,600 in Year 0 ($1,600 = 0.4 × $4,000). The company expects to have an operating loss of $14,000 in Year +1; thus, it will be able to get an income tax refund of up to $5,600 ($5,600 = 0.4 × $14,000) if it has sufficient taxable income in the previous two years. Conrades' taxable income for the previous two years was only $6,000; thus, the company can carry back only $6,000 of the operating loss to previous years, resulting in a $2,400 income tax refund in Year +1. In Exhibit 3.17, we present schedules showing Conrades' NOLs and taxes due.

Since the company had an expected operating loss of $14,000 but could only carry back $6,000 of that amount to the previous two years, it has an NOL carryforward of $8,000 ($8,000 = $14,000 − $6,000) at the end of Year +1. Thus, the company can shelter $8,000 of taxable income in Year +2 onward. The company's taxable income in Year +2 is $6,000, which can all be shielded from income taxes with the NOL carryforward. At the end of Year +2, the company will have a $2,000 NOL carryforward remaining, which it can use to shelter $2,000 of the $16,000 in projected taxable income in Year +3.

In addition to the income tax and NOL carryforward calculations in this exhibit, we also show the company's average income tax rate. We observe that although the company's income tax rate is 40%, its average income tax rate is less than 40% for Years +1 to +3. The NOL carryback and carryforward are the cause of this difference. The company's average income tax rate is 40% in Years −1 and 0, for it is profitable in those years, and it had no NOL carryforward that it could use to shelter income in those years. In Year +1, the company was not profitable, but since it could carry back part of its loss, it was able to get an income tax refund at an average of 17.1% of its taxable loss. Even though the company was profitable in the subsequent years, its average income tax rate does not reach 40% until Year +4 due to the NOL carryforward in Years +2 and +3.

EXHIBIT 3.17	The George Conrades Company's Income Tax and Net Operating Loss Carryforward Calculations								
	Actual			**Forecast**					
Levered Company	Year –1	Year 0	Year +1	Year +2	Year +3	Year +4	Year +5	Year +6
Earnings before interest and taxes......	$8,000	$10,000	$ –8,000	$12,000	$22,000	$25,000	$27,500	$30,250
Interest.........................	6,000	6,000	6,000	6,000	6,000	6,000	6,000	6,000
Taxable income	$2,000	$ 4,000	$–14,000	$ 6,000	$16,000	$19,000	$21,500	$24,250
Income taxes	800	1,600	–2,400	0	5,600	7,600	8,600	9,700
Earnings........................	$1,200	$ 2,400	$–11,600	$ 6,000	$10,400	$11,400	$12,900	$14,550
Average income tax rate............	40.0%	40.0%	17.1%	0.0%	35.0%	40.0%	40.0%	40.0%
Net Operating Loss Carryforward Balance								
Beginning NOL carryforward	$ 0	$ 0	$ 0	$ 8,000	$ 2,000	$ 0	$ 0	$ 0
Change in NOL....................	0	0	8,000	–6,000	–2,000	0	0	0
Ending NOL carryforward.............	$ 0	$ 0	$ 8,000	$ 2,000	$ 0	$ 0	$ 0	$ 0
Calculation of Income Taxes								
Taxable income before NOL carryforward adjustment............	$2,000	$ 4,000	$–14,000	$ 6,000	$16,000	$19,000	$21,500	$24,250
NOL carryforward...................	0	0	0	–6,000	–2,000	0	0	0
Taxable income after NOL carryforward adjustment............	$2,000	$ 4,000	$–14,000	$ 0	$14,000	$19,000	$21,500	$24,250
Income taxes	800	1,600	–2,400	0	5,600	7,600	8,600	9,700
Earnings........................	$1,200	$ 2,400	$–11,600	$ 0	$ 8,400	$11,400	$12,900	$14,550

The Effect of Net Operating Loss Carryforwards on Interest Tax Shields

If we assume that a company's income tax rate is a flat statutory rate and that it has positive taxable income (after deducting its interest expense), then the appropriate income tax rate with which to calculate the company's interest tax shields, T_{INT}, is equal to that flat statutory income tax rate. This is because the company's marginal and average income tax rates are equal to the statutory rate. For such a company, the interest tax shield is equal to T_{INT} multiplied by the interest expense deduction. However, this is not always the case.

A company's NOL carryforward can affect the timing of when the company receives the benefit of potential interest tax shields. Here, it would be inappropriate to use our simple interest tax shield formula from earlier. Fortunately, we can still calculate a company's interest tax shield when it has NOLs. The most straightforward, but sometimes cumbersome, way to calculate a company's interest tax shield when it has NOLs is to calculate the company's income tax payments under the assumption that it is unlevered; in other words, the company has no debt and no interest expense deductions. The difference between the company's income tax payments assuming it is unlevered (without consideration of the interest expense) and its income tax payments assuming it is levered (after deducting interest expense) equals the company's interest tax shield. We show this calculation for the George Conrades Company in Exhibits 3.18 and 3.19.

In Exhibit 3.18, we assume Conrades is unlevered. Notice that we do not change the interest deductions for the actual years of history but only change them for the years we are forecasting. To explain further, the company's situation at the end of Year 0 is a fact; it is the history of the company as of the valuation date. We would not make any changes to the actual years of history regardless of whether or not the company had preexisting NOL carryforwards (even if those were partially attributable to interest expense). We use the last period of actual data—whatever that happens to be—as the starting point in the calculation. In all of the years we forecast, however, we eliminate the interest expense to put the company on an unlevered basis to calculate what its taxes would be if it were unlevered after the valuation date.

EXHIBIT 3.18	The George Conrades Company's Income Tax and Net Operating Loss Carryforward Calculations Assuming the Company Is Unlevered							

	Actual		Forecast					
Unlevered Company	**Year −1**	**Year 0**	**Year +1**	**Year +2**	**Year +3**	**Year +4**	**Year +5**	**Year +6**
Earnings before interest and taxes........	$8,000	$10,000	$−8,000	$12,000	$22,000	$25,000	$27,500	$30,250
Interest.............................	6,000	6,000						
Taxable income	$2,000	$ 4,000	$−8,000	$12,000	$22,000	$25,000	$27,500	$30,250
Income taxes	800	1,600	−2,400	4,000	8,800	10,000	11,000	12,100
Earnings............................	$1,200	$ 2,400	$−5,600	$ 8,000	$13,200	$15,000	$16,500	$18,150
Average income tax rate.............	40.0%	40.0%	30.0%	33.3%	40.0%	40.0%	40.0%	40.0%
Net Operating Loss Carryforward Balance								
Beginning NOL carryforward	$ 0	$ 0	$ 0	$ 2,000	$ 0	$ 0	$ 0	$ 0
Change in NOL.......................	0	0	2,000	−2,000	0	0	0	0
Ending NOL carryforward..............	$ 0	$ 0	$ 2,000	$ 0	$ 0	$ 0	$ 0	$ 0
Calculation of Income Taxes								
Taxable income before NOL carryforward adjustment..............	$2,000	$ 4,000	$−8,000	$12,000	$22,000	$25,000	$27,500	$30,250
NOL carryforward......................	0	0	0	−2,000	0	0	0	0
Taxable income after NOL carryforward adjustment..............	$2,000	$ 4,000	$−8,000	$10,000	$22,000	$25,000	$27,500	$30,250
Income taxes	800	1,600	−2,400	4,000	8,800	10,000	11,000	12,100
Earnings............................	$1,200	$ 2,400	$−5,600	$ 6,000	$13,200	$15,000	$16,500	$18,150

We can see that the company's NOL in Year +1 will be lower if the company is projected to be unlevered ($8,000 versus $14,000), and the difference is equal to the interest expense we assume to not exist. Since the NOL is lower, though the previous two years (of history) are unchanged, the company has an NOL carryforward at the end of Year +1 that is lower by $6,000 ($6,000 = $8,000 − $2,000). The reason that the NOL carryforward is only $2,000 at the end of Year +1 is the company uses $6,000 of its $8,000 loss to receive a refund of $2,400 based on the taxes it paid in Years −1 and 0. This is the same refund it would have received if it were levered. The company's taxable income is higher in subsequent years because it has no interest expense. The result is that the company uses up its NOL carryforward sooner (Year +2 instead of Year +3). Now that we know the company's income tax payments assuming it is unlevered, we can calculate the company's interest tax shield as the difference between the company's income tax payments on an unlevered basis and its income tax payments on a levered basis. We show this calculation in Exhibit 3.19.

If we were to use the simple method to calculate interest tax shields, $T_{INT} \times$ Interest Expense, the company's interest tax shields would be calculated as $2,400 for each year ($2,400 = 0.4 \times $6,000). From the exhibit, we can see that $2,400 is the incorrect interest tax shield in every year during which the company has a NOL carryforward affecting the company's income tax payments. In reality, the company has no interest tax shields in Year +1, and the Year +1 potential interest tax shield is deferred until Years +2 and +3, increasing the interest tax shields in those years above $2,400.

More specifically, in Year +2, the company captures all of the potential interest tax shield from Year +2 interest plus $1,600 of the $2,400 potential interest tax shield from Year +1 interest for a total interest tax shield equal to $4,000. In Year +3, the company captures the remaining $800 of the potential interest tax shield from Year +1 plus all of the potential interest tax shield from Year +3 for a total interest tax shield equal to $3,200. By Year +4, the company has no NOL carryforward, and its average and marginal income tax rate is 40%. The company's interest tax shield, therefore, is equal to $2,400.

EXHIBIT 3.19	The George Conrades Company's Forecasted Interest Tax Shields					
Interest Tax Shield	**Year +1**	**Year +2**	**Year +3**	**Year +4**	**Year +5**	**Year +6**
Income taxes (unlevered firm)	$-2,400	$ 4,000	$ 8,800	$10,000	$11,000	$12,100
Income taxes (with interest deduction)	-2,400	0	5,600	7,600	8,600	9,700
Correct interest tax shield	$ 0	$ 4,000	$ 3,200	$ 2,400	$ 2,400	$ 2,400

Implied Income Tax Rate for Interest Tax Shields	**Year +1**	**Year +2**	**Year +3**	**Year +4**	**Year +5**	**Year +6**
Interest tax shield	$ 0	$ 4,000	$3,200	$ 2,400	$ 2,400	$ 2,400
Interest	$ 6,000	$ 6,000	$6,000	$ 6,000	$ 6,000	$ 6,000
Implied income tax rate for interest tax shields	0%	67%	53%	40%	40%	40%

This exhibit also shows the implied income tax rate for interest tax shields for each year. The implied tax rate for interest tax shields is equal to the interest tax shield divided by interest. The company has a 0% implied tax rate in Year +1 because it captured no interest tax shield in that year. Its implied tax rate is greater than 40% in Years +2 and +3 from capturing the deferred interest tax shield from Year +1. In Year +4, the implied tax rate for interest finally reaches 40% because the NOLs are now gone.

Valuation Key 3.6

Net operating loss carryforwards (NOLs) can be an important consideration when valuing a company. NOLs can reduce a company's future income tax payments relative to what they would have otherwise been. They can also defer the benefits of interest tax shields. We can often glean useful information about NOLs from a company's financial statements in its income-tax-related footnote disclosures.

While this discussion focuses on the cash flow implications of NOLs, it is useful to point out a related valuation consideration. Recall that the weighted average cost of capital DCF method embeds the value of the interest tax shields by adjusting the discount rate, whereas the adjusted present value method discounts the tax shields year by year as they occur. If we have a levered company with NOL carryforwards, there is no way that the weighted average cost of capital DCF method can correctly incorporate the value of the tax shields into the valuation, for the timing of the interest payments is dislodged from the timing of the tax deductions for interest. In this case, we would have to use the adjusted present value method to ensure that the timing of the interest tax shields is correct in our valuation.

REVIEW EXERCISE 3.4

Net Operating Loss Carryforwards and Interest Tax Shields

A startup company in the United States issues $50,000 of 10% debt at its inception; interest is $5,000 per year. The company has a 40% income tax rate on all income. Use the earnings before interest and taxes (EBIT) forecasts for Years 1 through 4, the company's first four years of operations, to calculate the company's taxable income, income taxes, average income tax rate (income taxes to taxable income), marginal income tax rate on $1 of additional taxable income, and the expected interest tax shield, ITS.

	Year 1	**Year 2**	**Year 3**	**Year 4**
EBIT =	$0	$1,000	$20,000	$20,000

Solution on pages 121–122.

SUMMARY AND KEY CONCEPTS

Free cash flows are cash flows available for distribution to all of a company's security holders. In this chapter we discuss the concept of free cash flows and how to measure them. They are the cash flows we use in discounted cash flow models that measure a company's value. Equity free cash flows are free cash flows adjusted for all cash flows to and from non-equity investors and represent the amount that could be distributed to the equity investors.

We also discuss the preparation of a cash flow statement in this chapter. We use most of the calculations and adjustments in the cash flow statement in order to calculate free cash flows and then reconcile free cash flows to the change in the company's cash balance. Constructing a cash flow statement from a company's balance sheets, income statement, statement of shareholders' equity, and supplemental schedules serves as an introduction to the creation of financial models, which we will discuss in the next chapter. The flow of information from the income statement and balance sheet into the cash flow statement, and the flow of all of that information into a free cash flow schedule, is the same flow we use in financial modeling.

ADDITIONAL READING AND REFERENCES

Barth, M., D. Cram, and K. Nelson, "Accruals and the Prediction of Future Cash Flows," *The Accounting Review* vol. 76, no. 1 (January 2001), pp. 27–58.
Sloan, R., "Do Stock Prices Fully Reflect Information in Accruals and Cash Flows About Future Earnings?" *The Accounting Review* (July 1996), pp. 289–315.

EXERCISES AND PROBLEMS

P3.1   **Tim Schlindwein & Company (Cash Flow Statement and Free Cash Flow Schedule):** We provide income statements and balance sheets for Tim Schlindwein & Company (Schlindwein) in Exhibit P3.1. All of the cash flows occur at the end of each year, including capital expenditures and any financing transactions. The company distributes all equity free cash flows to equityholders in the form of dividends; in other words, it does not hold any excess cash. Its income tax rate is 30% on taxable income up to $2,000 and 40% on all additional taxable income. The interest rate the company pays on debt is 8%, and its preferred stock dividend rate is 9% (both based on the company's book value of debt and preferred stock). The company has no sales or retirements of property, plant, or equipment during the period covered by the exhibit. The cash line represents required cash.

   a.   Calculate Schlindwein & Company's unlevered free cash flow and equity free cash flows for Years 0 through 4.

   b.   Compare the stability of the company's earnings before interest and taxes, net income, unlevered free cash flows, and equity free cash flows.

EXHIBIT P3.1   Tim Schlindwein & Company Income Statement and Balance Sheet Forecasts

TIM SCHLINDWEIN & COMPANY Income Statement and Balance Sheet Forecasts	Actual Year −1	Actual Year 0	Forecast Year 1	Forecast Year 2	Forecast Year 3	Forecast Year 4
Income Statement						
Revenue	$ 7,960	$ 8,119	$ 8,931	$ 9,556	$ 9,939	$10,137
Operating expenses	−5,094	−5,196	−5,537	−5,256	−5,466	−5,576
Depreciation expense	−889	−1,005	−1,207	−1,411	−1,610	−1,642
Earnings before interest and taxes	$ 1,977	$ 1,918	$ 2,187	$ 2,889	$ 2,862	$ 2,919
Interest expense	0	−400	−392	−360	−288	−208
Income before taxes	$ 1,977	$ 1,518	$ 1,795	$ 2,529	$ 2,574	$ 2,711
Income tax expense	−593	−455	−538	−812	−830	−885
Net income	$ 1,384	$ 1,062	$ 1,256	$ 1,718	$ 1,745	$ 1,827
Balance Sheet						
Cash	$ 80	$ 81	$ 89	$ 96	$ 99	$ 101
Net operating working capital	318	325	357	382	398	405
Property, plant, and equipment (net)	8,119	8,931	9,556	9,939	10,137	10,340
Total assets	$ 8,517	$ 9,337	$10,003	$10,416	$10,634	$10,847
Debt	$ 5,000	$ 4,900	$ 4,500	$ 3,600	$ 2,600	$ 2,652
Preferred stock	1,000	1,050	1,170	1,430	1,740	1,775
Equity	2,517	3,387	4,333	5,386	6,294	6,420
Total liabilities and equities	$ 8,517	$ 9,337	$10,003	$10,416	$10,634	$10,847
Statement of Retained Earnings						
Beginning-of-year balance	$ 701	$ 1,517	$ 2,387	$ 3,333	$ 4,386	$ 5,294
Net income	1,384	1,062	1,256	1,718	1,745	1,827
Preferred stock dividends	−68	−90	−95	−105	−129	−157
Common equity dividends	−500	−102	−216	−559	−708	−1,544
End-of-year balance	$ 1,517	$ 2,387	$ 3,333	$ 4,386	$ 5,294	$ 5,420

Exhibit may contain small rounding errors

P3.2   **Jake and Phil Company (Cash Flow Statement and Free Cash Flow Schedule):** We provide financial statement forecasts for the Jake and Phil Company in Exhibit P3.2 (comparative balance sheets, an income statement, and statement of retained earnings). During Year 3, the company sold property, plant, and equipment with an acquisition cost of $5,000. Its income tax rate is 40%. The company needs an increase in cash of $1,000 to operate next year. Prepare a Statement of Cash Flows, a Free Cash Flow Schedule using the Earnings Before Interest and Taxes method and a Free Cash Flow Schedule using the Cash Flow from Operations method for Year 3.

EXHIBIT P3.2   Income Statement and Balance Sheet Forecasts for the Jake and Phil Company

Income Statement	Year 2	Year 3	Balance Sheet	Year 2	Year 3
Net revenues	$ 80,000	$100,000	Cash and short-term investments	$ 19,500	$ 22,420
Gain on sale (other revenues).	0	700	Accounts receivable.	8,000	18,000
			Inventories	2,000	1,500
Total revenues	$ 80,000	$100,700	Total current assets	$ 29,500	$ 41,920
Cost of goods sold.	$–40,000	$–50,000			
Selling, general and administrative . .	–20,000	–20,000	Property, plant and equipment.	$100,000	$125,000
Depreciation expense—total	–10,000	–13,000	Less: accumulated depreciation	–10,000	–22,000
Total expenses	$–70,000	$–83,000	Net property, plant, and equipment	$ 90,000	$103,000
Income before interest and taxes. . . .	$ 10,000	$ 17,700	Pre-paid expenses (non-current)	$ 0	$ 3,000
Interest expense.	–1,000	–3,000	Total assets.	$119,500	$147,920
Income before taxes.	$ 9,000	$ 14,700			
Income tax expense.	–1,200	–5,880	Accounts payable—trade.	$ 4,200	$ 8,200
Net income.	$ 7,800	$ 8,820	Accrued liabilities (expenses).	6,000	3,500
			Interest payable	1,000	1,100
Beginning retained earnings.		7,800	Income taxes payable	500	2,500
Dividends	0	–4,000	Dividends payable	0	1,000
Ending retained earnings	$ 7,800	$ 12,620	Total current liabilities.	$ 11,700	$ 16,300
			Long-term debt-A.	$ 20,000	$ 20,000
			Long-term debt-B	0	15,000
			Long-term liabilities	$ 20,000	$ 35,000
			Total liabilities.	$ 31,700	$ 51,300
			Common stock at par.	$ 80,000	$ 85,000
			Additional paid-in capital	0	0
			Foreign currency translation adj.	0	0
			Retained earnings	7,800	12,620
			Treasury stock, at cost	0	–1,000
			Total shareholders' equity	$ 87,800	$ 96,620
			Total liabilities and equity	$119,500	$147,920

P3.3   **The Missing Data Company (Working Backwards—Cash Flow Statement and Free Cash Flow Schedule):** We provide partially completed calculations for the income statements, balance sheets, retained earnings, and free cash flows for the Missing Data Company in Exhibit P3.3. All of the cash flows occur at the end of each year, including capital expenditures and any financing transactions. The company distributes all equity free cash flows to equityholders in the form of dividends; in other words, it does not hold any excess cash. The interest rate it pays on debt is 7%, and its preferred stock dividend rate is 8% (of the company's book value of preferred stock). All cash flows occur at the end of each year. The tax rate is 25% on the first $4,000 of income and 45% on all income above $4,000. Complete the Missing Data Company's income statements, balance sheets, retained earnings, and free cash flow calculations for Years 0 and 1.

EXHIBIT P3.3	Income Statements, Balance Sheets and Free Cash Flow Schedules for the Missing Data Company

Income Statement and Balance Sheet				Free Cash Flow and Equity Free Cash Flow		
	Actual Year −1	Actual Year 0	Forecast Year 1		Actual Year 0	Forecast Year 1
Income Statement				Earnings before interest and taxes (EBIT)	$3,180	$3,935
Revenue	$ 9,568	$9,759	$10,735	– Income taxes paid on EBIT	−795	−984
Operating expenses........	−5,262	−5,368	−5,368			
Depreciation expense.......	−1,091	−1,212	−1,433	Earnings before interest and after taxes	$2,385	$2,951
Earnings before interest and taxes	$ 3,215	$3,180	$ 3,935	+ Depreciation expense	1,212	1,433
Interest expense...........	0	?−1	?−1	– Change in required cash	?−15	?−15
Income before taxes........	$ 3,215	?−2	?−2	– Change in net operating working capital....	?−16	?−16
Income tax expense........	−804	?−3	?−3	– Capital expenditures	−2,432	−2,372
Net income..............	$ 2,411	?−4	?−4	Unlevered free cash flow	?−17	?−17
				– Interest paid in cash	?−18	?−18
Statement of Retained Earnings				+ Interest tax shield	158	151
Beginning-of-year balance...	$ 209	$2,060	$ 3,557	– Preferred stock dividends	?−19	?−19
Net income..............	2,411	?−5	?−5	+ Change in debt financing...............	−400	−1,300
Preferred stock dividends ...	−60	?−6	?−6	+ Change in preferred stock financing	140	380
Common equity dividends...	−500	?−7	?−7	Equity free cash flow	?−20	?−20
End-of-year balance........	$ 2,060	?−8	?−8			
Balance Sheet						
Cash....................	$ 96	$ 98	$ 107			
Net operating working capital	765	781	429			
Property, plant, and equipment (net)..........	12,199	?−9	?−9			
Total assets..............	$13,060	?−10	?−10			
Debt	$ 9,000	?−11	?−11			
Preferred stock............	1,000	?−12	?−12			
Equity	3,060	?−13	?−13			
Total liabilities and equities	$13,060	?−14	?−14			

Exhibit may contain small rounding errors

P3.4 **The Unknown Company (Permanent Tax Differences):** A company owns a municipal bond that pays $30,000 interest annually. The company's financial reporting (book) income before income taxes and municipal bond interest is $200,000, which is also equal to the company's taxable income (interest on the municipal bond is not taxable). The company's statutory income tax rate is 30%. Calculate the company's current income tax payable to the taxing authority, its financial reporting or book income before income taxes and provision for income taxes, and its effective income tax rate.

P3.5 **The Second Unknown Company (Permanent Tax Differences):** A company's financial reporting (book income) and taxable income (taxable income) before income taxes, municipal bond interest, and warranty expense is $120,000. A company owns a municipal bond that pays $20,000 interest annually, which is not taxable. The company had an accrued warranty expense equal to $40,000 and a warranty tax deduction equal to $25,000. The company accrues warranty expenses based on expected warranty expenses for current year revenues, resulting in an increase in a warranty accrued liability. The company's warranty liability at the end of the year was equal to $135,000. For income taxes, the company can only deduct warranty expenses when it incurs actual warranty expenditures. The company's statutory income tax rate is 40%. Calculate the company's current income tax payable to the taxing authority, its financial reporting or book income before income taxes and provision for income taxes, and its effective income tax rate.

P3.6   **The Equipment Company (Deferred Income Taxes):** Assume a company originally paid $400,000 for an asset three years ago. The asset has a ten-year life and zero salvage value at the end of the ten years. During the past three years, the company deducted depreciation on this asset for income tax purposes according to the MACRS depreciation schedule using the half-year convention from Exhibit 3.13. It uses straight-line depreciation for financial reporting purposes. In the past, the company had $100,000 of taxable income and book income before deducting depreciation expense, and it expects to have that same income for the foreseeable future. The company has a 40% income tax rate. Calculate the following for Year 4: the amount of tax the company will pay, the depreciation expense and cumulative depreciation expensed for tax and book purposes, the income tax expense shown on the income statement, the net income shown on the income statement, and the balance in its deferred tax asset and liability accounts.

P3.7   **The Warranty Company (Deferred Income Taxes):** At the end of Year 1, a company records a $5,000 warranty expense and pays $3,000 to fulfill its warranty commitments for that year. The balance for the warranty liability at the beginning of Year 1 was $20,000. At the end of Year 2, the company records an $8,000 warranty expense and pays $9,000 to fulfill its warranty commitments for that year. The company's income tax rate is 40%, and income before warranty expenses is $10,000 for both income tax and financial reporting purposes. For income taxes, the company can only deduct warranty expenses when it incurs actual warranty expenditures. Calculate the following: the amount of tax the company will pay, the income tax expense shown on the income statement, the net income shown on the income statement, and the balance in its deferred tax asset and liability accounts for Year 1 and Year 2.

P3.8   **Google Inc. (Statutory Tax Rate Reconciliation):** Use the information in Exhibit P3.4 for Google Inc. and discuss the components of its statutory income tax rate reconciliation for Years 2 and 3. For each year, calculate Google's effective tax rate and the marginal tax rate for its interest tax shields. Also discuss the tax rates you would use in forecasting Google's after-tax earnings and interest tax shields for income and interest in the United States. Also using just the Federal statutory tax rate line and the foreign rate differential line, what is your estimate of the tax rate paid on foreign income if 50% of their income is from outside the United States.

EXHIBIT P3.4	Statutory Income Tax Rate Reconciliation for Google	
	Google Inc.	
($ in millions)	**Year 2**	**Year 3**
Federal statutory tax rate (35%)......................................	$2,933	$2,049
State taxes, net of federal benefit	302	263
Stock-based compensation expense	63	91
Change in valuation allowance...	–41	313
Foreign rate differential..	–1,339	–1,020
Federal research credit..	–56	–52
Tax exempt interest	–15	–52
Other permanent differences...	14	34
Provision for income taxes...	$1,861	$1,626

P3.9   **The Unknown Company (Net Operating Losses and Interest Tax Shield):** A company has an income tax rate of 40% on all taxable income. It issued $50,000 of 10% debt at its inception; interest is $5,000 per year. The company is a start-up company in the United States. Management has created three scenarios of possible earnings before interest and taxes (EBIT) for the first four years of the company's operations. Management does not expect to change any of its external financing (the company will not issue or repurchase securities). For each scenario, calculate the company's taxable income, income taxes, and interest tax shield.

		Year 1	Year 2	Year 3	Year 4
a.	Scenario #1, EBIT =	$10,000	$ 0	$10,000	$10,000
b.	Scenario #2, EBIT =	$ 0	$3,000	$10,000	$20,000
c.	Scenario #3, EBIT =	$ 4,000	$4,000	$ 7,000	$10,000

SOLUTIONS FOR REVIEW EXERCISES

Solution for Review Exercise 3.1: Frits Seegers, Inc. Free Cash Flow Schedule

Below, we present the free cash flow schedule for Frits Seegers that includes unlevered free cash flows, equity free cash flows, and a reconciliation to the change in the company's cash balance using the EBIT method. (Note, the problem in the chapter only provided data for you to solve Year 0. The additional years of data are contained in Problem 1.7.)

FRITS SEEGERS INC. Free Cash Flow Forecasts (for the years ended December 31)							
	Year 0	Year 1	Year 2	Year 3	Year 4	Year 5	Year 6
Earnings before interest and taxes (EBIT)	$ 297.0	$ 445.5	$ 623.7	$ 810.8	$ 891.9	$ 918.6	$ 946.2
– Income taxes paid on EBIT	–118.8	–178.2	–249.5	–324.3	–356.8	–367.5	–378.5
Earnings before interest and after taxes	$ 178.2	$ 267.3	$ 374.2	$ 486.5	$ 535.1	$ 551.2	$ 567.7
– Change in accounts receivable	–16.7	–91.7	–110.0	–115.5	–50.1	–16.5	–17.0
– Change in inventory	–11.9	–65.2	–78.3	–82.2	–35.6	–11.8	–12.1
+ Change in accounts payable	5.1	28.0	33.6	35.2	15.3	5.0	5.2
+ Change in current other liabilities	3.5	19.3	23.1	24.3	10.5	3.5	3.6
– Change in required cash balance	–5.0	–27.5	–33.0	–34.7	–15.0	–5.0	–5.1
Unlevered cash flows from operations	$ 153.3	$ 130.1	$ 209.6	$ 313.6	$ 460.2	$ 526.5	$ 542.3
– Capital expenditures	–275.0	–330.0	–346.5	–150.2	–49.5	–51.0	–52.6
Unlevered free cash flow	$–121.7	$–199.9	$–136.9	$ 163.5	$ 410.7	$ 475.4	$ 489.7
– Interest paid	–96.0	–112.0	–128.0	–136.0	–144.0	–152.0	–160.0
+ Interest tax shield	38.4	44.8	51.2	54.4	57.6	60.8	64.0
Cash flow before changes in financing	$–179.3	$–267.1	$–213.7	$ 81.9	$ 324.3	$ 384.2	$ 393.7
+ Change in debt financing	200.0	200.0	100.0	100.0	100.0	100.0	100.0
Free cash flow to common equity	$ 20.7	$ –67.1	$–113.7	$ 181.9	$ 424.3	$ 484.2	$ 493.7
+ Change in common equity financing	$ 0.0	$ 67.1	$ 113.7	$ 0.0	$ 0.0	$ 0.0	$ 0.0
– Common equity dividends paid	–20.7	0.0	0.0	–181.9	–424.3	–484.2	–493.7
Change in excess cash	$ 0	$ 0	$ 0	$ 0	$ 0	$ 0	$ 0
+ Change in required cash balance	5.0	27.5	33.0	34.7	15.0	5.0	5.1
Change in cash balance	$ 5.0	$ 27.5	$ 33.0	$ 34.7	$ 15.0	$ 5.0	$ 5.1
Change in cash balance on the balance Sheet	$ 5.0	$ 27.5	$ 33.0	$ 34.7	$ 15.0	$ 5.0	$ 5.1

Exhibit may contain small rounding errors

Solution for Review Exercise 3.2: Frits Seegers, Inc. Cash Flow Statement

Below, we present the cash flow statement and use cash flow from operations in order to calculate the company's unlevered free cash flow. (Note, the problem in the chapter only provided data for you to solve Year 0. The additional years of data are contained in Problem 1.7.)

FRITS SEEGERS INC.
Cash Flow Statement Forecasts
(for the years ended December 31)

	Year 0	Year 1	Year 2	Year 3	Year 4	Year 5	Year 6
Cash flows from operations:							
Net income	$ 120.6	$ 200.1	$ 297.4	$ 404.9	$ 448.7	$ 460.0	$ 471.7
– Change in accounts receivable	–16.7	–91.7	–110.0	–115.5	–50.1	–16.5	–17.0
– Change in inventory	–11.9	–65.2	–78.3	–82.2	–35.6	–11.8	–12.1
+ Change in accounts payable	5.1	28.0	33.6	35.2	15.3	5.0	5.2
+ Change in current other liabilities	3.5	19.3	23.1	24.3	10.5	3.5	3.6
Cash flow from operations	$ 100.7	$ 90.4	$ 165.8	$ 266.7	$ 388.8	$ 440.2	$ 451.4
Investing Activities:							
– Capital expenditures	$–275.0	$–330.0	$–346.5	$–150.2	$ –49.5	$ –51.0	$ –52.6
Financing activities:							
+ Change in debt financing	$ 200.0	$ 200.0	$ 100.0	$ 100.0	$ 100.0	$ 100.0	$ 100.0
+ Change in common equity financing	0.0	67.1	113.7	0.0	0.0	0.0	0.0
– Common equity dividends paid	–20.7	0.0	0.0	–181.9	–424.3	–484.2	–493.7
Cash flows from financing activities	$ 179.3	$ 267.1	$213.7	$–81.9	$–324.3	$–384.2	$–393.7
Change in cash balance	$ 5.0	$ 27.5	$ 33.0	$ 34.7	$ 15.0	$ 5.0	$ 5.1
Change in cash balance on balance sheet	$ 5.0	$ 27.5	$ 33.0	$ 34.7	$ 15.0	$ 5.0	$ 5.1

Exhibit may contain small rounding errors

FRITS SEEGERS INC.
Free Cash Flow Forecasts
(for the years ended December 31)

	Year 0	Year 1	Year 2	Year 3	Year 4	Year 5	Year 6
Cash flow from operations	$ 100.7	$ 90.4	$ 165.8	$ 266.7	$ 388.8	$ 440.2	$ 451.4
Change in required cash balance	–5.0	–27.5	–33.0	–34.7	–15.0	–5.0	–5.1
Adjusted cash flow from operations	$ 95.7	$ 62.9	$ 132.8	$ 232.0	$ 373.8	$ 435.3	$ 446.3
Interest expense	96.0	112.0	128.0	136.0	144.0	152.0	160.0
Interest tax shield	–38.4	–44.8	–51.2	–54.4	–57.6	–60.8	–64.0
Unlevered cash flow from operations	$ 153.3	$ 130.1	$ 209.6	$ 313.6	$ 460.2	$ 526.5	$ 542.3
Capital expenditures	–275.0	–330.0	–346.5	–150.2	–49.5	–51.0	–52.6
Unlevered free Cash flow	$–121.7	$–199.9	$–136.9	$ 163.5	$ 410.7	$ 475.4	$ 489.7

Exhibit may contain small rounding errors

Solution for Review Exercise 3.3: Deferred Tax Liabilities and Depreciation

Below, we show the calculation of tax and book depreciation for this asset.

	MACRS	Tax (40%)	Straight-Line	Book
Amount paid for asset		$600,000		$600,000
Year 1 depreciation	33.33%	$199,980	33.33%	$200,000
Year 2 depreciation	44.45%	$266,700	33.33%	$200,000
Year 3 depreciation	14.81%	$ 88,860	33.33%	$200,000
Year 4 depreciation	7.41%	$ 44,460		$ 0
	100.00%	$600,000	100.00%	$600,000

We measure tax and book accumulated depreciation as of the beginning and end of Year 3. The difference in the tax and book accumulated depreciation is equal to the difference in the tax basis of the asset, which—when multiplied by the income tax rate—measures the deferred tax liability.

Year 3	Tax Basis	Book Value	Difference (Book Value – Tax Basis)	Deferred Income Tax Liability (Asset)
Original amount paid (acquisition cost)	$ 600,000	$ 600,000	$ 0	$ —
Depreciation deducted or expensed as of the beginning of the year . . .	−466,680	−400,000	66,680	26,672
Taxable basis or book value as of the beginning of the year	$ 133,320	$ 200,000	$ 66,680	$ 26,672
Depreciation deducted or expensed during the current year	−88,860	−200,000	−111,140	−44,456
Taxable basis or book value as of the end of the year.	$ 44,460	$ 0	$ −44,460	$ −17,784

We can now measure income tax for tax and book purposes. For financial reporting (books), the current income tax is equal to 40% of the taxable income for tax purposes; the deferred tax is equal to the change in the balance of the deferred income tax liability. In Year 3, deferred income taxes reduces tax expense relative to the tax owed because the deferred tax liability decreased this year (and actually became a deferred tax asset). The deferred tax liability became a deferred tax asset at the end of Year 3 because the asset was fully depreciated on the books but it was not fully depreciated on the tax records. In Year 4, $44,460 of depreciation will be deducted on the tax return, but zero depreciation expense will be recorded on the books (income statement).

	Tax (40%)	Book
Net income before depreciation.	$ 400,000	$ 400,000
Depreciation.	−88,860	−200,000
Taxable income or income before taxes.	$ 311,140	$ 200,000
Provision for income taxes:		
Currrent	$−124,456	$−124,456
Deferred		44,456
Provision for income taxes—total	$−124,456	$ −80,000
Net income.	$ 186,684	$ 120,000
Effective income tax rate	40.0%	40.0%

Solution for Review Exercise 3.4: Net Operating Loss Carryforwards and Interest Tax Shields

In Year 1, the first year of the company's operations, it has a pre-tax loss of $5,000, which creates an NOL of $5,000, and the company pays no income tax in Year 1. In Year 2, the company has another pre-tax loss of $4,000, which increases the NOL balance to $9,000, and the company also pays no income tax in Year 2. In Year 3, the company has a pre-tax income of $15,000. It uses its NOL of $9,000 to reduce its taxable income to $6,000, on which it pays taxes of $2,400 ($2,400 = 0.4 × $6,000). In Year 4, it pays taxes at the 40% rate. We present these calculations for the levered company on the left-hand-side of the table below. On the right-hand-side of the table, we present the same calculations for the unlevered company. The company would pay taxes of 40% in each year if it were unlevered.

Income tax rate:	40.0%	
Debt / interest rate:	$50,000	10.0%

	Levered Company				Unlevered Company			
	Year 1	Year 2	Year 3	Year 4	Year 1	Year 2	Year 3	Year 4
Earnings before interest and taxes.....	$ 0	$ 1,000	$20,000	$20,000	$ 0	$1,000	$20,000	$20,000
Interest.........................	–5,000	–5,000	–5,000	–5,000				
Earnings before taxes...............	$–5,000	$–4,000	$15,000	$15,000	$ 0	$1,000	$20,000	$20,000
Income taxes	0	0	2,400	6,000	0	400	8,000	8,000
Earnings.........................	$–5,000	$–4,000	$12,600	$ 9,000	$ 0	$ 600	$12,000	$12,000
Average income tax rate.............			16.0%	40.0%		40.0%	40.0%	40.0%

Net Operating Loss Carryforward Balance	Year 1	Year 2	Year 3	Year 4	Year 1	Year 2	Year 3	Year 4
Beginning NOL carryforward	$ 0	$5,000	$ 9,000	$ 0	$ 0	$ 0	$ 0	$ 0
Change in NOL....................	5,000	4,000	–9,000	0	0	0	0	0
Ending NOL carryforward............	$ 5,000	$9,000	$ 0	$ 0	$ 0	$ 0	$ 0	$ 0

Calculation of Income Taxes	Year 1	Year 2	Year 3	Year 4	Year 1	Year 2	Year 3	Year 4
Earnings before taxes...............	$–5,000	$–4,000	$15,000	$15,000	$ 0	$ 1,000	$20,000	$20,000
NOL carryforward adjustment	0	0	–9,000	0	0	0	0	0
Earnings before taxes...............	$–5,000	$–4,000	$ 6,000	$15,000	$ 0	$ 1,000	$20,000	$20,000
Income taxes	0	0	2,400	6,000	0	400	8,000	8,000
Earnings........................	$–5,000	$–4,000	$ 3,600	$ 9,000	$ 0	$ 600	$12,000	$12,000

We calculate interest tax shields as the difference between the income taxes paid and the income taxes the company would have paid if it were unlevered. In Years 1 and 2, the company saved $0 and $400 in income taxes because of the interest deductions. These amounts are less than the $2,000 ($2,000 = 0.4 × $5,000) interest tax shield we would normally expect for a company generating positive pre-tax earnings. The interest tax shields not captured in Years 1 and 2 are deferred until Year 3, when the company has an interest tax shield of $5,600. The $5,600 is equal to the $2,000 interest tax shield from interest in Year 3 plus the interest tax shields deferred from Years 1 ($2,000) and 2 ($1,600). In Year 4, the company is in a profitable pre-tax position and captures the $2,000 interest tax shield from interest deducted in that year. We present this calculation and the implied marginal tax rate for the interest tax shields below.

Interest Tax Shield	Year 1	Year 2	Year 3	Year 4
Income taxes (unlevered firm)	$ 0	$ 400	$8,000	$8,000
Income taxes (with interest deduction)	0	0	2,400	6,000
Interest tax shield....................................	$ 0	$ 400	$5,600	$2,000

Implied Income Tax Rate for ITS	Year 1	Year 2	Year 3	Year 4
Interest tax shield.....................................	$ 0	$ 400	$5,600	$2,000
Interest..	$5,000	$5,000	$5,000	$5,000
Implied income tax rate for interest tax shields	0%	8%	112%	40%

After mastering the material in this chapter, you will be able to:

1. Learn the steps in the process of creating a financial model (4.1–4.2)

2. Identify and measure the forecast drivers and create the operating model (4.3–4.4)

3. Test the model, incorporate the company's capital structure, and assess forecast reasonableness (4.5–4.8)

4. Forecast revenues and capital expenditures at a more detailed level (4.9)

Creating a Financial Model

4

Companies often make public announcements about their future performance, called guidance. These forecasts are usually short term, forecasting no more than the next 12 to 24 months. For example, Estée Lauder disclosed the following:

THE ESTÉE LAUDER COMPANIES INC.

Net sales for the first half of next year are expected to grow between 3% and 4% in constant currency. Foreign currency translation is estimated to negatively impact first half sales by approximately one percent, versus the first half of last fiscal year. . . . The Company expects diluted earnings per share from continuing operations for the first half of between $.83 and $.88, including the $.07 impact from expensing stock-based compensation and $.04 impact of the Federated and May merger.

For the Company's coming full-year results, net sales are expected to grow between 3% and 4% in constant currency. The Company expects foreign currency to negatively impact its reported results by approximately 1.5% versus last fiscal year. At the same time the Company expects to achieve diluted earnings per share from continuing operations of between $1.87 and $1.94 for the coming fiscal year, which includes the above mentioned approximately $.22 per share impact from expensing stock-based compensation as well as the potential impact of the Federated and May merger. Full-year expectations also include approximately $.12 related to the Company's incremental savings initiatives.[1]

In this chapter, we discuss how to build a financial model that culminates in forecasts of free cash flows. The forecasts in a valuation setting are typically for many years in the future.

---

[1] Estée Lauder manufactures, markets, licenses, and sells various personal care products that include skin care, makeup, fragrance, and hair care products. See the investors section of the company's website for this and other announcements as well as various financial report and U.S. Securities and Exchange Commission (SEC) disclosures at http://www.elcompanies.com/investor_relations/financial_news_events.

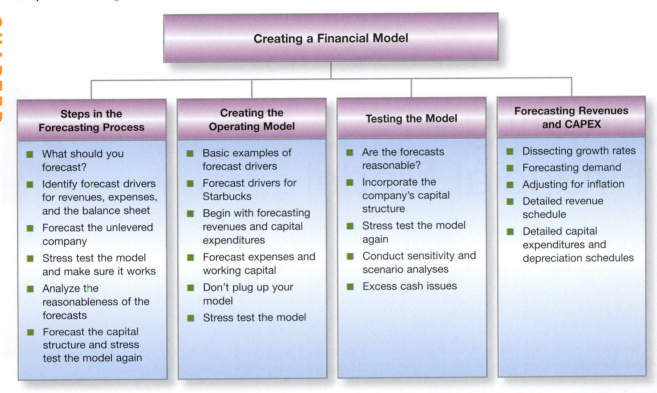

Creating a Financial Model			
Steps in the Forecasting Process	**Creating the Operating Model**	**Testing the Model**	**Forecasting Revenues and CAPEX**
■ What should you forecast?	■ Basic examples of forecast drivers	■ Are the forecasts reasonable?	■ Dissecting growth rates
■ Identify forecast drivers for revenues, expenses, and the balance sheet	■ Forecast drivers for Starbucks	■ Incorporate the company's capital structure	■ Forecasting demand
■ Forecast the unlevered company	■ Begin with forecasting revenues and capital expenditures	■ Stress test the model again	■ Adjusting for inflation
■ Stress test the model and make sure it works	■ Forecast expenses and working capital	■ Conduct sensitivity and scenario analyses	■ Detailed revenue schedule
■ Analyze the reasonableness of the forecasts	■ Don't plug up your model	■ Excess cash issues	■ Detailed capital expenditures and depreciation schedules
■ Forecast the capital structure and stress test the model again	■ Stress test the model		

INTRODUCTION

Since a company's value is equal to the present value of its expected free cash flows (adjusted appropriately for any value created from financing), forecasts of its free cash flows and the inputs that we use to measure them—for example, financial statements—are important elements in a company's valuation. Forecasts have other uses as well; for example, managers use forecasts for financial planning, bankers and other creditors use forecasts to make credit decisions, and managers, investors, and analysts use forecasts to evaluate various types of investment opportunities. A common way to forecast a company's financial statements and free cash flows is to create a financial model. In this chapter, we discuss how to a create a financial model with sufficient detail to provide all of the inputs needed to value a company using the discounted cash flow (DCF) and market multiple based valuation methods. In this chapter, we also discuss methods with which to assess the reasonableness of the forecasts in a financial model and to stress test that model.

A **financial model** is a set of assumptions (or forecast drivers) and relations (or formulas) that produces predictions regarding the future performance of a company. We call these predictions either **forecasts**, **projections**, or **pro forma (financial) statements**. In most valuation contexts, we recommend developing a sufficiently detailed financial model that includes a company's income statement, balance sheet, cash flow statement, free cash flow schedule, and appropriate supporting schedules (for example, debt, fixed assets, and income tax schedules). Sometimes, we create a financial model that is more detailed than what the company reports in its publicly available information (to the extent we have access to such information). For example, we may disaggregate selling, administrative, and general expenses into its components if they are important value drivers for the company, or we may forecast at the divisional level or by geographic region as opposed to the consolidated company level.

Managers of companies, such as Estée Lauder, sometimes make public forecasts of future results. In the United States, a company is protected if its actual performance is below its forecasts. According to the Private Securities Litigation Reform Act of 1995, a company or its management can make "forward-looking statements" (forecasts) and have "safe harbor" protection as long as the statements are not false (at the time the forecast is made). The company must also clearly identify the statement as forward-looking and accompany it with meaningful cautionary statements that identify important factors that could cause actual results to differ materially from those in the statement.

4.1 AN OVERVIEW OF THE PROCESS OF CREATING A FINANCIAL MODEL

We base our forecasts on a set of assumptions from which we forecast all aspects of a company's performance. We call these **forecast drivers**, for they are the inputs and relationships that underpin or "drive" the entire financial model. To facilitate changing the forecast drivers to either stress test the model or examine alternative assumptions or scenarios, we place all of the forecast drivers in a separate section of our spreadsheet, typically at the very top or in a separate sheet of the financial model.

LO1 Learn the steps in the process of creating a financial model

Steps in the Process of Creating a Financial Model

We show a summary of the steps we use to create a financial model in Exhibit 4.1. Naturally, the specific process we use to create a financial model depends on the valuation context. However, the basic process typically involves the steps we show in this exhibit. Before discussing that, it is important to remember the first two steps of the valuation process that we outlined in Chapter 1. Step 1 was identifying the company's direct, indirect, and potential competitors, and Step 2 was analyzing historical performance, strategy, and sources of competitive advantage. These two steps are useful in the creation of a financial model for a variety of reasons.

We conduct a competitive analysis of the company's industry and assess the company's competitive advantage in order to help us identify and forecast the forecast drivers; to help assess the role that general economic, industry, and comparable company factors could have in developing a financial model; and to assess the reasonableness of the forecasts. A competitive analysis might have a role in developing forecasts for a company's revenue or capacity needs; for example, a company's revenues might be linked to its predicted market share, and the size of that market might be linked to the general economy through such statistics as the size of the economy or population. Analyzing a company and its industry can also play a key role in developing forecasts of the forecast drivers. Recall from Chapter 2 that sometimes we are able to link a company's competitive advantage to certain financial statement relations. For example, we were able to link Nike's competitive advantage that it gets through advertising and promotion to its cost structure and profit margins. In some valuation assignments, we rely on management forecasts, common practice in fairness opinions, and sometimes we are able to use analyst forecasts as the basis of our forecasts.

	EXHIBIT 4.1 The Steps in the Process of Creating a Financial Model
1	Determine the appropriate items (financial statements, free cash flows, and supporting schedules) to forecast the level of aggregation and the horizon for the detailed forecasts
2	Identify the forecast drivers and forecast the forecast drivers to forecast revenues and capacity needs
3	Identify the operating expenses and balance sheet operating items in the model and identify and forecast the key factors necessary to forecast these items
4	Create the basic structure of the financial statements and supporting schedules; ignoring capital structure, forecast each item in the financial model related to the company's operations
5	Stress test the model by forecasting the company's operations—make sure the financial statements and schedules articulate, that assets equal liabilities plus equities, and correct calculation errors
6	Analyze the reasonableness of the forecasts of the company's operations; iterate to Step 2 if adjustments are appropriate
7	If needed for the valuation, forecast all capital structure items based on the company's capital structure strategy (type and amount of financing, amount of interest and dividends, etc.)
8	Stress test the model and analyze the reasonableness of the forecasts again; iterate to Step 2 if adjustments are appropriate

Assuming all of that background work is completed, we are ready to create a financial model. In Step 1, we make various decisions about the model's level of detail (line items in the financial statements), the model's level of aggregation (consolidated company, by subsidiary, etc.), and the horizon (number of years) over which we will forecast the explicit year-by-year cash flows. These decisions depend, in part, on the homogeneity of the parts of the company, the availability of information, and the valuation context.

Level of Aggregation

Given sufficient information, we prefer to create separate forecasts for the parts of the company that are not homogeneous. For example, suppose a company has two divisions that have different but constant growth rates—5% and 10%. Even though the two divisions have constant but different growth rates, the growth rate of the consolidated company is not constant. The growth rate of the combined divisions increases over time and approaches, but never reaches, the higher of the two divisional growth rates. It is also advantageous to disaggregate forecasts when two divisions have different but constant growth rates and different but constant margins. In this case, the growth rate and the margin will vary every year at the consolidated level, but forecasting at the divisional level will be quite easy. For similar reasons, we often forecast multinational companies at the country level or by geographic regions. Different countries or geographic regions can have different expected inflation rates and different exposure to exchange rate fluctuations and regional economic conditions, all of which can result in different growth rates, profit margins, rates of return, and so forth. As such, we often forecast at the "currency" level for multinational companies if we have sufficient data.

Real or Nominal Cash Flow Forecasts

We must also decide whether we want to create our forecasts in "real" or "nominal" currencies. Unless a company operates in a high-inflation economy, most analysts use nominal currency values and nominal costs of capital in valuation. It is sometimes more difficult to forecast a company's financial statements when the company operates in a highly inflationary economy, for it can be difficult to assess how various inputs or line items in the company's financial statements are affected by inflation.

Choice of Horizon for Explicit Year-by-Year Cash Flows

As we discussed in Chapter 1, when we use the DCF valuation method, we typically forecast free cash flows year by year for a finite forecast horizon and then use a cash flow perpetuity model or some other valuation method to measure the value of the firm as of the end of the finite forecast horizon (the continuing value date). Some practitioners use a fixed horizon for their year-by-year forecasts—say, five years, for every valuation they perform. We recommend preparing detailed forecasts year by year until the company reaches "steady state." Thus, we must decide when the company will reach steady state. We can define steady state in a variety of ways, and the definition depends, in part, on the valuation method we use to measure the continuing value. We will discuss this issue in more detail in later chapters when we discuss the alternative methods of estimating continuing value. As we shall see, the choice of horizon relates directly to the point in time in the future at which we will be comfortable performing a continuing value calculation, given the method used for that calculation.

Timing of Cash Flows Within a Year

A company's cash flows occur throughout the year; it collects revenues, pays expenses, issues and repays debt, and issues and redeems other securities on a continual basis. Even though cash flows are generated continuously throughout the year, it is not reasonable to forecast a company's cash flows without making an assumption that reduces the frequency of the cash flows (monthly, quarterly, yearly etc.) over a year. The most common assumption for the frequency of cash flows is that they occur annually. If we forecast a company's performance on an annual basis, we assume the cash flows occur at the same time each year. If we assume an annual frequency of cash flows, we need to decide when the forecasts occur during the year—for example, at the beginning of the year; at the end of the first, second, third, or fourth quarter; or continuously throughout the year.

A common way to address this issue is to assume that cash flows occur evenly throughout the year and approximate the present value of the cash flows by discounting them under the assumption that they occur at mid-year (called the **mid-year convention**). If a company's business is seasonal (for example, a retail toy store that sells most of its toys in the fourth quarter), we would likely assume that cash flows occur sometime after mid-year—maybe at the end of the third quarter. In this book, for both clarity and simplicity, we assume a company's cash flows occur at the end of the year even though the mid-year convention is more commonly used in practice. To implement the mid-year convention, we can simply take the value we derive from end-of-year discounting and multiply that value by $(1 + r)^{1/2}$, where r is the discount rate used.

The year-end discounting assumption not only affects free cash flow calculations, but it also affects the way we measure interest expense and interest tax shields. Since we assume that all cash flows occur at the end of the year, we therefore assume that a company will only issue or repay debt at the end of the year. We therefore calculate a company's interest expense based on the amount of debt issued as of the beginning of the year. In many issues we discuss throughout the book, basing interest expense for the year on the debt balance at the beginning of the year makes the examples much clearer with no loss of generality. In practice, it is common to use the company's average debt outstanding in a year in order to calculate interest expense. Thus, if a company has significant changes in its debt between the beginning and end of the year, or if it has seasonal debt variations for financing short-term working capital needs (for example, retail toy stores), it is common to calculate interest expense using the average amount of debt outstanding for the year.

4.2 FORECASTING STARBUCKS CORPORATION (STARBUCKS)

Recall that we used Starbucks in the previous chapter to illustrate how to calculate free cash flows. We extend that illustration to this chapter as we use Starbucks to illustrate how to create a financial model. Before we walk through the detailed steps of building a model, we show the outcome of that process. In Exhibits 4.2 through 4.4, we show the company's historical (Years 11 and 12) financial statements and our illustrative forecasts (Years 13 through 17). For brevity, we only show forecasts through Year 17, but we know that we would likely use a longer forecast horizon for a company with Starbucks' growth. Starbucks' income statements appear in Exhibit 4.2.

EXHIBIT 4.2	Income Statements for the Starbucks Corporation						
	STARBUCKS CORPORATION Income Statement Forecasts (for the fiscal years ended October)						
	Actual				**Forecast**		
($ in thousands)	**Year 11**	**Year 12**	**Year 13**	**Year 14**	**Year 15**	**Year 16**	**Year 17**
Revenue	$6,369,300	$7,786,942	$9,344,330	$11,680,413	$13,432,475	$14,775,722	$15,514,509
Cost of goods sold.	−2,605,212	−3,178,791	−3,831,175	−4,672,165	−5,372,990	−5,910,289	−6,205,803
Gross margin	$3,764,088	$4,608,151	$5,513,155	$ 7,008,248	$ 8,059,485	$ 8,865,433	$ 9,308,705
Store and other operating expenses	−2,362,935	−2,947,902	−3,550,846	−4,380,155	−5,037,178	−5,540,896	−5,817,941
General and administrative expenses	−357,114	−473,023	−560,660	−642,423	−738,786	−812,665	−853,298
Depreciation and amortization	−340,169	−387,211	−425,770	−531,568	−628,526	−724,960	−815,926
Other operating income	76,648	93,937	93,443	116,804	134,325	147,757	155,145
Operating income.	$ 780,518	$ 893,952	$ 1,069,323	$ 1,570,907	$ 1,789,319	$ 1,934,670	$ 1,976,686
Interest and other income	17,101	23,396					
Interest expense.	−1,272	−11,105	−42,163	−42,163	−42,163	−42,163	−42,163
Income before taxes.	$796,347	$906,243	$1,027,159	$ 1,528,743	$ 1,747,156	$ 1,892,507	$ 1,934,523
Provision for income taxes.	−301,977	−324,770	−369,777	−550,348	−628,976	−681,303	−696,428
Cumulative effect of accounting change . . .	0	−17,214					
Net earnings.	$ 494,370	$ 564,259	$ 657,382	$ 978,396	$ 1,118,180	$ 1,211,204	$ 1,238,095
Earnings Per Share							
Net earnings.	$ 494,370	$ 564,259	$ 657,382	$ 978,396	$ 1,118,180	$ 1,211,204	$ 1,238,095
Common shares outstanding—basic.	789,570	766,114	766,114	766,114	766,114	766,114	766,114
Earnings per share—basic	$ 0.63	$ 0.74	$ 0.86	$ 1.28	$ 1.46	$ 1.58	$ 1.62
Retained Earnings (and Other)							
Beginning balance	$1,444,617	$1,938,987	$2,151,084	$ 2,584,753	$ 3,036,888	$ 3,378,940	$ 3,568,421
Net income.	494,370	564,259	657,382	978,396	1,118,180	1,211,204	1,238,095
Dividends and stock repurchases	0	−352,162	−223,713	−544,693	−773,056	−1,018,140	−1,036,233
Ending balance.	$1,938,987	$2,151,084	$2,584,753	$ 3,018,455	$ 3,363,580	$ 3,556,644	$ 3,758,506

Exhibit may contain small rounding errors

In these forecasts, Starbucks' revenues almost double during this period; they increase from $7.8 billion in Year 12 to $15.5 billion in Year 17. Early in this period, its revenues grow by more than 20% annually, but by Year 17, its growth rate decreases to 5%. By Year 2017, Starbucks' net income is forecasted to exceed $1.2 billion relative to its net income of $564 million in Year 12. We see that the growth in Starbucks' operating income parallels the growth in its balance sheet. Notice that we eliminated interest and other income from the forecasts because we assume this income statement item results from excess assets that we distribute to shareholders at the beginning of Year 13. We see the effects of this distribution in the balance sheets in Exhibit 4.3 in our elimination of the company's short-term investments, for we assume these are the excess assets.

EXHIBIT 4.3 Balance Sheets for the Starbucks Corporation

STARBUCKS CORPORATION
Balance Sheet Forecasts
(for the fiscal years ended October)

($ in thousands)	Actual		Forecast				
	Year 11	Year 12	Year 13	Year 14	Year 15	Year 16	Year 17
Required cash	$ 173,809	$ 312,606	$ 467,217	$ 584,021	$ 671,624	$ 738,786	$ 775,725
Short-term investments	133,227	141,038					
Accounts receivable.	190,762	224,271	256,009	320,011	368,013	404,814	425,055
Inventories	546,299	636,222	766,235	934,433	1,074,598	1,182,058	1,241,161
Other current assets.	165,237	215,651	280,330	350,412	402,974	443,272	465,435
Total current assets	$1,209,334	$1,529,788	$1,769,791	$2,188,877	$2,517,209	$2,768,930	$2,907,376
Land, buildings, and equipment, net	1,842,019	2,287,899	2,920,103	3,358,119	3,693,931	3,878,627	4,072,558
Goodwill and other intangible assets.	127,883	199,433	199,433	199,433	199,433	199,433	199,433
Long-term investments	261,564	224,904	224,904	224,904	224,904	224,904	224,904
Other non-current assets	72,893	186,917	186,887	233,608	268,649	295,514	310,290
Total assets.	$3,513,693	$4,428,941	$5,301,117	$6,204,941	$6,904,126	$7,367,408	$7,714,562
Accounts payable.	$ 220,975	$ 340,937	$ 434,103	$ 530,451	$ 604,181	$ 659,479	$ 686,565
Accrued expenses and other	552,907	661,148	840,990	1,051,237	1,208,923	1,329,815	1,396,306
Interest payable	318	847	7,027	7,027	7,027	7,027	7,027
Deferred revenue	175,048	231,926	280,330	350,412	402,974	443,272	465,435
Short-term and current long-term debt	277,748	700,762	700,762	700,762	700,762	700,762	700,762
Total current liabilities.	$1,226,996	$1,935,620	$2,263,212	$2,639,890	$2,923,868	$3,140,355	$3,256,095
Long-term debt	2,870	1,958	1,958	1,958	1,958	1,958	1,958
Other non-current liabilities	193,565	262,857	373,773	467,217	537,299	591,029	620,580
Total liabilities.	$1,423,431	$2,200,435	$2,638,943	$3,109,064	$3,463,125	$3,733.342	$3,878,634
Common stock and surplus.	$ 130,361	$ 40,149	$ 40,149	$ 40,149	$ 40,149	$ 40,149	$ 40,149
Cumulative comprehensive income (loss)	20,914	37,273	37,273	37,273	37,273	37,273	37,273
Retained earnings	1,938,987	2,151,084	2,584,753	3,018,455	3,363,580	3,556,644	3,758,506
Total shareholders' equity	$2,090,262	$2,228,506	$2,662,175	$3,095,877	$3,441,002	$3,634,066	$3,835,928
Total liabilities and equities.	$3,513,693	$4,428,941	$5,301,117	$6,204,941	$6,904,126	$7,367,408	$7,714,562

Exhibit may contain small rounding errors

We show the free cash flow schedule in Exhibit 4.4. Recall from Chapter 3 that in its reported cash flow statement, Starbucks combined the change in receivables, change in other current assets, and change in other non-current assets into a single number (other, net). This is why the changes in those accounts show as zeroes in the Years 11 and 12 (the two prior actual years). Since we have line items in the balance sheet for each of those accounts that we are forecasting, we model the change in each of these separate accounts in the free cash flow forecasts. Not surprisingly, given all of our other forecasts, Starbucks has substantial growth in its unlevered free cash flows during this period. Its unlevered free cash flows grow from $121 million to $1.1 billion. Although we do not show it as an exhibit here, we also prepared a cash flow statement forecast, which we discuss later.

EXHIBIT 4.4   Free Cash Flow Statement Forecasts for the Starbucks Corporation

STARBUCKS CORPORATION
Free Cash Flow Forecasts
(for the fiscal years ended October)

($ in thousands)	Actual		Forecast				
	Year 11	Year 12	Year 13	Year 14	Year 15	Year 16	Year 17
Earnings before interest and taxes (EBIT)	$780,518	$893,952	$1,069,323	$1,570,907	$1,789,319	$1,934,670	$1,976,686
Income taxes paid on EBIT	−295,975	−320,365	−384,956	−565,526	−644,155	−696,481	−711,607
Earnings before interest and after taxes	$484,543	$573,587	$ 684,366	$1,005,380	$1,145,164	$1,238,189	$1,265,079
Depreciation and amortization	367,207	412,625	425,770	531,568	628,526	724,960	815,926
Asset impairment charges	19,464	19,622					
Receivables	0	0	−31,738	−64,002	−48,002	−36,801	−20,241
Inventories	−121,618	−85,527	−130,013	−168,198	−140,165	−107,460	−59,103
Other current assets.....................	0	0	−64,679	−70,082	−52,562	−40,297	−22,164
Accounts payable.......................	9,717	104,966	93,166	96,348	73,731	55,298	27,086
Accrued expenses and other	30,216	145,427	179,842	210,247	157,686	120,892	66,491
Deferred revenue	53,276	56,547	48,404	70,082	52,562	40,297	22,164
Other non-current assets	0	0	30	−46,722	−35,041	−26,865	−14,776
Other non-current liabilities			110,916	93,443	70,082	53,730	29,551
Other, net	70,204	−104,029					
Change in required cash balance...........	−28,756	−138,797	−154,611	−116,804	−87,603	−67,162	−36,939
Unlevered cash flow from operations	**$884,253**	**$984,421**	**$1,161,454**	**$1,541,261**	**$1,764,378**	**$1,954,780**	**$2,073,074**
Capital expenditures, net	−664,879	−862,964	−1,057,975	−969,583	−964,338	−909,656	−1,009,857
Unlevered free cash flow	**$219,374**	**$121,457**	**$ 103,480**	**$ 571,677**	**$ 800,040**	**$1,045,124**	**$1,063,217**
Interest expense........................	−1,272	−11,105	−42,163	−42,163	−42,163	−42,163	−42,163
Interest payable	80	529	6,180	0	0	0	0
Interest tax shield	482	3,980	15,179	15,179	15,179	15,179	15,179
CF before non-equity financing changes.......	$218,664	$114,861	$ 82,675	$ 544,693	$ 773,056	$1,018,140	$1,036,233
Change in debt, net	276,265	422,102	0	0	0	0	0
Equity free cash flow	**$494,929**	**$536,963**	**$ 82,675**	**$ 544,693**	**$ 773,056**	**$1,018,140**	**$1,036,233**
Interest and other income, after-tax...........	10,616	15,011	0	0			
Purchase of investments	444,264	21,924	141,038	0	0	0	0
Effect of exchange rate changes	283	3,530	0	0	0	0	0
Cash flow before CF to/from common.........	$950,092	$577,428	$ 223,713	$ 544,693	$ 773,056	$1,018,140	$1,036,233
Change in common stock, net..............	−950,092	−577,428	0	0	0	0	0
Common dividends			−223,713	−544,693	−773,056	−1,018,140	−1,036,233
Change in excess cash	$ 0	$ 0	$ 0	$ 0	$ 0	$ 0	$ 0
Change in required cash balance............	28,756	138,797	154,611	116,804	87,603	67,162	36,939
Change in cash balance....................	**$ 28,756**	**$138,797**	**$ 154,611**	**$ 116,804**	**$ 87,603**	**$ 67,162**	**$ 36,939**
Change in cash on balance sheet	$ 28,756	$138,797	$ 154,611	$ 116,804	$ 87,603	$ 67,162	$ 36,939

Exhibit may contain small rounding errors

4.3 SELECTING AND FORECASTING THE FORECAST DRIVERS FOR THE COMPANY'S OPERATIONS (STEPS 2 AND 3)

We now begin our walk through the steps in building the financial model for Starbucks. We assume that we already completed the first step in the process (decide on the level of aggregation, forecast horizon, etc.), and we begin our illustration with Step 2. In Steps 2 and 3 of the forecasting process, we develop a set of forecast drivers for our financial model. In Exhibit 4.5, we show some basic forecast drivers that may be used in a simple financial model to drive forecasts of various items in the financial statements and supporting schedules.

LO2 Identify and measure the forecast drivers and create the operating model

EXHIBIT 4.5 Some Example (Basic) Forecast Drivers

Item in Financial Statement or Supporting Schedule	Typical (Basic) Forecast Driver
Certain Income Statement Items	
Revenue	Growth rates, store openings, square feet, production capacity, and others
Cost of goods sold	Expense ratio, adjusted for fixed cost component
General and administrative	Expense ratio, adjusted for fixed cost component
Selling and marketing	Expense ratio, adjusted for fixed cost component; adjusted for specific costs in marketing plan
Depreciation and amortization	Based on a schedule that incorporates the company's depreciation and amortization methods for financial reporting purposes; might need another schedule for income taxes
Interest expense	Based on a debt schedule
Provision for income taxes	Based on an income tax schedule; might need another schedule for actual income taxes to be paid
Certain Balance Sheet Items—Assets	
Cash	Relationship with revenues; adjusted for potential economies of scale
Accounts receivable	Days to collect trade receivables
Inventory	Days to sell inventory
Property, plant, and equipment (cost)	Formula = Beginning + CAPEX – Dispositions = Ending
Capital expenditures	Based on a schedule that measures capital expenditures needed to maintain the current productive capacity and capital expenditures needed to support expected volume increases
Accumulated depreciation	Formula = Beginning + Depreciation Expense – Dispositions = Ending
Deferred tax assets	Based on a schedule that adjusts for the difference between revenue and expense recognition in the financial statements and income tax forms; might relate to the scale of the company or line items in the financial statements
Certain Balance Sheet Items—Liabilities	
Accounts payable	Days to pay accounts payable
Debt (short-term and long-term)	Based on a debt schedule that is driven by the company's capital structure strategy
Deferred tax liabilities	See deferred tax assets
Common stock (invested capital)	Increases with negative equity free cash flows (at least in the first pass); ultimately affected by the capital structure strategy of the company
Retained earnings	Formula = Beginning + Net Income – Dividends = Ending
Dividends	Positive equity free cash flows (at least in the first pass); ultimately affected by the capital structure strategy of the company

We can develop forecast drivers using a combination of general economic, industry, and company factors. For near-term forecasts, we sometimes rely more on the company's recent history (assuming we have no reason to not rely on its recent history, such as major economic shifts) or recent innovations. For longer-term forecasts, we would consider translating our analysis of both the competitive nature of the industry and the sustainability of a company's competitive advantage into the way in which our forecast drivers will evolve over time. Obviously, comparable companies play a role in this assessment.

Recall our discussion of Fort Howard in Chapter 2. Fort Howard appeared to have a competitive advantage—its deinking technology—that reduced its cost of goods sold expense ratio. When we forecast Fort Howard's cost of goods sold expense ratio, we might choose a ratio with a value close to its historical value (assuming no change in capacity utilization or industry pricing) for the beginning of the forecast period. As the forecast horizon increases, we might eventually trend the expense ratio toward the cost of goods sold expense ratios of comparable companies if we want to assume Fort Howard's competitive advantage would erode during this period.

In Step 2, we develop a set of forecast drivers for the company's revenues and capacity requirements. We forecast revenue and capacity using either an overall growth rate or a complex set of detailed calculations. We normally begin with the company's forecasted revenue and associated capacity requirements, for many operating expenses, assets, and liabilities are directly or indirectly linked to revenues or capacity. In Step 3, we identify and forecast the forecast drivers we will use for all of the other operating expenses, assets, and liabilities. For example, we might forecast cost of goods sold as a percentage of revenues or inventory as a function of costs of goods sold. We often use the same type of relation used for cost of goods sold—expense ratios—for the other operating expenses (selling and marketing, general and administrative).

Forecast Drivers for the Starbucks Corporation Financial Model

To make the Starbucks illustration as straightforward as possible, we use relatively simple forecast drivers for most of the items we forecast. Remember, our purpose here is to illustrate how to create a financial model; it is not to create the most sophisticated, detailed, and accurate forecasts of Starbucks' future operations. The key forecast drivers for Starbucks appear in Exhibit 4.6. We forecast revenues at the company level using a growth rate—$Revenue_{t+1} = Revenue_t \times (1 + g_{Rev})$. Revenue forecasts can, of course, result from a more complex calculation such as a forecast of store openings and closures for Starbucks or a buildup by division or even product (e.g., determining growth at the product or divisional level, which ultimately yields the consolidated company growth rate). For example, Starbucks sells its products through its own stores but then also sells its products through grocery stores and other outlets. We will illustrate a more detailed buildup for forecasting revenue growth later in the chapter. If you look at Exhibit 4.6, we project Starbucks' revenue to grow 20% in Year 13, grow 25% per year for the next year (revenues had grown 22% in Year 12), and then we fade Starbucks revenue growth rate down to 5.0% over the next three years. As we said before, at this stage in Starbucks' growth, we would likely need a longer horizon to forecast Starbucks to steady state, but for purposes of illustrating the creation of a financial model, that level of detail is not needed.

EXHIBIT 4.6	Forecast Drivers for the Starbucks Corporation Financial Model

STARBUCKS CORPORATION Forecast Drivers (for the fiscal years ended October)							
	Actual		**Forecast**				
	Year 11	Year 12	Year 13	Year 14	Year 15	Year 16	Year 17
Revenue growth rate		22.3%	20.0%	25.0%	15.0%	10.0%	5.0%
Cost of goods sold (% revenue, rev)	40.9%	40.8%	41.0%	40.0%	40.0%	40.0%	40.0%
Store and other operating expenses (% rev)	37.1%	37.9%	38.0%	37.5%	37.5%	37.5%	37.5%
General and administrative (% rev)	5.6%	6.1%	6.0%	5.5%	5.5%	5.5%	5.5%
Other operating income (% rev)	1.2%	1.2%	1.0%	1.0%	1.0%	1.0%	1.0%
Interest and other income			Assume income from excess assets, which we liquidate				
Depreciation (# of years).		9.36	10.00	10.00	10.00	10.00	10.00
Constant income tax rate.	37.9%	35.8%	36.0%	36.0%	36.0%	36.0%	36.0%
Required cash balance (% rev)	2.7%	4.0%	5.0%	5.0%	5.0%	5.0%	5.0%
Short-term investments	2.1%	1.8%	Assume to be excess assets, which we liquidate				
Accounts receivable (days to collect).	10.9	10.5	10.0	10.0	10.0	10.0	10.0
Inventory (days to sell)	76.5	73.1	73.0	73.0	73.0	73.0	73.0
Other current assets (% rev).	2.6%	2.8%	3.0%	3.0%	3.0%	3.0%	3.0%
Goodwill and other intangible assets.	2.0%	2.6%	No additional goodwill or other intangible assets acquired				
Long-term investments	4.1%	2.9%	No additional long-term investments acquired				
Other non-current assets (% rev).	1.1%	2.4%	2.0%	2.0%	2.0%	2.0%	2.0%
Accounts payable (days to pay).		38.1	40.0	40.0	40.0	40.0	40.0
Accrued expenses (% rev)	8.7%	8.5%	9.0%	9.0%	9.0%	9.0%	9.0%
Interest payable (% debt).	0.1%	0.1%	1.0%	1.0%	1.0%	1.0%	1.0%
Deferred revenue (% rev)	2.7%	3.0%	3.0%	3.0%	3.0%	3.0%	3.0%
Non-current liabilities (% Rev)	3.0%	3.4%	4.0%	4.0%	4.0%	4.0%	4.0%
Short-term debt—change from previous year ($).			$0	$0	$0	$0	$0
Long-term debt—change from previous year ($)			$0	$0	$0	$0	$0
Interest rate for debt (beginning balance—assumed)		5.6%	6.0%	6.0%	6.0%	6.0%	6.0%
Cumulative comprehensive income.			Assume no change in future years				
Revenues$_{t+1}$ to net property, plant, and equipment	4.2	4.1	4.0	4.0	4.0	4.0	4.0

As we stated earlier, we assume the company's short-term investments are excess assets, and we assume interest and other income represents the income from those excess assets. The company states that the market value of these investments equal $141,038 as of the end of Year 12. We do not show a DCF valuation for Starbucks based on our forecasts in this chapter, but if we did, we would not include the income from its excess assets, but we would add the value of the company's excess assets to our DCF valuation. In effect, we essentially liquidate these assets from the company's balance sheet, assume we distribute their value to the shareholders as of the valuation date (on an after-tax basis), and do not include any subsequent income from these assets in our forecasts.

We forecast most of the other items on the income statement—cost of goods sold, store and other operating expenses, general and administrative expenses, and other operating income—using a percentage of revenues. Looking at Exhibit 4.6, if we compare the actual percentages in Year 12 to our forecasted percentage projections, we see that some cost improvements are forecast for Year 14, which are then maintained for all future years. Being able to discern whether these are good assumptions is beyond what we are trying to accomplish in this chapter, but we do illustrate some tests of forecast reasonableness later in the chapter.

We calculate depreciation expense using straight-line depreciation over the number of years in the exhibit. We make the simplifying assumption that the company does not amortize any of its intangible assets, which is consistent with the company's practice. We measure interest expense using the beginning-of-year debt balance. Finally, we assume the company has a constant income tax rate for all income and expense, including interest.

We also forecast most items on the balance sheet as either a direct or indirect function of the company's revenues. We use "percentage of revenues" to forecast the required cash balance, other current assets, other non-current assets, accrued expenses, deferred revenue, and non-current liabilities. We use "average days to collect receivables" to forecast accounts receivable, "average days to sell inventory" to forecast inventory, and "average days of payables" to forecast accounts payable. Again, we see that all of these percentages and days calculations are kept constant through time at approximately the Year 12 levels.

Recall from Chapter 2 that we often use the average balance of balance sheet items (a stock) to measure financial ratios. For example, we use the average balance of accounts receivable to measure the average number of days it takes a company to collect its accounts receivable. We often use average balances for these ratios because they are the average investments needed to generate the flows (average accounts receivable needed to generate the year's revenues). As discussed earlier, using the average rather than ending balance does not have a significant effect on the financial ratio if the growth in the flow variable during the period is small. This same issue exists in a financial model. For simplicity, we only use ending balances in the Starbucks example, but we could utilize the financial ratios that use average balances discussed in Chapter 2.

We assume the company will not acquire any additional long-term investments or goodwill and other intangible assets. Even though the company may invest in such assets, our assumption is equivalent to assuming that any such assets acquired will create no additional value. This is a simplifying assumption considering Starbucks is partnering and creating joint ventures around the world—activities that are reported as long-term investments on its balance sheet. For land, buildings, and equipment, we assume that the forecasts include expenditures for new locations as well as the refurbishing and replacement of existing locations. For simplicity, we assume that expected inflation is constant and has been factored into our forecast driver for capital expenditures. In our calculations, we also ignore any retirements and dispositions the company may make; this implicitly assumes that retirements and dispositions would have no effect on expected cash flows.

Recall that we usually assume that a company does not change its capital structure when we first create a financial model; as such, our initial focus is on creating a model for the company's operations. In addition, this means the company will not issue or redeem any short-term or long-term debt. To simplify things further, we will assume that interest payable is a function of the amount of debt outstanding. We also assume that the company will not have any change in its cumulative comprehensive income line item under shareholders' equity.

Next, we assume the company will not accumulate any excess cash or other assets. The implication of this assumption is that the company uses equity free cash flow (either negative or positive) to balance the company's balance sheet. If Starbucks generates positive equity free cash flows, it will distribute these cash flows to its equityholders (for example, through dividends or a repurchase of equity). If Starbucks has negative equity free cash flow, its existing equityholders will invest the additional cash needed.

In other words, if we assume no change in debt financing, then distributions/contributions to/from the company's existing equityholders are equal to its equity free cash flows. Later in the chapter, after we review Starbucks' operating results, we will incorporate an illustrative capital structure strategy into the forecasts.

4.4 CREATING A FINANCIAL MODEL FOR THE COMPANY'S OPERATIONS (STEP 4)

After implementing the first three steps of the process, we have all of the forecast drivers and inputs we need in order to create a financial model to forecast the company's operations. We now create the formulas to forecast each item in the financial model. Since our focus is on the company's operations, we will ignore the company's capital structure strategy in this step of the process.

We can think of Step 4 as having three (sub-) steps. First, we collect all of the forecast drivers (like Exhibit 4.6) in a table at the top of the model or in a separate sheet of our model. Second, we create a basic structure for each of the financial statements and supporting schedules, and we link the financial statements and schedules to each other. Third, we create formulas that use both the relevant forecast drivers and any other forecasts already in the model in order to forecast all of the items in each supporting schedule and financial statement.

These last two substeps can be especially complex for someone who is creating a financial model for the first time. A financial model typically contains many linkages throughout the various supporting schedules and financial statements. Recall the lyrics from that old song that describe all of the bones in the body and how they are connected to each other: ". . . the hip bone connected to the back bone, and the back bone connected to the neck bone, and the neck bone connected to the head bone . . ."[2] Financial models essentially work in the same way; each part of a financial model is in some way connected to the other parts. We explain the process of building a financial model as a sequence of events, but it is much more of an iterative process. In general, we do not create an entire financial statement or schedule. Rather, we create part of a financial statement or schedule, and this part then feeds into another financial statement or schedule. Then, we "loop back" to complete the previous financial statement or schedule. This is somewhat complex the first time you see this, but you have already seen these linkages explained in Chapter 3 in the Bob Adams example. If you have never created a financial model, we urge you to create the Starbucks model on your own to fully understand these linkages. The chapter provides sufficient detail that you should be able to replicate the model exactly.

Starbucks' Income Statement Forecasts—Part 1

Given the forecast drivers in Exhibit 4.6, we begin creating the model by forecasting revenue. From revenue, we can then forecast cost of goods sold directly. Other items will follow. We summarize the initial calculations for the Year 13 income statement forecast in Exhibit 4.7 (subsequent years' calculations are similar—the formulas need only be copied to future years). We reference each calculation in the exhibit with a number in square brackets (e.g., [1]); we do not discuss references to subtotals and totals in the calculations. We begin creating the financial model by forecasting revenues [1]. Using a growth rate for total revenues, we can forecast revenues directly in the income statement. If the revenue forecasting procedure was more complex, we would use one or more separate schedules to forecast revenues, and revenues on the income statement would be linked to these supplemental schedules.

Next, to forecast the expenses that are directly related to revenue, we multiply revenue by the appropriate percentage rate in [2], [4], [5], and [6]. We also have sufficient information to forecast interest expense [7], and we do not require a forecast for interest and other income, because we assumed the company had liquidated its excess assets for the purposes of our forecasts. We cannot calculate operating income or income before taxes until we forecast depreciation and amortization. We could forecast this expense directly in the income statement, but we typically find it better to have a separate schedule for land, buildings, and equipment and accumulated depreciation; this schedule includes forecasts for capital expenditures and depreciation.

---

[2] See the lyrics to the song titled, "Dry Bones," composer unknown.

EXHIBIT 4.7	Income Statement Forecasts for Starbucks Corporation

($ in thousands)	Year 11	Year 12	Year 13	Calculation	Formulas and Explanation
		STARBUCKS CORPORATION **Income Statement Forecasts** **(for the fiscal years ended October)**			
Revenue	$6,369,300	$7,786,942	$9,344,330	[1] = 7,786,942 × 1.20	= Rev (Last Year) × (1 + g)
Cost of goods sold..................	−2,605,212	−3,178,791	−3,831,175	[2] = −.41 × 9,344,330	= Rev × [CGS / Rev]
Gross margin	$3,764,088	$4,608,151	$5,513,155	[3] = [1] + [2]	= Sum
Store and other operating expenses	−2,362,935	−2,947,902	−3,550,846	[4] = −.38 × 9,344,330	= Rev × [S&OO/Rev]
General and administrative expenses	−357,114	−473,023	−560,660	[5] = −.06 × 9,344,330	= Rev × [G&A/Rev]
Depreciation and amortization..........	−340,169	−387,211	−425,770	[12]	= See Exhibit 4.8, [12]
Other operating income	76,648	93,937	93,443	[6] = .01 × 9,344,330	= Rev × [OOI/Rev]
Operating income....................	$ 780,518	$ 893,952	$1,069,323	[15] = [3] + [4] + [5] + [12] + [6]	= Sum
Interest and other income	17,101	23,396		Income from liquidated excess asset	= Forecast not required
Interest expense.....................	−1,272	−11,105	−42,163	[7] = −.06 × (700,762 + 1,958)	= Interest Rate × Beg bal debt
Income before taxes..................	$ 796,347	$ 906,243	$1,027,159	[16] = [15] + [7]	= Sum
Provision for income taxes.............	−301,977	−324,770	−369,777	[17] = −.36 × [16]	= Tax rate × income before taxes
Cumulative effect of accounting change ..	0	−17,214		Assumed $0	= Forecast not required
Net earnings........................	$ 494,370	$ 564,259	$ 657,382	[18] = [16] + [17]	= Sum
Earnings Per Share					
Net earnings........................	$ 494,370	$ 564,259	$ 657,382	[18]	= [18]
Common shares outstanding—basic.....	789,570	766,114	766,114	[19] = 766,114	= Assumed constant
Earnings per share—basic.............	$ 0.63	$ 0.74	$ 0.86	[20] = [18] ÷ [19]	= Quotient
Retained Earnings (and Other)					
Beginning balance	$1,444,617	$1,938,987	$2,151,084	[65] = 2,151,084	= Ending balance (last year)
Net income..........................	494,370	564,259	657,382	[18]	= [18]
Common equity distributions...........	0	−352,162	−223,713	[62]	= See Exhibit 4.11, [62]
Ending balance......................	$1,938,987	$2,151,084	$2,584,753	[66] = [65] + [18] + [62]	= Sum

Exhibit may contain small rounding errors

Not All Items Depend Solely on Revenues

Naturally, when forecasting expenses, we consider other factors besides revenue (or revenue growth); for example, we may want to consider capacity utilization, changes in capacity utilization, and economies of scale. For a given change in revenues and demand, some expenses and balance sheet items may depend entirely on revenue and demand forecasts, some may depend partially on revenue and demand forecasts, and others may not depend on revenue and demand forecasts at all.

A company's operating expense ratios (for example, cost of goods sold as a percentage of its revenues) can change if the company has substantial fixed costs and if its capacity utilization changes during the forecast period. Assuming substantial fixed costs and all else equal, increasing the company's capacity utilization would decrease the company's ratio of cost of goods sold to revenue, and vice versa. The ratio of cost of goods sold to revenue can also change as a function of capacity utilization at the industry level. Prices typically rise when the industry is operating at full capacity, and they fall when there is excess capacity. The ratio of cost of goods sold to revenue can also change when the industry becomes more or less competitive, for such an event can cause changes in gross margins.

Even so-called fixed costs are not generally fixed over all ranges of output for all periods. A company's rent expense is fixed only until the company's scale increases such that it needs to rent additional assets. Such costs are fixed only until the company begins operating at full capacity with respect to those assets; and then it must rent more assets to expand capacity. Thus, such costs are only fixed over some relevant range of output. Some assets and related costs have an unlimited capacity, such as patents and copyrights; however, these assets typically have a limited life, so the related costs are fixed for unlimited changes in revenues but only for a limited period. Management policies can also affect, at least in part, the forecast drivers. Managers, for example, determine the credit risk that the company will accept from its customers. Managers also decide the terms of sale, such as the discount for quick payment or the cost of late payment. These policy decisions affect the company's bad debt expense, amount of accounts receivable, and likely also affect revenues. Thus, although changes in revenues can explain some of the variation in certain expenses and assets, that variation can also be affected by management policies.

REVIEW EXERCISE 4.1

Financial Model for the Bob Wardrop Company—Part 1

Forecast drivers, financial statements, and certain supporting schedules for the Bob Wardrop Company appear below. Assume that the company uses only common equity financing, raises more equity capital when equity free cash flows are negative, and distributes all positive equity free cash flows to common equityholders in the form of dividends. Forecast the company's income statement for Year 1. Calculate depreciation expense as the beginning balance in gross property, plant, and equipment, divided by the number of years of life.

B. WARDROP COMPANY—Forecast Drivers	Actual	Forecast			
	Year 0	Year 1	Year 2	Year 3	Year 4
Operating Drivers					
Revenue growth rate		40.0%	30.0%	20.0%	10.0%
Cost of goods sold (% of revenues).	60.0%	60.0%	60.0%	60.0%	60.0%
Depreciation (# of years, straight-line basis)	10	10	10	10	10
Constant income tax rate.	30.0%	30.0%	30.0%	30.0%	30.0%
Required cash (% of revenue)	10.0%	10.0%	10.0%	10.0%	10.0%
Accounts receivable (% of revenues).	20.0%	20.0%	20.0%	20.0%	20.0%
Capital expenditures	$670	$700	$610	$360	$200

Income Statement and Balance Sheet ($ in thousands)	Year 0
Income Statement	
Revenue (Rev)	$1,000
Cost of goods sold (CGS)	−600
Depreciation expense.	−167
Earnings before interest and taxes. . . .	$ 233
Interest expense	
Income before taxes.	$ 233
Income tax expense.	−70
Net income.	$ 163
Balance Sheet	
Cash.	$ 100
Accounts receivable.	200
Total current assets	$ 300
Property, plant, and equipment (net). . .	1,837
Total assets.	$2,137
Debt	$ 0
Capital stock	100
Retained earnings	2,037
Liabilities and shareholders' equity . .	$2,137

Statement of Retained Earnings ($ in thousands)	Year 0
Retained earnings—Beginning of year. . . .	$1,873
Net income.	163
Common equity dividends	0
Retained earnings—End of year.	$2,037

Cash Flow Statement ($ in thousands)	Year 0
Cash flows from operations	
Net income.	$ 163
+ Depreciation expense	167
− Change in accounts receivable	−20
Cash flow from operations.	$ 310
Investing activities	
− Capital expenditures	$ −670
Financing activities	
+ Change in debt financing	$ 0
+ Change in common equity financing . . .	0
− Common equity dividends paid.	0
Cash flows from financing activities.	$ 0
Change in cash balance.	$ −360

Exhibit may contain small rounding errors

continued

continued from prior page

Plant and Equipment (PPEQ) Schedule ($ in thousands)	Year 0
Beginning PPEQ—gross	$1,667
Capital expenditures	670
Ending PPEQ—gross...............	$2,337
Beginning accumulated depreciation....	$ 333
Depreciation expense...............	167
Ending accumulated depreciation	$ 500
Net property, plant, and equipment	$1,837

Exhibit may contain small rounding errors

Solution on page 159.

Starbucks' Property, Plant, and Equipment Forecasts

Next, we prepare a separate schedule to forecast the company's depreciation expense and capital expenditures; we also forecast the balance of its accumulated depreciation and of its net land, buildings, and equipment (see Exhibit 4.8). We begin this schedule by forecasting land, buildings, and equipment (gross). We add the beginning balance [8] to capital expenditures for the year [9] in order to calculate its ending balance [10].

EXHIBIT 4.8 Land, Buildings, and Equipment Forecasts for Starbucks Corporation

	STARBUCKS CORPORATION Land, Buildings, and Equipment Forecasts (for the fiscal years ended October)				
($ in thousands)	Year 11	Year 12	Year 13	Calculation	Formulas and Explanation
Land, Buildings, and Equipment (GPPEQ)					
Beginning balance (BB)	$2,802,704	$3,467,583	$4,257,703	[8] = 4,257,703	= Ending balance (last year)
Capital expenditures	664,879	862,964	1,057,975	[9] = [1]$_{t+1}$/4 – [14]$_{t-1}$ + [12]$_t$ = 11,680,413/4 – [14]$_{t-1}$ + [12]$_t$	= Rev$_{t+1}$/[Rev/NetPPEQ] – BBNetPPEQ + Dep
Retirements and dispositions...........		–72,844		Assumed to Equal $0	= Forecast not required
Ending balance (EB).................	$3,467,583	$4,257,703	$5,315,678	[10] = [8] + [9]	= Sum
Accumulated Depreciation: (AcDep)					
Beginning balance (BB)	$1,258,357	$1,625,564	$1,969,804	[11] = 1,969,804	= Ending balance (last year)
Depreciation expense.................	367,207	412,625	425,770	[12] = [10]$_{t-1}$/10 years = 4,257,703/10	= Gross PPEQ (last year)/# years
Retirements and dispositions...........		–68,385		Assumed to Equal $0	= Forecast not required
Ending balance (EB).................	$1,625,564	$1,969,804	$2,395,574	[13] = [11] + [12]	= Sum
Net property, plant, and equipment	$1,842,019	$2,287,899	$2,920,103	[14] = [10] – [13]	= Sum

Exhibit may contain small rounding errors

We forecast the ending balance of accumulated depreciation [13] by adding the beginning balance [11] to depreciation taken for the year [12]. Depreciation [12] is equal to the beginning balance of land, buildings, and equipment (gross), divided by the average number of years of depreciable life; in this case we use ten years. In order to forecast capital expenditures, we first forecast the total year-end net land, buildings, and equipment needed to generate next year's revenues. The net, land, buildings, and equipment balance is equal to revenues next year divided by our forecast driver—the ratio of next year's revenue to this year's ending balance of net land, buildings, and equipment. From this, we subtract the amount of net land, buildings, and equipment the company already owns before adding the depreciation taken this year. The result of this calculation is equal to our forecast of capital expenditures. Recall that we assume Starbucks will not have any retirements or dispositions of its assets.

This is a straightforward and top-level property, plant, and equipment schedule. We will show an example of a more detailed forecast of capital expenditures later in the chapter. Further, we often want to create a depreciation schedule that keeps track of each tranche of capital investment (as defined by the year purchased) and then depreciate each tranche separately. For the beginning balance of plant and equipment, we may or may not have detailed information on these tranches, so we may have to depreciate the existing stock of plant and equipment as one tranche. If we do have enough information, we can depreciate the different tranches of plant and equipment separately. In addition, companies often use different methods of depreciation for financial reporting and taxes, and we can build separate depreciation schedules for each. Thus, a model's set of depreciation schedules can be quite detailed and complex, and we illustrate some of the complexities of such a depreciation schedule later in the chapter.

Starbucks' Income Statement Forecasts—Part 2

Now that we have a forecast of depreciation and amortization [12], we can use this forecast in order to complete the income statement forecasts (see Exhibit 4.7). In this illustration, we calculate income taxes [17] by multiplying a constant income tax rate by income before taxes [16]. As you know from Chapter 3, income tax calculations can be quite complex. Here we assume no difference exists between financial reporting income and taxable income and thus intentionally ignore this complexity. We now have our forecast of Starbucks' net earnings [18]. We can also calculate the company's earnings per share [20] by dividing net earnings [18] by common shares outstanding, which we assume remain unchanged [19]. While we can begin our forecast for retained earnings, we cannot complete this calculation, for we do not know the company's distributions to equityholders. We will not know that amount until we calculate the company's equity free cash flow. We defer that calculation until then.

Starbucks' Balance Sheet Forecasts—Part 1

Once we have our income statement forecasts, we can begin forecasting the balance sheet (see Exhibit 4.9). Again, we begin creating our balance sheet forecasts by forecasting items that are directly or indirectly related to revenues. To start, we note that several of our balance sheet forecast drivers are directly related to revenues—required cash [21], other current assets [24], other non-current assets [26], accrued expenses and other [29], deferred revenue [30], and other non-current liabilities [31].

Several of our balance sheet forecast drivers are indirectly related to revenues—accounts receivable [22], inventories [23], and accounts payable [28]. In addition, we have our forecast for net, land, buildings, and equipment [14] from Exhibit 4.8. We can also forecast the debt balance (short-term [32] and long-term [33] debt) because, for now, we are assuming the company's debt balances remain constant. Based on the debt balance, we can also forecast interest payable [34]. Taking all of this into account, we can now forecast all of the asset and liability accounts.

> ### REVIEW EXERCISE 4.2
>
> **Financial Model for the Bob Wardrop Company—Part 2**
>
> Use the information in Review Exercise 4.1 to forecast the asset side of the company's balance sheet for Year 1.
>
> Solution on page 160.

Don't Plug Up Your Financial Model

We know the balance in the capital stock account is equal to the beginning balance plus the amount received for stock issued minus the amount paid for stock repurchases; however, we do not know the amount of the stock issued or repurchased. We know that the balance of retained earnings is equal to the beginning balance plus net income for the year minus any distributions to equityholders (such as dividends); however, we do not yet know the amount of the dividends (or other distributions) the company will pay to its equityholders.

EXHIBIT 4.9	Balance Sheet Forecasts for Starbucks Corporation

STARBUCKS CORPORATION
Balance Sheet Forecasts
(for the fiscal years ended October)

($ in thousands)	Year 11	Year 12	Year 13	Calculation	Formulas and Explanation
Required cash	$ 173,809	$ 312,606	$ 467,217	[21] = .05 x 9,344,330	= Rev x [cash/rev]
Short-term investments	133,227	141,038		Liquidated excess asset	= Forecast not required
Accounts receivable.	190,762	224,271	256,009	[22] = 9,344,330/365 x 10	= Rev/365 x [days AR]
Inventories	546,299	636,222	766,235	[23] = 3,831,175/365 x 73	= CGS/365 x [days inventory]
Other current assets.	165,237	215,651	280,330	[24] = .03 x 9,344,330	= Rev x [other current assets/rev]
Total current assets	$1,209,334	$1,529,788	$1,769,791	[25] = [21] + [22] + [23] + [24]	= Sum
Land, buildings, and equipment, net	$1,842,019	$2,287,899	$2,920,103	[14]	= See Exhibit 4.8, [14]
Goodwill and other intangible assets.	127,883	199,433	199,433	Assumed constant (GW)	= Forecast not required
Long-term investments	261,564	224,904	224,904	Assumed constant (LTI)	= Forecast not required
Other non-current assets	72,893	186,917	186,887	[26] = .02 x 9,344,330	= Rev x [other non-current assets/rev]
Total assets.	$3,513,693	$4,428,941	$5,301,117	[27] = [25] + [14] + [26] + GW + LTI	= Sum
Accounts payable.	$ 220,975	$ 340,937	$ 434,103	[28] = (3,831,175 + (766,235 – 636,222)) /365 x 40	= (CGS + change in inventory)/365 x [days AP]
Accrued expenses and other	552,907	661,148	840,990	[29] = .09 x 9,344,330	= Rev x [accrued expenses and other/rev]
Interest payable	318	847	7,027	[34] = .01 x (700,762 + 1,958)	= End bal debt x [interest payable/debt bal]
Deferred revenue	175,048	231,926	280,330	[30] = .03 x 9,344,330	= Rev x [deferred revenue/rev]
Short-term and current long-term debt	277,748	700,762	700,762	[32] = 700,762 + 0	= Ending balance (last year) + change
Total current liabilities.	$1,226,996	$1,935,620	$2,263,212	[35] = [28] + [29] + [34] + [30] + [32]	= Sum
Long-term debt	$ 2,870	$ 1,958	$ 1,958	[33] = 1,958 + 0	= Ending balance (last year) + change
Other non-current liabilities	193,565	262,857	373,773	[31] = .04 x 9,344,330	= Rev x [other non-current liabilities/rev]
Total liabilities.	$1,423,431	$2,200,435	$2,638,943	[36] = [35] + [33] + [31]	= Sum
Common stock and surplus	$ 130,361	$ 40,149	$ 40,149	[71] = 40,149 + [61]	= Beg bal + change, see Exhibit 4.11, [61]
Cumulative comprehensive income (loss)	20,914	37,273	37,273	Assumed constant (CCI)	= Forecast not required
Retained earnings	1,938,987	2,151,084	2,584,753	[66]	= See Exhibit 4.7, [66]
Total shareholders' equity	$2,090,262	$2,228,506	$2,662,175	[67] = [71] + [66] + CCI	= Sum
Total liabilities and equities.	$3,513,693	$4,428,941	$5,301,117	[68] = [36] + [67]	= Sum

Exhibit may contain small rounding errors

We could "plug" for the sum of these two amounts, but we recommend that you do not use such an approach, because that procedure can result in a financial model in which the financial statements and free cash flow schedule do not properly articulate (link). In the next section, we describe an alternative approach to calculating these balances that ensures the financial statements and free cash flow schedule will properly articulate. This approach uses the checks and balances embedded in the financial statements, which helps to reduce the errors in the financial model's calculations.

In this approach, we treat common equityholders as residual claimants of the company's free cash flows. In other words, if the company generates a positive equity free cash flow, it will distribute that cash—in some manner—to its existing equityholders. On the other hand, if the company generates a negative equity free cash flow, we assume that its existing equityholders will make an additional investment in the company to fund the negative free cash flow. We can make this assumption even though we do not actually expect the company to either distribute cash to or secure financing from its current equityholders. If the company does retain cash not needed for operations, we assume it will invest that cash in zero net present value projects or investments that earn their respective required rates of return. The assumption concerning securing financing from equityholders is valid as long as we can assume that the company will be able to raise any needed capital at its risk-adjusted cost of capital and with minimal transactions cost.

Starbucks' Cash Flow Statement Forecasts—Part 1

In this section, we create a cash flow statement in the financial model from the other financial statements and schedules in the same manner as we discussed in Chapter 3. In this way, we create forecasts of Starbucks' cash flow statement. At this point, we do not have all of the information needed to fully complete the statement of cash flows, but we can create most of the cash flow statement from what we already know. We already have the forecasts necessary to forecast cash flow from operations and investing cash flows, for all of the inputs for these calculations are forecasts in the other financial statements and schedules we have already created. We show the cash flow statement forecasts in Exhibit 4.10. We assume the company will not have any asset impairment charges or accounting changes.

EXHIBIT 4.10	Cash Flow Statement Forecasts for Starbucks Corporation

STARBUCKS CORPORATION
Cash Flow Statement Forecasts
(for the fiscal years ended October)

($ in thousands)	Year 11	Year 12	Year 13	Calculation	Formulas and Explanation
Cash Flows from Operations					
Net earnings..................................	$ 494,370	$ 564,259	$ 657,382	[18]	= See Exhibit 4.7, [18]
Depreciation and amortization....................	367,207	412,625	425,770	[12]	= See Exhbit 4.7, [12]
Cumulative effect of accounting change...........	0	17,214		Assumed $0	= Forecast not required
Asset impairment charges.....................	19,464	19,622		Assumed $0	= Forecast not required
Adjustments for operating working capital:					
Receivables..................................			−31,738	[37] = − (256,009 − 224,271)	= − Change in accounts receivable
Inventories	−121,618	−85,527	−130,013	[38] = − (766,235 − 636,222)	= − Change in inventory
Other current assets.........................			−64,679	[39] = − (280,330 − 215,651)	= − Change in other current assets
Accounts payable............................	9,717	104,966	93,166	[40] = + (434,103 − 340,937)	= + Change in accounts payable
Accrued expenses and other	30,216	145,427	179,842	[41] = + (840,990 − 661,148)	= + Change in accrued expenses and other
Interest payable	80	529	6,180	[42] = + (7,027 − 847)	= + Change in interest payable
Deferred revenue	53,276	56,547	48,404	[43] = + (280,330 − 231,926)	= + Change in deferred revenue
Other non-current assets			30	[44] = − (186,887 − 186,917)	= − Change in other non-current assets
Other non-current liabilities			110,916	[45] = + (373,773 − 262,857)	= + Change in other non-current liabilities
Other, net	70,204	−104,029		Not used	= Forecast not required
Cash flow from operations.....................	$ 922,915	$1,131,633	$ 1,295,261	[46] = [18] + [12] + [37] + … + [45]	= Sum
Investing Activities					
Purchase of investments, net....................	$ 444,264	$21,924		Not used	= Forecast not required
Sale (purchase) of short-term investments, net......			$ 141,038	[47] = − (0 − 141,038)	= − Change in short-term investments
Sale (purchase) of long-term investments, net.......			0	[48] = − (224,904 − 224,904)	= − Change in long-term investments
Capital expenditures, net......................	−643,296	−771,230	−1,057,975	−[9]	= See Exhbit 4.8, [9]
Acquisitions, net of cash acquired...............	−21,583	−91,734		Assumed $0	= Forecast not required
Net cash used by investing activities..............	$−220,615	$ −841,040	$ −916,937	[49] = [47] + [48] − [9]	= Sum
Financing Activities					
Change in common stock, net...................	$−950,092	$ −577,428	$0	[61]	= See Exhibit 4.11, [61]
Change in debt, net	276,265	422,102	0	[50] = + (770,762 − 770,762) + (1,958 − 1,958)	= + Change in short-term and long-term debt
Common equity distributions....................			−223,713	[62]	= See Exhibit 4.11, [62]
Cash flows from financing activities..............	$−673,827	$ −155,326	$ −223,713	[69] = [61] + [50] + [62]	= Sum
Effect of exchange rate changes	$283	$3,530		Assumed $0	= Forecast not required
Change in cash balance.......................	$ 28,756	$ 138,797	$ 154,611	[70] = [46] + [49] + [69]	= Sum

Exhibit may contain small rounding errors

Cash flow from operations is equal to net earnings [18], plus depreciation and amortization [12], adjusted for changes in all of the operating assets and liabilities as well as interest payable [37] through [45]. Cash flow for investing is equal to the change in short-term [47] and long-term investments [48] minus capital expenditures [9]. We do not, however, have sufficient information to calculate cash flow from financing for the same reason we could not complete the balance sheet forecasts—we do not know the common equity distributions or the change in common stock. We cannot complete the balance sheet or cash flow statement until we know the change in our common equity accounts (common stock and surplus and retained earnings). In our forecasts, we assume the company does not have any effect of exchange rate changes.

Starbucks' Free Cash Flow Forecasts

We show the free cash flow schedule in Exhibit 4.11. The free cash flow schedule begins with one input from the income statement—EBIT (operating income, [15]). We then deduct the income tax the company would pay on its EBIT [51]; again, we use the simplifying assumption of a constant income tax rate on all income with no other complexities. We use these two inputs to measure the company's unlevered earnings [52]. Next, we adjust EBIT for accounting accruals. These adjustments are mostly the same adjustments we made in the cash flow statement to measure cash flow from operations—[37] through [41] and [43] through [45]. The exception to this is interest payable [42]; we do not use the change in interest payable, for we exclude interest completely from our unlevered cash flow calculations. Said differently, since EBIT is before interest, we do not want to adjust it for changes in interest payable. In addition, we must take into consideration the change in required cash [53], which is just the change in required cash from the balance sheet.

EXHIBIT 4.11 Free Cash Flow Forecasts for Starbucks Corporation

STARBUCKS CORPORATION
Free Cash Flow Forecasts
(for the fiscal years ended October)

($ in thousands)	Year 11	Year 12	Year 13	Calculation	Formulas and Explanation
Earnings before interest and taxes (EBIT)	$ 780,518	$ 893,952	$ 1,069,323	[15]	= See Exhibit 4.7, [15]
Income taxes paid on EBIT	−295,975	−320,365	−384,956	[51] = −.36 × 1,069,323	= − Tax rate × EBIT
Unlevered earnings.	$ 484,543	$ 573,587	$ 684,366	[52] = [15] + [51]	= Sum
Depreciation and amortization	367,207	412,625	425,770	[12]	= See Exhbit 4.7, [12]
Asset impairment charges	19,464	19,622		Assumed $0	= Forecast not required
Receivables	0	0	−31,738	[37]	= See Exhibit 4.10, [37]
Inventories	−121,618	−85,527	−130,013	[38]	= See Exhibit 4.10, [38]
Other current assets.	0	0	−64,679	[39]	= See Exhibit 4.10, [39]
Accounts payable.	9,717	104,966	93,166	[40]	= See Exhibit 4.10, [40]
Accrued expenses and other	30,216	145,427	179,842	[41]	= See Exhibit 4.10, [41]
Deferred revenue	53,276	56,547	48,404	[43]	= See Exhibit 4.10, [43]
Other non-current assets	0	0	30	[44]	= See Exhibit 4.10, [44]
Other non-current liabilities			110,916	[45]	= See Exhibit 4.10, [45]
Other, net	70,204	−104,029		Not used	= Forecast not required
Change in required cash balance.	−28,756	−138,797	−154,611	[53] = −(467,217 − 312,606)	= − Change in required cash
Unlevered cash flow from operations	$ 884,253	$ 984,421	$ 1,161,454	[54] = [52] + [12] + [37] +...+ [41] + [43] + [44] + [45] + [53]	= Sum
Capital expenditures, net	−664,879	−862,964	−1,057,975	[55] = −[9] + [48]	= See Exhbit 4.8, [9], Exhibit 4.10 [48]
Unlevered free cash flow	$ 219,374	$ 121,457	$ 103,480	[56] = [54] + [55]	= Sum
Interest expense.	−1,272	−11,105	−42,163	[7]	= See Exhibit 4.7, [7]
Interest payable	80	529	6,180	[42]	= See Exhibit 4.10, [42]
Interest tax shield	482	3,980	15,179	[57] = .36 × [7]	= Tax rate × Exhibit 4.7 [7]
CF before non-equity financing changes	$ 218,664	$ 114,861	$ 82,675	[58] = [56] + [7] + [42] + [57]	= Sum
Change in debt, net	276,265	422,102	0	[50]	= See Exhibit 4.10, [50]
Equity free cash flow	$ 494,929	$ 536,963	$ 82,675	[59] = [58] + [50]	= Sum
Interest and other income, after-tax	10,616	15,011	0	Income from liquidated excess asset	= Forecast not required
Sale (purchase) of short-term investments.	444,264	21,924	141,038	[47]	= See Exhibit 4.10, [47]
Effect of exchange rate changes	283	3,530	0	Assumed $0	= Forecast not required
Cash flow before cash flows to/from common equityholders	$ 950,092	$ 577,428	$ 223,713	[60] = [47] + [59]	= Sum
Change in common stock, net	−950,092	−577,428	0	[61] = if [60] < 0, − [60], otherwise 0	= − Negative equity free cash flow, 0
Common dividends			−223,713	[62] = if [60] > 0, − [60], otherwise 0	= − Positive equity free cash flow, 0
Change in excess cash	$ 0	$ 0	$ 0	[63] = [60] + [61] + [62]	= Sum
Change in required cash balance.	28,756	138,797	154,611	− [53]	= − [53]
Change in cash balance	$ 28,756	$ 138,797	$ 154,611	[64] = [63] + [53]	= Sum

Exhibit may contain small rounding errors

To measure Starbucks' unlevered free cash flow [56], we subtract both capital expenditures and the change in long-term investments [55] from its unlevered cash flow from operations [54]. We calculate equity free cash flow by adjusting unlevered free cash flow [56] for after-tax cash interest paid—[7], [42], and [57]—and the change in non-equity financing [50].

We add the proceeds from the sale of short-term investments [47] to equity free cash flow [59] in order to measure the cash flow before cash flows to/from common equityholders [60]. If that amount is negative, we assume the company's existing stockholders invest more cash into the company [61], and if that amount is positive, we assume the company distributes the cash to its investors [62]. You can see the dividends are $223.7 million. In this treatment, we are not treating the sale of the excess asset as a free cash flow. That is an alternative, but if we did, we would be assuming that these assets are liquidated at the end of Year 13. Recall from our prior discussion that if we did conduct a DCF valuation, we would add the value of the excess assets to the discounted value of the free cash flows, implicitly assuming that the liquidation and distribution takes place at the valuation date.

At the end of the schedule, we reconcile our free cash flow schedule to the change in the cash balance [64] in order to make sure that these calculations articulate with the other financial statements.

Completing Retained Earnings, Balance Sheet and Cash Flow Statement—Part 2

Now that we know the amount of capital invested by the company's equityholders—if any—and the distributions to its equityholders, we can complete the retained earnings schedule (Exhibit 4.7, [65], [18], [62], and [66]). We can also use this information to complete the shareholders' equity section of the balance sheet (Exhibit 4.9, [71], [66] and [67]). Last, we can use this information to complete the financing section of the cash flow statement (Exhibit 4.10, [61], and [62]) and reconcile to the change in cash [70].

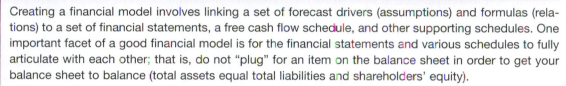

Valuation Key 4.1

Creating a financial model involves linking a set of forecast drivers (assumptions) and formulas (relations) to a set of financial statements, a free cash flow schedule, and other supporting schedules. One important facet of a good financial model is for the financial statements and various schedules to fully articulate with each other; that is, do not "plug" for an item on the balance sheet in order to get your balance sheet to balance (total assets equal total liabilities and shareholders' equity).

REVIEW EXERCISE 4.3

Financial Model for the Bob Wardrop Company—Part 3

Use the information in Review Exercise 4.1 to forecast the company's cash flow statement, free cash flow schedule, and statement of retained earnings for Year 1; afterward, complete the company's balance sheet (liabilities and shareholders' equity section) that you started in Review Exercise 4.2.

Solution on page 161.

4.5 STRESS TESTING THE MODEL AND ASSESSING THE REASONABLENESS OF THE FORECASTS (STEP 5 AND 6)

The next step in the forecasting process—Step 5—is to check the model for its calculation accuracy and to stress test the model to make sure the model works properly when we change the forecast drivers. We also repeat this step after Step 7 (capital structure integration) to make sure that we did not introduce any new errors when we integrated capital structure into the financial model. In Step 6, we analyze the reasonableness of the forecasts and revise the forecasts accordingly.

LO3 Test the model, incorporate the company's capital structure, and assess forecast reasonableness

Checking and Stress Testing the Model—Step 5

We check to ensure the financial model works properly in various ways. First, we check that total assets equal the sum of total liabilities and shareholders' equity. We check to make sure that the ending balance in retained earnings is equal to the beginning balance in retained earnings, plus net income, minus dividends and other adjustments (if relevant); that changes in balance sheet accounts are tied to changes in the cash flow statement where appropriate; that the change in the cash balance ties to the free cash flow schedule and statement of cash flows; that depreciation expense is deducted from net property, plant, and equipment and net income; and that depreciation is added back to net income in the operating section of the cash flow statement.

We can also use the financial statements to measure the forecast drivers and check our formulas. For example, if we use the "days to pay accounts payable" financial ratio as a forecast driver, we can calculate it based on the forecasted financial statements and check that it is the same as the forecast driver. If they are not the same, we have an error in our formulas. At this step, we also verify that even when we change the assumptions in the model, the model continues to work properly. It is sometimes helpful to make large changes in the assumptions for this purpose. For example, we might significantly change the growth rates and see if the model still works or we might change the capital structure significantly to see if the unlevered free cash flows remain unchanged.

Step Back and Ask, "Do the Forecasts Make Sense?"—Step 6, Part 1

We begin this step by looking at big-picture issues in order to assess whether the forecasts make sense based on our competitive analysis. For example, suppose our forecasts indicate an increase in revenues over the next five years. Are the increases reasonable when compared to the forecasts for the industry (for example, from industry associations or financial analysts)? Can we identify the factors that are driving the sales increase? Is the increase a result of price increases above inflation? If so, how can such price increases be justified? Does the new pricing make sense given the competition and cost structure of the company and its competitors? If demand for the company's products depends on certain macro conditions (for example, growth in the economy or population), are our forecasts consistent with the forecasts of these macro conditions?

Alternatively, is the increase in revenue a result of selling more volume of the same product(s)? If so, is the overall demand in the market going to increase, or are you assuming the company will take market share away from its competitors? In other words, do you have a foundation for the increase in volume, at least at an intuitive level? What other factors might affect revenues? For example, could changes in regulations, global competition, or innovations affect demand for the company's products? Questions regarding the source of an increase in revenues often lead to questions about cost structure and capital investments. For example, is an increase in volume achievable with the projected level of marketing expenses? Is the projected level of production consistent with planned staffing and capital expenditures? Are inventory and other working capital forecasts consistent with the sales increase?

Sometimes we can check the reasonableness of our forecasts by using our forecasting process on earlier years for which data is available—in other words, **back testing** the model. In particular, we might do this for the part of the model that forecasts revenue and capital expenditures if these are based on complex schedules. However, if we used these earlier years as the basis of developing our forecasting model—a common approach—back testing the model is unlikely to be very informative. However, if the model fails to forecast well in the earlier period, it is unlikely to work in the future unless you have assumed that some structural shift has occurred.

Comparing Historical Financial Ratios to the Financial Ratios Based on the Forecasts—Step 6, Part 2

Comparing forecasted financial ratios to a company's historical financial ratios and the financial ratios of comparable companies can be a useful way of analyzing the reasonableness of a set of forecasts. As we indicated previously, examining financial ratios—which were direct forecast drivers—is merely a check on the intended calculations in the model, but it is not an analysis of the reasonableness of the forecasts. However, we can use financial ratios that do not drive the model to help us analyze the reasonableness of the forecasts.

A good starting point for such an analysis is a comparison of the accounting rates of return that we discussed in Chapter 2—the return on assets, return on investment, and potentially the return on equity. We also examine many of the components that allow us to decompose these ratios (such as the unlevered profit margin and its components and sales to total assets and its components). Other useful financial ratios include various turnover ratios (for example, revenue to fixed assets), asset composition ratios (for example, current assets relative to total assets), liquidity ratios (for example, the current ratio), and various margins (for example, gross margin and operating margin)—assuming we did not use these to drive the forecasts. We would also examine projected growth rates in revenues and other important line items such as free cash flows.

We know that, on average, a company's profitability ratios are likely to move toward those of its comparable companies over some horizon. This is just the nature of a competitive economy. Over the long run, most companies will eventually approach the industry average in terms of profitability and revenue growth. We call this phenomenon **mean reversion.** The key issue here, of course, is how to estimate the time period over which this mean reversion will occur. Naturally, we can observe exceptions to this principle. For example, Microsoft Corporation has been able to sustain its competitive advantage longer than many companies have. Dell sustained a competitive advantage for quite some time, but it now appears to have lost that advantage. In addition, we can compare our forecasts for revenues, earnings, and other performance and operating measures to either financial analyst forecasts or forecasts based upon other forecasting methods (for example, statistical time-series models). At the end of this step, we can go back to Step 2 to adjust the model if it is appropriate to do so. We can revise the model until we conclude that the forecasts are reasonable for our intended purpose.

Assessing the Reasonableness of the Forecasts for the Starbucks Corporation's Operations

In Exhibit 4.12, we present some summary financial ratios for Starbucks' forecasts in order to provide a preliminary examination of the reasonableness of the forecasts. In these illustrative forecasts for Starbucks, we observe an initial jump in some of its financial ratios. In Year 14, the return on assets increases from 14.1% to 17.5%, largely due to an increase in its unlevered profit margin. Reviewing the forecast drivers in Exhibit 4.6, we see reductions in cost of goods sold, store and other operating expenses, and general and administrative expenses (all as a percentage of revenue); these changes explain the increase in the forecasted unlevered profit margin. Revenue to total assets also increases a little in Years 14 to 16, but it does not appear to be systematically drifting upward over time—often a sign of too little investment in a model. That said, some additional analysis of the property, plant, and equipment ratios appears in order. Note also that the "days calculations" for receivables, inventory, and payables do not match the forecasts driver for those items in Exhibit 4.6. That occurs because the forecasts use the drivers in Exhibit 4.6 to calculate the ending balance in receivables, inventory, and payables, and the calculations shown in Exhibit 4.12 are based on average balances.

EXHIBIT 4.12 Selected Financial Ratios Based on the Forecasts for Starbucks Corporation						
	Actual		**Forecast**			
Disaggregating the Rate of Return	Year 12	Year 13	Year 14	Year 15	Year 16	Year 17
Return on assets	14.4%	14.1%	17.5%	17.5%	17.4%	16.8%
Unlevered profit margin	7.4%	7.3%	8.6%	8.5%	8.4%	8.2%
Total asset utilization (turnover)	1.96	1.92	2.03	2.05	2.07	2.06
Return on equity.	26.1%	26.9%	34.0%	34.2%	34.2%	33.1%
Profit margin (to common)	7.2%	7.0%	8.4%	8.3%	8.2%	8.0%
Total asset utilization (turnover)	1.96	1.92	2.03	2.05	2.07	2.06
Financial leverage factor	1.84	1.99	1.99	2.00	2.01	2.01
ROE/ROA	1.809	1.911	1.945	1.958	1.973	1.976
Coverage Ratios	Year 12	Year 13	Year 14	Year 15	Year 16	Year 17
EBIT to interest.	80.50	25.36	37.26	42.44	45.89	46.88
EBITDA to interest	117.66	35.46	49.87	57.34	63.08	66.23
Working Capital Management Ratios	Year 12	Year 13	Year 14	Year 15	Year 16	Year 17
Current ratio (operating liabilities).	1.2	1.1	1.1	1.1	1.1	1.1
Days of purchases outstanding (payable)	31.4	35.7	36.4	37.6	38.3	39.2
Days of inventory held	67.9	66.8	66.4	68.2	69.7	71.3
Accounts receivable collection period	9.7	9.4	9.0	9.3	9.5	9.8
Trade cash cycle.	46.2	40.5	39.1	40.0	40.9	41.8
Property, Plant, and Equipment	Year 12	Year 13	Year 14	Year 15	Year 16	Year 17
Depreciable life of gross plant	9.36	11.24	10.91	10.77	10.63	10.62
Depreciable life of net plant	5.54	6.86	6.32	5.88	5.35	4.99
Capital expenditures to revenues.	11.1%	11.3%	8.3%	7.2%	6.2%	6.5%
Capital expenditures to EBIT	96.5%	98.9%	61.7%	53.9%	47.0%	51.1%
Capital expenditures to EBITDA.	66.0%	70.8%	46.1%	39.9%	34.2%	36.2%
Capital expenditures to depreciation	209.1%	248.5%	182.4%	153.4%	125.5%	123.8%

We will not analyze the reasonableness of these forecasts further, for we do not show a longer history for Starbucks, nor do we have comparable companies, both of which are things we would likely use in such an analysis. However, it should be apparent that a detailed financial analysis of the forecasts, such as the analysis we discussed of The Gap, Inc. in Chapter 2, could help assess the reasonableness of the forecasts.

Valuation Key 4.2

Assessing the reasonableness of a financial model and its forecasts involves stepping back from the numbers and conducting a competitive analysis, an analysis of competitive advantage, and a financial analysis of the forecasts relative to the company's recent history as well as the recent history and expected performance of its comparable companies.

4.6 INCORPORATING THE COMPANY'S CAPITAL STRUCTURE STRATEGY

It is possible to skip this step if the valuation model does not require specific forecasts for interest and debt balances, a point we discuss later in the book. However, we often incorporate an estimate of the company's capital structure into the financial model in order to better understand the company's financing needs and to assess how close the company will be to the financial-statement-based covenants in its debt contracts.

Fortunately, if we follow all of the first six steps in our forecasting process, the model will already include all, or at least most, of the necessary calculations to easily change the company's capital structure (as long as the company has some interest-bearing debt on the balance sheet). If we adjust the company's debt balances, interest rates on debt, and other relevant aspects of its capital structure strategy, the model will automatically adjust the forecasts for any change in capital structure.

Once we incorporate the company's capital structure strategy into the model, we again stress test the model and check it for calculation accuracy; naturally, at this juncture, we will focus more on the parts of the model affected by the capital structure strategy. We will continue to use the Starbucks example to illustrate this process.

Incorporating an Alternative Capital Strategy in the Financial Model

A careful reader will have noted that Starbucks has $700.8 million in debt that is due this coming year (see Exhibit 4.3, short-term and current long-term debt). You will also note that we did not assume that this debt was paid off in our projected balance sheet; we did this because at that point we ignored all capital structure issues. If the short-term and current long-term debt were paid off and if Starbucks did not issue new debt or preferred stock, its equity free cash flow will be negative by over $600 million (it is currently $82.7 million).

We assume that Starbucks wants to understand how much debt it can issue next year (Year 13) and still maintain an AAA debt rating. Since we already have the operating forecasts set up in the financial model, any change in the company's debt financing will affect the equity free cash flows and the cash it distributes to its equityholders. To illustrate this kind of analysis, we use Starbucks' interest coverage ratio (EBIT divided by Interest) to determine its debt rating. Naturally, qualifying for a debt rating is more complex than maintaining a certain coverage ratio, but using the company's coverage ratio allows us to illustrate how we can incorporate this type of capital structure strategy into a financial model (we discuss the intricacies of debt ratings in more detail in Chapter 9). At the time, the median EBIT coverage ratio of companies with an AAA rating was 21.4 and senior debt with an AAA rating carried an interest rate of 6%.

We assume that at the end of Year 13, Starbucks will retire all of its debt ($702.7 million) and issue enough long-term debt that its expected interest coverage ratio—based on the projected EBIT for Year 13—is equal to 22.0 (slightly above the median coverage ratio for companies with an AAA debt rating). Starbucks' debt will carry an interest rate of 6%.

We calculate the company's debt level in Year 13 with a two-step calculation that we combine into one calculation. First, we calculate the amount of interest Starbucks can have in Year 13, based on the company's EBIT in Year 13 and its target coverage ratio. Next, we calculate the maximum amount of debt the company can issue at the end of Year 13 based on that projected EBIT divided by the target coverage ratio at the presumed 6% interest rate. The combined calculation of the maximum amount of debt is as follows:

$$\text{Maximum Debt}_{\text{Year 13}} = \frac{\dfrac{\text{EBIT}_{\text{Year 13}}}{\text{Target Coverage Ratio}}}{\text{Interest Rate}} = \frac{\dfrac{\$1,069,323}{22.0}}{0.06} = \$810,093$$

The total maximum debt that allows Starbucks to maintain an interest coverage ratio of 22 (and an AAA rating) is $810,093 in Year 13. It will redeem its current debt ($702,720 = $700,762 + $1,958) and issue $810,093 in new long-term debt. While we don't present an exhibit illustrating the debt issuance, the newly issued debt is $107,373 higher than the previous debt balance ($107,373 = $810,093 − $700,762 − $1,958), resulting in an increase in equity free cash flows and an additional cash distribution to its equityholders of $107.3 million (assuming no change in interest payable with the increased debt). We note that in all years after Year 13, the company's EBIT continues to increase such that the maximum debt Starbucks could issue and maintain an AAA rating would increase each year. Of course, issuing additional debt has no impact on Starbucks' projected unlevered free cash flows.

This is just one potential capital structure strategy that a firm might pursue. For example, a company might choose to fund its entire cash shortfall before financing by issuing debt, without worrying about maintaining a particular bond rating. Another alternative is that a company might pursue a target debt-to-equity capital structure (e.g., fund itself with 20% debt and 80% equity). We discuss this latter alternative in more detail later in the book.

Valuation Key 4.3

Once we create a financial model that ignores a company's capital structure strategy (that is, assuming no change in non-equity financing), we can easily incorporate the company's capital structure strategy by changing the way we calculate the company's debt balances (and balances of all other non-equity financing items).

Since we only changed the parts of the model that relate to financing, the parts of the company's income statement related solely to its operations (through the Operating Income) do not change. In addition, the unlevered free cash flows should not change. If any of these parts do change, it is likely that we have an error in the model, for a company's operations are normally assumed independent of its financing decisions. Of course, if raising additional debt causes changes in required cash holdings, for example, then the unlevered free cash flows would change.

Before we leave the topic of modeling the capital structure, we note that investment bankers often build debt schedules that allow for an automatic pay down of debt in order of seniority when the cash available before financing (before changes in debt, preferred stock, and equity) is positive. In addition, these schedules also often allow for an automatic draw from a revolver, if the cash available before financing is negative. These schedules often calculate interest expense based on average debt outstanding during the year. We discuss whether creating detailed schedules like this is important for valuation later in the book.

REVIEW EXERCISE 4.4

Financial Model for the Bob Wardrop Company—Part 4

Use the information in Review Exercise 4.1 (except the information on the company's capital structure). For the company's capital structure, assume the company will issue debt to fund all of the financing needs it cannot fund with internally generated cash flow, and assume that its cost of debt is 10%. The company will pay down all of its debt before it begins to pay any dividends; then, it will distribute all positive equity free cash flows to common equityholders. Using this information, forecast the financial statements and supporting schedules, including a free cash flow schedule, for Year 1.

Solution on pages 162–163.

4.7 SENSITIVITY AND SCENARIO ANALYSES AND SIMULATIONS

Forecasts are predictions of the future, so they are, by nature, uncertain. Given this uncertainty, we often examine our forecasts under alternative scenarios—that is, sets of likely (and even unlikely, though possible) future outcomes. Sensitivity and scenario analyses can be useful tools to help us understand the impact that alternative strategies have on a company's forecasts and valuation. In addition, scenario analysis and simulations can provide a distribution of possible forecasts and valuations based on alternative assumptions we might use in the financial model. Further, a manager might want to know how "bad things can get" before the company violates its debt covenants or is unable to service its debt—as opposed to the company's expected performance (what we use in a DCF valuation).

In a **sensitivity analysis**, we change one or more of a financial model's forecast drivers and examine the impact that these changes have on the forecasts. We can then see how sensitive the value is to variation in specific forecast drivers. In a **scenario analysis**, we develop alternative scenarios in which we change a large number of assumptions in creating each scenario. For example, suppose we are valuing a biotech startup that is working on a single drug that could potentially cure a deadly form of cancer. We might develop a scenario where the drug undergoing testing is approved by the Food and Drug Administration (FDA), and the efficacy tests indicate that the drug has great benefits with little side effects—turning it into a blockbuster drug with strong demand and excellent pricing. Another scenario is that the drug is approved, but the tests indicate frequent side effects and positive results in a smaller number of patients. Thus, while the drug will be marketable to patients with little hope from any alternative treatments, its sales will not be as impressive. Finally, we could develop a scenario where the FDA does not approve the drug due to serious side effects and poor clinical results at an early stage of testing and further development is abandoned.

A Monte Carlo simulation is more complex than either a sensitivity or scenario analysis. In a **Monte Carlo simulation**, we place our financial model into a simulation software package (typically an Excel add-on). In addition, we input distributional parameters for each forecast driver in the model (for example, assume that the company's ratio of cost of goods sold to revenue is normally distributed with a mean of 55% and a variance of 1.5%) and the correlation among all of the forecast drivers. The simulation software package allows the user to choose from a wide variety of statistical distributions as well as allowing the user to customize the distribution. The simulation then generates distributions of the forecasts by repeatedly sampling across the forecast drivers, based on the distributional assumptions provided. Assuming our financial model calculates the present value of the future cash flows, the simulation will provide a distribution of firm values obtained from the distributional assumptions provided. The mean of the distribution will represent the value of the company at the expected value of the cash flows.

Valuation Key 4.4

Sensitivity analyses, scenario analyses, and simulations can be useful tools to help us understand the impact that various assumptions have on forecasts and valuations. In addition, these tools can provide a distribution of possible forecasts and valuations based on the distributions of the assumptions in the financial model. One advantage of uncovering which assumptions have the biggest impact on value is that we can then try to refine our information with respect to the most critical drivers of value.

4.8 ACCUMULATING EXCESS CASH

Sometimes, managers accumulate cash beyond what is necessary to operate the company at its current or anticipated level of operations. In other words, managers do not distribute all of the company's equity free cash flows to its equityholders. Managers might do this to take advantage of future investment opportunities or to avoid raising capital externally if the company might have cash needs in the near future. For example, during the financial crisis of 2008 and 2009, many companies accumulated cash as a cushion against uncertainty. Regardless of the reason, if the managers do not distribute all of the company's equity free cash flows to equityholders, the company's cash balance (or other investments) will be larger than necessary.

How we treat existing excess assets or undistributed future cash flows and the related income (or losses) generated by them depends on the assumption we make about those assets. If we assume that all of these assets earn just their required rate of return (that is, they do not create value), we do the following. If companies have already "hoarded" excess cash in the years before the valuation date, the assets resulting from this activity are excess assets. In this case, we assume the excess assets are liquidated and distributed to the shareholders as of the valuation date based on their after-tax value. For future equity free cash flows that are not needed for the business, we just pay them out as dividends even if we do not think the company will do that, as long as we can again assume that the company will invest those in zero net present value projects or assets. This treatment essentially assumes that the company invests these excess assets in investments that neither create nor destroy value.

Valuation in Practice 4.1

Integra LifeSciences Holdings Corporation's (Integra) Acquisition Strategy and Its Required Cash Balance At the end of 2000, Integra had a cash (and equivalent) balance of about $15.2 million, and its revenues for that year were $71.6 million. By the end of 2003, Integra's cash balance increased by more than 13 times to $206.7 million, and its revenues grew by about 2.6 times to $185.6 million. Why the large increase in cash relative to revenues? During this period, Integra adopted a strategy of growth by acquisitions. Consequently, it began to build up a large cash balance, enabling the company to take advantage of potential acquisition opportunities as they became available. In its annual filing with the U.S. SEC, Integra stated:

> Our goal is to become a global leader in the development, manufacturing and marketing of medical devices, implants and biomaterials in the neurosurgery, reconstructive surgery and general surgery markets. Key elements of our strategy include ... expanding our product portfolio and market reach through additional acquisitions . . .
>
> We have achieved this growth in our overall business through the development and introduction of new products, the development of our distribution channels and acquisitions.
>
> We regularly evaluate potential acquisition candidates in this market and in other specialty medical technology markets characterized by high margins, fragmented competition and focused target customers.

Thus, for Integra, its cash holdings in excess of its required cash balance for its existing businesses were not an excess asset, for Integra managers thought they needed the additional cash and financial flexibility to implement their acquisition growth strategy, which turned out to be quite successful. Management felt that it would not have been cost effective for Integra to distribute these funds and have to raise capital shortly afterward to fund acquisitions given the transactions costs of raising capital. One way to address the valuation of this cash and acquisition growth strategy is to separate the cash not needed to operate the company from the financial model and then assess the value of Integra's growth strategy through acquisition, given the reduced financing costs it would bear.

Source: See Part I of the 2004 Form 10-K report filed by the company with the U.S. SEC on March 16, 2005.

If, however, the company subsequently invests excess assets in existence as of the valuation date and future undistributed cash flows in investments that are non-zero net present value "projects," we would treat them as part of the company's investment strategy, for they affect the value of the firm. We would treat these investments the same way we treat any other investment. We would include any income from these assets as part of the free cash flows generated by the company and then value them accordingly. Thus if a company invests those excess assets in negative net present value projects, the value of the company will be reduced relative to distributing those excess assets to the shareholders. One complexity that this assumption may create is that the unlevered cost of capital of the company will change if the risk of these investments is different from the risk of the other assets of the company. We will return to this issue later in the book.

One final note about the accumulation of excess cash has to do with multinational companies. Multinational companies sometimes do not repatriate earnings (cash) back to their home country in order to defer taxation on that income. We discuss this issue in more detail in the last chapter of the book, but it is useful to mention here that the tax a multinational company faces is often affected by its repatriation policy. In this case, the accumulation of excess cash may create value for shareholders because of its interplay with the taxes the entity pays.

Valuation Key 4.5

Sometimes managers accumulate excess cash; in other words, they do not distribute all equity free cash flows to equityholders. Fortunately, we can ignore any subsequent income generated by equity free cash flows that are not distributed after the valuation date if we assume the company invests them in zero net present value projects. If we assume the company invests them in assets that have non-zero net present values, then we treat them like any other investment made by the company and include their earnings in subsequent free cash flows.

4.9 FORECASTING REVENUES AND CAPITAL EXPENDITURES

LO4 Forecast revenues and capital expenditures at a more detailed level

Naturally, forecasting revenues is an important part of most financial models, for as we have seen, revenue forecasts typically drive many of the other forecasts in a financial model. For example, cost of goods sold and selling, general, and administrative expenses are typically driven, at least in part, by revenue forecasts. The same can be said of the company's operating assets (accounts receivable and inventory) and operating liabilities (accounts payable and other accruals).

In a financial model, we sometimes use a simple single growth rate, g, to forecast revenues—for example, $\text{revenue}_t = (1 + g) \times \text{revenue}_{t-1}$—in much the same way we did in the Starbucks example. The magnitude of this growth rate, however, is the result of either an implicit or an explicit forecast of macroeconomic factors, industry factors, and company-specific factors that eventually forecast the company's market share (volume) and prices. In this section, we show how to disaggregate a simple growth rate into its volume and price components. We also provide an example of a more detailed revenue forecast and discuss capital expenditure forecasts and how they can be related to revenue forecasts. Many models build up a forecast by division, segment, or geographic area.

The Price and Quantity Components of the Revenue Growth Rate

Simply stated, revenue is equal to price multiplied by volume; thus, a revenue growth rate is the result of a growth in volume, a change in price, or both. Disaggregating the revenue growth into its components and other drivers can be helpful in understanding the factors that drive a company's value (value drivers). In this section, we disaggregate the revenue growth rate into its price change ($\Delta p/p = g_p$) and quantity (or volume) change ($\Delta q/q = g_q$) growth rate components.

Assume a company has revenue of $1,000 in Year 0 and $1,476 in Year 1. Its revenue growth rate is 47.6% ($0.476 = \$1,476/\$1,000 - 1$). We cannot disaggregate this growth rate unless we know either the number of units sold in each period (q_0 and q_1) or the price at which the units were sold for in each period (p_0 and p_1). Assume that in Year 0, this company sold 1,000 units of output at $1 per unit, and in Year 1, the company sold 1,200 units at $1.23 per unit. The growth rate for the change in price, g_p, is 23% ($0.23 = \$1.23/\$1.00 - 1$), and its growth rate for quantity, g_q, is 20% ($0.2 = 1,200/1,000 - 1$). How does a price growth rate of 23% and a quantity growth rate of 20% result in a revenue growth rate of 47.6%? We can figure this out by disaggregating the revenue growth rate formula:

$$g_{\text{rev, total}} = \frac{\Delta p}{p_o} + \left(1 + \frac{\Delta p}{p_o}\right) \times \frac{\Delta q}{q_o} = g_p + (1 + g_p) \times g_q = 0.23 + 1.23 \times 0.20 = 0.23 + 0.246 = 0.476$$

Thus, a company's revenue growth rate is equal to its percentage change in price plus its volume growth rate, adjusted for percentage price changes. We can also calculate the growth rate in revenues, $g_{\text{rev, total}}$, as $(1 + g_p) \times (1 + g_q) - 1$, which in this example is 47.6% ($0.476 = 1.23 \times 1.2 - 1$).

Adjusting Growth Rates for Inflation

We can disaggregate the previous growth formula further to adjust for inflation. To adjust total revenues for the effects of inflation, we can first divide revenues by 1 plus the inflation rate for the period in order to measure the effect of inflation on revenues. Assuming inflation was 2.5% in the previous example, what are the inflation-adjusted (or real) growth rates for revenue and price? We can calculate the real growth rate for revenues by dividing (1 plus) the growth rate for revenues by (1 plus) the inflation rate.

$$g_{rev,\ real} = \frac{1 + g_{rev,\ real}}{1 + i} - 1 = \frac{1.476}{1.025} - 1 = 0.44$$

Alternatively, we can calculate the real (inflation-adjusted) change in price and use our original formula to measure real growth in revenues:

$$g_{p,\ real} = \frac{1 + g_{price}}{1 + i} - 1 = \frac{1.23}{1.025} - 1 = 0.20$$

$$g_{rev,\ real} = g_p + (1 + g_p) \times g_q = 0.20 + 1.20 \times 0.20 = 0.20 + 0.24 = 0.44$$

Potential Forecast Drivers for Revenues and Capital Expenditures

While we think of revenues as being equal to price multiplied by volume, we often use capacity and capacity utilization as measures of volume and use the average price (revenue)—per unit of capacity available or capacity utilized—as a measure of price. For example, we sometimes use price and volume to forecast revenues in industries that produce clearly identifiable products with clearly identifiable prices. As such, in the auto industry, we might use the number of cars and the average price per car in order to measure revenue, or we might disaggregate our revenue forecast by brand or by class of car within a brand if the prices and product mixes vary within our forecast period. Companies in heavy manufacturing industries (for example, steel and paper) have different revenue forecast drivers but they are still measures of capacity and price. The measure used for capacity is the maximum number of tons output (production). In turn, capacity utilization is the actual number of tons of output divided by the maximum number of tons of capacity, and the average revenue per unit of capacity utilized is the average price per ton.

Valuation in Practice 4.2

Companies Sometimes Provide Forecasts About Capital Expenditures—The Gap, Inc. (GAP)
Below is a quote from GAP's 10-K filing with the U.S. Securities and Exchange Commission (U.S. SEC). It provides an example of the type of information that we can sometimes glean from a company's financial reports on its value drivers and short-term forecasts.

> . . . Our real estate strategy in fiscal 2005 includes plans to open about 175 new stores, weighted more toward Old Navy. We have announced the launch of a new brand targeted at women over the age of 35 and the expansion of Banana Republic into Japan. . . . We also plan to close about 135 stores in 2005, mainly from Gap brand in North America . . . These growth initiatives and moves will negatively impact operating expenses in fiscal 2005, but will position us to take advantage of future opportunities.
>
> In 2005, we expect earnings per share to grow to $1.41 to $1.45 per share on a fully diluted basis. . . . We expect operating margin to be about 13% and we also expect to generate at least $1 billion in free cash flow.

Note that although GAP plans to increase the number of stores it operates by 40, it plans to build 175 new stores and close 135 stores; thus, we would forecast capital expenditures for 175 new stores and not for 40 net new stores.

Source: Gap, Inc. 2004 10-K filing with the U.S. SEC.

For most companies in the retail industry (for example, GAP), we would likely use other determinants (forecast drivers) for revenues. Here, we might use either number of stores (capacity) in conjunction with average revenue per store (revenue per unit of capacity) or the number of square feet of retail space (capacity) in conjunction with average revenue (price) per square foot of retail space (revenue per unit of capacity). To better understand the driver of growth in a retail chain, we might further disaggregate a measure such as average revenue per square foot of retail space into average number of transactions (number of purchases) per square foot (which we could use to measure capacity and capacity utilization) and average revenue (price) per transaction. We might also decide to inflation adjust the revenue per unit of capacity numbers to understand whether prices are increasing in real terms or whether revenue per transaction or per square foot is rising solely due to inflation. We also will see forecasts in the retail industry separated into two components—increases in "same store" or "comparable store" sales (what is the increase in sales expected for stores open for two full consecutive years) and sales related to new locations. Sometimes, forecasts are adjusted by the number of days available—for example, a store that opens or closes during the year. In addition, some retailers adjust their forecasts for the number of days and weekends between the Thanksgiving and Christmas holidays (which varies across years). They do this to take into account the critically important holiday shopping season that generally occurs between these two holidays. In addition, many retailers use fiscal year-ends that cause the number of weeks per year to vary between 52 and 53.

Naturally, the way we measure the determinants of revenues varies across industries and, to some extent, even different companies within an industry. The restaurant industry, for example, has revenue forecast drivers that are similar to those we typically use in the retail industry. As for capacity and capacity utilization, we can use a variety of measures depending on the information available on the company. For example, we might use the number of restaurants, the number of tables served, the number of checks (a restaurant's invoices) issued, or the number of seats. For price, we would use average revenue (price) per unit of capacity; for example, if we used the number of checks as a measure of utilized capacity, we would use the average revenue per check.

Other industries have different measures of capacity, capacity utilization, and price. An industry such as the commercial airline industry has different ways of measuring revenue forecast drivers. For this industry, one measure of overall capacity is the number of available seat miles (essentially, the sum across all flights of the number of miles flown on a flight, multiplied by the number of seats on the plane). A corresponding measure for capacity utilization is the number of available seat miles with people in them (called revenue seat miles). Another widely discussed measure of capacity utilization is revenue seat miles divided by available seat miles (the load factor). The average revenue per unit of capacity utilized is the average revenue per seat mile.

Potential Forecast Drivers for Capital Expenditures (and Property, Plant, and Equipment)

We typically forecast revenues before we forecast capital expenditures. We base our capital expenditure forecasts on the productive capacity required to support the revenue forecasts. We can classify capital expenditures into four types: increasing the company's productive capacity; maintaining existing productive capacity—in other words, replacing worn out, expired, or inefficient assets; replacing or enhancing the operating infrastructure of the company (for example, purchasing information technology for ordering materials or scheduling production and distribution); and replacing or expanding the company's administrative offices and equipment (overhead).

When forecasting capital expenditures, we attempt to measure each type of capital expenditure. Using publicly available information, we sometimes must forecast all types of capital expenditures together and sometimes we have enough additional information that allows us to analyze the different types of capital expenditures (even from public disclosures).

Many companies make productive capacity decisions based on either short- or mid-term revenue forecasts or growth strategies. Short-term decision frameworks like these do not typically work for companies in capital-intensive industries, as it can take these companies years to add productive capacity, and often the incremental change in productive capacity is large (the minimum amount is the amount produced by an efficiently sized plant). Companies operating in these industries therefore must develop long-term industry demand forecasts in order to decide when to add additional productive capacity.

Revenue forecasts often drive capital expenditures as in the above example; a company determines what its revenues (volume and price) are likely to be—perhaps based on forecasts of industry demand and market share—and then adds productive capacity to be able to deliver the necessary products. In other cases, capital expenditures are at least a partial driver of forecasted revenues. For example, as in Valuation in Practice 4.2, managers of retail and restaurant chains often consider how many new locations they can open in a given year, and those forecasts of store openings partially drive both capital expenditures and revenues for that period.

Illustration of a More Detailed Revenue Forecast

In this section, we use Darden Restaurants Inc. (Darden) to illustrate how we can forecast revenues using a more detailed approach. Darden owns and operates casual dining restaurants in the United States and Canada under the names Red Lobster, Olive Garden, Bahama Breeze, and Seasons 52. In Darden's case, some of the restaurant chains it operates are more mature and slower growing, while others are new concepts with higher growth potential. Thus, it may be useful to forecast revenues separately for Darden's different restaurant concepts, as they are growing at substantially different rates. In our illustration, we focus on forecasting just one of its restaurant concepts—Olive Garden—using both information provided in Darden's financial statements and our own estimates.

To forecast revenues, we multiply the number of Olive Garden restaurants by the expected revenue per restaurant. Darden discloses much of this information in its financial statements for the last two years, but we estimate some of the required information to generate the forecasts. We show the revenue forecasts in Exhibit 4.13. In this model, the revenue growth rate is a function of the growth rate in revenue per restaurant—a function of price and the volume of food sold—and the growth rate for number of restaurants. We first forecast the number of restaurants by forecasting the number of restaurants that will open and the number that will close (see Valuation in Practice 4.2 for an example of such management forecasts). We then multiply the revenue generated per restaurant (for the year we are forecasting) by the number of restaurants open as of the end of the previous year. This calculation makes the simplifying assumption that all restaurants open and close on the last day of the year. Moreover, this assumes that new restaurants do not need to mature over several years before they are operating at normal capacity utilization. To forecast revenues in Year 1, the first year of our forecast, we multiply 561 restaurants (as of the end of Year 0) by average revenue per restaurant of $4.640 million in order to forecast revenues of $2,603 million.

EXHIBIT 4.13	Darden Restaurants Inc.—Olive Garden Revenue Forecasts					
	Actual	**Forecast**				
Olive Garden	**Year 0**	**Year 1**	**Year 2**	**Year 3**	**Year 4**	**Year 5**
Beginning number of restaurants..............	542	561	579	596	610	621
New restaurants...............................	24	24	24	22	20	18
Closed restaurants.............................	−5	−6	−7	−8	−9	−10
Ending number of restaurants	561	579	596	610	621	629
Growth rate in number of stores		3.2%	2.9%	2.3%	1.8%	1.3%
Sales per restaurant—previous year (× $1,000).......		$4,419	$4,640	$4,872	$5,116	$5,372
Growth in revenue per restaurant.................		5.0%	5.0%	5.0%	5.0%	5.0%
Sales per restaurant—current year (× $1,000)		$4,640	$4,872	$5,116	$5,372	$5,640
Total revenue (× $1,000,000)		$2,603	$2,821	$3,049	$3,277	$3,503
Revenue growth rate			8.4%	8.1%	7.5%	6.9%

In this illustration, the revenue growth rate for Olive Garden decreases from 8.4% to 6.9% even though the revenue generated per restaurant grows by 5% each year. This decrease results from a decrease in the number of new restaurants and an increase in the number of restaurants closed, resulting in a decrease in the growth rate of the number of restaurants open each year (the growth rate in number of restaurants goes from 3.2% down to 1.3%). Since Olive Garden restaurants are roughly the same size, we use average revenue per restaurant in our forecast. If the restaurants varied in size (number of seats), one refinement we might consider would be the number of seats multiplied by revenue generated per seat. An alternative approach for projecting revenues is to forecast the number of invoices or bills multiplied by the average revenue per invoice. Another modeling technique that we sometimes use is modeling the growth in revenue per restaurant as a function of real growth in revenue per restaurant and inflation.

Illustration of More Detailed Capital Expenditure and Depreciation Forecasts

In this section, we again use Darden to illustrate how we can forecast capital expenditures and depreciation using a more detailed approach. We first forecast capital expenditures, which we show in Exhibit 4.14. From the previous exhibit, we have a forecast of the number of restaurants Darden will open each year. We multiply this number by the cost per restaurant for land, buildings, and equipment (which Darden discloses for the most recent year in its 10-K) in order to measure capital expenditures for new restaurants. For Year 1, we measure capital expenditures for new restaurants by multiplying the 24 new restaurants built in Year 1 by the cost of constructing a new restaurant of $3.8 million in order to calculate total capital expenditures for new restaurants of $91.2 million. In subsequent years, we increase capital expenditures for land, building, and equipment using a 2.5% inflation rate.

EXHIBIT 4.14 Darden Restaurants Inc. Capital Expenditure Forecasts

	Actual	Forecast				
	Year 0	Year 1	Year 2	Year 3	Year 4	Year 5
Olive Garden—Capital Expenditures for New Restaurants						
Per restaurant—land (× $1,000)	$ 488	$ 500	$ 513	$ 525	$ 538	$ 552
Per restaurant—buildings (× $1,000)	2,244	2,300	2,358	2,416	2,477	2,539
Per restaurant—equipment (× $1,000)	976	1,000	1,025	1,051	1,077	1,104
Per restaurant—total (× $1,000)	$ 3,707	$ 3,800	$ 3,895	$ 3,992	$ 4,092	$ 4,194
Capital expenditures—land (× $1,000)	$ 11,707	$ 12,000	$ 12,300	$ 11,557	$ 10,769	$ 9,934
Capital expenditures—buildings (× $1,000)	53,854	55,200	56,580	53,162	49,537	45,698
Capital expenditures—equipment (× $1,000)	23,415	24,000	24,600	23,114	21,538	19,869
Capital expenditures—total (× $1,000)	$ 88,976	$ 91,200	$ 93,480	$ 87,832	$ 81,844	$ 75,501
Olive Garden—Capital Expenditures for Existing Restaurants						
Beginning number of restaurants	542	561	579	596	610	621
Closed restaurants	–5	–6	–7	–8	–9	–10
Number of existing restaurants	537	555	572	588	601	611
Per restaurant—buildings (× $1,000)	$ 107	$ 110	$ 113	$ 116	$ 118	$ 121
Per restaurant—equipment (× $1,000)	49	50	51	53	54	55
Per restaurant—total (× $1,000)	$ 156	$ 160	$ 164	$ 168	$ 172	$ 177
Capital expenditures—buildings (× $1,000)	$ 57,629	$ 61,050	$ 64,493	$ 67,954	$ 71,193	$ 74,187
Capital expenditures—equipment (× $1,000)	26,195	27,750	29,315	30,888	32,361	33,721
Capital expenditures—total (× $1,000)	$ 83,824	$ 88,800	$ 93,808	$ 98,843	$103,554	$107,909
Olive Garden—Total Capital Expenditures for Restaurants						
Capital expenditures—land (× $1,000)	$ 11,707	$ 12,000	$ 12,300	$ 11,557	$ 10,769	$ 9,934
Capital expenditures—buildings (× $1,000)	111,483	116,250	121,073	121,116	120,730	119,885
Capital expenditures—equipment (× $1,000)	49,610	51,750	53,915	54,002	53,898	53,590
Capital expenditures—total (× $1,000)	$172,800	$180,000	$187,288	$186,675	$185,397	$183,410
Capital expenditure growth rate		4.2%	4.0%	–0.3%	–0.7%	–1.1%

Exhibit may contain small rounding errors

In addition to capital expenditures for new restaurants, we also measure capital expenditures for existing restaurants. In this illustration, we do this by multiplying the number of existing restaurants (beginning number of restaurants minus the number closed) by an average capital expenditure per existing restaurant. Naturally, Darden does not arrive at its capital expenditures in this way, but if this relation is stable, such an approach is possible to use. For Year 1, we measure capital expenditures for existing restaurants by multiplying the 555 existing restaurants (555 = 561 – 6) by the capital expenditures per existing restaurant of $160 thousand in order to calculate a total capital expenditures for existing restaurants figure of $88.8 million. A more detailed analysis might have relied on the age of the restaurants to project the amount spent each year on refurbishing particular restaurant locations.

Capital expenditures for existing restaurants are growing each year based on an increase in capital expenditures per restaurant due to inflation and an increase in the number of existing restaurants; however, capital expenditures for new restaurants decrease during the period because the number of new restaurants decreases during the period.

Note that the revenue growth rate in Exhibit 4.13 is larger than the capital expenditure growth rate in Exhibit 4.14 for all years. Further, the growth rate for capital expenditures decreases and eventually becomes negative in Year 3. Recall that in this illustration, revenues are growing because of either an increase in revenues per restaurant (growing at 5% each year), an increase in the number of restaurants, or both. Growth due to an increase in revenues per restaurant might not be related to capital expenditures. Rather, it could be the result of increases in price or utilization, which are potentially unrelated to capital expenditures. Thus, having different growth rates for capital expenditures and revenues is feasible in this situation.

In Exhibit 4.15, we present depreciation schedules and a schedule for property, plant, and equipment. We present two depreciation schedules—one for buildings and one for equipment. The acquisition cost of the buildings as of the end of Year 0 is $813.5 million, and the buildings have an average life of 12 years; concurrently, newly constructed and renovated buildings have an average life of 20 years. Depreciation for existing buildings is equal to $813.5 million divided by 12 years of remaining life, or $67.8 million. In this illustration, depreciation begins the year after construction and is equal to capital expenditures (for a new building) divided by 20 years. For example, depreciation in Year 2 for buildings constructed in Year 1

EXHIBIT 4.15 Darden Restaurants Inc. Depreciation Forecasts and Property, Plant, and Equipment Schedules

Buildings	Depr Years	Initial Bal	Year 1	Year 2	Year 3	Year 4	Year 5
					Forecast		
Existing buildings	12.0	$ 813,474	$ 67,790	$ 67,790	$ 67,790	$ 67,790	$ 67,790
New buildings year 1	20.0	$ 116,250		5,813	5,813	5,813	5,813
New buildings year 2	20.0	121,073			6,054	6,054	6,054
New buildings year 3	20.0	121,116				6,056	6,056
New buildings year 4	20.0	120,730					6,037
Total buildings—depreciation			$ 67,790	$ 73,602	$ 79,656	$ 85,711	$ 91,748

Equipment	Depr Years	Initial Bal	Year 1	Year 2	Year 3	Year 4	Year 5
					Forecast		
Existing equipment	4.0	$ 365,460	91,365	91,365	91,365	91,365	
New equipment year 1	8.0	51,750		6,469	6,469	6,469	6,469
New equipment year 2	8.0	53,915			6,739	6,739	6,739
New equipment year 3	8.0	54,002				6,750	6,750
New equipment year 4	8.0	53,898					6,737
Total equipment—depreciation			$ 91,365	$ 97,834	$ 104,573	$ 111,323	$ 26,696
Total depreciation			**$ 159,154**	**$ 171,436**	**$ 184,229**	**$ 197,035**	**$ 118,444**

	Actual		Forecast			
	Year 0	Year 1	Year 2	Year 3	Year 4	Year 5
Property, Plant, and Equipment—Cost						
Beginning balance		$1,257,554	$1,415,873	$1,578,062	$1,744,051	$1,905,775 $2,062,401
Capital expenditures		172,800	180,000	187,288	186,675	185,397　183,410
Retirements and dispositions		−14,481	−17,811	−21,299	−24,951	−28,771　−32,767
Ending balance		$1,415,873	$1,578,062	$1,744,051	$1,905,775	$2,062,401 $2,213,044
Property, Plant, and Equipment—Accumulated Depreciation						
Beginning balance		$ 548,072	$ 585,879	$ 734,956	$ 894,341	$1,064,453 $1,245,209
Depreciation expense		46,000	159,154	171,436	184,229	197,035　118,444
Retirements and dispositions		−8,193	−10,077	−12,051	−14,117	−16,278　−18,539
Ending balance		$ 585,879	$ 734,956	$ 894,341	$1,064,453	$1,245,209 $1,345,113
Net property, plant, and equipment		$ 829,994	$ 843,106	$ 849,710	$ 841,322	$ 817,192 $ 867,930

Exhibit may contain small rounding errors

(which includes improvement to existing buildings) is equal to capital expenditures in Year 1 of $116.25 million divided by 20 years, which is equal to $5.8 million. We perform the same calculation to measure depreciation for equipment. Notice, however, that for existing equipment as of the end of Year 0 (assumed to have a four-year remaining life), we stop the depreciation after the end of Year 4.

At the bottom of this exhibit, we present the property, plant, and equipment schedule, which includes schedules for gross property, plant, and equipment and accumulated depreciation. These schedules have the same basic format—beginning balance plus increases minus decreases is equal to the ending balance. The increases are either capital expenditures or depreciation. The decreases result from the retirement or disposition of assets—for example, the closing of a restaurant. Retirements and dispositions are based on the number of closed restaurants and an estimate of the original acquisition cost per restaurant, assuming that the average closed restaurant is 10 years old and that construction costs increased by 2.5% per year (the assumed inflation rate). We assume that the buildings of the closed restaurants are half depreciated since they have a twenty-year life and that the equipment is fully depreciated since it has an eight-year life.

SUMMARY AND KEY CONCEPTS

In this chapter, we discussed the process used to create a financial model, which can involve many different types of analyses and decisions, as well as a multitude of calculations. We discussed the flow and structure of financial models and the identification of forecast drivers (or assumptions) used in our formulas to forecast each item in the financial statements and supporting schedules. We discussed ways in which to embed the company's capital structure strategy into the model. We also extended our discussion to an examination of topics such as excess cash, scenario analysis, sensitivity analysis, and simulations. In addition, we discussed the creation of detailed revenue, capital expenditure, and depreciation schedules.

ADDITIONAL READING AND REFERENCES

Minton, B., and C. Schrand, "The Impact of Cash Flow Volatility on Discretionary Investment and the Costs of Debt and Equity Financing," *Journal of Financial Economics* 54 (1999), pp. 423–460.

Verrecchia, R., "Essays on Disclosure," *Journal of Accounting and Economics* 32 (2001), pp. 97–180.

EXERCISES AND PROBLEMS

P4-1. Calculate the number for each of the missing parts to this problem.

	Quantity$_{t-1}$	Price$_{t-1}$	Total Revenue$_{t-1}$	Quantity$_t$	Price$_t$	Total Revenue$_t$	$g_{quantity}$	g_{price}	$g_{Rev, Total}$
a.	10,000	$10.00	?–1	11,000	?–2	?–3	?–4	20.00%	?–5
b.	?–1	?–2	$750,000	60,000	?–3	?–4	20.00%	10.00%	?–5
c.	10,000	?–1	?–2	?–3	$13.80	$151,800	?–4	?–5	26.50%
d.	5,000	?–1	?–2	?–3	$11.00	?–4	5.00%	?–5	15.50%
e.	?–1	?–2	?–3	7,350	?–4	$ 72,000	5.00%	20.00%	?–5

P4-2. Calculate the number for each of the missing parts to this problem.

	Quantity$_{t-1}$	Price$_{t-1}$	Total Revenue$_{t-1}$	Quantity$_t$	Price$_t$	Total Revenue$_t$	$g_{quantity}$	g_{price}	$g_{Rev, Total}$	Inflation rate	$g_{price, real}$	Revenue from Inflation	Price$_t$ with no Inflation
a.	10,000	?–1	?–2	?–3	$ 1.26	$13,230	?–4	?–5	28.0%	5.0%	?–6	?–7	$ 1.20
b.	5,000	?–1	?–2	?–3	$11.00	?–4	20.0%	?–5	38.6%	5.0%	?–6	?–7	$10.48
c.	?–1	$5.00	?–2	5,500	?–3	?–4	10.0%	23.0%	?–5	2.5%	?–6	$825	?–7
d.	?–1	?–2	$5,000	800	?–3	?–4	20.0%	17.0%	?–5	4.0%	?–6	$270	?–7
e.	?–1	?–2	?–3	1,800	?–4	$ 3,600	5.0%	14.4%	?–5	4.0%	?–6	?–7	$ 1.92

P4-3.   Respond to the following questions, assuming each part of the problem is independent of the other parts.

   a.   Company A has an expected revenue growth rate of 20%, and Company B has an expected revenue growth rate of 10%. Company A has an expected **increase** in its selling prices of 12%, and Company B has an expected **increase** in its selling prices of 10%. Which company has the higher expected increase in volume?

   b.   Company A has an expected revenue growth rate of 20%, and Company B has an expected revenue growth rate of 10%. Company A has an expected **increase** in its selling prices of 12%, and Company B has an expected **decrease** in its selling prices of −5%. Which company has the higher expected increase in volume?

   c.   Company A has an expected revenue growth rate of 15%, and Company B has an expected revenue growth rate of 12%. Company A has an expected **increase** in the number of units sold equal to 10%, and Company B has an expected **increase** in the number of units sold equal to 5%. Which company has the higher expected price change?

   d.   Company A has an expected revenue growth rate of 15%, and Company B has an expected revenue growth rate of 12%. Company A has an expected **decrease** in the number of units sold equal to −10%, and Company B has an expected **decrease** in the number of units sold equal to −5%. Which company has the higher expected price change?

   e.   Company A has an expected revenue growth rate of −10%, and Company B has an expected revenue growth rate of −5%. Company A has an expected **increase** in the number of units sold equal to 5%, and Company B has an expected **increase** in the number of units sold equal to 10%. Which company has the higher expected price change?

P4-4.   **Financial Model for the Bob Wardrop Company (All Equity Financed):** Forecast drivers, financial statements, certain supporting schedules, and other information for the Bob Wardrop Company appear in Review Exercise 4.1. Forecast the financial statements and supporting schedules, including a free cash flow schedule, for Year 2 through Year 4. Note: Year 1 is illustrated in Review Exercises 4.1 to 4.3.

P4-5.   **Financial Model for the Bob Wardrop Company (with Debt):** Use the information on the Bob Wardrop Company from the previous problem except for the information on the company's capital structure. For the company's capital structure, assume the company will issue debt to fund all of the financing needs it cannot fund with internally generated cash flow, and assume that its cost of debt is 10%. The company will pay down all of its debt before it begins to pay any dividends; then, it will distribute all positive equity free cash flows to common equityholders. Using the above information, forecast the financial statements and supporting schedules, including a free cash flow schedule for Year 2 through Year 4. Note: Year 1 is illustrated in Review Exercise 4.4.

P4-6.   **Financial Model for the Bruce Rigel Company (Debt Held Constant):** The Year 0 financial statements and supporting schedules for the Bruce Rigel Company appear in Exhibit P4-1. Forecast the financial statements and supporting schedules, including a free cash flow schedule, for Year 1 through Year 4. Use the following assumptions and the information in the exhibit as the basis of your forecasts.

   a.   **Revenue**—The company expects its revenues to grow 25% in Year +1, 30% in Year +2, 20% in Year +3, 10% in Year +4, and 2% thereafter. Expected inflation is 2% per year for the entire forecast horizon. The company expects its selling prices will grow at the expected inflation rate and inflation is already taken into consideration in the projected revenue growth rates.

   b.   **Cost of Goods Sold**—The company expects its cost of goods sold expense ratio to be 45% in all years.

   c.   **Depreciation**—The company depreciates its property, plant, and equipment over 20 years. None of the company's property, plant, and equipment will be retired or sold during the five-year forecast period.

   d.   **Income Taxes**—The company has a 40% income tax rate on all income.

   e.   **Cash**—The company expects its required cash balance to equal 5% of current year revenues during the entire forecast period. The company does not expect to accumulate any excess cash.

   f.   **Days to Collect Accounts Receivable**—The company expects to increase its days to collect accounts receivable to 50 days in Year +1 and to 60 days thereafter as a way to extend additional credit to its customers, which is needed to achieve its expected revenue growth (this driver is based on year-end receivables, not average receivables).

   g.   **Days to Sell Inventory (Inventory Held)**—The company expects to increase its days to sell inventory to 60 days during the forecast period, which is needed to achieve its expected revenue growth (this driver is based on year-end inventory, not average inventory).

   h.   **Days to Pay Accounts Payable**—The company expects to increase its days to pay its accounts payable to 50 days in all years in the forecast period (this driver is based on year-end payables, not average payables).

i. **Capital Expenditures**—The company must invest $2.5 for each $1 of expected revenue increase expected in the following year due to volume increases (in other words, revenue increases that result from price increases do not require capital expenditures). Hint: Reread the revenue assumption for this problem.

j. **Capital Structure**—The company will not change its debt financing from its balance in Year 0, and the interest rate on the debt remains at 8% for all years in the forecast period. Current equityholders will make any necessary investments in the company. Similarly, the company plans to distribute all positive equity free cash flows to its equityholders in the form of dividends.

EXHIBIT P4-1   The Bruce Rigel Company

Income Statement and Balance Sheet ($ in thousands)	Year 0
Income Statement	
Revenue (Rev)	$ 20,000
Cost of goods sold (CGS)	–10,200
Depreciation expense.	–1,875
Earnings before interest and taxes.	$ 7,925
Interest expense	
Income before taxes.	$ 7,925
Income tax expense	–3,170
Net income.	$ 4,755
Balance Sheet	
Cash.	$ 1,800
Accounts receivable.	2,192
Inventory.	1,397
Total current assets	$ 5,389
Property, plant, and equipment (net)	41,275
Total assets.	$ 46,664
Accounts payable.	$ 1,324
Debt	6,000
Total liabilities	$ 7,324
Capital stock	$ 2,000
Retained earnings	37,340
Shareholders' equity	$ 39,340
Liabilities and shareholders' equity	$ 46,664

Statement of Retained Earnings ($ in thousands)	Year 0
Retained earnings—beginning of year	$ 32,952
Net income.	4,755
Common equity dividends	-367
Retained earnings—end of year	$ 37,340

Cash Flow Statement ($ in thousands)	Year 0
Cash flows from operations	
Net income.	$ 4,755
+ Depreciation expense	1,875
– Change in accounts receivable	–789
– Change in inventory.	–182
+ Change in accounts payable.	33
Cash flow from operations	$ 5,692
Investing activities	
– Capital expenditures	$–11,275
Financing activities.	
+ Change in debt financing	$ 6,000
+ Change in common equity financing . . .	0
– Common equity dividends paid.	–367
Cash flows from financing activities.	$ 5,633
Change in cash balance.	$ 50

Plant and Equipment (PPEQ) Schedule ($ in thousands)	Year 0
Beginning PPEQ—gross	$ 37,500
Capital expenditures	11,275
Ending PPEQ—gross	$ 48,775
Beginning accumulated depreciation.	$ 5,625
Depreciation expense.	1,875
Ending accumulated depreciation	$ 7,500
Net Property, Plant and Equipment	$ 41,275

P4-7. **Financial Model for the Bruce Rigel Company (with Varying Debt):** Use all of the information on the B. Rigel Company that appears in the previous problem except for the information on the company's capital structure, including its dividend policy. Instead, use the following information on the company's capital structure strategy and dividend policy. The company knows that its planned capital expenditures over the next few years will require the company to raise additional capital. The company plans to raise all additional capital using debt financing. The company would like to keep its debt level as low as possible; however, the company would like its dividends to grow at least by 10% per year subsequent to the Year 0 dividends, even if the company must borrow additional debt to pay its dividends. The company believes that its interest rate will be 8% if its debt level is less than $10,000 and 9%, if it is between $10,000 and $25,000. Forecast the financial statements and supporting schedules, including a free cash flow schedule, for Year 1 through Year 4.

P4-8. **Financial Model for the Bruce Rigel Company (Capital Structure Based on Maintaining a Debt Rating):** Use all of the information on the B. Rigel Company that appears in Problem 4.6 except for the information on the company's capital structure, including its dividend policy. Instead, use the following information on the company's capital structure strategy and dividend policy. The company knows that its planned capital expenditures over the next few years will require the company to raise additional capital. Although the company would like to maintain an "AAA" credit rating, it is willing to decrease its debt rating for a few years in order to finance its growth. The company will finance all negative free cash flows before changes in financing by refinancing its debt with new debt. The amount of debt and the interest rate for this debt depend on the company's debt rating, which is determined by the interest coverage ratios in the following schedule. Use forecasted EBIT in year t divided by interest expense in year t+1 (based on the debt outstanding at the end of year t) to determine the rating.

	Credit Rating				
	AAA	**AA**	**A**	**BBB**	**BB**
Interest rate for credit rating class	8.0%	8.5%	9.0%	9.5%	10.0%
Minimum coverage ratio for credit rating class	22.0	10.0	6.0	4.0	2.0

Once the company begins generating positive free cash flows before changes in financing, the company plans to use them to repay its debt until it regains its AAA credit rating. Once the company regains its AAA credit rating, it plans to maintain that credit rating and distribute all positive equity free cash flows to its equityholders. Forecast the financial statements and supporting schedules, including a free cash flow schedule, for Year 1 through Year 4.

P4-9. **Assessing the Forecasts for the Bruce Rigel Company (Capital Structure Based on Maintaining a Debt Rating—Must complete P4-8 before attempting this problem):** Assess the reasonableness of the forecasts created in P4-8 using the time-series of various financial ratios.

SOLUTIONS FOR REVIEW EXERCISES

Solution for Review Exercise 4.1: Forecasts for Bob Wardrop Company—Part 1

B. WARDROP COMPANY
Income Statements

($ in thousands)	Actual Year 0	Forecast Year +1
Income Statement		
Revenue	$1,000	$1,400
Cost of goods sold.	−600	−840
Depreciation expense.	−167	−234
Earnings before interest and taxes.	$ 233	$ 326
Interest expense.		0
Income before taxes.	$ 233	$ 326
Income tax expense.	−70	−98
Net income.	$ 163	$ 228

Solution for Review Exercise 4.2: Forecasts for Bob Wardrop Company—Part 2

B. WARDROP COMPANY Income Statements and Balance Sheets	Actual	Forecast
($ in thousands)	Year 0	Year +1
Income Statement		
Revenue	$1,000	$1,400
Cost of goods sold.	−600	−840
Depreciation expense.	−167	−234
Earnings before interest and taxes.	$ 233	$326
Interest expense.		0
Income before taxes.	$ 233	$ 326
Income tax expense.	−70	−98
Net Income.	$ 163	$ 228
Balance Sheet		
Cash.	$ 100	$ 140
Accounts receivable.	200	280
Total current assets	$ 300	$ 420
Property, plant, and equipment (net)	1,837	2,303
Total assets.	$2,137	$2,723
Debt	$ 0	$ 0
Capital stock	100	458
Retained earnings	2,037	2,265
Liabilities and shareholders' equity	$2,137	$2,723

B. WARDROP COMPANY Statement of Retained Earnings	Actual	Forecast
($ in thousands)	Year 0	Year +1
Retained earnings—beginning of year	$1,873	$2,037
Net income.	163	228
Common equity dividends	0	0
Retained earnings—end of year.	$2,037	$2,265

B. WARDROP COMPANY Income Tax Schedule	Actual	Forecast
($ in thousands)	Year 0	Year+1
Earnings before income taxes	$ 233	$ 326
Income tax rate	30.0%	30.0%
Income tax expense.	$ 70	$ 98

B. WARDROP COMPANY Plant and Equipment (PPEQ) Schedule	Actual	Forecast
($ in thousands)	Year 0	Year +1
Beginning PPEQ—gross	$1,667	$2,337
Capital expenditures	670	700
Ending PPEQ—gross.	$2,337	$3,037
Beginning accumulated depreciation.	$ 333	$ 500
Depreciation expense.	167	234
Ending accumulated depreciation	$ 500	$ 734
Net property, plant and equipment	$1,837	$2,303

Exhibit may contain small rounding error

Note: Review Exercise 4.2 asked you to complete only the asset side of the balance sheet. You cannot complete the liability and shareholder's equity side of the Balance Sheet or the Statement of Retained Earnings before completing Review Exercise 4.3. For convenience, we show both the statement of retained earnings and liability and stockholders' equity side of the balance sheet (partial solution to Review Exercise 4.3) here.

Solution for Review Exercise 4.3: Forecasts for Bob Wardrop Company—Part 3

B. WARDROP COMPANY Cash Flow Statement		
($ in thousands)	Actual Year 0	Forecast Year +1
Cash flows from operations		
Net income	$ 163	$ 228
+ Depreciation expense	167	234
– Change in accounts receivable	–20	–80
Cash flow from operations	$ 310	$ 382
Investing activities		
– Capital expenditures	$–670	$–700
Financing activities		
+ Change in debt financing	$ 0	$ 0
+ Change in common equity financing	0	358
– Common equity dividends paid	0	0
Cash flows from financing activities	$ 0	$ 358
Change in cash balance	$–360	$ 40

B. WARDROP COMPANY Free Cash Flow and Equity Free Cash Flow		
($ in thousands)	Actual Year 0	Forecast Year +1
Earnings before interest and taxes	$ 233	$ 326
– Income taxes paid on EBIT	–70	–98
Earnings before interest and after taxes	$ 163	$ 228
+ Depreciation expense	167	234
– Change in accounts receivable	–20	–80
Unlevered operating cash flow	$ 310	$ 382
– Change in required cash balance	–50	–40
– Capital expenditures	–670	–700
Unlevered free cash flow	$–410	$–358
– Interest paid in cash	0	0
+ Interest tax shield	0	0
Cash Flow before changes in financing	$–410	$–358
+ Change in debt financing	0	0
Equity free cash flow	$–410	$–358
+ Change in common equity financing	410	358
– Common dividends	0	0
+ Change in required cash balance	50	40
Change in cash balance	$ 50	$ 40

Note: See the solution to Review Exercise 4.2 for the Statement of Retained Earnings and the Liability and Stockholders' Equity side of the Balance Sheet.

Solution for Review Exercise 4.4: Forecasts for Bob Wardrop Company—Part 4

B. WARDROP COMPANY
Income Statement

($ in thousands)	Actual Year 0	Forecast Year +1
Revenue	$1,000	$1,400
Cost of goods sold.	−600	−840
Depreciation expense.	−167	−234
Earnings before interest and taxes. . . .	$ 233	$ 326
Interest expense.		0
Income before taxes.	$ 233	$ 326
Income tax expense.	−70	−98
Net income.	$ 163	$ 228

B. WARDROP COMPANY
Income Tax Schedule

($ in thousands)	Actual Year 0	Forecast Year +1
Earnings before income taxes	$ 233	$ 326
Income tax rate	30.0%	30.0%
Income tax expense.	$ 70	$ 98

B. WARDROP COMPANY
Balance Sheet

($ in thousands)	Actual Year 0	Forecast Year +1
Cash.	$ 100	$ 140
Accounts receivable.	200	280
Total current assets	$ 300	$ 420
Property, plant, and equipment (net) . .	1,837	2,303
Total assets.	$2,137	$2,723
Debt		$ 358
Capital stock	$ 100	100
Retained earnings	2,037	2,265
Liabilities and shareholders' equity . . .	$2,137	$2,723

B. WARDROP COMPANY
Plant and Equipment (PPEQ) Schedule

($ in thousands)	Actual Year 0	Forecast Year +1
Beginning PPEQ—gross	$1,667	$2,337
Capital expenditures	670	700
Ending PPEQ—gross	$2,337	$3,037
Beginning accumulated depreciation. . . .	$ 333	$ 500
Depreciation expense.	167	234
Ending accumulated depreciation	$ 500	$ 734
Net property, plant and equipment	$1,837	$2,303

B. WARDROP COMPANY Cash Flow Statement		
($ in thousands)	Actual Year 0	Forecast Year +1
Cash flows from operations		
Net income	$ 163	$ 228
+ Depreciation expense	167	234
− Change in accounts receivable	−20	−80
Cash flow from operations	$ 310	$ 382
Investing activities		
− Capital expenditures	$ −670	$ −700
Financing activities		
+ Change in debt financing	$0	$ 358
+ Change in common equity financing	0	0
− Common equity dividends paid	0	0
Cash flows from financing activities	$0	$ 358
Change in cash balance	$ −360	$ 40

B. WARDROP COMPANY Statement of Retained Earnings		
($ in thousands)	Actual Year 0	Forecast Year +1
Retained earnings—beginning of year	$1,873	$2,037
Net income	163	228
Common equity dividends	0	0
Retained earnings—end of year	$2,037	$2,265

Exhibit may contain small rounding error

B. WARDROP COMPANY Free Cash Flow and Equity Free Cash Flow		
($ in thousands)	Actual Year 0	Forecast Year +1
Earnings before interest and taxes	$ 233	$ 326
− Income taxes paid on EBIT	−70	−98
Earnings before interest and after taxes	$ 163	$ 228
+ Depreciation expense	167	234
− Change in accounts receivable	−20	−80
Unlevered operating cash flow	$ 310	$ 382
− Change in required cash balance	−50	−40
− Capital expenditures	−670	−700
Unlevered free cash flow	$ −410	$ −358
− Interest paid in cash	0	0
+ Interest tax shield	0	0
Cash flow before changes in financing	$ −410	$ −358
+ Change in debt financing	0	358
Equity free cash flow	$ −410	$ 0
+ Change in common equity financing	410	0
− Common dividends	0	0
+ Change in required cash balance	50	40
Change in cash balance	$ 50	$ 40

After mastering the material in this chapter, you will be able to:

1. Know how financing can affect the value of the firm and its equity (5.1)

2. Measure value using the adjusted present value and weighted average cost of capital valuation models (5.2–5.5)

3. Measure value using the equity free cash flow and dividend valuation models (5.6–5.7)

4. Adjust the implementation of these valuation models for specific circumstances (5.8)

The Adjusted Present Value and Weighted Average Cost of Capital Discounted Cash Flow Valuation Methods

Emerging Communications' valuation using discounted cash flow valuation models—Emerging Communication Inc. (EmCom) owned various subsidiaries whose businesses provided local telephone service, sold and leased telecommunications equipment, and provided cellular telephone service in the U.S. Virgin Islands. During 1998, EmCom's chairman, CEO, and secretary began a process to acquire EmCom and take the company private. In the first step of the process, the chairman was to secure control of at least 80% of EmCom's shares. In order to accomplish that, a special committee drawn from EmCom's Board of Directors negotiated a $10.25 price per share, and its financial advisor issued a fairness opinion stating that the $10.25 price per share was fair from a financial point of view. EmCom's Board approved the $10.25 bid and EmCom gave notice to its shareholders of a special meeting to vote on the sale. On October 19, 1998, EmCom's shareholders approved the transaction.[1] According to Delaware law—the state in which the company was incorporated—shareholders not wishing to participate in the transaction can exercise their appraisal rights by petitioning the court to assess the fair value of their stock. Some of EmCom's minority shareholders opted to exercise their appraisal rights under Delaware law. The court decided on a share price of $38.05 per share based on a weighted average cost of capital valuation method.

EMERGING COMMUNICATIONS INC.

In this chapter, we will explore the intricacies of both the weighted average cost of capital discounted cash flow (DCF) method as well as the adjusted present value DCF method and see how the two methods are related to one another.

---

[1] See Emerging Communications Inc. Proxy Statement, filed with the Securities and Exchange Commission (SEC) on September 28, 1998.

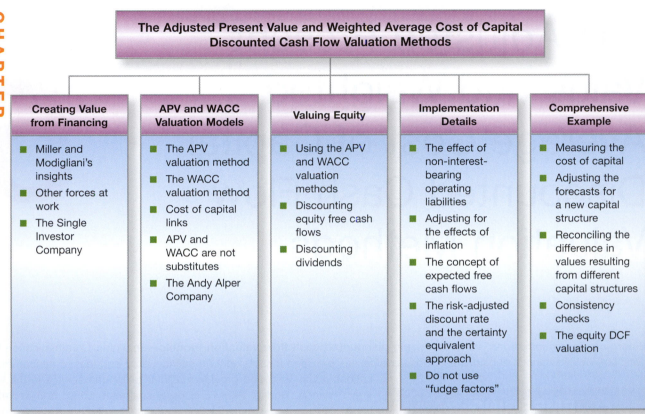

The Adjusted Present Value and Weighted Average Cost of Capital Discounted Cash Flow Valuation Methods

Creating Value from Financing	APV and WACC Valuation Models	Valuing Equity	Implementation Details	Comprehensive Example
■ Miller and Modigliani's insights ■ Other forces at work ■ The Single Investor Company	■ The APV valuation method ■ The WACC valuation method ■ Cost of capital links ■ APV and WACC are not substitutes ■ The Andy Alper Company	■ Using the APV and WACC valuation methods ■ Discounting equity free cash flows ■ Discounting dividends	■ The effect of non-interest-bearing operating liabilities ■ Adjusting for the effects of inflation ■ The concept of expected free cash flows ■ The risk-adjusted discount rate and the certainty equivalent approach ■ Do not use "fudge factors"	■ Measuring the cost of capital ■ Adjusting the forecasts for a new capital structure ■ Reconciling the difference in values resulting from different capital structures ■ Consistency checks ■ The equity DCF valuation

INTRODUCTION

In Chapter 1, we introduced the discounted cash flow (DCF) valuation model, but we only valued a company financed entirely by common equity. We also saw in Chapter 1 that the way a company finances itself may affect the value of the firm, and we showed the value created from financing as an asset on a company's economic balance sheet. This asset is not a physical asset, but a company may create value by financing itself in a particular way as long as the company's after-tax cost of capital on any financing instrument is less than the cost of capital required by the investors to invest in that security.

We use one of two forms of the DCF valuation model to value the company including the value from financing—the **adjusted present value method (APV)** or the **weighted average cost of capital method (WACC)**. Both methods measure the same value of a firm. The difference between the methods is the way in which the methods incorporate the value created from financing in the valuation. The APV method incorporates the benefit directly by discounting the expected tax benefits from a particular type of financing. The WACC method incorporates this benefit indirectly through an adjustment to the discount rate; for this reason, the WACC method is also called the **adjusted cost of capital valuation method**. The APV and WACC methods are *not* substitutes because the appropriateness of a particular method depends on the context of the valuation, in particular the capital structure strategy of the company.

We begin this chapter with a discussion of how the tax deductibility of interest can create value. We then discuss the APV and WACC valuation methods, which measure the value of the firm. We illustrate how to use these methods and how they relate to each other. We measure the value of a company's common equity by subtracting the value of the company's non-common equity claims from the value of the firm. We also discuss DCF valuation methods that measure the value of a company's equity directly—the equity discounted cash flow (Equity DCF) method and the dividend discounted cash flow valuation method (Dividend DCF).

Another way a company can create value from financing is by securing financing with a subsidized (lower than market rate) cost of capital. In general, investors do not knowingly give such subsidies to a for-profit company, but a government might. For example, a government, such as a state or municipal government, might provide subsidized debt financing to provide incentive for a company to build a plant within its jurisdiction.

5.1 CREATING VALUE FROM FINANCING

Debt financing can create value for the firm because of the tax deductibility of interest at the corporate level. In the United States, and in many other tax jurisdictions, interest paid to debtholders is generally tax deductible at the corporate level, and payments to equityholders (dividends) are not. A company that issues debt and has tax-deductible interest will generally have more cash flows to distribute to its investors (debt- and equityholders) than a company that does not issue debt. The government essentially subsidizes the cash flow paid to debtholders (interest) because it is tax deductible, unlike the flows paid to equityholders. We refer to the incremental cash flows arising from the tax savings from interest as **interest tax shields (ITS)**, and we call the potential value created by the interest tax shields the **value of interest tax shields (V_{ITS})**. The value of interest tax shields is a component of the value created by financing (V_{FIN}), and sometimes, it is the only component.

LO1 Know how financing can affect the value of the firm and its equity

Insights from Miller and Modigliani and Others

The framework for understanding the effect of a company's capital structure decisions on its value comes from the research of Miller and Modigliani (M-M).[2] M-M established the framework for analyzing how interest tax shields create value and how capital structure decisions affect the relationships among a company's costs of capital. M-M based their initial work in this area on various assumptions. We list some of these below.

- No one capital market participant (investor or company) sets security prices; everyone is a **price taker**.
- Everyone can transact without incurring any transaction costs (no transaction costs entails no fees for transacting, no costs of processing information, and no direct cost for transferring assets to debtholders in bankruptcy).
- No one can earn **arbitrage profits**.
- Investors and companies borrow and lend at the same rate.
- All capital market participants have the same information and knowledge (no asymmetric information) and investors and companies can write perfect, enforceable contracts that eliminate all agency costs (agency costs between the owner and manager and agency costs between the owners/manager and debtholders).
- Neither investors nor companies pay income taxes.

M-M showed that, if all of their assumptions were correct, capital structure decisions would not affect the value of the firm; in other words, capital structure decisions would be irrelevant as long as the firm did not change its investment decisions because of the change in the capital structure. M-M demonstrated that if this result was not true, investors could buy the mispriced company and personally borrow or lend in order to create an investment that would earn arbitrage profits. They showed that an investor could always buy the equity of an unlevered company by borrowing money to recreate a levered company's financial leverage; thus, both the unlevered company and levered company would have the same value. To explain this concept in a non-academic setting, Professor Miller used a joke attributed to the famous baseball player Yogi Berra: "You better cut the pizza in four pieces because I'm not hungry enough to eat six." Professor Miller would then explain that like Yogi Berra's pizza, no matter how you sliced up the claims on a company's assets (in other words, no matter how many different types of securities

---

[2] See the following research on this topic: Modigliani, F., and M. H. Miller, "The Cost of Capital, Corporate Finance and the Theory of Investment," *American Economic Review* 48 (1958), pp. 261–297; Modigliani, F., and M. H. Miller, "Corporate Income Taxes and the Cost of Capital: A Correction," *American Economic Review* 53 (June 1963), pp. 433–443; Modigliani, F., and M. H. Miller, "Some Estimates of the Cost of Capital to the Electric Utility Industry, 1954–1957," *American Economic Review* 56 (June 1966), pp. 333–391.

a company issued and no matter what capital structure it adopted), its size (value) would not change as long as the company held the investments it made constant.

M-M also showed that a levered firm's equity cost of capital—that is a firm with debt or preferred in its capital structure—would be higher than that of an unlevered firm because of the additional risk to the equity caused by the issuance of debt and preferred. The additional risk of the equity comes because the debtholders and preferred holders are paid a fixed amount each period (interest payments or preferred dividends) and their claims are given priority over the claims of the common equityholders. M-M showed that the equity cost of capital is equal to the company's unlevered cost of capital, plus a premium for the company's financial leverage. Although M-M based their work on assumptions that are not reflective of the real world, their capital structure irrelevance proposition provides an anchor for our thinking about capital structure decisions and how they could affect the value of the firm. To analyze the effect of capital structure on the value of the firm, we can systematically change M-M's assumptions and examine the effect on both the value of the firm and the relationships between a company's costs of capital. In fact, M-M did this in a subsequent paper by changing the corporate income tax assumption.

In their subsequent research, M-M assumed that companies paid income taxes and that interest expense was tax deductible while dividends were not, which roughly mirrored the tax code in the United States and many other countries at the time and to this day. They kept all other assumptions the same, including their assumption of no personal income taxes. M-M showed that the tax deductibility of interest reduced the income taxes paid by a company. This, in turn, increased the cash flows the company could pay to its investors (by the amount of the interest tax shields) and decreased the company's overall cost of capital (weighted average cost of capital). The effect of the interest tax shields was that they decreased a company's corporate taxes and increased the value of the firm because of the additional payouts possible to claimholders.

Many other researchers have analyzed issues related to the value of interest tax shields.[3] Some researchers have extended M-M's work by making the original assumptions more robust. For example, M-M assumed that all companies had the same risk and debt was risk-free, but subsequent research showed that neither is necessary for M-M's results to hold. Other researchers extended M-M's work to companies that refinanced their debt both annually and continuously, and to companies that were not zero-growth perpetuities. Finally, other researchers, including Miller himself, have added additional factors to consider, such as personal income taxes, signaling, agency costs, and financial distress and bankruptcy costs, all of which may mitigate the benefits of financial leverage. First, we illustrate how the tax deductibility of interest can create value, and then we will return to discuss the potential countervailing forces.

The Single Investor Company

To illustrate the value created from financing, we use a simple example of a sole owner deciding whether to finance a company with all equity, with equity and debt when interest is not tax deductible, and with equity and debt when interest is tax deductible. Our company is the Single Investor Company, which has a single investor and manager, regardless of whether equity or equity and debt are issued. We use an example with one investor to avoid any agency costs for a firm with different investors. The Single Investor Company is a startup company that needs $50,000 of financing. All of the company's transactions are in cash, and it does not require other investments in the future other than the initial capital. The company

---

[3] For example, Shackelford, D., and T. Shevlin, "Empirical Tax Research in Accounting," *Journal of Accounting and Economics*, 31 (2001), pp. 321–387; and Graham, J. R., "Taxes and Corporate Finance: A Review," Working Paper (July 2001), Fuqua School of Business, Duke University, Durham NC 27708-0120; Hamada, R. S., "Portfolio Analysis, Market Equilibrium, and Corporation Finance," *Journal of Finance* (March 1969), pp. 13–31; Hamada, R. S., "The Effect of the Firm's Capital Structure on the Systematic Risk of Common Stocks," *Journal of Finance* (May 1972), pp. 435–452; Rubinstein, M. E., "A Mean-Variance Synthesis of Corporate Financial Theory," *Journal of Financial and Quantitative Analysis* (March 1973), pp. 167–181; Stiglitz, J. E., "A Re-Examination of the Modigliani-Miller Theorem," *American Economic Review* (December 1969), pp. 187–193; Stiglitz, J. E., "On the Irrelevance of Corporate Financial Policy," *American Economic Review* (December 1974), pp. 851–866; Rubinstein, M. E., "A Mean-Variance Synthesis of Corporate Financial Theory," *Journal of Financial and Quantitative Analysis* (March 1973), pp. 167–181; Conine, T. E., "Corporate Debt and Corporate Taxes: An Extension," *Journal of Finance* (September 1980), pp. 1033–1037; Miles, J. A., and J. R. Ezzell, "The Weighted Average Cost of Capital, Perfect Capital Markets, and Project Life: A Clarification," *Journal of Financial and Quantitative Analysis* vol. 15, no. 3 (1980), pp. 719–730; Miles, J. A., and J. R. Ezzell, "Reformulating Tax Shield Valuation: A Note," *Journal of Finance* vol. 40 (1985), pp. 1485–1492; and Harris, R. S., and J. J. Pringle, "Risk-Adjusted Discount Rates—Extensions from the Average Risk Case," *Journal of Financial Research* vol. 8, no. 3 (1985), pp. 237–244.

expects to generate earnings before interest and taxes (EBIT) of $10,000 in perpetuity. The company has a 40% income tax rate on all income.

The manager-owner is considering whether to finance the company with $50,000 of equity financing or with $30,000 of equity financing and $20,000 of perpetual debt financing with a 10% interest rate. In either case, the manager-owner is investing $50,000. The manager-owner will select the capital structure that results in a higher firm value. We analyze two income tax cases (regimes). In both cases, the income tax rate is 40%, but in the first case, interest and dividends are not tax deductible to the company, and in the second case, interest is tax deductible but dividends are not.

Since the Single Investor Company has only one investor (who will hold all securities issued by the company), the only way one financing alternative can be better than the other is if it results in a higher perpetual total cash flow (the combined cash flows paid to debtholders and equityholders). If the total perpetual cash flow is larger, then the value of the firm will be larger, and the single investor will be better off. If the total payoff is the same, then the value of the firm will be the same, and none of the alternatives will make the single investor better off.

In Exhibit 5.1, we examine the effect of using all equity financing and some equity and some debt financing when interest is not tax deductible. The two financing alternatives have identical **revenues**, operating expenses, and **earnings before interest and taxes (EBIT)**. Since interest is not tax deductible, income taxes are also the same, as is the total cash flow generated by the company to distribute to its investor. Here, the only effect of issuing debt is that some of the company's total cash flows are paid to the debtholder (the single investor) in the form of interest. The value of the firm does not change and the equityholder (the single investor) is not better off than without debt.

EXHIBIT 5.1	Single Investor Company's Initial Investment, Income Statement, and Cash Flows When Interest Is Not Tax Deductible

SINGLE INVESTOR COMPANY Income Statement Forecast		
	All Equity	**Interest Not Deductible**
Initial Investment		
Debt (10% interest rate)	$ 0	$20,000
Equity	50,000	30,000
Total investment	$50,000	$50,000
Income Statement (All Items Are Cash)		
Revenue	$50,000	$50,000
Operating expenses	−40,000	−40,000
Earnings before interest and taxes (EBIT)	$10,000	$10,000
Tax deductible interest	0	0
Earnings before tax	$10,000	$10,000
Income taxes (40%)	−4,000	−4,000
Earnings before non-tax deductible interest	$ 6,000	$ 6,000
Non-tax deductible interest	0	−2,000
Earnings to equityholders.	$ 6,000	$ 4,000
Cash flow to debtholders (interest)	0	2,000
Total cash flow to all investors	$ 6,000	$ 6,000
Return on equity	12.0%	13.3%
Return on total investment.	12.0%	12.0%

We can clearly see this result for the Single Investor Company because of its one investor that owns all of the company's securities. If the company only uses equity financing, the single investor earns a return on total investment of 12% at the expected EBIT of $10,000. If the company issues debt, the single investor continues to earn a 12% return on total investment at the expected EBIT of $10,000, even though the cost of debt is 10%. The single investor earns 10% on the debt and a higher return on equity, but the return on total investment is still equal to the 12%. Thus, no value is created. Since the total cash flows paid to all investors do not increase after adding debt to the capital structure (when interest is not tax deductible), the single investor will not be better off.

Although issuing debt when interest is not tax deductible does not change either the total cash flows to all investors or the return on total investment, it does make the equity more risky. If the equity is made more risky when debt is issued, then the expected return on equity should increase. Although the earnings to equityholders at the expected EBIT of $10,000 are smaller when the company issues debt ($4,000 versus $6,000), the initial equity investment is also smaller ($30,000 versus $50,000) such that the expected return on equity is larger. In the all-equity case, the expected return on equity is 12%, but in the debt and equity financed case, the expected return on equity is 13.33%. As we said before, however, the single investor still holds a portfolio with an expected return of 12% (40% of the portfolio is debt yielding 10%, and 60% of the portfolio is equity returning 13.33%).

Why does the equity become more risky? The equity becomes more risky because we promised to pay the debtholders a fixed amount, and this payment has priority over flows to equityholders. We can see the increase in risk by comparing what happens to the return on equity in relation to variation in EBIT with and without debt in the capital structure. For example, if the actual EBIT is $5,000 instead of the expected EBIT of $10,000, then the return on equity decreases more in the case with debt and equity financing (ROE for all equity is 6% versus 3.3% for debt and equity). Conversely, if the actual EBIT is $15,000 instead of the expected EBIT of $10,000, then the return on equity increases more in the case with debt and equity financing (ROE for all equity is 18% versus 23.3% for debt and equity).

Thus, the return on equity varies more with a given variation in EBIT if there is debt financing, making the equity more risky. Thus, the higher expected return on equity merely reflects the fact that the equity is made more risky when we add debt to the capital structure, but it has not made the single investor better off. Why? When interest is not tax deductible, adding debt to the capital structure does not increase the total cash flow to the single investor, nor does it increase the total return on the single investor's portfolio of debt and equity.

Our conclusions are different from the above when a company's interest is tax deductible. In Exhibit 5.2, we show the company's initial investment and income statement for the two financing alternatives (all equity and debt and equity) and for the two income tax regimes (interest is not tax deductible and

| EXHIBIT 5.2 | Single Investor Company's Initial Investment, Income Statement, and Cash Flows When Interest Is Tax Deductible |

SINGLE INVESTOR COMPANY Income Statement Forecast			
	All Equity	**Interest Not Deductible**	**Interest Deductible**
Initial Investment			
Debt (10% interest rate).	$ 0	$20,000	$20,000
Equity	50,000	30,000	30,000
Total investment	$50,000	$50,000	$50,000
Income Statement (All Items Are Cash)			
Revenue	$50,000	$50,000	$50,000
Operating expenses	−40,000	−40,000	−40,000
Earnings before interest and taxes (EBIT)	$10,000	$10,000	$10,000
Tax deductible interest	0	0	−2,000
Earnings before tax	$10,000	$10,000	$ 8,000
Income taxes (40%)	−4,000	−4,000	−3,200
Earnings before non-tax deductible interest	$ 6,000	$ 6,000	$ 4,800
Non-tax deductible interest	0	−2,000	0
Earnings to equityholders.	$ 6,000	$ 4,000	$ 4,800
Cash flow to debtholders (interest)	0	2,000	2,000
Total cash flow to all investors	$ 6,000	$ 6,000	$ 6,800
Return on equity	12.0%	13.3%	16.0%
Return on total investment.	12.0%	12.0%	13.6%

interest is tax deductible). Neither the financing alternative nor the tax regime affects the company's revenues, operating expenses, or EBIT. However, having an income tax regime in which interest is tax deductible has the effect of increasing the earnings to equity holders by $800 ($800 = $4,800 − $4,000) relative to the income tax regime in which interest is not tax deductible. Likewise, the total payoff paid to all investors and the rate of return on the total investment increases from 12% to 13.6%. Since the return on total investment has increased, value has been created. The $800 increase in total payoff to all investors goes to the equityholders ($4,800 − $4,000), for both the amount of debt and the interest rate are fixed in both income tax regimes. Thus, equityholders are better off with the debt and equity alternative when interest is tax deductible.

We can also see the same effect by examining the return on equity. Notice how the return on equity has gone up relative to the case in which interest is not deductible. Since the promised payments to debtholders do not change when moving to the case where interest is deductible, there will be an increase in the return on equity with no further increase in risk as the return on equity increases to 16%. Indeed, the return on the single investor's portfolio will increase from 12% (12% = $6,000/$50,000) to 13.6% (13.6% = $6,800/$50,000). The single investor now holds a portfolio composed of 40% debt that yields 10% and 60% equity with a return of 16%.

For every $1 of tax-deductible interest, income tax expense will decrease by $1 multiplied by the company's **income tax rate applicable to interest expense** (T_{INT}). The government, in essence, subsidizes the cash flow paid to debtholders (interest) because the cash flow is tax deductible relative to the flows paid to equityholders. This subsidy, called an **interest tax shield (ITS)**, is equal to the income tax rate applicable to the interest deduction, multiplied by the **interest expense deducted (INT)**.

$$ITS = T_{INT} \times INT$$

The corporation's average and marginal tax rates can differ from the income tax rate for interest tax shields, T_{INT}, for a variety of reasons that include progressive income tax rates, net operating loss carryforwards, non-deductible interest, and alternative minimum tax calculations (a company might have to pay a minimum amount of income tax based on income items unrelated to interest). We discuss all of these more fully elsewhere in the book.

In valuing a company, the value of the interest tax shields is, not surprisingly, the discounted value of the expected interest tax shields for the company based on its capital structure strategy. If the Single Investor Company expected to never retire the $20,000 in debt it had issued nor issue additional debt, the value of the interest tax shields would be $800 per year in perpetuity discounted at an appropriate risk-adjusted discount rate, a topic we discuss in more detail later in the chapter.

Countervailing Forces

For a company with just one investor, the choice appears to be clear. The company should issue as much debt as possible to that single investor. In this way, the investor has converted payments that he or she might receive in the form of dividends to interest and the company can deduct those payments on its tax return. It is not surprising, then, that governments restrict the owners of small companies from lending the company money. Governments will often not allow a company to deduct interest expense attributable to loans from its owners, or they will at least restrict the amount that can be deducted. For companies with a large number of diverse owners, these same restrictions do not apply.

The fact that we do not observe companies, even those with a large number of diverse owners, maximizing the amount of debt they have suggests that countervailing forces must offset some, or perhaps all, of the value created by interest tax shields. These countervailing forces include the transactions cost of enforcing bond covenants, the cost of financial distress, the cost of bankruptcy, agency costs, and the potential for the value of interest tax shields to be offset by personal income taxes paid by the company's investors.

When a company has many investors, the interests of the shareholders, debtholders, and managers often come into conflict. We call the costs associated with managing these conflicts of interest **agency costs**. Debt contracts are used to help mitigate the potential agency costs between the debtholders and managers and shareholders and provide the debtholders with rights to protect their principal if the company ever fails to make required **debt service** payments (interest and principal) or violates other provisions of the loan contract. One of these rights is to accelerate the due date of the loan and demand immediate payment. If the amount owed cannot be immediately paid, the debtholders can force the company into bankruptcy. The bankruptcy process can be expensive, and it has both indirect and direct costs associated with it. The more debt a company has, the more incentive the managers and shareholders have to take actions that will benefit themselves yet harm the debtholders. Examples of actions managers and shareholders can take that would hurt the debtholders include investing in riskier projects than anticipated, not investing in projects that create value (because the value created would go to the debtholders), or liquidating assets and distributing the cash to the shareholders.[4] The increase in agency costs associated with more debt in the capital structure mitigates the benefit of the interest tax shields generated by the debt. If we believe that the amount of leverage is sufficiently high that there are some states of the world where the firm would incur financial distress or bankruptcy costs, we would have to take those costs into account in estimating the future expected free cash flows of the firm.

While there are agency costs arguments for why debt in the capital structure may affect the value of the firm negatively, there are also agency costs arguments that suggest debt may increase the value of the firm in some circumstances. In Chapter 1, we said that a large debt overhang could be an incentive for managers to operate the firm efficiently because they are so focused on generating sufficient cash flows to pay off the debt. This is an argument often given in favor of firms undergoing a debt recapitalization or a leveraged buyout.[5]

Personal income taxes may also have an effect on the value of the interest tax shields. Naturally, investors care about the amount of cash they earn on their investments after all income taxes are paid (both corporate and personal taxes). If the personal income taxes paid on interest from debt investments differ from the personal income taxes paid on earnings from equity investments (dividends and appreciation in value), then this different income tax treatment can affect the value of the company's interest tax shields. This issue is somewhat complicated because the tax laws are complex and not all investors face the same income tax rates. However, under the correct circumstances, personal income taxes can mitigate or eliminate the value of interest tax shields.[6]

As a result, the value created from financing is equal to the value of a company's interest tax shields plus the value of any subsidized financing minus the other expected costs that result from using non-equity financing. The current view held by most scholars, managers, and investors is that debt creates some value for a company if the company has a reasonably high probability of generating sufficient taxable income to capture the benefit of its interest tax shields and if the probability of bankruptcy is not too high.[7] In this chapter, we assume that the value from financing is equal to the value of a company's interest tax shields, (V_{ITS}). In other words, $V_{FIN} = V_{ITS}$. In effect, we ignore the other potential benefits and costs of debt financing, such as positive management incentives, the transaction costs of issuing debt, and the expected costs of financial distress and bankruptcy.

Valuation Key 5.1

If interest is tax deductible, a manager can potentially create value by financing the company with debt. Measuring the value from debt financing is potentially a more complex issue than merely discounting expected interest tax shields at the appropriate risk-adjusted discount rate. We must consider adjustments for the potential effects of personal income taxes, agency costs, and financial distress and bankruptcy, all of which can reduce the value created from debt financing.

---

[4] See Jensen and Meckling (1976) for an important discussion about the agency conflicts between managers, shareholders, and debtholders that result from our inability to write perfect contracts; Jensen M. C., and W. Meckling, "Theory of the Firm: Managerial Behavior, Agency Costs and Capital Structure," *Journal of Financial Economics* 3 (1976), pp. 305–360.

[5] See Jensen (1986); Jensen, M. C., "Agency Costs of Free Cash Flow, Corporate Finance, and Takeovers," *American Economic Review* 2 (1986), pp. 323–329.

[6] See Miller, M. H. "Debt and Taxes," *Journal of Finance* 32 (May 1977), pp. 261–276.

[7] See Rajan and Zingales (1995) and Miller (1989) for reviews of this literature; Rajan, R. G., and L. Zingales, "What Do We Know About Capital Structure? Some Evidence from International Data," *Journal of Finance* 50 (December 1995), pp. 1421–1460; Miller, M. H., "The Modigliani-Miller Propositions After Thirty Years," *Journal of Applied Corporate Finance* vol. 2, no, 1 (Spring 1989), pp. 6–18.

5.2 THE ADJUSTED PRESENT VALUE AND WEIGHTED AVERAGE COST OF CAPITAL VALUATION MODELS

Recall that the value of the firm is equal to the discounted value of the company's free cash flows (FCF). Since, conceptually, a company has an infinite life, we discount the company's cash flows through infinity using an appropriate risk-adjusted discount rate (r). We implement the infinite discounting of a company's cash flows by discounting the company's free cash flows for a finite period, then estimate its continuing (residual or terminal) value (CV) as of the end of the finite period and discount that continuing value back to the present. One way to measure the company's continuing value is with a free cash flow perpetuity formula. This formula, as taken from Chapter 1, is as follows:

LO2 Measure value using the adjusted present value and weighted average cost of capital valuation models

$$V_F = \sum_{t=1}^{\infty} \frac{FCF_t}{(1+r)^t} = \sum_{t=1}^{C} \frac{FCF_t}{(1+r)^t} + \frac{CV_{F,C}}{(1+r)^C} = \sum_{t=1}^{C} \frac{FCF_t}{(1+r)^t} + \frac{FCF_{C+1}}{(r-g)} \times \frac{1}{(1+r)^C}$$

The above formula is generic, for we have not yet filled in all the details regarding the discount rate. For example, if the company is entirely financed with equity, the formula would measure both the value of the firm and the value of the equity, for they would be the same. If the company's value changes as a result of using another type of financing such as debt or preferred stock, then we must adjust either the cash flows or the discount rate in the above DCF valuation model. We now turn to a discussion of the APV and WACC valuation models, both of which incorporate the value of interest tax shields in the value of the firm.

Adjusted Present Value (APV) Method

Recall that the value of the firm is equal to the sum of the value of the unlevered assets (V_{UA}) and the value from financing. For now, we assume that the value from financing is just due to the value of the interest tax shields (V_{ITS}). In the APV method, we measure these two components of the value of the firm separately. We measure the value of the unlevered assets, V_{UA}, by discounting the free cash flows at the cost of capital that reflects the risk of these assets, called the **unlevered cost of capital (r_{UA})** or **asset cost of capital**.

Then, to the value of the unlevered firm, we add the value of the company's interest tax shields (V_{ITS}), which is equal to the discounted value of the company's expected interest tax shields (ITS). The appropriate risk-adjusted discount rate for the interest tax shields (r_{ITS}) depends on a variety of factors, but for now, we assume that it is appropriate to discount interest tax shields at the unlevered cost of capital ($r_{ITS} = r_{UA}$). We defer a more detailed discussion of this topic to a later chapter, but we just note here that it is not uncommon to discount interest tax shields at the cost of debt. Using the assumption that we discount interest tax shields at the unlevered cost of capital, the formula for the APV method using the continuing value of the company's unlevered assets ($CV_{UA,C}$) and the continuing value of the interest tax shields ($CV_{ITS,C}$) as of the end of Year C appears in Equation 5.1.

$$V_F = \sum_{t=1}^{C} \frac{FCF_t}{(1+r_{UA})^t} + \frac{CV_{UA,C}}{(1+r_{UA})^C} + \sum_{t=1}^{C} \frac{ITS_t}{(1+r_{UA})^t} + \frac{CV_{ITS,C}}{(1+r_{UA})^C} \qquad (5.1)$$

Using a constant growth perpetuity formula for the continuing values, the equation becomes

$$V_F = \sum_{t=1}^{C} \frac{FCF_t}{(1+r_{UA})^t} + \frac{FCF_{C+1}}{(r_{UA}-g)} \times \frac{1}{(1+r_{UA})^C} + \sum_{t=1}^{C} \frac{ITS_t}{(1+r_{UA})^t} + \frac{ITS_{C+1}}{(r_{UA}-g)} \times \frac{1}{(1+r_{UA})^C} \qquad (5.2)$$

Valuation Key 5.2

The adjusted present value (APV) valuation method measures the value of the firm by adding the value created by financing to the value of the unlevered firm. The inputs into the APV valuation method are a company's free cash flows, its interest tax shields, the unlevered cost of capital, and the risk-adjusted discount rate for interest tax shields.

Weighted Average Cost of Capital (WACC) Method

In the WACC method, instead of measuring the value of the interest tax shields as a separate component of the value of the firm, we incorporate the value of a company's interest tax shields by adjusting the discount rate we use to discount the company's free cash flows. In other words, the WACC method measures the value of the unlevered firm and the value of the interest tax shields jointly. When we use the WACC method, we also discount the same expected unlevered free cash flows as in the APV method, but we discount these cash flows by the weighted average cost of capital rather than the unlevered cost of capital. If interest tax shields create value, the weighted average cost of capital is lower than the unlevered cost of capital. The formula for the WACC method that uses the continuing value of the company's levered assets ($CV_{F,C}$) appears in Equation 5.3.

$$V_F = \sum_{t=1}^{C} \frac{FCF_t}{(1 + r_{WACC})^t} + \frac{CV_{F,C}}{(1 + r_{WACC})^C} \tag{5.3}$$

Using a constant growth perpetuity formula for the continuing value, we get

$$V_F = \sum_{t=1}^{C} \frac{FCF_t}{(1 + r_{WACC})^t} + \frac{FCF_{C+1}}{(r_{WACC} - g)} \times \frac{1}{(1 + r_{WACC})^C} \tag{5.4}$$

The WACC method is sometimes called the adjusted cost of capital method because it "adjusts" the unlevered cost of capital downward to reflect the benefit of the interest tax shields. It is helpful to compare the WACC method in Equation 5.4 to the APV method in Equation 5.2. Both valuation methods discount the same unlevered free cash flows. The difference between the two methods is that the APV method adds the discounted value of the year-by-year interest tax shields to the discounted value of the unlevered free cash flows, whereas the WACC method embeds the value of the interest tax shields into the valuation through a lower discount rate (r_{WACC}). This is not a simple concept to understand immediately, but we will explain it at a big-picture level in this chapter and we will explain it in much more depth in a later chapter. For now, it is important to recognize that the WACC method embeds the value of interest tax shields by adjusting the discount rate.

Calculating the Weighted Average Cost of Capital

Since we embed the value created by the company's interest tax shields in the weighted average cost of capital, the weighted average cost of capital must be less than the unlevered cost of capital ($r_{WACC} < r_{UA}$)—if interest tax shields create value. The unlevered cost of capital (r_{UA}) is determined by the risk of the cash flows of the company's assets. Further, for now, we assume that $r_{ITS} = r_{UA}$. Recall the economic balance sheet. The returns generated on the company's assets must be allocated to the investors with claims on those assets (equity, r_E; debt, r_D; preferred, r_{PS}).

$$r_{UA} \times V_{UA} + r_{UA} \times V_{ITS} = r_{UA} \times V_F$$

$$r_{UA} \times V_F = r_D \times V_D + r_{PS} \times V_{PS} + r_E \times V_E$$

From the above formula, the return on the company's assets (r_{UA}) must be equal to the weighted average returns on the company's financing instruments (equity, debt, preferred) as measured by the market value weights in the capital structure.

$$r_{UA} = r_E \times \frac{V_E}{V_F} + r_D \times \frac{V_D}{V_F} + r_{PS} \times \frac{V_{PS}}{V_F} \tag{5.5}$$

The common way to measure a company's weighted average cost of capital is to measure the after-tax cost of capital of each of the company's securities (sources of financing) and calculate the weighted average of its after-tax costs of capital, using the proportion of the company (proportion of firm value, not book value) financed with each security. Since companies can deduct interest expense when calculating income taxes, the **after-tax debt cost of capital** is equal to the debt cost of capital, multiplied by one minus the corporate tax rate that is applicable to the interest deduction, $(1 - T_{INT}) \times r_D$. Note in the following expression that only the cost of debt is multiplied by 1 minus the company's appropriate tax rate, for payments to the common and preferred equityholders are not tax deductible for the corporation in most tax regimes.

$$r_{WACC} = r_E \times \frac{V_E}{V_F} + (1 - T_{INT}) \times r_D \times \frac{V_D}{V_F} + r_{PS} \times \frac{V_{PS}}{V_F} \qquad (5.6)$$

The difference between the weighted average cost of capital and the unlevered cost of capital ($r_{WACC} - r_{UA}$) is equal to the following (subtract Equation 5.5 from Equation 5.6):

$$r_{WACC} - r_{UA} = -T_{INT} \times r_D \times \frac{V_D}{V_F}$$

Thus, we see that the weighted average cost of capital is equal to the unlevered cost of capital, minus the tax savings ($T \times r_D$) from the proportion of the firm financed with debt (V_D/V_F). If the tax rate applicable to interest is zero or the firm uses no debt financing, then of course the weighted average cost of capital is just equal to the unlevered cost capital. Equation 5.7 shows why the adjusted cost of capital valuation method is another name for the weighted average cost of capital valuation method.

$$r_{WACC} = r_{UA} - T_{INT} \times r_D \times \frac{V_D}{V_F} \qquad (5.7)$$

Note that in this chapter, we assume that the debt cost of capital is equal to the promised yield on the debt and that the expected interest deduction is equal to the yield on the debt multiplied by the value of the debt. In a later chapter, we discuss the complications that arise when this is not the case.

Valuation Key 5.3

The weighted average cost of capital (WACC) method discounts the unlevered free cash flows of the firm at the weighted average cost of capital. This method incorporates the value of the interest tax shields in the valuation by using a discount rate that is lower than the unlevered cost of capital (when interest tax shields create value).

5.3 THE LINK BETWEEN THE UNLEVERED, EQUITY, DEBT, AND PREFERRED STOCK COSTS OF CAPITAL

We know that the risk of a company's assets determines the unlevered cost of capital. We also know that the return on the company's assets is allocated to the investors who finance the company (see Equation 5.5). The risk of the company's equity, however, depends on the risk of the company's assets—operating risk—and the risk from the company using non-equity financing—financial leverage risk. We can rewrite Equation 5.5 to measure the equity cost of capital by isolating the equity cost of capital on the left-hand-side of Equation 5.5.

$$r_E = r_{UA} \times \left(1 + \frac{V_D}{V_E} + \frac{V_{PS}}{V_E}\right) - r_D \times \frac{V_D}{V_E} - r_{PS} \times \frac{V_{PS}}{V_E}$$

We can gain some of the basic intuition that underlies the above formula by examining each of its components. The return required by equityholders is equal to the unlevered cost of capital, multiplied by a leverage factor from which we subtract an adjustment for the return paid to the non-equity security holders. We can also rearrange the terms in the above formula to provide another equation for the equity cost of capital:

$$r_E = r_{UA} + (r_{UA} - r_D) \times \frac{V_D}{V_E} + (r_{UA} - r_{PS}) \times \frac{V_{PS}}{V_E} \qquad (5.8)$$

This form of the formula shows that a company's equity cost of capital is equal to its unlevered cost of capital, which reflects the company's operating risk, plus a premium to reflect the risk from financial leverage—one factor due to debt in the capital structure and another due to preferred. We do not show time subscripts in Equation 5.8 because each of the terms in this formula has the same time subscript. In other words, we measure each input at the same point in time. Just as for the weighted average cost of capital, we must remember that the equity cost of capital and the variables to the right of the equal sign need not be constant over time. The equity cost of capital changes if we expect the company's business risk or financial risk to change or if we expect economy-wide shifts in required rates of return.[8]

Valuation Key 5.4

Since equityholders are the residual claimants for a company's assets, a company's equity cost of capital is always greater than or equal to its unlevered cost of capital. If a company only issues equity, then its equity cost of capital will be equal to its unlevered cost of capital. If a company issues equity and non-equity securities, then its equity cost of capital will be equal to its unlevered cost of capital plus a premium related to each non-equity security it uses.

5.4 THE ADJUSTED PRESENT VALUE AND WEIGHTED AVERAGE COST OF CAPITAL METHODS ARE NOT SUBSTITUTES

The APV and WACC methods are not substitutes. Depending on the information available and the valuation assumptions you make, only one of the two methods will be an appropriate starting point for a particular valuation analysis. As we will later show, if you already know all of the information you need to use both the APV and WACC valuation methods, you will already know the value of the firm, and you will not even need to conduct a valuation analysis. Even though only one method is technically the correct starting point, the degree of error that results from starting with the wrong method depends on the degree to which the assumptions underpinning that valuation method are violated.

We can understand why these methods are not substitutes by comparing the inputs we need to implement each one. For the APV method, we need to measure the company's free cash flows, interest tax shields, and unlevered cost of capital. To calculate interest tax shields, we need to know the company's debt cost of capital, the tax rate for the interest tax shields, and the amount of debt (dollar magnitude) for each future year. For the WACC method, we need to know the free cash flows and the weighted average cost of capital. To calculate the weighted average cost of capital, we need to know the equity cost of capital, the debt cost of capital, the tax rate, the cost of preferred stock, and the company's capital structure strategy—as measured by the proportion of the firm financed with each security (measured in terms of market values). We do not need to know the value of the individual securities; we only need to know the company's target capital structure or capital structure strategy, stated as proportions of the firm financed with each of the securities. If we knew the values of each of the individual securities for the company, our task would be over. We would not need to value the firm, for we would already know it (since $V_F = V_D + V_{PS} + V_E$). A company might not have a formal strategy or even a plan for financing itself. Still, we must make an assumption about how the company will finance itself when we value it, which we refer to as the company's capital structure strategy even though it might not be a formal strategy.

The key difference between the inputs for the two methods is the type of information we know about the company's capital structure. For the APV method, we need to know the actual magnitude (dollar or other currency amount) of the debt, and for the WACC method, we need to know the proportion (stated in terms of market values) of the company financed with each type of security. When valuing a company, it is unlikely for us to know both the amount of debt and proportion of debt at the same time, for then, we would implicitly know the value of the firm. For example, if you know that a company has $1,000 in debt and that the company always finances itself with 25% debt, you implicitly know that the value of the firm is $4,000 ($4,000 = $1,000/0.25).

The primary factor for choosing either the APV or WACC valuation method is the information available on, or the assumptions made, about the company's capital structure. If you assume the company has a target capital structure strategy stated in terms of the proportion of the company financed with each

---

[8] Equation 5.8 is also the correct formula for calculating the equity cost of capital if interest is not tax deductible. We will discuss this issue in detail in a later chapter of the book.

type of security, then use the WACC valuation method. On the other hand, if you assume the company has a capital structure strategy stated in terms of specified dollar amounts of the company financed with debt securities at future points in time (that is you have forecasts of the magnitude of the debt in each future period), then use the APV valuation method. It is also possible to switch from the APV valuation method to the WACC valuation method within a given valuation if we anticipate the company will switch its capital structure strategy from known magnitudes of the debt outstanding to a constant proportion of debt outstanding to firm value.

Valuation Key 5.5

The adjusted present value and weighted average cost of capital valuation methods are not substitutes. The key factor for choosing between the two methods is the information available on or the assumptions made about the company's capital structure. You should use the method that best fits the information or assumptions available. Use the WACC method if the company has a target capital structure strategy stated in terms of the proportion of the company financed with non-equity securities; otherwise, use the APV method when you have forecasts of the dollar magnitude of the debt in future periods.

In practice, managers, analysts, and investors use the WACC valuation method most often and assume that the discount rate is constant. They assume that the company will adopt a target capital structure stated in terms of the proportion of the company financed with non-equity securities. Such an assumption is not appropriate if a company will have significant changes in its capital structure over time (for example, companies that have just undergone a highly leveraged transaction, such as an LBO or a debt recapitalization) or if it intends to pay down its debt according to a specified schedule. In many of these cases, the companies are operating at a capital structure far different from the industry norm and often intend to bring their capital structures back in line with their industry counterparts over time. The WACC method will also not be the preferred method if a company does not have sufficient taxable income to capture the benefits of its interest tax shields when it pays the interest (for example, startup companies incurring losses in their early years or companies with significant net operating loss carryforwards). In Chapter 3, we discussed the complexity of determining the timing and amount of the interest tax shields for companies with net operating loss carryforwards. In these situations, the APV valuation method is more appropriate to use.

5.5 THE ANDY ALPER COMPANY

We use the Andy Alper Company (Alper) to illustrate the APV and WACC valuation methods. Mr. Alper started his company at the end of Year 0 by investing $3,000, issuing $1,000 of preferred stock (with a cost of capital of 12%), and borrowing $4,000 from the bank (with a cost of capital of 10%). At the end of Year 0, Mr. Alper purchased two machines, paying $1,000 for one machine and $3,000 for the other. He also invested $3,000 in operating working capital (for example, inventory). Mr. Alper believes he needs to keep the remaining $1,000 in cash in order to operate the business (required cash). Mr. Alper believes the company's revenues, free cash flows, and interest tax shields will grow at 5% per year in perpetuity. In addition, all balance sheet items will increase by the 5% growth rate in every year, including the amount of debt and preferred financing. Free cash flow forecasts and summary financial statements for Year +1 appear in Exhibit 5.3. Based on an analysis of publicly traded comparable companies, the appropriate unlevered cost of capital for Alper is 15%. Alper faces a 40% corporate tax rate.

Which Valuation Method Do We Use to Value Andy Alper Company?

Deciding on what valuation method to use depends on the information we have available. For Alper, we know its capital structure in terms of the amount of capital issued, and we know the cost of capital for its debt and preferred stock. We also know its unlevered cost of capital and interest tax shield (see Exhibit 5.3). We do not, however, know Alper's capital structure ratios, for the relevant capital structure ratios are based on market values—not book values—and we do not know the value of the company. As such, we have sufficient information to value Alper using the APV method but not the WACC method.

EXHIBIT 5.3 Andy Alper Company's Financial Statement and Free Cash Flow Forecasts

Balance Sheet Forecast	Actual Year 0	Forecast Year +1
Cash.	$1,000	$ 1,050
Net operating working capital	3,000	3,150
Net property, plant, and equipment	4,000	4,200
Total assets.	$8,000	$ 8,400
Debt (10% interest rate)	$4,000	$ 4,200
Preferred stock (12% dividend rate).	1,000	1,050
Common equity	3,000	3,150
Total liabilities and equities.	$8,000	$ 8,400

Income Statement Forecast	Forecast Year +1
Revenue	$10,000
Depreciation expense.	–2,000
Operating expenses	–5,933
Earnings before interest and taxes.	$ 2,067
Interest expense.	–400
Earnings before tax	$ 1,667
Income taxes (40% tax rate)	–667
Earnings after tax	$ 1,000
Preferred stock dividends	–120
Earnings available to equity	$ 880

Free Cash Flow Schedule	Forecast Year +1
Earnings before interest and taxes.	$2,067
Income taxes (40% tax rate, T_{INT}).	–827
Unlevered earnings after tax	$1,240
Depreciation.	2,000
Change in required cash	–50
Change in net working capital	–150
Capital expenditures	–2,200
Unlevered free cash flow (FCF)	$ 840
Interest paid in cash ($r_D \times V_{D,0}$)	–400
Interest tax shield ($T_{INT} \times r_D \times V_{D,0}$)	160
Preferred stock dividend ($r_{PS} \times V_{PS,0}$)	–120
Change in debt ($V_{D,0} \times g$)	200
Change in preferred stock ($V_{PS,0} \times g$)	50
Equity free cash flow (EFCF)	$ 730
Common dividends	–730
Change in common equity	0
Change in required cash	50
Change in cash balance.	$ 50

Adjusted Present Value Valuation

Since Mr. Alper expects all key dimensions of the business to grow at 5% in perpetuity, we can use the constant-growth perpetuity formula to measure the value of Alper using the APV method. Recall, in this chapter, we assume that the appropriate risk adjusted discount rate for the interest tax shields is the unlevered cost of capital (e.g., $r_{ITS} = r_{UA}$). The APV valuation of Alper is as follows, assuming a constant growth perpetuity for both the free cash flows and interest tax shields.

$$V_{F,0} = \frac{FCF_1}{r_{UA} - g} + \frac{ITS_1}{r_{UA} - g}$$

$$= \frac{\$840}{0.15 - 0.05} + \frac{\$160}{0.15 - 0.05}$$

$$= \$8,400 + \$1,600 = \$10,000$$

The value of the unlevered firm is $8,400, and the value of the interest tax shields is $1,600, yielding a total firm value of $10,000. Recall that the investors initially invested $8,000. Since the value of the firm is $10,000, the valuation implies that management will create $2,000 in value by implementing its business strategy and plan.

Capital Structure Ratios, Equity Cost of Capital, and Weighted Average Cost of Capital Implicit in the Adjusted Present Value Valuation of Andy Alper Company

Now that we know Alper's value, we can measure the capital structure ratios implicit in our valuation, which we show in Exhibit 5.4. We can use these capital structure ratios and other information we know from above to measure Alper's value using the WACC method. While this calculation is redundant, it illustrates that, given the same underlying inputs, both methods result in the same valuation.

EXHIBIT 5.4 Andy Alper Company's Implicit Capital Structure Ratios			
Valuation and Capital Structure Ratios	**Year 0**	**to V_F**	**to V_E**
Value of the firm	$10,000		
Value of the debt	4,000	40.0%	80.0%
Value of the preferred	1,000	10.0%	20.0%
Value of the equity	$ 5,000	50.0%	

Although we do not know Alper's equity cost of capital for this capital structure, we can calculate the weighted average cost of capital using Equation 5.7.

$$r_{WACC} = r_{UA} - T_{INT} \times r_D \times \frac{V_D}{V_F}$$

$$= 0.15 - 0.4 \times 0.1 \times 0.4 = 0.134$$

Alternatively, we could use the more common approach and first calculate Alper's equity cost of capital using Equation 5.8, and then calculate its weighted average cost of capital using Equation 5.6.

$$r_E = r_{UA} + (r_{UA} - r_D) \times \frac{V_D}{V_E} + (r_{UA} - r_{PS}) \times \frac{V_{PS}}{V_E}$$

$$= 0.15 + (0.15 - 0.1) \times 0.8 + (0.15 - 0.12) \times 0.2 = 0.196$$

$$r_{WACC} = r_E \times \frac{V_E}{V_F} + (1 - T_{INT}) \times r_D \times \frac{V_D}{V_F} + r_{PS} \times \frac{V_{PS}}{V_F}$$

$$= 0.196 \times 0.5 + (1 - 0.4) \times 0.1 \times 0.4 + 0.12 \times 0.1 = 0.134$$

We can measure Alper's value using the weighted average cost of capital method, which results in the same $10,000 valuation for Alper. Thus, the weighted average cost of capital valuation of Alper replicates the adjusted present value valuation.

$$V_{F,0} = \frac{FCF_1}{r_{WACC} - g} = \frac{\$840}{0.134 - 0.05} = \$10,000$$

This example illustrates two important points. First, the APV and WACC valuation methods are not substitutes for each other. Rather, we use the method that best fits the available information or assumption we are making about the company's capital structure strategy. Second, once we measure the value of the firm using one method, we can get the capital structure information we need to use the other method to value the firm, which will result in the same valuation.

REVIEW EXERCISE 5.1

The Stuart Essig Perpetuity Company—Part 1

The Stuart Essig Company has an unlevered cost of capital of 12% and an income tax rate of 40%. The company finances itself with 1/3 debt, which has a cost of capital equal to 8%; 1/6 preferred stock, which has a cost of capital of 8.5%; and the remainder with common equity. The company expects its unlevered free cash flows to remain constant in perpetuity. Assume that interest tax shields should be valued at the unlevered cost of capital and that the company holds no excess cash nor any other excess assets. Use this information and the information that follows to value the Stuart Essig Company (firm and equity) as of the end of Year 0 using the WACC valuation method.

Income Statement Forecast	Year 1
Revenue	$180,000
Depreciation expense	−25,000
Operating expenses	−84,000
Earnings before interest and taxes	$ 71,000

Asset Forecast	Year 1
Cash	$ 4,000
Net operating working capital	25,000
Net property, plant, and equipment	120,000
Total assets	$149,000

Unlevered Free Cash Flow Forecast	Year 1
Earnings before interest and taxes	$71,000
Income taxes	−28,400
Unlevered earnings after tax	$42,600
Depreciation expense (non-cash expenses)	25,000
Change in required cash	0
Change in net working capital	0
Capital expenditures	−25,000
Unlevered free cash flows	$42,600

Solution on page 208.

Alternative Capital Structure Assumption for the Andy Alper Company

Instead of financing the Alper Company with $3,000 of cash, $1,000 of preferred stock, and $4,000 of debt at the end of Year 0, assume Mr. Alper is going to finance the company with 60% debt financing, 10% preferred stock financing, and 30% equity financing. For simplicity in this example, we assume that the cost of debt and the cost of preferred capital stay the same at 10% and 12% respectively despite the more highly levered capital structure. Also, assume that Mr. Alper will continually refinance the company in order to maintain those capital structure ratios. Under this capital structure strategy, the dollar amount of debt to be issued cannot be calculated until the value of the firm is calculated.

Given this alternative capital structure strategy, we do not have sufficient information to value Alper using the APV method because we do not know how much debt Alper will issue; we only know that Alper will issue debt in an amount equal to 60% of the value of the firm. Thus, based on this information, the WACC valuation method is the method we would use. First, we calculate Alper's equity cost of capital for this capital structure using Equation 5.8, and then we calculate its weighted average cost of capital using Equation 5.6:

$$r_E = r_{UA} + (r_{UA} - r_D) \times \frac{V_D}{V_E} + (r_{UA} - r_{PS}) \times \frac{V_{PS}}{V_E}$$

$$= 0.15 + (0.15 - 0.1) \times \frac{0.6}{0.3} + (0.15 - 0.12) \times \frac{0.1}{0.3} = 0.26$$

$$r_{WACC} = r_E \times \frac{V_E}{V_F} + (1 - T_{INT}) \times r_D \times \frac{V_D}{V_F} + r_{PS} \times \frac{V_{PS}}{V_F}$$

$$= 0.26 \times 0.3 + (1 - 0.4) \times 0.1 \times 0.6 + 0.12 \times 0.1 = 0.126$$

Notice that the increase in leverage (from 40% to 60% debt) caused the equity cost of capital to rise from 0.196 to 0.26, and the weighted average cost of capital to decline from 0.134 to 0.126. We can (again) measure Alper's value using the weighted average cost of capital method, which results in a valuation for Alper of $11,052.63.

$$V_{F,0} = \frac{FCF_1}{r_{WACC} - g} = \frac{\$840}{0.126 - 0.05} = \$11,052.63$$

The value of the firm increases from $10,000 to $11,053 (an increase of $1,053 or about 11%). In Exhibit 5.5, we show Alper's alternative capital structure ratios and the value of Alper's various securities based on the above valuation. Why does Alper's value increase? Alper's unlevered free cash flows and unlevered cost of capital are not affected by the choice of capital structure; thus, the value of the unlevered firm is unchanged. The value of the firm increases, however, because of an increase in the value of Alper's interest tax shields as a result of additional debt financing ($6,632 versus $4,000 initially, and then both growing at 5%). Note that we are assuming that despite the increase in leverage, the firm does not bear higher agency costs or costs of financial distress or bankruptcy that would require an adjustment to value. In Exhibit 5.5, we show part of the free cash flow schedule for both the original capital structure and the alternative capital structure.

EXHIBIT 5.5	Andy Alper Company's Alternative Capital Structure and Resulting Free Cash Flow Schedule

Valuation and Capital Structure Ratios	Year 0	to V_F	to V_E
Value of the firm	$11,053		
Value of the debt	6,632	60.0%	200.0%
Value of the preferred.	1,105	10.0%	33.3%
Value of the equity	$ 3,316	30.0%	

	Capital Structure		
Free Cash Flow Schedule	Original Year +1	Alternative Year +1	Difference
Unlevered free cash flow (FCF)	$ 840	$ 840	$0
Interest paid in cash ($r_D \times V_{D,0}$)	−400	−663	−263
Interest tax shield ($T_{INT} \times r_D \times V_{D,0}$)	160	265	105
Preferred stock dividend ($r_{PS} \times V_{PS,0}$)	−120	−133	−13
Change in debt ($V_{D,0} \times g$)	200	332	132
Change in preferred stock ($V_{PS,0} \times g$)	50	55	5
Equity free cash flow (EFCF)	$ 730	$ 696	$ −34
Common dividends	−730	−696	34
Change in common equity.	0	0	0
Change in required cash	50	50	0
Change in cash balance.	$ 50	$ 50	$ 0

We see the increase in interest expense and interest tax shield from the increase in the amount of debt. The $2,632 increase in debt results in a $263 increase in interest ($263 = $2,632 \times 0.1$) and a $105 increase in the interest tax shield ($105 = 263×0.4). The difference in the value of the interest tax shields is equal to $1,053 ($1,053 = $105/(0.15 − 0.05)$), which is equal to the difference in the value of the firm ($1,053 = $11,053 − $10,000$). Given our WACC valuation, we now know Alper's interest tax shields under this new capital structure strategy and we can measure (again) Alper's value using the APV valuation method. The adjusted present value valuation is able to replicate the weighted average cost of capital valuation.

$$V_{F,0} = \frac{FCF_1}{r_{UA} - g} + \frac{ITS_1}{r_{UA} - g}$$

$$= \frac{\$840}{0.15 - 0.05} + \frac{\$265}{0.15 - 0.05}$$

$$= \$8,400 + \$2,653 = \$11,053$$

REVIEW EXERCISE 5.2

The Stuart Essig Perpetuity Company—Part 2

Use the information in and solution for Review Exercise 5.1 to value the Stuart Essig Company (firm and equity) using the APV valuation method.

Solution on page 208.

5.6 THE DISCOUNTED EQUITY FREE CASH FLOW VALUATION METHOD

LO3 Measure value using the equity free cash flow and dividend valuation models

We can measure the value of the equity by using either the APV or the WACC valuation methods to measure the value of the firm and then subtracting the value of the non-equity claims to value the equity. Alternatively, we can measure the value of the equity directly using the Equity DCF valuation method.

As we discuss below, properly using the Equity DCF valuation method can sometimes be complex. We discuss both of these approaches to measuring the value of the equity in this section of the chapter.

Valuing Common Equity by First Measuring the Value of the Firm

Common equityholders are the residual claimants of a company; that is, equityholders get what is left over when all other claims against the company's assets are satisfied. Using our economic balance sheet, we can express the value of the firm's equity as the value of the firm minus the value of each of the non-equity claims. For a company with debt, V_D, preferred stock, V_{PS}, and any other claims such as warrants and options, V_{OTHER}, this calculation is

$$V_E = V_F - V_D - V_{PS} - V_{OTHER} \qquad (5.9)$$

Alternatively, we can use either the Equity DCF or Dividend DCF method to value a company's equity value directly. In the Equity DCF method we discount the cash flows the company has available to pay its equityholders (**equity free cash flows**) at the equity cost of capital. Equity free cash flows are equal to a company's unlevered free cash flows adjusted for all after-tax cash flows paid to or received from all non-equity claimholders. We can also discount a company's expected dividend payments at the equity cost of capital. In general, a company's dividends typically do not equal its equity free cash flows. Companies usually adopt a dividend policy that smoothes dividends so that they are not equal to equity free cash flows period by period. In the long run, however, the sum of a company's dividends must be equal to the sum of its equity free cash flows (assuming no share repurchases). Thus, as long as the company earns the equity cost of capital on the difference between its dividends and equity free cash flows, these two valuation methods result in the same equity value.

For reasons that will become apparent later, we generally do not recommend using the Equity DCF or the Dividend DCF valuation methods. In most circumstances, we recommend valuing the company using either the APV or WACC valuation methods and then measuring the value of the equity by subtracting the value of the non-equity securities from the value of the firm.

Valuing the Equity Directly Using the Equity Discounted Cash Flow Method

The formula used in the Equity DCF valuation method is similar to the formula used in the WACC method. The differences between the two methods are in the calculations of the relevant cash flows and discount rate. In the WACC method, we discount the unlevered free cash flows at the weighted average cost of capital to measure the value of the firm. In the Equity DCF method, we discount the equity free cash flows at the equity cost of capital. The general formula for the Equity DCF method is

$$V_E = \sum_{t=1}^{\infty} \frac{EFCF_t}{(1 + r_E)^t}$$

If we construct detailed forecasts for the company for C years and measure the continuing value of the equity ($CV_{E,C}$) as of the end of Year C, the above formula becomes

$$V_E = \sum_{t=1}^{C} \frac{EFCF_t}{(1 + r_E)^t} + \frac{CV_{E,C}}{(1 + r_E)^C} \qquad (5.10)$$

If we use the constant growth perpetuity method to measure the continuing value, the above formula becomes

$$V_E = \sum_{t=1}^{C} \frac{EFCF_t}{(1 + r_E)^t} + \frac{EFCF_{C+1}}{(r_E - g)} \times \frac{1}{(1 + r_E)^C} \qquad (5.11)$$

Valuation Key 5.6

We can measure the value of a company's equity by valuing the firm using either the APV or WACC valuation methods and then subtracting the value of the company's non-equity claims. An alternative approach is to value the company's equity directly using the Equity DCF method, which discounts the company's equity free cash flows at the equity cost of capital.

Equity Discounted Cash Flow Model for the Andy Alper Company

We can use Equation 5.11 to measure the value of the equity using the Equity DCF method. We have sufficient information to value Alper Company's equity regardless of which capital structure strategy we use (original or alternative), given our previous valuations using the APV method (original capital structure) and WACC method (alternative capital structure).

Original Capital Structure Strategy.   Since we know the dollar amount of debt and preferred stock financing that Alper plans to use in its original capital structure strategy, we can measure its equity free cash flows directly (see Exhibit 5.3). However, we did not have sufficient information to measure Alper's equity cost of capital until we used the APV method to calculate the value of the firm so we could measure its capital structure ratios. Once we know Alper's equity cost of capital (19.6%, calculated previously), we can use Equation 5.11 to measure the value of Alper's equity directly (which agrees with the equity valuation in Exhibit 5.4):

$$V_E = \frac{EFCF_1}{(r_E - g)} = \frac{\$730}{0.196 - 0.05} = \$5,000$$

Alternative Capital Structure Strategy.   We know the capital structure ratios, and we can measure the equity cost of capital using the information we were given about the alternative capital structure strategy (60% debt, 10% preferred stock, and 30% equity). However, we did not have sufficient information to measure Alper's equity free cash flows until we used the WACC method to calculate Alper's value and measure the amount of debt and preferred stock it would have in its capital structure (see Exhibit 5.5). Once we know the dollar amounts of the capital structure, we can use the equity free cash flows from Exhibit 5.5 and again use Equation 5.11 to measure the value of Alper's equity directly (which agrees with the equity valuation in Exhibit 5.5):

$$V_E = \frac{EFCF_1}{(r_E - g)} = \frac{\$696.32}{0.26 - 0.05} = \$3,316$$

Complexities and Limitations of the Equity Discounted Cash Flow Method

To use the Equity DCF method, we need to know both the equity cost of capital and the equity free cash flows. Since a company's equity cost of capital changes with the amount of financial leverage a company uses, we need to know the company's capital structure ratios (e.g., debt to firm value) in each year. To measure a company's equity free cash flows, however, we need to know the company's after-tax interest expense and any other payments to and from non-equity security holders. That means that we need to know both a company's capital structure ratios and the amount of each of its non-equity securities issued, which of course means that we already know the value of the firm.

If we want to use the Equity DCF method, we have two ways to address this problem. In the first approach, we measure the value of the firm in order to then measure both the company's capital structure ratios and the amount of debt it has outstanding. To use this approach, we measure the value of the firm every year in order to have sufficient information to measure both inputs of the Equity DCF valuation method—equity free cash flows and equity cost of capital—for every year. Once we measure both the equity free cash flows and the equity cost of capital for every year, we can use the Equity DCF method. Note that we did not have to do this every year explicitly in the Alper example. The reason is that we assumed that everything would grow at 5% per year; thus, the debt and preferred stock grow by 5% per year, as do the interest tax shields and unlevered cash flows. As a consequence, the capital structure ratios stay constant over time.

Alternatively, we can begin at our continuing value date and iteratively solve for the equity free cash flows and equity cost of capital that are consistent with our assumptions. We continue this process backward until we arrive at the value of the equity as of the valuation date.

Note that neither the APV nor WACC valuation method requires knowledge of both the amount and the proportion of the firm financed with each non-equity security. The APV method requires forecasts of debt but not the proportion of the company financed by each non-equity security. The WACC method requires forecasts of the proportion of the company financed with each non-equity security but not the amount of debt or other non-equity securities. The Equity DCF method, however, requires knowledge of both, which is why it is not usually the best starting point for a valuation analysis. Why, then, would we bother to use the Equity DCF method if we already know the value of the firm and equity from the WACC or APV method? Truthfully, we probably would not use it in most circumstances except as a consistency check for the other DCF methods.

From a practical perspective, if the forecasts of the amounts of the non-equity securities are not too different from the amounts that would be needed to maintain the company's target capital structure, the difference in the equity value for a company between the Equity DCF and the APV- or WACC-based methods will be small. The issue, of course, is how to verify that they are not too different. In some situations, however, using the Equity DCF method as the starting point makes sense. For example, the Equity DCF method is often used for financial institutions, which have very little equity. If a company has very little equity, any inaccuracy in our valuation of the firm will likely translate into an inaccuracy in the value of the equity. Further, if there are a lot of non-equity claims, and if there is some uncertainty about their value, the value of the equity may be inaccurate due to the measurement error in the value of the non-equity claims—even if the value of the firm is completely appropriate. Thus, in such situations, any inaccuracy resulting from using the Equity DCF method might be less than the inaccuracy resulting from using either the WACC or APV valuation methods.

Valuation Key 5.7

Although we can measure the value of a company's equity by discounting the company's equity free cash flows at its equity cost of capital, this is not typically the best starting point in a valuation. Usually, the best starting point for a valuation is to use either the APV or the WACC valuation method to value the firm and then subtracting the value of the company's non-equity claims in order to measure the value of its equity.

Assumption About Distributing Equity Free Cash Flows to Equityholders

In the Equity DCF valuation method, we discount equity free cash flows at the equity cost of capital. For positive equity free cash flows, we assume either that the company distributes these cash flows to equityholders or, if the company retains them, that the company invests the equity free cash flows in zero net present value investments. In addition, if the equity free cash flows are invested in zero net present value projects, these investments neither change the value of the firm nor the equity, so we can ignore them. In general, it is easier to assume that the equity free cash flows are distributed. The most common form of a cash distribution to equityholders is a dividend; alternatively, the company could repurchase stock at its current market price.[9] For negative equity free cash flows, we implicitly assume that the equityholders are making additional cash investments in the company and that the new shares are sold to equity investors at their fair market value at the time of sale.

REVIEW EXERCISE 5.3

The Stuart Essig Perpetuity Company—Part 3

Use the information in and solutions to Review Exercises 5.1 and 5.2 to measure the company's equity free cash flow in Year 1; afterward, value Stuart Essig Company's equity by discounting the equity free cash flows at the equity cost of capital.

Solution on page 209.

[9] For a detailed review of the academic literature on how companies pay out cash to shareholders, see, Franklin, Allen, and Roni Michaely, "Payout Policy," in George Constantinides, Milton Harris, and Rene Stulz, eds., *Handbook of Economics and Finance* North-Holland Publishing (2003), pp. 337–429.

5.7 THE DISCOUNTED DIVIDEND VALUATION MODEL

The dividend discounted cash flow (Dividend DCF) valuation method is similar to the Equity DCF valuation method. In fact, if expected dividend distributions equal expected equity free cash flows, the two methods are identical. We know, however, that companies do not usually declare dividends equal to equity free cash flows; rather, companies tend to smooth dividend distributions.[10] Companies have other ways to distribute cash to their shareholders that can have certain advantages, such as share repurchases.

Valuation in Practice 5.1

Apple Inc. Decides to Distribute Cash to Shareholders On March 20, 2012, Apple Inc.'s (Apple) CEO Tim Cook announced that the company would begin to pay dividends and buy back shares. As of December 31, 2011, Apple had close to $100 billion in cash and marketable securities, the largest cash stockpile of any non-financial U.S. corporation at the time. Former CEO Steve Jobs had resisted returning cash to shareholders, arguing that the company needed it for future investments. Apple announced that over the next three years the dividends and share repurchase program would return $45 billion in cash to shareholders. Apple also indicated that approximately $64 billion of its cash holdings was overseas and that Apple would not be repatriating that cash back to the United States to make the cash payouts because of the U.S. taxes that would then be owed on that income. While Apple's announcement is certainly significant, this is not the largest *one-time* payout by a company. On December 2, 2004, Microsoft Corporation (Microsoft) paid a one-time special dividend of $32 billion—the biggest cash dividend in history.

Sources: Vascellaro, J., "Apple Pads Investor Wallets," *Wall Street Journal* (March 20, 2012), p. A1; and Oster, C., "Microsoft's $32 Billion Payout Sparks a New Interest in Dividends," *Wall Street Journal* (July 22, 2004), p. D2.

The formula for the Dividend DCF method is the same as the formula for the Equity DCF valuation method, except that we replace equity free cash flows with dividends (DIV). The general formula for the Dividend DCF method is

$$V_E = \frac{DIV_1}{(1 + r_E)^1} + \frac{DIV_2}{(1 + r_E)^2} + \dots + \frac{DIV_\infty}{(1 + r_E)^\infty} = \sum_{t=1}^{\infty} \frac{DIV_t}{(1 + r_E)^t}$$

If we construct detailed forecasts for the company for C years and measure the continuing value of the equity ($CV_{E,C}$) as of the end of Year C, the above formula becomes

$$V_E = \sum_{t=1}^{C} \frac{DIV_t}{(1 + r_E)^t} + \frac{CV_{E,C}}{(1 + r_E)^C} \tag{5.12}$$

Even though the Dividend DCF and Equity DCF valuation methods are likely to use different expected cash flows to value a particular company's equity (dividends versus equity free cash flows), the two methods can still arrive at the same value. The key assumption that equates the two valuation methods is that whatever the company does with the difference between equity free cash flows and dividends, it does not change the risk of the equity nor change the value of the equity or the firm. If the company's equity free cash flow is greater than its dividend distribution, the company invests in zero net present value projects that neither change the value and risk of the company nor its equity. If the company's equity free cash flow is less than its dividend distribution, the company raises additional equity capital that neither changes the value and risk of the company nor its equity. If this assumption is met, then the discount rate—the equity cost of capital—and the equity valuation are the same for the two methods. The Dividend DCF method has the same limitations as the Equity DCF method.

---

[10] See Lintner, John, "Distribution of Incomes of Corporations Among Dividends, Retained Earnings, and Taxes," *American Economic Review*, vol. 46, no. 2 (1956), pp. 97–113; and Fama, Eugene F., and Harvey Babiak, "Dividend Policy: An Empirical Analysis," *Journal of the American Statistical Association* vol. 63, no. 324 (1968), pp. 1132–1161.

5.8 IMPLEMENTATION DETAILS

LO4 Adjust the implementation of these valuation models for specific circumstances

We will discuss various implementation specifics in this section. We will begin with a discussion on the implicit assumption made in DCF valuation models about current and non-current operating liabilities. We will then discuss the way inflation should affect the DCF valuation model. Afterward, we will discuss the concept of expected free cash flows and the concept of risk-adjusted discount rates. Last, we will discuss the misuse of what we call "**fudge factors**," which result when someone arbitrarily adjusts the discount rate for any uncertainty that should only affect the calculation of expected free cash flows and not the risk-adjusted discount rate.

The Value of the Firm Is Net of Its Current Non-Interest-Bearing Operating Liabilities

In every DCF-based valuation, the value of the firm that we measure is the value of the company's assets (including growth opportunities) net of its non-interest-bearing operating liabilities. In other words, the value of the company's non-interest-bearing operating liabilities is already subtracted out when we value the firm using either DCF valuation method. Thus, the value of the firm includes the value of all interest-bearing debt, preferred stock, common equity, and any options or warrants issued by the firm; however, it excludes non-interest-bearing operating liabilities.

For example, suppose that you value a firm using a DCF valuation method and find that the value of the firm is $100 million with $30 million of debt and $5 million of accounts payable. The $100 million firm value represents the value of the company net of its $5 million in accounts payable. The value of the equity is $70 million ($70 = $100 − $30). If the company sells its assets, and if the buyer does not assume the company's non-interest-bearing operating liabilities, then the value of the firm should be adjusted to reflect the netting of the non-interest-bearing operating liabilities. In other words, if the company sells the assets but retains all of the liabilities, including accounts payable, the value of the company's assets will equal $105 million ($105 = $100 + $5). If in selling the assets, the purchaser agrees to assume the accounts payable, the purchase price would be $100 million. If the purchaser assumes both the accounts payable and the debt, the purchase price would be $70 million.

The reason we do not treat non-interest-bearing operating liabilities like debt is that we generally do not know their implicit financing charge; hence, we cannot easily treat them like interest-bearing debt. Suppliers of goods and services typically provide a grace period in which invoices can be paid without interest; therefore, any implicit financing charge is embedded in the cost of the good or service. Thus, when the entire cost is charged to various operating expenses, it reduces a company's EBIT that, in turn, reduces a company's free cash flows. In the end, the entire amount is treated as an operating activity, which reduces the value of the firm. As such, non-interest-bearing operating liabilities have already been netted out in valuing the firm.

Right now, the important point to understand is that the value of the firm as measured by the DCF methods is net of its non-interest-bearing operating liabilities. Later, we will see that there will be times when we can choose to treat some items as either operating activities or financing activities, and our choice will impact what the value of the firm will encompass but not affect the value of the equity. Before leaving this topic, there is one more thing that we should discuss; if we were liquidating a firm, things would be a little different. In this case, the firm would not operate any longer, so we would not use a DCF method. Instead, we would sell all the assets and pay off all liabilities (including any non-interest-bearing operating liabilities and corporate taxes due because of the liquidation) and any preferred stock. Whatever cash remains (if any) could then be distributed to equityholders and potentially option holders if their options are in-the-money.

Using Nominal or Real (Inflation-Adjusted) Cash Flows and Discount Rates

When forecasting cash flows, we can either include the effects of expected inflation (**nominal forecasts**) or exclude them (**real forecasts** or **constant dollar forecasts**). We can also measure discount rates in either nominal or real terms. **Nominal discount rates** (nominal cost of capital estimates) include compensation for expected inflation and **real discount rates** do not. Naturally, we must use discount rates that are consistent with our forecasts; we use nominal discount rates with nominal forecasts and real discount rates with real or constant dollar forecasts.

Real growth implies that the company is growing at a rate faster than the rate of inflation. A company's free cash flows can grow as a result of inflation, even if it is not experiencing real growth. Since the effect of inflation is included in the company's nominal cost of capital, we must also consider the effect of inflation on the company's free cash flows when we use a nominal cost of capital.

Assume our company's expected free cash flows grow at the rate of inflation (i), which is constant in perpetuity. We can value the company using either nominal free cash flow forecasts and nominal discount rates or real (inflation free) cash flow forecasts and real discount rates. We can express the relationship between the nominal ($r_{nominal} = r$) and real (r_{real}) rates of return as

$$r = r_{nominal} = (1 + r_{real}) \times (1 + i) - 1$$

$$r_{real} = \frac{(1 + r)}{(1 + i)} - 1$$

where i is the rate of inflation.

Assume a company's free cash flow for Year 0 is $100 and its expected outlook for the future is that its cash flows will grow with inflation (i = 2.9%); thus, it will not have any real growth. If the company's nominal cost of capital is 12.5%, we can measure the value of the firm using our perpetuity formula:

$$V_{F,0} = \frac{FCF_0 \times (1 + i)}{r - i}$$

$$V_{F,0} = \frac{\$100 \times (1 + 0.029)}{0.125 - 0.029} = \$1{,}071.88$$

If the company's nominal cost of capital is 12.5%, and if the constant inflation rate is 2.9%, its real cost of capital is

$$r_{real} = \frac{(1 + r)}{(1 + i)} - 1$$

$$r_{real} = \frac{(1.125)}{(1.029)} - 1 = 0.0933$$

We can then measure the value of the firm using our perpetuity formula and a real discount rate (r_{real}) and real cash flows:

$$V_{F,0} = \frac{FCF_1}{r_{real}}$$

$$V_{F,0} = \frac{\$100}{0.0933} = \$1{,}071.88$$

If we have all of the information we need to precisely convert nominal forecasts and nominal discount rates to real forecasts and real discount rates, then the choice of using either nominal or real forecasts and discount rates is irrelevant, for we end up measuring the same value. The key to deciding which approach to use rests in identifying the approach that will result in forecasts that are more accurate. Using a nominal approach is more common for valuation contexts that do not include high rates of expected inflation. In hyperinflationary economies where many contracts and tax regulations are indexed by the rate of inflation, it is common to use real discount rates and real cash flow forecasts.

Valuation Key 5.9

We can forecast cash flows and use discount rates that either include inflation (nominal) or exclude inflation (real). The key is to keep forecasts of cash flows and discount rates consistent—nominal and nominal or real and real. The more common approach for low-inflation situations is to use nominal forecasts and discount rates.

The Concept of Expected Free Cash Flows

Since companies typically face various business and financial risks, most assets (such as the stocks or bonds issued by companies) have uncertain future cash flows. In the DCF valuation model, we use the concept of **expected cash flow**. Using expected cash flows allows us to perform present value calculations when there are numerous possible outcomes for an investment. We have discussed this to some extent in previous chapters, but we will now develop this concept in more detail and draw links to relevant issues.

We can readily see the concept of expected value in the context of a game of chance. Assume a casino has a bowl containing 50 red, 40 white, and 10 green balls. You, the player, pay (bet) to play the game and pick one ball from the bowl; you cannot see inside the bowl, and the balls are identical except for color. The relative number of balls of a certain color represents the probability of picking a color; in addition, playing the game multiple times does not affect the **outcome** of any game. You will receive $22 if you pick a red ball, $75 if you pick a white ball, and $690 if you pick a green ball.

How much would you expect to win, on average (before deducting the cost of playing the game), from playing one round of the game? The answer is $110. To calculate the **expected payoff** from playing the game, we multiply the probability of each outcome (0.5, 0.4, and 0.1) by the payoff from that outcome ($22, $75, and $690) and add all of those products together (see Exhibit 5.6).

EXHIBIT 5.6	Calculating Expected Values				
Color of Ball		**Number of Balls in Bowl**	**Payoff**	**Probability of Payoff**	**Expected Payoff**
Red..		50	$ 22	0.5	$ 11
White		40	$ 75	0.4	30
Green		10	$690	0.1	69
		100		1.0	$110

How can $110 be the expected value if you will never receive $110, regardless of which ball you pick? The payoff will be either $22, $75, or $690, but it will never be $110. To answer, the $110 represents the average payoff you would get if you made a sufficient number of bets.

We can calculate expected cash flows in the same way we calculated the expected payoff in the casino game of chance. We multiply the probability of each outcome (sometimes called a **state of nature**, such as the state of the economy) by the cash flow that will occur along with that outcome before adding all of these products together. In other words, an expected cash flow is the probability-weighted sum of the cash flows from all of the possible outcomes that might occur. In truth, we do not often calculate expected cash flows in this way in a valuation setting.

Instead, valuation specialists often construct their forecasts based on a single scenario they view as being the most likely as of the date of the forecast. Another common approach is to calculate the forecast as the average of several scenarios. For example, our scenarios can be pessimistic, most likely, or optimistic, with each scenario being weighted by its respective probability. When only one scenario or a few probability-weighted scenarios are used in our valuation models, we implicitly assume that the individual scenario or the expected outcome of a few scenarios represents the expected value of the multiple states of nature. We discussed scenario analysis briefly in Chapter 4.

Sometimes, a project or a firm can be characterized as a chronological sequence of events, where some of these events result in a decision point for a manager or firm. In such cases, we sometimes use decision trees to help guide and structure our analysis. For example, we can use a decision tree to analyze the cash flows of a startup company that is developing a new product. If product development is successful, the company will invest in production facilities; if it is not successful, it will go bankrupt at zero cost and zero liquidation value. A decision tree helps us to better understand the potential cash flow outcomes, better identify the decisions to be made, and better analyze the options available to the company at various points in time. These options are often called "real options." Below we provide a decision tree example.

The company invests $1,000 at the end of Year 0 to develop the product. In one year, the company will either market the product or not, and each outcome has an equal probability of occurring. If the company successfully develops the product, the company will invest $2,000 at the end of Year 1, and it expects the new product to generate a cash flow at the end of Year 2 of either $10,000 if the economy is doing well or $3,000 if the economy is doing poorly. The probability of the economy doing well is 40%, and the probability of the economy doing poorly is 60%. If the company does not develop the project, the company will go bankrupt at zero cost and zero liquidation value at the end of Year 1. For simplicity, we assume that the new product can only be sold in Year 2 and that the company liquidates costlessly at the end of Year 2—even if the product is successful. We can use the following decision tree to help us analyze this investment:

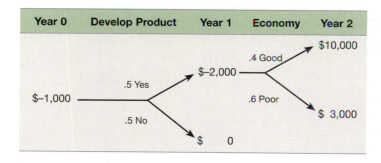

When measuring expected cash flows for each year, we must remember that at the end of Year 0, the company does not yet make the investment decision for the end of Year 1. It will not do so until it observes the outcome of the product development. This is a type of real option. The company can choose to abandon the project at the end of Year 1 if the product development is unsuccessful—an abandonment option.

Let us see what the expected cash flows are for each year. If the company makes the investment at the end of Year 1, the expected cash flow in Year 2 is $5,800 ($5,800 = 0.4 × $10,000 + 0.6 × $3,000). However, since there is only a 50% chance that it will make the investment in Year 1, the expected cash flow in Year 2 is $2,900. For Year 1, the expected cash flow is −$1,000 (−$1,000 = 0.5 × −$2,000). For Year 0, the expected cash flow is −$1,000 as well. If we assume that the appropriate discount rate for valuing the company is 10%, the value of the company will be $487.60 ($487.60 = −$1,000 − $1,000/1.1 + $2,900/1.1²).

An alternative approach that will yield the same value is to calculate the present value of the three possible scenarios and probabilistically weight them. The first scenario is to spend $1,000 at Year 0 and abandon the company. This scenario has a probability of 0.5 and a net present value of −$1,000. The second scenario is to spend $1,000 at Year 0, spend $2,000 at Year 1, and receive $3,000 at Year 2. This scenario has a probability of 0.3 (0.3 = 0.5 × 0.6) and has a present value of −$338.84 (−$338.84 = −$1,000 − $2,000/1.1 + $3,000/1.1²). The third scenario is to spend $1,000 at Year 0, spend $2,000 at Year 1, and receive $10,000 at Year 2. This scenario has a probability of 0.2 (0.2 = 0.5 × 0.4) and a present value of $5,446.28 ($5,446.28 = −$1,000 − $2,000/1.1 + $10,000/1.1²). Considering the scenarios together, the value of the company is $487.60 ($487.60 = −$1,000 × 0.5 − $338.84 × 0.3 + $5,446.28 × 0.2). Thus, discounting the expected cash flows from each period or calculating the present value of each scenario and probabilistically weighting them yields exactly the same valuation.

To appropriately measure expected cash flows, we use all of the available information to create the most precise, unbiased forecasts possible. Sometimes managers and investors are too optimistic and include all of the good outcomes but leave out one or more of the very bad outcomes—for example, financial failure or some catastrophic event. This error results in forecasts that are too high, creating an upward bias in the forecasts. Alternatively, some managers and investors implicitly consider all of the possible outcomes and then reduce the expected cash flow to be conservative. This approach results in forecasts that are too low, creating a downward bias. The key is to be realistic (remain objective) and neither bias the forecasts by unintentionally ignoring possible outcomes nor intentionally attempting to be conservative.

Valuation Key 5.10

The cash flows we use to value companies are typically expected cash flows. Expected cash flows represent the probability-weighted cash flows of all of the possible outcomes the company faces (for example, high growth, normal growth, low growth, zero growth, negative growth, etc.). The key is to be realistic (remain objective) and not bias the forecasts by unintentionally ignoring possible outcomes or intentionally attempting to be conservative.

The Risk-Adjusted Discount Rate (Cost of Capital)

We use a company's **risk-adjusted discount rate**—also commonly referred to as a **required rate of return**, an **expected rate of return**, **a hurdle rate**, or **the cost of capital**—to discount the relevant cash flows. A key concept underpinning the measurement of a company's risk-adjusted discount rate is diversification. Investors can reduce or diversify away some of the risk of a single investment by owning a portfolio of investments instead of just a single investment. Investors cannot diversify away all risk, for the outcomes companies face in a country—or even within the world—are not independent.

The reason investors cannot diversify away all of their risk is that while investments do not have identical risks, they do have some of the same risks—for example, the health of the general economy affects many businesses similarly. Risk that investors can diversify away is referred to as **diversifiable risk**, and the risk that they cannot diversify away is **undiversifiable risk**. The models we typically use to measure a company's risk-adjusted discount rate assume that diversifiable risk does not affect the company's discount rate; that is, investors will not expect to receive compensation for that form of risk because they can easily eliminate it from their portfolios by holding multiple securities. However, risk that is not diversifiable will increase the company's risk-adjusted discount rate.

Since diversification is so important to the measurement of a company's risk-adjusted discount rate, we will discuss it in some detail here and again later in the book. We introduce the concept of diversification with the same game of chance example we used in our discussion of measuring expected cash flows. To make our game of chance example more closely reflect the concept of expected cash flow from an investment (which includes a time element), assume the casino pays winners exactly one year after the player makes a bet and plays the game. We assume it costs $100 to play the game and be eligible for the payoffs previously discussed, but we also assume that a player can bet any amount (with a minimum bet of $1) and that the payoffs of $22, $75, and $690 are proportionally adjusted for the amount of the bet. The cost of playing the game includes the fee (bet) to play the game plus other costs to play the game such as the opportunity cost of time incurred for playing. It might also include non-monetary costs or benefits that result from the act of playing the game such as the entertainment value. However, in this example, we assume that the value of all costs and benefits other than the fee (bet) and winnings are zero.

If we assume the risk-free rate is 10%, we can see the value of placing the bet is zero ($0 = -$100 + $110/1.1) if the bet is riskless. However, the bet is not without risk. Assuming you prefer less uncertainty over more uncertainty (in other words, you are **risk averse**), the more uncertain the expected payoff, the less willing you will be to make a $100 bet to play the game. However, note that you can minimize the uncertainty of the payoff by betting the minimum amount for each bet. As long as you can play the game a sufficient number of times at no cost other than the cost of the bet, and as long as you can play all of the games simultaneously, and as long as the casino is certain to pay off the winners, you are essentially certain to win the expected payoff. Thus, you essentially eliminate all of the uncertainty from your outcome. We call this reduction in risk **diversification**. By playing the game over and over again, you are able to **diversify** away essentially all of the risk of playing the game. You can do this because the outcome each time you play is independent of the outcomes of the other times you play. As the number of times you play increases, you reduce the uncertainty of not winning the expected cash flow. For example, if you plan to bet $100,000 in total, you can minimize your uncertainty by betting the minimum for each bet ($1), which maximizes the number of bets you make (100,000). Your expected payoff for betting $100,000 (100,000 bets of $1) is $110,000, and the uncertainty is close to zero. If the expected payoff is close to certain, the value of your total bet is $100,000 ($100,000 = $110,000/1.1). Because you can virtually eliminate all the uncertainty, the appropriate discount rate we would use to value the bet is the risk-free rate.

The risk-adjusted discount rate used in a present value calculation of risky cash flows is equal to the risk-free rate, plus a risk premium for an investment's undiversifiable risk. Even though this explanation is far from complete in that we do not discuss the specific risk factors and ways of measuring them, it is a sufficient definition for our purposes right now. We will discuss the specific risk factors and the ways of measuring them in a later chapter.

Assume you have the opportunity to make an investment that has the same expected cash flow as the game of chance and that the payment is a year from now. The expected cash flow of the investment is $110; you will receive this cash flow one year after making the investment; this is the only cash flow you will receive; and the risk-free rate is 10%. Assume you hold a diversified portfolio of investments, and the appropriate risk premium to adjust for the undiversifiable risk of this investment is 5%, then the risk-adjusted discount rate is 15%. Using our time-value-of-money formula, the value of the investment is equal to $95.65.

$$\$95.65 = \frac{\$110}{1.15}$$

If the investment's payoff is certain, its value will be $100 ($100 = $110/1.1). The difference between the $100 and the $95.65 is the adjustment in value due to undiversifiable risk. It should be clear that if two investments have identical expected cash flows with one having a higher risk-adjusted discount rate, the one with the lower risk-adjusted discount rate would be more valuable. If the expected cash flows are not identical, then you can no longer decide which investment has a higher value unless you can compare the present values of the two investments.

Certainty Equivalent Approach

There is an alternative way we can adjust our discounted value calculation for the undiversifiable risk investors face when making risky investments. Instead of adjusting the denominator (the discount rate), we can adjust the numerator (the expected cash flow). Using this alternative, we adjust the expected cash flows directly by reducing the expected cash flow by an amount that converts the expected cash flow into its risk-free equivalent. This adjusted expected cash flow is the **certainty equivalent cash flow**. If we discount a certainty equivalent cash flow at the risk-free rate, then by definition, the result will be the same as discounting the expected cash flow at the risk-adjusted rate. We can adjust the expected cash flow of the investment in the previous example to measure its **certainty equivalent**. The certainty equivalent cash flow is equal to the expected cash flow of $110 minus a risk adjustment of $4.78, which equals $105.22. We know this because we know that the present value of $105.22 paid in one year and discounted at the 10% risk-free rate is $95.65:

$$\$95.65 = \frac{\$105.22}{1.1}$$

We calculated the certainty equivalent by reverse engineering. We already knew both the expected cash flow and the present value of the cash flow, so it was easy to measure the expected cash flow's certainty equivalent. We began with the discounted value of $95.65 and calculated the certainty equivalent adjustment (CEA) we must make to the $110 expected cash flows so that when we discount the certainty equivalent cash flow at the risk-free rate, we get the same answer:

$$\$95.65 = \frac{\$110 - CEA}{1.1}$$

$$CEA = \$4.78$$

Measuring an expected cash flow's certainty equivalent is substantially more difficult when we do not know the present value of the expected cash flow. Although this alternative is conceptually identical to the risk-adjusted discount rate method of adjustment, it is not widely used in practice, and we do not discuss it further in this book.[11]

Valuation Key 5.11

To calculate the value of a risky investment, we discount *expected* cash flows with *risk-adjusted* discount rates. We take into consideration both diversifiable and non-diversifiable risk in computing expected cash flows, but risk-adjusted discount rates only rise above the risk-free rate when there is non-diversifiable risk.

---

[11] See Grinblatt and Titman (2002) for a good exposition on using the certainty equivalent approach; Grinblatt, M., and S. Titman, *Financial Markets and Corporate Strategy*, 2nd ed., McGraw-Hill Companies, Inc. (2002).

Don't Use "Fudge Factors"

When we create forecasts for use in a DCF valuation, the forecasts should represent the expected value of the company's future free cash flows. As discussed previously, we measure expected values by probability weighting all potential outcomes that might occur. Naturally, we typically face what appears to be an infinite number of potential outcomes, so probability weighting all of these outcomes is generally not feasible. However, we can select a finite number of potential outcomes in order to approximate the expected value.

Suppose that a company's free cash flow—in perpetuity—will be $133 if the economy is bad, $500 if it is good, and $1,200 if it is booming, and that the probability of a bad, good, and booming economy is 30%, 40%, and 30%, respectively. The expected value of the company's free cash flow is $600 ($600 = 0.3 × $133 + 0.4 × $500 + 0.3 × $1,200). If the company's discount rate is 10%, the value of the company is $6,000 ($6,000 = $600/0.1).

How would we adjust the above valuation—expected free cash flow and discount rate—of the company if we now learn that the success of the company is entirely dependent on the company being awarded a patent next year and that the probability of the company being awarded that patent is 80%? Further, if the patent is awarded to the company, the expected cash flows will be $600 in perpetuity and $0 otherwise.

Initially, we used the probabilities of outcomes in the general economy to measure the company's expected free cash flows. Do we now include the probability of getting the patent in our expected value calculation? Yes. The outcomes we use to measure the expected values of free cash flows include all potential outcomes, regardless of whether they are related to the general economy (systematic effects) or are company specific (idiosyncratic effects). Thus, in addition to the potential outcomes for the general economy and industry, we—at least implicitly—consider such events as the success of various research and development programs, the approval of drugs, the approval of patents, the weather, the death of a key employee, and so on. Our company has a 20% chance of having $0 free cash flows and an 80% chance of having an expected free cash flow of $600 (in perpetuity). Adjusting the company's expected free cash flow for this uncertainty, we get $480 ($480 = 0.2 × $0 + 0.8 × $600 = 0.8 × $600). An alternative way to calculate this expected value is to incorporate both the probability of the company not obtaining the patent—and the resulting zero free cash flow—and then adjust the probability of each state of the economy for the probability of the company not obtaining the patent; $480 = 0.2 × $0 + (0.8 × 0.3) × $133 + (0.8 × 0.4) × $500 + (0.8 × 0.3) × $1,200.

Should we also adjust the discount rate for this new information? No. Unless the probability of getting the patent is somehow related to the economy and affects the company's non-diversifiable risk, we do not include this uncertainty (company-specific risk) into the discount rate. Thus, adding this uncertainty to the example does not change the discount rate (10%), but it does change the value of the company to $4,800 ($4,800 = $480/0.1) from $6,000.

Arbitrarily changing the discount rate to adjust for these potential uncertainties—arguing that they are additional "risk factors"—is conceptually flawed. As we discussed earlier, the discount rate should not reflect unsystematic or idiosyncratic risks (risks that can be diversified away). Adjusting the discount rate for these effects will undervalue the company if the expected free cash flows are already adjusted for these uncertainties. If an adjustment is not made when measuring the expected free cash flows, adjusting the discount rate is merely an arbitrary adjustment. For example, if someone were to guess and use an adjustment of 5% for the discount rate, the resulting "adjusted" discount rate would be 15%. The resulting value would then be $4,000 ($4,000 = $600/0.15), which is an error of more than 16%.

Is it possible to make such an adjustment to the discount rate such that the valuation is correct? Algebraically, the answer is yes, but conceptually, the answer is no. If we make this adjustment to the discount rate, we will no longer be using a discount rate that measures value by discounting the company's expected free cash flows, and the free cash flows will no longer be expected free cash flows. In addition, and more important, we typically need the correct value of the company before we can calculate the correct adjustment to the discount rate, as there is no theory we can rely on to tell us how to make this particular discount rate adjustment. The only way to accurately adjust the discount rate for this type of risk is to first measure the appropriate value of the company based on the expected cash flows. Once you do this, you can then determine what discount rate—applied to cash flows that differ from the expected value cash flows—will yield the same valuation.

Using our example, we can illustrate how to make such an adjustment. We know the correct value of the firm is $4,800, and the value ignoring the additional uncertainty is $6,000; thus, the correct value is 80% of the value ignoring the additional uncertainty (0.8 = $4,800 / $6,000). Using this information, we can adjust the discount rate by this ratio in order to measure the discount rate that we will use to discount the free cash flow that ignores the additional uncertainty. That discount rate is 12.5% (0.125 = 0.1/0.8). Discounting the $600 free cash flow by 12.5%, we get $4,800 ($4,800 = $600/0.125). Note that calculating the adjustment to the discount rate will not be so simple in situations in which the cash flows are not simple perpetuities. That said, it would be simple to solve for that discount rate in a financial model using software such as Excel. Nevertheless, you still need to know the value of the company before you can calculate the discount rate that will yield the correct valuation when applied to cash flows that differ from the expected values.

Adding an adjustment to the discount rate that does not have a conceptual foundation is nothing more than a **fudge factor**. Thus, although adjusting the discount rate for idiosyncratic risks can result in the correct valuation, it is unlikely to do so unless we already know the value of the firm. As you might have guessed, we do not recommend using the "fudge factor" approach.

Valuation Key 5.12

When we create forecasts to use in a DCF valuation, they should represent the expected value of the company's future free cash flows. We measure expected values by probability weighting all of the potential outcomes that might occur. Ignoring the unlikely outcomes and attempting to consider them by adjusting the discount rate in the valuation—arguing that they are additional risk factors for the discount rate—is conceptually flawed and cannot be directly implemented, which is why we call such adjustments "fudge factors."

5.9 COMPREHENSIVE EXAMPLE—DENNIS KELLER, INC.

We use a company—Dennis Keller, Inc. (Keller)—to illustrate how to use the various DCF valuation methods discussed in this chapter. Keller is a privately owned company with one owner, Dennis Keller, who is also the company's chief executive officer (CEO). Dennis Keller is going to sell the company to his current chief financial officer (CFO). Based on the company's current strategic plan, the CEO and CFO prepared forecasts for the company's unlevered free cash flows that are shown in Exhibit 5.7. After Year 3, they believe the company's unlevered free cash flows will keep pace with the estimated long-run annual inflation rate of 3% per year. They agree that these forecasts are not only attainable by the company but are also reasonable to use to value the company. The company does not hold any excess cash and it faces a tax rate of 40%, T_C, on all income.

EXHIBIT 5.7 Unlevered Free Cash Flow Forecasts for Dennis Keller, Inc.

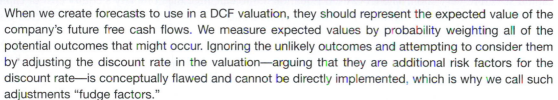

($ in thousands)	Actual Year 0	Forecast Year 1	Forecast Year 2	Forecast Year 3	Forecast Year 4
Earnings before interest and taxes (EBIT)	$6,200	$5,300	$6,100	$6,017	$6,197
– Income taxes paid on EBIT ($T_C \times$ EBIT).	–2,480	–2,120	–2,440	–2,407	–2,479
Earnings before interest and after taxes	$3,720	$3,180	$3,660	$3,610	$3,718
+ Depreciation expense	2,600	3,100	3,700	4,077	4,200
– Change in required cash	0	0	–80	–8	–9
– Change in net operating working capital.	–500	900	–220	–55	–56
– Capital expenditures	–5,000	–6,000	–3,775	–4,899	–5,046
Unlevered free cash flow	$ 820	$1,180	$3,285	$2,726	$2,807

Exhibit may contain small rounding errors

The Dennis Keller comprehensive example will use two different capital structure strategies to review how financing can affect the value of the firm and its equity, and how to measure firm and equity values using the adjusted present value (APV) and weighted average cost of capital (WACC) valuation models. The Keller example will also show how the APV and the WACC valuation methods, as well as the Equity DCF method, can be used as "consistency checks." The first capital structure strategy will be that of a constant capital structure ratio strategy of 20% debt and 80% equity, which will be called the *20% debt capital structure*. The second capital structure strategy, called the *$20 million debt capital* *structure*, will be to borrow $20 million and invest $10 million. After the original financing, any available cash will be used to repay debt for the first three years, and after Year 3, a constant capital structure will be maintained at the end of Year 3's debt-to-value ratio.

Dennis Keller, Inc.'s—20% Debt Capital Structure Valuation Using the Weighted Average Cost of Capital Method

The CFO measured Keller's costs of capital on a regular basis so that he could evaluate its investment opportunities. Using information on several comparable companies, the CFO concluded that the best estimate of Keller's unlevered cost of capital is 12%. The CFO re-levered Keller's unlevered cost of capital—based on Keller's 8% cost of debt and a constant capital structure ratio of 20% debt and 80% equity—in order to measure Keller's equity cost of capital. The company's current debt outstanding—$2,000 of 8% debt—does not reflect this capital structure strategy, but the company had expected to get back to its target capital structure very soon. The CFO used Equation 5.8 to calculate the company's equity cost of capital from the unlevered cost of capital, which assumes interest tax shields are valued using the unlevered asset cost of capital:

$$r_E = 0.12 + (0.12 - 0.08) \times \frac{0.2}{0.8} = 0.13$$

Based on Keller's 20% capital structure strategy, 8% cost of debt, 40% income tax rate, and 13% equity cost of capital, the CFO calculated Keller's weighted average cost of capital (r_{WACC}):

$$r_{WACC} = 0.13 \times 0.8 + (1 - 0.4) \times .08 \times 0.2 = 0.1136$$

Using the free cash flow forecasts in Exhibit 5.7, a 3% growth rate for free cash flows after Year 3, and an 11.36% weighted average cost of capital, the WACC method valuation of the company was $30 million, which we present in Exhibit 5.8. Given the $30 million valuation of the firm and $2 million in debt outstanding, the value of the equity is $28 million. Note that in order for this $30 million valuation to be correct, it must be that Keller would immediately recapitalize the company to 20% debt if he did not sell it, since the WACC valuation assumes that the capital structure is composed of 20% debt, not 6.67% debt (6.67% = $2,000/$30,000). If the company did not recapitalize to its target capital structure, the value of the interest tax shields would not be as high as is being assumed in the valuation.

EXHIBIT 5.8	CEO's Weighted Average Cost of Capital Valuation of Keller (20% Debt Capital Structure)					
($ in thousands)		Year 0	Year 1	Year 2	Year 3	CV$_{Firm}$ Year 3
Unlevered free cash flow for continuing value						$ 2,807
Continuing value capitalization factor (r_{WACC} − g)$^{-1}$						11.962
Unlevered free cash flow and continuing value			$1,180	$3,285	$2,726	$33,582
Discount factor (1 + r_{WACC})$^{-t}$			0.898	0.806	0.724	0.724
Present value			$1,060	$2,649	$1,974	$24,317
Value of the firm		$30,000				

Exhibit may contain small rounding errors

$20 Million Debt Capital Structure Valuation Using the Adjusted Present Value Method

The CFO was arranging the following financing in order to purchase Keller. The CFO plans to personally invest $10 million and borrow the remaining amount needed, $20 million, in debt with a 9% interest rate. The $30 million in raised capital would be used to repay the existing debt ($2 million with an 8% interest rate) and to purchase the CEO's equity for $28 million.

Sources of Funds ($ in thousands)		Uses of Funds	
New equity invested.................	$10,000	Value of the equity purchased	$28,000
New debt (9%)	20,000	Existing debt (8%)	2,000
Total sources of funds	$30,000	Total uses of funds	$30,000

For the next three years, the CFO plans to use any free cash flow the company generates to pay interest and repay debt. After the end of Year 3, the CFO plans to maintain a constant proportion of debt to equity at whatever that proportion is at the end of Year 3. In other words, the CFO intends to use the debt-to-value ratio expected at the end of the third year and then maintain the capital structure at that target ratio beyond Year 3.

The increase in the interest rate for the new debt (from 8% to 9%) reflects the additional risk of having more debt in the capital structure. To make the calculations less complex, we assume that the interest rate on the debt is equal to the debt cost of capital. We also assume that the company's debt cost of capital of 9% will not change, even though the CFO expects the company to reduce the amount of debt it has outstanding to some degree in Years 1 through 3.

Forecasts for Keller with the $20 Million Debt Capital Structure

The CFO is confident that the company can achieve the free cash flow forecasts in Exhibit 5.7. Given the CFO's plan to reduce the debt with all available cash flows each year through the end of Year 3, the CFO needed more detailed forecasts of the company's financial statements and equity free cash flows. Based on both the forecasts for the company's free cash flows in Exhibit 5.7 and the plan to reduce debt with all available cash flows, the CFO prepared complete forecasts of the financial statements and free cash flows. The income and balance sheet forecasts appear in Exhibit 5.9. The balance sheet as of the end of Year 0 includes the effects of purchasing the equity for $28 million. As stated previously, the CFO will invest $10 million in equity and issue $20 million of debt. The company will use these funds to pay down the existing debt of $2 million and pay the CEO $28 million for his equity. The net effect of this is an outstanding debt balance of $20 million and a common equity balance of $7.1 million (we will explain the latter after we discuss the free cash flow forecasts).

EXHIBIT 5.9 Income Statement and Balance Sheet Forecasts for Dennis Keller, Inc.
($20 Million Debt Capital Structure)

($ in thousands)	Actual Year –1	Actual Year 0	Forecast Year 1	Forecast Year 2	Forecast Year 3	Forecast Year 4
Income Statement						
Revenue..........................	$10,000	$11,000	$12,000	$14,000	$14,420	$14,853
Operating expenses................	–2,000	–2,200	–3,600	–4,200	–4,326	–4,456
Depreciation expense...............	–2,100	–2,600	–3,100	–3,700	–4,077	–4,200
Earnings before interest and taxes......	$ 5,900	$ 6,200	$ 5,300	$ 6,100	$ 6,017	$ 6,197
Interest expense....................	–160	–160	–1,800	–1,791	–1,592	–1,433
Income before taxes................	$ 5,740	$ 6,040	$ 3,500	$ 4,309	$ 4,424	$ 4,764
Income tax expense................	–2,296	–2,416	–1,400	–1,724	–1,770	–1,906
Net income........................	$ 3,444	$ 3,624	$ 2,100	$ 2,585	$ 2,655	$ 2,859
Balance Sheet						
Cash.............................	$ 200	$ 200	$ 200	$ 280	$ 288	$ 297
Net operating working capital	2,000	2,500	1,600	1,820	1,875	1,931
Property, plant, and equipment (net)	22,000	24,400	27,300	27,375	28,196	29,042
Total assets.......................	$24,200	$27,100	$29,100	$29,475	$30,359	$31,270
Debt	$ 2,000	$20,000	$19,900	$17,689	$15,919	$16,396
Common equity	500	10,500	10,500	10,500	10,500	10,500
Retained earnings	21,700	–3,400	–1,300	1,285	3,940	4,373
Total liabilities and equities...........	$24,200	$27,100	$29,100	$29,475	$30,359	$31,270

Exhibit may contain small rounding errors

Starting with the unlevered free cash flows in Exhibit 5.7, the CFO also prepared forecasts for the company's expected equity free cash flows and reconciliations to the change in cash, both of which appear in Exhibit 5.10. Since the company does not hold any excess cash, the dividend paid each year is equal to the equity free cash flow. Now that we know the company's dividend in Year 0, we can reconcile the common equity accounts on the Year 0 balance sheet. The common equity balance is equal to $10.5 million, which is equal to the $0.5 million balance from Year -1, plus the $10 million invested in Year 0. The retained earnings balance is $21.7 million at the end of Year -1. To that, we add $3.624 million in Net Income for Year 0 and subtract both the $28 million paid to the CEO and the $0.724 million equity free cash flow (equals dividends paid in Year 0, excluding the increase in debt issued), in order to measure the retained earnings balance as of the end of Year 0 of -3.4 million ($-\$3,400 = \$21,700 + \$3,624 - \$28,000 - \$724$).

EXHIBIT 5.10	Equity Free Cash Flow Forecasts for Dennis Keller, Inc. ($20 Million Debt Capital Structure)				
($ in thousands)	Actual Year 0	Forecast Year 1	Forecast Year 2	Forecast Year 3	Forecast Year 4
Equity Free Cash Flow (EFCF)					
Unlevered free cash flow (FCF)	$ 820	$1,180	$3,285	$2,726	$2,807
Interest expense paid ($r_D \times V_{D,t-1}$).	−160	−1,800	−1,791	−1,592	−1,433
Interest tax shield (ITS = $T_{INT} \times r_D \times V_{D,t-1}$)	64	720	716	637	573
Free cash flow minus after-tax interest	$ 724	$ 100	$2,211	$1,770	$1,948
Change in debt.	18,000	−100	−2,211	−1,770	478
Equity free cash flow (EFCF)	$18,724	$ 0	$ 0	$ 0	$2,425
Reconciliation to Change in Cash					
Equity free cash flow (EFCF)	$18,724	$ 0	$ 0	$ 0	$2,425
− Common equity dividends paid	−28,724	0	0	0	−2,425
+ Change in common equity financing	10,000	0	0	0	0
Change in excess cash	$ 0	$ 0	$ 0	$ 0	$ 0
Change in required cash	0	0	80	8	9
Change in cash balance.	$ 0	$ 0	$ 80	$ 8	$ 9

Exhibit may contain small rounding errors

Calculating equity free cash flows will help the CFO better understand the company's ability to repay its debt and forecast the company's interest tax shields. Since the CFO plans to reduce the debt balance using all available cash flow for the first three years, equity free cash flows will be zero until Year 4. The equity free cash flows will grow at a constant rate after Year 4, as the company will have a constant target capital structure after Year 4. The CFO knows the initial amount of debt ($20 million), the debt cost of capital (9%), and the income tax rate for interest (40%). Thus, the interest tax shield in Year 1 is $0.72 million ($720 = \$20,000 \times 0.09 \times 0.4$). The change in debt in Years 1 through 3 equals the unlevered free cash flow minus the after-tax interest because the CFO plans to use all available cash to repay debt. Thus, the CFO can calculate the change in debt and subsequent after-tax interest through Year 3. After Year 3, the CFO plans to use the debt-to-value ratio at the end of Year 3 as the target ratio for all future years. As such, the change in debt in Year 4 is equal to the growth rate of 3% multiplied by the end of Year 3's debt forecast ($478 = \$15,919 \times 0.03$) since this will result in a constant debt-to-value ratio.

Adjusted Present Value Valuation of Keller with the $20 Million Debt Capital Structure

The CFO knows that given this new capital structure, the APV method—and not the WACC method—is the best valuation method to use to value the company. The CFO used the unlevered cost of capital to discount its interest tax shields for all years. Using the APV method and a 12% cost of capital for the company's unlevered assets, the CFO calculated the value of the firm as of the end of Year 0 to be equal to $34.015 million, which we present in Exhibit 5.11. The CFO assumed that the company would maintain its capital structure ratios in perpetuity from the end of Year 3, and that debt, interest, and interest tax shields would grow at the company's long-term growth rate after that year. The CFO calculated the value of Keller's equity by subtracting the values of each of the non-equity claims from the value of the firm.

Since Keller finances itself with debt and equity only, the value of the CFO's equity as of the end of Year 0 is $14.015 million ($14,015 = $34,015 − $20,000).

| EXHIBIT 5.11 | CFO's Adjusted Present Value Valuation of Keller ($20 Million Debt Capital Structure) |

($ in thousands)	Year 0	Year 1	Year 2	Year 3	CV Year 3
Value of the Unlevered Firm					
Unlevered free cash flow for continuing value					$ 2,807
Continuing value capitalization factor $(r_{UA} - g)^{-1}$					11.111
Unlevered free cash flow and continuing value		$1,180	$3,285	$2,726	$31,194
Discount factor $(1 + r_{UA})^{-t}$		0.893	0.797	0.712	0.712
Discounted value		$1,054	$2,619	$1,940	$22,203
Value of the unlevered firm.	$27,816				
Value of the Interest Tax Shields					
Interest tax shield for continuing value.					$ 573
Continuing value capitalization factor $(r_{UA} - g)^{-1}$					11.111
Interest tax shield and continuing value of the interest tax shield		$ 720	$ 716	$ 637	$ 6,368
Discount factor $(1 + r_{UA})^{-t}$		0.893	0.797	0.712	0.712
Present value		$ 643	$ 571	$ 453	$ 4,532
Value of the interest tax shields	$ 6,200				
Value of the firm	**$34,015**				

Exhibit may contain small rounding errors

How Can Keller Create So Much Value by Using Debt Financing?

The CFO calculated the difference between the 20% debt capital structure and the $20 million debt capital structure valuations as $4.015 million ($4,015 = $34,015 − $30,000)—an increase of 13%. The CFO knows that his equity investment of $10 million is now worth $14.015 million—an increase of more than 40%. The CFO also knows that both valuations assumed that the company did not have significant expected costs of financial distress or bankruptcy. The CFO, however, felt comfortable with this assumption, even with the additional debt the company was going to issue, because the CFO was comfortable with and confident that the company would meet these forecasts.

Since the value of the unlevered firm is independent of financing, the entire difference between the 20% debt capital structure valuation and $20 million debt capital structure valuation results from the difference in the value of the interest tax shields in the capital structure scenarios. We can reconcile this difference by calculating the interest tax shields implied by the WACC method and comparing the discounted value of the interest tax shields embedded in the WACC valuation to the value of the interest tax shields in the APV valuation. The discounted value of the difference between the interest tax shields must equal the difference between the two valuations.

The value of the interest tax shields in the $20 million debt capital structure valuation is $6,200 from Exhibit 5.11. To measure the value of the interest tax shields embedded in the WACC valuation, we calculate the amount of debt in each year as implied by both the valuation and the assumed capital structure strategy of 20% debt. From Exhibit 5.8, we know the value of the firm at the end of Year 0, $30,000, and at the end of Year 3, $33,582 equals the continuing value before discounting it back to Year 0. We can also measure the value of the firm at the end of Years 1 and 2 by using the WACC method. We measure the value of the firm in Year 2 by discounting both the value of the firm at the end of Year 3 (the continuing value) and the free cash flow in Year 3 for one year by the weighted average cost of capital. The resulting calculation is the value of the firm as of the end of Year 2. The general formula for this calculation is

$$V_{F,t} = \frac{FCF_{t+1}}{1 + r_{WACC}} + \frac{V_{F,t+1}}{1 + r_{WACC}}$$

Using this approach, the value of Keller at the end of Year 2 and Year 1 is

$$V_{F,2} = \frac{\$33,582 + \$2,726}{1.1136} = \$32,604$$

$$V_{F,1} = \frac{\$32,604 + \$3,285}{1.1136} = \$32,228$$

Now that we know the value of the firm in each year, we can use the constant target debt to value ratio in order to calculate both the amount of debt and the interest tax shields imbedded in the WACC valuation, which we show in Exhibit 5.12. This exhibit also shows the increase in the interest tax shields resulting from the $20 million debt capital structure.

EXHIBIT 5.12	Interest Tax Shields Implied in the 20% Debt Capital Structure WACC Valuation Compared to the $20 Million Debt Capital Structure for Dennis Keller, Inc.

($ in thousands) As of the Beginning of the Year	Year 1	Year 2	Year 3	Year 4
Value of the firm	$30,000	$32,228	$32,604	$33,582
Constant target debt to value ratio	20%	20%	20%	20%
Amount of debt	$ 6,000	$ 6,446	$ 6,521	$ 6,716
Interest rate for debt.	8.0%	8.0%	8.0%	8.0%
Interest on debt for Year ($r_D \times V_D$)	$ 480	$ 516	$ 522	$ 537
Tax rate for interest (T_{INT})	40%	40%	40%	40%
ITS implied in WACC valuation (20% debt)	$ 192	$ 206	$ 209	$ 215
ITS in APV valuation ($20 million debt) (Ex. 5.10).	720	716	637	573
Difference	$ −528	$ −510	$ −428	$ −358

We can see from this exhibit that the interest tax shields imbedded in the WACC valuation (20% debt capital structure) are smaller than the interest tax shields in the APV valuation ($20 million debt structure) for every year. While the exhibit only presents this difference for Years 1 to 4, we must remember that the difference in Year 4 will grow 3% annually in perpetuity—the assumed perpetuity growth rate. We can measure the value of the interest tax shields imbedded in the WACC valuation shown in Exhibit 5.12 by discounting them at the unlevered cost of capital:

$$V_{ITS} = \frac{ITS_1}{(1 + r_{UA})} + \frac{ITS_2}{(1 + r_{UA})^2} + \frac{ITS_3}{(1 + r_{UA})^3} + \frac{ITS_4}{(r_{UA} - g)} \times \frac{1}{(1 + r_{UA})^3}$$

$$\$2,184.1 = \frac{\$192}{(1.12)} + \frac{\$206}{(1.12)^2} + \frac{\$209}{(1.12)^3} + \frac{\$215}{(0.12 - 0.03)} \times \frac{1}{(1.12)^3}$$

The difference between the $20 million debt capital structure and 20% debt capital structure valuations of the interest tax shields is $4.015 million ($4,015 = $6,199.5 − $2,184.1), which is equal to the difference between the $20 million debt capital structure and 20% debt capital structure valuations of Keller. Thus, the entire difference between these valuations is due to the capital structure assumption made in each valuation, and the resulting interest tax shields. As an aside, another way to compute the interest tax shields in the WACC valuation of the 20% capital structure would have been to take the difference between the valuation of the 20% debt capital structure using the WACC method from Exhibit 5.8 ($30 million) and subtract from that the value of the unlevered firm in Exhibit 5.11 ($27.816 million). The advantages of our more elaborate calculation, which lets us see the implied capital structure in the WACC valuation, are that we can determine if the company will need additional financing or violate any debt covenants.

Using the Adjusted Present Value Method as a "Consistency Check"—20% Debt Capital Structure

We can use the APV method as a consistency check for the WACC valuation. In order to do this, we need to know the interest tax shield forecasts implied in the WACC valuation for each year; thus, we need to know the forecasts of the amount of debt the company will have in each year as implied by the WACC valuation. To generate these forecasts, we first measure the value of the firm in each year using the WACC method. Then, we generate our debt forecasts by multiplying our constant capital structure ratio by the value of the firm in order to measure the amount of debt the company will have at the beginning of the period; from this debt, we can measure the company's interest tax shield for each year. These are the calculations we have already performed in Exhibit 5.12. Once we know the interest tax shields, we have all the information we need to value the company using the APV valuation. We show the APV valuation using the 20% debt capital structure in Exhibit 5.13.

| EXHIBIT 5.13 | Adjusted Present Value Valuation of the 20% Debt Capital Structure for Dennis Keller, Inc. |

($ in thousands)	Year 0	Year 1	Year 2	Year 3	CV Year 3
Value of the Unlevered Firm					
Unlevered free cash flow for continuing value					$ 2,807
Discount factor for continuing value					11.111
Unlevered free cash flow and continuing value		$1,180	$3,285	$2,726	$31,194
Discount factor.		0.893	0.797	0.712	0.712
Discounted value		$1,054	$2,619	$1,940	$22,203
Value of the unlevered firm.	$27,816				
Value of the Interest Tax Shields					
Interest tax shield for continuing value.					$ 215
Discount factor for continuing value					11.111
Interest tax shield and continuing value.		$ 192	$ 206	$ 209	$ 2,388
Discount factor.		0.893	0.797	0.712	0.712
Present value		$ 171	S 164	$ 149	$ 1,700
Value of the interest tax shields	$ 2,184				
Value of the firm	**$30,000**	$1,225	$2,783	$2,089	$23,903

Exhibit may contain small rounding errors

Since we used the same cash flow and discount rate assumptions in the APV and WACC valuations of the 20% debt capital structure, both valuations are identical. In addition, as with all APV valuations, this valuation has two parts—the value of the unlevered firm and the value of the interest tax shields. Notice, however, that the section computing the value of the unlevered firm is exactly the same as the section computing the value of the unlevered firm in the CFO's valuation of the company with the $20 million debt capital structure. This, of course, is not coincidence.

Using the Weighted Average Cost of Capital Method as a "Consistency Check"—$20 Million Debt Capital Structure

We can also use the WACC method as a consistency check for an APV valuation. In an APV valuation, we do not know a company's capital structure ratios, but we do have forecasts of the amount of debt the company will have each year. We can calculate the value of the firm for each year using the APV method, and then we can calculate the company's capital structure ratio for each year. Once we have the capital structure ratios for each year, we can measure the company's equity cost of capital and weighted average cost of capital in each year and then use the weighted average cost of capital to value the firm. Since the capital structure ratios are changing, both the equity cost of capital and weighted average cost of capital will change each year. The first step in the process is to use the APV method to measure the value of the firm in each year using the data presented in the APV valuation (Exhibit 5.11). We show these calculations in Exhibit 5.14.

EXHIBIT 5.14	Year-by-Year Adjusted Present Value Valuation of the $20 Million Debt Capital Structure for Dennis Keller, Inc.

($ in thousands) As of the Beginning of the Year	Year 1	Year 2	Year 3	CV Year 3
Value of Unlevered Firm				
Unlevered free cash flow for continuing value				$ 2,807
Continuing value capitalization factor ($r_{UA} - g$)$^{-1}$				11.111
Unlevered free cash flow	$ 1,180	$ 3,285	$ 2,726	
Value of the unlevered firm at year end	29,974	30,285	31,194	
Unlevered value at year end plus unlevered free cash flow	$31,154	$33,571	$33,920	
Discount factor for one year (1 + r_{UA})$^{-1}$	0.893	0.893	0.893	
Beginning of year value of unlevered firm	$27,816	$29,974	$30,285	$31,194
Value of the Interest Tax Shields (ITS)				
Interest tax shield for continuing value.				$ 573
Continuing value capitalization factor ($r_{UA} - g$)$^{-1}$				11.111
Interest tax shields	$ 720	$ 716	$ 637	
Value of the interest tax shields at year end.	6,223	6,254	6,368	
End of year ITS plus current year ITS.	$ 6,943	$ 6,970	$ 7,004	
Discount factor for one year (1 + r_{UA})$^{-1}$	0.893	0.893	0.893	
Beginning of year value of interest tax shields.	$ 6,200	$ 6,223	$ 6,254	$ 6,368
Beginning of year value of the firm.	**$34,015**	**$36,197**	**$36,539**	**$37,561**

Exhibit may contain small rounding errors

To understand the exhibit's calculation, note that we are doing the same type of calculation that we did in the context of the WACC valuation, where we computed the value of the firm at the beginning of each year. For example, to calculate the value of the unlevered firm at the beginning of Year 3, we take the continuing value of the unlevered firm ($31,194), add it to the Year 3 unlevered free cash flow ($2,726), and discount the sum back one period at the unlevered cost of capital to arrive at $30,285. We do the same type of calculation with the interest tax shields and find that the value of the firm at the beginning of Year 3 is $36,539. To calculate the value of the unlevered firm at the beginning of Year 2, we take the value of the unlevered firm at the beginning of Year 3 ($30,285), add it to the Year 2 unlevered free cash flow ($3,285), and discount the sum back one period to arrive at $29,974. Doing the same type of calculation with the interest tax shields, we find that the value of the firm at the beginning of Year 2 is $36,197.

Once we know the value of the firm at the beginning of each year, we use the debt forecasts to measure the company's capital structure ratios in each year, which we show in the top panel of Exhibit 5.15. Afterward, we can use our levering formula (Equation 5.8) to measure the equity cost of capital in each year, which we show in the bottom panel of Exhibit 5.15.

Note that the equity cost of capital is decreasing each year starting at 16.3% and going down to 14.2% by the beginning of Year 4. Assuming market conditions do not change, it will remain at 14.2% thereafter, for the company's capital structure strategy is to adopt a constant capital structure ratio after Year 3 of whatever that capital structure happens to be at that time (from Exhibit 5.15, you can see that the debt-to-value ratio is forecasted to be 42.4%). Given that the equity cost of capital is decreasing, how should we expect the weighted average cost of capital to change? On the one hand, a decrease in the equity cost of capital will cause a decrease in the weighted average cost of capital, but on the other hand, the decrease in the equity cost of capital is due to a decrease in the use of financial leverage. A decrease in the use of financial leverage puts more weight on the equity cost of capital and less weight on the after-tax debt cost of capital in the weighted average cost of capital calculation. As it turns out, the net effect increases the weighted average cost of capital, which we show in Exhibit 5.16. This should not come as a surprise to you given the work of M-M.

EXHIBIT 5.15 Year-by-Year Capital Structure Ratios Based on the Adjusted Present Value Valuation of the $20 Million Debt Capital Structure for Dennis Keller, Inc.

($ in thousands) As of the End of the Year	Year 0	Year 1	Year 2	Year 3
Value of the firm (V_F)	$34,015	$36,197	$36,539	$37,561
Value of debt (V_D)	20,000	19,900	17,689	15,919
Value of equity (V_E)	$14,015	$16,297	$18,850	$21,643
Value of debt (V_D) to value of the firm (V_F)	58.8%	55.0%	48.4%	42.4%
Value of equity (V_E) to value of the firm (V_F)	41.2%	45.0%	51.6%	57.6%
Value of debt (V_D) to value of equity (V_E)	1.4270	1.2211	0.9384	0.7355

$r_E = r_{UA} + (r_{UA} - r_D) \times \dfrac{V_D}{V_E}$	Beg of Year 1	Beg of Year 2	Beg of Year 3	Beg of Year 4
Unlevered cost of capital, r_{UA}	12.0%	12.0%	12.0%	12.0%
Cost of debt, r_D	9.0%	9.0%	9.0%	9.0%
Value of debt to value of equity	1.43	1.22	0.94	0.74
Equity cost of capital, r_E	16.3%	15.7%	14.8%	14.2%

Exhibit may contain small rounding errors

EXHIBIT 5.16 Year-by-Year Weighted Average Costs of Capital Based on the Adjusted Present Value of the $20 Million Debt Capital Structure for Dennis Keller, Inc.

$r_{WACC} = r_E \times \dfrac{V_E}{V_F} + (1 - T_{INT}) \times r_D \times \dfrac{V_D}{V_F}$	Beg of Year 1	Beg of Year 2	Beg of Year 3	Beg of Year 4
Equity cost of capital, r_E	16.3%	15.7%	14.8%	14.2%
Value of equity to value of the firm	41.2%	45.0%	51.6%	57.6%
Cost of the debt r_D	9.0%	9.0%	9.0%	9.0%
Value of debt to value of the firm	58.8%	55.0%	48.4%	42.4%
Income tax rate	40.0%	40.0%	40.0%	40.0%
Weighted average cost of capital, r_{WACC}	9.9%	10.0%	10.3%	10.5%

We now have all of the information we need to use the WACC method in order to measure the value of the firm with a changing capital structure. Note that since the weighted average cost of capital is changing over time, we discount the cash flows using the appropriate present value calculation allowing for varying discount rates.

$$V_F = \frac{FCF_1}{(1 + r_{WACC,1})} + \frac{FCF_2}{(1 + r_{WACC,1}) \times (1 + r_{WACC,2})} + \frac{FCF_3 + \dfrac{FCF_4}{(r_{WACC,4} - g)}}{(1 + r_{WACC,1}) \times (1 + r_{WACC,2}) \times (1 + r_{WACC,3})}$$

$$\$34,015 = \frac{\$1,180}{1.099} + \frac{\$3,285}{1.099 \times 1.1} + \frac{\$2,726 + \dfrac{\$2,807}{0.105 - 0.03}}{1.099 \times 1.1 \times 1.103}$$

The continuing value of the firm in this WACC valuation is equal to $37.561 million [= FCF_4 ÷ ($r_{WACC,4}$ − g)], which is equal to the continuing value from the APV valuation (see Exhibit 5.14; $37,561 = $31,194 + $6,367).

Keller Inc.'s Valuation Using the Equity Discounted Cash Flow Valuation Method

Recall that in order to implement the Equity DCF method, we need to know both the company's capital structure ratios (to compute the equity cost of capital) and the amount of each of its non-equity securities issued (to measure equity free cash flows). Consequently, we must measure the value of the firm in every year in order to have sufficient information to know both inputs—equity free cash flows and equity cost of capital—for each year. Since we already know the value of the firm needed to use this method, this might seem like a pointless exercise; however, it is often useful to analyze the equity free cash flows implied by a particular capital strategy, as they provide information on the company's ability to distribute dividends in the future or potentially to require additional capital. In addition, monitoring the equity cost of capital can potentially provide useful information on the riskiness of the equity.

Using the Equity Discounted Cash Flow Method for the 20% Debt Capital Structure

In the 20% debt capital structure valuation of Keller, the CEO assumed that Keller was going to maintain a constant target capital structure of 20% debt and, in turn, Keller's equity cost of capital, which we calculated previously to be 13%, would not change over time. Although we know the equity cost of capital, we do not know the equity free cash flows based on this capital structure. To measure equity free cash flows, we need to know the amount of debt the company will have in each year. However, we cannot know this unless we know the value of the firm in each year (the value of the debt each year is equal to the target capital structure ratio, multiplied by the value of the firm each year). Thus, we can use the Equity DCF method only if we first measure the value of the firm in every year, then measure the amount of debt the firm will have, and then calculate the equity free cash flow forecasts.

In our reconciliation of the WACC valuation of the 20% debt capital structure using the APV method, we already calculated the value of the firm and the value of debt in each year (Exhibit 5.12). The change in debt for Year 4 is not shown in Exhibit 5.12, but we know it equals the debt balance at the beginning of Year 4 multiplied by the growth rate ($201 = $6,716 \times 0.03$). Based on this information and the unlevered free cash flow forecasts, we can measure the equity free cash flows implied by the WACC valuation. We show this calculation in Exhibit 5.17. Note that in this case, the company will be able to pay dividends every year and will require no additional financing.

EXHIBIT 5.17	Equity Free Cash Flows Implied in the CEO's Valuation of Dennis Keller, Inc. (20% Debt Capital Structure)				

		Forecast			
($ in thousands)		**Year 1**	**Year 2**	**Year 3**	**Year 4**
Unlevered free cash flow (FCF)		$1,180	$3,285	$2,726	$2,807
Interest expense paid ($r_D \times V_D$).		−480	−516	−522	−537
Interest tax shield (ITS = $T_{INT} \times r_D \times V_D$).		192	206	209	215
Change in debt.		446	75	196	201
Free cash flow to common equity (EFCF)		$1,338	$3,051	$2,608	$2,687

Exhibit may contain small rounding errors

To measure the value of Keller's equity by discounting the equity free cash flows implied in the CEO's 20% debt capital structure, we perform the following calculation.

$$V_E = \frac{EFCF_1}{(1 + r_E)} + \frac{EFCF_2}{(1 + r_E)^2} + \frac{EFCF_3}{(r_E - g)} \times \frac{1}{(1 + r_E)^2}$$

$$\$24,000 = \frac{\$1,338}{1.13} + \frac{\$3,051}{1.13^2} + \frac{\$2,608}{0.13 - 0.03} \times \frac{1}{1.13^2}$$

Note that the equity free cash flows were discounted individually for Years 1 and 2, and the continuing value began in Year 3. We were able to start the continuing value in Year 3 rather than Year 4 because the Year 4 and subsequent free cash flows are assumed to increase annually by the growth rate.[12] The amount calculated using the equity discounted cash flow method of $24 million equals the value of the equity using the WACC valuation method ($24,000 = $30,000$ firm value $\times 0.8$ equity/firm value).

---

[12] The same equity value will be obtained if you discount Years 1 through 3 individually, and begin the continuing value in Year 4, as shown below:

$$\$24,000 = \frac{\$1,338}{1.13} + \frac{\$3,051}{1.13^2} + \frac{\$2,608}{1.13^3} + \frac{\$2,687}{0.13 - 0.03} \times \frac{1}{1.13^3}$$

Notice that because we used the implied capital structure in the WACC valuation to measure the equity free cash flows, the equity value we measure here presumes that Keller is at its target capital structure, which would mean it has $6 million of debt ($6,000 = $30,000 \times 0.2$) and thus has an equity value of $24 million ($24,000 = $30,000 - $6,000$).

Equity Discounted Cash Flow Method for the $20 Million Debt Capital Structure

In the APV valuation of the $20 million debt capital structure, the CFO prepared forecasts for all of the company's financial statements (Exhibit 5.9) as well as its equity free cash flows (Exhibit 5.10). Although we have forecasts for the company's equity free cash flows given its capital structure strategy, we know that its capital structure ratio (debt to firm value) is changing over time. If this is the case, then the company's equity cost of capital is changing over time and we would need to measure its equity cost of capital in each year. To measure the equity cost of capital in each year, we must know the company's capital structure ratios at the beginning of each year; thus, we need to know the value of the firm in each year. We have already measured the value of the firm in each year using the APV valuation method, and we have already measured the company's capital structure ratios and its equity costs of capital (Exhibit 5.15) in each year. Thus, we have all the information we need to value the company using the Equity DCF method for the $20 million debt capital structure:

$$V_E = \frac{EFCF_1}{(1 + r_{E,1})} + \frac{EFCF_2}{(1 + r_{E,1}) \times (1 + r_{E,2})} + \frac{EFCF_3 + \dfrac{EFCF_4}{(r_{E,4} - g)}}{(1 + r_{E,1}) \times (1 + r_{E,2}) \times (1 + r_{E,3})}$$

$$\$14,015 = \frac{\$0}{1.163} + \frac{\$0}{1.163 \times 1.157} + \frac{\$0 + \dfrac{\$2,425}{0.142 - 0.03}}{1.163 \times 1.157 \times 1.148}$$

The value of the equity calculated above equals the value of the equity calculated using the APV valuation method ($14,015 = $34,015 firm value - $20,000 debt$).

The Equity Discounted Cash Flow Valuation Model Also Serves as a "Consistency Check"

Recall that we can use one DCF valuation method to value the firm (WACC or APV) and then use the other method to check the consistency of our valuation. Similarly, as we have demonstrated, we can use the Equity DCF valuation method as a consistency check on our initial valuation. The Equity DCF valuation was able to replicate both the CEO's and CFO's valuations of Keller, for we used the same information and assumptions that the CEO and CFO used when they valued the firm.

SUMMARY AND KEY CONCEPTS

In this chapter, we discussed how the tax deductibility of interest could affect the value of the firm, and we then learned how the different valuation methods measure this effect. The cash flows created by the tax deductibility of interest, or interest tax shields, are equal to the reduction in income taxes a company pays as a result of the tax deductibility of interest.

In addition, we learned about the relationships between the equity cost of capital and a company's other costs of capital under the assumption that interest tax shields are valued at the unlevered cost of capital. As we will see later in the book, those relationships change if we want to make other assumptions about valuing interest tax shields. We also learned how to compute the weighted average cost of capital.

Further, we illustrated how to implement the APV and WACC discounted cash flow methods. We saw that the method that is the best starting point for our valuation depends on the capital structure strategy of the company and the information we have on its capital structure. In addition, we saw that the Equity DCF method is not a particularly useful starting point in most valuation situations. Although most of the formulas presented in this chapter assumed a company had only three types of financing—debt, preferred stock, and common stock—all of the formulas can easily be adjusted if the company has other sources of financing.

ADDITIONAL READING AND REFERENCES

Myers, S. C., "Interactions of Corporate Financing and Investment Decisions—Implications for Capital Budgeting," *Journal of Finance* 29 (1974), pp. 1–25.

Ruback, R. S., "Downsides and DCF: Valuing Biased Cash Flow Forecasts," *Journal of Applied Corporate Finance*, vol. 23, no.2 (2011), pp. 8–17.

EXERCISES AND PROBLEMS

P5.1   **Which Valuation Method to Use:** Assume you were going to value the companies described below. State which valuation method you would use to value the company and discuss why you would use that method.

    a.   A privately held company has had a stable capital structure strategy using 20% debt financing and 20% preferred stock financing and is expected to use the same capital structure in the future. Value the company as of today.

    b.   A publicly traded company, which has had no debt for many years, is planning to undergo a debt recapitalization. The plan calls for the company to issue a large amount of debt—about 90% of the value of the firm—and distribute the cash to its equityholders. Over the next ten years, the company plans to repay its debt so that the company will have 20% debt financing at the end of ten years. The company's long-run (after year ten) capital structure strategy is to maintain 20% debt financing. Value the company as of the date of the anticipated debt recapitalization.

    c.   Company P is acquiring Company S in a cash transaction. Company P has a capital structure strategy of 30% debt financing. Company S is in a different industry than Company P and has a capital structure strategy of 10% debt financing. Company P plans to continue to use its capital structure strategy on a consolidated basis after the transaction. Value Company S for this transaction.

    d.   A publicly traded company has been changing its capital structure over the past few years as it acquired various companies operating in various industries. The company plans to refinance itself with 20% debt financing. Value the company as of the refinancing.

P5.2   **Basic Valuation Calculations—The APV Perpetuity Company—Interest Is Tax Deductible:** The APV Perpetuity Company does not expect to grow. In other words, it expects its cash flows to remain constant, and it expects to distribute all equity free cash flows to the equityholders in the form of dividends and not hold any excess cash. The company is expected to generate an unlevered free cash flow of $3,000 per year in perpetuity. The company is initially financed with $10,000 equity, $12,000 debt, and $8,000 preferred stock. The company's income tax rate on all income statement items is 40%, and interest is tax deductible. The company does not intend to change the amount of financing it has currently. The company's interest rate, which is equal to its debt cost of capital, is 8%. The company's preferred stock dividend rate (paid on the book value of preferred stock), which is equal to the cost of capital of preferred stock, is 9%. The company's unlevered cost of capital is 10%. The appropriate discount rate for interest tax shields is the unlevered cost of capital for this company.

    a.   Value the company—the value of the firm and the value of the equity—as of the end of Year 0 using the APV valuation method.

    b.   Calculate the company's capital structure ratios as of the end of Year 0. Given the company's capital structure strategy, how will these capital structure ratios vary in the future?

    c.   Calculate the company's weighted average cost of capital as of the end of Year 0.

    d.   Value the company—the value of the firm—as of the end of Year 0 using the WACC valuation method.

    e.   Value the equity as of the end of Year 0 using the Equity DCF valuation method.

P5.3   **Basic Valuation Calculations—The APV Perpetuity Company—Interest Is Not Tax Deductible:** In this problem, we value the APV Perpetuity Company from Problem 5.2 in an income tax regime in which interest expense is **not** tax deductible. The underlying information for the APV Perpetuity Company appears in Problem 5.2 with the following exceptions—interest is not tax deductible. If you also completed the previous problem for the APV Perpetuity Company, compare your responses for this problem to your responses for Problem 5.2.

    a.   Value the company—the value of the firm and the value of the equity—as of the end of Year 0 using the APV valuation method.

    b.   Calculate the company's capital structure ratios as of the end of Year 0. Given the company's capital structure strategy, how will these capital structure ratios vary in the future?

    c.   Calculate the company's weighted average cost of capital as of the end of Year 0.

    d.   Value the company—the value of the firm—as of the end of Year 0 using the WACC valuation method.

    e.   Value the equity as of the end of Year 0 using the Equity DCF valuation method.

P5.4   **Basic Valuation Calculations—The WACC Perpetuity Company—Interest Is Tax Deductible:** The WACC Perpetuity Company does not expect to grow. In other words, it expects its cash flows to remain constant, and it expects to distribute all equity free cash flows to the equityholders in the form of dividends; the company does not hold excess cash. The company is expected to generate an unlevered free cash flow of $3,000 per year in perpetuity. The company's income tax rate on all income statement items is 40%, and interest is tax deductible. The company does not have forecasts for the dollar values of its financing but knows it is going to finance itself with 50% debt, 10% preferred stock, and 40% equity. The company does not intend to change the proportions of financing it will have. The company's interest rate, which is equal to its debt cost of capital, is 9%. The company's preferred stock dividend rate (paid on the book value of preferred stock), which is equal to the cost of capital of preferred stock, is 10%. The company's unlevered cost of capital is 11%. The appropriate discount rate for interest tax shields is the unlevered cost of capital for this company.

    a.   Value the company—the value of the firm and the value of the equity—as of the end of Year 0, using the WACC valuation method and assuming its capital structure strategy was in place at the end of Year 0.

    b.   Calculate the amount of debt and preferred stock the company would have as of the end of Year 0 based on your WACC valuation.

    c.   Value the company—the value of the firm—as of the end of Year 0 using the APV valuation method.

    d.   Calculate the company's equity free cash flow for Year 1, assuming its capital structure strategy was in place at the end of Year 0.

    e.   Value the equity as of the end of Year 0 using the Equity DCF valuation method, assuming its capital structure strategy was in place at the end of Year 0.

P5.5   **Basic Valuation Calculations—The WACC Perpetuity Company—Interest Is Not Tax Deductible:** In this problem, we value the WACC Perpetuity Company from Problem 5.4 in an income tax regime in which interest expense is **not** tax deductible. The underlying information on the WACC Perpetuity Company appears in Problem 5.4, with the following exception—interest is not tax deductible. If you also completed the previous problem for the WACC Perpetuity Company, compare your responses for this problem to your responses for Problem 5.4.

    a.   Value the company—the value of the firm and the value of the equity—as of the end of Year 0, using the WACC valuation method, assuming its capital structure strategy was in place at the end of Year 0.

    b.   Calculate the amount of debt and preferred stock the company would have as of the end of Year 0 based on your WACC valuation.

    c.   Value the company—the value of the firm—as of the end of Year 0 using the APV valuation method.

    d.   Calculate the company's equity free cash flow for Year 1, assuming its capital structure strategy was in place at the end of Year 0.

    e.   Value the equity as of the end of Year 0 using the Equity DCF valuation method assuming its capital structure strategy was in place at the end of Year 0.

P5.6   **Adjusted Present Value Valuation—The Joel Germunder Company:** The Joel Germunder Company (Germunder) is a privately held family business that currently uses no debt in its capital structure. The owner-managers have a plan to expand the operations of the company over the next two years. Some of Germunder's younger owner-managers proposed a plan to issue a large amount of debt to not only expand the company's operations but to also pay the owners a one-time, special dividend. The younger owner-managers' plan is to finance the entire transaction by issuing $15 million of 10% debt.

    After the company completes its expansion, the plan of the younger owner-managers is to use some of the free cash flows to repay the debt until the end of Year 3, but they will continue to pay some dividends in Years 1 through 3. As of the beginning of Year 4, they expect the company's cash flows to grow at the long-run inflation rate, which they expect to be 2.5%. At the end of Year 3, they believe that the company will have paid down a sufficient amount of debt so that the remaining debt will be used as the basis of a stable target capital structure, and the debt will grow at the overall growth rate of 2.5%. While the leverage of the company will decline some over the first three years, it will not fall enough to change the cost of debt. Moreover, since the debt-to-value ratio will stay the same after Year 3, the cost of debt will remain at 10%. The company does not hold any excess cash, and all equity free cash flows will be paid out as a dividend to shareholders. The company's chief financial officer prepared a set of financial forecasts that reflects this plan. The income statement, balance sheet, and cash flow statement forecasts appear in Exhibit P5.1. The forecasts assume the company will issue the debt at the end of Year 0, which is reflected in the balance sheet for that year. Germunder's income tax rate for all revenues and expenses (including interest) is 40%, and its unlevered cost of capital is 12%.

    a.   Use the financial statements in Exhibit P5.1 to measure Germunder's unlevered free cash flows in Years 1 through 4.

    b.   Value Germunder—the entire firm and equity—as of the end of Year 0, using the APV valuation method. Assume that the appropriate discount rate for interest tax shields is the unlevered cost of capital of the company.

    c.   As of the end of Year 0, what amount and percent of firm value and what percent of equity value does Germunder derive from the value of its interest tax shields?

d. What issues would you suggest the company's management think about before moving forward with this capital structure strategy?

e. As a consistency check on your previous valuation, value Germunder as of the end of Year 0 using all of the above assumptions with the WACC valuation method. Again, assume that the appropriate discount rate for interest tax shields is the unlevered cost of capital for this company.

f. As a consistency check on your previous valuation, value Germunder's equity as of the end of Year 0 using the Equity DCF valuation method. Again, assume that the appropriate discount rate for interest tax shields is the unlevered cost of capital for this company.

EXHIBIT P5.1	Income Statement, Balance Sheet, and Cash Flow Statement Forecasts for the Joel Germunder Company					

($ in thousands)	Actual Year –1	Actual Year 0	Forecast Year 1	Forecast Year 2	Forecast Year 3	Forecast Year 4
Income Statement						
Revenue	$ 7,968	$ 8,765	$13,147	$14,462	$14,823	$15,194
Operating expenses.	–3,187	–3,506	–5,259	–5,785	–5,929	–6,078
Depreciation expense.	–1,000	–1,273	–1,875	–2,226	–2,494	–2,557
Earnings before interest and taxes.	$ 3,781	$ 3,986	$ 6,014	$ 6,451	$ 6,400	$ 6,560
Interest expense.	0	0	–1,500	–1,440	–1,320	–1,190
Income before taxes.	$ 3,781	$ 3,986	$ 4,514	$ 5,011	$ 5,080	$ 5,370
Income tax expense.	–1,512	–1,594	–1,805	–2,004	–2,032	–2,148
Net income.	$ 2,268	$ 2,392	$ 2,708	$ 3,006	$ 3,048	$ 3,222
Balance Sheet						
Cash.	$ 80	$ 88	$ 131	$ 145	$ 148	$ 152
Net operating working capital	1,514	1,665	1,972	2,169	2,224	2,279
Property, plant & equipment (net).	11,686	16,434	18,077	18,529	18,993	19,467
Total assets.	$13,280	$18,187	$20,181	$20,843	$21,364	$21,898
Debt	$ 0	$15,000	$14,400	$13,200	$11,900	$12,198
Equity	13,280	3,187	5,781	7,643	9,464	9,701
Total liabilities and equities.	$13,280	$18,187	$20,181	$20,843	$21,364	$21,898
Cash Flow Statement						
Cash flows from operations						
Net income.		$ 2,392	$ 2,708	$ 3,006	$ 3,048	$ 3,222
+ Depreciation expense		1,273	1,875	2,226	2,494	2,557
– Change in net operating working capital.		–151	–307	–197	–54	–56
Cash flow from operations.		$ 3,513	$ 4,276	$ 5,036	$ 5,488	$ 5,723
Investing activities						
– Capital expenditures		$–6,020	$–3,518	$–2,678	$–2,958	$–3,031
Financing activities						
+ Change in debt financing		$15,000	$ –600	$–1,200	$–1,300	$ 297
+ Change in common equity financing		0	0	0	0	0
– Common equity dividends paid.		–12,485	–114	–1,144	–1,227	–2,985
Cash flows from financing activities.		$ 2,515	$ –714	$–2,344	$–2,527	$–2,688
Change in cash balance.		$ 8	$ 44	$ 13	$ 4	$ 4

Exhibit may contain small rounding errors

P5.7 **Weighted Average Cost of Capital Valuation—The Joel Germunder Company:** Before you begin this problem, read the text and review the information in the previous problem for the Joel Germunder Company and use that information but incorporate the changes described below. Some of Germunder's older owner-managers are concerned about the younger owner-managers' plan to issue so much debt to expand the company and pay a large one-time dividend. They agree that the company's cash flows could easily support some debt, but they are concerned about the amount of debt proposed by the younger owner-managers. They hired a consultant who recommended a lower risk capital structure strategy of financing the company with a constant target capital structure of 20% debt (for a debt-to-firm value ratio equal to 20%). The consultant told them that with this target capital structure, their interest rate on debt (and debt cost of capital) would be equal to 8%. Based on this revised capital structure, the older owner-managers would pay out all equity free cash flows as dividends.

a. Use the financial statements in Exhibit P5.1 to measure Germunder's unlevered free cash flows in Years 1 through 4.

b. Value Germunder—the entire firm and its equity—as of the end of Year 0 using the WACC valuation method and the proposed capital structure strategy assuming that interest tax shields are valued at the unlevered cost of capital.

c. Calculate the company's equity free cash flows forecasts based on the older owner-managers' capital structure strategy.

d. Value Germunder's equity as of the end of Year 0 using the Equity DCF valuation method and the proposed capital structure strategy.

e. As a consistency check, value Germunder as of the end of Year 0 using the APV valuation method. Assume that the appropriate discount rate for interest tax shields is the unlevered cost of capital for this company.

f. You must complete the previous problem on the Joel Germunder Company to solve this part of the problem. Analyze the difference between the value of the firm based on the capital structure strategy in the previous problem and the value based on the capital structure strategy in this problem. Reconcile, mathematically, the difference in the value of the firm.

P5.8   **Adjusted Present Value Valuation with Debt Recapitalization at the Continuing Value Date—The Joel Germunder Company**: The Joel Germunder Company (Germunder) is a privately held, family business that currently uses no debt in its capital structure. The owner-managers have a plan to expand the operations of the company over the next two years. The owner-managers agreed on a plan to issue a large amount of debt to not only expand the company's operations but also pay the owners a one-time, special dividend. Their plan is to finance the entire transaction by issuing $15 million of 10% debt. After the company completes its expansion, their plan is to use some of the free cash flows to repay the debt until the end of Year 3; thus, they will pay some dividends in Years 1 through 3. At the end of Year 3, they plan to refinance the company to a constant target capital structure of 20% debt. As of the beginning of Year 4, they expect the company's cash flows to grow at the long-run inflation rate, which they expect to be 2.5%. The company's chief financial officer prepared a set of financial forecasts that reflects this plan. The income statement, balance sheet, and cash flow statement forecasts appear in Exhibit P5.1. The forecasts assume the company will issue the debt at the end of Year 0, which is reflected in the balance sheet for that year. The forecasts do not, however, reflect the debt recapitalization at the end of Year 3. The debt cost of capital will not change while the company is paying off its debt, but it will decrease to 8% when they recapitalize the company to 20% debt at the end of Year 3. Germunder's income tax rate for all revenues and expenses is 40%, and its unlevered cost of capital is 12%.

a. Use the financial statements in Exhibit P5.1 to measure Germunder's unlevered free cash flows in Years 1 through 4.

b. As of the continuing value date, what amount and percent of its firm value does Germunder derive from the value of its interest tax shields? Assume the appropriate discount rate for interest tax shields is the unlevered cost of capital for this company.

c. As of the continuing value date, what amount and percent of its equity value does Germunder derive from the value of its interest tax shields? Assume the appropriate discount rate for interest tax shields is the unlevered cost of capital for this company.

d. Value Germunder—the entire firm and equity—as of the end of Year 0 using the APV valuation method. Assume that the appropriate discount rate for interest tax shields is the unlevered cost of capital for this company.

e. As of the end of Year 0, what amount and percent of its firm value and equity does Germunder derive from the value of its interest tax shields?

f. What issues would you suggest the company's management think about before moving forward with this capital structure strategy (in other words, what factors related to issuing additional debt are not considered in your APV valuation that might affect the value of the firm and equity)?

g. Value Germunder—the entire firm and equity—as of the end of Year 0 using the WACC valuation method. Again, assume that the appropriate discount rate for interest tax shields is the unlevered cost of capital for this company.

h. Value Germunder's equity as of the end of Year 0 using the Equity DCF valuation method. Again, assume that the appropriate discount rate for interest tax shields is the unlevered cost of capital for this company.

SOLUTIONS FOR REVIEW EXERCISES

Solution for Review Exercise 5.1: The Stuart Essig Perpetuity Company—Part 1

$$r_E = r_{UA} + (r_{UA} - r_D) \times \frac{V_D}{V_E} + (r_{UA} - r_{PS}) \times \frac{V_{PS}}{V_E}$$

$$= 0.12 + (0.12 - 0.08) \times \frac{0.3333}{0.5} + (0.12 - 0.085) \times \frac{0.167}{0.5} = 0.158333$$

$$r_{WACC} = r_E \times \frac{V_E}{V_F} + (1 - T_{INT}) \times r_D \times \frac{V_D}{V_F} + r_{PS} \times \frac{V_{PS}}{V_F}$$

$$= 0.1583 \times 0.5 + (1 - 0.4) \times 0.08 \times 0.333 + 0.085 \times 0.167 = 0.1093$$

$$r_{WACC} = r_{UA} - T_{INT} \times r_D \times \frac{V_D}{V_F}$$

$$= 0.12 - 0.4 \times 0.08 \times 0.333 = 0.1093$$

$$V_{F,O} = \frac{FCF_1}{r_{WACC} - g} = \frac{\$42,600}{0.1093333 - 0} = \$389,634$$

$$V_{E,O} = V_{F,O} \times \frac{V_E}{V_F}$$

$$= \$389,634 \times 0.5 = \$194,817$$

Solution for Review Exercise 5.2: The Stuart Essig Perpetuity Company—Part 2

	Value	% Value
Debt	$129,878	33.3%
Preferred stock.	64,939	16.7%
Equity	194,817	50.0%
V$_F$	$389,634	100.0%

Interest Tax Shields	
	Year 1
Beginning of year debt.	$129,878
Cost of debt = interest rate	0.08
Interest expense.	$ 10,390
Income tax rate for interest	40%
Interest tax shield.	$ 4,156

$$V_{F,O} = \frac{FCF_1}{r_{UA} - g} + \frac{ITS_1}{r_{UA} - g}$$

$$= \frac{\$42,600}{0.12 - 0} + \frac{\$4,156}{0.12 - 0}$$

$$= \$355,000 + \$34,634 = \$389,634$$

Solution for Review Exercise 5.3: The Stuart Essig Perpetuity Company—Part 3

Equity Free Cash Flows	
	Year 1
Unlevered free cash flow	$ 42,600
Interest paid in cash	−10,390
Interest tax shield	4,156
Preferred stock dividend	−5,520
Change in debt	0
Change in preferred stock	0
Equity free cash flow (EFCF)	$ 30,846

$$V_E = \frac{EFCF_{C+1}}{(r_E - g)} = \frac{\$30,846}{0.158333 - 0} = \$194,817$$

After mastering the material in this chapter, you will be able to:

1. Calculate continuing value using the constant-growth perpetuity model (6.2–6.4)

2. Measure the base year free cash flow for the continuing value estimate (6.5–6.6)

3. Allow for real growth and value creation in the continuing value estimate (6.7)

4. Assess the reasonableness of the continuing value estimate (6.8)

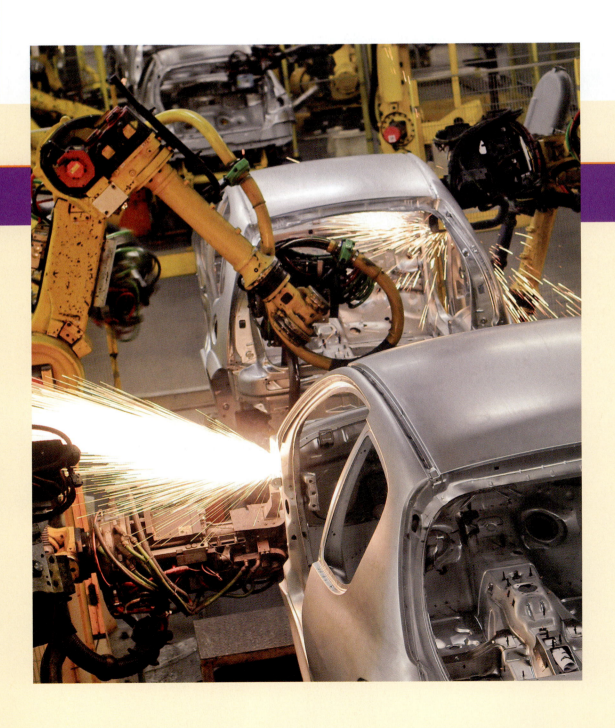

Measuring Continuing Value Using the Constant-Growth Perpetuity Model

Daimler-Benz, AG (Daimler) and Chrysler Corporation (Chrysler) merged in the late 1980s. Credit Suisse First Boston (CSFB) was Chrysler's financial advisor, and the financial advisor for Daimler-Benz was Goldman Sachs (Goldman). Both financial advisors provided a fairness opinion to their respective clients, and both investment banks used the discounted cash flow (DCF) valuation model as part of the basis for their fairness opinions. To use the DCF valuation model, CSFB and Goldman valued Chrysler on a standalone basis (before considering any potential synergies from the merger) using management forecasts that were prepared for 1998 through 2002. To measure the value of Chrysler's cash flows after 2002, CSFB used an earnings before interest, taxes, depreciation and amortization (EBITDA) multiple based on comparable companies. Goldman, on the other hand, applied a 2% growth rate to the 2002 management forecast for each of the years between 2003 through 2007, and then it used a perpetuity valuation model with growth rates between 0% and 4% to value cash flows after 2007.[1]

THE DAIMLER-BENZ AND CHRYSLER MERGER

The DaimlerChrysler merger is a typical example of how valuation experts use the DCF valuation model to value a company. It is also a good example of the alternative ways valuation experts implement the DCF valuation model. CSFB used an EBITDA multiple to measure the value of cash flows after 2002, and Goldman used a constant growth rate for five additional years before using a perpetuity valuation to measure the value of Chrysler's remaining cash flows.

In this chapter, we explore the intricacies of using the constant-growth cash flow perpetuity model to estimate the continuing value of a company.

---

[1] See the text as well as Annex C and Annex D in the DaimlerChrysler AG SEC Form F-4 (Registration Statement) available at the U.S. Securities and Exchange Commission website.

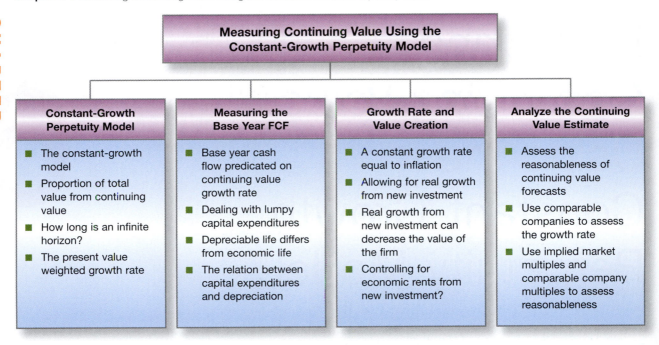

INTRODUCTION

Corporations do not have a predetermined finite life under law, and theoretically, they can continue to operate forever. While some companies liquidate, when viewing a company as a **going concern**, we typically assume that it will continue to operate. Therefore, we typically use a very long forecast horizon for a company's expected free cash flows when we implement a DCF valuation model. Such an assumption complicates DCF calculations because it is not practicable to forecast (and then discount) a very long series of explicit year-by-year cash flows without making some simplifying assumptions.

To address this complication, we develop detailed forecasts for a company's expected cash flows for some finite period of time—say, 10 years. Then, we measure the value of the firm at the end of this finite period. We call the value at the end of the finite period the company's **continuing value (CV)**; other terms used for this concept are **terminal value**, **residual value**, and **horizon value**. The continuing value component often ranges from 30% to more than 50% of the company's total value; thus, continuing value estimates are an important part of valuing companies, and they deserve careful consideration.

Although we suggest using the free cash flow constant-growth perpetuity method to measure a company's continuing value, another commonly used procedure is to estimate continuing value using the market multiple valuation method. Our suggested approach is to use the constant-growth perpetuity method to measure continuing value and then to calculate the market multiples implied by that continuing value estimate and the underlying forecasts. We then compare the implied market multiples to the market multiples of a set of comparable companies in order to help judge the reasonableness of the continuing value.[2]

It is less common to assume that a company will be liquidated (presumably, because most companies are worth less when liquidated than operating as a going concern) or that the company will be broken up into different parts and sold to various interested parties. This latter type of valuation is called a **breakup value** and presumes that at least some of the parts of the company will continue to operate

---

[2] In a 1998 survey of large corporations and financial advisors, Bruner et al. (1998) report that 30% of financial advisors use multiples only to assess continuing values, while 70% use both multiples and a perpetuity DCF analysis. See Bruner, R., K. Eades, R. Harris, and R. Higgins, "Best Practices in Estimating the Cost of Capital: Survey and Synthesis," *Financial Practice and Education* (Spring/Summer, 1998), pp. 13–28.

but under the auspices of multiple owners. A breakup value should be considered if the independent parts of the company can be utilized more effectively when sold to others than when operating as parts of a single conglomerate company.

We introduced the constant-growth perpetuity model in Chapter 1. In this chapter, we will focus on several key assumptions that we must satisfy in order to use the constant-growth perpetuity model for a continuing value calculation. First, we have to model the firm's year-by-year cash flows sufficiently far into the future so that we are willing to assume that the firm's rate of return on investment will remain constant in perpetuity; that the risks of its operations will be unchanged in the future; and that it is operating with a capital structure that could persist indefinitely given the nature of the business. If all of these hold, we say that the firm has reached steady state. Therefore, a key decision we must make is how far out we need to model the explicit year-by-year cash flows in order for the firm to reach steady state. Second, we have to create a base year cash flow that we believe can grow at the chosen constant proportionate growth rate. This involves ensuring that all aspects of the free cash flows are growing at the same rate as the assumed growth rate, that the relationship between capital expenditures and depreciation is appropriate, and that the returns embedded in the company's cash flows for both its existing scale of operations and for new investments for real growth are reasonable. In short, we must truly believe that the cash flows in the base year of our continuing value calculation can grow at the chosen constant rate in perpetuity.

As it turns out, satisfying all of these conditions is difficult, and getting a reasonable continuing value requires extensive analysis. Finally, we discuss different techniques for assessing the reasonableness of our continuing value estimates. Since the continuing value component of total firm value is large, it is worth taking the time to do this analysis. Throughout the chapter, we will illustrate many of the concepts we discuss with a detailed analysis of Yahoo! Inc.

6.1 YAHOO! INC.

We use a discounted cash flow valuation of Yahoo! Inc. (Yahoo) as of the end of 2006 to illustrate the various issues, analyses, and adjustments that we discuss.[3] We pick this particular time as it helps illustrate the important points we make in this chapter. Yahoo had very little debt in its capital structure and more than $2 billion in excess assets (marketable securities). In our illustration, we assume that at the end of 2006, Yahoo liquidated all of its excess assets, redeemed all of its debt, and distributed the remaining proceeds (approximately $2.1 billion). Yahoo had a total market capitalization (firm value) of about $34.7 billion around the end of its 2006 fiscal year (December 2006). We developed a set of forecasts that are consistent with this valuation and useful for our illustration. In Exhibit 6.1, we show Yahoo's historical and forecasted income statement and balance sheet forecasts.

In Exhibit 6.2, we show the free cash flow forecasts generated from operations for Yahoo. Since we assume that as of the date of our valuation, the company redeems all of its debt, liquidates all of its excess assets, and distributes the net proceeds to its equity holders, we do not include the distribution of $2.128 billion in the unlevered free cash flows in Exhibit 6.2.

We use a 12% unlevered cost of capital (discount rate) and a 2.5% constant free cash flow growth rate for years after 2017 to value Yahoo. We assume that 2.5% is a reasonable forecast for long-term inflation, so, for now, we are assuming no real growth for Yahoo after 2017. In Exhibit 6.3, we show Yahoo's DCF valuation. The valuation of Yahoo's operations is $32.6 billion. Yahoo's total value is equal to the sum of the value of its operations and the net excess assets of $2.1 billion, which is equal to its $34.7 billion market capitalization ($34.7 = $32.6 + $2.1) at that time.

We note that as of March 2012, Yahoo's market capitalization is only $18.5 billion, roughly half of what it was at the end of 2006. Yahoo's revenue in 2011 was $5 billion, much smaller than the $25.7 billion we forecasted in order to replicate Yahoo's value in the marketplace in 2006. We also forecasted net income of $4.0 billion for 2011 whereas its actual net income is $1.05 billion; no wonder that Yahoo was unable to maintain its 2006 value.

---

[3] Yahoo (and its consolidated subsidiaries) is a leading global Internet website portal. It generates revenue by providing marketing services to businesses across its properties and by establishing paying relationships with users of premium offerings. Yahoo was incorporated in 1995 and is a Delaware corporation headquartered in Sunnyvale, California.

EXHIBIT 6.1 Yahoo! Inc.—Historical and Forecasted Income Statements and Balance Sheets

YAHOO! INC.
Income Statement Forecasts
(for the years ended December 31)

($ in millions)	A2005	A2006	F2007	F2008	F2009	F2010	F2011	F2012	F2013	F2014	F2015	F2016	F2017
Revenue	$ 5,258	$6,426	$ 8,032	$10,442	$14,096	$19,735	$25,655	$30,786	$34,647	$36,406	$37,316	$38,249	$39,205
Cost of goods sold	−2,096	−2,676	−3,213	−4,177	−5,639	−7,894	−10,262	−12,315	−13,859	−14,562	−14,926	−15,300	−15,682
Gross margin	$ 3,161	$3,750	$ 4,819	$ 6,265	$ 8,458	$11,841	$15,393	$18,472	$20,788	$21,844	$22,390	$22,949	$23,523
Product development	−570	−833	−884	−1,149	−1,551	−2,171	−2,822	−3,387	−3,811	−4,005	−4,105	−4,207	−4,313
Selling, general, and administrative	−1,484	−1,976	−2,249	−2,924	−3,947	−5,526	−7,183	−8,620	−9,701	−10,194	−10,449	−10,710	−10,977
Operating income	$ 1,108	$ 941	$ 1,687	$ 2,193	$ 2,960	$ 4,144	$ 5,388	$ 6,465	$ 7,276	$ 7,645	$ 7,836	$ 8,032	$ 8,233
Interest expense			0	0	0	0	0	0	0	0	0	0	0
Other income and expenses	1,556	268	336	436	589	824	1,072	1,286	1,447	1,521	1,559	1,598	1,638
Income before taxes	$ 2,664	$1,209	$ 2,022	$ 2,629	$ 3,549	$ 4,969	$ 6,459	$ 7,751	$ 8,723	$ 9,166	$ 9,395	$ 9,630	$ 9,871
Income tax expense	−768	−458	−768	−999	−1,349	−1,888	−2,455	−2,945	−3,315	−3,483	−3,570	−3,659	−3,751
Net income	$ 1,896	$ 751	$ 1,254	$ 1,630	$ 2,200	$ 3,081	$ 4,005	$ 4,806	$ 5,408	$ 5,683	$ 5,825	$ 5,971	$ 6,120

YAHOO! INC.
Balance Sheet Forecasts
(for the years ended December 31)

($ in millions)	A2005	A2006	F2007	F2008	F2009	F2010	F2011	F2012	F2013	F2014	F2015	F2016	F2017
Cash plus marketable securities	$ 2,561	$ 321	$ 402	$ 522	$ 705	$ 987	$ 1,283	$ 1,539	$ 1,732	$ 1,820	$ 1,866	$ 1,912	$ 1,960
Accounts receivable	722	931	1,100	1,430	1,931	2,703	3,514	4,217	4,746	4,987	5,112	5,240	5,371
Other current assets	167	218	241	313	423	592	770	924	1,039	1,092	1,119	1,147	1,176
Total current assets	$ 3,450	$1,470	$ 1,743	$ 2,266	$ 3,059	$ 4,282	$ 5,567	$ 6,680	$ 7,518	$ 7,900	$ 8,097	$ 8,300	$ 8,507
Property, plant, and equipment	$ 1,267	$1,955	$ 2,758	$ 3,802	$ 5,212	$ 7,185	$ 9,751	$12,829	$16,294	$19,118	$22,047	$25,099	$28,228
Accumulated depreciation	−570	−853	−1,220	−1,737	−2,450	−3,428	−4,776	−6,604	−9,011	−11,250	−14,033	−16,885	−19,808
Property, plant, and equipment (net)	$ 698	$1,101	$ 1,538	$ 2,065	$ 2,761	$ 3,757	$ 4,975	$ 6,225	$ 7,284	$ 7,868	$ 8,014	$ 8,214	$ 8,420
Other assets*	$ 6,685	$6,662	$ 6,948	$ 7,622	$ 8,740	$10,459	$11,673	$12,161	$12,126	$11,650	$11,941	$12,240	$12,546
Total assets	$10,832	$9,233	$10,229	$11,953	$14,560	$18,499	$22,215	$25,066	$26,928	$27,418	$28,052	$28,754	$29,472

* Other assets equal equity investments, goodwill, and intangible and other assets

($ in millions)	A2005	A2006	F2007	F2008	F2009	F2010	F2011	F2012	F2013	F2014	F2015	F2016	F2017
Accounts payable	$ 70	$ 109	$ 161	$ 209	$ 282	$ 395	$ 513	$ 616	$ 693	$ 728	$ 746	$ 765	$ 784
Accrued expenses	1,134	1,365	2,008	2,610	3,524	4,934	6,414	7,697	8,662	9,101	9,329	9,562	9,801
Total current liabilities	$ 1,204	$1,474	$ 2,169	$ 2,819	$ 3,806	$ 5,328	$ 6,927	$ 8,312	$ 9,355	$ 9,830	$10,075	$10,327	$10,585
Long-term debt	750	0	0	0	0	0	0	0	0	0	0	0	0
Non-current liabilities	311	129	161	209	282	395	513	616	693	728	746	765	784
Total liabilities	$ 2,265	$ 1,603	$ 2,329	$ 3,028	$ 4,088	$ 5,723	$ 7,440	$ 8,928	$10,048	$10,558	$10,822	$11,092	$11,370
Common stock (and other)	$ 5,600	$ 5,443	$ 5,443	$ 5,443	$ 5,443	$ 5,443	$ 5,443	$ 5,443	$ 5,443	$ 5,443	$ 5,443	$ 5,443	$ 5,443
Retained earnings	2,966	2,187	2,456	3,482	5,029	7,333	9,332	10,695	11,437	11,417	11,787	12,218	12,660
Total shareholders' equity	$ 8,566	$ 7,630	$ 7,899	$ 8,925	$10,472	$12,776	$14,775	$16,138	$16,880	$16,860	$17,231	$17,661	$18,103
Total liabilities and equities	$10,832	$9,233	$10,229	$11,953	$14,560	$18,499	$22,215	$25,066	$26,928	$27,418	$28,052	$28,754	$29,472

Exhibit may contain small rounding errors

EXHIBIT 6.2 Yahoo! Inc.—Historical and Forecasted Free Cash Flow Schedules

YAHOO! INC.
Free Cash Flow Forecasts
(for the years ended December 31)

($ in millions)	A2005	A2006	F2007	F2008	F2009	F2010	F2011	F2012	F2013	F2014	F2015	F2016	F2017
Earnings before interest and taxes (EBIT)	$2,664	$1,209	$2,022	$2,629	$3,549	$4,969	$6,459	$7,751	$8,723	$9,166	$9,395	$9,630	$9,871
− Income taxes paid on EBIT	−768	−458	−768	−999	−1,349	−1,888	−2,455	−2,945	−3,315	−3,483	−3,570	−3,659	−3,751
Earnings before interest and after taxes	$1,896	$ 751	$1,254	$1,630	$2,200	$3,081	$4,005	$4,806	$5,408	$5,683	$5,825	$5,971	$6,120
+ Depreciation	224	302	367	517	713	977	1,348	1,829	2,406	3,056	3,586	3,675	3,767
+ Amortization	173	238	238	238	238	238	238	238	238	238	238	238	238
− Change in accounts receivable	−272	−185	−169	−330	−501	−772	−811	−703	−529	−241	−125	−128	−131
− Change in other current assets	0	0	−23	−72	−110	−169	−178	−154	−116	−53	−27	−28	−29
− Change in other assets	−35	−10	−523	−912	−1,355	−1,957	−1,451	−725	−203	239	−529	−536	−544
+ Change in accounts payable	32	30	52	48	73	113	118	103	77	35	18	19	19
+ Change in accrued expenses	212	175	643	602	914	1,410	1,480	1,283	965	440	228	233	239
+ Change in non-current liabilities	−518	70	32	48	73	113	118	103	77	35	18	19	19
− Change in required cash balance		−58	−80	−120	−183	−282	−296	−257	−193	−88	−46	−47	−48
Unlevered cash flow from operations	$1,711	$1,313	$1,788	$1,648	$2,063	$2,750	$4,571	$6,522	$8,131	$9,344	$9,186	$9,416	$9,651
− Capital expenditures (net)	−2,146	−816	−803	−1,044	−1,410	−1,973	−2,566	−3,079	−3,465	−3,641	−3,732	−3,876	−3,973
Unlevered free cash flow	$ −435	$ 496	$ 985	$ 604	$ 654	$ 777	$2,006	$3,443	$4,666	$5,703	$5,454	$5,540	$5,678

Exhibit may contain small rounding errors

EXHIBIT 6.3	Yahoo! Inc.—Discounted Cash Flow Valuation

YAHOO! INC.
Discounted Cash Flow Valuation

Cost of capital		12.0%
Growth rate for free cash flow for continuing value		2.5%

($ in millions)	2006	F2007	F2008	F2009	F2010	F2011	F2012	F2013	F2014	F2015	F2016	CV$_{Firm}$ F2016
Unlevered free cash flow for continuing value												$ 5,678
Discount factor for continuing value												10.526
Unlevered free cash flow and continuing value		$ 985	$ 604	$ 654	$ 777	$2,006	$3,443	$4,666	$5,703	$5,454	$5,540	$59,773
Discount factor		0.893	0.797	0.712	0.636	0.567	0.507	0.452	0.404	0.361	0.322	0.322
Present value		$ 879	$ 482	$ 465	$ 494	$1,138	$1,744	$2,111	$2,303	$1,967	$1,784	$19,245
Value of the firm (without excess cash)	$32,612											
Net excess assets	2,128											
Value of the firm	$34,741											

Exhibit may contain small rounding errors

6.2 THE CONSTANT-GROWTH PERPETUITY MODEL

We often use the constant-growth perpetuity model to estimate continuing value. We first discuss the model and its derivation and we then go on to discuss the assumptions we have to make about the company in order use the constant-growth cash flow perpetuity model to estimate a company's continuing value.

LO1 Calculate continuing value using the constant-growth perpetuity model

The formula to discount an infinite series of cash flows is as follows:[4]

$$V_0 = \sum_{t=1}^{\infty} \frac{FCF_t}{(1 + r)^t}$$

If we assume free cash flows grow at a constant rate, g, after Year 1, we can expand the infinite sum as follows:[5]

$$V_0 = \frac{FCF_1}{(1 + r)} \times \left(1 + \frac{(1 + g)}{(1 + r)} + \frac{(1 + g)^2}{(1 + r)^2} + \cdots + \frac{(1 + g)^{\infty - 1}}{(1 + r)^{\infty - 1}}\right)$$

We cannot directly calculate the result of this formula, for we cannot directly calculate an infinite series; however, we can nicely summarize the above formula if we make an assumption about the relative magnitudes of the discount rate and growth rate. If the discount rate is equal to the growth rate ($r = g$), then the last term in the formula is equal to infinity, for an infinite series of 1s is equal to infinity $[\infty = FCF_1/(1 + r) \times (1 + 1 + 1 + \ldots)]$. We also arrive at the same answer if the discount rate is less than the growth rate ($r < g$) because an infinite series of numbers greater than 1 is equal to infinity. If the discount rate is greater than the growth rate ($r > g$), the present value of the constant-growth perpetuity is less than infinity and greater than zero.[6] In this case, we can reduce the above formula to a simple and usable form—the constant-growth perpetuity formula.

$$V_0 = \frac{FCF_1}{(r - g)} \tag{6.1}$$

Using the Free Cash Flow in Year Zero (FCF$_0$)

Using the above assumptions, we can also adapt the above perpetuity formula to use the free cash flow in Year 0 ($FCF_1 = FCF_0 \times (1 + g_1)$) as follows:

$$V_{F.0} = \frac{FCF_0 \times (1 + g_1)}{r - g} \tag{6.2}$$

---

[4] The discount rate, r, is equal to the unlevered cost of capital for an all-equity company or the weighted average cost of capital for a company with debt.

[5] In most situations, the free cash flow in period 1 must be greater than zero in order to make the constant-growth assumption.

[6] Recall that we are assuming that the initial cash flow, FCF_1, is positive, that the constant growth rate is a finite number ($-\infty < g < \infty$), and that the discount rate is a finite positive number ($0 < \infty$).

The growth rate for Year 1, g_1, does not need to be the same as the growth rate for future years for the formula to work.

When We Can Apply the Cash Flow Perpetuity Model—A Company in Steady State

We must make certain assumptions in order to use the constant-growth perpetuity model. First, we assume the company's base year free cash flow is positive and grows at a constant expected growth rate in perpetuity. We also assume the company has a constant discount rate, which implies that it has a constant proportionate capital structure and constant expected operating risks as well as constant required rates of return in the economy. Further, the company's expected economic rate of return on its investment is constant through time. The point in time when the company in our financial model meets all of these assumptions—that is, when it is in steady state—is the point when we can use the constant-growth cash flow perpetuity model to measure the continuing value.

As discussed earlier, when valuing a company, we must choose the number of years for which we will prepare detailed forecasts. If we measure continuing value by discounting free cash flows using a perpetuity model, the choice is clear. We would prepare detailed year-by-year forecasts for the company until the company reaches steady state. You may need to value a company's cash flows for five years, ten years, or longer if the company is far from becoming a stable mature company as of the valuation date. As a result, the horizon for the continuing value calculation will vary across valuations as a function of company-specific characteristics as of the valuation date. Estimating the point in time when you expect a company to reach its steady state can be complex, especially for a company in a high-growth stage of its life at the valuation date. A common way to describe a business as it approaches its steady state is to describe it as maturing or matured. In other words, the point in time that a company will likely begin to grow at a steady rate in perpetuity is when its operations and business have matured.

How do we make these choices and address these issues? Let us think about a company like Starbucks to explore how we might approach these issues. To decide on when Starbucks reaches its steady state, we must decide how long it will take Starbucks to saturate the U.S. market with its locations. We must also select the countries to which its business model is transportable and decide on how long it will take to saturate those markets. We must also consider whether Starbucks will be able to create new revenue streams. For example, a number of years ago, Starbucks began selling its coffee beans in grocery stores and other retail outlets, which was a brand new revenue stream beyond revenues generated from its store locations.

The capital structure issue is reasonably straightforward to address. We simply consider the company's current capital structure strategy and assess whether it is operating at its long-run sustainable capital structure. If it is not, we then investigate the company's long-run sustainable capital structure as well as how long it will take the company to reach it. One way to think about a sustainable capital structure is to examine comparable companies to understand the typical capital structure for companies in that industry.

Additional Considerations—Companies in Cyclical Industries

A **cyclical industry** is an industry whose performance follows the general cycle of the economy—when the economy is doing well, the industry generally performs well, and when the economy is doing poorly, the industry generally performs poorly. The automobile and construction industries are typically considered cyclical industries, whereas food processing and mining industries are not. When forecasting a company in a cyclical industry, it is often useful to analyze what the cycle for the industry usually looks like and to identify the point in the cycle you are beginning your forecast. Naturally, fully understanding an industry's cycle is not an easy task.

Recall that when we are valuing a company, we typically develop detailed forecasts until the company reaches a "steady state." In addition to the factors we previously discussed, the steady state for a company in a cyclical industry should be at the midpoint of the cycle. Measuring the company's continuing value at the peak of a cycle will likely overstate the company's continuing value, and measuring it at the trough of a cycle will likely understate its value. An alternative to using the midpoint is to model the cycle in a spreadsheet and extend the detailed forecast for, say, 100 or more years. If you can model the cycle, the latter is a reasonable approach given the power of computers and the spreadsheet software available.

Valuation Key 6.1

When using the constant-growth perpetuity formula, we assume that the growth rate is smaller than the discount rate; otherwise, the resulting value is infinite. In a constant-growth perpetuity model, the continuing value is quite sensitive to the growth rate chosen. We apply the constant-growth cash flow perpetuity model at the point in time the firm is expected to reach steady state.

6.3 HOW IMPORTANT IS THE CONTINUING VALUE COMPONENT OF A COMPANY'S TOTAL VALUE?

In this section, we will illustrate that the proportion of total value that results from continuing value calculations is often more than 50%. Therefore, the continuing value calculation is going to be an important part of most of the valuations that you will perform. You might conclude that the reason for this is due to our assumption that a company will continue to operate in perpetuity. Using a simple example, we show that the first 50 or so years of a perpetuity drive almost all of its value. Thus, from a practical standpoint, we are not really assuming that a company will continue to operate indefinitely.

Proportion of Total Value Resulting from Continuing Value

To examine this issue, we assume that an investment will generate cash flows of $100 next year, and thereafter, we expect future cash flows to grow at 3% in perpetuity. For an investment with a 13% discount rate, the value of the investment is $1,000.[7] In Exhibit 6.4, we present a chart with proportions of the investment's value derived from various ranges of future periods. This exhibit shows that more than 60% of the value results from cash flows after Year 5 and that about 40% results from cash flows after Year 10. Thus, if you were to have a company with cash flows like this and modeled the explicit year-by-year cash flows for only the first five years, 60% of the value would be in the continuing value. Note, however, only 1% of the total value comes from the cash flows beyond Year 50. Therefore, in practical terms, given the parameters used in this example, we are essentially assuming that the firm would continue to generate cash flows for about 50 years.

EXHIBIT 6.4	Proportion of Constant-Growth Perpetuity Value for Subsets of Years in the Infinite Horizon

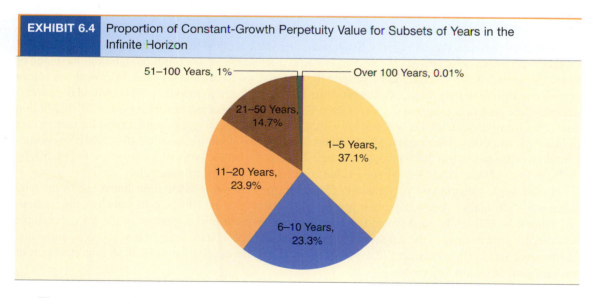

The percentage of value resulting from the cash flows after, say, Year 10 increases with the growth rate and decreases with the discount rate. In Exhibit 6.5, we show the percentage of value resulting from

---

[7] We calculated the value of this investment using the cash flow perpetuity formula. The value of the investment is calculated as $1,000 = $100/(0.13 − 0.03).

cash flows after Year 10 for various combinations of discount rates (varying between 8% and 15%) and growth rates (varying between 0% and 5%). This exhibit shows that the percentage of value derived from cash flows after Year 10 has a low of 25% (with a growth rate of 0% and a discount rate of 15%) and a high of 75% (with a growth rate of 5% and a discount rate of 8%). For growth rates between 2% and 4% and discount rates between 8% and 10%, the percentage of value from the cash flows after Year 10 ranges from 47% to 69%. Thus, in many valuations, more than 50% of the total value of the firm is likely to come from the continuing value calculation, even when you model the year-by-year cash flows out for 10 years. Many practitioners only model the year-by-year cash flows for five years, which means that an even greater proportion of the total value will result from the continuing value estimate.

EXHIBIT 6.5	Percentage of Constant-Growth Perpetuity Value Derived from Years 11 Through Infinity for Various Combinations of Discount and Growth Rates					
			Constant-Growth Rate in Perpetuity			
	0%	**1%**	**2%**	**3%**	**4%**	**5%**
8%	46%	51%	56%	62%	69%	75%
9%	42%	47%	51%	57%	63%	69%
10%	39%	43%	47%	52%	57%	63%
11%	35%	39%	43%	47%	52%	57%
12%	32%	36%	39%	43%	48%	52%
13%	29%	33%	36%	40%	44%	48%
14%	27%	30%	33%	36%	40%	44%
15%	25%	27%	30%	33%	37%	40%

(Discount Rate labels the left axis.)

Yahoo's Continuing Value as a Percentage of Its Total Value

The DCF model we use for Yahoo contains 11 years of detailed forecasts. We use the 11th year, 2017, to measure Yahoo's continuing value. Its free cash flow in 2017 is $5.678 billion. With a 12% discount rate and a 2.5% perpetual growth rate after 2017, Yahoo's continuing value as of the end of 2016 is $59.8 billion.

$$V_{Yahoo, 2016} = \frac{FCF_{2017}}{r - g} = \frac{\$5.678}{0.12 - 0.025} = \$59.8$$

The 2006 present value of Yahoo's 2016 continuing value is equal to $19.2 billion ($19.2 = $59.8 × $(1.12)^{-10}$). This value is almost 60% of Yahoo's total 2006 value of $32.6 billion, ignoring the value of its excess assets (0.59 = $19.2/$32.6), despite the fact that we forecasted 10 years of cash flows before performing the continuing value calculation. Note that we further assumed that Yahoo would not experience any real growth subsequent to 2017. Given Yahoo's 2007 expected free cash flow of $0.985 billion and 12% cost of capital, we know that its free cash flows will have to grow at high rates for many years in order for its 2006 value to equal $32.6 billion. In our illustration, we assumed that Yahoo's revenues would grow by more than 20% annually through 2012, and then we reduced its growth rate to 2.5% by 2015; in spite of this, Yahoo's continuing value is still almost 60% of its total value.

In the Apple valuation we performed in Chapter 1, the continuing value contributed less of the total value when we again forecasted explicit year-by-year cash flows for 10 years. In that case, the continuing value was 42% of the total value; this is still substantive but not as great as in the Yahoo example because the growth rates in the Apple valuation are not as high as they were in the Yahoo example and the discount rate is slightly larger (12.5%). Suffice it to say, the continuing value is an important part of the valuation of almost any company.

Does an Infinite Horizon Really Mean the Company Exists Forever?

We might conclude that it is the perpetuity assumption that causes continuing values to have such a large effect on a company's total value. Moreover, you might be concerned that it is an inappropriate assumption to assume a company will last forever. If we again review Exhibit 6.4, we see, however, that cash flows after 100 years contribute less than 0.01% of the total value and that cash flows after 50 years contribute only 1% of the total value. The cash flows between Years 11 and 50 contribute about 39% of the total value. Thus, in most situations, a company derives most of its economic value from the first 50 years of its forecasted cash flows.

Valuation Key 6.2

The cash flows beyond Year 50 typically have a small effect on value when we make an infinite horizon assumption in the continuing value calculation. However, in a typical valuation of a company the continuing value often drives more than 50% of the total value.

In Exhibit 6.6, we show the percentage of value derived from the first 50 years of the perpetuity for various combinations of discount rates and growth rates. For discount rates of at least 8% and growth rates of no more than 5%, the first 50 years account for at least 76% of the perpetuity's value. For growth rates between 2% and 4% and discount rates between 10% and 13%, the first 50 years account for at least 94% of the perpetuity's value. Thus, in economic terms, we are not really assuming an infinite life.

| EXHIBIT 6.6 | Percentage of Constant-Growth Perpetuity Value Derived from the First 50 Years of Cash Flows for Various Combinations of Discount Rates and Growth Rates |

Discount Rate	Constant-Growth Rate in Perpetuity					
	0%	**1%**	**2%**	**3%**	**4%**	**5%**
8%	98%	96%	94%	91%	85%	76%
9%	99%	98%	96%	94%	90%	85%
10%	99%	99%	98%	96%	94%	90%
11%	99%	99%	99%	98%	96%	94%
12%	100%	99%	99%	98%	98%	96%
13%	100%	100%	99%	99%	98%	97%
14%	100%	100%	100%	99%	99%	98%
15%	100%	100%	100%	100%	99%	99%

6.4 THE PRESENT VALUE WEIGHTED AVERAGE GROWTH RATE

Although we eventually assume that a company reaches a steady state to use a cash flow perpetuity model, we might conclude that it will be a long period before the company reaches its steady state growth rate. Given today's computing power and the usefulness of software used to create financial models, extending the continuing value date out to 20, 30, 50, or 100 years is not an unreasonable undertaking in some circumstances. Regardless, either for presentation purposes or for other reasons, valuation models sometimes incorporate a continuing value date that is before the date when the company is expected to reach its steady state. In order to do that, we still need to model what the future growth rates will be; once we do that, we can use a perpetuity model and a present value weighted average growth rate.

Even if the year-to-year growth rates in cash flows for a company vary widely over time, we can always express the value of a firm as a function of single growth rate in a constant-growth perpetuity model as long as the first cash flow is positive and the discount rate is constant through time. More specifically, if we know the value of an investment, its discount rate, and its free cash flows in Year 1, we can modify Equation 6.1 to measure the present value weighted average growth rate for this investment, g_A.

$$g_A = r - \frac{FCF_1}{V_{F,0}}$$

(6.3)

This relation allows us to measure the constant growth assumption that would yield an equivalent valuation to an assumption about varying growth rates. In particular, you might assume that a company will have high growth for a few years and that its growth will then slow until it reaches some modest long-run sustainable growth rate. For such a company, there will be some constant growth assumption across all years that will provide the same valuation.

For example, assume a company's Year 0 free cash flow is $100, and its expected growth rates are 50% for Year 1, 30% for Year 2, 10% for Year 3, and 3% thereafter. If the company's cost of capital is 12%, the value of the company is $2,189.36 as of the end of Year 0. We measure its value using the expected free cash flows, which is effectively the same as using both the free cash flow in Year 0 and the expected future growth rates.

$$V_{F,0} = \frac{\$100 \times (1.5)}{(1.12)} + \frac{\$100 \times (1.5) \times (1.3)}{(1.12)^2} + \frac{\$100 \times (1.5) \times (1.3) \times (1.1)}{(1.12)^3} + \frac{\$100 \times (1.5) \times (1.3) \times (1.1) \times (1.03)}{.12 - .03} \times \frac{1}{(1.12)^3} = \$2,189$$

Once we know both the value of the firm at Year 0 and the Year 1 free cash flow, we can measure the company's present value weighted average growth rate for Year 2 onward as

$$g_A = r - \frac{FCF_1}{V_{F,0}} = .12 - \frac{\$150}{\$2,189} = 0.0515$$

In other words, the anticipated cash flow growth rates for Year 2 onward are 30%, 10%, and then 3% in perpetuity, which is equivalent to assuming a 5.15% growth rate in perpetuity for Year 2 onward (assuming a discount rate of 12%). Of course, since this is a present value weighted average growth rate, this calculation depends on the discount rate and not just the growth rates.

Being able to calculate the present value weighted average growth rate can be very useful for presentation purposes, as many times cash flow forecasts are only shown for six years (the sixth year for the perpetuity calculation). Calculating the present value weighted average growth rate for the cash flow growth rates for Years 6 through infinity allows you to do a perpetuity cash flow calculation at the end of the fifth year using the sixth year's cash flow. Of course, you still have to model the cash flows out beyond Year 5 in order to calculate the present value weighted average growth rate. Note that we are not advocating that you only forecast five years of cash flows and then guess the continuing value growth rate!

If we use Year 0 as our base year and use its free cash flow (see Equation 6.2), we measure the present value weighted average growth rate, g_A—which includes the effect of the growth rate for Year 1—using the following formula:

$$g_A = \frac{1 + r}{1 + \frac{FCF_0}{V_{F,0}}} - 1 \tag{6.4}$$

For our example, we also measure the company's present value weighted average growth rate for Year 1 onward as

$$g_A = \frac{1 + r}{1 + \frac{FCF_0}{V_{F,0}}} - 1 = \frac{1.12}{1 + \frac{\$100}{\$2,189}} - 1 = 0.0711$$

The company's present value weighted average growth rate for Year 1 onward is about 2% larger than it is for Year 2 onward, because we included the effect of its Year 1 growth rate, which at 50% is much larger than the subsequent growth rates.

Yahoo's Present Value Weighted Average Growth Rate

We use the DCF valuation to measure Yahoo's present value perpetual weighted average growth rate as of 2006. We know that its 2006 value is $32.6 billion after the distribution of excess assets and that its 2007 free cash flow is $0.985 billion. With a discount rate of 12%, Yahoo's present value weighted average growth rate for 2008 onward is equal to 8.98%.

$$g = r - \frac{FCF_1}{V_{F,0}} = 0.12 - \frac{\$0.985}{\$32.612} = 0.0898$$

Growth Rate Using Five Years of Free Cash Flow Forecasts

As discussed previously, for presentation purposes, one can present a limited number of free cash flow forecasts and then use the present value weighted average growth rate in a perpetuity model for the cash flow subsequent to those being detailed in order to simplify the presentation of the valuation. We demonstrate this approach here with Yahoo! Inc. by showing only six years of free cash flow forecasts from 2007 to 2012, with the 2012 forecast being used for the continuing value calculation.

At the top of Exhibit 6.7, we calculate the value of Yahoo! Inc. as of year-end 2011 based on the forecasts for 2012 to 2017 in conjunction with the perpetuity growth assumption of 2.5% after 2017. As you can see in the exhibit, the value at the end of year 2011 is $51.4 billion. Next, we calculate the present value weighted average growth rate that yields the $51.4 billion valuation using the 2012 free cash flow of $3.443 billion in conjunction with Yahoo's 12% cost of capital.

$$g = r - \frac{FCF_{2012}}{V_{F, 2011}} = 0.12 - \frac{\$3,443}{\$51,380} = 0.0530$$

Now that we know the present value weighted average growth rate to apply to the 2012 cash flow, we can present a version of Yahoo's valuation using only six years of forecasts, which we present at the bottom of Exhibit 6.7. The resulting value of the firm of $32.6 billion (without excess cash) is equal to the value calculated using all 11 years of forecasts (Exhibit 6.3).

EXHIBIT 6.7	Calculation of Yahoo! Inc.'s 2011 Value and Present Value Weighted Average Growth Rate for 2012 Onward

YAHOO! INC.
Discounted Cash Flow Valuation

Cost of capital			12.0%				
Growth rate for free cash flow for continuing value			2.5%				

($ in millions)	F2011	F2012	F2013	F2014	F2015	F2016	CV$_{Firm}$ F2016
Unlevered free cash flow for continuing value							$ 5,678
Discount factor for continuing value							10.526
Unlevered free cash flow and continuing value		$3,443	$4,666	$5,703	$5,454	$5,540	$59,773
Discount factor		0.893	0.797	0.712	0.636	0.567	0.567
Present value		$3,074	$3,720	$4,060	$3,466	$3,144	$33,917
Value of the firm as of 2011	$51,380						
Present value weighted average growth rate		5.30%					

YAHOO! INC.
Discounted Cash Flow Valuation

Cost of capital			12.0%				
Present value weighted average growth rate			5.3%				

($ in millions)	2006	F2007	F2008	F2009	F2010	F2011	CV$_{Firm}$
Unlevered free cash flow for continuing value							$ 3,443
Discount factor for continuing value							14.922
Unlevered free cash flow and continuing value		$ 985	$ 604	$ 654	$ 777	$2,006	$51,380
Discount factor		0.893	0.797	0.712	0.636	0.567	0.567
Present value		$ 879	$ 482	$ 465	$ 494	$1,138	$29,155
Value of the firm (without excess cash)	$32,612						

Exhibit may contain small rounding errors

REVIEW EXERCISE 6.1

Present Value Weighted Average Growth Rate

Assume an investment will generate cash flows at the end of Years 1 through 5 equal to $2,200, $3,240, $3,300, $3,820, and $4,280, respectively. After Year 5, the cash flows will grow at 3% per year in perpetuity. Calculate the present value of these cash flows at the end of Year 0, assuming a discount rate of 12%. Then calculate the present value weighted average growth rate for this investment for Year 2 onward.

Solution on page 247.

Two-Stage Growth Rates

As we indicated, we can adjust our free cash flow perpetuity valuation model to incorporate the effects of multiple growth rates for a company by using the present value weighted average growth rate. For example, at some point, it might be possible to assume that a company will experience two growth rates—a growth rate higher than the company's steady state growth rate for a finite period and, in a subsequent year, the company's steady state growth rate.[8] If we make this assumption, the present value weighted average growth rate used in a constant-growth perpetuity formula to encompass both of these stages would be larger than the company's steady state growth rate. We do not recommend using a constant-growth perpetuity formula for a multi-stage growth rate assumption unless you explicitly determine the constant-growth perpetuity assumption that is justified by the multi-stage growth rate assumption that we now demonstrate.

In the prior section, we showed how to calculate the present value weighted average growth rate irrespective of how much variation there is in the growth rate over time. However, in order to use Equations 6.3 or 6.4, you needed to assess the value of the firm. Below, we show how to calculate the present value weighted average growth rate of a free cash flow stream using a two-stage growth rate assumption. We begin with two free cash flow growth rates, g_1 and g_2; we assume that the free cash flows will grow at the first growth rate through Year N and then grow at the second growth rate thereafter in perpetuity. Note that the cash flows grow at g_1 for $N - 1$ years because the first year to which the growth rate applies is the second year. We use our present value framework to derive the present value weighted average growth rate that we could use in the constant-growth perpetuity cash flow model to measure the present value of the free cash flows with these two growth rates. We begin with the formula to measure the present value of the free cash flows with two growth rates; this formula combines the present value of an N-year annuity with constant growth (g_1) and the present value of a constant-growth perpetuity (g_2).

$$PV_0 = FCF_1\left[\left(\frac{1}{r - g_1} - \frac{1}{r - g_1} \times \frac{(1 + g_1)^N}{(1 + r)^N}\right) + \left(\frac{1 + g_2}{r - g_2} \times \frac{(1 + g_1)^{N-1}}{(1 + r)^N}\right)\right]$$

For example, assume that a company with a risk-adjusted discount rate equal to 13% has an expected free cash flow next year (FCF_1) equal to $1,000, which is expected to grow at 15% for Years 2 through 4 and thereafter grow at 3% in perpetuity. Using the above formula, we measure the present value of this four year annuity and the subsequent perpetuity as follows:

$$\$13,243 = \$1,000\left[\left(\frac{1}{0.13 - 0.15} - \frac{1}{0.13 - 0.15} \times \frac{(1.15)^4}{(1.13)^4}\right) + \left(\frac{1.03}{0.13 - 0.03} \times \frac{(1.15)^3}{(1.13)^4}\right)\right]$$

$$\$13,243 = \$1,000[(-50 - (-50 \times 1.0727) + (10.3 \times 0.933)]$$

$$\$13,243 = \$1,000[13.243]$$

---

[8] Naturally, we do not need to limit our multi-stage growth rates to two growth rates. Instead of using two discrete growth rates, we might also add a transition period between the first (high) and second (steady state) growth rates.

Once we know the value, we can calculate the present value weighted average growth rate using Equation 6.3, which we discussed previously.

$$g_A = 0.13 - \frac{\$1,000}{\$13,243} = 0.05449$$

We check the answer we obtained from the two approaches by using this growth rate in the constant-growth perpetuity formula.

$$\$13,243 = \frac{\$1,000}{0.13 - 0.05449}$$

The potential disadvantage of this approach is that you have to solve for the value. However, you can avoid that step if there are just two growth rates by adapting the previous formulas to measure the present value weighted average growth rate. We do that for the previous company.[9] Using the equation in the footnote, we again calculate the present value weighted growth rate equal to 5.449%. The potential disadvantage of this approach relative to using Equation 6.3 is that it can only allow for two different growth rates, whereas Equation 6.3 works with any number of different growth rates.

In Exhibit 6.8, we show the present value weighted average growth rate for various combinations of growth rates, two horizons for the first growth rate, and a discount rate of 12%. The first growth rate can have a large effect on the present value weighted average growth rate. For example, we show that a company with free cash flows growing at 20% for five years and 3% thereafter will have a present value weighted average growth rate of more than 7% with a discount rate of 12%.

EXHIBIT 6.8	**Present Value Weighted Average Growth Rate for a Two-Stage Growth Rate Perpetuity**					
Discount Rate is 12% (r = 12%)		**g_2 after Year 5**			**g_2 after Year 10**	
g_1 (through Year N)	**0%**	**3%**	**5%**	**0%**	**3%**	**5%**
10%	3.1%	4.8%	6.0%	5.1%	6.1%	6.9%
15%	4.3%	5.8%	6.9%	6.9%	7.7%	8.3%
20%	5.3%	6.6%	7.6%	8.2%	8.8%	9.3%
25%	6.2%	7.3%	8.2%	9.2%	9.7%	10.1%

The larger the discount rate, the larger the effect of the first growth rate on the present value weighted average growth rate, because the present value of the cash flows coming from the years of the second growth rate is smaller. In addition, the longer the time the first growth rate persists, the larger the weighted average growth rate if g_1 is greater than g_2.

---

[9] The formula is equal to

$$g_A = r - \left[\frac{1}{\left[\left(\frac{1}{r - g_1} - \frac{1}{r - g_1} \times \frac{(1 + g_1)^N}{(1 + r)^N} \right) + \left(\frac{1 + g_2}{r - g_2} \times \frac{(1 + g_1)^{N-1}}{(1 + r)^N} \right) \right]} \right]$$

where $N - 1$ is the number of years that g_1 will persist. For our example company, we see that the present value weighted average annual growth rate is equal to 5.449%.

$$0.05449 = 0.13 - \left[\frac{1}{\left(\frac{1}{0.13 - 0.15} - \frac{1}{0.13 - 0.15} \times \frac{(1.15)^4}{(1.13)^4} \right) + \left(\frac{1.03}{0.13 - 0.03} \times \frac{(1.15)^3}{(1.13)^4} \right)} \right]$$

Valuation Key 6.3

It is always possible to express the value of a firm in terms of a single growth rate within a constant-growth free cash flow perpetuity model, as long as the first cash flow is positive and the discount rate is constant through time, even if the year-to-year cash flow growth rates are expected to vary over time.

REVIEW EXERCISE 6.2

Two-Stage Growth Rates

Calculate the present value weighted average growth rate for an investment with a discount rate of 12% and cash flows that grow at g_1 through Year 10 and at g_2 thereafter in perpetuity; use every combination of g_1 (5%, 10%, 15% and 20%) and g_2 (−3%, 0%, 3%).

Solution on page 247.

6.5 MEASURING THE BASE YEAR CASH FLOW FOR THE PERPETUITY

LO2 Measure the base year free cash flow for the continuing value estimate

We consider a variety of different issues when measuring the base year cash flow for a perpetuity calculation. First, we must consider the growth rates of all the components of the free cash flow forecasts relative to the assumed perpetual growth rate. This may require modeling the company's year-by-year cash flows a few more years than you originally thought necessary. The key here is to make sure that the investments that you are making in the business are appropriate for the growth rate you intend to use in your perpetuity model. This also means that if you want to examine the sensitivity of your valuation to different assumptions about the perpetuity cash flow growth rate, you will want to calculate a different base year cash flow that is consistent with each growth rate assumption you make.

Another issue to consider related to the base year cash flow is the relation between depreciation and capital expenditures. We explore whether the growth in both of these components is sustainable over the long run. We consider potential issues associated with a company's capital expenditures being lumpy as opposed to growing smoothly due to having to replace major investments (say, a production facility or headquarters building). A related issue to consider is the use of accelerated depreciation for tax purposes and when an asset's useful life for tax purposes is shorter than its underlying economic life. We will discuss these issues in a subsequent section of the chapter.

We also consider the reasonableness of the base year cash flows. This entails several analyses. First, we examine the profitability and rates of returns that the company is generating from its existing operations at the continuing value date. From this analysis, we assess whether the level of profitability and rates of return embedded in the forecasts as of the continuing value date are reasonable. We face difficulties when we conduct such analyses due to the limitations of using accounting profitability and rates of return rather than economic profits and returns. Second, we consider the amount of real growth that we think the company can achieve in perpetuity—if any—and whether the company can earn an economic rate of return on its new investments that exceeds its cost of capital. These analyses lead to decisions about the expected constant growth rate to use in the continuing value perpetuity as well as an understanding of investments needed to generate this growth. We discuss this issue in a later section of the chapter, but we mention it here, as it is part of the overall work that we do in measuring the base year cash flow.

Valuation Key 6.4

There are many critical issues associated with using a free cash flow perpetuity method to measure continuing value. We must determine when a firm will reach "steady state," judge the reasonableness of the base year free cash flow, and determine the perpetuity growth rate.

Preparing the Base Year Cash Flow for the Assumed Constant Perpetuity Growth Rate

The assumption underlying the free cash flow perpetuity model is that free cash flows grow at a constant rate. To satisfy this assumption, analysts often use varying revenue growth rates for the year-by-year detailed cash flow forecasts in a financial model, and at the end of the year-by-year detailed forecasts period (the continuing value date), they assume that revenues and free cash flows grow at the same constant rate in perpetuity as of the continuing value date. While not all of the free cash flow components need to grow at that rate in every period, any deviations from the assumed constant growth rate for one component must be offset by deviations in another component. The equivalence of the revenue and free cash flow growth rates is not a natural result of the typical relationships in a financial model, since some of the free cash flow components are based on changes in balances on the balance sheet (for example, changes in working capital accounts). In general, by the continuing value date, we want all related operating asset and liability balances growing at the revenue growth rate.

It is typically incorrect to assume that future cash flows will grow at a constant rate in the year that the revenue growth rate decreases from a high growth rate to the constant growth rate. In the year that the growth rate decreases, the growth rate for capital expenditures and the increase in working capital—both of which reduce free cash flows—are typically less than the constant growth rate assumed for revenue. Thus, it is likely that free cash flows grow at a rate higher than the revenue growth rate when the growth rate in revenues first declines.

In Exhibit 6.9, we provide a simple illustration of the effect of changing revenue growth rates on free cash flow growth rates. This company has no capital expenditures and finances itself with 100% equity. Its only expense is an operating expense that is equal to 60% of revenues, and it has a constant income tax rate equal to 30%. The company has only one asset—accounts receivable—that is equal to 40% of revenues. The company's revenues grow by 50% in Year +1 and by 5% thereafter. We show one year of actual results and three years of forecasts. We also show the annual growth rates for each line item in the financial model on the right-hand side of the exhibit. First, we confirm the revenue growth rates in this exhibit (50% for Year + 1 and 5% thereafter). Since all of the items in the income statement and all of the assets on the balance sheet are proportional to revenue, the growth rate for every item on the income statement and balance sheet is equal to the revenue growth rate in each year.

EXHIBIT 6.9	Effect of Changing Revenue Growth Rates on Free Cash Flows						
Income Statement, Balance Sheet, and Free Cash Flow Forecasts					**Growth Rates**		
	Actual Year 0	**Forecast Year +1**	**Forecast Year +2**	**Forecast Year +3**	**Forecast Year +1**	**Forecast Year +2**	**Forecast Year +3**
Income Statement							
Revenue	$1,000	$1,500	$1,575	$1,654	50.0%	5.0%	5.0%
Operating expenses	−600	−900	−945	−992	50.0%	5.0%	5.0%
Income before taxes.	$ 400	$ 600	$ 630	$ 662	50.0%	5.0%	5.0%
Income tax expense	−120	−180	−189	−198	50.0%	5.0%	5.0%
Net income	$ 280	$ 420	$ 441	$ 463	50.0%	5.0%	5.0%
Balance Sheet							
Total assets = Accounts receivable	$ 400	$ 600	$ 630	$ 662	50.0%	5.0%	5.0%
Shareholders' equity	$ 400	$ 600	$ 630	$ 662	50.0%	5.0%	5.0%
Free Cash Flows							
Earnings before interest and taxes (EBIT)	$ 400	$ 600	$ 630	$ 662	50.0%	5.0%	5.0%
Income taxes paid on EBIT	−120	−180	−189	−198	50.0%	5.0%	5.0%
Earnings before interest and after taxes	$ 280	$ 420	$ 441	$ 463	50.0%	5.0%	5.0%
Change in accounts receivable	−36	−200	−30	−32	450.0%	−85.0%	5.0%
Unlevered free cash flow = Equity FCF	$ 244	$ 220	$ 411	$ 432	−9.7%	86.8%	5.0%

Exhibit may contain small rounding errors

The free cash flow growth rate, however, is not equal to the revenue growth rate in Year 1 and 2 because the free cash flows are determined, in part, by changes in the balance sheet. When the revenue growth rate increased from 10% in Year 0 (not shown in the exhibit but calculable) to 50% in Year +1, the free cash flow growth rate was -9.7%, and when the revenue growth rate decreased from 50% to 5% in Year +2, the free cash flow growth rate was 86.8%. An examination of the free cash flow components indicates that the growth rates for all of the free cash flow components are equal to the revenue growth rate—except for the growth rate for the change in accounts receivable. The growth rates for all of the other free cash flow components (except the change in accounts receivable) are equal to the revenue growth rate because the other components included in this simple model are proportional to revenues.

If you look carefully at Exhibit 6.9 you can see that once you model the free cash flow for Year +2, which equals $411, you can then safely grow the cash flow forecasts at 5% per year thereafter, because all of the components of the free cash flows are growing at 5 percent subsequent to Year +2. In other words, you will note that the free cash flow for Year +3 of $432 is 5% greater than the free cash flow forecast for Year +2 ($432 = $411 × 1.05).

In the simple example in Exhibit 6.9, the valuation consequences of erroneously growing the free cash flow forecasts for Year +1 at 5% and using that to determine the continuing value instead of using the free cash flow forecasts for Year +2 are extremely large. Assuming a cost of capital of 10%, the correct valuation of the company would be $7,672.7 based on growing the Year +2 forecasts at 5%. Growing the Year +1 forecast at 5% yields a value of $4,400, which is only 57% of the correct value. The correct valuation is

$$V_{F,0} = \frac{\$220}{1.1} + \frac{\$411}{1.1^2} + \frac{\$411 \times (1.05)}{(0.1 - 0.05)} \times \frac{1}{1.1^2} = \$7,672.7$$

Whereas the incorrect valuation stemming from applying a 5% growth rate to the Year 1 forecast would be

$$V_{F,0} = \frac{\$220}{1.1} + \frac{\$220 \times (1.05)}{(0.1 - 0.05)} \times \frac{1}{1.1} = \$4,400$$

While we used a simple example and the change in accounts receivable to illustrate why the free cash flow growth rate will not always equal the revenue growth rate, any cash flow component based on changes in balances on the balance sheet (all working capital components, capital expenditures, etc.) will have a similar effect. In addition, since we calculate depreciation based on historic capital expenditures, depreciation can also cause a difference between the revenue and free cash flow growth rates, a topic we discuss in the next section of the chapter.

Some cash flow components may take even longer to reach steady state than we show in this simple example. For example, if in a financial model we assume that accounts payable is a percent of total purchases, and total purchases is equal to cost of goods sold plus the change in inventory, then the growth rate for the change in accounts payable will take three years to equal the constant revenue growth rate. Why? It will take two years for the change in inventory to equal the constant revenue growth rate, and the growth rate for the change in accounts payable will take one additional year to equal the constant revenue growth rate.

Thus, it is typically helpful to extend the horizon of the year-by-year explicit forecasts until the free cash flow growth rate "settles down" to something that is close to a reasonably constant rate. While it is not necessary to have every component of the free cash flows growing at a constant rate in order to accomplish this goal, analyzing every line item provides useful insights into the model. It should also be apparent that if we wanted to examine the sensitivity of our valuation to different perpetuity growth rates, the base year free cash flow from which the perpetuity is calculated should be different for each different growth rate assumption. We do this because we want to ensure that the appropriate amount of investment is embedded in the free cash flows for each possible growth rate scenario we want to consider.

Valuation Key 6.5

It is often useful to extend the horizon of the financial model—using the growth rate you plan to use as the constant perpetual growth rate—and test whether the free cash flow growth rate is equal to the assumed growth rate in a free cash flow perpetuity valuation. If this is not done and the firm's growth rate is slowing, it is likely that you will understate the continuing value and therefore the value of the firm.

Yahoo's Revenue and Free Cash Flow Growth Rates

In Exhibit 6.10, we present Yahoo's annual growth rates for both its revenue forecasts and the components of its free cash flow forecasts. We can quickly observe that Yahoo's revenue and free cash flow growth rates are never the same until 2017 even though its revenue growth rate is at the long-term inflation rate of 2.5% beginning in 2015. Yahoo's expense ratios stabilize in 2008, and after that, its EBIT growth rate is the same as its revenue growth rate because the financial model forecasts each earnings component as a percentage of revenues (or something else that is directly related to revenues).

The growth rates for the adjustments that convert EBIT to free cash flow, however, are not the same as the revenue growth rates for many years. The working capital items, such as accounts receivable, grow in the way we discussed earlier in this chapter. We have two key points to glean from this analysis. First, when the revenue growth rate increases (decreases), the free cash flow growth rate is often smaller (larger) than the revenue growth rate, indicating that it is not likely to be a good point in the forecast horizon to select as the continuing value date. Second, it can take multiple years with a constant long-term revenue growth rate before the free cash flow growth rate will equal the revenue growth rate. The number of years it takes depends on the forecast drivers embedded in the financial model.

EXHIBIT 6.10 Yahoo! Inc.—Revenue and Free Cash Flow Growth Rates

YAHOO! INC.
Annual Growth Rates for Revenues and Components of Free Cash Flow Forecasts
(for the years ended December 31)

($ in millions)	A2006	F2007	F2008	F2009	F2010	F2011	F2012	F2013	F2014	F2015	F2016	F2017
Revenue	22.2%	25.0%	30.0%	35.0%	40.0%	30.0%	20.0%	12.5%	5.1%	2.5%	2.5%	2.5%
Earnings before interest and taxes (EBIT)	−54.6%	67.2%	30.0%	35.0%	40.0%	30.0%	20.0%	12.5%	5.1%	2.5%	2.5%	2.5%
− Income taxes paid on EBIT	−40.3%	67.8%	30.0%	35.0%	40.0%	30.0%	20.0%	12.5%	5.1%	2.5%	2.5%	2.5%
Earnings before interest and after taxes	−60.4%	66.9%	30.0%	35.0%	40.0%	30.0%	20.0%	12.5%	5.1%	2.5%	2.5%	2.5%
+ Depreciation	34.9%	21.3%	41.1%	37.9%	37.1%	37.9%	35.7%	31.6%	27.0%	17.3%	2.5%	2.5%
+ Amortization	37.4%	0.0%	0.0%	0.0%	0.0%	0.0%	0.0%	0.0%	0.0%	0.0%	0.0%	0.0%
− Change in accounts receivable	−32.0%	−8.6%	94.9%	51.7%	54.3%	5.0%	−13.3%	−24.8%	−54.4%	−48.3%	2.5%	2.5%
− Change in other current assets			211.8%	51.7%	54.3%	5.0%	−13.3%	−24.8%	−54.4%	−48.3%	2.5%	2.5%
− Change in other assets	−72.9%	5369.9%	74.3%	48.5%	44.5%	−25.9%	−50.0%	−72.0%	−217.4%	−321.5%	1.4%	1.4%
+ Change in accounts payable	−3.7%	69.4%	−6.4%	51.7%	54.3%	5.0%	−13.3%	−24.8%	−54.4%	−48.3%	2.5%	2.5%
+ Change in accrued expenses	−17.7%	268.4%	−6.3%	51.7%	54.3%	5.0%	−13.3%	−24.8%	−54.4%	−48.3%	2.5%	2.5%
+ Change in non-current liabilities	−113.5%	−54.9%	52.7%	51.7%	54.3%	5.0%	−13.3%	−24.8%	−54.4%	−48.3%	2.5%	2.5%
− Change in required cash balance		37.5%	50.0%	51.7%	54.3%	5.0%	−13.3%	−24.8%	−54.4%	−48.3%	2.5%	2.5%
Unlevered cash flow from operations	−23.3%	36.2%	−7.8%	25.2%	33.3%	66.2%	42.7%	24.7%	14.9%	−1.7%	2.5%	2.5%
− Capital expenditures (net)	−62.0%	−1.6%	30.0%	35.0%	40.0%	30.0%	20.0%	12.5%	5.1%	2.5%	3.9%	2.5%
Unlevered free cash flow	−214.1%	98.4%	−38.6%	8.1%	18.8%	158.2%	71.7%	35.5%	22.2%	−4.4%	1.6%	2.5%

Another important consideration in the base year cash flow is to deal appropriately with capital expenditures, depreciation, and the relationship between them. We discuss that in detail in the next section.

6.6 CAPITAL EXPENDITURE AND DEPRECIATION ISSUES

In this section, we examine four other issues associated with the base year cash flow. All of these issues deal with capital expenditures and depreciation. All of the concepts presented here are equally applicable to investments in intangibles and the amortization of intangibles (if deductible for tax purposes), but we only discuss these issues in the context of tangible investments and depreciation.

First, capital expenditures are often "lumpy"; that is, the growth rate for capital expenditures changes from year to year and differs from the revenue growth rate. For example, a company that requires large manufacturing facilities in order to be efficient will have large capital expenditures when it builds a new plant and subsequently replaces it. However, it will experience lower capital expenditures in other years.

Second, a related issue occurs with depreciation expense when the depreciable useful life of an asset differs from its economic useful life. The **depreciable useful life** (or **useful life**) of an asset is the number of years over which the company depreciates the asset, and the **economic useful life** of an asset is the number of years the company uses the asset. For tax purposes, companies generally have an incentive to use as short a depreciable life as possible. If the depreciable life for tax purposes is shorter than the economic useful life, the company will not have any depreciation expense for tax purposes for the years between the end of the depreciable life for taxes and the end of the economic useful life. Thus, the growth rate for depreciation will not be constant, and this will affect the free cash flows because of the effect of depreciation on taxes. While this occurs at the individual asset level in most cases, the key issue is whether it occurs in aggregate across all assets the company depreciates.

Third, a company's depreciation for book accounting and tax accounting purposes can differ—sometimes substantially. The book depreciation is not relevant to the matters we discuss in this chapter; rather, it is the tax depreciation that is of importance to us. Since companies generally use accelerated depreciation for tax purposes, the growth rate for depreciation tax shields will not be constant over the life of an asset and more importantly may not be constant across all depreciable assets of the company as a whole. Finally, over the long run—that is, in "steady state"—the ratio of a company's capital expenditures to its depreciation may tend to converge to some constant ratio, but this depends on the growth rate of the company's capital expenditures and the useful life of the company's assets. The constant ratio can be less than, equal to, or greater than one. It is helpful to develop a reasonable rationale for the relation between capital expenditures and depreciation for the base year cash flow used in the perpetuity calculation.

"Lumpy" Capital Expenditures Result in "Lumpy" Free Cash Flows

In this section, we will illustrate the effect of "lumpy" capital expenditures on free cash flows. In Exhibit 6.11, we show the financial forecasts and growth rates for the Lumpy CAPEX Company over 24 years, Year +1 to Year +24. The company uses a three-year useful life and straight-line depreciation to amortize

EXHIBIT 6.11 The Lumpy CAPEX Company's Financial Forecasts and Growth Rates

	Year 0	Year +1	Year +2	Year +3	Year +4	Year +5	Year +6	...	Year +22	Year +23	Year +24
Income Statement											
Revenue		$150.0	$210.0	$252.0	$252.0	$252.0	$252.0	...	$252.0	$252.0	$252.0
Depreciation expense		−75.0	−105.0	−126.0	−126.0	−126.0	−126.0	...	−126.0	−126.0	−126.0
Income before taxes		$ 75.0	$105.0	$126.0	$126.0	$126.0	$126.0	...	$126.0	$126.0	$126.0
Income tax expense (provision)		−22.5	−31.5	−37.8	−37.8	−37.8	−37.8	...	−37.8	−37.8	−37.8
Net income		$ 52.5	$ 73.5	$ 88.2	$ 88.2	$ 88.2	$ 88.2	...	$88.2	$ 88.2	$ 88.2
Balance Sheet											
Total assets	$ 225.0	$240.0	$198.0	$297.0	$261.0	$198.0	$297.0	...	$261.0	$198.0	$297.0
Shareholders' equity	$ 225.0	$240.0	$198.0	$297.0	$261.0	$198.0	$297.0	...	$261.0	$198.0	$297.0
Free Cash Flows											
Earnings before interest and taxes		$ 75.0	$105.0	$126.0	$126.0	$126.0	$126.0	...	$126.0	$126.0	$126.0
Income taxes paid on EBIT		−22.5	−31.5	−37.8	−37.8	−37.8	−37.8	...	−37.8	−37.8	−37.8
Earnings before interest and after taxes		$ 52.5	$ 73.5	$ 88.2	$ 88.2	$ 88.2	$ 88.2	...	$88.2	$ 88.2	$ 88.2
Depreciation		75.0	105.0	126.0	126.0	126.0	126.0	...	126.0	126.0	126.0
Unlevered cash flow from operations		$127.5	$178.5	$214.2	$214.2	$214.2	$214.2	...	$214.2	$214.2	$214.2
Capital expenditures	$−225.0	−90.0	−63.0	−225.0	−90.0	−63.0	−225.0	...	−90.0	−63.0	−225.0
Unlevered free cash flow		$ 37.5	$115.5	$−10.8	$124.2	$151.2	$−10.8	...	$124.2	$151.2	$−10.8

			Year +2	Year +3	Year +4	Year +5	Year +6	...	Year +22	Year +23	Year +24
Growth Rates											
Revenue growth rate			40%	20%	0%	0%	0%	...	0%	0%	0%
Earnings before interest and after taxes growth rate			40%	20%	0%	0%	0%	...	0%	0%	0%
Depreciation growth rate			40%	20%	0%	0%	0%	...	0%	0%	0%
Unlevered operating cash flow growth rate			40%	20%	0%	0%	0%	...	0%	0%	0%
Unlevered free cash flow growth rate			208%	−109%	NMF	22%	−107%	...	NMF	22%	−107%
Capital expenditure growth rate			−30%	257%	−60%	−30%	257%	...	−60%	−30%	257%

its assets for both book and tax purposes, and we assume the three-year useful life is equal to the economic life of the assets. To keep the example simple, we assume that the company has no working capital assets or any other assets apart from the depreciable assets; that the company has no working capital liabilities or debt; and that the company will not experience inflation. Again, in order to keep it simple, we also assume the company only has three assets. Real companies typically have many more assets, but we can still face the same situation illustrated in this simple example.

From this exhibit, we see that revenues grow at 40% in Year +2, 20% in Year +3, and 0% thereafter. The company's earnings before interest and after taxes, depreciation expense, and unlevered cash flow from operations all grow at the revenue growth rate. The company's free cash flows, however, do not grow at the revenue growth rate; further, the free cash flow growth rate never converges to a zero growth rate even though the revenue growth rate is zero after Year +3. The cause of the varying free cash flow growth rate is the lumpiness of the company's capital expenditures.

We assume that the company must invest $1.5 in Year t to generate $1 of additional revenues in Year t + 1. For Years 0, 1, and 2, the company must invest for the growth in revenues it will experience in Years 1, 2, and 3. At the end of Year 0—the first year of the company's operations—the company has $225 of assets that generate revenues of $150 in Year +1. Revenues grow by $60 (40%) in Year +2, which requires the company to invest $90 at the end of Year +1. Revenues grow by $42 (20%) in Year +3, which requires the company to invest $63 at the end of Year +2. Although the company's revenues are growing in Year +2, its capital expenditures are decreasing (from $90 to $63, or −30%) because revenues grow less in Year +3 ($42 = $252 − $210) than they do in Year +2 ($60 = $210 − $150).

Since revenues stop growing in Year +4, the company does not need to make any new investments in Year +3 to grow the company's revenues. However, since the company's assets purchased at the end of Year 0 are fully depreciated and have no remaining economic useful life, the company must replace the assets purchased in Year 0. The capital expenditures in Year +3 replace the assets the company purchased in Year 0. Similarly, in Year +4, the company must replace the assets purchased in Year +1, and in Year +5, the company must replace the assets purchased in Year +2. This pattern repeats in perpetuity; thus, the company's capital expenditures and, hence, free cash flow growth rates never converge to the company's "steady state" revenue growth rate (0%). In this case, depreciation is constant from Year +3 on even though the capital expenditures are lumpy, for the company uses straight-line depreciation. If accelerated depreciation were used instead, the depreciation number would not become constant, which complicates the issue further. We will discuss that complication in the next sub-section.

In Exhibit 6.12, we show different valuations of the Lumpy CAPEX Company by varying the continuing value date (at which we use a perpetuity valuation method) using a 10% discount rate and a 0% growth rate. The correct value of the firm is equal to $816. The valuation we show under the Year +3 column assumes that the continuing value date is Year +3; thus, to measure the value of the firm at the end of Year 0, we discount the free cash flow for Years +1 through +3 and the continuing value at the end of Year +3 (based on the Year +4 free cash flow) discounted back to Year 0; specifically:

$$V_{F,0} = \frac{FCF_1}{1+r} + \frac{FCF_2}{(1+r)^2} + \frac{FCF_3}{(1+r)^3} + \frac{FCF_4}{(r-g)} \times \frac{1}{(1+r)^3}$$

$$V_{F,0} = \frac{\$37.5}{1.1} + \frac{\$115.5}{1.1^2} + \frac{-\$10.8}{1.1^3} + \frac{\$124.2}{(0.1-0)} \times \frac{1}{1.1^3} = \$1,055$$

This valuation of $1,055 is larger than the company's actual valuation of $816 (29% larger). Since we know that the free cash flows for each year are correct, the reason this valuation exceeds the actual valuation is because the free cash flow we use in the continuing value ($FCF_4 = \$124.2$) is too large to use as the base period free cash flow in the perpetuity valuation. If we extend the continuing value date to Year +4, the error is larger (52%) because the base year free cash flow is even larger than the previous base year free cash flow ($FCF_5 = \$151.2$). If we extend the continuing value date to Year +5, the absolute value of the error is even larger (71%), but in this case, the valuation is too low because the base year free cash flow in the continuing value calculation is negative ($FCF_6 = -\$10.8$).

After Year +6, the free cash flows repeat in the same three-year sequence as they did in Years +4 through +6. Because the free cash flows series repeats, the error in the perpetuity valuation as of the continuing value date repeats in the same sequence. However, the error in the value of the continuing value as of Year 0, and consequently the error in the value of the firm in absolute value, becomes smaller and smaller. It becomes smaller as we postpone the continuing value calculation further out into the future, for the continuing value becomes a smaller percentage of the value of the firm.

EXHIBIT 6.12	The Lumpy CAPEX Company Valuation with Varying Continuing Value Dates

| | Discounted Cash Flow Valuation Using Actual Free Cash Flows | | | | | | | | | | |
Year (t)	Year 0	Year +1	Year +2	Year +3	Year +4	Year +5	Year +6	...	Year +22	Year +23	Year +24
Free cash flow		$37.5	$115.5	$–10.8	$124.2	$151.2	$–10.8	...	$124.2	$151.2	$–10.8
Continuing value at Year 0				$ 933	$1,033	$ –67	$ 701	...	$ 186	$ –12	$ 126
Present value of FCF Year +1 to Year (t).				121	206	300	294	...	706	723	722
Value of the firm at Year 0.	$816			$1,055	$1,239	$ 233	$ 995	...	$ 892	$ 711	$ 848
Error in the valuation				29%	52%	–71%	22%	...	9%	–13%	4%
Continuing value (% of total)				88%	83%	–29%	70%	...	21%	–2%	15%
Present value of FCF (% of total)				12%	17%	129%	30%	...	79%	102%	85%
Value of the firm at Year 0.				100%	100%	100%	100%	...	100%	100%	100%

Exhibit may contain small rounding errors

To correct this problem, we can either run or model out for, say, 100 columns or we can convert the lumpy capital expenditure time-series into an equivalent present value annuity time-series as of the end of Year +3. The repeating capital expenditure time-series is $90, $63, and $225. The present value (using a 10% discount rate) of these capital expenditures is equal to $302.9 ($302.9 = $90/1.1 + $63/1.1^2 + $225/1.1^3). We then convert this present value into a three-year annuity with the same present value by substituting capital expenditures of $121.8 per year ($121.8 = $302.9/2.487, where 2.487 is the present value factor of an ordinary annuity for 3 years at 10% interest; the sum of 0.909, 0.828, and 0.751).

We adjust the free cash flows in each period for the difference between the actual capital expenditure and the capital expenditure annuity. We show this calculation in Exhibit 6.13. We also show the different valuations of the Lumpy CAPEX Company for varying continuing value dates. All of the valuations equal $816—the correct value of the firm.

EXHIBIT 6.13	Using an Annuity to Eliminate the Lumpiness in the Capital Expenditures

| | Discounted Cash Flow Valuation Using Adjusted Free Cash Flows, Adjusted for Annuity Capital Expenditures | | | | | | | | | | |
Year (t)	Year 0	Year +1	Year +2	Year +3	Year +4	Year +5	Year +6	...	Year +22	Year +23	Year +24
Capital expenditure in FCF.					$ 90.0	$ 63.0	$225.0	...	$ 90.0	$ 63.0	$225.0
Annuity for capital expenditures.					121.8	121.8	121.8	...	121.8	121.8	121.8
Adjustment to free cash flow					$–31.8	$–58.8	$103.2	...	$–31.8	$–58.8	$103.2
Adjusted free cash flow		$37.5	$115.5	$–10.8	$ 92.4	$ 92.4	$ 92.4	...	$ 92.4	$ 92.4	$ 92.4
Continuing value at Year 0				$ 694	$ 631	$ 574	$ 522	...	$ 113	$ 103	$ 94
Present value of FCF Year +1 to Year (t).				121	185	242	294	...	702	712	722
Value of the firm at Year 0.	$ 816			$ 816	$ 816	$ 816	$ 816	...	$ 816	$ 816	$ 816
Error in the valuation				0%	0%	0%	0%	...	0%	0%	0%
Continuing value (% of total)				85%	77%	70%	64%	...	14%	13%	12%
Present value of FCF (% of total)				15%	23%	30%	36%	...	86%	87%	88%
Value of the firm at Year 0.				100%	100%	100%	100%	...	100%	100%	100%

Exhibit may contain small rounding errors

Thus, we correct for the lumpiness in capital expenditures by converting the lumpy series into an annuity with the same present value. First, we must identify the capital expenditure cycle—that is, the period during which capital expenditures are lumpy and the repeating pattern of the lumpiness. The example we used had a three-year cycle, which is likely shorter than most that you will encounter. Our example also assumed a zero growth rate in perpetuity. The issue becomes more complex for a non-zero growth rate; however, converting the lumpy capital expenditure series into either an annuity or an annuity with growth mitigates this problem. If we expect the capital expenditures to increase because of changes in prices at the assumed perpetual growth rate, then we can calculate the annuity with the formula for an annuity with a constant growth rate.

Valuation Key 6.6

We correct for the lumpiness in capital expenditures by converting the lumpy series into an annuity. First, we identify the capital expenditure cycle. Then, we convert the capital expenditures in that cycle to an annuity with the same present value. The alternative is to run the model out, say, 100 years.

REVIEW EXERCISE 6.3

Lumpy Capital Expenditures

A company has $1,200 in annual revenues that are expected to continue in perpetuity with no growth. The company's only expenses are depreciation and income taxes (40% tax rate). The company uses straight-line depreciation with no salvage value and a three-year life for its single fixed asset. The fixed asset has an acquisition cost of $1,200 and must be replaced every three years. The replacement cost of the fixed asset is not expected to change in the future. Below we present the company's income statement and balance sheet for Years 0 and 1. The company was formed on the last day of Year 0 when it invested $1,200 in its fixed asset. The company is all-equity financed, will hold no cash, and has no working capital requirements. The company's cost of capital is 10%. Measure the company's free cash flow for Years 1 through 3. Measure the value of the company at the end of Year 0 using a cash flow perpetuity.

	Actual Year 0	Forecast Year 1
Income Statement		
Revenue		$1,200
Depreciation expense.		−400
Income before taxes.		$ 800
Income tax expense (provision)		−320
Net income.		$ 480
Balance Sheet		
Total assets = Fixed asset	$1,200	$ 800
Shareholders' equity	$1,200	$ 800

Solution on pages 247–249.

Depreciable Life Differs from the Economic Useful Life

We can also run into situations where the depreciable life differs from the economic useful life. Given current tax codes in the United States and elsewhere, this is not unusual. While depreciation does not represent a cash flow itself, the fact that the depreciation growth rate for tax purposes is not equal to the revenue growth rate is relevant to the free cash flow calculations in a perpetuity because depreciation reduces income taxes due. The company's income taxes due in this case would not be the same every year because of the year-to-year difference in depreciation expense for tax purposes. This can also occur when the company uses accelerated depreciation for tax purposes because then again the depreciation expense will vary every year. While these differences almost always occur at the individual asset level, the key again is whether these differences occur at the aggregate level for the company.

Thus, in an example like the Lumpy CAPEX Company where the revenues and EBITDA are constant after Year 3, we could now have two factors driving the difference in the revenue and free cash flow growth rates. The first factor is, again, lumpy capital expenditures, and the second is varying income taxes due to varying depreciation. We can use an annuity to adjust a company's free cash flows for the non-constant growth rate resulting from the depreciable life of the assets not equaling the economic life of the assets just as we adjusted the capital expenditures in the Lumpy CAPEX example. In other words, we calculate the equivalent annuity value of the depreciation tax shields. The alternative is to run your model out for, say, 100 years.

Valuation Key 6.7

If the depreciable life of a company's assets is not equal to the economic life of its assets or if the company uses accelerated depreciation for tax purposes, the company's continuing value free cash flows may not have a constant growth rate. We adjust the free cash flows to have a constant growth rate by converting the lumpy income tax and capital expenditure series into an annuity.

Relationship Between Capital Expenditures and Depreciation

We now examine the issue of the relationship between capital expenditures and depreciation in our base year cash flow. A number of factors determine whether capital expenditures are greater than, equal to, or less than depreciation in the continuing value free cash flows. Three such factors are price level changes, productivity changes, and the company's expected real growth after the continuing value date. In addition, whether the company uses straight-line depreciation and uses a depreciable life equal to the economic useful life of the asset will be of importance to us. For the purposes of this discussion, we assume that the company uses straight-line depreciation and that the depreciable life and economic useful life are the same, which is more likely the case for financial reporting than for tax reporting purposes, but it is easier to illustrate the basic point we are making using this assumption.

If we assume the company will have no real growth after the continuing value date and the assets it purchases have no change in productivity, then price level changes—either increases or decreases—will affect the relation between capital expenditures and depreciation. If the company is in steady state with no lumpy capital expenditure series, and if prices have remained constant since the initial purchase date of the worn out physical assets, the capital expenditures required to replace those assets will equal depreciation. If prices increased during this period, capital expenditures will be greater than depreciation; if prices decreased during this period, capital expenditures will be less than depreciation. Again, this presumes no changes in productivity.

In Exhibit 6.14, we compute continuing value capital expenditure to depreciation ratios for varying levels of price level changes (−3% to +3%) and varying years of useful life for the asset (5, 10, 15, ..., 40 years). The exhibit shows how this ratio increases when price levels increase and decreases when price levels decrease. We assume that the firm is in steady state for purposes of these calculations. In particular, if the company uses assets with a five-year life, it replaces one-fifth of these assets every year. If the assets have a 10-year life, we assume the company replaces one-tenth of these assets every year. The effects of the price level changes are magnified as the number of years of useful life increases and as the inflation rate increases. This exhibit indicates that the ratio of capital expenditure to depreciation can easily be more than 1.25 for many assets even with inflation at just 3% (and ignoring all other factors). Of course, the relation between depreciation and capital expenditures at the firm level will depend on the mix of the useful lives of the assets that the firm uses in its operations. Assuming 3% inflation, that a company had only assets

EXHIBIT 6.14	Ratios of Continuing Value Capital Expenditure to Depreciation for Varying Levels of Inflation and Varying Years of Useful Life

	Price Level Changes for Each Year in the Life of the Asset				
Years of Life	−3.0%	−1.5%	0.0%	1.5%	3.0%
5	91%	96%	100%	105%	109%
10	84%	92%	100%	108%	117%
15	78%	88%	100%	112%	126%
20	72%	85%	100%	116%	134%
25	66%	82%	100%	121%	144%
30	60%	78%	100%	125%	153%
35	55%	75%	100%	129%	163%
40	50%	72%	100%	134%	173%

with a 5-, 10-, and 40 year life, and that each type represented one-third of the assets of the company, then the company would have a ratio of capital expenditures to depreciation of 1.33 (1.33 = 1.09/3 + 1.17/3 + 1.73/3).

If the company is experiencing real growth and is investing in capital expenditures to achieve that real growth, the ratio of capital expenditures to depreciation will be even greater than shown in the previous table for various inflation rates. On the other hand, increases in productive capacity can offset the effects of inflation and real growth on the ratio of capital expenditure to depreciation at the continuing value date. In this context, productivity means the ability to purchase the same productive capacity at a lower cost (for example, productivity increases in computing power). If productivity increases are larger than inflation, the ratio of continuing value capital expenditure to depreciation will be less than one with no real growth.

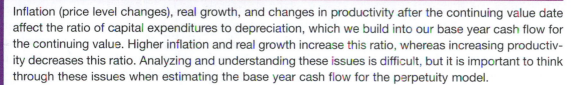

Valuation Key 6.8

Inflation (price level changes), real growth, and changes in productivity after the continuing value date affect the ratio of capital expenditures to depreciation, which we build into our base year cash flow for the continuing value. Higher inflation and real growth increase this ratio, whereas increasing productivity decreases this ratio. Analyzing and understanding these issues is difficult, but it is important to think through these issues when estimating the base year cash flow for the perpetuity model.

The Relationship Between CAPEX and Depreciation in the Yahoo Example

In our continuing value of Yahoo, it is important to consider the relationship between capital expenditures and depreciation and to be certain that we are comfortable with that relationship in the base year cash flow. If you look back at Exhibit 6.2, you will see that capital expenditures equal $3.973 billion and depreciation is $3.767 billion, resulting in a ratio of capital expenditures to depreciation of 1.055. Remember that the growth rate we assumed for the perpetuity was 2.5%, which was just the expected inflation rate. As such, we are not allowing for any real growth. In addition, we are not modeling any book/tax differences in the depreciation expense in this example. Given that, it seems reasonable to assume a ratio of capital expenditures to depreciation just slightly in excess of one given the low expected inflation, the generally short life of many of Yahoo's capitalized investments, and the productivity increases in computer-related fields.

6.7 THE CONSTANT GROWTH RATE AND VALUE CREATION

The constant growth rate is, of course, an important input into the constant-growth perpetuity model. Most of the time, the growth rate is positive, but it can be either positive or negative depending on the economic context underpinning the valuation. If it is positive, and if we are forecasting nominal (including inflation) free cash flows, it can reflect expected long-term inflation and it can reflect growth higher than inflation (real growth).

LO3 Allow for real growth and value creation in the continuing value estimate

One way for a company to experience real long-term growth is by expansion through new investment. For example, the growth rate may be linked to growth in an economy or population growth, both of which can result in a growth rate that is higher than inflation (real growth). If we expect a company to exactly keep pace with the real growth of the economies in which it operates, the real growth component of the company's perpetual growth rate is equal to the expected real growth of the economies in which it operates. We might also expect the company to grow with the population to which it sells its goods or services or a sub-group of that population, such as a certain age group.

The growth rate may be linked to long-term product or service market penetration in various markets, including global markets. In this case, real growth cannot occur in perpetuity because all markets will eventually be penetrated, but the growth from expanded market penetration can be sufficiently long enough—say 50 or more years—that including it in the perpetuity valuation is appropriate. Another way to achieve real growth is to find completely new products and services to offer; think of the new products and services that Apple has introduced since the introduction of the iPod in 2001. It is possible to link real growth to taking away market share from competing companies, but this is less likely to occur year after year over the long run. If we expect real growth from new investment, we include the expected new investment in the calculation of the base year free cash flow used in the perpetuity valuation.

Another way for a company to grow is by increasing its unlevered operating cash flows without increasing its investment beyond what it has already made; in other words, it uses its excess capacity. An example of this might be excess capacity in a company's production facilities. While growth like this can occur over a few years, it is less likely to continue in perpetuity or for a long enough period to include in a perpetuity valuation. Thus, we should be wary of a continuing value estimate based on this premise.

Not all positive real growth rates increase the value of the firm. We know that if a company invests in negative net present value projects, its free cash flows might grow, but the value of the firm will decrease. Thus, we must also consider the rate of return the company earns on its investments.

In the remainder of this section, we develop the constant-growth perpetuity model for use on the continuing value date based on two sets of conditions. We first develop the model under the assumption that a company faces inflation but has no real growth opportunities after the continuing value date. Next, we develop the model with an allowance for inflation and an assumption for real growth that may create value, have no effect on value, or actually decrease value, depending on the return earned on the new investment. As we shall see, one advantage of this approach is that you can precisely control the extent to which a company earns a rate of return above its cost of capital on new investment in perpetuity.

A Constant Growth Rate Equal to Inflation (No Real Growth)

Recall from earlier chapters that in DCF models, we either forecast free cash flows in nominal amounts and discount the free cash flows at the appropriate nominal risk-adjusted discount rate, or we forecast real free cash flows and discount the free cash flows at the appropriate real risk-adjusted discount rate. Done properly, these two approaches result in the same valuation. If nominal free cash flows, FCF, are growing at inflation, then discounting the nominal free cash flow at the appropriate risk-adjusted nominal discount rate, r, using inflation as the constant growth rate, $g = i$, is equivalent to discounting real free cash flows, FCF^{Real}, at the real discount rate, r^{Real}.

$$V_0 = \frac{FCF_1}{r - i} = \frac{FCF_0 \times (1 + i)}{r - i} = \frac{FCF_1^{Real}}{r^{Real}} = \frac{FCF_0^{Real}}{r^{Real}}$$

If nominal free cash flows grow at inflation and have no real growth, then the appropriate growth rate for the constant-growth perpetuity model is inflation, $g = i$. Including inflation in the growth rate in the perpetuity formula does not imply that the company will experience real growth. If the company's nominal cash flows will grow with inflation, omitting the effect of expected inflation from the growth rate will understate value if nominal discount rates are used. Of course, the world is not so simple that you can automatically assume that the cash flows will grow with inflation and that the company has no real growth.

The appropriate growth rate can be greater or less than inflation, and it can even be negative. For example, assume we expect computer chip manufacturers to continue to have technological innovations in the design and manufacture of microchips such that product prices are reduced throughout the industry. In this case, the nominal cash flow per unit for these companies can grow at less than inflation; in fact, it can have a negative growth rate per unit, and total nominal cash flows will have a growth rate lower than inflation unless the companies either increase the number of units sold to offset decreasing prices or expand to other products. In other words, the effect of inflation on the growth of nominal cash flows can be offset, in part, by technological advances so that neither revenues nor costs increase as fast as inflation. Competitive pressures can also reduce cash flow growth rates below inflation as well if profit margins are squeezed.

Valuation Key 6.9

Even if the company has zero real growth, the growth rate in the perpetuity model will not be zero if the company's nominal cash flows grow as a result of a decline in the purchasing power of the currency.

Real Growth from New Investment Can Decrease the Value of the Firm[10]

We typically expect real growth in free cash flows to increase firm value, but this is not always the case. A company that invests in negative net present value projects can experience real growth in its free cash flows, but such investments will decrease the value of the firm. You may recall that although the preferred approach to evaluate projects is the net present value method, an alternative way to assess the effect of a new investment on the value of the firm is to compare the internal rate of return on the investment to the company's required rate of return for that investment. We know a company destroys value if it invests in negative net present value projects, which occurs if projects' internal rates of return are less than their required rates of return. However, negative net present value projects can result in positive real growth in the company's free cash flows.

We use the perpetuity valuation framework to illustrate two points. First, ignoring inflation, the nominal free cash flow growth rate is a function of two factors—the proportion of free cash flow invested in new investments to achieve real growth and the rate of return on that new investment. Second, the effect of new investment on the value of the firm depends on the rate of return on the new investment relative to the required rate of return on that new investment. Positive real growth destroys value if the return on the new investment is less than the investment's required rate of return. Growth in free cash flows from new investment only creates value if the return on the new investment is greater than the investment's required rate of return—in other words, if it has a positive net present value.

For the purposes of our analysis, we assume that new investments have the same risk and, hence, the same required rate of return, r, as the company's existing investments. We use the term "new investment" for investments that result in positive (real) growth in free cash flows. We include new investments in the model by assuming that the company has new investment opportunities in perpetuity equal to a percentage, $I\%$, of its free cash flows without new investments, $FCF_{t+1}^{w/o\ NewI}$. Free cash flow is equal to the free cash flow without new investment multiplied by 1 minus the investment percentage (the plowback ratio). Although the free cash flows without new investment do not include a deduction for new investment, they do include the capital expenditures and working capital investments needed to maintain the company's scale as of the continuing value date given some amount of inflation. Without these investments, the company's free cash flows would decrease over time because of decreasing capacity. The real return on new investment, ROI^{Real}, is equal to the cash flow generated by new investment in the following year divided by the amount of the new investment adjusted for inflation, i. The nominal return on investment, ROI, is equal to the real return on investment adjusted for inflation, $(1 + ROI^{Real}) \times (1 + i) - 1$. Finally, if a company has not made any new investments, we assume its free cash flows grow at the rate of inflation, i.

$$FCF_{t+1}^{w/o\ NewI} = FCF_t^{w/o\ NewI} \times (1 + i)$$

$$FCF_{t+2}^{w/o\ NewI} = FCF_{t+1}^{w/o\ NewI} \times (1 + i) = FCF_t^{w/o\ NewI} \times (1 + i)^2$$

The growth rate of free cash flows is equal to the ratio of two consecutive free cash flows minus 1. If we make investments for real growth, the free cash flow in Year 1 is equal to the free cash flow without new investment multiplied by 1 minus the investment percentage (often called the plowback ratio). The free cash flow in Year 2 has two components, both of which are multiplied by 1 minus the plowback ratio. The first component is the free cash flow without investment in Year 2, and the second component is the return on the new investment in Year 1, adjusted for one year of inflation.

$$1 + g = \frac{FCF_2}{FCF_1} = \frac{(FCF_2^{w/o\ NewI} + FCF_1^{w/o\ NewI} \times I\% \times (1 + i) \times ROI^{Real}) \times (1 - I\%)}{FCF_1^{w/o\ NewI} \times (1 - I\%)}$$

We can rewrite the free cash flow without investment in Year 2 as the free cash flow without investment in Year 1 adjusted for one year of inflation.

$$1 + g = \frac{(FCF_1^{w/o\ NewI} \times (1 + i) + FCF_1^{w/o\ NewI} \times I\% \times (1 + i) \times ROI^{Real}) \times (1 - I\%)}{FCF_1^{w/o\ NewI} \times (1 - I\%)}$$

---

[10] For a more detailed examination of this issue, see Bradley, M., and Jarrell, G. A., "Expected Inflation and the Constant-Growth Valuation Model," *Journal of Applied Corporate Finance* 20 (2008), pp. 66–78.

The resulting growth rate has two components. The first component is equal to the plowback ratio multiplied by the nominal return on new investment. The second component is equal to the inflation rate multiplied by 1 minus the plowback ratio, which reduces the inflation adjustment for the percentage of the cash flow due to inflation that is invested in new investments.

$$g = I\% \times ROI + i \times (1 - I\%) \tag{6.5}$$

If inflation is equal to zero, the second component disappears and the growth rate (which is now the real growth rate) is equal to the plowback ratio multiplied by the real return on investment ($I\% \times ROI^{Real}$).

If we substitute Equation 6.5 for the growth rate in the constant-growth cash flow perpetuity model, we get

$$V_{CV} = \frac{FCF_{CV}^{w/o\ NewI} \times (1 + i) \times (1 - I\%)}{r - I\% \times ROI - i \times (1 - I\%)} \tag{6.6}$$

Although the implication of the above formula might not be readily obvious, it shows that new investment only increases the company's value if its return is greater than its required return. We can restate this formula to make this point a little clearer by partitioning the above formula into two parts—a free cash flow without new investment perpetuity growing at inflation and the effect of new investment on value. The second component is greater than 1; that is, the new investment creates value only if the nominal return on new investment is greater than the nominal required rate of return.

$$V_{CV} = \frac{FCF_{CV}^{w/o\ NewI} \times (1 + i)}{r - i} \times \frac{1 - I\%}{1 - I\% \times \left(\dfrac{ROI - i}{r - i}\right)}$$

This formula shows that if the company's nominal return on investment is equal to its nominal cost of capital, the last term in our formula is equal to 1, and making new investments—or plowing back free cash flow into the company for real growth—has no effect on the company's value. If the company's nominal return on its investment is less than its nominal cost of capital, the last term in our formula is less than 1, and the value of the company is less than the value of the company with zero real growth. On the other hand, if the company's nominal return on its investment is greater than its nominal cost of capital, the last term in our formula is greater than 1, and the value of the company is greater than the value of the company with zero real growth.

This analysis provides certain insights to guide our modeling of the growth rate to be used in the perpetuity valuation. Assume we developed a base year free cash flow to represent the company's free cash flow based on the current scale of its operations, its expected performance, and some assumed inflation rate—the no real growth free cash flow forecast. Thus, we expect the company's growth rate to equal expected long-term inflation if the company makes no investment for real growth. In addition, if we expect the company to have ongoing new investment opportunities, then we would increase the growth rate in the perpetuity calculation based on Equation 6.5. The major advantage of applying Equation 6.6 is that we can explicitly control for the difference between the rate of return on new investment and the company's cost of capital that we are willing to embed in the company's free cash flow forecasts and valuation. In other words, you have total control over the size of the economic rents (the difference between the return on investment and the required rate of return on investment) that the company earns on new investment opportunities every year in perpetuity.

Valuation Key 6.10

If we assume that a company's continuing value free cash flows are increasing from real growth due to new investment, we can calculate both the percentage of the company's continuing value free cash flow that can be invested and the rate of return on the new investment. We use these two factors in conjunction with inflation to measure the company's growth rate above inflation.

For example, assume a company has expected free cash flows without new investment equal to $120 in Year 0. It has a required real rate of return of 12%, and the inflation rate is 2.5%. The expected free cash flow without new investment in Year 1 is equal to the free cash flow in Year 0, $120, multiplied by 1 plus the inflation rate, $123 ($123 = $120 × 1.025). Since we include inflation in the free cash flows (nominal free cash flows), we also include inflation in the required real rate of return since we use the nominal required rate of return. The nominal required rate of return is equal to 12% adjusted for inflation, which is 14.8% ($0.148 = 1.12 \times 1.025 - 1$). If the company has no new investments and thus no real growth, the free cash flows will grow at the inflation rate, and the value of the firm without any new investments will be $1,000 ($1,000 = \$123/(0.148 - 0.025)$).[11]

Now, assume the company can invest for real growth, in perpetuity, 20% of its free cash flow without new investment. Should the company make this investment? If we assume the nominal return on the new investment is equal to 10%, ROI = 10%, using Equation 6.5 we find that the growth rate for the free cash flows is equal to 4% [$0.04 = 0.2 \times 0.1 + 0.025 (1 - 0.2)$], which is 1.5% higher than the inflation rate (1.5% is the real growth). Applying Equation 6.6, we see that the new value of the firm decreases to $911.1 (an 8.9% decrease).

$$V_0 = \frac{FCF_0^{w/o\ NewI} \times (1 + i) \times (1 - I\%)}{r - I\% \times ROI - i \times (1 - I\%)} = \$120 \times \frac{(1.025) \times (1 - 0.2)}{0.148 - 0.2 \times 0.1 - 0.025 \times (1 - 0.2)} = \frac{\$98.4}{0.108} = \$911.1$$

Why did the value of the company decrease when the growth rate increased? It decreased because the nominal return on the new investment, 10%, is less than the nominal required rate of return of 14.8%. Using Equation 6.6, we show various combinations of the plowback ratio (I%) and the nominal return on new investment in Exhibit 6.15. As you can see in all the tabulated examples, there is real growth with new investment. However, whether or not a company creates or destroys value with that new investment depends on the relationship between the required rate of return and the return on investment.

	EXHIBIT 6.15	Value Created or Destroyed (Real Cost of Capital = 12%, Initial Free Cash Flow Without New Investment = $120, and Inflation = 2.5%)						
I%	ROI	Inflation (i)	FCF$_1$	g$_{FCF}$	$[r - g_{FCF}]^{-1}$	V$_0$	% Change in V$_0$
0%		2.5%	$123	2.5%	8.1	$1,000	
20%	10.0%	2.5%	98	4.0%	9.3	911	−8.9%
20%	14.8%	2.5%	98	5.0%	10.2	1,000	0.0%
20%	18.0%	2.5%	98	5.6%	10.9	1,070	7.0%
40%	10.0%	2.5%	74	5.5%	10.8	794	−20.6%
40%	14.8%	2.5%	74	7.4%	13.6	1,000	0.0%
40%	18.0%	2.5%	74	8.7%	16.4	1,210	21.0%

How Do We Judge the Reasonableness of ROI in the Base Year Cash Flow?

Since we assume that the base year free cash flow forecast will grow in perpetuity, it is often useful to examine the reasonableness of the base year free cash flow. One way to do this is to compare the company's implicit projected rate of return of its cash flows to its cost of capital (discount rate). If the company were in a steady state by the continuing value date, then we would expect it to earn a constant (economic) rate of return on its invested capital in perpetuity. Since we are going to hold this rate of return constant in perpetuity, we have to ask ourselves how great of a difference we are prepared to allow between the company's economic rate of return and its cost of capital. If the economic rate of return exceeds the cost of capital in the base year cash flow, then we are effectively projecting that the company will earn an excess return in perpetuity, or for at least 50 years or so. In other words, we are assuming that the company will be able to earn economic rents for a very long time and that competition in the industry will not drive the firm's economic rate of return to its cost of capital. As part of this analysis, we would examine the company's competitive advantages and their sustainability.

Evaluating the economic rate of return on old investment is difficult, for we cannot observe a company's actual economic rate of return. We can observe the accounting-based rates of return in our

---

[11] We can use the real free cash flow and real required rate of return to calculate the same value of the firm, $1,000 ($1,000 = $120/0.12$).

projections, which is informative, but these rates of return do not necessarily equal the economic rate of return on capital at the continuing value date. We know that accounting-based rates of return do not measure a company's actual economic return, but empirical evidence indicates that a company's accounting-based rates of return are significantly correlated with its economic rates of return.

We have already shown how to explicitly control for the economic rents in the new investments that the firm makes for real growth in the continuing value calculation. However, what do we do about the potential rents we might have embedded into the free cash flows we measured without new investment? Here, the issue is more challenging. The good news is that we have a partial solution to this. We can produce forecasts for what the firm would look like if it maintained its current productive capacity and just grew due to inflation. We would then evaluate those forecasts using the various analyses discussed in Chapter 2 and compare it to other companies.

Are Yahoo's No Real Growth Forecasts Reasonable?

We assume a 2.5% growth rate in Yahoo's continuing value calculation, which is roughly equal to expected long-run inflation as of the valuation date; consequently, we assume that Yahoo will not experience any real growth from new investments after 2016 in our base year cash flow. Using a 2.5% continuing value growth rate assumes, however, that Yahoo's financial performance in 2017 will continue in perpetuity and grow at the inflation rate. We will begin a preliminary investigation of Yahoo's performance at the continuing value date by examining Yahoo's (accounting) rate of returns throughout the forecast horizon up to 2017.

We show Yahoo's return on assets and return on investment in Exhibit 6.16. Recall that we are using a 12% required rate of return for Yahoo. In this exhibit, the accounting rates of return increase during the forecast horizon, reach their highest point in 2015, and remain at that level through 2017. By 2017, Yahoo's return on assets is 21% and its return on investment is 32.8%, both of which are considerably higher than its 12% cost of capital. Before we discuss these accounting rates of return relative to Yahoo's required return, we should first recall the potential issues that can arise when we compare accounting rates of return to the economic required return.

| EXHIBIT 6.16 | Yahoo! Inc.—Return on Assets, Return on Investment with Profit Margin and Asset Utilization (Turnover) Components |

Rate of Return Ratios	A2006	F2007	F2008	F2009	F2010	F2011	F2012	F2013	F2014	F2015	F2016	F2017
Return on assets (ROA)	7.5%	12.9%	14.7%	16.6%	18.6%	19.7%	20.3%	20.8%	20.9%	21.0%	21.0%	21.0%
Unlevered income to revenue. . .	11.7%	15.6%	15.6%	15.6%	15.6%	15.6%	15.6%	15.6%	15.6%	15.6%	15.6%	15.6%
Revenue to total assets	0.640	0.825	0.941	1.063	1.194	1.260	1.302	1.333	1.340	1.345	1.347	1.347
Return on investment (ROI)	8.9%	16.1%	19.4%	22.7%	26.5%	29.1%	31.1%	32.8%	33.7%	34.2%	34.2%	34.2%
Unlevered income to revenue. . .	11.7%	15.6%	15.6%	15.6%	15.6%	15.6%	15.6%	15.6%	15.6%	15.6%	15.6%	15.6%
Revenue to investment.	0.758	1.034	1.241	1.453	1.698	1.862	1.992	2.099	2.158	2.189	2.192	2.192

We have to remember that accounting rates of return do not equal economic rates of return for many reasons. For our DCF valuation of Yahoo that uses Yahoo's current market value as the initial investment, Yahoo's economic return in the financial model (over its life) is 12% per year given its valuation at the time. We know this because discounting the free cash flows we forecasted by 12% yields Yahoo's market value. This does not mean that the return in each year (defined as free cash flow to its 2006 market value) is equal to 12% every year; it only means that the internal rate of return (based on both the value and the cash flow forecasts) is equal to 12%.

The investment used in calculating accounting rates of return (total assets or capital invested) likely does not represent the investment in the economic rate of return unless the investment was just made. As of 2006, Yahoo's market value is $32.6 billion after the payout of the excess assets (Exhibit 6.3) but its total assets are only $9.2 billion and its invested capital is only $7.6 billion. Accounting numbers are largely based on historical costs and not current values, and this partially explains the difference between the accounting and economic measurement of the denominator. So when we calculate a rate of return from the accounting statements, the denominator is not based on economic value. Further, we are computing just the return on a single year, not a yearly return over the life of the asset. In addition, in Yahoo's case, expenditures for investments in brand development or company-developed intellectual property are generally expensed and thus reduce accounting book values. In effect, the accounting system does not treat these as part of invested capital. However, these investments undoubtedly create value for many companies like Yahoo, and the market value of Yahoo reflects these values.

Because of the potential difference between accounting rates of return and the unobservable true economic rate of return for Yahoo on its past investments, we are unable to make meaningful comparisons between Yahoo's accounting returns and its cost of capital. This is why we rely on comparable companies to assess the reasonableness of the base year cash flows. Of course, with a company like Yahoo, assessing what its ratios or the ratios of its competitors should look like at the continuing value date is difficult to do if there are currently no mature companies in this space. We would not generally expect the industry's accounting rates of return at the continuing value date to look like the accounting rates of return we observe now, as the company would have been expected to mature by the continuing value date. They could be higher, or they could be lower. In Yahoo's case, one could argue that they might be higher, for currently, Yahoo is investing heavily in its future growth and profitability, and the accounting system writes off many of those investments. Thus, its accounting rates of return could very well increase over time. In many industries, it is not a problem to find a reasonable set of comparable companies for the continuing value date, as there is usually a continuum of companies in various stages of their life cycles; thus, we can often find mature comparable companies to assess the reasonableness of the base year cash flow.

Yahoo with New Investments as of the Continuing Value Date

To illustrate how new investment opportunities affect continuing value, we assume that Yahoo's management believes that in 2017, and thereafter, it will have additional opportunities to invest a certain percentage of its free cash flow in new investments (a certain percentage of $5.678 billion in 2017 and of each subsequent free cash flow before new investments). Should Yahoo make this additional investment each year? The answer, of course, depends on the rate of return that Yahoo can earn on these new investments.

In Exhibit 6.17, we illustrate the effect resulting from three alternative assumptions regarding Yahoo's new investment opportunities as of the continuing value date. We use the same free cash flow, discount rate, and inflation rate that we used in the continuing value calculation of $59.8 billion (Exhibit 6.3), which we show in the first column of this exhibit. In the second column of the exhibit, we assume that Yahoo invests 20% of its free cash flow of $5.7 billion and that the nominal return on the new investment is 12% as a result of a real rate of return on new investment of 9.27% and inflation of 2.5% (12% nominal, $0.12 = 1.0927 \times 1.025$). Applying Equation 6.5, we see that this investment strategy is value neutral; even though Yahoo's growth rate increases to 4.4%, which is 1.9% above inflation, its value is unchanged by this investment regardless of the percentage invested in the new investment, for the return on new investment is equal to the required rate of return.

EXHIBIT 6.17 Yahoo! Inc.—Alternative New Investment Opportunities				
	No New Investment	**Value Neutral New Investment**	**Value Creating New Investment**	**Value Destroying New Investment**
Free cash flow (Before investment), Year CV+1	$5.678	$5.678	$5.678	$5.678
Nominal required rate of return	12.00%	12.00%	12.00%	12.00%
Inflation.	2.50%	2.50%	2.50%	2.50%
Return on new investment (Real)		9.27%	11.00%	8.00%
Return on new investment (Nominal)		12.000%	13.775%	10.700%
% New investment.		20.00%	20.00%	20.00%
Growth rate.	2.50%	4.40%	4.76%	4.14%
Continuing value.	$ 59.8	$ 59.8	$ 62.7	$ 57.8
% Change in value.		0.00%	4.90%	-3.31%

In the third column of the exhibit, we increase the real return on the new investment to 11% (13.8% nominal) but maintain all other assumptions. Since the inflation-adjusted return on new investment is larger than Yahoo's cost of capital by 1.8%, this investment increases Yahoo's continuing value to $62.7 billion (a 4.9% increase). The growth rate also increases to 4.8% as a result of the increase in the return on investment. In the last column, we show what would occur if the real return on new investments was only 8%. Although Yahoo's growth rate (4.1%) would be greater than inflation, its continuing value would decrease to $57.8 billion (−3.3%) because the inflation-adjusted return on investment is lower than Yahoo's cost of capital.

These examples illustrate how we can include new investment opportunities into our continuing value calculation as well as the impact they can have on value—positive, negative, or neutral. As we stated earlier, such value-creating growth only results if the company can identify new investment opportunities in perpetuity (or at least for a substantial number of years) and if the rate of return on these new investments is greater than the company's required rate of return; in other words, the investments must have a positive net present value. Perhaps most important, the examples show the potential usefulness of this approach. As we have seen, applying Equation 6.6 gives us the ability to precisely control the spread between the cost of capital and the return on new investment on the investments the company makes for real growth.

Valuation Key 6.11

One technique for trying to control for the economic rents allowed in a continuing value measure is to create a base year cash flow for the continuing value calculation that does not allow for real growth from new investment, but does allow for the investment necessary to maintain the company's scale given expected inflation. We then assess the reasonableness of the base year cash flow forecasts by performing a financial statement analysis relative to a set of comparable companies. We then explicitly control for any allowable economic rents from new investment intended to achieve real growth.

REVIEW EXERCISE 6.4

Real Growth and Value

Assume a company has expected free cash flows without new investment equal to $1,000 in Year 0. It has a required discount rate of 10%, and the inflation rate is 0%. If the company does not invest any of its free cash flows without new investment in Year 0, its cash flows will not grow. The company believes that it could invest 40% of its free cash flows without new investment in perpetuity. Measure the value of the company and its perpetual growth rate for the free cash flows in four scenarios: no new investment is made, and the company makes the new investment each year and earns an 8%, 10%, or 12% return on its investment annually and in perpetuity.

Solution on page 249.

6.8 TESTING THE REASONABLENESS OF THE CONTINUING VALUE

LO4 Assess the reasonableness of the continuing value estimate

In the prior section of the chapter, we suggested performing a financial analysis of key accounting ratios in an attempt to determine the reasonableness of the base year cash flow. In other prior sections, we also talked about making sure that the investments in the base year cash flow are predicated on the perpetual growth rate to be assumed, to closely examine the relationship between depreciation and capital expenditures and if you want to allow for real growth, that you consider explicitly controlling for the extent to which the return on new investment will exceed the company's cost of capital. In this section, we discuss two other ways to assess reasonableness. One technique is to benchmark the perpetual growth rate that you intend to use against implicit growth rates in market prices. Another technique is to benchmark implied price multiples from your continuing value estimate against comparable companies.

Using Comparable Companies to Assess the Long-Term Perpetual Growth Rate

We can use information for comparable companies to estimate the long-term perpetual growth rate if we have sufficient information on an appropriate group of comparable companies. In this discussion, we will assume that the weighted average cost of capital DCF method is the most useful method for valuing a set of firms. If, for a comparable company, we can measure its value and the weighted average cost of capital, and obtain free cash flow estimates for a series of years, we can estimate the perpetual growth rate for that company, by solving for g in the following formula. The growth rate that we measure is the present-value weighted average growth rate for years after T.

$$V_{F,0} = \sum_{t=1}^{T} \frac{FCF_t}{(1 + r_{WACC})^t} + \frac{FCF_T \times (1 + g)}{(r_{WACC} - g)} \times \frac{1}{(1 + r_{WACC})^T}$$

We can solve for g using an iterative process (such as "goal seek" or "solver" functions in spreadsheet software), or we can solve it directly using the following formula:

$$g = r_{WACC} - \frac{FCF_T}{(1 + r_{WACC})^{T-1} \times \left[V_{F,0} - \sum_{t=1}^{T-1} \frac{FCF_t}{(1 + r_{WACC})^t}\right]}$$

We measure the comparable company's firm value from the observed value of its securities in the marketplace and its cost of capital using the methods we discuss in this book. In most valuations, we would have already measured the value of the firm and unlevered cost of capital for the relevant comparable companies, so it is generally easy to calculate the weighted average cost of capital from the inputs used in the measurement of the unlevered cost of capital. For most comparable companies followed by financial analysts, we can use financial analyst forecasts to measure free cash flows for several years. Once we collect this information, we can measure the growth rate using the above formula.

For example, assume we measured the following inputs for a computer technology consulting company: a weighted average cost of capital equal to 9.06%; a firm value equal to $3,578.8 million; and free cash flow forecasts for the following three years equal to $259.0 million, $254.9 million, and $255.1 million, respectively. Using the above formulas, this company's present value weighted average growth rate for Year 4 and beyond is equal to 2.2%.

$$\$3,578.8 = \frac{\$259.0}{(1.0906)^1} + \frac{\$254.9}{(1.0906)^2} + \frac{\$255.1}{(1.0906)^3} + \frac{\$255.1 \times (1 + g)}{(0.0906 - g)} \times \frac{1}{(1.0906)^3}; g = 0.022$$

$$g = r_{WACC} - \frac{FCF_T}{(1 + r_{WACC})^{T-1} \times \left[V_{F,0} - \sum_{t=1}^{T-1} \frac{FCF_t}{(1 + r_{WACC})^t}\right]}$$

$$g = 0.0906 - \frac{\$255.1}{(1.0906)^2 \times \left(\$3,578.8 - \frac{\$259.0}{(1.0906)^1} - \frac{\$254.9}{(1.0906)^2}\right)} = 0.022$$

The perpetual growth rate for this company is around the long-run inflation rate expected at that time. Below, we show the resulting growth rate for this and five other computer technology consulting companies. As we show in Exhibit 6.18, this company (labeled Comparable Company 6) has the highest growth rate among these companies.

EXHIBIT 6.18   Measuring the Implied Growth Rate for Technology Consulting Companies

Technology Consulting Companies ($ in millions)	WACC	Unlevered Free Cash Flow Forecasts Year 1	Year 2	Year 3	Firm Value	Growth Rate
Comparable Company 1	9.83%	$2,442.5	$2,619.2	$2,547.5	$23,310.3	−1.33%
Comparable Company 2	9.45%	$ 336.6	$ 380.1	$ 367.3	$ 3,513.5	−1.16%
Comparable Company 3	9.19%	$ 191.3	$ 171.9	$ 169.2	$ 1,847.4	−0.10%
Comparable Company 4	9.01%	$ 891.6	$ 941.1	$ 924.1	$10,423.6	0.18%
Comparable Company 5	9.83%	$1,443.7	$1,500.4	$1,522.2	$17,507.0	1.39%
Comparable Company 6	9.06%	$ 259.0	$ 254.9	$ 255.1	$ 3,578.8	2.20%
25th percentile						−0.90%
Median						0.04%
75th percentile						1.09%

This analysis shows that the present value weighted average growth rate for Year 4 onward for the selected comparable companies is negative for three of the six comparable companies. The median growth rate is essentially zero, and the 25th and 75th percentiles are −0.9 and 1.1%. These growth rates suggest that, over the long-term, free cash flows will be steady or modestly expanding or declining in this industry. Even a negative long-term free cash flow growth rate, however, does not necessarily mean that the size of this industry will decrease as measured by revenues. The industry may be growing, but increased competition could cause profit margins and, hence, free cash flows to decrease. For example, the microcomputer industry experienced declining margins of this sort for many years.

Naturally, in order to use this approach, the weighted average cost of capital valuation method must be appropriate for the comparable company (for example, constant capital structure strategy and business risk). We must also adjust the calculations for excess assets to the extent that they exist by subtracting them from the value of the comparable companies and then measuring the growth rates on the adjusted values. We also know that financial analysts are slightly optimistic in their forecasts, on average. If free cash flow forecasts are optimistic, we should adjust them appropriately.

One last caveat or adjustment that one might have to make to this analysis is to consider the timing of the continuing value calculation in the firm you are valuing and the horizon of the cash flow forecasts for the comparable companies. If you are performing your continuing value calculation based on an assumption about the perpetual growth in cash flows after Year 5 and you only have comparable company cash flow forecasts for three years, you have a timing issue to consider with respect to the growth rates. The reason is that the implied growth rate that you are measuring for the comparable companies is based on the growth in cash flows beyond Year 3 while the growth rate for the company you are valuing is for years beyond Year 5. Even with all these caveats in mind, this approach can be an informative guideline with which to assess the long-term growth rate of an industry (or company) as assessed by the market-place.

REVIEW EXERCISE 6.5

Estimating Growth Rates from Comparable Companies

A comparable company has a 10% weighted average cost of capital. Its equity value is currently $12,000, and the value of its debt—the only other financing it uses—is $6,000. It has unlevered free cash flow forecasts for the next three years equal to $1,000, $1,200, and $1,500, respectively. The company is anticipated to maintain a constant proportionate capital structure. Measure the present value weighted average growth rate for the company's continuing value for Year 4 and beyond.

Solution on page 249.

Using Market Multiples to Assess the Reasonableness of the Continuing Value

Although we will discuss market multiples later in the book, here it will be helpful to introduce the notion that we can use market multiples to assess the reasonableness of the constant-growth cash flow perpetuity continuing value. In the valuation process we described in Chapter 1, we collect and analyze information on a company's comparable companies. A part of this process entails a calculation of the market multiples for those comparable companies. We often use these market multiples as an alternative way to value the subject company. We can also use multiples, however, to assess the reasonableness of the perpetuity-based continuing value.

When we use the perpetuity-based continuing value formula, we must know the company's expected free cash flow for the year after the continuing value date. We recommend that we measure this free cash flow based on a detailed forecast from our financial model. If we use a financial model, we also have a forecast of the company's income statement and balance sheet for the year of and the year after the continuing value date. Thus, we have sufficient information to calculate market multiples implied by the financial forecasts and the continuing value calculated using the perpetuity formula. For example, the implied earnings before interest and taxes (EBIT) multiple as of the continuing value date is equal to the continuing value divided by the EBIT in the financial model. We then compare the implied multiple to the multiples of appropriately selected comparable companies.

This analysis is useful for examining the perpetuity-based continuing value calculation, but it is not definitive. Two issues arise in this analysis. The first is the same as it is for all market multiple-based valuations; that is, have we identified the correct set of comparable companies, and are we measuring the multiples correctly? The second issue is concerned with whether a particular multiple measured today is appropriate for the continuing value estimate. Market multiples of competitors measured as of the valuation date may not be appropriate as a benchmark for the continuing value date. For example, if the comparable companies are all at the beginning of a high-growth period as of the valuation date, we know the market multiples of these companies will decline at the end of the high-growth period, and this will likely be near the time of the continuing value date. As such, it may be appropriate to use a different set of comparable companies' multiples as the benchmark at the continuing value date versus the set of comparable companies used to value the company as of the valuation date. If all of the comparable companies are at the same stage of development, none of the existing comparable companies will reflect the likely multiples at the continuing value date and thus there may not be a good set of comparable companies from this industry for assessing the continuing value calculation. The good news is that in many industries, we can find companies at very different stages of their life cycle, so this is often not a problem. If no good comparable companies exist in this industry, then we may need to look at closely related industries.

Yahoo's Implied Market Multiples

We demonstrate here how to calculate implied market multiples based on both the DCF valuation and the forecasts in the financial model. We illustrate this calculation using one of many alternative market multiples and one of many ways to measure them. The market multiple we will use is the ratio of total market capitalization (firm value) to earnings before interest and taxes (EBIT) in the following year. The implied EBIT multiple for Yahoo's $59.8 billion continuing value is 6.1, which we calculate as follows (using data from Exhibits 6.2 and 6.3):

$$\frac{V_{\text{Yahoo, 2016}}}{\text{EBIT}_{2017}} = \frac{\$59.773}{9.871} = 6.1$$

Note that if we have assumed that Yahoo could reinvest 20% of its base year cash flow for new growth at a return on investment of 13.775%, Yahoo's continuing value would have been $62.7 billion (see Exhibit 6.17). In that case, the implied multiple of its continuing value would be 6.4 (6.4 = $62.7/$9.871). We would use this implied EBIT multiple by comparing it to the market multiples of comparable companies. However, as we stated above, the multiples you observe today for a company need not be the appropriate multiples for the continuing value calculation. Yahoo's multiple—calculated based on its value as of 2006 divided by our forecasted EBIT for 2007—is over 17 (17.2 = $34.741/$2.022), far from the implied multiple at the continuing value date. Given all the growth we had to forecast for Yahoo in order to justify its valuation as of 2006, it is no wonder that the multiple at the time of the valuation far exceeds our implied multiple at the continuing value date when the growth rate is assumed to be just 2.5%.

Valuation Key 6.12

There are a variety of techniques available for assessing the reasonableness of the continuing value used in a valuation. One such technique is to calculate implied growth rates from publicly traded comparable companies. Another is to calculate the implied multiple from a continuing value and compare that to multiples of appropriate comparable companies.

SUMMARY AND KEY CONCEPTS

In this chapter, we discussed how to use the constant-growth perpetuity model to measure a company's continuing value. The continuing value component of the total value of a firm is usually very large. Even so, most of the continuing value results from the first 50 years after the continuing value date, so using the constant-growth perpetuity model is not really dependent on the firm lasting forever. Given this large effect on value, it is critically important that we carefully analyze each of the inputs in the perpetuity model. This chapter has reviewed important issues related to the horizon (number of years of explicit year-by-year cash flow forecasts) until we rely on a continuing value calculation, how to create a reasonable base year free cash flow, how to control for economic rents embedded in the continuing value calculation, and how to assess the perpetual growth rate used for the perpetuity calculation and the overall continuing value estimate.

ADDITIONAL READING AND REFERENCES

Levin, J., and P. Olsson, "Terminal Value Techniques in Equity Valuation–Implications of the Steady State Assumption," SSE/EFI Working Paper Series in Business Administration No. 2000:7 (June 2000).

EXERCISES AND PROBLEMS

P6.1   **Present Value Weighted Growth Rate:** Assume an investment will generate cash flows at the end of Years 1 through 5 equal to $200, $240, $300, $420, and $480, respectively; from that point, the investment begins to generate a series of constant-growth perpetual cash flows.

   a.   Calculate the present value of these cash flows at the end of Year 0, assuming a discount rate of 10% and a 3% constant growth rate for the perpetuity. Calculate the present value weighted growth rate for this investment.

   b.   Calculate the present value of these cash flows at the end of Year 0, assuming a discount rate of 10% and a −3% constant growth rate for the perpetuity. Calculate the present value weighted growth rate for this investment.

P6.2   **Present Value Weighted Growth Rate:** Assume an investment will generate cash flows at the end of Years 1 through 5 equal to $2,000, −$3,000, $3,000, $3,900, and $5,000, respectively; from that point, the investment begins to generate a series of constant-growth perpetual cash flows.

   a.   Calculate the present value of these cash flows at the end of Year 0, assuming a discount rate of 10% and a 3% constant growth rate for the perpetuity. Calculate the present value weighted growth rate for this investment.

   b.   Calculate the present value of these cash flows at the end of Year 0, assuming a discount rate of 10% and a −3% constant growth rate for the perpetuity. Calculate the present value weighted growth rate for this investment.

P6.3   **Present Value Weighted Growth Rate:** A company's current, Year 0, free cash flow is $231, and its expected growth rates are 60% for Year 1, 20% for Year 2, 10% for Year 3, 5% for Years 4 and 5, and 3% thereafter. The company's cost of capital is 10%.

   a.   Measure the present value of the cash flows as of Year 0, and measure the present value weighted average growth rate for the cash flows after Year 0.

   b.   Measure the present value weighted average growth rate for the cash flows after Year 1.

   c.   Discuss the change in the present value weighted growth rate from Year 0 to Year 1.

P6.4   **Multi-Stage Growth Rate:** Calculate the present value weighted average growth rate for an investment with a discount rate of 9% and cash flows that grow through Year 10 at g_1 and at g_2 thereafter in perpetuity, using every combination of g_1 (5%, 10%, and 15%) and g_2 (−3%, 0%, and 3%).

P6.5   **Estimating a Perpetual Growth Rate from Comparable Companies:** Straight Shooter Inc.'s CFO is using the DCF valuation model to value his company. The company's CFO collected information about six comparable companies as shown in Exhibit P6.1. Estimate the perpetual growth rate for each of the comparable companies based on this information.

EXHIBIT P6.1	Straight Shooter, Inc.'s Comparable Company Information				
		Unlevered Free Cash Flow Forecasts			**Firm**
($ in millions)	**WACC**	**Year 1**	**Year 2**	**Year 3**	**Value**
Comparable Company 1	10.50%	$2,000.0	$2,400.0	$2,600.0	$30,000.0
Comparable Company 2	10.20%	$ 340.0	$ 350.0	$ 360.0	$ 4,200.0
Comparable Company 3	10.10%	$ 200.0	$ 210.0	$ 240.0	$ 2,800.0
Comparable Company 4	9.80%	$1,200.0	$1,400.0	$1,500.0	$20,000.0
Comparable Company 5	9.50%	$ 260.0	$ 250.0	$ 250.0	$ 2,870.0

P6.6   **Lumpy Capital Expenditures:** A company has $1.6 million in annual revenues in Year 1. The company expects revenues to increase by $0.6 million in Years 2 and 3 before remaining constant. Expected inflation is 0% in perpetuity. The company's only expenses are depreciation and income taxes (40% tax rate). The company uses straight-line depreciation with no salvage value and a three-year life for its assets. The fixed asset purchased at the end of Year 0 has an acquisition cost of $3.2 million. All fixed assets purchased must be replaced every three years and depreciation on fixed assets purchased begins the year after they are purchased. The replacement cost of all fixed assets is expected to remain constant in perpetuity. The company will have to invest $1.2 million in fixed assets at the end of Years 1 and 2 to support its revenue growth in Years 2 and 3. The company is all-equity financed, will hold no cash, and has no working capital requirements. The company's cost of capital is 12%. Measure the company's free cash flow for Years 1 through 4. Measure the value of the company as of the end of Year 0.

P6.7 **Growth and Value Creation:** Assume a company has expected free cash flows equal to $12,000 in Year 0, before making any new investments. It has a discount rate of 15%, and the inflation rate is 3%. If the company does not invest any of its free cash flows without new investment in Year 0, its cash flows will grow at the inflation rate. The company believes it could invest 20% of its free cash flows before new investment in perpetuity. Measure the value of the company under four scenarios: no new investment is made; the company makes a new investment each year and earns a 10%, 15%, and 20% nominal return on its investment annually and in perpetuity. What if the company invested 40% of its free cash flows before new investment and earned a 10%, 15%, or 20% nominal return?

P6.8 **Growth Rates and Continuing Value—Ed Kaplan, Inc.:** A young analyst is valuing Ed Kaplan, Inc. as of the end of Year 0. The forecast drivers underpinning the financial statement and free cash flow forecasts for four years appear in Exhibit P6.2, and the resulting income statement, balance sheet, and free cash flow forecasts for three years appear in Exhibits P6.3 and P6.4. The company's unlevered cost of capital is 13% and interest tax shields are valued using the unlevered cost of capital. The company's revenue growth rate is expected to equal 3% in perpetuity beginning in Year 4. The company intends to increase the amount of debt outstanding every year beginning at the end of Year 4 by 3%. To measure the company's continuing value at the end of Year 3, the analyst assumed the Year 3 free cash flow grew at 3% in Year 4 and then continued at that growth rate in perpetuity. The analyst calculated the company's continuing value at the end of Year 3 (CV_3) using the following formula:

$$CV_3 = \frac{FCF_3 \times (1 + g)}{r_{UA} - g} + \frac{ITS_3}{r_{UA}}$$

$$CV_3 = \frac{\$852.5(1.03)}{0.13 - 0.03} + \frac{\$320.0}{0.13} = \$8,780.75 + \$2,461.5 = \$11,242.3$$

a. Identify the errors the analyst made in the continuing value calculation.
b. Forecast the company's unlevered free cash flow in Year 4 using the information in the exhibits for this problem.
c. Discuss the difference between the Year 4 growth rates for revenue and the unlevered free cash flow.
d. Calculate the correct value of the firm as of the end of Year 0 and the continuing value of the firm as of the end of Year 3 using the perpetuity valuation.
e. Forecast the company's equity free cash flow in Year 4 using the information in the exhibits for this problem.
f. Calculate the correct value of the equity as of the end of Year 0 and the continuing value of the equity as of the end of Year 3 using the perpetuity valuation.

EXHIBIT P6.2 | Ed Kaplan, Inc.—Forecast Drivers

Ed Kaplan, Inc.—Foreast Drivers					
	Actual	**Forecast**			
	Year 0	**Year 1**	**Year 2**	**Year 3**	**Year 4**
Expected inflation..............................	3.0%	3.0%	3.0%	3.0%	3.0%
Revenue growth rate	10.0%	20.0%	20.0%	20.0%	3.0%
Cost of goods sold (% revenue)......................	20.0%	20.0%	20.0%	20.0%	20.0%
Selling, general and administrative (% revenue)	12.0%	12.0%	12.0%	12.0%	12.0%
Constant income tax rate...........................	40.0%	40.0%	40.0%	40.0%	40.0%
Required cash balance (% revenue)...................	2.5%	2.5%	2.5%	2.5%	2.5%
Accounts receivable (days to collect)...............	60.0	60.0	60.0	60.0	60.0
Inventory (days to sell)	70.0	70.0	70.0	70.0	70.0
Accounts payable (days to pay).....................	30.0	30.0	30.0	30.0	30.0
Other current operating liabilities (% revenue)..........	3.5%	3.5%	3.5%	3.5%	3.5%
Land based on revenue to land	0.50	0.50	0.50	0.50	0.50
Interest rate on debt............................	8.0%	8.0%	8.0%	8.0%	8.0%

EXHIBIT P6.3   Ed Kaplan, Inc.—Income Statement and Balance Sheet Forecasts

Ed Kaplan, Inc.—Income Statement and Balance Sheet Forecasts					
	Actual		Forecast		
	Year −1	Year 0	Year 1	Year 2	Year 3
Income Statement					
Revenue	$10,000.0	$11,000.0	$13,200.0	$15,840.0	$19,008.0
Cost of goods sold.	−2,000.0	−2,200.0	−2,640.0	−3,168.0	−3,801.6
Gross margin	$ 8,000.0	$ 8,800.0	$10,560.0	$12,672.0	$15,206.4
Selling, general and administrative	−1,200.0	−1,320.0	−1,584.0	−1,900.8	−2,281.0
Operating income.	$ 6,800.0	$ 7,480.0	$ 8,976.0	$10,771.2	$12,925.4
Interest expense.	−640.0	−800.0	−800.0	−800.0	−800.0
Income before taxes.	$ 6,160.0	$ 6,680.0	$ 8,176.0	$ 9,971.2	$12,125.4
Income tax expense.	−2,464.0	−2,672.0	−3,270.4	−3,988.5	−4,850.2
Net income.	$ 3,696.0	$ 4,008.0	$ 4,905.6	$ 5,982.7	$ 7,275.3
Balance Sheet					
Cash balance	$ 250.0	$ 275.0	$ 330.0	$ 396.0	$ 475.2
Accounts receivable.	1,666.7	1,833.3	2,200.0	2,640.0	3,168.0
Inventory.	388.9	427.8	513.3	616.0	739.2
Total current assets	$ 2,305.6	$ 2,536.1	$ 3,043.3	$ 3,652.0	$ 4,382.4
Land.	20,000.0	22,000.0	26,400.0	31,680.0	38,016.0
Total assets.	$22,305.6	$24,536.1	$29,443.3	$35,332.0	$42,398.4
Accounts payable.	$ 166.7	$ 183.3	$ 220.0	$ 264.0	$ 316.8
Other current operating liabilities	350.0	385.0	462.0	554.4	665.3
Total current liabilities.	$ 516.7	$ 568.3	$ 682.0	$ 818.4	$ 982.1
Debt	10,000.0	10,000.0	10,000.0	10,000.0	10,000.0
Total liabilities.	$10,516.7	$10,568.3	$10,682.0	$10,818.4	$10,982.1
Common stock.	$10,419.3	$10,419.3	$10,419.3	$10,419.3	$10,419.3
Retained earnings	1,369.6	3,548.5	8,342.0	14,094.3	20,997.0
Total shareholders equity	$11,788.9	$13,967.8	$18,761.3	$24,513.6	$31,416.3
Total liabilities and equities.	$22,305.6	$24,536.1	$29,443.3	$35,332.0	$42,398.4

Exhibit may contain small rounding errors

EXHIBIT P6.4   Ed Kaplan, Inc.—Free Cash Flow Forecasts

Ed Kaplan, Inc.—Free Cash Flow Forecasts				
	Actual	Forecast		
	Year 0	Year 1	Year 2	Year 3
Earnings before interest and taxes (EBIT)	$7,480.0	$8,976.0	$10,771.2	$12,925.4
− Income taxes paid on EBIT	−2,992.0	−3,590.4	−4,308.5	−5,170.2
Earnings before interest and after taxes	$4,488.0	$5,385.6	$ 6,462.7	$ 7,755.3
− Change in accounts receivable.	−166.7	−366.7	−440.0	−528.0
− Change in inventory.	−38.9	−85.6	−102.7	−123.2
+ Change in accounts payable.	16.7	36.7	44.0	52.8
+ Change in current other liabilities	35.0	77.0	92.4	110.9
− Change in required cash balance	−25.0	−55.0	−66.0	−79.2
Unlevered cash flow from operations.	$4,309.1	$4,992.0	$ 5,990.5	$ 7,188.5
− Capital expenditures	−2,000.0	−4,400.0	−5,280.0	−6,336.0
Unlevered free cash flow	$2,309.1	$ 592.0	$ 710.5	$ 852.5
− Interest paid.	−800.0	−800.0	−800.0	−800.0
+ Interest tax shield	320.0	320.0	320.0	320.0
Free cash flow before changes in financing.	$1,829.1	$ 112.0	$ 230.5	$ 372.5
+ Change in debt financing	0.0	0.0	0.0	0.0
Free cash flow to common equity	$1,829.1	$ 112.0	$ 230.5	$ 372.5

Exhibit may contain small rounding errors

SOLUTIONS FOR REVIEW EXERCISES

Review Exercise 6.1: Present Value Weighted Average Growth Rate

Discounted Cash Flow Valuation							
Cost of capital				12.0%			
Growth rate for free cash flow for continuing value				3.0%			

($ in millions)	Year 0	Year 1	Year 2	Year 3	Year 4	Year 5	CV_{Firm} Year 5
Unlevered free cash flow for continuing value							$ 4,408
Discount factor for continuing value							11.111
Unlevered free cash flow and continuing value		$2,200	$3,240	$3,300	$3,820	$4,280	$48,982
Discount factor.		0.893	0.797	0.712	0.636	0.567	0.567
Present value		$1,964	$2,583	$2,349	$2,428	$2,429	$27,794
Value of the firm as of Year 0	$39,546						
Present value weighted average growth rate.		6.44%					

$$g = r - \frac{FCF_1}{V_0} = 0.12 - \frac{\$2,200}{\$39,546} = 0.0644$$

Exhibit may contain small rounding errors

Review Exercise 6.2: Multi-Stage Growth Rates

Discount Rate is	12%		
		g_2 after Year 10	
g_1 (through Year N)	−3%	0%	3%
5%	2.0%	2.9%	4.0%
10%	4.4%	5.1%	6.1%
15%	6.3%	6.9%	7.7%
20%	7.7%	8.2%	8.8%

Review Exercise 6.3: Lumpy Capital Expenditures

Capital expenditures occur in a three-year sequence: $0, $0, and $1,200. Unlevered cash flow from operations is equal to $880, and thus, unlevered free cash flow occurs in the following three-year sequence: $880, $880, −$320. We can convert the capital expenditure to an annuity of $363 by dividing the present value of the three-year capital expenditure cash flows by the annuity present value factor formula (we previously showed the annuity present factor formula for an annuity with growth, but the growth rate is zero in this exercise).

$$A = \frac{PV_{CAPEX,\,0}}{PV \text{ of Annuity (3 years, 10\%)}} = \frac{PV_{CAPEX,\,0}}{\dfrac{1}{(r-g)} - \dfrac{1}{(r-g)} \times \dfrac{(1+g)^3}{(1+r)^3}} = \frac{\dfrac{\$1,200}{1.1^3}}{\dfrac{1}{(0.1-0)} - \dfrac{1}{(0.1-0)} \times \dfrac{1.0^3}{1.1^3}} = \$363$$

We can now adjust the free cash flows by the amount of the annuity, and the cash flows become a constant $517 per year.

Below, we present various schedules providing more detailed calculations. Note that if we value the company using the actual unlevered free cash flow, the company's value will be overstated for years in which it does not have capital expenditures and understated for years it has capital expenditures. The company's value is correct when the cash flows are adjusted for the capital expenditures annuity. The continuing value at Year 3 using the adjusted cash flows is $3,888 with a present value of the actual cash flows for Years 1 through 3 of $1,287. The total of the two present values yields the correct firm value of $5,175.

Income Statement, Balance Sheet, and Free Cash Flow Forecasts							
	Year 0	Year 1	Year 2	Year 3	Year 4	Year 5	Year 6
Income Statement							
Revenue		$1,200	$1,200	$1,200	$1,200	$1,200	$1,200
Depreciation expense.		−400	−400	−400	−400	−400	−400
Income before taxes.		$ 800	$ 800	$ 800	$ 800	$ 800	$ 800
Income tax expense (Provision)		−320	−320	−320	−320	−320	−320
Net income.		$ 480	$ 480	$ 480	$ 480	$ 480	$ 480
Balance Sheet							
Total assets = Fixed asset	$1,200	$ 800	$ 400	$1,200	$ 800	$ 400	$1,200
Shareholders' equity	$1,200	$ 800	$ 400	$1,200	$ 800	$ 400	$1,200
Free Cash Flow							
Earnings before interest and taxes.		$ 800	$ 800	$ 800	$ 800	$ 800	$ 800
Income taxes paid on EBIT		−320	−320	−320	−320	−320	−320
Earnings before interest and after taxes		$ 480	$ 480	$ 480	$ 480	$ 480	$ 480
Depreciation.		400	400	400	400	400	400
Unlevered cash flow from operations.		$ 880	$ 880	$ 880	$ 880	$ 880	$ 880
Capital expenditures	$−1,200	0	0	−1,200	0	0	−1,200
Unlevered free cash flow = Equity FCF		$ 880	$ 880	$ −320	$ 880	$ 880	$ −320

Property, Plant, and Equipment and Accumulated Depreciation Forecasts							
	Year 0	Year 1	Year 2	Year 3	Year 4	Year 5	Year 6
Beginning property, plant, and equipment. . . .		$1,200	$1,200	$1,200	$1,200	$1,200	$1,200
Capital expenditures	$1,200	0	0	1,200	0	0	1,200
Retirements				−1,200	0	0	−1,200
Ending property, plant, and equipment	$1,200	$1,200	$1,200	$1,200	$1,200	$1,200	$1,200
Beginning accumulated depreciation.		$ 0	$ 400	$ 800	$ 0	$ 400	$ 800
Depreciation expense.		400	400	400	400	400	400
Retirements		0	0	−1,200	0	0	−1,200
Ending accumulated depreciation	$ 0	$ 400	$ 800	$ 0	$ 400	$ 800	$ 0
Net property, plant, and equipment	$1,200	$ 800	$ 400	$1,200	$ 800	$ 400	$1,200

Discounted Cash Flow Valuation Using Actual Free Cash Flows							
Year (t)	Year 0	Year 1	Year 2	Year 3	Year 4	Year 5	Year 6
Free cash flow		$ 880	$ 880	$ −320	$ 880	$ 880	$−320
Continuing value at Year 0		$8,000	$−2,645	$6,612	$6,011	$−1,987	
Present value of FCF Year +1 to Year t . . .	Correct	800	1,527	1,287	1,888	2,434	
Value of the firm at Year 0.	$5,175	$8,800	$−1,117	$7,898	$7,898	$ 447	
Error in the valuation		70%	−122%	53%	53%	−91%	

Exhibit may contain small rounding errors

continued

Discounted Cash Flow Valuation Using Adjusted Free Cash Flows, Adjusted for Annuity Capital Expenditures

Year (t)		Year 0	Year 1	Year 2	Year 3	Year 4	Year 5	Year 6
Actual capital expenditure			$ 0	$ 0	$1,200	$ 0	$ 0	$1,200
Annuity for capital expenditures.			363	363	363	363	363	363
Adjustment to free cash flow			$ –363	$ –363	$ 837	$ –363	$ –363	$ 837
Actual free cash flow			880	880	–320	880	880	–320
Adjusted free cash flow			$ 517	$ 517	$ 517	$ 517	$ 517	$ 517
Continuing value at Year 0			$4,704	$4,277	$3,888	$3,534	$3,213	
Present value of FCF Year +1 to Year t . . .	Correct		470	898	1,287	1,640	1,962	
Value of the firm at Year 0.	$5,175	$5,175	$5,175	$5,175	$5,175	$5,175	
Error in the valuation			0%	0%	0%	0%	0%	

Exhibit may contain small rounding errors

Review Exercise 6.4: Real Growth and Value

	No New Investment	Value Neutral New Investment	Value Creating New Investment	Value Destroying New Investment
Free cash flow (Before Investment), Year CV+1 . .	$ 1,000.0	$ 1,000.0	$ 1,000.0	$1,000.0
Nominal required rate of return	10.0%	10.0%	10.0%	10.0%
Inflation.	0%	0%	0%	0%
Return on new investment (Real)		10.0%	12.0%	8.00%
Return on new investment (Nominal)		10.0%	12.0%	8.0%
% New investment.		40.0%	40.0%	40.0%
Growth rate.	0.0%	4.0%	4.8%	3.2%
Continuing value.	$10,000.0	$10,000.0	$11,538.5	$8,823.5
% Change in value.		0.00%	15.4%	–11.8%

Review Exercise 6.5: Estimating Growth Rates from Comparable Companies

$$\$18,000 = \frac{\$1,000}{(1.1)^1} + \frac{\$1,200}{(1.1)^2} + \frac{\$1,500}{(1.1)^3} + \frac{\$1,500 \times (1+g)}{(0.1-g)} \times \frac{1}{(1.1)^3}; g = 0.023$$

$$g = r_{WACC} - \frac{FCF_T}{(1 + r_{WACC})^{T-1} \times \left[V_{F,0} - \sum_{t=1}^{T-1} \frac{FCF_t}{(1 + r_{WACC})^t} \right]}$$

$$g = 0.1 - \frac{\$1,500}{(1.1)^2 \times \left(\$18,000 - \frac{\$1,000}{(1.1)^1} + \frac{\$1,200}{(1.1)^2} \right)} = 0.023$$

After mastering the material in this chapter, you will be able to:

1. Understand how the excess earnings model works (7.1–7.2)

2. Measure firm value using the WACC and APV forms of the excess earnings model (7.3–7.4)

3. Measure equity value using the equity form of the excess earnings model (7.5)

4. Learn about adjustments to both earnings and invested capital that are made when excess earnings are used to evaluate performance (7.6–7.7)

The Excess Earnings Valuation Method

The use of the excess earnings (residual earnings or residual income) valuation method is natural for some Wall Street analysts who forecast long-term estimates of earnings and book value. For example, in an analyst report on electronics manufacturing service (EMS) companies, Morgan Stanley Dean Witter states:

MORGAN STANLEY DEAN WITTER

Residual income valuations depend on the sustainable returns companies generate on current invested capital and the expected returns they will generate on incremental invested capital from the free cash they generate. . . . revenues, costs, and invested capital are linked through ROE, so that the tie into the valuations should be relatively transparent. . . . revenue growth, operating margins, and operating asset turns are key inputs to understanding profitability. As the EMS companies begin to leverage their recent investments, they should start to generate more free cash flow. Thus, valuations also depend on our assumptions regarding how this free cash gets used. As electronic manufacturing service (EMS) companies drive profitability through economies of scale and scope, we see them as natural candidates for a residual income valuation analysis, which focuses on the actual invested capital, plus the related return on that invested capital, specifically operating margins and operating asset turnover (efficiency).[1]

In this chapter we will learn the ins and outs of residual income valuation models, as these are sometimes used as an alternative to the discounted cash flow model.

---

[1] Morgan Stanley Dean Witter, "Technology: Electronics Manufacturing Service," Equity Research—Industry, Morgan Stanley Dean Witter, New York (March 28, 2001), pp. 1, 7.

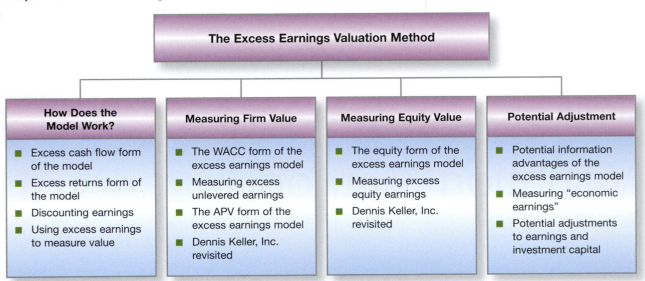

INTRODUCTION

The excess earnings (residual earnings or residual income) valuation method is a specific form of a more general valuation model we call the excess flow model. While it might not be apparent at first glance, all excess flow valuation models—including the excess earnings form—result directly from our fundamental valuation principles and concepts, and they are algebraically equivalent to the discounted cash flow (DCF) valuation models. Like the DCF valuation models, each excess flow valuation model has an adjusted present value (APV), weighted average cost of capital (WACC), and equity discounted flow (Equity) form. From Chapter 5, we know that, if implemented properly, the APV, WACC, and Equity DCF valuation methods all result in the same valuation. The same statement is true for all forms of the excess flow model; that is, if implemented properly, all forms of the excess flow valuation model result in the same valuation, and this valuation is equal to the DCF-based valuation.

If excess flow models are algebraically equivalent to the DCF model, you might be wondering why someone would bother using an excess flow model. The reason is that it sometimes conveys additional information that is potentially informative. The **excess flow valuation model** separates the value of the firm into two parts—the amount invested as of the valuation date and the value of the firm in excess of its invested capital. The value of the firm in excess of its invested capital is equal to the discounted value of the company's forecasted excess flows or earnings. The additional information provided by the excess flow model consists of the excess flows or earnings a company earns every period.

The most popular form of the excess flow model is the excess earnings model due to the widespread use of earnings as a measure of performance and given that earnings forecasts are a primary output of equity analysts. Consulting companies often advise using excess earnings valuation models as part of a value-based management system. Stern Stewart & Company, for example, uses its economic value added (EVA®) and market value added (MVA®) approaches. CSFB HOLT LLC uses its cash flow return on investment approach (CFROI®). McKinsey & Company uses a variety of approaches to help managers create value and become "value managers." We will discuss the potential information benefits of the excess flows model later in the chapter after first demonstrating exactly how these models work.

7.1 THE BASIC FRAMEWORK

LO1 Understand how the excess earnings model works

We begin our discussion of the excess flow valuation model with its most basic form—the **excess free cash flow** form. In this form, the value of the firm is equal to the invested capital as of the valuation date plus the value of the company's discounted excess free cash flows. We will then discuss the excess operating cash flow model before discussing the popular **excess earnings** (**residual earnings** or **residual income**) valuation model. It is important to emphasize that each of these forms of the excess flow model is algebraically equivalent to the DCF valuation model.

Excess Free Cash Flow Form

If we make an investment with an expected return equal to its risk-adjusted required rate of return, r, the value of the investment will be equal to the amount invested. For a no-growth perpetuity, if the investment's expected free cash flow is equal to its required return multiplied by the amount of the investment ($FCF = r \times I_0$), then the value of the investment will equal the amount invested ($V_0 = I_0$). For example, assume Mr. J. Stern purchased an all-equity-financed company with an investment of $100, I_0. When Mr. Stern purchased the company—now called the J. Stern Company—it had an expected annual free cash flow (FCF) of $10 in perpetuity and a required rate of return of 10%; thus, its expected return of 10% ($0.1 = \$10/\$100$) is equal to its required rate of return. The company distributes its free cash flow at the end of each year to investors, so Stern's investment will always remain at $100.

Since the company's expected rate of return is equal to its required rate of return (10%), the value of the company must be equal to the amount invested by Stern, $100. We can also phrase this statement in terms of amounts—since the company's expected free cash flow of $10 is equal to the company's required cash flow ($\$10 = 0.1 \times \$100$), the value of the company is equal to the value of the investment. We can use the zero-growth DCF perpetuity formula to show this result.

$$V_0 = \frac{FCF_1}{r} = \frac{r \times I_0}{r} = I_0$$

For reasons we will explain below, this is an important concept, for it underpins all of the excess flow models. Instead of discounting the entire free cash flow stream, the excess flow models discount the flows in excess of the required free cash flows—called **excess flows**. Since the value of the required free cash flows is equal to the value of the investment, we can calculate the value of the firm by adding the amount of the investment as of the valuation date to the discounted value of the forecasted excess flows. In essence, the excess flow model adds and subtracts the value of the investment from the DCF model valuation, which of course results in the same value as the DCF valuation.

We can illustrate this concept with the J. Stern Company. We know that Mr. Stern could create value if the company's free cash flows were greater than the required free cash flow return of $10. If Mr. Stern found a way to use the company's assets to generate expected free cash flows of $12 per year in perpetuity without changing the risk of the company, the value of the company would increase to $120.

$$V_0 = \frac{FCF_1}{r} = \frac{\$12}{0.1} = \$120$$

In the excess flow model, we calculate the value of the firm as being the investment plus the present value of the discounted excess free cash flows.

$$V_0 = \frac{r \times I_0}{r} + \frac{FCF_1 - r \times I_0}{r} = I_0 + \frac{FCF_1 - r \times I_0}{r}$$

$$V_0 = \frac{0.1 \times \$100}{0.1} + \frac{\$12 - 0.1 \times \$100}{0.1} = \$100 + \frac{\$12 - 0.1 \times \$100}{0.1} = \$120$$

It is important to note that while we added back and subtracted initial investments from the DCF model, we could have added and subtracted any value from the DCF model. For example, we could have multiplied the initial investment by 2. As long as we subtract the required return multiplied by the amount we added (investment multiplied by 2), we are merely adding and subtracting the same amount from the DCF valuation. The reason for using the amount invested instead of another amount (e.g., investment multiplied by 2) is that the excess return has a potential economic meaning and interpretation. For example, although it would have no economic meaning, we could have added $200 and subtracted r $\times$ $200 in every subsequent period, and we would have still arrived at the same value.

$$V_0 = I_0 + \frac{FCF_1 - r \times I_0}{r} = \$200 + \frac{\$12 - 0.1 \times \$200}{0.1} = \$200 + \frac{\$12 - \$20}{0.1} = \$200 - \$80 = \$120$$

An Excess Returns Presentation of the Excess Flow Model

We can also implement the excess flow model in a returns form, which is merely an alternative way of showing the calculation of an investment's excess flow. In the J. Stern Company example, the $12 free cash flow is a 12% return on investment (0.12 = $12/$100). The company's **excess return**, xr, is equal to its expected return, ER, minus its required return, r. The excess return in this example is 2% (0.02 = 0.12 − 0.1). Using an excess returns approach, the value of a company with a 12% expected return is equal to the initial investment plus the value of the excess return (xr) multiplied by the amount of the investment.

$$V_0 = I_0 + \frac{(ER_1 - r) \times I_0}{r} = I_0 + \frac{xr_1 \times I_0}{r}$$

For the above example, we can value the investment as

$$V_0 = \$100 + \frac{(0.12 - 0.1) \times \$100}{0.1} = \$100 + \frac{0.02 \times \$100}{0.1} = \$120$$

The excess returns form of the excess flow valuation model is an alternative, but equivalent, approach to implementing the excess flow valuation methods. The choice is purely based on analyst preference. Again, by discounting excess returns, the excess flow model essentially extracts the amount of the investment's return (the required return) that, when discounted, is equal to the value of the invested capital as of the valuation date. The value of the excess returns is equal to the firm's value in excess of the initial investment or, in essence, the net present value of the firm's investments.

Valuation Key 7.1

The discounted excess flow valuation methods value a firm or investment as the value of the initial investment plus the value of the discounted future returns in excess of the required returns. Properly implemented, all forms of the excess flow valuation methods are equivalent to DCF-based valuations.

REVIEW EXERCISE 7.1

Excess Free Cash Flow Model

A group of investors formed a company at the end of Year 0 by investing $10.0 million in equity, which was used to purchase assets and provide working capital for the company's operations. The company is financed with only equity and has a 12% cost of capital. The company expects to generate $1.44 million in annual free cash flows in perpetuity, and the company holds no excess cash. Measure the value of the company using the excess free cash flow model.

Solution on page 278.

7.2 THE EXCESS ACCOUNTING EARNINGS METHOD

To use the excess earnings valuation method, we discount excess accounting earnings (residual earnings or residual income) instead of excess free cash flows. We measure excess earnings the same way that we measure excess free cash flows, but instead of using free cash flows and cash investment, we use accounting earnings and total invested capital based on the financial statements. The concept of excess or residual earnings is not new. As early as 1890, an economist by the name of Alfred Marshall defined profits in terms of excess earnings and the value of a company in terms of its capitalized excess earnings:

When a man is engaged in business, his profits for the year are the excess of his receipts from his business during the year over his outlay for his business. The difference between the value of his stock of plant, material, etc. at the end and at the beginning of the year is taken as part of his receipts or as part of his outlay, according as there has been an increase or decrease of value. What remains of his

continued

continued from prior page

> profits after deducting interest on his capital at the current rate (allowing, where necessary, for insurance) is generally called his earnings of undertaking or management. . . .
>
> He would not be, however, willing to continue the business unless he expected his total net gains from it to exceed interest on his capital at the current rate. These gains are called profits. [2]

It took quite a few years before Edwards and Bell (1961) explicitly discussed measuring residual earnings using financial statements.[3] The consulting company, Stern Stewart & Company, also popularized an adjusted excess earnings valuation method, called economic value added (EVA®).[4] Ohlson (1989, 1995) provided a rigorous development of these models and popularized this valuation method as a research topic and its use in the investment community.[5]

If implemented consistently, the various excess earnings valuation methods result in the same valuation as the DCF valuation method. At first, this assertion might seem confusing. Everyone who knows how to read a financial statement knows that accounting earnings do not equal free cash flows, so understanding why the discounted excess earnings method results in the same valuation as the DCF models is not straightforward. The equivalence of the excess earnings and DCF valuation models, however, is neither a coincidence nor a mystery; the algebra underlying the two valuation methods is simply equivalent, though that equivalence is not transparent at first.

How can the excess earnings and DCF valuation methods result in the same valuation? The sneak preview answer is simply that the excess earnings valuation method adjusts for the timing difference between a company's free cash flows and its earnings. A company begins with cash (initial investment) and ends with cash (liquidating dividend). Over the life of the company, the sum of its earnings is equal to the sum of its free cash flows. Thus, if we want to discount earnings instead of free cash flows, we need to make an adjustment in our calculations to adjust for the timing differences between the two. The mechanics of the discounted excess earnings valuation method implicitly adjust for these timing differences on a present value basis. The result is that the present value of the difference between excess earnings and excess cash flows is equal to zero.

Excess Earnings Model—Part 1—General Form of the Excess Free Cash Flow Model

We begin our development of the excess earnings model with a more general form of the excess free cash flow model. For now, assume that r measures an appropriate discount rate based on the riskiness of the cash flows—later in the chapter we will make clear what cost of capital we use in specific forms of the model. The excess free cash flow model for an all-equity company is

$$V_F = I_0 + \sum_{t=1}^{\infty} \frac{FCF_t - r \times I_0}{(1 + r)^t}$$

We can show that the above model is nothing more than adding and subtracting the investment (I_0) from the DCF model.

$$V_F = \sum_{t=1}^{\infty} \frac{FCF_t}{(1 + r)^t} + I_0 - \sum_{t=1}^{\infty} \frac{r \times I_0}{(1 + r)^t}$$

$$V_F = \sum_{t=1}^{\infty} \frac{FCF_t}{(1 + r)^t} + I_0 - \frac{r \times I_0}{r}$$

---

[2] Marshall used the term "interest" more broadly than interest on debt. He used it in the same way we use the term "cost of capital." Marshall, A., *Principles of Economics*, first published in 1890, London: Macmillan and Co., Ltd. (1920), retrieved on April 28, 2003 from http://www.econlib.org/library/Marshall/marP8.html, Book II, Chapter IV, paragraph 11, 9.

[3] Edwards, E. and P. Bell , *The Theory and Measurement of Business Income*, Berkeley: University of California Press (1961).

[4] See, for example, Stewart (1991) for a detailed discussion of this approach; Stewart, B. B. III, *The Quest for Value*, Harper Collins Publishers, Inc. (1991).

[5] Ohlson, J. A., "Accounting Earnings, Book Value, and Dividends: The Theory of the Clean Surplus Equation Part I," Columbia University Working Paper, 1989; reprinted in Brief, R. P., and K. V. Peasnell, *Clean Surplus: A Link Between Accounting and Finance*, Garland Publishing, Inc. (1996); and Ohlson, J. A., "Earnings, Book Values and Dividends in Equity Valuation," *Contemporary Accounting Research* vol. 11, no. 2 (1995), pp. 661–688.

Excess Earnings Model—Part 2—Excess Operating Cash Flow Model

We can convert the excess free cash flow model to an excess operating cash flow (CFO) model. For an all-equity-financed company, the key difference between operating cash flows and free cash flows is capital expenditures or the change in investment, ΔI. For our discussion, we assume that free cash flow is equal to operating cash flow minus the change in cash investments ($FCF_t = CFO_t - \Delta I_t$).

We can also use operating cash flow to measure the value of the firm as long as we subtract the present value of all expected investments (Years 1, 2, . . ., ∞) from the calculation. The operating cash flow form of the excess free cash flow model makes this adjustment, and is as follows:

$$V_F = I_0 + \sum_{t=1}^{\infty} \frac{CFO_t - r \times I_{t-1}}{(1 + r)^t}$$

We will spend a little time working through the intuition behind how this works, for if you understand this model, you will realize that the same types of adjustments occur in the other models that we will develop. The difference between the excess free cash flow model and excess cash flow from operations model is that we replace free cash flow with cash flow from operations, and since we do not deduct the change in cash investments when we calculate operating cash flow, we must deduct—in present value terms—the change in cash investments for each year in another way. We deduct the present value of these investments by adjusting the required flow each year for the change in the investment; in other words, the required cash flow is equal to the required rate of return multiplied by the beginning-of-year investment ($r \times I_{t-1}$)—and not the initial investment that we used in the excess free cash flow model. That is, all we need to do is deduct the present value of the additional investments from the valuation.

We can rewrite the excess operating cash flow model to show that it is equal to the DCF model. Although the model is complicated by deducting the required return based on the beginning of the period investment ($r \times I_{t-1}$), the basic approach is the same. The excess operating flow model is equal to the DCF model plus and minus the investments, but now, we add and deduct the investment for every year (0, 1, 2, . . ., ∞).

Since operating cash flow is equal to free cash flow plus the change in investment (CFO = FCF + ΔI from FCF = CFO $-$ ΔI), we can restate the excess operating cash flow model with a free cash flow component by adding and subtracting the change in investments.

$$V_F = I_0 + \sum_{t=1}^{\infty} \frac{CFO_t - \Delta I_t + \Delta I_t - r \times I_{t-1}}{(1 + r)^t} = I_0 + \sum_{t=1}^{\infty} \frac{FCF_t + \Delta I_t - r \times I_{t-1}}{(1 + r)^t}$$

We can now state the above form of the excess operating cash flow model as a DCF model with additional components.

$$V_F = \sum_{t=1}^{\infty} \frac{FCF_t}{(1 + r)^t} + \left[I_0 + \sum_{t=1}^{\infty} \frac{\Delta I_t - r \times I_{t-1}}{(1 + r)^t} \right]$$

The first term on the right-hand side of the above equation is equal to the DCF model; thus, the excess operating cash flow model is equal to the DCF model if

$$0 = I_0 + \sum_{t=1}^{\infty} \frac{\Delta I_t - r \times I_{t-1}}{(1 + r)^t}$$

Showing that the right-hand side of the above equation reduces to I_0 is more complex than showing the analogous result for the excess free cash flow model. It is more complex, for we have an infinite series of investments in this equation, and we cannot deduct the investments as part of the free cash flow calculation as we did in the excess free cash flow model. Regardless, the underlying algebra is the same. We add back each investment and then subtract it out by subtracting the present value of the required returns on that investment. To show this result, we first begin by expanding the above equation:

$$0 = I_0 + \left[\frac{\Delta I_1}{(1 + r)^1} - \frac{r \times I_0}{(1 + r)^1} \right] + \left[\frac{\Delta I_2}{(1 + r)^2} - \frac{r \times I_1}{(1 + r)^2} \right] + \left[\frac{\Delta I_3}{(1 + r)^3} - \frac{r \times I_2}{(1 + r)^3} \right] + \cdots$$

Next we expand each of the changes in the investments and combine like terms.

$$0 = I_0 + \left[\frac{I_1 - I_0}{(1 + r)^1} - \frac{r \times I_0}{(1 + r)^1} \right] + \left[\frac{I_2 - I_1}{(1 + r)^2} - \frac{r \times I_1}{(1 + r)^2} \right] + \left[\frac{I_3 - I_2}{(1 + r)^3} - \frac{r \times I_2}{(1 + r)^3} \right] + \cdots$$

$$0 = I_0 + \left[\frac{I_1}{(1 + r)^1} - \frac{(1 + r) \times I_0}{(1 + r)^1} \right] + \left[\frac{I_2}{(1 + r)^2} - \frac{(1 + r) \times I_1}{(1 + r)^2} \right] + \left[\frac{I_3}{(1 + r)^3} - \frac{(1 + r) \times I_2}{(1 + r)^3} \right] + \cdots$$

We restate the above equation as follows:

$$0 = I_0 + \left[\frac{I_1}{(1+r)^1} - I_0 \right] + \left[\frac{I_2}{(1+r)^2} - \frac{I_1}{(1+r)^1} \right] + \left[\frac{I_3}{(1+r)^3} - \frac{I_2}{(1+r)^2} \right] + \cdots$$

Each term in the previous equation has an additive inverse such that the value of this equation is zero; in other words, the investment is both added and then subtracted in the excess valuation model.

Excess Earnings Model—Part 3—The Excess (or Residual) Earnings Model

Accountants record revenues and expenses based on generally accepted accounting principles (GAAP) and not based on cash receipts and cash expenses. The difference between cash-basis accounting and GAAP-based accrual accounting is called **accounting accruals**. Examples of accruals include revenues recorded by the company but not yet collected in cash—resulting in an account receivable—or expenses recorded by the company but not paid in cash—resulting in an account payable. Another type of accrual is the result of expensing a previously capitalized investment over its useful life; this is called **depreciation** if the investment is for plant or equipment or **amortization** if the investment is for an intangible asset.

Accounting accruals affect both the income statement and the balance sheet. The balance sheet contains the cumulative amount of the accruals recorded by the company, A. The income statement, on the other hand, contains the change in the company's cumulative accruals, ΔA_t. Thus, we can state the difference between accounting earnings and free cash flows as the change in accounting accruals and new cash investments. In other words, free cash flow is equal to accounting earnings, adjusted for the change in accounting accruals and new investment. As long as we use clean-surplus accounting, accruals and investments do not cause a permanent difference between cumulative accounting earnings and cumulative free cash flows. That is, over the life of the firm, the sum of the free cash flows is equal to the sum of the earnings. Eventually, all accruals and investments reverse through the income statement and affect earnings. For example, a company collects its receivables, pays its payables, and expenses its previously capitalized cash expenditures. The difference is only a matter of timing.[6]

Recall the basic free cash flow formula in which free cash flow is equal to earnings before interest and taxes, EBIT, minus cash income taxes on EBIT, TAX, plus non-cash expenses, NCX (an accrual), minus non-cash revenues, NCR (an accrual), minus the change in required cash, ΔRC, minus the change in non-cash operating working capital, ΔNWC (an accrual), minus capital expenditures, CAPEX.

$$FCF = EBIT - TAX + NCX - NCR - \Delta RC - \Delta NWC - CAPEX$$

Since we are assuming the company is all-equity financed, earnings, E, is equal to earnings before interest and taxes less income taxes (E = EBIT – TAX). We can assume that the new cash investment is equal to the change in required cash plus capital expenditures ($\Delta I_t = \Delta RC + CAPEX$), and we can assume that the remainder of the terms in the above free cash flow formula represent the change in accounting accruals ($\Delta A_t = \Delta NWC + NCR - NCX$). Thus, we can rewrite the free cash flow formula as follows:

$$FCF_t = E_t - \Delta A_t - \Delta I_t$$

The assumptions are not precise, for we assume the change in working capital is only an accrual when, in fact, it contains both accruals (such as the changes in accounts receivable and wages payable) and new investment (such as investments in inventory and prepaid expenses). We could have used a more precise mapping of the terms in the initial free cash flow formula, but the additional precision would have no effect on proving the equivalence of the excess earnings and DCF valuation methods.

We need one more relation before we can show the equivalence of the DCF model and excess earnings model. That is to note that the book value of a company's equity, BVE_t, is equal to its cumulative investment, I_t, plus its cumulative accruals, A_t, or $BVE_t = I_t + A_t$.

---

[6] See Ohlson, J. A., "Earnings, Book Values and Dividends in Equity Valuation," *Contemporary Accounting Research* vol. 11, no. 2 (1995), pp. 661–688.

One way to understand this relation is to consider an all-equity-financed company that pays dividends equal to its free cash flows. In this case, it should be straightforward to see that the book value of equity is equal to the level of investment made plus the level of accruals. If the company paid out fewer dividends than free cash flows, it would imply that investment in the company increased because it retained excess cash. That additional investment would then increase the book value of equity because, in fact, the actual investment was greater than what had been used in determining free cash flows.

The excess earnings model is equal to

$$V_F = BVE_0 + \sum_{t=1}^{\infty} \frac{E_t - r \times BVE_{t-1}}{(1 + r)^t} \tag{7.1}$$

We can rewrite the excess earnings model to show that it is equal to the DCF. Although, like the excess operating cash flow model, the excess earnings model is complicated by the deduction of the required return based on the beginning of period investment ($r \times I_{t-1}$), the basic approach is the same. We can restate Equation 7.1 by replacing earnings with its equivalent, $E_t = FCF_t + \Delta A_t + \Delta I_t$, and book value with cash investments plus accruals. Since earnings is equal to free cash flow plus the change in investment plus the change in accruals, we can restate the excess earnings model with a free cash flow component by adding and subtracting the changes in investments and accruals.

$$V_F = (I_0 + A_0) + \sum_{t=1}^{\infty} \frac{[FCF_t + \Delta I_t + \Delta A_t] - r \times (I_{t-1} + A_{t-1})}{(1 + r)^t}$$

We can now restate the above equation in terms of the DCF model plus two other components.

$$V_F = \sum_{t=1}^{\infty} \frac{FCF_t}{(1 + r)^t} + \left[I_0 + \sum_{t=1}^{\infty} \frac{\Delta I_t - r \times I_{t-1}}{(1 + r)^t} \right] + \left[A_0 + \sum_{t=1}^{\infty} \frac{\Delta A_t - r \times A_{t-1}}{(1 + r)^t} \right]$$

The first term on the right-hand side of above equation is the DCF model. The second term is the same investment term from the excess operating cash flow model, which we know is equal to zero. The third term is the accrual term, and it has the same format as the investment term. We know that the value of this term, regardless of whether it is investments or accruals—or even some random number—is equal to zero.

As we stated in the introduction to this section, we do not need to know very much about accounting in order to understand the simple mechanics that make the excess earnings valuation method equivalent to the DCF valuation method. We need to know that accounting rules result in differences between free cash flows and accounting net income (accruals and investments for the period), and that this difference is recorded in the company's balance sheet. Further, we know that over the life of a company, the cumulative difference between free cash flows and earnings (cumulative accruals and investments) net to zero. The mechanics of the model ensure that the present value of the accruals in the excess earnings model is equal to zero.

Extending the J. Stern Company Example to the Excess Earnings Valuation Method

Recall our simple excess cash flow example concerning the J. Stern Company, which is an all-equity-financed company. After Stern purchases the company, the expected free cash flows of the company are equal to $12 per year, and the company's discount rate is 10%. The company will not grow and will distribute all of its free cash flow to its investors. Thus, the value of the company is $120. Now, we are going to add some accruals to the J. Stern Company example.

We first extend our example by adding an accrual to the initial balance sheet—that is, the investment (assets and common equity) on the balance sheet will no longer equal the cash investment. We do this by assuming that J. Stern invested $100, but for whatever reason, the company recorded the investment on both the asset side and equity side of the balance sheet at $110 ($BVE_0 = \$110$). We can characterize this difference as an accrual of $10. We also assume that the company's expected earnings is equal to its expected free cash flows for every year—$12; that is, the company does not have any additional accruals or new investments.

We do not need to know why we recorded this accrual (the difference between the cash invested and the book value of the company). In fact, it could even be an error. The mechanics of the excess flow valuation model are such that such accruals do not affect the valuation of the company; again, it's not magic—only a little algebra at work. Seeing is believing, so here is the valuation with the $10 accrual that increases the book value of equity ($BVE_0 = \$110$).

$$V_F = BVE_0 + \frac{E_1 - r \times BVE_0}{r}$$

$$V_F = \$110 + \frac{\$12 - 0.1 \times \$110}{0.1} = \$120$$

The valuation of the company is still $120. The accrual not only increased the initial book value of the investment by $10 (from $100 to $110), but it also reduced the excess earnings for every year in the future; because the required return ($r \times BVE$) became larger, so the excess earnings became smaller. The present value of the decrease in excess earnings in future years is equal to $10, which exactly offsets the $10 accrual, so the valuation is unchanged by adding an accrual to the initial book value. We know that we could have chosen any number for the accrual because the model merely adds back and subtracts that number. That is why having an economic underpinning to the accrual number is important—so that the present value of the excess earnings has some economic meaning.

Now, accruals can also affect earnings such that earnings no longer equal free cash flow every period. The company's expected free cash flows continue to be $12 per year. The company's expected earnings, however, no longer equal its free cash flows. We expect the company to have a $10 earnings increasing accrual in Year 1 that reverses in Year 3, and in all other years, its expected earnings are equal to its expected free cash flow. Thus, the company's expected earnings no longer equal its free cash flows in every year ($12 per year). Earnings will increase by $10 in the year the accrual is taken (Year 1) and will decrease by $10 in the year the accrual reverses (Year 3). Thus, forecasted earnings are equal to $22 in Year 1, $12 in Year 2, $2 in Year 3, and $12 thereafter. Note that the income increasing accrual also increases the book value of equity at the end of Year 1 by $10 to $120, and the reversal will decrease it by $10 to $110 at the end of Year 3.

The mechanics work in the same way as when we added an accrual to the initial book value of the investment. The accrual either increases or decreases earnings relative to cash flows from operations in that year, and it similarly affects the book value of the company's assets (investment plus cumulative accruals). Thus, applying the cost of capital to the company's book value exactly offsets the accrual in the earnings when we calculate the present value, even though we had an accrual that created a difference between earnings and cash flow. The calculation is a little more complex because we need to value the excess earnings for Years 1 through 3 separately from the perpetuity, which begins in Year 4.

$$V_E = V_F = BVE_0 + \frac{E_1 - r \times BVE_0}{1 + r} + \frac{E_2 - r \times BVE_1}{(1 + r)^2} + \frac{E_3 - r \times BVE_2}{(1 + r)^3} + \frac{E_4 - r \times BVE_3}{r} \times \frac{1}{(1 + r)^3}$$

$$V_E = V_F = \$110 + \frac{\$22 - 0.1 \times \$110}{1.1} + \frac{\$12 - 0.1 \times \$120}{(1.1)^2} + \frac{\$2 - 0.1 \times \$120}{(1.1)^3} + \frac{\$12 - 0.1 \times \$110}{0.1} \times \frac{1}{(1.1)^3}$$

$$V_E = V_F = \$110 + \frac{\$22 - \$11}{1.1} + \frac{\$12 - \$12}{(1.1)^2} + \frac{\$2 - \$12}{(1.1)^3} + \frac{\$12 - \$11}{0.1} \times \frac{1}{(1.1)^3} = \$120$$

REVIEW EXERCISE 7.2

Excess Earnings Model

Use the information from Review Exercise 7.1 and assume that in addition to the initial $10 million investment in the company, the company also recorded a $1 million intangible asset, which has a perpetual life. Also assume that the company's free cash flow is equal to its accounting earnings (for example, depreciation is equal to capital expenditures and that there is no change in working capital). Measure the value of the company using the excess earnings model.

Solution on page 278.

Summary

The equivalence of the excess earnings valuation method and the DCF valuation methods is not magical—it is only algebra. The sum of accounting accruals and investment during a period is essentially the difference between free cash flows and accounting earnings. Accountants record the difference between free cash flows and accounting earnings on the balance sheet. The mechanics of the excess earnings valuation method are such that any set of accounting rules results in the same valuation of a company, because the excess earnings valuation method automatically adjusts the valuation for the present value of the difference between the company's free cash flows and earnings as long as we use clean-surplus accounting.

More specifically, in the excess flow valuation model, we subtract a capital charge to calculate the excess flow. When we compute the capital charge in the excess earnings model, we use the book value of total invested capital as the investment base (book value of equity for an all-equity-financed company), which includes the effects of the accruals and investment. Using the book value of total invested capital or equity as the investment base automatically adjusts for the timing difference between earnings and free cash flows. The end result is that the discounted value of the difference between the free cash flows and the excess earnings is always equal to the beginning total invested capital (or book value of equity for an all-equity-financed firm).

The Articulation of the Income Statement and the Balance Sheet

In order for the sums of accounting earnings and free cash flows to be equivalent over the life of a company, a company's earnings must be comprehensive; that is, net income must reconcile to the change in the book value of equity excluding the effects of the issuance or repurchase of equity or equity distributions (e.g., dividends)—called the **articulation of the income statement and the balance sheet** or the **clean surplus accounting** principle. As we showed earlier, the exact accounting rules or principles accountants use to measure accounting earnings are irrelevant to making the model work. Accountants could use any set of accounting principles and the value from the excess earnings valuation method would still be the same as the value from the DCF model so long as the sum of a company's accounting earnings equals the sum of its free cash flows over the life of the company.

If the company's earnings on its income statement are not comprehensive, we need to adjust the earnings in order to make them comprehensive. Thus, forecasts of the financial statements would have to be comprehensive in order to use them in an excess earnings valuation model. It is not necessary to restate the historical financial statements on a comprehensive basis, but the forecasts must be comprehensive.

Comprehensive income is defined by *Statement of Financial Accounting Concepts No. 6* as "the change in equity of a business enterprise during a period from transactions and other events and circumstances from non-owner sources. It includes all changes in equity during a period except those resulting from investments by owners and distributions to owners."[7]

Valuation Key 7.2

As long as the accounting system adheres to clean surplus accounting, the use of accounting earnings instead of cash flows results in the same valuation when using the excess earnings valuation technique. Clean surplus requires that the net income must reconcile to the change in the book value of equity excluding the effects of the issuance or repurchase of equity or equity distributions (e.g., dividends).

Under U.S. GAAP, deviations from clean surplus accounting occur for a variety of reasons, including foreign currency translation adjustments, gains and losses on foreign currency transactions that are economic hedges of a net investment in a foreign entity, a change in the market value of a futures contract that qualifies as a hedge of certain assets reported at fair value, unrealized holding gains and losses on available-for-sale securities, and unrealized holding gains and losses that result from a debt security being transferred from the held-to-maturity category to the available-for-sale category.[8] The items that do not flow through income under U.S. GAAP are generally not the kinds of items we forecast anyway, but if you do forecast them, just remember to run them through net income.

---

[7] Financial Accounting Standards Board, *Statement of Financial Accounting Concepts No. 6: Elements of Financial Statements (A Replacement of FASB Concepts Statement No. 3—Incorporating an Amendment of FASB Concepts Statement No. 2)*, December 1985, p. 70.

[8] Financial Accounting Standards Board, *Statements of Financial Accounting Standards 130: Reporting Comprehensive Income*, June 1997.

Valuation in Practice 7.1

HSBC Investment Bank plc Version of the Excess Earnings Valuation Method and Continuing Value To develop excess earnings, HSBC has detailed forecasts for an "explicit forecast period." Then,

> After the explicit forecast period we fade the ROIC down towards the cost of capital and growth down to long-run sustainable levels. The length of the fade period is a judgment based on the sustainability of competitive advantage. . . . The terminal value is a one-off representation of the value of the "continuing period;" i.e., the value of the . . . residual income that the business will generate beyond the end of the "fade" period. By definition the assumption in the continuing period is that the ROIC will be equal to the cost of capital; super-normal returns will have been competed away . . . If using continuing economic residual income in perpetuity to value the continuing period, then, by definition, it should be set at nil.

Thus, HSBC implements the excess flow method by adding the discounted value of the excess earnings, for as long as it believes the ROIC will exceed the company's cost of capital, to current book value. HSBC bases the length of supernormal returns on a judgment of the ability of the company to maintain a competitive advantage. Of course, keep in mind that what is important here is whether the ROIC (based on the book value of the company's investments) exceeds the company's cost of capital. A company's new investments could earn just their cost of capital, but the ROIC, which is based on the historical cost book value of all prior investments, could exceed the company's cost of capital for a very long time.

Source: HSBC Investment Bank plc (HSBC), headquartered in London, is one of the world's largest banking and financial services companies. See www.HSBC.com for information about this company; see "Innogy Uncovering Hidden Value," Company Report, HSBC Investment Bank plc, London (September 1, 2000), pp. 82–83; ROIC is the return on invested capital.

7.3 THE WEIGHTED AVERAGE COST OF CAPITAL FORM OF THE MODEL

To value a company using the WACC form of the excess earnings valuation method, we discount the company's excess earnings and the continuing value of its excess earnings at the weighted average cost of capital and add its book value of total invested capital as of the valuation date. In this case, excess earnings is equal to unlevered earnings minus the required earnings calculated as total invested capital as of the beginning of the period multiplied by the weighted average cost of capital ($UE_t - r_{WACC} \times TIC_{t-1}$). Conceptually, unlevered earnings are equal to earnings (net income) plus any after-tax interest deducted in calculating earnings. Unlevered earnings can be measured in various ways, which we now discuss.

LO2 Measure firm value using the WACC and APV forms of the excess earnings model

For a company financed with claims beyond common equity, the book value of a company's **total invested capital (TIC)** is equal to the book value of its debt (D), preferred stock (PS), and common equity (BVE), but it does not include non-interest-bearing operating liabilities (accounts payable, deferred income taxes, etc.). As in the case of an all-equity financed company, we can also define total invested capital using the other side of the balance sheet as well—that is, total assets (TA), net of the company's non-interest-bearing operating liabilities (OPL).

$$TIC = D + PS + BVE = TA - OPL$$

The general formula for the WACC-based excess earnings valuation method, using a constant growth perpetuity formula to measure the continuing value of excess earnings, is

$$V_F = TIC_0 + \sum_{t=1}^{C} \frac{UE_t - r_{WACC} \times TIC_{t-1}}{(1 + r_{WACC})^t} + \frac{UE_{C+1} - r_{WACC} \times TIC_C}{r_{WACC} - g} \times \frac{1}{(1 + r_{WACC})^C} \quad \textbf{(7.2)}$$

An alternative but equivalent way of measuring the continuing value of a company's excess earnings is to set it equal to the continuing value of the firm, $CV_{F,C}$, minus the book value of total invested capital as of the continuing value date, TIC_C. Using this approach, our formula is

$$V_F = TIC_0 + \sum_{t=1}^{C} \frac{UE_t - r_{WACC} \times TIC_{t-1}}{(1 + r_{WACC})^t} + \frac{CV_{F,C} - TIC_C}{(1 + r_{WACC})^C} \quad \textbf{(7.3)}$$

A useful feature of the continuing value calculation in Equation 7.3 is that we can use a different valuation method for the continuing value—such as an assumed sales price, a value based on a market multiple, or a liquidation value.

Note that in either formula, we can also calculate excess earnings in every year by taking the difference between the return on invested capital, ROIC (unlevered earnings divided by beginning of year total invested capital), and the weighted average cost of capital and then multiply that difference by the beginning-of-year total invested capital.

Dennis Keller, Inc. Revisited—Weighted Average Cost of Capital Form of the Model

In Chapter 5, we used Dennis Keller, Inc. to illustrate the WACC, APV, and Equity DCF valuation models. In this section, we again use the Keller company to illustrate how to use the various forms of the excess earnings model and to show that this model calculates the same value as the DCF valuation model. In Exhibit 7.1, we present summary information related to Keller's WACC DCF valuation from Chapter 5. Recall that the company's unlevered cost of capital is 12%, that its debt cost of capital is 8%, and that its capital structure strategy is made up of 20% debt and 80% equity financing. Based on this capital structure and a 40% income tax rate, the company's equity and weighted average cost of capital are 13% and 11.36%, respectively. The growth rate after Year 3 is estimated to be 3% per year.

EXHIBIT 7.1	Summary of Dennis Keller, Inc. Weighted Average Cost of Capital DCF Valuation from Chapter 5—20% Debt Capital Structure Strategy				
($ in thousands)	**Year 0**	**Year 1**	**Year 2**	**Year 3**	**Year 4**
Earnings before interest and after taxes	$ 3,720	$ 3,180	$ 3,660	$ 3,610	$ 3,718
Unlevered free cash flows	$ 820	$ 1,180	$ 3,285	$ 2,726	$ 2,807
Debt	$20,000	$19,900	$17,689	$15,919	$16,396
Retained earnings	–3,400	–1,300	1,285	3,940	4,373
Common stock.	10,500	10,500	10,500	10,500	10,500
Total invested capital	$27,100	$29,100	$29,475	$30,359	$31,270
Value of the firm	$30,000	$32,228	$32,604	$33,582	
Value of the debt	$ 6,000	$ 6,446	$ 6,521	$ 6,716	
Interest		$ 480	$ 516	$ 522	$ 537
Equity free cash flow (Exhibit 5.17)		$ 1,338	$ 3,051	$ 2,608	$ 2,687
Restated equity balance.	$21,100	$22,654	$22,954	$23,643	$31,270

Exhibit may contain small rounding errors

To measure the company's excess earnings, we first measure its unlevered earnings—or earnings before interest and after taxes—which we know is independent of the company's capital structure. We also measure the company's total invested capital for each year in the forecasts. While the financing of the company's total invested capital depends on the capital structure, total invested capital, itself, does not; thus, we can use the total invested capital from the CFO's financial projections in Chapter 5 (see Exhibit 5.9) even though the 20% debt capital structure is based on a different mix of debt and equity. To understand that more fully, remember that we can define total invested capital as total assets less non-interest-bearing operating liabilities. Since the CFO and CEO agreed on the operations of the company, the total invested capital is the same, regardless of the capital structure strategy.

We measure the company's required earnings by multiplying the beginning-of-year total invested capital by the weighted average cost of capital. In Year 1, the required earnings are $3,079, or 11.36% of $27,100. We measure excess earnings as the difference between the unlevered earnings forecasts and required earnings. Note that the unlevered income is equal to earnings before interest and after taxes from Exhibit 5.7. For Year 1, excess earnings is equal to $101 ($101 = $3,180 − $3,079). We present the calculation of excess earnings for Years 1 through 4 in Exhibit 7.2. Alternatively, we could measure excess earnings as the difference in the forecasted rates of return on total invested capital and the weighted average cost of capital multiplied by the beginning balance of total invested capital.

EXHIBIT 7.2	Calculation of Excess Earnings Based on the Weighted Average Cost of Capital— Dennis Keller, Inc.

($ in thousands)	Year 1	Year 2	Year 3	Year 4
Unlevered net income	$ 3,180	$ 3,660	$ 3,610	$ 3,718
Beginning of Year Invested Capital				
Common stock	$10,500	$10,500	$10,500	$10,500
Retained earnings	–3,400	–1,300	1,285	3,940
Debt	20,000	19,900	17,689	15,919
Total invested capital	$27,100	$29,100	$29,475	$30,359
Weighted average cost of capital	11.36%	11.36%	11.36%	11.36%
Required unlevered net income	$ 3,079	$ 3,306	$ 3,348	$ 3,449
Excess unlevered earnings	$ 101	$ 354	$ 262	$ 269

Exhibit may contain small rounding errors

Now that we have measured the expected excess earnings, we discount the excess earnings at the weighted average cost of capital. We calculate the company's continuing value using a constant-growth perpetuity formula as follows:

$$CV_{Year\ 3} = \frac{\text{Excess Earnings}_4}{(r_{WACC} - g)} = \frac{\$269}{(0.1136 - 0.03)} = \$3,223$$

The company's total invested capital at the end of Year 3 is equal to $30,359. If we add the continuing value of the company's excess earnings as of the end of Year 3—$3,223 to the beginning value of the total invested capital at the end of Year 3 ($30,359)—we measure the continuing value of the firm as being $33,582 (Exhibit 7.1). This is the same continuing value based on the WACC DCF valuation (Exhibit 5.8). As we will discuss later in the chapter, the $3,223 continuing value of excess earnings provides information on the expectations for the company. If the company's total invested capital and accounting earnings reasonably represent the company's underlying economic investment and performance, then this continuing value assumes the company will be able to earn a return in excess of its required rate of return (weighted average cost of capital) in perpetuity. This may or may not be a reasonable assumption, for we know from Chapter 2 that for reasonably competitive markets, a company is likely to only earn its required rate of return in the long run. However, it is important to also remember that excess earnings is based on the book value of total invested capital—not on the market value of the capital—and that excess earnings is based on accounting earnings—not economic earnings. Total invested capital and earnings are accounting numbers based on accounting rules. At best, they measure economic value and performance with error. Thus, it is plausible that rates of return computed based on accounting numbers will be greater than the company's economic cost of capital in perpetuity.

To complete our valuation of Keller, we discount each year's excess earnings to measure the value of the company's excess earnings as of the end of Year 0, which we calculate to be $2,900. We add that amount to the value of the company's total invested capital at the end of Year 0 of $27,100 in order to measure Keller's firm value of $30,000. We show these calculations in Exhibit 7.3. This value is equal to the WACC DCF valuation we calculated in Chapter 5 (Exhibit 5.8) and is shown in the summary information in Exhibit 7.1.

EXHIBIT 7.3	Excess Earnings Weighted Average Cost of Capital Valuation—Dennis Keller, Inc.

($ in thousands)	Year 0	Year 1	Year 2	Year 3	CV_Firm Year 3
Excess earnings for continuing value					$ 269
Discount factor for continuing value					11.962
Excess earnings and continuing value		$ 101	$ 354	$ 262	$ 3,223
Discount factor		0.898	0.806	0.724	0.724
Present value		$ 91	$ 286	$ 189	$ 2,334
Present value of excess earnings	$ 2,900				
Book value of total invested capital	27,100				
Value of the firm	$30,000				

Exhibit may contain small rounding errors

REVIEW EXERCISE 7.3

WACC Form of the Excess Earnings Model

Use the income statement, balance sheet, and free cash flow forecasts for State Line Farm, Inc. to value the firm as of the end of Year 0 using the WACC form of the excess earnings model. The company's unlevered cost of capital is 12%, it has a target capital structure of 1/3 debt (which is reflected in the forecasts provided below), it has a cost of debt of 8%, and it has a perpetual growth rate of 2% for excess earnings. Assume interest tax shields are valued using the unlevered cost of capital.

STATE LINE FARM, INC.
Income Statement and Balance Sheet Forecasts

($ in thousands)	Year 0	Year 1	Year 2	Year 3	Year 4
Income Statement					
Revenue		$10,000	$11,000	$11,550	$11,781
Operating expenses		−6,200	−6,820	−7,161	−7,304
Depreciation expense		−833	−1,000	−1,146	−1,169
Earnings before interest and taxes		$ 2,967	$ 3,180	$ 3,243	$ 3,308
Interest expense		−425	−481	−502	−515
Income before taxes		$ 2,542	$ 2,699	$ 2,741	$ 2,793
Income tax expense		−1,017	−1,080	−1,096	−1,117
Net income		$ 1,525	$ 1,619	$ 1,645	$ 1,676
Balance Sheet					
Cash	$ 500	$ 500	$ 550	$ 578	$ 589
Inventory	1,000	2,300	2,530	2,657	2,710
Total current assets	$1,500	$ 2,800	$ 3,080	$ 3,234	$ 3,299
Property, plant, and equipment (net)	8,333	9,167	9,625	9,818	10,014
Total assets	$9,833	$11,967	$12,705	$13,052	$13,313
Debt	$5,313	$ 6,011	$ 6,279	$ 6,432	$ 6,561
Equity	4,521	5,955	6,426	6,619	6,752
Total equities	$9,833	$11,967	$12,705	$13,052	$13,313

STATE LINE FARM, INC.
Free Cash Flow and Equity Free Cash Flow Forecasts

($ in thousands)	Year 1	Year 2	Year 3	Year 4
Earnings before interest and taxes (EBIT)	$ 2,967	$ 3,180	$ 3,243	$ 3,308
− Income taxes paid on EBIT	−1,187	−1,272	−1,297	−1,323
Earnings before interest and after taxes	$ 1,780	$ 1,908	$ 1,946	$ 1,985
+ Depreciation expense	833	1,000	1,146	1,169
− Change in inventory	−1,300	−230	−127	−53
− Change in required cash balance	0	−50	−28	−12
− Capital expenditures	−1,667	−1,458	−1,338	−1,365
Unlevered free cash flow	$ −353	$ 1,170	$ 1,599	$ 1,724
− Interest paid in cash ($r_D \times V_D$)	−425	−481	−502	−515
+ Interest tax shield ($T_{INT} \times r_D \times V_D$)	170	192	201	206
+ Change in debt financing	699	267	153	129
Equity free cash flow	$ 90	$ 1,148	$ 1,451	$ 1,544

Exhibit may contain small rounding errors

Solution on pages 278–279.

7.4 THE ADJUSTED PRESENT VALUE FORM OF THE MODEL

To value a company using the APV form of the excess earnings model, we start with the book value of the company's total invested capital, TIC, at the valuation date. Then, we add the discounted value of the company's excess earnings and the continuing value of its excess earnings (all discounted at the company's unlevered cost of capital), and then we add the value of its interest tax shields, V_{ITS} (exactly

Valuation in Practice 7.2

Whole Foods Market, Inc.'s (Whole Foods) Use of the EVA® Excess Earnings Model
Whole Foods explains the use of EVA as follows:

> We use Economic Value Added ("EVA") to evaluate our business decisions and as a basis for determining incentive compensation. . . . We believe that one of our core strengths is our decentralized culture, where decisions are made at the store level, close to the customer. We believe this is one of our strongest competitive advantages, and that EVA is the best financial framework that team members can use to help make decisions that create sustainable shareholder value.
>
> We use EVA extensively for capital investment decisions, including evaluating new store real estate decisions and store remodeling proposals. We are turning down projects that do not add long-term value to the Company. . . . Our emphasis is on EVA improvement, as we want to challenge our teams to continue to innovate and grow EVA in new ways. We believe that opportunities always exist to increase sales and margins, to lower operating expenses and to make investments that add value in ways that benefit all of our stakeholders. . . .
>
> The Company provides information regarding EVA as additional information about its operating results. EVA is a measure not in accordance with, or an alternative to, generally accepted accounting principles ("GAAP"). The Company's management believes that this additional EVA information is useful to shareholders, management, analysts and potential investors in evaluating the Company's results of operations and financial condition. In addition, management uses these measures for reviewing the financial results of the Company and for budget planning and incentive compensation purposes. . . .
>
> Capital charge is calculated by multiplying weighted average EVA capital by our weighted average cost of capital.

Source: Whole Foods Market, Inc., headquartered in Austin, Texas, is a large grocery store chain in the United States. See www.wholefoodsmarket.com for information about the company.

as calculated using the APV form of the DCF model). Excess earnings is equal to unlevered earnings minus the required earnings, where the required earnings are now based on the unlevered cost of capital (total invested capital as of the beginning of the period multiplied by the unlevered cost of capital), or $UE_t - r_{UA} \times TIC_{t-1}$.

The general formula for the APV-based excess earnings valuation method, using a constant growth perpetuity formula to measure the continuing value of the excess earnings, is

$$V_F = TIC_0 + \sum_{t=1}^{C} \frac{UE_t - r_{UA} \times TIC_{t-1}}{(1 + r_{UA})^t} + \frac{UE_{C+1} - r_{UA} \times TIC_C}{r_{UA} - g} \times \frac{1}{(1 + r_{UA})^C} + V_{ITS,0} \quad \textbf{(7.4)}$$

Again, we can use an alternative method to compute the continuing value of the unlevered firm, such as a market multiple or liquidation value. In this case, we measure the continuing value of the unlevered firm, $CV_{UA,C}$, and we subtract the book value of its total invested capital as of the continuing value date, TIC_C. Using this approach, our formula in Equation 7.4 becomes

$$V_F = TIC_0 + \sum_{t=1}^{C} \frac{UE_t - r_{UA} \times TIC_{t-1}}{(1 + r_{UA})^t} + \frac{CV_{UA,C} - TIC_C}{(1 + r_{UA})^C} + V_{ITS,0} \quad \textbf{(7.5)}$$

Here again, with either of these two formulas, we can calculate excess earnings every year by taking the difference between return on invested capital and the unlevered cost of capital multiplied by the beginning-of-year total invested capital.

Dennis Keller, Inc. Revisited—Adjusted Present Value Form of the Model

Recall that we used the APV valuation method for the Keller Company in Chapter 5 when we changed the capital structure strategy from 20% debt to an initial amount of debt equal to $20 million and used all available cash flow to reduce the debt over the next three years. For this capital structure strategy, the company's unlevered cost of capital is 12%, and its debt cost of capital is 9%. Since we do not know the company's capital structure ratios for this capital structure strategy, but instead know the expected amount of debt the company will have outstanding at each point in time, we use the APV form of the model to value the company. The additional financial leverage resulted in an increase in the value of the firm from $30,000 to $34,015 (Exhibit 5.11), ignoring financial distress costs and other costs related to the increase in financial leverage. The value of the interest tax shields with this new capital structure strategy is $6,200. In Exhibit 7.4, we present summary information related to Keller's APV DCF valuation from Chapter 5.

EXHIBIT 7.4	Summary of Dennis Keller, Inc. Adjusted Present Value Valuation from Chapter 5—$20,000 Debt Capital Structure Strategy				
($ in thousands)	**Year 0**	**Year 1**	**Year 2**	**Year 3**	**Year 4**
Earnings before interest and after taxes	$ 3,720	$ 3,180	$ 3,660	$ 3,610	$ 3,718
Debt	$20,000	$19,900	$17,689	$15,919	$16,396
Retained earnings	–3,400	–1,300	1,285	3,940	4,373
Common stock.	10,500	10,500	10,500	10,500	10,500
Total invested capital	$27,100	$29,100	$29,475	$30,359	$31,270
Value of the firm	$34,015	$36,197	$36,539	$37,561	
Value of the debt	$20,000	$19,900	$17,689	$15,919	
Value of the equity	$14,015	$16,297	$18,850	$21,643	
Value of the ITS	$ 6,200	$ 6,223	$ 6,254	$ 6,368	
Equity cost of capital		16.3%	15.7%	14.8%	14.2%

Exhibit may contain small rounding errors

We measure the company's required earnings in the top panel of Exhibit 7.5. The only difference between this calculation and the calculation for the WACC form of the model is the required return used. The unlevered earnings and total invested capital in this exhibit are the same as in Exhibit 7.2; thus, the only difference in the calculation of excess unlevered earnings is the cost of capital. We use the unlevered cost of capital for the APV form of the model and weighted average cost of capital for the WACC form of the model. Since the unlevered cost of capital is higher than the weighted average cost of capital, the excess earnings are smaller in the APV form of the model relative to the WACC form of the model.

EXHIBIT 7.5	Excess Earnings Adjusted Present Value Valuation				
($ in thousands)		**Year 1**	**Year 2**	**Year 3**	**Year 4**
Unlevered net income		$ 3,180	$ 3,660	$ 3,610	$ 3,718
Beginning of year total invested capital		$27,100	$29,100	$29,475	$30,359
Unlevered cost of capital		12.00%	12.00%	12.00%	12.00%
Required unlevered net income		$ 3,252	$ 3,492	$ 3,537	$ 3,643
Excess unlevered earnings.		$ –72	$ 168	$ 73	$ 75

APV Valuation	**Year 0**	**Year 1**	**Year 2**	**Year 3**	**CV$_{Firm}$ Year 3**
Excess earnings for continuing value.					$ 75
Discount factor for continuing value					11.111
Excess earnings and continuing value.		$ –72	$ 168	$ 73	$ 835
Discount factor (unlevered cost of capital).		0.893	0.797	0.712	0.712
Present value		$ –64	$ 134	$ 52	$ 594
Present value of excess earnings.	$ 716				
Book value of total invested capital	27,100				
Value of the unlevered firm.	$27,816				
Value of interest tax shields	6,200				
Value of the firm	$34,015				

Exhibit may contain small rounding errors

In the bottom part of the exhibit, we measure the value of the firm using the APV form of the model by calculating the value of the unlevered firm and adding the value of the interest tax shields. We measure the value of the interest tax shields in the same way we measured them in Chapter 5, but we do not show that calculation in this chapter. We discount each year's excess earnings at the unlevered cost of capital to measure the value of the company's excess earnings as of the end of Year 0, which equals $716. We add that amount to the book value of the company's total invested capital at the end of Year 0 to measure the company's unlevered value of $27,816, which is the same valuation we calculated in Chapter 5 (Exhibit 5.11). To measure the value of the firm, we add the value of the interest tax shields—measured in Chapter 5 (Exhibit 5.11) and summarized in Exhibit 7.4—to the value of the unlevered firm, yielding a firm value of $34,015, which agrees with the DCF valuation from Exhibit 5.11.

REVIEW EXERCISE 7.4

Adjusted Present Value Form of the Excess Earnings Model

Use the income statement, balance sheet, and free cash flow forecasts, and other information in Review Exercise 7.3 for State Line Farm, Inc., to value the firm as of the end of Year 0 using the APV form of the excess earnings model.

Solution on pages 280–281.

7.5 THE EQUITY DISCOUNTED EXCESS EARNINGS MODEL

If implemented correctly, the equity excess earnings valuation method results in the same equity valuation as the WACC or APV forms of the DCF models. To measure the value of a company's equity using the equity excess earnings valuation method, we discount both the company's excess earnings to the equityholders and the continuing value of its equity excess earnings—at its equity cost of capital—and add the book value of its equity, BVE, as of the valuation date. Excess earnings to common equityholders is equal to earnings available to common (earnings after preferred dividends) minus required earnings calculated as the book value of the common equity as of the beginning of the period multiplied by the equity cost of capital ($E_t - r_E \times BVE_{t-1}$). The general formula for the equity excess earnings valuation method, assuming we construct detailed forecasts for the company for C years and use a constant growth perpetuity formula to measure the continuing value of the excess earnings, is

LO3 Measure equity value using the equity form of the excess earnings model

$$V_E = BVE_0 + \sum_{t=1}^{C} \frac{E_t - r_E \times BVE_{t-1}}{(1 + r_E)^t} + \frac{E_{C+1} - r_E \times BVE_C}{r_E - g} \times \frac{1}{(1 + r_E)^C} \quad (7.6)$$

Again, an alternative way to measure the continuing value of the company's equity excess earnings is to take the company's continuing equity value, CV_E, based on perhaps a market multiple or some other method, and to then subtract the book value of its equity as of the continuing value date. Using this approach, our formula is

$$V_E = BVE_0 + \sum_{t=1}^{C} \frac{E_t - r_E \times BVE_{t-1}}{(1 + r_E)^t} + \frac{CV_{E,C} - BVE_C}{(1 + r_E)^C} \quad (7.7)$$

In both of the above formulas, we could compute excess earnings every year by taking the difference between the return on equity (net income available to common divided by beginning-of-period book value of equity) and the equity cost of capital and multiply the difference by the beginning-of-period book value of equity.

In Chapter 5, we discussed the calculations we need to perform in order to use the Equity DCF valuation method in both the constant target capital structure and changing capital structure valuation contexts. As we had discussed, the Equity DCF method is difficult to implement directly; either the cost of equity capital is changing each period when the capital structure proportions are not constant, or the implied debt levels—and hence, the interest tax shields—are not readily apparent if the capital structure proportions are constant. The same issues arise when implementing the equity excess earnings valuation method.

To implement the equity excess earnings valuation method correctly, we need to forecast both the income statement and balance sheet in order to measure the company's excess earnings to equityholders. Earnings to equityholders are directly affected by a company's capital structure. To measure earnings to equityholders, we deduct after-tax interest and preferred stock dividends from unlevered earnings. Thus, the earnings forecasts will not be the correct forecasts for use in our valuation unless they match our assumptions about the target capital structure of the firm.

Just like the DCF valuation method, there are three different forms of the excess earnings valuation model: the weighted average cost of capital form, the adjusted present value form, and the equity excess earnings form. Properly implemented, all three techniques provide consistent valuations.

If we assume a constant proportionate target capital structure in our valuation—the valuation context when we typically use the WACC valuation method—our initial forecasts will likely not reflect the constant target capital structure correctly. Usually, to measure the earnings to equityholders and the book value of equity that are consistent with the constant target capital structure assumption, we must measure the value of the firm in each year first. If we know the value of the firm in each year, we can use the target capital structure to measure amounts of non-equity financing and update our forecasts with these new amounts. This allows us to update our forecasts for earnings to equityholders and the book value of equity in order to make them consistent with the target capital structure. If instead, we have forecasts of the amount of debt—the valuation context when we typically use the APV valuation method—the equity cost of capital will vary over time, so we must value the firm every period to compute the varying cost of equity capital.

Dennis Keller, Inc. Revisited—Equity Discounted Excess Earnings Form of the Model

We can use the equity discounted excess earnings form of the model for both of the capital structure strategies we examined in the previous two sections of the chapter. However, just as we did in the Equity DCF valuations in Chapter 5, we cannot use the equity form of the excess earnings model for either capital structure—20% debt or $20,000 in debt—unless we know the value of the firm in every period.

Capital Structure Strategy of 20% Debt.

For the capital structure strategy based on constant capital structure ratios (20% debt and 80% equity), we know the equity cost of capital is 13%. The original forecasts, however, are based on a capital structure with $20,000 of debt with a 9% interest rate. The $20,000 debt capital structure—not the 20% debt capital structure—is the basis of the common equity balances (on the balance sheet) and the net income (on the income statements) in the original forecasts. We must recalculate the forecasts based on the 20% debt capital structure as follows. We calculate the value of the firm in each year, measure the amount of debt the company will have outstanding (20% of the firm value), measure the amount of interest paid in each year, and then measure both the common equity balance and the company's net income in each year. We present these calculations in Exhibit 7.6, using information from Chapter 5 that we summarized in Exhibit 7.1.

We begin these calculations with a restatement of the common equity balance. The 20% debt capital structure strategy has $6,000 of debt outstanding at the end of Year 0, because the value of the firm is equal to $30,000 at the end of Year 0 ($6,000 = 0.2 × $30,000). We calculate the amount of debt outstanding each year in the same way. We measure the value of the firm each year using our WACC valuation method, which we discussed in Chapter 5. Since the book value of the assets is unchanged by the capital structure strategy, the *initial* book value of the common equity (based on $6,000 of debt) is equal to the book value of the total assets of $27,100 less the $6,000 of debt ($21,100 = $27,100 − $6,000). We use this value as the beginning book value of the common equity based on the 20% capital structure. Net income for this capital structure is equal to the year's unlevered income minus after-tax interest. We know the unlevered income from the original forecasts. Interest is equal to the outstanding debt balance multiplied by the interest rate. The interest tax shield is equal to interest multiplied by the income tax rate. In Year 1, unlevered earnings are $3,180. Interest expense is equal to 8% of the $6,000 in debt outstanding as of the beginning of the year ($480), and the interest tax shield is equal to 40% of the interest ($192). Thus, net income to common equity in this year is equal to $2,892 ($2,892 = $3,180 − $480 + $192). We measure the required equity earnings as the beginning book value of equity multiplied by the equity cost of capital ($2,743 = $21,100 × 0.13). We measure excess equity earnings as the difference between the actual equity earnings and the expected equity earnings ($149 = $2,892 − $2,743).

To calculate the book value of equity in subsequent years, we must take the beginning balance in the book value of equity for that year, add the net income, and subtract the common equity dividends. The common equity dividends equal unlevered free cash flow minus interest paid plus the interest tax shield minus the change in debt (Exhibit 5.17). We continue these calculations for each year in our forecasts.

In Exhibit 7.7, we discount the excess equity earnings at the 13% equity cost of capital. The discounted value of the excess equity earnings is $2,900. We add the beginning book value of equity of $21,100 to the discounted value of the excess equity earnings in order to measure a value of equity of $24,000, which agrees with our DCF valuation of the equity.

EXHIBIT 7.6 Equity Excess Earnings—20% Debt and 80% Equity Capital Structure Strategy

DENNIS KELLER, INC.
(20 Percent Constant Capital Structure Assumption)
Equity Excess Earnings Valuation

Growth rate for free cash flow for continuing value . . .			3.0%		
Equity cost of capital			13.0%		

($ in thousands)	Year 0	Year 1	Year 2	Year 3	Year 4
Restated Earnings and Equity for Target Capital Structure					
Book value of total assets	$27,100				
Debt based on 20% debt to value	6,000				
Book value of equity	$21,100				
Unlevered net income		$ 3,180	$ 3,660	$ 3,610	$ 3,718
Interest expense.		−480	−515	−522	−537
Interest tax shield.		192	206	209	215
Net income to common equity.		$ 2,892	$ 3,351	$ 3,297	$ 3,396
Net income to common equity.		$ 2,892	$ 3,351	$ 3,297	$ 3,396
Common equity at beginning of year.		21,100	22,654	22,954	23,643
Common equity dividends (EFCF) (see Exhibit 5.17). .		−1,338	−3,051	−2,608	−2,687
Total common equity	$21,100	$ 22,654	$ 22,954	$ 23,643	$ 24,352
Total common equity at beginning of year.		21,100	22,654	22,954	23,643
Common equity cost of capital		13.0%	13.0%	13.0%	13.0%
Required net income to common equity		$ 2,743	$ 2,945	$ 2,984	$ 3,074
Excess earnings to common equity.		$ 149	$ 406	$ 313	$ 322

EXHIBIT 7.7 Discounted Equity Excess Earnings—20% Debt and 80% Equity Capital Structure Strategy

($ in thousands)	Year 0	Year 1	Year 2	Year 3	CV$_{Equity}$ Year 3
Excess equity earnings for continuing value					$ 322
Discount factor for continuing value					10.000
Excess equity earnings and continuing value		$ 149	$ 406	$ 313	$ 3,223
Discount factor.		0.885	0.783	0.693	0.693
Present value		$ 132	$ 318	$ 217	$ 2,234
Present value of excess equity earnings	$ 2,900				
Book value of equity.	21,100				
Value of the equity	$24,000				

Exhibit may contain small rounding errors

Capital Structure Strategy of $20,000 in Debt.

For the capital structure strategy with $20,000 in debt, the common equity balances on the balance sheets and the net incomes on the income statements in the original forecasts are correct. However, we do not know the equity cost of capital based on this capital structure strategy, because we do not know the debt ratios (stated in terms of market values) for this capital structure strategy. To measure the equity cost of capital, we measure the value of the firm in each year, subtract the value of the outstanding debt to measure the value of the equity in each year, and then measure the company's resulting capital structure ratios in order to measure the company's equity cost of capital in each year. We measured the equity cost of capital in this way in Chapter 5 (Exhibit 5.15), and we present summary information in Exhibit 7.4, including the varying cost of equity capital.

We present this valuation in Exhibit 7.8. This valuation has the same format as the previous valuation. However, here, we use the book value of the common equity and the net income from the original forecasts, and we use the changing equity cost of capital that results from the $20,000 capital structure strategy. The total common equity is equal to the total invested capital less the value of the debt. Since the equity cost of capital is changing each year, the discount factor for each year is a cumulative factor based upon the annual equity cost of capital (e.g., the Year 3 discount factor of $0.648 = 1/[(1 + 0.163) \times (1 + 0.157) \times (1 + 0.148)]$). The resulting value of the equity of $14,015 equals the value of the firm of $34,015 from Exhibit 7.5 less the value of the debt of $20,000.

EXHIBIT 7.8 Discounted Equity Excess Earnings—$20,000 Debt Capital Structure Strategy				
($ in thousands)	Year 1	Year 2	Year 3	Year 4
Net income to common equity.	$2,100	$2,585	$ 2,655	$ 2,859
Total common equity at beginning of year.	$7,100	$9,200	$11,785	$14,440
Common equity cost of capital	16.3%	15.7%	14.8%	14.2%
Required net income to common equity	$1,156	$1,441	$ 1,746	$ 2,051
Excess earnings to common equity.	$ 944	$1,144	$ 909	$ 807
Equity cost of capital	16.3%	15.7%	14.8%	14.2%

	Year 0	Year 1	Year 2	Year 3	CV$_{Equity}$ Year 3
Excess equity earnings for continuing value					$ 807
Discount factor for continuing value					8.923
Excess equity earnings and continuing value . . .		$ 944	$ 1,144	$ 909	$ 7,202
Discount factor.		0.860	0.744	0.648	0.648
Present value		$ 812	$ 851	$ 588	$ 4,664
Present value of excess equity earnings	$ 6,915				
Book value of equity	7,100				
Value of the equity	$14,015				

Exhibit may contain small rounding errors

REVIEW EXERCISE 7.5

Equity Discounted Excess Earnings Model

Use the income statement, balance sheet, and free cash flow forecasts, and other information in Review Exercise 7.3 for State Line Farm, Inc., to value the company's equity as of the end of Year 0 using the equity discounted excess earnings model.

Solution on pages 281–282.

7.6 POSSIBLE INFORMATION ADVANTAGES OF THE EXCESS EARNINGS VALUATION METHOD

LO4 Learn about adjustments to both earnings and invested capital that are made when excess earnings is used to evaluate performance

Since the DCF-based and excess-earnings-based valuations are identical, the only possible advantages the excess earnings valuation method may have over the DCF-based valuation method are that it requires fewer forecast inputs, that it may be easier to implement, or that it provides different information. As we observed in this chapter, the inputs are essentially the same for the DCF-based and excess-earnings-based models, and both approaches are equally easy (or difficult) to implement; thus, the potential advantages of the excess-earnings-based models are informational. This appears to be the major motivation for consultants and managers who use excess-earnings-based models.

Indeed, the commercialized forms of the excess flow models make adjustments to both earnings figures and book values in an attempt to make the excess earnings calculated even more informative with respect to deciding whether a manager adds value to a firm's investments in a given period. The commercialized forms are most often implemented for use in compensation systems for managers. The intuition for these models is simple. Given an investment that the firm has made (as measured by the accounting system with some modifications), did the managers create flows during the current period (again, as measured by the accounting system with some modifications) that exceeded the required flows? That is, did they create excess flows or excess earnings? If they did, the firm's investment has added value. As such, the accounting system is adjusted in order to arrive at a measure of the value delivered in a given period, which is then tied to the compensation system for managers. It is a subject of debate as to how close these measures are to a true measure of the value created in a given period, but that is the intent of these systems. Whether or not they measure value created in a period, these systems do focus on the importance of earning returns on investment in excess of a company's cost of capital. For example, G. Bennett Stewart, III, a founding partner of Stern Stewart & Company, stated,

> EVA® [an excess earnings-based valuation method] is a practical method of estimating the economic profit that is earned, as opposed to the accounting profit. . . . It's really a finance tool for non-finance executives. Finance execs don't need EVA.[9]

Valuation in Practice 7.3

Using EVA® in Compensation Contracts—Crane Co. Crane Co. (Crane) is a typical example of how companies use EVA® as a basis for compensation:

> The Company's annual incentive compensation program utilizes the principles of economic value added ("EVA"). EVA is defined as the difference between the return on total capital invested in the business (net operating profit after tax, or NOPAT, divided by total capital employed) and the cost of capital, multiplied by total capital employed. . . .
>
> The Committee believes that, compared to such common performance measures as return on capital, return on equity, growth in earnings per share and growth in cash flow, EVA has the highest correlation with the creation of value for shareholders over the long term. . . . Awards are generally uncapped to provide maximum incentive to create value and, because awards may be positive or negative, executives can incur penalties when value is reduced.
>
> . . . Thus, the EVA formula requires the executive to focus on improvement in the Company's balance sheet as well as the income statement. Awards are calculated on the basis of year end results, and award formulas utilize both a percentage of the change in EVA from the prior year, whether positive or negative, and a percentage of the positive EVA, if any, in the current year. EVA awards are calculated for the Company as a whole for the corporate executives.

Source: Crane is a diversified manufacturer of engineered industrial products and operates in the aerospace, engineered materials, merchandising systems, fluid handling, and controls business segments. For more information on Crane Co., see http://www.craneco.com/ and its filings with the U.S. Securities and Exchange Commission (SEC). To read more about Crane Co.'s compensation, see its DEF 14A (Proxy Statement) filing with the U.S. SEC, dated March 7, 2003, pp. 11–12. For the specific compensation contract based on EVA®, see its 10-K filing for the year ended December 31, 2002, Exhibit 7 (a), "CRANE CO. CORPORATE EVA INCENTIVE COMPENSATION PLAN."

Karl-Hermann Baumann, Chairman of the Supervisory Board of Siemens AG, stated,

> We tested discounted cash-flow—it was not much of a success. It is too abstract . . . too far from the current reporting system and our annual financial statements. EVA® removes the confusion, arising from the existence of the several planning measures and creates a common language for everyone – for the simple employee and for the top manager.[10]

---

[9] Taub, S., "Which Companies Created the Most Wealth for Shareholders Last Year? Enter MVA—or Market Value Added," *CFO.com* of *CFO Magazine* (July 1, 2003), http://www.cfo.com/Article?article=9854, retrieved November 8, 2003.

[10] Stern Stewart & Company, "EVA® Implementation at Siemens AG," October 2000, available at Stern Stewart & Company's website at http://www.eva.com/, p. 6, retrieved November 8, 2003.

Naturally, support for excess earnings valuation models is not unanimous. Armstrong Holdings Inc., the floor-and-ceiling materials company, replaced EVA® with a cash flow measure of performance. E. Follin Smith, CFO, gave the following reason for the switch:

> . . .because we want to reward growth and accuracy and meeting budget commitments, which EVA doesn't capture.[11]

7.7 ADJUSTMENTS TO EARNINGS AND BOOK VALUE MADE TO MEASURE "ECONOMIC EARNINGS"

As we just discussed, various consulting companies have commercialized the excess earnings valuation method. Each of the refinements attempts to provide more economic content to the measures of excess earnings and the excess return of earnings. The refinements adjust both the calculation of the investment and the measure of earnings, affecting the calculation of the required earnings, actual earnings, and therefore the excess earnings. These commercial forms have the same underpinning concepts as the excess earnings valuation methods.[12]

We sometimes see the term "economic earnings" when reading about these models. The concept of economic earnings to which such writings refer is not the same concept that economists use when using the same term. Most economists discuss **economic earnings** in terms of the cash flow distribution plus the change in the value of an investment (or capital gains)—that is, the value you can consume during a period that will make you as well off at the end of the period as you were at the beginning of the period.[13]

It is possible to use any valuation method that is consistent with the DCF valuation models to measure economic earnings as economists define it. We would measure economic earnings for a period as the difference in the valuations at two different points in time plus any cash paid out. When we read about economic earnings in practice, the authors are typically referring to an improved measurement of investments or returns relative to that normally measured by the accounting system. By devising a series of adjustments to the financial statements, consultants attempt to create excess earnings that have more economic meaning.

The analysts implementing the commercialized forms of the excess earnings valuation method generally make two types of adjustments to a company's financial statements. The first type of adjustment affects the beginning balance of the balance sheet. These adjustments typically adjust the beginning balance of the balance sheet for the effect of some previous income statement adjustments. For example, these analysts will often partially capitalize research and development (R&D) expenditures instead of just expensing them as is required by GAAP. The second type of adjustment affects the income statement in current and subsequent years and therefore affects the ending balances of the balance sheet in current and subsequent years. For example, the analyst might continue to capitalize future R&D expenditures and then amortize the capitalized value of the R&D over time.

The goal of the adjustments to the income statement and balance sheet is to make the adjusted earnings and book value more closely reflect the determinants of the changes in the value of the company.[14] While these adjustments may be important in compensation contracts or for measuring performance in a particular year (see Valuation in Practice 7.3), they do not affect the value of the firm or equity we might calculate. The mechanics of the excess earnings valuation method will adjust the calculations to measure the same value, irrespective of the accounting rules used, as long as earnings are comprehensive.

---

[11] Taub, S., "On Further Reflection—Do EVA and Other Value Metrics Still Offer a Good Mirror of Company Performances?" *CFO.com* of the *CFO Magazine*, March 1, 2001, http://www.cfo.com/Article?article=2182, retrieved November 8, 2003.

[12] See Myers (1996, 1997) for a discussion of how companies are adopting these approaches and choosing among them; Myers, R., "Metric Wars," *CFO: The Magazine for Senior Financial Executives* vol. 12, no. 10 (October 1996), pp. 41–50; Myers, R., "Measure for Measure," *CFO: The Magazine for Senior Financial Executives* vol. 13, no. 11 (November 1997), pp. 41–50.

[13] For seminal work on this topic, see Hicks (1938), who was awarded the Nobel Prize in economics in 1972; Hicks, J. R., *Value and Capital*, Oxford: Clarendon Press (1938), reprinted in Parker, R. H., G. C. Harcourt, and G. Whittington, eds., *Readings in the Concept and Measurement of Income*, 2nd ed., Deddington, Oxon.: Philip Allan, (1986).

[14] Whether or not EVA® accomplishes this goal is an empirical issue. For a review of the literature examining this issue, see Biddle, Gary, R. Bowen, and J. Wallace, "Evidence on EVA®," *Journal of Applied Corporate Finance* (Summer 1999), pp. 8–18. The general conclusion is that these adjustments do provide some additional information related to stock price changes.

Potential Adjustments for Implementing the Excess Earnings Model

Analysts attempting to implement the excess earnings model for use in, say, a compensation plan must use their best judgment as to how to adjust a company's financial statements. Regardless of the specific adjustments, the analysts must adjust both the income statement and the balance sheet (beginning and subsequent balances). It is important to adjust the initial balances of the balance sheet, for that is the base used to measure required earnings. In Exhibit 7.9, we summarize some of the types of adjustments an analyst might consider making when implementing the excess earnings model. The goal of the summary in this exhibit is to provide a list of the types of issues that analysts might address when attempting to implement an economic-value-added approach. We do not, however, review these issues in detail, but most of the issues are similar to the intangible asset example we discussed previously in the chapter.[15]

	EXHIBIT 7.9	Possible Income Statement and Balance Sheet Adjustments When Implementing Excess Earnings Valuation Models

	Possible Issue	**Possible Adjustments**
1	Management stock options	If company does not expense these options, then expense the value of the options when issued.
2	Income taxes	Either eliminate or use present value tools to recalculate deferred income taxes. If eliminated, then income tax expense is equal to income taxes paid (other than a short-term income taxes payable).
3	Research and development	Capitalize expenditures on the balance sheet and amortize when used in future years.
4	Depreciation (amortization and depletion)	Adjust depreciation to reflect depreciation deducted for income tax purposes or adjust to better reflect economic depreciation (actual loss in value).
5	Goodwill	If directly written off against equity, reverse write-off and amortize over useful life. If capitalized and amortized, use appropriate amortization period that reflects economic life.
6	Expense accruals	Either eliminate or adjust expense accrual to reflect actual economic situation—examples include accruals for warranties, allowance for uncollectible accounts, and loan loss reserves.
7	Pensions	Adjust value of pension assets and pension liabilities to reflect market values; adjust pension expense for cash flow or actual economic cost to company.
8	Off-balance-sheet financing	Capitalize off-balance-sheet financing instruments—for example, operating leases and special-purpose vehicles, recognizing an expense based on the capitalized value.
9	Restructuring charges and other write-downs	Capitalize expense on the balance sheet and amortize over the original life of the assets (and liabilities) restructured.
10	Accounting for mergers	Reverse any excess expense accruals recorded as part of the merger; if an old merger was recorded using the pooling-of-interests (recorded merger using book values) method, restate to purchase (market value at date of transaction) method.
11	Successful efforts oil & gas accounting	Capitalize exploration-related expenditures on the balance sheet and amortize when used in future years.
12	Inventory accounting	Restate inventory on the balance sheet to reflect current value; for example, eliminate LIFO reserve by increasing inventory value and adjusting cost of goods sold.

It is important to remember that any of the excess-earnings-based valuation methods require that everything affecting equity accounts other than events affecting the investment of the equityholders—for example, the issuance or repurchase of equity or distributions to equityholders—must flow through the income statement (called comprehensive income or clean surplus accounting). An example is the write-off of goodwill directly to equity instead of expensing it through the income statement first. Such effects must be reversed and then adjustments must be made so that all items flow through the income statement.

It is also important to remember that these adjustments would not change the amount of income taxes paid by the company because the adjustments would be made on the analyst's worksheet and would not change what the company reports to the taxing authority. Also, since these adjustments are accounting accruals and not cash flows, they do not affect any of the company's cash flows.

---

[15] For a more detailed discussion of these adjustments, see Stewart, G. B. III, "Accounting Is Broken—Here's How to Fix It—A Radical Manifesto," *EVAluation* vol. 5, no. 1 (September 2002), available at Stern Stewart & Company's website at http://www.eva.com/; and Young, D., and S. O'Byrne, *EVA and Value-Based Management*, New York: McGraw-Hill (2001), especially Chapter 6.

SUMMARY AND KEY CONCEPTS

In this chapter we have learned how to implement excess earnings valuation methods. In this context, we have seen that there are WACC and APV forms of the model based on unlevered earnings and that there is also an equity excess earnings valuation model that is based on earnings available to common shareholders. All of these forms of the excess earnings valuation model will yield the same answer as their DCF counterparts if they are properly implemented. In addition, we have seen that the advantages and disadvantages of each of the forms of the excess earnings valuation methods are exactly the same as those of their DCF counterparts.

ADDITIONAL READING AND REFERENCES

Lundholm, R., and T. O'Keefe, "Reconciling Value Estimates from the Discounted Cash Flow Model and the Residual Income Model," *Contemporary Accounting Research* 18 (Summer 2001), pp. 311–335.

Ohlson, J. A., "Earnings, Book Values and Dividends in Equity Valuation," *Contemporary Accounting Research* vol. 11, no. 2 (1995), pp. 661-688.

EXERCISES AND PROBLEMS

P7.1   **Excess Earnings Valuation—Two-Year Investment Life—The One-Shot Tee-Shirt Company:** At the end of Year 0, an investor creates a company by investing $1,500 in cash for stock, and the company uses all of the cash to buy t-shirts (inventory). At the end of Year 1, the company sells the t-shirts to a vendor for $2,420 but does not collect the revenue in cash until the end of Year 2. At the end of Year 2, the company liquidates itself by paying a liquidating dividend. The company has no operating expenses other than those related to the inventory (cost of goods sold) and does not pay income taxes. We show the company's income statement and balance sheet forecasts in Exhibit P7.1. For all parts of this problem, assume a discount rate of 10%.

EXHIBIT P7.1	Income Statement and Balance Sheet Forecasts for the One-Shot Tee-Shirt Company		

ONE-SHOT TEE-SHIRT COMPANY Income Statement and Balance Sheet	Year 0	Year 1	Year 2
Income Statement			
Revenue		$2,420	$ 0
Expenses		−1,500	0
Earnings		$ 920	$ 0
Balance Sheet			
Cash	$ 0	$ 0	$ 0
Receivable	0	2,420	0
Inventory (t-shirts)	1,500	0	0
Total assets	$1,500	$2,420	$ 0
Common stock	$1,500	$1,500	$1,500
Retained earnings		920	−1,500
Total equities	$1,500	$2,420	$ 0

  a.   Value the company as of the end of Year 0 using the discounted cash flow valuation model.
  b.   Value the company as of the end of Year 0 using the excess cash flow valuation method.
  c.   Value the company as of the end of Year 0 using the residual earnings valuation method.

P7.2   **Excess Earnings Valuation with an Intangible Asset—Two-Year Investment Life—The One-Shot Tee-Shirt Company:** At the end of Year 0, an investor creates a company by investing $1,500 in cash for stock, and the company uses all of the cash to buy t-shirts (inventory). The company also issues $200 of stock to another investor who gave the company a customer list (the name of the vendor). The company records a $200 intangible asset at the end of Year 0 for this transaction. At the end of Year 1, the company sells the t-shirts to a vendor for $2,420 but does not collect the revenue in cash until the end of Year 2. At the end of

Year 2, the company liquidates itself by paying a liquidating dividend. The company has no operating expenses other than those related to the inventory (cost of goods sold) and does not pay income taxes. We show the company's income statement and balance sheet forecasts in Exhibit P7.2. For all parts of this problem, assume a discount rate of 10%.

EXHIBIT P7.2 Income Statement and Balance Sheet Forecasts for the One-Shot Tee-Shirt Company with an Intangible Asset

ONE-SHOT TEE-SHIRT COMPANY
Balance Sheet and Income Statement

	Year 0	Year 1	Year 2
Income Statement			
Revenue		$2,420	$ 0
Amortization of intangible		−100	−100
Expenses		−1,500	0
Earnings		$ 820	$ −100
Balance Sheet			
Cash	$ 0	$ 0	$ 0
Receivable	0	2,420	0
Inventory (t-shirts)	1,500	0	0
Intangible asset	200	100	0
Total assets	$1,700	$2,520	$ 0
Common stock	$1,700	$1,700	$1,700
Retained earnings		820	−1,700
Total equities	$1,700	$2,520	$ 0

a. Value the company as of the end of Year 0 using the discounted cash flow valuation model.
b. Value the company as of the end of Year 0 using the excess cash flow valuation method.
c. Value the company as of the end of Year 0 using the residual earnings valuation method.

P7.3 Adjusted Present Value Form of the Excess Earnings Valuation Method—Joel Germunder Company (see Problem 5.6): Use the information and exhibits in Problem 5.6 for the Joel Germunder Company to answer the questions in this problem.

a. Use the adjusted present value form of the excess earnings valuation method to value the Joel Germunder Company (the entire firm and the equity).
b. Use the equity excess earnings form of the excess earnings model to value the common equity of the company.

P7.4 Weighted Average Cost of Capital Form of the Excess Earnings Valuation Method—Joel Germunder Company (see Problem 5.7): Use the information and exhibits in Problem 5.7 for the Joel Germunder Company to answer the questions in this problem.

a. Use the weighted average cost of capital form of the excess earnings valuation method to value Germunder and Company (the entire firm and the equity).
b. Use the equity excess earnings form of the excess earnings model to value the common equity of the company.

P7.5 Weighted Average Cost of Capital Form of the Excess Earnings Valuation Method—B. Stewart Company: A small group of equity investors plans to start the B. Stewart Company (Stewart). The company needs $10.33 million in initial financing to start the company and another $2.22 million in the second year. The investors arranged for an initial debt financing of $6 million and another $1 million in the following year, all with a 10% cost of debt (interest rate). The equity investors plan to initially invest $4.33 million and $1.22 million in the following year.

The investors hired a consultant to prepare forecasts for the company and to then value it. The forecasts of the company's income statement and balance sheet appear in Exhibit P7.3, and the forecasts of free cash flow appear in Exhibit P7.4. These exhibits show detailed forecasts for the first four years of the company's life. The company's income tax rate is 30% for all taxable income items. The investors believe that beginning in Year 4, the company will grow at the expected long-run inflation rate, which is 3% and that the debt will grow at the same rate from then on as well. Based on an analysis of both comparable companies and other information, the investors concluded that the company's unlevered cost of capital is 12%. Based on the analysis used to measure the company's unlevered cost of capital, the investors concluded that companies similar to Stewart have a target capital structure of one-third debt. The investors asked their valuation consultant to value Stewart using this target capital structure. The valuation consultant explained that the financing in the forecasts might not be consistent with the target capital structure, so they might have to revisit the financing assumptions after the valuation of Stewart using the WACC based method. Assume that regardless of the capital structure strategy, interest tax shields are valued at the unlevered cost of capital.

EXHIBIT P7.3 Income Statement and Balance Sheet Forecasts for the B. Stewart Company

B. STEWART CORPORATION
Income Statement and Balance Sheet Forecasts

($ in thousands)	Actual Year 0	Forecast Year 1	Year 2	Year 3	Year 4
Income Statement					
Revenue		$10,000	$15,000	$17,250	$17,768
Operating expenses		−6,000	−9,000	−10,350	−10,661
Amortization		−500	−500	0	0
Depreciation expense.		−833	−1,333	−1,654	−1,704
Earnings before interest and taxes.		$ 2,667	$ 4,167	$ 5,246	$ 5,403
Interest expense.		−600	−700	−700	−700
Income before taxes.		$ 2,067	$ 3,467	$ 4,546	$ 4,703
Income tax expense		−620	−1,040	−1,364	−1,411
Net income.		$ 1,447	$ 2,427	$ 3,182	$ 3,292
Balance Sheet					
Cash	$ 1,000	$ 1,000	$ 1,500	$ 1,725	$ 1,777
Inventory.	1,000	3,000	4,500	5,175	5,330
Total current assets	$ 2,000	$ 4,000	$ 6,000	$ 6,900	$ 7,107
Intangible asset	1,000	500	0	0	0
Property, plant, and equipment (net)	8,333	12,500	14,375	14,806	15,250
Total assets.	$11,333	$17,000	$20,375	$21,706	$22,357
Accounts payable.	$ 0	$ 2,000	$ 3,000	$ 3,450	$ 3,554
Debt	6,000	7,000	7,000	7,000	7,000
Equity	5,333	8,000	10,375	11,256	11,804
Total equities	$11,333	$17,000	$20,375	$21,706	$22,357

Exhibit may contain small rounding errors

EXHIBIT P7.4 Free Cash Flow Forecasts for the B. Stewart Company

B. STEWART CORPORATION
Free Cash Flow and Equity Free Cash Flow Forecasts

($ in thousands)	Year 1	Year 2	Year 3	Year 4
Earnings before interest and taxes (EBIT)	$ 2,667	$4,167	$5,246	$5,403
− Income taxes paid on EBIT	−800	−1,250	−1,574	−1,621
Earnings before interest and after taxes	$ 1,867	$2,917	$3,672	$3,782
+ Depreciation expense	833	1,333	1,654	1,704
+ Amortization expense	500	500	0	0
− Change in inventory	−2,000	−1,500	−675	−155
+ Change in accounts payable	2,000	1,000	450	104
− Change in required cash balance	0	−500	−225	−52
− Capital expenditures	−5,000	−3,208	−2,085	−2,148
Unlevered free cash flow	$−1,800	$ 542	$2,791	$3,235
− Interest paid in cash ($r_D \times V_D$)	−600	−700	−700	−700
+ Interest tax shield ($T_{INT} \times r_D \times V_D$)	180	210	210	210
+ Change in debt financing.	1,000	0	0	0
Equity free cash flow	$−1,220	$ 52	$2,301	$2,745

a.   Value the company using the weighted average cost of capital form of the discounted cash flow model and the company's target capital structure.

b.   Value the company using the weighted average cost of capital form of the excess earnings model and the company's target capital structure.

c.   Value the common equity of the company using the equity free cash flow form of the discounted cash flow model and the company's target capital structure.

d.   Value the common equity of the company using the equity excess earnings form of the excess earnings model and the company's target capital structure.

7.6   **Adjusted Present Value Form of the Excess Earnings Valuation Method—B. Stewart Company:**   Use the information in Problem 7.5 to respond to the questions in this problem.

a.   Value the company using the adjusted present value form of the discounted cash flow model and the company's capital structure as forecasted in the exhibits and assume that the debt will grow at the long-run growth rate beginning in Year 4.

b.   Value the company using the adjusted present value form of the excess earnings model and the company's capital structure as forecasted in the exhibits.

c.   Value the common equity of the company using the equity free cash flow form of the discounted cash flow model and the company's capital structure as forecasted in the exhibits.

d.   Value the common equity of the company using the equity excess earnings form of the excess earnings model and the company's capital structure as forecasted in the exhibits.

7.7   **Adjusting the Financial Statements for the Excess Earnings Valuation Method—The Phillip Zee Company:**   The Phillip Zee Company financial statements for the first three years of its life which began as of the end of Year 0 are shown in Exhibit P7.5. The company initially recorded an intangible asset for $10,000, and amortized 50% of this intangible asset in each of the first two years of its operation. Assume the company uses equity financing only and does not pay income taxes. The company has a 10% cost of capital. Assume an analyst in devising a compensation plan decides that the intangible asset has an infinite life instead of a two-year life. In other words, the intangible asset does not decrease in value over time.

a.   Measure the company's excess earnings in Years 1 through 3 using the company's financial statements.

b.   Adjust the company's Year 0 through Year 3 income statements and balance sheets based on the analyst's view of the life of the intangible asset.

c.   Discuss the effect that these adjustments have on the company's equity free cash flows.

d.   Measure the company's excess earnings in Years 1 through 3 using the company's restated financial statements.

e.   Compare the excess earnings calculated in parts a and d.

EXHIBIT P7.5	Income Statements and Balance Sheets for the Phillip Zee Company			
Reported Financial Statements	**Year 0**	**Year 1**	**Year 2**	**Year 3**
Income Statement				
Revenue		$10,000	$15,000	$17,250
Operating expenses		–6,000	–9,000	–10,350
Amortization		–5,000	–5,000	
Net income		$–1,000	$ 1,000	$ 6,900
Balance Sheet				
Net operating working capital	$ 2,000	$ 3,000	$ 4,500	$ 5,175
Intangible asset	10,000	5,000	0	0
Total assets.	$12,000	$ 8,000	$ 4,500	$ 5,175
Equity	$12,000	$ 8,000	$ 4,500	$ 5,175
Total equities	$12,000	$ 8,000	$ 4,500	$ 5,175

SOLUTIONS FOR REVIEW EXERCISES

Solution for Review Exercise 7.1: Excess Free Cash Flow Model

In the excess flow model, we calculate the value of the firm as the investment plus the present value of the discounted excess free cash flow.

$$V_0 = I_0 + \frac{FCF_1 - r \times I_0}{r} = \$10 + \frac{\$1.44 - 0.12 \times \$10}{0.12} = \$10 + \frac{\$0.24}{0.12} = \$10 + \$2 = \$12$$

We can also implement the excess flow model in a returns form, which is merely an alternative way to show the calculation of an investment's excess flow. The rate of return is equal to $\$1.44 / \$10$ or 14.4%.

$$V_0 = I_0 + \frac{(ER_1 - r) \times I_0}{r} = I_0 + \frac{xr_1 \times I_0}{r}$$

$$V_0 = \$10 + \frac{(0.144 - 0.12) \times \$10}{0.12} = \$10 + \frac{0.024 \times \$10}{0.12} = \$12$$

We can use the DCF valuation model to measure the value of the firm as

$$V_0 = \frac{FCF_1}{r} = \frac{\$1.44}{0.12} = \$12$$

Solution for Review Exercise 7.2: Excess Earnings Model

Instead of using the dollar investment and free cash flow, we use the book value of the investment and accounting earnings in the excess earnings model.

$$V_F = BVE_0 + \frac{E_1 - r \times BVE_0}{r}$$

$$V_F = \$11 + \frac{\$1.44 - 0.12 \times \$11}{0.12} = \$11 + \frac{\$0.12}{0.12} = \$11 + \$1 = \$12$$

The firm value of $12 from the excess earnings model equals the firm value calculated in Review Exercise 7.1 using the excess free cash flow model.

We can also implement the excess earnings model in a returns form—the rate of return is equal to $\$1.44 / \$11$ or 13.09%.

$$V_0 = BVE_0 + \frac{(ER_1 - r) \times BVE_0}{r} = BVE_0 + \frac{xr_1 \times BVE_0}{r}$$

$$V_0 = \$11 + \frac{(0.1309 - 0.12) \times \$11}{0.12} = \$11 + \frac{0.0109 \times \$11}{0.12} = \$12$$

Solution for Review Exercise 7.3: Weighted Average Cost of Capital Form of the Excess Earnings Model—State Line Farm, Inc.

The equity cost of capital is equal to:

$$r_E = r_{UA} + (r_{UA} - r_D) \times \frac{V_D}{V_E} = 0.12 + (0.12 - 0.08) \times 0.5 = 0.14$$

The weighted average cost of capital is equal to:

$$r_{WACC} = r_E \times \frac{V_E}{V_F} + (1 - T_{INT}) \times r_D \times \frac{V_D}{V_F} = 0.14 \times \frac{2}{3} + 0.08 \times \frac{1}{3} \times (1 - 0.4) = 0.10933$$

The discounted cash flow WACC valuation is equal to:

($ in thousands)	Year 0	Year 1	Year 2	Year 3	CV$_{\text{Firm}}$ Year 3
Unlevered free cash flow for continuing value					$ 1,724
Discount factor for continuing value					11.194
Unlevered free cash flow and continuing value		$–353	$1,170	$1,599	$19,296
Discount factor.		0.901	0.813	0.733	0.733
Present value		$–319	$ 950	$1,172	$14,135
Value of the firm	$15,938				

Exhibit may contain small rounding errors

To use the excess earnings model, we first calculate the excess unlevered earnings:

($ in thousands)	Year 1	Year 2	Year 3	Year 4
Earnings before interest and taxes (EBIT)	$ 2,967	$ 3,180	$ 3,243	$ 3,308
Income tax rate (assuming one tax rate, T$_C$)	40%	40%	40%	40%
Income taxes	$–1,187	$–1,272	$–1,297	$–1,323
Unlevered earnings, UE	$ 1,780	$ 1,908	$ 1,946	$ 1,985

($ in thousands)	Year 1	Year 2	Year 3	Year 4
Total invested capital (book value) beginning balance.	$ 9,833	$11,967	$12,705	$13,052
Required rate of return, r$_{\text{WACC}}$.	10.93%	10.93%	10.93%	10.93%
Required unlevered earnings	$ 1,075	$ 1,308	$ 1,389	$ 1,427
Unlevered earnings, UE	$ 1,780	$ 1,908	$ 1,946	$ 1,985
Required unlevered earnings	1,075	1,308	1,389	1,427
Excess unlevered earnings.	$ 705	$ 600	$ 557	$ 558
Return forecast (expectation).	18.1%	15.9%	15.3%	15.2%
Required rate of return	10.9%	10.9%	10.9%	10.9%
Excess return	7.2%	5.0%	4.4%	4.3%

Now we can calculate the value of the firm:

($ in thousands)	Year 0	Year 1	Year 2	Year 3	CV$_{\text{Firm}}$ Year 3
Excess unlevered earnings for continuing value					$ 558
Discount factor for continuing value					11.194
Excess unlevered earnings and continuing value		$ 705	$ 600	$ 557	$ 6,245
Discount factor.		0.901	0.813	0.733	0.733
Present value		$ 635	$ 487	$ 408	$ 4,574
Value of excess flows.	$ 6,105				
Initial total invested capital.	9,833				
Value of the firm	$15,938				

Exhibit may contain small rounding errors

The values of the debt and equity are 1/3 of the value of the firm ($5,313) and 2/3 of the value of the firm ($10,625), respectively. Note, this is the same value of the debt on the balance sheet as of the end of Year 0. This is not a coincidence. We created the forecasts for the company based on the target capital structure.

Solution for Review Exercise 7.4: Adjusted Present Value Form of the Excess Earnings Model—State Line Farm, Inc.

The discounted cash flow APV valuation is equal to:

($ in thousands)	Year 0	Year 1	Year 2	Year 3	CV$_{Firm}$ Year 3
Value of the Unlevered Firm					
Unlevered free cash flow for continuing value					$ 1,724
Discount factor for continuing value					10.000
Unlevered free cash flow and continuing value		$–353	$1,170	$1,599	$17,238
Discount factor.		0.893	0.797	0.712	0.712
Discounted value		$–315	$ 932	$1,138	$12,270
Value of the unlevered firm.	$14,025				
Value of the Interest Tax Shields					
Interest tax shield for continuing value.					$ 206
Discount factor for continuing value					10.000
Interest tax shield and continuing value of the interest tax shield		$ 170	$ 192	$ 201	$ 2,058
Discount factor.		0.893	0.797	0.712	0.712
Present value		$ 152	$ 153	$ 143	$ 1,465
Value of the interest tax shields	$ 1,913				
Value of the firm	$15,938				

Exhibit may contain small rounding errors

To use the excess earnings model, we first calculate the excess unlevered earnings, which we calculated in Review Exercise 7.3. The difference in this calculation is that we use the unlevered cost of capital rather than the weighted average cost of capital.

($ in thousands)	Year 1	Year 2	Year 3	Year 4
Total invested capital (book value) beginning balance.	$ 9,833	$11,967	$12,705	$13,052
Required rate of return, r_{UA}.	12.00%	12.00%	12.00%	12.00%
Required unlevered earnings	$ 1,180	$ 1,436	$ 1,525	$ 1,566
Unlevered earnings (See Review Exercise 7.3)	$ 1,780	$ 1,908	$ 1,946	$ 1,985
Required unlevered earnings	1,180	1,436	1,525	1,566
Excess unlevered earnings.	$ 600	$ 472	$ 421	$ 419
Return forecast (expectation).	18.10%	15.94%	15.32%	15.21%
Required rate of return	12.00%	12.00%	12.00%	12.00%
Excess return	6.10%	3.94%	3.32%	3.21%

We then measure the value of the firm using the APV form of the excess earnings model:

($ in thousands)	Year 0	Year 1	Year 2	Year 3	CV_Firm Year 3
Value of the unlevered Firm Using Excess Earnings Valuation					
Unlevered excess earnings for continuing value					$ 419
Discount factor for continuing value					10.000
Excess earnings and continuing value.		$ 600	$ 472	$ 421	$ 4,186
Discount factor.		0.893	0.797	0.712	0.712
Present value		$ 536	$ 376	$ 300	$ 2,980
Value of unlevered excess earnings.	$ 4,192				
Initial total invested capital.	$ 9,833				
Value of the unlevered firm.	$14,025				
Value of the Interest Tax Shields					
Interest tax shield for continuing value.					$ 206
Discount factor for continuing value					10.000
Interest tax shield and continuing value of the interest tax shield . .		$ 170	$ 192	$ 201	$ 2,058
Discount factor.		0.893	0.797	0.712	0.712
Present value		$ 152	$ 153	$ 143	$ 1,465
Value of the interest tax shields	$ 1,913				
Value of the firm	$15,938				

Exhibit may contain small rounding errors

Solution for Review Exercise 7.5: Equity Discounted Excess Earnings Model—State Line Farm, Inc.

The Equity DCF valuation is equal to:

($ in thousands)	Year 0	Year 1	Year 2	Year 3	CV_Equity Year 3
Equity free cash flow for continuing value					$ 1,544
Discount factor for continuing value					8.333
Equity free cash flow and continuing value		$ 90	$1,148	$1,451	$12,864
Discount factor.		0.877	0.769	0.675	0.675
Present value		$ 79	$ 884	$ 980	$ 8,683
Discounted equity free cash flow V_E	$10,625				

Exhibit may contain small rounding errors

To use the **excess earnings model**, we first calculate excess equity earnings:

($ in thousands)	Year 1	Year 2	Year 3	Year 4
Common equity (book value, BVE) beginning balance	$ 4,521	$ 5,955	$ 6,426	$ 6,619
Required rate of return, r_E.	14.00%	14.00%	14.00%	14.00%
Required earnings	$ 633	$ 834	$ 900	$ 927
Earnings.	$ 1,525	$ 1,619	$ 1,645	$ 1,676
Required earnings	633	834	900	927
Excess earnings.	$ 892	$ 786	$ 745	$ 749
Return forecast (expectation).	33.73%	27.19%	25.59%	25.32%
Required rate of return.	14.00%	14.00%	14.00%	14.00%
Excess return	19.73%	13.19%	11.59%	11.32%

Exhibit may contain small rounding errors

Now, we can measure the value of the equity using the equity form of the excess earnings model:

($ in thousands)	Year 0	Year 1	Year 2	Year 3	CV$_{Equity}$ Year 3
Equity excess earnings for continuing value					$ 749
Discount factor for continuing value					8.333
Excess equity earnings and continuing value		$ 892	$ 786	$ 745	$6,245
Discount factor.		0.877	0.769	0.675	0.675
Present value		$ 783	$ 605	$ 503	$4,215
Discounted excess equity flow.	$ 6,105				
Initial book value of common equity	4,521				
Common equity value	$10,625				

Exhibit may contain small rounding errors

The resulting value of the common equity of $10,625 equals the value of the equity calculated using the excess earnings model in Review Exercise 7.3 ($10,625 = 2/3 equity × $15,938 firm value).

After mastering the material in this chapter, you will be able to:

1. Understand the underpinnings and implications of the Capital Asset Pricing Model (8.1–8.2)

2. Estimate the required inputs for the Capital Asset Pricing Model (8.3–8.10)

3. Estimate the Capital Asset Pricing Model adjusted for market capitalization and other potential attributes (8.11–8.12)

4. Estimate the equity cost of capital using the three-factor model or implied cost of capital estimates (8.13–8.14)

Estimating the Equity Cost of Capital

Aviva plc, a large life insurance company in Europe, uses the Capital Asset Pricing Model (CAPM) to calculate the discount rate it uses in certain disclosures it provides to the investing public. Those disclosures are:

AVIVA & VODAFONE

... based on an assessment of the Group's weighted average cost of capital (WACC) using well established capital asset pricing model (CAPM) methodology. The Group WACC has been calculated by reference to the cost of equity and the cost of debt based on the actual relative weighting at the relevant date. In arriving at the cost of equity, we have used an equity risk premium of 3% and a market assessed risk rate (beta) averaged over 2 years.[1]

Vodafone Group plc (Vodafone), a British multinational telecommunications company headquartered in London, uses the CAPM to calculate the discount rate it uses to assess the potential impairment of its assets:

... the Group undertook a detailed review of the carrying value of its fixed assets, including the Group's goodwill and intangible asset balances. This review assessed whether the carrying value of assets was supported by the net present value of future cash flows ... The discount rates used were all derived within a Capital Asset Pricing Model framework, using a risk free rate obtained using long-dated government bonds, equity market risk premia ... .[2]

In this chapter, we discuss how to estimate the cost of equity capital using alternative techniques.

---

[1] Aviva plc press release, "Aviva plc—Restatement for EEV Part 1," *Regulatory News Service*, January 13, 2005, RNS No. 3197H Aviva plc 13 January 2005.

[2] Vodafone Group plc press release, "Vodafone Group plc Interim Results," *PR Newswire*, November 13, 2001.

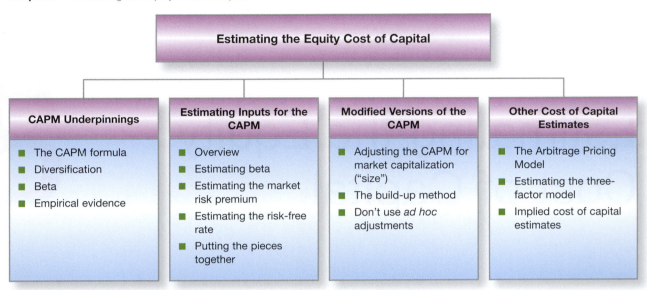

INTRODUCTION

When valuing a company, the end result of the process of estimating the cost of capital is estimating either the unlevered cost of capital (if we are using the adjusted present value method) or the weighted average cost of capital (if we are using the weighted average cost of capital method). We usually begin that process by estimating the equity cost of capital for the appropriate comparable companies, and if possible, estimating it directly for the company we are valuing.

The Capital Asset Pricing Model (CAPM) is the method used most often to estimate a company's equity cost of capital. In a recent survey, 95% of the corporations responded that they used the CAPM to estimate the equity cost of capital, and the other 5% responded that they used a modified version of the CAPM. Investment banks also responded that they relied primarily on the CAPM or a modified version of the CAPM to estimate the equity cost of capital.[3]

In this chapter we introduce the CAPM and discuss how to implement the CAPM to estimate the cost of equity capital. Estimating the CAPM is not as straightforward as one might expect based on its basic formula. It is more complex to implement because scholars and practitioners have varying views on the specific methods they favor in estimating the inputs for the CAPM. We discuss these issues and the trade-offs among alternative methods.

We then examine some alternative methods for estimating the cost of equity capital. The primary alternative to the CAPM used in practice is the CAPM modified for the potential effect of market capitalization, although use of the three-factor model is increasing. A large part of our discussion is on the practical implementation of the CAPM, and those issues are as germane for the CAPM, the CAPM modified for market capitalization, and the three-factor model. Beyond the CAPM, modified CAPM, and three-factor model, there are other, less used models, such as the Arbitrage Pricing Model, the Gordon Constant Growth Dividend Model, implied cost of capital models, and the so-called "build-up" method.

8.1 THE CAPITAL ASSET PRICING MODEL

LO1 Understand the underpinnings and implications of the Capital Asset Pricing Model

The **Capital Asset Pricing Model (CAPM)** was developed in the 1960s.[4] It describes how individual securities (assets) are priced in the market under the assumption that investors care about the trade-off

---

[3] See Bruner, R., K. Eades, R. Harris, and R. Higgins, "Best Practices in Estimating the Cost of Capital: Survey and Synthesis," *Financial Practice and Education* (Spring/Summer, 1998), pp. 13–28. This survey was conducted on corporations that have reputations as leaders in financial management, according to their peers, and on 10 investment banks that had the greatest deal flow over the 1993–1995 period according to *Institutional Investor*. The primary version of the modified CAPM used by the respondents was the CAPM modified for the effect of market capitalization.

[4] The CAPM is generally attributed to William Sharpe, John Lintner, and Jack Treynor (though Treynor never published his paper). See W. F. Sharpe, "Capital Asset Prices: A Theory of Market Equilibrium Under Conditions of Risk," *Journal of Finance* 19 (1964), pp. 425–442; and J. Lintner, "The Valuation of Risky Assets and the Selection of Risky Investments in Stock Portfolios and Capital Budgets," *Review of Economics and Statistics* 47 (1965), pp. 13–37. The CAPM is often referred to as the Sharpe-Lintner Capital Asset Pricing Model. Lintner, Markowitz, and Sharpe all won the Nobel Prize in Economics for their work on portfolio theory and the Capital Asset Pricing Model.

they experience between expected return and risk—specifically, given a specified level of risk, investors prefer more expected return to less expected return. In its standard form, the CAPM describes the relationship between an asset's (or security's) expected return, $E(\tilde{R}_i)$ (which we use as an estimate of the security's cost of capital), and the factors that determine it—the risk-free rate of return, r_F, a measure of the risk of a security, β_i, and a risk premium (or price of risk) per unit of risk, $[E(\tilde{R}_m) - R_F]$, measured against the return on the risk-free asset. A typical form of the CAPM is:

$$E(\tilde{R}_i) = r_F + \beta_i[E(\tilde{R}_m) - R_F]$$ (8.1)

We first begin with a discussion of the benefits of diversification and then go on to discuss the development of the CAPM.

The Effects of Diversification

It was the seminal work of Harry Markowitz that addressed the benefits of diversification by deriving the effect of diversification on the expected return and variance of return of a portfolio.[5] This work presumes that the measure of reward that investors care about is the expected return on a portfolio and also presumes that variance (or standard deviation) of returns is an appropriate measure of risk for investors to assess the risk of their portfolios. We can use observed stock returns to measure the historical mean and variance of an individual security. We can also combine stocks into portfolios and use observed portfolio returns to measure the historical mean and variance of any portfolio. If we randomly pick securities for our portfolio, as we increase the number of securities in a portfolio, we should observe a reduction in the variance without affecting the mean return. We show this effect in Exhibit 8.1. To create Exhibit 8.1, we randomly select portfolios that vary in size from 1 to 125 companies from the New York, American, and NASDAQ stock exchanges that had monthly return data available from January 2001 to December 31, 2010.[6] For each size of portfolio, we repeat this random selection 1,000 times. In this exhibit, we plot the average monthly standard deviation of the return of the 1,000 equally weighted portfolios as a function of the number of securities in the portfolio, and we also report the average mean monthly return for the same portfolios.

| **EXHIBIT 8.1** | Effects of Adding Stocks to a Portfolio on the Standard Deviation and Mean Return of the Portfolio's Stock Returns |

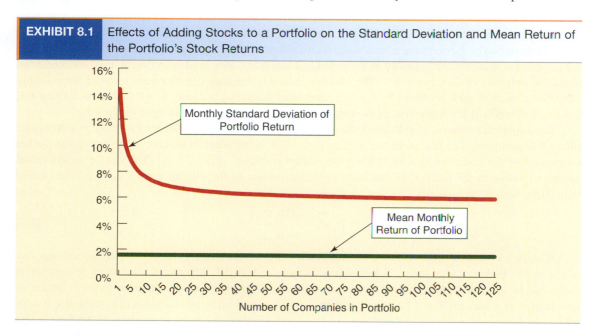

The standard deviation of returns falls rapidly as you add securities to the portfolio. The first security in the 1,000 portfolios has an average standard deviation of 14.4% per month. With three securities the portfolio average standard deviation has fallen to 10%, and at seven securities the portfolio average

---

[5] See H. M. Markowitz, "Portfolio Selection," *Journal of Finance* 7 (1952), pp. 77–91.

[6] The name of the American Stock Exchange (AMEX) was changed to NYSE Amex when NYSE Euronext bought the AMEX in 2008. In May of 2012, the name was changed to NYSE MKT.

standard deviation has fallen to 8%. At 15 securities the average standard deviation has fallen under 7%, and at 90 securities the average standard deviation is 6%. Thus, by the time 15 firms have entered the portfolio, the portfolio's standard deviation has dropped to one-half of the standard deviation with only one security in the portfolio. One can achieve faster benefits of diversification by optimally choosing companies as opposed to random selection. [7]

Given this drop in standard deviation, what do we expect to happen to the expected return to the portfolio as we add securities to it? Remember that we randomly picked securities to add to the portfolio; thus, on average, we would expect the stocks to earn the expected return on the market. Thus, we anticipate that the expected return on the portfolio will remain (roughly) constant and (roughly) equal to the expected return on the market as we add securities to the portfolio. As you can see in the diagram, the mean return of the portfolios is constant.

Valuation Key 8.1

Investors trade off expected return (reward) and standard deviation of returns (risk) in deciding on the portfolio to hold. The benefits of diversification (holding multiple securities in a portfolio instead of a single stock) are that you can reduce the risk of your portfolio without affecting the expected return (reward).

Beta as a Measure of Security Risk

While we do not discuss the derivation of the CAPM, the CAPM assumes that investors are concerned about the risk–return trade-off in assessing their portfolios, where risk is determined by the standard deviation of the portfolio's return and return is the expected return of the portfolio. The CAPM, among other things, describes how individual securities are priced (as well as inefficient portfolios and efficient portfolios). In other words, the question resolved by the CAPM is, given that the relevant measure of risk for an investor's portfolio is the standard deviation of portfolio return, what is the relevant measure of risk for an individual security in an investor's portfolio? As it turns out, the relevant measure of risk for an individual security is not the standard deviation of return of that security; rather, it is the contribution of that security to the standard deviation of the portfolio return, which is measured by β_i in Equation 8.1. In other words, investors are not compensated for the volatility of the individual assets that they hold even though they are concerned about the volatility of their portfolios. The intuitive reason is that they can eliminate some of the volatility or variance of individual securities by holding diversified portfolios because, as we showed in Exhibit 8.1, holding a diversified portfolio reduces the risk of the portfolio relative to holding a single stock.

The expected return of an individual security in the CAPM is equal to the return on the risk-free asset plus a risk premium. The risk premium is equal to the risk of the security relative to the risk in the market multiplied by the risk premium for holding the market portfolio, $[E(\tilde{R}_m) - r_F]$. The risk of an individual security relative to the market (or the security's contribution to the overall market risk) is often called beta (β), which is defined as

$$\beta_i = \frac{\text{cov}(\tilde{R}_i, \tilde{R}_m)}{\sigma^2(\tilde{R}_m)} \tag{8.2}$$

A stock's beta measured against a market index indicates the stock's risk relative to the average risk of the stocks in that market index. Whether it adds more or less risk than the average stock to the market index can be inferred by whether the stock's beta measured against that same market index is greater or less than 1. If a security has a beta greater than 1 when measured against a particular portfolio, it adds relatively more risk to the overall riskiness of that portfolio than the average security. If the beta is less than 1, it adds relatively less risk to that portfolio than the average security adds to that portfolio.

For example, if a stock moves up and down the same amount as the market portfolio on average, then it should have a beta equal to 1. If a stock has a beta of 1, we would expect it to earn a return of 5% above the risk-free return on a day the market earned 5% above the risk-free return. We would expect it to earn 5% below the risk-free return on a day the market earned 5% below the risk-free return. If another stock

---

[7] There have been many studies that examine this question. For example, see M. Statman, "How Many Stocks Make a Diversified Portfolio?" *Journal of Financial and Quantitative Analysis* 22 (September, 1987), pp. 353–364.

has a beta of 2, we would expect it to earn a return of 10% above the risk-free return on a day the market earned 5% above the risk-free return. Of course, securities will not track the market's return exactly, but beta measures how we expect it to move with the market, on average.

When you hear someone talking about **systematic risk** or **non-diversifiable risk** in the context of the CAPM, they are talking about beta or market risk. This is risk that cannot be avoided through diversification. It can only be controlled by choosing a portfolio with a given beta. As an example, an investor could choose to invest in a portfolio with a beta of 2.0 or a beta of 0.25—thus controlling the amount of market risk to bear. You will also hear people use the term **diversifiable risk** or **idiosyncratic risk**—this is the risk that can potentially be eliminated through diversification. So while idiosyncratic risk is part of the volatility of a security's return, it can be eliminated in a portfolio through diversification. As a consequence, investors are not rewarded for that form of risk, but are rewarded for systematic risk according to the CAPM.

While the CAPM prices any risky asset in theory, the CAPM is mostly used in practice to assess the expected returns (estimate the cost of capital) of equity securities. We can rewrite the CAPM formula to reflect this use

$$r_{E,i} = r_F + \beta_{E,i} \times MRP \tag{8.3}$$

where $r_{E,i}$ is the expected return on equity security i, r_F is the rate of return earned on an asset that is completely risk-free, $\beta_{E,i}$ is the equity beta of security i, and MRP is the expected market risk premium (the difference between the expected return on the value-weighted market portfolio of all risky assets less the return earned on the risk-free asset).

The CAPM is a model of expected returns, not the actual returns an investor earned historically or will necessarily earn in any given period. In other words, because this is a model of the returns expected to be earned by risky assets, in any given time period, an investor might earn more or less than the expected return. However, if the model is correct, over the long run and over a large number of assets, the model should describe the mean return an investor will earn.

REVIEW EXERCISE 8.1

Calculating Beta

Information is provided below for three companies. The standard deviation of the market return is .05 and the expected market risk premium $(E(R_m) - r_F)$ equals .06.

Standard deviation of the market return	0.05
Expected market risk premium	0.06

	Firm 1	Firm 2	Firm 3
Standard deviation of firm's return...................	0.12	0.06	0.10
Covariance of firm's return and market return	0.003	0.0025	0.004

For each company, calculate each firm's beta and the relative risk of the firm's security return to the market return based upon their relative standard deviations. Are beta and the relative standard deviations both measures of the firm's risk?

Solution on page 333.

Valuation Key 8.2

Beta is a measure of how much more or less a particular stock's return moves with the market portfolio. It measures the risk of that stock relative to the market. The volatility of an individual security's return is not the relevant measure of risk of an individual stock. A security with a high variance of its returns could add relatively little risk to a portfolio, which is the risk relevant for determining its expected return and equity cost of capital according to the CAPM.

A Quick Look at Some Betas

Think about some industries and how the returns of stocks in those industries are likely to move with the overall market return. Would you expect the betas of grocery store chains to have more or less risk than the overall market (have a beta above or below 1)? To answer this question, we would think about how grocery store businesses are affected by upturns and downturns in the economy. Certainly business cycles affect the profitability of grocery stores. In an economic downturn, people probably do not go to the gourmet aisle as often, or eat the finest cuts of meat and fish, and probably buy fewer pre-prepared foods (all of which generally have higher margins), but people still eat. Thus, after thinking about the issue for a few moments, you might not be surprised that grocery stores are generally less risky than the market and have betas that are less than 1.

Companies in the "high-end" consulting services industry face a different situation. When the economy turns down and the profits of corporations begin to drop, those corporations often delay non-essential spending. They will delay the purchases of services that are not of an immediately critical nature. We generally observe betas for companies in the business services industry that are greater than 1 because their revenue streams fluctuate more with general economic conditions than those of average companies.

In Exhibit 8.2 we provide estimates of industry equity betas estimated using 60 months of data ending March 31, 2010. The industry betas are equally weighted and include all companies that were listed on the New York Stock Exchange, American Stock Exchange, and NASDAQ. In all cases, betas were estimated against the S&P 500. The industry betas in the exhibit range from a low of 0.67 for electric, gas, and sanitary services to a high of 1.72 for furniture and fixtures. If you look down the list of industries and you think about their respective systematic risks, the betas should generally make sense to you. Rate of return regulated utilities have relatively little systematic risk despite their very high leverage. Food stores have a risk that is below the average (folks continue to eat even when the economy is depressed), while industries such as hotels and other lodging places have relatively high betas, as travel is impacted significantly by overall economic conditions. Finally, industries such as chemicals and trucking and warehousing have betas that are around 1.

| EXHIBIT 8.2 | Equity Betas for U.S. Companies in Various Industries |

Industry Name	Beta	# of Firms	Industry Name	Beta	# of Firms
Electric, gas, and sanitary services	0.67	122	Communication	1.32	110
Insurance agents, brokers, and service	0.70	10	Water transportation	1.35	17
Educational services	0.76	10	Real estate	1.41	25
Holding and other investment offices	0.77	460	Automotive dealers and service stations	1.42	15
Food stores	0.81	13	Electronic and other electric equipment	1.42	265
Depository institutions	0.85	395	Eating and drinking places	1.42	33
Food and kindred products	0.90	77	Industrial machinery and equipment	1.43	168
Health services	1.07	49	Heavy construction, except building	1.45	11
Trucking and warehousing	1.08	22	Oil and gas extraction	1.46	104
Engineering and management services	1.09	59	Non-depository institutions	1.46	26
Instruments and related products	1.11	179	Miscellaneous retail	1.46	41
Wholesale trade—nondurable goods	1.13	30	Rubber and misc. plastics products	1.48	21
Leather and leather products	1.14	13	Paper and allied products	1.49	25
Chemicals and allied products	1.18	254	Printing and publishing	1.49	27
Petroleum and coal products	1.20	25	Furniture and home furnishings stores	1.52	11
Transportation by air	1.20	17	Misc. manufacturing industries	1.55	23
Business services	1.21	281	Amusement and recreation services	1.56	24
Insurance carriers	1.23	86	Apparel and other textile products	1.57	21
Wholesale trade—durable goods	1.25	58	Apparel and accessory stores	1.59	33
General merchandise stores	1.26	18	Stone, clay, and glass products	1.62	11
Lumber and wood products	1.27	11	Transportation equipment	1.62	63
Personal services	1.27	11	Hotels and other lodging places	1.67	10
Fabricated metal products	1.30	38	General building contractors	1.70	15
Metal mining	1.30	35	Primary metal industries	1.70	36
Security and commodity brokers	1.32	42	Furniture and fixtures	1.72	18

A Portfolio Beta Is a Weighted Average of the Betas of the Securities in the Portfolio

For a portfolio of N securities, the return of the portfolio is simply the weighted average of the returns to the individual securities in the portfolio. The weights, x_i, are calculated as the market value of security i divided by the total market value of the securities in the portfolio.

$$\tilde{R}_p = \sum_{i=1}^{N} x_i \tilde{R}_i$$

A portfolio beta is the weighted average of the betas of the securities in the portfolio, where the weights are again based on the market values of each security relative to the total market value of the portfolio.

$$\beta_p = \sum_{i=1}^{N} x_i \beta_i \qquad (8.4)$$

The implication is that the beta of a portfolio is the weighted average of the betas of the individual securities in the portfolio. If you had two securities in your portfolio and one stock had a beta of 0.4 and the other had a beta of 2.0, and you held equal values of both, your portfolio beta would be 1.2 ($1.2 = 0.4 \times 0.5 + 2.0 \times 0.5$).

The beta of the portfolio with respect to a market portfolio can be written as

$$\beta_p = \frac{\text{cov}(\tilde{R}_p, \tilde{R}_m)}{\sigma^2(\tilde{R}_m)} \qquad (8.5)$$

This expression looks just like the expression for the beta of an individual security except the numerator is now the covariance of the return of the portfolio with the market instead of the covariance of the return of an individual security with the market.

Valuation Key 8.3

The beta of a portfolio is a weighted average of the betas of the individual securities that comprise that portfolio. The weights for each security are determined by the proportion of the portfolio's value stemming from that security.

REVIEW EXERCISE 8.2

Calculating Portfolio Return and Portfolio Beta

In the table below, the market value, beta, and equity security return are listed for four individual equity securities that are contained in a portfolio. Calculate the return to the portfolio and the beta for the portfolio.

	Firm 1	Firm 2	Firm 3	Firm 4
Total equity market value in portfolio (in millions).	$1,000	$3,500	$2,300	$700
Firm beta	0.90	1.07	1.20	1.46
Stock return	5.0%	7.0%	9.0%	10.0%

Solution on page 333.

8.2 FURTHER OBSERVATIONS AND EMPIRICAL EVIDENCE

In addition to describing the risk and return relationship for individual securities, the CAPM has certain implications. The first implication is that investors should hold well-diversified portfolios. If they do not, they will bear risk for which they are not compensated. Why? If the portfolio isn't sufficiently well diversified, then the variance of the portfolio will be driven by idiosyncratic risk, and investors are not compensated for idiosyncratic risk according to the CAPM. They are only compensated for systematic risk.

The second implication is that corporations should not pursue pure diversification as a strategy. By diversification, we mean investing in different businesses when there are no synergies or cash flow effects associated with operating multiple businesses. Why? Because investors can diversify themselves, this is not a value-creating strategy unless there are positive cash flow ramifications. In practice, diversification across industries for investors is usually simple and practically costless because there are many index funds available that track broad-based indices, such as the S&P 500, as well as many other major indices, including international indices.

The third implication of the CAPM is the main reason we discuss it in this book. The CAPM is a model about the returns that investors demand in expectation for the risk that they are bearing. As such, it provides a method for estimating a company's cost of capital.

Valuation Key 8.4

The Capital Asset Pricing Model is widely used to estimate the cost of equity capital. In addition, the model has important implications for investors and corporations. For investors, the model indicates that it is important to hold well-diversified portfolios. For corporations, the model implies that diversification is not a value-added activity unless it is associated with positive cash flow effects.

Evidence on the Capital Asset Pricing Model

Is the CAPM a reasonable model to use to calculate the cost of capital? That is, does it explain differences in expected returns empirically? Substantial, but certainly not all, scholarly research on this topic suggests that the primary predictions of the CAPM are consistent with the data. However, academicians have identified two generic issues. First, we observe that stock returns appear to be related to measures other than beta (other factors are important), and second, the CAPM-based predicted returns of the high- (low-) beta portfolios are too low (high).

While some relatively early evidence investigating the CAPM showed that returns were related to betas and that measures such as the variance of returns were unrelated to returns, subsequent evidence began to show departures from the predictions of the CAPM. For example, an early study by Black, Jensen, and Scholes provided evidence that returns were linearly related to beta. A study by Fama and Macbeth[8] indicated that variables such as beta squared and idiosyncratic risk were not priced. However, both of these studies indicated that the relationship between expected return and beta was somewhat "flat" relative to the predictions of the CAPM using data back to the 1930s. The more recent experience has also been that while the relationship between return and beta is positive, it is still flatter than the CAPM predicts. That is, the returns to low-beta stocks are too high and the returns to high-beta stocks are too low relative to the predictions of the CAPM.[9]

One problem, discussed by Richard Roll and others, is that a true test of the CAPM would require us to know the market portfolio, defined as the value-weighted portfolio of all risky assets in the world. Of course, such an index does not exist and is unlikely to ever exist. Since most tests of the CAPM rely only on portfolios of common stock or include a few other types of securities (bonds, preferred stock and real estate but then only with U.S. data), one could argue the CAPM has never been fairly tested, nor likely will it ever be.[10] However, from a practical perspective, what is important to estimating the equity cost of capital is that so far, we have not been able to define a proxy for the market return that totally describes expected returns to common equities using the CAPM.

The other problematic issue for the CAPM is that there have been a series of academic papers that suggest that measures other than beta explain the returns of firms in a systematic way. For example,

---

[8] See Black, F., M. Jensen, and M. Scholes, "The Capital Asset Pricing Model: Some Empirical Tests," in M. Jensen, ed., *Studies in the Theory of Capital Markets,* New York: Praeger Publishing (1972), pp. 79–121; and Fama, E., and J. MacBeth, "Risk, Return and Equilibrium: Empirical Tests," *Journal of Political Economy* 81 (1973), pp. 607–636.

[9] See Fama, E., and K. French, *Journal of Economic Perspectives* 18 (Summer 2004), pp. 25–46.

[10] See R. Roll, "A Critique of the Asset Pricing Theory's Tests; Part I: On Past and Potential Testability of the Theory, *Journal of Financial Economics* 4 (March, 1977), pp. 129–176.

small firms (in terms of market capitalization of the equity) have, on average, outperformed large firms on a CAPM risk-adjusted basis. In other words, smaller firms over long historical periods had returns that were higher than the CAPM predicted and large firms had returns that were smaller than the CAPM predicted.[11] This is often referred to as the "**size effect**." Interestingly, a large portion (and maybe all) of the size effect occurs in the month of January. The other months do not indicate nearly as severe departures from the CAPM. In fact, some researchers have concluded that there is little or no size effect other than in the month of January.[12] Researchers refer to this phenomenon as the "**January effect**." A variety of explanations for the size effect have been considered, such as issues arising from bid-ask spreads and turn-of-the-year trading; issues in estimating betas; and the effect of taxes, and transactions costs, and more. To date, we have no completely satisfactory explanation for the phenomenon.

Some individuals interpreted this evidence to indicate the existence of a trading rule based on firm size (that is, if you want to beat the market, just buy small stocks). But this interpretation presumes that the risk adjustment in the CAPM is correct. Another interpretation is that the CAPM is not a perfect descriptor of the return-generating process and somehow we are not measuring risk completely with the CAPM beta. In that interpretation, size is a proxy for some element of priced risk that is not captured by beta as we measure it. Academicians generally interpret the evidence on firm size to infer that the CAPM is not a perfect descriptor of the return-generating process.

Despite the uncertainty with regard to interpreting this evidence, the evidence has led some valuation experts to estimate a firm's cost of capital using the traditional CAPM with an adjustment factor based on the firm's approximate market equity capitalization. We discuss the alternatives to the CAPM based on firm size later in the chapter.

Besides the evidence on the so-called size effect, there are other variables that appear to be potentially important in explaining the cross-section of expected returns beyond the CAPM; this evidence led to the three-factor model, which we also discuss later in the chapter. All of this evidence suggests that the CAPM is not a perfect descriptor of expected returns. That said, it has something to say about risk and return, and until we have an alternative model that clearly dominates the CAPM, people will continue to use it. We next discuss how to implement the CAPM in practice, and later in the chapter we examine some of the alternatives to the CAPM. We explore the implementation issues associated with the CAPM in depth, as it is still the most commonly used method to estimate a company's cost of equity capital. Moreover, all of the implementation issues we discuss for the CAPM exist for the CAPM modified for the effect of market capitalization and the three-factor model. As such, the issues associated with implementing the CAPM are illustrative of the issues associated with many alternative models.

Valuation Key 8.5

The evidence on the Capital Asset Pricing Model is mixed. While we observe the basic risk–return relationship predicted by the model, the evidence suggests that it is not a perfect descriptor of expected returns. Regardless, however, it is still the most popular model used to estimate expected returns.

8.3 AN OVERVIEW ON ESTIMATING THE EQUITY COST OF CAPITAL USING THE CAPITAL ASSET PRICING MODEL

In order to estimate the cost of equity capital using the CAPM, we need estimates of the three components of the CAPM: the risk-free rate, the company's beta, and the market risk premium. As we shall see in our discussion, we can estimate those three components in many ways. While the CAPM is widely used, the method used to estimate these components varies significantly in practice.

In the next few sections, we discuss many of the alternative methods used to estimate the three components of the CAPM and discuss some of the trade-offs to consider in making those decisions. In

LO2 Estimate the required inputs for the Capital Asset Pricing Model

---

[11] See Banz, R., "The Relationship Between Return and Market Values of Common Stock," *Journal of Financial Economics* 9 (March, 1981), pp. 3–18.

[12] Keim, Donald B., "Size-Related Anomalies and Stock Return Seasonality: Further Evidence," *Journal of Financial Economics* 9 (June 1983), pp. 13–32.

the end, like many steps in the valuation process, we must use our professional judgment as to how to estimate each component of the CAPM. If you work for an investment bank or consulting firm or other company that conducts frequent valuations, it may have certain standard practices to follow to estimate these components. Even then, however, the specific company and valuation context usually requires some refinement to standard practices requiring professional judgment.

In Exhibit 8.3, we outline the steps required to estimate the cost of equity capital using the CAPM. The first step is to decide, which, if any, comparable companies we will use to estimate the equity cost of capital needed in the valuation, which is generally determined in part by the suitability of the available comparable companies. We begin with this step because this decision affects subsequent decisions we make and analyses we perform. The second step is to assess the stability of the company's operating assets and capital structure as well as any comparable companies being considered. Next, we must decide if we are going to use commercially available CAPM-based estimates of the equity cost of capital or develop our own estimate. If we are using a commercially available estimate, we also must identify the assumptions and choices underlying the estimation process used in the commercially available estimates to make sure that it is consistent with our assessment in Steps 1 and 2. If we use commercially available estimates, we stop the process here. If we are going to develop our own estimate, we continue to estimate the CAPM components.

EXHIBIT 8.3	Steps in Estimating the Cost of Equity Capital Using the CAPM
1	Decide, which, if any, comparable companies to use to estimate the equity cost of capital needed in the valuation
2	Assess the stability of the operating assets (asset risk or unlevered company risk) and capital structure (financial leverage risk) of the company we are valuing and comparable companies, if any
3	Decide to use commercially available CAPM-based estimates or develop own estimates (if using commercially available estimates, stop process here)
4	Estimate the beta of each company's common stock
5	Estimate the market risk premium
6	Estimate the risk-free rate (yield on a risk-free asset at the valuation date)
7	Substitute your estimates in the CAPM and solve for the cost of equity

In Steps 4, 5, and 6 of the process, we estimate the three components of the CAPM—beta, the market risk premium, and the risk-free rate of return. Each of these steps has its own process with various steps, which we discuss in subsequent sections of the chapter. The last step is to calculate the CAPM equity cost of capital using the components estimated from the previous three steps.

Before we discuss the many choices that we make when estimating each component, it is useful to understand at a conceptual level that the choices we make across the components are not independent of one another. Thus, there are interdependencies between estimating beta and estimating the market risk premium. There are also interdependencies between estimating the risk-free rate and estimating the market risk premium. We will discuss these interdependencies as we discuss estimating the three components of the CAPM.

8.4 ESTIMATING BETA: OVERVIEW

Beta, as we already discussed, is a measure of the risk of an asset or security relative to a certain portfolio, which, according to the CAPM, is the market portfolio. When we implement the CAPM, we estimate the beta by measuring the risk of an asset relative to some proxy that we choose for the market portfolio. The most common method used to estimate betas is the estimation of the parameters of a regression model called the market model. Virtually all estimates of beta start with an estimate from a market model regression because the statistical formula for the slope parameter of the market model is the same as the formula for beta in the CAPM (Equation 8.2). Instead of conducting our own analyses to estimate beta, it is also possible to use a commercially available estimate of beta for many companies.

We show the primary steps in the process to estimate beta in Exhibit 8.4. The first step is to decide whether to use a commercially available estimate or develop your own estimate. If you are developing your own estimate, the next step is to choose the independent variable, the chosen proxy for the market index, to estimate the market model regression. Steps 3 and 4 involve choices for the time period and return holding period for the stock returns used to estimate the market model. Then, we estimate the model and adjust the beta estimate for such effects as mean reversion. When implementing this process, we must be cognizant of the second step in the cost of equity estimation process in Exhibit 8.3, which is evaluating the stability of the companies' operating risk and financial leverage risk, as it informs us about the time period we should use to estimate beta.

EXHIBIT 8.4	Steps in Estimating Beta of the Company's Common Stock
1	Decide to use commercially available beta estimate or develop own estimate (if using commercially available estimate, stop sub-process here; however, you should identify underlying assumptions that link to the market risk premium and risk-free rate estimates, as well as understand the period over which beta is estimated)
2	Choose a market index (links to the market risk premium estimation process)
3	Choose an estimation period (length of period and specific dates)
4	Choose the periodicity for the stock return (daily, weekly, or monthly interval)
5	Collect the necessary data and estimate the market model
6	Make adjustments, if any, for mean reversion and other effects

The Equity Cost of Capital Used in Valuation is Forward Looking but Estimated Using Historical Data

When we estimate a company's cost of capital for purposes of valuing it, we require a **forward-looking** estimate of that cost of capital, that is, a cost of capital relevant for discounting future free cash flows. Unfortunately, the regression approach used to measure beta uses historical information, and therefore represents the historical beta. As we discuss next, the estimate of beta can shift from one estimation period to another for the same company. This effect can be due to just the noise in estimated betas or it can be due to shifts in economic fundamentals, which change the systematic risk of the company or its industry. Below, we discuss ways that we can adjust betas estimated using historical data so they better represent more forward-looking betas, but it is useful to remember that by necessity we start with something that is historical, not forward looking.

The Market Model

The **market model** represents a direct way to estimate the beta of an asset or security using historical information. It can also further strengthen our intuition for why beta is the measure of risk that is priced in the CAPM. Since we are focused on estimating the cost of equity capital, we focus our discussion on using the market model to estimate equity betas using stock returns; however, it is possible to use the market model for any asset or security if the necessary data are available. We estimate the parameters of the **market model**, one of which is beta, using regression analysis. Such regressions are typically referred to as **market model regressions**. **Regression analysis** is a statistical method that explains the variation in a **dependent variable** with other variables called **independent variables**. A regression model has one dependent variable and can have one or more independent variables.

The standard market model regression has one independent variable; it is a "simple" regression where the stock return of the company for which we are estimating beta is the dependent variable (left-hand-side variable) and the contemporaneous return on a proxy for the market portfolio is the independent variable (right-hand-side variable). We estimate the regression using a time-series (from $t = 1$ to $t = T$) of the stock returns, R_{it}, and the contemporaneous returns on the market index, R_{mt}. The equation for the market model is:

$$R_{it} = \alpha_i + \beta_i R_{mt} + \varepsilon_{it} \quad t = 1 .... T \tag{8.6}$$

The market model specifies that the return of a stock is equal to a constant, α_i, plus the asset's beta, β_i, multiplied by the return on the market, plus a shock or noise term. The estimate of β_i is the slope of the fitted regression line, and is an estimate of the beta of the CAPM. The estimated α_i is the intercept of the regression line on the vertical axis.

Assuming the data meet the assumptions required for ordinary least squares regression (primarily normality, stationarity, and serial independence of the error terms), the estimate of beta, $\hat{\beta}_i$, from a regression is an unbiased estimate of the true beta, β_i; in other words, the expected value of the estimated beta is equal to the true beta. The good news is that market model regressions are generally well specified so that all the properties that a regression should have are generally observed for market model regressions. This is not true universally, however. Of course, even though the expected value of the estimated beta is the true beta, the estimated beta from any particular regression could be above or below the true beta. The standard error of the beta estimate from the regression analysis describes the sampling variability of the beta estimate and thus measures the precision of the estimate (how precisely it is measured).

Return Dichotomization in the Market Model

The market model dichotomizes or disaggregates a company's stock return into two components—the part of the company's stock return explained by movements in the market index and the part of the company's stock return that is not explained by the movements in the market index. We typically describe the latter component as a firm-specific return. The firm-specific component is equal to $\alpha_i + \varepsilon_{it}$ and the market related component is equal to $\beta_i R_{mt}$. Similarly, the market model implies that the stock return variance can also be disaggregated into two parts. The expression for the stock return variance derived in terms of the market model equation is

$$\sigma^2(\tilde{R}_i) = \beta_i^2 \sigma^2(\tilde{R}_m) + \sigma^2(\tilde{\varepsilon}_i)$$

The first component represents the stock return variance related to the variance of the market return, which we call non-diversifiable risk or systematic risk. The second component is variance not explained by the market, which we call non-systematic risk, unsystematic risk, or idiosyncratic risk. Recall that we used all those terms previously in providing some intuition for the CAPM. If we divide both sides of the above formula by the variance of the stock's returns, we can measure the proportion of a company's stock return explained by the market.

$$\frac{\sigma^2(\tilde{R}_i)}{\sigma^2(\tilde{R}_i)} = 1 = \beta_i^2 \frac{\sigma^2(\tilde{R}_m)}{\sigma^2(\tilde{R}_i)} + \frac{\sigma^2(\tilde{\varepsilon}_i)}{\sigma^2(\tilde{R}_i)}$$

The first term on the right-hand side in the above formula, $\beta_i^2 \sigma^2(\tilde{R}_m)/\sigma^2(\tilde{R}_i)$, is the proportion of the variance of the return of the security that can be explained by variation in the market. The r-squared statistic from a market model regression is an estimate of this proportion.

Market Model Estimates for Four Example Companies

In Exhibit 8.5, we show scatter plots of the time-series observations of the monthly with-dividend stock returns of Hewlett Packard Development Company (HP), Wal-Mart Stores, Inc. (Wal-Mart), General Electric Company (GE), and Microsoft Corporation (Microsoft) paired with the contemporaneous with-dividend returns on the S&P 500 from January 2006 to December 31, 2010 (60 months of return data in all). We also show the estimated regression lines from estimating a market model regression of the return on each security against the return on the S&P 500.

These are fairly typical scatter plots for market model regressions. Since the market does not explain all of the variation of the stock returns of any company, the data points do not all lie on the estimated regression lines. The vertical deviation between each data point and the fitted regression line is the error term, ε_{it}, in the market model equation.

In Exhibit 8.6, we provide certain summary statistics for the market model regressions for these companies. We report the estimated beta, the standard error of the beta estimate, the t-statistic to test if beta is significantly different from zero, the 95% confidence interval for the estimated beta, and the adjusted r-squared of the regression. The betas for the individual companies range from a low of 0.31 for Wal-Mart to a high of 1.61 for GE. All of the betas are statistically significantly different from zero based on the t-statistics,[13] and the adjusted r-squareds of the regressions for the individual companies range from a low of 11% for Wal-Mart to a high of 64% for GE—the latter is very high for a market model regression on an individual company, but GE is a highly diversified company in its own right.

While all of these beta estimates are statistically different from zero, this exhibit shows that estimates of beta can have large confidence intervals. For example, the smallest standard error is 0.11 for Wal-Mart.

---

[13] With 60 observations, any t-statistic greater than 2.0 or less than −2.0 indicates that we can reject the hypothesis that the true beta is equal to zero at the 5% significance level (which means that there is only a 5% chance that we are wrong). Consistent with that, note that zero does not fall within the 95% confidence interval for any of these stocks.

EXHIBIT 8.5   Scatter Plots and Market Model Regression Lines for Four Companies

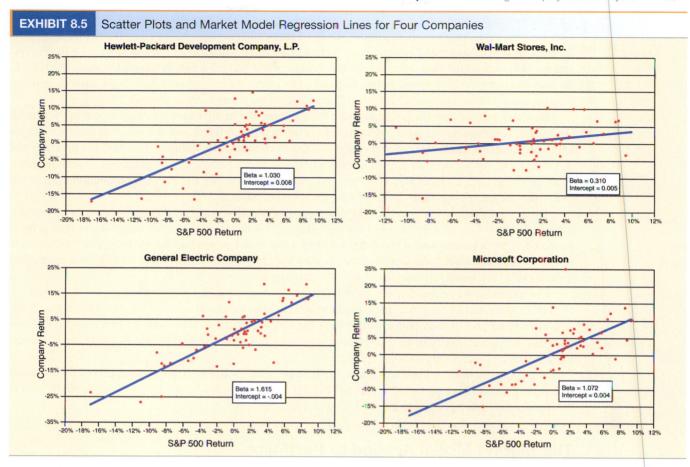

EXHIBIT 8.6   Market Model Regression Statistic for Four Companies

	Beta Estimate	Standard Error of Beta	t-statistic	95% Confidence Interval Lower Bound	95% Confidence Interval Upper Bound	Adjusted r-squared
Wal-Mart Stores, Inc.	0.31	0.11	2.74	0.09	0.53	0.11
General Electric Company	1.61	0.16	10.25	1.31	1.92	0.64
Microsoft Corp.	1.07	0.15	7.24	0.78	1.36	0.47
Hewlett-Packard Development Co.	1.03	0.12	8.38	0.79	1.27	0.55
Equally weighted portfolio	1.01	0.07	15.08	0.88	1.14	0.80

But even for Wal-Mart, the 95% confidence interval is from about 0.1 to 0.5. For GE, which has the largest standard error among the four companies (0.16), the 95% confidence interval ranges from 1.3 to 1.9. It should be noted, and we'll see more evidence on standard errors later in the chapter, that these are reasonably small standard errors when estimating market model regressions at the individual company level. You should also note that the standard error for the beta estimate of the equally weighted portfolio is lower, a topic we return to later in the chapter.

Equity Betas Capture Systematic Financial Risk and Business Risk

While we have talked about the statistics of measuring a beta in the context of a market model regression, let's talk about the underlying economics of a company that determines its equity beta. A company's equity beta, or systematic risk, comes from two different sources of risk—financial risk and business or operating risk. This notion has been the topic of research for many years.[14] Financial risk is the risk that results from

---

[14] See, for example, Brenner, M., and S. Smidt, "Asset Characteristics and Systematic Risk," *Financial Management* (Winter 1978), pp. 33–39, who model the relation between systematic risk and fixed costs, contribution margin, and the covariance of revenues with the market. Also see Mandelker, G., and S. Rhee, "The Impact of the Degrees of Operating and Financial Leverage on Systematic Risk of Common Stock," *Journal of Financial and Quantitative Analysis* (March 1984), pp. 45–57, who empirically document the relation between a company's systematic risk and its operating and financial risk.

the fixed cost associated with financial leverage (interest payments or preferred stock dividends—payments with priority over distributions to equityholders). **Financial leverage** results from fixed financing costs (interest on debt). A company with a higher degree of leverage will have a common stock with higher systematic risk, or a higher beta, relative to what its beta would be with lower levels of leverage. We refer to the beta of a company's operating or business risk as its unlevered beta or asset beta. We discuss the relation between equity betas, unlevered betas, and financial leverage extensively in Chapter 10.

Business risk or operating risk has two components.[15] The first component is operating leverage. **Operating leverage** results from having fixed operating costs. A **fixed cost** is a cost that does not change with volume and a **variable cost** is a cost that directly changes with volume. The world is naturally not that simple. A cost is rarely only fixed or only variable—over a sufficiently large change in volume, most costs vary; and over a sufficiently short time interval, many costs are fixed. Fixed production costs result in a higher degree of operating leverage and, thus, higher business risk.

The second component is **cyclicality** or **revenue cyclicality**, which is the sensitivity of a company's revenue (or how sensitive the demand for the company's products and product prices are) to the general economy. The more sensitive a company's revenues are to the general economy, the more business risk it has; thus, all else equal, more cyclical companies have more business risk than non-cyclical companies if their cycles are positively correlated with the economy.

For example, we know that the automobile and construction industries are more cyclical than the food processing and mining industries; thus, the automobile and construction industries have higher business risk. Examples of factors that might drive the revenue cyclicality component of a company's business risk are its sensitivity to general economic growth, inflation, the cost of borrowing in the economy, input prices, and the ability to adjust prices.

If a company does not use any financial leverage, then its equity beta is a measure of its operating or business risk and is equal to its unlevered beta. If a company uses financial leverage, its equity beta is determined by both its business risk and financial risk.

The Market Model Applied to Portfolios

Just as the CAPM is applicable to both individual securities and portfolios of securities, the market model is applicable to both also. The market model regression in terms of portfolio p is written as

$$\tilde{R}_{pt} = \alpha_p + \beta_p \tilde{R}_{mt} + \tilde{\varepsilon}_{pt} \quad t = 1......T \tag{8.7}$$

And the variance of the portfolio's return based on the market model is

$$\sigma^2(\tilde{R}_p) = \beta_p^2 \sigma^2(\tilde{R}_m) + \sigma^2(\tilde{\varepsilon}_p)$$

What happens to $\sigma^2(\tilde{\varepsilon}_p)$ as the number of securities in the portfolio increases, that is, approaches the securities in the market portfolio used to estimate the market model? In the limit, $\sigma^2(\tilde{\varepsilon}_p)$ approaches zero, implying that all of the variation in a portfolio's return can be explained by variation in the market in conjunction with the beta of the portfolio. Consequently, the r-squared of a market model regression approaches 1.0 (100%) as the portfolio becomes more diversified and more similar to the market used to estimate the market model.

REVIEW EXERCISE 8.3

Systematic Risk and Unsystematic Risk

Assume a portfolio has monthly stock returns with a standard deviation of 0.155, and the standard deviation of the market portfolio of monthly returns is 0.06. The portfolio has an estimated beta of 1.3. Calculate the proportion of the portfolio's stock return variance that represents systematic risk and the proportion that represents unsystematic risk. Is the portfolio well diversified?

Solution on page 333.

---

[15] For a discussion of this issue, see Brenner, M., and S. Smidt, "Asset Characteristics and Systematic Risk," *Financial Management* (Winter 1978), pp. 33–39.

Market Model Regression for a Portfolio of the Four Companies

In the last line of Exhibit 8.6, we show the results of a market model regression for an equally weighted portfolio of the four companies (add the four companies' stock returns together for a period and divide by 4). The portfolio beta is equal to 1.01, which is equal to the sum of the betas of the companies divided by 4. This is what we would expect because we know from Equation 8.4 that a portfolio beta is the weighted average of the individual security betas. Also as we expect, the market explains more of the variance of the portfolio of the four security portfolio (the r-squared is 80%) than any individual stock. In addition, the standard error of the four-stock portfolio beta is lower, indicating the 95% confidence interval has a smaller range.

These results are not surprising. As we increase the number of securities in a portfolio we reduce the amount of idiosyncratic risk in the portfolio, and that generally decreases the standard error of the beta estimates of the portfolio. That is why using comparable companies can increase the precision of our beta estimate (reduces the standard error). While we can never eliminate all of the uncertainty, the use of comparable companies can reduce the degree of uncertainty. Of course, the comparable companies must truly be comparable if this technique is to actually improve our estimates of the cost of capital.

From the market model, we know that the variance in the return of a portfolio is equal to beta squared multiplied by the variation in the return on the market plus the variance of the portfolio's idiosyncratic term. In a well-diversified portfolio, if the idiosyncratic error term approaches zero, then all the variation in the portfolio's return is determined almost entirely by the market return and the portfolio's beta. Individual investors cannot choose the variance of the market, but they do get to choose the beta of their portfolio. Within the assumptions of the CAPM, since the risk (variance) of a well-diversified portfolio is proportional to its beta and the portfolio beta is just the weighted average of the betas of the securities in the portfolio, the risk premium earned on an individual stock is also proportional to beta.

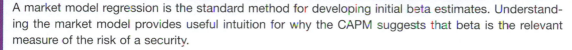

Valuation Key 8.6

A market model regression is the standard method for developing initial beta estimates. Understanding the market model provides useful intuition for why the CAPM suggests that beta is the relevant measure of the risk of a security.

8.5 BETA ESTIMATION: ASSUMPTIONS AND CHOICES

In the previous section of the chapter we introduced the market model. In this section of the chapter, we discuss the specific steps we follow and decisions we make to estimate beta using a market model. We discuss the choice of a market index, which links to the market risk premium estimation process, an estimation period (length of period and specific dates, which links to the period of time over which the company's business and financial risk were constant), the periodicity for measuring stock returns (daily, weekly, or monthly interval, which links to the amount of data available when the company's business and financial risk were stable), and certain adjustments we might make to the market model, depending on the circumstances. Even if we are using commercially available betas, it is important to understand the issues we discuss here, as these issues are important to decide what commercial estimate to use and how to adjust it, if necessary.

Choice of Proxy for the Market Portfolio (Market Index)

The market portfolio in the theoretical derivation of the CAPM is the value-weighted index of all risky assets in the world. While that is the theoretical construct, in practice, we implement the model differently as we have no estimates of the returns to such a market portfolio. Thus, one factor to consider in the choice of an index is what securities to include in the index. Since we use the CAPM to price equity securities, we typically use a broad-based stock market index and do not include other types of assets such as bonds, real estate, and so forth. The primary reason for not including these other assets is the abundance of stock return data and the relative paucity of return data for other types of assets.

One important factor to consider when choosing a market index to estimate beta is what market index you will choose to estimate the market risk premium. The two choices are linked to each other in that the same index must be used for estimating both beta and the market risk premium. For example, assume we can use either a broad market index of stocks to estimate the beta for a company and market risk premium or an index of these same stocks and a broad index of corporate bonds. We know that the risk (volatility) of a broad-based stock index is higher than the risk (volatility) of that same broad-based stock index combined with a bond index because bonds have less risk than stocks. We also know that the expected return on a stock-only index will be greater than the expected return on the combined stock and bond index.

As such, the market risk premium estimated using the stock-only index would be larger than the market risk premium estimated using the combined stock and bond index. We would also expect a company's estimated stock beta to be higher using the stock and bond combined index than when using the stock-only index because beta is a measure of relative risk, that is, an asset's risk judged relative to a particular portfolio or index. If we use one index to estimate a company's beta and use a different index to estimate the market risk premium, the estimates will be inconsistent. While using a stock index versus using a combined stock and bond index is a somewhat extreme example, the same issues arise when mixing other indices. For example, we would not want to estimate a company's beta against the Wilshire 5000 and then estimate the market risk premium from the S&P 500.

Two additional factors to consider are whether to include dividends in the calculation of the returns to a stock index and whether to use a value-weighted or equal-weighted average index. Since the stock returns investors earn include the effect of dividends, we recommend using a market index that also includes the effect of dividends to estimate beta. Some indices, such as the S&P 500 as it is normally calculated, do not include the dividend component in the calculation of the return on the index. We recommend including dividends. Whenever we use the returns to the S&P 500 in this book, we have calculated the returns with dividends. The last factor we discuss regarding the construction of the index is the weighting of the firms in the market index, usually either an equal or a value weighting. The CAPM assumes that the market portfolio is a value-weighted index of all risky assets, but practitioners use both equal-weighted and value-weighted indices, though value-weighted indices such as the S&P 500 are most commonly used.[16]

Domestic or World Index.

An issue that we discuss later in the book (see Chapter 17) is whether one should use a domestic index or a world index, or some other index altogether. As we explain in much more detail later, the decision depends on the appropriate reference portfolio for the shareholders of the company you are valuing. If we are valuing a U.S. company with almost all U.S. investors who primarily hold U.S. securities, we would choose a domestic index like the S&P 500. However, if we believed that investors in that U.S. company held a diversified world portfolio regardless of where they resided, we would use a world index. The former view of the world assumes that capital markets are segmented while the latter view assumes that capital markets are integrated and that capital flows freely around the world. We discuss this issue in greater detail in Chapter 17, and for now we just assume that markets are segmented, meaning that if we are interested in valuing a U.S. company, we would use a U.S. stock market index. Analogously, if we were valuing a Japanese firm, we would use a Japanese stock market index.

Number of Observations, Time Interval (Periodicity) for Measuring Returns, and Chronological Time Period

When we measure returns, we can measure them over virtually any time interval—hourly (or even shorter intervals), daily, weekly, monthly, quarterly, annually, and more. The most commonly used intervals for estimating betas are monthly, weekly, and, to a lesser extent, daily returns. The precision of regression parameters tends to increase with more observations; hence, all else equal, we prefer to use more observations.

Using more recent data might better reflect a company's current (and more forward-looking) systematic risk. Betas can shift because of changes in capital structure or because of changes in the underlying business risk of the company, or because of fundamental changes in the overall market. Using monthly

---

[16] On March 21, 2005, the weighting in the S&P 500 was changed to be based on the market value of the public float (shares held by the public) as opposed to the total number of shares outstanding. Wal-Mart and Microsoft have the biggest number of shares not in the public float and will accordingly now have less of an impact on the S&P 500. Had the S&P 500 index been calculated using the new rule from September 2003 to March 16, 2005, the difference in the return would have been 0.13%. See M. Krantz, *USA Today*, March 21, 2005 at http://www.usatoday.com/money/markets/us/2005-03-21-sp-usat_x.htm.

data, it is quite common to use 60 monthly observations, if the data are available and if there is no obvious indication that the beta has shifted. Some scholarly research indicates that 60 months of data is a reasonable time period over which to measure beta.[17] But we can sometimes get reasonable estimates of beta with as few as 30 observations, depending on the company and the circumstances. If we do not have a sufficient stable history of monthly returns, we would use a shorter return interval (for example, weekly or daily data).[18]

Many commercial services use monthly data; however, Bloomberg,[19] for example, uses weekly data as a default (although the user can specify the use of monthly data). The advantage of using data measured over a shorter interval is that we can generally estimate betas over a shorter and more recent time period, because given the same period of time we get more observations when each return is computed over a shorter interval. For example, the services that use monthly data generally use 60 monthly observations or five years of data, whereas Bloomberg uses 104 weeks of weekly observations or two years of data. Depending on the company and its characteristics, using more recent data might provide a better forward-looking estimate. However, if the company's operating risk and financial leverage have been stable for five years, the longer time period might provide a better forward-looking estimate.

The shorter the periodicity we choose to measure each return, the more likely that we will encounter statistical issues when we estimate the market model. One statistical issue is that over shorter return intervals, such as daily returns, the returns are more likely to be auto-correlated (last period's return is related to the next period's return). This is much less of an issue for monthly returns. Another issue is that the shorter the return interval, the greater the likelihood that the period over which the return on the stock is measured will not match the period over which the return on the market is measured because stocks might not trade precisely at the end of each interval. When this occurs we say that the returns are non-synchronous. In order to estimate the beta properly, the period over which the stock returns and index returns are measured must be matched. The more infrequently a stock trades, the more likely we encounter non-synchronous returns. We observe this effect for daily return intervals for many stocks. For stocks trading infrequently, this effect can even occur in monthly return intervals to some extent, and it is more likely to occur in emerging markets where trading is less frequent.

One method we can use to correct for non-synchronous trading is to include both lead and lagged market returns in the market model regression.[20] In other words, we estimate the following regression:

$$R_{it} = \alpha_i + \beta_{i,lag}R_{mt-1} + \beta_iR_{mt} + \beta_{i,lead}R_{mt+1} + \varepsilon_{it} \quad t = 1.......T \qquad (8.8)$$

The advantage of this technique is that if the returns are non-synchronous, the lead and lag terms help correct for the non-synchronicity. To calculate the estimated beta from this version of the market model, we simply add the three beta terms together, $\beta_{i,lag} + \beta_i + \beta_{i,lead}$.

Using Daily and Weekly Data to Adjust for Changes in Operations and Capital Structure

We indicated that monthly returns may have advantages relative to daily or weekly data if we believe infrequent trading potentially exists. However, a company's risk characteristics are more likely to shift the

---

[17] See Alexander, G., and N. Chervany, "On the Estimation and Stability of Beta," *Journal of Financial and Quantitative Analysis* 15 (1980), pp. 123–137. They show that four- and six-year estimation periods are superior to alternative estimation periods varying between one and nine years.

[18] While using 60 months is common in practice, Eugene Fama and Ken French provide some indirect and preliminary evidence that a longer estimation period, in fact substantially longer than 60 months, may work better. In their study, they estimate industry costs of equity capital (not firm-specific estimates of the cost of capital). They document that, when estimating CAPM betas for industries, estimation periods of up to 26 years work best for longer forecast horizons of a year or longer. This evidence suggests that industry betas are mean reverting and using the longer time period dampens the effect of any wanderings the industry beta may take from its underlying mean. However, for short-term forecasts of one month, they find using the past 60 months of returns works best. This approach has not been studied at the company level as of yet. See Fama, E., and K. French, "Industry Costs of Equity," *Journal of Financial Economics* 43 (1997), pp. 153–193.

[19] Bloomberg L. P. is a company that produces and sells various types of market and financial data. See http://about.bloomberg.com/pressctr/index.html for more information and a description of the company, its products, and its services.

[20] See M. Scholes and J. Williams, "Estimating Betas from Nonsynchronous Data," *Journal of Financial Economics* 5 (1977), pp. 309–327; Dimson, E., "Risk Measurement When Shares Are Subject to Infrequent Trading," *Journal of Financial Economics* 7 (1979), pp. 197–226.

longer the time period used for estimating beta. The underlying business risk can shift because of major acquisitions, divestitures, shifts in the company's primary business, or simply because of structural shifts in the economy that cause the underlying business to have a different systematic risk with the overall market. To address this issue, we might use either weekly or daily returns so we can estimate the beta over a shorter time period. Alternatively, we may be able to measure beta prior to the structural shift and then adjust the beta for the structural shift.

Valuation in Practice 8.1

Estimating Laureate Education, Inc.'s Beta After a Major Divestiture Laureate Education, Inc. ("the Company" or "Laureate") is focused exclusively on providing a superior higher education experience through a leading global network of accredited campus-based and online universities and other higher education institutions ("higher education institutions" or "schools").

On June 30, 2003, Sylvan Learning Systems, Inc. sold the principal operations that comprised its K–12 educational services segments. As a result, the Company changed its name from Sylvan Learning Systems, Inc. to Laureate Education, Inc. The selling price of the K–12 segment on June 30, 2003, was $283.4 million dollars, which was roughly 35% of Sylvan Learning Systems' total firm value prior to the sale. In addition to the significant divestiture, Laureate reduced its market value debt to equity ratio from approximately 25% to 6%.

Suppose you were interested in valuing Laureate as of March 31, 2005. How would you estimate its beta given its new business mix? The significant divestiture and change in leverage make it difficult to use monthly data because we have only 21 monthly returns since the changes took place. If we estimate Laureate's beta using the 21 monthly returns, we obtain a beta estimate of 0.31 with a standard error of 0.70 for a 95% confidence interval of −1.15 to 1.77, not a particularly useful result. If we use daily returns, the company's beta estimated from January 1, 2000, to June 30, 2003, is 0.51 (prior to the transaction, when it was still Sylvan Learning Systems, Inc.). Laureate's beta post-transaction, estimated from July 1, 2003, to March 31, 2005, is 1.02. Thus, despite the decline in leverage, Laureate's equity beta approximately doubled with the shift in operations. The estimated beta of 1.02 utilizing daily data between July 1, 2003, and March 31, 2005, has a standard error of 0.09 for a 95% confidence interval from 0.85 to 1.20. This example illustrates the potential benefit of using a shorter time period for estimation in conjunction with higher-frequency data for estimating beta when there has been a shift in a company's operations.

Source: See Laureate Education, Inc.'s December 31, 2004 10-K Report, p. 3.

When using daily data, a common rule of thumb is to use one to two years of data (a typical year has approximately 260 trading days). When using weekly data, it is a fairly common practice to use two years of data (104 observations). The advantage of daily and weekly data relative to monthly data is that we use a more recent history of returns to estimate beta, but we have to make sure we do not run into statistical issues such as asynchronous returns.

Valuation Key 8.7

Before attempting to estimate a company's equity beta, first assess the stability of the company's business risk and risk from financial leverage. Changes in operations or capital structure can cause instability in beta estimates measured in periods that span such changes. Using a shorter return interval (weekly or daily) may provide a sufficient number of observations to estimate beta after such shifts occur.

Mean Reversion in Estimated Betas and Adjusted Betas

In examining estimated betas, we find that estimated betas have a tendency to revert back toward the mean of the market beta, which is 1. This effect is often referred to as **mean reversion** in estimated betas. The betas we estimate from a market model equal the true beta plus noise (measurement error). In other words, we cannot observe a company's true beta. By examining the behavior of estimated betas over time, we can infer that, on average, estimated betas that are greater than 1 have positive noise terms (or positive measurement error), and estimated betas that are less than 1 have negative noise terms (negative measurement error). Thus, on average, but not for every company, beta estimates that are greater than 1 tend to be upward biased and estimated betas that are less than 1 tend to be downward biased, even though, on average, beta is an unbiased estimate of the true beta.

An early study of this phenomenon was undertaken by Marshall Blume in 1971.[21] He divided his observations up into six different time periods and examined how betas moved between one time period and the next time period. For each adjacent two time periods, he estimated a regression using the second period's beta for each security i as the dependent variable and the first period's beta for each security i as the independent variable (which we refer to as $\beta_{i,2}$ and $\beta_{i,1}$). On average across all of his regressions of adjacent time periods, he found that:

$$\beta_{i,2} = 0.371 + 0.635\ \beta_{i,1}$$

That finding is of course consistent with the mean reversion phenomena discussed earlier. This formula implies that the best prediction of the beta you will observe in the second period if the first period's beta is 2.0 is equal to 1.641 ($1.641 = 0.371 + 0.635 \times 2.0$). If the first period's estimated beta is 0.4, the best prediction of that beta in period 2 is 0.625 ($0.625 = 0.371 + 0.635 \times 0.4$). Thus, the best prediction of next period's beta is that it is closer to one.

Valuation in Practice 8.2

Commercially Available Estimated Betas Exhibit Considerable Variation Commercially available beta estimates vary. The variation results from different assumptions and choices, such as a different market index, return interval, number of observations for estimation, and how to adjust, if at all, for mean reversion. The chart below presents five different sources of betas on our four example companies available as of August 10, 2011.

	General Electric	Microsoft	Wal-Mart	Hewlett Packard
Bloomberg—Unadjusted[a].	1.407	0.872	0.468	1.116
Bloomberg—Adjusted[a].	1.272	0.915	0.646	1.077
FactSet[b]	1.413	0.870	0.460	1.112
Value Line[c]	1.200	0.800	0.600	0.950
Yahoo! Finance[d]	1.860	0.980	0.370	1.030

[a] The user can specify the type of returns, the index, and the number of observations used, but the default is two years of weekly data against the S&P 500 index, and adjusted betas are available using 0.33 + 0.67 × unadjusted beta.

[b] The user can specify the type of returns, the index, and the number of observations. FactSet defaults depend on the screen used; above betas calculated using two years of weekly return regressed against the S&P 500 index.

[c] Calculated using five years of weekly returns against the New York Stock Exchange Composite Index and betas are adjusted for mean reversion using 0.35 + 0.67 × unadjusted beta.

[d] Calculated using one year of weekly data against the S&P 500 index.

Blume's results could be just a statistical issue (the measurement error we have been discussing) or it could simply be that over time, firms choose projects that naturally move them closer to 1. Subsequent work shows that we still observe substantial mean reversion whether we run the regression as discussed earlier or when we perform the regression in reverse ($\beta_{i,2}$ becomes the independent variable and $\beta_{i,1}$ becomes the dependent variable). The result also stands for portfolios or for individual securities.[22] The same pattern exists if we use every other day to estimate betas or even and odd months. Thus, this result appears to be a statistical issue, not an economic one; fortunately, we have procedures to adjust for this effect if necessary.

---

[21] See Blume, M. E., "On the Assessment of Risk," *Journal of Finance* 26 (1971), pp. 1–10.

[22] See Elgers, P. T., J. R. Haltiner, and W. H. Hawthorne, "Beta Regression Tendencies: Statistical and Real Causes," *Journal of Finance* 34 (March, 1979), pp. 261–263.

Many practitioners and suppliers of commercial estimates adjust their betas and provide so-called **adjusted betas**. For many, the technique they use follows closely from the work of Blume. Bloomberg, for example, provides both historical and adjusted betas. Bloomberg's adjusted beta is

$$\text{Bloomberg Adjusted Beta} = 0.33 + 0.67 \times \text{Historical Beta}$$

Valuation Key 8.8

Beta estimates appear to regress toward the mean beta of 1.0 because of statistical reasons. Thus, if the regression estimate of beta is above 1.0, we might adjust it downward; if it is below 1.0, we might adjust it upward. There is also evidence of reversion back to the mean industry beta. Various adjustment processes are available to adjust for these effects.

8.6 ADJUSTING ESTIMATED BETAS FOR CHANGES IN RISK (NON-STATIONARY BETAS)

A company's betas will change if either financial or operating risk changes. For example, IBM's beta was around 0.8 for most of the 1980s and then declined in the early 1990s to approximately 0.6. Starting in the mid-1990s, IBM's beta increased, eventually to the 1.4 to 1.6 range. Two fundamental economic factors appear to have impacted IBM's beta. First, in the mid-1990s, IBM's market debt to equity leverage ratio increased from the 5% to 10% range to over 40%, reaching 62% at the end of 1993. In addition, IBM was turning from primarily a computer hardware company to a company that sold services. The service business (which was more risky than IBM's hardware business) had become increasingly important to IBM over time. While the leverage levels declined back to the 10% to 15% range since 2000, services and software became increasingly important to IBM. By 2004, services represented 48% of IBM's revenues and about 32% of its gross profit. In 1994, services accounted for 15% of IBM's revenue and only 4.4% of its gross profit.

Direct Adjustments to Beta for Changes in Operations

If we have sufficient information, we can make direct adjustments for changes in certain types of operations and for changes in capital structure. We discuss how to adjust betas for changes in capital structure in Chapter 10. Here we discuss how to adjust betas for changes in operations. Generally when this is done, we adjust a company's unlevered betas, but that is not always the case, as we shall see.

Recall from Equation 8.4 that the beta of a portfolio is simply the weighted average of the betas of the securities in the portfolio, where the weights are relative market values. So the equity beta of a portfolio is just the weighted average of the equity betas of the individual securities in the portfolio. This same principle is also applicable to the composition of a company's unlevered beta or asset beta. An unlevered beta is the weighted average of the betas of the firm's assets (or projects). As it turns out, this is a useful result and sometimes can help us adjust betas for changes in operations.

To see how we might use this relation, assume that we were interested in trying to estimate what America OnLine (AOL) and Time Warner, Inc.'s (Time Warner) beta would be after they merged in January of 2001. In other words, assume it is early in the year 2000, but the merger will not close until early 2001. We could forecast what AOL/Time Warner's beta would be after the merger as follows. First, we would estimate Time Warner's beta and AOL's beta separately. Then, we would calculate the weighted average beta based on the relative weights. In this case, the companies merged in a stock-for-stock transaction, so the balance sheets were essentially just merged together. The merging of the balance sheets is what allows us to assume that the equity beta after the merger will be the weighted average of the pre-merger equity betas of the two companies, along with an assumption that value will neither be created nor destroyed by the merger. Had this not been the case, we would have had to have worked with unlevered betas of the two companies in this example and then relevered the unlevered beta for the anticipated capital structure.

In the case of AOL and Time Warner, the equity beta of the combined company should equal the market value weighted average of the equity betas, assuming there are no subsequent changes in capital structure. Of course, this presumes that the merger has no significant effect on value. If the total amount of debt stays the same after the merger but the value of the firm increases from synergies, then the amount of financial leverage will decrease. Also, in some transactions, capital structures might be anticipated to change and appropriate adjustments would have to be made for that. For purposes of this analysis, we assume the leverage of the company is expected to stay the same.

At the time of the merger announcement, AOL's equity was 42% of the total equity value of AOL and Time Warner, and Time Warner was 58% of the total. AOL's pre-merger beta was approximately 2.7 and Time Warner's pre-merger beta was 1.2. Weighting the pre-merger betas by the market values at the time of announcement yields an estimate of the combined firm's beta of 1.83 ($1.83 = 0.42 \times 2.7 + 0.58 \times 1.2$). Hence, we would anticipate a combined beta of approximately 1.8. It turns out that the post-merger beta was in the 2.1 range, higher than we anticipated.

Our analysis did not predict the post-merger beta correctly because two changes occurred that our calculation did not anticipate. First, AOL/Time Warner issued more debt subsequent to the transaction and thus the amount of debt of the combined firm was slightly greater than our calculation anticipated. Second, by the time of the close of the merger, the market values of both companies had decreased by approximately one-third and the new company was now much more highly levered than expected. The value of the combined company continued to fall subsequent to the close, thus making the company even more highly levered in the months and years after the closing. As such, it is not a surprise that the beta of AOL/Time Warner would be greater than our prediction of 1.8 since that calculation presumed there would be no increase in leverage, which proved to be incorrect.

In the case of AOL and Time Warner, we made our prediction by working with the equity betas directly. Had we known that the capital structures were going to change, we could have first calculated unlevered betas, weighted the unlevered betas based on the market values of AOL and Time Warner, and then adjusted the unlevered betas for the capital structure of the merged entity. In that case, we would unlever each company's beta, calculate the unlevered beta of the combined company, and then lever back up for the capital structure of the combined company. We discuss levering and unlevering betas in Chapter 10, but it is analogous to levering and unlevering cost of capital estimates as discussed in Chapter 5.

Direct Adjustments to Unlevered Betas for Excess Assets and Divestitures

The basic principle that a company's unlevered asset beta is equal to the weighted average unlevered betas of its projects is also useful to make adjustments for excess assets or for divestitures. For example, Microsoft's equity beta in Exhibit 8.6 is 1.07. Since Microsoft did not have any significant debt during this period, its unlevered beta was also around 1.07. During this time period, Microsoft had about 20% of its market value in various types of cash instruments and marketable securities, which we will assume were all excess assets and have a beta of .15. Using this principle, we can estimate Microsoft's unlevered beta for its operations. Its unlevered beta for its operations would be $\beta_{\text{unlevered operations}}$ in the following formula

$$\beta_{\text{unlevered company}} = 0.2 \times \beta_{\text{marketable securities}} + (1 - .2) \times \beta_{\text{unlevered operations}}$$

$$1.07 = 0.2 \times .15 + (1 - .2) \times \beta_{\text{unlevered operations}}$$

Solving the above formula for $\beta_{\text{unlevered operations}}$, we estimate the unlevered beta of Microsoft's operations to be approximately 1.30.

We could perform a similar calculation for a company that was going to divest itself of a division or spin it off, if we wanted to estimate the beta of the remaining assets. Similarly, if we have sufficient information, we can use this same principle to estimate the unlevered beta of one of the business segments of a company.

Valuation Key 8.9

The beta of a portfolio is equal to the weighted average beta of the securities that make up that portfolio. Similarly, the beta of a company's assets—the company's unlevered beta—is equal to the weighted average beta of the assets (or projects) in which the company invests. We can use this relationship to make adjustments to beta for changes in the company's assets and to exclude the effect of a company's excess assets on its beta.

Shifting Betas in the Future

It is possible that we might anticipate beta shifting in the future because of expected changes in the underlying economics. For example, suppose you are valuing a firm that produces jets for the government and has a five-year backlog for those planes, sold on a "cost plus" basis. Business beyond five years depends on the company obtaining additional contracts. It is possible that the risk of the first five years of cash flows is different from the risk of the cash flows beyond five years. The government may purchase more planes when the economy is good and tax revenues are high than when the economy is poor and tax receipts are down. In that case, the relevant beta for the first five years of cash flows for this company could be smaller than the beta of the cash flows starting in Year 6.

REVIEW EXERCISE 8.4

Adjusting Estimated Betas

Part 1—Assume Company A that operates in the transportation equipment industry and has an estimated equity beta of 1.7 is planning to merge with Company B that operates in the trucking and warehousing industry and has an estimated equity beta of 1.0. At the time of the announcement of the merger, Company B's equity was twice the market value of Company A's equity. Estimate the combined firm's equity beta after the merger, assuming that debt in the merged entity will be equal to the pre-merger debt of Company A and Company B combined and the merger is not expected to create or destroy value.

Part 2—Company C has an estimated beta of 1.5 and does not have any debt or other non-common-equity financing. The company has 30% of its total market value invested in marketable securities that have an estimated beta of 0.4 and are assumed to be excess assets. Estimate the unlevered beta for Company C's operations.

Solution on page 334.

8.7 USING COMPARABLE COMPANIES TO ESTIMATE BETAS

One of the reasons we use comparable companies, even when a firm is publicly traded, is to increase the precision of our estimates. We did not report this earlier, but we estimated the standard errors of the portfolio betas of the portfolios we described in Exhibit 8.1 (remember that we constructed portfolios with the number of firms in the portfolio ranging from 1 to 125 and we constructed 1,000 portfolios of each size of portfolio). When we estimate the portfolio betas, the average standard error across the 1,000 replications for the portfolio of just one firm was 0.26 (think about what that implies about a 95% confidence interval—the point estimate plus or minus 0.52). Increasing the portfolio to just five firms brought the average standard error of the portfolio beta down to 0.13—a drop of 50%. With a portfolio of 10 firms, the average standard error of the portfolio beta was 0.10. Thus, if we have a set of truly comparable companies, we feel we can gain precision in our estimate of the cost of capital by using multiple companies.

The business risk of a company is determined by its revenue cyclicality and its operating leverage. When we choose comparable companies for measuring the cost of capital, we are implicitly assuming that the comparable companies have the same revenue cyclicality and operating leverage as the company we are valuing. In other words, the revenues of those companies should all react similarly to changes in overall economic conditions and they should have similar cost structures.

We begin the process of choosing comparable companies by choosing close competitors and then asking whether there is any indication that any of the comparable companies might have a different degree of revenue cyclicality or degree of operating leverage. For example, the degree of operating leverage could be different if two firms use very different production processes or have different business models. For example, a restaurant chain that leases all of its locations is likely to have a much higher fixed cost structure than a restaurant chain that uses a franchise model for its business where the company owns none of the restaurant locations. We do not generally worry about the degree to which the financial leverage is the same across the companies, as we control for differences in financial leverage through the levering and unlevering process.

Use Individual Betas Not Portfolio Betas to Achieve Precision Improvements

When we use comparable companies, we generally do not estimate the portfolio beta. Rather, we estimate each company's betas separately. We would not estimate a portfolio beta for the portfolio of the comparable companies or for all the companies in an industry unless we can assume that the capital structure of the company we are valuing is close to the average capital structure embedded in the portfolio. Instead, after estimating each company's beta, we use the unlevering process on each of the comparable companies to adjust each company for its own capital structure. Once we have the unlevered betas of the comparable companies, we use the distribution of the unlevered betas to measure the unlevered beta of the company we are valuing. Even though we do not estimate portfolio betas directly in this method, we achieve a similar reduction in the standard error as indicated by the standard error of the portfolio beta.

Of course, when we use comparable companies, we are assuming that the business risk (unlevered cost of capital) is the same for each of the comparable companies. If the comparable companies have different business risks than the company we are valuing, then using comparable companies would not result in more precise beta estimates. One of the trade-offs we make in choosing comparable companies is that generally, the standard error of the portfolio beta declines by increasing the number of comparable companies, but as we add comparable companies, the degree of comparability (e.g., the similarity of the business risk) may decrease.

What does the standard error of the beta estimate actually tell us about the imprecision of the estimated beta? It is possible for a company's beta to shift over time due to changes in operations, changes in capital structure, or changes in market conditions. The standard error provides information about the imprecision of the beta estimate based on the historical data, which could be the result of such shifts or the inability of the market to explain the company's stock return. The standard error does not provide definitive information that a shift occurred. For example, if we estimated a company's beta using data through December 2012, and the company significantly changed its operations or capital structure toward the end of that time period, the standard error that we estimated would provide information about the degree of imprecision we had in estimating the historical beta, but would provide little or no information about the potential imprecision we would face because of the recent change in the company's operations or capital structure if we were to apply that beta to determine a forward-looking cost of capital estimate. We analyze the companies whose betas we plan to estimate in order to ensure that shifts in operations or capital structure have not occurred—or if they have occurred, we make appropriate adjustments for those changes when possible. If shifts in operations or capital structure have occurred and appropriate adjustments are not possible, we will likely eliminate that firm as a comparable company.

Determining the Company's Unlevered Beta from the Comparable Companies' Unlevered Betas

After we unlever all of the comparable company betas, we can use alternative ways to assess the unlevered beta we use for the company we are valuing. We have a distribution of unlevered betas and can use the mean, median, a range of betas, a point on the distribution (if we believe the company's unlevered beta is higher or lower than the median or average beta), or we can calculate a weighted average. The weights we use depend on our professional judgment. For example, we might use market values to weight betas or we might decide to assign more weight to companies that are similar in size. We could also use some other characteristic that we believe is correlated with the degree of comparability.

In addition, if we believe the comparable companies are equally comparable, we could also use the precision of the unlevered beta estimates to weight the betas, using the standard errors of the unlevered betas for weights, called a **precision weighted beta**:

$$\beta_{\text{Precision Weighted}} = \frac{\sum_{i=1}^{N} \beta_i \left(\frac{1}{\sigma_{\text{SE}, \beta_i}} \right)}{\sum_{i=1}^{N} \left(\frac{1}{\sigma_{\text{SE}, \beta_i}} \right)} \qquad (8.9)$$

where $\sigma_{SE,\,\beta_i}$ is the standard error of company i's beta. For example, assume we had two companies that had the following unlevered betas and standard errors of the unlevered betas.

Firm	β_i	$\sigma_{SE,\,\beta_i}$	$\dfrac{1}{\sigma_{SE,\,\beta_i}}$
A	1.0	0.4	2.5
B	2.0	0.1	10.0

An equally weighted average of those two betas would give us an estimated beta of 1.5. But a precision weighted average of those two betas would yield a beta of 1.8 [1.8 = (1.0 × 2.5 + 2.0 × 10.0)/ (2.5 + 10.0)]. As can be seen, the beta that is estimated more precisely is given more weight in the calculation.

The above calculation assumes we calculated the unlevered betas of the companies as well as the standard errors of the unlevered betas. However, when we estimate the market model, we observe the equity betas and the standard errors of the equity betas (assuming the company has leverage), but we don't observe unlevered betas and the standard errors of the unlevered betas directly. In Chapter 10, we describe how to calculate unlevered betas from equity betas. In addition, under a reasonable set of assumptions it can be shown that the standard error of the unlevered beta for a company is the standard error of the equity beta multiplied by the equity to value ratio (V_E/V_F). Note that if the company has no leverage (i.e., $V_E = V_F$), the standard error of the unlevered beta and equity beta are the same. To the extent the company has leverage, the standard error of the unlevered beta will be smaller than the standard error of the equity beta.

Oldrich Vasicek developed another adjustment technique.[23] This method allows one to adjust toward the mean of any specified portfolio's beta (a market beta or peer group beta or industry beta). The adjustment is a function of how noisy the beta estimate is for the individual firm relative to how much variation there is in the betas from a peer group, the market, or an industry.

$$\text{Vasicek Adjusted } \beta_i = \frac{\sigma_{\beta_P}^2}{\sigma_{SE,\,\beta_i}^2 + \sigma_{\beta_P}^2}\beta_i + \frac{\sigma_{SE,\,\beta_i}^2}{\sigma_{SE,\,\beta_i}^2 + \sigma_{\beta_P}^2}\beta_P \qquad (8.10)$$

where:

β_i = the beta for security i

β_P = the mean beta of some peer group, the market, or the industry

$\sigma_{SE,\,\beta_i}^2$ = the square of the standard error of the historical beta estimate for security i

$\sigma_{\beta_P}^2$ = the variance of the betas in the peer group, market, or industry.

Using this adjustment method, the adjusted beta is a weighted average of the beta estimate for the firm and the mean beta estimate for a benchmark portfolio of firms, such as a market, industry, or peer group. Suppose that we estimated the betas of 10 firms in a peer group and they were very close to one another with little variation. On the other hand, when we estimated the beta of the company of interest, its standard error was large. In this case, the Vasicek method would weight the mean beta of the peer group more heavily than the estimated beta of the firm of interest.

Valuation Key 8.10

Choosing comparable companies can increase the precision of our beta estimates. We must make the trade-off between more precise beta estimates with more comparable companies and the degree of comparability of the firms. We typically do not estimate a portfolio equity beta for the comparable companies because of capital structure differences. We estimate individual company equity betas, unlever the equity betas, and use the distribution of unlevered betas to measure the unlevered beta of the company we are valuing. We have discussed a variety of different techniques for weighting the individual unlevered betas.

---

[23] See Vasicek, O. A., "A Note on Using Cross-Sectional Information in Bayesian Estimation of Security Betas," *Journal of Finance* 28 (1973), pp. 1233–1239.

Valuation in Practice 8.3

Ibbotson Associates Estimates Beta in Multiple Ways Ibbotson Associates produces several alternative estimates of beta. One of its estimates uses a lag term, which Ibbotson calls a Sum Beta (similar to our Equation 8.8 without the lead term). Ibbotson also uses the Vasicek method to adjust beta estimates back to a peer industry group. Ibbotson Associates uses monthly data and generally uses 60 months of observations.

> For the CAPM model, we provide several equity beta statistics including traditional levered and unlevered ordinary least squares (OLS) estimates, levered and unlevered Sum Beta (including lag) estimates, peer group betas and levered and unlevered adjusted betas. Each of these statistics is intended to provide the user with additional information regarding the actual equity beta of each individual company.
>
> To estimate the beta of a company, monthly total returns of the company's stock, in excess of the risk-free asset, are regressed against the monthly total returns of the stock market in excess of the return on the risk-free asset.
>
> In all of the beta regressions the total returns of the S&P 500 are used as the proxy for the market returns. The series used as a proxy for the risk-free asset is the yield on the 30 day T-bill. Total returns for both individual stocks and the market proxy are determined by calculating price appreciation and dividend reinvestment. A sixty-month time frame is used for the regression. If less than sixty months of data are available for a company, the beta is then calculated using the months of data that are available with a minimum of thirty-six months as acceptable.

Source: See the website for Morningstar, where the company's beta book methodology is described at http://ccrc.morningstar .com/PDF/Methodology/(Methodology)%20Company%20Betas_08.pdf.

REVIEW EXERCISE 8.5

Bloomberg, Precision, and Vasicek Adjusted Betas

Calculate the Bloomberg adjusted beta for each of the comparable companies and the portfolio of comparable companies that appear in the table below. Also calculate the precision weighted beta for the four comparable companies and the company being valued as well as the equally weighted beta of the five companies using the unadjusted beta estimates. Last, calculate the Vasicek adjusted beta for the company being valued using its unadjusted beta estimate and the unadjusted betas of the four comparable companies. Assume all companies are unlevered.

	Beta Estimate	Standard Error of Beta	t-statistic
Comparable Company #1	0.900	0.50	1.80
Comparable Company #2	1.100	0.40	2.75
Comparable Company #3	1.350	0.60	2.25
Comparable Company #4	1.500	0.45	3.33
Comparable company average beta	1.213		
Company being valued	1.100	0.56	1.96

Solution on page 334.

8.8 ESTIMATING THE MARKET RISK PREMIUM

The market risk premium represents the expected return, above the return on the risk-free asset, demanded by the market to induce investors to invest in the market portfolio. More practically, it is the difference between the expected return on a proxy for the overall market less the return offered on a risk-free investment. At the current time, there is considerable debate about the most accurate way to estimate the market risk premium. While there is some debate about the most appropriate proxy for the market portfolio and the proxy for the risk-free rate, the major controversy for implementing the CAPM is how to estimate the expected market risk premium once the proxies are chosen for the market and the risk-free rate. For years, the most common approach was to calculate the historical average market risk premium over some long prior historical period. While this method is still used, other methods have been developed and are being used. Many of these methods use historical data, but some do not.

In Exhibit 8.7, we summarize the steps in estimating the market risk premium, and discuss them in this section of the chapter.

EXHIBIT 8.7	Steps in Estimating the Market Risk Premium
1	Decide to use a commercially available market risk premium estimate or develop own estimate (if using commercially available estimate, stop sub-process here; but make sure that the underlying assumptions link to the beta and risk-free rate estimates)
2	Decide which statistic to use to measure the market risk premium (average, geometric mean, or some other procedure)
3	Choose a market index (links to the beta estimation process) and a proxy for the risk-free asset (links to estimating the risk-free yield)
4	Choose an estimation period (how long of a period and specific beginning and ending dates)
5	Make adjustments, if any, for survivorship bias or other effects

The 1926 to 2011 U.S. Return Experience

Before we discuss the market risk premium, we first examine some historical security returns. Our goal is to glean some general information about the magnitude of the returns of different kinds of assets to help you understand some of the debates about estimating the market risk premium. Exhibit 8.8 presents the annual returns on various classes of assets measured over the 1926–2011 period.[24]

EXHIBIT 8.8	Total Annual U.S. Returns 1926–2011		
Return Series	**Geometric Mean**	**Arithmetic Mean**	**Standard Deviation**
S&P 500	9.8%	11.8%	20.3%
Small stocks.	11.9%	16.5%	32.5%
Long-term corp bonds	6.1%	6.4%	8.4%
Long-term gov't bonds	5.7%	6.1%	9.8%
Intermediate-term gov't bonds.	5.4%	5.5%	5.7%
U.S. Treasury Bills	3.6%	3.6%	3.1%
Inflation.	3.0%	3.1%	4.2%

Each line in the exhibit represents the return for a different class of assets traded in the United States between 1926 and 2011. The S&P 500 is the with-dividend returns earned on the Standard and Poor's 500, which tend to be very large capitalization stocks. Small stocks represent the returns to a portfolio of small stocks, but the construction of that series has changed somewhat over time.[25] The long-term corporate bonds are the returns earned on the Salomon Brothers High-Grade Corporate Bond Index. The long-

---

[24] See p. 32 of *Stocks, Bonds, Bills and Inflation* by Morningstar, Inc., 2012, Chicago, IL.

[25] From 1926 until 1981, the series was the value-weighted index of the lowest quintile of the New York Stock Exchange. Between 1982 and March, 2001, the series represents the performance of Dimensional Fund Advisors (DFA) Small Company Fund, which is a value-weighted portfolio of the lowest quintile of the NYSE plus any stocks on the AMEX or NASDAQ with market capitalization less than or equal to the highest-valued company in the lowest quintile of the NYSE. Starting in April 2001, the series represents the performance of DFA's Micro Cap Fund, which is a portfolio composed of the stocks with the smallest 4% of market capitalization across the NYSE, AMEX, and NASDAQ. DFA manages passive small company stock funds that take the passive side of transactions for their benchmark portfolios. Thus, the performance of their funds includes the transactions costs they receive for always taking the passive side of a transaction. See *Stocks, Bonds, Bills and Inflation*, Ibbotson Associates (2005), p. 61. Reprinted with permission.

term government bonds are 20 year bonds (bonds issued by the U.S. Treasury with a maturity of 20 years, or as close to that as possible). The bonds are held for a year, sold, and the proceeds are reinvested in a new 20-year bond (assuming no taxes). The intermediate government bond, which is also issued by the U.S. Treasury, is similar to the long-term government bond except that the bonds are bought when they have a maturity of five years, are held for a year, and the proceeds are reinvested in a new five-year bond (again, assuming no taxes). The U.S. Treasury Bill series is obtained by buying a U.S Treasury Bill with one month to go until it matures, holding it for a month, and then reinvesting in another Treasury bill with a one-month maturity (again with no taxes).[26] Inflation is measured by the Consumer Price Index (CPI).

Exhibit 8.8 presents the arithmetic mean annual return, the geometric mean annual return, and the standard deviation of the annual returns for each type of asset. The arithmetic mean return, $\overline{R}_A$, is the simple average annual return and is calculated as

$$\overline{R}_A = \frac{1}{T}\sum_{t=1}^{T} R_t \qquad\qquad (8.11)$$

Thus, it measures the simple average yearly return over the period 1926–2011.

The geometric mean return, R_G, is estimated as

$$R_G = \left[\prod_{t=1}^{T}(1 + R_t)\right]^{1/T} - 1 \qquad\qquad (8.12)$$

The geometric mean return, say, for the S&P 500, indicates the annually compounded return over the 1926–2011 time period if someone would have invested $1 in the S&P 500 on January 1, 1926, and held that position until December 31, 2011 (and reinvested all cash distributions without taxes). One dollar invested in the S&P 500 in the beginning of 1926 would have grown to $3,045.22 by the end of 2011, which is equivalent to an annual return every year of 9.8%, the geometric mean. The geometric mean return is always less than the arithmetic mean return as long as the time-series experiences both up and down movements. We focus our discussion on the arithmetic mean return for now.

From the information in Exhibit 8.8, we can estimate the real risk-free rate of return earned over this period as the difference between the average annual return on one-month U.S. Treasury Bills and the average annual increase in the CPI, which is 0.5% (0.5% = 3.6% − 3.1%). We would not use longer-term U.S. debt securities for this calculation because the return on these securities includes a maturity premium.

We can measure the average maturity premium as the difference in the average annual returns of long-term government bonds and short-term Treasury bills. Measured this way, on average, investors earned 2.5% more per year by holding U.S. securities that matured in 20 years as opposed to a one-month maturity. Since investors holding a 20-year bond bear the risk of unanticipated inflation and shifts in required real risk-free returns, it is not surprising that they demand a premium for holding long-term bonds relative to short-term bills. The maturity premium measured between intermediate-term government bonds and Treasury bills is 1.9%.

In addition to the maturity premium, the returns on long-term corporate bonds also include a default premium. The default premium compensates investors for the possible default on the bonds. One measure of the default premium is the difference between the average annual return on high-grade long-term corporate bonds and long-term government bonds. The average difference is 0.3% per year. Of course, default premiums relative to non-investment-grade (more risky) bonds would be larger, and we discuss this further in Chapter 9.

Two proxies for the market risk premium are the difference in the average annual returns between the S&P 500 and U.S. Treasury Bills and the difference in the average annual returns between the S&P 500 and U.S. long-term government bonds. From Exhibit 8.8, we can calculate both of these proxies for this period. The average market risk premium measured using the S&P 500 and U.S. Treasury Bills has been 8.2%. Using the S&P 500 and U.S. long-term government bonds, the average market risk premium has been 5.7%. We can also calculate a market risk premium relative to intermediate-term government bonds, which would result in a market risk premium estimate of 6.3%.

The mean difference in average annual returns between small stocks and the S&P 500 has been 4.7% during this period. The returns of small stocks are much more volatile than the returns of large stocks as well. The standard deviation of annual returns is 20.3% for large stocks and 32.5% for small stocks.

---

[26] U.S. Treasury Bills are a debt obligation of the U.S. Treasury that have maturities of one year or less (typically issued with maturities of 91 days, 182 days, or 52 weeks).

Choice of the Proxy for the Market Portfolio (Market Index)

Recall from our earlier discussion that, generally, we should estimate beta using the same market index that we use to measure the market risk premium. Thus, the issues regarding the choice of index for measuring the market risk premium are essentially the same as the issues we discuss regarding beta estimation. The key issues are what securities to include in the index, what weighting method to use, and whether to include dividends. Recall from our discussion about estimating beta that we generally include dividends to calculate the index returns and generally use a value-weighted index. We also generally use an index composed of stocks rather than stocks and other assets. That is why some authors and practitioners often refer to the market risk premium as the equity risk premium. We use the term market risk premium to keep in mind that we use a portfolio of common stocks as a proxy for the market portfolio.

Choice of Proxy for the Risk-Free Return to Measure the Market Risk Premium

In the CAPM, we use an expected (forward-looking) risk-free rate—that is, the yield on the risk-free asset as of the date of our valuation—the expected return of a riskless security at the date of our valuation, or the expected return before we add a risk premium. However, we also use historical risk-free rates of return to estimate the market risk premium if we estimate the market risk premium using a history of returns. As you might expect, our choice of the yield on the risk-free asset we use to measure the yield (which we discuss in the next section of the chapter) affects the risk-free rate we use to estimate the market risk premium.

In the United States, the most common choices for the historical risk-free rate returns to measure the market risk premium are U.S. government bonds (intermediate-term or long-term) and U.S. Treasury Bills. Advocates of using U.S. Treasury Bills often make the argument that while long-term U.S. government bonds might be free of default risk, they are not free of risk due to variation in expected inflation and variation in real required risk-free returns. The risk of unexpected inflation or shifts in real rates that an investor must bear increases with the maturity of a bond that has a fixed coupon rate. Suppose an investor buys a 10-year government bond at its face value, when expected inflation is 2% per year. After purchasing the bond, an economic shock occurs, increasing expected inflation to 5%. If that occurs, the price of the bond will fall to reflect the increase in the required nominal rate of return that investors demand because of the increase in expected inflation. The price falls because the coupon is fixed and the only way that a new investor in the bond can earn the new higher required nominal return is to purchase the bond below face value. Thus, the purchaser of a long-term government bond is not really buying a completely risk-free security; it may be free of default risk, but it is not free of all risk as its price will fluctuate over time.

On the other hand, short maturity U.S. Treasury Bills are reasonable proxies for the risk-free return over a very short period. A strategy of rolling over one-month Treasury bills yields a return series that is very close to risk-free, assuming the risk of the U.S. government defaulting within a month is remote. Moreover, while changes in expected inflation or shifts in real required rates of return can occur within a month, the amount of risk that an investor would bear due to either factor is quite small given a one-month maturity. At the end of the month, the investor gets to buy a new one-month Treasury bill, which should reflect current expectations of inflation and investors' required rates of return on a risk free asset.

Despite the fact that government bonds are more risky than Treasury bills, using long-term or intermediate-term government bonds to measure the market risk premium has many advocates. Fortunately, this choice does not have a large impact, because there is a corresponding and offsetting adjustment made in estimating the risk-free yield. In fact, we will see later that for a security whose beta is exactly equal to 1, the choice between using one-month Treasury bills and long-term government bonds to measure the market risk premium will have no impact on the cost of capital estimated.

If we choose to use government bonds, we must choose between using the long-term or intermediate-term government bond. If we are valuing a long-term investment, such as a company, we would generally measure the market risk premium using a long-term bond. If we are valuing a project that generated cash flows for, say, five years, we would measure the market risk premium using intermediate-term government bonds. This choice of long-term versus intermediate-term bonds is based on the bond that we want to use to measure the risk free yield as of the date of the valuation.

When calculating the returns on government bonds, we often use the total return on the government bond. Ibbotson Associates, however, advocates using the income return on government bonds instead of the total return. If you buy a 20-year bond at face value and hold it for a year and then sell it, there will be two components to your return. One component is the income return (the interest rate on the bond multiplied by the face value) and the other return component will be the capital gain or loss you will generally experience when you sell the bond at the end of the year as it still has 19 years until it matures (shifts in real rates or expectations of inflation will cause the price of the bond to change, thus providing a capital gain or loss component). If you measure the market risk premium by subtracting the income return on long-term government bonds from the S&P 500, the market risk premium measured over the 1926 to 2011 period is 6.6%, almost a full percentage point higher than the market risk premium estimated using the total return on the long-term government bond.[27]

If we choose to use a long-term government bond to estimate the market risk premium and the yield, how long a bond should we use? Many advocate using a 20- or 30-year bond, because it more closely captures the duration of the cash flows when valuing a company. However, as a matter of practice, the U.S. government does not always issue bonds with a long maturity. For example, the U.S. government did not issue 30-year bonds before 1977. The U.S. Treasury stopped issuing them in 2001. Beginning in February, 2006, the U.S. government began issuing 30-year bonds again. In addition, for a time, the U.S. government did not issue bonds with more than a 10-year maturity. Remember that no matter what term to maturity you choose, you must match the maturity of the bond for purposes of estimating both the yield and the market risk premium.

Another alternative some advocate is using the return on a very-high-grade long-term corporate bond instead of the return on a government bond. The justification of this alternative is that U.S. government bonds are tax-free at the state level (although they are taxed at the federal level). The argument is that the returns on government bonds are affected by their preferential tax status, suggesting they are priced to return a lower, pre-state-tax rate of return. U.S. corporate bonds are taxable at both the federal and state level, and hence they do not have that tax advantage. However, even high-grade corporate bonds, such as an AAA-rated bond, have some default risk, which would be embedded in the bond returns.

The Historical Approach to Estimating the Market Risk Premium

One way to estimate the market risk premium is to calculate annual returns on the chosen market portfolio and risk-free asset for some historical time period and then calculate the "mean" difference between the return on the market portfolio and the return on the risk-free asset. To use this approach, we must choose the time period over which to measure the "average" and how to measure the "mean" (arithmetic mean versus geometric mean).

In using this approach, the arithmetic mean return is generally used because it is the conceptually correct estimate if annual returns are independent through time (knowing last period's return does not help you predict next period's return). Since evidence indicates that annual returns are generally independent over time, the arithmetic mean is typically adopted in lieu of the geometric mean estimate.

A common technique is to use all of the data available since 1926 because 1926 is the oldest readily available year for which we have data that we believe is quite accurate. This approach assumes that the expected market risk premium has not changed over approximately 85 years, and therefore using more data provides a more precise estimate. Using a long time period ensures that the estimation period encompasses all types of economic and political conditions, such as war, peace, expansions, contractions, rampant inflation, oil price shocks, assassinations, natural disasters, and so forth.

An alternative to using all the data back to 1926 is to estimate the market risk premium over shorter time periods, say, the last 20 or 30 years. One effect of using a shorter time period is that the estimated market risk premium varies more from one year to the next because the addition of one new observation and the dropping of the oldest observation has a larger effect when using 20 years of observations than it does using 80 years of observations. Of course, just because the market risk premium estimated this way is volatile, it does not mean that the estimates are incorrect or inappropriate.

From Exhibit 8.8, we can use the historical arithmetic average based on data from 1926–2011, utilizing the return on the S&P 500 and the return on one of the government bond or Treasury bill series. Using the total return on long-term government bonds, the expected market risk premium is 5.7%, using the intermediate-term government bonds, the expected market risk premium is 6.3%, and using U.S. Treasury Bill returns, the expected market risk premium is 8.2%. While the difference between the expected

---

[27] See *Stocks, Bonds, Bills and Inflation: 2012 Valuation Yearbook* by Morningstar, Inc., 2012, Chicago, IL, p. 54.

market risk premium using the long-term government bonds and the U.S. Treasury Bill returns is 2.5%, for reasons we explain in the following section on estimating the risk-free yield, its net effect on the CAPM expected return is substantially less than 2.5%.

Not everyone who uses the historical approach uses estimates back to 1926. Stern Stewart & Co. estimates the market risk premium using the S&P 500 index in excess of the long-term government bond to be approximately 5.0% since 1950. It advocates using data since 1950 because it believes the markets are less risky now and that risk premiums should be smaller now than they were in the first half of the twentieth century. Stern Stewart makes other adjustments to the market risk premium.[28]

Another issue associated with using realized returns to compute the market risk premium is that the estimated risk premium could be upward biased because of "survivorship bias" in our proxy for the market portfolio. An example of survivorship bias is to use historical returns of the companies that were listed continuously for the past 20 years. That sample would obviously exclude companies that were listed for some time during the period but failed and were delisted, which would upward bias our historical returns.

Some have applied similar logic to estimating the market risk premium using only U.S. data (even though that data does include companies which have failed and delisted). They argue that the U.S. stock market has been wildly successful. Thus, because the U.S. market survived and prospered, using historical data on only the U.S. market overstates the premium an investor should expect, as there have been stock markets that literally disappeared. Of course in 1926, no one knew for certain that the U.S. stock market would survive and prosper. For example, the U.S. stock market earned a real return of 4.3% during the twentieth century versus a median real return of 0.8% for other countries. Academic evidence suggests that an adjustment for such survivorship bias is probably between 30 and 70 basis points—that is, take the historical market risk premium and subtract 0.3% to 0.7%.[29]

A major assumption made when using the historical approach is the assumption that the risk premium has remained constant over a relatively long time period. Some argue that the market risk premium varies over time and, in particular, that it has declined since the depression in the first half of the twentieth century. One way to accommodate that belief is to use a shorter time period that does not extend all the way back to 1926.

Time Variation in Estimating the Market Risk Premium

Recent research suggests that the expected market risk premium decreased during the second half of the twentieth century. Mayfield (2004) provides evidence of a structural shift in the underlying volatility process occurring after the depression in the 1930s and concludes that average historical estimates of the market risk premium using data back to 1926 overstate the expected premium. Mayfield argues that as investors recognized that expected volatility decreased, stock prices rose because of the declining market risk premium. Since that rise in stock prices is embedded in historical returns but was due to a decline in risk, those returns should be backed out in estimating the expected market risk premium. Using data through 2000, Mayfield claims that the average market risk premium (measured relative to Treasury bills) since 1940 is 5.6% in contrast to the historical premium relative to Treasury bills of 8.2% going back to 1926, indicating that the historical estimates are approximately 2.6% too high.[30]

Pastor and Stambaugh as well as Fama and French come to somewhat similar conclusions using different approaches. Pastor and Stambaugh use a longer history of data and a different methodology than Mayfield. Using data back to 1834, they provide evidence that the market risk premium (again, measured relative to U.S. Treasury Bills) has fluctuated between 4% and 6%. As of the end of 1999, Pastor and Stambaugh estimated the market risk premium at 4.8%, suggesting the historical risk premium relative to Treasury bills (measured back to 1926 and ending at that same time) was about 3.7% too high.[31] Fama and French, similar to Mayfield, argue that the high average return observed using data back to 1926 is due to a decline in the market risk premium, which in turn produced a large capital gain. Using data from

[28] See Petit, J., I. Gulic, and A. Park, "The Equity Risk Measurement Handbook," *Stern Stewart Research EVAluation* (March, 2001).

[29] See Jorion, P., and W. Goetzmann, "Global Stock Markets in the Twentieth Century," *Journal of Finance* 54 (June, 1999), pp. 953–974.

[30] See Mayfield, E. Scott, "Estimating the Market Risk Premium," *Journal of Financial Economics* 73 (2004), pp. 465–496.

[31] See Pastor, L., and R. Stambaugh, "The Equity Premium and Structural Breaks," *Journal of Finance* 56 (August, 2001), pp. 1207–1239. The change in prices since 1999 would likely change Pastor and Stambaugh's estimate of the market risk premium since 1999, but they have not updated their study at this time.

1872 to 2000, they estimate that the historical average excess return overstates the market risk premium substantially, by between 2.65% and 3.6% (depending on the model used).[32]

Suffice it to say that this evidence is beginning to attract some interest. While these three articles do not come to the same conclusion regarding the exact point estimate of the market risk premium, nor do they provide evidence about which of the alternatives is the best measure of the market risk premium, they all suggest that estimates of the market risk premium using the historical approach are too high, when using data back to 1926. Using Mayfield's estimates, an estimate of the market risk premium relative to Treasury bills is 5.6% and from that we can infer that the market risk premium relative to long-term government bonds would be about 4.2%.[33] Those numbers lie within the range produced by Fama and French.

Estimates of the Market Risk Premium from Chief Financial Officers

Graham and Harvey have surveyed CFOs every quarter from June of 2000 asking them their current estimate of the market risk premium (judged relative to the 10-year U.S. Treasury Bond). Over the 13 years of their survey, the risk premium estimates have varied widely. At the end of the first quarter of 2012 survey, the mean risk premium estimate for the S&P 500 relative to the 10-year U.S. government bond across all CFOs who responded to the survey was 4.9%.[34]

Estimates of the Market Risk Premium from Implied Cost of Capital Estimates

Another approach for estimating the market risk premium is to measure implied cost of capital estimates using forecasts of earnings or cash flows in conjunction with currently observed stock prices. The way this approach is implemented is to use analysts' forecasts or forecasts derived from a model to estimate short-term and intermediate-term growth rates for a company's free cash flows or excess earnings. For a long-term growth rate, this approach typically uses either long-term industry growth rates or forecasted growth rates for the economy. Once we know a company's price, its current free cash flows or excess earnings, and short- and long-term growth rates of free cash flows or excess earnings, we can solve for the internal rate of return that equates discounted expected free cash flows or excess earnings to the company's current stock price. This yields an implied cost of capital for a company.

To use this approach to estimate the market risk premium for an index of stocks such as the S&P 500, we would average the individual company's implied cost of capital estimates based on market capitalizations for all stocks in the S&P 500 to solve for the value-weighted average expected return on the S&P 500. To then estimate the market risk premium, say relative to long-term government bonds, you would then subtract the current yield on the long-term government bond, and the resulting difference is an estimate of the market risk premium. Bloomberg uses a procedure like this to estimate market risk premiums for different countries. Several academic papers have also utilized this approach. The estimates from these models depend in part on the price levels seen in the market. In the late 1990s and early 2000, when values were quite high relative to current earnings, these models often gave estimates of the market risk premium under 3%.[35] We discuss implied cost of capital estimates more thoroughly in a subsequent section of the chapter, as they are a standalone alternative to using the CAPM.

Uncertainty in Estimates of the Market Risk Premium

One of the difficulties in estimating the CAPM revolves around our uncertainty about the expected market risk premium. While there is uncertainty about estimated betas, the economic importance of the uncertainty about the estimated market risk premium dominates any uncertainty about estimation errors in beta

---

[32] See Fama, E., and K. French, "The Equity Premium," *Journal of Finance* 57 (April, 2002), pp. 637–659.

[33] Mayfield does not discuss the market risk premium relative to long-term government bonds. To estimate the 4.2%, we calculated the difference in returns between long-term government bonds and U.S. Treasury Bills between 1940 and 2000 (Mayfield's estimation period). That difference is 1.4%.

[34] The results of the CFO surveys can be found at http://www.cfosurvey.org/.

[35] J. Claus and J. Thomas, "Equity Premia as Low as Three Percent? Evidence from Analysts' Earnings Forecasts for Domestic and International Stock Markets," *Journal of Finance* 56 (2001), pp. 1629–1666; and Gebhardt, W., C. Lee, and B. Swaminathan, "Toward an Implied Cost of Capital," *Journal of Accounting Research* 39 (2001), pp. 135–176.

(assuming, for now, that the CAPM is a perfect model). Fama and French conclude that the uncertainty about the market risk premium alone translates into a standard error of industry cost of capital estimates in their study of approximately 3.01% per year, while including uncertainty about an industry's true beta increases the standard error by only 0.14% to 3.15%.[36]

Where Does All of the Evidence Leave Us?

Recent evidence suggests that the expected market risk premium is overstated using the historical approach back to 1926. However, this empirical work is not definitive. Mehra and Prescott discuss these issues as well as alternative rationales for why we may have observed such large historical market risk premiums. Those explanations include factors such as changes in taxes and regulation, compensation for the chance of a cataclysmic event, and more. None of their explanations, however, can completely explain the magnitude of the observed market risk premiums to date. Without an explanation, Mehra and Prescott conclude: "In the absence of this [a plausible explanation for the high market risk premium], and based on what we currently know, we can make the following claim: over the long horizon the equity premium is likely to be similar to what it has been in the past. . . ."[37] Thus, there is far from a unanimous view on this important issue.

Valuation Key 8.11

Estimating the market risk premium is an important part of implementing the Capital Asset Pricing Model. At the current time, there is not a broad consensus concerning the best way to estimate the market risk premium, and estimates of the market risk premium vary widely. More recent evidence suggests that using the long-term average historical market risk premium may overstate the expected market risk premium; however, the "jury is still out" on this issue.

8.9 ESTIMATING THE RISK-FREE RATE OF RETURN TO USE IN THE CAPM

We can estimate the risk-free rate in the CAPM using the yield on a risk-free security, measured as of the date of our valuation. The good news is that for most U.S. government securities, we can observe this yield. In Exhibit 8.9, we summarize the steps in estimating the forward-looking risk-free rate of return, and discuss them in this section of the chapter. The first two choices we make are choosing the proxy for the risk-free asset and the maturity of that proxy. Then, depending on our choice for the proxy and the maturity of the proxy, we may have to adjust the proxy for any risk-premium embedded in it.

EXHIBIT 8.9	Steps in Estimating the Risk-Free Rate of Return (Yield on a Risk-Free Asset at the Valuation Date)
1	Choose a proxy for the risk-free asset (U.S. government bond or corporate AAA bond)
2	Choose a maturity for the risk-free asset proxy based on the length of the cash flow forecasts being utilized
3	Make adjustments, if any, for risk premium embedded in the risk-free asset proxy
4	Use one rate to discount all periods or different rates for each period

As we discussed earlier, these choices are linked to the choices that we make when estimating the market risk premium. Generally, the choice of the proxy (U.S. government bonds versus AAA corporate bonds) and the choice of maturity (short-term, intermediate-term, and long-term maturity) are linked to our choices for the market risk premium. The driver of both choices however is based on the duration of the cash flows that we are valuing, which governs the maturity that we use for estimating the risk-free yield.

[36] See Fama, E., and K. French, "Industry Costs of Equity," *Journal of Financial Economics* 43 (1997), pp. 153–193.

[37] See Mehra, R., and E. Prescott, "The Equity Premium in Retrospect," in G. Constantinides, M. Harris, and R. Stulz, eds., *Handbook of the Economics of Finance*, Elsevier B.V. (2003), pp. 887–936.

If we are discounting nominal free cash flow forecasts in our valuation model, we need to capture investors' expectations for inflation, and this is captured in the risk-free rate we use. We can use different risk-free rates for each period by choosing a risk-free estimate of the expected return for each future period using the yield curve or we might just simply measure the time-weighted average rate of return that investors' demand over the relevant horizon. The latter approach is more popular. Of course, if the **term structure of interest rates** as of the valuation date is such that the **yield curve**[38] is very steep (rates changing with maturity), we might choose to estimate the cost of capital period by period.[39]

The most common practice is to match, as closely as practicable given the asset that is being valued, the maturity (or duration) of the proxy for the risk-free asset to the duration of the cash flows being discounted. For example, if we are discounting cash flows for five years, we would use the yield on an intermediate-term bond. When we value a firm, we generally assume the firm has an infinite life and has a long duration. As such, when measuring the risk-free rate for valuing a firm, we generally use the yield on a long-term bond.

Recall from the previous section that we observe a maturity premium between different maturities of government bonds. For example, the maturity premium is 2.5% based on the difference between the average long-term U.S. government bond return and the average U.S. Treasury Bill return. For the intermediate-term U.S. government bond, the maturity premium is 1.9% (see the arithmetic mean difference between the intermediate-term government bond returns and U.S. Treasury Bill returns). We must adjust for this maturity premium if we use a different proxy for the risk-free asset to measure the market risk premium and the yield on the risk-free asset.

As such, if we estimate the market risk premium using one-month U.S. Treasury Bills, we must adjust the yield on the risk-free asset if it is not a one-month U.S. Treasury Bill yield (which it typically is not, because we want the yield to be appropriate for the duration of the cash flows we are valuing). In such situations, we subtract an estimate of the maturity premium from the yield on the bond. For example, assume we used the historical approach and measured the market risk premium as the difference between the returns on the S&P 500 and the return on U.S. Treasury Bills between 1926 and 2011. Further assume that we also used the yield on a long-term government bond as of the valuation date for the risk-free yield. In that case, we would use a market risk premium of 8.2% and a yield on the risk-free asset equal to the yield on the long-term government bond less the historical maturity premium of 2.5%. If we were using the yield on an intermediate-term government bond for the yield on the risk-free asset, we would subtract the historical maturity premium for intermediate-term bonds of 1.9% from the yield on the intermediate-term bond.

Valuation Key 8.12

When valuing a company, the risk-free rate of return in the CAPM is normally measured as the yield on a long-term government bond as of the date of the valuation. We would adjust that yield for the expected maturity premium if the market risk premium is measured against a short maturity security, such as U.S. Treasury Bills. The maturity premium adjustment to the risk-free yield is not required when the market risk premium is measured against long-term government bonds.

8.10 PUTTING THE PIECES TOGETHER

Using the CAPM to estimate the expected return of a security requires estimates of three inputs—the yield on the risk-free asset, beta, and the market risk premium. We can estimate each of these inputs in various ways, and we generally use data from different time periods to estimate the different inputs for the CAPM. We use the observed yield on a proxy for the risk-free asset as of the valuation date. We usually estimate beta using historical data (two to five years are common, but we may use other periods depending on the valuation context). We might use a very long time-series of data to estimate the historical market risk premium or we might use more current data from implied cost of capital estimates.

---

[38] The term structure of interest rates is the relationship between interest rates and maturity of debt securities with the same default risk. The yield curve is a graph of the term structure of interest rates. The yield curve is generally rising with maturity.

[39] In addition, we would also estimate a different cost of capital if we had reason to expect the company's systematic risk were changing through time, for example, because of a planned divestiture.

Judgment and Guiding Principles (Links)

Estimating the cost of capital using the CAPM requires a certain amount of judgment. Fortunately, we have a few guiding principles we can use when we are making our choices. The inputs are linked to each other in certain ways. The first link is between the proxy we use for the market index to estimate beta and the proxy we use to measure the market risk premium; generally, we use the same proxy in the estimation process for both inputs. The second link is between the proxy for the return on the risk-free asset we use to estimate the market risk premium and the proxy we use for the yield on the risk-free asset as of the valuation date. Generally, this link is based in part on the duration of the cash flows we are valuing. The type of security (government bond versus corporate bond) and the maturity of the security (long-term, intermediate-term, or short-term maturity) must be consistent or we need to make adjustments to maintain consistency, such as the maturity premium adjustment discussed previously.

CAPM Example Using Our Four Companies

Assume that we estimated the following inputs for the CAPM to determine the cost of equity capital for our four companies: HP, Wal-Mart, GE, and Microsoft. The assumptions we use to implement the CAPM for these four companies are:

- Proxy for the yield on the risk-free asset is the yield on the long-term government bond on our valuation date, 5.0%
- Two estimates of beta for each company in Exhibit 8.6 based on the S&P 500
  - Betas in Exhibit 8.6 (based on the S&P 500)
  - Betas in Exhibit 8.6 (based on the S&P 500) using the Bloomberg adjustment, Bloomberg Adjusted Beta = 0.33 + 0.67 × Historical Beta
- Three estimates of the market risk premium
  - 8.2%, based on 1926 through 2011 returns on the S&P 500 and U.S. Treasury Bills
  - 5.7%, based on 1926 through 2011 returns on the S&P 500 and the long-term government bonds
  - 4.2%, based on Mayfield's research, which is based on the difference between the returns on the S&P 500 and long-term government bonds
- A maturity premium equal to 2.5% for U.S. long-term government bonds relative to U.S. Treasury Bills, based on the 1926–2011 returns

Based on the above assumptions, we can calculate six different CAPM-based equity cost of capital estimates (2 alternative betas × 3 alternative market risk premiums). We show the calculation of each of the six estimates as well as the average estimate for each of our four companies in Exhibit 8.10. We use GE to discuss the exhibit. GE's beta is 1.615 in Exhibit 8.6. Applying the CAPM to the first set of assumptions (no Bloomberg adjustment and a market risk premium equal to 5.7%), GE's estimated cost of capital is 14.2% ($0.142 = 0.05 + 1.615 \times 0.057$). If we adjust GE's beta using the Bloomberg adjustment process, its adjusted beta is equal to 1.41 ($1.41 = 0.33 + 0.67 \times 1.615$), and its estimated equity cost of capital (holding the other inputs constant) is equal to 13.0% ($0.130 = 0.05 + 1.41 \times 0.057$). For GE, which had a beta more than 50% above the average beta, the Bloomberg adjustment procedure reduced the cost of equity capital estimate for GE by 1.2%.

Using the returns on the S&P 500 and U.S. Treasury Bills to estimate the market risk premium of 8.2%, our estimate of the risk-free yield would be 2.5% (5.0% current yield on the long-term government bond less the historical maturity premium on long-term government bonds of 2.5%). Our estimate of GE's cost of equity capital using adjusted betas is 14.1% ($0.141 = 0.050 - 0.025 + 1.41 \times 0.082$). Note that had GE's beta been exactly equal to one, the choice of the proxy for the yield on the risk-free asset would not have made any difference, but in this case since GE's beta is greater than 1, using U.S. Treasury Bills to estimate the market risk premium results in a higher cost of capital than when using long-term U.S. government bonds (14.1% vs. 13.0%). If we use the 4.2% market risk premium estimate inferred from Mayfield (the difference between the return on the S&P 500 and long-term government bonds), our estimate for GE's equity cost of capital using adjusted betas is equal to 10.9% ($0.109 = 0.05 + 1.41 \times 0.042$). In this case the difference in the estimate of the cost of capital relative to the historical approach using long-term government bonds is 2.1% [$0.021 = 0.13 - 0.109 = 1.41 \times (0.057 - 0.042)$].

EXHIBIT 8.10 Alternative CAPM-Based Equity Cost of Capital Estimates for Our Four Companies

Company	Equity Cost of Capital Estimate	Yield on Risk-Free Asset	Beta (Exhibit 8.6)	Beta (Bloomberg Adjusted)	Market Risk Premium — Historical Based on U.S. Treasury Bill	Market Risk Premium — Historical Based on U.S. Long-Term Gov Bond	Market Risk Premium — Mayfield	Maturity Risk Premium
Wal-Mart Stores, Inc.	6.8%	5.0%	0.310			5.7%		
	5.0%	5.0%	0.310		8.2%			2.5%
	6.3%	5.0%	0.310				4.2%	
	8.1%	5.0%		0.54		5.7%		
	6.9%	5.0%		0.54	8.2%			2.5%
	7.3%	5.0%		0.54			4.2%	
Average	6.7%							
General Electric Company . . .	14.2%	5.0%	1.615			5.7%		
	15.7%	5.0%	1.615		8.2%			2.5%
	11.8%	5.0%	1.615				4.2%	
	13.0%	5.0%		1.41		5.7%		
	14.1%	5.0%		1.41	8.2%			2.5%
	10.9%	5.0%		1.41			4.2%	
Average	13.3%							
Microsoft Corp.	11.1%	5.0%	1.072			5.7%		
	11.3%	5.0%	1.072		8.2%			2.5%
	9.5%	5.0%	1.072				4.2%	
	11.0%	5.0%		1.05		5.7%		
	11.1%	5.0%		1.05	8.2%			2.5%
	9.4%	5.0%		1.05			4.2%	
Average	10.6%							
Hewlett-Packard.	10.9%	5.0%	1.030			5.7%		
Development Co.	10.9%	5.0%	1.030		8.2%			2.5%
	9.3%	5.0%	1.030				4.2%	
	10.8%	5.0%		1.02		5.7%		
	10.9%	5.0%		1.02	8.2%			2.5%
	9.3%	5.0%		1.02			4.2%	
Average	10.3%							

Our six estimates of the cost of capital for GE range from 10.9% to 15.7%. The range for GE is larger than the range of the other companies because GE's beta is larger than the betas of the other companies.[40] Still you can see that variation in the way the CAPM is implemented can lead to substantial variation in the estimated cost of equity capital.

REVIEW EXERCISE 8.6

Alternative CAPM-Based Equity Cost of Capital Estimates for Four Comparable Companies in Review Exercise 8.5

Calculate the cost of equity capital for the four comparable companies in Review Exercise 8.5 using the alternative assumptions used to measure the equity cost of capital in Exhibit 8.10; in other words, create a table similar to Exhibit 8.10 for the four comparable companies in Review Exercise 8.5.

Solution on page 335.

---

[40] It is common for practitioners to use a range of up to ±2% when valuing a company.

8.11 ADJUSTING THE CAPITAL ASSET PRICING MODEL FOR MARKET CAPITALIZATION

LO3 Estimate the Capital Asset Pricing Model adjusted for market capitalization and other potential attributes

Earlier in the chapter, we discussed the empirical evidence that the CAPM overstates the returns to large firms and understates the returns to small firms. One reason for us to be interested in this evidence is that it represents another method for determining a firm's equity cost of capital. In order to more fully understand this approach, let's examine the data in Exhibit 8.11.

EXHIBIT 8.11	Size Premium Relative to the Risk-Free Return and the CAPM from January 1926 Through 2011 for 10 Deciles of Firm Size.

Decile	Arithmetic Mean	Return in Excess of LT Govt Bond	Size Premium Relative to the CAPM	Common Stock Market Value (Largest Firm in Decile—Millions) @ Sept. 2011
1—largest	10.82%	5.67%	−0.38%	$354,351.9
2	12.78%	7.63%	0.78%	15,408.3
3	13.37%	8.22%	0.94%	6,896.4
4	13.78%	8.63%	1.17%	3,577.8
5	14.57%	9.42%	1.74%	2,362.5
6	14.76%	9.61%	1.75%	1,620.9
7	15.15%	10.00%	1.77%	1,090.5
8	16.27%	11.12%	2.51%	682.8
9	16.88%	11.73%	2.80%	422.8
10—smallest	20.56%	15.40%	6.10%	206.8

Source: See Morningstar Inc., *Ibbotson SBBI Valuation Yearbook 2012*, Chapter 7. Reprinted with permission.

The data is constructed by ranking New York Stock Exchange firms based on their market capitalization (market value of the common equity) as of the last trading day in March, June, September, and December of every year, ranking them from largest to smallest, and then putting the largest one-tenth of the firms in decile 1, the next largest one-tenth in decile 2, and so on, until the smallest one-tenth of the firms are put in decile 10. The quarterly decile cutoffs are based only on NYSE companies in existence at the end of every quarter, and then all companies on the NYSE, AMEX, and NASDAQ exchanges are assigned to the appropriate size decile based on the NYSE deciles. The return in excess of the long-term government bond is calculated as the value-weighted return for each decile portfolio every year less the income return from investing in a 20-year U.S. government bond for the year. The return in excess of the CAPM is calculated as the value-weighted return for each decile portfolio less the return predicted by the CAPM given the portfolio's beta. The last column provides information on the market value of the common stock of the largest firm in each decile as of September, 2011.

Add the Decile Risk Premium to the Risk-Free Rate.
Given the relation between size and returns, one technique for using this data to determine a firm's cost of equity capital is to add the historical return in excess of the long-term government bond for the size decile of which the firm is currently a member to the long-term government bond yield. That is

$$r_E = r_F + \text{Return in Excess of LT Govt Bond for Size Decile} \qquad (8.13)$$

This technique presumes that beta plays no role whatsoever in setting expected returns and that only size matters. This is not the most common usage of this data, but we will illustrate its implementation because some practitioners do use this technique.

To implement this technique one must have some approximate knowledge of how large the firm is. As such, if the firm were not publicly traded, one would probably have to use a price multiple technique to approximate the market value in the absence of any other indication. In addition, if the firm grows through time sufficiently to change deciles, this technique suggests that the required rate of return would decline through time. Of course implementing that would be difficult because you would need to forecast the path of the market capitalization cutoffs for each of the deciles through time.

As an example, the arithmetic mean return on firms in the eighth decile has been 16.27%. More importantly, the eighth decile risk premium relative to long-term U.S. government bonds has been 11.1%. If long-term government bonds were yielding 5.0%, this would suggest that the equity cost of capital for firms in the eighth decile of firm size (defining the market risk premium relative to long-term government bonds) is 16.1% (0.161 = 0.05 + 0.111).

Adjusting the CAPM for the Historical Size Mispricing.

The more commonly used technique for estimating the cost of equity capital using this data is to estimate the cost of capital from the standard CAPM and add or subtract the historical deviation from CAPM pricing for a firm of that approximate market capitalization.

$$r_E = r_F + \beta_E \times MRP + \text{Adjustment for CAPM Size Mispricing} \qquad (8.14)$$

Using this data one could calculate the CAPM return and then add the size premium relative to the S&P 500 as the adjustment. Again, you need to have some idea of the market value of a firm's equity to be able to use this technique.

For example, suppose we had a $500 million company whose beta is 1.2. A firm with a market value of $500 million is in decile 8 in Exhibit 8.11. What would you do if you wanted to use the CAPM with a size adjustment to estimate the cost of equity capital? If long-term government bonds were yielding 5.0%, this would suggest an equity cost of capital (estimating the market risk premium relative to long-term government bonds as 5.7%) of 14.35% [0.1435 = (0.05 + 1.2 * 0.057 + 0.0251). The 2.51% that is added in this calculation is the adjustment for CAPM size mispricing for the eighth decile per Exhibit 8.11.

The same issue exists here as for the previous method if the firm is expected to grow or decline through time. That is, as the value moves up or down, the size decile might differ, resulting in a different cost of capital.

An alternative technique discussed by Ibbotson Associates is to use fewer groupings than the 10 deciles shown in Exhibit 8.11. In this technique, adjustments are constructed for three different portfolios, a mid-cap (stocks in deciles 3 to 5), low-cap (stocks in deciles 6 to 8), and micro-cap (stocks in deciles 9 and 10) portfolio, with no adjustment made to the CAPM for stocks that are in decile portfolios 1 and 2. Note that the companies in the first two deciles, for which no adjustment is made, represent approximately 75% of the market capitalization of the NYSE, AMEX, and NASDAQ markets. This data is contained in Exhibit 8.12.

EXHIBIT 8.12	Size Premium Relative to the Risk-Free Return and the CAPM from January 1926 Through 2011 for Three Portfolios of Firm Size.

Decile	Arithmetic Mean	Return in Excess of LT Govt Bond	Size Premium Relative to the CAPM	Common Stock Market Value (Largest Firm in Decile—Millions) @ Sept. 2011
Mid-cap	13.70%	8.55%	1.14%	$6,896.4
Low-cap.........................	15.16%	10.01%	1.88%	1,620.9
Micro	18.04%	12.88%	3.89%	422.8

Source: See Morningstar Inc., *Ibbotson SBBI Valuation Yearbook 2012*, Chapter 7. Reprinted with permission.

If we were to apply this data to our example of a company with an approximate market capitalization of $500 million and a beta of 1.2 (continuing to assume that the risk-free rate is 5% and the market risk premium is 5.7%), we would estimate the equity cost of capital to be 13.72% (0.1372 = 0.05 + 1.2 * 0.057 + 0.0188).

Valuation in Practice 8.4

Dimensional Fund Advisors Invests Based on the Size Anomaly and the Three-Factor Model
Dimensional Fund Advisors (DFA), with over $100 billion under management, utilizes research about asset pricing that contradicts the CAPM. When DFA started out in 1982, it used the research discussed previously of Rolf Banz and Don Keim that showed that small firms outperformed the predictions of the CAPM. As such, DFA's first fund held the bottom two deciles of the New York Stock Exchange in terms of market capitalization. In its first year, DFA's small-cap fund appreciated nearly 100%. After that year, small stocks performed poorly compared to the S&P 500 for approximately seven years (practically the worst seven years in their history), but DFA still outperformed most of the other small-cap funds.

Based on the research of Eugene Fama and Ken French that led to the three-factor model (discussed later in this chapter), DFA started to manage funds based on both market capitalization and low price-to-book ratios in 1992. Their research indicated that low-price-to-book companies outperformed high-price-to-book companies regardless of whether they were small-cap or large-cap companies. DFA has both a small-cap and large-cap fund but both hold only stocks with low price-to-book ratios.

Source: See Banz, R., "The Relationship Between Return and Market Values of Common Stock," *Journal of Financial Economics* 9 (March, 1981), pp. 3–18; Keim, Donald B., "Size-Related Anomalies and Stock Return Seasonality: Further Evidence," *Journal of Financial Economics* 9 (June 1983), pp. 13–32; Fama, E., and K. French, "The Cross-Section of Expected Stock Returns," *Journal of Finance* 47 (1992), pp. 427–463; and Fama, E., and K. French, "Multifactor Explanations of Asset Pricing Anomalies," *Journal of Finance* 51 (1996), pp. 55–84. Dimensional Fund Advisors has a series of companies around the world, including Dimensional Fund Advisors, Inc., DFA Australia Limited, Dimensional Fund Advisors, Ltd., and Dimensional Fund Advisors Canada, Inc. See http://www.dfa.us.com .

A significant question to ask is whether we should use data all the way back to 1926 to determine whether and how much to adjust the CAPM for size. The original article documenting this phenomenon was published by Rolf Banz in 1981 and DFA was formed in 1982. From 1982 through 2011, the size premium for the mid-cap portfolio has been 0.8%, 0.9% for the low-cap portfolio, and 1.2% for the micro-cap portfolio. Hence, since the publication of the original Banz study, the size effect has been much more modest (compare those numbers to the 1.1%, 1.9%, and 3.9% in Exhibit 8.12). The difference is especially noticeable for the smaller companies.

As such, there is much weaker evidence of a size effect since the original Banz article was published. This is consistent with three interpretations. The first interpretation is that the size premium represented a prior capital market inefficiency that was corrected once the research made it clear that the inefficiency existed. The second interpretation is that the size premium represented an element of risk that was formerly priced, but is no longer priced or is much more modest in magnitude (perhaps because capital markets have become more efficient and the liquidity of small-cap stocks has improved sufficiently to eliminate some prior risk factor or cost of trading). Under either interpretation, the addition of the historical size adjustment to the CAPM estimated using data back to 1926 to estimate the equity cost of capital would be unwarranted, but we would use the more recent data, say since 1982, to estimate the magnitude of the effect. The third interpretation is that the size premium still exists, but by chance, it has not been observed with the same strength over the past 30 years, which would mean that all the data in Exhibits 8.11 and 8.12 going back to 1926 are still relevant.

Since the original Banz article, U.S. capital markets have fundamentally changed. Small stocks are more liquid than they used to be and there are many funds that manage portfolios of small-cap stocks. As such, it may be that the size effect discussed here no longer exists or is more modest. Valuation specialists examine this evidence and disagree as to whether to adjust the CAPM for size and if they chose to do so, whether to use data back to 1926 or to just use some more recent period, such as data only back to 1982.

Valuation Key 8.13

Evidence on the historically observed size premium is used by some practitioners to adjust the CAPM by the amount the CAPM has historically misestimated the returns earned by portfolios of differently sized securities. The size adjustment is negligible for the firms that are as large as the firms in the top two deciles of the NYSE.

8.12 THE BUILD-UP METHOD

The build-up method is another method used for estimating the cost of capital. Unfortunately, many implementations of the build-up method that we see in practice are extremely *ad hoc* because many practitioners just pick rates for various components of the build-up method that are not based on scientific evidence.

Typical Formulation of the Build-Up Method

A common formulation for the build-up method starts with the risk-free rate, adds a general equity risk premium, and adds (or subtracts) an industry risk premium depending on whether the industry is considered to be more or less risky than the average industry. It then may add a premium for size and finally may add a company-specific risk factor. So the build-up method might look like the following:

$$r_E = r_F + \text{MRP} + \text{ISRP} + \text{Adjustment for CAPM Size Mispricing} + \text{CSRP} \qquad (8.15)$$

where ISRP is an industry-specific risk premium and CSRP is a company-specific risk premium.

The addition of the industry-specific risk premium can be sensible if it is done properly. For example, Ibbotson Associates essentially calculates industry-specific risk premiums by estimating industry-specific betas and subtracting 1 from them. The resulting difference is then multiplied by the market risk premium. If the industry-specific beta minus 1 is positive (negative), the industry-specific risk premium is positive (negative). Ibbotson Associates then says to add this industry-specific risk premium to the risk-free rate and the market risk premium (not a company-specific beta times the market risk premium, just the market risk premium).[41] If you think about it, this is tantamount to estimating the CAPM with an industry beta and multiplying the industry beta times the market risk premium and then adding the risk-free rate. Note, however, that in this case the industry beta is determined in part by the typical capital structure that exists in any given industry. So this method would incorporate the average industry capital structure into the cost of equity capital for every firm, regardless of actual capital structure.

Not every practitioner who adds an industry-specific risk premium bases the estimate of the industry-specific premium on any hard evidence. Instead, these are often based on subjective assessments and thus are open to question.

We have already discussed the adjustment to the CAPM for market capitalization and the evidence in favor of and against making that adjustment. As such, there is little to be added here, except for one point. To the extent that you are going to add an industry-specific risk premium, you have to be sure that the manner in which you calculate the industry risk premium does not also incorporate a size adjustment. The same caveat would be appropriate if you intend to add a company-specific risk premium.

The potential subjectivity in the build-up method increases greatly when practitioners start to add company-specific risk premiums because the rationalizations for company-specific premiums are often tenuous and there is no hard evidence on the veracity of these company-specific risk premiums. As such, they are essentially just subjective judgments. We have seen cases where a company-specific premium of more than 10% has been added to the CAPM adjusted for market capitalization.

The reasons often given for these company-specific factors are based on a wide variety of items, such as leverage; dependence on a key executive, key supplier, or important customer; risk of competition; and more. The reasons for a company-specific risk premium are only limited by one's imagination. If you think about many of the reasons that we listed for a company-specific risk premium, they largely reflect idiosyncratic risks. Idiosyncratic risks should be accounted for in the expected cash flows, not in the cost of capital, as diversifiable risk should not affect the cost of capital according to the theory underlying all asset pricing models in modern finance. For example, assume that there is one key executive and if that individual dies, the company will cease to exist. That risk should be accounted for in assessing the expected cash flows. If the company would cease to exist, there would be a probability of zero future cash flows at every future year based on the probability that the death of the executive would take place by that year. An alternative scenario might be that if the key executive dies the company will be worth $5 million less from that point forward. If the company would be worth $5 million less, we could insure the executive's life for $5 million and subtract the annual insurance premium from the

---

[41] See Ibbotson Associates, *Stocks Bonds, Bills and Inflation: Valuation Edition 2010 Yearbook*, 2010, pp. 27–41.

expected cash flows based on the premise that the death of the CEO had not occurred each year in order to determine the relevant expected cash flows for our valuation that were adjusted for the possibility that the CEO might die.

Don't Use *Ad Hoc* Models

There are many complexities and alternatives with respect to estimating the cost of capital. Obviously, valuation experts may make a variety of different judgment calls in estimating the cost of capital. Many will use the CAPM, but they will implement it differently. Others may use an alternative model such as the Fama-French model, which we discuss later in this chapter. Despite the differences in these models, there is some scientific basis for many of the alternative models and many of the alternative ways in which the models are implemented in practice. One thing we would strongly urge is that you not use *ad hoc* models. In our opinion, the build-up method can lead to completely *ad hoc* and unsupportable estimates of the cost of capital if done improperly. While some versions of the build-up method can be supported, we would not advocate the use of company-specific risk premiums, at least not based on the scientific evidence that we have to date.

Valuation Key 8.14

The build-up method is often used in practice, especially for valuing small companies. We urge caution in the use of the build-up method and to be sure that you have some scientific basis for how you implement that approach, if you use it all.

8.13 THE THREE-FACTOR MODEL

LO4 Estimate the equity cost of capital using the three-factor model or implied cost of capital estimates

Arbitrage Pricing Theory (APT) is a theoretical equilibrium pricing model that is a competitor to the CAPM.[42] The APT starts with the premise that there are multiple macroeconomic factors that affect the actual returns that assets will experience. Further, it assumes that different assets will respond differently to these macroeconomic forces. For example, the returns earned by some businesses may be more sensitive to shifts in expected inflation rates than others. Or perhaps some businesses are more sensitive to the cost of energy than others. In addition, the model assumes, like the CAPM, that there are idiosyncratic shocks that also affect an asset's return. Like the CAPM, the APT assumes that all of the idiosyncratic risk can be diversified away by holding well-diversified portfolios. Because the idiosyncratic risk can be eliminated, it will not be priced. Sound familiar? But unlike the CAPM, because there are multiple macroeconomic forces that affect the pricing of assets and that affect companies differently, more than one factor will appear in the pricing equation, whereas in the CAPM there was only one risk factor, market risk. In the remainder of this section we discuss a three-factor model.

Besides the evidence on the size effect documented by Banz and Keim, there are other variables that appear to be potentially important in explaining the cross-section of expected returns beyond beta from the CAPM. For example, Basu documented that returns for stocks with high ratios of earnings to price exceeded the return predicted by the CAPM, and Statman documented that stocks with high book-to-market ratios (the book value of the common stock divided by the market value of the common stock) had higher returns than predicted by the CAPM.[43]

Fama and French updated the evidence on these and other earlier studies that had documented the empirical shortcomings of the CAPM. In particular, they showed that there is significant explanatory power for predicting expected returns from size, earnings-to-price ratios, book-to-market ratios, and debt-to-equity ratios even in the presence of beta.[44] As such, Fama and French propose a three-factor model

---

[42] See Ross, S., "The Arbitrage Theory of Capital Asset Pricing," *Journal of Economic Theory* 13 (1976), pp. 341–360.

[43] See Basu, S., "Investment Performance of Common Stocks in Relation to Their Price-Earnings Ratios: A Test of the Efficient Market Hypothesis," *Journal of Finance* 12 (1977), pp. 129–156; and Statman, D., "Book Values and Stock Returns," *The Chicago MBA: A Journal of Selected Papers* 4 (1980), pp. 25–45.

[44] See Fama, E., and K. French, "The Cross-Section of Expected Stock Returns," *Journal of Finance* 47 (1992), pp. 427–463; and Fama, E., and K. French, "Multifactor Explanations of Asset Pricing Anomalies," *Journal of Finance* 51 (1996), pp. 55–84.

that includes market risk, size, and book-to-market factors.[45] This model is not based on any underlying theory for why size and book-to-market might represent risks that are undiversifiable and might be priced. Instead, the model is motivated from the previously described empirical work that shows that size and the market-to-book ratio help explain the cross-section of expected returns even in the presence of the CAPM beta. You can think of the three-factor model as an alternative attempt to specify the APT. However, it does not rely on standard macroeconomic factors as is more typical of implementations of the APT.

The Model and Its Estimation

Fama and French start with the CAPM (risk-free rate plus sensitivity [beta] multiplied by the market risk premium) and add two other factors: the sensitivity of a stock's return to the difference in returns between diversified portfolios of small and large market capitalization companies multiplied by the small minus big firm risk premium, and the stock's sensitivity to the difference in returns between diversified portfolios of high and low book-to-market stocks multiplied by the expected risk premium on high minus low book-to-market portfolios.

The equation of the three-factor model is as follows:

$$r_E = r_F + \beta_{MRP}[MRP] + \beta_{SMB}[SMB] + \beta_{HML}[HML] \tag{8.16}$$

where r_E is the return on equity, r_F is the risk free rate, β_{MRP} is the sensitivity of a stock's return to the market risk premium (MRP), β_{SMB} is the sensitivity of a stock's return to the small minus big risk premium (SMB), and β_{HML} is the sensitivity of a stock's return to the high minus low book-to-market risk premium (HML). In estimating their model, Fama and French construct the portfolios of big and small stocks using the median size of all NYSE companies and construct the portfolios of high and low book-to-market portfolios based on the top and bottom 30% of the book-to-market distribution of NYSE companies. Firms are placed in these portfolios at the beginning of every quarter.

SMB measures the difference in returns between small and big companies. Certain firms may prosper more when the environment for small firms is better than that for large firms and vice-versa. This would be reflected in different sensitivities to the SMB factor. In addition, if HML is negative, it means that high-book-to-market firms have performed worse than low-book-to-market firms. Firms with high sensitivity to the HML factor are likely to perform poorly and distressed firms may perform particularly poorly when the HML factor is negative. Again, this would be reflected in the company's sensitivity to the HML factor. We illustrate this calculation in Exhibit 8.13 for the same four stocks in Exhibit 8.6.

To estimate the three-factor model we must estimate the sensitivity of a stock's return to each of the three risk factors, which means we need a time series of the returns on a company's stock and the return on each of the risk premiums on a periodic basis, such as monthly return data. Fortunately, Ken French maintains the returns to the three factors on his website[46] and thus it is simply a matter of regressing a company's monthly stock returns on monthly returns associated with the three factors to determine a stock's sensitivity to each of the factors. We then use estimates of the historical risk premiums in conjunction with the sensitivities. Next, we compare the three-factor risk premium to the risk premium calculated using the CAPM. Note that to estimate the cost of equity capital, we would have to add an appropriate estimate of the risk-free rate to the risk premium estimates shown in Exhibit 8.13.

Examining the results in Exhibit 8.13, one can see that for this time period, the estimates from the two different models yield reasonably similar results for Wal-Mart and Hewlett Packard (a difference of 0.5% or less). General Electric's risk premium estimates using the two models are different by 1.8%, and Microsoft's two risk premium estimates are quite different, with the three-factor risk premium being 3.4% less than the CAPM risk premium (5.4% vs. 8.8%). It is not uncommon for the estimates from the two models to be different, especially at the firm level.

Even when estimating risk premiums for entire industries we can observe substantially different estimates between the CAPM and the three-factor model. In Exhibit 8.14, we report industry risk premiums using the three-factor model and the CAPM. For some industries the risk premium estimates obtained from the two models are quite close but in other industries they are quite different. For example, the risk

---

[45] See Fama, E., and K. French, "Common Risk factors in the Returns on Stocks and Bonds," *Journal of Financial Economics* 33 (1993), pp. 3–56; and Fama, E., and K. French, "Multifactor Explanations of Asset Pricing Anomalies," *Journal of Finance* 51 (1996), pp. 55–84.

[46] See http://mba.tuck.dartmouth.edu/pages/faculty/ken.french/data_library.html.

premium estimates vary by more than 4% between the two models for pharmaceuticals, real estate, and automobiles and trucks. In some cases, the three-factor model produces higher risk premium estimates and in other cases it is the CAPM that produces the higher estimate. For example, the CAPM estimate is higher for pharmaceuticals, computers, electronic equipment, and alcoholic beverages. For the remaining industries shown, the three-factor model produces the higher estimate.

EXHIBIT 8.13   Firm-Specific Risk Premiums from the Three-Factor and CAPM Models for Our Four Companies

	Three-Factor Model			CAPM
	MRP	SMB	HML	MRP
Risk Premiums	0.0804	0.0378	0.0470	0.0820

	Three-Factor Model Sensitivities[a]			Three-Factor Risk Premium[b]	CAPM β[c]	CAPM Risk Premium[d]
	β_{MRP}	β_{SMB}	β_{HML}			
Wal-Mart Stores, Inc.	0.422	−0.434	0.091	2.2%	0.31	2.5%
General Electric Corp.	1.296	−0.311	0.463	11.4%	1.61	13.2%
Microsoft Corp.	1.163	−0.201	−0.686	5.4%	1.07	8.8%
Hewlett Packard Corp.	1.255	0.385	−0.556	8.9%	1.03	8.4%

[a] Factor sensitivities for each stock are estimated using monthly data from January 2000 to March 2010 by regressing the monthly returns on the stock against the monthly returns associated with the three factors.

[b] We calculate the three-factor risk premium based on the company's sensitivities to each factor multiplied by the historical average realized risk premiums based on 1927–2010 data for each of the other three factors—MRP equals 8.04%, SMB equals 3.79%, and HML equals 4.70%. The sample of firms used to construct MRP, SMB, and HML includes all NYSE, AMEX, and NASDAQ companies, which is why the MRP is slightly different than that used for the CAPM.

[c] CAPM β is estimated using monthly data from January 2000 to March 2010 by regressing the monthly returns on the stock against the monthly returns on the S&P 500.

[d] We use the CAPM risk premium of 8.2% based on the S&P 500 less the returns on one-month U.S Treasury Bills from 1926 to 2010. CAPM betas are measured against the S&P 500.

EXHIBIT 8.14   Industry Risk Premiums from the Three-Factor and CAPM Models[a]

	Three-Factor Model Sensitivities[b]			Three-Factor Risk Premium[c]	CAPM β[d]	CAPM Risk Premium[e]
	β_{MRP}	β_{SMB}	β_{HML}			
Pharmaceuticals	0.84	−0.25	−0.63	0.09%	0.92	4.71%
Computers	0.90	0.17	−0.49	2.49%	1.04	5.29%
Electronic equipment	1.15	0.69	−0.39	6.01%	1.38	7.04%
Alcoholic beverages	0.90	−0.13	−0.22	2.99%	0.92	4.69%
Entertainment	1.17	0.83	−0.04	8.43%	1.35	6.91%
Precious metals	0.71	0.40	0.08	5.35%	0.78	3.98%
Recreational products	1.17	0.97	0.17	10.01%	1.34	6.83%
Banking	1.13	0.13	0.35	8.08%	1.09	5.55%
Telecommunications	0.79	−0.23	0.35	5.17%	0.66	3.39%
Real estate	1.01	1.18	0.40	11.16%	1.17	5.99%
Automobiles and trucks	1.10	0.17	0.60	9.39%	1.01	5.13%

[a] Selected industry risk premiums from Fama, E., and K. French, "Industry Costs of Equity," *Journal of Financial Economics* 43 (1997), pp. 172–173.

[b] Factor sensitivities for each industry are estimated using monthly data from July 1968 to December 1994 by regressing the value-weighted industry monthly returns against the monthly returns associated with the three factors.

[c] The three-factor risk premium is calculated based on the industry's sensitivities to each factor multiplied by the historical realized risk premiums from July 1963 to December 1994 for each of the three factors, where MRP (judged relative to one-month U.S. Treasury Bills) equals 5.1%, SMB equals 3.2%, and HML equals 5.4%.

[d] CAPM β is estimated using monthly data from July 1968 to December 1994 by regressing the value-weighted industry monthly returns on the stock against the monthly returns on the market.

[e] The CAPM risk premium is calculated based on the industry's CAPM β multiplied by the historical realized return on the market in excess of the one-month U.S. Treasury Bills estimated from July 1963 to December 1994, equal to 5.1%.

Almost all of the estimation issues that arise for the CAPM are relevant for the three-factor model, only now we are estimating the risk premiums associated with three risk factors instead of one and the sensitivity of a company's stock to three factors instead of one. For example, what is the best way to estimate the risk premiums for the three different factors? Should we use the historical approach? If so, should we use the arithmetic or geometric mean? Should we use data all the way back to 1926 as we did in Exhibit 8.13 or only use more recent data as was done in Exhibit 8.14? Should we use some approach other than the mean historical approach? How many observations do we need to estimate factor sensitivities? (Exhibit 8.13 uses 123 monthly observations while Exhibit 8.14 uses over 25 years of monthly observations.) Should we use monthly data, weekly data, or daily data? The list goes on.

The imprecision in our estimates of the cost of capital that are obtained from the three-factor model is similar to what we discussed earlier in the chapter regarding the CAPM. Fama and French again conclude that the imprecision in the factor risk premiums is the major cause of error even if the three-factor model is the correct model. Again, they find that the standard errors of the overall risk premium introduced by uncertainty about the risk premiums associated with the three factors, assuming one knew the sensitivities with certainty and that the three-factor model was correct, amount to 3.17% per year.

Valuation Key 8.15

The three-factor model is an alternative method for estimating a company's cost of capital. The three-factor model is widely used in academic studies and is seeing increasing use in practice. Use of the three-factor model requires estimating the sensitivity of a stock's return to the three different factors and estimating the risk premiums for each of the factors.

REVIEW EXERCISE 8.7

Three-Factor Risk Premiums for Four Comparable Companies in Review Exercise 8.5

Use the information in Review Exercise 8.5, assumptions in Exhibit 8.13, and the information that appears below to calculate the three-factor and CAPM risk premiums for the four comparable companies; in other words, create a table similar to Exhibit 8.13 for the four comparable companies in Review Exercise 8.5.

	Three-Factor Model Sensitivities		
	β_{MRP}	β_{SMB}	β_{HML}
Comparable Company #1	0.900	0.300	0.250
Comparable Company #2	0.800	0.100	0.900
Comparable Company #3	1.500	−0.200	0.500
Comparable Company #4	1.100	0.600	0.200

Solution on page 335.

8.14 IMPLIED COST OF CAPITAL ESTIMATES

Earlier in the chapter, we briefly discussed estimating the market risk premium by first estimating the expected rate of return on a stock from the current price and forecasts of earnings or free cash flows and then aggregating those individual estimates of expected returns across all firms in a market to determine an estimate of the expected return on the market. Essentially, given a set of forecasts of cash flows or excess earnings derived from forecasts of analysts or from a model, we solve for the discount rate that equates that stream of projected cash flows or excess earnings with the currently observed price. The discount rate or internal rate of return is an implied cost of capital for the firm—implied by current prices and forecasts. These implied cost of capital estimates can be used as a measure of a company's equity cost of capital. We discuss this technique in further detail here and start with a simple model to develop the intuition.

The Constant Dividend Growth Model

If we assume that a company's dividends and share repurchases will grow by a constant proportion each year and if we assume that the cost of equity capital is constant through time, then the price per share of the company is equal to

$$P_0 = \frac{DIV_1}{(r_E - g)} \qquad\qquad (8.17)$$

where

P_0 = the price per share of the company's stock today.
DIV_1 = the expected dividend and share repurchases per share for the next year.
r_E = the cost of equity capital.
g = the expected annual growth rate in dividends and share repurchases.

This is nothing more than a constant growth perpetuity model applied to dividends and share repurchases.

Rearranging this formula suggests that the cost of equity capital is equal to

$$r_E = g + \left(\frac{DIV_1}{P_0}\right)$$

where $\frac{DIV_1}{P_0}$ is often referred to as the firm's dividend yield (including share repurchases).

This formulation is obviously a simplification in that it assumes that the company's dividends and amounts spent on share repurchases will grow by the same proportionate amount each year. As such, this model only has any chance of producing reasonable estimates of the cost of equity capital for companies that are very stable, mature, growing slowly, and paying dividends or repurchasing shares. As such, we don't generally recommend the use of the constant dividend growth model as a means of estimating the cost of equity capital. Despite our lack of faith in this model, on occasion you will see it used to derive estimates of the cost of equity capital in valuation work. However, if you understand the constant growth model, it is conceptually easy to understand the varying growth models.

Implied Cost of Capital Estimates from Forecasts of Excess Earnings or Cash Flows

A variation of the constant growth model would be to develop short-term, intermediate-term, and long-term free cash flow or excess earnings forecasts in an effort to solve for the expected return, which when used to discount the projected cash flow or excess earnings forecasts yields the currently observed stock price. In this case, the models are not typically applied to assumptions about dividend growth, but are instead applied to either free cash flows or excess earnings. However, the intuition is similar to the constant dividend growth rate. We solve for the rate of return that equates the cash flow forecasts or forecasts of excess earnings with the publicly observed price. Unlike the constant growth dividend model, there is no closed-form solution to estimate the cost of equity capital when allowing for varying growth rates. Thus, the solution is an iterative one, just like determining the internal rate of return on a bond or a project.

There are quite a few variants on this procedure, and we will not discuss them in detail here. All of the models either discount estimates of free cash flows or discount excess earnings. Many of the variations in this method relate to how far out to forecast explicit year-by-year free cash flows or excess earnings, how to determine the intermediate and long-term growth rates (for example, use long-term industry outlooks or expected inflation), and how and when to transition between the intermediate- and long-term growth rates.[47]

All of those variations can be applied to either analyst forecasts or forecasts that come from some kind of model. A disadvantage of using analyst forecasts has to do with the biases of analysts and the staleness of analyst forecasts. Another disadvantage is that analysts tend to not follow small market capitalization companies, so the sample of companies for which we can measure implied cost of capital estimates from analysts' forecasts is limited. Academic research suggests that if you control for some of

---

[47] See Appendix A of Hou, K., M. van Dijk, and Y. Zhang, "The Implied Cost of Capital: A New Approach," *Journal of Accounting and Economics* 53 (2012), pp. 504–526, for a discussion of some of the alternative ways of estimating implied costs of capital.

the known biases of analysts and if you control for the fact that some analyst forecasts are "stale" at any given point in time, implied cost of capital measures have desirable properties. However, without controls for the known biases and staleness, the estimates do not exhibit these desirable properties.[48]

Recent research suggests that estimating the implied equity cost of capital from earnings forecasts derived from a simple cross-sectional model has superior properties to using analysts' forecasts—the implied cost of capital estimates are a better proxy for expected returns using the forecasts from the cross-sectional model.[49] As such, there is promise for this technique and we expect research to continue to attempt to exploit this technique to estimate the cost of capital. There are several potential advantages to estimating implied costs of capital. First, it is totally forward looking, as it does not depend on any historical data. Second, we do not have to make any presumption about which asset pricing model is best, nor do we have to worry about estimating parameters such as the market risk premium. However, we do have to assume that observed prices in the market are rational, that we can estimate reliable forecasts of free cash flows or excess earnings, and that the market correctly estimates the equity cost of capital in pricing the security.

SUMMARY AND KEY CONCEPTS

In this chapter, we have discussed the Capital Asset Pricing Model and how to implement it in practice. As we have discussed, the CAPM is the most commonly used model to estimate the cost of equity capital in practice, but that does not mean that the CAPM is necessarily more accurate than the other models. We have discussed the issues associated with estimating a company's beta as well as the risk-free rate and market risk premium. One should always remember that the CAPM is a model; it is not a perfect statement of how the world works. In addition, even if the model were perfect, there is still noise in our estimates of the parameters of the CAPM. We have also seen that there are a variety of ways that practitioners and academics implement the CAPM, and some of the differences in estimation can lead to substantial differences in the estimated equity cost of capital. Suffice it to say that two individuals working independently might not agree on a company's cost of capital even if both individuals were using the CAPM.

We also have discussed alternatives to the CAPM for estimating the equity cost of capital. Such alternatives include the size adjustment to the CAPM, the build-up method, arbitrage pricing theory, the three-factor model, and implied cost of capital models. The CAPM is still the most commonly used model to estimate the cost of equity capital in practice, but that does not mean that the CAPM is more accurate than the other models, as there is some scientific basis for most of these models. Thus, there is uncertainty about which is the best model to use. Moreover, as we have discussed, all of these models have a large number of estimation issues associated with them, and all of this introduces uncertainty into our estimates of the cost of capital.

One important caveat to our discussion of estimating the cost of equity capital is worth noting before concluding this chapter. The methods discussed in this chapter for estimating the cost of capital are not directly relevant for valuing private companies as private companies, since these methods all presume that investors hold well-diversified portfolios and that the assets are readily marketable. As such, we often must make adjustments to the valuation of private companies when using these methods for estimating the cost of equity. We discuss these adjustments later in the book. Of course, we sometimes value a private company as if it were a public company, such as for an initial public offering, in which case the kinds of adjustments we discuss later are unnecessary.

ADDITIONAL READING AND REFERENCES

Fama, E., and K. French, "The Capital Asset Pricing Model: Theory and Evidence," *Journal of Economic Perspectives* 18 (Summer, 2004), pp. 25–46.

Fama, E., and K. French, "Multifactor Explanations of Asset Pricing Anomalies," *Journal of Finance* 51 (1996), pp. 55–84.

EXERCISES AND PROBLEMS

P8.1   **Calculating Beta:** Information is provided below for three companies. The standard deviation of the market return is .055 and the expected market risk premium $[(E(R_m) - r_F]$ equals .065. For each company, calculate

---

[48] See Guay, W., S. P. Kothari, and S. Shu, "Properties of Implied Cost of Capital Estimates Using Analysts' Forecasts," *Australian Journal of Management* 36 (2011), pp. 125–149.

[49] See Hou, K., M. van Dijk, and Y. Zhang, "The Implied Cost of Capital: A New Approach," *Journal of Accounting and Economics* 53 (2012), pp. 504–526.

the firm beta, and the relative risk of the firm's security return to the market return based upon their relative standard deviations. Are beta and the relative standard deviations both measures of the firm's risk?

	Firm 1	Firm 2	Firm 3
Standard deviation of firm's return.....................	0.108	0.066	0.101
Covariance of firm's return and market return............	0.0027	0.0032	0.0042

P8.2   **Calculating Portfolio Return and Portfolio Beta:** In the table below, the total equity market value, beta, and equity security return is listed for four individual equity securities. Assume you create a portfolio with these four securities. Calculate the return to the portfolio and the beta for the portfolio.

	Firm 1	Firm 2	Firm 3	Firm 4
Total firm equity market value (in millions)	$ 990	$3,675	$2,714	$ 581
Firm beta	0.78	1.06	0.96	1.47
Firm security return	5.8%	6.5%	7.7%	8.3%

P8.3   **Systematic Risk and Unsystematic Risk:** Assume a portfolio has monthly stock returns with a standard deviation of 0.12, and the standard deviation of the market portfolio of monthly returns is 0.05. The portfolio has an estimated beta of 1.2. Calculate the proportion of the portfolio's stock return variance that represents systematic risk and the proportion that represents unsystematic risk. Is the portfolio well diversified?

P8.4   **Adjusting Beta for an Anticipated Merger:** Assume Company A that operates in the retail industry and has an estimated beta of 1.6 is planning to merge with Company B that produces food related products and has an estimated beta of 0.8. At the time of the announcement of the merger, Company A was three times the size of Company B. Estimate the combined firm's beta after the merger assuming that the merger is not expected to create or destroy value and that the pre-merger debt of the two companies will remain outstanding after the merger occurs.

P8.5   **Adjusting Beta for Non-Operating Assets:** Company C has an estimated beta of 1.3 and uses no debt or other non-common equity financing. The company has 20% of its total market value invested in marketable securities that have an estimated beta of 0.1 and are assumed to be excess assets. Estimate the unlevered beta for Company C's operations.

P8.6   **Bloomberg, Precision, and Vasicek Adjusted Betas:** Calculate the Bloomberg adjusted beta for each of the comparable companies and the portfolio of comparable companies that appear in the table for this problem. All of the companies are unlevered. Also calculate the precision weighted beta for the four comparable companies and the company being valued based on the unadjusted betas as well as the equally weighted beta of the five companies. In addition, compute the Vasicek adjusted beta for the company being valued based on the unadjusted betas. Compare the comparable company average beta (based on the unadjusted betas), comparable company precision weighted beta, and Vasicek adjusted beta.

	Beta Estimate	Standard Error of Beta	t-statistic
Comparable Company #1	0.970	0.500	1.94
Comparable Company #2	1.310	0.550	2.38
Comparable Company #3	1.420	0.710	2.00
Comparable Company #4	1.580	0.700	2.26
Comparable company average beta	1.320		
Company being valued	1.110	0.600	1.85

P8.7   **Alternative CAPM-Based Equity Cost of Capital Estimates for Four Comparable Companies in Problem 8.6:** Calculate the cost of equity capital for the four comparable companies in Problem 8.6 using the alternative assumptions used to measure the equity cost of capital in Exhibit 8.10; in other words, create a table similar to Exhibit 8.10 for the four comparable companies in the previous problem.

P8.8   **Three-Factor Risk Premiums for Four Comparable Companies in Problem 8.6:** Use the information in Problem 8.6, assumptions in Exhibit 8.13, and the information that appears below to calculate the three-factor and CAPM Risk Premiums for the four comparable companies; in other words, create a table similar to Exhibit 8.13 for the four comparable companies in Problem 8.6.

	Three-Factor Model Sensitivities		
	β_{MRP}	β_{SMB}	β_{HML}
Comparable Company #1	0.820	0.340	0.930
Comparable Company #2	1.250	0.090	0.890
Comparable Company #3	1.320	−0.200	1.260
Comparable Company #4	1.650	0.670	0.320

P8.9   **Estimating Beta Using Monthly Stock Return Data:** Exhibit P8.1 presents monthly stock returns and the market capitalization of the equity for four companies, as well as the monthly returns for the S&P 500 and the three factors of the three-factor model.

   a.   Estimate the CAPM betas for each of the four stocks using regression analysis and 60 months of stock return data and an equally weighted portfolio of the four stocks.

   b.   Discuss the various statistics from the regression analysis including the statistical significance and 95% confidence interval of each beta.

   c.   Identify any of the companies that have a beta which is reliably (at the 95% confidence interval) different from the market beta.

   d.   Calculate the Bloomberg adjusted beta for each company.

EXHIBIT P8.1   Stock Returns for the Honeywell International, Inc. (HON), Boeing Company (BA), McDonalds Corporation (MCD), Oracle Systems Corporation (ORCL), S&P 500, and the Three Fama-French Factors

S&P 500 = S&P 500 value–weighted return with dividends   FF – HML = Fama-French HML Factor
FF $R_m - R_f$ = Fama–French Market Factor   Ticker Ret = Stock Return for Ticker
FF – SMB = Fama–French SMB Factor

DATE	HON RET	BA RET	MCD RET	ORCL RET	S&P 500	FF $R_m - R_f$	FF – SMB	FF – HML
1/31/07	1.0%	0.8%	0.0%	0.1%	1.5%	1.4%	−0.4%	−0.4%
2/28/07	2.1%	−2.2%	−1.5%	−4.3%	−1.9%	−1.9%	1.1%	0.7%
3/30/07	−0.7%	1.9%	3.1%	10.3%	1.1%	0.7%	−0.1%	−0.6%
4/30/07	17.6%	4.6%	7.2%	3.7%	4.4%	3.5%	−2.1%	−0.7%
5/31/07	7.3%	8.6%	4.7%	3.1%	3.4%	3.2%	0.1%	0.0%
6/29/07	−2.8%	−4.4%	0.4%	1.7%	−1.7%	−2.0%	0.8%	−1.5%
7/31/07	2.2%	7.6%	−5.7%	−3.0%	−3.1%	−3.8%	−2.6%	−4.4%
8/31/07	−1.9%	−6.2%	2.9%	6.1%	1.5%	0.8%	−0.2%	−1.6%
9/28/07	5.9%	8.6%	10.6%	6.8%	3.7%	3.2%	−2.2%	−3.3%
10/31/07	1.6%	−6.1%	9.7%	2.4%	1.7%	1.7%	0.4%	−4.7%
11/30/07	−5.9%	−5.8%	0.4%	−9.0%	−4.1%	−4.9%	−2.5%	−1.8%
12/31/07	8.7%	−5.5%	0.8%	11.9%	−0.6%	−0.8%	0.6%	−3.1%
1/31/08	−4.1%	−4.9%	−9.0%	−9.0%	−6.1%	−6.3%	−1.3%	8.2%
2/29/08	−2.1%	0.0%	1.7%	−8.5%	−3.1%	−3.2%	0.1%	−4.3%
3/31/08	−1.9%	−10.2%	3.1%	4.0%	−0.3%	−0.9%	0.8%	−1.1%
4/30/08	5.3%	14.1%	6.8%	6.6%	4.9%	4.6%	−2.5%	−0.4%
5/30/08	0.8%	−2.0%	−0.4%	9.5%	1.3%	1.9%	3.2%	−4.3%
6/30/08	−15.7%	−20.6%	−4.6%	−8.1%	−8.3%	−8.4%	−0.1%	−8.8%
7/31/08	1.1%	−7.0%	6.4%	2.5%	−0.7%	−0.7%	2.5%	6.2%
8/29/08	−0.8%	7.9%	4.3%	1.9%	1.5%	1.5%	3.3%	2.3%
9/30/08	−17.2%	−12.5%	−0.5%	−7.4%	−8.5%	−9.6%	0.2%	3.3%
10/31/08	−26.7%	−8.6%	−6.1%	−9.9%	−16.7%	−17.2%	−2.9%	−7.5%
11/28/08	−7.6%	−18.0%	2.3%	−12.0%	−7.4%	−7.8%	−4.3%	−5.7%
12/31/08	17.8%	0.1%	5.9%	10.2%	1.2%	1.8%	2.9%	−0.1%
1/30/09	−0.1%	−0.8%	−6.7%	−5.1%	−8.3%	−7.9%	0.9%	−5.4%
2/27/09	−17.4%	−24.9%	−9.1%	−7.7%	−10.4%	−9.9%	−0.8%	−8.3%
3/31/09	3.8%	13.2%	4.4%	16.3%	8.8%	8.8%	0.9%	5.1%
4/30/09	12.0%	12.6%	−2.3%	7.3%	9.4%	10.2%	10.6%	19.7%
5/29/09	7.2%	13.0%	10.7%	1.3%	5.5%	5.3%	−1.5%	7.3%
6/30/09	−5.3%	−5.2%	−1.7%	9.3%	0.2%	0.4%	2.0%	−4.8%

continued

continued from prior page

EXHIBIT P8.1	Stock Returns for the Honeywell International, Inc. (HON), Boeing Company (BA), McDonalds Corporation (MCD), Oracle Systems Corporation (ORCL), S&P 500, and the Three Fama-French Factors

S&P 500 = S&P 500 value–weighted return with dividends   FF – HML = Fama-French HML Factor
FF R_m – R_f = Fama–French Market Factor   Ticker Ret = Stock Return for Ticker
FF – SMB = Fama–French SMB Factor

DATE	HON RET	BA RET	MCD RET	ORCL RET	S&P 500	FF R_m – R_f	FF – SMB	FF – HML
7/31/09	10.5%	1.0%	–4.2%	3.6%	7.4%	7.8%	2.4%	3.4%
8/31/09	6.9%	16.9%	3.1%	–1.1%	3.5%	3.2%	–1.1%	7.3%
9/30/09	1.1%	9.0%	1.5%	–4.8%	3.7%	4.2%	2.9%	0.6%
10/30/09	–3.4%	–11.7%	2.7%	1.5%	–1.8%	–2.5%	–4.1%	–1.7%
11/30/09	8.0%	10.6%	8.8%	4.6%	6.0%	5.6%	–3.1%	–0.1%
12/31/09	1.9%	3.3%	–1.3%	11.1%	1.9%	2.8%	5.7%	–0.2%
1/29/10	–1.4%	12.0%	0.0%	–5.8%	–3.6%	–3.5%	0.4%	3.5%
2/26/10	4.7%	4.9%	3.1%	6.9%	3.0%	3.4%	1.2%	0.6%
3/31/10	12.7%	15.0%	4.5%	4.3%	6.1%	6.3%	1.8%	1.6%
4/30/10	4.9%	–0.2%	5.8%	0.8%	1.6%	2.1%	4.4%	2.6%
5/28/10	–9.3%	–10.9%	–4.5%	–12.7%	–8.0%	–7.9%	0.3%	–1.8%
6/30/10	–8.7%	–2.2%	–1.5%	–4.9%	–5.4%	–5.7%	–1.9%	–1.7%
7/30/10	9.8%	8.6%	5.9%	10.4%	7.2%	7.3%	–0.5%	1.0%
8/31/10	–8.2%	–9.7%	5.6%	–7.6%	–4.5%	–4.8%	–2.8%	–1.7%
9/30/10	12.5%	8.8%	2.0%	22.9%	9.0%	9.6%	3.6%	–2.7%
10/29/10	7.2%	6.2%	4.4%	9.6%	3.9%	4.0%	0.4%	–1.5%
11/30/10	6.2%	–9.2%	1.5%	–7.9%	0.0%	0.6%	3.5%	–0.5%
12/31/10	6.9%	2.3%	–2.0%	15.7%	6.7%	6.8%	0.8%	4.7%
1/31/11	5.4%	6.5%	–4.0%	2.5%	2.3%	2.1%	–2.1%	0.6%
2/28/11	4.0%	4.2%	3.6%	2.7%	3.2%	3.5%	1.6%	0.0%
3/31/11	3.1%	2.7%	0.5%	1.6%	0.1%	0.6%	2.1%	–1.6%
4/29/11	2.5%	7.9%	2.9%	7.8%	2.9%	3.0%	–0.8%	–1.7%
5/31/11	–2.2%	–1.7%	4.9%	–4.8%	–1.1%	–1.3%	–0.6%	–0.7%
6/30/11	0.1%	–5.3%	3.4%	–3.8%	–1.6%	–1.7%	–0.6%	–1.0%
7/29/11	–10.9%	–4.7%	2.6%	–6.9%	–2.0%	–2.3%	–1.2%	–1.2%
8/31/11	–9.3%	–4.4%	5.2%	–8.2%	–5.5%	–6.0%	–2.8%	–2.3%
9/30/11	–8.2%	–9.5%	–2.9%	2.4%	–7.0%	–7.5%	–2.9%	–2.0%
10/31/11	19.3%	8.7%	5.7%	14.3%	10.9%	11.3%	3.6%	3.2%
11/30/11	4.1%	5.1%	3.6%	–4.3%	–0.3%	–0.3%	0.2%	–1.8%
12/30/11	0.4%	6.8%	5.0%	–18.2%	0.9%	0.9%	–0.8%	0.9%

P8.10 **Alternative CAPM-Based Equity Cost of Capital Estimates for the Four Companies in Problem 8.9:** Calculate the cost of equity capital for the four comparable companies in Problem 8.9 using the alternative assumptions used to measure the equity cost of capital in Exhibit 8.10; in other words, create a table similar to Exhibit 8.10 for the four companies in the previous problem. However, do not use the Mayfield estimate of the market risk premium in this example (for each company you will have four different cost of capital estimates—two betas (adjusted and unadjusted) and two market risk premium estimates).

P8.11 **Estimating Three-Factor Risk Factor Betas and Risk Premiums for the Four Companies in Problem 8.9:** Use the information in Problem 8.9 to estimate the three-factor risk factor betas for the four companies in Problem 8.9. Use the assumptions in Exhibit 8.13 and the other information for this problem and calculate the three-factor risk premiums and the CAPM risk premiums for the four companies. Compare these risk premiums to the risk premiums from the CAPM and Bloomberg adjusted betas estimated in Problem 8.10.

SOLUTIONS FOR REVIEW EXERCISES

Review Exercise 8.1: Calculating Beta

Standard deviation of the market return	0.05
Expected market risk premium	0.06

	Firm 1	Firm 2	Firm 3
Standard deviation of firm's return.	0.12	0.06	0.10
Covariance of firm's return and market return	0.003	0.0025	0.004
Firm beta	1.20	1.00	1.60
Firm standard deviation/market std. dev..	2.40	1.20	2.00

The betas are calculated by dividing the covariance of the individual security return and the market return by the variance (standard deviation squared) of the market return. The relative risk of the individual security to the market as measured by standard deviations is calculated by dividing the individual security standard deviation by the market return standard deviation. Beta is a measure of how much more or less an individual stock's return moves with the market portfolio (a measure of risk) whereas the volatility of an individual security's return does not measure risk. Firm 3 has the highest beta or risk measure of 1.6, but Firm 1 has the highest relative standard deviation as compared to the market of 2.4. The relative standard deviation measure indicates the relative volatility of the individual firm's return and the market, but does not measure risk. Firm 2 happens to have the lowest beta of 1.0 and lowest relative standard deviation measure of 1.2.

Review Exercise 8.2: Calculating Portfolio Return and Portfolio Beta

	Firm 1	Firm 2	Firm 3	Firm 4
Total equity market value in portfolio (in millions).	$1,000	$3,500	$2,300	$ 700
Firm beta	0.90	1.07	1.20	1.46
Stock return	5.0%	7.0%	9.0%	10.0%
Firm market value/total market value.	13.3%	46.7%	30.7%	9.3%
Return to the portfolio	7.6%			
Portfolio beta	1.124			

To compute the weights, we simply determine the proportion of each firm's market value to the total value of the portfolio. We then use the weighted average returns and weighted average betas to compute the portfolio return of 7.6% and the portfolio beta of 1.12.

Review Exercise 8.3: Systematic Risk and Unsystematic Risk

Portfolio standard deviation of returns.	0.155
Market portfolio standard deviation of returns.	0.060
Portfolio estimated beta.	1.300
Systematic risk.	25.3%
Unsystematic risk.	74.7%

We can use the following formula to measure systematic risk

$$\frac{\sigma^2(\tilde{R}_i)}{\sigma^2(\tilde{R}_i)} = 1 = \beta_i^2 \frac{\sigma^2(\tilde{R}_m)}{\sigma^2(\tilde{R}_i)} + \frac{\sigma^2(\tilde{\varepsilon}_i)}{\sigma^2(\tilde{R}_i)}$$

(Keep in mind that standard deviations were given in the problem so those amounts must be squared to arrive at variances that are used in the formula.) The proportion of the variance of the security return that is systematic is calculated to be 25%. The unsystematic proportion is therefore 75% (= 1 − .25). The portfolio is not well diversified.

Review Exercise 8.4: Adjusting Estimated Betas

Part 1	Company A	Company B
Beta	1.70	1.00
Percentage of the merged company	33.3%	66.7%
Estimated beta after the merger.	1.233	

The estimated beta for the combined company is 1.23. This is just a value-weighted average of the pre-merger betas. Note this calculation presumes that the merger neither creates nor destroys value and that the pre-merger debt of the companies remains with the merged entity.

Part 2	
Beta (levered = unlevered) for the company	1.500
% of market value in excess assets.	30.0%
Beta for marketable securities	0.400
Beta for unlevered operations (excludes excess assets).	1.971

The estimated beta for unlevered operations is 1.97. To calculate it, we solve for the beta of the operations knowing the unlevered beta of the company is 1.5 and that the excess assets have a beta of 0.4 and represent 30% of the market value of the firm.

Review Exercise 8.5: Bloomberg, Precision, and Vasicek Adjusted Betas

Precision Weighted Beta	Beta Estimate	Standard Error of Beta	1/ Standard Error	Bloomberg Adjusted Beta
Comparable Company #1	0.90	0.50	2.00	0.933
Comparable Company #2	1.10	0.40	2.50	1.067
Comparable Company #3	1.35	0.60	1.67	1.235
Comparable Company #4	1.50	0.45	2.22	1.335
Company being valued	1.10	0.56	1.96	1.067
Comparable company average beta	1.213			1.142
Average beta of comps and company being valued	1.190			
Precision weighted comparable company beta.	1.208			
Sum of 1/standard error.	8.389			
Vasicek adjusted beta—company being valued	1.196			
Variance of the comparable company betas	0.0530			
Standard error squared—company being valued	0.3136			
Weight for company being valued	0.1445			
Weight for comparable company portfolio beta.	0.8555			

The Bloomberg adjusted beta is $0.33 + 0.67 \times$ unadjusted beta.

The comparable company average beta and average beta of the comparable companies and the company being valued are just equally weighted averages.

The precision weighted beta is calculated using Equation 8.9 and the Vasicek adjusted beta is based on Equation 8.10. In this case the average beta, precision-weighted beta and Vasicek adjusted beta are all quite close to one another with a range of 1.19 to 1.21.

Review Exercise 8.6: Alternative CAPM-Based Equity Cost of Capital Estimates for Four Comparable Companies in Review Exercise 8.5

| Company | Equity Cost of Capital Estimate | Yield on Risk-Free Asset | Beta | | Market Risk Premium | | | Maturity Risk Premium |
			Review Exercise 8.5	Bloomberg Adjusted	Historical Based on U.S. Treasury Bill	Historical Based on U.S. Long-Term Gov Bond	Mayfield	
Comparable Company #1 ...	10.1%	5.0%	0.900			5.7%		
	9.9%	5.0%	0.900		8.2%			2.5%
	8.8%	5.0%	0.900				4.2%	
	10.3%	5.0%		0.933		5.7%		
	10.2%	5.0%		0.933	8.2%			2.5%
	8.9%	5.0%		0.933			4.2%	
Average	9.7%							
Comparable Company #2 ...	11.3%	5.0%	1.100			5.7%		
	11.5%	5.0%	1.100		8.2%			2.5%
	9.6%	5.0%	1.100				4.2%	
	11.1%	5.0%		1.067		5.7%		
	11.2%	5.0%		1.067	8.2%			2.5%
	9.5%	5.0%		1.067			4.2%	
Average	10.7%							
Comparable Company #3 ...	12.7%	5.0%	1.350			5.7%		
	13.6%	5.0%	1.350		8.2%			2.5%
	10.7%	5.0%	1.350				4.2%	
	12.0%	5.0%		1.235		5.7%		
	12.6%	5.0%		1.235	8.2%			2.5%
	10.2%	5.0%		1.235			4.2%	
Average	12.0%							
Comparable Company #4 ...	13.6%	5.0%	1.500			5.7%		
	14.8%	5.0%	1.500		8.2%			2.5%
	11.3%	5.0%	1.500				4.2%	
	12.6%	5.0%		1.335		5.7%		
	13.4%	5.0%		1.335	8.2%			2.5%
	10.6%	5.0%		1.335			4.2%	
Average	12.7%							

The betas of the companies come from review exercise 8.5. The market risk premium measured from the S&P 500 less one-month U.S. Treasury Bills is 8.2%, the market risk premium measured from the S&P 500 less U.S. Long-Term Government Bonds is 5.7%, the market risk premium per Mayfield is 4.2% and the maturity premium is 2.5%.

Review Exercise 8.7: Three-Factor Risk Premiums for Four Comparable Companies in Review Exercise 8.5

| | Three-Factor Model | | | CAPM MRP |
	MRP	SMB	HML	
Risk Premiums	0.0804	0.0378	0.0470	0.0820

| | Three-Factor Model Sensitivities | | | Three-Factor Risk Premium | CAPM β | CAPM Risk Premium |
	β_{MRP}	β_{SMB}	β_{HML}			
Comparable Company #1	0.900	0.300	0.250	9.5%	0.900	7.4%
Comparable Company #2	0.800	0.100	0.900	11.0%	1.100	9.0%
Comparable Company #3	1.500	-0.200	0.500	13.7%	1.350	11.1%
Comparable Company #4	1.100	0.600	0.200	12.1%	1.500	12.3%

The three-factor risk premiums and CAPM risk premiums are reasonably close to one another in this example. The smallest difference is for Comparable Company #4 with a difference of 0.2%, whereas the greatest difference is for Comparable Company #3 with a difference of 2.6%.

After mastering the material in this chapter, you will be able to:

1. Understand how companies finance their operations and the effect of these decisions on credit ratings, yields, and default and recovery rates (9.1–9.2)

2. Identify both the cost of debt and default premium components in promised yields on debt and preferred stock (9.3)

3. Understand the process for measuring the costs of non-equity capital (9.4)

4. Use credit rating and financial distress statistical models (9.5–9.6)

5. Understand the importance of measuring the cost of capital for equity-linked securities (9.7)

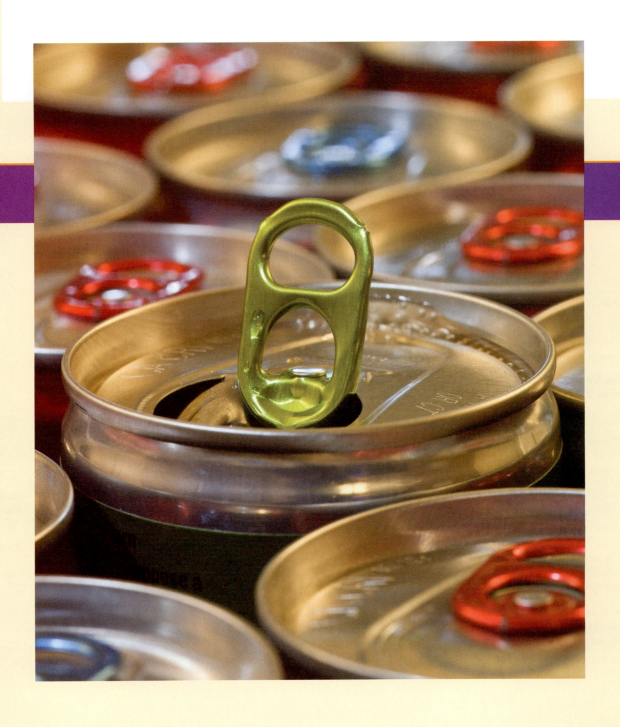

Measuring the Cost of Capital for Debt and Preferred Securities

In February 2009, the credit rating of Alcoa Inc.[1] was downgraded. In its 10-K filing, the company discussed the downgrade as follows:

ALCOA INC.

Alcoa's cost of borrowing and ability to access the capital markets are affected not only by market conditions but also by the short- and long-term debt ratings assigned to Alcoa's debt by the major credit rating agencies. . . .

In February 2009, Standard & Poor's Ratings Services (S&P) and Fitch Ratings (Fitch) each lowered Alcoa's long-term debt rating to BBB–; . . . and both indicated that the current outlook is negative. Also in February 2009, Moody's Investors Service lowered Alcoa's long-term debt rating to Baa3 . . .

Although the company has available to it committed revolving credit facilities to provide liquidity, these recent downgrades in Alcoa's credit ratings, as well as any additional downgrades, will increase Alcoa's cost of borrowing and could have a further adverse effect on its access to the capital markets, . . . An inability to access the capital markets could have a material adverse effect on Alcoa's financial condition, results of operations or cash flow.

In this chapter, we examine the ways in which companies finance their operations with debt and preferred financing, how we estimate the cost of that financing, and the role that credit ratings play in that analysis.

---

[1] Alcoa Inc. produces primary aluminum, fabricated aluminum, and alumina. See the company's 2008 10-K filing at page 21 and other pages for a discussion of its credit rating downgrade.

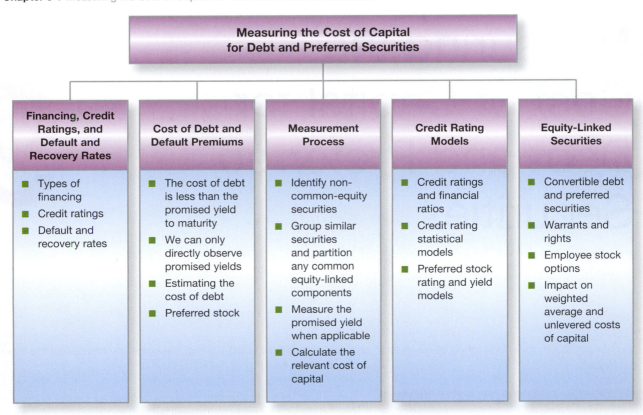

Measuring the Cost of Capital for Debt and Preferred Securities

Financing, Credit Ratings, and Default and Recovery Rates	Cost of Debt and Default Premiums	Measurement Process	Credit Rating Models	Equity-Linked Securities
■ Types of financing ■ Credit ratings ■ Default and recovery rates	■ The cost of debt is less than the promised yield to maturity ■ We can only directly observe promised yields ■ Estimating the cost of debt ■ Preferred stock	■ Identify non-common-equity securities ■ Group similar securities and partition any common equity-linked components ■ Measure the promised yield when applicable ■ Calculate the relevant cost of capital	■ Credit ratings and financial ratios ■ Credit rating statistical models ■ Preferred stock rating and yield models	■ Convertible debt and preferred securities ■ Warrants and rights ■ Employee stock options ■ Impact on weighted average and unlevered costs of capital

INTRODUCTION

In the previous chapter, we discussed how to measure the equity cost of capital. After common equity, the most widely used source of financing is debt financing; however, companies also use other sources of financing such as preferred stock and securities that are convertible into another security (for example, debt or preferred that are convertible into equity as well as **warrants** and **employee stock options**). These other financing sources are relevant to our valuation analysis because the levering, unlevering, and weighted average cost of capital formulas include a component for each type of financing used by the company in its capital structure. The focus of this chapter is on measuring the cost of capital for straight debt and preferred securities (debt and preferred without conversion privileges). In Chapter 12, we discuss measuring the cost of capital in detail for equity-linked securities such as **convertible debt**, **convertible preferred**, warrants, **rights**, and employee stock options.

We can measure the costs of non-common equity capital in various ways. Recall the Capital Asset Pricing Model (CAPM) and the other asset pricing models used to measure the equity cost of capital. We can use models similar to these models along with other asset pricing models, such as option pricing models, or other techniques to measure the cost of capital for non-common-equity securities. We also often use comparable companies to measure various costs of capital. To do the latter, we identify comparable companies whose debt and preferred stock have similar risk characteristics as the debt and preferred claims of the company for which we are measuring the cost of capital. After making any appropriate adjustments, we then use the observed costs of capital for the comparable companies. We can use statistical models (credit rating and bankruptcy prediction models) to assess the risk of a company's debt and preferred securities in order to help select the comparable companies.

An important caveat to our discussion in this and the previous chapter on measuring the cost of capital is that the models and methods available to measure costs of capital are evolving, and none of them fully explains the variation we observe in returns. Factors such as liquidity, regulation, and other factors, including some that are likely yet to be discovered, affect security prices and thus affect the cost of capital. On the state of our understanding of discount rates, Cochrane (2011) concludes "Discount rates vary a lot more than we thought. Most of the puzzles and anomalies that we face amount to discount-rate variation we do not understand. Our theoretical controversies are about how discount rates are formed.

We need to recognize and incorporate discount-rate variation in applied procedures. We are really only beginning these tasks."[2]

9.1 TYPES OF NON-COMMON-EQUITY SECURITIES

In this section of the chapter, we provide a summary of alternative sources of financing. We present a list of the alternative sources of financing in Exhibit 9.1. This list is not meant to be exhaustive, but rather, it presents the most prevalent sources of financing companies use.

LO1 Understand how companies finance their operations and the effect of these decisions on credit ratings, yields, and default and recovery rates

EXHIBIT 9.1 Alternative Sources of Financing	
Debt	**Equity**
Short-Term Debt	**Preferred or Preference Stock**
Bank debt (secured or unsecured)	Fixed or variable dividend rate (usually fixed)
Revolving line of credit	Callable
Commercial paper	Convertible (into common stock)
	Publicly traded or privately placed
Long-Term Debt	Cumulative dividends (if not paid)
Mortgage (secured)	Required redemption (redemption price)
Notes (secured or unsecured)	Liquidation price
Capital lease (secured)	
Debentures or bonds	**Common Stock**
Senior or subordinated (junior)	Class A (voting)
Sinking fund or no sinking fund	Class B
Callable	Voting (more rights or fewer rights than Class A)
Putable	or non-voting
Convertible (into preferred stock or common stock) or with warrants	Higher priority or same priority (as Class A)
Publicly traded or privately placed	Fixed or variable or no dividend rate
Fixed or floating interest rate (with/without a collar or cap, inflation adjusted, income based, equity linked)	**Equity Derivatives**
Covenants (performance hurdles or restricting actions)	Convertible components of debt and preferred stock
Zero-coupon and pay-in-kind debt (see debentures for characteristics)	Employee stock options
	Warrants
	Rights offering
Quasi Long-Term Debt	
Operating leases	
Swaps	
Interest rate and other swaps	

We see from this exhibit that companies have many alternative sources of financing available to them. Naturally, one of the company's goals is to finance itself at the lowest possible cost in order to maximize the value of the firm and the value of its common equity. Recall that a company's unlevered free cash flows represent the cash flow available for distribution to all of the company's investors—in other words, to the investors of every source of financing used by a company (excluding non-interest-bearing operating liabilities)—before consideration of any benefits from interest tax shields. Based on the contracts for the different forms of financing, investors in different securities have different claims, and the varying claims have different rights and priorities on the company's unlevered free cash flows. These, as well as other, differences result in different costs of capital for different sources of financing. Claims that are more senior or have higher priority over other claims generally have a lower cost of capital.

---

[2] Cochrane, John, "Presidential Address: Discount Rates," *The Journal of Finance* vol. LXVI, no. 4 (August 2011), pp. 1047–1108.

How Do Companies Finance Their Balance Sheets?

In Exhibit 9.2, we show the distribution of the different types of financing that companies use based on book values reported in their financial statements.[3] In this chart, we present the distribution in terms of the percentage of the average company's balance sheet that is financed with various types of debt, operating liabilities, and equities (excluding employee stock options, warrants, and rights). Note that this chart does not represent these percentages in terms of market values. Recall that in estimating the weighted average cost of capital, we use weights based on market values, not book values, and we do not include operating liabilities in measuring the capital structure. The exhibit does, however, show the relative book values of the various liability and equity claims for the average company. We will discuss estimated market-value-based percentages in a subsequent chapter when we discuss the weighted average cost of capital.

| **EXHIBIT 9.2** | How Companies Finance Their Balance Sheets |

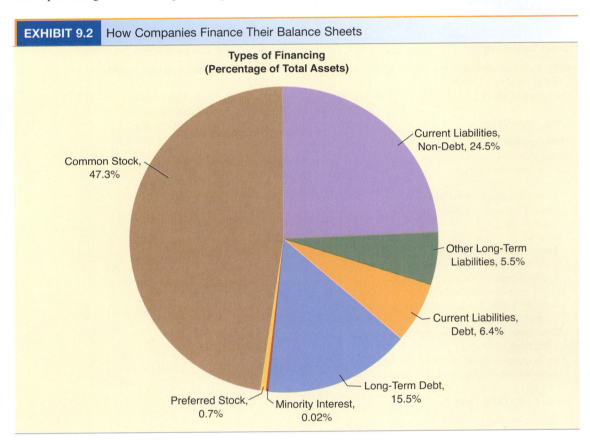

**Types of Financing
(Percentage of Total Assets)**

Current Liabilities, Non-Debt, 24.5%
Other Long-Term Liabilities, 5.5%
Current Liabilities, Debt, 6.4%
Long-Term Debt, 15.5%
Minority Interest, 0.02%
Preferred Stock, 0.7%
Common Stock, 47.3%

On average, common stock financing (on a book value basis) accounts for 47.3% of the companies' total liabilities and stockholders' equity, and long-term debt represents 15.5% of the total. Current debt (bank debt and the current portion of long-term debt) accounts for 6.4% of the total, and preferred stock accounts for less than 1% of the total. Current non-interest-bearing operating liabilities and other long-term non-interest-bearing operating liabilities account for 24.5% and 5.5% of the total, respectively. Thus, on average, non-interest-bearing operating liabilities finance 30% of the companies' assets.

Valuation Key 9.1

Companies can use many different types of non-common-equity securities to finance their operations. Non-common-equity claims can have different maturity dates, different rights, and different priorities on a company's unlevered free cash flows. These differences can result in varying costs of capital for different sources of financing.

---

[3] To be included in the sample, the company needed complete information for its 2010 fiscal year available in the Compustat® North American Industrial Annual File. The resulting sample consisted of 5,439 U.S. companies.

Preferred stock is a different form of non-common-equity financing than debt. Like common equity, it pays dividends rather than interest, but it often does not have a maturity date. In general, it legally has equity status—thus, it cannot force a company into bankruptcy—and has priority on claims over common equity but below debt. Its dividends are either cumulative or non-cumulative. If dividends are cumulative, missed dividends become dividends in arrears that must be paid before the company makes distributions to common shareholders. Preferred stock can be convertible (typically into common stock), be callable by the company, be redeemable (at the option of the company or be required after certain events), have a floating dividend rate, and even participate in a company's profits. Companies can issue preferred stock directly or through a special-purpose vehicle (trust).

On average, preferred stock accounts for a small portion of the total financing of companies, less than 1%. Further, we know that preferred stock is not used by all companies and that it is used more often in certain industries. In this sample, over 80% of the companies use debt financing, but only 10% of the companies use preferred stock financing. However, this exhibit does not show that preferred stock financing is more likely to be used in the oil and gas extraction, chemicals and allied products, communications, electric, gas and sanitary services, and business services industry groups.

Valuation in Practice 9.1

Washington Mutual, Inc. Issuance of 7.75% Series R Non-Cumulative Perpetual Convertible Preferred Stock Washington Mutual, Inc.* announced that it was going to increase its public offering to 3,000,000 shares of 7.75% Series R Non-Cumulative Perpetual Convertible Preferred Stock, priced at $1,000 per share, resulting in a $3.0 billion issuance before transactions costs. In its amended prospectus, dated December 12, 2007, Washington Mutual described this security as follows:

Washington Mutual, Inc. is offering 3,000,000 shares of our 7.75% Series R Non-Cumulative Perpetual Convertible Preferred Stock, referred to as the Series R Preferred Stock.

Dividends on the Series R Preferred Stock will be payable quarterly in arrears, when, as and if declared by our board of directors, at a rate of 7.75% per year on the liquidation preference of $1,000 per share. . . . Dividends on the Series R Preferred Stock will be non-cumulative. If for any reason our board of directors does not declare full cash dividends on the Series R Preferred Stock for a dividend period, we will have no obligation to pay any dividends for that period, . . . However, . . ., we may not declare or pay dividends on or redeem or purchase our common stock or other junior securities during the next succeeding dividend period.

Each share of the Series R Preferred Stock may be converted at any time, at the option of the holder, into 47.0535 shares of our common stock (which reflects an approximate initial conversion price of $21.25 per share of common stock) plus cash in lieu of fractional shares, subject to anti-dilution adjustments. . . .

On or after December 18, 2012, if the closing price of our common stock exceeds 130% of the conversion price for 20 trading days during any consecutive 30 trading day period . . ., we may at our option cause some or all of the Series R Preferred Stock to be automatically converted into common stock at the then prevailing conversion rate.

Investing in the shares of Series R Preferred Stock involves risks. See "Risk Factors" beginning on page S-11.

* Washington Mutual, Inc. was a financial services company that served consumers and small to medium-sized businesses. Its assets were eventually sold to JPMorgan Chase.

Balance Sheet Liabilities and Other Equities Not Included in Non-Common-Equity Financing

Although we show all of the typical liabilities and equities we see on balance sheets in Exhibit 9.2 (including non-interest-bearing operating liabilities), our focus in this chapter is on measuring the cost of capital for straight debt and preferred stock. Recall that when valuing a company, we implicitly "net" non-interest-bearing operating liabilities against the value of the company's operations and excess assets; in other words, the value of the firm is measured net of its non-interest-bearing operating liabilities.

We "net" non-interest-bearing liabilities against the value of the company because financing costs related to non-interest-bearing-operating liabilities are embedded in the company's operating expenses, and we do not have an easy way of disentangling them. For example, when a company buys a product or service on account from a vendor, the vendor charges the company for the product or service plus an implicit financing charge for not paying at the time the good or service is received. Hence, the financing charge is embedded in the cost of the product or service and cannot be easily partitioned from the value of the operations.

Thus, we do not include all of a company's liabilities as part of its capital structure. We use the term *debt* to represent certain types of financing such as notes, mortgages, and bonds (debentures). From a valuation perspective, we define debt to be an amount contractually owed to another party that has an explicit or implicit interest payment *that we can measure*. This definition excludes such liabilities as deferred income taxes, unearned revenue, and most operating liabilities (for example, accounts payable, wages payable, accruals, etc.).

9.2 CREDIT AND PREFERRED STOCK RATINGS, DEFAULTS, AND YIELDS

Unlike common equity, debt and preferred stock have contractually promised payments. Thus, measuring the cost of capital requires an assessment of both the promised payments and the company's ability to make the payments promised in the debt or preferred stock contract. The likelihood of default and the recovery in case of default is a function of the riskiness of the firm's unlevered cash flows, the leverage ratio the firm maintains, the magnitude and timing of the payments that the firm is required to make to all of its non-common-equity investors, the extent to which the debt is secured by the firm's assets, and the value of its non-secured assets. Different securities issued by the same company can have different costs of capital due to differences in the terms of the contracts; these include maturity, seniority, and security or collateral features. In addition, restrictions that the issuing corporation agrees upon when issuing debt can affect the cost of debt. For example, a corporation may agree to limit the amount of indebtedness that it can take on, or it may agree to restrict the amount of its asset sales, common stock repurchases, and dividends. In addition, it may agree to let certain financial measures or ratios determine when it has had a "technical default" (even though it hasn't missed any required payments), forcing the company to renegotiate the terms of the agreement with the creditors or receive a waiver for the technical default. These restrictions or covenants tend to reduce the cost of debt.

Fortunately, credit rating agencies provide assessments of the ability of a company to meet the obligations of its debt and preferred stock. These ratings and the market data associated with them provide useful information for measuring the costs of debt and preferred capital of a company. In this section of the chapter, we discuss credit and preferred stock ratings as well as relevant associated data.

Credit Rating Agencies

Ratings on the debt securities of companies, municipalities, and governments are issued by various credit rating agencies. These rating agencies include, among others, Moody's Investors Service, Inc. (Moody's); Standard & Poor's (S&P); Fitch, Inc. (Fitch); and Dominion Bond Rating Services, Limited (DBRS)—a Canadian company. In the United States, all of these credit rating agencies are designated by the U.S. Securities and Exchange Commission as **Nationally Recognized Statistical Rating Organizations** (NRSROs) and they operate in many markets around the world (as of May 2012, there were nine NRSROs in total). In addition to these global credit rating agencies, many rating agencies have their focus in a single country or region. For example, Asia, China, Japan, Malaysia, Indonesia, Korea, Thailand, and the Philippines all have local credit rating agencies, as do some countries in Latin America such as Columbia, Chile, Ecuador, Panama, and Peru.

Credit ratings indicate the likelihood of timely repayment of principal and interest by the borrower. Higher probabilities of repayment are associated with higher ratings. Ratings measure default risk and also incorporate recovery rates in the event of default. However, they do not measure overall market interest rate risk—that is, the risk that the value of the bond may change due to fluctuations in market-wide interest rates.

S&P rates bonds AAA, AA, A, BBB, BB, B, CCC, CC, C, and D. The D rating is reserved for bonds that have defaulted. Ratings between AA and CCC are assigned gradients of + or − to show their relative standing within the major rating classifications. For example, an A-rated bond can be rated A+, A, or A−. Bonds rated BBB− or above are generally considered **investment-grade bonds**, and those rated below BBB− are **non-investment grade**, and may be referred to as speculative or **junk bonds**. Some institutions and funds are prohibited from holding bonds that are not investment grade.

Moody's has a similar ranking system: Aaa, Aa, A, Baa, Ba, B, Caa, Ca, and C with gradations of 1, 2, and 3 within the rating categories of Aa to B. Thus, an Aa-rated bond can be rated Aa1, Aa2, or Aa3. Much like S&P, Dominion Bond Rating Services uses rating categories of AAA to D and denotes three gradations between AA and C. Fitch's also has rating categories that are similar to those of S&P.[4]

In Exhibit 9.3, we show the distribution of credit ratings for a sample of 1,148 publicly traded companies for which S&P had a current credit rating in 2008 (we will describe this sample in more detail later in the chapter).

EXHIBIT 9.3	Distribution of Company Credit Ratings from Standard and Poor's in 2008

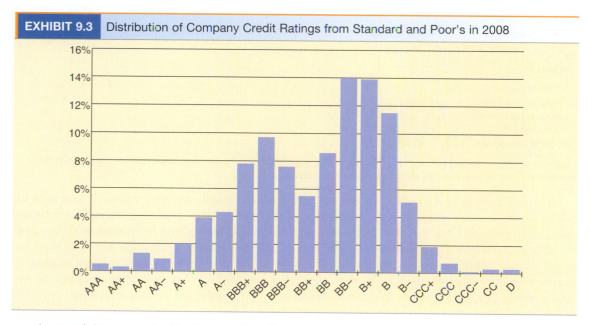

As we might expect, the distribution of credit ratings shows that fewer companies have credit ratings in the highest (AAA and AA) and lowest (CCC, CC, C, and D) categories. The proportion of ratings in each class, especially those in the middle of the distribution, changes over time, depending on the state of the economy. If the economy is weaker, as it was in 2008 (the time period of this sample), we observe more companies in the B categories; conversely, if the economy is strong, we observe a shift in the ratings as more ratings exist in the BB categories.

Valuation Key 9.2

Debt and preferred stock ratings measure the likelihood of default and incorporate information on expected recovery in the event of default. Rating agencies use factors such as the riskiness of the firm's cash flows, the firm's leverage ratio, the payments that the firm is required to make to all of its lenders, and the extent to which the debt is secured by assets in order to develop these ratings.

Ratings and Recovery and Default Rates

As stated earlier, credit ratings are intended to reflect both the likelihood of default and the anticipated **recovery rates** in the event of default; the lower the rating, the more likely the company will default on its promised payments and, generally, the lower the recovery will be. Although we use the term "default" for both debt and preferred stock, the term "dividend omission" is often used instead of "default" when discussing preferred stock because not paying or omitting a preferred stock dividend payment is not a violation of its associated contract.

---

[4] For more information on the credit agencies and their ratings methodologies as well as some statistics on ratios for various credit ratings, check out http://www.standardandpoors.com/ratings/ and http://www.moodys.com.

Empirically, we observe that the higher the rating, the higher the recovery rate. Therefore, the percentage of the promised payments on a security that is recovered when a company defaults is negatively correlated with default rates.[5] In Exhibit 9.4, we present recovery rates for debt, which are measured by Moody's as functions of seniority and security.

EXHIBIT 9.4	Average Recovery Rates for Various Types of Debt Securities (1982–2007) from Moody's Investors Service*		
Type of Security		**Based on Trading Prices after Default**	**Ultimate Recovery**
Bank Loans			
Senior secured		70.5%	
Senior unsecured		54.0%	
All			82.0%
Bonds			
Senior secured		51.9%	65.8%
Senior unsecured		36.7%	39.0%
Senior subordinated		32.4%	29.1%
Subordinated		31.2%	26.5%
Junior subordinated		24.0%	16.3%

* See Exhibits 8 and 9 in Emery, K., S. Ou, J. Tennant, F. Kim, and R. Cantor, *Corporate Default and Recovery Rates*, 1920–2007, Moody's Investors Service, February 2008, reprinted with permission.

The first column of recovery rates presents recovery rates based on market prices 30 days after the default event; in other words, it is the percentage of the amount owed (including accrued interest and outstanding principal) that would be received if the investor sold the security in the market 30 days after the default. Bank loan prices are taken from the secondary loan market, where bank and other loans are traded on both public and private companies. The second column of recovery rates is based on the ultimate outcome; in other words, it is the percentage of the amount owed (including accrued interest and outstanding principal) that an investor ultimately received from holding the security until it was redeemed or liquidated. These two columns do not represent "apples-to-apples" comparisons because the ultimate recovery rates in the second column typically require the investor to wait longer than 30 days to receive the recovered amount. Since the recovery rates are not adjusted for the time value of money, they cannot be directly compared to one another. As we would expect, this exhibit shows that secured debt and more senior debt have higher recovery rates.

In Exhibit 9.5, we present recovery rates—based on market prices 30 days after the default event—for senior unsecured bonds partitioned by the bond's credit rating as measured by Moody's. This exhibit presents average recovery rates by rating class within a given number of years until default. The Year 1 column in this exhibit is the recovery rate after the bond was rated in the rating class for that row if it defaulted in the first year; the Year 2 column is the recovery rate after the bond was rated in the rating class for that row if it defaulted in the first or second year; and so forth. In this sample, no AAA bond defaulted in the first three years after it had been given an AAA rating. Of the AAA bonds defaulting in the fourth year subsequent to being rated as an AAA-rated bond, the recovery rate was 97% of principal and interest. For those AAA bonds defaulting within five years subsequent to being rated an AAA bond, the recovery rate was 74%. This exhibit shows that for a given column (number of years after the bond was rated), higher ratings generally have higher recovery rates, but the difference narrows as the number of years increases. For example, recovery rates on investment-grade debt are greater than the recovery rates on speculative-grade debt in the first few years but are more similar by years 4 and 5.

In Exhibit 9.6, we show recovery rates for preferred stock—based on market prices 30 days after the default event—as measured by Moody's. The rows in the exhibit represent different "default" events or impairments and subsequent or contemporaneous events relative to the default event. In addition, we also present recovery rates based on whether the dividends are cumulative or not. The two columns of recovery rates represent the recovery rates for preferred stock issued directly by the company (Corporate or Non-Trust) and through a special-purpose vehicle (Trust). The exhibit shows that preferred stock recovery rates are higher with dividend omissions than in the case of distress exchanges, which have a higher

---

[5] See the discussion on page 10 in *Corporate Default and Recovery Rates*, 1920–2007, Moody's Investors Service, February 2008, reprinted with permission.

EXHIBIT 9.5	Average Recovery Rates for Various Types of Credit Ratings of Senior Unsecured Bonds by Year Prior to Default (1982–2007) from Moody's Investors Service*

Senior Unsecured Bond Rating	Year 1	Year 2	Year 3	Year 4	Year 5	Average
Aaa				97.0%	74.1%	85.6%
Aa	95.4%	62.1%	30.8%	55.3%	41.6%	57.0%
A	46.2%	54.8%	50.2%	47.7%	47.8%	49.4%
Baa	46.3%	44.8%	46.0%	42.0%	43.8%	44.6%
Ba	42.8%	40.8%	39.8%	43.1%	41.9%	41.7%
B	37.6%	37.2%	40.2%	43.4%	47.0%	41.1%
Caa–C	36.7%	36.3%	36.8%	38.9%	32.6%	36.2%
Investment grade	47.5%	48.9%	47.1%	45.6%	45.2%	46.9%
Speculative grade.	37.9%	37.6%	39.5%	42.8%	44.5%	40.4%
All ratings	38.7%	39.2%	41.0%	43.5%	44.7%	41.4%

* See Exhibit 23 in Emery, K., S. Ou, J. Tennant, F. Kim, and R. Cantor, *Corporate Default and Recovery Rates*, 1920–2007, Moody's Investors Service, February 2008, reprinted with permission.

recovery rate than Chapter 11 bankruptcy filings. Corporate or non-trust preferred shares have a higher recovery rate than preferred stock issued by a special-purpose entity, and cumulative preferred stock has a higher recovery rate than non-cumulative preferred stock. Not surprisingly, the recovery rates on debt are generally higher than the recovery rates on preferred stock.

EXHIBIT 9.6	Average Recovery Rates for Various Types of Preferred Stock (1983–2007) from Moody's Investors Service*

	Corporate (Non-Trust)	Trust
All issuances	23%	12%
Dividend omission	35%	18%
Distress exchange	22%	
Chapter 11	16%	11%
Missed payment.	19%	9%
Other.	2%	6%
Preferred Impairment Contemporaneous with Bond Default		
Cumulative dividends.	20%	
Non-cumulative	13%	
Dividend Omission with Subsequent Bond Default		
Cumulative dividends.	34%	
Non-cumulative	26%	
Dividend Omission with no Subsequent Bond Default		
Cumulative dividends.	42%	
Non-cumulative	33%	
All Issuances		
Cumulative dividends.		18%
Non-cumulative		7%

*See Exhibits 8, 45, and 46 in Emery, K., S. Ou, J. Tennant, F. Kim, and R. Cantor, *Corporate Default and Recovery Rates*, 1920–2007, Moody's Investors Service, February 2008 , reprinted with permission.

In Exhibit 9.7, we provide data on the cumulative weighted average default rate of bonds that default N years into the future (N-year horizon) from Moody's Investors Service. Moody's recognizes a default if the company misses or delays payment of interest or principal, if the company files for bankruptcy or experiences other legal impediments to making timely interest or principal payments, or if a distressed exchange occurs. A distressed exchange occurs when a debt security is exchanged for another security (or securities) that diminishes the company's financial obligation and helps the company avoid default.

EXHIBIT 9.7	Average Cumulative Issuer-Weighted Global Default Rates (1983–2007) from Moody's Investors Service*

Rating	Cumulative Percent of Companies in Rating Class that Defaulted N Years in the Future							
	1	2	3	4	5	6	7	8
Aaa	0.0%	0.0%	0.0%	0.0%	0.1%	0.1%	0.2%	0.2%
Aa1	0.0%	0.0%	0.0%	0.1%	0.1%	0.2%	0.2%	0.2%
Aa2	0.0%	0.0%	0.0%	0.1%	0.2%	0.3%	0.3%	0.4%
Aa3	0.0%	0.0%	0.1%	0.1%	0.2%	0.2%	0.3%	0.3%
A1	0.0%	0.1%	0.2%	0.3%	0.4%	0.4%	0.5%	0.5%
A2	0.0%	0.1%	0.2%	0.4%	0.6%	0.7%	0.9%	1.1%
A3	0.0%	0.2%	0.3%	0.4%	0.6%	0.7%	0.9%	1.1%
Baa1	0.1%	0.4%	0.7%	0.9%	1.1%	1.3%	1.6%	1.8%
Baa2	0.1%	0.4%	0.8%	1.4%	1.9%	2.4%	2.9%	3.3%
Baa3	0.3%	0.8%	1.5%	2.2%	3.0%	3.8%	4.4%	5.1%
Ba1	0.7%	1.8%	3.2%	4.6%	6.0%	7.4%	8.4%	9.1%
Ba2	0.8%	2.2%	4.0%	5.9%	7.6%	8.8%	10.0%	11.2%
Ba3	1.8%	5.0%	9.1%	13.1%	16.5%	19.7%	22.6%	25.3%
B1	2.6%	7.1%	11.9%	16.4%	20.9%	25.1%	29.4%	33.2%
B2	4.3%	9.9%	15.0%	19.3%	22.8%	25.9%	29.0%	31.3%
B3	8.5%	16.1%	23.2%	29.7%	35.5%	41.3%	45.4%	48.9%
Caa1	10.5%	20.9%	30.4%	38.4%	44.8%	49.0%	50.8%	51.1%
Caa22	18.4%	27.7%	34.8%	41.0%	44.8%	48.8%	52.2%	56.4%
Caa3	25.6%	37.6%	44.5%	49.6%	54.7%	55.0%	55.0%	55.0%
Ca–C	32.9%	43.1%	51.5%	56.9%	63.3%	66.2%	70.9%	75.5%
Investment-grade	0.1%	0.2%	0.4%	0.6%	0.8%	1.0%	1.2%	1.4%
Speculative-grade	4.5%	9.0%	13.4%	17.3%	20.6%	23.6%	26.1%	28.3%
All-rated	1.6%	3.2%	4.7%	6.0%	7.0%	7.9%	8.7%	9.3%

*See Exhibit 29 in Emery, K., S. Ou, J. Tennant, F. Kim, and R. Cantor, *Corporate Default and Recovery Rates*, 1920–2007, Moody's Investors Service, February 2008, reprinted with permission.

Moody's measures the cumulative weighted average default rates in Exhibit 9.7 by first forming a cohort of similarly rated bonds for each year, 1920 to 2007, in the analysis. Moody's tracks each cohort and measures the annual default rate for annual horizons of up to a 20-years;[6] for example, the 1988 cohort of B3 rated bonds has annual default rates for each year from 1988 through 2007, or for one to 20-year horizons. After Moody's measures the default rates for each horizon for each cohort, it measures the weighted average annual default rate for each horizon across all cohorts with the same rating. Moody's uses the weighted average annual default rates to calculate the cumulative default rates in Exhibit 9.7 for an N-year horizon by multiplying the series of one minus each default rate for each year from year-one to year-N and then subtracts the resulting number from 1. For example, the cumulative weighted average eight-year default rate is equal to $1 - (1 -$ first-year weighted average default rate) $\times$ $(1 -$ second-year weighted average default rate) $\times \ldots \times (1 -$ eighth-year weighted average default rate). Thus, we can use the cumulative weighted average default rates in Exhibit 9.7 to measure the weighted average default rate for a specific year by dividing one-minus the cumulative weighted average default rate for that horizon by one-minus cumulative weighted average default rate for the previous horizon and then subtract the resulting number from 1; for example, the weighted average default rate for the eighth year for B3 rated debt is equal to the 6.4% $[.064 = 1 - (1 - .489)/(1 - .454)]$.

Valuation Key 9.3

We can use the recovery rates and default percentages of debt and preferred stock (published by various rating agencies) to help measure the expected cash flows of securities of a given type and rating.

---

[6] The number of bonds in the cohort decreases in the subsequent horizons if Moody's no longer rates the bond, however, the bond remains in its cohort even if Moody's changes its rating. A debt rating can be withdrawn by Moody's for various reasons such as the debt matures or Moody's no longer has adequate information to rate the debt security. For the details of these calculations see, J. Tung and A. Metz, Glossary of Moody's Ratings Performance Metrics – Special Comment, Moody's Investors Service, September 30, 2011, pp. 2 – 4.

Cumulative Percent of Companies in Rating Class that Defaulted N Years in the Future											
9	**10**	**11**	**12**	**13**	**14**	**15**	**16**	**17**	**18**	**19**	**20**
0.2%	0.2%	0.2%	0.2%	0.2%	0.2%	0.2%	0.2%	0.2%	0.2%	0.2%	0.2%
0.2%	0.2%	0.2%	0.2%	0.4%	0.6%	0.8%	0.9%	0.9%	0.9%	0.9%	0.9%
0.4%	0.5%	0.6%	0.7%	0.8%	0.8%	0.8%	0.9%	1.1%	1.4%	1.7%	1.7%
0.3%	0.3%	0.4%	0.6%	0.8%	0.9%	1.0%	1.1%	1.3%	1.5%	1.5%	1.5%
0.6%	0.7%	0.8%	1.0%	1.1%	1.4%	1.7%	2.0%	2.1%	2.1%	2.1%	2.1%
1.2%	1.3%	1.4%	1.4%	1.5%	1.6%	1.6%	1.8%	2.3%	2.8%	3.2%	3.3%
1.2%	1.2%	1.3%	1.3%	1.4%	1.5%	1.9%	2.3%	2.8%	3.5%	3.9%	4.4%
2.0%	2.1%	2.3%	2.5%	2.9%	3.5%	4.1%	4.8%	5.4%	5.7%	5.7%	5.7%
3.9%	4.6%	5.5%	6.4%	7.2%	7.9%	8.7%	9.3%	10.0%	11.2%	12.3%	12.5%
5.6%	5.9%	6.1%	6.3%	7.1%	7.9%	8.2%	8.2%	8.6%	9.0%	9.4%	9.9%
9.6%	10.3%	11.1%	12.2%	12.9%	13.6%	14.5%	16.0%	18.0%	20.2%	22.8%	24.5%
12.4%	13.5%	15.0%	17.0%	18.9%	20.8%	23.1%	25.1%	26.9%	27.1%	27.6%	27.6%
27.8%	30.3%	32.4%	34.1%	36.2%	38.9%	40.4%	41.4%	42.0%	42.4%	42.4%	43.2%
36.2%	38.5%	40.5%	42.3%	44.0%	46.6%	48.3%	49.5%	49.5%	49.5%	49.5%	49.5%
33.8%	36.0%	37.5%	39.0%	40.7%	43.0%	46.3%	47.8%	49.4%	51.3%	51.3%	51.3%
51.3%	53.0%	55.7%	58.9%	60.9%	61.8%	62.1%	62.1%	62.5%	63.4%	63.4%	63.4%
51.1%	51.1%	51.1%									
62.9%	70.0%	73.3%	73.3%	75.2%	77.5%	79.2%	82.5%	83.4%	83.4%	83.4%	83.4%
55.0%	55.0%										
75.5%	75.5%	75.5%	75.5%	75.5%	75.5%	75.5%	75.5%	75.5%			
1.6%	1.7%	1.9%	2.0%	2.3%	2.5%	2.7%	3.0%	3.3%	3.7%	3.9%	4.1%
30.2%	31.8%	33.4%	34.9%	36.4%	38.0%	39.4%	40.7%	41.8%	42.9%	43.8%	44.6%
9.8%	10.2%	10.6%	11.0%	11.4%	11.9%	12.3%	12.7%	13.1%	13.5%	13.9%	14.1%

9.3 THE DEBT COST OF CAPITAL IS LESS THAN THE PROMISED YIELD TO MATURITY

Usually, at this point in a chapter, we would discuss the process to implement the concepts in the chapter. Before we do that, however, we must first discuss a topic that is not well understood and affects the process we use. A potentially important issue to consider when estimating the cost of capital for debt and preferred securities is the difference between the promised yield and the cost of capital. The **debt cost of capital** we use in our valuation formulas is equal to the required or expected rate of return based on the riskiness of the expected cash flows. The **promised yield** is equal to the rate of return the investor would realize if the debt is fully paid and the company does not default, but those are not the expected cash flows unless the default risk is non-existent.

A debt contract specifies the magnitude and timing of the agreed-upon cash payments, which we call promised payments. However, recall that the expected cash flows for a given period equal the sum of the cash flows in each possible state (or outcome that might occur) for that period, each multiplied by its respective probability of occurring. Naturally, when investors make investments in debt securities, they assess the likelihood of the debtor defaulting on the agreed-upon cash payments, and they then forecast the amount they expect to recover in default. We measure expected cash flows by adjusting the promised payments for both the probability of default and the amount expected to be recovered in each possible state. Thus, the promised yield to maturity, which is based on the magnitude and timing of the promised cash flows, is larger than the debt cost of capital that is based on the expected cash flows. (Although we will discuss preferred stock later in the chapter, this issue also pertains to it; that is, the cost of capital for preferred stock is less than the promised dividend yield on preferred stock unless the default risk is zero.)

We use a simple example to illustrate this calculation. Assume there is a one-period debt agreement with two possible outcomes—default and no default. The terms of this debt agreement are as follows. One year after the execution of the contract, the company will pay the investor 9% annual interest—called the coupon rate—on the face (or par) value of the loan plus the $1,000 face (or par) value. The promised

LO2 Identify both the cost of debt and default premium components in promised yields on debt and preferred stock

payments for this debt agreement, all to be made at the end of one year, are $90 of interest plus $1,000 of principal, or $1,090 ($1,090 = $1,000 × 0.09 + $1,000). These promised payments are the maximum payments the company would ever pay under the contract. If the investor's expected cash flows are equal to the maximum promised payments (in other words, there is no chance of default), then the 9% rate of interest (which is also the promised yield, assuming the bond is valued at $1,000) is the cost of capital for this security. However, if the expected cash flows are less than the promised cash flows, then the cost of capital must be less than the promised yield.

To illustrate this point, we assume that investors assess a 4% probability of the company defaulting on the promised payments, and if the company defaults, the investor will be paid $0 interest and 60% of the principal (or $600 = $1,000 × 0.6). We can measure the expected cash flows as follows. The expected interest payment is equal to $86.40 ($86.40 = $1,000 × 0.09 × 0.96), which is $3.60 (or 4%) less than the $90 promised interest payment. The expected principal payment is equal to $984.00 [$984.00 = $1,000 × 0.96 + $1,000 × 0.6 × (1 − 0.96)], which is $16.00 (or 1.6%) less than the $1,000 promised principal payment. The total expected cash flow (expected interest and principal) is $1,070.40, which we show below.

	Promised	No-Default State	Default State	Expected	
Debt (coupon) interest rate.	9.0%				
Face value	$1,000.00				
Probability		96.0%	4.0%		
Recovery rate—interest		100.0%	0.0%		
Recovery rate—principal		100.0%	60.0%		
Interest	$ 90.00	$ 86.40	$ 0.00	$ 86.40	96.0%
Principal	1,000.00	$960.00	$24.00	984.00	98.4%
Total	$1,090.00			$1,070.40	98.2%
Interest rate (9%)	0.9174				
Debt cost of capital (10.0%).				0.9091	
Present value	$1,000.00			$ 973.09	97.3%

Exhibit may contain small rounding errors

If investors require an expected annual rate of return (in other words, a debt cost of capital) of 10% for a debt security with this risk (remember there is a 4% chance of default), then the investors would be willing to pay $973.09 for the debt. We calculate this value by discounting the sum of the expected interest payment of $86.40 and the expected principal payment of $984.00 by the cost of debt of 10%.

$$\$973.09 = \frac{(\$1,000 \times 0.09 \times 0.96) + [\$1,000 \times 0.96 + \$1,000 \times 0.6 \times (1 - 0.96)]}{1.10}$$

$$\$973.09 = \frac{\$86.40 + \$984.00}{1.10}$$

Valuation Key 9.4

Expected cash flows from debt or preferred stock are equal to the probability weighted cash flows under different states of the world. These consist of the cash flows the investor expects to receive if the company defaults times the probability of default, plus the promised cash flows the investor will receive if the company does not default times the probability of no default.

The issue we face when valuing a company, however, is that we neither directly observe the debt cost of capital nor do we observe the expected cash flows. However, we can often observe or measure the price of the debt issue. If we did know the price, promised payments, probability of default, and expected recovery rates, we could calculate the debt cost of capital, r_D, which is equivalent to calculating an internal rate of return based on the expected payments and the price of the debt.

$$\$973.09 = \frac{\$86.40 + \$984.00}{1 + r_D}$$

$$r_D = \frac{\$86.40 + \$984.00}{\$973.09} - 1 = 0.1$$

Valuation Key 9.5

The debt cost of capital we use in valuation formulas—like the weighted average cost of capital and levering and unlevering formulas—is equal to the required or expected rate of return, which is based on the timing, magnitude, and riskiness of the expected cash flows. We can calculate the debt cost of capital using an internal rate of return formula if we know the price and expected cash flows. Expected cash flows are based on the promised payments, the probability of default, and the expected recovery rates in the event of default. Simply calculating the internal rate of return from the promised payments and the current price will not yield the debt cost of capital unless the default probability is zero.

Typically, we cannot use the simple formula above to measure the debt cost of capital, because most debt agreements have a longer term to maturity and other complicating characteristics; we can, however, use the more general form of the internal rate of return formula:

$$0 = \frac{E_0(CF_1)}{(1 + r_D)} + \frac{E_0(CF_2)}{(1 + r_D)^2} + \frac{E_0(CF_3)}{(1 + r_D)^3} + \ldots + \frac{E_0(CF_T)}{(1 + r_D)^T} - Price_0 \qquad (9.1)$$

where $E_0(CF_t)$ is the expected cash flow for period t as of time 0, and $Price_0$ is the price of the bond at time 0. Measuring the expected cash flows from the investment requires that we know the promised cash flows, which we can observe from the contract, but it also requires that we know the default and recovery rates. Note that the default and recovery rates from Exhibits 9.4 to 9.7 are averages over many years, and while these statistics may be good approximations for a normal state of the economy, they may not be good approximations for either a boom or bust economy. For example, in times of a recession, default probabilities may be higher and recovery rates may be lower than those portrayed in the exhibits.

Measuring the expected cash flow in the one-period example is straightforward, but it is more complex for multi-period securities. This complexity arises from the fact that the company may default on the debt in any period. If the company does not default, the cash flow is equal to the interest payment; however, if the company defaults, the expected cash flow is equal to the amount of principal and interest expected to be recovered. As we will illustrate in a multi-period example in just a few pages, we have to take into consideration the probability that the company does not default in a prior period as we estimate subsequent expected cash flows.

REVIEW EXERCISE 9.1

Debt Cost of Capital

Assume the company has a $1,000 debt agreement that will pay the investor at the end of one year the coupon interest rate of 12% plus the $1,000 face value of the debt. Assume the investor believes the company has a 3% probability of defaulting on the promised payments. If the company defaults, the investor will be paid no interest and 50% of the face value of the debt at the end of year 1.

    a. Calculate the expected cash flows for the debt.

    b. Assume the investor requires an expected annual rate of return of 14% for a debt security with this level of risk. Calculate the amount the investor would be willing to pay for this debt security.

    c. Ignore part b, and instead assume the debt security is sold for $1,019.81. Calculate the debt cost of capital implied by this price. Why is the issue price greater than the face value of the debt?

Solution on page 377.

We Observe Promised Yields and Not the Debt Cost of Capital

We can often observe prices and promised yields to maturity for publicly traded and sometimes even for privately held debt securities (for privately held debt this occurs at the date of issue or when traded in a secondary loan market). For all debt securities, we can also observe the timing and magnitude of the promised payments. We are not, however, able to directly observe the debt cost of capital. With the readily observable data, investors and the financial press calculate the promised yield to maturity or, more simply, the **yield to maturity** (**YTM**). In the earlier example, we observe a promised interest payment of $90, a promised principal payment of $1,000, and a price of $973.09. The investment's internal rate of return when based on the price of the bond and the promised cash flows is, of course, larger than the debt cost of capital, and in our example, it is equal to 12%. This is the promised yield to maturity; it is not the debt cost of capital.

$$\$973.09 = \frac{\$1,000 \times 0.09 + \$1,000}{1 + \text{YTM}}$$

$$\text{YTM} = \frac{\$1,090}{\$973.09} - 1 = 0.12014$$

As we discussed earlier in our example regarding the cost of capital, we typically cannot calculate the yield to maturity using the simple formula above, but rather, we must use the more general form of the internal rate of return formula:

$$0 = \frac{\text{PrInt}_1}{(1 + \text{YTM}_0)} + \frac{\text{PrInt}_2}{(1 + \text{YTM}_0)^2} + \frac{\text{PrInt}_3}{(1 + \text{YTM}_0)^3} + \dots + \frac{\text{PrInt}_T + \text{PrPrinc}_T}{(1 + \text{YTM}_0)^T} - \text{Price}_0 \quad \textbf{(9.2)}$$

where PrInt_t and PrPrinc_t are, respectively, promised payments in period t for interest and principal, respectively.

We can quickly see that since we measured the promised yield using promised payments rather than expected payments (the latter are lower than promised payments), the yield to maturity is larger than the debt cost of capital. We call this difference between the yield to maturity and the debt cost of capital the **expected default loss**, E(DL).

$$\text{E(DL)} = \text{YTM} - r_D$$

$$0.02014 = 0.12014 - 0.10$$

The expected default loss is the amount of the promised yield to maturity that an investor does not expect to receive, for the investor knows that the expected cash flows are less than the promised cash flows. We can use one or more alternative methods to measure expected default losses and the cost of debt, depending on the data available. Once we measure both the promised yield and the expected default loss, we can measure the debt cost of capital with the following formula:

$$r_D = \text{YTM} - \text{E(DL)} \quad \textbf{(9.3)}$$

$$0.10 = 0.12014 - 0.02014$$

Valuation Key 9.6

We measure the promised yield to maturity or yield to maturity (YTM) using promised interest payments rather than expected interest payments; thus, the promised yield to maturity is larger than the debt cost of capital. The difference between the promised yield to maturity and the debt cost of capital is called the expected default loss.

REVIEW EXERCISE 9.2

Yield to Maturity and Expected Default Loss

Using the information in Review Exercise 9.1, calculate the yield to maturity and expected default loss for parts b and c.

Solution on pages 377–378.

American Axle's Promised Yield to Maturity and Debt Cost of Capital[7]

In this section we examine an extreme situation to clearly make the point that the promised yield to maturity is not equal to the cost of debt. In 2008, the credit rating for the unsecured senior debt issued by American Axle & Manufacturing Holdings, Inc. (AXL) declined to CCC+ with a negative outlook. A credit rating of this type indicates that the company has a high probability of defaulting on its obligations—Exhibit 9.7 indicates the average cumulative default probability is 45% by Year 5. One of AXL's unsecured senior debt securities was its "5.25% Notes," which matured in roughly five years according to AXL's 2008 10-K filing. The 2008 principal of this note was $250 million, and its fair value was $68.8 million as disclosed in the 10-K. The difference between the principal and fair value represents a discount of 72.5%. We can measure the promised yield to maturity for this note using Equation 9.2. The annual promised interest payments were $13.1 million ($13.1 = 0.0525 \times 250$), and the promised principal payment (to be paid in roughly five years) was $250 million. Given this, the yield to maturity for this note was

$$0 = \frac{\$13.1}{(1 + \text{YTM}_0)} + \frac{\$13.1}{(1 + \text{YTM}_0)^2} + \frac{\$13.1}{(1 + \text{YTM}_0)^3} + \frac{\$13.1}{(1 + \text{YTM}_0)^4} + \frac{\$13.1 + \$250}{(1 + \text{YTM}_0)^5} - \$68.8$$

$$\text{YTM}_0 = 42.2\%$$

Clearly, investors in AXL's debt were uncertain that they would receive these promised payments. Therefore, AXL's debt cost of debt capital for this note was not 42.2%, for the yield to maturity did not consider the expected cash flows given expected recovery rates and the likelihood of default. To measure the cost of debt for this note, we will use Equation 9.1. In order to use that formula, we must know the probability of default and recovery rate for each year. To illustrate this calculation, we assume a constant recovery rate of 25% for each year, and we assume that the conditional probabilities of default (that is, conditional on not defaulting until that point in time) equal 70%, 60%, 40%, 20%, and 10% for 2009 through 2013, respectively.[8] You might be wondering why the probability of default decreases over time for this note. For such a low credit rating, we observe that if a company does not default in the first year, it is less likely to default in the second year; and if a company does not default for two years, it is even less likely to default in the third year, and so forth. Given the promised payments, the probabilities of default, and the recovery rates at each point in time, we can calculate the expected cash flows (versus promised cash flows) for each year. Once we calculate the expected cash flows, we can calculate the cost of debt using Equation 9.1.

In this illustration, each year has two possible outcomes—default and no default. If the company defaults, the company pays the investor the expected recovery rate multiplied by the sum of the principal and interest for that year; if the company does not default, the company pays the investor the promised interest payment, but if it is the final year, the company pays the promised principal in addition to the

---

[7] American Axle Manufacturing Holdings, Inc. (AXL) is the principal supplier of driveline components to General Motors Corporation (GM) for its rear-wheel drive light trucks and SUVs manufactured in North America. See AXL's 2008 Form 10-K filing for information relevant to this section.

[8] The default probabilities and recovery rates in Exhibits 9.5 and 9.7 can provide empirical estimates of the probabilities and recovery rates we use in this illustration, keeping in mind the descriptive statistics in those exhibits are measured over several years and various industries.

interest payment. To calculate the expected cash flow in a year, we multiply each outcome by its respective probability in that year.

$$E_0(CF_t) = prob_{no\ default,\ t} \times (PrInt_t + PrPrinc_t) + prob_{default,\ t} \times recov_t(PrInt_t + PrPrinc_t) \quad \textbf{(9.4)}$$

Here, $prob_{default,t}$ and $prob_{no\ default,t}$ are the probabilities that the company will and will not default in period t, respectively; $recov_t$ is the expected recovery rate (percentage collected) in period t for interest and principal if the company defaults in period t; finally, $PrInt_t$, and $PrPrinc_t$ are as we defined earlier.

For example, in 2009, the company had a default probability of 70%, and the recovery rate was equal to 25%; thus, the expected cash flow was equal to

$$\$50.0 = 0.7 \times 0.25 \times (\$13.1 + \$250) + (1 - 0.7) \times \$13.1$$

Note that the expected cash flow of $50.0 million is larger than the promised payment of $13.1 million. To explain, the promised payment is the promised interest payment. However, the expected cash flow considers the expected cash flows in both the no-default (promised interest payment only) and default (recovered interest and principal payments) states—the latter of which can have a cash flow that is larger than the promised interest payment if the probability of default is as large as it is for AXL. Of course, after the amount is recovered subsequent to default, there are no further payments.

We continue to use this same approach for 2010 through 2013, but we also adjust the expected cash flows in these years for the probability that the company will not default prior to that point in time. The company has a probability of not defaulting in 2009 of 30%. In 2010, the company has a 60% probability of defaulting. Hence, the probability of the company not defaulting in 2009 and defaulting in 2010 is 18% $(0.18 = 0.6 \times 0.3)$. Similarly, the probability of the company not defaulting in both 2009 and 2010 is 12% $[0.12 = (1 - 0.6) \times 0.3]$. Thus, for 2010, the expected cash flow is equal to

$$\$13.4 = 0.18 \times 0.25 \times (\$13.1 + \$250.0) + 0.12 \times \$13.1$$
$$\$13.4 = \$11.8 + \$1.6$$

We show a calculation of the expected cash flows for all years in Exhibit 9.8. Depending on the assumptions you make about the different possible outcomes and the timing of those outcomes for the different states (default and no-default), the decision tree for measuring expected cash flows can be even more complex.

Now that we have the expected cash flows, we can use Equation 9.1 to calculate AXL's cost of debt.

$$0 = \frac{\$49.98}{(1 + r_D)^1} + \frac{\$13.42}{(1 + r_D)^2} + \frac{\$4.10}{(1 + r_D)^3} + \frac{\$1.70}{(1 + r_D)^4} + \frac{\$14.02}{(1 + r_D)^5} - \$68.8$$

$$r_D = 10.6\%$$

The expected default loss is 31.6% $(0.316 = 0.422 - 0.106)$, which is 80.6% of the spread between AXL's yield to maturity (42.2%) and the U.S. government bond rate at the time of 3% $[0.806 = 0.316 \div (0.422 - 0.03)]$. We typically measure expected recovery rates and year-by-year default probabilities with the information published by credit rating agencies adjusted potentially for any company-specific and economy-specific information. We can use models to estimate the default probability (sometimes called financial distress or financial failure or bankruptcy probabilities). A summary of the yield to maturity and cost of debt calculations for American Axle is as follows.

	Yield to Maturity		Cost of Debt
2008	−$ 68.8		−$68.8
2009	$ 13.1		$50.0
2010	$ 13.1		$13.4
2011	$ 13.1		$ 4.1
2012	$ 13.1		$ 1.7
2013	$263.1		$14.0
Internal rate of return	42.2%		10.6%
Risk-free YTM, $R_{f,\ YTM}$	3.0%	Default loss.	31.6%
Spread = YTM − $R_{f,\ YTM}$.	39.2%	% of spread	80.6%

EXHIBIT 9.8 Expected Cash Flows for American Axle & Manufacturing Holdings, Inc.

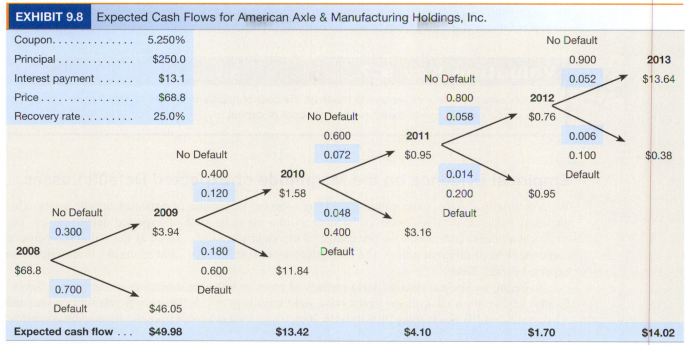

Coupon............	5.250%
Principal...........	$250.0
Interest payment......	$13.1
Price..............	$68.8
Recovery rate........	25.0%

Exhibit may contain small rounding errors

REVIEW EXERCISE 9.3

Debt Cost of Capital for Debt with Maturity Greater than One Year

Assume the company issues debt with the following characteristics:

Face value of debt..	$600
Coupon interest rate (paid annually).............................	8%
Years to maturity..	5
Issue price...	$460
Recovery rate (all years).....................................	50%
(Recovery rate is for the principal plus interest for the year of default)	
Probability of default—Year 1.................................	30%
Probability of default—Year 2.................................	20%
Probability of default—Year 3.................................	15%
Probability of default—Year 4.................................	5%
Probability of default—Year 5.................................	5%

Calculate the yield to maturity, the cost of debt, and the expected default loss for this debt issue.

Solution on page 378.

Preferred Stock and the Adjusted Promised Yield Approach

We use the same conceptual framework to measure the cost of capital for preferred stock as we use to measure the debt cost of capital. The primary differences between debt and preferred stock securities are that debt typically has required interest payments and a defined term to maturity, whereas preferred stock often has no mandatory dividend payments and no maturity. Dividend payments must be paid before common shareholders receive distributions if the dividends are cumulative, but not paying preferred dividends only results in an arrearage (dividends in arrears), not a default. For non-cumulative preferred, not paying preferred dividends generally just means that you cannot pay common dividends for some time period (see Valuation in Practice 9.1). Not paying interest results in a default on the debt issue, consequently resulting in a renegotiation of the debt or the company filing for bankruptcy. Thus, for preferred stock, we may have to use the perpetuity formulas instead of Equations 9.1 and 9.2.

Valuation Key 9.7

The conceptual framework we use to measure the cost of capital for preferred stock is essentially the same as the one we use to measure the debt cost of capital.

Empirical Evidence on the Magnitude of Expected Default Losses

We now briefly discuss some empirical evidence on the magnitude of expected default losses. This empirical evidence provides some useful insights into the magnitude of expected default losses. The empirical evidence indicates what percentage of the yield spread (measured as the difference between corporate debt of different ratings and U.S. government bonds of the same maturity) is attributable to expected default losses.

To begin, we look at data on yield spreads in order to learn something about their properties. In Exhibit 9.9, we show the average annual bond yield spreads over U.S. Treasury Bonds for two-year and 30-year AA and BB bonds from 1999 through 2008 (using data available from the Bloomberg composite database). This chart shows several things. First, we see that bond yield spreads change over time. We also see that higher-rated bonds have smaller spreads and that bonds with a longer maturity generally have larger spreads. In addition, when spreads change for bonds in one rating category, they do not necessarily change in the same way for bonds in other rating categories. For example, the spreads for BB bonds increased significantly during the 2000–2003 period, but the spreads for AA bonds changed relatively little; in other words, there was a significant increase in the default risk attached to BB bonds but no such impact was observed for AA bonds. The spreads on all bonds increased in 2008 during the financial crisis.

| **EXHIBIT 9.9** | Average Promised Yield Spread over U.S. Treasury Bonds, 1999 through 2008 |

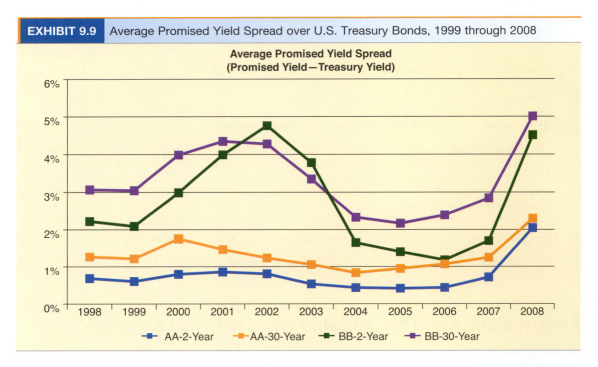

In a study conducted by Elton et al. (2001),[9] the authors analyzed the difference between the yield to maturity on corporate bonds and U.S. government bonds of the same maturity using three factors—expected default losses, state income taxes, and systematic risk factors. The authors used a sample of

---

[9] Elton, Edwin J., M. Gruber, D. Agrawal, and C. Mann, "Explaining the Rate Spread on Corporate Bonds," *The Journal of Finance* vol. LVI, no. 1 (February 2001), pp. 247–277.

over 90,000 monthly bond prices from the Lehman Brothers Fixed Income Database with the sample period ending in 1998. Unfortunately, this empirical evidence on expected default losses does not provide information on bonds rated below BBB (but we know expected default losses increase in the lower rating categories); however, this is the best empirical evidence we have at this point in time.

The authors calculated the proportion of the yield spread attributable to the expected default loss for AA-, A-, and BBB-rated bonds for a maturity between 2 and 10 years. The calculation of the expected default losses was based on both default probabilities and recovery rates—similar to the calculations we presented earlier in the chapter. For each combination of credit rating and maturity, the authors calculated the expected default loss and the yield spread. In Exhibit 9.10, we show the percentage of the yield spread that is attributable to the expected default loss for every rating/maturity combination the authors examined. Note that the authors were careful not to include any effects of systematic risk in their estimates of expected default losses. This is important, as we then leave the systematic risk component in the cost of debt (as it should be) when we take the yield to maturity and subtract these estimated expected default losses to estimate the cost of debt. Looking at the exhibit, you can see that holding the rating constant, the expected default loss becomes a larger percentage of the spread as the maturity increases. Furthermore, holding the maturity constant, the expected default loss becomes a larger percentage of the spread as the rating decreases. In addition, as you observed in Exhibit 9.9, the spreads themselves increase with longer maturities and with more poorly rated debt. All of this implies that expected default losses increase with longer maturities and lower ratings.

EXHIBIT 9.10	Expected Default Losses as a Percentage of the Spread of Industrial Bonds over U.S. Government Bonds (Elton et al. [2001])

Maturity	AA	A	BBB
2	1.0%	8.5%	12.4%
3	1.9%	9.3%	15.0%
4	2.6%	10.3%	17.9%
5	3.4%	11.4%	20.9%
6	4.4%	12.6%	23.9%
7	5.1%	13.9%	26.7%
8	5.9%	15.1%	29.5%
9	7.0%	16.4%	32.1%
10	8.0%	17.8%	34.7%

The empirical evidence on expected default losses indicates that they are not large for highly rated debt; thus, the promised yield and the cost of debt will be quite close. However, we can see that even within investment-grade debt, decreasing the rating and increasing the maturity of the debt results in a greater percentage of the yield spread being attributable to the expected default loss. The expected default loss for AA bonds will be very small when these percentages (8% or less) are multiplied by the AA yield spreads (usually around 1%—see Exhibit 9.9). Thus the expected default losses for AA bonds are generally 8 basis points or less. For A-rated debt (BBB-rated debt) maturing in 10 years, the expected default loss is 18% (35%) of the spread. As such, even for A- and BBB-rated debt, there will be a measurable difference between the promised yield and the cost of debt. As the rating declines further and as the maturity lengthens, the percentage of the spread that is the expected default loss increases and the promised yield becomes an even more biased estimate of the cost of debt.

Suppose that we wanted to use this data to estimate the cost of debt for a BBB-rated bond with 10 years to maturity. Assume that a 10-year U.S. government bond is yielding 5% and a BBB-rated bond is yielding 8%. The expected default loss is then 1.04% $[0.0104 = 0.347 \times (0.08 - 0.05)]$ and the cost of debt would be 6.96% $(0.0696 = 0.08 - 0.0104)$.

Recall that the expected default loss we computed previously for AXL was 80.6% of the spread between AXL's yield to maturity and the U.S. government bond rate. This percentage exceeds the largest expected default loss percentage in Exhibit 9.10 for a five-year maturity, which is 20.9% for BBB debt. The percentages in this exhibit, however, are calculated for debt rated BBB or higher; thus, these percentages are unlikely to be useful for the AXL example given its CCC+ rating. Since we know that the ratio of the expected default loss to the spread increases as the credit rating decreases, we would expect that AXL's expected default loss as a proportion of its spread (in relation to U.S. government bonds) would be much larger than those reported in this exhibit. However, we do not have any empirical evidence to calibrate it precisely. We will now turn to other ways to estimate the cost of debt.

Empirical Adaptation of the Capital Asset Pricing Model

An alternative way to measure the debt and preferred stock costs of capital is to use an asset pricing model like the CAPM, the three-factor model, or an empirical variation of these models—such as the model in Fama and French (1993).[10] The specific process used to implement one of these asset pricing models varies depending on the specific model. We know that even highly rated debt is risky and includes both default and liquidity risk, because its promised yield is larger than the yield on a risk-free security, but the risk premium for highly rated debt is quite small.

In Exhibit 9.11, we show the beta (measured against the S&P 500 index) for various bond rating categories based on the Lehman Brothers Global Family of Indices.[11] We examine three different periods; the first is from 1999 through March 2009. During a period beginning sometime in 2007 and ending in March of 2009, we had what has been called a "crisis" in the world's financial markets. To exclude and isolate the effects of this period, we also examine the sub-periods of 1996 through 2006 and 2007 through March 2009. The first observation from this exhibit is that betas consistently increase as the bond ratings decrease.

EXHIBIT 9.11	Betas and Incremental Betas and Costs of Capital for Alternative Bond Ratings

Panel A: Beta Estimates for Bond Indices Based on Certain Bond Ratings and Using the S&P 500 Index

Estimation Period	AAA	AA	A	Baa	Ba	B	Caa	Ca–D
1999–March 2009. . .	−0.026	0.007	0.063	0.117	0.246	0.370	0.548	0.707
1999–2006	−0.060	−0.059	−0.034	0.026	0.164	0.259	0.361	0.356
2007–March 2009. . .	0.038	0.107	0.213	0.263	0.379	0.550	0.835	1.265

Incremental Betas for Ratings Below the AA Rating

Estimation Period		AA	A	Baa	Ba	B	Caa	Ca–D
1999–March 2009. . .		0.000	0.055	0.110	0.238	0.363	0.541	0.699
1999–2006		0.000	0.024	0.085	0.223	0.318	0.420	0.415
2007–March 2009. . .		0.000	0.106	0.156	0.272	0.443	0.728	1.158

Panel B: Incremental Cost of Capital for Ratings Below an AA Rating

Estimation Period	Market Risk Premium	A	Baa	Ba	B	Caa	Ca–D
1999–March 2009. . .	4.0%	0.2%	0.4%	1.0%	1.5%	2.2%	2.8%
	6.0%	0.3%	0.7%	1.4%	2.2%	3.2%	4.2%
	8.0%	0.4%	0.9%	1.9%	2.9%	4.3%	5.6%
1999–2006	4.0%	0.1%	0.3%	0.9%	1.3%	1.7%	1.7%
	6.0%	0.1%	0.5%	1.3%	1.9%	2.5%	2.5%
	8.0%	0.2%	0.7%	1.8%	2.5%	3.4%	3.3%
2007–March 2009. . .	4.0%	0.4%	0.6%	1.1%	1.8%	2.9%	4.6%
	6.0%	0.6%	0.9%	1.6%	2.7%	4.4%	6.9%
	8.0%	0.8%	1.2%	2.2%	3.5%	5.8%	9.3%

Recall that a beta of 1.0 indicates a risk that is equal to the average risk in the overall market (recall that the market index used in this exhibit is the S&P 500 index). For the entire period of 1999 through March 2009, the betas for the AAA, AA, and A ratings are all less than 0.1; however, the beta increases to 0.25 for the Ba rating, to more than 0.5 for the Caa rating, and to 0.7 for the lowest combined group of ratings—Ca−D.[12] The betas that predate the global financial crisis are all lower than the betas of the same rating measured over the entire period and the betas for a rating for the period of the global financial crisis

---

[10] For example, for debt securities, see Fama, E., and French, K., "Common Risk Factors in the Returns on Stocks and Bonds," *Journal of Financial Economics* 33 (1993), pp. 3–56.

[11] See Lehman Brothers, "A Guide to the Lehman Brothers Global Family of Indices," *Fixed Income Research*, March 2008.

[12] Lehman Brothers groups the ratings from Ca through D because of the small number of bonds with these ratings.

(2007–March 2009) are higher than those of the other two periods we report in the exhibit. For example, for all rating categories, the global financial crisis period has betas that are at least twice as large as their respective counterparts for the pre-financial-crisis period.

An adaptation of the CAPM that is sometimes used in practice to estimate the cost of debt assumes that debt with a rating of AA or higher has a zero expected default loss; in other words, the promised yield to maturity for such debt is equal to its cost of capital, which seems reasonable given the evidence in Exhibit 9.9 and 9.10 on expected default losses for AA bonds in conjunction with the typical spread between government bonds and AA bonds. Then, for a company with a credit rating below AA, we can add a risk premium to the AA-rated debt's cost of capital based on the CAPM. The justification underpinning this approach is that the CAPM measures systematic risk and therefore the measured cost of capital does not include the effect of unsystematic risk (which should not be included in the cost of debt), but would include the systematic risk component, which should be part of the cost of debt.

We can use the results in Exhibit 9.11 to illustrate how we can adjust the yield to maturity of an AA-rated debt security for the risk premium of a lower-rated bond. In the lower part of Panel A of Exhibit 9.12, we present the difference between the betas of bonds with ratings lower than AA and the betas of bonds that are AA rated for the three different estimation periods. These differences are all positive and increase as the rating decreases. For example, for the Baa rating, the differences in betas range between 0.085 and 0.156, depending on the estimation period. For the lowest rating group, Ca−D, the differences range between 0.415 and 1.158. We can use these incremental betas and an estimate of the market risk premium of the S&P 500 (since that was the market index we used to measure the bonds' betas) to measure the incremental debt cost of capital for a lower-rated debt security. Panel B presents the premiums that have to be added to the AA promised yields for each rating class, for different estimates of the market risk premium (4%, 6% and 8%), and for the three different estimation periods.

Valuation Key 9.8

We can use the CAPM to help measure the cost of debt. In essence, we assume that the promised yields on AA-rated debt measure the cost of debt appropriately for AA bonds and then we add a premium to the AA yield based on the incremental betas of a rating class (relative to AA-rated bond betas) multiplied by an estimate of the market risk premium.

American Axle & Manufacturing Holdings, Inc. (AXL) Revisited. We can use this adaptation of the CAPM for AXL. At the end of 2008, the yield to maturity of AA rated debt was around 6%, which we assume to be equal to its cost of debt. From Panel B of Exhibit 9.11, the incremental cost of capital for the Caa-rated debt for the 2007–March 2009 estimation period ranges from 2.9% to 5.8%, depending on the market risk premium estimate chosen. [13] This results in estimates for the cost of debt that range from 8.9% to 11.8%. Assuming a market risk premium of 6%, the cost of debt for AXL is 10.4% (0.104 = 0.06 + 0.044), which is very close to the 10.6% cost of capital we calculated using estimated default rates and recovery rates.

REVIEW EXERCISE 9.4

Debt Cost of Capital Estimated Using the CAPM

The LLJ Company had debt on its books at the end of 2008 with a credit rating of Ba. The yield to maturity of AA-rated debt at that time was approximately 6%, which we assume is equal to its cost of debt. Use the data in Exhibit 9.11 to estimate the debt cost of capital for the LLJ Company *at the end of 2008*. Assume the market risk premium is 4%.

Solution on page 379.

---

[13] The AXL example occurred during the global financial crisis, and we used the 2007 through March 2009 estimation period, which may not be the best estimation period to use for the period after the global financial crisis.

Using Credit Default Swaps to Measure Default Risk and Recovery Rates

A **credit default swap** (**CDS**) is a contract in which the issuer provides the purchaser of the credit default swap protection against the risk of default on one or more debt obligations issued by a country or company, called a **reference entity**; thus, a CDS is essentially an insurance policy that protects the purchaser against the loss of principal resulting from the default by the issuer. If certain pre-specified default events occur, the premium payments stop and the issuer of the CDS pays the buyer the par value for the bond and the CDS issuer receives the bond. If no default event occurs during the term of the contract, the purchaser of the protection continues to pay the premium for the term of the contract. The insurance premium paid by the purchaser is a periodic premium over the life of the contract, which is often called the CDS spread, and is quoted in basis points per annum of the contract's notional (or par) value. These contracts were first issued in the late 1990s for sovereign debt but expanded to corporate bonds, mortgage-backed securities, and local government debt. The notional capital covered by CDSs in 1997 was around $180 billion and grew to $17.1 trillion in 2005 and $26 trillion by mid-2006.[14]

The CDS spread is, in part, a measure of the premium required by investors to bear a firm's default risk. Default risk has two components, the probability of default and the expected recovery rate. To the extent CDS spreads measure the default risk premium, we can potentially use them to help measure a company's debt cost of capital. In Exhibit 9.12, we present average CDS spreads for different credit ratings, maturities, and durations. These results show that CDS spreads increase with lower credit ratings, longer maturities, and longer durations.

EXHIBIT 9.12	Credit Default Spreads for Different Bond Ratings, Maturities, and Durations for January 2001 to December 2008*							
Credit Rating	CDS Spread	Std Dev of Spread	Maturity	CDS Spread	Std Dev of Spread	Duration	CDS Spread	Std Dev of Spread
AAA	0.16	0.17	Short	0.31	0.79	Short	0.35	0.82
AA	0.32	0.51	2	0.51	0.84	2	0.55	0.86
A	0.45	0.74	3	0.62	0.79	3	0.79	0.92
BBB	0.86	0.94	4	0.79	0.83	4	0.81	0.81
			Long	0.83	0.79	Long	0.75	0.52

* This exhibit is taken from Li, Haitao, Weina Zhang, and Gi Hyun Kim, "The CDS-Bond Basis Arbitrage and the Cross Section of Corporate Bond Returns," Working Paper, December 2011, Stephen M. Ross School of Business, University of Michigan, Ann Arbor, MI 48109.

Callen, Livnat, and Segal (2007) document that CDS spreads are related to credit ratings but they vary substantially within a given rating.[15] Hull, Predescu, and White (2004) examine the relationship between bond yields and CDS spreads, and whether changes in CDS spreads anticipate credit rating announcements.[16] The authors document that the CDS spreads anticipate negative credit events such as a downgrade, negative watch, or negative outlook, but they do not find evidence that they anticipate positive rating events.

More specific to our adjustment of a company's promised yield, Das and Hanouna (2009) developed a model to estimate a forward-looking probability of default and expected recovery rate using a company's stock price and its volatility in conjunction with the company's CDS spread.[17] The authors developed a methodology to estimate the present value of premiums paid on the CDS for a given maturity given no default and the losses if the reference entity defaults based on an estimated recovery rate and the probability of default. Their results indicate that recovery rates are inversely related to expected default rates, just as we observed in Exhibits 9.5 and 9.7. Such models are an alternative to using historical default and recovery rates to estimate expected cash flows and are potentially useful since they are forward looking and

---

[14] International Swaps and Derivatives Association press release of September 19, 2006 , available at http://www.isda.org/press/press_releases2006.html.

[15] Callen, J. L., J. Livnat, and D. Segal, "The Impact of Earnings on the Pricing of Credit Default Swaps," *The Accounting Review* vol. 84, no. 5 (2009), pp. 1363–1394.

[16] Hull, J. C., M. Predescu, and A. White, "The Relationship Between Credit Default Swap Spreads, Bond Yields, and Credit Rating Announcements," *Journal of Banking & Finance* vol. 28, no. 11 (November 2004), pp. 2789–2811.

[17] Das, Sanjiv, and Paul Hanouna, "Implied Recovery," *Journal of Economic Dynamics and Control* vol. 33, no. 11 (2009), pp. 1837–1857.

presumably would measure appropriate default and recovery rates irrespective of the state of the economy. Once we know the expected cash flows and the price of a bond, we can measure the cost of debt.

CDS spreads are driven in part by both idiosyncratic and systematic expected default losses. Since CDS spreads include the systematic component of expected default losses, the adjustment to the yield to maturity is not as simple as subtracting the observed CDS spread for the bond. Moreover, CDS spreads are not driven solely by default losses. For example, there is some counterparty risk (the risk that the seller of the protection cannot cover the buyer's losses), and that is priced in the CDS spread as well. Thus, we cannot merely adjust the yield to maturity by the entire CDS spread to estimate the cost of debt, as we have to isolate the component of the CDS spread that is not related to counterparty risk or systematic risk. Given the factors reflected in the CDS spread, we know that the adjustment for the expected default loss should be no larger than the CDS spread if credit default swaps are priced accurately and if the length of the contract matches the maturity of the debt.

Summary

We have discussed multiple ways to estimate the cost of debt when the default risk is non-zero and the recovery rate is less than 100%. The first approach was to estimate expected cash flows using information about default probabilities and recovery rates. Then, given the price of the bond and the expected cash flows, we estimate the internal rate of return of the bond, which provides an estimate of the cost of the debt. The second approach discussed was to use the historical evidence on the percentage of the yield spread between like-maturity U.S. government bonds and corporate debt that is attributable to the expected default loss for bonds of a particular rating and maturity. Once we estimate the expected default loss, we subtract it from the corporate debt's promised yield to estimate the cost of debt. The third approach was to estimate betas of debt of various rating categories, compute the incremental beta for that rating category relative to AA bonds, and then take the yield on the AA bonds and add it to the incremental beta multiplied by an estimate of the relevant market risk premium. We also discussed the potential to use information from CDS spreads to calculate expected cash flows from a debt instrument so we could calculate the cost of debt in conjunction with the price of the bond or to adjust the yield to maturity for expected default losses. Unfortunately, neither of these techniques using CDS spreads is particularly straightforward.

9.4 AN OVERVIEW OF THE PROCESS OF MEASURING THE COST OF CAPITAL OF NON-COMMON-EQUITY SECURITIES

The process of measuring the cost of capital depends on both the type of security and the measurement approach we use. In this section, we describe the overall process that generally applies to all non-equity securities. We show these steps in Exhibit 9.13. The first step in the process is to identify all the sources of non-common-equity financing. These are the securities we expect the company to use to finance itself in the future, which may or may not be the same mix of securities it currently uses. While the process we discuss includes a discussion of non-common equity financing with option-like characteristics (convertible debt, convertible preferred, warrants, and options), we postpone our discussion of measuring the value and cost of capital of those types of securities until Chapter 12.

LO3 Understand the process for measuring the costs of non-equity capital

A useful starting point for this process is to prepare a financing schedule that lists all of the securities a company currently uses. A non-common-equity financing schedule is a list of all of the non-common-equity financing instruments used by a company. Our goal is to prepare such a schedule for every source of non-equity financing we expect the company to use in the future, but a useful starting point for this schedule is to prepare it simply for the securities the company uses currently or that a particular transaction, such as a leveraged buyout, contemplates. After preparing this list, we adjust and update it for the non-equity financing we expect the company to use subsequently. The debt financing schedule includes such information on each security as its description, book value, face value, coupon rate of interest, maturity, current promised yield to maturity, rating, market value, proportion of capital structure, and any other key features. The long-term debt footnote in a company's 10-K is a good starting point for collecting information on a company's existing debt. A schedule of other forms of non-equity financing—such as preferred stock, warrants, and options—includes pertinent information on these securities as well. Again, the 10-K is a valuable source of information for these securities as well.

EXHIBIT 9.13	Overview Summary of Steps to Measure the Non-Common-Equity Costs of Capital

1   For each company being valued and comparable companies, identify each source of non-common-equity financing used or expected to be used to finance the company (debt, preferred stock, warrants, convertible securities, etc.)

2   For convertible securities, partition the value of the convertible feature (if material)

3   Group similar securities that have the same cost of capital (for example, convertible debt partitioned into "straight" debt and grouped with debt and a conversion feature grouped with common-equity-based derivative securities)

4   If appropriate, measure the yield to maturity (for debt) and dividend yield (for preferred stock) and adjust the promised yields for expected default losses to measure the cost of capital for debt and preferred stock directly

5   If appropriate, use an asset pricing model to measure the cost of capital for the non-common-equity securities, such as debt, preferred stock, warrants, convertible features, and other common-equity-based derivative securities

6   Use the estimates in the previous two steps to measure the cost of capital for each non-common-equity security

Since securities with convertible features—such as convertible debt and convertible preferred stock—have features of multiple types of securities, in Step 2, we partition such securities into their non-equity and equity-linked components. For example, we would partition a convertible debt issue into a non-convertible debt security and an equity-based option security. In the third step, we cluster or group securities of the same type that have similar features. For example, we would cluster non-convertible debt securities with the same seniority, maturity, and so forth into one group. We can use maturity, seniority, credit rating, call, and other features to group debt securities.

In the fourth and fifth steps, we use one or more methods to measure the cost of capital for each group of securities. In the fourth step, for securities with a promised yield, we measure the promised yields on securities and adjust them for expected default losses that are not part of the cost of debt or cost of preferred. The fifth step in the process, if relevant, is to use an asset pricing model to estimate the cost of capital directly. Naturally, we might use one method for one group of securities and another method (or even multiple methods) for another group of securities. The last step in the process is to use the information from the previous two steps to measure the cost of capital for each group of securities.

Measuring the Debt and Preferred Stock Costs of Capital

We can use Equation 9.3 to adjust the promised yield of either debt or preferred stock for the expected default loss to measure their respective costs of capital. Using this approach, we measure both the promised yield and the expected default loss, and then we measure the cost of capital as the difference between the two. Earlier in the chapter, we discussed a variety of ways to measure the expected default loss. Alternatively, we discussed measuring the cost of debt by using the CAPM to estimate a risk premium to add to the promised yield on AA-rated bonds. Now, we will outline ways to estimate the promised yields when they are not readily available for a company and to determine a company's likely bond rating when it is also not available.

Publicly Traded Debt and Preferred Stock Securities.   If the company has publicly traded debt or preferred stock, we can often observe the promised yield or the price of the security from which we can then calculate the promised yield. In addition, publicly traded debt and preferred stock are often rated by credit rating agencies, so we can often observe the rating for the security as well. We can use the methods we discussed earlier to adjust the promised yield for expected default losses or to add a risk premium using the CAPM based on a known credit rating. If we cluster multiple publicly traded debt or preferred stock securities into the same group, we can compare promised yields as a check on our grouping, as we should observe generally similar promised yields for securities within the same group. If the rating is not available, then we can estimate it by using a rating model or any of the other methods we discuss in the following section.

Debt and Preferred Stock That Are Not Publicly Traded.   We can observe the promised yield and value of a security even if the company's securities are not publicly traded at the time the company issues the security and after issuance if the debt trades in the secondary loan market. Naturally, how useful the issuance price is depends on how recent it is, whether the company had or anticipates material changes in its financial leverage or operating risk, and whether the economy-wide interest rates have changed since the debt was issued. We can adjust for such changes using the various methods we discuss in this chapter, but the historical yields will not be particularly helpful if there have just been or will be material changes. If only the risk-free interest rates changed and general economy-wide default premiums did not change, we can adjust the date of issuance information for the change in the risk-free rate as long as the company's risk did not change (that is, its financial leverage and operating risk did not change).

If the company did not issue all its securities recently, then we can measure the promised yields using another approach. One approach is the grouping approach that we discussed earlier in which we group similar securities. If one of the securities in a group is publicly traded or was issued recently, we would use the same cost of capital for the other securities in that group, assuming there were no changes in financial or operating risk.

If none of the approaches just described is feasible, an alternative approach is to estimate the rating for the security and to then measure the promised yields from the current promised yields for bonds of that rating, maturity, and so forth.

Expected Changes in Capital Structure or Operating Risk.

We use the expected capital structure—not the current capital structure—when we value a company. Thus, we base the costs of capital on the company's expected capital structure and expected operating risk. When we expect that a company's capital structure or operating risk will change, we estimate the company's rating based on the new capital structure and operating risk, and we measure its cost of capital based on that rating. In this situation, we use forecasts of the company's financial statements in addition to other information based on the new capital structure and potential change in operations in order to estimate its rating.

We can approach changes in capital structure in two ways. In one approach, we can establish how much debt (and preferred stock) the company must issue to fund its activities and forecast the financial statements based on that capital structure in order to estimate the rating. In the other approach, we can begin by specifying a minimally accepted rating, and based on this rating and the company's projected operating results, we can estimate how much debt and preferred stock the company can issue and still maintain that rating. In either approach, we use pro-forma financial statement forecasts to measure the relevant financial ratios and other information to arrive at the credit rating. We illustrated this procedure in Chapter 4 when we added debt to the financial model we created for Starbucks.

When constructing the forecasts, we integrate the new capital structure into all of the components of the financial statements—balance sheet, income statement, statement of free cash flows, and other schedules—in order to understand all of the effects of the new capital structure. The income statement effects include a change in interest expense and the resulting change in income taxes; the balance sheet effects include a change in both long-term debt and, most likely, short-term debt. Total assets may or may not be affected by the new capital structure depending on whether the change in capital structure is tied to a change in investing activities. If the company is issuing new debt and/or preferred and all of the proceeds are being used to repurchase shares or pay a one-time dividend, then the assets of the company will not change.

If we expect a major change in operations, we would do the same thing that we would do for a change in capital structure; that is, we create pro-forma financial statements that reflect the changes in operations and then assess the likely rating based on our pro-forma forecasts. For example, if a company makes a major acquisition or is engaged in a major divestiture, we can create pro-forma financial statement forecasts to see the impact of these changes on the company's various financial ratios in comparison to the historical financials.

Valuation Key 9.9

One way to measure the debt or preferred stock cost of capital is to measure the promised yield and adjust it for the expected default loss. We can often measure promised yields for publicly traded securities or debt traded in the secondary loan market directly. For securities that are not publicly traded, we can estimate a rating and use published yields for that rating to measure the promised yield for a company and then adjust it for the expected default loss. Knowing or estimating the rating allows us to also implement the CAPM-based approach for estimating the cost of debt.

9.5 CREDIT OR DEBT RATING MODELS

LO4 Use credit rating and financial distress statistical models

Using a company's credit rating in combination with its current promised yields to maturity provides useful information for measuring the company's cost of capital. Not all companies have a current credit rating or have promised yields to maturity that are observable. In such cases, we can use estimation methods to first measure the company's likely credit rating. For example, we know from our discussion of financial ratios in Chapter 2 that those ratios provide information on a company's financial performance, financial condition, and risk. We also know that credit rating agencies use financial ratios, various other metrics, and qualitative information to assign credit ratings. In this section of the chapter, we illustrate how we use financial ratios and a statistical model to assess a company's credit rating. These estimated credit ratings can, in turn, be used to estimate the cost of debt.

Credit rating models combine various financial ratios and other factors into a metric to classify a company into a credit rating category. The ultimate goal of a credit rating model is to develop a model that mimics the assessments of the rating agencies. Since such models only attempt to reproduce the ratings of rating agencies, the model can only be as good as the work of the rating agencies. Before we illustrate how to develop and use such a model, we will examine the relation between credit ratings and certain financial ratios, and we will illustrate how to estimate a credit rating with the same set of financial ratios as published by rating agencies.

Credit Ratings and Financial Ratios

In Exhibit 9.14, we present the averages of the median financial ratios from 2005 through 2007 for different credit ratings as published by S&P.[18] The financial ratios generally vary monotonically across the rating classes.

Financial ratios that measure profitability or coverage generally decrease as the rating decreases, and ratios that measure the degree of financial leverage used by the company generally increase as the rating decreases. Although the first two ratios (operating margin and return on capital)[19] are performance measures, S&P states, "Investors should continue to note that the strength of operating income (before D&A) as a percentage of revenues, also known as operating margin, is not indicative of a particular rating category and is best used when analyzing specific industries."[20]

EXHIBIT 9.14	Adjusted Key U.S. Industrial Companies' Financial Ratios for Different Credit Ratings, Standard &Poor's*						
Average of 2005–2007 Medians	**AAA**	**AA**	**A**	**BBB**	**BB**	**B**	**CCC**
Operating margin (before D&A) (%)	22.2%	26.5%	19.8%	17.0%	17.2%	16.2%	10.5%
Return on capital (%)	27.0%	28.4%	21.8%	15.2%	12.4%	8.7%	2.7%
EBIT interest coverage (x)	26.2	16.4	11.2	5.8	3.4	1.4	0.4
EBITDA interest coverage (x)	32.0	19.5	13.5	7.8	4.8	2.3	1.1
Free cash flow to debt (%)	155.5%	79.2%	54.5%	35.5%	25.7%	11.5%	2.5%
Free operating cash flow to debt (%)	129.9%	40.6%	31.2%	16.1%	7.1%	2.2%	–3.6%
Debt to EBITDA (x)	0.4	0.9	1.5	2.2	3.1	5.5	8.6
Debt to debt + equity (%)	12.3%	35.2%	36.8%	44.5%	52.5%	73.2%	98.9%
Number of observations	6	14	111	213	306	354	22

* See Table 1 in Lugg, D., A. Balasubramanian, N. Pradhan, and V. Vishwanathan, *CreditStats: 2007 Adjusted Key U.S. Industrial and Utility Financial Ratios*, September 10, 2008, Standard & Poor's, a division of the McGraw-Hill Companies, reprinted with permission.

In Exhibit 9.15, we present a time-series of the ratios of EBIT to interest coverage across four of the ratings. The important observation to glean from this exhibit is that the ratio for a rating class can vary

---

[18] See *CreditStats: 2007 Adjusted Key U.S. Industrial and Utility Financial Ratios*, Standard & Poor's, September 10, 2008. According to S&P, U.S. industrials include telecoms, aerospace and defense, chemicals, health care, metals and mining, auto parts, retail, consumer goods, paper and forest products, oil and gas, and technology—among other industrial sectors. Beginning in 2005, it also includes railroads, airlines, trucking companies, and other transportation-related companies.

[19] Return on capital is defined as unlevered net income divided by total invested capital.

[20] See *CreditStats: 2007 Adjusted Key U.S. Industrial and Utility Financial Ratios*, Standard & Poor's, September 10, 2008, p. 8.

over time, which indicates that it is useful to update these benchmarks from time to time. For example, the median ratio of EBIT to interest coverage for the A rating group was about 8 in 2001 and almost 14 in 2006, while the median ratio for the BBB-rated debt was also about 8 during the years 2004 through 2007 but lower prior to that. Note that the various financial ratios also vary by industry and most of the rating agencies publish industry data as well.

EXHIBIT 9.15	Time-Series of the Ratio of EBIT to Interest Coverage for U.S. Industrial Companies with Different Credit Ratings, Standard & Poor's*

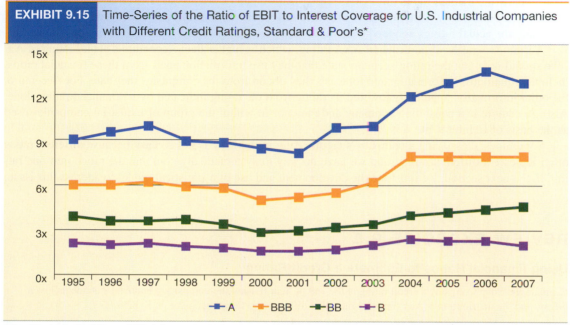

* See Chart 1 in *CreditStats: 2007 Adjusted Key U.S. Industrial and Utility Financial Ratios*, Standard & Poor's, September 10, 2008.

One way to estimate a company's credit rating is to compare certain financial ratios to the average of the relevant median financial ratios of specific ratings published by rating agencies. In Exhibit 9.16, we show the financial ratios as of the end of the 2008 fiscal year for two companies—General Motors and Accenture Limited (Accenture).[21] We conduct the analysis for two points in time for General Motors— September 30, 2008 (when its credit rating was B), and December 31, 2008 (when its credit rating was CCC+ after being downgraded on November 7, 2008). During this time, Accenture's credit rating stayed constant at A+.

EXHIBIT 9.16	Key Standard & Poor's Financial Ratios for General Motors Corporation and Accenture Limited

	General Motors				Accenture	
	30-Sep-08		**31-Dec-08**		**Accenture**	
Financial Ratio/Metric	Ratio	Rating	Ratio	Rating	Ratio	Rating
Return on capital (%)	4.3%	B – CCC	−207.2%	< CCC	68.7%	AAA
EBIT interest coverage (x)	0.87	B – CCC	−6.14	< CCC	32.66	AAA
EBITDA interest coverage (x)	1.51	B – CCC	−3.25	< CCC	38.00	AAA
Free cash flow to debt (%).	2.2%	< CCC	−35.6%	< CCC	27245.3%	AAA
Free operating cash flow to debt (%).	−5.5%	< CCC	−43.3%	< CCC	26523.4%	AAA
Debt to EBITDA (x)	8.64	CCC	−4.02	< CCC	0.00	AAA
Debt to debt + equity (%)	94.6%	B – CCC	751.5%	< CCC	0.3%	AAA
Actual rating		**B**		**CCC+**		**A+**

---

[21] Accenture Limited is a management consulting, technology services, and outsourcing company. It has the following operating groups: Communications & High Tech, Financial Services, Products, Public Service and Resources.

We compare each of the ratios for General Motors and Accenture to the distribution of the respective ratio across credit ratings in Exhibit 9.14, and we show what rating corresponds to the ratios of the companies. The exhibit shows that the September 30 ratios for General Motors are consistently either between the B and CCC credit rating ratios or below the CCC credit rating ratios. The December 31 ratios show deterioration in General Motors', financial condition; its rates of returns were lower, interest coverage ratios were lower, and leverage ratios were higher. As a result, the December 31 ratios for General Motors are all below the median ratios for a CCC rating. Unfortunately, we do not have financial ratios for CC- and C-rated bonds, so we are unable to precisely tell where we would have classified General Motors. That said, the actual ratings assigned General Motors are slightly higher than the ratios alone suggest.

Accenture's ratios all indicate an AAA rating, which is higher than Accenture's actual rating of A+ . We should note that the rating agencies state that they use information apart from these financial ratios, including qualitative information and forecasts they obtain from the companies they rate. For Accenture, the other information apparently lowered its rating from the rating indicated by its financial ratios alone. Also, Accenture is a consulting company and may not fit within the group of industrial companies used as the basis of Exhibit 9.14.

Sometimes, classifying a company's credit rating in this way is not so easy because different ratios often indicate a different rating, and we have no way to systematically combine the ratios into one rating. In the next section, we illustrate the development and use of a statistical model to address this issue.

REVIEW EXERCISE 9.5

Using Financial Ratios to Estimate a Credit Rating

Estimate the Snap Company's credit rating at the end of Year 0 using the company's financial statements given below, and the distribution of key financial ratios for different credit ratings given in Exhibit 9.14.

SNAP COMPANY Balance Sheets and Income Statement		
($ in thousands)	Year –1	Year 0
Income Statement		
Revenue		$26,243
Operating expenses		–9,447
Depreciation expense		–1,939
Earnings before interest and taxes		$14,857
Interest expense		–1,028
Income before taxes		$13,829
Income tax expense		–5,532
Net income		$ 8,297
Balance Sheet		
Total current assets	$ 4,974	$ 6,460
Property, plant, and equipment (net)	31,275	30,262
Total assets	$36,249	$36,722
Account payable	$ 1,037	$ 1,347
Debt	12,845	13,487
Total liabilities	$13,882	$14,834
Capital stock	$12,000	$12,000
Retained earnings	10,367	9,888
Shareholders' equity	$22,367	$21,888
Liabilities and shareholders' equity	$36,249	$36,722

SNAP COMPANY Unlevered Free Cash Flow Statement	
($ in thousands)	Year 0
Unlevered operating cash flow	$9,796
– Change in required cash balance	–119
– Capital expenditures	–926
Unlevered free cash flow	$8,751

Solution on page 379.

The HZ Credit Rating Model

Credit rating models have been studied for more than 40 years. For example, Horrigan (1966), Pinches, and Mingo (1973), and Kaplan and Urwitz (1979) are early examples that document such models being used to classify credit ratings.[22] All of these and many subsequent models use a company's financial ratios and other metrics to predict (or classify) its credit rating. More recent models have attempted to use artificial intelligence and neural net estimation methods to better predict the ratings assigned by credit rating agencies. Various commercial versions of bond rating models exist. Some of these models use financial ratios and other metrics and some of them use models based on option-theoretic approaches using prices from credit default swaps.

In this section, we develop a financial-ratio-based credit rating model to illustrate how such a tool is developed and used. We use the sample of 1,148 companies for which S&P had a current senior unsecured credit rating for the company and for which we could compute the necessary financial ratios. We show the distribution of company credit ratings for the sample and how we aggregate these into a smaller number of broader rating categories in Exhibit 9.17.

EXHIBIT 9.17	Distribution of Company Credit Ratings for the HZ Credit Rating Model Sample				
	Original Sample			**Aggregated HZ Sample**	
S & P Rating	**Number**	**%**		**Number**	**%**
AAA.	6	0.5%			
AA+.	3	0.3%			
AA.	15	1.3%			
AA–.	10	0.9%	AA– to AAA	34	3.0%
A+.	23	2.0%			
A.	45	3.9%			
A–.	49	4.3%	A– to A+	117	10.2%
BBB+	90	7.8%			
BBB	111	9.7%			
BBB–	87	7.6%	BBB– to BBB+	288	25.1%
BB+	63	5.5%			
BB.	99	8.6%			
BB–.	161	14.0%	BB– to BB+	323	28.1%
B+.	159	13.9%			
B.	132	11.5%			
B–.	58	5.1%	B– to B+	349	30.4%
CCC+	22	1.9%			
CCC	8	0.7%			
CCC–	1	0.1%			
CC	3	0.3%			
D.	3	0.3%	CCC+ & Below	37	3.2%
Total	1,148	100.0%		1,148	100.0%

Because of the small number of observations in certain categories, we aggregated the 21 different credit ratings into six broader rating groups in order to have a reasonable number of observations in each group.[23] For example, we combined the 3 companies with a D credit rating, the 3 companies with a CC rating, and the 31 companies with various CCC ratings into one rating category (CCC+ & below) with 37

[22] Horrigan, J. O. "The Determination of Long-Term Credit Standing with Financial Ratios," *Empirical Research in Accounting: Selected Studies, Supplement to V.4. Journal of Accounting Research* (1966); Kaplan, R. S., and G. Urwitz, "Statistical Models of Bond Ratings: A Methodological Inquiry," *Journal of Business* 52 (1979), pp. 231–261; and Pinches, G. E., and K. A. Mingo, "A Multivariate Analysis of Industrial Bond Ratings," *Journal of Finance* 28 (1973), pp. 1–18.

[23] The 21 credit ratings are D, CC, CCC–, CCC, CCC+, B–, B, B+, BB–, BB, BB+, BBB–, BBB, BBB+, A–, A, A+, AA–, AA, AA+, and AAA.

observations. At the other end of the rating scale, we combined the 6 companies with an AAA rating and the 28 companies with various AA ratings into one rating category (AA− to AAA) with 34 observations. We aggregated the remaining ratings by overall rating; in other words, we ignored the +/− designations of the rating. The largest group is the B− to B+ group with 349 (or 30% of the) observations, followed by the BB− to BB+ group with 323 (or 28% of the) observations, which is then followed by the BBB− to BBB+ group with 288 (or 25% of the) observations. The A− to A+ group has 117 (or 10% of the) observations. Thus, our dependent variable has six groups ranging from CCC+ & below to AA− & above.

We use five independent (or explanatory) variables used in other credit rating models. The five variables are a performance measure (EBIT to the Average of Total Debt plus Shareholders' Equity), the inverse of interest coverage (Interest to EBITDA), the inverse of debt coverage (Total Debt to Cash Flow from Operations minus Capital Expenditures), financial leverage (Total Debt to Total Debt plus Shareholders' Equity), and capital expenditures coverage (Capital Expenditures to EBITDA). We present the parameter estimates and summary statistics for the model in Exhibit 9.18.

EXHIBIT 9.18	The HZ Credit Rating Model			
Variable (Logit Model Estimation)	**Coefficients***	**Standard Error**	**Chi-Square Statistic**	**Probability**
Intercept for CCC+ & below.....................	−5.632	0.301	350.616	0.000
Intercept for B− to B+	−1.669	0.237	280.591	0.000
Intercept for BB− to BB+	−0.072	0.251	489.255	0.000
Intercept for BBB− to BBB+.....................	1.663	0.270	727.915	0.000
Intercept for A− to A+.........................	3.447	0.317	820.815	0.000
EBIT to average total debt + shareholders' equity.....	−5.387	0.540	99.546	0.000
Interest to EBITDA	2.441	0.300	66.262	0.000
Total debt to CFO − capital expenditures	−0.002	0.001	1.505	0.220
Total debt to total debt + shareholders' equity	2.092	0.202	107.058	0.000
Capital expenditures to EBITDA.................	−0.182	0.091	3.982	0.046

CFO = Cash flow from operations

EBITDA = Earnings before interest, taxes, depreciation, and amortization

*The reported intercept coefficients represent the coefficients for a rating class. The difference between the intercept coefficients for a rating class and those of the lowest rating class provides the incremental intercept coefficient for that rating class, which is the relevant coefficient for the standard error, chi-square, and probability statistics.

The overall model is statistically significant, and all but one of the coefficients for the independent variables are statistically significant (the column labeled probability indicates the statistical significance of each variable). The one explanatory variable that is not statistically significant in this sample (but is used in other credit rating models) is Total Debt to Cash Flow from Operations minus Capital Expenditures, which has a coefficient that is essentially zero.

A positive coefficient in this model indicates that, holding everything else constant, the larger the value of the variable, the lower the debt rating; a negative coefficient indicates that, holding everything else constant, the larger the value of the variable, the higher the debt rating. As such, the positive coefficient for the inverse of the coverage ratio (Interest to EBITDA) indicates that as interest rises relative to EBITDA, the company is likely to have a lower rating. Further, the negative coefficient for company performance (EBIT to average Total Debt + Shareholders' Equity) indicates that a higher-performing company is more likely to have a higher credit rating, as expected. Similarly, if a company has a lot of investment opportunities and is plowing a larger proportion of its EBITDA into capital expenditures, it is likely to have a higher credit rating. The positive coefficient on the leverage ratio (Total Debt to Total Debt + Shareholders' Equity) indicates that as leverage goes up, the company is likely to have a lower rating. The remaining variable (Total Debt to CFO − Capital Expenditures) is insignificant given its near-zero coefficient.

Note that the results of the logistic model include five intercepts—one intercept for each category with the exception of the AA− to AAA category. These intercepts are important when we use the model to classify a company's credit rating, but for now the key observation is that all of the intercept coefficients are reliably different from zero, indicating that the estimated model can distinguish companies' credit ratings across groups. The statistical test for the intercept is actually a test of whether or not the difference between adjacent intercepts is statistically significant. We present the predictive (classification) ability of our model in Exhibit 9.19.

| EXHIBIT 9.19 | Classifications from the HZ Credit Rating Model on the 1,148 Sample Observations |

| | Sample Classifications | | | | | | | |
Actual	CCC+ & Below	B– to B+	BB– to BB+	BBB– to BBB+	A– to A+	AA– to AAA	Total % Correct
CCC+ & below	19%	78%		3%			
B– to B+	2%	63%	26%	8%	0%	1%	
BB– to BB+	0%	28%	41%	28%	3%	1%	
BBB– to BBB+		11%	36%	51%	2%		
A– to A+		5%	15%	73%	6%	2%	
AA– to AAA		9%	6%	74%	12%		
Total % correct							45%

Exhibit may contain small rounding errors

The model predicts about 45% of the credit ratings correctly and the vast majority of the predictions (over 90%) are within one rating class of the actual rating. The model correctly classifies 19% of the CCC+ & below group, 63% of the B– to B+ group, 41% of the BB– to BB+ group, 51% of the BBB– to BBB + group, only 6% of the A– to A+ group, and 0% of the AA– to AAA group.

In Exhibit 9.20, we show the calculation of the credit rating score for General Motors as of September 30 and December 31, 2008. As discussed before, its credit rating as of September 30, 2008, was B; in the following quarter, its financial condition deteriorated, and its credit rating was downgraded to CCC+. The model calculates a probability for each of the credit rating groups. The credit rating group with the highest probability is the predicted credit rating for the company. We measure the probability by first calculating the credit rating score for each of the credit ratings using its associated intercept. We calculate a credit rating score by adding the intercept for that rating to the product of each of the model's financial ratios for the company and the respective coefficient for each financial ratio. The resulting credit rating score is a number that can theoretically vary between +/− infinity. Given the logistic regression estimation method we use, we convert the credit rating score, which we label HZ, into a probability using the following formula, where $\exp^{-HZ}$ is the exponential function of –HZ.

$$\text{Cumulative Probability} = \frac{1}{1 + \exp^{-HZ}}$$

This probability is the cumulative probability that the credit rating is lower than or equal to the credit rating for that group. The probability for a credit rating group is equal to the difference between its cumulative probability and the cumulative probability of the adjacent lower credit rating group. Doing this, we calculate probabilities for five of the six credit ratings. The probability for the remaining credit rating is equal to 1 minus the sum of the other five probabilities.

We calculate the probabilities for General Motors as of September 30, 2008, as follows. For the CCC+ group with a credit rating score of −1.404, we measure its probability to be 0.1972. For the B– to B+ group with a credit rating score of 2.559, we measure its cumulative probability to be 0.9282, which we interpret as the company having a 92.8% probability that its credit rating is no higher than B– to B+. The probability for the B– to B+ group is the difference between these two cumulative probabilities, or 73.1% (0.7310 = 0.9282 − 0.1972). The cumulative probability for the BB– to BB+ group is 0.9846, and its probability is 5.6% (0.0564 = 0.9846 − 0.9282). The probability of the last group, AA– to AAA, is equal to 1 minus the cumulative probability of the previous rating class, A; this difference is equal to 0.05% for General Motors (0.0005 = 1 − 0.9995).

For the September ratios, the credit rating with the highest probability is the B– to B+ group, which is General Motors' actual rating. The next most likely rating is the lowest rating—the CCC+ & below group—with a probability of 19.7%. As we had discussed earlier, the financial condition of General Motors deteriorated in the following quarter (as evinced in Panel B). The effect of this deterioration in financial condition on the debt rating model was an increase in the probability of the lowest rating group from 19.7% to 84.1%, making this rating group the one with the highest probability. Thus, the model classifies General Motors in the correct categories for both periods.

| EXHIBIT 9.20 | The HZ Credit Rating Model Applied to General Motors Corporation as of September 30 and December 31, 2008* |

Panel A: September 30, 2008, Actual Credit Rating = B

Variable (Logit Model Estimation)	Coefficients	General Motors Corporation (Credit Rating = B)					
		CCC+ & Below	B– to B+	BB– to BB+	BBB– to BBB+	A– to A+	AA– to AAA
Intercept for CCC+ & below.........................	–5.632	–5.632					
Intercept for B– to B+	–1.669		–1.669				
Intercept for BB– to BB+	–0.072			–0.072			
Intercept for BBB– to BBB+........................	1.663				1.663		
Intercept for A– to A+..............................	3.447					3.447	
EBIT to average total debt + shareholders' equity.........	–5.387	0.118	0.118	0.118	0.118	0.118	
Interest to EBITDA	2.441	0.233	0.233	0.233	0.233	0.233	
Total debt to CFO – capital expenditures	–0.002	234.598	234.598	234.598	234.598	234.598	
Total sebt to total debt + shareholders' equity	2.092	2.283	2.283	2.283	2.283	2.283	
Capital expenditures to EBITDA.....................	–0.182	0.605	0.605	0.605	0.605	0.605	
HZ credit rating score..............................		–1.404	2.559	4.156	5.891	7.675	
Cumulative probability		0.197	0.928	0.985	0.997	0.9995	1.000
Probability of this credit rating		**19.72%**	**73.10%**	**5.64%**	**1.27%**	**0.23%**	**0.05%**

Panel B: December 31, 2008, Actual Credit Rating = CCC+

Variable (Logit Model Estimation)	Coefficients	General Motors Corporation (Credit Rating = CCC+)					
		CCC+ & Below	B– to B+	BB– to BB+	BBB– to BBB+	A– to A+	AA– to AAA
Intercept for CCC+ & below.........................	–5.632	–5.632					
Intercept for B– to B+	–1.669		–1.669				
Intercept for BB– to BB+	–0.072			–0.072			
Intercept for BBB– to BBB+........................	1.663				1.663		
Intercept for A– to A+..............................	3.447					3.447	
EBIT to average total debt + shareholders' equity.........	–5.387	–0.141	–0.141	–0.141	–0.141	–0.141	
Interest to EBITDA	2.441	–0.307	–0.307	–0.307	–0.307	–0.307	
Total debt to CFO – capital expenditures	–0.002	–2.311	–2.311	–2.311	–2.311	–2.311	
Total debt to total debt + shareholders' equity	2.092	3.424	3.424	3.424	3.424	3.424	
Capital expenditures to EBITDA.....................	–0.182	–0.668	–0.668	–0.668	–0.668	–0.668	
HZ credit rating score..............................		1.665	5.628	7.225	8.960	10.744	
Cumulative probability		0.841	0.996	0.999	1.000	1.000	1.000
Probability of this credit rating		**84.1%**	**15.6%**	**0.3%**	**0.1%**	**0.0%**	**0.0%**

Exhibit may contain small rounding errors
* Note: The financial ratios are listed in the table, and the HZ credit rating score is the sum of each ratio multiplied by the applicable coefficient and the appropriate intercept.

Note that given the sample used, senior unsecured debt ratings, one would have to adjust the rating for debt issues that are secured or collateralized or for debt issues that are junior or junior subordinated. It is not unusual for a company with many different kinds of debt instruments outstanding to have different ratings on its debt as a function of security, seniority, and maturity.

Note that all such classification or prediction models of this kind make an assumption about the relative cost of misclassifying a company. In our illustration, we assumed that the misclassification cost was constant for each credit rating group, and we chose the credit rating group with the highest probability. If we assume the misclassification costs are not equal, we must adjust the model for the unequal misclassification costs.

In Exhibit 9.21, we show this same analysis for Accenture, which had an actual rating of A+. The highest probability rating group for Accenture is the highest rating group—AA– to AAA. Like the individual financial ratio analyses we discussed earlier, the debt rating model classifies Accenture as having a rating higher than its actual rating.

EXHIBIT 9.21	The HZ Credit Rating Model Applied to Accenture Limited as of October 31, 2008—Actual Credit Rating Is A+

		Accenture Limited (Credit Rating = A+)					
Variable (Logit Model Estimation)	Coefficients	CCC+ & Below	B– to B+	BB– to BB+	BBB– to BBB+	A– to A+	AA– to AAA
Intercept for CCC+ & below	–5.632	–5.632					
Intercept for B– to B+	–1.669		–1.669				
Intercept for BB– to BB+	–0.072			–0.072			
Intercept for BBB– to BBB+	1.663				1.663		
Intercept for A– to A+	3.447					3.447	
EBIT to average total debt + shareholders' equity	–5.387	1.294	1.294	1.294	1.294	1.294	
Interest to EBITDA	2.441	0.026	0.026	0.026	0.026	0.026	
Total debt to CFO – capital expenditures	–0.002	0.004	0.004	0.004	0.004	0.004	
Total debt to total debt + shareholders' equity	2.092	0.003	0.003	0.003	0.003	0.003	
Capital expenditures to EBITDA	–0.182	0.174	0.174	0.174	0.174	0.174	
HZ credit rating score		–12.565	–8.601	–7.005	–5.269	–3.485	
Cumulative probability		0.000	0.000	0.001	0.005	0.030	1.000
Probability of this credit rating		**0.0%**	**0.0%**	**0.1%**	**0.4%**	**2.5%**	**97.0%**

* Note: The financial ratios are listed in the table, and the HZ credit rating score is the sum of each ratio multiplied by the applicable coefficient and the appropriate intercept.

REVIEW EXERCISE 9.6

Using the HZ Credit Rating Model to Estimate a Credit Rating

Apply the HZ Credit Rating Model to the Snap Company given in Review Exercise 9.5. What is the probability that Snap's credit rating falls within each of the six credit rating categories used in the HZ model in Year 0?

Solution on page 379.

Valuation Key 9.10

We can use credit rating models to estimate the credit rating of a company that does not have a current credit rating or for one that is planning to change its capital structure or operations. We then use the estimated credit rating as an input in the process of measuring the promised yield and debt cost of capital.

Preferred Stock Rating Models

We observe fewer companies with preferred stock, and information such as that in Exhibit 9.16 is not as readily available; the same is true of preferred stock rating models like the credit rating model we just illustrated. One approach we can use to estimate a preferred stock rating is to adjust the company's credit rating. To adjust a company's credit rating, we must, of course, begin with either observing or estimating the company's credit rating. Since preferred stock generally has a lower priority of claims, deferral of dividend payments, and other characteristics specific to preferred stock, we lower the credit rating to estimate the company's preferred stock rating.

A reduction of one rating (one notch, not an entire rating) is typically the minimum reduction for preferred stock. Factors considered include the deferral of dividends (which are optional as opposed to those required by either covenants of other securities or regulators), cumulative versus non-cumulative dividends, subordination, payment risk, specific default and distress risk, and potential government support. For example, in 2005, MetLife Inc. issued $2.1 billion of non-cumulative perpetual preferred. This security was rated BBB, which was three notches below the company's A credit rating. One reason provided for this reduction was that the preferred security had both optional and mandatory dividend deferrals.[24]

---

[24] For additional information on this issue, see "Criteria: Assigning Ratings to Hybrid Capital Issues," *Standard & Poor's Viewpoint*, Standard & Poor's, May 8, 2006, 10:02 EST, available at http://www2.standardandpoors.com/portal/site/sp/en/us/page.article/3,1,1,0,1145718364711.html.

Yield Prediction Models

The alternative to using a credit rating model is to use a yield prediction model. In a yield prediction model, we create a model that explains cross-sectional variation in yield spreads with a procedure similar to that of a bond rating model. In other words, we use variables such as leverage, size, profitability, interest coverage, and specific bond terms to estimate yields. The potential advantage of a yield prediction model is that it is a more direct approach.

9.6 BANKRUPTCY PREDICTION AND FINANCIAL DISTRESS MODELS

Recall from earlier in the chapter that assessing a company's probability of bankruptcy or financial distress may be useful for assessing a company's risk of default. Financial distress, financial failure, or bankruptcy prediction models attempt to combine various financial ratios and other factors into a financial distress metric that can be used to predict the likelihood of companies entering bankruptcy or a state of financial distress within a specified period (usually over roughly the next 12 months). The financial ratios are typically measures of company performance and financial leverage.

The HZ Financial-Ratio-Based Bankruptcy Prediction Model

Financial-ratio-based bankruptcy prediction models have as long a history as debt rating models. Edward Altman conducted one of the first studies of this sort in 1968.[25] He developed his model using a sample of 33 bankrupt and 33 non-bankrupt manufacturing companies. He used the following five financial ratios in his model: working capital/total assets; retained earnings/total assets; earnings before interest and taxes/total assets; market value of equity/book value of total debt; and sales/total assets. Altman's model correctly classified 94% of the bankrupt companies and 97% of the non-bankrupt companies, one year prior to a company filing for bankruptcy. Altman tested his model on another (hold-out) sample of 25 bankrupt and 66 non-bankrupt companies and was able to correctly classify 94% of the bankrupt companies and 79% of the non-bankrupt companies in this sample, again one year prior to a company filing for bankruptcy.

Depending on where in the business cycle the economy is, 0.1% to 4% of publicly traded companies file for bankruptcy in a typical year. Between 1986 and 2008, approximately 1.2% of U.S. publicly traded companies went bankrupt, with a high of 4.0% and a low of 0.27% in a single year. Thus, Altman's hold-out sample of 25 (27.5%) bankrupt companies and 66 non-bankrupt companies (72.5%) is not representative of the actual population and overstates the ability of the model to make correct predictions.[26] Regardless, Altman's study began a long history of the development of financial distress models, and numerous authors (including Altman) have refined Altman's original approach. These refinements include extending the model to other industries and privately held companies, using a sample that is more representative of the population of companies (to avoid problems that may arise if some underlying characteristic of the sampled companies differs from that of the population), addressing the problems that arise if the proportion of companies in the sample (bankrupt v. non-bankrupt) is not representative of the population, carefully collecting the historical data to represent a predictive context, and making various adjustments to the financial ratios and other metrics in the model.

In this section we illustrate the development and use of a financial-ratio-based bankruptcy prediction model, which we call the HZ Bankruptcy Prediction Model. We use a sample of 2,719 companies composed of 354 (13%) bankrupt companies and 2,365 (87%) non-bankrupt companies, somewhat oversampling the bankrupt group. We use five financial ratios in the model, which we show in Exhibit 9.22. The dependent variable is coded one for bankrupt companies and zero for non-bankrupt companies; thus, a positive (negative) coefficient for a financial ratio indicates that the larger the financial ratio, the higher

[25] See Altman, E. I "Financial Ratios, Discriminant Analysis and Prediction of Corporate Bankruptcy," *Journal of Finance* (September 1968), pp. 589–610.

[26] See Zmijewski, M. E. "Methodological Issues Related to the Estimation of Financial Distress Prediction Models," *Journal of Accounting Research* 22 (Supplement 1984), pp. 59–82.

(lower) the probability of bankruptcy. We use a logistic regression model as we did for the debt rating model, but we now have a dependent variable with only two outcomes (bankrupt/not bankrupt) versus the six debt rating categories in the debt rating model. The financial statements for the bankrupt companies are the annual financial statements made available up to 12 months prior to when the company files for bankruptcy. Thus, the model is predicting the probability of bankruptcy within 12 months of the financial statement date.

EXHIBIT 9.22	The HZ Bankruptcy Prediction Model				
Bankruptcy sample		354	13.0%		
Non-bankrupt sample		2,365	87.0%		
Total sample.		2,719	100.0%		
Variable	**Coefficients**	**Standard Error**	**Chi-Square Statistic**	**Probability**	
Intercept.	−3.099	0.302	105.350	0.000	
Net income to total assets	−0.756	0.227	11.080	0.001	
Current assets to current liabilities.	−0.176	0.063	7.733	0.005	
CFO to total liabilities.	−1.192	0.388	9.425	0.002	
EBITDA to interest (10 if no debt).	−0.029	0.007	17.343	0.000	
Total liabilities to total assets.	2.326	0.330	49.746	0.000	
Pseudo R-squared.	26.7%				

CFO = Cash flow from operations
EBITDA = Earnings before interest, taxes, depreciation and amortization

The overall model is statistically significant, and the coefficient for each of the independent (or explanatory) variables is statistically significant as well (see the probability column). All of the coefficients in this model are negative except for one. The coefficients are consistent with our discussion of how to interpret financial ratios in Chapter 2. The performance measure (net income to total assets), liquidity measure (current assets to current liabilities), debt coverage (cash flow from operations to total liabilities), and interest coverage (EBITDA to interest) all have negative coefficients. The negative coefficient indicates that a company with a higher financial ratio (higher performance, liquidity, cash flow to debt, and coverage) has a lower probability of bankruptcy. The positive coefficient for the ratio of total liabilities to total assets (financial leverage) is also consistent with our previous discussion—companies with higher financial leverage have a higher probability of bankruptcy.

Altman's model had a very high prediction rate for the sample used in that study; however, the sample in that study greatly overrepresented the bankruptcy group and the methodology did not control for that oversampling. Increasing the relative size of the non-bankruptcy group will result in lower overall prediction rates. While our sample is more representative, we also have a sample that somewhat overrepresents bankrupt companies (13% versus the lower than 2% in the population). We present the predictive (classification) ability of our model in Exhibit 9.23. We show that the model predicts about 80% of both the bankrupt and non-bankrupt companies over the next 12 months.[27]

---

[27] When making these predictions, we assume that our goal is to maximize the number of correct predictions; in other words, we assume that the cost of incorrectly predicting each group is equal. It may be more likely that the cost of incorrectly predicting a bankrupt company is more than the cost of incorrectly predicting a non-bankrupt company. For example, consider the extreme example of a financial institution not making a one-year loan to a company because it thought the company was going to go bankrupt. Assume that the financial institution does not have another customer to lend this money to and that it loses the interest on the loan (and only the interest) relative to investing the money in government securities. Also, assume that if the financial institution makes the loan and that the company does go bankrupt, the financial institution will lose both the interest and principal of the loan. We can quickly see that the relative cost of incorrectly predicting no bankruptcy when a company goes bankrupt—principal plus interest—is substantially larger (probably by more than 20 times) than the cost of not making a loan when the company does not go bankrupt but we predicted it would—the spread between the interest rate on the loan and the government rate of return.

EXHIBIT 9.23	Classifications from the HZ Bankruptcy Prediction Model on the 2,719 Sample Observations

	Sample Classifications		
Actual	**Non-Bankrupt**	**Bankrupt**	**Overall**
Non-bankrupt...	80%	20%	
Bankrupt..	17%	83%	
Overall			81%

Using a cutoff value of −0.99 for the financial distress metric maximizes the number of correct predictions for this sample.

In Exhibit 9.24, we provide more details on the output of this model. We partition the companies into five groups based on the financial distress metric—lowest probability of bankruptcy to highest probability of bankruptcy. The percentage of bankrupt companies increases in each group from 0% bankrupt for the group with the lowest probability of bankruptcy to 1%, to 4%, to 17%, and finally to 43% for the group with the highest probability of bankruptcy.

EXHIBIT 9.24	Probability of Bankruptcy Groupings Using the HZ Bankruptcy Prediction Model on the 2,719 Sample Observations

	Sample Classifications		
Probability	**% Non-Bankrupt**	**% Bankrupt**	**Cutoff Value**
Lowest	100%	0%	−3.63
Lowest + ...	99%	1%	−2.24
Medium	96%	4%	−1.46
Medium + ...	83%	17%	−1.05
Highest...	57%	43%	> −1.05

Like we did for the debt rating models, we show in Exhibit 9.25 the calculation of the bankruptcy prediction score for General Motors at two points in time—September 30, 2008, and December 31, 2008—and for Accenture at its fiscal year-end—October 31, 2008. We measure the bankruptcy prediction score for a company by adding the intercept to the product of each of the model's financial ratios for the company and its respective coefficient. We convert the bankruptcy prediction rating score, which we again label HZ, into a probability using the formula below, where $\exp^{-HZ}$ is the exponential function of $-HZ$.

$$\text{Cumulative Probability} = \frac{1}{1 + \exp^{-HZ}}$$

According to the model, as of September 2008, General Motors had a 66.7% probability of filing for bankruptcy within the next 12 months. In the following quarter, its financial condition continued to deteriorate, and its probability of filing for bankruptcy within a year increased to 85.1% by December 2008. It is worth noting that General Motors filed for bankruptcy on June 1, 2009. Accenture has a substantially lower probability of bankruptcy of 4% because of its higher rates of return, higher current ratio, higher interest coverage, and lower financial leverage.

EXHIBIT 9.25	The HZ Bankruptcy Prediction Model Applied to General Motors Corporation and Accenture Limited

		General Motors		
Variable	**Coefficients**	**30-Sep-08**	**31-Dec-08**	**Accenture**
Intercept..	−3.099			
Net income to total assets	−0.756	−0.20	−0.34	0.14
Current assets to current liabilities..................	−0.176	0.73	0.56	1.34
CFO to total liabilities.............................	−1.192	−0.04	−0.07	0.30
EBITDA to interest	−0.029	−5.69	−3.25	38.00
Total liabilities to total assets......................	2.326	1.53	1.94	0.74
HZ bankruptcy prediction score....................		0.695	1.741	−3.178
Probability of bankruptcy in 12 months..............		66.7%	85.1%	4.0%

Valuation Key 9.11

Bankruptcy or financial distress prediction models can be used to assess the probability that a company will be in a state of financial distress within a certain period of time. We can use these models to help assess a company's debt cost of capital.

REVIEW EXERCISE 9.7

Using the HZ Bankruptcy Prediction Model to Estimate the Probability of Bankruptcy

Using the financial information for the Snap Company given in Review Exercise 9.5, and the HZ Bankruptcy Prediction Model, calculate the probability that Snap will file for bankruptcy in the next 12 months.

Solution on page 380.

Financial Distress Models Based on Option Pricing Models

Another type of financial distress prediction model is an option-pricing-based model, which is based on the Merton model and its variations.[28] These models consider such company factors as financial leverage, market value, and volatility of the market value of the equity. Using this and other information, the model estimates the volatility of the underlying assets and predicts the probability of financial distress. We will discuss this approach and its applications in Chapter 12.

9.7 THE COST OF CAPITAL FOR WARRANTS, EMPLOYEE STOCK OPTIONS, AND OTHER EQUITY-LINKED SECURITIES

Recall that the levering, unlevering, and weighted average cost of capital formulas require us to know the cost of capital and the capital structure ratio for each of the securities used by a company to finance itself. These securities include such equity-linked securities as warrants, employee stock options, convertible debt, and other similar securities. We simply introduce these securities in this chapter, but we will discuss them in greater detail, including how to value them and measure their cost of capital, in Chapter 12. They have characteristics that are similar, but are not identical, to the stock option contracts for which the Black-Scholes Option Pricing Model was developed.[29] For example, a warrant is similar to a call option; generally, it is a security issued by the company that gives the holder the right to purchase a certain number of shares of the company's stock at a fixed price on or before a specified date.

One important feature of these securities is that they are dilutive; if the holder of such a security exercises the option in the security, the company issues additional shares of stock, which dilutes the ownership interest of the pre-existing shares. In general, equity-linked securities have a longer term to maturity than options traded on option exchanges. Various researchers have extended the Black-Scholes Option Pricing Model to measure the value and cost of capital of warrants, employee stock options, convertible debt, and other similar equity-linked securities.

It is important to measure the value and cost of capital for equity-linked securities. The cost of equity is typically reduced by the issuance of securities such as stock options and warrants. Moreover, options and warrants typically have a higher cost of capital than the equity cost of capital. If we do not measure the cost of capital of the equity-linked components, we will not measure the unlevered or weighted average costs of capital properly. We discuss and illustrate this issue further in Chapter 12.

Convertible debt is a security that has a coupon interest rate and maturity date (among other provisions) just like a straight-debt security. However, it also has an option for the holder to convert the bond into

LO5 Understand the importance of measuring the cost of capital for equity-linked securities

---

[28] Merton, R., "On the Pricing of Corporate Debt: The Risk Structure of Interest Rates," *Journal of Finance* vol. 29, no. 2 (May 1974), pp. 449–470.

[29] Black, F., and M. Scholes, "The Pricing of Options and Corporate Liabilities," *Journal of Political Economy* vol. 81, no. 3 (May/June 1973), pp. 637–654.

common stock (or sometimes even into preferred stock). Referring to the sample of companies in Exhibit 9.2, 13% have convertible debt. Of the companies that have any debt, 16% have convertible debt, and on average, 9% of the book value of the debt outstanding is convertible debt. This percentage, of course, is 0% for the 87% of the companies that do not have convertible debt. For the companies that have convertible debt, convertible debt is less than 35% of the total debt for about a third of these companies, between 35% and 85% of the total debt for another third, and between 85% and 100% of the total debt for the last third.

Valuation in Practice 9.2

General Motors Corporation Issues $4.0 Billion in Debt General Motors Corporation (General Motors) amended its prospectus to issue up to $4.0 billion in 30-year, 6.250% Series C Convertible Senior Debentures Due 2033. In its amended prospectus, dated June 19, 2003, the company described this debenture, to be publicly traded, as follows:

> We are offering $4,000,000,000 principal amount of 6.250% Series C Convertible Senior Debentures Due 2033. . . . The Series C debentures are **convertible into shares** of our $1 2/3 par value common stock, at your option, under any of the following circumstances: (1) the closing sale price of our $1 2/3 par value common stock exceeds specified thresholds, (2) the trading price of the Series C debentures falls below specified thresholds, (3) the Series C debentures are called for redemption or (4) upon the occurrence of other specified corporate events. **The Series C debentures are convertible** at a conversion price of $47.62 per share, which is equal to a conversion rate of 0.525 shares per $25.00 principal amount of Series C debentures, subject to adjustment. We may pay you an amount of cash equivalent to the shares of our $1 2/3 par value common stock otherwise required to be delivered upon conversion. **We will pay interest** on the Series C debentures on January 15 and July 15 of each year, beginning January 15, 2004. **We may redeem** the Series C debentures, in whole or in part, on or after July 20, 2010 for an amount in cash equal to the redemption prices set forth herein. **You may require us to repurchase** your Series C debentures on July 15 of 2018, 2023 and 2028, or, if any of those days is not a business day, on the next succeeding business day, for an amount equal to the principal amount plus accrued and unpaid interest. **We may elect to pay the repurchase price** in cash, shares of our $1 2/3 par value common stock or any combination thereof. **We have listed** the Series C debentures on the New York Stock Exchange under the symbol 'GPM' and expect trading of the debentures to commence on June 27, 2003. . . . Investing in the debentures involves risks. See 'Risk Factors' beginning on page S-5.

If we turn our attention to convertible preferred stock, we know from Exhibit 9.2 that preferred stock financing is used less often; recall that only 10% of the companies in the overall sample have any type of preferred stock. Of the companies that have preferred stock, about 50% have convertible preferred stock (or 5% of the companies in the entire sample). Of the companies that have convertible preferred stock, 90% have only convertible preferred stock. The analysis and methods we describe in Chapter 12 for valuing and measuring the cost of capital for convertible debt are generally applicable for convertible preferred stock as well.

Measuring the Value and Cost of Capital for Employee Stock Options

Employee stock options are similar to warrants in that they provide the employee with the option to purchase the common stock of the employer at a fixed price over some period of time. However, employee stock options diverge from the assumptions underpinning option pricing theory. For example, option pricing theory assumes that options are traded and that holders can hedge the risk of options by means of short-selling stock or other such actions; however, employee stock options are not traded, and the employee generally cannot hedge the risk. Thus, the value of employee stock options has two different values—the economic cost to the company and the economic value to the employee.[30]

---

[30] For a discussion of this issue, see Hall, B. J., and K. J. Murphy, "Stock Options for Undiversified Executives," *Journal of Accounting and Economics* vol. 33, no. 1 (February 2002), pp. 3–42.

For a company, the cost of granting an option to an employee is about equal to the value the company could have received by issuing the option to an outside investor. Fortunately, since our focus is on the company's capital structure and not on the value to the employee, we can still measure the value and cost of capital of employee stock options, but we have to keep in mind the specific provisions in employee stock options (for example, employee stock options typically have provisions that do not allow trading and include forfeiture).

Valuation Key 9.12

It is important to consider all of the equity-linked securities in estimating a company's capital structure and cost of capital. As such, we must value and estimate the cost of capital for securities such as convertible debt, convertible preferred, warrants, and employee stock options.

SUMMARY AND KEY CONCEPTS

The levering, unlevering, and weighted average cost of capital formulas we use to measure the cost of capital in a valuation analysis include a component for each type of financing used by a company in its capital structure. In this chapter, we discussed how to measure the costs of capital for a company's straight debt and preferred claims. The most frequently issued non-common-equity security is debt financing; however, even debt financing varies considerably based on the terms and provisions of its contract.

For a straight or pure debt contract, we measure the value of the debt by discounting the promised payments (interest and principal) at the promised yield to maturity. We can observe the promised payments from the terms of the contract, and we can observe the promised yield to maturity directly if the debt is traded. If the debt is not traded, we can measure the promised yield by using the company's credit rating, which we can either observe or directly measure from the company's underlying financial and market data. The promised yield is not, however, the company's cost of capital for the debt. The promised yield is equal to the cost of debt plus the expected default loss. Alternatively, we can use an asset pricing model like the CAPM to measure the cost of debt directly. We can use similar methods for preferred stock.

Companies also issue equity-linked securities such as warrants, employee stock options, and debt and preferred stock that are convertible into common equity. We can use models based on option pricing theory to measure the value and cost of capital for these securities. We delay discussion of those topics to Chapter 12.

ADDITIONAL READING AND REFERENCES

Kaplan, R. S., and G. Urwitz, "Statistical Models of Bond Ratings: A Methodological Inquiry," *Journal of Business* 52 (1979), pp. 231–261.

Merton, R. C., "On the Pricing of Corporate Debt: The Risk Structure of Interest Rates," *Journal of Finance* vol. 29, no. 2 (May 1974), pp. 449–470.

Zmijewski, M. E. "Methodological Issues Related to the Estimation of Financial Distress Prediction Models," *Journal of Accounting Research* 22 (Supplement 1984), pp. 59–82.

EXERCISES AND PROBLEMS

P9.1   **Debt Cost of Capital and Promised Yield** Assume the company has a debt agreement with the following characteristics:

Face value of the debt	$1,000
Debt coupon interest rate (paid annually)	10%
Debt term (# years)	1
Probability of default	20%
Recovery rate—Interest paid upon default	0%
Recovery rate—Principal paid upon default	40%

    a.   Calculate the expected cash flows for the debt.

    b.   Assume the investors require an expected annual rate of return of 13% for a debt security with this level of risk. Calculate the amount the investors would be willing to pay for this debt security.

    c.   Ignore part b, and instead assume the debt security is sold for $880.73. Calculate the debt cost of capital implied in this price.

P9.2   **Yield to Maturity and Expected Default Loss** Using the information in P9.1, calculate the yield to maturity and expected default loss for parts b and c.

P9.3   **Debt Cost of Capital for Debt with Maturity Greater than One Year** Assume the company issues debt with the following characteristics:

Face value of debt (in millions)	$100
Coupon interest rate (paid annually)	12%
Years to maturity	5
Issue price	$75
Recovery rate (all years)	40%
(Recovery rate is for the principal plus interest for the year of default)	
Probability of default—Year 1	40%
Probability of default—Year 2	30%
Probability of default—Year 3	20%
Probability of default—Year 4	10%
Probability of default—Year 5	5%

Calculate the yield to maturity, the cost of debt, and the expected default loss for this debt issue.

P9.4   **Debt Cost of Capital Estimated Using the CAPM** The PMJ Company had debt on their books at the end of 2005 with a credit rating of B. The yield to maturity of AA rated debt at that time was approximately 5%, which we assume is equal to its cost of debt. Use the data in Exhibit 9.11 to estimate the debt cost of capital for the PMJ Company at the end of 2005. Assume the market risk premium is 8%.

P9.5   **Using Financial Ratios to Estimate a Credit Rating** Estimate the Viking Company's credit rating at the end of Year 0 using the company's financial statements given below, and the distribution of key financial ratios for different credit ratings given in Exhibit 9.14.

Viking Company Balance Sheets and Income Statement		
($ in thousands)	Year –1	Year 0
Income Statement		
Revenue		$12,290
Operating expenses		–4,793
Depreciation expense		–1,920
Earnings before interest and taxes		$ 5,577
Interest expense		–1,148
Income before taxes		$ 4,429
Income tax expense		–1,329
Net income		$3,100
Balance Sheet		
Total current assets	$ 1,904	$ 2,044
Property, plant & equipment (net)	30,894	29,553
Total assets	$32,798	$31,596
Account payable	$ 626	$ 672
Debt	16,399	16,563
Total liabilities	$17,025	$17,235
Capital stock	$ 8,000	$ 8,000
Retained earnings	7,773	6,361
Shareholders' equity	$15,773	$14,361
Liabilities and shareholders' equity . . .	$32,798	$31,596

Viking Company Unlevered Free Cash Flow Statement	
($ in thousands)	Year 0
Unlevered operating cash flow	$5,735
– Change in required cash balance	–5
– Capital expenditures	–578
Unlevered free cash flow	$5,152

Exhibit may contain small rounding errors

P9.6 **Using the HZ Credit Rating Model to Estimate a Credit Rating** Apply the HZ Credit Rating Model to the Viking Company given in P9.5. What is the probability that Viking's credit rating falls within each of the six credit rating categories used in the HZ model in Year 0?

P9.7 **Using the HZ Bankruptcy Prediction Model to Estimate the Probability of Bankruptcy** Using the financial information for the Viking Company given in P9.5, and the HZ Bankruptcy Prediction Model, calculate the probability that Viking will file for bankruptcy in the next twelve months.

SOLUTIONS FOR REVIEW EXERCISES

Review Exercise 9.1: Debt Cost of Capital

Assume the company has a one-period $1,000 debt agreement that will pay the investor at the end of one year the coupon interest rate of 12% plus the $1,000 face value of the debt. Assume the investors believe the company has a 3% probability of defaulting on the promised payments. If the company defaults, the investors will be paid no interest and 50% of the face value of the debt at the end of Year 1.

	Promised	No Default State	Default State	Expected	
Debt (coupon) interest rate.	12.0%				
Face value	$1,000.00				
Probability		97.0%	3.0%		
Recovery rate—interest		100.0%	0.0%		
Recovery rate—principal		100.0%	50.0%		
Interest	$ 120.00	$116.40	$ 0.00	$ 116.40	97.0%
Principal	$1,000.00	$970.00	$15.00	$ 985.00	98.5%
Total	$1,120.00			$1,101.40	98.3%
Debt cost of capital	14.0%			0.877	
Present value				$ 966.14	96.6%
Part C—Implied debt cost of capital					
Assumed debt issue price	$1,019.81				
Total expected cash flows	$1,101.40				
Implied debt cost of capital	8%				

Exhibit may contain small rounding errors

a. The expected cash flows for the debt equal $116.40 for interest plus $985 for the principal or a total of $1,101.40.

b. The investors would be willing to invest $966.14 in this security (= $1,101.40 expected cash flows × 0.8772 present value factor for one year at 14%).

c. The implied debt cost of capital is 8% (0.08 = $1,101.40 expected cash flows/$1,019.81 issue price of the debt – 1). The issue price is higher than the face value of the debt (issued at a premium) because the expected cash flows result in a return that exceeds the debt cost of capital when valued using the face value of the bond, even after taking into account the default risk. Thus, in order to earn just the debt cost of capital, the bond has to be selling at a premium to its face value.

Review Exercise 9.2: Yield to Maturity and Expected Default Loss

Part b: $YTM = \dfrac{\$1,120}{\$966.14} - 1 = 0.15925$

where $1,120 is the promised payments and $966.14 is the price of the bond

$E(DL) = YTM - r_D$

$E(DL) = 0.159 - 0.14 = 0.019$

Part c: $\text{YTM} = \dfrac{\$1,120}{\$1,019.81} - 1 = 0.098$

where $1,120 is the promised payments and $1,019.81 is the price of the bond

$E(DL) = YTM - r_D$

$E(DL) = 0.098 - 0.08 = 0.018$

Review Exercise 9.3: Debt Cost of Capital for Debt with Maturity Greater than One Year

Face value of debt	$600
Coupon interest rate (paid annually)	8%
Years to maturity	5
Issue price	$460
Recovery rate (all years).................	50%

(Recovery rate is for the principal plus interest for the year of default)

Probability of default—Year 1	30%
Probability of default—Year 2	20%
Probability of default—Year 3	15%
Probability of default—Year 4	5%
Probability of default—Year 5	5%

Coupon................	8%
Principal	$600.0
Interest payment	$48.0
Price..................	$460.0
Recovery rate...........	50.0%

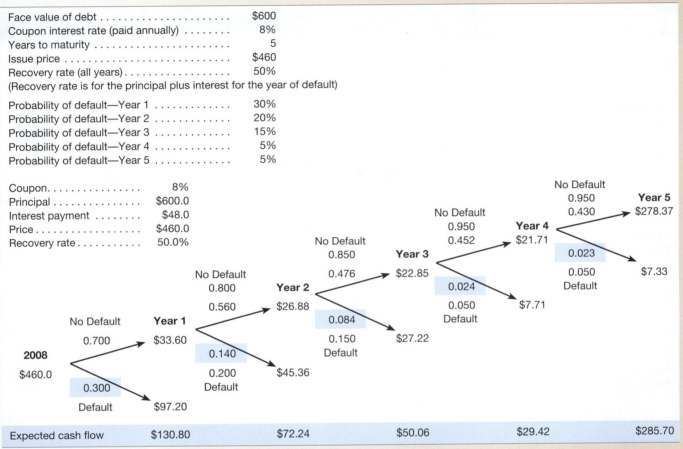

Expected cash flow	$130.80	$72.24	$50.06	$29.42	$285.70

Exhibit may contain small rounding errors

Using Equation 9.2 with the promised cash flows, the YTM is

$$0 = \frac{\$48}{(1 + r_D)^1} + \frac{\$48}{(1 + r_D)^2} + \frac{\$48}{(1 + r_D)^3} + \frac{\$48}{(1 + r_D)^4} + \frac{\$48 + \$600}{(1 + r_D)^5} - \$460$$

$\text{YTM} = 15\%$

Using Equation 9.1 with the expected cash flows, the cost of debt is

$$0 = \frac{\$130.80}{(1 + r_D)^1} + \frac{\$72.24}{(1 + r_D)^2} + \frac{\$50.06}{(1 + r_D)^3} + \frac{\$29.42}{(1 + r_D)^4} + \frac{\$285.70}{(1 + r_D)^5} - \$460$$

$r_D = 6.5\%$

The expected default loss is 8.5% $(0.085 = 0.15 - 0.065)$.

Review Exercise 9.4: Debt Cost of Capital Estimated Using the CAPM

Debt cost of capital for AA rated debt	6.0%
Market risk premium	4.0%
Incremental cost of capital for Ba rating	1.1%
Estimated debt cost of capital for Ba rating.	7.1%

The estimated debt cost of capital is 7.1% ($0.071 = 0.06 + 0.011$).

Review Exercise 9.5: Using Financial Ratios to Estimate a Credit Rating

Financial Ratios:	Ratio	Rating
Operating margin (before D&A) (%)	64.0%	AAA
Return on capital (%)	25.3%	A to AA
EBIT interest coverage (x)	14.46	A to AA
EBITDA interest coverage (x)	16.34	A to AA
Free cash flow to debt (%)	66%	A to AA
Free operating cash flow to debt (%)	74%	A to AA
Debt to EBITDA (x)	0.78	AA to AAA
Debt to debt + equity (%)	38%	BBB to A

The financial ratios for the Snap Company correspond with credit ratings ranging from AAA to BBB which illustrates the fact that using financial ratio distributions to estimate a credit rating can be difficult. Five of the ratios are between the median financial ratios for credit ratings between A and AA and the debt to debt plus equity ratio is very close to the cutoff for an A rating (ratio of 38% versus a cutoff of 36.8%). One of the eight ratios is associated with a credit rating between AA and AAA and another is an AAA rating. Given just the information in the financial ratios, we would anticipate that Snap Company would have an A rating.

Review Exercise 9.6: Using the HZ Credit Rating Model to Estimate a Credit Rating

Variable (Logit Model Estimation)	Coefficients	CCC+ & Below	B– to B+	BB– to BB+	BBB– to BBB+	A– to A+	AA– to AAA
Intercept for CCC+ & below	−5.632	−5.632					
Intercept for B– to B+	−1.669		−1.669				
Intercept for BB– to BB+	−0.072			−0.072			
Intercept for BBB– to BBB+	1.663				1.663		
Intercept for A– to A+	3.447					3.447	
EBIT to average total debt + shareholders' equity	−5.387	0.421	0.421	0.421	0.421	0.421	
Interest to EBITDA	2.441	0.061	0.061	0.061	0.061	0.061	
Total debt to CFO – capital expenditures	−0.002	1.484	1.484	1.484	1.484	1.484	
Total debt to total debt + shareholders' equity	2.092	0.381	0.381	0.381	0.381	0.381	
Capital expenditures to EBITDA.	−0.182	0.055	0.055	0.055	0.055	0.055	
HZ credit rating score.		−6.965	−3.002	−1.405	0.330	2.114	
Cumulative probability		0.001	0.047	0.197	0.582	0.892	1.000
Probability of credit rating.		0.1%	4.6%	15.0%	38.5%	31.0%	10.8%

The credit rating with the highest probability is the BBB− to BBB+ group with a probability of 38.5%, but the probability for the A− to A+ group is quite close at 31%. This result indicates that the range of most likely credit ratings is quite wide—from A+ to BBB−.

Review Exercise 9.7: Using the HZ Bankruptcy Prediction Model to Estimate the Probability of Bankruptcy

Variable	Coefficients	Year 0
Intercept.	−3.099	
Net income to total assets	−0.756	0.23
Current assets to current liabilities.	−0.176	4.80
CFO to total liabilities	−1.192	0.68
EBITDA to interest	−0.029	16.34
Total liabilities to total assets	2.326	0.40
HZ bankruptcy prediction score.		−4.465
Probability of bankruptcy in 12 months		1.1%

The HZ Financial Distress Model predicts only a 1.1% probability that Snap will file for bankruptcy in the next twelve months.

After mastering the material in this chapter, you will be able to:

1. Understand the process of levering and unlevering and its use in valuation (10.1)

2. Choose the appropriate discount rate for a company's interest tax shields (10.2)

3. Lever a company's unlevered cost of capital and unlevered beta (10.3–10.4)

4. Unlever a company's equity cost of capital and equity beta (10.5–10.6)

5. Avoid common errors in the levering and unlevering process (10.7–10.8)

The Effects of Financial Leverage on the Cost of Capital

LAN Airlines S.A. (LAN), a Chilean Company, and TAM S.A. (TAM), a Brazilian company, along with their respective controlling shareholders entered into an exchange offer agreement (prospectus dated May 10, 2012) to combine LAN and TAM to form

LATAM AIRLINES GROUP, S.A.

the airline with the largest fleet of aircraft of any airline in Latin America. The combined companies will be known as LATAM Airlines Group, S.A. when the proposed combination is completed. BTG Pactual, which served as the financial advisor for TAM, is an internationally recognized investment banking firm with experience in providing strategic advisory services for transactions in Latin America. Among other analysis, BTG Pactual conducted a discounted cash flow analysis. BTG's estimates of the cost of capital for TAM, "were determined based on (i) an unlevered beta of TAM, (ii) a target capital structure of 50% debt to total capital, (iii) country risk in Chile and (iv) the long-horizon expected equity premium." Banco Bradesco BBI S.A. (Bradesco) was elected by TAM's minority shareholders to file an independent appraisal report. In its appraisal report, Bradesco describes in detail how the equity betas for LAN and TAM were computed and the exact method used to unlever those betas and then relever them for the relevant target capital structure.[1]

In this chapter, we explore the levering and unlevering process in detail. In addition, we investigate the alternative relationships between the equity cost of capital, the unlevered cost of capital, and the company's other costs of capital that are determined by the company's capital structure strategy and the inherent risk of the interest tax shields.

---

[1] See the Offer to Exchange Each Common Share, Preferred Share and American Depositary Share of TAM S.A. for 0.90 of a Common Share of LAN Airlines, S.A., dated May 10, 2012.

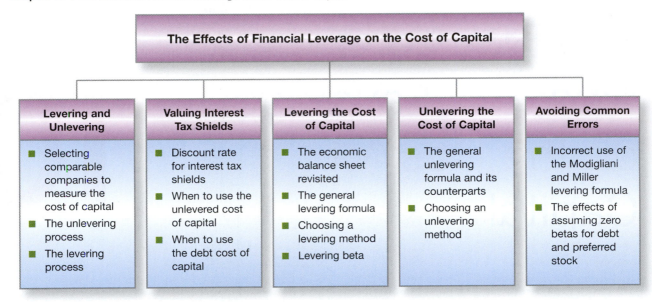

INTRODUCTION

In Chapter 5, we discussed the rudiments of the levering and unlevering process and introduced one specific form of the relationship between a company's equity cost of capital, its unlevered cost of capital, and the company's other costs of capital. In this chapter, we explore the levering and unlevering process in more detail. As it turns out, there are multiple forms of the relationship among the various costs of capital—all of which depend on the risk (as well as the magnitude and timing) of the company's interest tax shields, which in turn depends on the company's capital structure strategy. In other words, there are alternative assumptions we can make about how to value the interest tax shields, and that affects the relationship among the various costs of capital. In this chapter, we provide a framework for assessing the riskiness of the company's interest tax shields based on the company's capital structure strategy, which in turn leads to a specific form of the relationship between the various costs of capital for the levering and unlevering process.

More specifically, we can measure a company's unlevered cost of capital from its equity and other costs of capital, given its capital structure strategy. We call this the **unlevering process** because we remove the effects of financial leverage from the equity cost of capital in order to measure the unlevered cost of capital. We can also use these relationships to measure a company's equity cost of capital from its unlevered and non-equity costs of capital given its capital structure strategy. We call this the **levering process** because we adjust the company's unlevered cost of capital for the company's capital structure strategy. It is rare to conduct a valuation without using either the unlevering or levering process, or both processes.

In this chapter, we also show how to use these same relationships to lever and unlever the beta (or systematic risk) from the Capital Asset Pricing Model (CAPM). We demonstrate that if we use the CAPM to measure the cost of capital, using the levering and unlevering relationships that are stated in terms of CAPM betas and then applying the CAPM results in the same costs of capital that we would have calculated had we used the levering and unlevering relationships based on the costs of capital directly.

As part of our discussion, we will learn that the weighted average cost of capital discounted cash flow (DCF) method is capable of embedding the value of a company's interest tax shields into a company's valuation based on varying assumptions about their risk, magnitude, and timing. As we shall see, an important reason why the weighted average cost of capital DCF method can value the interest tax shields correctly under different assumptions is the choice of the levering formula that indicates how we want to value the interest tax shields.

10.1 AN OVERVIEW OF THE UNLEVERING AND LEVERING PROCESS

LO1 Understand the process of levering and unlevering and its use in valuation

We typically use either the weighted average cost of capital (WACC) or the adjusted present value (APV) valuation method to measure a company's value when using a discounted cash flow (DCF) valuation method. The weighted average cost of capital is the discount rate for the WACC DCF method, and it requires measuring a company's after-tax costs of capital for its equity and each of its non-equity securities. To use the APV valuation method, we need two discount rates—the unlevered cost of capital and the cost of capital for the company's interest tax shields.

We typically use comparable companies to measure the unlevered and equity costs of capital for the company we are valuing for two reasons. First, if the company we are valuing does not have publicly traded equity, we cannot estimate the company's equity cost of capital directly with an asset pricing model (such as the Capital Asset Pricing Model). Second, even if we can use an asset pricing model directly for the company we are valuing, we often use comparable companies to measure the unlevered or equity cost of capital for the company we are valuing in order to reduce the measurement error in our estimates, a topic we previously discussed in Chapter 8.

Selecting Comparable Companies

How do we choose comparable companies for estimating the cost of capital? To begin, let us think about what we are trying to achieve. We know that the unlevered cost of capital measures the risk of the unlevered assets of a firm. When we unlever the equity cost of capital for our comparable companies, we use these to estimate the appropriate unlevered cost of capital for the unlevered assets of the firm we are valuing. Therefore, we select comparable companies whose underlying business risk is the same as that of the company we are valuing. We know that the equity cost of capital is affected by both a company's business risk and its financial risk. However, the unlevering process removes the effect of capital structure risk (the financial risk) from the equity cost of capital, allowing us to estimate the unlevered cost of capital.

To choose comparable companies that we believe have the same underlying business risk, we typically search for companies in the same line of business as the company we are valuing. In addition, they should have similar production processes and cost structures—in particular, the extent to which they have similar proportions of variable and fixed costs (operating leverage). We are not concerned with whether their capital structures are the same, for the unlevering process allows us to undo the effects of differences in capital structure across firms.

Once we have selected the comparable companies, how do we use them in the unlevering and levering process? We start by measuring the equity cost of capital for each comparable company and for the company we are valuing, if possible. We then unlever the equity cost of capital of each company to measure each company's unlevered cost of capital. Based on our analysis of the unlevered costs of capital for these companies, we select a value or range of values for the unlevered cost of capital for the company we are valuing. We discussed different ways to weight the unlevered cost of capital estimates in Chapter 8. If we are using the adjusted present value method, we would now have the cost of capital that we need.

If we are using the weighted average cost of capital method, we would lever the unlevered cost of capital for the target capital structure of the company we are valuing in order to measure the company's equity cost of capital. That estimate, in conjunction with the company's other costs of capital, allows us to measure the company's weighted average cost of capital. As we shall see later, when we pick a formula to lever the unlevered cost of capital, we are basically informing the weighted average cost of capital method of how we want to value the interest tax shields.

We can use essentially this same process on the beta or systematic risk of the various companies. For example, we can unlever the equity betas of each company to estimate each company's unlevered beta and then use the CAPM to measure the unlevered cost of capital. If we need to measure the company's equity cost of capital, we lever the unlevered beta to obtain the equity beta of the firm we are valuing based on its target capital structure and then use the CAPM to measure the equity cost of capital. Unlevering the equity cost of capital that is based on the CAPM directly or unlevering the equity beta and then applying the CAPM results in the same unlevered cost of capital estimate. The same is true for levering the unlevered cost of capital or levering an unlevered beta to estimate the equity cost of capital—as long as the CAPM is used in both processes.

The Steps in the Unlevering Process

We can unlever a company's cost of capital using estimates of its equity cost of capital, the costs of capital of each of its non-equity securities, and its capital structure strategy. Instead of unlevering the equity cost of capital directly, we can also unlever the equity beta. We call this process the unlevering process, and we summarize both approaches in Exhibit 10.1.

EXHIBIT 10.1   The Steps in the Unlevering Process

Unlevering the Equity Cost of Capital Directly	Unlevering the Capital Asset Pricing Model Beta, β
For each comparable company (and perhaps the company you are valuing):	
1 Measure the company's equity cost of capital using an asset pricing model	Measure the company's equity beta, β_E, using the Capital Asset Pricing Model
2 Measure the cost of capital for each of its non-equity securities (e.g., r_D, r_{PS})	Measure the beta for each of its non-equity securities (e.g., β_D, β_{PS})
3 Measure the capital structure ratios or the value of each security (e.g., V_E/V_F, V_D/V_F, V_{PS}/V_F or V_E, V_D, V_{PS})	Same
4 Measure the income tax rate for interest tax shields, T_{INT}, discount rate, r_{ITS}, and any other information needed to measure the value of the company's interest tax shields, V_{ITS}	Same
5 Choose the appropriate unlevering formula for each company	Same
6 Measure the unlevered cost of capital, r_{UA}, for each company	Measure the unlevered beta, β_{UA}, for each company
Based on the distribution of comparable companies' unlevered costs of capital or betas:	
7 Measure the unlevered cost of capital (or range of the unlevered costs of capital) that best reflects the operating risk of the company you are valuing, r_{UA}	Measure the unlevered beta (or range of unlevered betas) that best reflects the operating risk of the company you are valuing, β_{UA}
8 Not relevant	Measure the company's unlevered cost of capital using the Capital Asset Pricing Model, if needed for the valuation

The Steps in the Levering Process

Once we measure the unlevered cost of capital for the company we are valuing, perhaps utilizing comparable companies, we can then measure its equity cost of capital using our estimate of the unlevered cost of capital, the costs of capital of the company's non-equity securities, and the capital structure strategy that is relevant for the valuation we are conducting. Again, instead of calculating the equity cost of capital directly from the unlevered cost of capital, we can first calculate the equity beta from the unlevered beta. Either way, we call this the levering process, and we summarize both approaches in Exhibit 10.2. We can then use the equity cost of capital and the other information used in this process to measure a company's weighted average cost of capital.

EXHIBIT 10.2   The Steps in the Levering Process

Levering the Unlevered Cost of Capital Directly	Levering the Unlevered Capital Asset Pricing Model Beta, β_{UA}
For the company you are valuing:	
1 Measure the company's unlevered cost of capital or range of unlevered costs of capital, r_{UA} (see Exhibit 10.1)	Measure the company's unlevered beta, β_{UA}, or range of unlevered betas (see Exhibit 10.1)
2 Measure the cost of capital for each of the company's non-equity securities (e.g., r_D, r_{PS})	Measure the beta for each of the company's non-equity securities (e.g., β_D, β_{PS})
3 Measure the capital structure ratios or the value of each security (e.g., V_E/V_F, V_D/V_F, V_{PS}/V_F or V_E, V_D, V_{PS})	Same
4 Measure the income tax rate, T_{INT}, discount rate, r_{ITS}, and any other information needed to measure the value of the company's interest tax shields, V_{ITS}	Same
5 Choose the appropriate levering formula for the company	Same
6 Measure the equity cost of capital, r_E, for the company	Measure the equity beta, β_E, for the company
7 Not relevant	Measure the equity cost of capital, r_E, for the company using the Capital Asset Pricing Model

Before we can discuss the formulas for levering and unlevering the cost of capital, we need to better understand both the risk of a company's interest tax shields and the discount rate used to value them.

> ## Valuation Key 10.1
>
> The unlevering and levering processes are used in almost every DCF valuation. If we are valuing a company using the APV method, we use the unlevering process to measure the unlevered cost of capital for the company being valued (if it is publicly traded) as well as for the relevant publicly traded comparable companies. If we are valuing a company using the WACC method, we often begin by using the unlevering process to measure the company's unlevered cost of capital if we have comparable companies to work with or if the company is considering a change in capital structure; then, we use the levering process to measure the company's equity cost of capital and weighted average cost of capital.

10.2 ASSESSING THE RISK AND VALUE OF INTEREST TAX SHIELDS

We need to assess the risk of a company's interest tax shields in order to measure the discount rate with which—either explicitly or implicitly—we value the company's interest tax shields. Companies adopt various types of capital structure strategies. Some companies adopt a target capital structure stated in terms of a target debt to total value ratio that is defined in terms of market values. For example, a past survey of chief financial officers (CFOs) indicated that about 10% of the CFOs surveyed had a strict target debt ratio, 34% had "a somewhat tight target range," 37% had a "flexible target range," and the remaining 19% had "no target."[2] Some companies—for example, companies that undergo a debt recapitalization—may have a strategy of paying down their outstanding debt for a certain number of years until the debt level reaches a certain long-run target capital structure ratio. Regardless of which capital structure strategy a company chooses, the capital structure strategy (how a company intends to manage its capital structure) affects the risk, as well as the magnitude and timing, of the interest tax shields and therefore, their value.

LO2 Choose the appropriate discount rate for a company's interest tax shields

Discount Rate for Interest Tax Shields Is the Cost of Debt

If the risk of a company's interest tax shields is solely determined by the company's ability to generate sufficient taxable income to capture the benefits of its interest tax shields, then the risk of the underlying debt is a reasonable measure of the risk of the interest tax shields. Why? Presumably, the debt's required rate of return—as set by lenders in an arms'-length transaction—indicates the company's ability to generate sufficient cash flows to meet its required payments. Further, this risk should be similar to the risk that the company can generate sufficient taxable income to be able to use the interest tax shields (to utilize those tax deductions). In such cases, we can use the debt cost of capital as the discount rate for the interest tax shields.

In the formulas we present in this chapter, we assume that the cost of debt, r_D, can be used to calculate a company's expected interest expense deduction for income tax purposes. This may not, however, be the case for all firms. The cost of debt at the date of issuance may not equal the current cost of debt, for the company's cost of debt can change over time because of shifts in the real risk-free rate of return or expected inflation as market conditions change. We discuss the implications of this difference later in the chapter, but for now, we assume that the current cost of debt multiplied by the value of the debt equals a company's expected interest expense deduction for income tax purposes.

Given these assumptions, the value of the interest tax shields at time 0, when the discount rate for all interest tax shields is equal to the cost of debt, $V_{ITS@r_D,0}$, can be stated as

$$V_{ITS@r_D,0} = \sum_{t=1}^{\infty} \frac{ITS_t}{(1 + r_{D,t})^t} = \sum_{t=1}^{\infty} \frac{r_{D,t} \times V_{D,t} \times T_{INT,t}}{(1 + r_{D,t})^t}$$

When might we want to value the interest tax shields at the cost of debt? For one, it can occur for already outstanding debt if the amount of the outstanding debt that the firm will keep in the future is independent of the value of the firm and the amount of debt is modest relative to the value of the firm. If

[2] See Graham, J. R., and C. R. Harvey, "The Theory and Practice of Corporate Finance: Evidence From the Field," *Journal of Financial Economics* 60 (2001), pp. 187–243.

we already know the amount of debt a company has outstanding and that it won't be changed if the value of the firm changes, the only risk is related to the company's ability to generate sufficient taxable income to take advantage of its interest tax shields; as such, the cost of debt is a reasonable discount rate to use for the company's interest tax shields.

An extreme example of this situation is a company with zero expected growth in perpetuity, a fixed amount of perpetual debt outstanding, and facing a constant tax rate in perpetuity.[3] The value of the interest tax shields in this case can be measured as

$$V_{ITS@r_D} = \frac{ITS}{r_D} = \frac{r_D \times V_D \times T_{INT}}{r_D} = T_{INT} \times V_D \tag{10.1}$$

Valuation in Practice 10.1

Companies Can Increase Financial Leverage by Repurchasing Equity: Philip Morris International, Inc. (PM) The Board of Directors of Philip Morris International Inc. (NYSE/Euronext Paris: PM) announced a new three-year share repurchase program of $18 billion on June 13, 2012. It was anticipated that the new program would be initiated August 1, 2012, following completion of the existing three-year program of $12 billion that began in May 2010 and that would conclude ahead of schedule. As previously announced, Philip Morris had a share repurchase target for 2012 of $6.0 billion.

Because of the recent share repurchases, the book value of shareholders' equity as of March 31, 2012, was only $112 million, so that share repurchases could drive the book value of shareholders' equity negative. The scheduled repurchases will also increase the company's debt-to-equity ratio (as measured in market values).

Source: For more information, visit Philip Morris' website at www.pmi.com/investors.

Discount Rate for Interest Tax Shields Is the Unlevered Cost of Capital[4]

A company's interest tax shields can be riskier than the risk of the underlying debt. If the company has a constant target capital structure (in terms of the proportion of debt to equity), then the amount of its debt—and in turn, the amount of its interest tax shields—depends on the value of the firm in each future period. Since the amount of the interest tax shields is directly linked to the value of the firm, the risk of a company's interest tax shields is approximately the risk of the company's underlying assets—the unlevered cost of capital. The presumption here is that a firm will adjust its leverage in order to maintain a constant proportionate capital structure—if the value of the firm goes down, it will reduce debt; if the value of the firm goes up, it will increase debt.

An extreme example of this situation is when a company has a strategy of a constant debt to value capital structure and issues debt with a very short maturity such that it must continually refinance its debt. As the company's value changes, the company changes the amount of debt it has outstanding. The risk of the interest tax shields depends on not only the ability of the company to capture the benefits of its interest tax shields but also on the amount of debt the company will have outstanding. The amount of debt the company will have outstanding depends directly on the value of the firm.[5] In this case, the value of the interest tax shields is based on the unlevered cost of capital, $V_{ITS@r_{UA},0}$, and is equal to

$$V_{ITS@r_{UA},0} = \sum_{t=1}^{\infty} \frac{ITS_t}{(1 + r_{UA,t})^t} = \sum_{t=1}^{\infty} \frac{r_D \times V_{D,t} \times T_{INT,t}}{(1 + r_{UA,t})^t}$$

---

[3] Recall that this is the assumption made by Modigliani, F., and M. H. Miller, "Corporate Income Taxes and the Cost of Capital: A Correction," *American Economic Review* 53 (June 1963), pp. 433–443.

[4] For a discussion of this approach see, Ruback, R. S., "A Simple Approach to Valuing Risky Cash Flows," *Financial Management* vol. 31, no. 2 (Summer, 2002), pp. 85–103.

[5] See Harris, R. S., Pringle, J. J. "Risk-adjusted Discount Rates—Extensions from the Average Risk Case," *Journal of Financial Research* vol. 8, no. 3 (1985), pp. 237–244, which examines the continuous financing assumption thoroughly; for an additional explanation and a discrete time version of the Harris and Pringle model, see Taggart Jr., R. A., "Consistent Valuation and Cost of Capital Expressions with Corporate and Personal Taxes," *Financial Management* vol. 20 (1991), pp. 8–20.

Discount Rate for Interest Tax Shields with Annual Refinancing

Some firms follow a strict target capital structure strategy, but, of course, even these companies do not refinance continually. Even if a company pursues a target capital structure policy in terms of some fixed target debt-to-equity ratio, such capital structures are "sticky" because of adjustment costs. In other words, the transactions costs of adjusting the capital structure are not zero. Whether a company issues debt, issues equity, calls debt, or repurchases shares, it will incur transactions costs. As such, managers do not instantaneously adjust their debt levels for every fluctuation in the value of a company's equity.

If a company only adjusts to its target capital structure *annually* because of the transactions costs of adjustments, we know the exact amount of debt the company will have for the first year subsequent to the valuation date because it will not make adjustments during that year. If the company sets the amount of debt outstanding as of the valuation date based on the value of the firm and the target debt-to-equity ratio, the only risk of the interest tax shields for the first year is the company's ability to generate sufficient taxable income to take advantage of its interest tax shields. There is no risk related to changes in the company's outstanding debt due to fluctuations in the value of the firm during the first year, because the company does not adjust its capital structure until the end of the year. For subsequent years, however, the amount of debt (and therefore the magnitude of the interest tax shields) will depend on the value of the firm at each successive year. At the end of each year, we assume the firm will refinance itself to maintain a constant target capital structure, so the amount of debt the company will issue (or retire) will depend on the value of the firm at the end of each subsequent year (each annual refinancing date).[6]

As of Year 0, we know the interest tax shield that is available in Year 1, but as of Year 0, future interest tax shields depend on the value of the firm at each subsequent year-end. As such, the risk of the Year 1 interest tax shield is less than the risk of the later interest tax shields. Thus, it is reasonable to use the cost of debt to discount the interest tax shield in Year 1 and to use the unlevered cost of capital to discount the value of all remaining interest tax shields as of the end of Year 1, back to Year 0. So the value of all the interest tax shields at Year 0, $V_{ITS,0}$, is

$$V_{ITS,0} = V_{ITS@r_D,0} + V_{ITS@r_{UA},0} = \frac{r_D \times V_{D,0} \times T_{INT}}{1 + r_D} + \frac{V_{ITS,1}}{1 + r_{UA}} \qquad (10.2)$$

Discount Rate for Interest Tax Shields for Existing Debt, Refinanced Debt, and Additional Debt

None of the discussed capital structure strategies is reflective of the actual capital structure strategies of real companies. These examples, however, provide a useful framework for thinking about the selection of a discount rate for interest tax shields that is bounded between the cost of debt and unlevered cost of capital $(r_D \leq r_{ITS} \leq r_{UA})$.[7] One intuitive rule of thumb we can glean from our framework is that if a company has existing debt and if management does not intend to adjust the debt (for example, early repayment) as a function of the company's performance, a reasonable cost of capital for the debt's interest tax shields prior to maturity is the debt cost of capital $(r_{ITS} = r_D$ for debt outstanding), which approximates the risk that the company's taxable income will be sufficiently high that it will be able to use the interest tax shields. In addition, consider the survey on capital structure strategies discussed previously in which 10% of the companies indicated they had a very strict target debt ratio and 34% said they had a strict target range. For these companies, it is probably reasonable to value their interest tax shields at the unlevered cost of capital.

Our framework is not as clear for debt a company expects to issue to either replace existing debt once it matures or to finance growth if the firm does not have a target debt ratio. If a company is already using a lot of financial leverage and does not have much additional debt capacity, the amount of new or replacement debt the company can issue is likely dependent on the value of the firm. If this is the case, a

---

[6] Miles and Ezzell extended Modigliani and Miller's original work for a company that refinances itself annually to maintain a constant capital structure. See: Miles, J. A., and J. R. Ezzell, "The Weighted Average Cost of Capital, Perfect Capital Markets, and Project Life: A Clarification," *Journal of Financial and Quantitative Analysis* vol. 15, no. 3 (1980), pp. 719–730; and Miles, J. A., and J. R. Ezzell, J.R. (1985), "Reformulating Tax Shield Valuation: A Note," *Journal of Finance* vol. 40 (1985), pp. 1485–1492.

[7] This range of discount rates for interest tax shields is reasonable for most companies, but it is argued that even the cost of debt is too high for discounting the interest tax shields of some companies—or at least some of the interest tax shields of some companies. For example, if a company has a policy of not increasing (or even decreasing) its debt when it is performing well, it might be the case that the discount rate for interest tax shields is lower than the cost of debt. See: Grinblatt, M., and S. Titman, *Financial Markets and Corporate Strategy*, 2nd ed., McGraw-Hill Companies, Inc. (2002).

reasonable cost of capital for such a company's interest tax shields from new or replacement debt is the unlevered cost of capital. On the other hand, if the company is not using a lot of financial leverage and has a lot of additional debt capacity, and if the value of the firm is unlikely to fluctuate greatly, the debt a company might issue in the future might not be as dependent on the value of the firm. It might be possible for such a company to have a policy of having some amount of debt—that may even be modestly increasing—that is largely independent of its value for some finite period of time. In this case, we could use the cost of debt to value the tax shields.

Our framework also provides the following additional intuition—in the long run, it is unlikely that the amount of debt a company will issue will be independent of the company's value. Eventually, the risk of the interest tax shields approaches the risk of the unlevered cost of capital of the company. As such, we typically discount the interest tax shields at the unlevered cost of capital in continuing value calculations.

We might note that when we use the weighted average cost of capital DCF method and apply a constant weighted average cost of capital, we are essentially assuming that the company is pursuing a constant debt-to-value capital structure strategy. In other words, the valuation assumes that if the value of the company goes up (or goes down), the firm adjusts the amount of debt outstanding to have a constant proportionate capital structure.

Valuation Key 10.2

The selection of a discount rate for interest tax shields is a complex issue. For outstanding debt (and even for low levels of debt), when the amount of debt is independent of the value of the firm, the cost of debt is a reasonable discount rate for the interest tax shields ($r_{ITS} = r_D$). When the amount of outstanding debt is closely tied to the value of a firm, such as an assumption of a constant proportionate capital structure, the unlevered cost of capital is a reasonable discount rate for interest tax shields ($r_{ITS} = r_{UA}$).

10.3 LEVERING THE UNLEVERED COST OF CAPITAL

LO3 Lever a company's unlevered cost of capital and unlevered beta

In this section of the chapter, we develop a framework for levering the cost of capital. It is important to note that for the purposes of this chapter, we assume that the value from financing is equal to the value of a company's interest tax shields, V_{ITS} ($V_{FIN} = V_{ITS}$), and any potential effects of financial distress, bankruptcy costs, agency costs, and personal income taxes have no significant impact on the value of debt financing. In other words, we assume that the present value of a company's expected interest tax shields—discounted at the appropriate discount rate—captures the entire effect of financial leverage on the value of the firm. In addition, we assume that there have been no shifts in economy-wide expected rates of return due to changes in economic conditions, such as shifts in inflation or shifts in the required real rate of return on a riskless asset demanded by investors. Finally, while we start out with a more generic derivation of these relations, we ultimately assume that the risk of a company's interest tax shields is captured by either its debt cost of capital or its unlevered cost of capital (or a combination of the two).

The Economic Balance Sheet

The starting point for developing the various ways we can lever a company's cost of capital is the economic balance sheet, which we introduced in Chapter 1. On the economic balance sheet, the value of a company's resources (or its assets) is equal to the value of the claims on those assets (or its securities such as debt, preferred and common equity). The value of a company's assets is composed of the value of its unlevered assets, V_{UA}, and the value of its interest tax shields, V_{ITS} (remember, we are assuming that interest tax shields are the only valuation impact of financing). The values of the claims on these assets that we discuss in this chapter are the value of its debt, V_D, the value of its preferred stock, V_{PS}, and the value of its equity, V_E. For such a company, we can represent the economic balance sheet with the following formula:

$$V_{UA} + V_{ITS} = V_D + V_{PS} + V_E$$

Since the value of a company's assets is equal to the value of its securities, the dollar returns on its assets and securities—measured as the beginning value of an asset or security multiplied by its respective cost of capital or return—should also follow this relationship. That is, the dollar return on a company's resources is equal to the dollar return of the company's securities. The company has a value and cost of capital for each of its assets and securities. The cost of capital for the unlevered assets is r_{UA}. For now, we use a cost of capital for the interest tax shields, r_{ITS}, but we do not make any assumptions regarding its relationships to other costs of capital. The economic balance sheet equation expressed in terms of dollar returns is equal to

$$r_{UA} \times V_{UA} + r_{ITS} \times V_{ITS} = r_D \times V_D + r_{PS} \times V_{PS} + r_E \times V_E$$

Using the above formula as our starting point, we develop a fairly general relationship between a company's equity cost of capital and its other costs of capital (the unlevered cost of capital and the costs of capital for its non-equity securities). Note that if there were securities other than debt and preferred that the company had issued, such as warrants or stock options, there would be terms for each of those non-equity securities as well, which would carry through the rest of the formulas in this chapter. Since flows to warrant holders and rights holders are not tax deductible, we would just include additional terms on the right-hand side of the above equation for the cost of capital for each of those non-equity securities multiplied by their value (just like the preferred term on the right-hand side of that equation). Note that in all the levering and unlevering equations that follow that are derived from this expression, there would be a term like the preferred stock term on the right-hand side of each equation that captures the extent to which the firm is financed with warrants or rights and the cost of capital of those warrants or rights.[8]

The General Levering Formula

If we rearrange the terms in the above formula so that the equity cost of capital is on the left side, we can derive a formula to measure the equity cost of capital.[9]

$$r_E = r_{UA} + (r_{UA} - r_D) \times \frac{V_D}{V_E} + (r_{UA} - r_{PS}) \times \frac{V_{PS}}{V_E} - (r_{UA} - r_{ITS}) \times \frac{V_{ITS}}{V_E} \qquad \textbf{(10.3)}$$

The key insight to glean from this levering formula is that a company's equity cost of capital is always greater than its unlevered cost of capital when the company uses debt or preferred financing, since both the cost of debt and cost of preferred are less than the unlevered cost of capital. If a company only issues equity, its equity cost of capital is equal to its unlevered cost of capital, for all of the other components are equal to zero. Two components of the formula add premiums to the unlevered cost of capital for the debt and preferred financing issued by the company, the implication being that a company's equity cost of capital must be riskier than the unlevered cost of capital as the company issues debt and preferred stock. The two components reflect the fact that the equity becomes riskier as the firm promises to pay greater fixed amounts to the debtholders and preferred equityholders who have seniority over the common equityholders. The last term in the formula, however, decreases the equity cost of capital when the discount rate for interest tax shields is less than the unlevered cost of capital—in other words, when

---

[8] In Chapter 12, we discuss warrants and rights and various forms of equity-based compensation such as stock options, restricted stock, and stock appreciation rights. In most cases, the equity-based compensation yields tax benefits for the firm. We discuss levering and unlevering with these types of securities in more detail then.

[9] We derive this formula by isolating the equity cost of capital on the left-hand side of the formula.

$$r_E = r_{UA} \times \frac{V_{UA}}{V_E} + r_{ITS} \times \frac{V_{ITS}}{V_E} - r_D \times \frac{V_D}{V_E} - r_{PS} \times \frac{V_{PS}}{V_E}$$

Then, from the economic balance sheet, we know that the sum of the value of a company's securities minus the value of its interest tax shields is equal to the value of the unlevered firm, $(V_{UA} = V_E + V_D + V_{PS} - V_{ITS})$. We substitute this relationship in the above formula and rearrange terms to get

$$r_E = r_{UA} \times \left(\frac{V_E + V_D + V_{PS} - V_{ITS}}{V_E} \right) - r_D \times \frac{V_D}{V_E} - r_{PS} \times \frac{V_{PS}}{V_E} + r_{ITS} \times \frac{V_{ITS}}{V_E}$$

$$r_E = r_{UA} \times \left(\frac{V_E}{V_E} + \frac{V_D}{V_E} + \frac{V_{PS}}{V_E} \right) - r_{UA} \times \frac{V_{ITS}}{V_E} - r_D \times \frac{V_D}{V_E} - r_{PS} \times \frac{V_{PS}}{V_E} + r_{ITS} \times \frac{V_{ITS}}{V_E}$$

$$r_E = r_{UA} \times \left(1 + \frac{V_D}{V_E} + \frac{V_{PS}}{V_E} \right) - r_D \times \frac{V_D}{V_E} - r_{PS} \times \frac{V_{PS}}{V_E} - (r_{UA} - r_{ITS}) \times \frac{V_{ITS}}{V_E}$$

$$r_E = r_{UA} + (r_{UA} - r_D) \times \frac{V_D}{V_E} + (r_{UA} - r_{PS}) \times \frac{V_{PS}}{V_E} - (r_{UA} - r_{ITS}) \times \frac{V_{ITS}}{V_E}$$

the company creates an asset through financing (the value of the interest tax shields)—that is potentially less risky than the company's business risk (the risk of the company's unlevered assets). The last term potentially mitigates the increase in the cost of equity from having debt in the capital structure.

We do not show time subscripts in the previous formula because we measure each input at the same point in time. Like we do for the weighted average cost of capital, we must remember that the equity cost of capital and the variables to the right of the equality sign need not be constant over time. The equity cost of capital will change within a valuation model if we predict that the company's business risk or financial risk will change or if we predict economy-wide shifts in required rates of return.

Valuation Key 10.3

Equityholders are the residual claimants for a company's assets, and hence a company's equity cost of capital is always greater than its unlevered cost of capital when the company issues debt or preferred. If a company issues debt and preferred securities, then its equity cost of capital is equal to its unlevered cost of capital plus a premium related to the amount of debt and preferred it uses, with a potential adjustment related to the risk of its tax shields.

We now take the general formula we developed and apply it to a series of special cases where we can write the present value of the interest tax shields, V_{ITS}, using expressions that rely on, say, the debt and unlevered costs of capital and the amount of debt.

Levering Formula When the Discount Rate for Interest Tax Shields Is the Unlevered Cost of Capital, r_{UA}, or When Interest Is Not Tax Deductible ($V_{ITS} = 0$)

If interest is not tax deductible, then the value of a company's interest tax shields, V_{ITS}, is, by definition, zero.[10] If the value of a company's interest tax shields is equal to zero, the last term in the levering formula (Equation 10.3) is equal to zero. Moreover, if the discount rate for a company's interest tax shields is equal to the unlevered cost of capital ($r_{ITS} = r_{UA}$), then the risk of the company's assets (operating assets and interest tax shields) is the same, and, again, the last term in Equation 10.3 is equal to zero.

Thus, if either the discount rate for all of a company's interest tax shields is equal to the unlevered cost of capital, or if interest is not tax deductible (in other words, the value of a company's interest tax shields is equal to zero), then the levering formula becomes

$$r_E = r_{UA} + (r_{UA} - r_D) \times \frac{V_D}{V_E} + (r_{UA} - r_{PS}) \times \frac{V_{PS}}{V_E}$$ (10.4)

Levering Formula When the Discount Rate for Interest Tax Shields Is the Cost of Debt, r_D

If the discount rate for a company's interest tax shields is the cost of debt, then the last term in Equation 10.3 reduces the equity cost of capital relative to what it would be for a company with the same capital structure and a zero value for the interest tax shields or if the discount rate for the interest tax shields is equal to the unlevered cost of capital. We can use the generalized version of Equation 10.3 when the discount rate for all of the interest tax shields is equal to the cost of debt or when the interest tax shields are discounted at both the cost of debt and the unlevered cost of capital. Remember that $V_{ITS@r_D}$ represents the present value of the interest tax shields that are discounted at the cost of debt.

$$r_E = r_{UA} + (r_{UA} - r_D) \times \frac{V_D - V_{ITS@r_D}}{V_E} + (r_{UA} - r_{PS}) \times \frac{V_{PS}}{V_E}$$ (10.5)

The intuition underpinning this formula is that with no tax shields or with tax shields valued at the unlevered cost of capital, the risk of all of the company's assets equals the unlevered cost of capital.

---

[10] See: Modigliani, F., and M. H. Miller, "The Cost of Capital, Corporate Finance and the Theory of Investment," *American Economic Review* 48 (1958), pp. 261–297.

If some of the interest tax shields are valued at the debt cost of capital, the equityholders have a claim to a portfolio of assets with less risk, on average, than a portfolio of assets with risk only equal to the unlevered cost of capital. This reduction in the average risk of the company's assets (operating assets and interest tax shields) mitigates the increase in the equity cost of capital resulting from the company's financial leverage relative to what it would have been if interest was not tax deductible or if all tax shields were valued at the unlevered cost of capital.

Valuation Key 10.4

If the appropriate discount rate for some of a company's interest tax shields is the debt cost of capital, the increase in the cost of equity capital from using financial leverage is partially mitigated because the company has an asset—the value of its interest tax shields—that is not as risky as the company's unlevered assets. This effect also lowers the weighted average cost of capital.

Equation 10.5 requires us to measure the present value of the company's interest tax shields that are discounted at the cost of debt, $V_{ITS@r_D}$, in order to measure its equity cost of capital. We can do this if we know the amount of debt for all future periods from a debt schedule that shows the anticipated amount of debt outstanding every year. We can also make some alternative simplifying assumptions about the valuation of the interest tax shields discounted at the cost of debt and substitute those expressions for $V_{ITS@r_D}$ in Equation 10.5 to obtain simpler forms of the levering formula to use. Whether it makes sense to use these formulas depends on the capital structure strategy of the firm.

Levering Formula for a Zero-Growth Company with a Fixed Amount of Perpetual Debt ($r_{ITS} = r_D$)

In the previous section of the chapter, we discussed the risk and valuation of interest tax shields for a zero-growth company with a fixed amount of perpetual debt and a discount rate for interest tax shields equal to the cost of debt (see Equation 10.1).[11] For a company with a fixed amount of perpetual debt, we can restate the levering formula for interest tax shields discounted at the cost of debt (Equation 10.5) by substituting the present value of the tax shield discounted at the cost of debt ($V_{ITS@r_D}$) in this case with the expression $[(T_{INT} \times V_D \times r_D)/r_D = T_{INT} \times V_D]$ for the value of interest tax shields discounted at the cost of debt. The result, after a little algebra, is

$$r_E = r_{UA} + (r_{UA} - r_D) \times (1 - T_{INT}) \times \frac{V_D}{V_E} + (r_{UA} - r_{PS}) \times \frac{V_{PS}}{V_E} \qquad (10.6)$$

Levering Formula When a Company Uses Annual Refinancing to Rebalance to Its Target Capital Structure

In the previous section of the chapter, we discussed the risk and valuation of interest tax shields for a company that refinances its debt annually (see Equation 10.2). For this type of company, we discount the interest tax shield for the first year after the valuation date at the cost of debt, and the risk of the remaining value of the interest tax shields as of the valuation date is measured using the unlevered cost of capital. We can restate our levering formula with the present value of the interest tax shields discounted at the cost of debt (Equation 10.5) by substituting an expression for the present value of the interest tax shields discounted at the cost of debt, which in this case is just $(r_D \times V_D \times T_{INT})/(1 + r_D)$.

$$r_E = r_{UA} + (r_{UA} - r_D) \times \left(1 - \frac{r_D \times T_{INT}}{1 + r_D}\right) \times \frac{V_D}{V_E} + (r_{UA} - r_{PS}) \times \frac{V_{PS}}{V_E} \qquad (10.7)$$

If we think about reasonable values that we might substitute into the expression in the large brackets we will see that the term in large brackets is very close to 1; for example, if the cost of debt is 10%, and if the tax rate is 40%, the term in the large brackets is equal to 0.9636. When the expression in the large

[11] See Modigliani, F., and M. H. Miller, "Corporate Income Taxes and the Cost of Capital: A Correction," *American Economic Review* 53 (June 1963), pp. 433–443; and Modigliani, F., and M. H. Miller, "Some Estimates of the Cost of Capital to the Electric Utility Industry, 1954–1957," *American Economic Review* 56 (June 1966), pp. 333–391.

brackets is close to 1 it is very close to assuming that all of the tax shields are discounted at the unlevered cost of capital. This should make sense, since only the first year's interest tax shield has a current discount rate equal to the cost of debt when we use the annual refinancing assumption.

Valuation Key 10.5

If we assume a company continually refinances its debt to a proportionate target capital structure, we value all of a company's interest tax shields at the company's unlevered cost of capital. This is an extreme assumption about capital structure strategy (one that no firm practices), but there is relatively little difference in the value of the tax shields (and hence the value of the firm) between this assumption and the assumption that management adjusts the firm's capital structure on an annual basis to its target capital structure. This is a reasonable presumption for many firms.

The Booth Company—Levering the Unlevered Cost of Capital

The Booth Company (Booth) is a privately held company and has adopted a capital structure strategy of financing itself with 60% debt, 10% preferred stock, and 30% equity. We assume that Booth's cost of debt is 8% and its cost of preferred stock financing is 9%. We further assume that Booth expects to maintain this capital structure in the future. The company has a 40% income tax rate on all income. Management expects Booth to generate free cash flows of $800 in perpetuity and plans to distribute all equity free cash flows each year (it will retain no excess cash). Since Booth is not growing, the dollar magnitude of debt and preferred stock it will have in its capital structure will stay constant. Booth's unlevered cost of capital is 10%. We now illustrate the use of each levering formula in determining the equity cost of capital and then the resulting weighted average cost of capital and valuation. Note that we are just illustrating the use of the various formulas. In a real valuation setting, we choose the formula that best fits the capital structure strategy of the firm that we are levering.

Value the Interest Tax Shields at the Unlevered Cost of Capital.   If we assume that the discount rate for interest tax shields is the company's unlevered cost of capital, then Booth's equity cost of capital (using Equation 10.4) and weighted average cost of capital are, respectively,

$$r_E = 0.1 + (0.1 - 0.08) \times \frac{0.6}{0.3} + (0.1 - 0.09) \times \frac{0.1}{0.3} = 0.1433$$

$$r_{WACC} = 0.1433 \times 0.3 + 0.08 \times (1 - 0.4) \times 0.6 + 0.09 \times 0.1 = 0.0808$$

Notice that the equity cost of capital is higher than the unlevered cost of capital because of the leverage and the weighted average cost of capital is less than the unlevered cost of capital because of the tax deductibility of interest. If we assume the company generates cash flows of $800 in perpetuity, we can value Booth using the WACC valuation method.

$$V_F = \frac{FCF_1}{r_{WACC}} = \frac{\$800}{0.0808} = \$9,901$$

Could we replicate this valuation with the adjusted present value (APV) method by discounting the tax shields at the unlevered cost of capital? Absolutely! At a value of $9,901, the company would have $5,940.6 of debt and the interest tax shield would be $190.1 ($190.1 = $9,901 × 0.6 × 0.08 × 0.4). The APV valuation is

$$V_F = \frac{FCF_1}{r_{UA}} + \frac{ITS_1}{r_{UA}} = \frac{\$800}{0.10} + \frac{\$190.1}{0.10} = \$9,901$$

From this example, we can see clearly that in this case the WACC DCF method valued the tax shields at the unlevered cost of capital. Note that we ignored the amount of preferred financing in utilizing the APV method, as it does not create any additional interest tax shields.

Assume Interest Is Not Tax Deductible.   If we had assumed that interest was not tax deductible, the equity cost of capital would have been identical to that above, or 14.33%, because the levering formula is identical to when all interest tax shields are valued at the unlevered cost of capital. However, the weighted average cost of capital would be equal to the unlevered cost of capital of 10% because the tax rate used in the weighted average cost of capital formula would be zero.

$$r_{WACC} = 0.1433 \times 0.3 + 0.08 \times (1 - 0) \times 0.6 + 0.09 \times 0.1 = 0.10$$

The value of the company would now only be $8,000 because there is no value from having debt in the capital structure. The difference of $1,901 ($1,901 = $9,901 − $8,000) is due solely to the value of the interest tax shields.

$$V_F = \frac{FCF_1}{r_{WACC}} = \frac{\$800}{0.10} = \$8,000$$

It should be obvious that an APV DCF valuation of the company would be exactly the same ($800/0.10). Thus, here the WACC DCF method assigned no value to the interest tax shields because the tax rate in the weighted average cost of capital formula was set to zero.

Value the Interest Tax Shields at the Cost of Debt.   Alternatively, if we assume the discount rate for interest tax shields is the company's cost of debt and that the debt is perpetual, then Booth's equity cost of capital (using Equation 10.5) and weighted average cost of capital are, respectively,

$$r_E = 0.1 + (0.1 - 0.08) \times (1 - 0.4) \times \frac{0.6}{0.3} + (0.1 - 0.09) \times \frac{0.1}{0.3} = 0.1273$$

$$r_{WACC} = 0.1273 \times 0.3 + 0.08 \times (1 - 0.4) \times 0.6 + 0.09 \times 0.1 = 0.076$$

Notice that Booth's equity cost of capital is now less than it was when tax shields were valued at the unlevered cost of capital. This is because the tax shields are valued at the cost of debt, thus mitigating the impact of debt on the cost of equity capital. As expected, Booth's weighted average cost of capital is now lower than it was before because the equity cost of capital is smaller. Again, assuming the company generates cash flows of $800 in perpetuity, we can value Booth using the WACC valuation method.

$$V_F = \frac{FCF_1}{r_{WACC}} = \frac{\$800}{0.076} = \$10,526$$

The valuation when we assume that the interest tax shields are valued at the cost of debt is $625 higher than it was when we valued the interest tax shields at the unlevered cost of capital ($625 = $10,526 − $9,901). This entire difference results from the assumption that the risk of the interest tax shields is now lower.

We can replicate this valuation with the adjusted present value method by discounting the tax shields at the debt cost of capital. At a value of $10,526, the company would have $6,315.6 of debt and the interest tax shield would be $202.1 ($202.1 = $10,526 × 0.6 × 0.08 × 0.4). The APV valuation is

$$V_F = \frac{FCF_1}{r_{UA}} + \frac{ITS_1}{r_D} = \frac{\$800}{0.10} + \frac{\$202.1}{0.08} = \$10,526$$

This example shows that in this case the WACC DCF method valued the tax shields at the debt cost of capital.

Assume Annual Refinancing.   Last, if we assume Booth refinances its capital structure annually (rather than issuing perpetual debt and preferred stock), then Booth's equity cost of capital (using Equation 10.7), weighted average cost of capital, and valuation are, respectively,

$$r_E = 0.1 + (0.1 - 0.08) \times \left(1 - \frac{0.08 \times 0.4}{1.08}\right) \times \frac{0.6}{0.3} + (0.1 - 0.09) \times \frac{0.1}{0.3} = 0.1421$$

$$r_{WACC} = 0.1421 \times 0.3 + 0.08 \times (1 - 0.4) \times 0.6 + 0.09 \times 0.1 = 0.080444$$

$$V_F = \frac{FCF_1}{r_{WACC}} = \frac{\$800}{0.080444} = \$9,945$$

Thus, the impact of assuming that the Booth Company adjusts to its target capital structure with an annual lag is similar to that of assuming that the company refinances itself continually and that the discount rate for all interest tax shields is the unlevered cost of capital—a weighted average cost of capital of 0.0804 compared to 0.0808 and valuation of $9,945 compared to $9,901.

As it turns out, to show that the WACC and APV methods yield the same answer takes a bit more explaining about the assumptions underlying the annual refinancing assumption. To use the APV valuation method we need forecasts of the company's interest tax shields. With a value of $9,945, Booth will have $5,967 of debt financing and annual interest tax shields of $191 ($191 = $5,967 × 0.6 × 0.08 × 0.4). The next step is to calculate the present value of the interest tax shields. This calculation involves some subtleties we have not explained. Recall that as of the valuation date, the end of Year 0, we know the amount of debt outstanding. As a result, we know the amount of the interest tax shield available for Year 1. The only uncertainty of the interest tax shield for Year 1 is the company's ability to use the interest tax shield in that year. Therefore, as we discussed earlier, a reasonable discount rate to use for the Year 1 interest tax shield is the cost of debt.

For the interest tax shield in Year 2, the situation is more complex. As of the end of Year 1, we know the amount of debt outstanding and the interest tax shield available for Year 2. This is a situation similar to the situation we have for the Year 1 interest tax shield, so we use the cost of debt to discount the Year 2 interest tax shield from Year 2 to Year 1. The risk of the Year 2 interest tax shield as of the end of Year 0, however, is greater than the risk as of the end of Year 1. At the end of Year 0, the amount of debt the company will have at Year 1 depends on the value of the firm at the end of Year 1, as does the interest tax shield we expect to have for Year 2. To account for this additional risk, we use the unlevered cost of capital to discount the Year 2 interest tax shield from Year 1 to Year 0.

Therefore, we discount the Year 2 interest tax shield from Year 2 to Year 1 at the cost of debt, and from Year 1 to Year 0 at the unlevered cost of capital. Putting these calculations together, we have the following formula for discounting the Year 2 interest tax shield.

$$\frac{ITS_2}{(1 + r_{UA}) \times (1 + r_D)}$$

Extending this logic forward to Year N, we discount the Year N interest tax shields from Year N to Year N − 1 at the cost of debt, and from Year N − 1 to Year 0 at the unlevered cost of capital.

$$\frac{ITS_N}{(1 + r_{UA})^{N-1} \times (1 + r_D)}$$

In other words, we discount each interest tax shield at the debt cost of capital for its last year and at the unlevered cost of capital for all remaining years.[12]

We often use perpetuity formulas to measure the continuing value of a company's interest tax shields. Since we do not discount all interest tax shields at the same discount rate, our standard perpetuity valuation formula does not work. The value of the interest tax shields would be too low if we used the unlevered cost of capital as the discount rate in the perpetuity formula. We need to adjust that formula so that

---

[12] Another way to think about this issue is as follows. We can measure the present value of the interest tax shields at Year 0 by discounting the interest tax shield for Year 1 at the cost of debt and discounting the value of all remaining interest tax shields as of the end of Year 1 at the unlevered cost of capital.

$$V_{ITS,\,0} = \frac{ITS_1}{1 + r_D} + \frac{V_{ITS,\,1}}{1 + r_{UA}}$$

We can perform the same calculation to measure the value of the interest tax shields as of the end of Year 1.

$$V_{ITS,\,1} = \frac{ITS_2}{1 + r_D} + \frac{V_{ITS,\,2}}{1 + r_{UA}}$$

If we substitute the above valuation of the interest tax shields as of the end of Year 1 into the valuation of the interest tax shields as of the end of Year 0, we get

$$V_{ITS,\,0} = \frac{ITS_1}{1 + r_D} + \frac{ITS_2}{(1 + r_D) \times (1 + r_{UA})} + \frac{V_{ITS,\,2}}{1 + r_{UA}}$$

If we extend this process forward, we can see that we are discounting each interest tax shield for one year at the cost of debt and for all remaining years at the unlevered cost of capital.

we discount each interest tax shield at the cost of debt for one year and at the unlevered cost of capital for the remaining years. Fortunately, the adjustment we need to make is quite simple

$$V_{ITS} = \frac{ITS_1}{r_{UA} - g} \times \frac{(1 + r_{UA})}{(1 + r_D)}$$

We now have all of the information we need to use the above approach to value Booth with annual refinancing using the APV method:

$$V_F = \frac{FCF_1}{r_{UA}} + \frac{r_D \times T_{INT} \times V_D}{r_{UA}} \times \frac{(1 + r_{UA})}{(1 + r_D)}$$

$$V_F = \frac{\$800}{0.1} + \frac{0.08 \times 0.4 \times \$5,967}{0.1} \times \frac{(1.1)}{(1.08)} = \$8,000 + \$1,945 = \$9,945$$

Thus, both the APV and WACC methods provide consistent estimates. Moreover, the WACC method embedded the value of the interest tax shields using the assumption that each yearly tax shield is discounted at the cost of debt for the last year and for the unlevered cost of capital for each prior year (in the case of the first year's tax shield, there is only the last year).

Summary.   By now it should be obvious that the WACC DCF method is capable of valuing the interest tax shields under a variety of assumptions. In this simple example, we have shown that we can assume there is no value to the tax shields, that they are valued using the unlevered cost of capital or the debt cost of capital, or that they are valued under the complicated assumptions of the annual refinancing case—a combination of the debt and unlevered costs of capital. The other key insight that should be obvious is that the levering formula chosen communicates to the weighted average cost of capital part of the information it needs to value the tax shields correctly—in particular, the levering formula indicates the riskiness of the interest tax shields.

One other point worth noting is that the Booth example is a simple no-growth perpetuity. As it turns out, although we don't demonstrate this, it is always possible to reconcile the WACC and APV valuation methods even for firms with varying growth rates as long as we continue to provide both valuation methods with the same assumptions about the valuation of the interest tax shields.

REVIEW EXERCISE 10.1

The Palm Company—Levering the Unlevered Cost of Capital

The Palm Company (Palm) is a privately held company and has adopted a capital structure strategy of financing itself with 30% debt, 20% preferred stock, and 50% equity. We assume that Palm's cost of debt is 7% and preferred stock cost of financing is 8%, that neither the debt nor preferred have a maturity, and that Palm expects to maintain this capital structure in the future. The company has a 45% income tax rate on all income. Management expects Palm to generate a free cash flow of $100 each year in perpetuity, and Palm plans to distribute all equity free cash flows each year (in other words, it will not have any excess cash). Since Palm is not growing, the dollar magnitude of debt and preferred stock it will have in its capital structure will stay constant. Palm's unlevered cost of capital is 12%. Measure Palm's equity cost of capital and weighted average cost of capital based on the following alternative assumptions for the discount rate for interest tax shields:

   a. discount the interest tax shields at the unlevered cost of capital,

   b. discount the interest tax shields at the cost of debt (assume this is a zero-growth company with a fixed amount of perpetual debt), and

   c. discount the interest tax shields assuming annual refinancing (using the debt cost of capital for one year and unlevered cost of capital for subsequent years).

Solution on pages 417–418.

Choosing a Levering Method

Now that we have all of these levering formulas, what do we do with them? The fifth step in the levering process (see Exhibit 10.2) is choosing the appropriate levering formula. The choice of the levering formula depends on the company we are valuing and the specific valuation context. As discussed earlier, the primary factor in this decision is the risk of the interest tax shields. The most reasonable method for levering the cost of capital depends on how closely both the company and the valuation context in which we are valuing the company meet the underlying assumptions for a particular levering method or formula. In particular, we need to determine the anticipated capital structure strategy of the firm. This is potentially important, because as we just explained, the choice of the levering formula, and the resulting cost of equity capital, communicates to the WACC DCF method how risky the interest tax shields are and how they should be valued.

If we believe a company pursues a constant target capital structure policy that is stated in terms of the proportion of debt to firm value, it is reasonable to use either the continuous refinancing assumption (all interest tax shields valued at the unlevered cost of capital) or the annual refinancing assumption since both yield very similar valuations. If a company has a lot of debt with a short maturity and has little room for additional debt capacity, it is again reasonable to use either the continuous refinancing assumption or the annual refinancing assumption. If the company does not have a lot of debt (and has a lot of room for additional debt capacity), if its debt has a long maturity that it will rollover when it matures, and if it has a very low or zero-growth rate and does not plan to issue additional debt, it is reasonable to use the formulas developed for situations in which a zero-growth company has a fixed amount of perpetual debt. If the company plans to pay down debt according to a schedule that does not depend on the value of the firm, we may just want to use the formula where we measure the present value of the interest tax shields discounted at the cost of debt. In practice, the valuation specialist has to make an informed judgment as to which of the various assumptions concerning the value of the tax shields is best suited for the situation.

Using the formula developed for the situation in which a zero-growth company has a fixed amount of perpetual debt is the most popular way to lever the unlevered cost of capital to determine the equity cost of capital, which is then used to estimate the weighted average cost of capital. We do not recommend using these formulas in situations that do not fit the underlying assumptions—for example, for highly levered transactions, for companies with even moderate expected growth rates, or for companies pursuing a fixed proportionate target capital structure ratio. The assumptions used in this method assume zero growth rates, and the relevant formulas are not appropriate to use for companies that are growing, even if that growth is just due to the effects of inflation. We will illustrate this point further in Section 10.7.

Valuation Key 10.6

The primary factor to consider when choosing a levering formula is the risk of the company's interest tax shields. Generally, the more financial leverage a company uses, the greater the effect the choice of levering formula may have on the resulting equity cost of capital. The levering formula that we choose is the manner in which the WACC DCF learns of the riskiness of the interest tax shields and how we want them valued.

10.4 LEVERING THE UNLEVERED (ASSET) BETA FROM THE CAPITAL ASSET PRICING MODEL

In this section of the chapter, we discuss an alternative, but equivalent, unlevering and levering process that we can use if we are using the Capital Asset Pricing Model (CAPM) to measure the cost of capital. In this approach, we first measure the CAPM betas of the comparable companies and potentially the company we are valuing (if it is publicly traded) and then unlever the relevant betas to measure the unlevered beta for the company we are valuing. Once we have the unlevered beta for the company we are valuing, we can use the CAPM to measure the unlevered cost of capital if we are using the APV DCF method, or we can lever the unlevered beta to determine the equity beta of the company we are valuing. Once we measure the equity beta we can plug it into the CAPM to determine the cost of equity capital and then measure the weighted average cost of capital.

Miller and Modigliani[13] (M-M) developed their theory of capital structure and levering and unlevering assuming, among other things, that all companies have the same risk, issue only debt and equity, and have debt that is risk-free. Other researchers—for example, Hamada, Stiglitz, and Rubinstein—extended this work. Hamada and Rubinstein show that M-M's work holds even if all companies do not have the same risk.[14] Stiglitz and Rubinstein show that M-M's work holds even if companies have risky debt.[15]

Unlevering and levering betas is the more popular alternative in practice than unlevering and levering the costs of capital directly, which is undoubtedly attributable to the popularity of the CAPM in practice. However, which approach we use (cost of capital approach or beta approach) is not important, because as long as we use consistent assumptions and data, the two approaches result in the same cost of capital for the company we are valuing. That said, practitioners often use shortcuts in the beta approach that induce errors in the levering and unlevering process and that result in violations of basic corporate finance theory. We discuss these shortcuts and their associated errors in Section 10.8. We summarize the steps in the levering process for beta, which are similar to the steps in the cost of capital levering process, in Exhibit 10.2.

Using the Capital Asset Pricing Model to Measure Beta from an Observed Cost of Capital

Recall from Chapter 8 that we can write the CAPM as

$$E(\tilde{R}_i) = r_F + \beta_i[E(\tilde{R}_m) - r_F]$$

Sometimes, we know the cost of capital (or discount rate) for an asset or security but do not know its CAPM beta, nor can we easily measure it. This situation often occurs when we observe the cost of debt or preferred but cannot easily measure the debt or preferred beta. In these cases, we can measure the implied CAPM beta from any cost of capital estimate by using the risk-free rate and the market risk premium that we are using in conjunction with the CAPM to estimate the cost of equity.

$$\beta_i = \frac{E(\tilde{R}_i) - r_F}{[E(\tilde{R}_m) - r_F]} \tag{10.8}$$

For example, assume we know that a company's debt cost of capital is 8%. In addition, assume that in order to estimate the equity cost of capital we are assuming that the risk-free rate of return is 4% and that the market risk premium is 6%. From this information, we can measure the company's implied debt beta as

$$\beta_D = \frac{E(\tilde{R}_i) - r_F}{[E(\tilde{R}_m) - r_F]} = \frac{0.08 - 0.04}{0.06} = 0.6667$$

It is important to understand that we are not saying that this would be the point estimate of the debt beta that we would measure if we were to estimate a company's debt beta using a market model regression (it is often difficult to estimate betas on specific debt instruments because they trade infrequently). All this calculation is doing is providing the levering and unlevering formulas stated in terms of betas

[13] See the following research on this topic: Modigliani, F., and M. H. Miller, "The Cost of Capital, Corporate Finance and the Theory of Investment," *American Economic Review* 48 (1958), pp. 261–297; Modigliani, F., and M. H. Miller, "Corporate Income Taxes and the Cost of Capital: A Correction," *American Economic Review* 53 (June 1963), pp. 433–443; and Modigliani, F., and M. H. Miller, "Some Estimates of the Cost of Capital to the Electric Utility Industry, 1954–1957," *American Economic Review* 56 (June 1966), pp. 333–391.

[14] See Hamada, R. S., "Portfolio Analysis, Market Equilibrium, and Corporation Finance," *Journal of Finance* (March 1969), pp. 13–31; Hamada, R. S., "The Effect of the Firm's Capital Structure on the Systematic Risk of Common Stocks," *Journal of Finance* (May 1972), pp. 435–452; and Rubinstein, M. E., "A Mean-Variance Synthesis of Corporate Financial Theory," *Journal of Financial and Quantitative Analysis* (March 1973), pp. 167–181.

[15] See Stiglitz, J. E., "A Re-Examination of the Modigliani-Miller Theorem," *American Economic Review* (December 1969), pp. 187–193; Stiglitz, J. E., "On the Irrelevance of Corporate Financial Policy," *American Economic Review* (December 1974), pp. 851–866; Rubinstein, M. E., "A Mean-Variance Synthesis of Corporate Financial Theory," *Journal of Financial and Quantitative Analysis* (March 1973), pp. 167–181; and Conine, T. E., "Corporate Debt and Corporate Taxes: An Extension," *Journal of Finance* (September 1980), pp. 1033–1037.

with the relative cost of capital for equity and debt (and preferred as well if the company has preferred). In order to do that, it is important to use the same estimate of the risk-free rate and the same estimate of the market risk premium in this calculation that we will use in estimating the equity cost of capital or unlevered cost of capital. If we do not use this technique, then the outcome of levering and unlevering the cost of capital and levering and unlevering betas will not be the same. We will discuss this in more detail in Section 10.8 when we discuss a common but inappropriate practice, setting debt and preferred betas to zero.

Integrating the Capital Asset Pricing Model into the Levering Formula

Since the CAPM return is equal to the risk-free rate plus a premium for risk (measured as beta multiplied by the market risk premium), we can substitute the CAPM formula for each cost of capital term in the general levering formula (Equation 10.3) and eliminate the redundant terms. After substituting the CAPM formula in the general levering formula, we obtain

$$\beta_E = \beta_{UA} + (\beta_{UA} - \beta_D) \times \frac{V_D}{V_E} + (\beta_{UA} - \beta_{PS}) \times \frac{V_{PS}}{V_E} - (\beta_{UA} - \beta_{ITS}) \times \frac{V_{ITS}}{V_E} \quad \textbf{(10.9)}$$

We can derive all of the other formulas in the previous section (Equations 10.4–10.7) with essentially the same derivation used in that section. We show a summary of the levering formulas in this and the previous section in Exhibit 10.3.

The Booth Company—Levering the Unlevered Beta

Continuing with our Booth Company example, we measure Booth's equity beta using its unlevered beta, debt beta, and preferred stock beta. We know the cost of capital for each of Booth's non-equity securities (debt with an 8% cost of capital and preferred stock with a 9% cost of capital) and the company's income tax rate for all income (40%). Management measures Booth's unlevered cost of capital to be 10%. We assume that the risk-free rate is 4% ($r_F = 0.04$) and that the market risk premium (MRP) is 6% (MRP $= 0.06$). Given this information, we can measure Booth's debt, preferred stock, and unlevered betas. Using Equation 10.8 to measure the implied betas, Booth's debt beta is 0.667 $[0.667 = (0.08 - 0.04)/0.06]$, its preferred stock beta is 0.833 $[0.833 = (0.09 - 0.04)/0.06]$, and its unlevered beta is 1.0 $[1.0 = (0.1 - 0.04)/0.06]$.

If we assume the discount rate for the interest tax shields is equal to the company's unlevered cost of capital, then Booth's equity beta is equal to 1.72, which results in an equity cost of capital equal to 14.33%, which is exactly what we calculated previously in levering the cost of capital estimates.

$$\beta_E = 1 + (1 - 0.667) \times \frac{0.6}{0.3} + (1 - 0.833) \times \frac{0.1}{0.3} = 1.72$$

$$r_E = 0.04 + 0.06 \times 1.72 = 0.1433$$

Alternatively, if we assume the discount rate for interest tax shields is equal to the company's cost of debt (zero-growth company with a fixed amount of perpetual debt), then Booth's equity beta is equal to 1.456, which results in an equity cost of capital equal to 12.73%, again exactly equal to what we obtained when we levered the cost of capital estimates.

$$\beta_E = 1 + (1 - 0.667) \times (1 - 0.4) \times \frac{0.6}{0.3} + (1 - 0.833) \times \frac{0.1}{0.3} = 1.456$$

$$r_E = 0.04 + 0.06 \times 1.456 = 0.1273$$

Last, if we assume Booth only refinances its capital structure annually (rather than refinancing continuously), then Booth's equity beta is equal to 1.702, which results in an equity cost of capital equal to 14.21%, again what we obtained previously.

$$\beta_E = 1 + (1 - 0.667) \times \left(1 - \frac{0.08 \times 0.4}{1.08}\right) \times \frac{0.6}{0.3} + (1 - 0.833) \times \frac{0.1}{0.3} = 1.702$$

$$r_E = 0.04 + 0.06 \times 1.702 = 0.1421$$

EXHIBIT 10.3 The Cost of Capital and Beta-Based Levering Formulas

Equity Cost of Capital	Equity Beta

Discount rate for interest tax shields is the unlevered cost of capital or interest is not tax deductible:

$$r_E = r_{UA} + (r_{UA} - r_D) \times \frac{V_D}{V_E} + (r_{UA} - r_{PS}) \times \frac{V_{PS}}{V_E} \qquad \text{(10.4)}$$

$$\beta_E = \beta_{UA} + (\beta_{UA} - \beta_D) \times \frac{V_D}{V_E} + (\beta_{UA} - \beta_{PS}) \times \frac{V_{PS}}{V_E} \qquad \text{(10.10)}$$

Discount rate for certain interest tax shields is the cost of debt:

$$r_E = r_{UA} + (r_{UA} - r_D) \times \frac{V_D - V_{ITS@r_D}}{V_E} + (r_{UA} - r_{PS}) \times \frac{V_{PS}}{V_E} \qquad \text{(10.5)}$$

$$\beta_E = \beta_{UA} + (\beta_{UA} - \beta_D) \times \frac{V_D - V_{ITS@r_D}}{V_E} + (\beta_{UA} - \beta_{PS}) \times \frac{V_{PS}}{V_E} \qquad \text{(10.11)}$$

Discount rate is the cost of debt for a zero-growth company with a fixed amount of perpetual debt:

$$r_E = r_{UA} + (r_{UA} - r_D) \times (1 - T_{INT}) \times \frac{V_D}{V_E} + (r_{UA} - r_{PS}) \times \frac{V_{PS}}{V_E} \qquad \text{(10.6)}$$

$$\beta_E = \beta_{UA} + (\beta_{UA} - \beta_D) \times (1 - T_{INT}) \times \frac{V_D}{V_E} + (\beta_{UA} - \beta_{PS}) \times \frac{V_{PS}}{V_E} \qquad \text{(10.12)}$$

Discount rate based on the annual refinancing assumptions:

$$r_E = r_{UA} + (r_{UA} - r_D) \times \left(1 - \frac{r_D \times T_{INT}}{1 + r_D}\right) \times \frac{V_D}{V_E} + (r_{UA} - r_{PS}) \times \frac{V_{PS}}{V_E} \qquad \text{(10.7)}$$

$$\beta_E = \beta_{UA} + (\beta_{UA} - \beta_D) \times \left(1 - \frac{r_D \times T_{INT}}{1 + r_D}\right) \times \frac{V_D}{V_E} + (\beta_{UA} - \beta_{PS}) \times \frac{V_{PS}}{V_E} \qquad \text{(10.13)}$$

REVIEW EXERCISE 10.2

The Palm Company—Levering Beta

Use both the information in Review Exercise 10.1 and the following information to measure Palm's equity beta. First, measure Palm's unlevered beta, debt beta, and preferred stock beta assuming that the market risk premium is 6% and that the risk-free rate is 4%. Then, measure Palm's equity beta and equity cost of capital based on the following alternative assumptions for the discount rate for interest tax shields:

a. discount the interest tax shields at the unlevered cost of capital,

b. discount the interest tax shields at the cost of debt (remember that this is a zero-growth company with a fixed amount of perpetual debt), and

c. discount the interest tax shields assuming annual refinancing (using the debt cost of capital for one year and unlevered cost of capital for subsequent years).

Solution on page 418.

10.5 UNLEVERING THE EQUITY COST OF CAPITAL AND EQUITY BETA

LO4 Unlever a company's equity cost of capital and equity beta

To measure the unlevered cost of capital, we unlever a company's equity cost of capital by using a formula that eliminates the effect of the non-equity securities the company uses that is embedded in the equity cost of capital. We call this process the unlevering process (or unlevering the cost of capital) because we calculate the unlevered cost of capital from both a company's (levered) equity cost of capital and other information about its capital structure. When we unlever betas, we unlever the equity beta to determine the unlevered beta that we then use in conjunction with the CAPM to determine the unlevered cost of capital or that we would then lever back up for the capital structure of the company we are valuing. The specific process and formula we use to measure a company's unlevered cost of capital or unlevered beta depends on the particular company we are unlevering.

Fortunately, the conceptual framework for developing the unlevering formulas is identical to the conceptual framework we used to develop each of the levering formulas. Again, we begin with the economic balance sheet formula expressed in terms of dollar returns—that is, the dollar return on the company's assets is equal to the dollar return on the company securities—and solve for the unlevered cost of capital (instead of solving for the equity cost of capital, which is what we did to develop the levering formulas). In other words, instead of solving for the equity cost of capital in each of the formulas we discussed earlier, we solve for the unlevered cost of capital. Thus, each levering formula has an unlevering formula counterpart, which we show in Exhibit 10.4. In this exhibit, we show two forms of the unlevering formulas. Depending on the inputs available, one or both of these forms may be calculable.[16]

Assume that a comparable company has the following information:

Income tax rate for interest (T_{INT})	40.0%
Value of debt	$10,000
Value of preferred stock	$ 4,000
Value of equity	$ 6,000
Debt cost of capital	6.0%
Preferred stock cost of capital	7.0%
Equity cost of capital	18.7%

Next, we use the unlevering formulas from Exhibit 10.4 to measure the unlevered cost of capital for the comparable company using different assumptions concerning the discount rate for interest tax shields. The unlevered cost of capital varies between 10% and 11%, depending on which assumption we make.

If we assume the discount rate for interest tax shields is equal to the company's unlevered cost of capital or that interest is not tax deductible, then the comparable company's unlevered cost of capital is equal to 10%.

---

[16] The reduced forms of the unlevering formulas are derived by multiplying the initial formulas by V_{UA}/V_E and then dividing by V_{UA}/V_E. In Equation 10.14, since $V_{ITS} = 0$ this leads to $V_{UA} = V_F = V_D + V_E + V_{PS}$. In the other two reduced forms of the unlevering formulas, V_{ITS} is not equal to zero, which results in more complex formulas, but the same process was used to derive them.

EXHIBIT 10.4   The Unlevering Formula Counterparts to the Levering Formulas for the Cost of Capital

Using the Value of the Securities as Inputs	Using the Capital Structure Ratios as Inputs

Discount rate for interest tax shields is the unlevered cost of capital or interest is not tax deductible:

(10.14)
$$r_{UA} = r_E \times \frac{V_E}{V_F} + r_D \times \frac{V_D}{V_F} + r_{PS} \times \frac{V_{PS}}{V_F}$$

(10.14')
$$r_{UA} = \frac{r_E + r_D \times \dfrac{V_D}{V_E} + r_{PS} \times \dfrac{V_{PS}}{V_E}}{1 + \dfrac{V_D}{V_E} + \dfrac{V_{PS}}{V_E}}$$

Discount rate for certain interest tax shields is the cost of debt:

(10.15)
$$r_{UA} = r_E \times \frac{V_E}{V_F - V_{ITS@r_D}} + r_D \times \frac{V_D - V_{ITS@r_D}}{V_F - V_{ITS@r_D}} + r_{PS} \times \frac{V_{PS}}{V_F - V_{ITS@r_D}}$$

Not Available

Discount rate is the cost of debt for a zero-growth company with a fixed amount of perpetual debt:

(10.16)
$$r_{UA} = r_E \times \frac{V_E}{V_F - T_{INT} \times V_D} + r_D \times (1 - T_{INT}) \times \frac{V_D}{V_F - T_{INT} \times V_D} + r_{PS} \times \frac{V_{PS}}{V_F - T_{INT} \times V_D}$$

(10.16')
$$r_{UA} = \frac{r_E + r_D \times (1 - T_{INT}) \times \dfrac{V_D}{V_E} + r_{PS} \times \dfrac{V_{PS}}{V_E}}{1 + (1 - T_{INT}) \times \dfrac{V_D}{V_E} + \dfrac{V_{PS}}{V_E}}$$

Discount rate based on the annual refinancing assumptions:

(10.17)
$$r_{UA} = r_E \times \frac{V_E}{Z} + r_D \times \left(1 - \frac{r_D \times T_{INT}}{1 + r_D}\right) \times \frac{V_D}{Z} + r_{PS} \times \frac{V_{PS}}{Z}$$

$$Z = V_F - \frac{r_D \times T_{INT}}{1 + r_D} \times V_D$$

(10.17')
$$r_{UA} = \frac{r_E + r_D \times \left(1 - \dfrac{r_D \times T_{INT}}{1 + r_D}\right) \times \dfrac{V_D}{V_E} + r_{PS} \times \dfrac{V_{PS}}{V_E}}{1 + \left(1 - \dfrac{r_D \times T_{INT}}{1 + r_D}\right) \times \dfrac{V_D}{V_E} + \dfrac{V_{PS}}{V_E}}$$

$$r_{UA} = 0.187 \times \frac{\$6,000}{\$20,000} + 0.06 \times \frac{\$10,000}{\$20,000} + 0.07 \times \frac{\$4,000}{\$20,000} = 0.10$$

$$r_{UA} = \frac{0.187 + 0.06 \times \frac{\$10,000}{\$6,000} + 0.07 \times \frac{\$4,000}{\$6,000}}{1 + \frac{\$10,000}{\$6,000} + \frac{\$4,000}{\$6,000}} = 0.10$$

Alternatively, if we assume the discount rate for interest tax shields is equal to the company's cost of debt (zero growth with a fixed amount of perpetual debt), then the comparable company's unlevered cost of capital is equal to 11%.

$$r_{UA} = 0.187 \times \frac{\$6,000}{\$20,000 - 0.4 \times \$10,000} + 0.06 \times (1 - 0.4) \times \frac{\$10,000}{\$20,000 - 0.4 \times \$10,000} + 0.07 \times \frac{\$4,000}{\$20,000 - 0.4 \times \$10,000} = 0.11$$

$$r_{UA} = \frac{0.187 + 0.06 \times (1 - 0.4) \times \frac{\$10,000}{\$6,000} + 0.07 \times \frac{\$4,000}{\$6,000}}{1 + (1 - 0.4) \times \frac{\$10,000}{\$6,000} + \frac{\$4,000}{\$6,000}} = 0.11$$

Last, if we assume the comparable company refinances its capital structure annually, then the comparable company's unlevered cost of capital is just over 10%.

$$r_{UA} = 0.187 \times \frac{\$6,000}{\$20,000 - \frac{0.06 \times 0.4}{1.06} \times \$10,000} + 0.06 \times \left(1 - \frac{0.06 \times 0.4}{1.06}\right) \times \frac{\$10,000}{\$20,000 - \frac{0.06 \times 0.4}{1.06} \times \$10,000} + 0.07 \times \frac{\$4,000}{\$20,000 - \frac{0.06 \times 0.4}{1.06} \times \$10,000} = 0.1005$$

$$r_{UA} = \frac{0.187 + 0.06 \times \left(1 - \frac{0.06 \times 0.4}{1.06}\right) \times \frac{\$10,000}{\$6,000} + 0.07 \times \frac{\$4,000}{\$6,000}}{1 + \left(1 - \frac{0.06 \times 0.4}{1.06}\right) \times \frac{\$10,000}{\$6,000} + \frac{\$4,000}{\$6,000}} = 0.1005$$

REVIEW EXERCISE 10.3

The Date Company—Unlevering the Equity Cost of Capital

Use the information in the table below to measure Date Company's unlevered cost of capital based on the following alternative assumptions for the discount rate for interest tax shields:

a. discount the interest tax shields at the unlevered cost of capital,
b. discount the interest tax shields at the cost of debt (assume this is a zero-growth company with a fixed amount of perpetual debt), and
c. discount the interest tax shields assuming annual refinancing (using the debt cost of capital for one year and unlevered cost of capital for subsequent years).

Income tax rate for interest (T_{INT})	45.0%
Value of debt	$5,000
Value of preferred stock	$3,000
Value of equity	$2,000
Debt cost of capital	8.0%
Preferred stock cost of capital	9.0%
Equity cost of capital	26.5%

Solution on pages 418–419.

Like we did for the unlevering formulas utilizing the various costs of capital in Exhibit 10.4, we can derive unlevering formulas utilizing the betas of the different securities. We summarize these formulas in Exhibit 10.5. Just as we observed for the levering formulas, the beta version of the unlevering formulas replaces various costs of capital from the formulas in Exhibit 10.4 with their respective betas.

EXHIBIT 10.5 The Unlevering Formula Counterparts to the Levering Formulas for the Capital Asset Pricing Model Beta

Using the Value of the Securities as Inputs		Using the Capital Structure Ratios as Inputs	

Discount rate for interest tax shields is the unlevered cost of capital or interest is not tax deductible:

(10.18)
$$\beta_{UA} = \beta_E \times \frac{V_E}{V_F} + \beta_D \times \frac{V_D}{V_F} + \beta_{PS} \times \frac{V_{PS}}{V_F}$$

(10.18′)
$$\beta_{UA} = \frac{\beta_E + \beta_D \times \dfrac{V_D}{V_E} + \beta_{PS} \times \dfrac{V_{PS}}{V_E}}{1 + \dfrac{V_D}{V_E} + \dfrac{V_{PS}}{V_E}}$$

Discount rate for certain interest tax shields is the cost of debt:

(10.19)
$$\beta_{UA} = \beta_E \times \frac{V_E}{V_F - V_{ITS@r_D}} + \beta_D \times \frac{V_D - V_{ITS@r_D}}{V_F - V_{ITS@r_D}} + \beta_{PS} \times \frac{V_{PS}}{V_F - V_{ITS@r_D}}$$

(10.19′) Not Available

Discount rate is the cost of debt for a zero-growth company with a fixed amount of perpetual debt:

(10.20)
$$\beta_{UA} = \beta_E \times \frac{V_E}{V_F - T_{INT} \times V_D} + \beta_D \times (1 - T_{INT}) \times \frac{V_D}{V_F - T_{INT} \times V_D} + \beta_{PS} \times \frac{V_{PS}}{V_F - T_{INT} \times V_D}$$

(10.20′)
$$\beta_{UA} = \frac{\beta_E + \beta_D \times (1 - T_{INT}) \times \dfrac{V_D}{V_E} + \beta_{PS} \times \dfrac{V_{PS}}{V_E}}{1 + (1 - T_{INT}) \times \dfrac{V_D}{V_E} + \dfrac{V_{PS}}{V_E}}$$

Discount rate is based on the annual refinancing assumptions:

(10.21)
$$\beta_{UA} = \beta_E \times \frac{V_E}{Z} + \beta_D \times \left(1 - \frac{r_D \times T_{INT}}{1 + r_D}\right) \times \frac{V_D}{Z} + \beta_{PS} \times \frac{V_{PS}}{Z}$$
$$Z = V_F - \frac{r_D \times T_{INT}}{1 + r_D} \times V_D$$

(10.21′)
$$\beta_{UA} = \frac{\beta_E + \beta_D \times \left(1 - \dfrac{r_D \times T_{INT}}{1 + r_D}\right) \times \dfrac{V_D}{V_E} + \beta_{PS} \times \dfrac{V_{PS}}{V_E}}{1 + \left(1 - \dfrac{r_D \times T_{INT}}{1 + r_D}\right) \times \dfrac{V_D}{V_E} + \dfrac{V_{PS}}{V_E}}$$

REVIEW EXERCISE 10.4

The Date Company—Unlevering Equity Beta

Use both the information in Review Exercise 10.3 and the following information to measure Date's unlevered beta. First, measure Date's equity beta, debt beta, and preferred stock beta, assuming the market risk premium is 6% and the risk-free rate is 4%. Then, measure Date's unlevered beta and unlevered cost of capital based on the following alternative assumptions for the discount rate for interest tax shields:

  a. discount the interest tax shields at the unlevered cost of capital,
  b. discount the interest tax shields at the cost of debt (assume the company will have zero growth with fixed amount of perpetual debt), and
  c. discount the interest tax shields assuming annual refinancing (using the debt cost of capital for one year and unlevered cost of capital for subsequent years).

Solution on page 419.

Choosing an Unlevering Method

As in the levering process, the most reasonable unlevering method to use depends on how closely a particular company we are unlevering meets the underlying assumptions for a particular unlevering method. If a company either maintains a target capital structure in terms of proportions of debt and equity or has a lot of debt with a short maturity with little room for additional debt capacity, then it is reasonable to use the relevant formulas that discount all interest tax shields at the unlevered cost of capital or that rely on the annual refinancing assumptions. If a company does not use a lot of debt (in other words, has a lot of additional debt capacity) and believes that it knows what its debt schedule will look like in terms of dollar values in the future, the general formula for discounting tax shields at the cost of debt might be the most relevant. If a company has relatively little debt with a long maturity and has a very low growth rate and does not plan to issue additional debt, then the relevant formulas developed for a zero-growth company with a fixed amount of perpetual debt might be reasonable to use.

There is no reason to apply the same unlevering formula to every comparable company that we unlever. Rather, we examine each comparable company separately to judge which of the assumptions underlying the alternative unlevering formulas best fits the capital structure strategy of a particular company. Thus, different unlevering formulas may be used in a single valuation, depending on the capital structure strategies of the chosen comparable companies.

Valuation Key 10.7

The conceptual framework for developing the unlevering formulas is identical to the conceptual framework we use to develop each of the levering formulas. For each of the sets of underlying assumptions we use to develop a levering formula, we can use the same underlying assumptions to develop an unlevering formula. In unlevering a company, we use the unlevering formula that best fits the capital structure strategy of the particular company being unlevered.

10.6 LIMITATIONS OF THE LEVERING AND UNLEVERING FORMULAS

In this section we briefly discuss a few limitations of the levering and unlevering formulas we derived. One issue results from deriving these formulas assuming the value of the debt financing is equal to the value of the interest tax shields. In other words, these formulas do not consider any of the countervailing effects from debt financing, such as financial distress costs. The other limitation results from assuming that the current cost of debt multiplied by the value of the debt is equal to the expected interest tax shields. We explore these two limitations and their effects further.

Considering Financial Distress Costs When Choosing Comparable Companies

Now that we understand the levering and unlevering process, we raise an issue regarding the choice of comparable companies. In deriving the levering and unlevering formulas, we assumed that there are no countervailing forces associated with issuing debt—in other words, issuing debt creates interest tax shields, but there are no costs of bankruptcy, financial distress, or agency costs. For example, if a highly levered capital structure results in non-negligible expected costs of financial distress and if those costs affect the cost of capital estimates, then the levering and unlevering formulas do not adjust for those financial distress effects because the formulas only adjust for the risk and value of the interest tax shields. In other words, if the company we are valuing has modest amounts of leverage, but we are using a highly levered comparable company with significant expected financial distress costs embedded in the cost of capital, the unlevered cost of capital we will estimate will include the effects of financial distress. This effect occurs because the levering and unlevering formulas only make adjustments for the value and riskiness of the interest tax shields—they do not make adjustments for the effects of financial distress costs on the cost of capital.

Until such time as we have levering and unlevering techniques that adjust for the effects of financial distress on the cost of capital, we suggest using comparable companies that do not have totally divergent expected financial distress costs. So, if the firm we are valuing has negligible expected financial distress costs, we probably do not want to choose comparable companies with significant expected financial distress costs embedded in their costs of capital. If we do, the resulting unlevered cost of capital—as well as the weighted average cost of capital—will contain the effects of those financial distress costs from the highly levered comparable companies. Similarly, if the firm we are valuing has high expected financial distress costs, we probably should not use comparable companies with minimal expected financial distress costs.

Valuation in Practice 10.2

Companies Can Reduce Financial Leverage by Issuing Equity: Noranda, Inc. (NRD) Noranda, Inc. (NRD) is a leading international mining and metals company. It is one of the largest producers of zinc and nickel and produces various other minerals and other products. NRD employs over 15,000 people and trades on both the Toronto and New York stock exchanges. On July 25, 2003, NRD announced a recapitalization plan, which included issuing $500 million of common shares (stock). The proceeds were to be used to reduce the amount of its debt and redeem its preferred shares. The company's press release stated, "The recapitalization plan and other recent transactions are expected to raise approximately $1 billion and should improve the Company's net-debt-to-total-capitalization ratio to 38% from 51% at year-end 2002 upon completion of these initiatives."

On August 18, 2003, NRD announced that it actually issued $613.8 million of common shares (the net proceeds were $599 million after underwriters' fees and estimated expenses).

Source: Noranda, Inc. The company's website at http://www.noranda.com lists all of its public announcements in the recent past.

Does the Cost of Debt Times the Value of the Debt Measure Expected Interest Tax Shields?

The formulas that we have derived presume that the current cost of debt times the value of the debt measures expected interest tax shields. That should be true for any newly issued debt, but need not be true for debt that was issued previously. Assume that no change in the company's default probability has occurred but that the company's cost of debt has changed since the existing debt was issued, for example, because the inflation rate has changed or the real risk-free rate of return demanded by investors has changed. In some cases, this can cause problems for the levering and unlevering formulas because the current cost of debt multiplied by the current value of the debt will not measure the expected interest tax shields.

We will briefly discuss the levering formulas to provide some intuition on this issue. First, the formula for valuing all of the interest tax shields at the unlevered cost of capital—the continuous refinancing assumption (or assuming interest is not tax deductible), Equation 10.4, is still correct because nowhere in that formula do we assume that the expected interest tax shields are equal to the cost of debt times the value of the debt. The same is true of Equation 10.5, where we calculate the present value of the tax shields discounted at the cost of debt, $V_{ITS@r_D}$, as long as we correctly measure the expected interest tax shields based on the original cost of debt and book value of the debt and discount them at the current cost of debt.

So far so good, but the same is not true for the perpetual debt, zero-growth assumption contained in the levering formula shown in Equation 10.6. The reason is that formula assumes that the current cost of debt times the value of the debt is the expected interest tax shield. That will not be the case if the cost of debt and value of the debt has changed since the debt was issued due to a change in inflation or a change in the real required rate of return on a risk-free instrument. The expected interest tax shield will be the effective rate of interest at the time of issuance multiplied by the book value of debt and not the current cost of debt multiplied by the value of the debt. The good news is that the effects are somewhat countervailing, so the error is not likely to be too large. Let's suppose inflation has gone up and the cost of debt is now higher than it was when the debt was issued. The countervailing effect is that the value of the debt will decrease. While the current cost of debt times the current value of the debt is not likely to yield the exact expected interest tax shield, and therefore the tax rate multiplied by the value of the debt will not yield the present value of the interest tax shields, the error is likely to be reasonably small.

The error in the annual refinancing formula (Equation 10.7) is likely to be trivial, as the only expected interest tax shield measured with error by assuming the current cost of debt multiplied by the current value of the debt is the first period's interest tax shield. We have already shown that the annual refinancing formula and continuous refinancing formula lead to essentially the same result, and also indicated that the problem we are discussing does not affect the continuous refinancing formula.

In summary, we do not believe this issue is likely to lead to a serious error in valuation in the levering and unlevering process for several reasons. First, we generally do not recommend the use of the perpetual debt zero-growth assumption where the error is likely to be the largest. Second, as we explained earlier, a change in the cost of debt from a change in the risk-free rate of return leads to a countervailing effect on the value of the debt. That said, it is useful to be aware of the issue to make sure that we do not encounter some situation where the error is potentially important.

10.7 LIMITATIONS OF MODIGLIANI AND MILLER'S LEVERING AND UNLEVERING FORMULAS

LO5 Avoiding common errors in the levering and unlevering process

Earlier in the chapter, we discussed the levering and unlevering formulas for a zero-growth company with a fixed amount of perpetual debt and a discount rate for interest tax shields that is equal to the cost of debt (see Equations 10.6, 10.12, 10.16, and 10.20).[17] These formulas do not apply to a growing company or to a company that is expected to change the dollar amount of debt it has outstanding.[18] Although this levering formula is widely used to lever and unlever the cost of capital, it is only appropriate to use in a very limited number of settings. Naturally, the extent of the error caused by using this formula in a valuation context in which it does not apply depends on the specific valuation context.

For example, assume a company with an unlevered cost of capital of 10% expects to follow a capital structure strategy with 70% debt and 10% preferred stock. The debt has an 8% cost of capital and the preferred stock has a 9% cost of capital. The company has an income tax rate equal to 40%. If we assume that the discount rate for interest tax shields is the cost of debt and that the present value of the interest tax shields is equal to the tax rate multiplied by the value of the debt ($T_{INT} \times V_D$)—which means that the debt is not expected to grow—the company's equity cost of capital and weighted average cost of capital are

$$r_E = 0.10 + (0.10 - 0.08) \times (1 - 0.4) \times \frac{0.7}{0.2} + (0.10 - 0.09) \times \frac{0.1}{0.2} = 0.147$$

$$r_{WACC} = 0.147 \times 0.2 + 0.08 \times (1 - 0.4) \times 0.7 + 0.09 \times 0.1 = 0.072$$

If we now assume the company has a Year 1 expected unlevered free cash flow of $1,000, which is expected to grow at 3.2% in perpetuity, the company's value according to the WACC valuation method is

$$V_{F,0} = \frac{FCF_1}{r_{WACC} - g} = \frac{\$1,000}{0.072 - 0.032} = \$25,000$$

---

[17] See Modigliani, F., and M. H. Miller, "Corporate Income Taxes and the Cost of Capital: A Correction," *American Economic Review* 53 (June 1963), pp. 433–443; and Modigliani, F., and M. H. Miller, "Some Estimates of the Cost of Capital to the Electric Utility Industry, 1954–1957," *American Economic Review* 56 (June 1966), pp. 333–391.

[18] Ehrhardt, M., and Daves, P. R., "Corporate Valuation: The Combined Impact of Growth and the Tax Shield of Debt on the Cost of Capital and Systematic Risk," *Journal of Applied Finance* vol. 12, no. 2 (Fall/Winter 2002).

However, the assumptions in this valuation are internally inconsistent. The company's free cash flows are growing at 3.2%; thus, the company's value will grow at 3.2%. The levering formula, however, assumes that the company will not issue additional debt, but the constant weighted average cost of capital formula assumes that the company will follow a constant capital structure strategy of 70% debt. This latter assumption assumes that the debt will grow since the value of the firm is growing. These assumptions are inconsistent with each other. Thus, an APV valuation of this company will not result in a value equal to the value from a WACC valuation.

The assumption underpinning the levering formula is that the company will not issue or retire debt, so if the previous WACC valuation is correct, the company will have 70% of $25,000 (or $17,500) in debt in perpetuity. The interest tax shield from this debt is $560 ($560 = $17,500 × 0.08 × 0.4). Assuming the amount of debt is fixed and that the interest tax shields are valued at the cost of debt, the APV valuation of the company is $21,706, which is less than the WACC valuation.

$$V_{F,0} = \frac{FCF_1}{r_{UA} - g} + \frac{r_D \times T_{INT} \times V_D}{r_D}$$

$$V_F = \frac{\$1,000}{0.1 - 0.032} + \frac{0.08 \times 0.4 \times \$17,500}{0.08} = \$14,706 + \$7,000 = \$21,706$$

The difference between the WACC and APV valuations is $3,294 ($3,294 = $25,000 − $21,706), or about 15%; thus, the valuation assumptions underpinning this valuation are not internally consistent.

What is the internal inconsistency in the two valuations? The WACC valuation assumes that the company's weighted average cost of capital of 7.2% is constant in perpetuity. However, given a 3.2% perpetual growth rate in the free cash flows, the value of the firm will grow over time at the same rate. Given a constant weighted average cost of capital, the debt therefore is implicitly assumed to be growing in the WACC valuation. However, in the APV valuation just done, the value of the firm is growing over time, but the amount of debt is held constant.

Suppose we used the APV method to measure the company's value and allowed the debt to grow at 3.2% per year such that the weighted average cost of capital stays constant. Would the WACC valuation and APV valuation result in consistent estimates? The answer is no.

$$V_{F,0} = \frac{FCF_1}{r_{UA} - g} + \frac{r_D \times T_{INT} \times V_D}{r_D - g}$$

$$V_F = \frac{\$1,000}{0.1 - 0.032} + \frac{0.08 \times 0.4 \times \$17,500}{0.08 - 0.032} = \$14,706 + \$11,667 = \$26,372$$

As we can see, the APV valuation now results in a valuation of $26,732, which is higher than the WACC valuation. Again, we cannot reconcile the WACC and APV methods, because the levering formula presumes the debt will stay fixed in magnitude. However, when we use the resulting weighted average cost of capital from this process and apply a 3.2% growth rate in the free cash flows, we implicitly are assuming the debt will grow by 3.2% per year because the weighted average cost of capital is held constant. The APV valuation immediately above now allows the amount of the debt to grow and still values all of the tax shields at the cost of debt. The reason the WACC valuation results in a lower value for the firm than the APV valuation is that the weighted average cost of capital that is computed using the levering formula for a no-growth perpetual debt company is too high relative to a scenario in which we let the tax shields grow year by year and still assume that all the tax shields can be valued at the cost of debt.

There is no way to use the M&M perpetual debt levering formula on a growing company with a constant weighted average cost of capital and get consistent valuations between the APV and WACC methods. Of course, we can always make the APV and WACC DCF methods give us the same answer if we provide the two methods with the same information. So we could assume the firm was not growing and then the two methods would yield the same valuation. Alternatively, we could use a different levering formula. If we really want to assume that the firm is expected to grow and that its debt-to-value ratio will be constant and that we believe it is appropriate to value the interest tax shields at the cost of debt, we can calculate the present value of the interest tax shields using a perpetuity and substitute into Equation 10.5. We do not think this is an appropriate assumption, but the resulting equation would be

$$r_E = r_{UA} + (r_{UA} - r_D) \times \left(1 - \frac{r_D \times T_{INT}}{r_D - g}\right) \times \frac{V_D}{V_E} + (r_{UA} - r_{PS}) \times \frac{V_{PS}}{V_E}$$

Given our example, we can then substitute into this equation and solve for the cost of equity capital and weighted average cost of capital.

$$r_E = 0.1 + (0.1 - 0.08) \times \left(1 - \frac{0.08 \times 0.4}{0.08 - 0.032}\right) \times \frac{0.7}{0.2} + (0.1 - 0.09) \times \frac{0.1}{0.2} = 0.12833$$

$$r_{WACC} = 0.12833 \times 0.2 + (1 - 0.4) \times 0.08 \times 0.7 + 0.09 \times 0.1 = 0.068267$$

Notice that the cost of equity and weighted average cost of capital are even lower now. The reason is that we have created even more interest tax shields at the cost of debt and allowed them to grow every year, which mitigates the effect of the leverage even more. The resulting value of the firm is

$$V_F = \frac{FCF_1}{r_{WACC}} = \frac{\$1,000}{0.0683 - 0.032} = \$27,573.5$$

Thus, the value of the firm is higher than before. Will the APV reconcile with this now? The answer is yes. The firm will now have $17,901.5 of debt, which is 70% of the value of the firm, generating tax shields of $401 in the first year ($401 = 27,573.5 \times 0.7 \times 0.08 \times 0.4$). Thus the APV valuation is

$$V_F = \frac{FCF_1}{r_{UA} - g} + \frac{ITS_1}{r_D - g} = \frac{\$1,000}{0.10 - 0.032} + \frac{\$401}{0.08 - 0.032} = \$27,573.5$$

Again, we note that we do not recommend this levering formula. We do not believe that it makes sense to assume that the debt-to-value ratio will remain constant, that the firm will grow, and that interest tax shields should be discounted at the cost of debt. In this scenario, we would value the interest tax shields at the unlevered cost of capital. If we made that assumption, the cost of equity would by 17.5%, the weighted average cost of capital would be 7.76%, and the value of the firm would be only $21,930 (we will leave it to the reader to check those calculations). The valuation immediately above of $27,573.5 results in an error of over 25% from valuing the growing tax shields at the cost of debt instead of the unlevered cost of capital. We might also note that the value of the unlevered firm is $14,706 and the value of the interest tax shields is $12,687.5 (47% of the value of the firm)—this is an extremely unreasonable assumption about the value created by interest tax shields.

Valuation Key 10.8

The assumptions that a company has a fixed amount of perpetual debt and that the discount rate for the company's interest tax shields is the company's debt cost of capital serve as the basis for the most widely used levering formula, which is often then used in conjunction with the assumption that the company will maintain a fixed proportionate capital structure strategy. Based on these assumptions, the value of the interest tax shields is simply the income tax rate for interest tax shields multiplied by the amount of debt ($T_{INT} \times V_D$). However, the levering formula based on these assumptions is inconsistent for most (if not all) companies because almost all companies expect to experience either an increase or decrease in value.

10.8 ASSUMING ZERO DEBT AND PREFERRED STOCK BETAS

We know that a company's debt and preferred stock securities are less risky than its equity, but we also know that even though the risk of these non-equity securities is lower than that of equity, these non-equity securities are not risk-free. In this section of the chapter, we explore the effect of assuming that these non-equity securities are risk-free. Assuming that debt and preferred betas are equal to zero ($\beta_D = \beta_{PS} = 0$), which is equivalent to assuming that the debt and preferred are risk-free, we develop levering and unlevering formulas, and illustrate the valuation errors that can result from such an assumption. The zero debt beta assumption might be reasonable to use for companies that have very highly rated debt (debt with low default risk) because the cost of such debt is close to the risk-free rate. However, it is not a reasonable assumption to use for many companies. Despite that, this assumption is commonly used in the practice community.

Levering Formulas with Zero Betas for Debt and Preferred Securities

Assuming zero betas for debt and preferred, we show the simplified levering and unlevering formulas in Exhibit 10.6. The effect of making this assumption on the levering formulas is that the equity beta resulting from the levering process becomes higher than it would be otherwise. To illustrate this, we use the levering formula that is relevant to the assumption that the discount rate for all interest tax shields is the unlevered cost of capital. Recall the original levering formula:

$$\beta_E = \beta_{UA} + (\beta_{UA} - \beta_D) \times \frac{V_D}{V_E} + (\beta_{UA} - \beta_{PS}) \times \frac{V_{PS}}{V_E}$$

If we assume both the debt and preferred stock betas equal zero, this formula becomes

$$\beta_E = \beta_{UA} + \beta_{UA} \times \frac{V_D}{V_E} + \beta_{UA} \times \frac{V_{PS}}{V_E}$$

$$\beta_E = \beta_{UA} \times \left(1 + \frac{V_D}{V_E} + \frac{V_{PS}}{V_E}\right)$$

EXHIBIT 10.6   The Levering and Unlevering Formulas for the Capital Asset Pricing Model Beta Assuming Debt and Preferred Securities Have a Zero Beta

Levering Formula		Unlevering Formula	
Discount rate for interest tax shields is the unlevered cost of capital or interest is not tax deductible:			
$\beta_E = \beta_{UA} \times \left(1 + \frac{V_D}{V_E} + \frac{V_{PS}}{V_E}\right)$	(10.22)	$\beta_{UA} = \dfrac{\beta_E}{1 + \frac{V_D}{V_E} + \frac{V_{PS}}{V_E}}$	(10.26)
Discount rate for certain interest tax shields is the cost of debt:			
$\beta_E = \beta_{UA} \times \left(1 + \frac{V_D - V_{ITS@r_D}}{V_E} + \frac{V_{PS}}{V_E}\right)$	(10.23)	$\beta_{UA} = \dfrac{\beta_E}{1 + \frac{V_D - V_{ITS@r_D}}{V_E} + \frac{V_{PS}}{V_E}}$	(10.27)
Discount rate is the cost of debt for a zero-growth company with a fixed amount of perpetual debt:			
$\beta_E = \beta_{UA} \times \left[1 + (1 - T_{INT}) \times \frac{V_D}{V_E} + \frac{V_{PS}}{V_E}\right]$	(10.24)	$\beta_{UA} = \dfrac{\beta_E}{1 + (1 - T_{INT}) \times \frac{V_D}{V_E} + \frac{V_{PS}}{V_E}}$	(10.28)
Discount rate based on the annual refinancing assumptions:			
$\beta_E = \beta_{UA} \times \left[1 + \left(1 - \frac{r_D \times T_{INT}}{1 + r_D}\right) \times \frac{V_D}{V_E} + \frac{V_{PS}}{V_E}\right]$	(10.25)	$\beta_{UA} = \dfrac{\beta_E}{1 + \left(1 - \frac{r_D \times T_{INT}}{1 + r_D}\right) \times \frac{V_D}{V_E} + \frac{V_{PS}}{V_E}}$	(10.29)

Since a company's true debt and preferred stock betas are lower than its unlevered beta but not equal to zero, assuming a zero beta for debt or preferred stock increases the equity beta above its true value given a properly measured unlevered beta. Since the capital structure ratios do not change as a result of this assumption, the higher equity cost of capital results in a higher weighted average cost of capital. In addition, the WACC and APV valuation methods will no longer result in the same valuation, confirming an inconsistency.

In Exhibit 10.7, we show an example of levering a company's unlevered beta assuming zero debt and preferred betas when, in fact, those betas are not equal to zero. The company's unlevered beta is 1.0. The risk-free rate of return is 5%, the market risk premium is 6%, and the income tax rate is 40%. We assume that the discount rate for all interest tax shields is the unlevered cost of capital. The company has an expected free cash flow for the next period equal to $1,000, which the company expects to grow at 3% in perpetuity.

EXHIBIT 10.7	Example of Levering Formulas for the Capital Asset Pricing Model Beta Assuming Debt and Preferred Securities Have a Zero Beta

Company We Are Valuing:

Free cash flow	$1,000.00
Growth rate (constant in perpetuity)	3.0%

Cost of debt	8.0%	Cost of preferred stock	9.0%
Debt beta	0.500	Preferred stock beta	0.667
Debt to firm value	50.0%	Preferred to firm value	20.0%

Using Betas for All Securities:		**Assuming Zero Non-Equity Betas:**	
$\beta_E = \beta_{UA} + (\beta_{UA} - \beta_D) \times V_D/V_E + (\beta_{UA} - \beta_{PS}) \times V_{PS}/V_E$	2.056	$\beta_E = \beta_{UA} \times (1 + V_D/V_E + V_{PS}/V_E)$	3.333
Equity cost of capital	17.33%	Equity cost of capital	25.00%
Weighted average cost of capital	9.400%	Weighted average cost of capital	11.700%
Value of the Firm—WACC Method	**$ 15,625**	**Value of the Firm—WACC Method**	**$11,494**
		Valuation error	−26.4%

The company we are valuing is a highly leveraged company. It uses 50% debt financing (with a cost of debt of 8%) and 20% preferred stock financing (with a cost of preferred of 9%). We first calculate the implied betas of the debt and preferred using the cost of debt and cost of preferred stock, the assumptions about the risk-free rate and market risk premium, and Equation 10.8. Then, using the unlevered beta of 1.0, a debt beta of 0.5, and a preferred stock beta of 0.667, we measure an equity beta of 2.056 [2.056 = 1 + (1 − 0.5) × 0.5/0.3 + (1 − 0.667) × 0.2/0.3], again assuming the discount rate for all interest tax shields is the unlevered cost of capital. Even though an equity beta of more than 2 is high (recall that the average beta is 1), it is reasonable for this company because it is so highly levered. The equity cost of capital for the company is 17.33% (0.1733 = 0.05 + 2.056 × 0.06). The company's weighted average cost of capital is 9.4% [0.094 = 0.1733 × 0.3 + 0.08 × (1 − 0.4) × 0.5 + 0.09 × 0.2].[19] The correct value of the company is equal to $15,625 [$15,625 = $1,000/(0.094 − 0.03)]. We present this valuation at the bottom of the left-hand side of the exhibit.

If we assume the company's non-equity betas equal zero, the equity beta is 3.333 [3.333 = 1 × (1 + 0.5/0.3 + 0.2/0.3)] instead of 2.056 from when we used the implied debt and preferred betas. The equity cost of capital for the company is 25% instead of 17.33% (0.25 = 0.05 + 3.333 × 0.06), and the company's weighted average cost of capital is 11.7% instead of 9.4% [0.117 = 0.25 × 0.3 + 0.08 × (1 − 0.4) × 0.5 + 0.09 × 0.2]. The higher weighted average cost of capital results in a value of $11,494 instead of $15,625 [$11,494 = $1,000/(0.117 − 0.03)], which is a valuation error of −26%.

The problems with this approach are twofold. First, the levered equity beta is too high and the resulting valuation is too low. Second, the assumption of zero betas causes violations of basic corporate finance theory. We can see this easily from the above example. With an unlevered beta of 1.0, a risk-free rate of 5%, and a market risk premium of 6%, the unlevered cost of capital is 11% (0.11 = 0.05 + 1 × 0.06). The value of the unlevered firm with $1,000 of free cash flow growing at 3% is $12,500 [$12,500 = $1,000/(0.11 − 0.03)]. However, note that the value of the company with debt and preferred financing assuming zero debt and preferred betas is less than that at $11,494 (see Exhibit 10.7). Thus, the measured value of the firm is lower with debt and the associated value of the interest tax shields than without debt—a clear violation of one of the very basic tenets of corporate finance. Since the value of the unlevered firm is $12,500, it should also be clear that the APV DCF method will not reconcile to the valuation of $11,494. Further, assuming a zero beta for preferred stock when it is not zero will result in preferred stock leverage affecting the value of the firm, which it should not. Similarly, assuming a zero beta for debt when it is not zero will result in debt leverage affecting the value of the firm even if income tax rates are zero (or if interest is not tax deductible).

---

[19] Again, we do not adjust the company's weighted average cost of capital or valuation for countervailing forces that could reduce the embedded value of the company's interest tax shields.

Unlevering Formulas with Zero Betas for Debt and Preferred Securities

As shown in Exhibit 10.7, levering betas under the assumption that the betas for a company's debt and preferred securities are equal to zero results in an equity beta that is higher than it would be if the levering were done properly. In Exhibit 10.8, we show an example of unlevering a comparable company's equity cost of capital assuming a zero beta for its debt and equity securities. The comparable company has an equity beta equal to 2.11, uses 60% debt financing and 10% preferred stock financing, and has a cost of debt of 8% and a cost of preferred stock of 9%. The risk-free rate of return is 5% and the market risk premium is 6%.

EXHIBIT 10.8	Example of Unlevering Formulas for the Capital Asset Pricing Model Beta Assuming Debt and Preferred Securities Have a Zero Beta

Comparable Company Capital Structure and Market Data:

Observed equity beta	2.11		
CAPM equity cost of capital	17.7%		
Equity to firm value	30.0%		
Cost of debt	8.0%	Cost of preferred stock	9.0%
Debt beta	0.500	Preferred stock beta	0.667
Debt to firm value	60.0%	Preferred to firm value	10.0%

Company We Are Valuing (Only Equity Financing):

Free cash flow	$1,000.00
Growth rate (constant in perpetuity)	3.0%

Unleverd Beta Using Betas for All Securities:		**Unlevered Beta Assuming Zero Non-Equity Betas:**	
$\beta_{UA} = \beta_E \times V_E/V_F + \beta_D \times V_D/V_F + \beta_{PS} \times V_{PS}/V_F$	1.000	$\beta_{UA} = \beta_E/(1 + V_D/V_E + V_{PS}/V_E)$	0.633
Unlevered cost of capital	11.00%	Unlevered cost of capital	8.80%
Value of Unlevered Firm—APV Method	$ 12,500	Value of Unlevered Firm—APV Method	$17,242
		Valuation error	38%

   Using the equity beta of 2.11 and the betas of the company's implied debt and preferred securities based on Equation 10.8 (a debt beta of 0.5 and a preferred stock beta of 0.667), we measure the comparable company's unlevered beta to be equal to 1, again assuming the discount rate for all interest tax shields is the unlevered cost of capital.[20] The unlevered cost of capital for the company is $11\%(0.11 = 0.05 + 1.0 \times 0.06)$. The value of the company we are valuing, which has free cash flows of $1,000 and a growth rate of 3% for the cash flows and no debt in its capital structure, is equal to $12,500 [$12,500 = $1,000/(0.11 - 0.03)]$. If we assume the betas of the comparable company's non-equity securities are equal to zero, the resulting unlevered beta is 0.633.[21] The resulting unlevered cost of capital for the company is 8.8% $(0.088 = 0.05 + 0.633 \times 0.06)$, and the estimated value of the company is now equal to $17,242 [$17,242 = $1,000/(0.088 - 0.03)]$—a valuation error of about 38%. Thus, when we unlever the equity beta while assuming that the debt and preferred betas are zero, the resulting unlevered cost of capital is too low.

---

[20] We calculate the unlevered beta as follows:

$$\beta_{UA} = \frac{2.11 + 0.5 \times \dfrac{0.6}{0.3} + 0.667 \times \dfrac{0.1}{0.3}}{1 + \dfrac{0.6}{0.3} + \dfrac{0.1}{0.3}} = 1.0$$

[21] We calculate the unlevered beta as follows:

$$\beta_{UA} = \frac{2.11}{1 + \dfrac{0.6}{0.3} + \dfrac{0.1}{0.3}} = 0.633$$

Valuation Key 10.9

Practitioners often assume that the betas of a company's debt and preferred securities are equal to zero. We do not recommend making this assumption because it implicitly assumes that the cost of debt and preferred are equal to the risk-free rate. For all but the most financially healthy companies with low amounts of financial leverage, this will lead to serious errors in the estimation of the cost of capital and, as we have shown, can lead to violations of the most basic principles of corporate finance.

SUMMARY AND KEY CONCEPTS

We discussed two processes that we use to help measure a company's cost of capital based on its capital structure strategy. The first process, called levering the cost of capital, is based on the relationship between the equity cost of capital and the other costs of capital, conditional on the company's capital structure strategy. The second process, called unlevering the cost of capital, is based on the relationship between the unlevered cost of capital and the other costs of capital, conditional on the company's capital structure strategy. These processes are important when we value companies because we often use one or both of them to measure the cost of capital required to value a company. In general, we use the unlevering process to measure the unlevered cost of capital for the comparable companies and the company being valued if it is publicly traded. If we are using the APV DCF method, we need not use the levering process as we already have measured the unlevered cost of capital. But if we are using the WACC DCF method, we lever back up based on the capital structure of the company being valued in order to determine the equity cost of capital, which we then use to compute the weighted average cost of capital.

The issues related to the effects of a company's capital structure decisions on its value are numerous and complex. We do not have a single method for levering a company's cost of capital, and as such, we do not have a single method for measuring a company's weighted average cost of capital from both its unlevered cost of capital and the cost of capital of each of its non-equity securities. We also do not have just a single unlevering method. We must, therefore, use our best judgment as to which approach is the most appropriate one to lever and unlever the cost of capital in a particular situation. We can use a similar approach to lever and unlever betas if we are using the CAPM to measure a company's equity or unlevered costs of capital. Just as for our levering and unlevering formulas for the cost of capital, we do not have a single method for levering and unlevering a company's beta.

We showed how the weighted average cost of capital can value the interest tax shields using alternative assumptions about the riskiness of the interest tax shields. We also discussed, and hopefully made salient, how it is that the weighted average cost of capital DCF method understands the riskiness of the interest tax shields when it values them—it is done through the choice of the levering formula, which determines the cost of equity. We also showed, in a variety of settings, what is required to get an APV valuation and a WACC valuation to agree. In essence, it is simple—we merely make sure that both methods are given the same information. But that requires that we value the interest tax shields in exactly the same way in the WACC and APV methods, which means that the levering formula has to be selected appropriately.

Finally, we have shown a few common mistakes that practitioners make in levering and unlevering. First, we showed that the use of the Miller and Modigliani perpetual debt formula applied to a growing firm is problematic. Second, we showed that the use of levering and unlevering formulas with the common assumption that debt and preferred betas are equal to zero leads to many problems, including violations of the most standard principles of corporate finance.

ADDITIONAL READING AND REFERENCES

Hamada, R. S., "Portfolio Analysis, Market Equilibrium, and Corporation Finance," *Journal of Finance* (March 1969), pp. 13–31.

Hamada, R. S., "The Effect of the Firm's Capital Structure on the Systematic Risk of Common Stocks," *Journal of Finance* (May 1972), pp. 435–452.

Miles, J. A., and J. R. Ezzell, "Reformulating Tax Shield Valuation: A Note," *Journal of Finance* vol. 40 (1985), pp. 1485–1492.

EXERCISES AND PROBLEMS

P10.1 **Levering the Unlevered Cost of Capital** A company's management is considering alternative ways of financing the company. Going forward, the company plans to adopt a target capital structure with some combination of short-term and long-term debt as well as preferred stock and common equity. Below, we show the three options management is considering.

	Option 1	Option 2	Option 3
Debt to firm value.	10.0%	10.0%	70.0%
Preferred stock to firm value	40.0%	10.0%	10.0%
Unlevered cost of capital	10.0%	10.0%	10.0%
Debt cost of capital	6.0%	6.0%	7.0%
Preferred stock cost of capital	9.0%	8.0%	8.0%
Equity cost of capital	???	???	???
Income tax rate for all income	40.0%	40.0%	40.0%

a. For each option, calculate the equity cost of capital and weighted average cost of capital under the assumption that interest is tax deductible and that (i) the discount rate for interest tax shields is the unlevered cost of capital, (ii) the discount rate for interest tax shields is the debt cost of capital (zero-growth with fixed amount of perpetual debt), and (iii) the company refinances itself annually to a target capital structure (use the debt cost of capital for the first year and the unlevered cost of capital for subsequent years).

b. For each option and each alternative assumption about valuing the tax shields:
   i. Value the firm and the equity using the WACC DCF method.
   ii. Value the firm using the APV DCF method.
   iii. Value the equity using the Equity DCF method.
   iv. Explain any discrepancies between the valuations.

P10.2   **Levering Unlevered Beta** Use the information from P10.1 and assume that the risk-free rate is 4% and that the market risk premium is 6%. Answer P10.1 (Part A only) but calculate the equity beta and then use the CAPM to calculate the equity cost of capital.

P10.3   **Levering the Unlevered Cost of Capital** A company is going to finance itself with the capital structure shown below. The company will generate a perpetual series of cash flows that will not grow. Management plans to measure the value of the firm and the value of each of its securities based on the information below and some additional assumptions outlined in each part of the problem. For each part of the problem, measure the value of the firm using the WACC valuation method and measure the value of each of the securities the company uses to finance itself. Then use the APV method to value the firm. Finally, measure the company's equity free cash flow and use the Equity DCF valuation method to value the company's equity.

Debt to firm value.	40.0%
Preferred stock to firm value	20.0%
Unlevered cost of capital	12.0%
Debt cost of capital	9.0%
Preferred stock cost of capital	10.0%
Equity cost of capital	???
Income tax rate for interest (T_{INT})	40.0%
Unlevered free cash flow	$1,000
Growth rate.	0.0%

a. Assume the company is going to issue short-term debt and continually refinance itself such that the discount rate for the company's interest tax shields is equal to the unlevered cost of capital.

b. Assume that the company is going to issue long-term debt and preferred stock such that the discount rate for the company's interest tax shields is equal to the debt cost of capital.

c. Assume that the company annually refinances itself to maintain a constant proportionate capital structure.

d. Compare the equity cost of capital, weighted average cost of capital, value of the firm, value of each of the company's securities, and equity free cash flow for parts (a), (b) and (c) of the problem. Explain how and why they differ.

P10.4   **Unlevering the Equity Cost of Capital** Below, we show the information for two potential comparable companies. Calculate the unlevered cost of capital based on the following assumptions. Neither company expects its free cash flows to grow.

	Low Leverage Company	High Leverage Company
Income tax rate for interest (T_{INT})	35.0%	45.0%
Value of debt	$ 4,000	$45,000
Value of preferred stock.......................	$ 1,000	$ 0
Value of equity	$15,000	$ 5,000
Maturity of debt (years)	Perpetual	Perpetual
Debt cost of capital	5.0%	8.0%
Preferred stock cost of capital...............	6.0%	
Equity cost of capital	11.8%	28.0%

    a.   Assume that interest is tax deductible and that the discount rate for all interest tax shields is the unlevered cost of capital.

    b.   Assume that interest is tax deductible and that the discount rate for all interest tax shields is the cost of debt.

    c.   Assume that interest is tax deductible but that the company refinances its debt at the end of each year (annual refinancing).

P10.5   **Unlevering the Equity Beta** Use the information from P10.4 and assume that the risk-free rate is 4% and that the market risk premium is 6%. Respond to each part of P10.4 but calculate the unlevered beta instead of the unlevered cost of capital.

P10.6   **Unlevering the Equity Cost of Capital** For each comparable company below, choose an unlevering method and measure the company's unlevered cost of capital. Explain why you chose the unlevering method you chose. Summary information appears below.

	Company A	Company B	Company C
Income tax rate for interest (T_{INT})	30.0%	40.0%	30.0%
Value of debt	$ 3,000	$28,000	$45,000
Value of preferred stock.......................	$ 1,000	$ 4,000	
Value of equity	$16,000	$ 8,000	$ 5,000
Maturity of debt (years)	1	50	5
Debt cost of capital	5.0%	8.0%	8.0%
Preferred stock cost of capital...............	8.0%	8.5%	
Equity cost of capital	11.8%	16.2%	28.0%

Company A is a company that has had a stable capital structure strategy; it generally adjusts its financing to its target capital structure on a regular basis. Company B is a company that had issued a very long-term bond to finance an expansion. This is the only debt the company ever issued. The company has a very low growth rate, it funds its investments internally, and has no plans to issue additional debt. Company C has had very little debt historically. About five years ago, the company went through a debt recapitalization. The company issued debt and repurchased some of its shares, and it announced a new capital structure strategy which was to repay all of the debt by the end of its ten-year maturity. Over the last five years, the company has repaid its debt as per its capital structure strategy. The company's current debt has a five-year maturity, and the company plans to repay 20% of this balance at the end of each of the next five years. The company plans to operate with no debt after it repays its current debt. The company's equity cost of capital reflects its current capital structure strategy and debt outstanding.

P10.7   **Assuming Zero Non-Equity Betas** For each part of the problem, measure the equity beta, equity cost of capital, and weighted average cost of capital under the assumptions that interest is tax deductible and that (i) the discount rate for interest tax shields is the unlevered cost of capital, (ii) the discount rate for interest tax shields is the debt cost of capital, and (iii) the company refinances itself annually to a target capital structure (use the debt cost of capital for the first year and the unlevered cost of capital for subsequent years).

    a.   Assume non-equity betas are equal to the betas implied by the cost of capital stated for each security.

    b.   Assume non-equity betas are equal to zero and use the debt and preferred stock costs of capital stated in the problem to measure the weighted average cost of capital. What violations of standard corporate finance theory do you observe?

	Company 1	Company 2	Company 3
Risk-free cost of capital	4.0%		
Market risk premium	6.0%		
Debt to firm value	10.0%	20.0%	60.0%
Preferred stock to firm value	40.0%	20.0%	20.0%
Unlevered CAPM beta	1.000	1.000	1.000
Debt cost of capital	6.0%	6.0%	7.0%
Preferred stock cost of capital	7.0%	6.5%	7.5%
Equity cost of capital	???	???	???
Income tax rate for interest (T_{INT})	40.0%	40.0%	40.0%

P10.8 **Incorrect Valuation Assumptions** A privately held company finances itself with long-term debt and preferred stock using the capital structure shown below. The company's current free cash flow is $100, and it expects to generate a series of cash flows that will grow at 3% per year in perpetuity. The company plans to maintain its current capital structure strategy of 50% debt and 20% preferred stock in perpetuity, refinancing the company on an ongoing basis.

Initial debt to firm value	50.0%
Initial preferred stock to firm value	20.0%
Unlevered cost of capital	12.0%
Debt cost of capital	8.0%
Preferred stock cost of capital	9.0%
Equity cost of capital	???

The company's chief financial officer (CFO) measured the company's equity cost of capital using the following formula.

$$r_E = r_{UA} + (r_{UA} - r_D) \times (1 - T_{INT}) \times \frac{V_D}{V_E} + (r_{UA} - r_{PS}) \times \frac{V_{PS}}{V_E}$$

The CFO valued the company and its equity using the WACC valuation method. The CFO wants to check the WACC valuation by using the APV valuation method but is unsure how to use this valuation method to check the WACC valuation. The CFO calculated a $15,152 firm value using the WACC valuation method.

a. Reproduce the CFO's equity cost of capital, weighted average cost of capital, and WACC valuation and compare it to an APV valuation. Are the valuations consistent?
b. Use the WACC valuation method to value the firm and the equity correctly by discounting the tax shields at the unlevered cost of capital. Use the APV valuation method to value the firm, and use the Equity DCF valuation method to value the company's equity. Are the valuations consistent?

SOLUTIONS FOR REVIEW EXERCISES

Review Exercise 10.1: The Palm Company—Levering the Unlevered Cost of Capital

a. If we assume the discount rate for interest tax shields is equal to the company's unlevered cost of capital, then Palm's equity cost of capital (using Equation 10.4) and weighted average cost of capital are, respectively,

$$r_E = 0.12 + (0.12 - 0.07) \times \frac{0.3}{0.5} + (0.12 - 0.08) \times \frac{0.2}{0.5} = 0.1660$$

$$r_{WACC} = 0.1660 \times 0.5 + 0.07 \times (1 - 0.45) \times 0.3 + 0.08 \times 0.2 = 0.1105$$

b. Alternatively, if we assume the discount rate for interest tax shields is equal to the company's cost of debt, then Palm's equity cost of capital (using Equation 10.5) and weighted average cost of capital are, respectively,

$$r_E = 0.12 + (0.12 - 0.07) \times (1 - 0.45) \times \frac{0.3}{0.5} + (0.12 - 0.08) \times \frac{0.2}{0.5} = 0.1525$$

$$r_{WACC} = 0.1525 \times 0.5 + 0.07 \times (1 - 0.45) \times 0.3 + 0.08 \times 0.2 = 0.1038$$

Notice that Palm's equity cost of capital is now less than it was before. The reason for this is that the tax shields in the formula are valued at the cost of debt, thus mitigating the impact of debt on the cost of equity capital.

c. Lastly, if we assume Palm refinances its capital structure annually (rather than issuing perpetual debt and preferred stock), then Palm's equity cost of capital (using Equation 10.7) and weighted average cost of capital are, respectively,

$$r_E = 0.12 + (0.12 - 0.07) \times \left(1 - \frac{0.07 \times 0.45}{1.07}\right) \times \frac{0.3}{0.5} + (0.12 - 0.08) \times \frac{0.2}{0.5} = 0.1651$$

$$r_{WACC} = 0.1651 \times 0.5 + 0.07 \times (1 - 0.45) \times 0.3 + 0.08 \times 0.2 = 0.1101$$

Thus, the impact of assuming that the Palm Company adjusts to its target capital structure with an annual lag is similar to that of assuming continual refinancing (i.e., a discount rate for interest tax shields equal to the unlevered cost of capital).

Review Exercise 10.2: The Palm Company—Levering Beta

Palm's debt beta is .5 $[0.5 = (0.07 - 0.04)/0.06]$, its preferred stock beta is 0.667 $[0.667 = (0.08 - 0.04)/0.06]$, and its unlevered beta is 1.333 $[1.333 = (0.12 - 0.04)/0.06]$.

a. If we assume the discount rate for interest tax shields is equal to the company's unlevered cost of capital, then Palm's equity beta is equal to 2.10, which results in an equity cost of capital of 16.66%.

$$\beta_E = 1.333 + (1.333 - 0.5) \times \frac{0.3}{0.5} + (1.333 - 0.667) \times \frac{0.2}{0.5} = 2.10$$

$$r_E = 0.04 + 0.06 \times 2.10 = 0.166$$

b. Alternatively, if we assume the discount rate for interest tax shields is equal to the company's cost of debt, then Palm's equity beta is equal to 1.875, which results in an equity cost of capital of 15.25%.

$$\beta_E = 1.333 + (1.333 - 0.5) \times (1 - 0.45) \times \frac{0.3}{0.5} + (1.333 - 0.667) \times \frac{0.2}{0.5} = 1.875$$

$$r_E = 0.04 + 0.06 \times 1.875 = 0.1525$$

c. Lastly, if we assume Palm refinances its capital structure annually (rather than issuing perpetual debt and preferred stock), its equity beta is 2.085.

$$\beta_E = 1.333 + (1.333 - 0.5) \times \left(1 - \frac{0.07 \times 0.45}{1.07}\right) \times \frac{0.3}{0.5} + (1.333 - 0.667) \times \frac{0.2}{0.5} = 2.085$$

$$r_E = 0.04 + 0.06 \times 2.085 = 0.1651$$

Review Exercise 10.3: The Date Company—Unlevering the Equity Cost of Capital

Below we use the unlevering formulas to measure the unlevered cost of capital for the Date Company based on several alternative assumptions for the discount rate for interest tax shields.

a. If we assume the discount rate for interest tax shields is equal to the company's unlevered cost of capital, then the comparable company's unlevered cost of capital is equal to 12%.

$$r_{UA} = 0.265 \times \frac{\$2,000}{\$10,000} + 0.08 \times \frac{\$5,000}{\$10,000} + 0.09 \times \frac{\$3,000}{\$10,000} = 0.12$$

$$r_{UA} = \frac{0.265 + 0.08 \times \dfrac{\$5,000}{\$2,000} + 0.09 \times \dfrac{\$3,000}{\$2,000}}{1 + \dfrac{\$5,000}{\$2,000} + \dfrac{\$3,000}{\$2,000}} = 0.12$$

b. Alternatively, if we assume the discount rate for interest tax shields is the company's cost of debt (zero-growth with fixed amount of perpetual debt), then the comparable company's unlevered cost of capital is equal to 13.2%.

$$r_{UA} = 0.265 \times \frac{\$2,000}{\$10,000 - 0.45 \times \$5,000} + 0.08 \times (1 - 0.45) \times \frac{\$5,000}{\$10,000 - 0.45 \times \$5,000} + 0.09 \times \frac{\$3,000}{\$10,000 - 0.45 \times \$5,000} = 0.132$$

$$r_{UA} = \frac{0.265 + 0.08 \times (1 - 0.45) \times \dfrac{\$5,000}{\$2,000} + 0.09 \times \dfrac{\$3,000}{\$2,000}}{1 + (1 - 0.45) \times \dfrac{\$5,000}{\$2,000} + \dfrac{\$3,000}{\$2,000}} = 0.132$$

c. Lastly, if we assume Date refinances its capital structure annually, then the comparable company's unlevered cost of capital is equal to just over 12.1%.

$$r_{UA} = 0.265 \times \frac{\$2,000}{\$10,000 - \dfrac{0.08 \times 0.45}{1.08} \times \$5,000} + 0.08 \times \left(1 - \frac{0.08 \times 0.45}{1.08}\right) \times \frac{\$5,000}{\$10,000 - \dfrac{0.08 \times 0.45}{1.08} \times \$5,000} + 0.09 \times \frac{\$3,000}{\$10,000 - \dfrac{0.08 \times 0.45}{1.08} \times \$5,000} = 0.121$$

$$r_{UA} = \frac{0.265 + 0.08 \times \left(1 - \dfrac{0.08 \times 0.45}{1.08}\right) \times \dfrac{\$5,000}{\$2,000} + 0.09 \times \dfrac{\$3,000}{\$2,000}}{1 + \left(1 - \dfrac{0.08 \times 0.45}{1.08}\right) \times \dfrac{\$5,000}{\$2,000} + \dfrac{\$3,000}{\$2,000}} = 0.121$$

Review Exercise 10.4: The Date Company—Unlevering Equity Beta

Below we use the unlevering formulas to measure the unlevered beta for the Date Company based on alternative assumptions for the discount rate for interest tax shields.

a. If we assume the discount rate for interest tax shields is the company's unlevered cost of capital, then the comparable company's unlevered cost of capital is equal to 12% $(0.12 = 0.04 + 1.333 \times 0.06)$.

$$\beta_{UA} = 3.750 \times \frac{\$2,000}{\$10,000} + 0.667 \times \frac{\$5,000}{\$10,000} + 0.833 \times \frac{\$3,000}{\$10,000} = 1.333$$

$$\beta_{UA} = \frac{3.750 + 0.667 \times \dfrac{\$5,000}{\$2,000} + 0.833 \times \dfrac{\$3,000}{\$2,000}}{1 + \dfrac{\$5,000}{\$2,000} + \dfrac{\$3,000}{\$2,000}} = 1.333$$

b. Alternatively, if we assume the discount rate for interest tax shields is the company's cost of debt (zero-growth with fixed amount of perpetual debt), then the comparable company's unlevered cost of capital is equal to 13.2% $(0.132 = 0.04 + 1.527 \times 0.06)$.

$$\beta_{UA} = 3.750 \times \frac{\$2,000}{\$10,000 - 0.45 \times \$5,000} + 0.667 \times (1 - 0.45) \times \frac{\$5,000}{\$10,000 - 0.45 \times \$5,000} + 0.833 \times \frac{\$3,000}{\$10,000 - 0.45 \times \$5,000} = 1.527$$

$$\beta_{UA} = \frac{3.750 + 0.667 \times (1 - 0.45) \times \dfrac{\$5,000}{\$2,000} + 0.833 \times \dfrac{\$3,000}{\$2,000}}{1 + (1 - 0.45) \times \dfrac{\$5,000}{\$2,000} + \dfrac{\$3,000}{\$2,000}} = 1.527$$

c. Lastly, if we assume Date uses annual refinancing of its capital structure, then the comparable company's unlevered cost of capital is equal to 12.1% $(0.121 = 0.04 + 1.345 \times 0.06)$.

$$\beta_{UA} = 3.750 \times \frac{\$2,000}{\$10,000 - \dfrac{0.08 \times 0.45}{1.08} \times \$5,000} + 0.667 \times \left(1 - \frac{0.08 \times 0.45}{1.08}\right) \times \frac{\$5,000}{\$10,000 - \dfrac{0.08 \times 0.45}{1.08} \times \$5,000} + 0.833 \times \frac{\$3,000}{\$10,000 - \dfrac{0.08 \times 0.45}{1.08} \times \$5,000} = 1.345$$

$$\beta_{UA} = \frac{3.750 + 0.667 \times \left(1 - \dfrac{0.08 \times 0.45}{1.08}\right) \times \dfrac{\$5,000}{\$2,000} + 0.833 \times \dfrac{\$3,000}{\$2,000}}{1 + \left(1 - \dfrac{0.08 \times 0.45}{1.08}\right) \times \dfrac{\$5,000}{\$2,000} + \dfrac{\$3,000}{\$2,000}} = 1.345$$

After mastering the material in this chapter, you will be able to:

1. Measure the weighted average cost of capital (11.1–11.2)

2. Make potential adjustments for the capitalization of contractual obligations (11.3)

3. Identify when to avoid using the WACC valuation method (11.4)

4. Measure the income tax rate for interest tax shields (11.5)

5. Identify the other factors that affect the value of financing (11.6–11.8)

Measuring the Weighted Average Cost of Capital and Exploring Other Capital Structure Issues

The Coca-Cola Hellenic Bottling Company S.A. (CCHBC) announced a debt recapitalization plan to increase the amount of debt it had outstanding and make a one-time distribution to shareholders. One reason the company gave for its plan was that it wanted to reduce its weighted average cost of capital.

COCA-COLA HELLENIC BOTTLING COMPANY S.A.

Coca-Cola HBC's Board of Directors approved the plan and believed the recapitalization was appropriate for the following reasons:

- Underlying business continues to be strong as evidenced by the company's performance in the first half of the year and the revised guidance for the full year also announced today.
- CCHBC's financial ratios remain strong post the leveraged recapitalization.
- S&P reaffirmed CCHBC's long-term credit rating of A and short-term rating of A-1.
- *Proposed recapitalization plan will lower CCHBC's Weighted Average Cost of Capital (WACC) by approximately 50 basis points.*
- CCHBC's operational activities, strategic priorities, and performance goals remain unaffected.[1]

In this chapter, we will discuss many of the intricacies associated with measuring the weighted average cost of capital. We will also explore the other effects of debt financing on the value of the firm.

---

[1] Source: Coca-Cola Hellenic Bottling Company S.A. The company's website is http://www.coca-colahellenic.com/home/ .

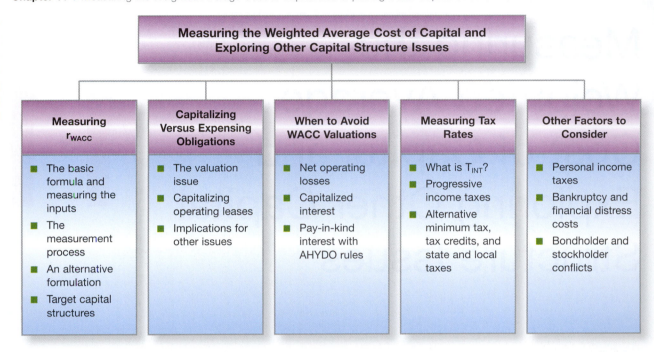

INTRODUCTION

In this chapter, we explore the process of, and the more complex issues related to, measuring the weighted average cost of capital. Recall that the two primary discounted cash flow methods are the weighted average cost of capital (WACC) and adjusted present value (APV) valuation methods. The value of the firm has two primary components: the value of the firm's unlevered assets and the value of the company's financing.

In many valuations, the primary valuation effect of the financing is the interest tax shields associated with the financing. The APV method measures the value of the unlevered assets and the interest tax shields separately by discounting a company's unlevered free cash flows at its unlevered cost of capital (which measures the unlevered value of the firm), and then adding the value of the interest tax shields, which is measured by discounting the company's interest tax shields at the appropriate discount rate. The WACC valuation method, on the other hand, measures the combined value of these two components by discounting a company's unlevered free cash flows—the same unlevered cash flows we discount in the APV method—at the weighted average cost of capital. The WACC method embeds the value of the interest tax shields into the valuation by using a discount rate—the weighted average cost of capital—that is smaller than the unlevered cost of capital used in the APV method. Using a lower discount rate results in a higher discounted value of the unlevered cash flows, and this increase in value is equal to the value of the interest tax shields. This is why the WACC valuation method is sometimes called the adjusted cost of capital valuation method. In Chapter 10, we explored how the weighted average cost of capital values the interest tax shields under various assumptions about their risk, timing, and magnitude.

In this chapter, we present a more detailed discussion of measuring a company's weighted average cost of capital, r_{WACC}, than our discussion in Chapter 5. Naturally, we need to follow this process only if we are using the WACC method. If we are using the APV method, we just measure the unlevered cost of capital as we discussed in Chapter 10. Here, we discuss the various cost of capital inputs in more detail. In addition, we discuss the measurement of a company's capital structure and capital structure ratios, the adjustment for excess assets, minority interest positions, unconsolidated affiliates, leases, and pensions (and similar benefits).

We also discuss topics related to measuring the value of debt financing in the capital structure. A review of the academic literature suggests that the benefits of debt associated with interest tax shields may be reduced by the effect of such items as personal taxes, agency costs, and the magnitude and likelihood of incurring financial distress costs. As such, the value of debt financing cannot be measured solely by valuing the interest tax shields. We also discuss circumstances in which the weighted average cost of capital method cannot measure the value of the interest tax shields correctly, whereas the adjusted present value method results in the correct value.

We know that the weighted average cost of capital is an appropriate discount rate for valuing the firm (that is, all of the company's assets), which is why it is of interest to us as valuation specialists. The weighted average cost of capital is also the appropriate discount rate for valuing "scale expansions" (increasing the size of the firm by scaling up all of its elements proportionately) or for valuing projects that have the "average" risk of existing operating assets, assuming the firm's capital structure strategy remains constant. However, the weighted average cost of capital is not an appropriate discount rate for all of the firm's projects. For example, it is not appropriate for projects that are either more or less risky than the average risk of the firm's existing operating assets or for projects that will result in changes in the company's capital structure. For many projects, it is more appropriate to use a project-specific cost of capital or hurdle rate that will differ from the weighted average cost of capital.

11.1 MEASURING THE WEIGHTED AVERAGE COST OF CAPITAL—OVERVIEW

The **weighted average cost of capital**, r_{WACC}, is the after-tax cost of capital the company must pay to finance itself, based on the company's expected or target capital structure. We summarize the process of measuring the weighted average cost of capital in Exhibit 11.1. We calculate a company's weighted average cost of capital by averaging its equity cost of capital and the cost of capital for each of its non-common-equity securities (debt, preferred stock, warrants, employee stock options, etc.), on an after-tax basis. Since companies usually do not have capital structures with equal amounts of debt, preferred stock, warrants, and equity, we cannot use a simple average to calculate the weighted average cost of capital. Instead, we weight each cost of capital by the proportion of the firm—measured using market values—that is financed with each respective security.

LO1 Measure the weighted average cost of capital

EXHIBIT 11.1   An Overview of the Process to Measure the Weighted Average Cost of Capital

1	Estimate the equity cost of capital, r_E
2	Estimate the cost of capital for each non-equity security (e.g., r_D, r_{PS})
3	Determine the proportions of a company's securities in its target capital structure (based on market values) (e.g., V_E/V_F, V_D/V_F, V_{PS}/V_F as well as warrants, options, etc.), making appropriate adjustments for excess assets, unconsolidated affiliates, minority interest, leases, etc.
4	Estimate the tax rate for interest (T_{INT}) and any other information needed to value the interest tax shields
5	Calculate the weighted average cost of capital, r_{WACC}, using the standard weighted average cost of capital formula

---

If we have all of the necessary inputs—the cost of capital for each of the company's securities, the income tax rate for interest, and the proportion of the firm financed with each security—we can measure the weighted average cost of capital with the standard formula for the weighted average cost of capital that we introduced in Chapter 5.

$$r_{WACC} = r_E \times \frac{V_E}{V_F} + r_D \times (1 - T_{INT}) \times \frac{V_D}{V_F} + r_{PS} \times \frac{V_{PS}}{V_F} + r_W \times \frac{V_W}{V_F} \qquad (11.1)$$

where: r_{WACC} = the weighted average cost of capital
   r_E = cost of equity capital
   r_D = cost of debt capital
   r_{PS} = cost of preferred stock capital
   r_W = cost of capital for warrants and/or rights offerings

$\dfrac{V_D}{V_F}$ = capital structure ratio for debt

$\dfrac{V_{PS}}{V_F}$ = capital structure ratio for preferred stock

$\dfrac{V_W}{V_F}$ = capital structure ratio for warrants and/or rights offerings

$\dfrac{V_E}{V_F}$ = capital structure ratio for equity

T_{INT} = the appropriate tax rate to measure the tax deduction for interest

Recall that we generally use the WACC method when we expect the managers of a company to manage the company's capital structure with constant proportions of debt, equity, preferred stock, and other issued claims. Thus, we measure all of the inputs in the previous formula by using market costs of capital and target capital structure ratios based on relative market values. For example, a company may have a stated capital structure strategy based on target capital structure ratios. As such, we do not need to know the values of the numerators and denominators separately to determine the capital structure ratios, for we only need the ratios. On the other hand, if we are measuring the weighted average cost of capital for a publicly traded company (with an ongoing capital structure), and if we know the values of all of its securities, then we have the values of the numerators and denominators we need to measure each of the capital structure ratios, assuming those values represent the target capital structure ratios. The debt cost of capital is multiplied by $(1 - T_{INT})$ to adjust the cost of debt capital for the tax deductibility of interest. None of the other terms for equity, preferred, and warrants are tax-adjusted because those generally do not lead to tax deductions at the corporate level. If they did lead to corporate tax deductions, we would have to adjust Equation 11.1 accordingly. The weights must represent the expected capital structure ratios, and the costs of capital must reflect the expected cost of capital based on the company's target capital structure, capital structure strategy, and business risk.

We do not show time subscripts in the weighted average cost of capital formula, for all of the terms in the formula share the same time subscript (in other words, we measure each input at the same point in time). We discussed estimating the cost of equity, the cost of debt, and the cost of preferred stock in Chapters 8 through 10, and we use the procedures from those chapters to get some of the inputs we need. It is important to remember, however, that a company's weighted average cost of capital is not necessarily constant over time. The weighted average cost of capital changes over time if we expect its inputs to change over time—for example, if we expect changes in a company's target capital structure ratios, costs of capital, or income tax rate for measuring the interest tax shields. The inputs would also change if we predict a company's business risk or financial risk will change. For example, if the company expects to sell off one or more of its businesses, its business risk will change if the businesses expected to be sold have a different business risk than the remaining businesses. In addition, shifts in required costs of capital can occur because of shifts in expected inflation, changes in required real risk-free rates of return, and variation in market risk premiums.

If we use a weighted average cost of capital that is constant over time, we assume that the firm will keep the proportions of debt, preferred stock, equity, and any other claims constant over time and that the operating risk and financial risk of the firm will remain constant. We also assume that the real risk-free rate of return, expected inflation, and market risk premium are constant. Under these assumptions, if the value of the equity increases or decreases, we assume management will adjust the capital structure to keep the proportions of the various claims constant (at least as an approximation). In Chapter 10, we discussed how we do not expect firms to continuously make these adjustments due to transactions costs. However, using a constant weighted average cost of capital presumes that management will manage the capital structure to achieve some perceived target, at least as a first approximation.

Of course, if a company anticipates changing its capital structure, then the company's current costs of capital will not be useful for calculating its weighted average cost of capital under the new capital structure. For example, a change in the proportion of debt used by a company will cause changes in the other costs of capital as well. Thus, conducting scenario analyses of alternative capital structures requires changing all of the costs of capital. Here, a common error is to not vary the costs of capital with different leverage ratios. We have already provided all of the necessary tools to estimate the effect of a change in a company's capital structure on its various debt, preferred, and equity costs of capital in Chapters 9 and 10.

Valuation Key 11.1

The weighted average cost of capital is used to value the firm and to value projects that are of average risk. It is based on the current after-tax cost of capital of each of the claims that the firm issues, weighted according to target capital structure weights as measured by market values.

It is useful to think about the weighted average cost of capital from a different perspective to understand exactly how it adjusts the unlevered cost of capital to embed the value of the interest tax shields in the WACC DCF method. We can illustrate this effect using the general levering formula we derived in Chapter 10 (Equation 10.3), which measures the equity cost of capital as a function of the unlevered cost of capital and the debt and preferred stock costs of capital. If we substitute this formula for the term for the equity cost of capital in the weighted average cost of capital formula (Equation 11.1), we can derive a weighted average cost of capital formula that is based on the company's unlevered cost of capital, debt cost of capital, and interest tax shields.

$$r_{WACC} = r_{UA} - r_D \times T_{INT} \times \frac{V_D}{V_F} - (r_{UA} - r_{ITS}) \times \frac{V_{ITS}}{V_F} \qquad \textbf{(11.2)}$$

The second term in the above weighted average cost of capital formula reduces the unlevered cost of capital for the tax deductibility of interest; in addition, if the company's interest tax shields have less risk than its operating assets (for example, if they are valued at the cost of debt), the third term reduces the weighted average cost of capital even further for this risk reduction. If the discount rate for interest tax shields is equal to the unlevered cost of capital, the third term is equal to zero. Further, if interest is not tax deductible, $T_{INT} = 0$, the last two terms of the formula equal zero, and the weighted average cost of capital is just equal to the unlevered cost of capital.

This formula does not contain terms for the equity cost of capital or preferred stock cost of capital. This is neither a coincidence nor a mystery. In Equation 11.2, we substituted the levering formula for the equity cost of capital term in Equation 11.1, and the equity cost of equity capital and the preferred stock cost of capital terms drop out of the formula. Recall that issuing preferred stock does not affect the weighted average cost of capital, for preferred stock dividends are not tax deductible and, thus, have no tax advantage over the equity cost of capital. Of course, if preferred stock dividends were tax deductible, then there would be an expression in the formula related to preferred stock and its tax effect.

We can derive an expression for the weighted average cost of capital for each of the special levering cases we discussed in Chapter 10. For example, the general levering formula for the situation where we are discounting some or all of the tax shields at the cost of debt (where $V_{ITS@r_D}$ is the present value of the interest tax shields discounted at the cost of debt) becomes

$$r_{WACC} = r_{UA} - r_D \times T_{INT} \times \frac{V_D}{V_F} - (r_{UA} - r_D) \times \frac{V_{ITS@r_D}}{V_F}$$

Further, if the discount rate for interest tax shields is the cost of debt for a company that is not growing and has perpetual debt, Equation 11.2 becomes (using $V_{ITS} = V_{ITS@r_D} = T_{INT} \times V_D$)

$$r_{WACC} = r_{UA} \times \left(1 - T_{INT} \times \frac{V_D}{V_F} \right)$$

On the other hand, if we were to solve for the expression where all interest tax shields are discounted at the unlevered cost of capital, the third term in Equation 11.2 is zero and the expression becomes

$$r_{WACC} = r_{UA} - r_D \times T_{INT} \times \frac{V_D}{V_F}$$

Finally, the annual refinancing levering formula substituted into Equation 11.2 becomes

$$r_{WACC} = r_{UA} - (1 + r_{UA}) \times \frac{r_D \times T_{INT}}{(1 + r_D)} \times \frac{V_D}{V_F}$$

As it turns out, there are situations, especially with warrants and options, where these expressions are useful and make our calculations simpler. We introduce them here since we are talking about the weighted average cost of capital and we will highlight their usefulness with warrants and options in Chapter 12.

REVIEW EXERCISE 11.1

Measuring the Weighted Average Cost of Capital

Calculate the weighted average cost of capital using Equations 11.1 and 11.2. Assume that the company's securities are publicly traded, that its debt is currently trading at 100% of book value, and that its preferred stock is currently trading at 95% of its book value. The company's stock price is currently $12 per share, and the company has 1,000 shares of stock outstanding, which is net of 100 treasury shares. The risk-free rate is 5%, and the market risk premium is 6%. The company issued the debt and preferred stock at par value. The company has an equity beta equal to 2.5. The company's debt has a yield to maturity equal to 8%, which includes a 1% expected default loss, and the cost of capital for the preferred stock is equal to 8.5%. The income tax rate on all income is 30%. The company plans to continually refinance itself to have a constant capital structure strategy based on its current capital structure ratios.

	Year 1	Year 2
Income Statement		
Revenue		$20,000
Operating expenses.		–8,000
Depreciation expense.		–5,200
Earnings before interest and taxes.		$ 6,800
Interest expense.		–800
Income before taxes.		$ 6,000
Income tax expense.		–1,800
Net income.		$ 4,200
Balance Sheet		
Total current assets	$ 4,000	$ 6,000
Property, plant, and equipment (net)	32,000	34,000
Total assets.	$36,000	$40,000
Account payable	$ 1,000	$ 1,200
Debt	10,000	12,000
Total liabilities.	$11,000	$13,200
Preferred stock.	$ 8,000	$ 8,000
Capital stock	2,000	2,000
Retained earnings	15,000	16,800
Shareholders' equity	$25,000	$26,800
Liabilities and shareholders' equity	$36,000	$40,000

Solution on page 467.

11.2 ASSESSING AND MEASURING TARGET CAPITAL STRUCTURES

Do companies have an optimal capital structure, and if so, how does one determine the optimal capital structure for a company? This question has been the subject of academic and practitioner research for more than 50 years.[2] This research provides important principles to guide our thinking about optimal capital structure, but the specific choice of an optimal capital structure remains largely unresolved. Different capital structure theories make different assumptions about the costs and benefits of issuing various securities, and as such, the different theories result in different optimal capital structures. We know that a company's optimal capital structure is contingent on many forces, some of which we discuss later in this chapter.[3] Moreover, the personal preferences of managers can impact the capital structure decision as well. Of course, in many valuations, it is only necessary to make an assumption about how the company will manage its capital structure, whether it is optimal or not.

---

[2] See, Modigliani, F., and M. H. Miller, "The Cost of Capital, Corporate Finance and the Theory of Investment," *American Economic Review* 48 (1958), pp. 261–297; Modigliani, F., and M. H. Miller, "Corporate Income Taxes and the Cost of Capital: A Correction," *American Economic Review* 53 (June 1963), pp. 433–443; and Modigliani, F., and M. H. Miller, "Some Estimates of the Cost of Capital to the Electric Utility Industry, 1954–1957," *American Economic Review* 56 (June 1966), pp. 333–391.

[3] See Myers (2001) and the various articles cited therein for a discussion of optimal capital structure; Myers, S. C., "Capital Structure," *Journal of Economic Perspectives* vol. 15, no. 2 (Spring 2001), pp. 81–102.

In using the weighted average cost of capital method, we implicitly assume that management chooses a target capital structure based on certain factors and we assume it will try to maintain this target capital structure unless changes in the economic situation create a reason to specify a new target. In this section, we discuss the process of assessing a company's target capital structure. We also discuss issues related to how the target capital structure is sometimes defined, what securities to include in the assessment, and what we can do when market values are not observable, as is the case with private companies. In addition, we discuss such complicating factors as excess assets, minority interests, and unconsolidated affiliates. Later in the chapter, we will discuss issues associated with leases.

VALUATION IN PRACTICE 11.1

How Do Companies Measure Cost of Capital Inputs? A survey of large U.S. companies, investment banks, and leading textbooks documents that

> The estimation approaches are broadly similar across the three samples in several dimensions.
>
> - Discounted Cash Flow (DCF) is the dominant investment-evaluation technique.
> - WACC is the dominant discount rate used in DCF analyses.
> - Weights are based on *market* not book value mixes of debt and equity.
> - The after-tax cost of debt is predominantly based on *marginal* pretax costs, and *marginal* or *statutory* tax rates.

Source: Bruner, R. F., K. M. Eades, R. S. Harris, and R. C. Higgins, "Best Practices in Estimating the Cost of Capital: Survey and Synthesis," *Financial Practice and Education* (Spring/Summer 1998), pp. 13–28; the specific quote is on page 15.

Use Target Weights and Market Values to Measure Capital Structure Ratios

As we stated previously, we use market values to measure capital structure ratios. In assessing the target capital structure, we typically examine how the company managed its capital structure in the recent past. This review provides useful information on whether the general assumption of a constant proportionate capital structure underlying the use of the WACC method is reasonable. In the absence of a stated company strategy or plan, using a recently observed capital structure as the target is often a viable option, especially if the capital structure proportions have been reasonably constant over the last few years.

If current capital structure weights do not reflect the target capital structure for the company, we assume that the company will adjust its financing to its target capital structure reasonably quickly as part of the company's ongoing capital structure strategy. If this is not the expectation, then using the target capital structure in the weighted average cost of capital method may not be appropriate. Rather, we might need to use an alternative capital structure until such time as we expect the company to refinance itself to its target capital structure. If the company expects to change capital structures over time—for example, if a company with high financial leverage plans to pay down its debt over a number of years in order to eventually achieve a long-run target capital structure—then the weighted average cost of capital will also vary over time. In this situation, the APV DCF method is likely the more appropriate method to use until the company reaches its target capital structure. At the point in time when the company reaches its target capital structure, we can switch from an APV valuation to a WACC valuation.

Operating Liabilities Are Not Part of a Company's Capital Structure

Capital structure ratios exclude operating liabilities that are included in operating working capital (such as accounts payable, wages payable, etc.). Most operating liabilities are current liabilities, but some are not (such as non-current deferred income tax liabilities). Any interest-bearing debt, such as bank debt, is part of the capital structure—as are common stock, preferred stock, warrants, rights offerings, and employee stock options.

Other contractual obligations—such as operating leases, capitalized leases, pensions, and post-retirement benefits—may or may not be part of the capital structure, depending on how we choose to treat them. We discuss the issue of including them or treating them as operating liabilities in more detail later in the chapter, but essentially, these liabilities can be treated as either an operating activity—affecting the company's operating risk—or a financing activity—affecting the company's financial risk.

Operating leases are a form of off-balance-sheet financing. However, companies use other types of off-balance-sheet financing such as special purpose entities (sometimes called special purpose vehicles), joint ventures, and partnerships. We also discuss this topic in more detail in a later section.

Industry Capital Structures

Companies in the same industry often have similar capital structures. Thus, companies sometimes use target capital structures that are observable in their industry as a guide to deciding on their own target capital structure. Further, we might choose to perform a valuation using a measure of the typical industry capital structure. For example, suppose we are advising a company on the value of a division it is considering selling. Rather than using the capital structure currently used by the selling company—which may reflect many different types of businesses—we would probably assign a typical industry capital structure for the business of the division when we measure its weighted average cost of capital, as potential buyers would likely believe it to be a reasonable capital structure strategy for the asset. This is also a common assumption to make when we cannot easily measure the value of a company's capital structure ratios, for example, with a private company. Naturally, this is only one alternative to consider when choosing a capital structure for valuing an entity. For example, if we decided that the cash flows of the entity were capable of supporting a leveraged buyout transaction, we might perform another valuation based on that capital structure and valuation method.

In Exhibit 11.2, we present data on average capital structure ratios by industry. These are the equally weighted average capital structures for these industries, averaged across all publicly traded firms in each respective industry from 2006 to 2010. For purposes of creating this exhibit, we measure debt and preferred stock using book values (given the relative paucity of data on the market values of debt and preferred) and we measure the equity using market values; all are measured at the fiscal year-end.[4] Market capitalization represents the sum of the book values of debt and preferred plus the market value of the equity.

In the exhibit, we sort the industries by total debt to market capitalization. As we can quickly see from this exhibit, the amount of debt financing used varies significantly across industries; the Metal Mining industry group finances itself, on average, with less than 10% debt, whereas other industries such as Amusement and Recreation Services; Paper and Allied Products; Electric, Gas, and Sanitary Services; Water Transportation; and Transportation by Air use 40% or more debt. One note of caution when examining this table: we have not included any off-balance-sheet financing in the calculated ratios. For example, we have not capitalized operating leases, and some of these industries use substantial operating leases (retail, airlines and more). In addition, we have not included other types of claims such as employee stock options or warrants.

Excess Cash and Other Excess Assets

Recall that we typically value a company's excess assets separately from its operating assets; the most typical example of this is a company holding more cash than it needs to operate its businesses (excess cash). In previous chapters, we discussed how to adjust the costs of capital for excess cash. To measure the weighted average cost of capital, we use both these adjusted costs of capital and the relevant capital structure ratios relevant for the assets we are valuing—that is, the capital structure ratios for the assets we are valuing (excluding excess assets) for the company's target capital structure. Of course, after we determine the value of the firm without the excess assets, we add the value of the excess assets back in order to determine the total firm value.

When we value a company, there may be circumstances where we believe that the company will retain the excess assets—such as excess cash. If this were the case, we would not adjust the costs of capital for the elimination of the excess cash, but rather, we would include the income flows from the excess

---

[4] To be included in the sample, the company needed complete information for its 2010 fiscal year available in the Compustat®North American Industrial Annual. The resulting sample consisted of 38,059 company-years. Standard & Poor's Compustat® is a standardized database delivering accounting and market data on over 54,000 securities to clients through a variety of databases and analytical software products.

cash in the free cash flows, and we would choose the target capital structure for the company with the retention of excess cash taken into consideration—companies may elect to hold more debt in their capital structure if they retain excess cash as opposed to if they had no excess cash.

EXHIBIT 11.2	Average Capital Structure Ratios for Selected Industries						
		Average Capital Structure Ratios of Companies by Industry					
Industry	Industry Description	Short-Term Debt to Market Cap	Long-Term Debt to Market Cap	Total Debt to Market Cap	Preferred Stock to Market Cap	Common Equity to Market Cap	Firm-Year Obs
	All companies in the sample	4.8%	23.0%	27.7%	1.2%	71.1%	38,059
10	Metal mining.	1.5%	5.8%	7.3%	0.2%	92.5%	2,211
38	Measuring, analyzing, and controlling instruments; photographic, medical, and optical goods; watches and clocks	2.5%	12.0%	14.5%	0.9%	84.7%	1,695
73	Business services.	2.4%	13.2%	15.6%	1.6%	82.7%	3,300
56	Apparel and accessory stores	2.6%	13.7%	16.3%	0.5%	83.2%	276
36	Electronic and other electrical equipment and components, except computer equipment	4.1%	13.1%	17.2%	0.9%	81.9%	2,516
87	Engineering, accounting, research, management, and related services	1.8%	15.6%	17.4%	1.0%	81.6%	528
28	Chemicals and allied products.	2.2%	15.4%	17.6%	0.9%	81.5%	2,940
35	Industrial and commercial machinery and computer equipment	3.3%	15.8%	19.2%	0.5%	80.4%	1,397
23	Apparel and other finished products made from fabrics and similar materials.	7.5%	12.8%	20.4%	0.2%	79.5%	239
13	Oil and gas extraction	3.8%	21.1%	24.9%	0.7%	74.4%	2,165
34	Fabricated metal products, except machinery and transportation equipment.	3.4%	23.5%	26.9%	0.6%	72.5%	334
33	Primary metal industries.	6.5%	21.1%	27.6%	0.6%	71.8%	407
50	Wholesale trade—durable goods.	8.8%	19.3%	28.0%	0.8%	71.1%	590
59	Miscellaneous retail	5.3%	24.0%	29.3%	0.8%	69.9%	481
62	Security and commodity brokers, dealers, exchanges, and services	13.5%	16.4%	29.9%	0.6%	69.4%	670
80	Health services.	1.7%	29.2%	30.8%	1.2%	67.9%	457
30	Rubber and miscellaneous plastics products	6.9%	24.6%	31.4%	0.8%	67.7%	223
20	Food and kindred products	5.6%	26.0%	31.6%	1.0%	67.3%	698
51	Wholesale trade—non-durable goods	5.6%	26.6%	32.2%	1.1%	66.7%	374
37	Transportation equipment	4.9%	27.4%	32.3%	0.9%	66.8%	601
58	Eating and drinking places.	1.2%	33.9%	35.1%	1.2%	63.7%	356
27	Printing, publishing, and allied industries.	2.4%	35.2%	37.6%	0.4%	62.1%	270
67	Holding and other investment offices.	4.4%	35.2%	39.6%	2.9%	57.6%	1,671
48	Communications	1.8%	38.0%	39.8%	0.9%	59.3%	1,065
79	Amusement and recreation services	2.5%	37.5%	40.0%	1.3%	58.6%	281
26	Paper and allied products	3.5%	39.3%	42.7%	0.9%	56.4%	296
45	Transportation by air.	1.8%	42.2%	44.0%	0.8%	55.2%	252
44	Water transportation.	1.1%	45.5%	46.6%	0.9%	52.5%	349
49	Electric, gas, and sanitary services	3.8%	44.1%	47.9%	0.8%	51.3%	1,777
	Across industry averages						
	1st percentile	1.1%	7.5%	9.3%	0.2%	51.6%	227
	10th percentile	1.6%	13.0%	16.2%	0.4%	56.2%	266
	25th percentile	2.2%	15.6%	19.2%	0.6%	62.1%	334
	50th percentile—median	3.4%	24.0%	29.9%	0.9%	69.4%	528
	75th percentile	5.3%	35.2%	37.6%	1.0%	80.4%	1,671
	90th percentile	7.0%	39.8%	43.0%	1.3%	82.8%	2,272
	99th percentile	12.2%	45.1%	47.5%	2.5%	90.3%	3,199

Minority Interest

If a parent company owns between 50% and 100% of a subsidiary, the parent almost always consolidates it. Consolidation means that the parent company reports 100% of the subsidiary's assets, liabilities, revenues, and expenses on its own financial statements. If the parent company owns less than 100% of the subsidiary, the parent company shows an allocation—a deduction for the parent company—of the subsidiary's income or loss and common equity attributable to the minority shareholders—called minority interest—on its financial statements for the proportion of the subsidiary not owned by the parent company.

Fortunately, relatively few companies have significant minority interest. For example, of the publicly traded firms in the United States with fiscal year-ends between July 2007 and June 2008, only about 22% reported any minority interest. Of those reporting minority interests, more than 50% reported a book value of minority interests to total assets of less than 0.8%. This result shows that, for the vast majority of companies, the effect of minority interest is likely to be quite small. About 10% of those reporting minority interests (about 2% of all publicly traded firms) had a book value of minority interest to total assets of 10% or more. Thus, when it is significant, we should consider the impact of minority interests when we value a company.

VALUATION IN PRACTICE 11.2

Altria Group, Inc. S.A. Minority Interest in Kraft Foods Inc. Prior to June 13, 2001, Kraft Foods Inc. (Kraft) was a 100% owned subsidiary of Altria Group, Inc. ("Altria"). On June 13, 2001, Kraft issued publicly traded common stock through an initial public offering (IPO) of 280 million shares. Altria's ownership in Kraft decreased to 89% as a result of the IPO. Altria continued to own 89% of Kraft for several years.

On its balance sheet dated December 31, 2006, Altria reported total assets of $104.3 billion. It also reported a minority interest of $3.5 billion or about 3.4% of its assets, which was composed mostly of the minority interest of non-Altria shareholders in Kraft. Kraft was a publicly traded company. On that date, the market value of the minority interest shares was $5.7 billion based on Kraft's stock price.

In 2007, Altria spun off its remaining interest (89.0%) in Kraft to Altria stockholders in a tax-free transaction.

Note: In 2006, before spinning off Kraft, Altria Group, Inc. owned 100% of Philip Morris USA Inc. and Philip Morris International Inc.—both of which manufacture and sell cigarettes and other tobacco products—and Philip Morris Capital Corporation—which is a direct finance leasing company. It also owned 89% of Kraft Foods Inc.—which manufactures and sells packaged foods and beverages—and 28.6% of SABMiller plc ("SABMiller")—which manufactures and sells various beer products.

Suppose that we are valuing a company with significant minority interests and that we believe we should adjust for that minority interest in our valuation. Conceptually, this adjustment is fairly straightforward. One way we can make the adjustment is to value the company, including the value of the minority interest, and then deduct the value of the minority interest, essentially treating it as a non-common-equity claim on the company's assets. However, it is sometimes very difficult to collect the information we need to make this adjustment.

To be more specific, if we can assume that the weighted average cost of capital for the less than 100% owned subsidiaries is the same as the parent company's weighted average cost of capital, we can then measure the weighted average cost of capital as follows. Since the consolidated company reports 100% of the subsidiaries' non-equity financing, we can add the market value of the minority interest claims to the value of the parent company's common equity. We measure the capital structure ratios using 100% of the debt, preferred stock, and equity (including minority interest); the latter is equal to 100% of the total parent company equity plus the value of the minority interest. If the subsidiary is publicly traded, this is a straightforward calculation, but if it is not, we have to use other valuation methods to value the minority interests depending on the information that is available. To measure the value of the firm, we discount the unlevered free cash flows (including cash flows that might be attributable to the minority interests) using the weighted average cost of capital, which measures the value of the firm plus the value of the minority interests. We then subtract the value of the minority interests to arrive at the value of the firm.

An alternative way to make this adjustment is to extract the effect of the part of the subsidiary that the parent company does not own from both the unlevered free cash flows and the components of the weighted average cost of capital. Naturally, depending on the level of information that is available, this exercise can be tedious or next to impossible.

Unconsolidated Affiliates

Generally, the term *unconsolidated affiliate* refers to a partially owned company that is not consolidated by the parent company; the ownership percentage is usually at least 20% but less than 50%. Investments of this sort are not consolidated but reported on the parent company's financial statements on one line, presenting the net effect of the investment in the appropriate financial statement. The income statement shows one line that represents the income effect of unconsolidated affiliates (the firm's proportionate share of the income or loss of its unconsolidated affiliates) for that period. The cash flow statement has a similar line item, but it converts the income effect into a cash effect. The balance sheet also shows the investment in one line, presenting the book value of the parent company's equity in the unconsolidated affiliate (the original investment plus the cumulative proportionate share of income since the original investment less any dividends received, adjusted for purchase premiums and discounts).

Using the same sample of companies we used in the minority interest section, we examine the percentage of companies that have unconsolidated affiliates. Of the sample, 18.5% report a value for unconsolidated affiliates. However, the ratio of equity in unconsolidated affiliates to total assets was 1.5% or less for about 50% of the companies with unconsolidated affiliates. Thus, more than 90% of publicly traded companies have unconsolidated affiliates representing 1.5% or less of their assets. In addition, of companies with unconsolidated affiliates, about 25% had a ratio of equity in unconsolidated affiliates to total assets of at least 4.8%, and 10% had a ratio of at least 12.8%.

To the extent information permits and if the amount of unconsolidated affiliates is considered material, we can treat unconsolidated affiliates in essentially the same way we treat excess assets. We measure the costs of capital as we discussed in previous chapters. In order to calculate the target weights for the weighted average cost of capital, we subtract the value of the company's ownership in the unconsolidated affiliate from the value of the equity, and hence the value of the firm. If the risk of the unconsolidated affiliate is different from the company's risk (without the unconsolidated affiliate), we would consider adjusting the company's equity beta using the techniques we discussed in Chapter 8 to adjust out the effect of excess assets—assuming we can measure the equity cost of capital of the unconsolidated affiliate. In order to make any of these adjustments, we must, of course, measure the value of the company's ownership in the unconsolidated affiliate either from market data if available, market multiples, or some other technique.

Once we measure the weighted average cost of capital and the unlevered free cash flows without the effect of the unconsolidated affiliates, we discount these free cash flows by the weighted average cost of capital. Doing so provides an estimate of the value of the firm without the value of the unconsolidated affiliate. To measure the total value of the firm, we add the value of the unconsolidated affiliates.

Off-Balance-Sheet Entities

Companies use certain types of off-balance-sheet entities such as **special-purpose entities** (sometimes called **special-purpose vehicles**) and partnerships for a variety of reasons. Companies can use special-purpose entities and limited partnerships for business ventures with other companies for tax or management incentives. For example, sometimes, companies set up limited partnerships to finance research and development activities.[5] A company typically uses special-purpose entities to either remove or separate assets or liabilities from its balance sheet in what is usually an attempt to mitigate some type of risk. The risk can be embedded in the transferred assets—thus removing that risk from the company—or embedded in the company—thus removing that risk from the transferred assets.

For these entities, one key issue we must consider is whether the creditors of the off-balance-sheet entity have claims against the company that set up the entity. An off-balance-sheet entity with creditors that do not have claims against the company is said to be bankruptcy remote. If the creditors of the off-balance-sheet entity do not have claims against the company that set it up, then we should not consider the debt of the off-balance-sheet entity when we measure the weighted average cost of capital of the company. If the off-balance-sheet creditors do have a claim against the company, then the financing of the entity (or at least the firm's proportionate share of the financing) should be considered as part of the company's capital structure. Further, even if the company is not contractually obligated to support the

---

[5] See, Beatty, A., P. Berger, and J. Magliolo, "Motives for Forming Research and Development Financing Organizations," *Journal of Accounting and Economics* 19 (1995), pp. 411–442.

entity, the company may voluntarily choose to support the entity's claims. Management may voluntarily support these claims to avoid a loss in investor confidence in the company, which could affect the company's ability to raise capital in the future.[6] This is called implicit recourse or moral recourse, and if this is the expectation, then the supported debt should be included in the company's capital structure. Last, income tax rules vary by the type of entity and by circumstances of the entity, which need to be considered when we include the financing of these entities in the company's capital structure.

One other issue is that if the off-balance-sheet entity is likely to produce cash flows that the company will receive, we must obviously include those cash flows in our valuation.

Valuation Key 11.2

The weighted average cost of capital is based on target market value weights. Care should be taken to include only the relevant claims in the cost of capital calculation and to make appropriate adjustments for such issues as excess assets, minority interests, and unconsolidated affiliates.

Target Long-Term Capital Structure and the Free Cash Flow Perpetuity Method

A company must have a target long-term capital structure in order to use the free cash flow perpetuity method to measure a continuing (terminal) value based on the WACC method. Recall that the free cash flow perpetuity formula assumes that the company has a constant discount rate and a constant growth rate. If we are using the weighted average cost of capital as the discount rate in the free cash flow perpetuity model, then we need a constant discount rate that, in turn, requires a constant weighted average cost of capital. From a practical perspective, this requires the company to use a target capital structure that it will adhere to over time. The assumption of a constant target capital structure at the continuing value date is an inherently reasonable one to make for most companies—especially when they have reached the steady state required for using the perpetuity method. In the absence of countervailing evidence, we often use a typical industry capital structure for this calculation. Of course, it is possible for a company's capital structure to change and for the weighted average cost of capital to remain the same if, for some reason, the costs of capital or income tax rate for interest changes in a way that offsets the effect of the change in the company's capital structure. Even though this is possible, this set of circumstances is unlikely to occur.

11.3 TREATING CAPITALIZING CONTRACTUAL OBLIGATIONS AS OPERATING VERSUS FINANCING—DOES IT MATTER?

LO2 Make potential adjustments for the capitalization of contractual obligations

Companies make various types of long-term contractual commitments, for example, leasing assets, pension obligations, and post-retirement health obligations. Accounting rules require companies to record the present value of some of these contractual commitments as liabilities, whereas for other contractual commitments, the accounting rules require companies to expense the cash payments when made. In addition, accounting rules require companies to treat some of these liabilities as debt-like and record interest expense—for example, certain lease obligations—and treat other of these liabilities as operating liabilities and record an operating expense with no interest component—for example, post-retirement health benefits. Regardless of how the accounting rules treat a contractual obligation, we must decide whether to treat the contractual obligation as an operating activity or a financing activity because this decision affects the unlevered cost of capital and unlevered free cash flows.

If we treat the contractual obligation as an operating activity, we assume the leverage from the contractual obligation is operating leverage and thus, affects the riskiness of the unlevered free cash flows. On the other hand, treating the contractual obligation as financing assumes the leverage from the contractual obligation is financial leverage, which does not affect the riskiness of the unlevered free cash flows. The different treatments do not affect the equity cost of capital or equity free cash flows. The riskiness

---

[6] For a discussion of special-purpose entities, see Gorton, G., and N. Souleles, "Special Purpose Vehicles and Securitization," *NBER Chapters, in: The Risks of Financial Institutions*, National Bureau of Economic Research, Inc. (2007), pp. 549–602.

of the equity free cash flows is unaffected by this decision because the effect of the leverage from the contractual obligation affects the riskiness of the equity free cash flows regardless of whether we treat it as operating or financial leverage.

As we illustrate with the following lease example, if we treat the contractual obligation as a financing activity, we record the present value of the contractual obligation as a debt-like security and treat it as debt in all of our cost of capital and free cash flow calculations. If we treat the contractual obligation as an operating activity, we treat the entire cash flow to pay or fund the contractual obligation as an expense that reduces unlevered free cash flow. Accounting rules require companies to record some contractual obligations as a liability but treat the related expense as an operating expense without any interest or other financing expense, for example, post-retirement health benefits. If we agree with this treatment—that is, treating the liability as an operating liability—then we do not make any adjustments to the financial statements. If we decide to treat this liability as a financing activity, then we would make adjustments to the expenses similar to those we discuss in the following lease example.

A company typically rents or leases some of its assets. For example, we know companies in certain industries—such as the airline, retail, and restaurant industries—lease many of their assets. The most straightforward way to record lease payments is to record an operating expense (rent or lease expense) for the amount of the lease payment; these operating leases are often considered off-balance-sheet financing. However, both U.S. and international accounting standards require companies to capitalize the present value of lease payments for leases that essentially transfer the ownership of the asset leased; we call these leases capitalized leases.[7]

Depending on the characteristics of the lease contract, a company may include the present value of the contractual lease payments on its balance sheet (a **capitalized lease** or **capital lease**), or it may merely record the periodic lease payments as rent expense (an **operating lease**) despite the company's contractual obligation to make lease payments over many years. If a company capitalizes a lease, the company initially records the capitalized value of the lease as an asset (capitalized lease asset or lease asset) and liability (capitalized lease obligation or lease obligation) on its balance sheet. Over the life of the lease, the company amortizes the capitalized value of the leased asset and expenses interest on the capitalized lease obligation. Over the life of the lease, the sum of the lease payments expensed (using the operating lease method) is equal to the sum of amortization of the the capitalized lease asset and the interest expense of the capitalized lease obligation (using the capitalized lease method). However, the timing of these expenses is not the same.

To illustrate the basic present value calculations underpinning capitalized leases, we present a simple three-year lease example in Exhibit 11.3. The lease contract begins on the first day of Year 1 and ends on the last day of Year 3. The lease has three annual payments equal to $1,000, and it has an 11.3% implicit interest rate. The present value of the three lease payments is $2,431, which is capitalized as the lease asset and lease liability.[8]

EXHIBIT 11.3 Simple Three-Year Lease Example

Annual payment	$1,000.0		
Implicit interest rate	11.3%	3.0	Life of Lease
Present value of lease payments	$2,431.0		

Year	Beginning Lease Obligation	Implicit Interest	Lease Payment	Ending Lease Obligation
Year 1	$2,431.0	$274.7	$1,000.0	$1,705.7
Year 2	$1,705.7	$192.7	$1,000.0	$ 898.5
Year 3	$ 898.5	$101.5	$1,000.0	$ 0

Exhibit may contain small rounding errors

The accounting for capitalized leases is relatively straightforward. The present value of the lease payments is put on the balance sheet as an asset and a liability. The asset is amortized (think

---

[7] See *Statement of Financial Accounting Standards No. 13*, "Accounting for Leases," November 1976, p. 7.

[8] The value of the lease payments is equal to the present value of a three-period annuity discounted at 11.3%.

$$\$2{,}431 = \$1{,}000 \times \left(\frac{1}{0.113} - \frac{1}{0.113} \times 1.113^{-3} \right)$$

depreciation) over the life of the lease. In this case, if we used straight-line amortization, the annual amortization would be $810.33 ($810.33 = $2,431/3$). The liability and payments on the lease work like a house mortgage. For each period, interest expense is equal to the beginning balance of the lease obligation multiplied by the implicit interest rate. The difference between the lease payment and interest is equal to the reduction in the lease obligation. For example, in Year 1, interest is equal to $274.7 ($274.7 = $2,431 \times 0.113$). The reduction in the lease obligation is $725.3, which is equal to the difference between the lease payment and interest ($725.3 = $1,000.0 - 274.7). Thus, in the next year the beginning lease obligation is $1,705.7 ($1,705.7 = $2,431 - 725.3) and the interest expense for the second year is $192.7 ($192.7 = $1,705.7 \times 0.113$). The reduction in the principal for Year 2 is $807.3 ($807.3 = $1,000 - 192.7). Over the life of the lease the sum of the interest expense ($568.9) and the lease amortization ($2,431) equal the $3,000 of lease payments. By the end of Year 3, the liability will be gone and the asset will be fully amortized.

REVIEW EXERCISE 11.2

A Simple Lease Example

A lease contract begins on the first day of Year 1 and ends on the last day of Year 3. The lease has three annual payments equal to $5,000. The appropriate discount rate for the lease is 8%. Prepare a lease amortization table similar to the one in Exhibit 11.3.

Solution on page 468.

Naturally, given our focus on valuation, we must answer the question of whether or not this choice matters when we are valuing a company. The short answer is that if we use comparable companies to measure the unlevered cost of capital before levering the unlevered cost of capital to measure the cost of equity, it does matter. As we will soon explain, when we use comparable companies to measure the unlevered cost of capital, we must use the same assumption with respect to the treatment of the leases for both the comparable companies and the company we are valuing. For example, if we capitalize all of the leases for the comparable companies, we must do the same for the company we are valuing. In addition, the treatment of the leases impacts the definition of the value of the firm—when leases are capitalized, the value of the firm includes the value of the capitalized leases.

As it turns out, the unlevering and levering issues related to this issue also apply to other quasi-financing instruments that might be treated as debt or as an operating expense—for example, post-retirement benefits and pensions. In brief, such quasi-financing instruments can be treated as either an operating activity or a financing activity. How we treat the items affects both the definition of the value of the firm and the levering and unlevering process.

The Valuation Issue with Leases

Consider a company with a perpetual lease on land. The company expects all of its cash flows to remain constant in perpetuity. The land has a value of $1,000, the cost of debt, r_D, for the company is 10%, and its annual lease payment is $100 per year. Since the lease is perpetual, the company's lease payment is equal to its interest expense, and the capitalized lease obligation does not change over time. The company has revenues from the use of the leased land of $1,000 per year (without any costs outside of the annual lease payment). The company has a 40% income tax rate on all income. All revenues and expenses are paid in cash. The company has no assets or liabilities other than those related to the lease. For the purposes of this example, assume that the lease transaction occurred and was recorded in some prior year. In Exhibit 11.4, we present the income statement and free cash flow schedule for this company using both the operating and capital lease methods. We do not present the balance sheet for this company. The balance sheet under the operating lease method would not show a capitalized lease asset or liability, whereas the balance sheet under the capitalized lease method would show a capitalized lease asset and liability of $1,000 (the capitalized value of the lease payments at 10% in perpetuity).

In the case of an operating lease, the income statement shows revenues of $1,000 and rent expense of $100 per year; in the case of a capitalized lease, the income statement shows the same revenues of $1,000, but the lease payment is now shown to be an interest expense of $100 per year. Thus, both cases have the same net income of $540, but their EBIT is not the same.

EXHIBIT 11.4 Perpetual Lease Example—Income Statement and Free Cash Flow Schedule		
	Operating Lease Method	**Capital Lease Method**
Income Statement		
Revenues	$1,000	$1,000
Rent expense	–100	n/a
Interest expense	n/a	–100
Pretax income	$ 900	$ 900
Income taxes	–360	–360
Net income	$ 540	$ 540
Free Cash Flow Schedule		
Earnings before interest and taxes	$ 900	$1,000
– Income taxes paid on EBIT	–360	–400
Earnings before interest and after taxes	$ 540	$ 600
– Increase in capital lease assets	n/a	0
Unlevered free cash flow	$ 540	$ 600
– Interest paid	n/a	–100
+ Interest tax shield	n/a	40
+ Change in non-common equity	n/a	0
+ Change in capital lease obligations	n/a	0
Free cash flow to common equity	$ 540	$ 540

With regard to the cash flows, the equity free cash flows are identical regardless of how the lease is treated—even in more complicated settings, the equity free cash flows are always identical whether the company capitalizes the leases or treats them as operating leases. However, the unlevered free cash flows are not the same for the two treatments. In this example, the unlevered free cash flows are higher when we capitalize the leases by the amount of the after-tax interest expense (remember, the company is not entering into additional leases). In more complicated settings, the unlevered cash flows in any given year can be higher or lower when we capitalize multiple leases over time. However, over the life of a lease of a single asset, the sum of the unlevered free cash flows is always higher when we capitalize the lease because we treat part of the cost of the lease as a financing activity (the implicit interest expense).

Now consider a valuation of this company. The market will understand that the company has a fixed obligation regardless of whether we treat this as an operating lease or as a capitalized lease. Remember, it has a fixed obligation to pay $100 a year and if it does not, then it loses the leased asset and its revenue. Thus, in either case, the market will assign the same equity cost of capital to the firm. We assume that the cost of equity capital, r_E, is 20%. Given that the company has constant and perpetual equity free cash flows of $540 and a constant equity cost of capital of 20%, the value of the equity, V_E, is equal to $2,700 ($2,700 = $540/0.2), irrespective of whether we treat the lease as operating or capitalized.

When we treat the lease as an operating activity, the company has no non-equity financing (debt); therefore, the unlevered cost of capital, r_{UA}, is equal to the equity cost of capital of 20%. (Recall that when a company only uses equity financing, the unlevered cost of capital and weighted average cost of capital both equal the equity cost of capital.) As such, the value of the firm is equal to the value of the equity, which we calculated to be $2,700 ($2,700 = $540/0.2). This result is not surprising considering we assume that the lease is an operating activity and that the company has no debt.

When we treat the lease as a financing activity (in other words, we capitalize the lease) the value of the firm is not the same, because the value of the firm now consists of both the value of the equity and the capitalized value of the lease obligation (the only debt this company has). The value of the lease obligation is equal to $1,000 ($1,000 = $100/0.1); thus, the value of the firm is now equal to $3,700 ($3,700 = $2,700 + $1,000). As must be the case given that the equity free cash flows and equity cost of capital are identical under both methods, the value of the equity is again $2,700 ($2,700 = $3,700 − $1,000). We can show the valuation of the firm using both the weighted average cost of capital (WACC) and adjusted present value (APV) valuation methods. The weighted average cost of capital is equal to 16.216%.

$$r_{WACC} = r_E \times V_E/V_F + r_D \times (1 - T) \times V_D/V_F$$
$$= 0.2 \times (\$2,700/\$3,700) + 0.1 \times (1 - 0.4) \times (\$1,000/\$3,700)$$
$$= 0.16216$$

Under the capitalized lease method, the unlevered free cash flow is equal to $600 and the value of the firm using the WACC valuation method is $3,700 ($3,700 = $600/0.16216), and the value of the equity is again $2,700 ($2,700 = $3,700 − $1,000). One key point to remember is that the claims that constitute the value of the firm change as we move from treating the lease as an operating activity to treating it as a financing activity.

Now consider the APV valuation of this company. To value the company using the APV method, we must first measure the unlevered cost of capital. When we treat the lease as a financing activity instead of an operating activity, we partially convert the lease payment from an operating activity to a financing activity, which we record as interest expense. These changes extract a fixed-cost lease cash payment (operating lease method with operating leverage) from the unlevered free cash flows and convert that fixed cost into a financing cost. As such, this conversion affects the unlevered free cash flows. Thus, the capital lease method has unlevered free cash flows with less operating risk, and thus an unlevered cost of capital that is lower than that of the operating lease method.

We show this effect by using our unlevering formula to unlever the 20% equity cost of capital. In this example, the debt (the capitalized lease obligation) is a no-growth perpetual debt financing instrument and the company also does not expect to grow; thus, the appropriate discount rate for the interest tax shield is the cost of debt. In this valuation context, we use the perpetual debt unlevering formula and the unlevered cost of capital is equal to

$$r_{UA} = r_E \times \frac{V_E}{V_F - V_D \times T_{INT}} + r_D \times \frac{V_D \times (1 - T_{INT})}{V_F - V_D \times T_{INT}} = r_E \times \frac{V_E}{V_E + V_D \times (1 - T_{INT})} + r_D \times \frac{V_D \times (1 - T_{INT})}{V_E + V_D \times (1 - T_{INT})}$$

$$r_{UA} = 0.2 \times \frac{\$2,700}{\$2,700 + \$1,000 \times (1 - 0.4)} + 0.10 \times \frac{\$1,000 \times (1 - 0.4)}{\$2,700 + \$1,000 \times (1 - 0.4)}$$

$$r_{UA} = 0.18182$$

Thus, as we indicated earlier, the unlevered cost of capital is now lower (remember that it was 20% when we treated the lease as an operating lease). We can now value the firm using the APV valuation. The value of the unlevered firm is $3,300 ($3,300 = $600/0.18182), and the value of the interest tax shields is $400 ($400 = $1,000 × 0.4 × 0.1/0.1); thus, the value of the firm is equal to $3,700, and the value of the equity is $2,700.

What have we learned from this simple example?

■ The value of the equity is not affected by the treatment of a lease as being either operating or capitalized, because the choice of the lease treatment does not affect the equity free cash flows of the company or the equity cost of capital.

■ The unlevered free cash flows are not equal under the two methods, because the operating lease method treats the lease cash payments as an operating activity whereas the capital lease method treats at least some of the lease cash payments as a financing activity. In more complicated settings, with leases being added in subsequent years, in any given year, the unlevered free cash flows can be higher or lower when you capitalize the leases.

■ The value of the firm under the capitalized lease method is greater than the value of the firm under the operating lease method by the value of the capitalized lease obligation.

■ The unlevered cost of capital is not the same under the two methods. Rather, the unlevered cost of capital for the capital lease method is smaller, because the capitalized lease method treats at least some of the lease cash payments as a financing activity instead of an operating activity.

One tempting conclusion to draw from this example is that given that the value of the equity is the same in both cases, it makes no difference whether we treat the lease as operating or capitalized, for the value of the equity is the same. All we have to remember is that if the leases are treated as capitalized, we must subtract the capitalized value of the leases from the value of the firm in order to calculate the value of the equity.

The above conclusion is appropriate if we can measure the equity cost of capital for the company we are valuing without using comparable companies and if the company's capital structure strategy is its existing capital structure. Our example shows that when we observe the equity cost of capital directly, both the adjusted present value and weighted average cost of capital valuation methods result in the same valuation for the value of the equity regardless of whether the company treated the lease as being capital-ized or operating. Suppose, however, that we do use comparable companies and that we first measure each comparable company's equity cost of capital and then unlever it to measure each company's unle-vered cost of capital. Even if the company we are valuing is publicly traded, this is the typical valuation context we face because we generally use comparable companies to reduce measurement error in our cost of capital estimates. Now, the situation becomes more complex because the unlevered cost of capital is affected by how the leases are treated at each firm, which has the following implications.

If the comparable companies use operating leases in the same proportions to each other and to the company we are valuing, we can ignore this issue. Any capitalized leases are part of the financing struc-ture of the company, and operating lease payments are part of the unlevered free cash flows. The fact that the companies have a mix of operating and capitalized leases causes no complication as long as the relative use of each type of leasing is the same across all companies. How do we know if the relative use of leases is the same? In order to make this assessment, we can capitalize the value of the operating leases for all relevant firms and see if the ratio of the total value of the operating leases capitalized to total firm value (including the capitalized value of the operating leases) is approximately the same across firms. However, if the comparable companies do not use operating leases in the same proportions as that of the company we are valuing, the only way to lever and unlever the cost of capital is to treat the leases of all companies as either all capitalized leases or all operating leases.

To be more specific, let us suppose that the company we are valuing uses mostly capitalized leases but also uses some operating leases, whereas the comparable companies use very different mixes of operating and capitalized leases. In this case, we would first capitalize the leases for all the companies and unlever the equity cost of capital estimates for all companies, including the company we are valuing, based on the capitalized lease treatment for all leases. To measure the *weighted average cost of debt* used in the unlever-ing, levering, and WACC formulas, we include the interest expense on the capitalized leases and treat the capitalized lease obligation as debt. To measure the value of the firm, we discount the unlevered free cash flows irrespective of whether we use the APV or WACC method, but we must calculate the unlevered free cash flows for the firm we are valuing based on the presumption that all of the leases are capitalized. Note that the value of the firm that we would measure using this process includes the capitalized value of all the lease obligations. We next demonstrate the adjustments that are necessary using AMR, Inc.

Valuation Key 11.3

Leases can be treated as being either operating or financing activities. When using comparable companies to estimate the cost of capital, it is important that we treat the leases for the comparable companies in the same way as the company being valued. It is also important to remember that the value of the firm includes the value of capitalized leases but does not include any value for operating leases. This issue also arises in other contexts whenever any cash flow can be treated as an operating activity by some companies and a financing activity by others.

REVIEW EXERCISE 11.3

Operating Versus Capitalized Leases and Valuation

In Year 0, a company entered into a perpetual lease on property. The property has a value of $5,000 at the end of Year 0, the implicit cost of debt is 9% (which is not expected to change over time), and the annual lease payment is $450 each year in perpetuity. The company expects to have revenues of $800 in Year 1 that will then grow at 2% in perpetuity and to have no other expenses apart from expenses related to the lease. In order to grow at 2% per year, the company expects to increase its leased property by 2% each year starting at the end of Year 1 (new leases will also be perpetual leases). The company's tax rate on all income is 30%. All revenues and expenses are paid in cash. The company has no assets or liabilities other than those related to the lease. Assume today is the end of Year 0. The company has an 18% equity cost of capital, and the discount rate for interest tax shields (including those from capitalized lease obligations) is equal to the unlevered cost of capital. Value the company as of the end of Year 0, assuming the company treats the lease as operating; value the company again, assuming the company treats the lease as capitalized. Prepare the company's income statement and free cash flow schedule for Year 1 for each lease treatment. Use the weighted average cost of capital, equity DCF, and APV valuation methods to value the company.

Solution on pages 468–469.

Converting from the Operating Lease Method to the Capital Lease Method

We illustrate two things. First, we illustrate how we would capitalize operating leases for the comparable companies that we might use. Second, for the company we are valuing, we demonstrate how to convert a company's financial statements and free cash flows from ones in which some of the leases are treated as operating leases and some are treated as capitalized leases to ones in which all of the leases are treated as capitalized leases. To illustrate this, we will use disclosures published by the AMR Corporation (see Valuation in Practice 11.3). We have already discussed one reason why this conversion might be important. We will discuss this conversion again in Chapter 14 when we cover market multiples. [9]

VALUATION IN PRACTICE 11.3

AMR Corporation (American Airlines)—Lease Footnote AMR's subsidiaries (American Airlines and other companies) lease various types of equipment and property—primarily aircraft and airport facilities. AMR outlined its capital and operating leases as follows.

The future minimum lease payments required under capital leases, together with the present value of such payments, and future minimum lease payments required under operating leases that have initial or remaining non-cancelable lease terms in excess of one year as of December 31, 2006, were (in millions):

Year	Capital Leases	Operating Leases
2007	$ 197	$ 1,098
2008	236	1,032
2009	175	929
2010	140	860
2011	142	855
After 2011	651	6,710
Total	$1,541	$11,484
Interest	614	
Present value	$ 927	

At December 31, 2006, the Company was operating 210 jet aircraft and 21 turboprop aircraft under operating leases and 89 jet aircraft and one turboprop aircraft under capital leases. The aircraft leases can generally be renewed at rates based on fair market value at the end of the lease term for one to five years. Some aircraft leases have purchase options at or near the end of the lease term at fair market value, but generally not to exceed a stated percentage of the defined lessor's cost of the aircraft or a predetermined fixed amount.

Source: The company operates as a scheduled passenger airline through its principal subsidiary, American Airlines, Inc. AMR Corporation is headquartered in Fort Worth, Texas, and was founded in 1934. For this footnote see AMR Corporation 2006 Form 10-K, Footnote 5, "Leases."

AMR as a Comparable Company. Let us first assume that AMR is serving as a comparable company in the valuation we are conducting. Using AMR's 2006 footnote disclosure for leases, we identify AMR's operating lease obligations for 2007 through 2011. The footnote disclosure also provides a lump sum for all lease obligations due in various years after 2011. In Exhibit 11.5, we also include the 2005 footnote disclosure for operating leases and illustrate how to measure the present value of the operating lease payments for both 2005 and 2006.[10]

---

[9] We cover the basics of lease accounting and how alternative lease treatments impact the financial statements and unlevered and equity free cash flows in the appendix to the chapter for the reader who wants more background on lease accounting before beginning the AMR example.

[10] The source of the information for the 2005 numbers is AMR Corporation 2005 Form 10-K, Footnote 5, "Leases," which we do not show in the chapter.

For the 2006 disclosure, we assume that the lease payments after 2011 will remain constant at $855 million annually until the year in which we use up the residual amount remaining of the total $6,710 million due after 2011. Thus, we assume that the lease payments are $855 million in each year from 2012 through 2018 and $725 million in 2019.[11] We assume that AMR's implicit interest rate for these leases is 7% and that the leases have an average life of 10 years. We make a similar assumption for the 2005 disclosures.

We can see from the exhibit that the present value of the lease obligations at 2005 and 2006, respectively, is $7,772.1 and $7,537.8. If AMR was a comparable company, that is all we would need to compute. We would then treat the capitalized values of the operating lease obligations as debt if we were going to unlever AMR and we would use the cost of debt of 7% we used to calculate the present value of the lease obligations. So this is straightforward and easy to do for multiple comparable companies.

EXHIBIT 11.5 | AMR Corporation (American Airlines)—Present Value of Lease Payments as of December 31, 2006, and December 31, 2005

Operating Lease Payments as of December 31, 2005 ($ in millions)				Operating Lease Payments as of December 31, 2006 ($ in millions)			
Year	**Payment**	**PV Factor**	**Present Value**	**Year**	**Payment**	**PV Factor**	**Present Value**
2006	$1,065	0.935	$ 995.3				
2007	1,039	0.873	907.5	2007	$1,098	0.935	$1,026.2
2008	973	0.816	794.3	2008	1,032	0.873	901.4
2009	872	0.763	665.2	2009	929	0.816	758.3
2010	815	0.713	581.1	2010	860	0.763	656.1
2011	815	0.666	543.1	2011	855	0.713	609.6
2012	815	0.623	507.5	2012	855	0.666	569.7
2013	815	0.582	474.3	2013	855	0.623	532.5
2014	815	0.544	443.3	2014	855	0.582	497.6
2015	815	0.508	414.3	2015	855	0.544	465.1
2016	815	0.475	387.2	2016	855	0.508	434.6
2017	815	0.444	361.9	2017	855	0.475	406.2
2018	815	0.415	338.2	2018	855	0.444	379.6
2019	815	0.388	316.1	2019	725	0.415	300.8
2020	118	0.362	42.8				
Present value as of 12/31/2005			$7,772.1	Present value as of 12/31/2006			$7,537.8
				2006 lease payment net of interest			521.0
Implicit interest rate			7.0%				$8,058.7
Implicit interest expense for 2006			$ 544.0	Present value as of 12/31/2005			7,772.1
				Present value of new leases in 2006			$ 286.64
Assumed remaining average life			10				
Lease asset amortization for 2006			$ 777.2	Rent in 2006			$1,065.0

In order to capitalize the operating leases, we must make an assumption about the implicit interest rate (cost of debt) to use for discounting the lease payments. Generally, we use a senior secured interest rate for a loan of a similar maturity (or something slightly less than that rate). As it turns out, in bankruptcy, a lessor is much more protected than a secured lender, as the lessor can take the asset back in bankruptcy, which is not necessarily true for a secured lender. We can use the interest rate that the company uses to capitalize its capitalized lease obligations.[12]

AMR as the Company Being Valued.

Now suppose that AMR was the company that we were valuing. We would need to do the same calculation for AMR again, capitalizing the leases. But we also need to determine AMR's unlevered free cash flows assuming that all leases are capitalized. One way to

---

[11] Total lease payments after 2012 are equal to $6,710 million; assuming constant $855 million lease payments, we expect the leases to continue at that amount for the next seven years (7.85 = $6,710/$855) before it becomes 0.85 of $855 million ($725 million) in the residual year, 2019.

[12] See Eisfeldt, A., and A. Rampini, "Leasing, Ability to Repossess and Debt Capacity," *Review of Financial Studies* 22 (2009), pp. 1621–1657.

do this is to recast the financial statements and recompute the unlevered free cash flows. We demonstrate this for 2006.

We use the present value of the leases as of the end of 2005 to measure both the amount of implicit interest on the leases and the amount of lease amortization in 2006. In 2006, interest on the lease obligation is equal to 7% multiplied by the December 31, 2005, present value of the leases ($544.0 = 0.07 \times$7,772.1$). Given a 10-year average life, the 2006 lease amortization is $777.2 million (see Exhibit 11.5).

We use the present value of the lease payments as of December 31, 2006 ($7,537.8 million), to measure the increase in the company's leased assets and lease obligations. We use the change in the present value of the leases—adjusted for lease payments net of implicit interest on the lease—in order to measure the present value of the new leases in 2006, which represent a capital investment in 2006. In other words the value of the new leases entered into in 2006 ($286.6) is equal to the present value of the leases as of December 31, 2006 ($7,537.8), plus the 2006 lease payments net of implicit interest ($521.0 = $1,065 − $544.0), less the present value of the leases as of December 31, 2005 ($7,772.1). The new leases will reduce the unlevered free cash flows, as they are treated as a capital expenditure.

REVIEW EXERCISE 11.4

Capitalizing Operating Leases—Part 1

Use the information in the following financial disclosures to measure the present value of the outstanding operating lease obligations as of the end of Year 0 and Year 1, assuming annual lease payments and an 8% discount rate. Also measure the present value of the additions to the lease obligations (new leases), the implicit interest on the capitalized lease obligations, and the lease asset amortization (assuming a 10-year life) for Year 1.

Year 0 Financial Disclosure				Year 1 Financial Disclosure		
Year	**Capital Leases**	**Operating Leases**		**Year**	**Capital Leases**	**Operating Leases**
Year 1	$ 800	$1,200		Year 2	$ 850	$1,100
Year 2	760	1,000		Year 3	810	990
Year 3	710	900		Year 4	760	770
Year 4	630	700		Year 5	670	660
Year 5	250	600		Year 6	270	630
After Year 5	2,000	5,400		After Year 6	2,160	5,670
Total	$5,150	$9,800		Total	$5,520	$9,820
Total interest	1,583			Total interest	1,703	
Present value	$3,567			Present value	$3,817	

Solution on page 469.

In Exhibit 11.6, we show AMR Corporation's 2006 summarized income statement and balance sheet. In the first column of the exhibit, we show the company's reported numbers. In the next five columns, we show the necessary adjustments to the company's income statement and balance sheet in order for us to capitalize its operating leases. We assume the lease interest adjustment and the lease amortization adjustment for 2006 are driven by the 2005 value of the leases upon capitalization; in other words, we assume the company capitalized its leases as of the end of 2005 by recording the capitalized lease assets and capitalized lease obligation as being the present value of the 2005 lease payments ($7772.1). This is the first adjustment we make in the exhibit, under the column labeled Beginning-of-Year Balance.

To convert the 2006 income statement so that all of the leases are capitalized, we first add back rent expense before recording interest expense and a reduction in the lease obligation (see Exhibit 11.5 for these calculations). Then, we amortize the capitalized lease asset (based on the ending 2005 balance and assuming an average 10-year remaining life), and we record the provision for income taxes, which includes adjusting for deferred income taxes (using a 38% marginal income tax rate). Even though the company has a zero income tax expense (it used its NOL carryforwards to shelter its income), we assume that the marginal tax rate for the change in the company's expenses is 38% in order to illustrate the effect of taxes in our example. That is, we will tax effect any difference in income between what AMR reported and its revised income based on the capitalization of its operating leases.

EXHIBIT 11.6 AMR Corporation—2006 Summary Income Statement and Balance Sheet with and Without Capitalizing Its Operating Leases

AMR Corporation Summarized Financial Statements ($ in millions)	2006 Reported	Beginning-of-Year Balance	Adjust Rent Expense	Amortization of Capital Lease Asset	Income Taxes	Acquistion of Additional Leases	2006 Adjusted
Income Statement							
Revenues	$22,563.0						$22,563.0
Rent expense	−1,065.0		$1,065.0				0.0
Depreciation and amortization	−1,157.0						−1,157.0
Amortization of operating leases				$−777.2			−777.2
All other operating expenses	−19,281.0						−19,281.0
Operating income	$ 1,060.0	$ 0.0	$1,065.0	$−777.2	$ 0.0	$ 0.0	$ 1,347.8
Interest expense, net	−722.0						−722.0
Miscellaneous, net	−107.0						−107.0
Lease interest			−544.0				−544.0
Income before taxes	$ 231.0	$ 0.0	$ 521.0	$−777.2	$ 0.0	$ 0.0	$ −25.3
Income taxes	0.0				97.4		97.4
Net income	$ 231.0	$ 0.0	$521.0	$−777.2	$ 97.4	$ 0.0	$ 72.1
Balance Sheet							
Current assets	$ 6,902.0						$ 6,902.0
Net property, plant, and equipment	17,941.0						17,941.0
Other assets	4,302.0						4,302.0
Deferred tax asset					$2,864.4		2,864.4
Capitalized operating leases		$7,772.1		$−777.2		$286.6	7,281.5
Total assets	$29,145.0	$7,772.1	$ 0.0	$−777.2	$2,864.4	$286.6	$39,290.9
Current operating liabilities	$ 7,156.0						$ 7,156.0
Other liabilities	9,205.0						9,205.0
Deferred tax liability					$2,767.0		2,767.0
Debt	13,390.0						13,390.0
Capitalized operating leases		$7,772.1	$ −521.0			$286.6	7,537.8
Total liabilities	$29,751.0	$7,772.1	$ −521.0	$ 0.0	$2,767.0	$286.6	$40,055.7
Shareholders' equity	−606.0		521.0	−777.2	97.4		−764.9
Total liabilities and shareholders' equity	$29,145.0	$7,772.1	$ 0.0	$−777.2	$2,864.4	$286.6	$39,290.9

Exhibit may contain small rounding errors

The income tax adjustment of $97.4 is the change in net income before tax of −256.2 (−256.2 = 521 − 777.2) multiplied by 38%. Note that in the restated financials there is a deferred tax liability of $2,767.0 ($2,767.0 = $7,281.5 ending 2006 capitalized operating lease asset × 0.38 tax rate) and a deferred tax asset of $2,864.4 ($2,864.4 = $7,537.8 ending 2006 capitalized lease liability × 0.38 tax rate), and the difference between the two is equal to the tax adjustment of $97.4, so there is no change in cash taxes paid.[13] Finally, we record the additional leases for 2006 (see Exhibit 11.5 for this calculation). Thus, as we showed previously, even though the total amount of capitalized leases at year-end decreased from $7,772.1 to $7,537.8, AMR obtained new assets under leases of $286.6 million.

We present a summary free cash flow schedule for AMR in Exhibit 11.7. This exhibit has the same columns as the previous exhibit. The first adjustment we make to the income statement and balance sheet—recording the beginning balance—is not relevant for measuring free cash flows because it does not represent a cash flow in 2006. The other adjustments all flow to the free cash flow statement. Converting from the operating lease method to the capitalized lease method has no effect on equity free cash

---

[13] Recall that a deferred tax liability exists whenever the book value of an asset for financial reporting purposes exceeds the tax basis of that asset. Since the value of the lease asset on the income tax records is zero, the value of the deferred income tax liability each year is equal to the value of the lease asset each year multiplied by the income tax rate. Similarly, a deferred tax asset exists whenever the book value of a liability for financial reporting purposes exceeds the tax basis of that asset. Here the value of the lease obligation for income tax records is zero, so the value of the deferred tax asset is equal to the value of the capitalized lease obligation multiplied by the income tax rate.

flows even though this affects net income, because the choice of method does not affect the company's equity free cash flows—however, notice that the unlevered cash flows increase from $1,296 to $1,867.6.

| **EXHIBIT 11.7** | AMR Corporation—2006 Summary Free Cash Flow Schedule | | | | | | |

AMR Corporation Summarized Free Cash Flow Schedule ($ in millions)	2006 Reported	Adjust Rent Expense	Amortization of Capital Lease Asset	Income Taxes	Acquistion of Additional Leases	2006 Adjusted
Earnings before interest and taxes (EBIT)	$ 953.0	$1,065.0	$−777.2			$1,240.8
− Income taxes paid on EBIT	0.0			$−109.4		−109.4
Earnings before interest and after taxes	$ 953.0	$1,065.0	$−777.2	$−109.4	$ 0.0	$1,131.4
+ Depreciation and amortization	1,157.0					1,157.0
+ Amortization of operating leases			777.2			777.2
− Change in net working capital	450.0					450.0
+ Change in non-current liabilities and other	101.0			−97.4		3.6
− Change in required cash balance	0.0					0.0
Unlevered cash flow from operations	$2,661.0	$1,065.0	$ 0.0	$−206.7	$ 0.0	$3,519.3
− Capital expenditures (net)	−1,365.0					−1,365.0
− Increase in capital lease assets					−286.6	−286.6
Unlevered free cash flow	$1,296.0	$1,065.0	$ 0.0	$−206.7	$−286.6	$1,867.6
− Interest paid	−722.0	−544.0				−1,266.0
+ Interest tax shield				206.7		206.7
+ Change in non-common equity	−821.0	−521.0				−1,342.0
+ Change in capital lease obligations					286.6	286.6
Free cash flow to common equity	$−247.0	$ 0.0	$ 0.0	$ 0.0	$ 0.0	$ −247.0
+ Change in common and other	230.0					230.0
− Common dividends and repurchases						0.0
Change in excess cash	$ −17.0	$ 0.0	$ 0.0	$ 0.0	$ 0.0	$ −17.0
+ Change in required cash balance	0.0					0.0
Change in cash balance	$ −17.0	$ 0.0	$ 0.0	$ 0.0	$ 0.0	$ −17.0

Exhibit may contain small rounding errors

These adjustments affect unlevered free cash flows because rent expense is an operating expense and decreases unlevered free cash flow, whereas interest and the repayment of the capitalized lease obligation are financing related and do not affect unlevered free cash flows. We also adjust the unlevered free cash flows for the increase in the capitalized lease asset, which we treat as a capital expenditure.

Effectively, what we do is increase the unlevered free cash flows for the lease expense and then decrease it for the increase in capitalized lease assets (essentially the present value of new leases) and then decrease it for the tax shield on the implicit interest expense. In our example, the unlevered free cash flows as adjusted are $1,867.6 ($1,867.6 = $1,296.0 + $1,065 − 0.38 × $544 − $286.6). As such, we need not recast the entire financial statements to make these adjustments. Since rent expense can be larger than or smaller than the present value of new leases when many assets are leased, the effect on unlevered free cash flows can be either positive (which it is for AMR) or negative.[14]

Valuation Key 11.4

When we unlever comparable companies to determine the cost of capital for the company of interest, we need to make sure that the treatment of the leases for the company being valued and the comparable companies is the same—if that is not true, we must make appropriate adjustments.

---

[14] We have seen most of the numbers in the table before, but it is worth discussing a few of the tax numbers. The adjustment to income taxes on EBIT (−109.4) is calculated as 38% multiplied by the net rent expense (1,065.0) minus amortization of the leased asset (777.2). The adjustment to the line "Non-Current Liabilities and Other" (−97.4) is the net change in the deferred tax asset and liability from Exhibit 11.6. The sum of these two tax adjustments (−109.4 and −97.4) is −206.7, which is equal to the absolute value of the interest tax shield on the implicit interest (544.0 × 0.38).

REVIEW EXERCISE 11.5

Capitalizing Operating Leases—Part 2

Use the information presented in Review Exercise 11.4 and the following financial information to restate the company's Year 1 income statement, balance sheet, and free cash flow schedule so that all operating leases are capitalized as of the end of Year 0 and onward. The company's income tax rate is 40% on all income.

Summarized Financial Statements	Year 1 Reported
Income Statement	
Revenues	$22,000.0
Rent expense	−2,000.0
Depreciation and amortization	−3,000.0
Amortization of operating leases	0.0
All other operating expenses	−10,000.0
Operating income	$ 7,000.0
Interest expense	−1,000.0
Lease interest	0.0
Income before taxes	$ 6,000.0
Income taxes	−2,400.0
Net income	$ 3,600.0
Balance Sheet	
Current assets	$ 8,000.0
Net property, plant, and equipment	20,000.0
Other assets	5,000.0
Deferred tax asset	0.0
Capitalized operating leases	0.0
Total assets	$33,000.0
Current operating liabilities	$ 7,000.0
Other liabilities	10,000.0
Deferred tax liability	0.0
Debt	13,000.0
Capitalized operating leases	0.0
Total liabilities	$30,000.0
Shareholders' equity	3,000.0
Total liabilities and shareholders' equity	$33,000.0

Summarized Free Cash Flow Schedule	Year 1 Reported
Earnings before interest and taxes (EBIT)	$7,000.0
− Income taxes paid on EBIT	−2,800.0
Earnings before interest and after taxes	$4,200.0
+ Depreciation and amortization	3,000.0
+ Amortization of operating leases	0.0
− Change in net working capital	500.0
+ Change in non-current liabilities and other	100.0
− Change in required cash balance	−50.0
Unlevered cash flow from operations	$7,750.0
− Capital expenditures (net)	−3,000.0
− Increase in capital lease assets	0.0
Unlevered free cash flow	$4,750.0
− Interest paid	−1,000.0
+ Interest tax shield	400.0
+ Change in non-common equity	0.0
+ Change in capital lease obligations	0.0
Free cash flow to common equity	$4,150.0

Solution on page 470.

The Lease Valuation Issue Applies to Other Circumstances

This same valuation issue arises whenever companies have a choice between characterizing a cash flow as either an operating activity or a financing activity—just as they do in the case of leases. Even if accounting rules require companies to use a specific accounting method in a given circumstance, companies still have some discretion. For example, conditional on the characteristics of a lease contract, accounting rules typically determine whether or not a lease must be capitalized. However, companies often have discretion over the characteristics of the lease contract, and hence they have discretion over whether or not a lease must be capitalized. In addition, cross-country differences in accounting rules may create situations in which the treatments are different.

We now consider the case of pensions under U.S. GAAP. Under U.S. GAAP, pension expense is treated as an operating expense even though it includes an implicit interest component. Thus, the interest component of pension expense is not reported as interest expense in the financial statements. As such, without adjusting the financial statements and free cash flows, the pension liability must be treated as an operating liability—not debt—in order to be consistent with the income statement treatment. However, consider a case where two companies are identical in all respects (including their pension obligations), but one company has a pension liability, and the other company fully funds its pension plan obligation by issuing debt. In essence, the latter company converts its operating liability into a financing liability. If we unlever the equity costs of capital for these two companies, the unlevered cost of capital will not be the same because for the company showing the pension liability, we treat the pension liability as an operating liability, not a financing activity.

If we adjust the reported numbers to treat the pension liability as a financing activity and unlever accordingly, the two companies will have the same unlevered cost of capital. In general, we cannot observe if a company makes this type of trade-off, so if this is an important issue, we make an adjustment similar to the adjustment we make for leases—in essence, we convert the operating liability into a financing liability to ensure consistent treatment between the comparable companies and the company we are valuing. As was the case in the lease example, this adjustment requires us to treat the pension liability as debt and back out the interest expense component of the pension expense and treat it as interest expense in order to calculate the weighted average cost of debt for any comparable companies. In addition, for the company we are valuing, we need to adjust the unlevered free cash flows by treating the interest expense component of the pension expense as interest expense—not as an operating expense as is done in the financial statements. For obvious reasons, this affects the unlevered free cash flows. A similar issue might arise with post-retirement benefits. While many companies do not even partially fund their post-retirement benefits (and unlike the case for pensions, even partial funding is not required by law), some companies at least partially fund these liabilities.

11.4 SITUATIONS WHEN THE WEIGHTED AVERAGE COST OF CAPITAL CANNOT VALUE THE INTEREST TAX SHIELDS CORRECTLY

LO3 Identify when to avoid using the WACC valuation method

In certain situations, the weighted average cost of capital method cannot correctly value the interest tax shields. In these situations, we can solve the problem by using the adjusted present value method. In this section, we discuss certain topics we have discussed before, but do so in the context of the weighted average cost of capital's inability to value the tax shields correctly. The issues we discuss are net operating losses, paid-in-kind interest subject to AHYDO (applicable high-yield discount obligation) rules, **capitalized interest**, and certain circumstances in which the current cost of debt is not equal to the cost of debt at the time of debt issuance.

Net Operating Losses

In Chapter 3, we discussed the treatment of net operating losses (NOLs) and how to identify when a company with NOLs will get the tax benefit of its interest deduction. Among other things, we learned that NOLs can cause a large timing difference between when the company receives its interest tax shield benefits and when it pays (or accrues) the interest. The weighted average cost of capital method cannot handle this complexity, and we cannot easily address this issue by making an assumption about the income tax rate used in the weighted average cost of capital formula. For example, if we assume that the tax rate is zero in periods when the company is using its NOL, we assume that the interest in these periods will never be deductible. If we set the tax rate at the marginal tax rate that the company will face when it returns to profitability, we are assuming the company is that profitable now. The easiest way to value a company in such situations is to use the techniques from Chapter 3 to model the period-by-period timing and magnitude of the interest tax shields and to use the adjusted present value method until the net operating losses have been used up. Once the net operating losses have been fully utilized, we can switch to a weighted average cost of capital valuation if it is desirable to do so.

In weighted average cost of capital DCF valuations, practitioners sometimes attempt to deal with NOL carryforwards by first using the weighted average cost of capital to discount the unlevered free cash flows that are not properly adjusted for the income tax effects of the NOL carryforwards. They then add the present value of the tax savings on the unlevered free cash flows from the NOL carryforwards. While this approach can be used to determine the effect of the NOLs on the unlevered free cash flows, it does not measure the value of the interest tax shields correctly and, as such, is just an approximation.

Capitalized Interest

Certain circumstances require interest to be capitalized, in which case it cannot be expensed in the period it is paid or accrued for both financial reporting and tax purposes. In this situation, the capitalized interest is attached to the value of an asset—for example, a building or work-in-process inventory. When interest is capitalized to the carrying value of a building during its construction phase, some of the subsequent depreciation expense on that building will be the result of the capitalized interest. For work-in-process inventory, the capitalized interest will be added to the carrying value of the inventory, and eventually, it will be expensed through cost of goods sold. For example, if it takes five years to build a yacht that is later sold, the interest is capitalized for five years and then is expensed as part of cost of goods sold.

It should be apparent that the capitalization of interest causes a timing difference between when the interest is paid or accrued and when the tax benefit from the interest is received. Note that the interest will never be shown as interest expense on the financial statements, but this is irrelevant. What is relevant is the timing difference between when the benefit of the interest is received relative to when it is paid or accrued. Since there is, again, a timing difference between when the interest is paid and when the interest is actually deductible, the weighted average cost of capital method cannot handle the timing appropriately; however, the adjusted present value method can. Of course, if the amount of the capitalized interest is small, it is unlikely that it will lead to a very large valuation error. On another note, we only need worry about interest that is capitalized in the forecast period of our valuation. Any capitalized interest from the past will simply show up in depreciation expense or cost of goods sold, but this is not a problem for the WACC method, for any capitalized interest from prior to the date of the valuation is just an asset that the firm has as of the valuation date, and it is not dependent on debt financing subsequent to the date of the valuation.

Paid-in-Kind Interest

In this section we discuss **paid-in-kind interest** (or **PIK interest**), which is when interest is simple accrued and not paid until a future period—which could be in a few years or not until the debt matures. The interest that is accrued, but not paid, is added to the principal amount of the loan. For financial reporting purposes, we charge the interest accrued on the **paid-in-kind debt** (or **zero coupon debt**) as interest expense in every period even though it is not paid. In many situations, paid-in-kind interest is tax deductible in the period in which it is expensed for financial reporting purposes. In these cases, the weighted average cost of capital has no problem valuing the tax shields correctly. We would simply include the PIK debt as part of the capital structure when we compute the weighted average cost of debt and capital structure ratios.

There are, however, certain circumstances where paid-in-kind interest is not tax deductible. The U.S. income tax code has a provision called the **AHYDO (applicable high-yield discount obligation)** rules. This provision potentially postpones the tax benefits of paid-in-kind interest until the interest is paid-in-cash (often at maturity, but possibly sooner) or can even convert the interest into dividends, meaning the interest will never be deductible.

If the rules apply, and the interest tax shield is postponed until it is paid in cash, the weighted average cost of capital method will not value the interest tax shields correctly. If we include the paid-in-kind debt in the capital structure as debt, and if the cost of that debt is used in calculating the weighted average cost of debt, the weighted average cost of capital will presume the interest is deductible in that period. Again, the adjusted present value method can handle this complexity based on when the interest deductions will actually be taken. Further, any PIK interest that will be treated as a dividend will not generate any interest tax shield and can just be ignored in an APV valuation.

Current Cost of Debt Is Not the Same as the Effective Interest Rate

The weighted average cost of capital method relies on the notion that the current cost of debt multiplied by the value of debt results in expected interest tax shields. If the cost of debt at the time of debt issuance differs from the current cost of debt due to shifts in inflation or due to shifts in required real returns on a risk-free asset, the WACC DCF method as normally applied may not value the interest tax shields correctly. We do not discuss this issue in detail here, as we discussed it to some extent in Chapter 10, but one can readily understand that when we measure the weighted average cost of capital using the current cost and value of debt, it may not properly reflect the value of the tax shields in these circumstances.

Generally, this error should be small since the change in the cost of debt is offset by a change in the market value of the debt if the cost of debt shifts. For example, if a company issues debt at face value and then inflation increases and investors demand a higher rate of return on the debt, the cost of debt will go up, but the value of the debt will fall. Conversely, if the cost of debt has fallen since the debt was issued, the market value of the debt will rise. As such, while the new cost of debt times the value of the debt may not exactly equal the expected interest tax shields, the error is likely to be small. If we ever think this issue could lead to significant errors in our valuation, the easiest approach is to use the APV valuation method and compute the period-by-period interest tax shields based on the true expected interest tax shields, not the current cost of debt multiplied by the value of debt. We would continue using the APV method until such time as all the affected debt is retired. At that point, one can switch to the WACC valuation method if it is desirable to do so.

Valuation Key 11.5

In situations such as when a company has net operating loss carryforwards, capitalized interest, pay-in-kind debt subject to AHYDO rules, and when the current cost of debt multiplied by the value of the debt does not equal the expected interest tax shields, the WACC valuation method cannot incorporate the present value of the interest tax shields correctly. In all of these cases, if the effect is likely to be material, we can value the interest tax shields correctly by using the APV valuation method.

11.5 THE INCOME TAX RATE

LO4 Measure the income tax rate for interest tax shields

As we discussed in previous chapters, in any given period, a company's interest tax shield is equal to the reduction in income taxes that results from the company's interest expense deduction for that period. Conceptually, it is the difference between the income tax a company would pay if it had no interest expense deduction and the actual income tax the company pays. Even though the concept is straightforward, we are unable to observe a company's interest tax shield directly; it does not appear in the company's financial statements or income tax filings. Since we cannot observe a company's interest tax shield directly, we typically estimate it by multiplying the company's interest expense deduction by an income tax rate we believe measures the company's interest tax shield, T_{INT}. This is an implicit income tax rate—not an income tax rate set by the government. This income tax rate depends on both the cumulative effect of complex tax laws and regulations and a company's particular income tax situation at a specific point in time. Ignoring issues that arise due to personal income taxes for a moment (more on this later), the same issues exist for the income tax rate used in the weighted average cost of capital calculation, and we typically assume that the rates measuring interest tax shields and the weighted average cost of capital are the same.

If we have the necessary information, we can measure the implied income tax rate that measures a company's interest tax shield, T_{INT}, by dividing a company's interest tax shield by its interest expense deduction. While we do not generally have the information to perform that hypothetical calculation, it is a useful frame of reference to help understand what we are trying to measure. The implied income tax rate that we use to measure a company's after-tax cost of debt depends on a variety of factors. Tax rules can create complexities in measuring the appropriate tax rate to use for estimating a company's interest tax shields, for example, complexities created by net operating losses. This tax rate may not be the marginal tax rate on the company's taxable income; in fact, it can even be a tax rate that exceeds the company's marginal tax rate if the tax code has graduated corporate tax rates and if the interest expense keeps the company out of the next highest tax bracket. Alternatively, these factors can reduce the income tax rate below the statutory income tax rate. In this section, we discuss some of these factors.[15]

Before we begin, we also note that many of these issues are relevant for assessing the taxes that the organization will pay on its overall taxable income. While we discussed many of these complications previously in Chapter 3, we will also relate these topics back to the issues discussed in Chapter 3 regarding the measurement of the relevant free cash flows.

---

[15] For an extensive review of the academic literature on this topic, see Shackelford, D., and T. Shevlin, "Empirical Tax Research in Accounting," *Journal of Accounting and Economics* 31 (2001), pp. 321–387; and Graham, J. R., "Taxes and Corporate Finance: A Review," *Review of Financial Studies* 16 (2003), pp. 1074–1128.

Additional Factors that Affect the Income Tax Rates

Various factors affect the implied income tax rate we use to measure a company's interest tax shields and taxes due. In this section, we discuss progressivity in corporate income tax rates, the alternative minimum tax, income tax credits, and state and local taxes.[16] In addition to these factors, we incorporate the probability of the company actually capturing the benefit of its interest tax shields when we forecast the company's interest tax shields. While foreign taxes are important and potentially confusing for valuing multinational companies, we postpone our discussion of that topic until the last chapter of the book, where we discuss valuing cross-border acquisitions and multinational valuation.

Progressive Corporate Income Tax Rates.

Currently, U.S. statutory tax rates are generally progressive at low levels of income; for example, the statutory income tax rate is 15% for taxable income up to $50,000 and 25% for taxable income greater than $50,000 and less than $75,000. A company with $60,000 of income would face a total tax bill of $10,000 [$10,000 = 0.15 (50,000) + 0.25 (10,000)]. Between $75,000 and $100,000 of taxable income, the tax rate is 34%, and between $100,000 and $335,000, the tax rate is 39%. The increased tax rate between $100,000 and $335,000 essentially means that if a company has $335,000 dollars in income, it is effectively paying 34% on all its income [0.34 = ($50,000 × 0.15 + $25,000 × 0.25 + $25,000 × 0.34 + $235,000 × 0.39)/$335,000] on all of its taxable income. Of course, the effect of this graduated rate means that, within certain ranges of income, a company might actually have a tax rate for its interest tax shields, T_{INT}, of 39%. For example if a company had $100,000 of taxable income and its deductions included $50,000 of interest expense, the interest tax shield would be $19,500 ($19,500 = 0.39 × 50,000).[17] It should also be obvious that we need to take into consideration the progressivity of the tax law in calculating the taxes we use in measuring the unlevered free cash flows.

Alternative Minimum Tax.

U.S. tax laws instituted the **alternative minimum tax (AMT)** in 1986 to ensure that all companies paid some minimum amount of income taxes.[18] To calculate the AMT, companies cannot deduct certain amounts of tax preference items, such as accelerated depreciation. Not allowing certain tax preference deductions increases a company's taxable income, which results in more companies having positive taxable income than under the regular definition of a corporation's taxable income. While the AMT computation of taxable income is higher, the AMT has a lower income tax rate, 20%. If a company pays income taxes as a result of any AMT owed (relative to what it would have paid under the regular tax system), it can offset the additional income taxes from the AMT calculation in future years against income taxes owed using the regular method (this AMT carryforward is indefinite). If a company's income tax due is based on the AMT, its federal statutory rate is only 20% instead of the usual 35% statutory tax rate, and thus its T_{INT} will be 20% in a year it is paying its taxes using the AMT. Moreover, to calculate the unlevered free cash flows for a firm subject to the AMT in some years, we would have to base the tax calculation for the year on the definition of taxable income under the AMT and the lower 20% tax rate.

Tax Credits.

Income tax credits reduce the amount of income taxes a company must pay on a dollar-for-dollar basis; that is, for every dollar of income tax credit, the taxpayer reduces income taxes due by a dollar. Examples of income tax credits allowed by U.S. tax law include research and development tax credits, foreign tax credits, various tax credits for investing in renewable energy (such as wind and solar power), and alternative minimum tax credits. Research and development tax credits provide incentives for companies to engage in these activities by providing a 20% tax credit for research and development

---

[16] For a more detailed discussion of these factors, see, Graham, J. R., and M. Lemmon, "Measuring Corporate Tax Rates and Tax Incentives: A New Approach," *Journal of Applied Corporate Finance* 11 (1998), pp. 54–65.

[17] The progressiveness of U.S. tax rates continues. For taxable income between $335,000 and $10 million, the tax rate is 34%; between $10 million and $15 million of taxable income, the tax rate is 35%; and between $15 million and $18.333 million of taxable income, the tax rate is 38% (which effectively means that the company pays a 35% tax rate on all taxable income if taxable income is at least 18.333 million). Again, in this range, T_{INT} would be 38%. Afterward, the statutory income tax rate is a constant 35%. The statutory tax rate is the income tax rate set by the government on taxable income. In most of our discussion, we assume that governments have one statutory tax rate in order to reduce the complexity of the calculations.

[18] Prior to this, the financial press publicized some instances in which companies used tax preference items such as accelerated depreciation to reduce their income taxes to or close to $0. For a more detailed discussion of this topic, see Manzon, G., "Earnings Management of Firms Subject to the Alternative Minimum Tax," *Journal of the American Taxation Association* 14 (1992), pp. 88–111.

expenditures above a certain base. Previously, U.S. tax laws also provided for investment tax credits. At one time, investment tax credits provided incentives for companies to purchase qualified assets by providing as high as a 10% tax credit on the amount spent on qualifying purchases (various types of fixed assets). Naturally, a company might not have sufficient income taxes to use its tax credits in the year it earns them. In most cases, tax credits can be carried forward against taxes in future years.

As we discussed in Chapter 3, tax credits reduce a company's effective tax rate, and these credits always affect the reconciliation between the federal statutory tax rate and the company's effective tax rate, which is what companies must report in their tax footnote. Tax credits do not generally affect the income tax rate used to value the interest tax shields unless they reduce the taxes that the company has to pay to zero (before the consideration of interest expense) or make the interest expense not fully deductible after they are considered. As we discussed in Chapter 3, the tax credits a company has and that are part of the reconciliation between the statutory and effective rate are important to consider in calculating the unlevered free cash flows.

State and Local Income Taxes. In most states and in some municipalities in the United States, companies pay state and local government income taxes. State and local income taxes have the effect of increasing a company's income taxes. This effect is less than a dollar for each dollar of tax paid to state and local governments, for in general, these income taxes are deductible when calculating federal income taxes. For example, a 10% state income tax rate that is deductible for federal income taxes, assuming the relevant federal income tax rate is 35%, is effectively a 6.5% income tax rate $[0.065 = 0.1 \times (1 - 0.35)]$ above the federal statutory tax rate. As discussed in Chapter 3, the reconciliation between the statutory and effective tax rates always shows the effects of state and local taxes net of the federal tax benefit.

Interest expense is generally tax deductible on state tax returns, so the tax rate used to calculate the after-tax cost of debt includes federal, state, and local taxes. In the absence of more detailed knowledge, many estimate the tax rate for the interest tax shields to be the federal statutory tax rate plus the effect of state and local income taxes, net of the federal tax benefit that is reported in the reconciliation of the federal statutory tax rate to the effective tax rate (ignoring foreign taxes for now). The state and local tax rates that are observable in the reconciliation represent average state and local tax rates—not marginal tax rates. Thus, if a company is doing business in states with a progressive corporate tax structure, it is feasible that using the effect of state and local tax rates that appears in the reconciliation undervalues the interest tax shields slightly, as it does not capture the marginal tax rate of the state and local taxes. In computing a company's unlevered free cash flows, we would of course take into consideration state and local taxes.

Valuation Key 11.6

The calculation of the appropriate tax rate with which to assess the benefit of interest tax shields, T_{INT}, is a potentially complex calculation. Because of progressive tax structures, state and local taxes, the alternative minimum tax, and tax credits, it is often appropriate to use a tax rate that differs from the federal statutory tax rate when estimating the weighted average cost of capital. These same items impact how we compute the taxes due when measuring the unlevered free cash flows.

Evidence on the Use of the Highest Federal Statutory Tax Rate to Estimate the Tax Rate for Interest Tax Shields, T_{INT}

Valuation practitioners often measure the tax rate for interest tax shields and the weighted average cost of capital, T_{INT}, using the highest federal statutory tax rate plus the after-tax effect of state and local taxes (which we call the combined statutory rate). If it is possible that the company may experience losses in future years (at least with some positive probability), the expected tax rate will be less than the combined statutory rate.

Shevlin (1987, 1990) and Graham (1996a, 1996b) conducted the early research on estimating a company's marginal income tax rate.[19] A recent article by Blouin, Core, and Guay (2010) provides more

---

[19] See Shevlin, T., "Taxes and Off-Balance Sheet Financing: Research and Development Limited Partnerships," *The Accounting Review* 62 (1987), pp. 480–509; Shevlin, T., "Estimating Corporate Marginal Tax Rates with Asymmetric Tax Treatment of Gains and Losses," *The Journal of the American Taxation Association* 12 (1990), pp. 51–67; Graham, J. R., "Debt and the Marginal Tax Rate," *Journal of Financial Economics* 41 (1996a), pp. 41–73; and Graham, J. R., "Proxies for the Corporate Marginal Tax Rate," *Journal of Financial Economics* 42 (1996b), pp. 187–221.

recent evidence on this issue and extends the earlier research of Shevlin and Graham.[20] These (and other) researchers provide extensive empirical evidence that marginal federal income tax rates are often less than the company's federal statutory income tax rate (it should be noted that these researchers ignore state and local taxes in performing their calculations).

The authors of these studies define the marginal tax rate differently than we do in this book; they define it "as the present value of the current plus future taxes to be paid on an additional dollar of current period income."[21] For example, if the company has an additional dollar of income this year and pays $0.35 with the expectation that it will not get back any part of this tax in the future, then the present value tax rate will be 35% (the statutory tax rate). However, suppose there is a possibility that in the following year, the company will have a large loss and that the company will use its loss to get a refund of its taxes from the prior year. In this case, the present value of the taxes paid on this income will be less than $0.35.

In discounted cash flow models, rather than calculate the present value of the income taxes separately, we measure the annual income tax effects and calculate the present value of the after-tax free cash flows. However, this definitional difference is not important to the implications of the overall findings we can glean from this research.[22]

Blouin, Core, and Guay (2010) find that the median publicly traded firm faces a present value weighted average tax rate of 32.2%; however, 10% of publicly traded firms face present value weighted tax rates of 8.8% or less, and another 15% of these firms face present value weighted average tax rates of 8.8% to 18.2%. As such, about one-fourth of the publicly traded firms have a present value weighted average tax rate that is approximately half the statutory rate or less. Smaller-size companies, companies reporting current losses, and companies with net operating losses are much more likely to not face the top marginal tax rates than large, profitable companies without net operating losses. Thus, at least for some firms, using the top federal statutory tax rate on all years to calculate the interest tax shields can misstate the value of the interest tax shields as well as the after-tax cash flows.

As stated earlier, we do not use present value weighted average tax rates like these, but the empirical evidence we just discussed is informative. In particular, this research suggests that a large number of companies will not pay taxes at the top marginal tax rate, and hence the value of the interest tax shields need not necessarily be estimated using the top marginal tax rates. This affects the taxes paid on other income as well. Thus, we should consider alternative scenarios, and at least for some companies, some of these scenarios will anticipate future losses, which will affect the calculation of the taxes, the value of the interest tax shields, and, as a result, the value of the firm.

Valuation Key 11.7

The extant empirical evidence suggests that for some companies, expected interest tax shields should not be based on the top statutory rate. Rather, the expected interest tax shield calculation for some companies should be based on scenarios where the interest is not deductible at the top statutory rate and may even be postponed because of NOLs. The same is true, of course, for measuring the unlevered free cash flows.

11.6 OTHER FACTORS THAT AFFECT A COMPANY'S COSTS OF CAPITAL

A review of both the extant research and the valuations of practitioners suggests that academic and practicing valuation experts believe that financial leverage increases the value of the firm. However, the effects of capital structure decisions on the value of a firm and its costs of capital are complex and far

LO5 Identify the other factors that affect the value of financing

---

[20] See Blouin, J., J. Core, and W. Guay, "Are Firms Under-Leveraged? Evidence from Improved Estimates of Marginal Tax Rates," *Journal of Financial Economics* (November 2010), pp. 195–213.

[21] See page 56 of Graham, J. R., and M. Lemmon, "Measuring Corporate Tax Rates and Tax Incentives: A New Approach," *Journal of Applied Corporate Finance* 11 (1998), pp. 54–65.

[22] The methodology of this research takes into consideration the complexity of the tax code, including such things as the progressiveness of the U.S. tax structure, net operating loss carrybacks and carryforwards (NOLs), tax credits, the alternative minimum tax, and other factors. In addition to the complexity of the tax code, the researchers also take into consideration forecasts of future income based on the volatility and mean reversion of a company's historical earnings. This allows these researchers to measure the present value of additional taxes paid on an additional dollar of current income.

from resolved. In the remainder of this chapter, we discuss factors other than interest tax shields that result from a company's capital structure decisions that may affect the value of the company. In this section, we provide an overview of these factors.[23]

- **Personal Income Taxes:** So far, we have assumed that personal income taxes do not affect our calculations. This assumption holds if investors do not pay income taxes on their investment income or if investors are taxed equally on all forms of income (interest, dividends, and capital gains). Since personal income taxes paid on investment income affects investor wealth, personal income taxes are relevant to the returns that investors will demand on different assets. Personal income taxes can also have an impact on the extent that debt in the capital structure increases the value of the firm. In particular, personal income taxes may reduce the benefits of debt. We discuss this issue in more detail in a later section.

- **Financial Distress Costs:** Financial distress costs take into account how the cash flows and costs of capital of a company are impacted by suppliers, customers, and capital suppliers for a company with a high probability of experiencing financial distress. If the financial distress leads to bankruptcy, the cost of going bankrupt is also part of these costs. The costs of bankruptcy equal the difference in the value of a company's assets before it goes bankrupt and after it emerges from bankruptcy or liquidates. The costs of bankruptcy include the impact of all the legal, accounting, consulting, and other fees involved in the bankruptcy process as well as the indirect costs of bankruptcy from operating inefficiently while in bankruptcy. We discuss this in more detail in a later section.

- **Agency Costs from Debt:** Conflicts of interest between debtholders and owners and managers can create costs from issuing debt, because those conflicts of interest need to be monitored and mitigated. For example, debtholders might be concerned that the firm will issue debt and then make a large distribution to shareholders instead of investing in the company. Or the company could decide to issue a lot of additional debt that will make the existing debt less valuable. Thus, the debtholders will be concerned that the equityholders can take actions that will reduce the value of their debt claims. Debtholders either charge for the expected losses from such actions or the company writes a contract (a bond indenture) that precludes it from taking certain actions (such as selling off assets and distributing the proceeds to the equityholders or issuing additional debt). These contracts restrict the actions the company can take to hurt the debtholders and result in a lower cost of debt. The agency costs associated with issuing debt increase with the amount of leverage, and these costs can reduce the net benefits of debt.[24]

- **Manager–Owner Conflicts (Agency Costs):** In Chapter 5, we focused our discussion on interest tax shields for a company with one investor/manager. Once we have different owners and managers, conflicts of interest can arise between them. It is possible that issuing debt is one way to reduce these conflicts. One way for managers to ensure that large free cash flows are paid out to shareholders instead of being invested in unprofitable projects is to issue a large amount of debt, pay a one-time dividend, or announce a share repurchase program; this way, the large free cash flows must go to service the debt. This provides managers with the incentive to make sure that the firm continues to produce free cash flows and to make decisions that will have positive effects on firm value.[25]

- **Information (Pecking Order), Product Market, and Industry Influences:**[26] If managers have more information than investors (asymmetric information in favor of managers), investors can interpret the managers' decision to issue more debt or equity as a signal of the future expected performance of the company. For example, issuing debt can imply that the managers believe the stock is undervalued, and issuing equity can indicate that the stock is overvalued. On the other hand, if

---

[23] See Rajan and Zingales (1995), Miller (1989), and Myers (2001) for reviews of this issue and literature; Rajan, R. G., and L. Zingales, "What Do We Know About Capital Structure? Some Evidence from International Data," *Journal of Finance* 50 (December 1995), pp. 1421–1460; Miller, M. H., "The Modigliani-Miller Propositions After Thirty Years," *Journal of Applied Corporate Finance* vol. 2, no. 1, (Spring 1989), pp. 6–18; and Myers, S. C., "Capital Structure," *Journal of Economic Perspectives* vol. 15, no. 2 (Spring 2001), pp. 81–102.

[24] See Jensen, M. C., and W. H. Meckling, "Theory of the Firm: Managerial Behavior, Agency Costs and Capital Structure," *Journal of Financial Economics* (1976), pp. 305–360.

[25] See Jensen, M. C., "Agency Costs of Free Cash Flow, Corporate Finance and Takeovers," *American Economic Review* 76 (1986), pp. 323–329.

[26] See Myers, S. C., and N. S. Majluf, "Corporate Financing and Investment Decisions When Firms Have Information That Investors Do Not Have," *Journal of Financial Economics* vol. 13, no. 2 (1984), pp. 187–221.

managers have more information than investors, all securities issued to external markets for additional financing may be undervalued. Thus, to the extent that it is practicable, managers tend to use internally generated funds first before issuing securities externally. Debt will then be the next source of funds, for the asymmetric information is likely to have a smaller effect on the pricing of debt than on the pricing of equity. One explanation for why capital structures differ across industries is that certain characteristics of a product, market, or industry can affect a company's choice of capital structure. For example, companies operating in industries with more stable cash flows or with assets that are relatively easy to secure will likely operate with greater leverage. To the extent that there is a tax advantage to debt, the differences in industry capital structure will be one reason for differences in the cost of capital across industries. For obvious reasons, differences in business risk are also an important factor.

11.7 THE EFFECT OF PERSONAL INCOME TAXES

So far, we have assumed that the income tax rate used to value a company's interest tax shields is equal to the company's income tax rate in the weighted average cost of capital formula, T_{INT}. In this section, we begin to introduce the effect of personal income taxes, which can result in different tax rates for measuring the value of interest tax shields than are used in measuring the weighted average cost of capital.

Before 1977, the literature on capital structure assumed personal income tax rates were zero or identical for all types of income. In 1977, Merton Miller published a study that added personal income taxes to the M-M framework.[27] In this section, we discuss the implications of Miller's research as well as that of others regarding the effect of personal income taxes on the value of a company's interest tax shields.[28] The effect of personal income taxes on the value of interest tax shields—and consequently, on the value of the firm—is still unresolved. We discuss this topic despite the fact that this issue is unresolved and despite the fact that we do not have very practical ways to implement the theory that exists. Even though we cannot provide a practical implementation for this topic, we believe given the current tax codes in the United States and in many other countries, it is important to understand that the value of interest tax shields may be mitigated by the effect of personal income taxes. Understanding the theory and implications provides a framework for thinking about how to value interest tax shields and provides a cautionary note to avoid being too aggressive in valuing interest tax shields. This is an area where future research will likely help to resolve this issue.

How do personal taxes affect the value of a company? Naturally, investors care about the returns on their investments after paying all income taxes, including personal income taxes. Miller showed, among other things, that investors will adjust rates of returns on different investments (e.g., equity, debt, preferred stock) so that investments with the same risk will have the same expected return to the investor (after adjusting for personal income taxes). If two investments have the same risk, but if the incomes from the investments have different personal income tax rates, then investors will gross-up (or increase) the expected return on the investment with the higher tax rate so that after personal income taxes, the two investments have the same expected return. For example, we know tax-exempt bonds (say, municipal or state bonds) have lower interest rates than taxable bonds with the same risk. The tax-exempt bonds have lower rates because the income received from tax-exempt bonds is not taxed to the investor; thus investors do not demand as high a rate of return as they do with taxable bonds. With this in mind, Miller shows that under certain assumptions, the tax advantage of debt can be mitigated or even become zero.

An Analysis of the Effect of Personal Taxes Based on Miller

With the introduction of personal taxes, we assume that investors are interested in after-tax wealth. Hence, the company is interested in structuring its capital structure to maximize the after-tax returns to its claimants for a given level of risk. Since interest is deductible at the corporate level, companies do not pay taxes

---

[27] Miller, M. H., "Debt and Taxes," *Journal of Finance* 32 (1977), pp. 261–275.

[28] See DeAngelo and Masulis (1980) and Kim (1989) for discussions of this point; DeAngelo, H., and R. W. Masulis, "Optimal Capital Structure Under Corporate and Personal Taxation," *Journal of Financial Economics* 8 (1980), pp. 3–29; and Kim, E. H., "Optimal Capital Structure in Miller's Equilibrium," in S. Bhattacharya and G. Constantinides, eds., *Financial Markets and Incomplete Information*, Totowa, NJ: Rowman and Littlefield (1989), pp. 36–48.

on tax-deductible interest expense. The only tax the debtholder pays is the personal income tax on the interest income. For every one dollar pre-corporate-tax cash interest distribution from the company, the after-tax amount debtholders retain is (1 − personal tax rate on interest) since the interest is tax deductible at the corporate level.

Income to equityholders is first taxed at the corporate level at the corporate tax rate and is then taxed again at the personal tax rate when the company distributes the income to the equityholders. For a one dollar pre-corporate-tax distribution from the company to the equityholders, the after-tax amount equityholders retain is (1 − corporate tax rate) × (1 − personal tax rate on equity).

Assume for illustrative purposes that the debt and equity are equally risky (or are both riskless). If

$$(1 - \textbf{personal tax rate on interest}) > (1 - \textbf{corporate tax rate}) \times (1 - \textbf{personal tax rate on equity})$$

the debt is tax advantaged, and the company should issue debt. Why? For every dollar of the corporate-level pre-corporate tax cash distribution, debtholders retain more than equityholders after corporate and personal taxes. If the inequality is reversed, debt is tax disadvantaged and the company should not issue debt. If the two are equal, then the capital structure is irrelevant, for debt has no tax advantage.

All Personal Income Is Taxed at the Same Rate.   If we assume that all personal income is taxed at the same rate, then the value of the interest tax shield is left intact and is equivalent to what we discussed earlier in the book when we ignored personal taxes. Why? The effect of personal income taxes is eliminated because investors pay the same personal tax rate no matter what type of income the investor earns. In this case, the debt is still a tax-advantaged form of financing, for distributions to debtholders are tax deductible at the corporate level whereas distributions to equityholders are not. Introducing personal taxes decreases the after-tax payments to both debtholders and equityholders in the same proportions, but there is still a tax advantage to debt, and the M-M view of the tax advantage of debt still stands.

Personal Tax Rates for Interest Are Higher than Personal Tax Rates for Dividends and Capital Gains.   Under this assumption, the effective personal tax rate on the cash flows to equityholders is less than that on the cash flows to debtholders. Further, if the equityholders receive some of their return in the form of capital gains, and if the realization of capital gains can be delayed by not selling appreciated shares, the effective tax rate on equity decreases even further because of the deferral of income taxes on the capital gain. The flows to debtholders escape corporate taxation but are taxed at the personal level. The cash flows to equityholders are taxed at the corporate level and at a lower rate rate at the personal level. However, simply knowing that interest income to debtholders can be taxed more heavily than income to equityholders at the personal level is not sufficient for determining whether debt retains its tax advantage. We also need to know the difference in the personal tax rates as well as the magnitude of the corporate tax rate.

To illustrate, consider the U.S. tax code as of December 2012 (though the U.S. tax laws may change soon). Generally, the top corporate tax rate is set at 35%, and the top personal tax rate on income is 39.6%. For our example, we *assume* that the tax rate for interest income is 39.6%. Dividends and realized capital gains are both taxed at 15%, but we *assume* that because capital gains can be postponed, the tax rate on equity is effectively 7.5%; in other words, the deferral of capital gains reduces the present value of the taxes such that the tax rate is 7.5%. Based on these assumptions, a dollar of pre-corporate tax interest paid to debtholders results in a $0.604 $[0.604 = 1 \times (1 - 0.396)]$ interest payment to the debtholders after corporate and personal income taxes (no corporate level taxes and 39.6% at the personal level). However, every dollar of pre-corporate tax distribution paid to equityholders results in a $0.60125 $[0.60125 = 1 \times (1 - 0.35) \times (1 - 0.075)]$ distribution to equityholders after corporate and personal income taxes. To distribute a pre-tax dollar to equityholders, the company must first pay a tax of 35%, thus distributing only $0.65 of the $1 to the equityholders after corporate taxes. Then, the equityholders pay an additional 7.5% in personal income taxes—a tax of $0.048—that results in a distribution of $0.60125 after corporate and personal taxes. In this scenario, the overall tax advantage of debt is small ($0.00275 = $0.604 − $0.60125) for a $1.00 flow. Thus, in this case the benefit of the interest tax shields would be close to zero—not the 35% corporate tax rate.

Thus, if everyone investing in debt and equity faced this tax structure, the debt would have very little tax advantage. However, before we conclude that debt has little to no tax advantage, we need to think about both the representative investor who sets security prices at the margin and the personal income tax rates that investors face (as not all investors face the same tax rates). Not-for-profit organizations (for example, university endowments) do not generally pay any income taxes. Income taxes on pension funds are generally paid by the beneficiary only after retiring and withdrawing funds from the pension fund. The tax this individual faces is the personal tax rate on the entire distribution from the pension fund (assuming the individual did not make any after-tax contributions to the pension) and is independent of how the pension fund earned its return. As such, the pension fund faces a zero personal income tax rate because it pays no taxes, and its holders pay tax on the distribution regardless of whether the pension earns dividends, capital gains, or interest income. Thus some "investors" face zero personal tax rates while others may face relatively high tax rates.

As it turns out, it is very difficult to measure the tax rate of the marginal or representative investor on debt and equity (the tax rate that represents how debt and equity are priced in the market). To understand why this is such a difficult issue to resolve, we turn to a discussion of the relevant tax rates for use in a calculation like this.

The Relevant Tax Rates to Use for Valuing Interest Tax Shields

Even though we can observe statutory tax rates and tax rules and laws, this is insufficient information to determine the effect of personal taxes on the value of interest tax shields for two reasons. First, we must understand the effect of postponing the recognition of capital gains on personal taxes paid on capital gains. This is not easy because investors have different holding periods. The longer capital gains are postponed, the lower the relevant tax rate on capital gains. It is also possible that an investor will never pay income taxes on capital gains; the investor only has to pay taxes when the gain is realized, which is when the investor sells the security while living. If the security goes into the investor's estate, a tax is never paid on the appreciation of the security. Thus, even if investors all face the same tax rate on capital gains when they are realized, the effective tax rates investors face can all be different due to different holding periods. Second, the relevant tax rate is the personal tax rate faced by the marginal or representative investor who buys either debt or equity, and sets the pricing in the market. Unfortunately, this is not observable.

To explain the latter point, we introduce progressive personal tax rates that are common in most countries. With progressivity introduced into the personal tax rate structure, it is not obvious which personal tax rates are implicitly priced in debt and equity securities in the market. In other words, the "gross-up" in the before-tax return each investor wants is a function of the investor's tax rate. Since investors face different tax rates under a progressive tax structure, what tax rate is used when the market reaches equilibrium and therefore how the cost of debt and equity are set is unknown. The implicit tax rate could be zero, the top marginal tax rate for that particular security, or something in between.

Consider the following. For simplicity, assume that the tax on all equity-related income (dividends and capital gains) is zero (it does not have to be this low to make the point), that debtholders have personal tax rates between 0% and 39.6%, and that the corporate tax rate is 35% on all corporations. We assume that we have certain "investors" that do not pay personal income taxes, just as we observe in the world—for example, not-for-profit organizations, university endowments, and pension funds. Also assume that companies are risk-free so that both debt and equity have no risk. (We can also relax this assumption, but the argument is much easier to understand if we ignore risk differences.)

In this economy, since not-for-profit organizations and pensions do not pay personal income taxes, companies will issue debt to these organizations because this debt will not be tax disadvantaged relative to equity for these investors. Therefore, the tax-exempt investors will not demand a premium above the equity return to hold the debt (remember that the personal tax rate on equity is assumed to be zero and that debt and equity have the same risk). Thus, debt has a tax advantage because there is a corporate tax deduction for interest and there is no gross-up in the cost of debt for personal taxes. All companies will follow this strategy. Once the tax-exempt investors purchase as much debt as they are willing to purchase (so that they are now fully invested), companies will consider issuing debt to investors in the very low tax brackets (recall that we assumed personal tax rates on interest vary between 0% and 39.6%).

Since some investors face low (but non-zero) personal income tax rates on debt, the company must pay these investors a higher rate of return than what it paid to the tax-exempt investors in order to entice them to hold debt instead of equity. Companies will pay them more, so that after tax, these investors are indifferent between debt and equity. For example, if these investors have a personal tax rate for interest of 15%, companies will pay them a premium that is about 17.6% $[0.17647 = 0.15/(1 - 0.15)]$ higher than the rate of return on equity (remember that there is no personal tax on equity). Thus, if the return on equity and the interest rate demanded by tax-exempt investors is 10%, the interest rate that companies must pay to investors taxed at the 15% tax rate is 11.76% $[0.1176 = 0.1 \times (1.176)]$. Even after paying the higher cost of debt, the company is better off because of the $0.041 ($0.041 = 0.117647×0.35) tax deduction on the interest paid on one dollar of additional debt. In other words, the after-corporate-tax cost of debt is still less than the after-corporate-tax cost of equity since the firm only has to pay a 17.6% premium to get a 35% tax deduction. Another way to think about this is that for every dollar of additional debt issued to the 15% tax bracket investors, the company paid a premium of $0.0176 ($1 \times 0.1176 - 0.10$) to get a deduction of $0.041 ($0.041 = 0.1176 \times 0.35$). However, when companies pay a premium to entice the investors taxed at a low personal tax rate to hold debt, they must pay the same premium to the tax-exempt investors.

Miller argues that in aggregate, companies will continue to entice more individuals to hold debt as long as the corporate tax savings from the interest deduction is greater than the premium the company must pay a taxed investor in order to entice the investor to hold debt over equity.

Consider the premium the company must pay to entice an investor to buy debt with a 35% tax rate on interest income. The company must pay that debtholder a 53.85% premium $[0.5385 = 0.35/(1 - 0.35)]$; thus, if the rate demanded by tax-exempt investors is 10%, companies must pay these investors a rate of 15.39% $[0.1539 = 0.1 \times (1.539)]$. For every one dollar of additional debt issued to the 35% tax bracket investors, the company must pay a premium of $0.0539 ($1 \times 0.1539 - 0.10$)—relative to the untaxed equity—to get a deduction of $0.0539 ($0.0539 = 0.1539 \times 0.35$). Thus, the company is indifferent about enticing this group of investors to hold debt, for the premium it must pay is exactly equal to the interest tax shield it will get. Here, there is no benefit associated with issuing this debt.

As we have just outlined, in Miller's model, companies issue debt until the personal tax rate on debt for the potential debt investors is equal to the maximum statutory corporate tax rate. If the two tax rates are equal, debt no longer has a tax advantage. To easily see this, consider a new company that enters the economy we have just described in which all investors with tax rates below 35% are enticed to hold debt. For this company, its debt-to-equity ratio is a matter of indifference, for the company will have to entice an investor with a 35% personal tax rate to purchase its debt at a rate that exactly offsets the corporate tax advantage of debt over equity. Miller argues that once the economy is in equilibrium, capital structure for the individual company is a matter of irrelevance. Hence, interest tax shields have no value to the equityholders because the before-tax interest rate has already been grossed up to compensate individuals for the personal tax they will bear.

Unfortunately, we cannot observe the tax rates faced by either the marginal or representative debtholder or the marginal or representative equityholder, both of which set the pricing of the debt and equity. As such, we do not know if corporations have issued debt to the point where the next debt investor will face a 35% tax bracket. If the tax-exempt or low-tax-bracket investors hold all of the debt and have the ability to invest more, then the economy may be at a point where debt is tax advantaged. To resolve this issue, we need to answer some questions about the tax rates for the marginal investors. Is the marginal investor who buys debt securities a tax-exempt investor or someone who pays the 35% tax rate, or somewhere in between? We must answer the same question for the marginal equityholder. In addition, we must measure the personal tax rate on equity after considering the mix of dividends, capital gains, and holding periods that affect the personal tax rate on equity.

What We Know About Personal Income Tax Rates

From the preceding discussion, it is clear that both corporate income tax rates for interest tax shields (T_{INT}) and personal income tax rates on debt and equity can affect the value of debt financing. Although this is a popular area of research, we have relatively little information on the relevant personal income tax rates of the marginal investors needed to resolve this issue. We can examine the tax laws and regulations; however, just knowing the income tax laws and regulations is not sufficient to resolve this issue unless we know the tax situation of the (marginal) investors in the marketplace, and this can change over time.

Based on what we know about personal income taxes, we might think that the relevant personal income tax rate on equity income is substantially lower than the personal income tax rate on debt income. The justification for this view is that individuals do not pay income taxes on equity gains until they realize (sell) them and that both the top statutory tax rates on dividend and capital gains income, 15%, are lower than the top statutory tax rate on ordinary income (which includes interest income), 39.6%. However, since not all investors are individuals, these factors may not be as important as we might at first think.

Graham[29] used the results of a research study on the exchange of traditional (dividend paying) preferred stock for monthly income preferred stock.[30] Based on the results of this study, Graham estimated a personal income tax rate on interest income of roughly 13%. While this conclusion is far from definitive, it is one estimate of the personal tax rate on interest income. A tax rate of 13% for the marginal investor for debt suggests that the tax advantage of debt is still substantive, even if the personal tax rate on equity is zero, and the latter is likely non-zero. Moreover, this evidence suggests that personal taxes do affect the value derived from debt financing to some extent.

Several research studies show that changes in the tax code, which have made debt less tax advantageous (assuming personal taxes matter), have affected the amount of debt that companies use. In particular, both the reduction in the capital gains tax rate and the dividends tax rate to 15% have reduced the personal tax rate on equity, and we have seen a shift from debt financing to equity financing that is consistent with personal taxes affecting the value of the interest tax shields. In addition, researchers who estimate forward-looking equity costs of capital have shown that the same two tax law changes reduced the equity cost of capital, which is again consistent with personal taxes affecting the pricing of securities.[31]

The paucity of information on these marginal investors leads us to agree with Graham, who summarizes the situation nicely: "The truth is that we know very little about the identity or tax-status of the marginal investor(s) between any two sets of securities, and deducing this information is difficult."[32]

The Effect of Personal Income Taxes on Levering and Unlevering Formulas

At first, we might think that we only need to substitute an adjusted tax rate for interest tax shields into our levering and unlevering formulas to adjust these formulas for personal income taxes. Unfortunately, such a substitution is incomplete. Making assumptions similar to Miller's, Taggart shows that in order to adjust the levering and unlevering formulas for the cost of debt, we not only need to make an adjustment for the income tax rate, but we also need to adjust the cost of debt for the difference between personal income tax rates on equity and debt.[33] In this article, Taggart presents the levering and unlevering formulas for both the continuous refinancing and perpetual debt assumptions. Taggart develops his formulas for the special case in which a company's debt is riskless. In other research, Dobbs and Miller discuss the nonlinear nature of the adjustment that has to be made in order to adjust the levering and unlevering formulas for personal income taxes.[34] Cooper and Nyborg develop levering and unlevering formulas for the continuous refinancing and annual refinancing cases with personal taxes and risky debt.[35]

Based on the state of the academic literature today, adjusting the levering and unlevering formulas for personal income taxes is unlikely to be useful because of the inherent difficulty in measuring the personal income tax rates of the marginal debt and equity investors, which we must know in order to make the adjustment. In addition, even the form of the Capital Asset Pricing Model likely changes with personal taxes, and one has to be able to specify the personal tax rates on dividends and capital gains (if they are different).[36] Until we develop a method to estimate the relevant personal tax rates, we will not be able to implement the approaches that have only been derived conceptually. Thus, currently we do not have the means to lever and unlever cost of capital estimates that include personal income taxes.

---

[29] Graham, J. R., "Taxes and Corporate Finance: A Review," *Review of Financial Studies* 16 (2003), 1074–1128.

[30] See Engel, E., M. Erickson, and E. Maydew, "Debt-Equity Hybrid Securities," *Journal of Accounting Research* 37 (1999), pp. 249–274.

[31] Dhaliwal, D. S., L. Krull, and O. Li. "The Effect of 2003 Tax Act on Cost of Equity Capital," *Journal of Accounting & Economics* (2007); and Dhaliwal, D. S., M. Erickson, and L. Krull, "The Effect of Personal Taxes on a Firm's Decision to Issue Debt vs. Equity," *Journal of the American Taxation Association* (2007).

[32] Graham, J. R., "Taxes and Corporate Finance: A Review," *Review of Financial Studies* 16 (2003), pp. 1074–1128.

[33] Taggart, R. A. Jr., "Consistent Valuation and Cost of Capital Expressions with Corporate and Personal Taxes," *Financial Management* 20 (1991), pp. 8–20.

[34] Dobbs, I. M., and A. D. Miller, "Capital Budgeting, Valuation and Personal Taxes," *Accounting and Business Research* 32 (2003), pp. 227–243.

[35] Cooper, I., and K. Nyborg, "Tax-adjusted Discount Rates with Investor Taxes and Risky Debt," *Financial Management* (Summer 2008), pp. 365–379.

[36] For a review of this issue, see Vandell, R. F., and J. L. Stevens, "Personal Taxes and Equity Security Pricing," *Financial Management* vol. 11, no. 1 (Spring, 1982), pp. 31–40.

The Bottom Line on Personal Taxes

Interestingly, if we did not have to lever and unlever, and if we knew how to estimate the cost of equity with personal taxes, the WACC method could correctly value the firm, even with personal taxes. The cost of debt will have increased due to the effect of personal taxes if necessary, but the corporate tax deduction will still be the observed cost of debt multiplied by the relevant corporate tax rate. The tax deductibility of interest at the corporate level will be mitigated by the premium paid for the debt due to personal taxes, and both of these effects would be incorporated using the weighted average cost of capital method. To use the adjusted present value method, however, we need to know how to calculate the unlevered cost of capital (which means we need to be able to unlever) and we need to incorporate the potentially mitigating effects of personal taxes when computing the value of debt financing—in other words, we measure the value of the interest tax shields as we always would but then offset that with the impact of the gross-up in the cost of debt for personal taxes.

So, what is the bottom line on personal taxes and the value of interest tax shields? Most managers and valuation experts believe that debt has some tax advantage. The evidence we have to date is consistent with that conclusion, but the evidence also suggests that personal taxes mitigate the benefits of interest tax shields—at least to some extent. At this point, we do not have the ability to conduct a valuation that explicitly takes into consideration the effect of personal taxes on the value of the firm. At the very least, valuation experts should be careful not to make overly aggressive assumptions about the value of debt financing (such as assuming that the tax shields are all discounted at the cost of debt and that all companies will receive tax savings at the top statutory tax rate adjusted for the effect of state, local, and foreign taxes). In addition, we should not forget the potential effects of financial distress costs that arise from using leverage—a topic we discuss next.

Valuation Key 11.8

Given a tax code that is similar to that in the United States, the effect of personal taxes, at least conceptually, is to potentially mitigate the benefit of the interest tax shields. Our inability to observe or empirically estimate the personal tax rates on debt and equity implicit in the pricing of these securities hampers our ability to perform a valuation that considers the effect of personal taxes on the value of the firm.

11.8 THE EFFECTS OF FINANCIAL DISTRESS COSTS ON CAPITAL STRUCTURE DECISIONS

In this section, we explore another effect of capital structure decisions; the magnitude of and likelihood that a firm will experience financial distress costs because of the use of debt financing. We will first describe what we mean by financial distress costs, then discuss the available empirical evidence on the magnitude of financial distress costs, and finally discuss its implications for valuation. The implications relate to how financial distress costs are incorporated into a valuation and into measuring the cost of capital. As a result, the value of the firm, V_F, is equal to the value of the unlevered firm, V_{UA}, plus the value of the interest tax shields, V_{ITS}, minus the present value of the expected costs of financial distress, PV(FD).

$$V_F = V_{UA} + V_{ITS} - PV(FD)$$

Financial Distress Costs

Financial distress costs are the expected costs that arise due to the possibility that a company will be unable to meet its principal and interest payments when a company has debt in its capital structure. Conceptually, we separate the costs of economic distress—that is, the expected costs of a company failing, even if it has no debt—from financial distress costs, but the two are intertwined. Even unlevered firms can experience economic distress if the company's business model starts to fail and if it begins to experience losses. At some point, the equityholders might decide that they will be better off if the company ceases running its business, sells off its assets, and distributes what is left to the equityholders. Financial distress costs are the costs a levered company incurs in addition to the costs of economic distress experienced by an unlevered firm. Examples of financial distress costs include the following:

- Loss of customers, employees, and suppliers when they become worried that the firm may go out of business due to the debt in the company's capital structure.

- Being denied access to the capital markets during some periods because of the existing debt in the company's capital structure.

- Costs of conflicts of interest between stockholders and debtholders, which increase with leverage (conflicts arise over changes in the risk of the firm's investments, the payment of dividends to shareholders or share repurchases, and increases in leverage that is not subordinate to the existing debt).

- Indirect costs of bankruptcy (i.e., the costs of inefficient operations while in bankruptcy proceedings).

- Direct costs of bankruptcy (i.e., the legal, accounting, and court costs associated with bankruptcy proceedings to determine how the assets are to be split among the claimants).

Unlevered firms can experience economic distress and face costs associated with the loss of customers, employees, and suppliers as well as with being denied access to capital markets. The financial distress costs we are discussing are the additional expected costs from having debt in the capital structure. A levered company that incurs a negative economic shock may well find itself renegotiating its lending terms with creditors in an effort to stave off bankruptcy. If these renegotiations fail, the company can be forced to file for bankruptcy by the creditors. Creditors may decide that they are better off liquidating the firm than allowing the firm to continue as a going concern. In these situations, the incentives of the debtholders and equityholders are likely to differ a great deal.

As discussed, issuing debt can cause conflicts between debtholders and equityholders, for the equityholders can take actions that impose costs on the debtholders. The agency costs associated with issuing debt increase as the amount of leverage increases, for the debtholders have more to lose as leverage increases (note that the leverage can increase because of a decline in the value of the equity). As these agency costs increase, the debtholders will charge the company a higher cost of debt in an effort to price protect themselves; in other words, the debtholders charge the company for actions they expect the company to take that are not in the debtholders' best interests. As a consequence, companies enter into contracts with debtholders that restrict the kinds of actions that managers might take to reduce their cost of debt.

For example, a company may voluntarily restrict the amount of dividends and share repurchases it can make, restrict how much additional debt it can issue, restrict the amount of assets that it can sell, and make commitments to maintain certain minimum interest coverage ratios, a minimum net worth, or certain maximum leverage ratios. If a company does not meet these restrictions, it is in default on its debt agreements—called a technical default. Not meeting these restrictions allows the lenders to renegotiate the terms of the contract and even demand immediate repayment of the loan. These restrictions can, in turn, impose costs on the company and reduce the value of the firm, for the company may be precluded from taking the appropriate actions to maximize firm value. The company, of course, trades off the cost of these restrictions against the borrowing costs it saves by restricting its actions. In some cases, the company must agree to such restrictions in order to obtain additional financing or renew its current financing.

In bankruptcy, the conflicts between debtholders and equityholders may be substantive. The debtholders will generally want to preserve capital and get back as much of their capital as possible. The equityholders, realizing that they are likely to get little or nothing out of bankruptcy, would be more inclined to take a very risky bet with the company's remaining assets to see if that would yield some return to them—essentially, they have nothing to lose in this situation.

Companies bear two types of bankruptcy costs when undergoing a bankruptcy process—direct bankruptcy costs and indirect bankruptcy costs. Direct bankruptcy costs arise because the bankruptcy process itself is expensive. A company going through bankruptcy must incur the costs of lawyers, accountants, and investment bankers, as well as incur the transactions costs of securing additional financing if needed. Indirect costs of bankruptcy arise because the firm may not operate as efficiently while in bankruptcy. In some bankruptcies, management is actually replaced, and in others, existing management may have to get court approval to engage in certain types of activities; all of which makes managing the business less efficient. At the very least, the bankruptcy process distracts management's focus. Various research studies examining bankruptcy costs suggest that bankruptcy costs can be up to 5% of the value of the firm.[37]

---

[37] See, for example, Warner, J., "Bankruptcy, Absolute Priority, and the Pricing of Risky Debt Claims," *Journal of Financial Economics* (May 1977a), pp. 239–276; Warner, J., "Bankruptcy Costs: Some Evidence," *Journal of Financial Economics* (May 1977b), pp. 337–347; White, M. J., "Bankruptcy Costs and the New Bankruptcy Code," *Journal of Finance* (May 1983), pp. 477–488; and Weiss, L., "Bankruptcy Resolution: Direct Costs and Violation of Priority of Claims," *Journal of Financial Economics* vol. 27, no. 2, (1990), pp. 285–314.

Bankruptcy costs vary by the type of company. An example of a company with low bankruptcy costs is a company with a single investment in real estate with a well-written mortgage contract. Ownership of an investment of this sort can pass from the pre-bankruptcy owners to the debtholders with relatively low transactions costs. Thus, in this case, the difference between the value of the company's assets immediately before and after the bankruptcy is likely to be small. At the other extreme, a company with mostly intangible assets (a service company or research and development intensive company) may not even survive bankruptcy unless the creditors believe the company's chances for success are substantial and consider it worthwhile to raise additional capital; thus, bankruptcy costs for these firms are higher.[38]

Andrade and Kaplan estimated the costs of financial distress for a sample of companies that underwent highly leveraged transactions and subsequently experienced financial distress.[39] Their sample underwent either a management buyout (leveraged buyout) or a leveraged recapitalization. Of 136 highly leveraged firms, 39 experienced some type of financial distress. Their estimates of financial distress costs varied depending on the specific tests and subsample examined. Some of the estimates were zero and some ranged between 10% and 20% of total firm value, conditional on the firm experiencing financial distress. They concluded from their analysis that the expected financial distress costs for firms that are healthy and not highly levered are very low since the probability of financial distress is quite low for these firms.

In Andrade and Kaplan's highly levered sample, approximately 30% of the firms suffered financial distress. However, in approximately 50% of these firms, negative economic shocks triggered the distress. The authors' cost estimates were unable to disentangle economic distress from financial distress, and thus their estimates incorporate the costs of both economic and financial distress. They attempted to control for economic distress by examining a subsample of companies that had no economic shock to their business—that is, no economic distress. These companies experienced no evidence of significant financial distress costs. However, since the companies in their sample willingly undertook highly levered transactions (management buyouts or leveraged recapitalizations), it is possible that this sample of firms may have had low expected costs of financial distress should distress even occur. Thus, firms with high expected costs of financial distress would likely not opt for high leverage.

More recently, Davydenko, Strebulaev, and Zhao (2011) examined a large sample of firms with observed prices of debt and equity that defaulted on their debt, and they conclude that the cost of default for an average defaulting firm is 22% of the market value of assets.[40] The costs are substantially higher for investment-grade firms (29%) than for highly levered bond issuers (20%). Glover (2011) concludes that previous research on observed financial distress costs understates the average firm's expected cost of default due to a sample selection bias.[41] Since credit markets price default costs, higher cost of default firms choose lower leverage, reducing the probability of default. Glover estimates the expected cost of financial distress and concludes that the average firm expects to lose as much as 45% of firm value in default, but that the sample of firms that actually default experiences default losses of 25% of firm value—firms with lower expected financial distress costs are more likely to take on more leverage and default.

Financial Distress Costs and the Costs of Debt and Equity Capital

An interesting question to consider is whether the costs of financial distress are incorporated into estimates of the costs of capital for debt, equity, and other securities. We briefly raised this issue in Chapter 10. It is certainly reasonable to believe that at least some financial distress costs are embedded in the cost of debt, for we know that the price of debt incorporates default premiums as perceived by the debtholders. However, it is less clear whether our estimates of the equity cost of capital include any premium for financial distress costs. The question to ask here is whether this is a priced risk.

If we use the CAPM and estimate the equity beta for a company that is already highly levered, the estimated beta could be impacted by the cost of financial distress to the extent that risk is priced and is

---

[38] For a discussion of the potential effects of salvage value on capital structure decisions, see Scott, J. H. Jr., "A Theory of Optimal Capital Structure," *Bell Journal of Economics* (Spring 1976), pp. 33–54.

[39] Andrade, G., and S. Kaplan, "How Costly Is Financial (Not Economic) Distress? Evidence from Highly Leveraged Transactions that Became Distressed," *The Journal of Finance* vol. 53, no. 5 (October 1998), pp. 1443–1493.

[40] Davydenko, S. A., I. A. Strebulaev, and X. Zhao, "A Market-Based Study of the Cost of Default," 2011 working paper, October 2011, University of Toronto.

[41] Glover, B., "The Expected Cost of Default," working paper, January 2011, The Wharton School.

incorporated in beta. Some academicians argue that the importance of the book-to-market factor in the Fama and French three-factor model (see Chapter 8) is due to the effects of financial distress (higher book-to-market firms are more financially distressed).[42] Thus, it is conceivable that the three-factor model more thoroughly includes at least some of the effects of financial distress in the equity cost of capital than the CAPM, but we have no clear empirical evidence on this issue at this time.

As we discussed in Chapter 10, the levering and unlevering methodology only adjusts for the effects of interest tax shields, and it makes no adjustment for any financial distress costs. As of right now, and to the extent financial distress affects the cost of capital, we have no means to remove or include the effects of financial distress costs on the equity cost of capital as we unlever and lever. Where does that leave us in thinking about comparable companies? We suggest that expected financial distress should be considered as a selection criterion for identifying comparable companies. Unlevering the equity cost of capital of highly levered comparable companies with high expected financial distress costs results in an unlevered cost of capital that includes the financial distress costs that are embedded in the equity costs of capital of the highly levered comparable companies (to the extent financial distress costs affect the cost of capital). If, for a weighted average cost of capital valuation, we are going to lever this estimate back up for the capital structure of the company being valued, including this effect in the unlevered cost of capital can be useful if we are valuing a highly levered company but not for valuing a company that is not highly levered. Why? Levering the unlevered cost of capital with embedded financial distress costs results in an equity cost of capital with similarly embedded financial distress costs. Thus, if the debt and other costs of capital include embedded financial distress costs, using an equity cost of capital with embedded financial distress costs results in a weighted average cost of capital with embedded financial distress costs. So if we are valuing a highly levered firm, we would not choose firms with low leverage as comparable companies, and if we are valuing a firm with little leverage, we would not choose highly levered comparable companies.

Adjusting Free Cash Flows for Financial Distress

When we discussed the various DCF valuation methods in Chapter 5, we discussed the concept of expected value and how to use this concept to measure expected free cash flows. Recall that expected free cash flows are equal to the sum of the probabilities of the potential outcomes multiplied by their respective free cash flows. Both economic distress and financial distress are possible outcomes, and those scenarios should naturally be a part of the calculation of expected free cash flows. If a valuation's expected free cash flow forecasts implicitly or explicitly incorporate the possible outcomes of economic distress and financial distress, we effectively will have incorporated financial distress costs into the valuation, assuming we have measured the cost of capital correctly. The financial distress prediction model of Chapter 9 (and one we will present in Chapter 12) can provide an assessment of the probability of financial distress.

If the probability of financial distress is not very close to zero, we want our expected cash flows to measure these potential costs. To do this, we suggest creating scenarios that consider what will happen to the firm if it experiences varying degrees of financial distress. This approach focuses on specific financial distress costs. What will be the loss of customers given the type of business we are valuing? Are we selling a durable good with a need for maintenance and parts, or are we selling a non-durable good with no service component? How will suppliers tighten their credit policies? Will we lose key employees? What will creditors do to us if we violate our lending agreements or miss a payment? If the distress the company experiences is bad enough and the company goes into bankruptcy, what kinds of costs will we face? We can calculate the value of the firm in these distressed scenarios and multiply these values by their respective probabilities. Note that these estimates of financial distress likely vary with the type of company and with general economic conditions.

An alternative approach for considering financial distress costs would be to use an estimate of the costs of financial distress from the empirical work we cited previously and multiply it by the probability of distress from one of the distress prediction models in Chapter 9 or 12. The disadvantage of this approach is that it does not take into account the likely variation in financial distress costs across firms that we just discussed.

---

[42] See Fama, E., and K. French, "Size and Book-to-Market Factors in Earnings and Returns," *Journal of Finance* 50 (March 1995), pp. 131–155.

Valuation Key 11.9

The costs of financial distress cause the value of debt financing to be less than the value of the interest tax shields. Financial distress scenarios should be taken into consideration when calculating expected cash flows. In addition, because the available levering and unlevering methodologies ignore the effects of financial distress costs, the choice of comparable companies should consider whether the firm being valued is subject to financial distress costs or not.

SUMMARY AND KEY CONCEPTS

In this chapter, we discussed how to measure the weighted average cost of capital in more detail, and we discussed issues related to specific valuation contexts—the existence of minority interests, unconsolidated affiliates, and excess assets. We also discussed the treatment of such financing alternatives as leases, which can be treated as either an operating or financing activity. In essence, we learned that it does not matter whether we treat a financing alternative as an operating or a financing activity, but we do need to use the same assumption for all of the comparable companies and the company we are valuing.

We also discussed certain situations in which the weighted average cost of capital cannot measure the value of the interest tax shields correctly. In most of these situations, the timing of when the interest deduction occurs differs from when the weighted average cost of capital assumes it to occur. The issues discussed include net operating losses, capitalized interest, paid-in-kind interest when AHYDO rules apply, and certain cases where the cost of debt has changed since the debt was issued.

We discussed complications associated with calculating the value of the interest tax shields. Some of this has to do with issues regarding the appropriate tax rate to use, but it is also associated with issues regarding how personal taxes might affect the benefits of using debt financing. Other issues that affect the value of debt financing include agency costs and financial distress costs. As stated previously, the value of the firm is equal to the value of the unlevered firm, plus the value of the interest tax shields adjusted for any impact from personal taxes minus the present value of the expected costs of financial distress and agency costs. Ignoring the effect of both personal taxes on interest tax shields and the countervailing forces of financial distress costs and agency costs can lead to upward-biased estimates of the value of debt financing.

ADDITIONAL READING AND REFERENCES

Miller, M. H., "Debt and Taxes," *Journal of Finance* 32 (1977), pp. 261–275.

Myers, S. C., and N. S. Majluf, "Corporate Financing and Investment Decisions When Firms Have Information That Investors Do Not Have," *Journal of Financial Economics* vol. 13, no. 2 (1984), pp. 187–221.

Taggart Jr., R. A., "Consistent Valuation and Cost of Capital Expressions with Corporate and Personal Taxes," *Financial Management* 20 (1991), pp. 8–20.

APPENDIX: Financial Statement and Free Cash Flow Effects of Leases

In this appendix, we demonstrate how the treatment of leases impacts the financial statements and free cash flows as a function of whether we treat the leases as capitalized or operating leases. To illustrate the impact of operating and capitalized lease treatments, we start with a simple three-year lease example in Exhibit A11.1 for the Hoplamasian Company. The lease contract begins on the first day of Year 1 and ends on the last day of Year 3. The lease has three annual payments equal to $4,000, and it has a 10% implicit interest rate. The present value of the three lease payments is $9,947.4, which is capitalized as the lease asset and lease liability.[43]

---

[43] The value of the lease payments is equal to the present value of a three-period annuity discounted at 10%.

$$\$9,947.4 = \$4,000 \times \left(\frac{1}{0.1} - \frac{1}{0.1} \times 1.1^{-3} \right)$$

EXHIBIT A11.1	Hoplamasian Company—Three-Year Lease Example				
Annual payment	$4,000.0				
Implicit interest rate	10.0%	3.0	Life of lease		
Present value of lease payments	$9,947.4				

	Beginning Lease Obligation	Implicit Interest	Lease Payment	Ending Lease Obligation
Year 1	$9,947.4	$994.7	$4,000.0	$6,942.1
Year 2	$6,942.1	$694.2	$4,000.0	$3,636.4
Year 3	$3,636.4	$363.6	$4,000.0	$0.0

Exhibit may contain small rounding errors

The accounting for capitalized leases works like a house mortgage. For each period, interest expense is equal to the beginning balance of the lease obligation multiplied by the implicit interest rate. The difference between the lease payment and interest is equal to the reduction in the lease obligation. For example, in Year 1, interest is equal to $994.7 ($9,947.4 multiplied by 10%). The reduction in the lease obligation is $3,005.3, which is equal to the difference between the lease payment and interest ($3005.3 = $4,000.0 − $994.7).

In Exhibit A11.2, we present Hoplamasian's income statements and balance sheets for both the operating and capital lease treatments of the three-year life of the lease. At the beginning of the example, the company has no assets aside from $1,000 in required cash, which remains constant over time. For each period, the company has a policy of distributing all equity free cash flows to its equityholders, and its income tax rate is 40% on all income. We present the operating lease treatment in the first set of columns in the exhibit. The company has revenues of $10,000.0 in each year and has no expenses other than rent. Thus, each year, its pre-tax income is equal to $6,000.0, its income tax is equal to $2,400.0, and its net income is equal to $3,600.0. Although we do not present the company's cash flows in this exhibit, given that the company has no non-cash assets or operating liabilities—and thus, no accruals—its equity free cash flows are equal to net income (see Exhibit A11.3, which we discuss later).

The capitalized lease treatment is more complex than the operating lease treatment for several reasons. First, over the life of the lease, the lease payments of $12,000.0 are expensed by amortizing the capitalized lease asset of $9,947.4 and expensing interest on the outstanding lease obligation, equal to $2,052.6 over the life of the lease (see Exhibit A11.1). The sum of the lease amortization and interest expense is never equal to $4,000 in any given year. As shown in Exhibit A11.2, the sum of the lease amortization and interest expense is greater than the lease payment in the early years of the lease and less than the lease payment in the later years of the lease.

Another complication arises because taxing authorities generally require use of the operating lease method for income taxes even if the lease is capitalized in the company's financial statements. As a result, deferred income taxes appear on the balance sheet, and the income tax expense is not equal to income taxes payable. A deferred income tax asset results whenever the book value of a liability for financial reporting purposes exceeds the value of that liability on the tax records (tax basis). The amount of the deferred tax asset is equal to that difference multiplied by the income tax rate. Since the value of the lease obligation on the income tax records is zero, the value of the deferred income tax asset is equal to the value of the capital lease obligation multiplied by the income tax rate; for example, at the end of Year 2, the deferred tax asset is equal to $1,454.5 ($1,454.5 = 0.40 × $3,636.4).

Also recall that a deferred tax liability exists whenever the book value of an asset for financial reporting purposes exceeds the tax basis of that asset. Since the value of the lease asset on the income tax records is zero, the value of the deferred income tax liability is equal to the value of the lease asset multiplied by the income tax rate; for example, the end of Year 2 deferred tax liability is equal to $1,326.3 ($1,326.3 = 0.40 × $3,315.8). Income tax expense for financial reporting purposes is equal to income taxes payable ($2,400.0 each year), minus the change in the deferred tax asset plus the change in the deferred tax liability; for example, the Year 2 income tax expense is equal to $2,396.0 [$2,396.0 = $2,400 − ($1,454.5 − $2,776.9) + ($1,326.3 − $2,652.6)].

Since our focus is on valuation, a key issue we must consider is whether capitalizing leases affects a company's free cash flows. We know that using the capitalized lease method affects neither the company's lease payments nor its income tax payments. However, the unlevered free cash flows are not equal between the two methods, for the capitalized lease method assumes the company essentially purchased the capitalized lease asset and financed that purchase with debt. Thus, both the magnitude and timing of the unlevered free cash flows change. We show this effect in Exhibit A11.3.

EXHIBIT A11.2   Hoplamasian Company—Income Statements and Balances Sheets

		Operating Lease			Capitalized Lease			Total Operating Lease	Total Capitalized Lease
Hoplamasian Company ($ in thousands)	Actual Year 0	Forecast Year 1	Forecast Year 2	Forecast Year 3	Forecast Year 1	Forecast Year 2	Forecast Year 3		
Income Statement									
Revenue		$10,000.0	$10,000.0	$10,000.0	$10,000.0	$10,000.0	$10,000.0	$30,000.0	$30,000.0
Rent		–4,000.0	–4,000.0	–4,000.0				–12,000.0	0.0
Capitalized lease amortization					–3,315.8	–3,315.8	–3,315.8	0.0	–9,947.4
Earnings before interest and taxes		$ 6,000.0	$ 6,000.0	$ 6,000.0	$ 6,684.2	$ 6,684.2	$ 6,684.2	$18,000.0	$20,052.6
Interest expense		0.0	0.0	0.0	–994.7	–694.2	–363.6	0.0	–2,052.6
Income before taxes		$ 6,000.0	$ 6,000.0	$ 6,000.0	$ 5,689.5	$ 5,990.0	$ 6,320.6	$18,000.0	$18,000.0
Income tax expense		–2,400.0	–2,400.0	–2,400.0	–2,275.8	–2,396.0	–2,528.2	–7,200.0	–7,200.0
Net income		$ 3,600.0	$ 3,600.0	$ 3,600.0	$ 3,413.7	$ 3,594.0	$ 3,792.3	$10,800.0	$10,800.0
Balance Sheet									
Cash	$1,000.0	$ 1,000.0	$ 1,000.0	$ 1,000.0	$ 1,000.0	$ 1,000.0	$ 1,000.0		
Capitalized lease asset					6,631.6	3,315.8	0.0		
Deferred tax asset					2,776.9	1,454.5	0.0		
Total assets	$1,000.0	$ 1,000.0	$ 1,000.0	$ 1,000.0	$10,408.5	$ 5,770.3	$ 1,000.0		
Deferred tax liability					$ 2,652.6	$ 1,326.3	$ 0.0		
Capitalized lease obligation					6,942.1	3,636.4	0.0		
Equity	$1,000.0	$ 1,000.0	$ 1,000.0	$ 1,000.0	813.7	807.7	1,000.0		
Total liabilities and equities	$1,000.0	$ 1,000.0	$ 1,000.0	$ 1,000.0	$10,408.5	$ 5,770.3	$ 1,000.0		
Sum of lease amortization and interest expense					$ 4,310.5	$ 4,010.0	$ 3,679.4		$12,000.0

Exhibit may contain small rounding errors

EXHIBIT A11.3   Hoplamasian Company—Free Cash Flow Schedule

Hoplamasian Company ($ in thousands)	Operating Lease			Capitalized Lease			Total Operating Lease	Total Capitalized Lease
	Forecast Year 1	Forecast Year 2	Forecast Year 3	Forecast Year 1	Forecast Year 2	Forecast Year 3		
Earnings before interest and taxes..........	$6,000.0	$6,000.0	$6,000.0	$ 6,684.2	$6,684.2	$6,684.2	$18,000.0	$20,052.6
– Income taxes paid on EBIT........	–2,400.0	–2,400.0	–2,400.0	–2,673.7	–2,673.7	–2,673.7	–7,200.0	–8,021.0
Earnings before interest and after taxes.....................	$3,600.0	$3,600.0	$3,600.0	$ 4,010.5	$4,010.5	$4,010.5	$10,800.0	$12,031.6
– Change in required cash.........	0.0	0.0	0.0	0.0	0.0	0.0	0.0	0.0
+ Lease amortization				3,315.8	3,315.8	3,315.8	0.0	9,947.4
+ Deferred tax adjustment				–124.2	–4.0	128.2	0.0	–0.0
– Capital lease increases (CAPEX)				–9,947.4	0.0	0.0	0.0	–9,947.4
Unlevered free cash flow	$3,600.0	$3,600.0	$3,600.0	$–2,745.3	$7,322.3	$7,454.5	$10,800.0	$12,031.6
Implicit interest on capitalized leases	0.0	0.0	0.0	–994.7	–694.2	–363.6	0.0	–2,052.6
Interest tax shield...............	0.0	0.0	0.0	397.9	277.7	145.5	0.0	821.0
Free cash flow minus after-tax interest	$3,600.0	$3,600.0	$3,600.0	$–3,342.1	$6,905.8	$7,236.4	$10,800.0	$10,800.0
Change in capital lease obligation (financing)............				6,942.1	–3,305.8	–3,636.4	0.0	0.0
Equity free cash flow	$3,600.0	$3,600.0	$3,600.0	$ 3,600.0	$3,600.0	$3,600.0	$10,800.0	$10,800.0

From this exhibit, we observe the following. First, whether we treat a lease as capitalized or operating does not affect the equity free cash flows. Second, if we use the capitalized lease method, the unlevered free cash flows over the life of the lease will be higher. The lease payments ($12,000) are all treated as operating expenses in the operating lease method, and they reduce unlevered free cash flows; however, the capitalized lease method treats the implicit interest embedded in the lease payments as a cost of financing and not a reduction of unlevered free cash flows. Thus, over the life of the lease the unlevered free cash flows under the capitalized lease method are larger than the unlevered free cash flows under the operating lease method by the amount of the after-tax implicit interest embedded in the lease payments.

Over the life of Hoplamasian's lease, the unlevered free cash flows under the capital lease method include deductions equal to the present value of the lease payments ($9,947.4)—not the sum of the lease payments ($12,000). The difference between the present value of the lease payments and the sum of the lease payments is $2,052.6, which is equal to the implicit interest expense. The after-tax effect of this on the unlevered free cash flows is $1,231.6 [$1,231.6 = 12,031.6 − $10,800 = (1 − 0.4) × $2,052.6]. Finally, under the capitalized lease method, the unlevered free cash flows are smaller for the initial year and larger for the later years of the lease. The capital lease method deducts the entire present value of the lease payments as a capital expenditure in the year the company enters the lease, whereas the operating lease method deducts the lease payments in the years these payments are made.

REVIEW EXERCISE A11.1

A Simple Lease Example

Prepare an income statement, balance sheet, and free cash flow schedule for the three years that the lease from Review Exercise 11.2 is in effect, using both the operating and capital lease methods (see Exhibits A11.2 and A11.3). Assume the company has $8,000 in revenue each year and that the income tax rate is 30% on all income. The company has a policy of distributing all equity free cash flows to its equityholders each period. The company has no assets other than $400 in required cash that remains constant over time.

Solution on page 471.

EXERCISES AND PROBLEMS

P11.1   **Measuring the Weighted Average Cost of Capital** Calculate the weighted average cost of capital using both Equations 11.1 and 11.2. Assume the company's securities are publicly traded, that its debt is currently trading at 100% of par value, and that its preferred stock is currently trading at 110% of its par value. The company's stock price is currently $8 per share, and the company has 5,000 shares of stock outstanding, which is net of 1,000 treasury shares. The risk-free rate is 4%, and the market risk premium is 6%. The company issued the debt and preferred stock at par value. The company has an equity beta equal to 1.5. The company has an effective interest rate equal to 7.5%, which includes an 0.5% default premium, and the cost of capital for the preferred stock is equal to 7.5%. The income tax rate on all income is 40%. The company plans to have a constant capital structure strategy based on its current capital structure ratios.

	Year 1	Year 2
Income Statement		
Revenue		$12,000
Operating expenses		–6,000
Depreciation expense		–5,200
Earnings before interest and taxes		$ 800
Interest expense		–450
Income before taxes		$ 350
Income tax expense		–105
Net income		$ 245
Balance Sheet		
Total current assets	$ 2,000	$ 3,000
Property, plant, and equipment (net)	12,000	12,000
Total assets	$14,000	$15,000
Accounts payable	$ 1,000	$ 1,000
Debt	6,000	6,000
Total liabilities	$ 7,000	$ 7,000
Preferred stock	$ 4,400	$ 4,600
Capital stock	5,000	5,000
Retained earnings	–2,400	–1,600
Shareholders' equity	$ 7,000	$ 8,000
Liabilities and shareholders' equity	$14,000	$15,000

P11.2   **Operating Versus Capitalized Leases and Valuation** In Year 0, a company entered into a perpetual lease on certain property. The property has a value of $25,000, the cost of debt is 12%, and its annual lease payment is $3,000. The company expects all of the cash flows to grow at 3% in perpetuity and it expects to increase the amount of leased property at the same rate beginning at the end of Year 1 (all new leases are perpetual leases). The company has revenues of $5,000 in Year 1 and has no other expenses other than those related to the lease. The company's tax rate on all income is 45%. All revenues and expenses are paid in cash. The company has no assets or liabilities other than those related to the lease. Assume today is the end of Year 0. The company has a 22% equity cost of capital, and the discount rate for interest tax shields is equal to the unlevered cost of capital. Value the company as of the end of Year 0 assuming the company treats the lease as an operating lease, and value the company again assuming the company treats the lease as a capital lease. As part of the valuation, prepare the company's income statement and free cash flow schedule for Year 1 under each lease treatment. Use the weighted average cost of capital, equity DCF, and APV valuation methods to value the company.

P11.3   **Capitalizing Operating Leases—Part 1** Use the information presented in the following financial disclosures to measure the present value of the outstanding operating lease obligations as of the end of Years 0 and 1, assuming annual payments and a 7% discount rate. Also measure the present value of the additions to the lease obligations (new leases), the implicit interest on the capitalized lease obligations, and the lease asset amortization (assuming a 10-year life) for Year 1.

Year 0 Financial Disclosure		
Year	**Capital Leases**	**Operating Leases**
Year 1	$ 1,200	$ 3,600
Year 2	1,160	3,480
Year 3	1,110	3,330
Year 4	1,030	3,090
Year 5	1,000	3,000
After Year 5	8,000	27,000
Total	$13,500	$43,500
Total interest	5,979	
Present value	$ 7,521	

Year 1 Financial Disclosure		
Year	**Capital Leases**	**Operating Leases**
Year 2	$ 1,400	$ 4,000
Year 3	1,400	3,900
Year 4	1,300	3,700
Year 5	1,200	3,400
Year 6	1,200	3,300
After Year 6	9,600	29,700
Total	$16,100	$48,000
Total interest	7,154	
Present value	$ 8,946	

P11.4   Capitalizing Operating Leases—Part 2 Use the information presented in Problem 11.3 and the following financial information to restate the company's Year 1 income statement, balance sheet, and free cash flow schedule so that all operating leases are capitalized as of the end of Year 0 and onward. The company's income tax rate is 35% on all income. The Year 1 operating lease payment of $3,600 reported in the footnote is included in the total rent expense reported of $10,000.

Summarized Financial Statements	Year 1 Reported
Income Statement	
Revenues	$40,000.0
Rent expense	−10,000.0
Depreciation and amortization	−6,000.0
Amortization of operating leases	0.0
All other operating expenses	−5,000.0
Operating income.	$19,000.0
Interest expense, net	−2,000.0
Lease interest	0.0
Income before taxes.	$17,000.0
Income taxes	−5,950.0
Net income.	$11,050.0
Balance Sheet	
Current assets	$20,000.0
Net property, plant, and equipment	60,000.0
Other assets.	10,000.0
Deferred tax asset	0.0
Capitalized operating leases	0.0
Total assets.	$90,000.0
Current operating liabilities.	$10,000.0
Other liabilities	20,000.0
Deferred tax liability	0.0
Debt	20,000.0
Capitalized operating leases	0.0
Total liabilities.	$50,000.0
Shareholders' equity	40,000.0
Total liabilities and shareholders' equity.	$90,000.0

Summarized Free Cash Flow Schedule	Year 1 Reported
Earnings before interest and taxes (EBIT)	$19,000.0
− Income taxes paid on EBIT	−6,650.0
Earnings before interest and after taxes	$12,350.0
+ Depreciation and amortization	6,000.0
+ Amortization of operating leases.	0.0
− Change in net working capital.	4,000.0
+ Change in non-current liabilities and other	1,000.0
− Change in required cash balance	−400.0
Unlevered cash flow from operations.	$22,950.0
− Capital expenditures (net)	−10,000.0
− Increase in capital lease assets.	0.0
Unlevered free cash flow	$12,950.0
− Interest paid	−2,000.0
+ Interest tax shield	700.0
+ Change in non-common equity.	0.0
+ Change in capital lease obligations	0.0
Free cash flow to common equity	$11,650.0

P11.5   Capitalizing Operating Leases Again—Part 1 Use the information presented in the following financial disclosures to measure the present value of the outstanding operating lease obligations as of the end of Years 0 and 1, assuming annual payments and a 7% discount rate. Also measure the present value of the additions to the lease obligations (new leases), the implicit interest on the capitalized lease obligations, and the lease asset amortization (assuming a 10-year life) for Year 1.

Year 0 Financial Disclosure		
Year	Capital Leases	Operating Leases
Year 1	$ 400	$ 1,200
Year 2	380	1,140
Year 3	360	1,080
Year 4	300	900
Year 5	250	750
After Year 5	2,000	6,750
Total	$3,690	$11,820
Total interest	1,088	
Present value	$2,602	

Year 1 Financial Disclosure		
Year	Capital Leases	Operating Leases
Year 2	$ 450	$ 1,400
Year 3	400	1,300
Year 4	400	1,200
Year 5	300	1,000
Year 6	300	800
After Year 6	2,400	7,200
Total	$4,250	$12,900
Total interest	1,280	
Present value	$2,970	

P11.6   **Capitalizing Operating Leases Again—Part 2** Use the information presented in Problem 11.5 and the following financial information to restate the company's Year 1 income statement, balance sheet, and free cash flow schedule so that all operating leases are capitalized as of the end of Year 0 and onward. The company's income tax rate is 45% on all income. The Year 1 operating lease payment of $1,200 from the footnote is included in the total rent expense reported of $5,000.

Summarized Financial Statements	Year 1 Reported
Income Statement	
Revenues	$10,000.0
Rent expense	−5,000.0
Depreciation and amortization	−2,000.0
Amortization of operating leases ...	0.0
All other operating expenses	−1,000.0
Operating income	$ 2,000.0
Interest expense, net	−500.0
Lease interest	0.0
Income before taxes	$ 1,500.0
Income taxes	−675.0
Net income	$ 825.0
Balance Sheet	
Current assets	$ 8,000.0
Net property, plant, and equipment	12,000.0
Other assets	2,000.0
Deferred tax asset	0.0
Capitalized operating leases	0.0
Total assets	$22,000.0
Current operating liabilities	$ 6,000.0
Other liabilities	2,000.0
Deferred tax liability	0.0
Debt	10,000.0
Capitalized operating leases	0.0
Total liabilities	$18,000.0
Shareholders' equity	4,000.0
Total liabilities and shareholders' equity	$22,000.0

Summarized Free Cash Flow Schedule	Year 1 Reported
Earnings before interest and taxes (EBIT)	$ 2,000.0
− Income taxes paid on EBIT	−900.0
Earnings before interest and after taxes	$ 1,100.0
+ Depreciation and amortization	2,000.0
+ Amortization of operating leases	0.0
− Change in net working capital	4,000.0
+ Change in non-current liabilities and other	1,000.0
− Change in required cash balance	−400.0
Unlevered cash flow from operations	$ 7,700.0
− Capital expenditures (net)	−10,000.0
− Increase in capital lease assets	0.0
Unlevered free cash flow	$−2,300.0
− Interest paid	−500.0
+ Interest tax shield	225.0
+ Change in non-common equity	0.0
+ Change in capital lease obligations	0.0
Free cash flow to common equity	$−2,575.0

P11.7   **Net Operating Carryforwards and Valuation** A company expects to have $5,000 in earnings before interest and taxes in perpetuity. The company has no capital expenditures or working capital such that its unlevered free cash flow is equal to EBIT minus taxes. The company's tax rate is 40% for all income. The company experienced operating losses in the past and has $9,000 in net operating loss carryforwards as of the date of the valuation that it can use to offset taxable income. The company has $20,000 in debt outstanding, which has a 10% cost of capital. The company's unlevered cost of capital is 12%. Measure the value of the firm with the adjusted present value valuation method, using the unlevered cost of capital to discount interest tax shields.

P11.8 **Appendix Problem—A Simple Lease Example—Part 1** A lease contract begins on the first day of Year 1 and ends on the last day of Year 3. The lease has three annual payments equal to $25,000. The appropriate discount rate for the lease is 9%. Prepare a lease amortization table similar to the one in Exhibit 11.3.

P11.9 **Appendix Problem—A Simple Lease Example—Part 2** Use the information in Problem P11.8 and the following information to prepare an income statement, balance sheet, and free cash flow schedule for the three years of the lease assuming the lease is an operating lease, and do this again assuming the lease is a capital lease (see Exhibits A11.2 and A11.3). Assume the company has $30,000 in revenue each year and that the income tax rate is 45% on all income. The company has a policy of distributing all equity free cash flows to equityholders each period. The company has no assets other than $1,500 in required cash that remains constant over time.

SOLUTIONS FOR REVIEW EXERCISES

Review Exercise 11.1: Measuring the Weighted Average Cost of Capital

Market Value of Debt	
Price	100%
Market value of debt	$12,000

Market Value of Preferred	
Price	95%
Market value of preferred	$ 7,600

Market Value of Equity	
Price	$ 12.00
Shares	1,000
Market value of equity	$12,000
Market value of firm	$31,600
Debt-to-firm value	38.0%
Preferred-to-firm value	24.1%
Equity-to-firm value	38.0%
	100.0%
Risk-free rate	5.00%
Market risk premium	6.00%
Equity beta	2.5
Equity cost of capital	20.00%
Yield on debt	8.00%
Less: Expected default loss	1.00%
Cost of debt	7.00%
Cost of preferred	8.50%
Income tax rate	30.00%
Weighted average cost of capital #1	11.50%

$$r_{WACC} = 0.20 \times 0.38 + 0.07 \times (1 - 0.3) \times 0.38 + 0.085 \times 0.241 = 0.115$$

Unlevered Cost of Capital	12.30%
Weighted Average Cost of Capital #2	11.50%

$$r_{WACC} = 0.123 - 0.07 \times 0.3 \times 0.38 - (0.1235 - 0.1235) \times 0 = 0.115$$

Review Exercise 11.2: A Simple Lease Example—Part 1

Annual Payment	$ 5,000.0		
Implicit Interest Rate	8.0%	3.0	Life of Lease
Present Value of Lease Payments..................	$12,885.5		

Year	Beginning Lease Obligation	Implicit Interest	Lease Payment	Ending Lease Obligation
Year 1	$12,885.5	$1,030.8	$5,000.0	$8,916.3
Year 2	$ 8,916.3	$ 713.3	$5,000.0	$4,629.6
Year 3	$ 4,629.6	$ 370.4	$5,000.0	$ 0.0

Exhibit may contain small rounding errors

Review Exercise 11.3: Operating versus Capitalized Leases and Valuation

Income Statement and Free Cash Flow Schedule for Year 1		Operating Lease Method	Capital Lease Method
Income Statement			
Revenues		$ 800	$ 800
Rent expense...		−450	
Interest expense..			−450
Pretax income		$ 350	$ 350
Income taxes	30.0%	−105	−105
Net income..		$ 245	$ 245
Free Cash Flow Schedule			
Earnings before interest and taxes..................................		$ 350	$ 800
− Income taxes paid on EBIT.......................................	30.0%	−105	−240
Earnings before interest and after taxes		$ 245	$ 560
− Increase in capital lease assets...................................	2.0%		−100
Unlevered free cash flow		$ 245	$ 460
− Interest paid		n/a	−450
+ Interest tax shield	30.0%	n/a	135
+ Change in non-common equity......................................		0	0
+ Change in capital lease obligations		n/a	100
Free cash flow to common equity		$ 245	$ 245

Values as of Year 0		Operating Lease Method	Capital Lease Method
Value of the property = Lease obligation.		$5,000	$5,000
Value of the equity	18.0%	$1,531	$1,531
Debt-to-firm value		—	76.6%
Unlevered cost of capital		18.0%	11.1%

$$r_{UA} = r_E \times \frac{V_E}{V_F} + r_D \times \frac{V_D}{V_F}$$

$$r_{UA} = 0.18 \times \frac{\$1,531}{\$1,531 + \$5,000} + 0.09 \times \frac{\$5,000}{\$1,531 + \$5,000} = 0.111$$

		Operating Lease Method	Capital Lease Method
Weighted average cost of capital		18.0%	9.0%
Value of the firm using WACC method		$1,531	$6,531
Value of debt		0	5,000
Value of equity		$1,531	$1,531
Value of the Firm Using APV Method			
Value of the unlevered firm		$1,531	$5,049
Value of the interest tax shields			1,482
Value of the firm		$1,531	$6,531
Value of debt		0	5,000
Value of equity		$1,531	$1,531

Review Exercise 11.4: Operating versus Capitalized Leases and Valuation

Operating Lease Payments as of end of Year 0			
Year	Payment	PV Factor	Present Value
Year 1	$1,200	0.926	$1,111.1
Year 2	1,000	0.857	857.3
Year 3	900	0.794	714.4
Year 4	700	0.735	514.5
Year 5	600	0.681	408.3
Year 6	600	0.630	378.1
Year 7	600	0.583	350.1
Year 8	600	0.540	324.2
Year 9	600	0.500	300.1
Year 10	600	0.463	277.9
Year 11	600	0.429	257.3
Year 12	600	0.397	238.3
Year 13	600	0.368	220.6
Year 14	600	0.340	204.3
Year 15			0.0
Present value as of end of Year 0			$6,156.7
Implicit interest rate			8.0%
Implicit Interest expense for Year 1			$ 492.5
Assumed remaining average life			10
Lease asset amortization for Year 1			$ 615.7

Operating Lease Payments as of end of Year 1			
Year	Payment	PV Factor	Present Value
Year 2	$1,100	0.926	$1,018.5
Year 3	990	0.857	848.8
Year 4	770	0.794	611.3
Year 5	660	0.735	485.1
Year 6	630	0.681	428.8
Year 7	630	0.630	397.0
Year 8	630	0.583	367.6
Year 9	630	0.540	340.4
Year 10	630	0.500	315.2
Year 11	630	0.463	291.8
Year 12	630	0.429	270.2
Year 13	630	0.397	250.2
Year 14	630	0.368	231.6
Year 15	630	0.340	214.5
Present value as of end of Year 1			$6,070.9
Year 1 interest			-492.5
Year 1 lease payment			1,200.0
			$6,778.3
Present value as of end of Year 0			6,156.7
Present value of new leases in Year 1			$ 621.7
Rent in Year 1			$1,200.0

Exhibit may contain small rounding errors

Review Exercise 11.5: Operating versus Capitalized Leases and Valuation

Summarized Financial Statements	Year 1 Reported	Beginning of Year Balance	Adjust Rent Expense	Amortization of Capital Lease Asset	Income Taxes	Acquisition of Additional Leases	Year 1 Adjusted
Income Statement							
Revenues	$22,000.0						$22,000.0
Rent expense	−2,000.0		$1,200.0				−800.0
Depreciation and amortization	−3,000.0						−3,000.0
Amortization of operating leases				$−615.7			−615.7
All other operating expenses	−10,000.0						−10,000.0
Operating income	$ 7,000.0	$ 0.0	$1,200.0	$−615.7	$ 0.0	$ 0.0	$ 7,584.3
Interest expense	−1,000.0						−1,000.0
Lease interest			−492.5				−492.5
Income before taxes	$ 6,000.0	$ 0.0	$ 707.5	$−615.7	$ 0.0	$ 0.0	$ 6,091.8
Income taxes	−2,400.0				−36.7		−2,436.7
Net income	$ 3,600.0	$ 0.0	$ 707.5	$−615.7	$ −36.7	$ 0.0	$ 3,655.1
Balance Sheet							
Current assets	$ 8,000.0						$ 8,000.0
Net property, plant, and equipment	20,000.0						20,000.0
Other assets	5,000.0						5,000.0
Deferred tax asset					$2,428.4		2,428.4
Capitalized operating leases		$6,156.7		$−615.7		$621.7	6,162.7
Total assets	$33,000.0	$6,156.7	$ 0.0	$−615.7	$2,428.4	$621.7	$41,591.0
Current operating liabilities	$ 7,000.0						$ 7,000.0
Other liabilities	10,000.0						10,000.0
Deferred tax liability					$2,465.1		2,465.1
Debt	13,000.0						13,000.0
Capitalized operating leases		$6,156.7	$ −707.5			$621.7	6,070.9
Total liabilities	$30,000.0	$6,156.7	$ −707.5	$ 0.0	$2,465.1	$621.7	$38,536.0
Shareholders' equity	3,000.0		707.5	−615.7	−36.7		3,055.1
Total liabilities and shareholders' equity	$33,000.0	$6,156.7	$ 0.0	$−615.7	$2,428.4	$621.7	$41,591.0

Summarized Free Cash Flow Schedule	Year 1 Reported	Adjust Rent Expense	Amortization of Capital Lease Asset	Income Taxes	Acquisition of Additional Leases	Year 1 Adjusted
Earnings before interest and taxes (EBIT)	$7,000.0	$1,200.0	$−615.7			$7,584.3
− Income taxes paid on EBIT	−2,800.0			$−233.7		−3,033.7
Earnings before interest and after taxes	$4,200.0	$1,200.0	$−615.7	$−233.7	$ 0.0	$4,550.6
+ Depreciation and amortization	3,000.0					3,000.0
+ Amortization of operating leases			615.7			615.7
− Change in net working capital	500.0					500.0
+ Change in non-current liabilities & other	100.0			36.7		136.7
− Change in required cash balance	−50.0					−50.0
Unlevered cash flow from operations	$7,750.0	$1,200.0	$ 0.0	$−197.0	$ 0.0	$8,753.0
− Capital expenditures (net)	−3,000.0					−3,000.0
− Increase in capital lease assets					−621.7	−621.7
Unlevered free cash flow	$4,750.0	$1,200.0	$ 0.0	$−197.0	$−621.7	$5,131.3
− Interest paid	−1,000.0	−492.5				−1,492.5
+ Interest tax shield	400.0			197.0		597.0
+ Change in non-common equity			−707.5			−707.5
+ Change in capital lease obligations					621.7	621.7
Free cash flow to common equity	$4,150.0	$ 0.0	$ 0.0	$ −0.0	$ 0.0	$4,150.0

Exhibit may contain small rounding errors

Review Exercise A11.1: A Simple Lease Example—Part 2

		Operating Lease			Capitalized Lease			Total Operating Lease	Total Capitalized Lease
	Actual Year 0	Forecast Year 1	Forecast Year 2	Forecast Year 3	Forecast Year 1	Forecast Year 2	Forecast Year 3		
Income Statement									
Revenue		$8,000.0	$8,000.0	$8,000.0	$ 8,000.0	$8,000.0	$8,000.0	$24,000.0	$24,000.0
Rent		−5,000.0	−5,000.0	−5,000.0				−15,000.0	0.0
Capitalized lease amortization					−4,295.2	−4,295.2	−4,295.2	0.0	−12,885.5
Earnings before interest and taxes		$3,000.0	$3,000.0	$3,000.0	$ 3,704.8	$3,704.8	$3,704.8	$ 9,000.0	$11,114.5
Interest expense.					−1,030.8	−713.3	−370.4	0.0	−2,114.5
Income before taxes.		$3,000.0	$3,000.0	$3,000.0	$ 2,674.0	$2,991.5	$3,334.5	$ 9,000.0	$ 9,000.0
Income tax expense.		−900.0	−900.0	−900.0	−802.2	−897.5	−1,000.3	−2,700.0	−2,700.0
Net income.		$2,100.0	$2,100.0	$2,100.0	$ 1,871.8	$2,094.1	$2,334.1	$ 6,300.0	$ 6,300.0
Balance Sheet									
Cash.	$400.0	$ 400.0	$ 400.0	$ 400.0	$ 400.0	$ 400.0	$ 400.0		
Capitalized lease asset.					8,590.4	4,295.2	0.0		
Deferred tax asset					2,674.9	1,388.9	0.0		
Total assets.	$400.0	$ 400.0	$ 400.0	$ 400.0	$11,665.2	$6,084.1	$ 400.0		
Deferred tax liability					$ 2,577.1	$1,288.5	$ 0.0		
Capitalized lease obligation . .					8,916.3	4,629.6	0.0		
Equity	$400.0	400.0	400.0	400.0	171.8	165.9	400.0		
Total liabilities and equities. . .	$400.0	$ 400.0	$ 400.0	$ 400.0	$11,665.2	$6,084.1	$ 400.0		
Sum of lease amortization and interest expense					$ 5,326.0	$5,008.5	$4,665.5		$15,000.0

	Operating Lease			Capitalized Lease			Total Operating Lease	Total Capitalized Lease
Free Cash Flow Schedule	Forecast Year 1	Forecast Year 2	Forecast Year 3	Forecast Year 1	Forecast Year 2	Forecast Year 3		
Earnings before interest and taxes. . .	$3,000.0	$3,000.0	$3,000.0	$3,704.8	$3,704.8	$3,704.8	$9,000.0	$11,114.5
− Income taxes paid on EBIT.	−900.0	−900.0	−900.0	−1,111.0	−1,111.0	−1,111.0	−2,700.0	−3,334.0
Earnings before interest and after taxes.	$2,100.0	$2,100.0	$2,100.0	$2,593.4	$2,593.4	$2,593.4	$6,300.0	$ 7,780.2
− Change in required cash.	0.0	0.0	0.0	0.0	0.0	0.0	0.0	0.0
+ Lease amortization				4,295.2	4,295.2	4,295.2	0.0	12,885.5
+ Deferred tax adjustment				−97.8	−2.5	100.3	0.0	−0.0
− Capital lease increases (CAPEX). . .				−12,885.5	0.0	0.0	0.0	− 12,885.5
Unlevered free cash flow	$2,100.0	$2,100.0	$2,100.0	$−6,094.7	$6,886.0	$6,988.9	$6,300.0	$ 7,780.3
Implicit interest on capitalized leases				−1,030.8	−713.3	−370.4	0.0	−2,114.5
Interest tax shield.				309.3	214.0	111.1	0.0	634.4
Free cash flow minus after-tax interest	$2,100.0	$2,100.0	$2,100.0	$−6,816.3	$6,386.7	$6,729.6	$6,300.0	$ 6,300.0
Change in capital lease obligation (financing).				8,916.3	−4,286.7	−4,629.6	0.0	0.0
Equity free cash flow	$2,100.0	$2,100.0	$2,100.0	$2,100.0	$2,100.0	$2,100.0	$6,300.0	$ 6,300.0

Exhibit may contain small rounding errors

After mastering the material in this chapter, you will be able to:

1. Use the Black-Scholes Option Pricing Model to value "plain vanilla" options (12.1)

2. Measure the value and cost of capital for warrants and make the appropriate adjustments for warrants in a valuation analysis (12.2)

3. Adjust a valuation and the various costs of capital for the effects of employee stock options and other similar equity-based compensation (12.3)

4. Analyze the straight debt and option components of convertible debt (12.4)

5. Measure the probability of financial distress using an option pricing framework (12.5)

Option Pricing Model Applications to Valuation Issues

International Business Machines (IBM) Corporation's Equity Incentive Plans[1]—IBM describes its incentive compensation plans as follows in its 10-K report:

IBM

Stock-based incentive awards are provided to employees under the terms of the company's plans (the "plans"). . . . Awards under the Plans principally include at-the-money stock options, premium-priced stock options, restricted stock units, performance stock units, stock appreciation rights or any combination thereof. . . .

. . . Stock options are granted at an exercise price equal to or greater than the company stock price on the date of grant. These awards, which generally vest 25 percent per year, are fully vested four years from the date of grant and have a contractual term of 10 years. In 2004, the company implemented a new stock-based program for its senior executives, designed to drive improved performance and increase the ownership executives have in the company. . . .

The company estimates the fair value of stock options using the Black-Scholes valuation model, . . . Key inputs and assumptions used to estimate the fair value of stock options include the grant price of the award, the expected option term, volatility of the company's stock, the risk-free rate and the company's dividend yield.

In this chapter, we discuss how to estimate the value and cost of capital of warrants, convertible debt, and convertible preferred and how to adjust all facets of a valuation for these securities. We also discuss various types of equity-based compensation and how to account for the impact of future grants of equity-based compensation in a valuation.

---

[1] IBM develops and sells products (computers, software, storage systems, and microelectronics) and services in the information technology industry; see IBM's 10-K reports filed with the U.S. Securities and Exchange Commission (SEC) and made available on the company's website, www.IBM.com.

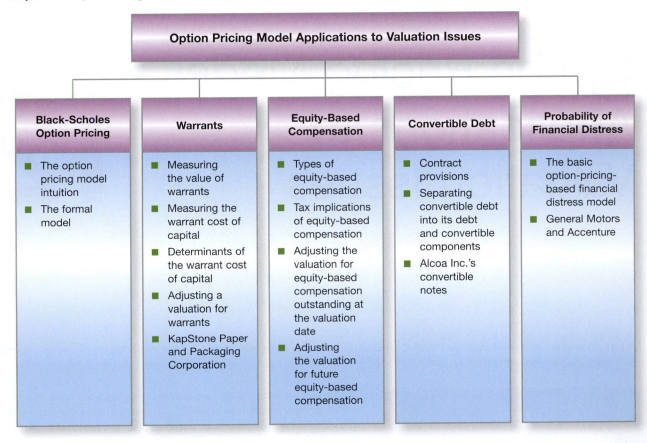

INTRODUCTION

Like all securities, an option is a contract. What differentiates options from many other securities is that an option provides the holder of the option contract the right (but not an obligation) to buy or sell the underlying security at a set price. The option is a **derivative security**, so called because its value depends in part on the value of another asset. There are two basic options—call and put options. A **call option** is an option to purchase an underlying security at a certain price for a specified period. The option may be exercisable on the date the option expires (**expiration date**)—a **European option**—or it may be exercisable any time before the expiration date—an **American option**. Examples of call options on common stock issued by companies and relevant to measuring firm value include employee stock options, warrants, convertible debt, and convertible preferred stock. A **put option** is an option to sell the underlying security at a certain price for a specified period, but companies generally do not issue put options on their common stock.

Option pricing theory is valuable in many different types of settings, but these are far too numerous to discuss in one chapter. In addition to company-issued options, investors issue options on a company's stock to other investors. These options not only include "plain vanilla" put and call options but also include "exotic" options. Exotic options include Asian options, which have payoffs that depend on the average prices of the underlying assets over a specified period, and rainbow options, which have payoffs that depend on multiple securities or events. Investors write option contracts on stocks, credit contracts, foreign currency, commodities, and even the weather. These options can be used by investors and corporations to hedge certain risks.

Another type of option is an option that is embedded within an investment opportunity. Any investment contains an embedded option if it can be changed during its life as an investor learns more about it; for example, if an investment can be deferred, contracted, expanded, or abandoned before completion. These options are called **real options**. They can be used in such various settings as research and development valuations, patent valuations, and natural resource investments. Discounted cash flow approaches cannot always capture all of the value derived from the embedded options. In such circumstances, an option pricing framework is more appropriate if the necessary information is available to utilize this approach.

The focus of the discussion in this chapter is on options written by a company on its common stock. These options include employee stock options, warrants, and convertible bonds and preferred stock. We discuss how to value these securities and how to estimate their cost of capital. We also discuss how these securities affect a valuation analysis. In so doing, we discuss the potential significance of ignoring these securities in assessing a company's cost of capital and value. Finally, we discuss how option pricing models can be used to measure the probability of financial distress.

12.1 THE BLACK-SCHOLES AND MERTON OPTION PRICING MODEL BASICS

The seminal works of Black and Scholes (1973) and Merton (1973) and other related works by these authors and others underpin many of the option pricing models used today.[2] We assume the reader already has some understanding of both option pricing theory and these models, so what follows is only a summary review of the Black-Scholes and Merton option pricing models. Just as with many models used in valuation, these option pricing models make certain assumptions about markets, information, and the characteristics of the options. Since these assumptions are unlikely to hold exactly in a specific circumstance, they are simply estimates of the value of the options. Nevertheless, these models are widely used in practice.

LO1 Use the Black-Scholes Option Pricing Model to value "plain vanilla" options

Key Factors that Determine the Value of an Option

Black and Scholes developed their option pricing model under the assumption that the option could not be exercised until the expiration date (**European option**). They assumed that markets are frictionless—that is, markets have no transactions costs or taxes—and that investors have the same instantaneous and cost-less access to information. They also assumed that investors have no restrictions on their ability to engage in short sales, that assets trade continuously, that the risk-free rate is known and stationary, and that the company does not pay dividends (Merton eliminated this last restriction). They also assume that it is not the company issuing the option; hence, there will be no dilution of the existing shareholders associated with the exercise of the option.

Based on these assumptions, we know two key factors relevant to option pricing, because they are part of the option's contract: the **strike** or **exercise price** (X_{Option}), at which the option can be exercised, and the length of the contract—or the amount of time to the expiration date (T_{Option}). We discuss these factors from the perspective of an investor who purchases a call option on a stock. All else equal, the investor prefers to have a lower exercise price because the investor will have to pay less for the stock. Similarly, all else equal, the investor prefers to have a longer time to expiration because the longer the time to expiration, the longer the stock price has to grow above the exercise price. In addition, since the difference between the stock price and the strike price determines the payoff at the expiration of the option, all else equal, the investor prefers a higher stock price (P_E). Thus, so far, we have identified three factors that clearly determine the value of an option—stock price, exercise price, and time to expiration.

The Black-Scholes option pricing model includes two additional factors that affect the option's value. The first factor is the variance of the stock price. Since the call is worth more the greater the spread between the stock price and the exercise price, the investor prefers a higher probability that the stock price will be higher than the exercise price. All else equal, the larger the variance of the stock price, the higher the probability that the stock price will be larger than the exercise price. Thus, all else equal, a call is worth more when written on a stock with a higher variance. The last factor in the Black-Scholes Option Pricing Model is the risk-free rate of return. The time value of money is relevant to option pricing because the investor pays the exercise price at the exercise date. Thus, the value of the option today takes the present value of the exercise price into consideration. Black and Scholes show that an investor can hedge an investment so that any adjustment for the time value of money will be at the risk-free rate of return. All else equal, the higher the risk-free rate of return, the lower the present value of the exercise price and thus the higher the value of the option. To summarize, all else equal, the value of an option increases with increases in the stock price, the variance of the stock price, the time to expiration of the option, and the risk-free rate; it decreases with increases in the strike price.

---

[2] Black, F., and M. Scholes, "The Pricing of Options and Corporate Liabilities," *Journal of Political Economy* vol. 81, no. 3, (May/June 1973), pp. 637–654; and Merton, R. C., "Theory of Rational Option Pricing," *Bell Journal of Economics and Management Science* vol. 4, no. 1 (Spring 1973), pp. 141–183.

Merton adds one additional factor: dividends. As we know, when a company pays a dividend, it reduces the company's assets and, thus, its equity value (ignoring any informational value of the dividend). All else equal, the stock price of a company that pays dividends will have a lower value by the amount of the dividends paid. The Black-Scholes model assumes dividends are not paid, but Merton includes dividend distributions. The higher the dividend yield, the lower the value of the option.

Valuation in Practice 12.1

Intel Corporation's Valuation of Its Equity Incentive Plan As described in its 10-K report, Intel Corporation (Intel) uses the Black-Scholes Option Pricing Model to measure the fair value of stock options and stock purchase rights granted:

. . . use the Black-Scholes option-pricing model for estimating the fair value of options granted under the company's equity incentive plans and rights to acquire stock granted under the company's stock purchase plan. The weighted average estimated values of employee stock option grants and rights granted under the stock purchase plan, as well as the weighted average assumptions that were used in calculating such values . . . , were based on estimates at the date of grant as follows:

	Stock Options			Stock Purchase Plan		
	2004	**2005**	**2006**	**2004**	**2005**	**2006**
Estimated value per option.	$10.79	$6.02	$5.21	$6.38	$0	$6.02
Expected life (in years)	4.2	4.7	4.9	0.5	0.5	0.5
Risk-free interest rate.	3.0%	3.9%	4.9%	1.4%	3.2%	5.0%
Volatility	50.0%	26.0%	27.0%	30.0%	23.0%	29.0%
Dividend yield.	0.6%	1.4%	2.0%	0.6%	1.3%	2.1%

Source: See Intel's 2006 10-K report filed with the U.S. SEC and available on the company's website, www.intel.com.

The Black-Scholes and Merton Option Pricing Models

We know that the value of a call option at the exercise date is equal to the price of the stock minus the exercise price. For example, if an investor exercises a call option at the expiration date when the stock price is $12 and the exercise price is $10, the investor will earn $2; thus, the value of this option immediately before it is expires is very close to $2. Naturally, valuing an option one year before the exercise date is more complex, for we do not know the value of the stock at the exercise date; however, we know the current stock price, the variability of the stock price, the length of the option contract, and the strike price. We can use these factors to estimate the expected payoff from the call option. The Black-Scholes Option Pricing Model, which is the continuous version of the discrete time binomial model for pricing options, does just that. The form of this model is

$$P_C = P_E \times N(d_1) - X_C \times e^{-r_F \times T_C} \times N(d_2) \tag{12.1}$$

where:

P_C = price of a European call option
P_E = common stock price per share
T_C = time to expiration of the call option (in years)
X_C = exercise or strike price of the call option

$$d_1 = \frac{\ln\left(\dfrac{P_E}{X_C}\right) + (r_F + \sigma_E^2/2) \times T_C}{\sigma_E \times \sqrt{T_C}}$$

$$d_2 = d_1 - \sigma_E \times \sqrt{T_C}$$

r_F = risk-free rate of return

$N(x)$ = the standard cumulative normal[3]

σ_E = the standard deviation of the company's continuously compounded annual returns

This formula might not be intuitive, but we can think of it as measuring the difference between the present value of the expected stock price at expiration minus the present value of the strike price.

Valuation Key 12.1

The Black-Scholes Option Pricing Model prices a European call option (option only exercisable at the expiration date) based on five factors. All else equal, the value of an option increases with increases in the stock price, variance of the stock price, time to expiration, and risk-free rate; it decreases with increases in the strike price.

As long as the option's underlying security does not pay dividends, Merton shows that the Black-Scholes option pricing formula can be used to value an American option even though it can be exercised before the expiration date. The intuition underpinning this conclusion is that the value of the option is always greater than the value of exercising the option and owning the stock; thus, the option will not be exercised early, and the value of the American option will be the same as the value of the European option. Merton also derives an adjustment for a European call option for a stock that pays dividends.

It is clear that, all else equal, if a company pays dividends, the value of the option decreases because the value of the stock at the exercise date will be lower. Merton adjusts the option pricing model for dividends by assuming the company pays a constant dividend yield (dividend divided by stock price, continuously compounded). He adjusts the pricing formula by essentially reducing the value of the first component in the option pricing formula by discounting the stock price by the dividend yield as follows:

$$P_C = P_E \times e^{-d_E \times T_C} \times N(d_1) - X_C \times e^{-r_F \times T_C} \times N(d_2) \tag{12.2}$$

All terms are as defined earlier with an adjustment to d_1 as follows:

$$d_1 = \frac{\ln\left(\dfrac{P_E}{X_C}\right) + (r_F - d_E + \sigma_E^2/2) \times T_C}{\sigma_E \times \sqrt{T_C}}$$

$$d_2 = d_1 - \sigma_E \times \sqrt{T_C}$$

d_E = annual continuously compounded dividend yield

Merton's formula for valuing a European call option is not applicable to an American call option for a dividend-paying stock. If an option holder can exercise an option before the expiration date, it may be more valuable to do so before the dividend reduces the stock price. In order to value the option, we must examine the value of the option before each expected dividend payment while considering such factors as the expected drop in stock price after the dividend and the time to expiration remaining after the dividend. The **binomial option method** can be used to value these options.

Valuation Key 12.2

Merton shows that the Black-Scholes option pricing formula can be used to value an American option as long as the underlying security does not pay dividends. He also develops an option pricing model for a European call option for a stock that pays dividends.

We do not walk through a detailed example using the Black-Scholes and Merton option pricing models, as we presume the reader already has familiarity with these models. However, Review Exercise 12.1 utilizes these models to value a European call option for those in need of a refresher.

---

[3] $N(x)$ is the probability that a normally distributed random variable will be less than x standard deviations above the mean. If x is, say, 2, then the probability will be close to 1.0 (.9972 to be exact).

REVIEW EXERCISE 12.1

Valuation of a Basic European Call Option

A European call option provides the holder of the option the right to purchase a share of a company's stock for $12 per share three years from today. The stock is currently trading at $10, does not pay dividends, and has a standard deviation on its annual return of 30%. The risk-free rate of return is 5%. What is the value of this option today? How will the value of the option change if the company changes its dividend policy and begins to pay a regular dividend (continuously compounded) equal to 5% of its stock price?

Solution on page 505.

12.2 THE VALUATION EFFECTS OF WARRANTS AND OTHER SIMILAR EQUITY-LINKED SECURITIES

LO2 Measure the value and cost of capital for warrants and make the appropriate adjustments for warrants in a valuation analysis

When valuing a company, we focus on securities used to finance the company—in other words, securities issued by the company that are part of the company's capital structure. Recall that the levering, unlevering, and weighted average cost of capital formulas require us to know the cost of capital and capital structure ratio for each of the securities used by a company to finance itself. These securities include such equity-linked securities as warrants, employee stock options, and convertible debt. Employee stock options can have free cash flow and income tax effects, which we discuss in the next section of the chapter.

Measuring the Price (Value) of Warrants

A warrant is similar to a call option. A warrant is a security issued by a company that gives the holder the right (but not the obligation) to purchase a certain number of shares of the company's stock at a fixed price on or before a specified date. One difference between a company issuing a warrant and investors issuing option contracts to each other is the dilution in the company's equity that occurs from issuing warrants that does not occur when investors issue options to each other.

Daves and Ehrhardt (2007) developed a pricing model and a cost of capital model for warrants, which we use in this section of the chapter.[4] In this analysis, we assume warrants are the only equity-linked security outstanding and that they are exercisable on their expiration date. If the company has other equity-linked securities outstanding, we would include all such securities in this analysis. As we might expect, the formula for the value of a warrant is similar to the Black-Scholes option pricing formula adjusted for dividends and the effect of the warrants on the number of shares of common equity oustanding.

$$P_W = \frac{n \times CR}{n + m \times CR} \times \left[\left(P_E \times e^{-d_E \times T_W} + P_W \times \frac{m}{n} \right) \times N(d_1) - X_W \times e^{-r_F \times T_W} \times N(d_2) \right] \quad (12.3)$$

All terms are as defined earlier, and

P_W = price per warrant
n = number of common shares outstanding
m = number of warrants outstanding
CR = conversion ratio or the number of common shares exchanged for each warrant
T_W = time to expiration of the warrant in years
X_W = the exercise or strike price of the warrant

$$d_1 = \frac{\ln\left(\dfrac{P_E \times e^{-d_E \times T_W} + P_W \times \frac{m}{n}}{X_W}\right) + (r_F + \sigma_Q^2/2) \times T_W}{\sigma_Q \times \sqrt{T_W}}$$

---

[4] Daves, P. R., and Ehrhardt, M., "Convertible Securities, Employee Stock Options and the Cost of Equity," *The Financial Review* vol. 42, no. 2 (May 2007), pp. 267–288, available at SSRN: http://ssrn.com/abstract=990906 or DOI: 10.1111/j.1540-6288.2007.00171.x.

$$d_2 = d_1 - \sigma_Q \times \sqrt{T_W}$$

σ_Q = the standard deviation of the expected annual return on the total value of the common stock and warrants, V_Q

We can measure the standard deviation, σ_Q, of the expected annual return on the total value of the common stock and warrants using Equation 12.4:

$$\sigma_Q = \sigma_E \times P_E \times \frac{n + m \times \omega_E}{n \times P_E + m \times P_W} \tag{12.4}$$

We can calculate the last term in the numerator of Equation 12.4 (which is equal to the partial derivative of the warrant price with respect to the stock price) using Equation 12.5:

$$\omega_E = \frac{n \times CR \times e^{-d_E \times T_W} \times N(d_1)}{n + m \times CR \times [1 - N(d_1)]} \tag{12.5}$$

As is apparent from Equation 12.3, the warrant price is a function of itself because it appears on both sides of Equation 12.3. In addition, Equation 12.3 depends on Equations 12.4 and 12.5 but Equation 12.4 depends on Equation 12.5; more specifically, ω_E in Equation 12.4 depends on d_1 (see Equation 12.5), which depends on σ_Q from Equation 12.4. Thus, the calculation of the warrant price is circular and we must solve for the warrant price numerically. While we could numerically calculate the warrant price manually, it is naturally easier to use spreadsheet software. Using spreadsheet software, we first enable the iterative function in the spreadsheet, which allows the calculation of indirect circular references like the one we have in the calculation of the warrant price. Then, using a solver or goal seek function, we choose a possible warrant price, use the chosen warrant price to calculate the warrant price using the above equations, and compare the chosen warrant price to the calculated warrant price. We use the solver or goal seek function to iterate the chosen warrant price numerically until we minimize the absolute value of the difference between the chosen and calculated warrant prices.

Measuring the Warrant Cost of Capital

The cost of capital for warrants is, in essence, a levered cost of equity because we invest less in a warrant than in a share of stock. The leverage effect of equity-linked securities relative to the underlying stock is not always immediately apparent. We often think of the common shareholders as the residual claimants, and that they hold the security with the highest amount of risk; however, warrants have more risk than the underlying equity.

What happens to the company's equity cost of capital (and beta) when it issues warrants? In Exhibit 12.1, we illustrate this effect on the beta (and hence on the equity cost of capital) of a hypothetical company. We assume the company in the exhibit is initially financed with common equity and has an equity beta equal to 2.0. The diamonds in the exhibit show a random set of market returns and corresponding stock returns for a company with a beta of 2.0, and a small normally distributed random error. The line through these diamonds represents the estimates of the market model and the slope of the line is equal to the company's beta, which is equal to 2.0.

The dots in the exhibit represent the equity returns of the company after it issues warrants. To hold the company's investments (assets) constant, we assume the company repurchases common equity with the proceeds from issuing the warrants. To more clearly show the effect of issuing warrants, we assume the stock price, $12, is above the exercise price. Since the warrants share in the upside and downside, the equityholders end up giving up some of the upside and downside. Thus, for a given change in the value of the assets, the warrants dampen the equity returns (the equity returns are closer to zero). In this case, the equity beta for the company with the warrants is 1.12—a reduction of 44%. Thus, issuing warrants—or other equity-linked securities—reduces the company's equity beta and reduces its equity cost of capital.

We show the effect of issuing warrants on the equity cost of capital in Equation 12.6. The term $r_{E\&W-WtdAvg}$ is the value-weighted average cost of capital for the warrants and equity combined, which is equal to the equity cost of capital if the company did not issue warrants.

$$r_E = r_{E\&W-WtdAvg} \times \frac{n \times P_E + m \times P_W}{n \times P_E + m \times P_E \times \omega_E} + r_F \times \frac{m \times P_E \times \omega_E - m \times P_W}{n \times P_E + m \times P_E \times \omega_E} \tag{12.6}$$

As it turns out, if we assume that the company repurchases shares with the proceeds from issuing warrants, the weighted average cost of capital of the equity and the warrants combined will equal the cost of equity prior to the issuance of the warrants.

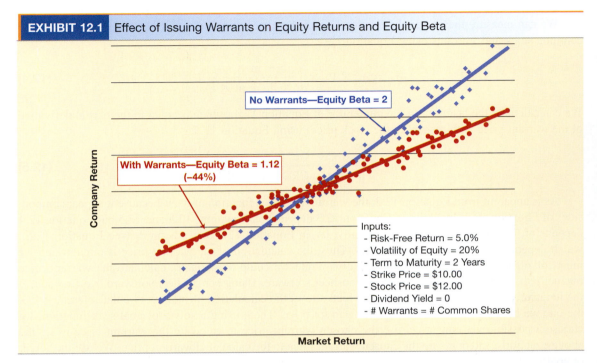

EXHIBIT 12.1 Effect of Issuing Warrants on Equity Returns and Equity Beta

No Warrants—Equity Beta = 2

With Warrants—Equity Beta = 1.12 (–44%)

Inputs:
- Risk-Free Return = 5.0%
- Volatility of Equity = 20%
- Term to Maturity = 2 Years
- Strike Price = $10.00
- Stock Price = $12.00
- Dividend Yield = 0
- # Warrants = # Common Shares

Company Return (vertical axis)

Market Return

For companies that have outstanding stock options or other equity-linked securities, the equity cost of capital we observe from models like the CAPM includes the effect of the equity-linked securities. As a result, for a comparable company with outstanding warrants, stock options, or other similar equity-linked securities, not including the equity-linked securities in the unlevering process will result in an unlevered cost of capital that is too low. We illustrate this point later in the chapter when we discuss the KapStone Paper and Packaging Corporation.

We show the relation between the warrant cost of capital and the equity cost of capital in Equation 12.7. The cost of capital for the warrants, r_W, is equal to the risk-free rate plus the stock's equity risk premium adjusted for the leverage from the warrant. The leverage adjustment is a function of two factors: the ratio of the stock price to the warrant price (which adjusts the return for the relative investments) and the last term in the equation (which is equal to the partial derivative of the warrant price with respect to the stock price and is defined in Equation 12.5). The leverage effect, which is the product of the last two terms, is always greater than or equal to 1; it is greater than 1 unless the stock price is substantially below the exercise price of the warrant.

$$r_W = r_F + (r_E - r_F) \times \frac{P_E}{P_W} \times \omega_E \qquad \textbf{(12.7)}$$

If we use the iterative process we describe to measure the warrant price, we have all of the inputs necessary to measure the warrant cost of capital using Equation 12.7. If we know the price of the warrant—for example, because it is publicly traded—we can measure the partial derivative, ω_E, directly using Equations 12.4 and 12.5.

Valuation Key 12.3

We can use option pricing models to measure the value and cost of capital for such equity-linked securities as warrants and other types of stock options.

Determinants (Inputs) of the Warrant Cost of Capital

From what we just discussed, it is clear that the warrant cost of capital is a function of such various determinants as the exercise price, the stock price, the volatility of the equity, the time to the expiration of the warrants, the dividend yield, the equity cost of capital, and the risk-free rate of return. In Exhibit 12.2, we summarize these relations. We know from option pricing theory that, holding everything else constant, the value of the option increases with increases in the stock price, the volatility of the equity, the risk-free rate, and the time to expiration; we also know it decreases with increases in the exercise price, and the dividend yield. The same is true for warrants, of course, as shown in the exhibit.

	Warrant	
Factor Increasing	**Value**	**Cost of Capital**
Stock price.	+	−
Volatility of common stock.	+	−
Risk-free rate	+	−
Time to expiration.	+	−
Exercise (strike) price	−	+
Dividend yield.	−	+
Equity cost of capital − r_F.	0	+

EXHIBIT 12.2 Effect of Various Factors on the Value and Cost of Capital of Warrants

Holding everything else constant, the value of an option does not depend on the equity cost of capital, but we can clearly see from Equation 12.7 that the warrant cost of capital is a function of the cost of equity spread (equity cost of capital minus the risk-free rate). As we can see from the exhibit, the warrant cost of capital is an increasing function of the equity cost of capital, but the value of the warrants is independent of (does not vary with) the equity cost of capital. For the other factors, the warrant cost of capital moves in the opposite direction of the value of the warrants; in other words, holding everything else constant, the warrant cost of capital decreases with increases in the stock price, the volatility of the equity, the risk-free rate, and the time to expiration; it increases with increases in the exercise price, and the dividend yield.

Valuation in Practice 12.2

KapStone Paper and Packaging Corporation's Warrants On August 19, 2005, the KapStone Paper and Packaging Corporation (KapStone) issued 20,000,000 units ("Units") for $6.00 per Unit as part of its initial public offering. Each Unit consisted of one share of the company's common stock and two warrants. According to the company, each warrant entitled the holder to purchase one share of common stock at an exercise price of $5.00 from the company, and the warrant expired on August 15, 2009. The warrants were also redeemable by the company at a price of $0.01 per warrant upon 30 days' notice after the warrants became exercisable, and their stock price is at least $8.50 per share for any 20 trading days within a 30-day trading period. The company included this provision to be able to force conversion.

Source: See KapStone Paper and Packaging Corporation (KapStone) 2008 10-K report.

The KapStone Paper and Packaging Corporation

Refer to Valuation in Practice 12.2. Assume we measured KapStone's various costs of capital and security values as of June 30, 2008, which we summarize in Exhibit 12.3. The company's observed equity cost of capital is 12%, and the company has 28,370,248 shares of common stock outstanding that are trading at $6.67 per share. These market data incorporate the effect of the warrants on the company's equity cost of capital and share price. Had KapStone not had these warrants outstanding, we would have observed a higher equity cost of capital. KapStone has 40,000,000 warrants outstanding that are trading at $2.30 and will expire in 1.125 years. The company does not pay dividends, the risk-free rate is 3%, and the annual volatility of the company's equity is 50%. Last, the market value of the company's debt is $390 million, which has a weighted average cost of capital of 8%. The company's marginal tax rate for interest tax shields is 40%. We assume for this illustration that the appropriate discount rate for interest tax shields is the unlevered cost of capital and we ignore the call feature of these warrants. We also assume the current capital structure reflects the company's long-run capital structure. Finally, while the company does have some employee stock options outstanding, we ignore them to simplify the illustration.

| EXHIBIT 12.3 | KapStone Paper and Packaging Corporation's Cost of Capital Excluding and Including the Effects of Warrants | | | | | | | |

	Shares/ Warrants	Price per Unit ($)	Valuation ($ in millions)	Capital Structure Weight	Cost of Capital	Unlevered Cost of Capital	Weighted Average Cost of Capital
Excluding (Ignoring) Warrants:							
Common...................	28,370,248	$6.670	$189.23	32.7%	12.0%	3.9%	3.9%
Debt			390.00	67.3%	8.0%	5.4%	3.2%
Total			$579.23	100.0%		9.3%	7.2%
Other Information:							
Income tax rate 40.0%							
Risk-free rate of return 3.0%							
Annual volatility of equity 50.0%							
Exercise price of warrants $5.00							
Expiration of warrants (in years)... 1.125							
Including Warrants:							
Common...................	28,370,248	$6.670	$189.23	28.2%	12.0%	3.4%	3.4%
Warrants...................	40,000,000	$2.300	92.00	13.7%	23.9%	3.3%	3.3%
Debt			390.00	58.1%	8.0%	4.6%	2.8%
Total			$671.23	100.0%		11.3%	9.5%

Exhibit may contain small rounding errors

KapStone as a Comparable Company.

We first calculate the company's unlevered cost of capital ignoring the warrants; in other words, we assume the only financing the company uses is common equity and debt and that interest tax shields are discounted at the unlevered cost of capital. As we show in the exhibit, when we ignore the warrants, the company's capital structure is 32.7% debt and 67.3% equity. The cost of debt and equity are, respectively, 8% and 12%. If we ignore the warrant financing in calculating the unlevered cost of capital, it is equal to 9.3%.

$$r_{UA} = r_E \times \frac{V_E}{V_F} + r_D \times \frac{V_D}{V_F}$$

$$.093 = .327 \times .12 + .673 \times .08$$

The above calculation is incorrect because we excluded the warrant component of the company's cost of capital, which also has the effect of overweighting the amount of debt in the company's capital structure. To measure the company's unlevered cost of capital that includes the effect of the warrants, we first measure the value of the warrants and the warrant cost of capital. The warrants are publicly traded at $2.30, resulting in a total value of the warrants of $92 million. When we include the warrants in the company's capital structure, the capital structure changes from 32.7% equity and 67.3% debt to 28.2% equity, 13.7% warrants, and 58.1% debt. Since we know that the warrant cost of capital is higher than the equity cost of capital, we know that the unlevered cost of capital that includes the warrants will be larger than the one that excludes the warrants. The warrant cost of capital is equal to 23.9%, which is almost twice as large as the equity cost of capital. The formula to measure the unlevered cost of capital now has three components (debt, equity, and the warrants), and the unlevered cost of capital that includes the warrants increases from 9.3% to 11.3%.

$$r_{UA} = r_E \times \frac{V_E}{V_F} + r_D \times \frac{V_D}{V_F} \quad \text{versus} \quad r_{UA} = r_E \times \frac{V_E}{V_F} + r_W \times \frac{V_W}{V_F} + r_D \times \frac{V_D}{V_F}$$

$$.093 = .12 \times .327 + .08 \times .673 \quad \text{versus} \quad .113 = .12 \times .282 + .239 \times .137 + .08 \times .581$$

KapStone's Weighted Average Cost of Capital.

Alternatively, assume that we are interested in valuing KapStone using the weighted average cost of capital discounted cash flow valuation method.

We illustrate the effect of excluding and including warrants in estimating KapStone's weighted average cost of capital in the last column of Exhibit 12.3. Using these same inputs and an income tax rate of 40%, KapStone's weighted average cost of capital is equal to 7.2% when we ignore the warrants. However, the weighted average cost of capital increases by almost a third to 9.5% once we include the warrants.

$$r_{WACC} = r_E \times \frac{V_E}{V_F} + (1 - T_{INT}) \times r_D \times \frac{V_D}{V_F} \quad \text{versus} \quad r_{WACC} = r_E \times \frac{V_E}{V_F} + r_W \times \frac{V_W}{V_F} + (1 - T_{INT}) \times r_D \times \frac{V_D}{V_F}$$

$$.072 = .12 \times .327 + (1 - .4) \times .08 \times .673 \quad \text{versus} \quad .095 = .12 \times .282 - .239 \times .137 + (1 - .4) \times .08 \times .581$$

In KapStone's case, not treating the warrants appropriately would lead to a large error in the valuation. If KapStone were a no-growth perpetuity, ignoring the warrants would lead to a valuation that is more than 30% too high. If KapStone were similar to a perpetuity with a 3% growth rate, ignoring the warrants would lead to a valuation that is more than 50% too high.

Naturally, we chose KapStone because its warrants had a large effect on its unlevered and weighted average cost of capital, and not all companies are affected as significantly by their equity-linked securities. However, we can readily see that for some companies with a significant number of warrants (or employee stock options or other equity-linked securities), the impact can be significant. Finally, we note that the equity and warrant cost of capital change over time as the warrants approach the expiration date. The only way for the company to have a constant equity or weighted average cost of capital is to assume the company will maintain its capital structure, which will include the characteristics of the warrants.

REVIEW EXERCISE 12.2

Cost of Capital for Warrants

A company has 20,000 shares of common stock and 1,000 warrants outstanding. Each warrant has the right to purchase five shares of the company's stock in five years at $12 per share, which is the current stock price. The value of a warrant is $8.775. The standard deviation of the stock's annual return is 24%. The company has a continuously compounded dividend yield of 5%. The company has $200,000 of outstanding debt with a 9% cost of capital. The company's equity cost of capital is 14%, the marginal tax rate for interest tax shields is 40%, and the risk-free rate is 4%. Ignore the warrants and calculate the company's unlevered cost of capital and weighted average cost of capital, assuming that the company's current capital structure (without the warrants) represents its long-run capital structure and that the discount rate for interest tax shields is the unlevered cost of capital. Using these same assumptions, calculate the company's unlevered cost of capital and weighted average cost of capital that includes the effect of the warrants.

Solution on page 506.

Adjusting the Valuation for Warrants and Other Similar Equity-Linked Securities

In order to measure the value of a company's common equity, we subtract the value of all the non-common equity securities from the value of the firm. These non-common equity securities include warrants and other common equity-linked securities. However, since the value of the equity-linked securities depends on the company's stock price, we must use numerical methods to simultaneously measure the value of the equity-linked securities and the value of the common equity. We use warrants to illustrate this issue and denote the value of the warrants as V_W. To measure the value of the equity we perform the following calculation:

$$V_E = V_F - V_D - V_{PS} - V_W$$

Since the value of the outstanding warrants is a function of the company's stock price, we must consider the simultaneous effect that the value of the equity has on the value of outstanding warrants. If we subtract the value of the non-convertible debt and preferred stock from the value of the firm, we measure the combined value of the equity and the outstanding warrants:

$$V_F - V_D - V_{PS} = V_E + V_W$$

The value of the equity is equal to the share price of the equity (P_E), multiplied by the number of shares of equity outstanding as of the valuation date (SO_E). The value of the outstanding warrants is equal to the price of a warrant on a per common share basis (P_W) multiplied by the number of common shares that can be purchased by the outstanding warrants (SO_W):

$$V_F - V_D - V_{PS} = P_E \times SO_E + SO_W \times P_W \qquad (12.8)$$

We can solve this equality using an iterative process. We choose alternative stock prices until we identify a stock price for which the value of the equity ($P_E \times SO_E$) plus the value of the outstanding warrants ($SO_W \times P_W$) is equal to the residual value of the firm ($V_F - V_D - V_{PS}$).

The Knuth Company

The Knuth Company has an expected unlevered free cash flow of $8,400 in Year 1 that is expected to grow at a 5% rate in perpetuity. As of the end of Year 0, the company has $40,000 in debt outstanding and $10,000 of preferred stock outstanding, which equals their respective market values. The debt and preferred are expected to grow with the value of the firm. The cost of debt is 10%, the cost of preferred stock is 12%, and its unlevered cost of capital is 15%, which is also the discount rate for interest tax shields. The company's income tax rate is 40% on all income. We do not know the company's capital structure ratios, but we do know the amount of debt it has outstanding; thus, we can value the company using the adjusted present value method:

$$V_F = \frac{\$8,400}{.15 - .05} + \frac{\$40,000 \times .10 \times .40}{.15 - .05} = \$100,000$$

The value of Knuth under its original capital structure is $100,000, and the value of the debt and preferred stock is $40,000 and $10,000, respectively. We measure the value of the equity to be $50,000 ($50,000 = $100,000 − $40,000 − $10,000). If Knuth has 10,000 shares of common stock outstanding and no equity-based compensation or other equity-based securities, the value of the common stock is $5 per share ($5 = $50,000/10,000). However, if Knuth has warrants outstanding, this price is overstated.

Measuring Knuth's Common Equity Value and Stock Price with Warrants. Now assume that Knuth has 5,000 outstanding warrants as of the valuation date. Each warrant allows the investor to purchase one share of the stock for $3 in three years. To measure the value of the common equity adjusted for the outstanding warrants, we first measure the value of all equity-based claims (common stock and warrants), which we already know is $50,000. We assume Knuth has a 50% annualized stock return standard deviation, the risk-free rate is 5%, and the company will pay dividends equal to the equity free cash flows of $7,300.

We can use the option-based warrant pricing model developed by Daves and Ehrhardt (2007) to value the warrants. Of course, the shares are no longer going to be worth $5 per share unless the warrants have no value as the sum of the equity value and the warrant value has to equal $50,000. In other words, the sum of the share price multiplied by the number of shares outstanding and the warrant price multiplied by the number warrants outstanding has to equal $50,000. We use an iterative process to identify the appropriate price per common share and price per warrant.

Since the value of the equity claims (stock and warrants) is too high at $5 per common share, we decrease the stock price and iterate until we identify the stock price that solves the equality in Equation 12.8. It turns out that the stock price that results in a combined stock and warrant value equal to $50,000 is $4.5513, which has a corresponding warrant price of $0.8975. The dividend yield is equal to the $7,300 equity free cash flow, divided by the value of the common equity evaluated at that stock price and calculated on a continuously compounded basis. At a value of $4.5513 per share, the continuously compounded dividend yield is 17.4%. We also note that the value of the stock and options is just $50,000 now.

$$\$100,000 - \$40,000 - \$10,000 = \$50,000 = \$4.5513 \times 10,000 + 5,000 \times \$0.8975$$

Using the Weighted Average Cost of Capital Method to Value Knuth. Since we know all of the capital structure inputs, we can measure Knuth's weighted average cost of capital and use the weighted average cost of capital valuation method to value Knuth. Knuth's debt-to-value capital structure ratio is 40% (.4 = $40,000/$100,000). With a 40% income tax rate, a 15% unlevered cost of capital, and using the unlevered cost of capital to discount interest tax shields, we can measure the weighted average cost of capital as follows (see Equation 11.2):

$$r_{WACC} = r_{UA} - r_D \times T_{INT} \times \frac{V_D}{V_F} - (r_{UA} - r_{ITS}) \times \frac{V_{ITS}}{V_F}$$

$$.134 = .15 - .10 \times .4 \times .4 - 0$$

$$V_F = \frac{\$8,400}{.134 - .05} = \$100,000$$

Note that to measure the weighted average cost of capital for a firm with warrants, we do not need to estimate either the value or the cost of capital for the warrants using this formula. We do need to know the unlevered cost of capital, the debt cost of capital, the proportion of debt in the capital structure, and the relevant tax rate for interest.

We could also measure Knuth's weighted average cost of capital using the more common formula, which measures the weighted average cost of capital by weighting the after-tax cost of capital for each type of security the company uses to finance itself. This calculation is not so straightforward. We do not know Knuth's equity cost of capital or its warrant cost of capital. We can solve for the equity and warrant cost of capital because we know the weighted average of the equity and warrant costs of capital after the warrants are issued. We can measure Knuth's weighted average equity and warrant costs of capital, $r_{E\&W-WtdAvg}$, as follows. First, we can measure the cost of capital for the combined equity and warrants using our standard levering formula for the equity cost of capital when interest tax shields are discounted at the unlevered cost of capital:

$$r_{E\&W-WtdAvg} = r_{UA} + (r_{UA} - r_{PS}) \times \frac{V_{PS}}{V_E} + (r_{UA} - r_D) \times \frac{V_D}{V_E}$$

$$.196 = .15 + (.15 - .12) \times \frac{\$10,000}{\$50,000} + (.15 - .1) \times \frac{\$40,000}{\$50,000}$$

Remember, however, that this is not the equity cost of capital after the warrants are issued, but is the weighted average cost of capital of the warrants and the equity. After we measure the value of the warrants, we can use Equation 12.4 to measure Knuth's common equity cost of capital:

$$r_E = r_{E\&W-WtdAvg} \times \frac{n \times P_E + m \times P_W}{n \times P_E + m \times P_E \times \omega_E} + r_F \times \frac{m \times P_E \times \omega_E - m \times P_W}{n \times P_E + m \times P_E \times \omega_E}$$

$$0.1838 = .196 \times \frac{10,000 \times \$4.5513 + 5,000 \times \$0.8975}{10,000 \times \$4.5513 + 5,000 \times \$4.5513 \times 0.3974}$$

$$+ .05 \times \frac{5,000 \times \$4.5513 \times 0.3974 - 5,000 \times \$0.8975}{10,000 \times \$4.5513 + 5,000 \times \$4.5513 \times 0.3974}$$

Now we can use Equation 12.6 to measure Knuth's warrant cost of capital:

$$r_W = r_F + (r_E - r_F) \times \frac{P_E}{P_W} \times \omega_E$$

$$0.3197 = .05 + (0.1838 - .05) \times \frac{\$4.5513}{\$0.8975} \times 0.3974$$

We now finally have all of the inputs to measure Knuth's weighted average cost of capital using the more common formula. Of course, this is a lot of work relative to just using Equation 11.2, so the formulas for the weighted average cost of capital based on Equation 11.2 are useful, especially for calculating the weighted average cost of capital for companies with option-like securities.

Capital Structure Including Warrants	Value	Weight	Cost of Capital	r_{WACC}
Value of the debt	$ 40,000	40.0%	10.0%	2.4%
Value of the preferred.	10,000	10.0%	12.0%	1.2%
Value of warrants	4,487	4.5%	32.0%	1.4%
Value of the equity	45,513	45.5%	18.4%	8.4%
Value of the firm	$100,000	100.0%		13.4%

REVIEW EXERCISE 12.3

The Stuart Essig Perpetuity Company

The Stuart Essig Company has an unlevered cost of capital of 10% and an income tax rate of 40%. The company finances itself with 50% debt, which has a cost of capital equal to 9%; with 20% preferred stock, which has a cost of capital of 9.5%; and the remainder with common equity. The company expects its unlevered free cash flows to remain constant in perpetuity. The company holds no excess cash or excess assets and expects to pay $3,600 in common dividends in Year 1. Interest tax shields are valued using the unlevered cost of capital.

Use the following information to measure the company's stock price, assuming it has 10,000 shares of common stock outstanding at the end of Year 0—the valuation date. Afterward, calculate the company's stock price, assuming the company issued 5,000 warrants as of the end of Year 0 (each warrant can buy one share) with an exercise or strike price of $1 and immediately paid the proceeds out to its shareholders. The company expects to follow a consistent dividend policy and to pay all available cash flow to its shareholders in the form of dividends. The warrants can be exercised at the end of five years, their expiration date. At the date of issuance, the risk-free rate was 5%, and the company's annualized standard deviation of its stock return was 45%.

Income Statement Forecast	Year 1
Revenue	$180,000.0
Depreciation expense.	−25,000.0
Operating expenses	−141,333.3
Earnings before interest and taxes. . . .	$ 13,666.7

Balance Sheet Forecast—Assets	Year 1
Cash	$ 4,000.0
Net operating working capital	25,000.0
Net property, plant, and equipment . .	120,000.0
Total assets.	$149,000.0

Unlevered Free Cash Flow Forecast	Year 1
Earnings before interest and taxes. . . .	$13,666.7
Income taxes	−5,466.7
Unlevered earnings after tax	$ 8,200.0
Depreciation expense (non-cash expenses).	25,000.0
Change in required cash	0.0
Change in net working capital	0.0
Capital expenditures	−25,000.0
Unlevered free cash flows	$ 8,200.0

Solution on page 506.

Valuation Key 12.4

The value of the firm includes the value of the common equity, the value of debt, and the value of preferred; in addition, it includes the value of a variety of such option-like securities as warrants and other similar equity-linked securities. When we value the firm, determining the combined value of the outstanding common equity and option-like securities is relatively straightforward. We must take additional steps to parse the combined value into the value of the outstanding common equity and the value of the option-like securities.

12.3 ADJUSTMENTS FOR THE TAX AND OTHER EFFECTS OF EMPLOYEE STOCK OPTIONS AND OTHER EQUITY-LINKED COMPENSATION

LO3 Adjust a valuation and the various costs of capital for the effects of employee stock options and other similar equity-based compensation

Companies often compensate employees using compensation plans that are either directly or indirectly related to the performance of the companies' common stock. The goal of such compensation plans is to better align the interests of the managers with those of the owners. We define such compensation plans as being either equity-based or share-based plans. In some of these plans, the company uses stock market performance or other measures believed to be related to stock market performance in order to pay cash bonuses to the employees. The cash bonus may be deferred and may require certain service or other performance requirements before it is paid. In equity-based compensation plans that are settled by issuing stock, the company does not pay the employee in cash; in fact, it may have a cash inflow as a result of paying an employee with this type of compensation (for example, when employees purchase stock by exercising stock options). Of course, many companies repurchase shares in anticipation of issuing shares to employees, and that results in a cash outflow for the company

When we value a company, we adjust our valuation for all forms of compensation paid to employees. If the company incurs an economic cost for compensating an employee, we adjust our valuation, financial model, and free cash flows for that economic cost even if it does not involve a direct cash outflow. As we discussed in Chapter 4, we adjust our valuation for cash compensation by including forecasts for all of its forms (annual salaries, bonuses, and hourly wages) in the free cash flow forecasts via the income statement and balance sheet forecasts. For equity-based compensation, we make equivalent adjustments, but they are not as straightforward as cash compensation adjustments.

We make two types of adjustments to our valuation model for equity-based compensation contracts. First, we adjust our valuation for equity-based compensation contracts outstanding as of the date of our valuation. We use the term "outstanding" to describe contracts that have been granted even if they have not vested with the employees. Second, we adjust the free cash flow forecasts for equity-based compensation contracts we expect the company to grant in the future.

Types of Equity-Based Compensation and the Accounting and Tax Implications

One form of equity-based compensation is a **stock option** compensation plan, where the company issues options to its employees—giving them rights to purchase a specified number of shares at a specific price (the **exercise** or **strike price**) during a certain period. A **stock appreciation right (SAR)** grants the employee the right to receive the value of the appreciation of a share of stock from the grant date to the expiration date of the SAR. The company can settle the amount owed the employee in cash, stock, or even preferred stock. Finally, the company may also give employees **restricted stock** or **restricted stock units (RSUs)**. In the case of restricted stock, the employee receives stock, but the stock is restricted and may not be transferred (or sold) until the restrictions are lifted, which is usually based on time and performance benchmarks. Depending on the specifics of the plan, the shares may or may not have dividend and voting rights while restricted. With restricted stock units, no stock is actually issued and the company often has the right to settle with the employee using stock or cash at the appropriate time.

The accounting for equity-based compensation consists of valuing the stock-based compensation and recording it as an expense over the vesting period, adjusting for any expected forfeitures or cancellations. A company usually values stock options or SARs using the Black-Scholes-based model adjusted for dividends as necessary, and it then records an expense over the vesting period equal to the value of the compensation at the date of grant. Companies can use either a straight-line or an accelerated form of amortization to expense the grant date value. A company values restricted stock or restricted stock units based on the number of shares, multiplied by their value at the date of grant. The company expenses this value over the vesting period of the restricted stock or RSU. In all cases, the valuation of the equity-based compensation at the grant date can be thought of as the present value of the ultimate expected cost the company will bear from having granted the equity-based compensation.

The tax effects of stock options and SARs are very similar. At the date of exercise for an option or settlement date for an SAR, the event triggers taxable income to the employee. The taxable income is based on the difference between the market value of the stock and the exercise price for an option and is based on the appreciation in the stock's value from the grant date for an SAR. The event also triggers a tax deduction for the corporation in the same amount. To be somewhat more precise, here we refer to non-qualified stock options that are issued out-of-the-money. There are also qualified stock options (also called incentive stock options) that are treated differently, and corporations can issue non-qualified options that are in-the-money.

Most corporations issue non-qualified stock options that are out-of-the-money or at-the-money (strike price is greater than or equal to the stock price when issued). With a qualified stock option, the corporation gets no tax deduction, and when the stock is sold, the employee only pays capital gains taxes on the difference between the market value of the stock and the exercise price. If an option is issued in-the-money, it is automatically non-qualified, but the employee pays a tax on the difference between the market value and the exercise price whenever the option vests (not at exercise). The corporation gets a tax deduction, but in-the-money options do not fall under performance-based compensation; rather, they become part of total non-performing compensation, the deduction of which is capped at $1 million per employee for the five highest-paid employees. For restricted stock or restricted stock units, the employee pays a tax based on the fair market value of the stock whenever the restricted stock or RSU vests, and the company gets a deduction for the same amount. Therefore, the timing of the tax deduction for the company is often earlier with restricted stock or restricted stock units than with options or SARs.

Measuring the Value and Cost of Capital for Employee Stock Options

Employee stock options are similar to warrants in that they provide an employee with the option to purchase the common stock of the employer at a fixed price over some period. Employee stock options diverge from the assumptions underpinning the valuation implied by option theory in some important ways. For example, option pricing theory assumes that options are traded and that the holder can hedge the risk of options by short-selling stock or by performing some other similar action; however, employee options are not traded, and the employee cannot typically hedge the risk. Thus, the value of employee stock options has two definitions—the economic cost to the company and the economic value to the employee.[5] The focus of our valuation is on the economic cost to the company.

The cost to the company of granting the option to the employee is similar to the value the company would have received by issuing a warrant to an outside investor. Fortunately, since our focus is on the company's capital structure and not on the value to the employee, we can use our formulas for warrants to measure the value and the cost of capital of employee stock options, keeping in mind that the provisions in employee stock options do not meet all of the assumptions underpinning these formulas. For example, employee stock options typically have provisions that do not allow trading and include forfeiture, and employees may have inside information on the company. Since employee stock options are not publicly traded, we can use the option-based warrant pricing model developed by Daves and Ehrhardt (2007) to numerically solve for the value and cost of capital of the employee stock options. Of course, we would want to adjust the number of options for anticipated forfeitures that occur, for example, if employees leave the company before their options vest.

Valuation Key 12.5

Employee stock options diverge from the assumptions underpinning the valuation implied by option theory. However, since our focus is on the company's value and hence the economic cost to the company, we can use our formulas for warrants to measure the value and the cost of capital of employee stock options.

Adjusting for Employee Stock Options Existing as of the Valuation Date

Since employee stock options can provide the company with an income tax deduction, we must ensure that the valuation of a company includes the tax benefit of the employee stock options outstanding as of the valuation date. When we measure the value of a company using publicly traded prices for the equity, debt, and preferred, as well as our estimate of securities that are not publicly traded such as some forms of debt and employee stock options, we would automatically include the market's assessment of value of this tax benefit in the value of the firm as it would be reflected in the value of the equity. This is often how we measure firm value for comparable companies when we are analyzing the cost of capital or market multiples. However, when we value a company using a discounted cash flow or other valuation model, we typically do not include the value of the tax benefits for employee stock options existing as of the valuation date in our measure of the value of the firm. When we do not include the tax benefit from employee stock options in our initial DCF valuation of the firm, we then must measure this tax benefit separately. In such situations, the value of the firm is equal to the value of the firm without the tax shelter from the options ($V_{F, \text{w/o OTS}}$), what we typically measure with our DCF valuation, plus the value of the option tax shelter (V_{OTS}). Hence, $V_F = V_{F, \text{w/o OTS}} + V_{OTS}$.

One way to measure the present value of the option tax shelter for existing options is to multiply the marginal tax rate for the option-related expense deduction by the value of the options. This calculation assumes that that the tax rate multiplied by the value of the options is a reasonable measure of the present

---

[5] For a discussion of this issue, see Hall, B., and K. Murphy, "Stock Options For Undiversified Executives," *Journal of Accounting and Economics* vol. 33, no. 11 (February 2002), pp. 3–42.

value of the tax benefit from the options, which is a reasonable assumption in most cases. Assuming the tax rate for the options is the same as the company's tax rate (T), the value of the tax shelter is equal to $T \times SO_{ESO} \times P_{ESO}$, where SO_{ESO} is the number of shares that can be purchased with the employee stock options and P_{ESO} is the value of the options on a per share basis. We adjust Equation 12.8 to include this tax effect and use the iterative process described previously to measure the stock price when employee stock options are outstanding at the valuation date.

$$V_{F, w/o \, OTS} + T \times SO_{ESO} \times P_{ESO} - V_D - V_{PS} = P_E \times SO_E + SO_{ESO} \times P_{ESO}$$

$$V_{F, w/o \, OTS} - V_D - V_{PS} = P_E \times SO_E + (1 - T) \times SO_{ESO} \times P_{ESO} \qquad (12.9)$$

The treatment of outstanding restricted stock or restricted stock units at the date of the valuation is somewhat different from that for options and warrants. In particular, we must merely adjust for the number of additional shares in the calculation of shares outstanding—adjusted, of course, for any expected forfeitures. Thus, in this case, no iterative process is required; we simply take the relevant amount of restricted stock and RSUs into consideration when we calculate shares outstanding. Both restricted stock and RSUs are included in the basic number of shares outstanding as soon as they vest. Footnote disclosures in a 10-K provide information on the number of restricted shares and restricted stock units that have been granted but not vested, which should be added to the basic shares outstanding—adjusted for expected forfeitures (see an example disclosure in Exhibit 14.5). If all of the restricted stock and RSUs have vested, the company should have already realized its tax benefit; remember that this occurs at the time of vesting. If some of the restricted stock or RSUs are not vested, we will also have to consider the expected tax benefit for the unvested restricted stock and restricted stock units.

The Knuth Company Revisited

Recall the Knuth Company example from the previous section of the chapter. Instead of assuming that Knuth has 5,000 outstanding warrants as of the valuation date, we instead assume that the company has 5,000 employee stock options outstanding as of the valuation date. Each stock option allows the employee to purchase one share of the stock for $3 in three years. To measure the value of the common equity adjusted for the outstanding options, we first measure the value of all equity-based claims (common stock and options) as we did before using a DCF valuation, $50,000. However, we know that this value does not include the tax benefit from the options.

If we use the option-based warrant pricing model developed by Daves and Ehrhardt (2007), we again iterate on the prices and solve the equality in Equation 12.9. It turns out that the stock price that results in a combined stock and after-tax value of the option equal to $50,000 is $4.7016, which has a corresponding option price of $0.9947, which naturally are both higher than the stock and warrant price we observed previously without the tax benefit ($4.5513 and $0.8975).

$$V_{F, w/o \, OTS} - V_D - V_{PS} = P_E \times SO_E + (1 - T) \times SO_{ESO} \times P_{ESO}$$

$$\$100,000 - \$40,000 - \$10,000 = \$50,000 = \$4.7016 \times 10,000 + (1 - .4) \times 5,000 \times \$0.9947$$

The value of the firm is equal to $101,989, which is equal to the original $100,000, plus a $1,989 tax shelter from the options ($1,989 = $0.9947 × 5,000 × 0.4). Since the value of the firm increases by $1,989 because of the tax benefit of the options, the value of the common equity shares and options increases relative to when we assumed that the Knuth Company had warrants outstanding that do not have any tax benefit.

$$V_{F, w/o \, OTS} - V_D - V_{PS} + T \times SO_{ESO} \times P_{ESO} = P_E \times SO_E + SO_{ESO} \times P_{ESO}$$

$$\$100,000 - \$40,000 - \$10,000 + .4 \times 5,000 \times \$0.9947 = \$51,989 = \$4.7016 \times 10,000 + 5,000 \times \$0.9947$$

Expected Issuance of Equity-Based Compensation After the Valuation Date

A company incurs an economic cost when it grants equity-based compensation to its employees even if no cash flows occur at the grant date. In the previous section, we only adjusted our valuation for the options already in existence at the date of valuation. Now, we consider how to include the economic cost of future grants of equity-based compensation into our valuation. In the United States and in many other countries, companies value equity-based compensation at the date of grant and then record an expense as the equity-based compensation vests. At a simplistic level, we can adjust the value of the company for expected equity-based compensation grants by adjusting the future expected free cash flows for each grant. These grants have two effects on the company's free cash flows—the economic cost of the equity-based compensation to the company and the income tax benefits the company receives from it. We discuss two alternative approaches to incorporate the effect of options granted after the valuation date—one complex and the other more easily implemented.

Valuation in Practice 12.3

Intel Corporation's 2006 Equity Incentive Plan Using Restricted Stock and Restricted Stock Units
In May 2006, Intel's stockholders approved an "Equity Incentive Plan," which it describes as follows:

> Under the 2006 Plan, . . . a maximum of 80 million shares can be awarded as non-vested shares (restricted stock) or non-vested share units (restricted stock units). The 2006 Plan allows for time-based, performance-based, and market-based vesting for equity incentive awards. . . . The company began issuing restricted stock units in the second quarter of 2006. . . . Awards granted to employees in 2006 under the company's equity incentive plans generally vest over 4 years and expire 7 years from the date of grant. Awards granted to key officers, senior-level employees, and key employees may have delayed vesting beginning 3 to 6 years from the date of grant and expire 7 to 10 years from the date of grant. . . .
>
> As of December 30, 2006, there was $380 million of unrecognized compensation costs related to restricted stock units granted under the company's equity incentive plans. The unrecognized compensation cost is expected to be recognized over a weighted average period of 1.8 years.

Source: Intel manufactures and sells semiconductor chips and related products throughout the world; see Intel's 10-K reports filed with the U.S. SEC and available at the company's website, www.Intel.com.

First, we discuss the more complex calculation to provide a sense of the difficulties in this approach. Consider a grant of stock options. At the date of an option grant, the company incurs an economic cost from granting the options but no cash flows occur. The cash flows do not occur until the exercise date. The cash flow effect of the income tax benefit from the equity-based compensation is a direct cash flow. At the exercise date, the company has a tax benefit equal to the difference between its stock price on the exercise date and the exercise price of the options. The tax benefit for SARs and restricted stock awards is based on the appreciation in price from the grant date. Thus, we must forecast the company's stock price to forecast the cash flow effect of the income tax benefit from the equity-based compensation contract. The other cash flow effect of equity-based compensation on the exercise date is not direct. The implicit effect on cash flow is the cost to the company to repurchase shares of stock so that it can reissue those shares to settle the equity-based compensation contract at the exercise date, net of any proceeds received from the exercise of the stock option. An alternative is to retire the shares repurchased and issue new shares, keeping the number of shares unchanged, but the economic effect is the same.

Those cash flow effects require a forecast of the company's stock price at both the grant date (in order to forecast the strike price) and exercise date (to forecast the cost to repurchase shares and compute the tax benefit). One, fairly complex, way to develop such forecasts is to value the company at the continuing value date, making an assumption about the effect on free cash flows of the equity-based compensation exercised in the base year of the continuing value calculation. Then, we can recursively work backwards each year until we value the firm at the valuation date. This is quite complex and we do not recommend this approach. In the remainder of this section, we describe an alternative to the more complex process we outline above to adjust our valuation for equity-based compensation plans. The alternative is that we value the options granted in each year and treat the value granted as an adjustment to the free cash flows in our financial model in the year of grant. This is a much simpler procedure and the one we recommend.

As we discussed earlier, accounting principles require companies to record an expense for the grant-date value of the equity-based compensation grants. The value of the equity-based compensation at the grant date represents the present value of the intrinsic value of the grant at the exercise date. Further, the intrinsic value of the grant at the exercise date is equal to the tax-deductible expense at the exercise date. Thus, the after-tax equity-based compensation grant value is an estimate of the present value of the expected economic effects of the equity-based compensation grants on an after-tax basis.

Since companies must include this expense in their income statements, forecasting all of a company's line items in its income statements in a financial model embeds the cash flow effects of equity-based compensation grants as long as we do not reverse those effects out in modeling the company's free cash flows. Depending on a company's disclosures, we may or may not be able to identify the exact location of equity-based compensation grants recorded in a company's income statement because the equity-based compensation grants do not appear as a separate line item on a company's income statements. Accounting principles require companies to include that expense in the line item in which the underlying employees' labor expense appears. Some companies do disclose the specific line-item effects of expensing equity-based compensation grants; for example, see Intel's disclosures that we summarize in Exhibit 12.4 and discuss in detail later in the chapter.

As such, the equity-based compensation grants expense for administration, marketing, and sales employees would appear in the selling, general, and administrative expense line item. The expense for research and development (R&D) employees would appear as part of the R&D expense line item. For employees manufacturing inventory, the cost of the equity-based compensation grants would follow the inventory and eventually be included in cost of goods sold. Thus, some of the cost of equity-based compensation grants might be included on the balance sheet as inventory. Other line items on the balance sheet also might include the cost of equity-based compensation grants (for example, if the company capitalizes labor costs for the construction of capital assets by the company's employees).

Assumptions Underpinning the Use of Grant-Date Value of the Equity-Based Compensation Contracts Expense

Naturally, we must make certain assumptions to use this approach. First, we assume that companies correctly value the equity-based compensation grants as of the grant date. If we do not have a reasonable estimate of the grant-date value for share-based compensation grants, our free cash flows will embed the effect of that issue. Companies typically use the valuation models discussed in the accounting standards to value stock options and stock appreciation rights. These models include the Black-Scholes Option Pricing Model and lattice models such as the binomial model. These valuation models are widely accepted models for valuing certain types of options. The models depend on certain factors (estimates of the volatility of the company's stock return, dividend yield, and risk-free rate), so we must assume that the company uses reasonable assumptions in the model.[6]

Another assumption is that we can identify reasonable forecast drivers of grant-date value for equity-based compensation grants. Forecast models will evolve as we have more time-series information on the relation between grant-date value for equity-based compensation grants and other forecast drivers.[7] Last, we assume that the companies do not amortize the expense over the vesting period but record the expense at the grant date. This is not strictly true, as accounting principles require companies to amortize the grant-date value for share-based compensation grants over the vesting period. Thus, using the expenses in the income statement will ignore the fact that a company can take the grant-date value and spread it ratably over the vesting period (often four years).

What is the effect of ignoring this amortization and assuming that the financial statements reflect the value of grant-date awards? The effect of the assumption is that there is a timing difference between the grant-date value for equity-based compensation and when that value is expensed over the vesting period. The result is that using the expense figures underestimates the value of the equity-based compensation to some degree. If the company is in a low-growth state and giving approximately equivalent new grants every year, or if the vesting periods are relatively short, this issue is not likely to be important. If the company is growing quickly or the vesting periods are long, then ignoring this issue will have a larger effect. The effect will also depend on whether the company uses an accelerated form of amortizing the grants to expense or uses a straight-line method (a larger error occurs with the straight-line method). One way to address this issue is by analyzing the company's footnote disclosure information about unamortized share-based compensation expenses to estimate the total value of the grant-date share-based compensation grant value and adjust the financial statements accordingly so that we reflect the grant-date share values appropriately. This calculation is easier to do with a few years of data from companies where the option expenses are included in their reported financial statements.

---

[6] While not yet a well-developed market, some investment banks are offering products to companies that allow the company to "sell" the liability to fulfill the equity-based compensation contracts to the bank. The product allows companies to hedge the potential cost of having to repurchase stock at higher prices and address the uncertain shareholder dilution caused by equity-based compensation. If this market develops, we may be able to use third-party valuations to value a company's equity-based compensation.

[7] See, for example, Bettis, J., J. Bizjak, and M. Lemmon, "Exercise Behavior, Valuation and the Incentive Effect of Employee Stock Options," *Journal of Financial Economics* vol. 76 (2005), pp. 445–470.

Intel Corporation's Disclosures on Equity-Based Compensation

In Exhibit 12.4, we show a summarized income statement and supplemental information for Intel Corporation. We show Intel's reported numbers in the first column of that exhibit, which include the share-based compensation expenses. In the second column, we show a common-sized income statement based on the reported numbers. In the third column, we show the share-based expenses and tax effects that Intel reports in its footnote disclosures, and in the fourth column, we show what percentage of the reported number for a given line on the income statement comes from share-based compensation expense. Intel includes share-based expenses in three expense categories—cost of sales (2% is share-based compensation), research and development (8.3% is share-based compensation), and marketing, general, and administrative (8.8% is share-based compensation). Although we do not report the number in the exhibit, Intel also includes costs related to share-based compensation in inventory. Overall, Intel's share-based expenses decrease its net income by about 16.4% (.164 = 987/ [5,044 + 987]) relative to what it would have reported had it not had to expense its share-based compensation. Obviously, the effect on Intel's income is economically significant.

EXHIBIT 12.4	Intel Corporation's Summarized Income Statement and Effect of Share-Based (Equity-Based) Compensation			
Intel Corporation—2006 Income Statement ($ in millions)	Reported (Including Share-Based Compensation Expense)	Reported (Including Share-Based Compensation Expense) %	Share-Based Compensation Expense	Share-Based Compensation Expense as % of Reported Amount
Revenue	$35,382	100.0%		
Cost of sales.	−17,164	−48.5%	$−349	2.0%
Research and development	−5,873	−16.6%	−487	8.3%
Marketing, general, and administrative	−6,096	−17.2%	−539	8.8%
Restructuring and asset impairment	−555	−1.6%		
Amortization	−42	−0.1%		
Operating income.	$ 5,652	16.0%	$−1,375	−24.3%
Gains (losses) on equity securities, net	214	0.6%		
Interest and other, net	1,202	3.4%		
Income before taxes.	$ 7,068	20.0%	$−1,375	−19.5%
Provision of income taxes	−2,024	−5.7%	388	−19.2%
Net income.	$ 5,044	14.3%	$ −987	−19.6%

We could use this information in several ways to develop a financial model for Intel, depending on the forecast drivers in our financial model and the characteristics of Intel's share-based compensation expense. The simplest approach would be to use Intel's historical information to develop expense ratios for each line on its income statement and use the expense ratios to forecast those expenses. That approach is likely to be reasonable for many companies. Alternatively, if we believe the grant-date value for share-based compensation grants is related to other forecast drivers, or a combination of forecast drivers, then we can forecast the amounts of share-based compensation in this exhibit using an approach different from the approach we use to forecast the expense line items. For example, if the grant-date value for share-based compensation grants is a function of certain types of labor costs and these labor costs will evolve differently than other costs, we would, if possible, partition those labor costs and forecast the labor costs and grant-date value for share-based compensation grants separately from the other costs.

No doubt, it is clear that this can be tedious and that no one would relish making these types of calculations. We investigate Intel's disclosures further to estimate the impact of the stock-based compensation on Intel's free cash flows, taking the numbers as reported by Intel to be a reasonable estimate of the economic impact of the equity-based compensation.

In Exhibit 12.5, we present Intel's summarized cash flow statement and our calculation of its free cash flows. The first column of the free cash flow calculation measures Intel's free cash flows using the treatment of the equity-based grant expense used by Intel's cash flow statement—that is, recognizing that the equity-based compensation is non-cash. The adjustments of the excess tax benefit from share-based compensation and share-based compensation come directly from the statement of cash flows. The

EXHIBIT 12.5 Intel Corporation's 2006 Summarized Statement of Cash Flows and Free Cash Flow Schedule*

Statement of Cash Flows ($ in millions)	2006
Cash Flows From Operations	
Net earnings	$ 5,044
Depreciation and amortization	4,912
Deferred income taxes	−325
Other, net	−191
Adjustments for operating working capital, net	−72
Excess tax benefit from share-based comp	−123
Share-based compensation	1,375
Cash flow from operations	$10,620
Investing Activities	
Purchase of investments, net	$ 153
Additions to property, plant, and equipment	−5,779
Proceeds from divestitures, net	752
Other, net	−33
Net cash used by investing activities	$−4,907
Financing Activities	
Change in common stock	
Proceeds from sale of stock to employees	$ 1,046
Excess tax benefit from share-based comp	123
Repurchase and retirement of stock	−4,593
Change in debt, net	−695
Common equity dividends paid	−2,320
Cash flows from financing activities	$−6,439
Effect of exchange rate changes	$ 0
Change in cash balance	$ −726
Assumed income tax rate	28.6%
Assumed deductible interest expense	$ 25

Free Cash Flow Schedule ($ in millions)	2006	2006 Adjusted	
Earnings before interest and taxes (EBIT)	$ 5,652	$ 5,652	
Income taxes paid on EBIT	−1,619	−1,619	
Earnings before interest and after taxes	$ 4,033	$ 4,033	
Depreciation and amortization	4,912	4,912	
Excess tax benefit from share-based comp	−123	−123	
Share-based compensation	1,375	0	
Deferred income taxes (share-based comp)	−388	0	
Deferred income taxes (without share-based comp)	63	63	
Other, net	−191	−191	
Adjustments for operating working capital, net	−72	−72	
Change in required cash balance (assumed)	−400	−400	
Unlevered cash flow from operations	$ 9,209	$ 8,222	−10.7%
Additions to property, plant and equipment	−5,779	−5,779	
Proceeds from divestitures, net and other	719	719	
Unlevered free cash flow	$ 4,149	$ 3,162	−23.8%
Interest expense	−30	−30	
Interest tax shield	9	9	
CF before non-equity financing changes	$ 4,128	$ 3,141	
Change in debt, net	−695	−695	
Equity free cash flow	$ 3,433	$ 2,446	−28.7%
Gains, interest and other, after tax	1,032	1,032	
Purchase of investments	153	153	
Effect of exchange rate changes	0	0	
Cash flow before cash flows to/from common	$ 4,618	$ 3,631	
Change in Common Stock			
Repurchase and retirement of stock	−4,593	−4,593	
Proceeds from sale of stock to employees	1,046	1,046	
Excess tax benefit from share-based comp	123	123	
Share-based compensation		1,375	
Deferred income taxes (share-based comp)		−388	
Common dividends	−2,320	−2,320	
Change in excess cash	$−1,126	$−1,126	
Change in required cash balance	400	400	
Change in cash balance	$ −726	$ −726	

* From Intel's 2006 10-K report filed with the U.S. SEC and available at the company's website, www.Intel.com and authors' estimates.

deferred income taxes (share-based comp) comes directly from the income statement. For purposes of this analysis, we treat the gains (losses) on equity securities, net and interest and other, net as coming from excess assets and do not include their effect in the free cash flow calculation.

In the second column of the free cash flows (labeled "2006 Adjusted"), we adjust free cash flows by removing the adjustments observed in the cash flow statement for share-based compensation, and the deferred tax effects of the share-based compensation. Thus, we treat the share-based compensation and its tax effect as having cash flow consequences in our calculation of Intel's unlevered cash flows from operations, unlevered free cash flows, and equity free cash flows. We do not reverse the adjustment for the excess tax benefit from share-based compensation, as this is from previously granted options that are being exercised, not from new grants of options, and we are illustrating the impact of the new grants. We then treat these items as adjustments to reconcile from equity free cash flows to the change in the company's cash balance. Our treatment of the share-based compensation reduces Intel's unlevered operating cash flow by $1.0 billion ($9.2 billion to $8.2 billion, or −10.7%). The dollar effect on Intel's unlevered free cash flow and equity free cash flow for 2006 is the same, −$1.0 billion, but the percentage decrease is larger (−23.8% and −28.7%, respectively).

Thus, we can see that the potential adjustments to free cash flows and the valuation are large. If Intel's numbers for this year are representative of the proportionate annual effect of Intel's stock-based compensation on its free cash flows, our valuation of Intel's equity would be roughly 25% lower than it would have been had we ignored these effects, a potentially serious error. Note that we have treated the amount that Intel expensed as the grant-date value of the stock-based compensation. As we indicated before, companies must amortize the grant-date value over the vesting period (mostly four years for Intel) and Intel reported that it still had $1.1 billion of unamortized compensation expense from prior option grants and $380 million of unamortized compensation expense related to restricted stock units. Had we treated this $1.48 billion as also reducing unlevered cash flows in the current year, the impact would be more significant.

Valuation Key 12.6

An approach to adjusting a valuation for equity-based compensation grants is to include a forecast of the grant-date value of the grants the company will issue in the future, based on the company's equity-based compensation. The free cash flow adjustment is equal to the after-tax grant-date value of the future grants. For some companies, these adjustments can be quite large.

12.4 CONVERTIBLE DEBT

LO4 Analyze the straight debt and option components of convertible debt

Convertible debt is a security that has a coupon interest rate and maturity date (among other provisions) just like a pure-debt security. However, it also has an option for the holder to convert the bond into common stock (or sometimes preferred stock). Based on the sample of companies we discussed in Chapter 11, we observe that 13% of the companies have convertible debt and 87% have no convertible debt. Of the companies that have debt, 16% have convertible debt. For the companies that have convertible debt, convertible debt is less than 35% of the total debt for about a third of these companies, between 35% and 85% of the total debt for another third, and between 85% and 100% of the total debt for the last third.

Convertible Debt Contract Provisions

Convertible debt (and convertible preferred stock) can have many different provisions (or conditions) in its contracts. Like straight debt, convertible debt has a coupon rate, coupon timing, a principal amount (or par value), and a maturity date. Furthermore, it can be issued at a premium (issued at a price above the par value) or at a discount (issued at a price below par value). Unlike straight debt, convertible debt has a conversion provision that gives an investor the right to convert the debt into a certain number of shares of common stock. The conversion ratio is the number of shares of stock into which a debt or preferred stock security can be converted. This ratio is typically adjusted for stock splits and stock dividends, so the underlying economics do not change with these events. However, the conversion ratio can change over time as specified in the contract—based on, for example, the passage of time or on some characteristic of the company (such as stock price). The conversion price is equal to par value (or the call price if it is callable) divided by the conversion rate. Depending on market conditions and the circumstances of the company issuing the convertible security, the conversion price is usually set 10% to 30% higher than the stock price on the issue date.

A call provision is very common in convertible debt securities. A call provision gives the company the right to call or repurchase its debt. In addition, it is common to have an initial period during which the company cannot call the debt—the hard non-call period (typically three to five years). The call provision also includes a call price that is often greater than the principal (or par) value and it often changes over time. Another type of call provision is one in which the call activates only after the company's stock price increases to a number specified in the contract, or if the company meets some other performance condition. On the investor side, a less common provision is the put provision, which gives the investor the right to sell back—or put—the debt to the company after a certain point in time at a certain price. The put provision has various characteristics that are similar to what we described for the call provision.

One measure of the intrinsic value of the convertible debt any time the conversion option is in-the-money is the price of the stock multiplied by the number of common shares that will be received if the debt is converted. This is often referred to as the "if-converted value." The value of the convertible debt is normally higher than that if the conversion option is in-the-money, as the option provides additional value over simply converting. Another common measure of intrinsic value is the ratio of the stock price to the conversion price—sometimes called the parity ratio. If the parity ratio is greater than 1, the conversion feature is "in-the-money"; if it is less than 1, the conversion feature is "out-of-the-money." Because the option to convert the bond into stock has value, we expect a convertible bond to always trade somewhere above the value of the straight debt component (what the debt would be worth without the conversion feature) or its value post-conversion—whichever is higher. In Exhibit 12.6, we show this relationship for an illustrative convertible note assuming there is no probability of default.

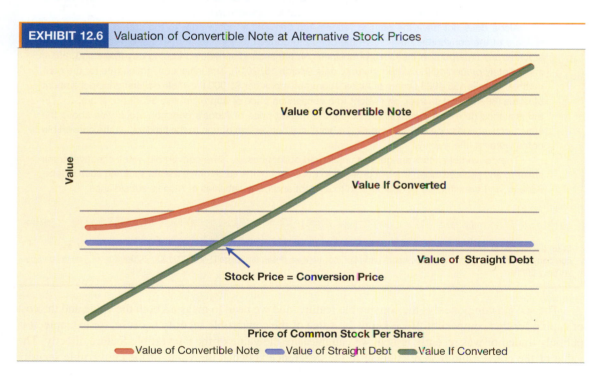

EXHIBIT 12.6 Valuation of Convertible Note at Alternative Stock Prices

Value of Convertible Note

Value If Converted

Value of Straight Debt

Stock Price = Conversion Price

Price of Common Stock Per Share

— Value of Convertible Note — Value of Straight Debt — Value If Converted

Value

Valuation Key 12.7

Convertible debt (and preferred stock) can have many different provisions (or conditions) in its contracts. Like straight debt, convertible debt has a coupon rate, coupon timing, a principal amount (or par value), and a maturity date, and it can be issued at a premium or discount. Unlike straight debt, convertible debt has a conversion provision that gives an investor the right to convert the debt into a certain number of shares of common stock. A call provision is very common in convertible debt securities, and it gives the company the right to repurchase its debt at a specified price.

Separating Convertible Debt into Its Straight Debt and Convertible Feature Components

We measure the value and cost of capital for a convertible security by separating it into two components—the value and cost of capital for the security if it were not convertible and the value and cost of capital for the convertible feature. For a convertible debt issue, we know from the terms of the contract what the contractual or promised payments for the interest and the principal are. Using the methods discussed in Chapter 9, we can measure the promised yield and cost of debt for straight debt with the same risk. We can often look to other debt instruments issued by the same company to determine the promised yield on a straight debt issue with similar risk; this is then assigned to the underlying straight debt component of the convertible security. We can then measure the value of this component by using the promised payments of the convertible security in conjunction with the promised yield for a straight debt instrument with the same default risk and maturity as the convertible debt.

Valuation in Practice 12.4

Alcoa Inc.'s Issuance of Convertible Notes (and Common Equity) In spite of a downgrade in its credit rating in February 2009, Alcoa Inc. (see the opening vignette to Chapter 9) was able to issue both common equity and convertible notes shortly afterward. In its 10-Q report for the quarter ending March 31, 2009 (Note H), the company stated:

> On March 24, 2009, Alcoa issued $575 [million] of 5.25% convertible notes due 2014 (the "convertible notes"). . . . Interest on the convertible notes is payable semi-annually . . .
>
> Alcoa does not have the right to redeem the convertible notes prior to the stated maturity date. Holders of the convertible notes have the option to convert their notes into shares of Alcoa's common stock at any time prior to the close of business on the second scheduled trading day (March 13, 2014) immediately preceding the stated maturity date (March 15, 2014). The initial conversion rate for the convertible notes is 155.4908 shares of Alcoa's common stock per $1,000 (in whole dollars) principal amount of notes (89,407,210 shares), equivalent to a conversion price of approximately $6.43 per share, . . . On the issuance date of the convertible notes, the market price of Alcoa's common stock was above the stated conversion price of $6.43 creating a beneficial conversion option to the holders, as the convertible notes were "in-the-money." . . .
>
> The convertible notes are general unsecured obligations. . . . The convertible notes effectively rank junior to any secured indebtedness of Alcoa to the extent of the value of the assets securing such indebtedness, and are effectively subordinated to all debt and other liabilities of Alcoa's subsidiaries.

Source: This text is taken from the company's press release made available on March 19, 2009, which is accessible on the company's website at http://www.alcoa.com/global/en/news/news_detail.asp?pageID=20090319005529en&detailType=invest&newsYear=2009.

The second component is the convertible feature, and we need to measure both the value and the cost of capital for this component. If we know the value of the convertible security because, for example, it is publicly traded or was recently issued, we can measure the value of the convertible feature directly. The value of the convertible feature is equal to the difference between the value of the convertible security and the value of the first component (the value of the underlying security if it were not convertible). If we do not know the value of the convertible security, we must use an option pricing model to value the convertible feature. Fortunately, we can usually use the same formulas and methods used for warrants to measure the value and cost of capital of the convertible feature.

Valuation Key 12.8

We measure the cost of capital for a convertible security by splitting it into two components—the cost of capital for the convertible feature and the cost of capital for the underlying security if it were not convertible. We can use the formulas and methods we used for warrants to measure the value and cost of capital of the convertible feature.

Alcoa Inc.'s Convertible Notes

We will use Alcoa's convertible note as described in Valuation in Practice 12.4 to illustrate how to measure the value and cost of capital for convertible debt. The total par value of the $1,000 notes is $575 million. The debt was issued for $641 million. The coupon rate is 5.25%, interest is paid semi-annually, and the maturity of the notes is five years from the date of issue. The conversion rate is 155.4908 common shares per $1,000 note, and the conversion price is $6.4312 per share of common stock ($6.4312 = $1,000/155.4908). On the day the debt was issued, the company's stock price was trading around $7.00 per share, so the conversion feature was "in-the-money." In total, the notes are convertible into 89.4 million shares of common stock (89,407,210 = [$575.0 million/$1,000] × 155.4908).

To value the conversion feature at issuance, we first separate the $641 million initial value of the notes into its straight debt and convertible feature components. To simplify the calculations, we ignore the fact that the term of the notes is a few days less than five years as well as certain features of the notes that make them more complex to value, such as the fact that the notes can be converted prior to the expiration date of the conversion feature. In Exhibit 12.7, we show two valuations for the straight debt component. In the first valuation, we value the notes using the coupon rate of interest. The promised interest payments, which occur every six months, equal $15.094 million ($15.094 = $575.0 × 2.625%). On the date of maturity, the promised payment is equal to the interest payment plus the repayment of the principal of $575 million. In the second valuation, we value the notes using the promised yield of Alcoa's unsecured straight debt with the same maturity, which we assume to be 9% at the time.

EXHIBIT 12.7	Alcoa Inc. Convertible Note—Issue Date		
($ in millions except per share amounts)		**Value Using Coupon Rate**	**Value Using Promised Yield**
Coupon (annual).		5.250%	9.000%
Coupon (semi-annual)		2.625%	4.500%
September 15, 2009.		$ 15.094	$ 15.094
March 15, 2010		$ 15.094	$ 15.094
September 15, 2010.		$ 15.094	$ 15.094
March 15, 2011		$ 15.094	$ 15.094
September 15, 2011.		$ 15.094	$ 15.094
March 15, 2012		$ 15.094	$ 15.094
September 15, 2012.		$ 15.094	$ 15.094
March 15, 2013		$ 15.094	$ 15.094
September 15, 2013.		$ 15.094	$ 15.094
March 15, 2014		$ 590.094	$ 590.094
Value of straight debt notes .		$ 575.000	$ 489.691
Market price of the notes.			$ 641.000
Value of the conversion provision.			$ 151.309
Number of shares.			89,407,210
Value of conversion feature per share			$ 1.692

($ in millions except per share amounts)	**Shares**	**Price per share**	**Value**
Value of notes (ignoring accrued interest)			$439.7
Value of conversion feature	89,407,210	$1.692	151.3
Value of convertible note			$641.0
Value if converted.	89,407,210	$7.000	625.9
Value of note in excess of converted value			$ 15.1

If we discount the same promised payments by the 9% discount rate, we find that the value of the straight debt component is equal to $489.7 million. Since the notes were issued for $641 million, the implied value of the conversion feature is $151.3 million ($151.3 = $641.0 − $489.7). The notes are convertible into 89,407,210 shares; thus, the per-share value of the conversion feature is $1.692 ($1.692

= \$151.3/89.407) as of the issuance date. At the bottom of the exhibit, we compare the value of the notes to the value of the notes if converted. As expected, the notes' \$641.0 million value (straight debt of \$489.7 million and conversion feature of \$151.3 million) is larger than the value of the notes if converted by \$15.1 million (\$15.1 = \$641 − 89.4 × \$7). We could use our option pricing model framework to measure the cost of capital for the convertible feature on the issue date as well.

Since many debt instruments do not trade very often, we often cannot measure the value of the conversion feature as we did as of the issue date and we must use the option pricing framework we used for the warrants to simultaneously estimate the value and cost of capital of the conversion feature. One year after Alcoa issued these notes, its stock price roughly doubled to \$14. At this time, its continuously compounded dividend yield decreased to 0.5%, its equity cost of capital was 12%, the standard deviation of its equity increased to 40%, and the risk-free rate was 3%. In Exhibit 12.8, we revalue the notes at this time and we show the various inputs used to measure the cost of capital for the note's conversion feature. Based on these inputs and the previously noted characteristics of the notes, the value of the conversion feature per share of common stock is \$8.47 and the cost of capital of the conversion feature is equal to 16.6%.

EXHIBIT 12.8 Alcoa Inc. Convertible Note—One Year After Issue Date

($ in millions)	Value Using Coupon Rate	Value Using Promised Yield
Coupon (annual)...	5.250%	9.000%
Coupon (semi-annual)	2.625%	4.500%
September 15, 2010..	$ 15.094	$ 15.094
March 15, 2011	$ 15.094	$ 15.094
September 15, 2011..	$ 15.094	$ 15.094
March 15, 2012	$ 15.094	$ 15.094
September 15, 2012..	$ 15.094	$ 15.094
March 15, 2013	$ 15.094	$ 15.094
September 15, 2013..	$ 15.094	$ 15.094
March 15, 2014	$ 590.094	$ 590.094
Value of straight debt notes............................	$ 575.000	$ 503.888

Other Information	Price	Valuation ($ in millions)
Risk-free rate of return.....................................	3.0%	
Equity cost of capital.......................................	12.0%	
Annual volatility of equity.................................	40.0%	
Dividend yield, continuously compounded	0.50%	
Expiration of warrants (in years)........................	4.0	
Face value per note	$ 1,000.00	
Conversion ratio per $1,000 note.........................	155.4908	
Exercise price of conversion feature	$ 6.4312	
Current stock price..	$ 14.000	
Parity ratio (stock price/conversion price)	2.18	
Cost of capital of conversion feature.....................	16.6%	
Common shares outstanding............................	974,372,426	
Value of notes (ignoring accrued interest)		$ 503.9
Value of conversion feature	89,407,210	$8.471	757.3
Value of convertible note		$1,261.2
Value If converted...	89,407,210	$14.000	1,251.7
Value of note in excess of converted value		$ 9.5

Now assume we are using Alcoa as a comparable company and want to unlever its equity cost of capital. Recall that Alcoa's equity cost of capital as measured using market data would reflect the impact of the conversion feature of the convertible debt. If we ignore the conversion feature of this debt and assumed the book value and market value of the debt were the same, we would include only one factor in the unlevered cost of capital calculation from the convertible debt; 5.25% cost of debt multiplied by the debt-to-value ratio of $575.0 million value of the debt divided by the value of the firm (see Exhibit 12.8—the valuation using the coupon rate). We know this factor contributes too little to the calculation of the unlevered cost of capital from the convertible debt because we know the cost of the debt is understated and we completely ignore the even higher cost of capital for the convertible feature. Thus, the unlevered cost of capital would be understated. To properly unlever the equity cost of capital, we would include two factors from the convertible debt; the straight-debt component of the convertible debt and the effect of the conversion feature after valuing the convertible debt appropriately (the valuation in Exhibit 12.8. The first factor is the 9% cost of debt multiplied by the debt-to-value ratio of $503.9 million value of the straight-debt component divided by the value of the firm, and the second factor is the 16.6% cost of capital for the convertible feature multiplied by the ratio of the $757.3 million value of the convertible feature to the value of the firm. Obviously, we would need to measure the value of the equity and cost of equity as well as the value and cost of capital for any other securities Alcoa has issued to perform the unlevering calculation. We would then unlever Alcoa's equity cost of capital just as we unlevered KapStone's equity cost of capital when we considered its warrants.

REVIEW EXERCISE 12.4

Convertible Debt

A company issued $2 million of $1,000 face-value convertible bonds with an 8% annual coupon payment. The bonds mature in six years. Each bond is convertible into 100 shares of the company's stock at the end of the six years. The company's straight debt has a yield to maturity and a cost of capital equal to 10%. The bonds are currently trading at $1,100. The company has 1 million shares of stock outstanding, and its stock is trading at $8.45 per share. Its equity cost of capital is 15%, the annual volatility of equity is 40%, the continuously compounded dividend yield is 5%, the income tax rate for interest tax shields is 40%, and the risk-free rate is 4%. This is the only financing the company uses to finance the company. Calculate the value of the conversion feature of these bonds based on a per convertible share value basis and the cost of capital for this conversion feature.

Solution on page 507.

12.5 OPTION-PRICING-BASED FINANCIAL DISTRESS MODELS

In Chapter 9, we discussed a financial-statement-based bankruptcy prediction model. Another type of financial distress prediction model is an option-pricing-based model, which is based on the Merton model and its variations.[8] These models consider such company factors as financial leverage, market value, and the volatility of a company's equity. Using this and other information, the model estimates the volatility of the underlying assets and predicts the probability of financial distress.

LO5 Measure the probability of financial distress using an option pricing framework

For a particular horizon (number of years in the future), this model measures the probability that the value of the company's assets will be less than the amount of the company's debt (the definition of financial distress or financial failure in the model). The debt maturity input, T, is unable to fully map the theoretical construct of the original model, as there is no option contract being settled up at this date. Even though we use this input to represent the horizon, it has a broader and more complex interpretation than a horizon or simple term to maturity. Note that this is not the same as going bankrupt, for a company can have the value of its assets fall below the principal value of its debt and not file for bankruptcy. The model below is based on the model in Hillegeist et al. (2004).[9] In this model, the value of the equity is measured using Equation 12.10.

$$V_E = V_A \times e^{-d_A \times T_D} \times N(d_1) - X_D \times e^{-r_F \times T_D} \times N(d_2) + (1 - e^{-d_A \times T_D}) \times V_A \quad \textbf{(12.10)}$$

where all terms are defined as previously and:

V_A = value of the company's assets

V_E = value of the company's common equity

d_A = continuously compounded dividend rate (rate based on V_A)

T_D = maturity of the company's debt

---

[8] Merton, R.C., "On the Pricing of Corporate Debt: The Risk Structure of Interest Rates," *Journal of Finance* vol. 29, no. 2 (May 1974), pp. 449–470.

[9] Hillegeist, S. A., E. K. Keating, D. P. Cram, and K. G. Lundstedt, "Assessing the Probability of Bankruptcy," *Review of Accounting Studies* 9 (2004), pp. 5–34.

X_D = amount due on the company's debt

$$d_1 = \frac{\ln(V_A/X_D) + [r_F - d_A + (\sigma_A^2/2)] \times T_D}{\sigma_A \times \sqrt{T_D}}$$

$$d_2 = d_1 - \sigma_A \times \sqrt{T_D}$$

r_A = the expected return on the company's assets (often the unlevered cost of capital)

σ_A = the volatility or standard deviation of the company's expected return on its assets

We can measure the probability that the value of the assets will be less than the debt claims for a certain horizon, T (for example, one year, three years, five years, etc.), and we define this to be the probability of financial distress in the model, $\text{Prob}_{\text{Financial Distress}}$.[10]

$$\text{Prob}_{\text{Financial Distress}} = N\left(-\frac{\ln(V_A/X_D) + [r_A - d_A(\sigma_A^2/2)] \times T_D}{\sigma_A \times \sqrt{T_D}}\right) \tag{12.11}$$

The probability of financial distress is a function of the expected growth in the value of the assets, r_A (the expected return on the assets, which is normally set to be equal to the unlevered cost of capital), the horizon, the volatility of the value of the company's assets, and the difference between the value of the assets and the amount due on the company's debt. Holding all else constant, the larger the difference between the value of the assets and amount due on the company's debt or the larger the expected growth in the value of the assets, the smaller the probability of financial distress; the longer the horizon or the larger the volatility of the value of the company's assets, the higher the probability of financial distress.

In the case of publicly traded companies, we can typically measure the following inputs for the model— the value of the equity, V_E; the standard deviation of the annual return on equity, σ_E; the amount due on the company's debt, X_D; the horizon, T_D; the risk-free rate of return, r_F; the expected dividends paid by the company, and the expected rate of return on the company's assets (often set equal to the unlevered cost of capital), r_A. We assume we cannot observe the value of the company's assets because we cannot measure the value of the company's non-equity claims; we also assume that we cannot measure the volatility of the assets. If we cannot measure the value of the assets, we also cannot observe the dividend rate based on the value of the company's assets, d_A; however, once we estimate the value of the company's assets as we describe below, we can calculate the continuously compounded dividend rate on the company's assets as the expected dividend divided by the value of the company's assets, continuously compounded.

If we cannot observe the value of the company's assets, V_A, and the volatility of the assets, σ_A, we can measure these two inputs by simultaneously solving the equity valuation formula (Equation 12.10) and the optimal hedge formula, which we show in Equation 12.12:

$$\sigma_E = \frac{\sigma_A \times N(d_1) \times V_A \times e^{-d_A \times T_D}}{V_E} \tag{12.12}$$

To simultaneously solve these two formulas, we choose values for the volatility of the company's assets, σ_A, and the value of the assets, V_A. For each iteration, we calculate the dividend rate as the expected dividends divided by the value of the assets, continuously compounded in that iteration. We then use these values in conjunction with the other inputs to calculate the results of Equation 12.12. Since we observe the value of the equity (which we can also calculate using Equation 12.10) and volatility of the equity (which we can also calculate using Equation 12.12), we can choose a value of the assets and volatility of the assets that solves Equation 12.12. Thus, we compare the observed values to the calculated values and use an iterative process as we did previously for warrants.

If we can observe either the value of the company's assets or the volatility of the assets, we can solve for the other term directly using one of the two formulas. If we know the value of the assets but not the volatility of the assets, we can use Equation 12.12 to calculate the volatility of the assets before measuring the probability of financial distress. If we know the volatility of the assets but not the value of the assets, we can use Equation 12.10 to calculate the value of the assets before measuring the prob-

---

[10] The model assumes that T is the maturity of a company's debt, which is assumed to be zero-coupon debt with the same maturity date. We illustrate the model for a shorter horizon—one or three years—to illustrate how to use this model even though this assumption varies from the theoretical model—see Hillegeist et al. (2004) for a discussion of this point. Other research studies develop more complex models that address this issue. See, for example, Black, F., and J. Cox, ''Valuing Corporate Securities: Some Effects of Bond Indenture Provisions,'' *Journal of Finance* vol. 31, no. 2 (1976), pp. 351–367; and Geske, R., ''The Valuation of Corporate Liabilities as Compound Options,'' *Journal of Financial and Quantitative Analysis* vol. 12, no. 4 (1977), pp. 541–552.

ability of financial distress. We can sometimes measure the volatility of the assets from a publicly traded, unlevered, comparable company.

Recall the financial distress analysis we conducted in Chapter 9 on General Motors and Accenture. In Exhibit 12.9, we show the results of estimating the option-theoretic financial distress prediction model for General Motors and Accenture using two different horizons (one year and three years) and two different expected returns on assets (we chose 5% and 0% in this example). We measure the other inputs as follows: we measure the value of the equity, V_E, as the number of shares outstanding multiplied by the price on the "as of date"; we measure the standard deviation of the annual return on equity, σ_E, using the daily returns for the 90 calendar days up to the as-of date (annualized); and we measure the dividend rate, d_A, as the dividend divided by the market value of the assets (value of the firm), continuously compounded. We use the book value of the company's debt reported in the company's financial statements for the amount due on the company's debt, X_D, and we use the one-year risk-free rate of return, r_F.

EXHIBIT 12.9 The Option-Pricing-Model-Based Financial Distress Model Applied to General Motors Corporation and Accenture

	General Motors		Accenture	
	5% Return	0% Return	5% Return	0% Return
	September 30, 2008		October 31, 2008	
Debt/(Debt + Equity)	85.6%		0.3%	
Standard deviation of equity	113.2%		60.0%	
1–Year probability of financial distress	35.6%	43.5%	0.0%	0.0%
3–Year probability of financial distress	78.5%	82.9%	3.2%	3.8%
	December 31, 2008			
Debt/(Debt + Equity)	94.8%			
Standard deviation of equity	186.0%			
1–Year probability of financial distress	79.6%	82.8%		
3–Year probability of financial distress	98.1%	98.4%		

For General Motors, as of September 30, 2008, the one-year horizon probability of financial distress was between 35.6% and 43.5%, depending on the assumed return on assets. This is less than the 66.7% probability we measured using the HZ financial-statement-based model. For December 31, 2008, the range of the probability of financial distress increases to between 79.6% and 82.8% because of the deterioration of General Motors' financial condition as well as the increase in the volatility of the equity. Recall that the bankruptcy probability from the HZ bankruptcy-prediction model is equal to 85.1% for the one-year horizon on this date. For Accenture, as of October 31, 2008, the one-year horizon probability of financial distress is zero. This is slightly less than the 4% probability of bankruptcy we measured using the HZ bankruptcy-prediction model.

We know that using a longer horizon results in a higher probability of financial distress. To illustrate this effect, we also use a three-year horizon for the two companies. For General Motors, as of September 30, 2008, the range of the probability increases from between 35.6% and 43.5% for the one-year horizon to between 78.5% and 82.9% for the three-year horizon. We also observe increases in the probability of financial distress for longer horizons for General Motors as of December 31, 2008. For Accenture, the range of the probability of financial distress also increases but it remains low at even the three-year horizon—between 3.2% and 3.8%.

Which Approach Works Better (Ratio-Based or Option-Pricing-Based Financial Distress Models)?

The study by Hillegeist et al. (2004) compared two approaches. It compared the option-pricing-based model we discussed earlier to updated versions of two financial ratio models—the model in Altman (1968)[11] and the model in Ohlson (1980).[12] The study reported that the option-pricing-based approach

[11] Altman, E., "Financial Ratios, Discriminant Analysis and the Prediction of Corporate Bankruptcy," *Journal of Finance* 23 (1968), pp. 589–609.

[12] Ohlson, J., "Financial Ratios and the Probabilistic Prediction of Bankruptcy," *Journal of Accounting Research* 19 (1980), pp. 109–131.

worked better than the financial ratio-based approach; however, both approaches work in that they both predict bankruptcy. Arora, Bohn, and Zhu (2005)[13] provide evidence that an option-theoretic-based model known as the K-V model[14]—which is now a proprietary model owned by Moody's and is now known as the KMV model—as well as option-theoretic-based models similar to those developed by Hull and White (2000)[15] outperform the Merton model.

Valuation Key 12.9

We can use option-pricing-theory-based models to develop financial distress prediction models. These models can be used to assess the probability that a company will be in a state of financial distress within a certain period of time.

SUMMARY AND KEY CONCEPTS

In this chapter, we focused on various aspects of valuing a company for which option pricing models are useful. Our focus is on option-like securities that are typically written by a company on its common stock. These options include employee stock options, warrants, and convertible bonds and preferred stock. We discuss how to value them and measure their cost of capital.

We showed how to use an option pricing model to estimate both the value and the cost of capital for warrants and the convertible feature of convertible debt or preferred. We also showed the potential importance of taking into consideration the value and cost of capital for option-like securities in unlevering the equity cost of capital or in computing the weighted average cost of capital discount rate.

We also discussed in detail the different forms of equity-based compensation that are paid to employees by companies—including stock options, stock appreciation rights, restricted stock, and restricted stock units. We discussed the accounting and tax treatments of this form of compensation and we discussed how to measure the economic value that the firm gives to employees when it provides equity-based compensation. Finally, we discussed in detail how to adjust a company's valuation for existing equity-based compensation as of the valuation date, as well as how to deal with grants of equity-based compensation that will occur after the valuation date.

Finally, we discussed how option pricing models can be used to measure the expected probability of financial distress. Estimates of the probability of financial distress can be an important consideration when thinking about the pricing of debt and whether it is important to incorporate financial distress costs into a valuation.

ADDITIONAL READING AND REFERENCES

Black, F., and M. Scholes, "The Pricing of Options and Corporate Liabilities," *Journal of Political Economy* vol. 81, no. 3 (May/June 1973), pp. 637–654.

Merton, R. C., "On the Pricing of Corporate Debt: The Risk Structure of Interest Rates," *Journal of Finance* vol. 29, no. 2 (May 1974), pp. 449–470.

EXERCISES AND PROBLEMS

P12.1 **Valuation of a Basic European Call Option** A European call option provides the holder the right to purchase a share of stock of a company at $15 per share three years from today. The stock is trading at $20, does not pay dividends, and has a standard deviation of its annual return equal to 40%. The risk-free rate of return is 4%. Based on the characteristics of the options, respond to each part of the question independently.

    a. Without doing any detailed calculations, what is the minimum price of the option?
    b. What is the value of this option today?
    c. How does the value of the option change if the stock price is $10?

---

[13] Arora, N., J. Bohn, and F. Zhu, "Reduced Form vs. Structural Models of Credit Risk: A Case Study of Three Models, "*Journal of Investment Management* vol. 3, no. 4 (2005), pp. 43–67.

[14] See Vasicek, O., *Credit Valuation*, 1984, Moody's KMV, for background on this model.

[15] See, Hull, J., and A. White, "Valuing Credit Default Swaps: No Counterparty Default Risk," working paper, 2000, University of Toronto.

    d.   How does the value of the option change if the strike price is $12?

    e.   How does the value of the option change if the standard deviation of the annual return is equal to 20%?

    f.   How does the value of the option change if the company changes its dividend policy and begins paying a regular dividend, continuously compounded, equal to 6% of its stock price?

    g.   How does the value of the option change if the expiration date is 10 years?

    h.   How does the value of the option change if the risk-free rate is 8%?

P12.2   **Valuation of a Basic European Call Option** A European call option provides the holder the right to purchase a share of stock of a company at $5 per share five years from today. The stock is trading at $5, pays dividends equal to 5% of the share price, continuously compounded, and has a standard deviation of its annual return equal to 50%. The risk-free rate of return is 5%. Based on the characteristics of the options, respond to each part of the question independently.

    a.   Without doing any detailed calculations, what is the minimum price of the option?

    b.   What is the value of this option today?

    c.   How does the value of the option change if the stock price is $10?

    d.   How does the value of the option change if the strike price is $10?

    e.   How does the value of the option change if the standard deviation of the annual return is equal to 10%?

    f.   How does the value of the option change if the company changes its dividend policy and stops paying dividends?

    g.   How does the value of the option change if the expiration date is 10 years?

    h.   How does the value of the option change if the risk-free rate is 10%?

P12.3   **Cost of Capital for Warrants 1** A company has 100,000 shares of common stock and 10,000 warrants outstanding. Each warrant has the right to purchase three shares of the company's stock at the end of five years at $9 per share. The value of a warrant is $3.50 per warrant, and the company's stock price is $8 per share. The standard deviation of the stock's annual return is 30%. The company has a continuously compounded dividend yield of 6%. The company has $100,000 of outstanding debt that has a 10% cost of capital. The company's equity cost of capital is 15%, and the risk-free rate is 5%. The company's income tax rate is 40% on all income.

    a.   Ignore the warrants and calculate the company's unlevered cost of capital and weighted average cost of capital, assuming that the company's current capital structure (without the warrants) represents its long-run capital structure, and that the discount rate for interest tax shields is the unlevered cost of capital.

    b.   Using these same assumptions, calculate the company's unlevered cost of capital and weighted average cost of capital, but now include the effect of the warrants.

P12.4   **Cost of Capital for Warrants 2** A company has 10,000 shares of common stock and 5,000 warrants outstanding. Each warrant has the right to purchase two shares of the company's stock at the end of ten years at $5 per share, which is the company's current stock price. The standard deviation of the stock's annual return is 40%. The company has a continuously compounded dividend yield of 2%. The company has $40,000 of outstanding debt that has an 8% cost of capital. The company's equity cost of capital is 10%, and the risk-free rate is 4%. The company's income tax rate is 30% on all income.

    a.   Ignore the warrants and calculate the company's unlevered cost of capital and weighted average cost of capital, assuming that the company's current capital structure (without the warrants) represents its long-run capital structure, and that the discount rate for interest tax shields is the unlevered cost of capital.

    b.   Using these same assumptions, calculate the company's unlevered cost of capital and weighted average cost of capital, but now include the effect of the warrants.

P12.5   **Equity with Warrants 1** A Company has an unlevered cost of capital of 10%, which is also the discount rate for interest tax shields; the company also has an income tax rate of 30%. The company finances itself with 40% debt, which has a cost of capital equal to 7%; finances itself with 10% preferred stock, which has a cost of capital of 7.5%; and the remainder with common equity. The company expects its unlevered free cash flows to remain constant in perpetuity. The company holds no excess cash or excess assets. Use the information that follows to calculate the company's stock price, assuming it has 2,000 shares of common stock outstanding at the end of Year 0—the valuation date. Afterward, calculate the company's stock price, assuming the company issued 1,000 warrants with an exercise or strike price equal to $5 and immediately paid out the proceeds to shareholders as of the end of Year 0. The warrants and the common equity together account for 50% of the capital structure. The company expects to follow a consistent dividend policy and pay all available cash flows to its shareholders in the form of dividends. The warrants can be exercised at the end of two years, their expiration date. At the date of issuance, the risk-free rate was 4%, and the company's annualized standard deviation of its stock return is 40%.

Income Statement Forecast	Year 1
Revenue	$120,000
Depreciation expense.	−20,000
Operating expenses	−96,859
Earnings before interest and taxes.	$ 3,141

Asset Forecast	Year 1
Cash.	$ 4,000
Net operating working capital	25,000
Net property, plant and equipment	120,000
Total assets.	$149,000

Unlevered Free Cash Flow Forecast	Year 1
Earnings before interest and taxes.	$ 3,141
Income taxes	−942
Unlevered earnings after tax	$ 2,198
Depreciation expense (non-cash expenses).	20,000
Change in required cash	0
Change in net working capital	0
Capital expenditures	−20,000
Unlevered free cash flows	$ 2,198

Exhibit may contain small rounding errors

P12.6   **Equity with Warrants 2**   A Company has an unlevered cost of capital of 12%, which is also the discount rate for interest tax shields; and the company has an income tax rate of 45%. The company finances itself with 40% debt, which has a cost of capital equal to 7%; finances itself with 10% preferred stock, which has a cost of capital of 8%; and the remainder with common equity. The company expects its unlevered free cash flows to grow at 6% in perpetuity. The company holds no excess cash or excess assets. Use the information that follows to calculate the company's stock price, assuming it has 20,000 shares of common stock outstanding at the end of Year 0—the valuation date. Next, calculate the company's stock price, assuming the company issued 5,000 warrants with an exercise or strike price equal to $3 and immediately paid the proceeds out to shareholders as of the end of Year 0. The warrants and the common equity together account for 50% of the capital structure. The company expects to follow a consistent dividend policy and pay all available cash flows to its shareholders in the form of dividends. The warrants can be exercised at the end of two years, their expiration date. At the date of issuance, the risk-free rate was 4%, and the company's annualized standard deviation of its stock returns is 40%.

Balance Sheet Forecast	Year 0	Year +1
Cash.	$ 12,000	$ 12,720
Net operating working capital	36,000	38,160
Net property, plant, and equipment	60,000	63,600
Total assets.	$108,000	$114,480
Debt	$ 80,000	$ 84,800
Preferred stock.	20,000	21,200
Common equity	8,000	8,480
Total liabilities and equities.	$108,000	$114,480

Income Statement Forecast	Year +1
Revenue	$120,000
Depreciation expense.	−24,000
Operating expenses	−66,982
Earnings before interest and taxes.	$ 29,018
Interest expense.	−5,600
Earnings before tax	$ 23,418
Income taxes	−10,538
Earnings after tax.	$ 12,880
Preferred stock dividends	−1,600
Earnings available to common equity . .	$ 11,280

Free Cash Flow Schedule	Year +1
Earnings before interest and taxes.	$29,018
Income taxes	−13,058
Unlevered earnings after tax	$15,960
Depreciation.	24,000
Change in required cash	−720
Change in net working capital	−2,160
Capital expenditures	−27,600
Unlevered free cash flow (FCF)	$9,480
Interest paid in cash ($r_D \times D$).	−5,600
Interest tax shield ($T_{INT} \times r_D \times D$).	2,520
Preferred stock dividend ($r_{PSDIV} \times PS$). . . .	−1,600
Change in debt.	4,800
Change in preferred stock	1,200
Equity free cash flow (EFCF)	$10,800
Common dividends	−10,800
Change in common equity.	0
Change in required cash	720
Change in cash balance.	$ 720

P12.7 **Convertible Bonds with an Observable Price** A company issues $1 million of $1,000 face value convertible bonds with a 6% annual coupon payment. The bonds mature in 5 years. Each bond is convertible into 200 shares of the company's stock at the end of the 5 years. If the company had straight debt outstanding, it would have a yield to maturity and a cost of capital of 9%. The bonds were issued today at $1,200. The company has 1 million shares of stock outstanding, and its stock is trading at $4.50 per share. Its equity cost of capital is 15%, the standard deviation of its annual stock return is 60%, its continuously compounded dividend yield is 4.75%, and the risk-free rate is 3.25%. This is the only financing the company uses to finance the company. Calculate the value of the conversion feature of these bonds on a per convertible share value and calculate the cost of capital for this conversion feature.

P12.8 **Convertible Bonds with an Unobservable Price** A few years ago, a company issued $1 million of $1,000 face value convertible bonds with a 7% annual coupon payment. Each bond is convertible into 100 shares of the company's stock at the end of 5 years from today. The company has 500,000 shares of stock outstanding and its stock is trading at $11 per share. Its equity cost of capital is 12%, the standard deviation of its annual stock return is 44%, it has a continuously compounded dividend yield of 3.90%, and the risk-free rate is 3.0%. If the company had straight debt outstanding, it would have a yield to maturity and cost of debt of 10%. This is the only financing the company uses to finance itself. Calculate the value of the conversion feature of these bonds on a per convertible share value and calculate the cost of capital for this conversion feature.

SOLUTIONS FOR REVIEW EXERCISES

Review Exercise 12.1: Valuation of a Basic European Call Option

With no dividends:

Assumptions for Option Valuation		
Stock price	$ 10.00	P_E
Exercise price	$ 12.00	X_C
Annualized standard deviation	30.00%	σ_E
Dividend yield, continuously compounded	0.00%	d_E
Maturity in years	3	T_C
Risk-free rate	5.0%	r_f

Key Calculations	
d_1	0.198
$N(d_1)$	0.578
d_2	−0.322
$N(d_2)$	0.374
Price of the call option	$1.923 P_C

With annual continuously compounded dividend yield = 5%

Assumptions for Option Valuation		
Stock price	$ 10.00	P_E
Exercise price	$ 12.00	X_C
Annualized standard deviation	30.00%	σ_E
Dividend yield, continuously compounded	5.00%	d_E
Maturity in years	3	T_C
Risk-free rate	5.0%	r_f

Key Calculations	
d_1	−0.091
$N(d_1)$	0.464
d_2	−0.611
$N(d_2)$	0.271
Price of the call option	$1.195 P_C
Change in value	−37.8%

Review Exercise 12.2: Cost of Capital for Warrants

	Shares/ Warrants	Price	Valuation ($ in thousands)	Capital Structure Weight	Cost of Capital	Unlevered Cost of Capital	Weighted Average Cost of Capital
Excluding (Ignoring) Warrants:							
Common.	20,000	$12.000	$240.00	54.5%	14.0%	7.6%	7.6%
Debt			200.00	45.5%	9.0%	4.1%	2.5%
			$440.00	100.0%		11.7%	10.1%

Other Information:

Income tax rate	40.0%
Risk-free rate of return	4.0%
Annual volatility of equity	24.0%
Exercise price of warrants	$12.00
Expiration of warrants (in years)	5.00
Dividend yield, continuously compounded	5.0%
Conversion ratio	5.0

	Shares/ Warrants	Price	Valuation ($ in thousands)	Capital Structure Weight	Cost of Capital	Unlevered Cost of Capital	Weighted Average Cost of Capital
Including Warrants:							
Common.	20,000	$12.000	$240.00	53.5%	14.0%	7.5%	7.5%
Warrants	1,000	$ 8.775	8.78	2.0%	33.6%	0.7%	0.7%
Debt			200.00	44.6%	9.0%	4.0%	2.4%
			$448.78	100.0%		12.2%	10.6%

σ_Q	25.66%
d_1	0.2797
d_2	−0.2941

Exhibit may contain small rounding errors

Review Exercise 12.3: The Stuart Essig Perpetuity Company

$$r_{WACC} = r_{UA} - r_D \times T_{INT} \times \frac{V_D}{V_F} - (r_{UA} - r_{ITS}) \times \frac{V_{ITS}}{V_F} \qquad (11.2)$$

$$.082 = .10 - .09 \times .4 \times .5 - 0$$

$$V_F = \frac{\$8,200}{.082} = \$100,000$$

Correct Valuation	Number	Price	Value
Equity	10,000	$2.662	$26,623
Warrants	5,000	$0.675	3,377
Total			$30,000

Valuation and Capital Structure Ratios		
Value of the debt	$ 50,000	50.0%
Value of the preferred	20,000	20.0%
Value of warrants	3,377	3.4%
Value of the equity	26,623	26.6%
Value of the firm	$100,000	100.0%

Assumptions for Option Valuation	
Dividend yield, continuously compounded	14.479%
Maturity in years	5
Risk-free rate	5.0%
Exercise price	$1.0000
Annualized standard deviation	45.0%
Stock price	$2.6623

Review Exercise 12.4: Convertible Debt

Inputs for Straight Debt

Total face value.	$2,000,000
Number of bonds	2,000
Face value per note	$ 1,000
Price per bond	$ 1,100
Coupon rate	8%
Straight debt promised yield	10%
Coupon payments per year	1
Maturity (years) from date of issue.	6
Conversion ratio per bond	100

Per Bond	Value Using Coupon Rate	Value Using Promised Yield
Coupon (annual).	8.000%	10.000%
Year 1	$ 80.00	$80.00
Year 2	$ 80.00	$80.00
Year 3	$ 80.00	$80.00
Year 4	$ 80.00	$80.00
Year 5	$ 80.00	$80.00
Year 6	$1,080.00	$1,080.00
Value of straight debt	$1,000.00	$ 912.89
Price of debt.		1,100.00
Value of the conversion provision.		$ 187.11
Number of shares.		100
Value of conversion feature per share		$ 1.871

	Price	Valuation
Income tax rate	40.0%	
Risk-free rate of return	4.0%	
Equity cost of capital	15.0%	
Annual volatility of equity	40.0%	
Dividend yield, continuously compounded	5.00%	
Expiration of warrants (in years).	6.0	
Face value per note	$1,000	
Conversion ratio per $1,000 agreement.	100	
Exercise price of conversion feature	$10	
Current stock price.	$8.45	
Parity ratio (stock price/conversion price)	0.845	
Cost of capital of conversion feature	25.7%	
Value of notes (ignoring accrued interest)	2,000	$912.895	$ 1,825,790
Value of conversion feature	200,000	$ 1.871	374,210
Value of convertible note			$2,200,000.0
Value if converted.	200,000	$ 8.450	1,690,000.0
Value of note in excess of converted value			$ 510,000.0
. . . .	41.66%	
d_1	0.3433	
d_2	−0.6771	

After mastering the material in this chapter, you will be able to:

1. Use market multiples to value a company and its equity (13.1–13.2)

2. Identify the characteristics that drive market multiples (13.3–13.4)

3. Choose comparable companies to use in a market multiple valuation (13.5)

4. Adjust for transitory changes when measuring market multiples (13.6)

5. Measure continuing values using market multiples (13.7)

Introduction to Market Multiple Valuation Methods

FIRST DATA CORPORATION

First Data Corporation (First Data) and Concord EFS, Inc. (Concord) issued a joint press release announcing the execution of a merger agreement on April 2, 2003. Each company hired two financial advisors to evaluate the transaction and issue a fairness opinion. All four of the financial advisors used the market multiple valuation method in addition to the discounted cash flow (DCF) valuation method in their assessments of the fairness of the merger. First Data's financial advisors used three valuation analyses—public market comparables analysis, comparable acquisitions analysis, and a DCF analysis. The first two analyses are both based on the market multiple valuation method. They also used a market multiple valuation method to measure the continuing value in their DCF analysis.

To select the comparable companies for the public market comparables analysis, they compared selected historical and projected financial data of First Data and Concord to corresponding data for publicly traded companies that they deemed to be relevant. The selected comparable companies engaged in businesses and had operating profiles reasonably similar to those of First Data and Concord.

They examined the following multiples: closing stock price to 2002 earnings per share, closing stock price to 2003 estimated earnings per share, closing stock price to 2004 estimated earnings per share, enterprise value to 2002 EBITDA, and enterprise value to 2003 estimated EBITDA. In their analyses, they used the mean and median multiples of the five comparable companies they selected.

In this chapter, you will learn the basics of market multiple valuation including the process used, the fundamental value drivers that affect variation in market multiples across firms and over time, and how to choose comparable companies.

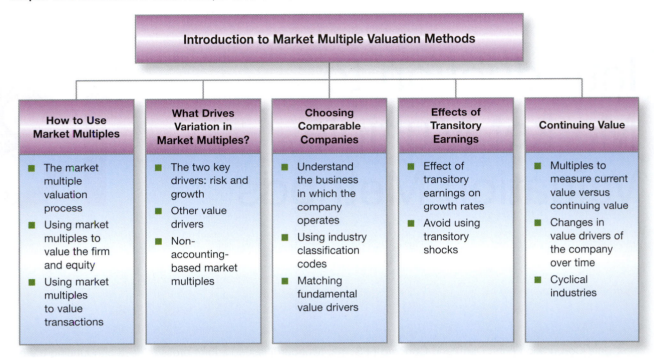

INTRODUCTION

In a **market multiple valuation**, we first identify comparable companies. We then measure the observed relation, or market multiple, between each comparable company's market value and the denominator of the multiple, typically an accounting-based measure, such as earnings or EBIT. This relation or market multiple represents the market value per unit of the denominator, and it is a measure of the amount the market is willing to "pay" relative to a current unit of the denominator of the multiple. We value the company of interest using its measures of the denominator of the chosen multiples and the comparable companies' market multiples. If the relation between the comparable companies' market values and current earnings is 15, and if the company we are valuing has current earnings of $1,000, we would multiply the earnings of the company we are valuing by the earnings market multiple of the comparable companies to measure the market value of the equity for the company of $15,000 ($15,000 = 15 × $1,000).

Don't be fooled by the seeming simplicity of the market multiple valuation method. If performed correctly, it is actually complex and time consuming due to various comparability and measurement issues. So while the first two lines in this introduction seem simple—"identify comparable companies" and "measure the observed relation or market multiple"—those two steps are difficult to do well. At one time, market multiple valuation was the predominant valuation method used by the investment banking community. Now, when valuing companies, investment bankers most often use a market multiple valuation in conjunction with a DCF valuation.[1]

We do not view market multiple valuation as an alternative but rather as a complement to a DCF valuation. We can use market multiple valuation as of the valuation date or as of the continuing (or terminal) value date for a DCF valuation. Some investment bankers use market multiple valuation to directly measure a company's continuing value in a DCF valuation. We recommend a somewhat different approach, which is to use market multiples as a tool to analyze the continuing value by examining various multiples implied by a constant-growth perpetuity model (see Chapter 6).

Alternative names for the market multiple valuation method include **comparable company valuation**, **multiple valuation**, **price multiple valuation**, **guideline company valuation**, **relative valuation analysis**, **direct comparison approach**, and **twin company approach**. As you can quickly see from

---

[1] See, DeAngelo, L., "Equity Valuation and Corporate Control," *Accounting Review* 65 (1990), pp. 93–112 for a discussion of the use of market multiples in rendering fairness opinions; and Kaplan, S., and R. Ruback, "The Valuation of Cash Flow Forecasts: An Empirical Analysis," *The Journal of Finance* vol. L, no. 4 (September, 1995), pp. 1093–1095 for evidence on the usefulness of using market multiples and DCF valuations.

the various names used to describe the market multiple valuation methods, comparable companies—or "**comps**"—are an important part of this valuation method. The key issues in valuing companies using market multiples are choosing appropriate comparable companies that would be priced similarly to the company being valued and then making adjustments to the financial numbers used so that distortions to the valuation do not arise from accounting differences or certain events that can affect the financial statements in ways that render the numbers less useful for a market multiple valuation.

We use market multiple valuation to measure both a company's firm value and common equity value assuming it were traded on a public exchange. We also use market multiple valuation to measure the value of an anticipated transaction (acquisition, leveraged buyout, IPO) by using similar transactions involving comparable companies that should be priced similarly to the company and transaction being valued. Alternative names for a market multiple analysis based on transactions are **comparable transaction analysis** and **comparable acquisitions analysis**.

The goals of this and the next chapter are to thoroughly discuss the conceptual underpinning and process of market multiple valuation. In this chapter, we focus on the conceptual framework of the market multiple valuation method and its relation to the DCF valuation method, and we highlight the implicit assumptions made when using the various market multiples. For now, we ignore many of the measurement and implementation issues faced in market multiple valuations, but we will discuss these issues in detail in the next chapter.

13.1 THE MARKET MULTIPLE VALUATION PROCESS

The basic approach in the market multiple valuation process is to first identify the relevant set of comparable companies for a particular valuation. We then measure the firm value and/or equity value of each comparable company. Then, we divide (or scale) each comparable company's market value by an appropriate denominator (for example, EBITDA) to measure the value of the multiple for each comparable company. After all of the multiples for comparable firms are estimated, we determine the appropriate value (or range of values) of the multiple for the company being valued. We then multiply the multiple estimated from the comparable companies by the measure that is the denominator of the multiple (say, EBITDA) for the company of interest. The result is a measure of the value of the firm or equity, depending on the multiple chosen. Of course, we often look at several different multiples when we perform this work. Further, we often measure the relevant denominators by using either very recent historical data or forecasts. We summarize the steps in the market multiple valuation process in Exhibit 13.1.

LO1 Use market multiples to value a company and its equity

EXHIBIT 13.1	An Overview of the Valuation Process Using Market Multiples
1	Identify potential comparable companies (key competitors and other companies in the same industry with similar value drivers)
2	Collect historical and forward-looking (forecasts) information for potential comparable companies and relevant market information
3	Identify the characteristics of the company being valued that drive variation in market multiples (risk, growth, profitability, required investments, etc.)
4	Assess the comparability of the financial statements for the comparable companies and the company being valued and make adjustments to the financial statements as needed (for differences in accounting principles, nonrecurring and unusual items, acquisitions and divestitures, etc.)
5	Assess the comparability of the potential comparable companies based on the characteristics that drive variation in the chosen market multiples and choose the comparable companies
6	Based on the comparability reviews, select the appropriate market multiples to use for the company being valued, given the specific valuation context
7	Measure the market value of the equity and firm, as well as the denominators of the market multiples selected, for the comparable companies at each relevant date
8	Measure the relevant multiples for each comparable company
9	Assess the relevant range and measure of central tendency (mean, median) of the multiples to be used
10	Measure the relevant denominator for the company being valued and value the company using the market multiples. Assess the reasonable range and consistency of valuations across the different multiples

Some steps in the market multiple valuation process overlap with steps in our overall valuation process. For example, the first two steps in the market multiple valuation process are to identify potential comparable companies and to collect and analyze historical information and forecasts for these companies. These steps are similar to the first two steps in the overall valuation process. The third step in a market multiple valuation, identifying the value drivers of the company being valued, is similar to what we do when we forecast a company's financial statements and free cash flows. Thus, in most cases, we will have already worked through the first three steps of the market multiple valuation process if we have completed a discounted cash flow valuation of the company prior to beginning our market multiple valuation analysis.

13.2 COMMONLY USED MARKET MULTIPLES

As you might expect, most of the common denominators of market multiples used by analysts, investment bankers, and valuation specialists are accounting-based. Some of these are based on the income statement and statement of cash flows—such as earnings; earnings before interest and taxes (EBIT); earnings before interest, taxes, depreciation, and amortization (EBITDA); revenue; sales; operating cash flows; and free cash flow (FCF). Others are based on the balance sheet—such as total invested capital, total assets, tangible assets, stockholders' equity, and net tangible equity. A multiple's denominator can also be non-accounting-based, such as a measure of productive capacity, number of employees, square feet of retail space, or population in an area served.

Firm Value Versus Enterprise Value

Many valuation specialists use multiples based on **enterprise value** instead of the value of the firm. The market value of the firm is the market value of the firm's common equity, options granted, preferred stock, long-term debt, short-term debt, and any other securities issued, such as warrants. Enterprise value is similar to the value of the firm, but instead of being based on total debt, it is based on debt minus cash and marketable securities, which is equal to net debt. When we measure a multiple based on enterprise value, we eliminate any income effect due to the cash and marketable securities that are netted against debt to arrive at net debt. If cash exceeds debt, the net debt will be negative.

By subtracting total cash and marketable securities from debt in order to measure net debt for computing enterprise value, we essentially assume that all cash is available to pay off debt, and hence the company does not require cash to run its business. This is unlikely to cause any problems as long as the comparable companies and the company we are valuing have comparable cash requirements that are proportional to value. Using enterprise value circumvents the issue of estimating required cash. In this book, we sometimes show multiples based on the value of the firm and at other times we use enterprise value.

To use the enterprise value approach, we multiply the market multiple based on the enterprise value and chosen denominator of the comparable companies by the relevant denominator of the market multiple for the company we are valuing. This calculation measures the enterprise value of the company we are valuing. To measure the value of the firm, we must add the value of the company's cash and marketable securities to its enterprise value.

Market Multiples Used to Value the Firm and Common Equity

We summarize some of the commonly used multiples in Exhibit 13.2. In the first panel of the exhibit, we list market multiples used to measure firm value or enterprise value, and in the second panel, we list market multiples used to value the equity.

Even though free cash flow is a logical denominator to use for a market multiple, it is not very popular, the reasons for which we discuss later in the chapter. We introduce it first because of its link to the DCF valuation model and its usefulness in identifying some of the key assumptions underlying the use of market multiples. The first of the earnings-based multiples is the unlevered earnings multiple—measured as earnings (net income) plus after-tax interest. We use unlevered earnings rather than straight earnings to measure the value of the firm. Since we are measuring the value of the firm, we do not want to deduct interest expense, for it is a flow available to the debtholders—similarly, we would not want to deduct preferred dividends, as it is a flow available to preferred holders. Unlevered earnings is similar to unle-

EXHIBIT 13.2	Some Commonly Used Market Multiples

Market Multiple Name	Denominator
Market Multiples to Value the Firm or Enterprise (Numerator Is Market Value of Firm or Enterprise Value)	
1 Free cash flow multiple	Unlevered free cash flow
2 Unlevered earnings multiple	Earnings after taxes plus after-tax interest
3 EBIT multiple	Earnings before interest and taxes
4 EBITDA multiple	Earnings before interest, taxes, depreciation, and amortization
5 Revenue (sales) multiple	Revenue or sales
6 Total invested capital (similar alternatives are tangible assets, total assets) multiple	Total invested capital
7 Non-accounting denominator (productive capacity, number of employees, square feet of retail space, population in area served)	Relevant non-accounting denominator
Market Multiples to Measure Equity Value (Numerator Is Market Value of Equity or Price per Share)	
1 Equity free cash flow multiple	Equity free cash flow
2 Price-to-earnings multiple	Earnings available to common shareholders (or earnings per share)
3 Market-to-book (similar alternative is tangible net equity) multiple	Book value of equity
4 Non-accounting denominator (productive capacity, number of employees, square feet of retail space, population in area served)	Relevant non-accounting denominator for equity

vered free cash flows but it does not include any adjustments for non-cash items (such as depreciation) and investments in fixed assets or working capital.

Two of the more popular earnings-based multiples used to value the firm are the EBIT and EBITDA multiples. Again, both EBIT and EBITDA are measures of earnings before interest, so they represent flows that relate to total firm value as opposed to the value of the equity. EBIT and EBITDA are of course even further removed from unlevered free cash flows than unlevered earnings. Revenue multiples are also used, though less popular, and by their nature cannot adjust for differences in the cost structure of the company and the comparable companies. Next in the panel are market multiples based on some measure of the investments made by the company—total assets, total invested capital, tangible assets, and so on. These are also used less often. In order to use market multiples based on total invested capital, we assume the comparable companies and the company we are valuing create the same value relative to the amount of invested capital. Financial institutions are sometimes valued based on total capital.

The last multiples in this panel are based on non-accounting measures. Based on our knowledge of the best predictor of a company's free cash flows, we must decide whether to use a non-accounting-based denominator. For example, assume that all of the companies in a certain industry have essentially the same investments, accruals, cost structure, and relation between revenues and some non-accounting measure, Z—say, the number of square feet of retail floor space. If the non-accounting measure, Z, is a better indicator of the company's future free cash flows than current or forecasted accounting-based measures, using a market multiple based on this non-accounting measure may be a more reasonable multiple to use to value the company. Naturally, this is a rather strong set of assumptions, but financial analysts, investment bankers, and investors often use non-accounting-based multiples that are specific to particular industries. We explore the logic underlying these multiples in more detail later in the chapter.

As long as we know or can estimate the value of each of the company's non-equity securities, we can use any of the market multiples in the first panel of Exhibit 13.2 to value a company's equity. Hence, the value of the company's equity is equal to the value of the firm less the value of the company's non-equity securities. For the multiples in the second panel of the exhibit, we measure each market multiple by dividing the value of the company's equity by a specific denominator. The denominators of these multiples are, for the most part, analogous to the denominators of multiples based on the value of the firm; however, in general, we only measure the denominator based on the claims of the equityholders. Thus, we use equity free cash flow, earnings (more specifically, net income available to common shareholders), and the book value of equity as the denominators.

While we use denominators that reflect the equityholders, claims for most of the equity value multiples, that is not true for either the multiple of equity value to sales or market multiples based on equity values to non-accounting measures. The denominators of these multiples measure the activity (for example, sales) that results from all of the company's investments—not from just its equity.

REVIEW EXERCISE 13.1

Basic Calculation of Market Multiples

Below, we present summary financial statements and a free cash flow schedule for an example company. Use this information to measure the free cash flow and financial-statement-based market multiples from Exhibit 13.2. Measure the market multiple using the end of Year 0 firm or equity value and the Year 0 denominator. The value of the company's equity at the end of Year 0 is $1,656.3, and the value of the firm is $2,070.3.

High-Growth Company Financial Statements and Free Cash Flows								
($ in millions)	Year −1	Year 0	Year 1	Year 2	Year 3	Year 4	Year 5	Year 6
Income Statement								
Revenue	$ 980.4	$1,000.0	$1,080.0	$1,231.2	$1,255.8	$1,280.9	$1,306.6	$1,332.7
Operating expenses	−686.3	−700.0	−756.0	−861.8	−879.1	−896.7	−914.6	−932.9
Depreciation expense	−62.8	−64.1	−69.2	−78.9	−80.5	−82.1	−83.8	−85.4
Interest expense	−29.2	−32.5	−33.1	−36.7	−37.8	−38.6	−39.3	−40.1
Income before taxes	$ 202.0	$ 203.4	$ 221.6	$ 253.7	$ 258.4	$ 263.6	$ 268.9	$ 274.3
Income tax expense	−80.8	−81.4	−88.7	−101.5	−103.4	−105.4	−107.6	−109.7
Net income	$ 121.2	$ 122.1	$ 133.0	$ 152.2	$ 155.1	$ 158.2	$ 161.3	$ 164.6
Balance Sheet								
Net working capital	$ 196.1	$ 200.0	$ 216.0	$ 246.2	$ 251.2	$ 256.2	$ 261.3	$ 266.5
Property, plant, and equipment (net)	967.8	1,006.3	1,130.9	1,083.5	1,035.2	986.0	935.7	884.5
Total assets	$1,163.9	$1,206.3	$1,346.9	$1,329.8	$1,286.4	$1,242.2	$1,197.0	$1,151.0
Debt	$ 405.9	$ 414.1	$ 458.7	$ 472.5	$ 481.9	$ 491.6	$ 501.4	$ 511.4
Equity	758.0	792.2	888.2	857.3	804.5	750.6	695.6	639.6
Total liabilities and equities	$1,163.9	$1,206.3	$1,346.9	$1,329.8	$1,286.4	$1,242.2	$1,197.0	$1,151.0
Free Cash Flows								
Earnings before interest and taxes (EBIT)		$ 235.9	$ 254.8	$290.4	$ 296.2	$ 302.2	$ 308.2	$ 314.4
– Income taxes paid on EBIT		−94.4	−101.9	−116.2	−118.5	−120.9	−123.3	−125.8
Earnings before interest and after taxes		$ 141.5	$ 152.9	$ 174.3	$ 177.7	$ 181.3	$ 184.9	$ 188.6
+ Depreciation expense		64.1	69.2	78.9	80.5	82.1	83.8	85.4
– Change in net working capital		−3.9	−16.0	−30.2	−4.9	−5.0	−5.1	−5.2
– Capital expenditures		−102.6	−193.8	−31.6	−32.2	−32.8	−33.5	−34.2
Unlevered free cash flow		$ 99.2	$ 12.2	$ 191.4	$ 221.1	$ 225.5	$ 230.1	$ 234.7
– Interest paid		−32.5	−33.1	−36.7	−37.8	−38.6	−39.3	−40.1
+ Interest tax shield		13.0	13.3	14.7	15.1	15.4	15.7	16.0
+ Change in debt financing		8.1	44.6	13.8	9.4	9.6	9.8	10.0
Free cash flow to common equity		$ 87.8	$ 37.0	$ 183.2	$ 207.9	$ 212.1	$ 216.3	$ 220.6

Exhibit may contain small rounding errors

Solution on page 540.

Time-Series Statistics for Typical Market Multiples

In order to gain some understanding of the magnitude of some typical market multiples, in Exhibit 13.3 we provide data on six of the firm value market multiples and four of the equity value market multiples described in Exhibit 13.2. We report the median market multiple for a sample of company-years. To be included in the sample in a particular year (1992 through 2010), a company must be in the Compustat®[2] database; have traded on the New York Stock Exchange, American Stock Exchange, or Nasdaq Exchange; and have sufficient information to calculate each of the 10 market multiples in Exhibit 13.3 in that year. Throughout the chapter, we refer to this dataset as the "Compustat® Based Market Multiple" dataset. The sample consists of 97,209 company-years, and the number of companies per year ranges from 3,964 to 5,683. To eliminate the effect of outliers, we "truncated" the market multiples (set the minimum and maximum values) at the 5th and 95th percentiles, and we do not include an observation for a market multiple if its denominator is negative.

In the exhibit, we present data for each year between 2000 and 2010 and for the overall 1992 to 2010 period. We show the medians for this sample because this is the approach often used by valuation experts. While there is some variation over time (for example, notice the effect of the 2008 financial crisis), the variation is somewhat suppressed relative to other presentations of these same data, which often report weighted averages (sometimes including negative denominators) instead of medians. The exhibit provides a general understanding of the central tendency of the multiples typically used by practitioners. For example, over this time period, the median P/E is 17.4, the median multiple of firm value to EBIT is 12.7, the median multiple of firm value to EBITDA is 9.1, the median multiple of firm value to revenue is 1.7, and the median multiple of firm value to total assets is 1.0. Note that enterprise value multiples will be somewhat smaller than those reported in Exhibit 13.3 because of the subtraction of all cash from the value of the firm in computing enterprise value.

| **EXHIBIT 13.3** | Time-Series of Some Typical Market Multiples—Median Value by Year |

Denominator	2000	2001	2002	2003	2004	2005	2006	2007	2008	2009	2010	1992–2010
Market Multiples Used to Measure the Value of the Firm (Numerator Is Market Value of the Firm)												
1 Unlevered free cash flow	15.2	14.7	12.5	17.1	19.7	19.3	20.5	18.1	12.2	12.6	14.7	16.9
2 Earnings after taxes plus after-tax interest ("Unlevered earnings")	16.1	19.9	17.7	21.3	21.5	20.8	20.4	19.9	15.5	18.7	18.6	18.7
3 Earnings before interest and taxes ("EBIT")	10.9	13.0	11.7	14.2	14.4	14.2	14.1	13.9	10.1	12.9	12.6	12.7
4 Earnings before interest, taxes, depreciation, and amortization ("EBITDA")	7.8	9.1	8.3	10.4	10.7	10.6	10.6	10.3	7.1	9.0	9.1	9.1
5 Revenue or sales	1.6	1.7	1.4	2.0	2.2	2.1	2.2	2.1	1.2	1.6	1.8	1.7
6 Total assets	0.9	0.9	0.8	1.1	1.2	1.2	1.2	1.1	0.7	0.9	0.9	1.0
Market Multiples to Measure the Value of the Equity (Numerator Is Market Value of the Equity)												
1 Equity free cash flow	16.0	18.1	13.4	19.2	18.8	18.1	19.7	16.4	10.6	13.4	14.6	16.9
2 Earnings available to common shareholders ("P/E")	14.4	17.4	15.6	19.5	19.9	19.1	19.2	18.5	13.7	17.6	17.5	17.4
3 Revenue or sales	1.2	1.3	1.2	1.8	1.9	1.9	1.8	1.6	0.9	1.2	1.4	1.4
4 Book value of equity	1.7	1.8	1.5	2.2	2.3	2.3	2.3	2.1	1.2	1.6	1.8	1.9

In addition to presenting the time-series of various multiples, this exhibit also allows us to compare the relative magnitudes of the multiples. We know that the unlevered earnings multiple is larger than the EBIT multiple, that the EBIT multiple is larger than the EBITDA multiple, and that the EBITDA multiple is larger than the revenue multiple. These relative magnitudes occur because the numerators in the multiples are the same, and we know the relative magnitudes of the denominators. Unlevered earnings is

---

[2] Standard & Poor's Compustat® is a standardized database that delivers accounting and market data on over 54,000 securities to clients via a variety of databases and analytical software products. Standard & Poor's Investment Services is a division of McGraw-Hill, Inc.

smaller than EBIT, EBIT is smaller than EBITDA, and EBITDA is smaller than revenue. Generally, we also know that total assets is larger than all of the earnings measures and that its multiple is smaller than the earnings multiples, though that is not universally true for all companies.

Valuation Key 13.1

One key factor in choosing a market multiple with which to value a company is how closely the denominator of the multiple maps to economic value. Some market multiples are based on earnings numbers or cash flows—such as earnings; earnings before interest and taxes (EBIT); earnings before interest, taxes, depreciation, and amortization (EBITDA); revenue or sales; and free cash flow (FCF). Others are based on balance sheet items—such as total invested capital, total assets, tangible assets, stockholders' equity, and net tangible equity. The denominator in a multiple can also be non-accounting-based—such as productive capacity, number of employees, square feet of retail space, and population in an area served.

13.3 RISK AND GROWTH VALUE DRIVERS

LO2 Identify the characteristics that drive market multiples

To understand the framework underpinning the market multiple valuation method, we begin by looking at the discounted cash flow (DCF) valuation model. We show how, by making certain assumptions, the market multiple valuation model can be related to a DCF valuation. Indeed, we see that they can be equivalent. Initially, we focus on multiples based on free cash flows, but later in the chapter, we extend our discussion to market multiples commonly used by analysts, investment bankers, and valuation specialists.

The Relation Between the Discounted Cash Flow Model and Free Cash Flow Multiples

From the DCF valuation model, we can measure the value of an *all-equity-financed firm* as

$$V_{F,0} = \frac{FCF_1}{1 + r} + \frac{FCF_2}{(1 + r)^2} + \frac{FCF_3}{(1 + r)^3} + \ldots + \frac{FCF_\infty}{(1 + r)^\infty}$$

As we know from our discussion of continuing value in Chapter 6, under certain assumptions, we can restate the DCF valuation as a constant-growth perpetuity—where $g_{1,\infty}$ is the present value weighted average growth rate for the company's free cash flows from Year 1 in perpetuity.

$$V_{F,0} = \frac{FCF_1}{r - g_{1,\infty}}$$

We can use this formula to rewrite our market multiple valuation formula for the free cash flow multiple, $MM[V_{F,0}/FCF_1]$, as

$$MM[V_{F,0}/FCF_1] = \frac{V_{F,0}}{FCF_1} = \frac{1}{r - g_{1,\infty}} \tag{13.1}$$

If we use free cash flow from Year 0 (instead of Year 1), then this formula must include the growth rate from Year 0 to Year 1.

$$MM[V_{F,0}/FCF_0] = \frac{V_{F,0}}{FCF_0} = \frac{(1 + g_{0,1})}{r - g_{1,\infty}} \tag{13.2}$$

Note that we are assuming an all-equity-financed firm, so the unlevered cost of capital is the same as the weighted average and equity costs of capital ($r_{UA} = r_{WACC} = r_E$). These formulas can be used to measure market multiples for a firm with debt, but the appropriate cost of capital would be the weighted average cost of capital in that case. The formulas can also be used to calculate equity market multiples, and in that case, you would use the value of the equity and the equity free cash flows and the appropriate discount rate would be the equity cost of capital.

As these formulas illustrate, the free cash flow multiple is equivalent to the capitalization factor in the constant growth perpetuity model. It is similar to a "price" that the market would pay for a current dollar of free cash flow for this company, conditional on the riskiness of the cash flows and expectations of the future growth of these cash flows. As is true with the perpetuity model, the base year free cash flow must be positive in order to use the market multiple valuation method. The clear implication from this formula is that we must match comparable companies on both risk and growth in order to use a free cash flow multiple. Equally important is the fact that the value drivers in this formula (growth and risk) underpin all market multiples—not just free cash flow multiples. No matter what market multiple we use, we must assess the comparability of potential comparable companies based on risk and free cash flow growth. As we will soon show, comparability for all multiples requires that characteristics beyond risk and growth must also be comparable, but the free cash flow multiple will be less sensitive to many of these other characteristics.

REVIEW EXERCISE 13.2

Risk and Growth Drivers of Market Multiples

Use the information in Review Exercise 13.1 and the company's costs of capital and growth rates to calculate the company's multiple of firm value to unlevered free cash flow and its multiple of equity value to equity free cash flow. The company's equity cost of capital is 13%, and its weighted average cost of capital is 11.36%. In order to solve this exercise, you will have to refer back to Equation 6.3 to solve for the present value weighted average growth rate.

Solution on page 541.

Valuation in Practice 13.1

Financial Analysts and Investors Know the Effect of Growth on Market Multiples: The "PEG" Ratio Many financial analysts and investors use the price-to-earnings (P/E) multiple as a basis for screening stocks (identifying potentially over- and undervalued stocks). One way they use the P/E multiple is in the calculation of the PEG (price-to-earnings-to-growth) ratio. The PEG ratio is equal to the P/E multiple divided by a measure of the company's growth rate (measured as a percentage). For example, if a company has a stock price of $15 per share and an earnings per share of $1.2, its P/E multiple is 12.5 (12.5 = $15/$1.2). We know that a company's growth rate affects all of its market multiples—the higher the growth rate, the higher the market multiple. The PEG ratio attempts to adjust for this growth rate effect.

If our example company has a growth rate of 10%, then its PEG ratio is 1.25 (1.25 = 12.5/10); if it has a growth rate of 25%, then its PEG ratio is .5 (.5 = 12.5/25). What does this calculation tell us? The financial analysts and investors who use PEG ratios suggest that a PEG ratio substantially greater than 1 might indicate an overvalued stock and that a PEG ratio substantially less than 1 might indicate an undervalued stock. No systematic studies document this alleged gold mine empirically, but research shows that this heuristic metric—the PEG ratio—is widely used by financial analysts.

Source: For a detailed discussion and derivation of the PEG ratio and the adjustments one might make to it, see, Easton, P., "PE ratios, PEG ratios, and Estimating the Implied Expected Rate of Return on Equity Capital," *The Accounting Review* vol. 79, no. 1 (January 2004).

Why Free Cash Flow Multiples Are Not Very Popular

Since free cash flow is directly linked to value, we might expect free cash flow multiples to be the most common type of multiple used. They are not, however, the most popular; in fact, free cash flow multiples are less popular than many of the other multiples shown in Exhibit 13.2. They are not as popular as other multiples for two related reasons: free cash flows are negative more often than earnings measures (such as EBITDA), and free cash flow multiples have more extreme observations (outliers) or transitory shocks than other multiples. The investments in capital expenditures, acquisitions, and working capital that companies make tend to vary from year to year, resulting in free cash flows that are more variable and more often negative than earnings-based measures. Thus, the choice of the appropriate measure of free cash flows for the denominator is often difficult.

One approach that one might take to implement a free cash flow multiple is to consider what a "normal level" of investment might be for the firm given its projected growth (thus removing the lumpiness of the investment series). This approach can produce a more reasonable base from which the growth rates are computed. In addition, normalizing the investment may make the free cash flows positive, thus allowing the use of that multiple. We are most likely to use one of the free cash flow multiples if the company we are valuing and our selected comparable companies have low and reasonably stable growth. In any event, free cash flow multiples are not popular in spite of their potential superior ability to control for variation in the value drivers of the company being valued and its associated comparable companies.

Valuation Key 13.2

In spite of their inherent conceptual superiority, free cash flow multiples are not very popular because of the frequency of negative denominators and the "lumpiness" of a company's investments (changes in net working capital and capital expenditures). The "lumpiness" causes free cash flows to vary more from year to year than earnings-based measures, which makes it difficult to judge the correct base to use for calculating the free cash flow multiple. One way to address this issue is to "normalize" the investments.

REVIEW EXERCISE 13.3

Free Cash Flow Market Multiples

Use the information in Review Exercise 13.1 to measure the free cash flow and financial-statement-based market multiples in Exhibit 13.2 for Year 1. Measure the market multiple using the end of Year 1 firm or equity value and the Year 1 denominator. Assume that the value of the company's equity at the end of Year 1 is $1,834.6 and that the value of the firm is $2,293.3. Compare the Year 0 multiples calculated in Review Exercise 13.1 to the Year 1 multiples.

Solution on page 541.

13.4 ADDITIONAL MARKET MULTIPLE VALUE DRIVERS

We know from the previous analysis that free cash flow multiples have two key underlying value drivers—risk and the free cash flow growth rate—and that these underlying value drivers affect all market multiples. The implication of this result is that we should match companies based on these two underlying factors in order to identify comparable companies, regardless of which multiple we use. In this section we investigate the potential value of considering additional factors—such as cost structure, working capital management, capital expenditure requirements, capital structure, and other components of value—when we identify comparable companies.

When Should We Consider Matching on a Value Driver?

If a factor affects both a multiple's numerator (market value) and denominator by the same percentage, it will have no effect on that market multiple. For example, assume a comparable company's income tax rate differs from the income tax rate of the company we are valuing—say, 40% for the comparable company versus 20% for the company we are valuing. If the two companies are exactly the same save for their income tax rates, then the comparable company will have lower free cash flows and a lower value relative to the company we are valuing.

In a simple perpetuity situation, the free cash flows and the value of the comparable company is 25% lower than that of the company we are valuing $[-0.25 = (1 - 0.4)/(1 - 0.2) - 1]$. Its free cash flow market multiple, however, is the same because the numerator and denominator are both 25% lower, so the ratio is unchanged. This is not, however, the case for EBIT. The companies have the same EBIT, but the value of the comparable company (numerator) is 25% lower. In this simple example, this difference results in a EBIT multiple for the comparable company that is 25% lower than the correct multiple for the company being valued. Naturally, the effects of income tax rates and other factors are more complex than the assumptions used in this simple example, so we cannot make such a straightforward adjustment for actual companies. However, you should be able to see that you would have to strive for comparability in the future tax rates faced by both the comparable companies and the company being valued when using EBIT, EBITDA, and revenue multiples.

In general, value drivers other than growth and risk are not as relevant for assessing comparability when using the free cash flow multiple as they are for other multiples; and they are likely to be more relevant for the revenue and total asset (and other balance-sheet-based) multiples. When we calculate free cash flows, we adjust the free cash flow for most of the important value drivers other than risk and growth. Both the free cash flow and therefore the value of the firm are often similarly affected, and thus the free cash flow multiple is often not as affected as other multiples for a difference in these other value drivers. This is not the case for other multiples, and hence other multiples are generally disadvantaged relative to the free cash flow multiples. The exact result depends on the financial model underpinning the company's free cash flows. For the free cash flow multiple to be unaffected by a change in a value driver, the effect on free cash flow and the effect on the value of the firm must change by the same proportion, which may not be the case, depending on the financial model. Unfortunately, as discussed earlier, the free cash flow multiple has various disadvantages that result mostly from the lumpiness of free cash flows.

What additional value drivers that affect multiples should we consider? By now, you are quite familiar with financial models that either explicitly or implicitly drive free cash flow forecasts and value. Each forecast driver is a potential value driver to consider. A value driver is important for assessing comparability if a change in the value driver results in a different proportionate effect on the market value (numerator) relative to the denominator used as the basis for the multiple. If a value driver affects both the market value and denominator by the same proportion, that value driver is irrelevant for assessing comparability because the ratio (multiple) is unchanged. The more a value driver affects one of the two inputs of a multiple (in relative terms), the more relevant it is to the selection of the comparable companies. Any value driver that can affect a multiple has to be controlled by choosing companies that are comparable to the firm being valued with respect to that factor. One thing to remember is that when we move to any earnings-based multiple (such as unlevered earnings, EBIT, EBITDA, or revenue), the denominator does not account for investment or non-cash revenues and expenses, which the free cash flow multiples explicitly incorporate.

Staples, Inc. Simulation

One way to examine the determinants of the different market multiples is to construct a model that algebraically specifies the relation between free cash flows and the denominator of the multiple of interest. While this is a useful exercise in its own right, the form of these relations for even a simple financial model become complex and do not provide insights beyond those provided by a simple simulation. Thus, instead of presenting the underlying algebra of a financial model, in this section we use a simple financial model for Staples, Inc. (Staples) to illustrate the effects of these relations on different market multiples. The goal of this simulation is not to create the ultimate financial model and DCF valuation for Staples, but to use a straightforward financial model and DCF valuation to illustrate the relations between different value drivers (assumptions in the financial model) and the commonly used market multiples. These relations provide guidance on how to assess comparability when selecting comparable companies for a market multiple valuation.

Overview of the Financial Model, Discounted Cash Flow Valuation, and Simulation.
At the end of its 2011 fiscal year (January 2012), Staples was trading with an equity market capitalization of approximately $10.4 billion. It had roughly $2 billion of debt and $1.2 billion of cash and equivalents. We eliminate assumed excess cash of $1 billion and use it to reduce Staples' debt to $1 billion. To simplify the effects of capital structure, we assume the company will maintain that level of debt in the future. After reducing its debt to $1 billion, the resulting enterprise value of Staples (market value of the debt and equity less the value of the cash) at the end of fiscal 2011 is approximately $11.2 billion ($11.2 = $10.4 + $1.0 − $0.2). We use a 12% discount rate and assume Staples does not hold any excess cash in the future.

We create a DCF valuation based on a financial model that results in a value equal to Staples' actual value as of the end of fiscal 2011. We do this through the choice of the fiscal 2012 initial revenue growth rate, 6.8%, which we assume decays by 10% annually until it decays to the assumed long-term inflation rate of 3%. For the other items on the income statement, the financial model assumes that Staples' cost of goods sold and selling, general, and administrative expenses in all future years are the same percentage of revenues as they were in 2011. It assumes straight-line depreciation based on the 2011 straight-line depreciation rate and a constant amortization of intangibles (no acquisitions). The model assumes a 34.5% income tax rate.

For Staples' balance sheet, the model assumes that all current assets and other non-current assets, as well as all current liabilities and non-debt non-current liabilities, are a percentage of revenues based on fiscal 2011. Net land, building, and equipment grow at the rate at which revenues grow and capital expenditures equal depreciation plus the growth in net land, building and equipment. The model sets goodwill and other intangible assets at the fiscal 2011 value less amortization taken on the income statement (no acquisitions). The free cash flows are calculated from the income statement and balance sheet forecasts.

In Exhibit 13.4, we present the calculation of most of the market multiples from Exhibit 13.2 based on Staples' actual enterprise value, equity value, and the forecasts of the relevant denominators. More specifically, the multiples equal the company's enterprise value or equity value as of January 2012 divided by the fiscal 2012 (January 2013) forecast for the denominator. As reported in the top panel of Exhibit 13.4, Staples' enterprise-value-based multiples include a free cash flow multiple of 11.7 and an unlevered earnings multiple of 9.9. The difference between the two multiples is primarily a result of having capital expenditures (included in unlevered free cash flows) that are larger than the depreciation expensed on the income statement (included in unlevered earnings). Naturally, since EBIT is larger than unlevered earnings, the EBIT multiple of 6.5 is lower than the unlevered earnings multiple. And the EBITDA multiple of 5.0 is lower than both the EBIT and unlevered free cash flow multiples for the same reason. The revenue multiple is 0.4, and the multiple of total invested capital (TIC) is 1.4.

EXHIBIT 13.4	Staples, Inc. Market Multiples (Using January 2012 Valuation Divided by January 2013 Forecast)		
	Numerator	**Denominator**	**Multiple**
Total Enterprise-Value-Based Multiples			
Unlevered free cash flow multiple	$11,210,184	$ 959,606	11.7
Unlevered earnings multiple.		$ 1,126,725	9.9
EBIT multiple		$ 1,720,192	6.5
EBITDA multiple		$ 2,253,044	5.0
Revenue (sales) multiple.		$26,712,327	0.4
Total invested capital multiple		$ 8,189,333	1.4
Equity-Capitalization-Based Multiples			
Equity free cash flow multiple	$10,436,153	$ 913,756	11.4
P/E or earnings multiple.		$ 1,080,875	9.7
Market-to-book multiple.		$ 7,189,333	1.5

In the bottom panel of Exhibit 13.4, we report the company's equity-value-based multiples. Since the amount of financial leverage is less than 10% of Staples' overall capital structure, its equity-value-based multiples are similar to the analogous enterprise-value-based multiples. The equity free cash flow multiple of 11.4 and net income (or P/E) multiple of 9.7 are similar to the unlevered free cash flow (11.7) and unlevered earnings (9.9) multiples. The market-to-book multiple is equal to 1.5, which is similar to the TIC multiple (1.4).

We use the Staples financial model to ask two questions. First, how does variation in certain value drivers—risk, growth, financial leverage, cost structure, and required investments in capital expenditures and working capital—cause variation in market multiples? Second, to what extent does variation in those value drivers affect different multiples—for example, does variation in cost structure affect all multiples to the same degree or not? As we illustrate next, when using a particular multiple, a value driver is relevant for assessing comparability across firms if a difference in the value driver affects the market value (numerator) of the multiple differently than it affects the denominator of that multiple in percentage terms. The more that variation in a value driver affects the numerator and denominator of the multiple differentially (in relative terms), the more important that value driver is for assessing comparability.

In Exhibits 13.5 and 13.6, we summarize the results of the Staples simulation of the effect of differences in value drivers on the multiples reported in Exhibit 13.4. These exhibits are organized in the following way. Each table consists of multiple sets of rows, with each set of rows presenting the effect of differences in a specific value driver on the different multiples shown in the columns of the tables. The first row in a set of rows presents the original value driver and value of each multiple based on the original value driver; the second row presents the revised value driver and value of each multiple based on the revised value driver; the third row presents the percentage change in enterprise value or equity value and the percentage change in the denominators of each of the multiples; and the last row presents the percentage change in the multiple resulting from the change in the value driver.

The percentage change in the multiple is equal to 1 plus the percentage change in the numerator divided by 1 plus the percentage change in the denominator. The more sensitive the multiple is to a change in a value driver, the more important that value driver is for assessing comparability. To partly standardize the effect across value drivers, the change in the value driver shown is the change necessary to increase the enterprise value of the firm by 10%, which for some assumptions requires a fairly large and not always realistic change in the assumption.[3] We begin our discussion by examining the effects of differences in risk and growth, and then discuss the impact of other value drivers on various market multiples.

EXHIBIT 13.5 Staples, Inc. Illustration of the Effects of Changes in Value Drivers on Enterprise-Value-Based Multiples

	Financial Model Assumption	% Change in Enterprise Value	Free Cash Flow Multiple	Unlevered Earnings Multiple	EBIT Multiple	EBITDA Multiple	Revenue Multiple	Total Invested Capital Multiple
Risk (discount rate)........................	12.0%		11.7	9.9	6.5	5.0	0.4	1.4
New assumption and multiples	11.2%		12.9	10.9	7.2	5.5	0.5	1.5
% Change in underlying variable		10.0%	0.0%	0.0%	0.0%	0.0%	0.0%	0.0%
% Change in multiples			10.0%	10.0%	10.0%	10.0%	10.0%	10.0%
Debt financing ($1 billion)....................	$1 billion		11.7	9.9	6.5	5.0	0.4	1.4
New assumption and multiples	$6 billion		12.9	10.9	7.2	5.5	0.5	1.5
% Change in underlying variable		10.0%	0.0%	0.0%	0.0%	0.0%	0.0%	0.0%
% Change in multiples			10.0%	10.0%	10.0%	10.0%	10.0%	10.0%
Initial revenue growth rate	6.8%		11.7	9.9	6.5	5.0	0.4	1.4
New assumption and multiples	8.8%		13.4	10.7	7.0	5.4	0.5	1.5
% Change in underlying variable		10.0%	−4.3%	2.3%	2.3%	1.9%	1.9%	0.8%
% Change in multiples			14.9%	7.5%	7.5%	7.9%	7.9%	9.1%
Cost of goods sold %	73.1%		11.7	9.9	6.5	5.0	0.4	1.4
New assumption and multiples	72.5%		11.7	10.1	6.6	5.1	0.5	1.5
% Change in underlying variable		10.0%	9.6%	8.2%	8.2%	6.3%	0.0%	0.0%
% Change in multiples			0.4%	1.6%	1.6%	3.5%	10.0%	10.0%
Income tax rate	34.5%		11.7	9.9	6.5	5.0	0.4	1.4
New assumption and multiples	28.3%		11.6	10.0	7.2	5.5	0.5	1.5
% Change in underlying variable		10.0%	11.0%	9.4%	0.0%	0.0%	0.0%	0.0%
% Change in multiples			−0.9%	0.6%	10.0%	10.0%	10.0%	10.0%
Net PPEQ growth as % of revenue growth rate....	100.0%		11.7	9.9	6.5	5.0	0.4	1.4
New assumption and multiples	32.7%		11.6	10.9	7.1	5.5	0.5	1.5
% Change in underlying variable		10.0%	10.4%	0.4%	0.4%	0.0%	0.0%	−1.2%
% Change in multiples			−0.3%	9.5%	9.5%	10.0%	10.0%	11.3%
Days to collect receivables....................	29.7		11.7	9.9	6.5	5.0	0.4	1.4
New assumption and multiples	12.7		11.3	10.5	6.8	5.2	0.4	1.5
% Change in underlying variable		5.0%	8.2%	0.0%	0.0%	0.0%	0.0%	−1.0%
% Change in multiples			−2.9%	5.0%	5.0%	5.0%	5.0%	6.1%

Differences in Risk (Discount Rate) and Capital Structure.

The first set of rows in Exhibit 13.5 illustrates the effect of a difference in the discount rate (risk) on the enterprise-value-based multiples. A reduction in the discount rate from 12% to 11.2% increases enterprise value by 10%. This is one of the easiest effects to understand. All else equal, a difference in the discount rate results in a difference in the

[3] The one exception is the change in the assumption of the days to collect receivables, which is a change to increase the enterprise value of the firm by 5%.

value of the firm but it has no effect on any of the denominators. The resulting percentage change in each of the enterprise-value-based multiples is thus equal to the percentage change in enterprise value, 10%.

The effect on equity multiples is similar. As shown in Exhibit 13.6, given the assumption of a fixed amount of debt that initially represents only 9% of the company's total value; the increase in the value of the equity is 10.7%. Again, since a difference in the discount rate has no effect on any of the equity multiple denominators, the percentage change in the respective multiples is equal to the percentage change in the equity value (numerator), or 10.7%. In sum, differences in risk affect all multiples, and therefore risk is an important value driver that should be comparable across all comparable companies and the company being valued.

EXHIBIT 13.6	Staples, Inc. Illustration of the Effects of Changes in Value Drivers on Equity-Value-Based Multiples				

	Financial Model Assumption	% Change in Equity Value	Equity Free Cash Flow Multiple	P/E or Earnings Multiple	Market-to-Book Multiple
Risk (discount rate).........................	12.0%		11.4	9.7	1.5
New assumption and multiples	11.2%		12.6	10.7	1.6
% Change in underlying variable		10.7%	0.0%	0.0%	0.0%
% Change in multiples			10.7%	10.7%	10.7%
Initial revenue growth rate	6.8%		11.4	9.7	1.5
New assumption and multiples	8.8%		13.2	10.4	1.6
% Change in underlying variable		10.7%	−4.5%	2.4%	0.9%
% Change in multiples			16.0%	8.1%	9.7%
Cost of goods sold %	73.1%		11.4	9.7	1.5
New assumption and multiples	72.5%		11.5	9.8	1.6
% Change in underlying variable		10.7%	10.1%	8.6%	0.0%
% Change in multiples			0.6%	2.0%	10.7%
Income tax rate	34.5%		11.4	9.7	1.5
New assumption and multiples	28.3%		11.4	9.8	1.6
% Change in underlying variable		10.7%	11.1%	9.4%	0.0%
% Change in multiples			−0.3%	1.2%	10.7%
Net PPEQ growth as % of revenue growth rate...	100.0%		11.4	9.7	1.5
New assumption and multiples	32.7%		11.4	10.6	1.6
% Change in underlying variable		10.7%	10.9%	0.4%	−1.3%
% Change in multiples			−0.1%	10.3%	12.2%
Days to collect receivables..................	29.7		11.4	9.7	1.5
New assumption and multiples	12.7		11.1	10.2	1.5
% Change in underlying variable		5.4%	8.6%	0.0%	−1.1%
% Change in multiples			−2.9%	5.4%	6.6%

We show a similar effect caused by differences in capital structure. One way that changing capital structure can affect the value of the firm is through a change in the value of the interest tax shields. Exhibit 13.5 shows the effect of a change in the capital structure by increasing the debt from $1 billion to $6 billion. An increase in debt of this magnitude increases enterprise value by 10% but, like changing the discount rate, it has no effect on any of the denominators of the enterprise-value-based multiples. Thus, the effect of a change in capital structure on the multiples is equivalent to the effect observed for the discount rate.[4] The resulting percentage change in each of the enterprise-value-based multiples is equal to the percentage change in enterprise value, 10%. Naturally, financial leverage has potentially more complicated relations with enterprise value (for example, financial distress costs) that we are ignoring here;

---

[4] We note that increasing the leverage is equivalent to reducing the discount rate assuming interest is tax deductible, as we know that the weighted average cost of capital declines with increases in leverage (assuming financial distress costs or other potential countervailing forces are not significant).

but even with this simplistic assumption, we are able to show that capital structure can be an important value driver to consider for assessing comparability.[5]

In summary, the Staples simulation illustrates that differences in risk (discount rate) and capital structure can have an important role in assessing the comparability for all multiples.

Differences in a Company's Growth Rate.

The next set of rows in Exhibits 13.5 and 13.6 illustrates the effect of differences in revenue growth rates for assessing comparability. We present the effect of changing the initial revenue growth rate from 6.8% to 8.8%. Changing the initial revenue growth rate increases many of the subsequent growth rates as the growth rate decays 10% annually from the initial revenue growth rate until it settles to the assumed long-term inflation rate of 3%. Unlike changes in the discount rate, changes in the revenue growth rate affect both the market multiple numerators and denominators. The effect of this change on the revenue and EBITDA denominators is the same, 1.9%, and thus the change in the respective multiples is 7.9% (0.079 = 1.1/1.019 − 1). EBIT and unlevered earnings both change by 2.3%. This larger percentage change (2.3% versus 1.9%) has the effect of reducing the percentage change of the respective market multiples, which increase by 7.5%.

Unlike the case of earnings-based multiples, the increase in the revenue growth rate actually has the effect of decreasing both unlevered and equity free cash flows in fiscal 2012 because of the additional investments required for the additional growth. While the starting point for the free cash flow calculation—that is, after-tax EBIT—increases, the increase in revenue from the higher growth rate results in even larger percentage increases in investments in working capital and net land, buildings, and equipment, which has the net effect of decreasing free cash flows in fiscal 2012. The overall effect on unlevered and equity free cash flows is a decrease of −4.3% and −4.5%, respectively, and this negative effect on the denominators results in an even larger effect on the respective multiples. The effects on the unlevered and equity free cash flow multiples are 14.9% and 16%, respectively. The denominators of the balance-sheet-based multiples (TIC and market-to-book), change less than any of the free cash flow and earning-based multiples, and thus the percentage change in these multiples is close to the percentage change in value (the numerator), 9.1% and 9.7%, respectively.

This simulation illustrates the importance of growth rates for assessing comparability. Moreover, depending on the characteristics of the firm, differences in revenue growth rates can affect free cash flow multiples more than other multiples because of their potential impact on capital expenditures and working capital investment, which do not affect (or have a very small effect on) earnings-based or balance-sheet-based multiples.

Differences in a Company's Cost Structure.

The next two sets of rows in Exhibits 13.5 and 13.6 illustrate the effects of differences in cost structures. We illustrate the effect of such differences by changing the cost of goods sold expense ratio and the income tax rate. The cost of goods sold expense ratio is assumed to fall from 73.1% to 72.5% for all future years. The tables also present the effect of changing the income tax rate from 34.5% to 28.3% for all future years. Since revenue and TIC are unaffected by these changes, the revenue and TIC multiples (Exhibit 13.5) change by the percentage change in enterprise value of 10%. Similarly, since the model assumes the company holds no excess cash and pays out all equity free cash flow as dividends, the market-to-book multiple (Exhibit 13.6) changes by exactly the percentage change in equity value of 10.7%.

The change in the cost of goods sold expense ratio increases EBITDA by 6.3%, and it increases EBIT and unlevered earnings by 8.2%. These changes in the denominators partially offset the effect of the increase in value of the numerators (Exhibit 13.5). The result is that the EBITDA multiple increases by 3.5%, and the EBIT and unlevered earnings multiples increase by 1.6%. Unlevered free cash flow increases more than the earnings-based denominators, 9.6%, because inventory and accounts payable also change as a result of the change in the cost structure. The result is that the unlevered free cash flow multiple is essentially unchanged (increase of 0.4%). We observe analogous affects for the equity free cash flow and P/E multiples (Exhibit 13.6).

The change in income tax rates has more of an effect on the EBIT, EBITDA, revenue, TIC, and market-to-book multiples than other multiples because the denominators of these multiples are unchanged by a change in the income tax rate. The change in the respective multiples is equal to the change in the

[5] We do not show the effect of a change in capital structure on the equity-value-based multiples because such an increase in the amount of debt results in a recapitalization of the equity, which is not as helpful for providing useful insights on the change in the equity-value-based market multiples.

enterprise value of the firm, 10%. Since unlevered earnings includes a deduction for income taxes, it increases by 9.4% as a result of the decrease in the income tax rate, which reduces the effect on the unlevered earnings multiple to 0.6%. Similarly, unlevered free cash flow also includes a deduction for income taxes but investments in working capital and net, land, buildings, and equipment are not tax deductible and are unaffected by the change in the income tax rate. As a result, the effect on unlevered free cash flow is 11%, and the unlevered free cash flow multiple decreases by −0.9%. We observe similar effects for the equity free cash flow and P/E multiples (Exhibit 13.6).

The simulation illustrates how differences in operating cost structure (such as cost of goods sold and selling, general, and administrative expenses) are most important for assessing comparability when using balance sheet and revenue multiples and, to a lesser extent, the EBITDA multiple. They are much less important for assessing comparability when using the unlevered and equity free cash flows, unlevered earnings, and P/E multiples. The simulation also illustrates that differences in income tax cost structure (e.g., income tax rates, net operating loss carryforwards, etc.) are important to take into account for assessing comparability when using balance sheet, revenue, EBITDA, and EBIT multiples, but are much less relevant for unlevered free cash flow, equity free cash flow, unlevered earnings, and P/E multiples.

Differences in Capital Expenditure Requirements and Investments in Working Capital.
The last two sets of rows in Exhibits 13.5 and 13.6 illustrate the effects of differences in required capital expenditures and working capital investments. Capital expenditures only affect income-statement-based denominators if the capital expenditures are depreciated or amortized over the asset's useful life and if the particular denominator includes the depreciation and amortization deduction. And even if the capital expenditure is depreciated, it will be depreciated over the life of the asset and not all in one year. Thus, the effect on income is smaller than the effect on free cash flows at least for the initial change in capital expenditure requirements.[6] Investments in working capital (in this case, days to collect receivables) have no effect on any component of earnings. As a result, differences in capital expenditure requirements and investments in working capital will affect the value of the firm, but have little or no effect on the components of earnings. The percentage change in earnings-based multiples will be equal to or close to the change in the market value of the numerator.

The base assumption for capital expenditures is that net land, buildings, and equipment grow at 100% of the revenue growth rate, and that capital expenditures equal depreciation expense plus the revenue growth rate multiplied by the balance in net land, buildings, and equipment. In this illustration, the new growth rate for net land, buildings, and equipment is assumed to be about one-third of the revenue growth rate for all future years. This change reduces capital expenditure requirements and increases the enterprise value of the firm by 10%. The financial model assumes the company expenses one year of depreciation in the year the company makes the capital expenditure. Revenue and EBITDA are unaffected by capital expenditures, and thus the percentage change in the respective multiples is equal to the percentage change in enterprise value.

Unlevered earnings and EBIT denominators are only slightly affected by one year of depreciation and increase by 0.4%. This increase in the denominators slightly offsets the increase in the numerators and the multiples increase by 9.5%. Free cash flows, by contrast, are dollar-for-dollar affected by capital expenditures. The free cash flows increase by 10.4%, and the net effect on the free cash flow multiple is only −0.3%. The balance-sheet-based multiples increase by more than the percentage increase in value because the effect of decreasing capital expenditures is to shrink the balance sheet. This decrease in the size of the balance sheet exacerbates the effect on the balance-sheet-based multiples. The TIC multiple increases by 11.3%, and the market-to-book multiple increases by 12.2%. The effects of working capital requirements are similar to the effect of capital expenditures. Decreasing the days to collect receivables from 29.7 to 12.7 increases the enterprise value of the firm by 5% but has no effect on the income statement; and as a result, all of the earnings-based and revenue multiples increase by the same percentage as the enterprise value of the firm—again, 5%. And once again, free cash flows increase as a result of the change in working capital requirements, which reduces the change in the free cash flow multiple to −2.9%.

The simulation illustrates how taking account of differences in investment requirements (both capital expenditures and working capital) can be important for assessing comparability when using

---

[6] A sustained difference in depreciable capital expenditure requirements—for example, two companies that are in steady state—would impact earnings more significantly than we are modeling in the Staples example, where the impact on depreciation is from a single year of additional capital expenditures.

earnings-based, balance-sheet-based, and revenue multiples. They are much less relevant for the free cash flow multiples.

Conclusions. It is well known that risk and growth are important for assessing the comparability of companies used in a market multiple valuation. Using the Staples simulation, we show that many multiples are affected by value drivers such as cost structure and working capital and capital expenditure requirements. Further, we have shown that not all multiples are equally affected by variations in particular value drivers. For example, when using a multiple in which expenditures (expenses or investments) are not deducted in the calculation of the denominator, that expenditure is more important for assessing comparability than when using a multiple in which it is deducted in the calculation of the denominator.

As a general rule, the unlevered free cash flow, equity free cash flow, unlevered earnings, and P/E multiples are less affected by changes in a company's cost structure than are other multiples. For example, income taxes are more important for assessing comparability when using multiples based on measures such as EBIT, EBITDA, revenue, and balance-sheet-based measures such as book value and total invested capital. Similarly, depreciation and amortization cost structure is more important for assessing comparability for EBITDA and revenue- and balance-sheet-based multiples than it is for other multiples. Since differences in capital expenditure and working capital requirements can have significant effects on the value of the firm and do not affect the denominator of certain multiples, taking account of such differences in these value drivers is relevant for improving comparability when using certain earnings-based or revenue multiples.

Interestingly, while the multiple of enterprise value to EBITDA is perhaps the most popular multiple in practice, it is not necessarily as invariant to differences in value drivers as some other multiples, such as enterprise value to unlevered earnings. One potential explanation of its popularity may be that because EBITDA is higher up in the income statement (closer to revenue), it is negative less often than either EBIT or unlevered earnings. However, in a valuation in which the unlevered earnings for the company being valued and the relevant comparable companies are positive and represent future growth and performance prospects as well as or better than EBITDA, the multiple of enterprise value to unlevered earnings may be a viable multiple to consider in a market multiple valuation.

Valuation Key 13.3

A company's growth, risk, cost structure, working capital management, capital expenditure requirements, and capital structure are all potentially relevant value drivers to consider when identifying comparable companies.

Does Firm Size Matter?

Controlling for the size of the comparable companies is popular in practice when selecting comparable companies. However, there is no theoretical model that we are aware of that includes size as a determinant of market multiples. The empirical research is mixed on whether or not controlling for size is helpful for choosing comparable companies after controlling for industry and other factors.[7] On the other hand, there is some evidence that firm size is correlated with some value-relevant aspects of a company, and we know from research in finance that size appears to be correlated with returns even after controlling for expected returns measured using the Capital Asset Pricing Model. Thus, the use of the CAPM alone may not be sufficient to control for risk (or the discount rate) completely.[8]

---

[7] See for example, Alford, A., "The Effect of the Set of Comparable Companies on the Accuracy of the Price Earnings Valuation Method," *Journal of Accounting Research* 30 (1992), pp. 94–108; and Beatty, R., S. Riffe, and R. Thompson, "The Method of Comparables and Tax Court Valuations of Private Firms: An Empirical Investigation," *Accounting Horizons* (September, 1999), pp. 177–199.

[8] See, for example, Banz, R., "The Relationship Between Return and Market Values of Common Stock," *Journal of Financial Economics* 9 (March, 1981), pp. 3–18; Fama, E., and K. French, "The Cross-Section of Expected Stock Returns," *Journal of Finance* 47 (1992), pp. 427–463; and Keim, D., "Size-Related Anomalies and Stock Return Seasonality: Further Evidence," *Journal of Financial Economics* 9 (June 1983), pp. 13–32.

REVIEW EXERCISE 13.4

Change in Market Multiples from a Change in Value Drivers

Use the information in Review Exercise 13.1 to examine the change in market multiples resulting from a change in the value drivers described below. For each of the changes in the value drivers, measure the changes in the multiples of firm value to free cash flow, unlevered earnings, EBIT, EBITDA, and revenue. Measure the market multiple using the end of Year 0 firm value and Year 0 denominator.

- The initial valuation of the company used a 2% perpetual growth rate. If the perpetual growth rate increases to 4%, the company's value increases by 4.7%.
- The initial valuation of the company used a 12% unlevered cost of capital. If the unlevered cost of capital decreases to 10%, the company's value increases by 29.6%.
- The company has a 70% operating expense ratio (% of revenue) in Year 0 and the forecasts. If the operating expense ratio decreases to 60% in Year 0 and the forecasts, the company's value increases by 37%. Assume this change has no effect on working capital.

Solution on page 541.

Assumptions Underlying Non-Accounting-Based Market Multiples

As we discussed earlier, analysts sometimes use non-accounting-based market multiples. Using non-accounting-based market multiples might not seem useful, but consider the following example. A friend tells you that she is going to buy a wireless telephone company and the price she is going to pay is $200 multiplied by the number of people living in the geographic region served by the company. You are shocked that she is going to buy a company based on a valuation model that ignores cash flows and risk, and you quickly challenge the reasonableness of her decision. Your friend tells you that she agreed to pay this price because $200 is well below the average multiple of market capitalization to population (sometimes called the **price-per-pop**) of all wireless telephone companies operating in regions with demographics that are similar to the company she is buying.

You begin to analyze her statement. You know that the market values of comparable companies reflect the market's expectations about future cash flows and risk, so at least using firm value provides a link to value. However, dividing firm value by population to calculate firm value per person in the relevant population seems to ignore the important drivers of value. Your friend then tells you that she knows that all wireless telephone companies make similar capital investments and have similar cost structures that are a function of the number of customers served. She also tells you that both the average revenue per customer and the percentage of the people in the population who are wireless customers are similar for all comparable companies.

You quickly realize that all companies of this type have essentially the same relations between the population and all of the factors related to cash flows—the percentage of the people who are customers, the average revenue per customer, the average cost per customer, and capital investments. As such, knowing the population is key to forecasting future cash flows. You conclude that your friend's analysis did not ignore cash flows and risk and that her valuation analysis might not be as crazy as you had first thought. You now conclude that this method might provide an accurate assessment of value, depending on the similarity of the comparable companies. Thus, properly done, market multiple valuations based on non-accounting-based denominators can implicitly incorporate fundamental valuation principles.

As it turns out, companies in the wireless communications industry often must purchase licenses from the government in order to have the right to service a population in a specific area. The government typically limits the number of licenses for each area. Since the population in an area for which a company has a license is a good measure of the company's potential customers in that area, the population in a service area (POP) is often used as a value driver. Naturally, this is not the only value driver investors examine. The number of subscribers, the penetration rate (number of subscribers divided by population), and the churn rate (average length of time a customer stays with the company) are all important non-accounting value drivers for companies in this industry. In fact, non-accounting value drivers appear to be better at explaining the value of companies in this industry than accounting value drivers.[9] However, the important

---

[9] See Amir, E., and B. Lev, "Value-Relevance of Nonfinancial Information: The Wireless Communications Industry," *Journal of Accounting and Economics* 2 (1996), pp. 3–30, for a discussion and empirical examination of the value drivers for this industry. Financial analysts sometimes use the ratio of market value to population to analyze wireless telecommunications companies. Another ratio they use is market value to number of subscribers.

value drivers of variation in non-accounting-based market multiples include all of the same drivers for accounting-based multiples, which we discussed earlier; in addition, they also share the assumption that the relation between the non-accounting-based value driver and free cash flow is the same.

Valuation in Practice 13.2

Non-Financial Drivers in the Telecommunications Industry The telecommunications industry often discusses values and deal prices in terms of price per subscriber or price divided by the size of the potential population that could be served, or "price-per-pop."

Deutsche Telekom's $50.7 billion bid for U.S. wireless service provider VoiceStream put a steep price tag on subscribers: about $22,000 per customer. The lofty price-per-subscriber figure underscores two trends: companies are intensely interested in wireless technologies for their ability to deliver voice and Internet services to customers nearly anywhere, and international carriers want to crack the lucrative U.S. communications market.

The high purchase price for VoiceStream raises questions about how Deutsche Telekom—and others that follow suit—will recoup the acquisition costs. . . .

Many analysts . . . believe a better metric is the price per "POP," or the total number of people within a wireless carrier's coverage area—all of which are potential customers, theoretically.

With a coverage area and licenses capable of serving more than 220 million people, VoiceStream went for about $265 per potential customer. Comparatively, the Vodafone-AirTouch deal was valued around $339 per potential customer, and the France Telecom-Orange deal went for about $675 per "POP"—both higher than the DT-VoiceStream deal.

Still, on a per-subscriber basis, Deutsche Telekom's bid represents more than $22,000 for each of VoiceStream's 2.29 million customers. In comparison, Vodafone paid approximately $7,000 per subscriber when it acquired AirTouch Communications.

Source: "Deutche Telekom Values VoiceStream at $22,000 per Customer," by Corey Grice, CNET News, July 26, 2000, available at http://news.cnet.com/Deutsche-Telekom-values-VoiceStream-at-22,000-per-customer/2100-1033_3-243637.html, accessed September 8, 2012.

13.5 IDENTIFYING COMPARABLE COMPANIES

Identifying comparable companies is an important step in many different facets of any valuation analysis. However, identifying comparable companies is usually the most important as well as the most difficult part of a market-multiple-based valuation. While selecting comparable companies might not appear to be too difficult, we often quickly conclude that not many, if any, companies are truly comparable to the company we are valuing for purposes of a market multiple valuation once we understand all the different dimensions of comparability and begin to analyze the potential comparable companies.

LO3 Choose comparable companies to use in a market multiple valuation

Understand the Businesses in Which the Company Operates

The first step in identifying potential comparable companies is to understand the businesses in which the company we are valuing operates. Analyzing a company's financial statements and filings with the government (such as its 10-K and proxy statements filed with the U.S. Securities and Exchange Commission) is often the best starting point to collect this information. The company always discusses its lines of business in these documents.

After understanding what the company does, we need to then identify its competitors. Fortunately, we have a variety of sources with which to identify a company's competitors. The company often identifies its primary competitors in its financial statements and other public filings. In addition, analyzing the industries (business segments) in which the company operates is another way we can identify the company's competitors. Keep in mind that because many companies operate in more than one industry, it is important to identify all of the industries in which the company has significant operations.

Industry association publications and financial analyst reports also often provide information about key competitors, even for private companies. Certain financial websites also contain information on competitors of companies. We can also examine companies that have the same industry code. While industry codes provide some indication of industry, there are many situations where firms with the same industry code are not direct competitors, and there are also situations where firms with different industry codes are direct competitors. In addition, the primary industry code may only indicate a portion of a company's business. It is not unusual for a company to sell products and services that fall under several different industry codes.

One popular classification system used to identify a company's industry is the Standard Industrial Classification (SIC) system maintained by the U.S. Department of Labor. The SIC system was developed in the 1930s, and it has been revised multiple times based on the economy's changing industrial composition. Current definitions come from the 1987 Standard Industrial Classification (SIC) Manual.[10] We can analyze SIC codes at the one-, two-, three-, or four-digit level. The one- and two-digit levels, however, are not very useful for many applications, including market multiples. It is usually best to start at the three- or four-digit level if you are relying on SIC codes. However, if you only had a handful of observations at the three-digit and four-digit levels, you could choose to analyze companies at the two-digit level. However, because there is a lot of "noise" in these industry classifications, it is often necessary to go beyond the use of SIC codes to identify direct competitors.

Recall that in order to use any of the market multiples, we need to at least control for the underlying risk and growth of the company's businesses. In addition, as the Staples example made clear, we need to control for a variety of additional value drivers, especially for the financial-statement-based multiples. Market multiples vary across industries (even at the four-digit level) because of differences in these value drivers across industries using the Compustat® Based Market Multiple dataset discussed previously. In Exhibit 13.7, we show the median market multiples for 10 industries at the four-digit level of aggregation. This exhibit shows how market multiples can vary across industries, suggesting that matching companies based on industry is important in identifying comparable companies. For example, the industry SIC = 1040: Gold and Silver Ores had consistently higher multiples than, say, SIC = 7389: Services—Business Services. The market multiples not only vary by industry but also by type. For example, SIC = 4412: Deep Sea Foreign Transportation of Freight has the fourth highest median EBIT multiple but only the eighth highest median P/E multiple.

EXHIBIT 13.7	Median Market Multiples for Selected Industries*									
Denominator	**1040**	**1311**	**2911**	**2836**	**4412**	**4813**	**6020**	**6311**	**6798**	**7389**
Market Multiples Used to Measure the Value of the Firm (Numerator Is Market Value of the Firm)										
1 Unlevered free cash flow	45.4	19.5	17.4	11.0	17.2	9.0	10.6	5.1	15.5	10.9
2 Earnings after taxes plus after-tax interest ("unlevered earnings")	25.8	26.7	13.6	15.2	18.1	14.7	25.7	10.3	27.9	15.2
3 Earnings before interest and taxes ("EBIT")	23.5	24.7	9.6	10.4	17.6	12.1	10.2	7.6	29.8	12.0
4 Earnings before interest, taxes, depreciation, and amortization ("EBITDA")	15.7	10.0	5.9	8.9	8.8	5.4	9.6	7.2	26.1	7.9
5 Revenue or sales	5.7	5.3	0.8	8.5	4.1	2.0	2.9	0.8	9.3	2.0
6 Total assets	1.9	1.3	0.8	2.6	0.7	1.0	0.2	0.2	1.0	1.2
Market Multiples to Measure the Value of the Equity (Numerator Is Market Value of the Equity)										
1 Equity free cash flow	41.4	19.1	15.7	13.9	20.7	9.6	5.6	4.4	8.9	12.3
2 Earnings available to common shareholders ("P/E")	26.9	25.3	11.7	16.1	12.8	13.6	14.7	10.9	29.3	18.3
3 Revenue or sales	5.7	4.6	0.6	9.2	1.7	1.0	1.6	0.7	4.9	2.1
4 Book value of equity	2.8	2.1	1.5	4.0	0.8	1.8	1.0	0.8	1.4	2.4

* The specific industries are:
1040   Gold and Silver Ores
1311   Crude Petroleum & Natural Gas
2911   Petroleum Refining
2836   Biological Products (No Diagnostic Substances)
4412   Deep Sea Foreign Transportation of Freight
4813   Telephone Communications (No Radiotelephone)
6020   Commercial Banks
6311   Life Insurance
6798   Real Estate Investment Trusts
7389   Services-Business Services

---

[10] You can find SIC industry definitions and a searchable manual at the U.S. Department of Labor's website at http://www.osha.gov/oshstats/sicser.html.

Identifying Competitors and Companies in the Same Industry Is Only the Starting Point

While determining a company's direct competitors is a good starting point for our analysis, it is usually insufficient for choosing the final set of comparables for a market multiple valuation. Choosing close competitors usually controls for business risk, for close competitors usually, but not always, have similar business risks. However, simply selecting close competitors is not sufficient to ensure the companies are comparable, as we observe a substantial amount of variation in multiples within an industry. This variation exists because of many of the factors we have been discussing. In Exhibit 13.8, we show the distributions of the firm value to EBITDA and P/E multiples across the 10 industries in Exhibit 13.7. The distributions in this exhibit show a substantial amount of variation within industries.

EXHIBIT 13.8	Distributions for Selected Market Multiples and Industries									
Denominator		**1040**	**1311**	**2911**	**2836**	**4412**	**4813**	**6020**	**6311**	**6798**	**7389**
Earnings Before Interest, Taxes, Depreciation, and Amortization (EBITDA) Multiple										
Average		17.0	13.8	6.8	14.5	11.3	5.9	12.1	8.4	27.8	11.5
Standard deviation		11.2	10.4	3.0	13.1	8.7	2.3	9.2	7.6	11.6	8.5
10th percentile		4.7	5.1	3.4	4.3	3.4	3.0	4.3	2.7	11.6	5.3
25th percentile		9.1	7.1	4.7	6.9	5.7	4.2	6.6	4.3	19.8	6.4
50th percentile		15.7	10.0	5.9	8.9	8.8	5.4	9.6	7.2	26.1	7.9
75th percentile		22.7	16.4	9.0	14.9	14.0	7.5	13.7	8.6	39.7	11.0
90th percentile		32.8	28.6	10.4	43.0	18.6	9.6	22.8	13.4	43.0	26.8
Earnings Available to Common Shareholders (P/E) Multiple										
Average		37.9	34.7	18.5	22.4	17.8	23.9	21.0	12.7	37.7	25.2
Standard deviation		28.3	25.8	16.5	21.9	16.4	25.0	17.9	7.5	27.5	19.2
10th percentile		6.0	9.9	6.6	6.8	4.7	6.0	8.8	6.8	6.3	9.4
25th percentile		14.9	15.5	9.6	10.2	8.2	9.5	11.5	8.5	16.8	14.6
50th percentile		26.9	25.3	11.7	16.1	12.8	13.6	14.7	10.9	29.3	18.3
75th percentile		69.5	49.8	20.9	21.0	22.6	24.8	20.7	14.9	62.1	26.8
90th percentile		82.2	82.2	43.2	73.9	33.4	80.0	41.6	17.2	82.2	53.5

Thus, a company's product lines, customer types, market segments, types of operation, and so forth are all important aspects to consider when we identify comparable companies. Even after these are taken into consideration, two companies can be in the same industry yet not be comparable on all of the characteristics that are important for a market multiple valuation. Choosing comparable companies is tantamount to trying to figure out where in the distribution of market multiples for an industry the company being valued is located. For example, if we are interested in valuing a company in the petroleum refining business (SIC 2911) based on its EBITDA multiple, we must decide where in the distribution the company lies. The 10th to 90th percentiles for this industry range from 3.4 to 10.4. Based on a company's characteristics, we need to determine whether it is more comparable to the median firm in the industry, or whether it is more likely to be closer to the 10th or 90th percentile of the distribution, or somewhere else.

The conceptual framework discussed in this chapter provides a guide for what value drivers we should examine when we identify comparable companies, even if they are competitors that operate in the same industry. Remember that the goal is to identify (comparable) companies that sell for the same multiple of earnings (or whatever multiple we decide to use) as the company being valued. Thus, we need to control for all of the relevant value drivers that we identified in our conceptual framework that affect a particular multiple by appropriately selecting comparable companies.

What does "control for all of the relevant value drivers that we identified in our conceptual framework" mean? Once we identify competitors, we analyze both the company being valued and the competitors with respect to characteristics that determine the variation in market multiples—such as future growth prospects, risk, future profitability, and future expected investment requirements. One trade-off will become apparent when we attempt this analysis. A valuation expert must achieve a balance between having a sufficient number of comparables for measuring the market multiples and the closeness of these comparables to the company being valued as far as the relevant value drivers affecting the multiples. Initially, it is useful to define "competitors" in broad terms in order to be in a position to make trade-offs between the closeness of the comparables' characteristics that drive variation in the market multiples to those same characteristics of the company being valued.

Since the choice of comparables necessitates analyzing such issues as growth and profitability, analysts' reports and historical financial statements of individual companies, in addition to analysts' reports on the industry, are extremely valuable. Financial statements allow one to determine the recent history of growth and profitability. In addition, analyzing the financial statements helps us understand the comparability of the financial statements across firms as well as the extent to which unusual or non-recurring items have affected the reported performance of the company (more on this latter topic in the next section).

Analysts' reports provide some insight into market expectations for near- and long-term growth prospects as well as into forecasts of future profitability as assessed by the analyst community. A valuation specialist obviously needs to have his or her own view of the company, the industry, and the potential comparable companies, but reading the reports of others can provide at least one set of expectations. That said, one does not want to rely entirely on the analyst community. Empirical evidence indicates that on average, analysts have an optimistic bias. In addition, for companies that are performing very well (very poorly), they also tend to believe that superior (inferior) performance will last longer than it actually will. In addition, empirical studies show that controlling for the historic growth rate is not very useful relative to controlling for expectations of future growth;[11] moreover, controlling for the known biases of analysts is useful.

Valuation Key 13.4

Identifying comparable companies is an important part of any market multiple analysis. We begin by identifying a company's competitors and other companies in the same industry. We then analyze future risk, growth, profitability, investment requirements, and other value drivers from our conceptual framework for the potential comparable companies in order to determine which firms have the best comparability with the firm being valued. It should be obvious that a market multiple valuation means that we need to have a view on the future growth and profitability of the comparable companies—not just the company being valued.

13.6 TRANSITORY SHOCKS AND MARKET MULTIPLES

LO4 Adjust for transitory changes when measuring market multiples

A company can experience temporary changes in its earnings and free cash flows. We call these changes transitory shocks. We know that the expected growth rate is important in selecting comparable companies. In this section, we explore the issue of transitory shocks and its effect on earnings and free cash flow growth rates, and hence its effect on market multiples.

Consider what happens to a potential comparable company that has a negative transitory shock to its earnings or free cash flow in the year in which we measure its market multiples. If the market believes that the transitory shock will only affect the firm for a single year, the value of the company is unlikely to decline substantially if at all, for the market expects the company to quickly recover. In this situation, the company's market multiples will rise temporarily, for earnings and free cash flow decrease temporarily, whereas value does not. In the following year, the transitory shock should disappear, and the company's earnings and free cash flows will grow because of the elimination of the transitory shock. Naturally, the opposite will occur for a firm that has a positive transitory shock to its earnings or free cash flow. This firm's market multiples will be low in the year that the positive transitory shock occurs, for its market value will not increase in proportion to the transitory shock. In the following year, when the positive transitory shock dissipates, earnings and free cash flow growth will be either low or perhaps even negative.

---

[11] Alford (1990) shows that controlling for historic growth rates is not important after controlling for industry. However, Zarowin (1990) shows that controlling for expected growth is important, for it dominates over other factors. See Alford, A., "The Effect of the Set of Comparable Companies on the Accuracy of the Price-Earnings Valuation Method," *Journal of Accounting Research* 30 (1992), pp. 94–108; and Zarowin, P., "What Determines Earnings-Price Ratios: Revisited," *Journal of Accounting, Auditing, and Finance* 5 (1990), pp. 439–457.

In Exhibit 13.9, we present actual free cash flows for Year −1 and Year 0 and free cash flow forecasts for Year 1 through Year 4 for two companies—the Bill Risen Company (Risen) and Habibi Corporation (Habibi). Risen and Habibi have the same cost of capital and are 100% equity financed, and we have sufficient information to value both of these companies using a DCF valuation method. Risen is one-half of the size of Habibi (see the relative Year 0 values). Assume that we plan to use Habibi as a comparable company for Risen. Given that the companies have the same risk (same unlevered cost of capital), we begin by assessing the growth rates of the two companies. Since we measured the value of both of these companies (which is not the typical valuation context), we can measure the present value weighted average growth rate subsequent to Year 1 ($r_{UA} - FCF_1/V_{F,0}$ from Equation 6.3) for the companies, which equals 2.3% for both. Based on this analysis, Habibi should be a good comparable company for Risen. If we use the Year 1 free cash flow to measure the free cash flow multiple for each company, we see that indeed the free cash flow multiples based on the Year 1 free cash flows are the same for both companies, 10.4. Thus, Habibi would be a perfect comparable company for Risen. Note that because both companies are 100% equity-financed, the firm value and equity value free cash flow multiples are the same for a given company.

EXHIBIT 13.9   The Effect of Transitory Shocks on Market Multiples

Bill Risen Company ($ in millions)	Year −1	Year 0	Year 1	Year 2	Year 3	Year 4 and Onward
Free cash flow	$40.0	$ 44.0	$ 47.5	$ 49.9	$51.4	$ 52.4
Growth rate		10.0%	8.0%	5.0%	3.0%	2.0%
Cost of capital		12.0%				
Value as of end of Year 0		$491.9				
Present value weighted average growth rate—Year 1		2.3%	inputs	12%	$47.5	$491.9
Present value weighted average growth rate—Year 0		2.8%	inputs	12%	$44.0	$491.9
Free cash flow multiple:						
Based on Year 1		10.4	inputs	$491.9	$47.5	
Based on Year 0		11.2	inputs	$491.9	$44.0	

Habibi Corporation ($ in millions)	Year −1	Year 0	Year 1	Year 2	Year 3	Year 4 and Onward
Free cash flow	$80.0	$ 20.0	$ 95.0	$ 99.8	$102.8	$104.8
Growth rate		−75.0%	375.2%	5.0%	3.0%	2.0%
Cost of capital		12.0%				
Value as of end of Year 0		$983.8				
Present value weighted average growth rate—Year 1		2.3%	inputs	12%	$ 95.0	$983.8
Present value weighted average growth rate—Year 0		9.8%	inputs	12%	$ 20.0	$983.8
Free cash flow multiple:						
Based on Year 1		10.4	inputs	$983.8	$ 95.0	
Based on Year 0		49.2	inputs	$983.8	$ 20.0	

However, if we were to use the Year 0 free cash flow to measure the firm value to free cash flow multiple, we see that the multiples are not the same—11.2 for Risen and 49.2 for Habibi. They are different because of the negative transitory shock in Habibi's free cash flow in Year 0. We can examine the cause of this difference in the multiples by comparing the present value weighted average growth rates of the two companies, using the Year 0 free cash flow as the base year. We measure the present value weighted average growth rate, using Year 0 as the base year, as follows (from Equation 6.4):

$$g_A = \frac{1 + r}{1 + \dfrac{FCF_0}{V_{F,0}}} - 1$$

Risen's present value weighted average growth rate, using Year 0 as the base year, is 2.8%, and the growth rate for Habibi is 9.8%. The difference in the present value weighted average growth rates results in a large difference between the market multiples of the two companies (49.2 vs. 11.2). When we use Year 0 as the base year, it is no longer sufficient for us to have comparable growth rates beginning in Year 1. This difference in the market multiples illustrates the potential effect of using a denominator that contains a transitory component. In this case, it should be clear that Habibi is not a good comparable for Risen when measuring the multiple based on the Year 0 free cash flow. In Chapter 14, we discuss techniques for looking for non-recurring items when making adjustments to the financial statements of the companies.

Valuation Key 13.5
When selecting comparable companies, we must ensure that the companies have the same short-run and long-run growth rates. Even if two companies have the same long-run growth rate, the market multiples of the companies can be substantially different if the short-run growth rates are different. We often observe this effect when one of the companies has a nonrecurring (one-time) or transitory shock to its current performance.

13.7 CONTINUING VALUE MULTIPLES

LO5 Measure continuing values using market multiples

In this section of the chapter, we discuss the measurement of a company's continuing value using market multiples. Using market multiples to measure a company's continuing or terminal value is not always the same as valuing a company (or its equity) as of the valuation date. Since the continuing value date is some number of years after the valuation date, the main question or challenge here is to forecast how the market multiples will have evolved by the continuing value date. Thus, to use market multiples to measure continuing value, the *future* growth and performance prospects (including capital expenditure and working capital requirements) at the continuing value date of the company being valued must be the same as the *current* growth and performance prospects of the comparable companies that will be used to measure the relevant continuing value market multiples from current data. As such, the best comparable companies for a market multiple valuation of a company on the valuation date can differ from the best comparable companies to assess the multiple at the company's continuing value date. For example, if the expected growth rate or the expected profitability is lower at the continuing value date than it is at the valuation date, the comparable companies for the current valuation and the continuing value calculation would be different.

We illustrate this effect by demonstrating the change in market multiples of a company with high initial revenue growth of 25% in Year 1, which declines to 20% and 8% in the next two years, and then to 2% thereafter. In Exhibit 13.10, we present summary financial statement and free cash flow forecasts for such a company along with a valuation of that company. The firm value to EBIT multiple declines from 10.9 to 8.0 during the forecast period, a decline of over 25%, as a result of the decreasing growth rate. The multiples of firm value to unlevered earnings and EBITDA decline by over 25% as well, while the firm value to free cash flow multiple declines even more, from 58.8 to 10.5. The decrease in the multiples directly corresponds to the decline in the present value weighted average growth rate that occurs during the forecast period. While this example illustrates the effect that decreasing growth rates can have on how we select comparable companies to estimate the continuing value, assessing comparability when using market multiples to measure the continuing value requires using comparable companies that currently have similar value drivers to the expected value drivers of the company of interest (on all relevant dimensions) at the continuing value date. These expected future value drivers could be quite different than the company's current value drivers, for example, if the company is currently growing rapidly and is very profitable due to some competitive advantage that will not be sustainable at the continuing value date.

Even though we illustrated this concept using a declining revenue growth rate, the same type of effect occurs as a result of declining profitability or any other change in a value driver that affects a market multiple used to assess value that occurs between the valuation date and the continuing value date. A related issue can arise for companies in cyclical industries in which market multiples vary over time depending on where the industry is in its cycle. Based on historical measures of the denominator, multiples tend to be the highest when the industry is coming out of the trough of the cycle, and the lowest soon after it passes the peak of the cycle. For example, if we use current information to value a company when the

EXHIBIT 13.10   Year-by-Year Valuation and Market Multiples

High-Growth Company
Financial Statements and Free Cash Flows

($ in millions)	Year −1	Year 0	Year 1	Year 2	Year 3	Year 4	Year 5	Year 6
Income Statement								
Revenue.	$490.2	$500.0	$625.0	$750.0	$810.0	$826.2	$842.7	$859.6
Operating expenses	−343.1	−350.0	−437.5	−525.0	−567.0	−578.3	−589.9	−601.7
Depreciation expense.	−16.3	−16.7	−20.8	−25.0	−27.0	−27.5	−28.1	−28.7
Interest expense.	−11.5	−12.8	−13.1	−14.3	−15.1	−15.5	−15.8	−16.1
Income before taxes.	$119.2	$120.5	$153.6	$185.7	$200.9	$204.8	$208.9	$213.1
Income tax expense	−35.8	−36.2	−46.1	−55.7	−60.3	−61.4	−62.7	−63.9
Net income	**$ 83.4**	**$ 84.4**	**$107.5**	**$130.0**	**$140.6**	**$143.4**	**$146.2**	**$149.2**
Balance Sheet								
Net working capital.	$ 98.0	$100.0	$125.0	$150.0	$162.0	$165.2	$168.5	$171.9
Property, plant, and equipment (net)	251.6	318.3	380.8	395.8	379.6	363.1	346.2	329.0
Total assets.	$349.7	$418.3	$505.8	$545.8	$541.6	$528.3	$514.8	$500.9
Debt	$142.3	$145.2	$159.3	$168.0	$172.2	$175.6	$179.1	$182.7
Equity	207.3	273.1	346.5	377.8	369.4	352.7	335.7	318.3
Total liabilities and equities.	$349.7	$418.3	$505.8	$545.8	$541.6	$528.3	$514.8	$500.9
Free Cash Flows								
Earnings before interest and taxes (EBIT)		$133.3	$166.7	$200.0	$216.0	$220.3	$224.7	$229.2
− Income taxes paid on EBIT		−40.0	−50.0	−60.0	−64.8	−66.1	−67.4	−68.8
Earnings before interest and after taxes		$ 93.3	$116.7	$140.0	$151.2	$154.2	$157.3	$160.5
+ Depreciation expense.		16.7	20.8	25.0	27.0	27.5	28.1	28.7
− Change in net working capital		−2.0	−25.0	−25.0	−12.0	−3.2	−3.3	−3.4
− Capital expenditures		−83.3	−83.3	−40.0	−10.8	−11.0	−11.2	−11.5
Unlevered free cash flow		**$ 24.7**	**$ 29.2**	**$100.0**	**$155.4**	**$167.5**	**$170.9**	**$174.3**

($ in millions)	Year 1	Year 2	Year 3	Year 4	Year 5	CV$_{Firm}$ Year 5
Unlevered free cash flow for continuing value (CV)						$ 174.3
Discount factor for continuing value						10.277
End of year value of firm.	$1,593.0	$1,679.9	$1,721.6	$1,756.0	$1,791.0	
Unlevered free cash flow	29.2	100.0	155.4	167.5	170.9	
	$1,622.2	$1,779.9	$1,877.0	$1,923.5	$1,962.0	
Discount factor.	0.895	0.895	0.895	0.895	0.895	
Beginning of year value of firm.	$1,451.9	$1,593.0	$1,679.9	$1,721.6	$1,756.0	$1,791.1
Beginning of year value of debt	145.2	159.3	168.0	172.2	175.6	179.1
Beginning of year value of equity	$1,306.7	$1,433.7	$1,511.9	$1,549.4	$1,580.4	$1,612.0

	Year 0	Year 1	Year 2	Year 3	Year 4	Year 5
Annual growth rates						
Revenue	2.0%	25.0%	20.0%	8.0%	2.0%	2.0%
Free cash flow		18.1%	242.9%	55.4%	7.8%	2.0%
Firm value market multiples						
Free cash flow multiple.		58.8	54.6	16.8	11.1	10.5	10.5
Unlevered earnings multiple.		15.6	13.7	12.0	11.4	11.4	11.4
EBIT multiple		10.9	9.6	8.4	8.0	8.0	8.0
EBITDA multiple.		9.7	8.5	7.5	7.1	7.1	7.1
Revenue (Sales) multiple—firm value.		2.9	2.5	2.2	2.1	2.1	2.1
Total assets multiple.		3.5	3.1	3.1	3.2	3.3	3.5

Exhibit may contain small rounding errors

industry is at the trough of its cycle, the market multiples we measure reflect the market multiples at the trough of the cycle, which could be appropriate for that valuation. However, for the continuing value calculation, we want to make sure that our valuation reflects the typical valuation of these companies. Thus, for our continuing value calculation, we probably want to estimate market multiples that are reflective of the midpoint of the cycle in conjunction with forecasts of the financial statements of the company being valued that are based on the midpoint of the cycle.

Market multiples also vary over time because of general economic conditions. Just as with cyclical industries, we expect market multiples to be higher as a slow- or negative-growth economy begins to recover and move into a period of high expected growth; again, this is based on historical measures of the denominator. Suppose current market valuations are quite high; by this we mean that the price-to-earnings ratios in the economy are on the high end of their historic distribution. If the price-to-earnings multiple is high relative to its long-run historical average, and if we are using market multiples to measure a company's continuing value, say, 10 years from now, we will have to decide whether or not the high current market valuations are permanent or whether multiples are likely to regress back toward their long-run average (perhaps because of diminished expectations of growth or because of increases in required rates of return for the economy). Thus, we have a variety of reasons why current market multiples may not reflect expected market multiples at the continuing value date.

Valuation Key 13.6

Current market multiples of comparable companies may not be appropriate to use in all situations, even if the comparable companies are indeed currently comparable. You might have to adjust the current market multiples when using them to measure continuing value because the company's prospects can be different at the continuing value date from what they are currently.

REVIEW EXERCISE 13.5

Evolution of Market Multiples

Use the information in Review Exercise 13.1 as well as the information below to measure the multiples of firm value to unlevered free cash flow and EBITDA, as well as the equity value to equity free cash flow and P/E multiples for Years 0 through 5, using the value as of the end of Year t divided by the value driver in Year t. Also calculate the company's unlevered free cash flow and equity free cash flow multiples using the company's costs of capital and growth rates. The company's equity cost of capital is 13%, and its weighted average cost of capital is 11.36%. The company's valuation as of the end of Years 0 through 5 appears below.

($ in millions)	Year 1	Year 2	Year 3	Year 4	Year 5	CV$_{Firm}$ Year 5
Unlevered free cash flow for continuing value (CV)						$ 234.7
Discount factor for continuing value						10.684
End-of-year value of firm	$2,293.3	$2,362.4	$2,409.7	$2,457.9	$2,507.0	
Unlevered free cash flow	12.2	191.4	221.1	225.5	230.1	
	$2,305.5	$2,553.8	$2,630.8	$2,683.4	$2,737.1	
Discount factor.	0.898	0.898	0.898	0.898	0.898	
Beginning-of-year value of firm	$2,070.3	$2,293.3	$2,362.4	$2,409.7	$2,457.9	$2,507.0
Beginning-of-year value of debt.	414.1	458.7	472.5	481.9	491.6	501.4
Beginning-of-year value of equity	$1,656.3	$1,834.6	$1,889.9	$1,927.7	$1,966.3	$2,005.6

Exhibit may contain small rounding errors

Solution on page 542.

SUMMARY AND KEY CONCEPTS

The market multiple valuation model is a widely used valuation method. We often use it in conjunction with DCF valuation methods as another way to value a company and its equity. This chapter provides a conceptual underpinning for the use of the market multiple technique, and it provides information regarding how to think about comparability as a function of company characteristics and different market multiples. DCF valuation methods rely heavily on the reasonableness of the assumptions (value drivers) underpinning the free cash flow forecasts of the company being valued and the discount rate used to discount the free cash flows. The market multiple valuation method, on the other hand, relies heavily on the choice of comparable companies and the observed valuations of those companies.

ADDITIONAL READING AND REFERENCES

Alford, A., "The Effect of the Set of Comparable Companies on the Accuracy of the Price-Earnings Valuation Method," *Journal of Accounting Research* 30 (1992), pp. 94–108.

Bhojraj, S., and C. Lee, "Who Is My Peer? A Valuation-Based Approach to the Selection of Comparable Companies," *Journal of Accounting Research* vol. 40, no. 2 (May, 2002), pp. 407–439.

EXERCISES AND PROBLEMS

P13.1   **Basic Market Multiple Calculations:** We present summary financial statements and a free cash flow schedule for the Growing Company in Exhibit P13.1 and present a valuation of the company and its equity in Exhibit P13.2. Use this information to measure the free cash flow and financial-statement-based market multiples in Exhibit 13.2 for Year 0 through Year 5, using the value of the firm or equity as of the end of Year t divided by the relevant denominators in Year t. Also calculate the company's unlevered free cash flow and equity free cash flow multiples, using the company's costs of capital and growth rates for each year.

EXHIBIT P13.1	The Growing Company Financial Forecasts

($ in millions)	Growing Company Financial Statements and Free Cash Flows							
	Year −1	Year 0	Year 1	Year 2	Year 3	Year 4	Year 5	Year 6
Income Statement								
Revenue.	$776.7	$800.0	$840.0	$1,050.0	$1,155.0	$1,189.7	$1,225.3	$1,262.1
Operating expenses	−543.7	−560.0	−588.0	−735.0	−808.5	−832.8	−857.7	−883.5
Depreciation expense.	−64.7	−66.7	−70.0	−87.5	−96.3	−99.1	−102.1	−105.2
Interest expense.	−17.1	−19.0	−19.5	−21.9	−23.4	−24.2	−24.9	−25.7
Income before taxes.	$151.2	$154.4	$162.5	$ 205.6	$ 226.8	$ 233.6	$ 240.6	$ 247.8
Income tax expense.	−52.9	−54.0	−56.9	−72.0	−79.4	−81.7	−84.2	−86.7
Net Income	$ 98.3	$100.3	$105.6	$ 133.6	$ 147.4	$ 151.8	$ 156.4	$ 161.1
Balance Sheet								
Net working capital.	$77.7	$80.0	$ 84.0	$ 105.0	$ 115.5	$ 119.0	$ 122.5	$ 126.2
Property, plant, and equipment (net)	472.5	439.2	544.2	544.2	476.8	407.4	335.9	262.3
Total assets.	$550.2	$519.2	$628.2	$ 649.2	$ 592.3	$ 526.4	$ 458.4	$ 388.5
Debt	$189.7	$195.4	$219.2	$ 234.3	$ 241.9	$ 249.2	$ 256.7	$ 264.4
Equity	360.4	323.7	408.9	414.9	350.3	277.2	201.8	124.1
Total liabilities and equities.	$550.2	$519.2	$628.2	$ 649.2	$ 592.3	$ 526.4	$ 458.4	$ 388.5

Exhibit may contain small rounding errors

continued

continued from previous page

EXHIBIT P13.1 The Growing Company Financial Forecasts

Growing Company
Financial Statements and Free Cash Flows

($ in millions)	Year 0	Year 1	Year 2	Year 3	Year 4	Year 5	Year 6
Free Cash Flows							
Earnings before interest and taxes (EBIT)	$173.3	$182.0	$ 227.5	$ 250.3	$ 257.8	$ 265.5	$ 273.5
– Income taxes paid on EBIT	–60.7	–63.7	–79.6	–87.6	–90.2	–92.9	–95.7
Earnings before interest and after taxes	$112.7	$118.3	$ 147.9	$ 162.7	$ 167.5	$ 172.6	$ 177.7
+ Depreciation expense.........................	66.7	70.0	87.5	96.3	99.1	102.1	105.2
– Change in net working capital	–2.3	–4.0	–21.0	–10.5	–3.5	–3.6	–3.7
– Capital expenditures	–33.3	–175.0	–87.5	–28.9	–29.7	–30.6	–31.6
Unlevered free cash flow.....	**$143.7**	**$ 9.3**	**$ 126.9**	**$ 219.5**	**$ 233.5**	**$ 240.5**	**$ 247.7**
– Interest paid	–19.0	–19.5	–21.9	–23.4	–24.2	–24.9	–25.7
+ Interest tax shield..........................	6.6	6.8	7.7	8.2	8.5	8.7	9.0
+ Change in debt financing.....................	5.7	23.8	15.0	7.7	7.3	7.5	7.7
Free cash flow to common equity	**$137.0**	**$ 20.4**	**$ 127.7**	**$ 212.0**	**$ 225.0**	**$ 231.8**	**$ 238.7**

Exhibit may contain small rounding errors

EXHIBIT P13.2 The Growing Company Valuation

Discounted Cash Flow Valuation

Growth rate for continuing value	3.000%
Unleverd cost of capital.....................	13.000%
Debt to value	10.000%
Equity cost of capital	13.333%
Weighted average cost of capital..............	12.650%

($ in millions)	Year 1	Year 2	Year 3	Year 4	Year 5	CV$_{Firm}$ Year 5
Unlevered free cash flow for continuing value (CV)						$ 247.7
Discount factor for continuing value						10.363
End of year value of firm......................	$2,192.2	$2,342.6	$2,419.4	$2,492.0	$2,566.8	
Unlevered free cash flow	9.3	126.9	219.5	233.5	240.5	
	$2,201.5	$2,469.5	$2,639.0	$2,725.5	$2,807.2	
Discount factor............................	0.888	0.888	0.888	0.888	0.888	
Beginning of year value of firm.................	$1,954.3	$2,192.2	$2,342.6	$2,419.4	$2,492.0	$2,566.8
Beginning of year value of debt	195.4	219.2	234.3	241.9	249.2	256.7
Beginning of year value of equity...............	$1,758.8	$1,973.0	$2,108.4	$2,177.5	$2,242.8	$2,310.1

Exhibit may contain small rounding errors

P13.2   **Measuring the Change in Market Multiples Resulting from a Change in Value Drivers:** Use the information in Problem 13.1 to examine the change in the firm value market multiples computed in Problem 13.1 resulting from a change in the value drivers described below. For each of the changes in the value drivers, measure the changes in the multiples of firm value to free cash flow, unlevered earnings, EBIT, EBITDA, and revenue. Measure the market multiple using the end of Year 0 firm value and Year 0 denominator.

   a.   The initial valuation of the company used a 3% perpetual growth rate. If the perpetual growth rate decreases to 2%, the company's value decreases by -4.1%.

   b.   The initial valuation of the company used a 13% unlevered cost of capital. If the unlevered cost of capital decreases to 12%, the company's value increases by 12.9%.

   c.   The initial valuation of the company used a 70% operating expense ratio (% of revenue). If the operating expense ratio decreases to 65%, the company's value increases by 18.3%.

   d.   The initial valuation of the company used a 1.2 ratio of revenue to gross property, plant and equipment. If the ratio of revenue to gross property, plant and equipment increases to 1.5, the company's value increases by 1.4%.

e. The initial valuation of the company used a 10% net working capital ratio (% of revenue). If the net working capital ratio increases to 15%, the company's value decreases by −1.3%.

f. The initial valuation of the company used a 35% income tax rate. If the income tax rate increases to 40%, the company's value decreases by −5.6%.

P13.3   **The Trouble with Market Multiple-Based Contracts:** You are a consultant and have been hired by the board of directors of P. R. Value, Inc.—a privately held firm—to evaluate the reasonableness of the proposed implementation of an employment contract for an employee, which describes a method for valuing the company's common stock. The employee owns 6,500 shares of the company's stock and decides that now is the best time to leave the company. The company uses the valuation method described in the employment agreement in order to determine the price at which it buys back shares of employees who retire, die, or leave for other reasons. The salient parts of the contract are as follows: the price-earnings ratio for each of the comparable companies (C&B, FH, M&M, and A&A) shall be measured by dividing the average trading price for a corporation's stock during the month of December preceding the date of death or retirement by such corporation's reported audited earnings per share for the fiscal year preceding the date of death or retirement; average the four price-earnings ratios and multiply by the earnings per share of P. R. Value to determine the buyout price per share. The relevant information for the four comparable companies follow:

Using Reported Earnngs	C&B	FH	M&M	A&A
Average selling price	$42.86	$47.30	$47.74	$43.54
Earnings per share	$2.220	$2.020	$2.490	$0.050

The A&A Company, had a loss associated with a change in accounting principles of $2.05 in the most recent year. The earnings per share for P. R. Value, Inc. is $1.25.

P13.4   **Free Cash Flow Multiple and Growth Rates 1:** You are valuing a company as of the end of Year 0. The company is privately owned and 100% equity financed. The company's free cash flow for the current year, Year 0, is $40 million, and management expects a free cash flow of $46.8 million next year (Year 1). Management expects the company's free cash flows to grow at a present value weighted average growth rate of 4%, using Year 0 as the base year. The company has one comparable company, which also uses only equity financing. The value of the comparable company is $1,283.3 million. Its free cash flow for the current year, Year 0, is $60 million, and management expects its free cash flow to be $115.5 million in the following year, Year 1. Management believes that the two companies have the same cost of capital of 12%.

a. What is the free cash flow multiple of the comparable company based on its Year 0 and Year 1 free cash flows? Why are they different?

b. Value the privately owned company using the free cash flow market multiples of the comparable company based on both the Year 0 and Year 1 free cash flows. Why are the valuations different, and which one is more likely to be the better valuation?

c. Measure the value of the privately owned company using the discounted cash flow valuation method, and compare it to the free cash flow multiple valuations.

P13.5   **Free Cash Flow Multiple and Growth Rates 2:** You are valuing a company as of the end of Year 0. The company is privately owned and 100% equity financed. The company's free cash flow for the current year, Year 0, is $10 million, and management expects a free cash flow of $11.5 million next year (Year 1). Management expects the company's free cash flows to grow at a present value weighted average growth rate of 3%, using Year 0 as the base year. The company has one comparable company which also uses only equity financing. The value of the comparable company is $3 billion. Its free cash flow for the current year, Year 0, is $200 million, and management expects its free cash flow to be $300 million in the following year, Year 1. Management believes that the two companies have the same cost of capital of 15%.

a. What is the free cash flow multiple of the comparable company based on its Year 0 and Year 1 free cash flows? Why are they different?

b. Value the privately owned company using the comparable company's free cash flow market multiple based on both the Year 0 and Year 1 free cash flows. Why are the valuations different, and which one is more likely to be the better valuation?

c. Measure the value of the privately owned company using the discounted cash flow valuation method, and compare it to the free cash flow multiple valuations.

P13.6   **Assessing Comparability—Unlevered Company:** Your company has been hired to value ValCo as of the end of Year 0. ValCo is a privately owned, 100% equity-financed company. A research analyst working at the company identified four potential publicly traded comparable companies: COMP A, COMP B, COMP C, and COMP D. The research analyst is confident that the free cash flows of ValCo and its comparable companies have the same risk (that is, all companies have an unlevered cost of capital equal to 12%) and the same growth rate (4%), but they do not have identical cost structures and investment requirements. The financial statements and free cash flows for ValCo and the four potential comparable companies appear in Exhibits P13.3 and P13.4. The research analyst calculates various firm value and equity value market multiples for each of the comparable companies, which also appear in these exhibits.

a. Discuss why the comparable companies have the same free cash flow market multiple even though they do not have the same cost structures or investment requirements.

b. For each comparable company, discuss why each of the accounting-based market multiples might not be the best market multiple for ValCo, and discuss whether the comparable company's market multiple is too high or too low.

EXHIBIT P13.3 Selected Data for ValCo and Potential Comparable Companies

	ValCo	COMP A	COMP B	COMP C	COMP D
Income Statement (Year 1)					
Revenue (sales)	$188.8	$1,067.2	$307.8	$271.4	$338.6
– Operating expenses (costs).	–85.0	–480.2	–110.8	–122.1	–152.4
– Depreciation	–37.8	–213.4	–61.6	–43.4	–84.7
Earnings before interest and taxes.	$ 66.1	$ 373.5	$135.4	$105.9	$101.6
– Interest.	0.0	0.0	0.0	0.0	0.0
Earnings before income taxes	$ 66.1	$ 373.5	$135.4	$105.9	$101.6
– Income tax expense	–26.4	–119.5	–54.2	–42.3	–40.6
Earnings	$ 39.7	$ 254.0	$ 81.3	$ 63.5	$ 61.0
Balance Sheet (Year 1)					
Total invested capital (net)	$261.9	$1,479.8	$426.8	$376.4	$587.0
Debt	$ 0.0	$0.0	$ 0.0	$ 0.0	$ 0.0
Equity	261.9	1,479.8	426.8	376.4	587.0
Debt and equity	$261.9	$1,479.8	$426.8	$376.4	$587.0
Balance Sheet (Year 0)					
Total invested capital (net)	$251.8	$1,422.9	$410.4	$361.9	$564.4
Debt	$ 0.0	$0.0	$ 0.0	$ 0.0	$ 0.0
Equity	251.8	1,422.9	410.4	361.9	564.4
Debt and equity	$251.8	$1,422.9	$410.4	$361.9	$564.4
Free Cash Flow (Year 1)					
Earnings before interest and taxes.	$ 66.1	$ 373.5	$135.4	$105.9	$101.6
– Income tax expense	–26.4	–119.5	–54.2	–42.3	–40.6
Unlevered earnings.	$ 39.7	$ 254.0	$ 81.3	$ 63.5	$ 61.0
Depreciation.	37.8	213.4	61.6	43.4	84.7
Investment	–47.8	–270.4	–78.0	–57.9	–107.2
Unlevered free cash flow	$ 29.6	$ 197.1	$ 64.8	$ 49.0	$ 38.4
After-tax interest.	0.0	0.0	0.0	0.0	0.0
New debt	0.0	0.0	0.0	0.0	0.0
Equity free cash flow	$ 29.6	$ 197.1	$ 64.8	$ 49.0	$ 38.4

Exhibit may contain small rounding errors

EXHIBIT P13.4 Selected Valuation and Multiples for ValCo's Potential Comparable Companies

	COMP A	COMP B	COMP C	COMP D
Market Multiples Based on the Value of the Firm				
Value of the firm	$2,463.4	$810.6	$612.9	$479.7
Free cash flow multiple.	12.5	12.5	12.5	12.5
Unlevered earnings multiple.	9.7	10.0	9.7	7.9
EBIT multiple	6.6	6.0	5.8	4.7
EBITDA multiple	4.2	4.1	4.1	2.6
Revenue (sales) multiple.	2.3	2.6	2.3	1.4
Total invested capital multiple	1.7	2.0	1.7	0.9

continued

continued from previous page

EXHIBIT P13.4	Selected Valuation and Multiples for ValCo's Potential Comparable Companies			
	COMP A	**COMP B**	**COMP C**	**COMP D**
Market Multiples to Measure the Value of the Equity (Numerator is Market Value of the Equity):				
Value of equity	$2,463.4	$810.6	$612.9	$479.7
Equity free cash flow multiple	12.5	12.5	12.5	12.5
Price-to-earnings multiple	9.7	10.0	9.7	7.9
Revenue (sales) multiple.	2.3	2.6	2.3	1.4
Market-to-book	1.7	2.0	1.7	0.9

P13.7   **Assessing Comparability—Levered Co.:** Your company has a consulting engagement to value Levered Co. as of the end of Year 0. Levered Co. is a privately owned, company. A research analyst working at the company identified four potential comparable companies: COMP A, COMP B, COMP C, and COMP D, all of which are publicly traded. The research analyst is confident that the free cash flows of Levered Co. and its comparable companies have the same risk (an unlevered cost of capital equal to 10%) and same growth rate (2%) but that they do not have identical cost structures or investment requirements. The financial statements and free cash flows for Levered Co. and the four potential comparable companies appear in Exhibit P13.5. The values and relevant multiples appear in Exhibit P13.6. Your research analyst calculated various firm value and equity value market multiples for each of the comparable companies, which also appear in these exhibits.

a.   For each comparable company, discuss why the free cash flow multiples are or are not the same.
b.   For each comparable company, discuss why each of the accounting-based market multiples might not be the best market multiple to value the Levered Co, and discuss whether the comparable company's market multiple is too high or too low.

EXHIBIT P13.5	Selected Data for Levered Co. and Potential Comparable Companies				
	Levered Co.	**COMP A**	**COMP B**	**COMP C**	**COMP D**
Income Statement (Year 1)					
Revenue (sales)	$246.5	$1,375.5	$530.4	$379.1	$374.5
– Operating expenses (costs).	–147.9	–825.3	–190.9	–227.5	–224.7
– Depreciation	–56.0	–312.6	–147.3	–51.7	–124.8
Earnings before interest and taxes.	$ 42.6	$ 237.6	$192.1	$ 99.9	$ 25.0
– Interest.	–6.8	–44.5	–33.2	–17.0	–2.0
Earnings before income taxes	$ 35.7	$ 193.1	$159.0	$ 82.9	$ 22.9
– Income tax expense	–10.7	–34.8	–47.7	–24.9	–6.9
Earnings	$ 25.0	$ 158.4	$111.3	$ 58.0	$ 16.1
Balance Sheet (Year 1)					
Total invested capital (net)	$228.6	$1,275.5	$601.1	$351.5	$509.3
Debt	$ 87.3	$ 566.8	$422.8	$217.3	$ 25.8
Equity.	141.3	708.7	178.3	134.2	483.5
Debt and equity	$228.6	$1,275.5	$601.1	$351.5	$509.3
Balance Sheet (Year 0)					
Total invested capital (net)	$224.1	$1,250.5	$589.3	$344.7	$499.3
Debt	$ 85.5	$ 555.7	$414.5	$213.1	$ 25.3
Equity.	138.5	694.8	174.8	131.6	474.0
Debt and equity	$224.1	$1,250.5	$589.3	$344.7	$499.3

Exhibit may contain small rounding errors

continued

continued from previous page

EXHIBIT P13.5 Selected Data for Levered Co. and Potential Comparable Companies

	Levered Co.	COMP A	COMP B	COMP C	COMP D
Free Cash Flow (Year 1)					
Earnings before interest and taxes.	$ 42.6	$ 237.6	$192.1	$ 99.9	$ 25.0
– Income tax expense	−12.8	−42.8	−57.6	−30.0	−7.5
Unlevered earnings.	$ 29.8	$ 194.8	$134.5	$ 70.0	$ 17.5
Depreciation	56.0	312.6	147.3	51.7	124.8
Investment	−60.5	−337.6	−159.1	−58.6	−134.8
Unlevered free cash flow	$ 25.3	$ 169.8	$122.7	$ 63.1	$ 7.5
After-tax interest.	−4.8	−36.5	−23.2	−11.9	−1.4
New debt	1.7	11.1	8.3	4.3	0.5
Equity free cash flow	$ 22.2	$ 144.5	$107.8	$ 55.4	$ 6.6

Exhibit may contain small rounding errors

EXHIBIT P13.6 Selected Valuation and Multiples for Levered Co.'s Potential Comparable Companies

	COMP A	COMP B	COMP C	COMP D
Market Multiples Based on the Value of the Firm				
Value of the firm	$2,222.7	$1,658.0	$852.3	$101.2
Free cash flow multiple.	13.1	13.5	13.5	13.5
Unlevered earnings multiple.	11.4	12.3	12.2	5.8
EBIT multiple	9.4	8.6	8.5	4.1
EBITDA multiple	4.0	4.9	5.6	0.7
Revenue (sales) multiple.	1.6	3.1	2.2	0.3
Total invested capital multiple	1.8	2.8	2.5	0.2
Market Multiples to Measure the Value of the Equity (Numerator is Market Value of the Equity)				
Value of equity	$1,667.0	$1,243.5	$639.2	$ 75.9
Equity free cash flow multiple	11.5	11.5	11.5	11.5
Price-to-earnings multiple	10.5	11.2	11.0	4.7
Revenue (sales) multiple.	1.2	2.3	1.7	0.2
Market-to-book	2.4	7.1	4.9	0.2

SOLUTIONS FOR REVIEW EXERCISES

Solution for Review Exercise 13.1: Basic Calculation of Market Multiples

Year 0 Market Multiples	Value	Denominator	Multiple
Firm Value Market Multiples			
Free cash flow multiple.	$2,070.3	$ 99.2	20.88
Unlevered earnings multiple.	$2,070.3	$ 141.5	14.63
EBIT multiple	$2,070.3	$ 235.9	8.78
EBITDA multiple	$2,070.3	$ 300.0	6.90
Revenue (sales) multiple—firm value	$2,070.3	$1,000.0	2.07
Total assets multiple.	$2,070.3	$1,206.3	1.72
Equity Value Market Multiples			
Equity free cash flow multiple	$1,656.3	$ 87.8	18.87
P/E or earnings multiple.	$1,656.3	$ 122.1	13.57
Revenue (sales) multiple—equity value	$1,656.3	$1,000.0	1.66
Book equity multiple.	$1,656.3	$ 792.2	2.09

Solution for Review Exercise 13.2: Risk and Growth Drivers of Market Multiples

Year 0 Market Multiples	Value	Denominator	Multiple
Firm value to free cash flow multiple	$2,070.3	$99.2	20.88
Present value weighted average growth rate unlevered FCF	10.77%	$= r_{WACC} - FCF_1/V_{F,0}$	
Growth rate $Year_0$ / $Year_1$	−87.65%		
Weighted average cost of capital	11.36%		
$(1+g_{0,1})/(r_{WACC} - g_{1,\infty})$	20.88		
Equity value to equity free cash flow multiple	$1,656.3	$87.8	18.87
Present value weighted average growth rate equity FCF	10.77%	$= r_E - EFCF_1/V_{E,0}$	
Growth rate $Year_0$ / $Year_1$	−57.90%		
Equity cost of capital	13.00%		
$(1 + g_{0,1})/(r_E - g_{1,\infty})$	18.87		

Note—The present value weighted average growth rate is calculated using Equation 6.3:

$$g_A = r - \frac{FCF_1}{V_{F,0}}$$

Solution for Review Exercise 13.3: Free Cash Flow Market Multiples

Firm Value Market Multiples	Year 0	Year 1
Free cash flow multiple	20.88	187.27
Unlevered earnings multiple	14.63	15.00
EBIT multiple	8.78	9.00
EBITDA multiple	6.90	7.08
Revenue (sales) multiple—firm value	2.07	2.12
Total assets multiple	1.72	1.70

Equity Value Market Multiples		
Equity free cash flow multiple	18.87	49.64
P/E or earnings multiple	13.57	13.80
Revenue (sales) multiple—equity value	1.66	1.70
Book equity multiple	2.09	2.07

The only market multiples that vary a great deal from Year 0 to Year 1 are those multiples that are based on free cash flows as the free cash flows vary much more than earnings or assets.

Solution for Review Exercise 13.4: Change in Firm Value Market Multiples from a Change in Value Drivers

Financial Model Forecast Driver	Forecast Driver Value	% Change in Value of Firm	Free Cash Flow Multiple	Unlevered Earnings Multiple	EBIT Multiple	EBITDA Multiple	Revenue Multiple
Continuing value growth rate	2.0%		20.88	14.63	8.78	6.90	2.07
New assumption and multiples	4.0%		21.86	15.32	9.19	7.23	2.17
% Change in multiples			4.7%	4.7%	4.7%	4.7%	4.7%
% Change in underlying variable		4.7%	0.0%	0.0%	0.0%	0.0%	0.0%
Unlevered cost of capital	12.0%		20.88	14.63	8.78	6.90	2.07
New assumption and multiples	10.0%		27.06	18.96	11.38	8.94	2.68
% Change in multiples			29.6%	29.6%	29.6%	29.6%	29.6%
% Change in underlying variable		29.6%	0.0%	0.0%	0.0%	0.0%	0.0%
Operating expenses (% rev)	70.0%		20.88	14.63	8.78	6.90	2.07
New assumption and multiples	60.0%		17.83	14.08	8.45	7.09	2.84
% Change in multiples			-14.6%	-3.8%	-3.8%	2.8%	37.0%
% Change in underlying variable		37.0%	60.5%	42.4%	42.4%	33.3%	0.0%
New denominator			$159.2	$201.5	$335.9	$400.0	$1,000.0

Solution for Review Exercise 13.5: Evolving Growth Rates and Market Multiples

	Year 0	Year 1	Year 2	Year 3	Year 4	Year 5
Firm value market multiples						
Free cash flow multiple..........................	20.88	187.27	12.34	10.90	10.90	10.90
EBITDA multiple................................	6.90	7.08	6.40	6.40	6.40	6.40
Equity market multiples						
Equity free cash flow multiple	18.87	49.64	10.32	9.27	9.27	9.27
P/E or earnings multiple........................	13.57	13.80	12.41	12.43	12.43	12.43
Present value weighted average growth rate unlevered FCF..........................	10.77%	3.01%	2.00%	2.00%	2.00%	2.00%
Growth rate Year t+1/Year t FCF	−87.65%	1462.74%	15.54%	2.00%	2.00%	2.00%
$(1 + g_{t,t+1})/(r_{WACC} - g_{t+1,\infty})$.....................	20.88	187.27	12.34	10.90	10.90	10.90
Present value weighted average growth rate equity FCF.............................	10.77%	3.01%	2.00%	2.00%	2.00%	2.00%
Growth rate Year t+1/Year t equity FCF	−57.90%	395.64%	13.49%	2.00%	2.00%	2.00%
$(1 + g_{t,t+1})/(r_E - g_{t+1,\infty})$......................	18.87	49.64	10.32	9.27	9.27	9.27

After mastering the material in this chapter, you will be able to:

1. Measure market multiples using first principles (14.1)

2. Measure market multiple numerators (14.2–14.3)

3. Measure market multiple denominators (14.4–14.5)

4. Make adjustments to market multiple numerators and denominators (14.6, 14.7, 14.10)

5. Choose an appropriate market multiple and range (14.8–14.9)

Market Multiple Measurement and Implementation

Coke (Coca Cola Company) and Pepsi (PepsiCo Inc.) are two competing brands of cola known throughout the world.[1] They are direct competitors, but are they comparable companies? As we can see from the graph of their enterprise value to EBITDA multiples, Coke's market multiples have been consistently higher than Pepsi's market multiples.

COCA COLA COMPANY PEPSICO INC.

Coke states that its business is nonalcoholic beverages; it generates almost all of its revenues from the sale of concentrates, syrups, and the sale of finished beverages. Pepsi, however, generates its revenues from a variety of snack and beverage products. It has four business units— Americas Foods, Americas Beverages, Europe, and Middle East and Africa.

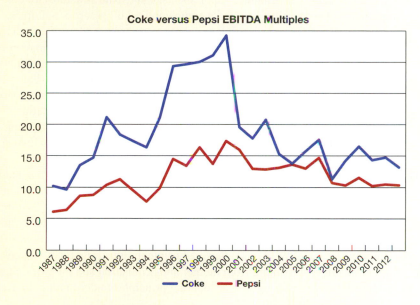

Coke versus Pepsi EBITDA Multiples

In the last chapter, we discussed why such differences in market multiples could exist for two companies. For example, Coke and Pepsi might not be perfect comparable companies because of their different operating strategies (concentrate versus finished beverages) and different lines of business that could lead to different fundamentals. As we discuss in this chapter, such differences could also exist because of certain measurement issues that arise when estimating market multiples.

---

[1] See the companies' respective 10-K filings with the U.S. Securities and Exchange Commission (SEC) for the 2011 fiscal year.

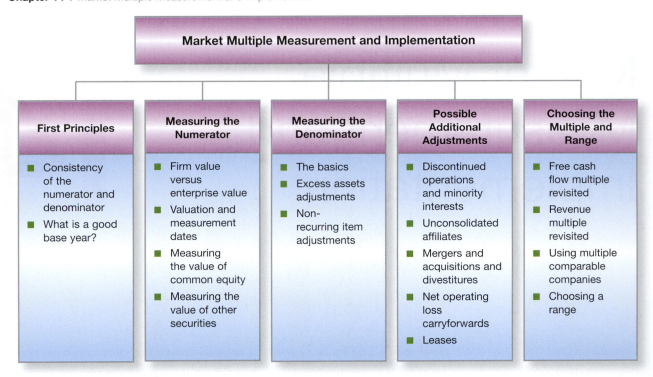

INTRODUCTION

In Chapter 13, we discussed both the market multiple valuation process and the conceptual framework underpinning it. We also described the commonly used market multiples and discussed some cross-sectional (across firms and industries) and time-series characteristics of the distributions of these multiples. We also emphasized the relevance of various dimensions of comparability (risk, growth, cost structure, working capital management, capital expenditure requirements, and capital structure) for comparable companies and how the importance of such value drivers for comparability differ across multiples.

In this chapter, we focus our discussion on how to measure and use these market multiples. Measuring market multiple inputs is more complex than merely observing the numerator and denominator of a multiple and performing simple division. Rather, we must often consider various issues when measuring both the numerator and denominator for a particular market multiple. The numerator is usually less complex to measure, but even this can become complicated, and both the numerator and denominator can require various adjustments to their basic calculations. The goals of these adjustments are twofold. First, we make adjustments to increase the consistency between the claims on the company's value as represented in the numerator and denominator. Second, we make adjustments to increase the comparability of the company we are valuing to its comparable companies.

These adjustments usually overlap. For example, making adjustments to exclude the effects of a company's excess (idle or non-operating) assets increases the consistency of the numerator and denominator and the comparability across companies. Similarly, adjustments that remove the effects of one-time or non-recurring items from a company's financial statements also increase consistency and comparability. Many of these adjustments relate to accounting treatments and accounting rules, both of which can affect comparability and consistency. We classify these adjustments into four types—excess assets, non-recurring effects, transaction effects (resulting from merger and acquisition and divestiture transactions), and effects resulting from differences or changes in accounting principles underpinning the financial statements.

14.1 FIRST PRINCIPLES FOR MEASURING MARKET MULTIPLES

LO1 Measure market multiples using first principles

In this section, we discuss three basic principles that guide how we measure market multiple inputs. The first principle is consistency in measuring a multiple's numerator and denominator. We measure a multiple's numerator based on the values of a certain set of securities—typically, either all of the securities (firm or enterprise value) or the common equity claims. We should therefore measure the denominator based on the same claims or securities that are represented in the numerator. Like many basic principles, this principle seems obvious; however, the subtleties in the way we measure earnings can make this principle difficult to follow.

The second principle is to measure a numerator that represents the value of the company's long-term operating performance. Thus, from a multiple's numerator, we exclude the value of such non-operating effects as the value of excess assets and the anticipated value from the expected sale of part of the business. The third principle follows from the second principle: use a denominator that represents the long-term performance of the company. In other words, choose a denominator that represents a good base year for measuring the company's long-term performance. The denominators we use to measure market multiples are typically operating-based, and they may require adjustments in order to reflect the company's long-run performance.

Consistency of Claims in the Numerator and Denominator

Even though it is simple in concept, consistency between the claims in the numerator and denominator is not always straightforward to discern. For example, a multiple that is measured by dividing the value of the firm by earnings before interest, taxes, depreciation, and amortization (the EBITDA multiple) has a reasonably consistent numerator and denominator because the numerator measures the claims related to all of the company's investors, and the denominator measures the flows that are potentially payable to all of the claimholders. However, two inconsistencies in the EBITDA multiple are that the denominator does not take into account the portion of EBITDA that is payable to the tax authorities and it does not consider required investments. As we discussed in Chapter 13, these value drivers then have to be controlled for through the use of comparable companies; that is, the company being valued and the comparable companies need to be in similar tax situations and require similar investments.

A multiple that really does not have a consistent numerator and denominator is the multiple measured by dividing the common equity value by revenue. This inconsistency arises because the numerator only represents equity claims and the denominator represents flows related to investors (debtholders, preferred stockholders, and common equityholders) as well as all suppliers, employees, and tax authorities. Two otherwise identical companies with different capital structures will have different multiples of equity value to revenue merely because they have different capital structures. It may be possible to use a market multiple that is defined as the market value of the firm to revenue, but doing so requires that all firms have the same cost structure, investment requirements, tax structure, and growth prospects. Finding comparable companies for such a multiple can be a daunting task. However, the degree of complexity in assessing comparability increases even more when we utilize a multiple of equity value to revenue, because it further mixes the claimholders represented in the numerator and denominator. Even though consistency between the numerator and the denominator is useful, assessing comparability can be a complex problem, as we saw in Chapter 13.

A multiple's numerator and denominator can also have more subtle inconsistencies. Measuring the earnings multiple as the market value of a company's equity to net income might seem to have a consistent numerator and denominator because the claimholders in both the numerator and denominator are the same—the common shareholders. However, if the company has preferred stock and pays preferred stock dividends, then the denominator does not represent the flow to common shareholders unless we use income available to common instead of net income. In addition, the numerator and denominator might not be consistent if a company has outstanding stock options, stock appreciation rights, or other securities (such as convertible debt) that can dilute the ownership interests of the common shareholders. In such cases, we must either adjust the numerator, the denominator, or both so that the value of the claims in the numerator and the flow in the denominator represent the same claimholders.

Use a Numerator that Represents the Value of the Company's Long-Run Operating Performance

The market value of a firm or its equity represents the value of the company's long-term performance, plus the value of any business being sold, plus the value of any excess assets. Unless the comparable companies and the company we are valuing have similar businesses being sold and similar excess assets, we typically adjust the numerator in a market multiple to exclude such effects. These adjustments to the numerator often lead to changes in the denominator. Including the effects of these items in the numerator and denominator can cause differences between the comparable companies and the company we are valuing, so we generally make the appropriate adjustments for these items.

Use a Denominator that Is a Good "Base Year" for Future Performance

Naturally, we cannot calculate a meaningful multiple if a company has a negative denominator. The ratio of firm or equity value to a negative denominator is nonsensical. This issue is similar to using a negative free cash flow in a constant growth perpetuity formula; that is, it does not fit the assumptions underlying the formula. Given that the numerator represents the value of the company's long-term performance, our denominator should represent a good base year for the company's long-term performance. This issue is somewhat similar to the base year issue for continuing values that are measured using a free cash flow perpetuity (recall this discussion in Chapter 6). We should therefore adjust the denominator for any effect that is not representative of the company's long-term performance. For example, the effect of any gain, loss, or cash proceeds from the sale of either a business or a non-recurring item would have to be adjusted out of the denominator.

Timing Issues

For market multiple denominators based on a stock (balance sheet value)—such as the book value of shareholders' equity or the book value of total invested capital—we usually rely on the last fiscal period (year or quarter) that is closest to the valuation date. Since the denominator is a balance sheet value, quarterly financial statements may provide the information needed as of, or closer to, the valuation date. We would have to adjust the denominator if a company has a major purchase (acquisition) or sale of a business after its last financial statement disclosure.

For market multiple denominators based on a flow (income or cash flow statement)—such as revenues, earnings, EBIT, and EBITDA—we have more choices as to what period we measure the denominator over. The typical alternatives include the last fiscal year, the **last twelve months (LTM)** or **trailing twelve months (TTM)**, the six-months-historic and six-months forecast, the next-fiscal-year forecast, or the forecast for the fiscal year two or more years out. Note that the timing convention used to measure the multiples has to match the measured denominator for the company being valued. For example, if we use EBIT measured over the TTM to calculate the multiple, we want to use the TTM of EBIT for the firm being valued in conjunction with that multiple. We discuss each of the timing alternatives next.

Last Fiscal Year. Measuring the variables from the last fiscal year entails identifying the relevant numbers from the most recent annual financial statement or 10-K filing. This is relatively straightforward. The problem with using the last fiscal year is that the information may be stale if the company's situation has changed. For example, if we are valuing a company with a December 31 year-end when it is late October, the last-fiscal-year results will be based on the performance of the company starting 22 months ago and ending 10 months ago. Another potential disadvantage of this alternative is that we might be measuring the denominator over different time periods for the comparable companies with different fiscal year-ends. Using different time periods results in different multiples if either the companies' situations or the conditions of the general economy or industry change substantially during the different measurement periods.[2]

Last Twelve Months (LTM) or Trailing Twelve Months (TTM). Most companies only issue quarterly (and not monthly) financial statements, so using the LTM generally means using the financial statements for the last four quarters available before the valuation date. If the valuation date falls after the date that annual financial statements are available and before the date that the year's first quarterly financial statements are available, then the LTM is equivalent to the last fiscal year.

In order to calculate the LTM that does not coincide with the fiscal year-end, we use a combination of quarterly and annual financial statements. For example, assume we are measuring the LTM of earnings

---

[2] One advantage of using annual versus quarterly financial statements is that they are audited, whereas quarterly financial statements are only reviewed by the auditor. We know that auditors sometimes require companies to restate their quarterly financial statements; see, Kinney, W. Jr., and L. McDaniel, "Characteristics of Firms Correcting Previously Reported Quarterly Earnings," *Journal of Accounting and Economics* 11 (February, 1989), pp. 71–93.

as of April 30, 2012, for a company that has a fiscal year-end of December 31. Assume that the quarterly financial statements for the quarter ending on March 31, 2012, are available by April 30. To measure the LTM of earnings as of April 30, 2012, we begin with the December 31, 2011, annual earnings. We then subtract the earnings for the March 31, 2011, quarter from the annual earnings (to measure the earnings for the last three quarters of that year) and add the earnings for the March 31, 2012, quarter. If we want to calculate the LTM of earnings as of June 30, 2012, we subtract the earnings for the six months ending June 30, 2011, from the annual earnings recorded on December 31, 2011, (to measure the earnings for the last two quarters of that fiscal year), and add the earnings for the six months ending June 30, 2012. The advantage of this approach is that the denominator is measured for a time period that is closer to the valuation date; in other words, the information is less stale.

Forecasts.   We can use a forecast for our denominator instead of the most recent historical result (assuming forecasts are available); in fact, using forecasts instead of the most recently observed value can have two potential advantages. First, forecasts might represent a better base with which to capture the long-run growth rates, for they are less likely to contain transitory or one-time effects. Second, market prices are based on expectations of the future, so it is natural to use forecasted-cash-flow- or earnings-based denominators of a market multiple. Like many things we have discussed, there are trade-offs to consider in using analyst forecasts. One problem with using financial analyst forecasts is that analysts do not always provide forecasts for the denominator we are interested in using. While most analysts forecast earnings per share, not all analysts make public their forecasts of revenues, EBIT, or EBITDA. Another problem is that analysts may not provide sufficient information on their forecasts to make some of the adjustments we describe in this chapter (for things such as minority interests, unconsolidated affiliates, excess assets, etc.).

As such, the most recently observed value might be better to use than one that is forecasted. As a result, we often have no clear choice as to whether we want to use the most recent actual value or a forecast. Limited empirical research suggests that, on average, using forecasts is better than using historic information, but we cannot generalize these results for all situations; this is especially true since the empirical evidence is not based on all of the adjustments we discuss in this chapter, which are more likely to improve multiples based on historical financial results than on forecasts.[3] This is undoubtedly why we observe analysts and others using a combination of multiples based on both historical results and forecasts.

Alternative forecast measures include using a six-month forecast (in conjunction with the most recent six months of actual results), a forecast of the next fiscal year, and a forecast for two or more fiscal years out. The next-fiscal-year forecast is only a complete one-year forecast at the beginning of a company's fiscal year. As a company's fiscal year progresses, the next-fiscal-year forecast becomes a combination of actual results reported for the year to date and the forecast for the remainder of the fiscal year (as analysts update their forecasts periodically during the year, often after quarterly results are released). Forecasts for two or more fiscal years out contain only forecast data.

Sources for forecasts include individual financial analyst reports or the consensus of many financial analysts' forecasts from companies such as I/B/E/S (Institutional Brokers Estimate Service), First Call, and Zach's Investment Research. I/B/E/S and First Call are owned by Thomson Reuters Corporation.

Valuation Key 14.1

For market multiples based on a stock (balance sheet) variable in the denominator, we usually rely on the fiscal period (year or quarter) that is closest to the valuation date. For market multiples based on a flow (income or cash flow statement) variable—variables such as sales, earnings, EBIT, and EBITDA— we typically choose from alternatives that include the last fiscal year, the last twelve months (or trailing twelve months), a combination of six months of historical results and six months of forecast results, the next-fiscal-year forecast, or the forecast for the fiscal year two or more years out.

---

[3] See, Liu, J., D. Nissim, and J. Thomas, "Equity Valuation Using Multiples," *Journal of Accounting Research* 40 (2002), pp. 135–172, who examine this and other issues for a large sample of companies; and, Kim, M., and J. Ritter, "Valuing IPOs," *Journal of Financial Economics* 53 (1999), pp. 409–437, who examine this and other issues for a sample of initial public offerings (IPOs).

Partial Fiscal Periods. Companies can report a partial fiscal period (part of a year or quarter) for several reasons. One reason is a change in the company's fiscal year-end. Companies do not change their fiscal year-end very often, but if a company changes its fiscal year-end, it will report a partial period (year or quarter) for one of its financial statements. We do not have an exact way to adjust for a partial period financial statement. We can extrapolate the missing part of the period from the following period, but this approach is not exact, especially with seasonal businesses.

Companies that come out of bankruptcy (or a reorganization) typically report a partial fiscal period for the part of the fiscal year or quarter prior to the date they come out of bankruptcy as well as for the period after they come out of bankruptcy. Again, the partial year limits our ability to calculate the market multiple denominators. A slightly different and less important issue occurs when a company uses a specified point in a year—for example, the last Saturday of August—rather than a fixed date. Fiscal years determined on this basis will not have the same number of days each year.

Valuation in Practice 14.1

UAL Corporation (United Airlines) Emergence from Bankruptcy UAL Corporation (United Airlines) reported a partial fiscal period for the first quarter of 2006 and the 2006 fiscal year. It came out of bankruptcy on February 1, 2006, and reported the month of January 2006 separately from its first quarter, making the first quarter only 2 months and the 2006 fiscal year only 11 months.

> In connection with its emergence from Chapter 11 bankruptcy protection, the Company adopted fresh-start reporting in accordance with SOP 90-7 and in conformity with accounting principles generally accepted in the United States of America ("GAAP"). As a result of the adoption of fresh-start reporting, the financial statements prior to February 1, 2006 are not comparable with the financial statements after February 1, 2006. References to "Successor Company" refer to UAL on or after February 1, 2006, after giving effect to the adoption of fresh-start reporting. References to "Predecessor Company" refer to UAL prior to February 1, 2006.

Source: United Airlines, Inc. 2006 10-K report, Item 6—Selected Financial Data.

14.2 MEASURING MARKET MULTIPLE "NUMERATORS"

LO2 Measure market multiple numerators

Measuring the numerator is usually less complex than addressing the other issues involved in using the market multiple valuation method. Although it is usually easier to measure, it still requires us to make several calculations and address various measurement issues. The first issue is specifying the concept of value we are measuring. The second issue is timing; for a given valuation date, we must decide on what date (or dates) to measure the market value of the comparable companies. The third issue, or series of issues, is measuring the components of the value of the firm. A fourth issue is knowing what adjustments need to be made to the numerator in order to maintain consistency between the numerator and denominator.

Value of the Firm's Operations and Enterprise Value as Alternative Numerators

Recall that the value of the firm is equal to the sum of the value of each of a company's securities (common equity, preferred equity, debt, options, and so forth), including off-balance-sheet financing but excluding current operating liabilities. We typically exclude excess or non-operating assets from our analysis and adjust the market multiple valuation separately for these assets. Thus, we adjust firm value by deducting the value of excess assets and any value that results from expected short-term, non-recurring events. For example, if a company announces that it is going to sell off one of its non-performing businesses, we would exclude the value of that business that is embedded in the value of the firm. The resulting calculation is the value of the firm's ongoing operations plus any value from financing. We make corresponding adjustments to the denominator to expunge any effect resulting from the business being sold.

However, since many companies hold excess cash, and since excess cash is not reported separately by the company, it is common to extract all cash from the company's value when calculating multiples. This is what investment bankers refer to as enterprise value, which they usually use as the numerator of many market multiples instead of firm value. For a company with no excess assets, the difference between the value of the firm and its enterprise value is required cash. Using enterprise value implicitly assumes that the company has no required cash or, alternatively, that all of the companies used in the analysis have the same relative cash requirements (that is, relative to enterprise value). Since enterprise value is the more common concept used, we focus the remainder of our examples on measuring enterprise value. Investment bankers often discuss the concept of net debt, which is the firm's debt less the company's cash and marketable securities. Thus, we will hear investment bankers talk about measuring enterprise value by adding the value of the equity to the value of the net debt and the value of any other claims. This calculation is identical to our calculation of enterprise value, but we will not discuss the concept of net debt any further.

There are also multiple ways to measure the value of equity. One way to measure the value of the equity is to measure the total value of the equity or a company's market capitalization; thus, using this approach, we measure the value of the numerator and denominator using the total value of the equity and total earnings to equityholders. An alternative approach is to use the price per share and earnings per share of the equity. In the latter approach, we face the issue of knowing how to measure per share earnings. For example, companies report basic earnings per share and fully diluted earnings per share. Ideally, we want to subtract the value of excess cash from the value of the equity when we compute multiples, but again, since excess cash is not reported, it is often easier to subtract all of the cash and marketable securities from the value of the equity.[4] We discuss this in more detail later.

Relation Between the Valuation Date and the Measurement Date for Value (Numerator)

Given a valuation date, we must decide on a date to measure the value of the company's securities. One might consider using the most recent value of the firm (or equity) for the comparable companies or measuring the average value over the last month, quarter, or year. In general, unless we have a clear reason to do otherwise, we measure the value of the firm (or equity) for the comparable companies as of the date the company is being valued (valuation date) or as reasonably close to that date as possible. With very thinly traded stocks that are subject to large bid-ask spreads, it may be useful to use an average over several days or to take the average of the bid and the ask prices.

In general, we do not recommend using an average value that is computed over a long time period. It is particularly difficult to argue that a market multiple valuation should be based on average values that include data prior to a large change in market value. For example, if we were using market multiples to value firms in the technology sector after the large decline in the value of technology stocks in April of 2000, it would have been hard to argue that the pre-April 2000 market multiples were the relevant multiples to use to assess the current value in, say, June of 2000. Similarly, arguing that we should use values from July of 2008 to measure the value of a security after October of 2008 when the economy was in the throes of the credit crisis would have been equally problematic; the S&P 500 index fell from 1284.91 on July 1, 2008, to 848.92 on October 27, 2008, a decline of 33%.

While we do not generally recommend using an average value when using market multiples to estimate value as of the valuation date, we have a somewhat different view when market multiples are used to measure the continuing value (terminal value, residual value). It may be the case that an average of market multiples over a historical period is appropriate for measuring continuing value. For example, if we have a company in a cyclical industry, rather than choose a multiple at the peak or trough of the cycle, it is more sensible to calculate the average multiple over the cycle in order to measure continuing value. Thus, the multiple we choose to measure a company's continuing value can be quite different from the multiple we use to measure the same company's current value.

---

[4] We note that some valuation experts do not subtract out the value of the cash and marketable securities from the value of the equity in computing multiples where the numerator is the value of the equity.

Measuring the Value of the Common Equity Shares

Measuring the value of the common equity shares at a point in time for a publicly traded comparable company is one of the easier calculations we can perform. To measure the value of the equity, we typically multiply the number of **shares outstanding** by the market price per share. It is incorrect to use the number of **shares issued** instead of the number of shares outstanding, because the number of shares issued includes shares that the company originally issued but later bought back to be held as **treasury stock** or **treasury shares**. Companies often hold treasury shares for employee or shareholder stock purchase plans and employee equity-based compensation, such as employee stock options. A company typically reports the number of shares issued, the number of treasury shares, and the number of shares outstanding in its financial statements. Sometimes companies issue more than one type (class) of common equity. In such cases, we calculate the value of each class of equity and add these values together to measure the value of the equity.

Since most companies issue their financial statements quarterly (at least in the United States), we do not know the exact number of shares outstanding between the quarterly financial statements. In both a company's 10-K and 10-Q filings with the U.S. SEC, we can obtain the number of shares outstanding on two dates—a date close to the date on which the company filed its report with the U.S. SEC and the date of the fiscal period end. By researching a company's website for public announcements, we can typically identify large issuances and repurchases of stock and adjust the shares outstanding accordingly when necessary.

Measuring the Value of Debt and Preferred Stock

We measure the value of the debt and preferred stock based on the market value of these claims as of the date we are measuring the market multiples. If these claims are publicly traded, we can observe their values. If such securities are not publicly traded, we have to review the company's financial statements for useful information and possibly value the securities ourselves. Fortunately, companies must provide an assessment of the "fair" value of their financial instruments in their 10-Ks, which includes most types of debt but does not include preferred stock. Thus, when confronted with this issue, the starting point is analyzing the company's 10-K and 10-Q filings. We also discussed a variety of techniques for valuing debt and preferred stock in Chapter 9.

Once we have reasonable values for a subset of the debt and preferred stock securities, we can sometimes use these values as the basis for valuing other securities while making adjustments for differences in the contracts, time to maturity, and so forth. For example, if a firm has some publicly traded debt with observable prices and yields, we can use this information to help us value the non-publicly traded claims.

We can also use a company's book values to value securities that were issued recently, making adjustments for changes in the economic conditions underlying the securities' value. Thus, we can use the book value of these securities as a proxy for the market value of these claims if market conditions and the company's financial situation did not change substantially since the date the claims were issued. On the other hand, if market conditions or the company's financial situation have changed substantially since the date the securities were issued, we cannot rely on book values.

Measuring the Value of Stock Options and Other Equity-Based Securities

Companies can have a variety of equity-based securities that may or may not be publicly traded. The most common examples of such securities are employee stock options and stock appreciation rights. Companies can also attach an option feature to other securities, such as convertible preferred stock or convertible debt. Such option features may be linked to the security for its entire term to maturity or may detach (become separate securities) after the company issues it. For example, a company may issue a bond with an attached warrant (option), and depending on the contract, the warrant may or may not be detachable after the investor purchases the security. Finally, companies also issue equity-based securities to raise capital (warrants). We discussed the valuation of convertible securities and warrants in Chapter 12.

As discussed in Chapter 12, we can estimate the value of stock options and other equity-based securities using an option pricing model. It is common for companies to use option pricing models such as the Black-Scholes Option Pricing Model in order to value employee stock options and related securities.

It is not uncommon for market multiple valuations to exclude the value of stock options and other equity-based securities. For example, one might calculate the enterprise value of a company by summing the value of the common equity, preferred equity, and debt and ignoring the value of stock options and other equity-based securities. The underlying assumption in such valuations is that the relative value of the stock options and other equity-based securities is the same for the comparable companies as the company we are valuing. Thus, when we use this approach to measure the enterprise value of a company, the enterprise value will not include the value of these other securities. To measure the value of the equity of the company, we do not subtract the value of the stock options and other equity-based securities from the market-multiple-based enterprise value that excluded the value of these securities. However, before choosing to exclude the value of stock options and other equity-based securities in measuring market multiples, we must check the underlying assumption that the relative values of these claims are similar for the company being valued and the comparable companies. That, of course, means we need to make some valuation assessments of these claims.

Measuring the Value of Other Securities and Off-Balance-Sheet Financing

Companies issue securities other than equity, debt, preferred stock, and stock options. The list of other securities a company may offer is quite long; the key is to identify the existence of these securities—typically through an examination of the company's financial statements and filings with the government—and measure their value. Companies sometimes issue claims that are not reported on their financial statements; we call these claims **off-balance-sheet claims**. A careful review of the company's financial statement footnotes—in particular, footnotes about leases, commitments, related transactions, and contingencies—often provides useful information on these claims.

Adjustments to the Numerator as a Result of Adjustments to the Denominator

We want to measure the denominators of market multiples in a manner that we think best reflects the long-run performance of the comparable companies and the firm being valued. Because of this, we often make adjustments to the denominator, such as extracting the effects of excess assets. Any time we adjust the denominator to exclude the effects of a portion of earnings or cash flows for the effect of an asset or liability, we will often have to adjust the numerator for that same effect. For example, if we exclude the effects of an excess asset from the denominator, we must also subtract the value of the excess asset from the numerator. An example of when we would add value to the numerator is when we capitalize operating leases. If we are capitalizing operating leases, we make the adjustments to the income statement and balance sheet when we measure the denominator, and, similarly, we add the value of the operating leases that we capitalized to the numerator. We discussed the capitalization of operating leases in Chapter 11, and we illustrate the concept later in this chapter in the context of market multiples.

Valuation Key 14.2

We measure the enterprise value for each comparable company by summing the values of each comparable company's securities and subtracting the respective cash and marketable securities. We identify a company's issued securities by examining its financial statements and other filings with the government and by researching the company in both the financial press and analyst reports. We measure the value of a company's securities in a variety of ways; sometimes we can use quoted values, sometimes we can use the company's fair value disclosure, and sometimes we must conduct our own valuation (and in some circumstances, we may be able to use book values for debt and preferred stock).

14.3 THE UNIVERSAL CORPORATION—PART 1— MEASURING ENTERPRISE AND EQUITY VALUE

We use the Universal Corporation (Universal)[5] to illustrate the calculation of the inputs for various market multiples. In Exhibit 14.1, we show Universal's income statements and balance sheets for its 2006 and 2007 fiscal years based on its reported financial statements.

EXHIBIT 14.1 Universal Corporation—Summarized Income Statements and Balance Sheets

Income Statement ($ in thousands, as of March 31)	2006	2007
Revenues	$1,781,312	$2,007,272
Operating expenses	–1,664,585	–1,812,791
Restructuring and impairment costs	–57,463	–30,890
Operating income	$ 59,264	$ 163,591
Equity in pretax earnings of unconsolidated affiliates	14,140	14,235
Interest income	2,056	10,845
Interest expense	–60,787	–53,794
Income before income taxes and other items	$ 14,673	$ 134,877
Provision for income taxes	–21,933	–61,126
Minority interest (net of tax)	4,287	6,660
Income (loss) from continuing operations	$ –2,973	$ 80,411
Income (loss) from discontinued operations (net of tax)	10,913	–36,059
Net income	$ 7,940	$ 44,352
Dividends on preferred stock		–14,685
Earnings available to common shareholders	$ 7,940	$ 29,667
Weighted average shares outstanding—basic	25,707.0	25,935.0
Weighted average shares outstanding—fully diluted	25,707.0	26,051.0
Earnings per share—basic	$ 0.309	$ 1.144
Earnings per share—fully diluted	$ 0.309	$ 1.139
Excess cash	$ 0	$ 287,750
Interest income on excess cash (pre-tax)	$ 0	$ 8,789

Balance Sheet ($ in thousands, as of March 31)	2006	2007
Assets		
Cash and equivalents	$ 62,486	$ 358,236
Current operating assets	1,134,666	1,144,692
Current assets of discontinued operations	609,028	42,437
Total current assets	$1,806,180	$1,545,365
Property, plant, and equipment, net	411,457	360,158
Other non-current assets	579,039	318,983
Investments in unconsolidated affiliates	95,988	104,316
Total assets	$2,892,664	$2,328,822
Liabilities and Shareholders' Equity		
Current operating liabilities	$ 316,464	$ 384,501
Short-term debt	318,710	131,159
Current portion of long-term debt	8,537	164,000
Current liabilities of discontinued operations	285,418	13,314
Total current liabilities	$ 929,129	$ 692,974
Long-term debt	762,201	398,952
Other long-term liabilities	218,664	200,341
Total liabilities	$1,909,994	$1,292,267
Minority interest	$ 17,799	$ 5,822
Series B 6.75% convertible perpetual preferred stock[1]	$ 193,546	$ 213,024
Common stock, no par value[2]	120,618	176,453
Retained earnings	697,987	682,232
Accumulated other comprehensive loss	–47,280	–40,976
Total shareholders' equity	$ 964,871	$1,030,733
Total liabilities and shareholders' equity	$2,892,664	$2,328,822

[1] Series B 6.75% Convertible Perpetual Preferred Stock, no par value, 5,000,000 shares authorized, 220,000 shares issued and outstanding (200,000 at March 31, 2006).

[2] Common Stock, no par value, 100,000,000 shares authorized, 26,948,599 shares issued and outstanding (25,748,306 at March 31, 2006).
 On the first page of the 10-K report, Universal states, "As of May 25, 2007, the total number of shares of common stock outstanding was 27,026,971."

Using Universal, we illustrate the calculation of the following multiples. For enterprise-value-based multiples, we measure the unlevered earnings, EBIT, EBITDA, and revenue multiples. For equity-based multiples, we measure the net income (P/E) multiple. In order to reduce the complexity of the calculations, we do not illustrate the kinds of adjustments required for either free cash flow multiples or for balance-sheet-based multiples in detail, but the concepts are similar to the adjustments we discuss for the more common earnings-based multiples.

Our goal is to measure various market multiples for Universal as of June 1, 2007, in order to measure the value of W. K. Cheng, a privately held company, as of that date, as we concluded that Universal is a good comparable company for this purpose. Very often, we use forecasts or a combination of historic results and forecasts, but here, we focus our analysis on the most recent fiscal year, which is the year

---

[5] Universal Corporation purchases, processes, and sells leaf tobacco to global tobacco product manufacturers. It was founded in 1888 and is headquartered in Richmond, Virginia.

ending on March 31, 2007. Thus, our market multiple valuation date is two months after the company's most recent fiscal year-end and two days after it filed its 10-K report with the U.S. SEC. We use the information in Exhibit 14.1 as well as supplemental information from Universal's 10-K and market data in order to measure the value of the firm and equity in the following parts of this section.

Total Cash (and Cash Equivalents)

Universal's cash balance in 2006 of $62.5 million was its required cash in 2006, and its required cash increased by $8 million in 2007 (approximately by the percentage increase in its revenue); thus, Universal has about $287.8 million in excess cash ($287.75 = $358.24 − $62.49 − $8.00). We assume the interest income in 2006 of $2.1 million was recurring income from required cash, but the $8.8 million of additional interest income in 2007 resulted from Universal's excess cash.

Value of Universal's Securities

In this section, we value Universal's securities to measure the enterprise value, and the value of its equity. We begin by valuing the equity before valuing the debt and preferred shares. Universal also has employee stock options and restricted stock, which we also value.

Value of the Common Equity Shares.   Universal does not have any treasury shares. From Exhibit 14.1, we see that it had 26.949 million shares issued and outstanding on March 31, 2007—its fiscal year-end. Companies always present this information on the balance sheet and in footnotes. Since we are measuring Universal's multiples as of June 1, 2007, we want to use the number of shares outstanding on that date. We can get close to that date from the supplemental information in Exhibit 14.1, which indicates that its shares outstanding were equal to 27.027 million as of May 25, 2007. Universal's stock price was equal to $64.78 per share on June 1, 2007; thus the value of its common equity shares was equal to its share price of $64.78, multiplied by the number of shares outstanding of 27,026,971, which equals $1.75 billion.

Universal—Value of Debt.   Universal had both short-term and long-term debt outstanding in 2007. From Exhibit 14.2, which contains excerpts from Note 8 in its 10-K filing, we see that Universal had various medium-term notes outstanding (maturing from 2007 through 2013). The book value of these notes was $563.0 million, $164 million of which was due within the next year. Universal assessed the value of this debt to be $550 million as of March 31, 2007. Interest rates did not change between that date and June 1; thus, we use $550 million as the value of Universal's long-term debt. Universal also had short-term notes of $131.2 million in addition to its long-term debt (see current liabilities in Exhibit 14.1).

EXHIBIT 14.2	Universal Corporation—Excerpts from Note 8—Long-Term Obligations		
Long-term obligations consist of the following: ($ in thousands)		**2006**	**2007**
Notes			
Medium-term notes due from 2007 to 2013 at various rates.		$570,602	$562,952
Private placement notes, due May 2008, at LIBOR + 1.25%, repaid November 2006. . . .		200,000	0
Other.		136	0
		$770,738	$562,952
Less current portion		−8,537	−164,000
Long-term obligations		$762,201	$398,952

Notes:

The Company has $563 million in medium-term notes outstanding. These notes mature at various dates from September 2007 to October 2013 and were all issued with fixed interest rates. At March 31, 2007, interest rates on the notes ranged from 5.00% to 8.50%.

Other Information:

The fair value of the Company's long-term obligations, including the current portion, was approximately $550 million at March 31, 2007, and $752 million at March 31, 2006.

Universal—Value of Convertible Preferred Stock.

Universal had one type of preferred stock outstanding that was issued at the end of its 2006 fiscal year and the beginning of its 2007 fiscal year (March and April 2006). Universal described the key characteristics of this security as follows (see note 11 in its 10-K filing):

> The Company is also authorized to issue up to 5,000,000 shares of preferred stock. In March and April 2006, 220,000 shares of Series B 6.75% Convertible Perpetual Preferred Stock (the "Preferred Stock" or "Preferred Shares") were issued under this authorization. The Preferred Stock has a liquidation preference of $1,000 per share and generated approximately $213 million in net cash proceeds, which were used to reduce short-term debt. Holders of the Preferred Shares are entitled to receive quarterly dividends at the rate of 6.75% per annum . . .
>
> The Preferred Shares are convertible, at the option of the holder, at any time into shares of the Company's common stock at a conversion rate that is adjusted each time the Company pays a dividend on its common stock that exceeds $0.43 per share. The conversion rate at March 31, 2007 was 21.40442 shares of common stock per preferred share, which represents a conversion price of approximately $46.72 per common share . . .
>
> During the period from March 15, 2013 to March 15, 2018, the Company may, at its option, convert the Preferred Shares into shares of common stock at the prevailing conversion rate. . . . On or after March 15, 2018, the Company may, at its option, redeem all or part of the outstanding Preferred Shares for cash at the $1,000 per share liquidation preference.

We can quickly conclude from reading the above summary of the terms of the preferred stock contract that valuing this preferred stock is complex (we discussed valuing convertible securities in Chapter 12).[6] This preferred stock is convertible, with a conversion price that depends on the magnitude of the quarterly common dividend declared. The company can also force conversion between 2013 and 2018 under certain circumstances, and the company can call (redeem) the preferred stock for $1,000 per share after 2018. While valuing this security is complex, in this case, we can make certain assumptions to reasonably estimate its value by using a less complex approach than we illustrated in Chapter 12. Since the company issued these securities fairly recently, we first analyze the issuance price. We can calculate the issuance price (net of issuance costs) by using the change in the value on the balance sheet and the change in the number of shares outstanding, which we show in Exhibit 14.3.

EXHIBIT 14.3	Universal Corporation—Issuance Price of Preferred Stock (net of issuance costs)				
Series B 6.75% Convertible Perpetual Preferred Stock	**Units**	**Total Value ($ in thousands)**	**Per Unit Value**	**Average Common Stock Price in Month Issued**	**Average Rate on 30-Year Government Bond**
Issuance in March 2006.	200,000	$193,546	$967.73	$37.66	4.72%
Issuance in April 2006	20,000	19,478	$973.90	$37.12	5.06%
Balance as of March 31, 2007	220,000	$213,024	$968.29		

	Dividend Rate	**Total**	**$ Estimation Error**	**% Estimation Error**
Preferred stock dividends—from 10-K.		$14,685		
Preferred stock dividends—calculated	6.75%	$14,850	$165.0	1.12%

Universal issued 200,000 shares of preferred stock in March 2006 for $193.5 million and 20,000 shares of preferred stock in April 2006 for $19.5 million (net of issuance costs). The prices for these securities at the date of issue were $967.73 and $973.90, respectively. We can also look up the issuance price from the financial press or, as we did in this case, from the face page of the prospectus for this offering (Form 424 filed with the U.S. SEC on March 17, 2006). From Form 424, we know that the company issued the securities at about $1,000 per share:

---

[6] For a discussion of alternative ways to value convertible preferred stock, see Ramanlal, P., S. Mann, and W. Moore, "Convertible Preferred Stock Valuation: Tests of Alternative Models," *Review of Quantitative Finance and Accounting* 10 (1998), pp. 303–319.

	Per Share	Total
Public offering price	$1,000	$200,000,000
Underwriting discounts and commissions	$ 30	$ 6,000,000
Proceeds, before expenses, to Universal Corporation	$ 970	$194,000,000

We have granted the underwriters a 30-day option to purchase up to 20,000 additional shares of preferred stock solely to cover over-allotments.

We now have to decide whether these prices are reasonable to use as the value of these securities on June 1, 2007. We know that certain factors will affect the value of this security, including the interest rate in the economy, the risk underlying the company's cash flows, the company's quarterly dividend on its common shares, and (since the preferred shares are convertible) the common share price. Interest rates did not change between the issuance dates and June 1, 2007; the long-term government bond rate was in the 4.8% to 5% range between the issuance dates and June 1. We will also assume that the underlying risk of the company did not change during this period. During this period, the company increased its quarterly common dividend from about $0.41 per common share to $0.43 per share. Most important, Universal's stock price increased from the $37 to $38 range at the end of its 2007 fiscal year to $64.78 on June 1. The change in the company's stock price results in a substantial increase in the values of the common equity and the preferred.

On March 31, 2007, the conversion price was $46.72 ($46.72 = $1000/21.40442), and the stock price was in the $37 to $38 range. The convertible feature of the preferred shares was "out-of-the-money" by about $8.72 ($8.72 = $46.72 − $38.00). On June 1, however, the convertible feature of the preferred shares was "in-the-money" by about $18 ($18.06 = $64.78 − $46.72), which increased the value of the preferred stock. We can use this and other information to calculate a simple valuation of Universal's convertible preferred stock. To use this approach, we assume that the company will force conversion of the preferred stock in 2013 and that the company's equity cost of capital is 15%. We assume that the company will force conversion since the company knows that all convertible preferred shareholders will convert to common shares before March 15, 2018, when the company can redeem the preferred because the convertible feature is so in-the-money. Thus, the company will force conversion as soon as it can, March 15, 2013, so that it does not have to pay the preferred dividends. We show this valuation in Exhibit 14.4.

EXHIBIT 14.4   Universal Corporation—Simple Valuation of Convertible Preferred Stock

Series B 6.75% Convertible Perpetual Preferred Stock ($ in thousands)

Conversion factor per preferred share	21.40442
Number of preferred shares	220,000
Common shares if converted	4,708,972
Stock price (ignoring dilution) on June 1, 2007	$ 64.780
Value if converted on June 1, 2007	$ 305,047
Liquidation value (issuance price) of preferred stock	$ 220,000
Preferred stock dividend rate	6.75%
Annual preferred dividends	$ 14,850
Common shares if converted	4,708,972
Current common dividend per share (DPS) and yield	$ 1.740
Total common dividends if converted	$ 8,194
Excess preferred dividends annually	$ 6,656
Present value of excess preferred dividends at 15% (equity cost of capital); assumming actual conversion in 2013, 6 years	$ 25,191
Value if converted on June 1, 2007	305,047
Total estimated value	$ 330,238

Based on these assumptions, we value the preferred shares as the sum of the value of the shares (if converted into common shares on June 1) and the present value of the excess dividends received by the preferred shares between 2007 and 2013 (the assumed forced conversion date). The number of converted shares is equal to the conversion factor (21.40442) multiplied by the number of preferred shares (220,000). We multiply the number of common shares (if converted) by the June 1 stock price ($64.78) to measure the value of the preferred shares (if converted on June 1) of $305 million. In addition, we know that the preferred shares receive a higher dividend than the common shares; the preferred shares have a 6.75% dividend yield and the common shares have a 2.69% (.0269 = $1.74 dividend per share/$64.78 share price) dividend yield. The total dividend on the preferred shares is $14.9 million ($14.9 = $220 × 0.0675), whereas the total dividend on the common shares resulting from a conversion is $8.2 million ($8.2 = 4.709 × $1.74 annual dividend in 2007). The difference in the dividends is $6.7 million per year. Using a discount rate of 15%, the present value of that difference over six years is $25.2 million. Thus, the value of the preferred shares is $330.2 million. This valuation will be a little lower than the actual valuation, for we did not include the value of the option. However, since this option is well into-the-money, we know the difference will not be large (see Chapter 12).

Universal—Value of Stock Options and Other Equity-Based Securities.

Other than its convertible preferred stock, Universal has no equity-based securities that are issued to non-employees. However, it grants several types of equity-based securities to its employees—stock options, stock appreciation rights (SARs), restricted stock units (RSUs), and restricted stock. We previously indicated that under certain conditions it may be acceptable to exclude the value of these securities, but we will include their value to illustrate the valuation. The company uses the Black-Scholes Option Pricing Model to value its stock options and stock appreciation rights at the grant date. For options granted in 2007, the company made the following assumptions (excerpts as taken from Note 12, executive compensation plans and stock-based compensation):

The grant date fair value of the SARs awarded in fiscal year 2007 and stock options awarded in fiscal years 2006 and 2005 was estimated using the Black-Scholes pricing model and the following assumptions:

Expected term	6.00 years
Expected volatility	31.60%
Expected dividend yield.	4.77%
Risk-free interest rate.	4.67%
Resulting fair value of SARs and stock options granted	$8.11

The expected term was based on the company's historical stock option exercise data for instruments with comparable features and economic characteristics. The expected volatility was estimated based on historical volatility of the Company's common stock using weekly closing prices. The expected dividend yield was based on the annualized quarterly dividend rate and the market price of the common stock at grant date. The risk-free interest rate was based on the U.S. Treasury yield curve in effect at the grant date for securities with a remaining term equal to the expected term of the SARs or stock options.

The fair value of the RSUs and restricted stock was based on the market price of the common stock on the grant date.

We summarize certain characteristics of these securities in Exhibit 14.5 (using excerpts from Note 12). In 2005, the company stopped granting stock options and began granting stock appreciation rights that had the same terms as the stock options. The company combined the information for these two securities.

For the purposes of this example, we use the Daves and Ehrhardt (2007) option-based warrant pricing model (see Chapter 12) to value Universal's stock options and stock appreciation rights, updating the inputs in the model to the values as of June 1, 2007. We use Universal's stock price of $64.78 as of June 1. We recalculate the continuously compounded annual dividend yield using the June 1 stock price, and we update the risk-free rate to 4.88%, which is the rate in effect on June 1. We increase the expected volatility of the stock to 32.1% based on updated information. We show these assumptions and the resulting Daves and Ehrhardt valuation of $27.4 million for the stock options and stock appreciation rights in Exhibit 14.6. We value the restricted stock units and the restricted stock using the stock price on June 1, which results in a value of $10.5 million. The total valuation of all of the stock options and other equity-based securities is $38 million ($37,967 = $27,428 + $10,539).

EXHIBIT 14.5	Universal Corporation—Summary of Stock Options and Other Equity-Based Securities

	Options and SARs		Restricted Stock Units		Restricted Stock	
Options and Stock Appreciation Rights (SARs), Restricted Stock Units (RSUs), and Restricted Stock, as of March 31, 2007	**Shares**	**Weighted Average Exercise Price**	**Shares**	**Weighted Average Exercise Price**	**Shares**	**Weighted Average Exercise Price**
Outstanding at beginning of year.............	2,011,782	$43.34	67,915	$46.21	28,900	$38.16
Granted	265,500	$36.03	71,909	$36.57	10,000	$35.26
Exercised (options and SARs) –						
vested (RSUs)........................	−1,232,967	$43.81	−7,503	$46.00		
Cancelled/expired	−17,000	$38.94				
Forfeited.............................	−69,500	$38.21	−8,530	$41.20		
Outstanding at end of year................	957,815	$41.16	123,791	$40.96	38,900	$37.42

	Exercise Price Range			
Options and Stock Appreciation Rights (SARs), as of March 31	**$20-$30**	**$30-$40**	**$40-$50**	**Total**
Number outstanding........................	26,217	465,470	466,128	957,815
Weighted average remaining contractual life....	2.81	6.83	6.82	6.72
Weighted average exercise price, per share	$25.09	$ 36.49	$ 46.72	$ 41.16
Intrinsic value (stock price − exercise price)	$ 951	$ 11,573	$ 6,818	$ 19,342

EXHIBIT 14.6	Universal Corporation—Valuation of Stock Options and Other Equity-Based Securities

	Exercise Price Range			Options and SARs Total	Restricted Stock Units and Stock
Options and Stock Appreciation Rights (SARs), Restricted Stock Units (RSUs), and Restricted Stock, as of June 1, 2007 ($ in thousands)	**$20-$30**	**$30-$40**	**$40-$50**		
Number outstanding......................	26,217	465,470	466,128	957,815	162,691
Resulting fair value of SARs and stock options per security				$ 28.64	$ 64.780
Total value of SARs and stock options........................				$27,428.0	$10,539.1
Total value of options, SARs, RSUs, and restricted stock, as of June 1, 2007				$37,967	

Enterprise Value and Value of the Common Equity. In Exhibit 14.7, we combine the previous calculations to measure both Universal's enterprise value and the value of the common equity as of June 1, 2007. Recall that we are going to deduct the value of Universal's cash ($358.2 million) in order to measure both the enterprise value and the value of the common equity. To measure Universal's enterprise value, we take the sum of the value of the debt ($681.2 million), the value of the preferred ($330.2 million), the value of all stock-based compensation granted ($38.0 million), and the value of the common equity claims ($1,750.8 million) before subtracting cash ($358.2 million). The resulting enterprise value is equal to $2.44 billion.

EXHIBIT 14.7	Universal Corporation—Value of the Firm, Enterprise Value, and Value of the Common Equity				
($ in thousands)		Units	Unit Price	Enterprise Value	Equity
Short-term debt				$ 131,159	
Long-term debt (including current portion)				550,000	
Total debt				$ 681,159	
Series B 6.75% convertible perpetual preferred stock		220,000		330,238	$ 330,238
Options and stock appreciation rights (SARs), restricted stock units (RSUs), and restricted stock, as of June 1, 2007				37,967	37,967
Value of common stock		27,026,971	$64.78	1,750,807	1,750,807
Cash and marketable securities.				−358,236	−358,236
Value (without cash)				$2,441,935	$1,760,776

In order to avoid having to identify what part of total cash is required cash and what part is excess cash, we subtract the total cash from the value of the equity in order to calculate the multiples. This is analogous to the enterprise value calculation. Removing all cash is a simplification to avoid having to estimate required cash for all of the comparable companies. The assumption underpinning the removal of total cash is that required cash is proportional to equity value. Excluding excess cash is important because the equity-based multiple should be measured for the company's operations and not include the multiple implicit in excess cash (essentially excess cash divided by the interest on the excess cash—we discuss this issue in more detail later when we discuss the denominator adjustment).

Another issue that makes measuring the value of the common equity less straightforward than measuring the enterprise value is that other securities may have equity value embedded in them. The equity component of these securities should be considered when measuring equity-based market multiples. Examples of such securities are convertible preferred stock, convertible debt, warrants, and stock-based compensation. For Universal, it is relatively clear how the convertible preferred stock and stock-based compensation should be treated, for these securities are so far "in-the-money" that they are essentially equivalent to equity because of their claim on part of the company's earnings. Thus, for Universal, we value the common equity by including the value of the convertible preferred ($330.2 million), the value of the stock-based compensation ($38 million), and the value of the common shares ($1,750.8 million) for a total equity value of $2,119 million (before removing the value of the cash and marketable securities). This treatment may not be as clear in other situations when the option component of the securities is not so far "in-the-money."

Since we assume for Universal that the convertible preferred stock is equivalent to common equity, we add back the preferred stock dividends that were originally deducted from the income statement when we calculate the relevant earnings to be allocated among these claimants. An alternative is to exclude this value from the numerator, but we would then need to remove the claim that the equity component of these securities has on the company's earnings. If such an adjustment is practicable, we can use the value of the common shares and divide it by the earnings that remain for the common shareholders after the claims of the other securities are deducted from the earnings of the company. Given that we have no easy way to do this in Universal's case, we define common equity so that it includes both stock-based compensation and convertible preferred stock. However, if the convertible preferred stock is way "out-of-the-money" and if the option component has almost no value, a more appropriate approach is to exclude the convertible preferred from the calculation of the value of the equity and then to subtract the preferred dividends and use earnings available for common in the denominator.

REVIEW EXERCISE 14.1

Measuring Market Multiple Numerators

Below we present an income statement and balance sheet for the Multiple Company. The company's debt and preferred stock are recorded on the balance sheet at par value. The debt and preferred stock are currently trading at 102% and 98% of their respective par values. The company's debt has a 7% interest rate and the dividend yield for its preferred stock is 8%. The company has 10,000 shares of outstanding stock trading at $10 per share. The company also has 2,000 employee stock options outstanding, which the company valued at $2 per option. The company's income tax rate on all income is 40%. Calculate the company's enterprise value and equity value as discussed in the previous sections of this chapter. Without making any adjustments to the income statement, also calculate the company's unlevered earnings, EBIT, EBITDA, revenue, and P/E multiples. HINT: Measure the unlevered earnings as net income plus after-tax interest expense and measure EBIT as net income plus interest expense plus income tax expense. EBITDA is just EBIT plus depreciation and amortization.

Year 2			Year 1	Year 2
Revenue	$30,000	Cash	$12,000	$12,000
Operating expenses	–21,000	Other current assets	5,000	5,000
Depreciation expense	–8,000	Equity in unconsolidated affiliates	11,000	11,000
Operating earnings	$ 1,000	Property, plant, and equipment (net)	36,000	38,000
Earnings from unconsolidated affiliates	2,000	Total assets	$64,000	$66,000
Investment income (on cash)	600			
Interest expense	–840	Account payable	$ 3,000	$ 4,000
Income before taxes	$ 2,760	Debt	12,000	12,000
Income tax expense	–1,104	Total liabilities	$15,000	$16,000
Minority interest (net of tax)	–400	Minority interest	$ 5,000	$ 6,000
Net income	$ 1,256	Preferred stock	$ 5,000	$ 5,000
		Capital stock	3,000	3,000
		Retained earnings	36,000	36,000
		Shareholders' equity	$44,000	$44,000
		Liabilities and shareholders' equity	$64,000	$66,000

Solution on pages 593–594.

14.4 MEASURING MARKET MULTIPLE "DENOMINATORS"

Measuring the denominator is often much more complex than measuring the numerator. Here, we discuss the basic measurement of various denominators, adjustments for the effects of removing cash when measuring enterprise value, adjustments related to other excess assets, and adjustments for non-recurring items.

LO3 Measure market multiple denominators

Measuring the Denominators—Basic Calculations

In this section, we discuss how to measure denominators for various market multiples. The specific calculation depends on the specific circumstances of the company, but the basic underlying calculations are the same.

Unlevered Earnings-Based and Unlevered Cash-Flow-Based Denominators. We use unlevered earnings-based multiples to measure enterprise value. Earnings measures that are used with enterprise value numerators include unlevered earnings, EBIT, and EBITDA. We also sometimes use unlevered free cash flows in conjunction with enterprise value. To measure unlevered earnings, we begin with net income and add back after-tax interest expense, all of which are from the income statement. To measure EBIT, we begin with net income and add back interest expense and income taxes, all of which are again from the income statement. To measure EBITDA, we begin with EBIT and add back depreciation and amortization (from the cash flow statement). When we measure the denominator for an enterprise value multiple, we adjust the unlevered earnings for the after-tax income on all cash and marketable securities. For the EBIT and EBITDA multiples, we adjust out all of the interest income, but we do not take out the tax effect on the interest income, as these earnings measures exclude the effects of income taxes.

We can also use revenues to measure enterprise value. We usually use net revenues from the income statement for the denominator, and this does not require any adjustments for interest income from cash and marketable securities.

Earnings-Based and Equity-Free-Cash-Flow-Based Denominators.
We use earnings-based and equity-free-cash-flow-based multiples to measure equity value. The most commonly used multiple is based on earnings to common shareholders, often referred to as the P/E ratio.

Per Share Calculations.
Companies report two sets of earnings-per-share figures in the income statement—basic and fully diluted earnings per share. Regarding the denominators, the weighted average shares outstanding that is used in basic earnings per share assumes no dilution and is based on the actual weighted average number of shares outstanding during the year. The weighted average shares outstanding that is used in the fully diluted earnings-per-share calculation includes—based on accounting rules—the effects of the dilution of earnings as a result of outstanding securities that are convertible into common stock—such as employee stock options, convertible debt, and convertible preferred stock. It is always the case that fully diluted per share multiples are no smaller than basic per share multiples, because fully diluted earnings per share is no larger than basic earnings per share. For most companies, however, the difference between the fully diluted and basic number of shares is not large.

The total-equity-based multiples may not have the same values as per-share-based multiples, for they are often based on different numbers of shares. The total-equity-based multiples are usually based on the share price and shares outstanding at the valuation date and earnings or cash flows for the prior year, whereas per share multiples are based on the share price at the valuation date divided by the per share earnings, which are based on a weighted average number of shares outstanding. There is no definitive relation between the total-equity-based multiples and the share-based multiples. Rather, it depends on whether the company increases or decreases the number of shares outstanding over the year, and it depends on other adjustments that are made.

Naturally, since these alternatives may result in different answers, a question remains: Which alternative is best? In truth, all three alternatives provide a different perspective on value, and which alternative is best depends on the situation. Total-equity-value multiples implicitly use the actual number of shares outstanding at the valuation date even though they are not per share multiples. Of course, this is the correct value for the numerator, but it may not be the correct value for the denominator; for example, assume that a company with a December fiscal year-end issued a large number of shares on December 31 to acquire another company on that date. The equity value reflects the acquisition, but the earnings do not; thus, using a weighted average number of shares outstanding might be more appropriate here (unless we adjust the earnings for the acquisition, which we argue is the more appropriate adjustment to make).

Balance-Sheet-Based Denominators.
Valuation analysts use various balance-sheet-based denominators to measure enterprise value and common equity value. For enterprise value, they usually use total invested capital. Total invested capital is equal to the sum of the book values of debt, preferred stock, and common equity. For common equity values, they measure the book value of equity, and this is sometimes done on a per share basis. For denominators used in enterprise value and common equity value multiples, they subtract total cash and marketable securities from the total invested capital and book value of the equity.

Adjusting Market Multiple Inputs for Excess Assets

A company may own an asset that is neither necessary for the company's current operations nor for the execution of its strategy. We call such an asset an excess asset. Since comparable companies typically do not have the same excess assets, and since excess assets are not part of current operations or strategy, we remove the effects of excess assets from a market multiple's numerator and denominator. A common excess asset is excess cash and marketable securities, but companies can have a variety of other excess assets as well. For example, a company may decide that it no longer needs certain assets or parts of the company for its current operations and strategy. Such assets might even involve an entire division.

The value of a company's excess assets is embedded in its value (both the value of the firm and the value of its equity). The company's income statement and cash flow statement may or may not reflect the effect of its excess assets depending on whether those excess assets affect cash flows and income. Even if a company's financial statements reflect the effect of its excess assets, the relation between the value of these excess assets and their effect on the company's financial statements—in other words, the market multiple for the excess assets—is likely to be different from the market multiple for the company's operations (see Valuation in Practice 14.2). If we do not eliminate the effect of the excess assets on the comparable companies' numerators and denominators, we are either assuming that the effect is the same for all comparable companies and the company we are valuing or that the market multiple for the excess assets is the same as the market multiple for the companies' operations. Neither assumption is likely to be correct.

For example, assume a company owns unused land that it does not need for its business. Assume that the land has no effect on the company's income statement and that the company records the land on its balance sheet at its historic cost. Since the value of the company includes the market value of its excess assets, any earnings-based market multiple will be higher than an earnings-based market multiple of the same company without that excess asset. Balance-sheet-based multiples will be affected as well. Thus, unless the market multiple for the excess asset is the same as the market multiple for the company's operations, including excess assets in measuring a company's market multiples results in market multiples that do not properly reflect the market multiples for its operations.

In general, we adjust for most types of excess assets in the same way. For comparable companies, we eliminate the effect of a company's excess assets on the enterprise value of the firm (or equity) as well as the effect of excess assets on any denominator that we might be using. We then measure the comparable companies' market multiples using the adjusted numerators and denominators. When it comes to cash, because it is difficult to disentangle excess cash from required cash, we usually remove all of the cash when calculating enterprise value and common equity value and remove any interest income attributable to cash from the denominator.

Valuation in Practice 14.2

Microsoft's Market Multiples with and Without Its Excess "Cash" As of December 31, 2002, Microsoft Corporation (Microsoft) reported that it had about $38.6 billion in cash and short-term investments (cash). Its market capitalization (the value of its equity) on this date was about $268 billion. Microsoft had essentially no debt at this time, so the value of the firm was more or less equal to the value of its equity. Thus, about 14% of Microsoft's value was the value of its cash, most of which was not needed for its operations ($0.144 = \$38.6/\$268$). Its EBITDA for the last 12 months was $13.584 billion (excluding any interest income from the cash), and its interest income was $1.647 billion. If we include cash and interest income when we measure Microsoft's EBITDA multiple, it is 17.6 ($17.6 = \$268/(\$13.584 + \$1.647)$); however, if we exclude its cash and interest income, its EBITDA multiple is 16.9 ($16.9 = (\$268 - \$38.6)/\$13.584$)—about 4% lower.

If we want to use Microsoft as a comparable company, we want to eliminate the effect of its large cash holdings on the numerators and denominators of the multiples we calculate. If we do not adjust Microsoft's multiple for its large cash holdings, the resulting multiple will be too high (by about 4%), for the multiple of its cash and marketable securities relative to the income from cash and marketable securities of 23.4 ($23.4 = \$38.6/\$1.647$) is so high in relation to its EBITDA operating multiple of 16.9. Microsoft continued to accumulate cash for several more years, further exacerbating this issue.

Adjusting the Value of a Company with Excess Assets.

To value a company with excess assets, we remove all of the effects of excess assets on the numerator and denominator for all of the comparable companies, and we remove the effect of excess assets on the measured denominator of the company we are valuing. We then apply these multiples to the measured denominator of the company we are valuing in order to value the company without its excess assets. To measure the enterprise value of the company, we add the value of the company's excess assets (other than cash and marketable securities) to the value obtained from the multiple calculations. To value the firm, we add the value of all of the cash and marketable securities to the enterprise value.

Valuation Key 14.3

Adjusting market multiple inputs for excess assets requires that we remove the value of the excess assets from the numerators. For flow-based multiples, we must also remove the effect of the excess assets on the flow, appropriately adjusting for taxes where necessary. For balance-sheet-based multiples, we must remove the reported value of the excess assets from the balance sheet.

Adjusting Market Multiple Inputs for Non-Recurring Items

By definition, a one-time expense that results in a one-time negative effect on earnings or free cash flows has no effect on a company's future performance. Non-recurring items are similar, but not as exact as the pure one-time effect we just described. In general, we remove the effects of all non-recurring items on a market multiple's denominator, appropriately adjusting for taxes where necessary. Most often, non-recurring items do not cause us to adjust the numerators, as we normally would be measuring value subsequent to the disclosure of a non-recurring charge. As such, any impact on value will already be reflected in the values used to estimate the numerator of the multiples.

We discussed transitory shocks and non-recurring items in Chapter 13 at a conceptual level. If we have a large, negative non-recurring item, then the multiple is likely to be very large relative to the true underlying multiple we want to measure to capture a company's long-term future performance. The opposite is the case for a positive non-recurring item.

The first step is to try to identify non-recurring effects, but this is not always straightforward. We examine the income statement, footnotes, the management discussion and analysis (MD&A), conference call presentations, company press releases, and analysts' reports to try to uncover non-recurring effects. One problem with trying to identify non-recurring items is that there is no requirement to disclose them.

The second step is that once we identify something that we think might be non-recurring, we then must make a determination as to whether that is true or not. For example, we might think that a restructuring charge on a company's income statement is non-recurring, but this may or may not be the case. We make the non-recurring assessment by analyzing the company's historical performance; does it usually have some type of restructuring charge? We may determine that only part or none of the restructuring charge is non-recurring. Another example of a potential non-recurring item is the write-down of an asset or impairment cost. We might not always think of asset impairments as being non-recurring. For example, retail store chains and restaurants often write down the values of underperforming locations. A retail chain with continuing impairments is unlikely to be worth as much as a retail chain with almost no impairments. Continuing impairments may suggest deterioration in the business plan of the retailer and that future impairments may be expected.

Valuation Key 14.4

In general, adjusting market multiple inputs for non-recurring items does not require an adjustment to market multiple numerators. For flow-based denominators, we remove the effect of the non-recurring item on the flow and appropriately adjust for taxes where necessary. For balance-sheet-based multiples (such as total invested capital or the book value of shareholders' equity), no adjustment is normally made.

Adjusting the Value of a Company with Non-Recurring Items. To value a company with non-recurring items, we remove the effects of the non-recurring items on the comparable companies and the company we are valuing. We then apply the market multiples of the comparable companies to the adjusted measure of the denominator of the company we are valuing. Usually, no further adjustments are necessary.

Valuation in Practice 14.3

Coca-Cola Enterprises Inc.'s Write-Down of Its Franchise License Intangible Assets—A Non-Recurring Item In 2005, Coca-Cola Enterprises Inc. wrote down its franchise license intangible assets, which it described as follows:

We do not amortize our goodwill and franchise license intangible assets. Instead, we test these assets for impairment annually (as of the last fiscal day of October), or more frequently if events or changes in circumstances indicate they may be impaired. . . .

We performed our 2006 annual impairment tests of goodwill and franchise license intangible assets as of October 27, 2006. . . . The results of the impairment test of our North American franchise license intangible assets indicated that their estimated fair value was less than their carrying amount. As such, we recorded a $2.9 billion ($1.8 billion net of tax, or $3.80 per common share) non-cash impairment charge to reduce the carrying amount of these assets to their estimated fair value. . . .

($ in millions)	2004	2005	2006
Revenues	$18,190	$18,743	$19,804
Cost of sales	−10,771	−11,185	−11,986
Selling and administrative expenses	−5,983	−6,127	−6,391
Franchise impairment charge			−2,922
Operating (loss) income	$ 1,436	$ 1,431	$−1,495
Interest and other, net	−618	−641	−623
Income (loss) before income taxes	$ 818	$ 790	$−2,118
Income tax expense (benefit)	−222	−276	975
Net income (loss)	$ 596	$ 514	$−1,143

This write-down is a potential non-recurring item. The factors the company attributes to this write-down are a reduction in the expected growth rate, increased costs, pricing pressures, and increased interest rates. We would consider these factors to decide the amount of this write-down that we would classify as non-recurring; for example, will the slowing growth rate and shrinking margins stabilize or continue to worsen?

Source: Coca-Cola Enterprises, Inc. 2006 Form 10-K, Consolidated Statement of Operations and Footnote 1—Significant Accounting Policies—Goodwill and Franchise License Intangible Assets.

14.5 THE UNIVERSAL CORPORATION—PART 2—THE DENOMINATORS

Before we calculate the various denominators (unlevered earnings, EBIT, EBITDA, etc.), we first adjust the company's financial statements as we discussed earlier. We present a summary of these adjustments in Exhibit 14.8. By the end of the chapter, we will have made adjustments for a total of five different items in the income statement. In this section of the chapter, we make two of these adjustments. The first is an adjustment for Universal's restructuring charges, which we assume to be a non-recurring charge. The second adjustment is for cash and cash equivalents.

Universal Corporation's Restructuring and Impairment Costs

Universal recorded various restructuring and asset impairment costs in fiscal 2007. We assume these costs are non-recurring, and thus we remove their effects in measuring the relevant denominators from the company's financial statements. In its 10-K report, Universal describes these costs as follows:

> The Company recorded impairment costs during the fiscal year-ended March 31, 2007, totaling approximately $30.9 million before tax. . . .
> . . . Substantially all of the restructuring liability at March 31, 2007, will be paid during the next twelve months. (Source: 10-K, Note 34, pp. 47–50)

To adjust unlevered earnings for Universal's impairment costs, we add back the restructuring and asset impairment costs of $30,890, which Universal presents on a pre-tax basis on its income statement. We also adjust earnings for taxes ($10,812 = $30,890 × 0.35). We make this adjustment using the marginal tax rate; however, the appropriate tax rate is likely to be smaller than this effect.[7] The total adjustment to earnings is an add-back of $20,079.

EXHIBIT 14.8	Universal Corporation—Income Statement Adjustments—Basic Calculations			
Income Statement ($ in thousands, as of March 31)	**2007 Reported**	**Restructing Charges**	**Cash and Equivalents**	**2007 Adjusted**
Revenues	$2,007,272			$2,007,272
Operating expenses	−1,812,791			−1,812,791
Restructuring and impairment costs	−30,890	$30,890		0
Operating income	$ 163,591	$30,890	$ 0	$ 194,481
Equity in pretax earnings of unconsolidated affiliates	14,235			14,235
Interest income	10,845		−10,845	0
Interest expense	−53,794			−53,794
Income before income taxes and other items	$ 134,877	$30,890	$−10,845	$ 154,922
Provision for income taxes	−61,126	−10,812	3,796	−68,142
Minority interest (net of tax)	6,660			6,660
Income (loss) from continuing operations	$ 80,411	$20,079	$ −7,049	$ 93,440
Income (loss) from discontinued operations (net of tax)	−36,059			−36,059
Net income	$ 44,352	$20,079	$ −7,049	$ 57,381
Dividends on preferred stock	−14,685			−14,685
Earnings available to common	$ 29,667	$20,079	$ −7,049	$ 42,696
Unlevered earnings (net income + after-tax interest)	$ 79,318			$ 92,347
Marginal tax rate for all income	35.0%			

Exhibt may contain small rounding errors

These adjustments to the income statement are made in an effort to create denominators of the multiples that best represent the long-run future performance of the company. We assume Universal's restructuring and impairment costs are non-recurring, and since the disclosure was made prior to June 1, any impact on the numerators had already taken place in the market. Hence, we do not need to adjust the equity or enterprise value for the restructuring charge.

Required Cash, Excess Cash, and Total Cash (and Cash Equivalents)

As discussed earlier, we assume that the 2006 cash balance of $62.5 million is its required cash in 2006 and that this increased by $8.0 million in 2007 (approximately the percentage increase in its revenue). However, since we are using enterprise-value-based multiples, we exclude all of the company's cash (and equivalents) and its respective interest income. Interest income reported on the company's income statement is $10.845 million; in Exhibit 14.8, we reduce interest income by that amount, and we reduce the provision for taxes for the tax effect of $3.796 million ($3.796 = $10.845 × 0.35).

---

[7] The tax adjustments we make for Universal are all equal to the underlying amount multiplied by the marginal tax rate of 35%. Various footnote disclosures indicate that the relevant tax rates for some of these costs equal zero; however, such a refinement is beyond the scope of our discussion.

14.6 ADDITIONAL ADJUSTMENTS TO THE NUMERATOR AND DENOMINATOR

In this section, we discuss additional adjustments that usually necessitate changes to a multiple's denominator and may necessitate changes to a multiple's numerator. We discuss discontinued operations, minority interests, unconsolidated affiliates, mergers and acquisitions, and divestitures.

LO4 Make adjustments to market multiple numerators and denominators

Discontinued Operations

Once a company adopts a plan to sell an entire business such as a division, accounting principles require the company to isolate the assets held for sale as discontinued operations on all financial statements. Thus, on the balance sheet, the assets and liabilities of the discontinued operations are segregated from the assets and liabilities of the continuing operations. In addition, the income from discontinued operations is segregated from the revenues and expenses of the continuing operations. Further, the company must indicate both the value it expects to get from the sale of the business and the income or loss it expects the discontinued operations to generate until the sale date. If a company is, indeed, intending to sell such assets, then we must treat these assets as excess assets, for they will not have a long-term effect on the performance of the company.

We treat discontinued operations as an excess asset in order to improve both consistency and comparability. It is often the case that companies sell operations because they are no longer profitable or because they are not an integral part of the overall business operations. The market value of the company will reflect both the present value of the expected after-tax net proceeds from the sale of the discontinued operations and the anticipated cash flows from the discontinued operations up to the date of sale. It is unlikely that the earnings of the discontinued operations reflect this value. Thus, discontinued operations are likely to have a different multiple from that of the company's continuing operations. Moreover, the discontinued operation is often in a different line of business or geographic region, making it incomparable to either the company's other operations or the operations of the comparable companies. Since we want to measure the long-term performance of the company, we want to eliminate the discontinued operations from the numerator and denominator.

If we have a comparable company with discontinued operations, we remove the value of the discontinued operations from the numerator of any multiple we calculate (enterprise value or equity value) on a present value and after-tax basis, and we also make sure to exclude the discontinued operations in any denominators we measure. As such, we will have a multiple that is solely based on the comparable company's continuing operations. Ideally, we will also adjust the numerator for the present value of the cash flows expected to be received between the valuation date and the date the discontinued operations are sold (exclusive of the sale proceeds). Sometimes, we know the expected income or loss, but we often do not know the expected cash flows or the timing of these cash flows; although that information is sometimes reported in the footnotes.

Adjusting the Value of a Company with Discontinued Operations.   If the company we are valuing has discontinued operations, we calculate any relevant denominators without the effect of the company's discontinued operations. We multiply the company's adjusted denominators by the multiples of the comparable companies (as measured based solely on these companies' continuing operations) in order to determine the value of the continuing operations of the company being valued. To value the firm, we have to then add the present value of the expected sale proceeds of our company's discontinued operations on an after-tax basis, which should be disclosed in the company's 10-K; this amount is not, however, disclosed on a present value basis and may need to be adjusted for the time value of money. We also need to add in the present value of any after-tax cash flows up to the date of the sale.

Minority Interests (Noncontrolling Interest)

Many companies own one or more other companies by purchasing and holding their stock. If a company (which we will call the P Company) owns more than 50% of another company (which we will call the S Company), the P Company will generally consolidate the S Company's financial statements with its own financial statements, for S is a subsidiary of the P Company. **Minority interest** or **noncontrolling interest** on a company's consolidated financial statements represents the ownership interest in the subsidiary's stock that is not owned by the parent company; thus, we generally observe minority interest or noncontrolling interest line items on a company's financial statements any time the company owns at least 50% and less than 100% of the stock of a subsidiary. Owners of the S Company's shares other than the P Company are called minority shareholders.

In the consolidation process, the parent company (P Company) that owns less than 100%—say, z%—of its subsidiary (S Company) will add 100% of S Company's assets to its assets, 100% of S Company's liabilities to its liabilities, and z% of S Company's stockholders' equity to its equity. The consolidation process, however, is incomplete at this point, for P Company's consolidated assets (which include 100% of S Company's assets) are greater than its consolidated liabilities and shareholders' equity (which include 100% of S Company's liabilities but only z% of its shareholders' equity). This difference is equal to $(1-z)\%$ of S Company's shareholders' equity. The company records this amount as a noncontrolling interest and presents it on its balance sheet as a separate line item as part of consolidated shareholders' equity.[8]

When less than 100% of a subsidiary is acquired, the parent company records the subsidiary's assets and liabilities at fair value as of the purchase date, and it records goodwill if the fair value of the assets minus the fair value of the liabilities is less than the purchase price paid. The parent company records the noncontrolling interest in that subsidiary without any adjustments for the difference between book value and fair value or for the goodwill implied in the transaction. Thus, the noncontrolling interest on P Company's consolidated balance sheet represents the claims of the minority shareholders on the book value of S Company's shareholders' equity.

In the consolidation process for the income statement, the P Company will add 100% of S Company's revenues to its own revenues and 100% of S Company's expenses to its own expenses. The resulting earnings, therefore, include 100% of the earnings of S Company even though the P Company only owns—and thus only has claims on—z% of S Company's earnings. To adjust the consolidated earnings for S Company's earnings, on which P Company has no claims, P Company records a reduction (or allocation) of the profit or loss of $(1-z)\%$ of S Company's net income or loss for the noncontrolling interest in the earnings of S Company. P Company's consolidated net income is equal to its own net income from its businesses plus z% of S Company's income. Thus, the noncontrolling interest on P Company's consolidated income statement represents the claims of the minority shareholders on the net income of S Company.

Since companies typically do not present the financial statements of their subsidiaries, we generally do not have enough information to remove $(1-z)\%$ of S Company's operations from every line item of P Company's consolidated financial statements. Thus, to adjust a company's market multiple denominators, we normally remove the minority interest from the income statement, balance sheet, and cash flow statement. By this, we mean that we measure the income statement and cash flow statement as if the parent owns 100% of the subsidiary, and on the balance sheet, the noncontrolling interest will be treated as part of shareholders' equity. This is usually a straightforward task. When we do this, however, we implicitly assume that both the subsidiary and the parent should have similar market multiples. There may be cases in which we wish to remove the subsidiary's impact from every line item on the balance sheet, income statement, and cash flow statement (as if the subsidiary was not owned by the parent) in order to measure the parent's value without the subsidiary. This will occur if we think that the multiples of the subsidiary and of the parent are different and if we feel that the parent's multiple is the appropriate multiple to use

---

[8] See Statement of Financial Accounting Standard No. 160, "Noncontrolling Interests in Consolidated Financial Statements," December, 2007.

for valuing some other company. Unfortunately, we seldom have enough data from public filings to make this kind of adjustment.

The parent company's market value does not include the market value of the minority interest claims. Thus, to adjust a company's market multiple numerators, we add the market value of the minority interest shareholders' stock in the subsidiary to the numerator since we used 100% of the relevant income number, cash flow number, or balance sheet number in the denominator. This adjustment is straightforward if the subsidiary's stock is publicly traded (so that its market value is equal to the subsidiary's price per share multiplied by the shares outstanding that are not owned by the parent company). If the subsidiary is not publicly traded, valuing the minority interest can be quite complex. We can use both the available information on the subsidiary and the valuation methods in this book to value the subsidiary's common equity.

If we are using a net income or earnings-per-share multiple to value the minority interest claim, we can sometimes use the equity value and net income of the parent company (after a deduction for the income attributable to the noncontrolling interest), assuming that the businesses of the parent and subsidiary companies are similar. The numerator and denominator are consistent in this case, for the parent company's value does not include the value of the minority shares, and the net income (after deducting minority interest on the income statement) removes the net income allocated to the minority shareholders. For the most part, we cannot use this approach for other multiples (unlevered earnings, EBIT, EBITDA), for we usually do not have enough information to remove the minority-interest-related revenues, expenses, interest, taxes, debt, preferred stock, and other income statement and balance sheet items. However, since we want to measure the value of the common stock of the minority shareholders, a multiple of the market value of the equity to earnings is generally appropriate to use.

Adjusting the Value of a Company with Minority Interest.   Let's assume that the subsidiary is in the same line of business as the parent company and that as a consequence, it should have a similar multiple. In this case, in order to value the company with minority interests, we remove all of the effects of the minority interests from the numerator and denominator of all of the comparable companies (effectively measuring the multiples as if the subsidiary is 100% owned by the parent) and from the relevant denominator measures of the company we are valuing. In other words, we add the value of the minority interest position to the numerator, and we include the relevant income or cash flow that is attributable to the minority shareholders in the denominator. We then apply these multiples to the relevant measure of the denominator of the company we are valuing in order to arrive at a valuation of the company that includes the value of the minority interest, which it does not own. To measure the enterprise value of the company, we subtract the value of the minority interest claims on the company's subsidiaries.

Unconsolidated Affiliates

If the P Company owns an investment in another company (which we will call the Z Company), and does not consolidate Z Company's financial statements with its own financial statements, Z Company is an unconsolidated affiliate. Typically, companies consolidate investments in other companies if they have more than a 50% ownership in a company; thus, the difference between a consolidated subsidiary and an unconsolidated affiliate is the amount of ownership interest.

On a company's financial statements, line items related to unconsolidated subsidiaries or unconsolidated affiliates indicate that the company has equity investments in other companies (affiliates) that it does not consolidate. The most likely—but not the only—reason the company chooses not to consolidate an equity investment is that it has a 50% or less ownership interest in that company.[9] The effect of unconsolidated affiliates on the company's income statement represents an allocation of the affiliate's income based on the company's equity ownership; that is, it is the affiliate's net income multiplied by the company's percentage ownership of that affiliate. Companies normally use this treatment when they own between 20% and 50% of a company.

---

[9] Under certain limited conditions, a company does not have to consolidate an equity investment of greater than 50% ownership—such as lack of control of the company because of regulation or government control. For example, Universal does not consolidate one of its investments even though it owns more than a 50% interest, which it describes as follows:

> We deconsolidated our operations in Zimbabwe as of January 1, 2006, under U.S. accounting requirements that apply under certain conditions to foreign subsidiaries that are subject to foreign exchange controls and other government restrictions. ... The investment is now accounted for using the cost method and is reported on the balance sheet in investments in unconsolidated affiliates. (Source: Universal 2007 10-K, p. 20.)

Since the company's income statement does not reflect the revenues or expenses of the affiliate (the only effect on the income statement is the one line item that represents the company's allocation of the affiliate's net income or loss), we cannot measure the unlevered earnings, EBIT, or EBITDA of the affiliate. Therefore, we treat unconsolidated affiliates in a way that is similar to how we treat excess assets.

The value of a company's unconsolidated affiliates is embedded in its value (in both the enterprise value and the value of its equity). We remove the value of the unconsolidated affiliates from the enterprise value and the common equity value. We also remove the after-tax effect of the unconsolidated affiliates on the company's income statement and cash flows—as well as such balance sheet denominators as total invested capital or shareholder's equity.

Adjusting the Value of a Company with Unconsolidated Affiliates. To value a company with unconsolidated affiliates, we remove all of the effects of the unconsolidated affiliates from the numerator and the denominator for all of the comparable companies and from the relevant measures of the denominators of the company we are valuing. We then apply these multiples to the denominator measures of the company we are valuing in order to value the company without its unconsolidated affiliates. To measure the enterprise value of the firm, we add the value of the company's unconsolidated affiliates.

Valuation Key 14.5

Adjusting market multiple inputs for unconsolidated affiliates requires that we remove the value of the unconsolidated affiliates from the numerators. For flow-based multiples, we remove the after-tax effect of the unconsolidated affiliates on the flow. For balance-sheet-based multiples, we remove the book value of the unconsolidated affiliates from the balance sheet.

Mergers and Acquisitions

Mergers and acquisitions are similar to each other. They represent a company's purchase of another company's assets or equity. A divestiture, on the other hand, is somewhat like the opposite of a merger or acquisition. Divestitures represent the sale of a company's business (division or subsidiary). The common feature of these transactions in relation to measuring market multiples is that they can result in financial statement inputs in the denominators that are inconsistent with the market values used in the numerators. When we measure a company's market value after one of these transactions, it will represent the value of the post-transaction company. The financial statements, however, generally represent a hybrid of the pre- and post-transaction company in the year of the acquisition. Let us be more specific.

When a company acquires another company, it usually records the assets and liabilities of the acquired company on its financial accounting records at the appraised value of the company's assets and liabilities. If the company pays more for the acquired company than the appraised value of its assets minus the value of its liabilities, the company will record goodwill on its books in the amount of the difference. This is the purchase method of accounting, which is the required method in the United States as of 2002.

As of the purchase date, the company's market value represents the post-acquisition market value of the company. Similarly, the company's balance sheet represents the post-acquisition balance sheet. Its income statement and cash flow statements, however, only include the flows (revenues, expenses, cash flows, and so forth) of the target after the transaction closes. Thus, if a company purchases another company, say, nine months into the acquirer's fiscal year, then the acquirer's annual income statement and cash flow statement in the year of the acquisition will only include the last three months of the acquired company's flows, and would exclude the first nine months of flows. Income statement or cash-flow-based market multiples will then have inconsistent denominators that are not only inconsistent with the numerators but that also are not representative of what the company looks like post-transaction.

Fortunately, we can often find information to at least partially adjust a company's financial statements. The acquiring company typically shows pro forma information in its financial statements. The pro forma information shows the company's income statements (and possibly other financial statements) as if the two companies were combined as of the beginning of the fiscal year. Most companies do not provide pro forma cash flow statements; thus, we will need to create cash flow statements from pro forma income statements and balance sheets if we are using a cash-flow-based multiple.

We can use pro forma information to adjust the denominator so that it is more consistent with the numerator (post-transaction company), but note that the pro forma results do not include expected synergies or transaction-related financing effects. The management's discussion of the transaction is sometimes useful for understanding the expected synergies that may be embedded in the company's market value. Transaction-related financing is usually disclosed as well. If the acquired company was publicly traded, it may be possible to use its pre-acquisition financial statements to create pro forma financial statements.

Valuation in Practice 14.4

The Bon-Ton Stores, Inc.'s Purchase of Carson Stores from Saks Inc. Bon-Ton Stores, Inc. purchased certain subsidiaries of Saks Inc. as of March 5, 2006, which the company described as follows:

> . . . the Company acquired all of the outstanding securities of two subsidiaries of Saks . . . Under the terms of the purchase agreement, the Company paid $1,040,188 in cash. The Company financed the Carson acquisition, . . . through the issuance of 10 ¼% Senior Notes due 2014 in the aggregate principal amount of $510,000, entry into a $1,000,000 senior secured revolving credit facility . . ., and entry into a $260,000 mortgage loan facility . . .
>
> The Company's consolidated financial statements for 2006 include Carson's operations for the period from March 5, 2006 through February 3, 2007. Carson's operations reflect purchase accounting in accordance with SFAS No. 141, "Business Combinations," whereby the purchase price was allocated to the assets acquired and liabilities assumed based upon their estimated fair values on the acquisition date. . . . Goodwill in the amount of $24,412 has been recorded in conjunction with the acquisition. The Company expects that substantially all goodwill will be deductible for income tax purposes.

Below, we compare the company's reported 2006 results to its 2006 pro forma results, which restates its income statement as if the acquisition occurred on the first day of fiscal 2006. This comparison shows an increase in revenues of 5% but a decrease in net income of 38%.

($ in thousands)	2006 Reported	2006 Pro Forma	% Difference
Net sales	$3,362,279	$3,543,886	5%
Costs of merchandise sold	−2,118,762	−2,251,416	
Selling, general and administrative	−1,056,472	−1,115,313	
Depreciation and amortization	−103,189	−110,062	
Amortization of lease-related interests	−3,720	−3,546	
Income from operations	$ 80,136	$ 63,549	−21%
Interest expense, net	−107,143	−116,960	
Other income	93,531	94,558	
Income before income taxes	$ 66,524	$ 41,147	−38%
Income tax provision	−19,641	−12,155	
Net income	$ 46,883	$ 28,992	−38%

Source: The company operates more than 250 department stores in more than 20 U.S. states. Its brand names include Bon-Ton, Bergner's, Boston Store, Carson Pirie Scott, Elder-Beerman, Herberger's, Younkers, and Parisian. The company's headquarters is in York, Pennsylvania, and it was founded in 1898. See the Bon-Ton Stores, Inc., February 3, 2007, Form 10-K, Consolidated Statements of Income and Footnote 2—Carson's Acquisition.

Divestitures

A divestiture is the sale of a part of a company; in other words, a company sells one or more (but not all) of its businesses. Earlier in this section, we discussed discontinued operations. If a company decides to sell one of its businesses and issues financial statements before the sale is completed, it will identify the assets, liabilities, and income from this business as a discontinued operation. In these situations, divestitures do not cause an inconsistency between the numerator and the denominator in the pre-divesture period because the company has already isolated the divestiture as a discontinued operation; this is true as long as the company isolated the discontinued operation for the entire year and as long as we use the information related to the discontinued operations to make the adjustments that we described earlier.

Of course, as indicated before, the numerator needs to be adjusted downward for the value of the discontinued operations. Once the company completes the disposition of the discontinued operation, we do not need to adjust the numerator for the multiples, for the cash proceeds have already been received. If the company is holding cash from the disposition, the cash will be removed when we calculate the enterprise value.

Companies may divest a business without deciding beforehand that the business was for sale and, therefore, without isolating it as a discontinued operation. In this situation, the company's income statement will include the operations of the divested company for the part of the year during which it owned the divested company. We generally review the footnote and other disclosures included with the financial statements in order to identify information so that we can back out the operations of the divested company for that partial year. This is often hard to do.

Valuation Key 14.6

Divestitures and mergers and acquisitions can result in a combination of pre- and post-transaction income statements and cash flow statements. We adjust these financial statements in order to make them consistent with the post-transaction company.

14.7 THE UNIVERSAL CORPORATION—PART 3— OTHER ADJUSTMENTS

In this section, we continue to adjust Universal's financial statements. We present a summary of these adjustments in Exhibit 14.9, which also includes the two adjustments we made previously for both the restructuring charge and the cash and cash equivalents. We make three additional adjustments in this section. The first adjustment is for Universal's discontinued operations, and the second adjustment is for its unconsolidated subsidiaries; we treat each of these items as an excess asset. The last adjustment is for the minority interest in Universal's subsidiaries.

Universal Corporation's Discontinued Operations (Excess Asset)

We already removed the effect of Universal's excess and required cash from the market multiples, but Universal has other excess assets as well. These excess assets are businesses that Universal no longer wants as part of its business strategy. In its 10-K report, Universal describes its decision as follows:

In December 2006, we adopted a plan to sell the remaining agri-products operations. One of those agri-products businesses was sold in January 2007, and one was sold in May 2007. The remaining agri-product operations are held for sale. We report the assets and liabilities of the lumber and building products and agri-products businesses as discontinued operations for all periods in the accompanying financial statements. (Source: 10-K, p. 3) . . .

Balances for agri-products operations not yet sold, but classified as "held for sale" at March 31, 2007, are reported as current assets and current liabilities in the consolidated balance sheet at that date. (Source: 10-K, pp. 46–47). . . .

Universal had negative income from its discontinued operations in 2007 (see the income statement in Exhibit 14.1), and it presents the loss from discontinued operations on the income statement on an after-tax basis; thus, we only need to eliminate this amount—$36.0 million—from the income statement. See the adjustment in Exhibit 14.9

EXHIBIT 14.9　　Universal Corporation—Income Statement Adjustments

Income Statement ($ in thousands, as of March 31)	2007 Reported	Restructing Charges	Cash and Equivalents	Discon- tinued Operations	Uncon- solidated Affiliates	Minority Interest	2007 Adjusted
Revenues	$2,007,272						$2,007,272
Operating expenses	−1,812,791						−1,812,791
Restructuring and impairment costs	−30,890	$30,890					0
Operating income	$ 163,591	$30,890	$ 0	$ 0	$ 0	$ 0	$ 194,481
Equity in pretax earnings of unconsolidated affiliates	14,235				−14,235		0
Interest income	10,845		−10,845				0
Interest expense	−53,794						−53,794
Income before income taxes and other items	$ 134,877	$30,890	$−10,845	$ 0	$−14,235	$ 0	$ 140,687
Provision for income taxes	−61,126	−10,812	3,796		1,495		−66,647
Minority interest (net of tax)	6,660					−6,660	0
Income (loss) from continuing operations	$ 80,411	$20,079	$ −7,049	$ 0	$−12,740	$−6,660	$ 74,040
Income (loss) from discontinued operations (net of tax)	−36,059			36,059			0
Net income	$ 44,352	$20,079	$ −7,049	$36,059	$−12,740	$−6,660	$ 74,040
Dividends on preferred stock	−14,685						−14,685
Earnings available to common	$ 29,667	$20,079	$ −7,049	$36,059	$−12,740	$−6,660	$ 59,355
Unlevered earnings (net income + after-tax interest)	$ 79,318						$ 109,006
Marginal tax rate for interest expense and income	35.0%						
Dividend Exclusion % on Intercompany Dividends	70.0%						

Exhibit may contain small rounding errors

Even though these operations are being sold at a loss, the company disclosed in its footnotes that it does not expect to realize any tax benefit on the sale; thus we do not need to tax adjust the sales proceeds.

Since this is an excess asset that is valued separately from the market multiple valuation, we subtract the value of the discontinued operations from the value of the common equity and the enterprise value. In Exhibit 14.10, we show the adjustment of $29,123, which is calculated as the difference between the current assets in discontinued operations and the current liabilities in discontinued operations ($29,123 = $42,437 − $13,314), for Universal indicated in its footnote that it had written these assets down to their net realizable sale value by year-end. In some circumstances, we might want to present value these proceeds, but Universal indicated that it anticipated that the sale of these businesses would be completed very quickly, so we do not present value this amount.

EXHIBIT 14.10　　Universal Corporation—Enterprise and Common Equity Value Adjustments

Market Value ($ in thousands)	Enterprise Value	Equity Value
Valuation before adjustments (from Exhibit 14.7)	$2,441,935	$1,760,776
Restructing charges	N/A	N/A
Cash and equivalents (already adjusted in Exhibit 14.7)	N/A	N/A
Discontinued operations	−29,123	−29,123
Unconsolidated affiliates	−121,000	−121,000
Minority interest	19,000	19,000
Adjusted value	$2,310,812	$1,629,653

Universal Corporation's Unconsolidated Affiliates (Excess Asset)

Universal's financial statements (as seen in Exhibit 14.1) include various disclosures regarding its investments in unconsolidated affiliates. On its income statement, Universal shows $14.2 million in income from these affiliates as Equity in Pretax Earnings of Unconsolidated Affiliates.

We adjust the income statement by eliminating this $14.2 million. We assume that any taxable earnings from these investments will be in the form of dividends to Universal that are subject to a 70% dividend exclusion from income tax, effectively reducing the income tax rate to 10.5% ($0.105 = 0.35 \times [1 - 0.7]$). We also adjust income taxes for the pretax earnings adjustment by using this income tax rate in order to arrive at a tax adjustment of $1.5 million ($1.5 = 14.2×0.105). These adjustments are presented in Exhibit 14.9. From various disclosures, we determine that the market value of Universal's interest in these subsidiaries is $121 million, and we reduce the value of the equity and the enterprise value by this amount in Exhibit 14.10.

Universal Corporation's Minority Interest

Universal lists 55 subsidiaries in its 2007 10-K report. We do not know which of these subsidiaries are wholly owned and which have a minority interest, but from Universal's income statement and balance sheet, we know that at least some of these subsidiaries are not wholly owned. We assume that the multiples of the subsidiaries are similar to the multiples for the parent and that, in aggregate, they have a value of $19 million.

The book value of the minority interest on Universal's balance sheet (Exhibit 14.1) is $5.8 million as of the end of 2007. We know that these subsidiaries had a net loss in 2007, for Universal shows a positive adjustment to its net income of $6.6 million to account for the share of the subsidiary losses that was allocated to the minority shareholders. The fact that these subsidiaries had a net loss suggests that the multiple of these businesses will differ from the multiples of the other parts of Universal. In this situation, we would ideally want to remove the effect of these subsidiaries on all of the multiples. However, we do not have sufficient information to do this, so we illustrate the more common adjustment for minority interests, which leaves their effect in the multiples, even though it may not be appropriate in this case. The income statement adjustment is straightforward. We eliminate the $6.6 million line item—net of income taxes—from the income statement. After this adjustment, the income statement reflects 100% of the income from consolidated subsidiaries—even those that are not 100% owned (see Exhibit 14.9).

Based on an analysis of the subsidiaries, we assume that the value of the minority interest in Universal's subsidiaries is $19 million, and we increase the value of the equity and the enterprise value by this amount in Exhibit 14.10. Since we prepare the denominators under the assumption that there are no minority interests, we want to increase the enterprise value and the value of the common equity by the value of the minority interest claims.

Universal's Market Multiples

We show the calculation of Universal's enterprise-value-based market multiples in Exhibit 14.11 and its share price and equity-value-based market multiples in Exhibit 14.12. The inputs in these exhibits are taken from previous exhibits in this chapter. In the first two columns, we present market multiples based on the 2007 reported financial statements, and in columns three and four, we present market multiples based on the 2007 adjusted financial statements. The last two columns show both the percentage change in the inputs and the percentage change in the multiples resulting from using the reported numbers versus the adjusted numbers. As we will discuss, some of these changes are quite large.

Enterprise Value-Based Market Multiples

The first line in Exhibit 14.11 presents Universal's enterprise value. Under the reported column, the enterprise value is equal to $2.44 billion (as calculated in Exhibit 14.7). For the adjusted column, the enterprise value is equal to $2.31 billion (as calculated in Exhibit 14.10). As a result of the adjustments, the enterprise value decreased by 5.4%. Unlevered earnings (see Exhibit 14.9) increased from $79.3 million to

$109.0 million (a 37.4% increase). The increase in unlevered earnings and the decrease in enterprise value result in an overall decrease in the unlevered earnings multiple from 30.79 to 21.20 (−31.1% change).

| EXHIBIT 14.11 | Universal Corporation—Enterprise-Value-Based Market Multiples |

Market Multiples Based on Enterprise Value	2007 Reported		2007 Adjusted		% Change in Input	% Change in Multiple
($ in thousands)	Inputs	Multiple	Inputs	Multiple		
Enterprise value	$2,441,935		$2,310,812		−5.4%	
Unlevered earnings.	$ 79,318	30.79	$ 109,006	21.20	37.4%	−31.1%
Earnings before interest and taxes (EBIT)	$ 163,591	14.93	$ 194,481	11.88	18.9%	−20.4%
Depreciation and amortization	48,305		48,305			
Earnings before interest, taxes, depreciation, and amortization (EBITDA).	$ 211,896	11.52	$ 242,786	9.52	14.6%	−17.4%
Revenue	$2,007,272	1.22	$2,007,272	1.15	0.0%	−5.4%

Because of their larger bases, the EBIT and EBITDA multiples change less than the unlevered earnings multiples. In this example, we set EBIT equal to operating income, and EBITDA is equal to EBIT plus depreciation and amortization. Depreciation and amortization in 2007 was $48.305 million. We show all of the inputs for the EBIT and EBITDA multiples in Exhibit 14.11. EBIT increases from $163.6 million to $194.5 million (18.9% change). The increase in EBIT and the decrease in enterprise value result in an overall decrease in the EBIT multiple from 14.93 to 11.88 (−20.4% change). EBITDA increases from $211.9 million to $242.8 million (14.6% change). The increase in EBITDA and the decrease in enterprise value result in an overall decrease in the EBITDA multiple from 11.52 to 9.52 (−17.4% change).

The last income statement or flow-based multiple in this exhibit is the revenue multiple. None of our adjustments affect Universal's revenue; thus, the revenue multiple solely decreases as a result of the decrease in enterprise value (−5.4%), and the revenue multiple decreases from 1.22 to 1.15. Suffice it to say that the adjustments we have made have caused material changes in some of the multiples, which of course translate directly into material changes in the valuation of the company being valued. As such, it is important to take the time to carefully make the necessary adjustments.

Common-Equity-Value-Based Market Multiples

The first line in Exhibit 14.12 presents Universal's market value of common equity (which, if you remember, includes convertible preferred stock and stock-based compensation). Under the reported column, equity value is equal to $1.76 billion (as calculated in Exhibit 14.7). Under the adjusted column, equity value is equal to $1.63 billion (as calculated in Exhibit 14.10). Because of the adjustments, common equity value decreased by 7.4%.

| EXHIBIT 14.12 | Universal Corporation—Equity-Value-Based Market Multiples |

Market Multiples Based on Equity Value	2007 Reported		2007 Adjusted		% Change in Input	% Change in Multiple
($ in thousands)	Inputs	Multiple	Inputs	Multiple		
Market value of common equity.	$1,760,776		$1,629,653		−7.4%	
Net income.	$44,352	39.70	$74,040	22.01	66.9%	-44.6%

The net income multiple is the one we will focus on (remember, we are not using net income available to common because we are treating the convertible preferred stock as common equity). If we use the market value of equity, the earnings multiple equals 39.70 if we use reported net income, and it equals 22.01 if we use adjusted earnings (−44.6% change). The decrease is a result of the decrease in equity value (−7.4%) and the increase in earnings (66.9%).

As we saw with enterprise value multiples, the adjusted value of the net income multiple also experiences significant change, again highlighting the importance of this adjustment process.

REVIEW EXERCISE 14.3

Adjusting Market Multiple Numerators and Denominators

Use the information from Review Exercise 14.1, Review Exercise 14.2, and the following information to adjust the company's financial statements for effects related to its Unconsolidated Affiliates and Minority Interest similar to the adjustments in Exhibit 14.9. Also calculate the company's unlevered earnings, EBIT, EBITDA, revenue, and P/E multiples using the adjusted financial statements. Assume earnings from the unconsolidated affiliates are taxed at a 40% tax rate. The market value of the Multiple Company's interest in the unconsolidated affiliates is $28,000. The market value of the minority interest in the Multiple Company's subsidiary is $5,600. HINT: Calculate unlevered earnings, EBIT, and EBITDA as in Review Exercise 14.1 using the adjusted financial statements.

Solution on pages 595–596.

14.8 SELECTING AMONG ALTERNATIVE MARKET MULTIPLES AND ESTABLISHING A RANGE

LO5 Choose an appropriate market multiple and range

Most likely, the perfect comparable company will not exist when we are using market multiple valuation methods. Thus, we naturally face trade-offs across alternative market multiples. From Chapter 13, we know that the importance and dimensions of comparability increase as we move up the line items on the income statement. Similarly, the importance and dimensions of comparability are larger for balance-sheet-based multiples than they are for most income-statement-based multiples. Free cash flow multiples, on the other hand, have the fewest relevant dimensions of comparability (primarily growth, risk, and capital structure).

Even though this pushes us toward the use of free-cash-flow-based or unlevered-earnings-based multiples, we still face trade-offs when we use free cash flow and unlevered earnings multiples. These trade-offs can then push us to move up the line items on the income statement (EBIT, EBITDA, and revenue) when calculating multiples. The other trade-offs are related to the likelihood that the measure in the denominator of the multiple is a good base year for a market multiple valuation, which also encompasses the issue of negative denominators. In the end, the decision as to which multiple to use in a valuation depends on the particular valuation context, the comparable companies, and the company being valued.

Even after we complete the arduous process of measuring the multiples and identifying the best comparable companies, our work is still not completed. We must use the multiples from the comparable companies to identify a range of values for each multiple and/or a measure of central tendency to be used to value the company. If we are able to identify comparable companies that are exactly comparable to the company we are valuing and make all of the necessary adjustments, all of the market multiples should work equally and perfectly well. In that case, we would not have to choose a subset of market multiples, we would not need a range or measure of central tendency, and we would not have to accept comparable companies that are not truly comparable. By now, it should come as no surprise that such a perfect situation does not arise. Thus, we almost always make trade-offs by selecting comparable companies that are not truly comparable, and that in turn affects the range of market multiple values we observe from our work.

Moving Up the Lines in the Income Statement Increases the Need for Comparability

As discussed in Chapter 13, when we move up the lines in the income statement, we increase the number of dimensions needed for comparability. For example, adding back interest and taxes in the EBIT multiple means we implicitly assume that the company's capital structure and income tax structure are comparable to those of the comparable companies. Even though EBIT is unaffected by interest and taxes, the EBIT multiple depends directly on these value drivers. Similarly, using a revenue multiple means we implicitly assume that the company's cost structure is comparable to that of the comparable companies.

Negative Denominators Can Eliminate a Multiple from Consideration

Naturally, we cannot use a denominator to measure a market multiple if it has a negative value. When we have a negative denominator, we either make an adjustment to it (for example, add back a non-recurring item) so that it is positive, use a forecast of it two or three years into the future when it is positive, or use a different multiple. For example, we might be able to salvage an unlevered earnings multiple by adjusting it for unusual or non-recurring items. If the denominator remains negative, then we are forced to move up the lines in the income statement and not use that particular multiple. Of course, if all of a company's earnings-based numbers are negative, we can use revenue multiples, for revenues are never negative. We know, however, that revenue multiples are more sensitive to differences in comparability—particularly differences in cost structures—than earnings-based multiples.

Free Cash Flow Multiples

We know that free cash flow multiples have certain advantages over other market multiples. In particular, free cash flow multiples rely on fewer dimensions of comparability than other multiples; however, free cash flows also have negative values more frequently and have greater variation in growth rates, making it more difficult to identify a good base year. We may not face these issues for free cash flow multiples for companies that are more mature and have more stable growth. For some other companies, we might be able to "normalize" the free cash flow measure so that it reflects the long-run prospects for the company.

Revenue Multiples Can Be Appropriate When We Believe the Cost Structure Will Change

Since revenue multiples assume that the cost structures of the comparable companies and the company we are valuing are identical, they can be useful when we believe a company's cost structure will change to that of a comparable company's cost structure. For example, if we believe that we can purchase a company and change its cost structure to that of the comparable companies, revenue multiples will be able to provide valuations consistent with this belief. Naturally, changing cost structures in this way is not always easy, but if we want to make such an assumption, revenue multiples may be appropriate to use. Consider companies such as Laboratory Corporation of America (LabCorp) or Quest Diagnostics that do medical testing. Both of these companies have acquired many smaller labs over the years and they know that most of their cost structure—with their enormous scale economies—will be in place in the acquired labs within a matter of days. In this case, they may actually be able to use a revenue multiple to value these acquisitions. Of course, they have to worry (and they do) about whether any of the revenue of the labs will be lost because of the acquisition.

Valuation Key 14.7

Choosing the most appropriate multiples is usually done after we make adjustments and assess comparability. If we have comparable companies that are perfectly comparable on all dimensions and make all of the necessary adjustments, all of the multiples will result in the same valuation. Realistically, however, that is not the situation we typically encounter, and we must choose multiples based on the particular valuation context for a company at the time we are valuing it (which includes the characteristics of the available comparable companies).

Using Multiple Comparable Companies to Offset Differences

We always make trade-offs when we select comparable companies. One comparable company might be more comparable on certain dimensions than another comparable company, and that comparable company might be more comparable on other dimensions. We might also use two companies that are not exactly comparable to the company we are valuing but have differences that are expected to be offsetting. For example, we might use two companies that are comparable on many dimensions—one with slightly lower growth prospects than the company being valued and the other with slightly better growth prospects. If we include both companies, on average, our portfolio of companies could be comparable and will capture the growth prospects of the company we are valuing.

All else equal, we prefer to use more comparable companies, but all else is rarely equal. Typically, we must make trade-offs between the number of comparable companies we include in our analysis versus the comparability of the comparable companies—including a greater number of comparable companies generally reduces the comparability of the firms we are using.

Does the Variation in Multiples Across Companies Line Up According to Expectations?

An interesting analysis to do before we compute the multiples for each of our comparable companies is to think about which companies' multiples are likely to be the highest, which will be in the middle of the range, and which will be at the low end. We would determine this based on our understanding of the risk, growth, profitability, and investment requirements of the comparable companies. If the multiples line up according to our expectations, it means that we have a good understanding of the characteristics of the comparables and that we have managed to make the necessary adjustments to the financial statements such that these characteristics are visible in the multiples. If we are successful in doing this, we also probably have a pretty good idea of where in the range of the multiples the company we are valuing belongs. Of course, if we are unsuccessful in this regard, it may mean that the companies are not very comparable or that we have not made the necessary adjustments we need to make.

Establishing a Reasonable Range of Values and Measuring Central Tendency

If we have a reasonable number of comparable companies, we can choose a reasonable range of values and calculate a measure of central tendency for each market multiple being used in our valuation. This task is easier if we have a large number of comparable companies, which again is often not the case. With respect to establishing a range of market values, we begin by assessing the reasonableness of the distribution of values. For example, is the range reasonably narrow or is there is a large variation across companies? If there is large variation, we might revisit our adjustment process or conclude that one or more of the companies we chose are not truly comparable to the company being valued.

Possible measures of central tendency include the equally weighted mean (called the mean or average), the value weighted mean, and the median. If we have some extreme outliers in our distribution of market multiples or if the distribution is not symmetric, the mean may be a poor measure of central tendency. An alternative approach is to truncate or trim the distribution of market multiples before calculating the mean; for example, we might truncate the distribution at the 5th and 95th percentiles and set all market multiples above (below) the 95th (5th) percentile equal to the 95th (5th) percentile. The median (50th percentile) is not influenced by outliers if the distribution is relatively symmetric.

Selecting the Range of Values (or Value) to Use in Our Valuation

Once we have narrowed the range of values to a reasonable degree and have a measure of central tendency, we can select the final range of values (or value) to use in our valuation. This is an easy task if our comparable companies have a high degree of comparability to the company we are valuing. In this situation, the measure of central tendency is a reasonable value to use in our valuation. If the comparable companies are not equally comparable, we would have to consider eliminating some of the less comparable of the companies or use a weighted approach, in which we weight the comparable companies by their degree of comparability—the more comparable, the more weight. Finally, if the multiples line up across the comparable companies as anticipated, we may be able to simply use a subset of the comparable companies in order to choose a range or measure of central tendency.

Valuation Key 14.8

We almost always need to make trade-offs when we select our portfolio of comparable companies, market multiples, and range of values to use in our valuation. We usually have little choice but to use our informed, personal judgment when making these decisions. Our goal is to select a portfolio of comparable companies, specific market multiples, and range of values that are appropriate for the company we are valuing.

14.9 VALUING W. K. CHENG COMPANY USING UNIVERSAL'S MARKET MULTIPLES (BEFORE ADDITIONAL ADJUSTMENTS)

W. K. Cheng Company (Cheng) is a privately held company. Even though Universal is much larger than Cheng, our analyst believes that Universal Corporation is a reasonable comparable company to use to value Cheng. In Exhibit 14.13, we show abbreviated financial statements for Cheng. About 75% of Cheng's cash and marketable securities is an excess asset. All of the dividend and interest income listed on the company's income statement relate to the required and excess cash. The market value of its cash and marketable securities is equal to the value listed on the balance sheet, which is also true of the market value of Cheng's debt and preferred stock. Cheng has a 40% income tax rate on all income.

EXHIBIT 14.13	W. K. Cheng Company—Abbreviated Financial Statements

Income Statement ($ in thousands, as of March 31)	2007
Revenues	$ 60,000.00
Operating expenses	−53,271.92
Depreciation expense	−3,000.00
Operating income	**$ 3,728.08**
Interest expense	−952.38
Interest income (cash and equivalents)	436.36
Income before income taxes and other items	**$ 3,212.07**
Provision for income taxes	−1,284.83
Net income	**$ 1,927.24**
Dividends on preferred stock	−372.81
Earnings available to common shareholders	**$ 1,554.43**

Balance Sheet ($ in thousands, as of March 31)	2007
Assets	
Cash and equivalents	$ 2,000.00
Net (non-cash) working capital	3,000.00
Total current assets	$ 5,000.00
Property, plant, and equipment, net	28,125.00
Total assets	**$ 33,125.00**
Liabilities and Shareholders' Equity	
Non-current operating liabilities	$ 12,000.00
Long-term debt	10,000.00
Total liabilities	**$ 22,000.00**
Perpetual preferred stock	$ 5,000.00
Common stock	6,125.00
Total shareholders' equity	**$ 11,125.00**
Total liabilities and shareholders' equity	**$ 33,125.00**

Exhibit may contain small rounding errors

We measure Cheng's denominators for the various market multiples in Exhibit 14.14. The adjustment to unlevered earnings for after-tax interest income includes all interest, $261.81 ($261.81 = $436.36 − $174.55), because all interest income has been included in unlevered earnings. The adjustment for EBIT subtracts interest income ($436.36), and the adjustment to EBITDA is the same as the one for EBIT. To measure adjusted net income to common shareholders, we must remember to subtract preferred stock dividends ($372.81) from net income. We also reduce the net income available to common shareholders by the after-tax interest income.

EXHIBIT 14.14   W. K. Cheng Company—Calculation of Market Multiple Denominators

Fiscal Year 2007 ($ in thousands)	Unlevered Earnings	EBIT	EBITDA	Net Income to Common
Net income.	$1,927.24	$1,927.24	$1,927.24	$1,927.24
Preferred stock dividends				–372.81
Interest expense.	952.38	952.38	952.38	
Interest tax shield.	–380.95			
Income taxes		1,284.83	1,284.83	
Depreciation and amortization			3,000.00	
Total (before adjustment for excess cash)	$2,498.67	$4,164.45	$7,164.45	$1,554.43
Interest income (cash and equivalents)	–436.36	–436.36	–436.36	–436.36
Income taxes	174.55			174.55
Total (after all adjustments).	$2,236.85	$3,728.08	$6,728.08	$1,292.62

Exhibit may contain small rounding errors

In Exhibit 14.15, we calculate Cheng's firm value and equity value by using Universal's enterprise-value-based and equity-based market multiples. To measure Cheng's firm value, excluding its excess assets and using Universal's enterprise-value-based multiples, we multiply the various measures of the denominator for Cheng (from the previous exhibit) by Universal's corresponding market multiple that we measured using adjusted inputs (from Exhibits 14.11 and 14.12). To measure enterprise value using the equity-based multiples, we add the value of Cheng's debt and preferred stock to the initial equity valuation based on Universal's market multiple. Now we have a measure of Cheng's enterprise value based on each of the market multiples. To enterprise value, we add the value of Cheng's cash and equivalents in order to measure the value of the firm that includes its excess assets.

EXHIBIT 14.15   W. K. Cheng Company—Enterprise Value and Equity Value Based on Universal Corporation's Market Multiples

Fiscal Year 2007 ($ in thousands)	Unlevered Earnings	EBIT	EBITDA	Revenue	Net Income to Common
W.K. Cheng value driver for market multiple . .	$ 2,236.85	$ 3,728.08	$ 6,728.08	$60,000.00	$ 1,292.62
Universal market multiple.	21.20	11.88	9.52	1.15	22.01
	$47,418.87	$44,296.89	$64,037.23	$69,073.22	$28,451.07
Long-term debt					10,000.00
Perpetual preferred stock.					5,000.00
Enterprise value	$47,418.87	$44,296.89	$64,037.23	$69,073.22	$43,451.07
Cash and equivalents.	2,000.00	2,000.00	2,000.00	2,000.00	2,000.00
Value of firm with excess assets	$49,418.87	$46,296.89	$66,037.23	$71,073.22	$45,451.07
Long-term debt	–10,000.00	–10,000.00	–10,000.00	–10,000.00	–10,000.00
Perpetual preferred stock.	–5,000.00	–5,000.00	–5,000.00	–5,000.00	–5,000.00
Common equity value with excess assets. . . .	$34,418.87	$31,296.89	$51,037.23	$56,073.22	$30,451.07
% Difference from Unlevered Earnings Valuation:					
Value of firm with excess assets	0.0%	–6.3%	33.6%	43.8%	–8.0%
Equity value with excess assets.	0.0%	–9.1%	48.3%	62.9%	–11.5%

As we can see, there is wide variation across the multiples in terms of the value of the firm with excess assets and the value of the equity with excess assets. For each multiple, we show the percentage difference in the value obtained from it relative to the unlevered earnings multiple valuation—not because this is necessarily the correct valuation but because it gives some sense of the differences across multiples. The value of the firm with excess assets varies from $45.5 million to $71.1 million, and the average value of the firm is $55.7 million. The average common equity with excess assets is $40.7 million, with a range from $30.5 million to $56.1 million. Keep in mind that we only used one comparable company and that this may give rise to some of the variation across the different multiples.

Which market multiple is the best one to use? We have not done a sufficient analysis to definitively answer this question, nor have we provided sufficient data to do the analysis. Answering this question requires us to use the various tools discussed in other chapters—such as the chapter discussing financial ratios and the chapter discussing the determinants of different market multiples. We do not review this analysis in detail here (as we did in the prior chapter), but we might ask, for example, whether the cost structures are very similar between the two companies. We know that the tax rates of the two companies differ (Cheng's is 40% and Universal's is 35%), which all else equal makes the EBIT and EBITDA multiples less useful than the unlevered earnings multiple.

The revenue multiple is also affected by the tax rate difference as well as other differences in the cost structure. For example, Cheng's EBIT/total invested capital (adjusted as in Exhibit 14.14) is 19.5% (19.5% = $3,728.1/$19,125), which is higher than Universal's 15.7% as adjusted per Exhibit 14.11 (15.7% = $194,481/$1,238,991). Thus, Cheng has a cost structure advantage and a tax rate disadvantage. Thus, for Cheng, based on this preliminary analysis, we are more likely to use the unlevered earnings multiple over the EBIT, EBITDA, or revenue multiple. There is also no reason to not use the net income multiple in this case, and we note that the unlevered earnings and net income multiples give reasonably similar estimates of value, whereas the EBITDA and revenue multiples are quite different from the others, as we might expect from the Staples simulation in Chapter 13.

We have now gone through the full process of making adjustments to the comparable company and the company being valued, and we have done a multiples valuation. As you can see, this is a very detailed and labor-intensive activity that requires a reasonable knowledge of the basis on which the financial statements are prepared. Also, in this example, we only examined one comparable company, but in a typical valuation, we would be looking at a greater number of comparable companies.

REVIEW EXERCISE 14.4

Valuing a Company Using Market Multiples

Below, we present an income statement and balance sheet for the ValueIT Company. The company's debt and preferred stock balance sheet values are approximately equal to their market values. ValueIT Company has a 30% income tax rate on all income. The company has land in its Net Property, Plant, and Equipment that is not used in its operations, and the land has no effect on the company's revenues or expenses. The current market value of the land is $6,000. Use the market multiples from Review Exercise 14.3 to measure ValueIT's enterprise value and equity value as of the end of Year 1.

Income Statement	Year 1	Balance Sheet	Year 1
Revenues	$5,000.0	**Assets**	
Operating expenses	–2,500.0	Cash and equivalents	$ 1,000.0
Depreciation expense	–1,300.0	Net (non-cash) working capital	2,000.0
Operating income	$1,200.0	Total current assets	$ 3,000.0
Interest expense	–480.0	Property, plant, and equipment, net	30,000.0
Interest income (cash and equivalents)	200.0	Total assets	$33,000.0
Income before income taxes and other Items	$ 920.0		
Provision for income taxes	–276.0	**Liabilities and Shareholders' Equity**	
Net income	$ 644.0	Non-current operating liabilities	$ 8,000.0
Dividends on preferred stock	–350.0	Long-term debt	8,000.0
Earnings available to common shareholders	$ 294.0	Total liabilities	$16,000.0
		Perpetual preferred stock	$ 5,000.0
		Common stock	12,000.0
		Total shareholders' equity	$17,000.0
		Total liabilities and shareholders' equity	$33,000.0

Solution on pages 596–597.

14.10 ADDITIONAL TOPICS—NET OPERATING LOSS CARRYFORWARDS AND ACCOUNTING DIFFERENCES

We discussed net operating loss (NOL) carryforwards in Chapter 3 in the context of their effect on measuring interest tax shields and free cash flows. NOLs can also affect the way we measure market multiples because of their potential affect on comparability. Using pre-tax multiples (EBIT, EBITDA, and revenue) does not eliminate the effect of NOLs. Also recall that NOL carryforwards have a limited number of years for which they can shelter taxable income. The number of years depends on the specific taxing authority. In the United States, NOLs can be carried forward for up to 20 years.

NOL carryforwards are specific to a taxing authority (a country or even state/province within a country). In addition, NOL carryforwards can be specific to a part of a company, for example, certain subsidiaries rather than the consolidated company. Thus, a company may have substantial NOL carryforwards but still pay income taxes, because the NOL carryforwards cannot shelter income from all parts of the company and from all tax jurisdictions.

Sometimes, accounting principle choices or changes in accounting principles limit the comparability of our comparable companies and the company we are valuing in spite of similar growth prospects and profitability. Generally, for a given company, the choice or use of particular accounting principles for financial reporting purposes (not tax purposes) does not directly affect its cash flows (or free cash flows). It does, however, affect the line items on the company's income statement and balance sheet. In addition, the choice of different accounting methods across companies may indicate other differences that are related to cash flow effects. Naturally, since such differences can affect market multiple denominators, adjusting financial statements for differences in accounting principles may be useful in a market multiple valuation. If differences in accounting methods do not relate to differences in the underlying valuation, then we will consider adjusting the financial statements for such differences in order to increase comparability. However, this is not always the case. For example, if two firms report depreciation based on different useful lives for depreciable assets, that difference may indicate differences in expected capital expenditures to replace assets, and in this case we would probably not adjust for the differences in depreciation.

Net Operating Loss Carryforwards as an Excess Asset to Increase Comparability

We can treat NOL carryforwards as an excess asset in order to increase the comparability of our comparable companies and the company we are valuing. In order to make our discussion more straightforward, we assume that a company will be able to use its NOL carryforwards to shelter all of its taxable income (before applying the NOLs) for the next 10 years and that it will have sufficient income to use all of its carryforwards before they expire. We also ignore any differences between a company's taxable income (for the taxing authority) and its book pre-tax income (as listed on its financial statements), or we assume that we will adjust the company's deferred taxes for any difference. To value a company with NOL carryforwards, we remove all of the effects of the NOLs on the numerator and denominator—as if they were excess assets for all of the comparable companies—and on the measure of the denominator of the company we are valuing.

To adjust the denominator, we restate the company's income taxes to what they would be if the company did not have NOL carryforwards. To adjust the numerator, we subtract the value of the NOL carryforwards from the enterprise value and common equity value. We value the NOL carryforwards as we value any asset—we discount the expected cash flows (the taxes that will not have to be paid because of the NOL carryforwards) at the appropriate cost of capital. Therefore, to value NOL carryforwards, we project both the company's taxable income and the dates that the company will use its NOL carryforwards. We then discount the expected benefits of the NOL carryforward in order to measure its value. The discount rate for expected cash flows from the NOL carryforwards is related to the company's asset or unlevered cost of capital, for the underlying risk of these cash flows depends in part on the cash flows generated by the company's assets. Of course, we have to assume that even with a company's NOLs, the future growth prospects are the same for the comparable companies as well as the company we are valuing; however, it won't be taxed as heavily in the first few years because of its NOLs.

Valuation in Practice 14.5

The Escalon Medical Corp. and Subsidiaries' Net Operating Loss Carryforwards As of June 30, 2007, Escalon Medical Corp. and Subsidiaries (Escalon) had net operating loss carryforwards (NOLs) of more than $30 million. The potential tax shelter from these NOLs was about $11 million, which was the amount the company recorded as an NOL deferred tax asset. The company discussed its NOLs as follows:

> As of June 30, 2007, the Company had deferred income tax assets of $12,347,516. The deferred income tax assets have been reduced by a $10,607,531 valuation allowance. The valuation allowance is based on uncertainty with respect to the ultimate realization of net operating loss carryforwards. . . .
>
> The Company has available federal and state net operating loss carryforwards of approximately $31,856,000 and $2,643,000, respectively, of which $26,487,000 and $1,048,000, respectively, will expire over the next ten years, and $5,369,000 and $1,595,000, respectively, will expire in years eleven through twenty. . . .

The company's $34.5 million ($34.5 = $31.9 + $2.6) in NOLs make up most of its deferred tax assets of $12.3 million and almost all of its valuation allowance of $10.6 million.

Source: Escalon develops and manufactures medical devices and pharmaceuticals for medical institutions, educational institutions, ophthalmologists, physician and veterinary office laboratories, and surgeons. The company was founded in 1987, and its headquarters is in Wayne, Pennsylvania. For this footnote, see Escalon Medical Corp. 2007 Annual Report, Footnote 8—Income Taxes.

We apply NOL-adjusted multiples to the NOL-adjusted denominator of the company we are valuing in order to value the company without the value of its NOL carryforwards. To measure the enterprise value of the firm, we add the value of the company's NOL carryforwards to the value obtained from the multiple calculations, and we then add the cash and marketable securities in order to measure the value of the firm.

Deferred Tax Valuation Allowance Related to Net Operating Loss Carryforwards

Companies record the potential tax benefits from NOL carryforwards—ignoring the time value of money—as a deferred tax asset. Based on its historic and expected taxable income, the company reduces its NOL deferred tax asset for the amount of the asset that it may not be able to capture through the use of a valuation allowance. While neither a probabilistic (expected value) nor a present value calculation, the valuation allowance can provide information that may be useful in valuing a company's NOL carryforwards (see Valuation in Practice 14.5).

Valuation Key 14.9

We can treat NOL carryforwards as an excess asset to increase the comparability of our comparable companies and the company we are valuing. We would restate a comparable company's income taxes to what they would be if the company did not have NOL carryforwards, and we would subtract the value of the NOL carryforwards when calculating the enterprise value and common equity value.

Capital Versus Operating Leases and Off-Balance-Sheet Financing

A company may not include all of its financing on its financial statements. We refer to such financing as **off-balance-sheet financing**. We often adjust a company's financial statements to include all of its off-balance-sheet financing activities in order to increase the comparability of the companies. A simple example of off-balance-sheet financing is a non-capitalized operating lease, which we discussed in Chapter 11.

Most companies rent or lease some of their assets. We know that companies in certain industries—such as the airline, retail, and restaurant industries—lease many of their assets. Since a company does not own a leased asset, the most straightforward way to record lease payments is to record an operating (rent) expense for the amount of the lease payment—we call such leases **operating leases**, and they are a form of off-balance-sheet financing.

However, U.S. GAAP requires companies to capitalize the present value of their lease payments for leases with certain characteristics that essentially transfer the ownership of the asset leased; we refer to these leases as **capitalized leases** or **capital leases**.[10] When a company capitalizes the present value of the lease payments for a leased asset, it records an asset (leased asset) and liability (lease liability) equal to the present value of these payments. Every period, the company depreciates (expenses) the leased asset and recognizes interest expense on the lease liability. Over the life of the lease, the sum of the expenses for a capitalized lease (depreciation and interest) will equal the sum of the lease payments. In the early years of a lease, however, a capitalized lease has higher expenses than an operating lease, which reverses in later years even though the cash flows (lease payments) are identical for both.

The AMR Corporation.

Using the AMR Corporation, we illustrate the effect that capitalizing leases can have on a company's market multiples.[11] Using a 7% discount rate, we calculate the present value of the company's operating lease obligations as of the end of 2005 and 2006, which are equal to approximately $7,772.1 million and $7,537.8 million, respectively. We do this by discounting the reported future lease payments as we illustrated for AMR in Chapter 11 (see Exhibit 11.5 for the details of these calculations).

In Exhibit 14.16, we show AMR Corporation's 2006 summary income statement and balance sheet. In the first column of the exhibit, we show the company's reported numbers. In the second column, we show the necessary adjustments to the company's income statement and balance sheet for the capitalization of its operating leases (these adjustments are also detailed in Exhibit 11.6). We assume that the lease interest adjustment and the lease amortization adjustment for 2006 are driven by the 2005 value of the leases when capitalized. To the income statement, we add back the amount of rent expense ($1,065) included in the reported income statement, and we subtract interest expense and amortization on the capitalized operating lease before adjusting the taxes. The interest expense is $544.0 million ($544.0 = $0.07 \times $7,772.1$). We assume that the operating leases have a remaining life of 10 years and that the annual lease amortization is $777.2 million ($777.2 = $7,772.1/10$). Even though the company had a zero income tax expense (it used its NOL carryforwards to shelter its income), we assume that the marginal tax rate for the change in the company's expenses is 38%. The tax adjustment is $97.4 [$97.4 = 0.38 \times ($1,065 − $777.2 − 544)]. Moreover, booking the leases gives rise to a deferred income tax asset of $2,864.4 and deferred tax liability of $2,767.0. In the bottom panel of the exhibit, we also show AMR's equity value and enterprise value with and without the value of the capitalized leases.

In Exhibit 14.17, we show the effect that capitalizing AMR's operating leases has on its denominators, numerators, and multiples for five market multiples—P/E, unlevered earnings, EBIT, EBITDA, and revenue. In the first section (set of rows) of the exhibit, we calculate the denominator of each multiple with and without capitalizing the company's operating leases. In the following two sections, we calculate the company's multiples with and without capitalizing its operating leases. At the very bottom of the exhibit, we compute the percentage change in the multiple from capitalizing the leases.

The company's P/E ratio increases by 220.3% as a result of capitalizing its operating leases, and the unlevered earnings multiple increases by 4.1%. The EBIT multiple hardly changes, but the EBITDA multiple decreases by 12.6% and the revenue multiple increases by 31.4%. AMR has relatively more operating leases than most other companies, but in general, this example illustrates the potentially large and varying effect that capitalizing operating leases can have on a company's market multiples and, hence,

---

[10] See *Statement of Financial Accounting Standards No. 13*, "Accounting for Leases," November 1976, ¶ 7.

[11] The company operates as a scheduled passenger airline through its principal subsidiary, American Airlines, Inc. AMR Corporation is headquartered in Fort Worth, Texas, and was founded in 1934.

how it can affect comparability. The key is that we need to treat the leases of the comparable companies and the company being valued in a similar fashion in order to ensure comparability.

EXHIBIT 14.16	AMR Corporation—2006 Summary Income Statement and Balance Sheet with and Without Capitalizing Its Operating Leases

AMR Corporation Summarized Financial Statements ($ in millions)	2006 Reported	Adjustments to Capitalize Operating Leases	2006 Adjusted
Revenues.	$22,563.0		$22,563.0
Rent expense	−1,065.0	$ 1,065.0	0.0
Depreciation and amortization	−1,157.0		−1,157.0
Amortization of operating leases		−777.2	−777.2
All other operating expenses	−19,281.0		−19,281.0
Operating income.	$ 1,060.0	$ 287.8	$ 1,347.8
Interest expense, net	−722.0		−722.0
Miscellaneous, net	−107.0		−107.0
Lease interest		−544.0	−544.0
Income before taxes.	$ 231.0	$ −256.3	$ −25.3
Income taxes	0.0	97.4	97.4
Net income	$ 231.0	$ −158.9	$ 72.1
Current assets	$ 6,902.0		$ 6,902.0
Net property, plant, and equipment	17,941.0		17,941.0
Other assets	4,302.0	$ 2,864.4	7,166.4
Capitalized operating lease asset		7,281.5	7,281.5
Total assets.	$29,145.0	$10,145.9	$39,290.9
Current operating liabilities.	$ 7,156.0		$ 7,156.0
Other liabilities	9,205.0	$ 2,767.0	11,972.0
Debt	13,390.0		13,390.0
Capitalized operating lease liability		7,537.8	7,537.8
Total liabilities.	$29,751.0	$10,304.7	$40,055.7
Shareholders' equity	−606.0	−158.9	−764.9
Total liabilities and shareholders' equity	$29,145.0	$10,145.9	$39,290.9

Valuation ($ in millions, except per share amounts)	Equity Value	Enterprise Value	
Shares outstanding	239.896	239.896	
Price/share	$ 37.49	$ 37.49	
Market value of equity	$ 8,993.7	$ 8,993.7	
Options and other securities	1,705.3	1,705.3	
Debt		13,390.0	
Cash	−121.0	−121.0	
Market value without capitalizing leases	$10,578.0	$23,968.0	
Capitalized operating leases		7,537.8	
Market value with capitalizing leases.	$10,578.0	$31,505.8	

Exhibit may contain small rounding errors

EXHIBIT 14.17   AMR Corporation—Market Multiples with and Without Capitalizing Its Operating Leases

($ in millions)	P/E	Unlevered Earnings Multiple	EBIT Multiple	EBITDA Multiple	Revenue Multiple
Denominator					
Earnings	$ 231.0	$ 231.0	$ 231.0	$ 231.0	
Interest		722.0	722.0	722.0	
Tax adjustment		−274.4	0.0	0.0	
Depreciation and amortization				1,157.0	
Earnings without capitalizing operating leases	$ 231.0	$ 678.6	$ 953.0	$ 2,110.0	
Rent expense	1,065.0	1,065.0	1,065.0	1,065.0	
Interest on leases	−544.0				
Amortization of leases	−777.2	−777.2	−777.2		
Tax adjustment	97.4	−109.4			
Earnings with capitalizing leases	$ 72.1	$ 857.1	$ 1,240.8	$ 3,175.0	
Multiple without capitalizing leases					
Value without capitalizing operating leases	$10,578.0	$23,968.0	$23,968.0	$23,968.0	$23,968.0
Denominator without capitalizing operating leases	231.0	678.6	953.0	2,110.0	22,563.0
Multiple without capitalized operating leases	**45.79**	**35.32**	**25.15**	**11.36**	**1.06**
Multiple with capitalizing leases					
Value with capitalizing operating leases	$10,578.0	$31,505.8	$31,505.8	$31,505.8	$31,505.8
Denominator with capitalizing operating leases	72.1	857.1	1,240.8	3,175.0	22,563.0
Multiple with capitalized operating leases	**146.67**	**36.76**	**25.39**	**9.92**	**1.40**
Percentage change	**220.3%**	**4.1%**	**1.0%**	**−12.6%**	**31.4%**

Exhibit may contain small rounding errors

REVIEW EXERCISE 14.5

Market Multiple and Operating Leases

For the LeaseIT Corporation, use the following information to measure the P/E, unlevered earnings, EBIT, EBITDA, and revenue multiples, with and without capitalizing its operating leases. Assume a marginal tax rate of 40% applies to all income.

Present value of operating leases—beginning balance	$ 1,996.3
Present value of operating leases—ending balance	$ 2,100.0
Annual lease payment	$ 500.0
Amortization period in years	5
Lease discount rate	8.0%
Market value of equity	$ 5,000.0
Market value of firm	$ 9,500.0

continued

LeaseIT Corporation Summarized Income Statement	Reported	LeaseIT Corporation Summarized Balance Sheet	Reported
Revenues.	$7,000.0	Cash.	$ 400.0
Rent expense	−500.0	Other current assets.	2,000.0
Depreciation and amortization	−2,000.0	Net property, plant, and equipment	8,000.0
Amortization of operating leases	—	Other assets.	2,000.0
All other operating expenses	−3,000.0	Capitalized operating leases	—
Operating income.	$1,500.0	Total assets.	$12,400.0
Interest expense, net	−400.0		
Lease interest.	—		
		Current operating liabilities.	$ 1,000.0
Income before taxes.	$1,100.0	Other liabilities	1,500.0
Income taxes	−440.0	Debt	4,500.0
Net income	$ 660.0	Capitalized operating leases	—
		Total liabilities.	$ 7,000.0
		Shareholders' equity	5,400.0
		Total liabilities and shareholders' equity. . . .	$12,400.0

Solution on pages 597–598.

Changes in Accounting, Correction of Errors, and Restated Financial Statements[12]

A company may change accounting principles voluntarily or because of changes in generally accepted accounting principles (GAAP). A company may also change accounting estimates (for example, the usable life of its assets). Mandatory changes in GAAP typically provide a transition process for companies to change to the new accounting method. Voluntary changes in accounting principles require a retrospective adjustment of the financial statements in the year of the change.

In a retrospective adjustment, the company adjusts its financial statements for the different accounting principles in prior accounting periods as if that principle had always been used. To make a retrospective adjustment, the company records the cumulative effect of the change in the book value of the assets and liabilities as of the beginning of the first period presented in the financial statements. The company then makes an offsetting adjustment to retained earnings (or to other appropriate components of equity).

If a company identifies an unintentional error made in its financial statements for previous years, the company follows essentially the same process as the one to address a change in accounting principles. If the error or misstatement was intentional, then the company will restate its previous financial statements. Regardless of whether a company provides restated financial statements or corrects errors in its financial statements, we should examine the effect of the restatement or correction on our assessment of the recurring earnings of the company.

---

[12] An accounting change is a change in an accounting principle or an accounting estimate, or an accounting entity; see *Statement of Financial Accounting Standards No. 154*, "Accounting Changes and Error Corrections: a Replacement of APB Opinion No. 20 and FASB Statement No. 3," May 2005.

SUMMARY AND KEY CONCEPTS

The market multiple valuation method is widely used. We use market multiple valuation methods to value the company and its equity as of both the valuation date and the continuing value date. The market multiple valuation method relies heavily on the comparability of the comparable companies.

We make adjustments to increase the consistency of the numerator and denominator of the market multiples we might use as well as to increase the comparability across companies. Adjusting the numerators and denominators of the market multiples is time-consuming and detailed work. However, if we do not make appropriate adjustments to the multiples, the usefulness of the estimated market multiples is usually sacrificed and the market multiple valuations are likely to contain errors. We demonstrated the adjustment process in detail using Universal Corporation and AMR Corporation for typical adjustments that are made. As is probably obvious, many kinds of adjustments are potentially important, and making such adjustments requires a detailed reading of the company's financial statements.

If we were able to identify a company that is comparable on all dimensions to the company we are valuing and if we make all of the necessary adjustments to the multiples and the company being valued, all of the common market multiples will work equally well. The perfect comparable company, however, does not exist, so we are always trading off the number of comparable companies we use with how comparable the companies are to the company being valued, and we are always considering which of the market multiples are best suited for the situation we face.

ADDITIONAL READING AND REFERENCES

Liu, J., D. Nissim, and J. Thomas, "Equity Valuation Using Multiples," *Journal of Accounting Research* 40 (2002), pp. 135–172.

Ramanlal, P., S. Mann, and W. Moore, "Convertible Preferred Stock Valuation: Tests of Alternative Models," *Review of Quantitative Finance and Accounting* 10 (1998), pp. 303–319.

EXERCISES AND PROBLEMS

P14.1 **Measuring Market Multiple Numerators:** Below, we present an income statement and balance sheet for the Multiple Company. The company's debt and preferred stock are recorded on the balance sheet at par value. The debt and preferred stock are currently trading at 95% and 105% of their respective par values. The company's debt has an 8% interest rate and the dividend yield for its preferred stock is 9%. The company has 50,000 shares of outstanding stock trading at $8 per share. The company also has 10,000 employee stock options outstanding that the company valued at $3 per option. The company's income tax rate on all income is 30%. Calculate the company's enterprise value and equity value in order to measure the company's market multiples as discussed in the previous sections of this chapter. Calculate the company's enterprise value to unlevered earnings, EBIT, EBITDA, revenue, and P/E multiples without making any adjustments to the income statement. HINT: Measure the unlevered earnings as net income plus after-tax interest expense and measure EBIT as net income plus interest expense plus income tax expense.

	Year 2		Year 1	Year 2
Revenue	$200,000	Cash	$ 80,000	$ 80,000
Operating expenses	−120,000	Other current assets	30,000	32,000
Depreciation expense	−50,000	Equity in unconsolidated affiliates	70,000	72,000
Operating earnings	$ 30,000	Property, plant, and equipment (net)	240,000	250,000
Earnings from unconsolidated affiliates	14,000	Total assets	$420,000	$434,000
Investment income (on cash)	5,000			
Interest expense	−6,400	Accounts payable	$ 20,000	$ 24,000
Income before taxes	$ 42,600	Debt	80,000	80,000
Income tax expense	−12,780	Total liabilities	$100,000	$104,000
Minority Interest (net of tax)	−17,000	Minority interest	$ 84,000	$ 87,000
Net income	$ 12,820	Preferred stock	$ 32,000	$ 32,000
		Capital stock	20,000	20,000
		Retained earnings	184,000	191,000
		Shareholders' equity	$236,000	$243,000
		Liabilities and shareholders' equity	$420,000	$434,000

P14.2 **Measuring Market Multiple Denominators:** Use the information from Problem 14.1 as well as the following information to adjust the company's financial statements for effects related to its cash balance and its nonrecurring items. In Year 2, the company incurred a non-recurring operating expense of $24,000, which is included in operating expenses. Also calculate the company's enterprise value to unlevered earnings, EBIT, EBITDA, revenue, and P/E multiples using the adjusted financial statements. HINT: Measure the unlevered earnings as net income plus after-tax interest expense and measure EBIT as net income plus interest expense plus income tax expense using the adjusted financial statements.

P14.3 **Adjusting Market Multiple Numerators and Denominators:** Use the information from Problem 14.1 and Problem 14.2 as well as the following information to adjust the company's financial statements for effects related to its unconsolidated affiliates and minority interest. Also calculate the company's enterprise value to unlevered earnings, EBIT, EBITDA, revenue, and P/E multiples using the adjusted financial statements. Earnings from the unconsolidated affiliates are taxed at a rate of 30%. The market value of the Multiple Company's interest in the unconsolidated affiliates is $196,000. The market value of the minority interest in Multiple Company's subsidiary is $238,000. HINT: Measure the unlevered earnings as net income plus after-tax interest expense and measure EBIT as net income plus interest expense plus income tax expense using the adjusted financial statements.

P14.4 **Valuing a Company Using Market Multiples:** Below, we present an income statement and balance sheet for the Multiple Value Company. The company's debt and preferred stock balance sheet values are approximately equal to their market values. The Company has a 40% income tax rate on all income. The company has land included in its Property, Plant, and Equipment, Net that it does not use in its operations, and the land has no effect on the company's revenues or expenses. The current market value of the land is $15,000. Use the market multiples from Problem 14.3 to measure the company's enterprise value and equity value as of the end of Year 1.

Income Statement	Year 1	Balance Sheet	Year 1
Revenues	$50,000.0	**Assets**	
Operating expenses.	–25,000.0	Cash and equivalents.	$ 5,000.0
Depreciation expense.	–15,000.0	Net (non-cash) working capital.	10,000.0
Operating income.	$10,000.0	Total current assets	$15,000.0
Interest expense.	–2,160.0	Property, plant, and equipment, net.	75,000.0
Interest income (cash and equivalents)	200.0	Total assets.	$90,000.0
Income before income taxes and other items . . .	$ 8,040.0		
Provision for income taxes.	–3,216.0	**Liabilities and Shareholders' Equity**	
Net income.	$ 4,824.0	Non-current operating liabilities.	$ 8,000.0
Dividends on preferred stock.	–680.0	Long-term debt	27,000.0
Earnings available to common shareholders	$ 4,144.0	Total liabilities.	$35,000.0
		Perpetual preferred stock.	8,000.0
		Common stock.	47,000.0
		Total shareholders' equity	$55,000.0
		Total liabilities and shareholders' equity. .	$90,000.0

P14.5 **Market Multiple and Operating Leases:** For the Leasing Company, use the following information to measure the P/E, and enterprise value to unlevered earnings, EBIT, EBITDA, and revenue multiples with and without capitalizing its operating leases.

Present value of operating leases—beginning balance.	$ 70,235.8
Present value of operating leases—ending balance	$ 74,000.0
Annual lease payment	$ 10,000.0
Amortization period in years.	10
Lease discount rate	7.0%
Market value of equity	$266,760.0
Market value of firm	$320,760.0

Leasing Company Summarized Income Statement	Reported	Leasing Company Summarized Balance Sheet	Reported
Revenues.	$150,000.0	Cash	$ 15,000.0
Rent expense	–10,000.0	Other current assets.	37,500.0
Depreciation and amortization	–8,000.0	Net property, plant, and equipment	120,000.0
Amortization of operating leases	—	Other assets.	7,500.0
All other operating expenses	–97,500.0	Capitalized operating leases	—
Operating income.	$ 34,500.0	Total assets.	$180,000.0
Interest expense, net	–4,860.0		
Lease interest.	—	Current operating liabilities.	$ 26,000.0
		Other liabilities	15,000.0
Income before taxes.	$ 29,640.0	Debt	54,000.0
Income taxes	–11,856.0	Capitalized operating leases	—
Net income	$ 17,784.0	Total liabilities.	$ 95,000.0
		Shareholders' equity	85,000.0
		Total liabilities and shareholders' equity. . . .	$180,000.0

P14.6 **Tina H's Dog Toys, Inc. Market Multiple Valuation:** Tina H's Dog Toys, Inc. is a privately held company. You have been hired to value the company's firm value and equity using market multiple valuation methods. An analyst already identified potential comparable companies for your analysis—Mike's Dog Wonderland, Inc., Matt's Pet Supply Company, and Jeff's Dog Heaven, Inc. The analyst also prepared a summary of some accounting and market information, as well as some forecast data for your analysis as shown in Exhibit P14.1. Some of the companies own various marketable securities that they do not need to operate their businesses. These companies record such investments at cost and show dividend income from these investments as a separate line item on the income statement. Operating income is equal to operating revenues minus all operating expenses but excludes interest expense, income taxes, and any extraordinary items (which the company shows as a separate line item in the income statement net of income taxes). Net income is measured after deducting all expenses, includes other income (dividends from investments) and includes the effect of extraordinary items. All of the companies have the same income tax rate, 35%, and all income is taxed at the same rate.

a. Calculate each comparable company's unlevered earnings, EBIT, EBITDA, revenue, and P/E multiples using the adjusted financial statements.

b. Value Tina H's Dog Toys, Inc. and its equity using market multiple valuation methods.

c. Assess the pros and cons of using each comparable company.

P14.7 **F. Hill Enterprises Market Multiple Valuation:** F. Hill Enterprises (Hill) is a privately held company that records and distributes musical recordings in a variety of formats. It is a reasonably large company for a privately held company and has several direct competitors that are publicly traded. You have been engaged to value Hill (its firm value and its equity value) using market multiple valuation methods. An analyst has already prepared a summary of some accounting and market information, as well as some forecast data for your analysis shown in Exhibit P14.2. In addition, the analyst identified three publicly traded potential comparable companies for Hill, all of which are its direct competitors—T. McGraw Corporation (McGraw), W. Nelson Company (Nelson), and T. Keith, Inc. (Keith). Further, the analyst reviewed the financial leverage of Hill and its three competitors and concluded that their capital structures were similar. Finally, the analyst found that the companies all had the same income tax rate, 40%, and that this rate applies to all forms of income.

a. Calculate each comparable company's unlevered earnings, EBIT, EBITDA, revenue, and P/E multiples using the adjusted financial statements.

b. Value Hill and its equity using market multiple valuation methods.

c. Assess the pros and cons of using each comparable company.

P14.8 **Comprehensive Market Multiple Calculation, the L. Messaglia Company:** In Exhibit P14.3, we present an income statement and balance sheet for the L. Messaglia Company. The company's debt and preferred stock are recorded on the balance sheet at par value and were issued a few years ago. The preferred stock is currently trading at its par value. The company's convertible bonds have a 6% interest rate. The company's straight debt has a 9% cost of capital and interest rate. The convertible bonds mature in 5 years. The equity cost of capital is 12%. The company's outstanding stock is trading at $12 per share. The company's income tax rate is 35% on all income. The company's income from unconsolidated affiliates is from dividends received; 70% of the intercompany dividends are excluded from income taxes. The value of the company's investments in its unconsolidated affiliates is $171,600, and the value of the minority interests is equal to $84,000. The current risk-free rate is 4%, and the company's stock has a 40% annual volatility. Depreciation and amortization expense was $48,305 in Year 1. The value of the company's discontinued operations is $18,000.

a. Making all of the appropriate adjustments, calculate the company's enterprise value and equity value as of the end of Year 1 for the purpose of measuring the company's market multiples.

b. Making all of the appropriate adjustments, calculate the company's enterprise value to unlevered earnings, EBIT, EBITDA, revenue, and P/E multiples.

EXHIBIT P14.1 Summary Information for Tina H's Dog Toys, Inc. and Comparable Companies

($ in thousands, except per share amounts)	Mike's Dog Wonderland Actual Year 0	Forecast Year 1	Forecast Year 5	Matt's Pet Supply Co. Actual Year 0	Forecast Year 1	Forecast Year 5	Jeff's Dog Heaven, Inc. Actual Year 0	Forecast Year 1	Forecast Year 5	Tina H's Dog Toys, Inc. Actual Year 0	Forecast Year 1	Forecast Year 5
Primary Income Statement Items												
Revenue (sales)	$614.5	$643.7	$880.2	$101.6	$112.7	$280.2	$179.6	$180.4	$299.4	$126.5	$127.1	$176.6
Operating income	$130.5	$126.5	$161.7	$ 32.0	$ 36.2	$ 89.2	$ 31.9	$ 34.9	$ 54.7	$ 31.0	$ 33.1	$ 44.2
Net income	$ 33.3	$ 33.7	$ 92.4	$ 22.0	$ 24.1	$ 54.3	$ 18.0	$ 19.8	$ 32.0	$ 18.3	$ 19.5	$ 26.2
Other Items in the Income Statement												
Depreciation expense	$ 41.5	$ 47.3	$ 60.1	$ 10.7	$ 11.7	$ 28.4	$ 9.4	$ 10.3	$ 14.7	$ 6.9	$ 7.6	$ 9.1
Interest expense	$ 14.7	$ 16.2	$ 19.6	$ 6.0	$ 6.8	$ 9.5	$ 4.2	$ 4.4	$ 5.6	$ 4.3	$ 4.5	$ 5.3
Dividends from investments	$ 0	$ 0	$ 0	$ 10.8	$ 10.8	$ 10.8	$ 0	$ 0	$ 0	$ 1.4	$ 1.4	$ 1.4
Extraordinary item (net of income taxes)	$-42.0	$-38.0	$ 0	$ 0	$ 0	$ 0	$ 0	$ 0	$ 0	$ 0	$ 0	$ 0
Preferred stock dividends	$ 6.5	$ 7.3	$ 8.9	$ 2.3	$ 2.6	$ 3.7	$ 2.8	$ 3.1	$ 3.9	$ 2.1	$ 2.4	$ 2.8
Primary Balance Sheet Items												
Cash balance	$ 2.5	$ 3.3	$ 5.1	$ 1.3	$ 1.6	$ 2.9	$ 0.6	$ 0.7	$ 0.8	$ 0.5	$ 0.6	$ 0.7
Marketable securities	$ 0	$ 0	$ 0	$ 94.5	$ 94.5	$ 94.5	$ 0	$ 0	$ 0	$ 19.2	$ 19.2	$ 19.2
Total assets	$321.9	$354.0	$442.3	$151.4	$173.0	$241.0	$ 82.0	$ 94.3	$128.5	$ 76.9	$ 82.1	$ 94.9
Common equity	$ 49.4	$ 65.6	$102.1	$ 25.2	$ 32.5	$ 58.8	$ -6.9	$ -1.7	$ 12.5	$ -3.5	$ -2.6	$ -2.5
Free Cash Flows (Before Extraordinary Items and Dividends from Investments)												
Unlevered free cash flow	$ 55.6	$ 50.0	$ 92.2	$ 13.1	$ 0.1	$ 49.3	$ 16.9	$ 10.4	$ 31.8	$ 17.4	$ 16.3	$ 26.5
Equity free cash flow	$ 61.1	$ 48.2	$ 80.5	$ 20.4	$ 7.7	$ 45.2	$ 16.4	$ 11.5	$ 27.6	$ 16.3	$ 15.3	$ 23.1
Market Values												
Marketable securities	$ 0			$131.2			$ 0			$ 32.5		
Debt	$190.7			$ 92.5			$ 53.3			$ 53.6		
Preferred stock	$ 81.7			$ 33.6			$ 35.5			$ 26.8		
Common equity:												
Shares authorized	183.35			315.36			214.52			23.12		
Shares issued	121.01			208.14			141.58			18.50		
Shares outstanding	108.91			187.32			127.42			17.02		
Price at end of Year 0	$5.838			$1.572			$1.627					
Average price per share in December of Year 0	$6.422			$1.729			$1.790					

EXHIBIT P14.2 Summary Information for F. Hill and Comparable Companies

($ in thousands, except per share amounts)	T. McGraw Corporation Actual Year 0	Forecast Year 1	Forecast Year 5	W. Nelson Company Actual Year 0	Forecast Year 1	Forecast Year 5	T. Keith, Inc. Actual Year 0	Forecast Year 1	Forecast Year 5	F. Hill Company Actual Year 0	Forecast Year 1	Forecast Year 5
Primary Income Statement Items												
Revenue (sales)	$235.8	$259.3	$642.4	$630.3	$664.4	$819.9	$366.5	$400.2	$825.4	$260.5	$286.5	$684.7
Operating income	$ 54.0	$ 61.0	$149.7	$ 89.1	$ 94.7	$114.8	$ 89.4	$ 99.7	$210.0	$ 66.3	$ 75.5	$170.5
Net income	$−13.2	$ −5.5	$ 82.0	$ 56.3	$ 59.5	$ 70.3	$ 47.7	$ 53.5	$116.4	$ 37.1	$ 42.2	$ 95.4
Other Items in the Income Statement												
Depreciation expense	$ 45.0	$ 49.2	$120.1	$131.5	$144.4	$164.0	$ 73.3	$ 80.0	$152.4	$ 52.2	$ 56.3	$137.7
Interest expense	$ 6.1	$ 6.8	$ 13.1	$ 7.1	$ 7.4	$ 9.4	$ 10.0	$ 10.5	$ 16.1	$ 7.5	$ 8.2	$ 14.4
Dividends from investments	$ 0	$ 0	$ 0	$ 11.8	$ 11.8	$ 11.8	$ 0	$ 0	$ 0	$ 3.0	$ 3.0	$ 3.0
Extraordinary item (net of income taxes)	$−42.0	$−38.0	$ 0	$ 0	$ 0	$ 0	$ 0	$ 0	$ 0	$ 0	$ 0	$ 0
Preferred stock dividends	$ 2.8	$ 3.1	$ 6.0	$ 2.6	$ 2.9	$ 3.7	$ 6.7	$ 7.5	$ 11.5	$ 3.9	$ 4.4	$ 7.7
Primary Balance Sheet Items												
Cash balance	$ 5.3	$ 8.3	$ 17.7	$ 29.2	$ 30.3	$ 34.6	$ 3.1	$ 5.3	$ 13.2	$ 7.6	$ 10.8	$ 19.4
Marketable securities	$ 0	$ 0	$ 0	$144.2	$144.2	$144.2	$ 0	$ 0	$ 0	$ 69.4	$ 69.4	$ 69.4
Total assets	$240.1	$331.4	$618.4	$721.9	$753.1	$871.4	$307.9	$384.8	$654.0	$323.0	$424.4	$696.8
Common equity	$105.6	$165.2	$353.8	$583.2	$606.4	$692.8	$ 61.8	$105.4	$264.8	$151.2	$216.2	$388.7
Free Cash Flows (Before Extraordinary Items and Dividends from Investments)												
Unlevered free cash flow	$ 6.7	$−54.7	$ 71.8	$ 23.8	$ 25.6	$ 54.6	$ 39.0	$−17.2	$106.9	$ 18.2	$−56.1	$ 84.0
Equity free cash flow	$ 18.8	$−30.2	$ 65.7	$ 24.1	$ 26.3	$ 48.8	$ 45.3	$ 2.5	$ 97.2	$ 30.4	$−29.0	$ 76.7
Market Values												
Marketable securities	$ 0			$144.2			$ 0			$ 69.4		
Debt	$ 94.1			$101.7			$147.6			$114.5		
Preferred stock	$ 40.3			$ 37.0			$ 98.4			$ 57.2		
Common equity:												
Shares authorized	153.35			315.36			214.52			23.12		
Shares issued	101.21			208.14			141.58			18.50		
Shares outstanding	91.09			187.32			127.42			17.02		
Price at end of Year 0	$3.445			$1.727			$4.505					
Average price per share in December of Year 0	$3.790			$1.900			$4.955					

EXHIBIT P14.3 Summary Information for the L. Messaglia Company

Income Statement	Year 0	Year 1
Revenues	$100,000	$120,000
Operating expenses.	−50,000	−57,600
Restructuring and impairment costs		−9,600
Operating income.	$ 50,000	$ 52,800
Equity in pretax earnings of		
unconsolidated affiliates.	10,000	13,200
Income on cash and equivalents	600	840
Interest expense.	−10,200	−10,680
Income before income taxes and other items	$ 50,400	$ 56,160
Provision for income taxes.	−15,120	−16,848
Minority interest (net of tax)	−5,000	−6,000
Income (loss) from continuing operations	$ 30,280	$ 33,312
Income (loss) from discontinued operations		
(net of tax)	0	−7,200
Net income.	$ 30,280	$ 26,112
Dividends on preferred stock.	−5,310	−5,310
Earnings available to common shareholders	$ 24,970	$ 20,802
Common dividends	$ 9,882	$ 10,402

Balance Sheet	Year 0	Year 1
Assets		
Cash and equivalents.	$ 15,000	$ 16,800
Current operating assets	18,000	20,400
Discontinued operations current assets. . . .		4,800
Total current assets	$ 33,000	$ 42,000
Property, plant and equipment, net	300,000	348,000
Other non-current assets	15,000	15,600
Investments in unconsolidated affiliates . . .	20,000	21,600
Total assets.	$368,000	$427,200
Liabilities and Shareholders' Equity		
Current operating liabilities.	$ 9,000	$ 13,200
Short-term debt	40,000	56,000
Discontinued operations liabilities		14,400
Total current liabilities.	$ 49,000	$ 83,600
Convertible bonds[1].	150,000	150,000
Other long-term liabilities.	9,000	13,200
Total liabilities.	$208,000	$246,800
Minority interest	$ 50,000	$ 60,000
Series A 9% perpetual preferred stock	$ 59,000	$ 59,000
Common stock[2]	10,000	10,000
Retained earnings	41,000	51,400
Total shareholders' equity	$110,000	$120,400
Total liabilities and shareholders; equity. . . .	$368,000	$427,200

[1] 6% Convertible Bond, each bond issued and outstanding at $1,000 par value. Each bond is convertible into 100 shares of common stock.

[2] Common Stock, 60,000 shares authorized, 40,000 shares issued and outstanding as of the end of Year 1.

SOLUTIONS FOR REVIEW EXERCISES

Solution for Review Exercise 14.1: Measuring Market Multiple Numerators

Market Value of Debt		
Price.		102
Market value of debt		$ 12,240
Market Value of Preferred		
Price.		98
Market value of preferred		$ 4,900
Market Value of Options		
Price.		$ 2.00
Shares		2,000
Market value of options		$ 4,000
Market Value of Common Equity		
Price.		$ 10.00
Shares		10,000
Market value of common equity.		$100,000

Market Value	Enterprise Value	Equity Value
Debt	$ 12,240	
Preferred stock.	4,900	
Options.	4,000	$ 4,000
Common equity	100,000	100,000
Subtotal	$121,140	$104,000
Cash and equivalents.	−12,000	−12,000
Total	$109,140	$ 92,000

Market Multiples	Numerator	Denominator	Multiple
Net income..		$ 1,256	
Interest expense....................................		840	
Interest tax shield..................................		−336	
Unlevered earnings	$109,140	$ 1,760	62.0
EBIT	$109,140	$ 3,200	34.1
Depreciation.......................................		8,000	
EBITDA	$109,140	$11,200	9.7
Revenue..	$109,140	$30,000	3.6
Net income...		$ 1,256	
Preferred stock dividends		−400	
Net income to common	$ 92,000	$ 856	107.5

EBIT of $3,200 = Net Income $1,256 + Interest Expense $840 + Income Taxes $1,104

Solution for Review Exercise 14.2: Measuring Market Multiple Denominators

	Year 1	Year 2	Cash and Equivalents	Non-recurring Expenses	Year 2 Adjusted
Revenue		$30,000			$30,000
Operating expenses............................		−21,000		$4,000	−17,000
Depreciation expense...........................		−8,000			−8,000
Operating earnings.............................		$ 1,000	$ 0	$4,000	$ 5,000
Pre-tax earnings from unconsolidated affiliates......		2,000			2,000
Interest income (on cash and equivalents)..........		600	−600		0
Interest expense................................		−840			−840
Income before taxes...........................		$ 2,760	$ −600	$4,000	$ 6,160
Income tax expense.............................		−1,104	240	−1600	−2,464
Minority interest (net of tax)		−400			−400
Net income.....................................		$ 1,256	$ −360	$2,400	$ 3,296
Cash and equivalents...........................	$12,000	$12,000	$−12,000		$ 0
Other current assets............................	5,000	5,000			5,000
Investments in unconsolidated affiliates	11,000	11,000			11,000
Property, plant, and equipment (net)	36,000	38,000			38,000
Total assets....................................	$64,000	$66,000	$−12,000	$ 0	$54,000
Accounts payable..............................	$ 3,000	$ 4,000			$ 4,000
Debt	12,000	12,000			12,000
Total liabilities.................................	$15,000	$16,000	$ 0	$ 0	$16,000
Minority interest	$ 5,000	$ 6,000			$ 6,000
Preferred stock................................	$ 5,000	$ 5,000			$ 5,000
Capital stock	3,000	3,000			3,000
Retained earnings	36,000	36,000	$−12,000		24,000
Shareholders' equity	$44,000	$44,000	$−12,000	$ 0	$32,000
Liabilities and shareholders' equity	$64,000	$66,000	$−12,000	$ 0	$54,000

Market Multiples	Numerator	Denominator	Multiple
Net income.		$ 3,296	
Interest expense.		840	
Interest tax shield		−336	
Unlevered earnings	$109,140	$ 3,800	28.7
EBIT	$109,140	$ 6,600	16.5
Depreciation		8,000	
EBITDA	$109,140	$14,600	7.5
Revenue.	$109,140	$30,000	3.6
Net income.		$ 3,296	
Preferred stock dividends		−400	
Net income to common	$ 92,000	$ 2,896	31.8

EBIT OF $6,600 = Net Income $3,296 + Interest Expense $840 + Income Taxes $2,464

Solution for Review Exercise 14.3: Adjusting Market Multiple Numerators and Denominators

	Year 1	Year 2	Cash and Equivalents	Non-recurring Expenses	Unconsolidated Affiliates	Minority Interest	Year 2 Adjusted
Revenue		$30,000					$30,000
Operating expenses		−21,000		$4,000			−17,000
Depreciation expense.		−8,000					−8,000
Operating earnings.		$ 1,000	$ 0	$4,000	$ 0	$ 0	$ 5,000
Pre-tax earnings from unconsolidated affiliates.		2,000			−2,000		0
Interest income (cash and equivalents)		600	−600				0
Interest expense.		−840					−840
Income before taxes.		$ 2,760	$ −600	$4,000	$ −2,000	$ 0	$ 4,160
Income tax expense.		−1,104	240	−1600	800		−1,664
Minority interest (net of tax)		−400				400	0
Net income.		$ 1,256	$ −360	$2,400	$ −1,200	$ 400	$ 2,496
Cash and equivalents.	$12,000	$12,000	$−12,000				$ 0
Other current assets.	5,000	5,000					5,000
Investments in unconsolidated affiliates	11,000	11,000			$−11,000		0
Property, plant, and equipment (net)	36,000	38,000					38,000
Total assets.	$64,000	$66,000	$−12,000	S 0	$−11,000	$ 0	$43,000
Account payable	$ 3,000	$ 4,000					$ 4,000
Debt	12,000	12,000					12,000
Total liabilities.	$15,000	$16,000	$ 0	S 0	$ 0	$ 0	$16,000
Minority interest	$ 5,000	$ 6,000				$−6,000	$ 0
Preferred stock.	$ 5,000	$ 5,000					$ 5,000
Capital stock	3,000	3,000					3,000
Retained earnings	36,000	36,000	$−12,000		$−11,000	$ 6,000	19,000
Shareholders' equity	$44,000	$44,000	$−12,000	S 0	$−11,000	$ 6,000	$27,000
Liabilities and shareholders' equity	$64,000	$66,000	$−12,000	S 0	$−11,000	$ 0	$43,000

Market Value	Enterprise Value	Equity Value
Debt	$ 12,240	
Preferred stock.	4,900	
Options.	4,000	$ 4,000
Common equity	100,000	100,000
Subtotal	$121,140	$104,000
Cash and equivalents.	−12,000	−12,000
Previous total	$109,140	$ 92,000
Unconsolidated affiliates	−28,000	−28,000
Minority interest	5,600	5,600
Total	$ 86,740	$ 69,600

Market Multiples	Numerator	Denominator	Multiple
Net income.		$ 2,496	
Interest expense.		840	
Interest tax shield.		−336	
Unlevered earnings	$86,740	$ 3,000	28.9
EBIT.	$86,740	$ 5,000	17.3
Depreciation		8,000	
EBITDA	$86,740	$13,000	6.7
Revenue.	$86,740	$30,000	2.9
Net income.		$ 2,496	
Preferred stock dividends		−400	
Net income to common.	$69,600	$ 2,096	33.2

$$\text{EBIT of } \$5{,}000 = \text{Net Income } \$2{,}496 + \text{Interest Expense } \$840 + \text{Income Taxes } \$1{,}664$$

Solution for Review Exercise 14.4: Valuing a Company Using Market Multiples

Year 1	Unlevered Earnings	EBIT	EBITDA	Net Income to Common
Net income.	$644.0	$ 644.0	$ 644.0	$644.0
Preferred stock dividends				−350.0
Interest expense.	480.0	480.0	480.0	
Interest tax shield.	−144.0			
Income taxes		276.0	276.0	
Depreciation and amortization.			1,300.0	
Total (before adjustment for excess cash)	$980.0	$1,400.0	$2,700.0	$294.0
Interest income (cash and equivalents)	−200.0	−200.0	−200.0	−200.0
Income taxes	60.0			60.0
Total (after all adjustments).	$840.0	$1,200.0	$2,500.0	$154.0

Year 1	Unlevered Earnings	EBIT	EBITDA	Revenue	Net Income to Common
ValueIT Company's value drivers	$ 840.0	$ 1,200.0	$ 2,500.0	$ 5,000.0	$ 154.0
Market multiple (Review Exercise 14.3)	28.91	17.35	6.67	2.89	33.21
	$24,287.2	$20,817.6	$16,680.8	$14,456.7	$ 5,113.7
Long-term debt					8,000.0
Perpetual preferred stock.					5,000.0
Enterprise value	$24,287.2	$20,817.6	$16,680.8	$14,456.7	$18,113.7
Cash and equivalents.	1,000.0	1,000.0	1,000.0	1,000.0	1,000.0
Excess asset (land).	6,000.0	6,000.0	6,000.0	6,000.0	6,000.0
Value of firm with excess assets	$31,287.2	$27,817.6	$23,680.8	$21,456.7	$25,113.7
Long-term debt	−8,000.0	−8,000.0	−8,000.0	−8,000.0	−8,000.0
Perpetual preferred stock.	−5,000.0	−5,000.0	−5,000.0	−5,000.0	−5,000.0
Common equity value with excess assets	$18,287.2	$14,817.6	$10,680.8	$ 8,456.7	$12,113.7
% Difference from Unlevered Earnings Valuation					
Value of firm with excess assets	0.0%	−11.1%	−24.3%	−31.4%	−19.7%
Equity value with excess assets.	0.0%	−19.0%	−41.6%	−53.8%	−33.8%

Solution for Review Exercise 14.5: Market Multiple and Operating Leases

	Reported	Adjustments	Adjusted
Revenues	$ 7,000.0		$ 7,000.0
Rent expense	−500.0	$ 500	0.0
Depreciation and amortization	−2,000.0		−2,000.0
Amortization of operating leases		−399.3	−399.3
All other operating expenses	−3,000.0		−3,000.0
Operating income.	$ 1,500.0	$ 100.7	$ 1,600.7
Interest expense, net	−400.0		−400.0
Lease interest		−159.7	−159.7
Income before taxes.	$ 1,100.0	$ −59.0	$ 1,041.0
Income taxes	−440.0	23.6	−416.4
Net income	$ 660.0	$ −35.4	$ 624.6
Cash	$ 400.0		$ 400.0
Other current assets.	2000.0	$ 840.0	2,840.0
Net property, plant, and equipment	8,000.0		8,000.0
Other assets.	2,000.0		2,000.0
Capitalized operating leased asset		2,041.0	2,041.0
Total assets.	$12,400.0	$2,881.0	$15,281.0
Current operating liabilities.	$ 1,000.0		$ 1,000.0
Other liabilities	1,500.0	$ 816.4	2,316.4
Debt	4,500.0		4,500.0
Capitalized operating lease obligations		2,100.0	2,100.0
Total liabilities.	$ 7,000.0	$2,916.4	$ 9,916.4
Shareholders' equity	5,400.0	−35.4	5,364.6
Total liabilities and shareholders' equity.	$12,400.0	$2,881.0	$15,281.0

	Capitalized Lease Balance
Lease liability—beginning balance.	$1,996.3
Interest expense.	159.7
Lease payment.	−500.0
Subtotal	$1,656.0
Lease liability—ending balance.	2,100.0
Present value of new leases.	$ 444.0
Lease asset—beginning balance	$1,996.3
Amortization	−399.3
Present value of new leases.	444.0
Lease asset—ending balance	$2,041.0

Valuation	Equity Value	Enterprise Value
Market value of equity	$5,000.0	$ 5,000.0
Debt		4,500.0
Market value of equity and firm	$5,000.0	$ 9,500.0
Cash.	−400.0	−400.0
Market value without capitalizing leases	$4,600.0	$ 9,100.0
Capitalized operating leases		2,100.0
Market value with capitalizing leases.	$4,600.0	$11,200.0

	P/E	Unlevered Earnings Multiple	EBIT Multiple	EBITDA Multiple	Revenue Multiple
Denominator					
Earnings	$ 660.0	$ 660.0	$ 660.0	$ 660.0	
Interest		400.0	400.0	400.0	
Tax adjustment.		−160.0	440.0	440.0	
Depreciation and amortization				2,000.0	
Earnings without capitalizing operating leases	$ 660.0	$ 900.0	$ 1,500.0	$ 3,500.0	
Rent expense	500.0	500.0	500.0	500.0	
Interest on leases	−159.7				
Amortization of leases	−399.3	−399.3	−399.3		
Tax adjustment.	23.6	−40.3			
Earnings with capitalizing leases	$ 624.6	$ 960.4	$ 1,600.7	$ 4,000.0	
Multiple Without Capitalizing Leases					
Value without capitalizing operating leases	$4,600.0	$ 9,100.0	$ 9,100.0	$ 9,100.0	$ 9,100.0
Denominator without capitalizing operating leases	660.0	900.0	1,500.0	3,500.0	7,000.0
Multiple without capitalized operating leases	6.97	10.11	6.07	2.60	1.30
Multiple With Capitalizing Leases					
Value with capitalizing operating leases.	$4,600.0	$11,200.0	$11,200.0	$11,200.0	$11,200.0
Denominator with capitalizing operating leases.	624.6	960.4	1,600.7	4,000.0	7,000.0
Multiple with capitalized operating leases	7.36	11.66	7.00	2.80	1.60
Percentage change	5.7%	15.3%	15.3%	7.7%	23.1%

After mastering the material in this chapter, you will be able to:

1. Understand LBO activity and LBO deal characteristics (15.1–15.2)

2. Decide when it is appropriate to consider an LBO transaction (15.3–15.4)

3. Learn about the role of financial sponsors in an LBO transaction (15.5)

4. Understand the steps for analyzing and valuing an LBO transaction (15.6)

5. Use an LBO model to analyze and value an LBO transaction (15.7)

Leveraged Buyout Transactions

15

RJR Nabisco, Inc. (RJR) was a manufacturer of cigarettes and food products (such as Oreo Cookies and Ritz Crackers). It was created by the merger of RJ Reynolds Tobacco Company and Nabisco Brands in the mid-1980s. By the late 1980s, RJR's stock price was "languishing," and in 1989, Kohlberg Kravis & Roberts (KKR), a private equity firm, purchased RJR Nabisco in a highly leveraged buyout transaction for close to $25 billion, which at the time was the largest leveraged buyout transaction on record.[1]

RJR NABISCO

Analysts thought that RJR was a good LBO candidate because it had stable cash flows, steady growth in both up and down business cycles (its unlevered beta was 0.7), low capital expenditure requirements, low financial leverage, and a high likelihood of being able to improve its operating cost structure. KKR funded the equity investment of $1.5 billion, and it issued various forms of debt securities and preferred stock with equity "kickers" for the remainder of the financing. The issuance of the additional debt increased RJR's debt-to-value ratio from roughly 5% to approximately 95%, and the increased debt increased its equity beta from roughly 1 to over 9.5.

In this chapter, we delve into the world of leveraged buyouts to understand the motivations for undertaking an LBO, how they are structured, and how to analyze an LBO transaction.

---

[1] KKR did not start the bidding for this company. The company's chief executive officer offered $74 per share in an attempt to take the company private. This initial bid was characterized as a "low-ball bid" and KKR responded with a $90 bid. As a result of a bidding war that was primarily between the chief executive officer and KKR, KKR bought the company for more than $100 per share. The premium paid to RJR's stockholders was over $9 billion. For a more detailed discussion, see Michel, A., and I. Shaked, "RJR Nabisco: A Case Study of a Complex Leveraged Buyout," *Financial Analysts Journal* (September–October 1991), pp. 15–27.

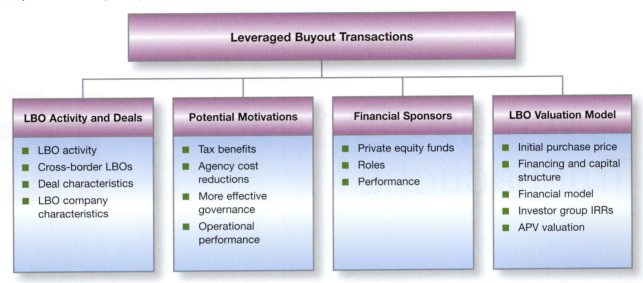

INTRODUCTION

This chapter focuses on a certain type of acquisition transaction that is financed with a large proportion of debt financing—**leveraged buyout** (**LBO**) and **management buyout** (**MBO**) transactions. The unsecured debt issued in these transactions is typically high-yield debt (below investment grade)—also called **junk bonds**. Another characteristic of these transactions is that the post-transaction company's equity securities are privately held even though its debt and preferred stock may be publicly traded. In a **going private** transaction, publicly held companies become privately held after the transaction, and they often use this type of financial structure. Investors also use this type of financial structure to acquire companies that are already privately owned.

As expected, the difference between LBOs and MBOs is that MBOs are leveraged transactions in which the current management continues to manage the post-transaction company and the term is generally reserved for situations where the management team is the party that initiates the transaction. Aside from conflicts of interest that occur when current managers participate in the purchase of the company, the valuation issues for LBOs and MBOs are generally the same. Note that current management often continues to manage the post-transaction company, even if the transaction was initiated by a **financial sponsor** or a **private equity firm**. Thus, even though the focus of our discussion is mostly on LBOs, the analyses, financial models, and valuation methods we discuss for LBOs also apply for MBOs.

The extent of LBO activity at any time depends on conditions in the credit market. When credit is "hard" to get and when interest rates are high, leveraged buyout activity dwindles. When credit is readily available and relatively cheap, leveraged buyout activity increases. We do not know when the first LBO transaction occurred, but LBOs became popular in the late 1970s and early 1980s. By 1990, the strategy for creating value using these transactions was well known and understood. Despite this understanding, a downturn in the business cycle in combination with a tightening of the credit markets after the collapse of the junk-bond market made it difficult to both find companies that were viable LBO candidates and arrange suitable financing. At times, leveraged buyout activity has accounted for a large proportion of merger and acquisition activity, as much as 20% in 2007. At other times, it has accounted for less than 5% of M&A activity, such as in 2009. Leveraged buyouts occur throughout most of the world now, but historically the predominant centers of activity have been in the United States, the United Kingdom and the countries that make up the European Union.

In this chapter, we discuss how leveraged buyout transactions are structured and what types of firms are normally candidates for a leveraged buyout. We discuss how leveraged buyouts increase the incentives of both management and monitors—such as the board of directors—and can potentially create wealth for the investors. We also discuss the extant empirical evidence on the performance of leveraged buyout transactions and the role of financial sponsors in these transactions. Finally, we discuss how to analyze these transactions, and we highlight the key factors in this analysis. As it turns out, the option for a company to go private in a leveraged buyout transaction is often an alternative strategy for a company, one that it examines when it is looking into ways it might create more value for shareholders. This is why an LBO analysis is sometimes used as another valuation method. It is common for an investment bank that is serving as a financial advisor to a target of an acquisition to examine a variety of different valuation methods—such as a discounted cash flow (DCF) valuation, various forms of market multiple analyses, a premium analysis, and a leveraged buyout analysis.

15.1 LEVERAGED BUYOUT ACTIVITY

As we document in the exhibits that follow, the extent of LBO activity varies over time and across global regions. (We do not distinguish MBO transactions from LBO transactions in this section.) Regardless of the country, LBO transactions are more common during certain time periods than they are in others. The United States, the United Kingdom, and the countries in the European Union have historically been the dominant countries for both the number and value of LBO transactions. In recent history, however, we have observed an increase in LBO transactions in new regions of the world. In addition, cross-border LBO transactions are more common now than they have been in the past.

LO1 Understand LBO activity and LBO deal characteristics

In the remainder of this section, we present descriptive characteristics of LBO transactions overall and by global region. We use the FactSet Merger database to collect the sample of transactions we examine.[2] We select transactions that were completed or were still pending between 1996 and 2010, that had a value (enterprise value) of at least $10 million, and we included both publicly traded and privately held acquirers and targets. We provide descriptive information on the number of transactions and the enterprise value of these transactions both globally and for 13 countries/regions: Africa, Australia, Canada, China, China—Hong Kong, the European Union (E.U.), Japan, Latin America, the Middle East, the United Kingdom (U.K.), United States (U.S.), Asia—Other, and Europe—Other (the last two of which include all countries in the respective regions other than those that are listed separately).[3] Based on these criteria, we examine 3,454 completed public and private LBO transactions.

Time-Series of Leveraged Buyout Transactions

In Exhibit 15.1, we present the time-series of both the size (enterprise value) of global LBO transactions and the percentage of global merger and acquisition transactions that were LBO transactions. Between 1996 and 2003, annual global LBO transactions ranged from $11.5 billion (in enterprise value) to $51.3 billion. LBO transactions were a small part—between 1% and 5.2%—of the merger and acquisition transactions during this period. In 2004, the enterprise value of LBO transactions increased to $91.0 billion and increased in each of the next three years to $158.5, $466.5, and $552.3 billion, respectively. During this period, LBO transactions as a percentage of merger and acquisitions transactions increased as well and peaked in 2007 at 20.5%. Some have argued that low interest rates and low stock prices (relative to

| EXHIBIT 15.1 | Time-Series of Global Leveraged Buyout Transactions and the Percentage of Global Mergers and Acquisitions |

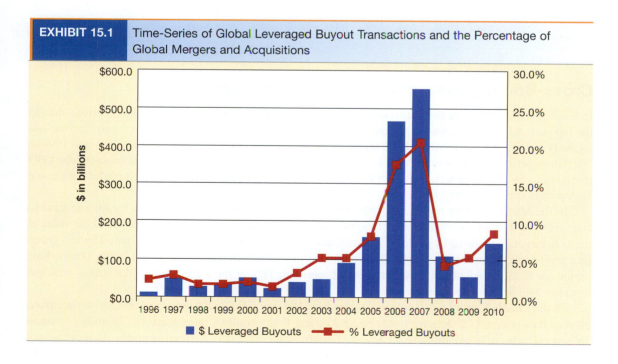

---

[2] We report results from FactSet Research Systems Inc. (FactSet), which is a U.S. financial data and software company. The various data we report are summary data from the FactSet Mergers database, which combines data from FactSet's Mergerstat and MergerMetrics products.

[3] To clarify, "Latin American Countries" are any countries in the Americas that are not the United States or Canada. Europe—Other represents all Eastern and Western European countries that are not in the E.U.

rising corporate profits) created ideal conditions for the LBO market in 2006 and 2007.[4] LBO transactions plummeted with the financial crisis and recession in 2008, decreasing to $109.9 billion (just 4.2% of all merger and acquisition transactions). They decreased again in 2009 as the recession continued and as the credit markets remained in flux, but increased to $143.7 billion in 2010 as the global economy began to recover slowly from the recession.

In Exhibit 15.2, we present measures of regional market shares of the value of global LBO transactions based on the country of the acquirer. We measure the market share metric as the value of the LBO transactions in that country or region for a given year, divided by the total market value of all global LBO transactions in that year. If we examine this time-series, we observe that the U.S., U.K., and E.U. generally have the largest market shares over the period. The market share of these countries decreased somewhat at the end of this period, while the market shares of the countries and regions in much of Asia (including Australia, Asia—Other, and Japan) and Latin America increased during this period. Of course, there was little, if any, LBO activity in these latter regions at the start of this period.

EXHIBIT 15.2		"Market Share" of the Leveraged Buyout Transactions for Global Regions														
	"Market Share"	**1996**	**1997**	**1998**	**1999**	**2000**	**2001**	**2002**	**2003**	**2004**	**2005**	**2006**	**2007**	**2008**	**2009**	**2010**
Acquirer Region	Africa	0%	0%	0%	0%	0%	0%	0%	1%	1%	0%	1%	5%	1%	0%	1%
	Asia—Other	0%	0%	0%	0%	0%	0%	0%	0%	0%	1%	1%	3%	2%	2%	2%
	Australia	0%	0%	0%	1%	0%	1%	0%	1%	2%	4%	3%	4%	11%	3%	20%
	Canada	6%	0%	0%	0%	1%	1%	0%	3%	4%	3%	9%	2%	2%	22%	5%
	China	0%	0%	0%	0%	0%	0%	0%	0%	0%	0%	0%	0%	0%	0%	1%
	China—Hong Kong . .	0%	0%	0%	0%	0%	4%	0%	0%	0%	1%	0%	1%	1%	0%	1%
	Europe—Other	2%	4%	1%	0%	0%	0%	0%	3%	2%	1%	1%	3%	3%	1%	1%
	European Union	3%	25%	14%	9%	7%	25%	16%	12%	14%	24%	6%	14%	25%	8%	10%
	Japan	0%	0%	0%	0%	2%	1%	0%	1%	6%	2%	1%	0%	2%	6%	3%
	Latin America	2%	0%	2%	0%	0%	1%	0%	5%	2%	1%	2%	3%	7%	1%	
	Middle East.	2%	0%	1%	0%	0%	0%	0%	0%	0%	1%	2%	1%	2%	0%	3%
	United Kingdom	32%	24%	22%	23%	31%	40%	20%	48%	19%	11%	11%	10%	13%	9%	5%
	United States	53%	46%	59%	67%	59%	27%	62%	31%	47%	51%	63%	54%	36%	40%	48%
	Total	100%	100%	100%	100%	100%	100%	100%	100%	100%	100%	100%	100%	100%	100%	100%

Exhibit may contain small rounding errors

Cross-Border Leveraged Buyout Transactions

In Exhibit 15.3, we present the distribution of cross-border LBO transactions based on enterprise value. In the top part of the exhibit, we anchor on acquirers (where the purchaser—often a private equity firm—is located) and present cross-border LBO transactions by acquirer country/region for the combined 1996 to 2010 time period. In the bottom part of the exhibit, we anchor on targets and present cross-border LBO transactions by target country/region for the same time period. As we will soon see, it is useful to examine both panels simultaneously.

In the Middle Eastern region, the value of the Middle Eastern targets purchased by Middle Eastern acquirers was 17% of the total value of targets acquired by Middle Eastern acquirers, whereas the value of the U.S. targets purchased by Middle Eastern acquirers was 26% of the total value acquired by this group (see top panel). Even though only 17% of the value of the LBO targets of acquirers in the Middle East region are in the Middle East, these transactions represent 71% of the value of all of the targets acquired from the Middle East (see bottom panel).

Of the Middle Eastern target companies purchased by non–Middle Eastern acquirers, Japan purchased 20% of their value, U.S. acquirers purchased 7%, and E.U. acquirers purchased 3%. In addition, while 26% of the value of acquisitions of the Middle Eastern acquirers was U.S. targets (top panel), these targets represented less than 1% of the value of all U.S. targets acquired during this time period (bottom panel).

In the U.S., 92% of the value of the targets of U.S. acquirers was U.S. targets; thus, only 8% of the value of the targets of U.S. acquirers was non-U.S. targets. E.U. and U.K. targets made up the next larg-

---

[4] See, for example, http://money.cnn.com/2007/08/06/markets/privateequitybubble.fortune/index.htm (cited as of June 20, 2011).

EXHIBIT 15.3 Cross-Border Leveraged Buyout Transactions by the Global Region of the Acquirer and Target

Target Region

Enterprise Value of Acquirer Transactions by Region	Africa	Asia —Other	Australia	Canada	China	China— Hong Kong	Europe— Other	European Union	Japan	Latin America	Middle East	United Kingdom	United States	Total
Africa	16.4%	0.0%	0.0%	0.0%	0.0%	0.0%	0.0%	2.1%	0.0%	0.0%	0.0%	81.5%	0.0%	100%
Asia—Other	0.0%	48.2%	0.3%	0.0%	0.1%	0.0%	8.5%	2.0%	0.0%	0.0%	0.0%	39.7%	1.2%	100%
Australia	0.0%	0.4%	31.9%	0.0%	0.0%	0.0%	0.0%	23.3%	0.0%	0.1%	0.0%	31.7%	12.5%	100%
Canada	0.0%	0.0%	7.7%	25.8%	0.0%	0.0%	0.2%	1.1%	0.0%	0.1%	0.0%	41.3%	23.8%	100%
China	0.0%	0.0%	0.0%	0.0%	100.0%	0.0%	0.0%	0.0%	0.0%	0.0%	0.0%	0.0%	0.0%	100%
China—Hong Kong	0.0%	61.0%	0.0%	0.0%	10.0%	15.7%	0.0%	7.0%	0.0%	4.2%	0.0%	0.0%	2.1%	100%
Europe—Other	0.1%	0.4%	0.0%	0.0%	0.0%	0.0%	53.1%	21.3%	0.0%	1.6%	0.0%	15.1%	8.4%	100%
European Union	2.1%	0.0%	0.1%	0.2%	0.0%	0.0%	7.1%	73.6%	2.3%	0.0%	0.1%	4.1%	10.5%	100%
Japan	3.1%	0.2%	0.0%	0.0%	0.0%	0.0%	0.0%	0.0%	60.8%	0.0%	3.9%	11.4%	20.6%	100%
Latin America	1.2%	7.8%	0.0%	0.0%	1.9%	2.9%	12.0%	0.9%	15.7%	28.5%	0.0%	23.2%	5.9%	100%
Middle East	0.4%	0.0%	0.0%	19.3%	0.0%	0.0%	23.9%	4.9%	0.0%	4.8%	17.0%	3.3%	26.4%	100%
United Kingdom	0.0%	0.0%	0.1%	0.3%	0.0%	0.6%	0.9%	13.9%	0.0%	0.0%	0.0%	70.6%	13.5%	100%
United States	0.3%	0.1%	0.6%	1.3%	0.0%	0.0%	0.1%	3.5%	0.5%	0.0%	0.0%	1.8%	91.5%	100%

Target Region

Enterprise Value of Target Transactions by Region	Africa	Asia —Other	Australia	Canada	China	China— Hong Kong	Europe— Other	European Union	Japan	Latin America	Middle East	United Kingdom	United States
Africa	36.2%	0.0%	0.0%	0.0%	0.0%	0.0%	0.0%	0.3%	0.0%	0.0%	0.0%	8.6%	0.0%
Asia—Other	0.0%	58.8%	0.2%	0.0%	1.1%	0.0%	5.0%	0.2%	0.0%	0.0%	0.0%	3.6%	0.0%
Australia	0.0%	1.4%	68.6%	0.0%	0.0%	0.0%	0.0%	7.4%	0.0%	1.0%	0.0%	8.6%	1.1%
Canada	0.0%	0.0%	15.7%	53.8%	0.0%	0.0%	0.4%	0.3%	0.0%	0.7%	0.0%	10.7%	2.0%
China	0.0%	0.0%	0.0%	0.0%	35.9%	0.0%	0.0%	0.0%	0.0%	0.0%	0.0%	0.0%	0.0%
China—Hong Kong	0.0%	25.2%	0.0%	0.0%	29.1%	38.2%	0.0%	0.2%	0.0%	3.3%	0.0%	0.0%	0.0%
Europe—Other	0.2%	0.5%	0.0%	0.0%	0.0%	0.0%	32.9%	2.3%	0.0%	3.9%	0.0%	1.4%	0.3%
European Union	32.7%	0.2%	0.4%	1.0%	0.0%	0.0%	34.7%	63.8%	16.4%	0.7%	2.8%	3.1%	2.5%
Japan	5.7%	0.2%	0.0%	0.0%	0.0%	0.0%	0.0%	0.0%	51.9%	0.0%	19.8%	1.0%	0.6%
Latin America	2.7%	11.1%	0.0%	0.0%	19.6%	24.9%	8.3%	0.1%	15.9%	77.2%	0.0%	2.5%	0.2%
Middle East	0.6%	0.0%	0.0%	11.3%	0.0%	0.0%	11.3%	0.4%	0.0%	8.9%	70.8%	0.2%	0.6%
United Kingdom	0.0%	0.1%	0.5%	1.7%	0.0%	36.9%	4.7%	12.6%	0.0%	0.7%	0.0%	55.0%	3.4%
United States	21.8%	2.5%	14.5%	32.2%	14.3%	0.0%	2.8%	12.4%	15.7%	3.6%	6.7%	5.3%	89.3%
Total	100%	100%	100%	100%	100%	100%	100%	100%	100%	100%	100%	100%	100%

Exhibit may contain small rounding errors

est groups of targets acquired by U.S. acquirers, respectively representing 4% and 2% of the value of the targets of U.S. acquirers. For U.S. targets (see the bottom panel), U.S. acquirers purchased 89% of the value of these target companies. Of the U.S. target companies purchased by non-U.S. acquirers, E.U. acquirers purchased less than 3% of the value of U.S. target companies, and the U.K. acquirers purchased just over 3% of the value of U.S. targets.

In the U.K., 71% of the value of the targets of U.K. acquirers was U.K. targets. U.S. and E.U. targets made up the next largest group of targets acquired by U.K. acquirers, each representing approximately 14% of the value of the targets of U.K. acquirers. For U.K. targets, U.K. acquirers purchased 55% of the value of these target companies. Of the U.K. target companies purchased by non-U.K. acquirers, Canadian acquirers purchased 11% of the value of the target companies, and U.S. acquirers purchased 5% of the value of the target companies.

Private Versus Public Targets and Acquirers

In Exhibit 15.4, we present the percentage of the number of global LBO transactions as well as the percentage of enterprise value that were transactions of privately held and publicly traded acquirers as well as privately held and publicly traded targets. The first set of bars reports the breakdown of privately held and publicly traded acquirers, and the second set of bars reports the breakdown of privately held and publicly traded targets.

EXHIBIT 15.4	Leveraged Buyout Transactions for Public Versus Private Targets and Acquirers

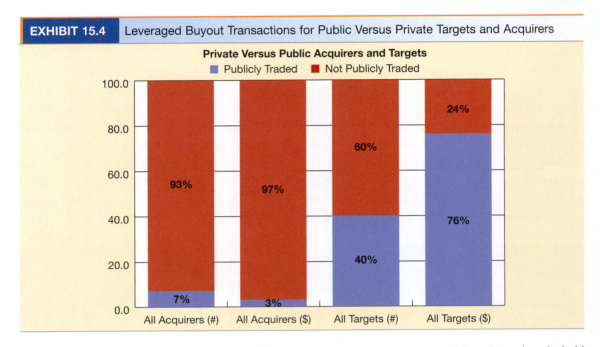

Given that most LBO funds are privately held partnerships, it is not surprising that privately held acquirers purchased 93% of the transactions and 97% of the value of the transactions. Further, even though 60% of the LBO transactions were acquisitions of privately held companies, they only represented 24% of the value of the targets purchased.

In the 1970 to 2007 sample of LBOs in Kaplan and Strömberg (2008), 27% of the total enterprise value of LBO transactions was comprised of public-to-private transactions. In addition, 23% consisted of independent private companies, 30% consisted of divisions of other companies, 20% consisted of secondary LBOs (a private equity firm buying a company from another private equity firm), and 1% was purchased out of distress.[5]

Premiums Paid and Transaction Market Multiples

In this section, we present the premiums paid to target shareholders in LBO transactions and the transaction multiples implied by the LBO transactions. FactSet measures transaction premiums in terms of changes in the publicly traded market prices of target companies; thus, we only report results for publicly traded target companies. In Exhibit 15.5, we report the average five-day transaction premiums.[6] Across all targets, the average premium is 22%, and the premiums range from 11% (China—Hong Kong) to 30% (Japan). The average premiums in the U.S., E.U., and U.K. are 25%, 16%, and 16%, respectively. The differences across regions are not the result of differences in the timing of the LBO transactions, since some regions have relatively fewer transactions in the beginning of the analyzed

---

[5] See Kaplan S., and P. Strömberg, "Leveraged Buyouts and Private Equity," *Journal of Economic Perspectives* vol. 22, no. 4 (2008), pp. 1–27.

[6] FactSet divides the closing price of the target company—immediately after the merger announcement—by the target's closing price five days earlier. FactSet also reports a 1-day and 30-day merger premium. Although the 1-day premiums are, on average, smaller than the 30-day premiums, which are, on average, larger than the 5-day premiums, overall, the results across global regions using either the 1-day or the 30-day premiums are qualitatively the same as those being reported in this exhibit. We trimmed the sample at the 5th and 95th percentiles to eliminate the effect of outliers.

time period. We compared the average five-day transaction premiums between the 1996–2010 and 2009–2010 time periods. The results for 2009–2010 are qualitatively the same as those for 1996–2010. Although it is beyond the scope of our discussion, economic factors that might drive the differences in premiums across regions include differences in industry composition of the targets, systematic differences in the value of expected efficiencies that might be gained, the degree of competition for targets among acquirers, and regulatory differences.

EXHIBIT 15.5	Average Target Company Five-Day LBO Transaction Premiums by Global Region

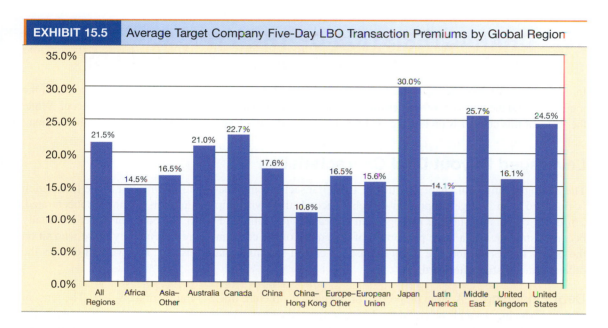

In Exhibit 15.6, we present three average enterprise-value-based LBO transaction multiples by global regions—earnings before interest and taxes (EBIT); earnings before interest, taxes, depreciation, and amortization (EBITDA); and revenue. The ranges for the EBIT, EBITDA, and revenue multiples are 7.3 to 15.0, 6.4 to 10.9, and 0.9 to 2.6, respectively. The rank orderings of the transaction multiples across the regions have some similarities for the three transaction multiples, but they are not the same (even though we restrict the set of transactions used in the exhibit to be the same for all three multiples).

EXHIBIT 15.6	Average Enterprise-Value-Based LBO Transaction Multiples by Global Region

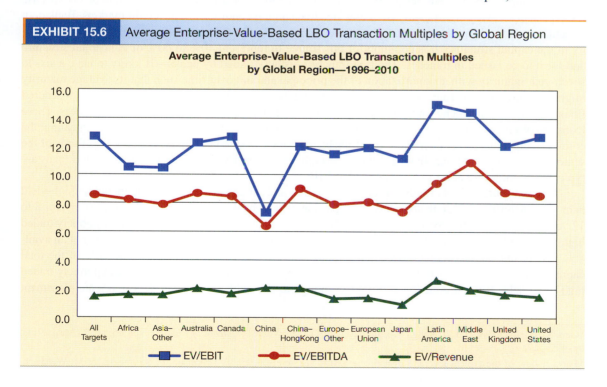

15.2 CHARACTERISTICS OF THE TYPICAL LEVERAGED BUYOUT DEAL AND COMPANY

In this section, we describe the characteristics of leveraged buyouts in terms of both the deal structure of the transaction and the types of companies for which leveraged buyout transactions most commonly occur. While the focus of this chapter is on leveraged buyouts, we also discuss leveraged recapitalizations in this section.

Leveraged Buyout Deal Characteristics

The distinguishing deal characteristics of LBO transactions include the following. First, the transaction is financed with a large proportion of debt. Second, the ownership in the firm becomes concentrated. Third, the ownership stake of management increases substantially. Fourth, the board of directors usually becomes smaller, and a large proportion of the equity of the company is represented by those who sit on the board. In this section, we focus on just the capital structure characteristics, and we will discuss the other characteristics afterward.

Debt Financing. A large proportion of the capital structure in LBO transactions is debt. The amount of debt financing depends on credit market conditions, the characteristics of the company (for example, the stability of the cash flows), the quality of the management team, and the quality of the financial sponsor. Guo, Hotchkiss, and Song (2011) report that for their 1990 to 2006 sample, the ratio of debt to total capital for the average firm increased from 23.7% prior to the LBO to 69.9% at the close of the transaction. For the average firm in their sample, 39% of the capital was bank debt, 10% was private debt, 16% was publicly traded debt, and 4% was pay-in-kind debt.[7] Pay-in-kind or PIK debt contracts do not pay interest in the first few years after an LBO, but the accrued interest increases the principal amount due as time passes.

Companies issue various forms of debt when undergoing an LBO. The proportions of the specific types of debt can vary significantly over time due to changing conditions in the credit markets. Bank debt or senior loan funds are loans secured with the company's assets. These claims have the highest priority in the capital structure. It is common for this source to represent 40% to 60% of the capital structure and for it to be issued in tranches. The first tranche—usually issued by banks—is likely to have a six- to seven-year maturity with an amortization of the principal amount over time such that its average maturity might be approximately four years. This tranche typically represents about one-third of the senior secured financing. The next tranche (or two) may be securitized and is often sold to institutional investors. These loans are often not amortizing, but rather, they have so called **bullet payments** on maturity (meaning the entire principal amount is then due). This tranche (or tranches) often accounts for about two-thirds of the senior secured debt and may have a maturity of eight or nine years. All of these senior secured loans are typically floating-rate notes that are pegged to LIBOR.[8]

The next source of debt funding is unsecured senior and senior subordinated debt, including high-yield debt. The maturity of these instruments is longer than that of bank debt and is usually in the range of 8 to 12 years. These securities represent 15% to 30% of the total capital structure. Offerings for publicly traded high-yield debt typically must be a minimum of $200 million; thus, public high-yield debt is not an available part of the capital structure for smaller transactions. If high-yield debt were to be 20% of the total capital structure, the transaction price would have to be roughly $1 billion in order to use publicly traded high-yield debt. If the transaction is not large enough to use public high-yield debt, a private placement

---

[7] Guo, S., E. Hotchkiss, and W. Song, "Do Buyouts (Still) Create Value?" *Journal of Finance* vol. 66, no. 2 (April 2011), pp. 479–517.

[8] For a review of the typical leverage structure in LBOs, see Axelson, U., T. Jenkinson, P. Strömberg, & M. Weisbach, "Borrow Cheap, Buy High? The Determinants of Leverage and Pricing in Buyouts," NBER working paper, 2010.

might be required. In some cases, a warrant is attached to enhance the debtholder's expected rate of return. These are usually cash pay (meaning the interest is paid in cash).

The next source of funding is mezzanine financing, which can be in the form of either debt or preferred stock. Mezzanine financing is often convertible into equity and can be a combination of PIK for some time followed by a cash pay. It is important to be aware that the rules regarding high-yield discount obligations adopted by various taxing authorities (including the United States) may delay or nullify the interest deduction on zero-coupon or paid-in-kind debt. Suffice it to say that the debt and preferred equity portion of the capital structure can be very complicated, with numerous different securities issued with varying contractual terms.

Although a discussion of the alternative corporate structures used in these transactions is beyond the scope of this chapter, sponsors often form a **holding company** to purchase the company's stock. The holding company owns the operating company and has no other assets other than the stock of the operating company. Equity investors in the transaction own shares in the holding company. Sometimes, sponsors use the holding company to issue subordinated debt. Since the loan covenants on the debt issued by the operating company generally prohibit dividend payments to the holding company, the holding company has no cash to make interest and principal payments. In this case, the notes will have to be zero-coupon notes in which the periodic interest that is earned simply increases the outstanding principal amount due. In order to pay off the holding company notes, the operating company has to either be sold or go public so that the holding company receives a cash infusion from the sale of its stock in the operating company.

Common Equity. The remainder of the capital structure is common equity. Obviously, since the amount of debt that can be issued fluctuates over time with changes in credit market conditions, and since leveraged buyout transactions try to utilize as much debt in the deal as possible, the amount of common equity varies over time as well. For example, in 1989, common equity represented, on average, 13% of the capital structure of the LBOs. In 2006 and 2007, the average common equity portion was 33%, down from roughly 40% in the early 2000s. In 2009, after the credit crisis unfolded, on average, 52% of the capital structure was common equity. The credit markets recovered to some extent subsequently—for 2010, the average equity component was 43% and in the first quarter of 2011, the average equity portion of the capital structure was 38%.

The common equity includes both new common equity and **rollover equity**, which is equity from the pre-LBO company (typically owned by the management team) that is then rolled over into the new entity. Rollover equity is usually a very small percentage of the total capital structure. The new common equity comes from a variety of sources. The management team often invests in the company beyond its rollover equity; a **private equity fund** raised by the financial sponsor (to which the sponsor contributes capital) also invests in the company; and the private equity firm may sometimes seek other direct investors who are not part of their fund (including other financial sponsors). The financial sponsor's fund may purchase different types of equity or equity-linked securities than management (such as convertible preferred) that ensure that the fund earns some minimum return on its investment before management participates in part or full.

Guo, Hotchkiss, and Song (2011) report that, in their sample, management is a part of the equity contribution in over 60% of the deals and that the average (median) management equity piece to total equity is 12.8% (6.5%). Management also receives additional incentives for good performance as time goes on. Kaplan and Strömberg (2008) report that in 43 U.S. leveraged buyouts that took place from 1996 to 2004, the CEO received 5.4% of the equity upside via stock and options, and the management team, as a whole, received 16%. Similar structures have been reported for leveraged buyouts in the U.K. as well.

As suggested earlier, two or more different private equity firms will sometimes both contribute to buy a company. This often happens when the size of the deal is too large for one private equity firm to write the equity check necessary for the transaction. Guo, Hotchkiss, and Song (2011) report that more than one private equity firm is involved in 27.7% of their sample from 1990 to 2006.

Valuation Key 15.2

LBO transactions are financed by large increases in debt, an investment in the company by management, and usually an equity investment from a private equity firm. There are many different forms of debt that may be issued to finance these transactions, including senior secured debt, unsecured senior debt, and senior subordinated debt, which includes high-yield debt, zero-coupon or paid-in-kind debt, and more.

Deal Characteristics: Leveraged Buyouts Versus Leveraged Recapitalizations

LBOs and **leveraged recapitalizations** (**leveraged recaps**) have one important characteristic in common: they result in a large increase in the amount of financial leverage used in a company's capital structure. While the focus of this chapter is on LBOs, it is useful to discuss leveraged recapitalizations in order to identify the key characteristics on which they differ. In a leveraged recap, the company borrows against the assets and cash flows of the company and then distributes that cash to its shareholders by either paying a large one-time dividend to the shareholders or through stock buybacks from shareholders who want to tender their shares. In a leveraged recap, the managers sometimes do not participate in the share repurchases and they sometimes get shares in lieu of cash when there is a one-time dividend (see Valuation in Practice 15.1). In some cases, the company also issues new shares in exchange for old shares.

Both leverage recaps and LBOs result in a substantial increase in leverage for the company. However, in an LBO, new equity investors purchase the company from the pre-LBO equity investors, whereas leveraged recaps do not result in new equity investors unless there is a specific equity sale component associated with the transaction. If the leveraged recap involves a public company, the company will continue to be publicly traded after the transaction, whereas a publicly traded company will become private after an LBO transaction.

Leveraged recapitalizations can be used for a variety of purposes. If a company wants to buy out a particular investor, investor group, or family member, the company can raise debt and buy back the shares of that individual or group. If the founders of a private company want to cash out some of their shares in order to better diversify their wealth, the founders can raise debt and have the corporation buy back some of their shares or pay them (and other shareholders, if any) a one-time dividend. A leveraged transaction can also be used to return capital to all shareholders. Finally, a leveraged recapitalization can be used as a defense against a **hostile takeover**. In some transactions, management significantly increases its proportionate share of the equity and offers shareholders a large cash dividend in order to thwart a hostile takeover (see Valuation in Practice 15.1).

Valuation in Practice 15.1

FMC Corporation Leveraged Recapitalization FMC is a diversified chemical company with leading positions in agricultural, consumer, and industrial markets. In late 1985, FMC management sensed a possible hostile takeover as it became clear that someone was accumulating shares of the company. At the time, FMC shares were trading for approximately $70 per share. On February 20, 1986, it offered its shareholders a cash distribution as well as an exchange of shares. The offer identified three distinct investor groups and treated each one differently. For each old share, public shareholders were offered $70 per share plus one new share. The employee thrift plan was offered $25 in cash and four new shares, and the management team was offered no cash and five and two-thirds shares. If the post-debt recap price of the new shares was $15 per share, all three offers were worth $85. Given the deal structure, if the stock price fell below (rose above) $15, management stood to lose (gain) the most from this transaction, and thus it had a strong incentive to improve the company's performance.

At the time of the FMC announcement, the old shares jumped to $85, implying a post-deal value of $15 for each new share. It turned out that a Mr. Ivan Boesky had been accumulating the shares, and the market apparently sensed that the bidding for FMC was not complete. Consequently, the price climbed to $100. Eventually, in order to thwart Boesky, FMC gave the public shareholders $80 per share plus a new share. As a result of the transaction, insiders at FMC increased their ownership from 14% to 41%, making it virtually impossible for Boesky to take over the firm. However, do not feel too bad for Mr. Boesky, the value of the old shares rose by $30 per share (or 40% relative to the value of FMC's shares prior to the recap announcement). Finally, FMC's cash flows increased considerably in the years immediately following the leveraged recap.

Characteristics of Potential Leveraged Buyout Candidates

What kinds of companies are good candidates for an LBO transaction? One major issue for an LBO transaction is the ability of the company to service its debt in order to avoid default or bankruptcy. What kinds of characteristics might help with this potential problem? One characteristic that helps mitigate default is stable cash flows. This means that we generally do not see LBO transactions taking place in highly cyclical industries or with companies that have highly volatile cash flows. In addition, most LBO companies have little debt prior to the transaction. Many times, LBOs will have excess cash that can be used to pay off the debt. If the company has a non-core business or excess assets that can be sold at a reasonable price, the post-LBO company can use these assets as an additional safety net or simply plan to sell these assets to help service or pay down the debt. Guo, Hotchkiss, and Song (2011) report that over one-third of the firms in their sample sold at least $10 million of assets in the first three years following the LBO transaction.

In most LBOs, the existing management team stays on—at least at the beginning. Thus, if a company has a strong management team that is risk tolerant and will respond positively to high-powered incentives, it increases the likelihood of a successful transaction. It is true that the existing management team (or subset thereof) is usually part of the transaction initially, but we also know that a large number of CEOs depart relatively quickly after a transaction closes. Acharya, Hahn, and Kehoe (2010) found that one-third of the CEOs in their sample of Western European LBO transactions between 1995 and 2005 were replaced in the first 100 days after the transaction.[9]

It is also helpful for the potential LBO company to have modern, up-to-date plant and equipment. The reason why this characteristic is useful is that if cash gets tight, the replacement of capital equipment, buildings, and other infrastructure can be delayed in order to increase the available cash flow to service the debt. If the plant, equipment, and other infrastructure need substantial maintenance or replacement at the time of the transaction, this option may not be available.

The potential for expense reductions or other efficiencies—such as improved working capital management—is also beneficial. The basic strategy is to buy an asset that can be worth more if it is managed more efficiently, buy it at a purchase price that largely reflects the inefficient operations, and then put incentives in place in order to drive management to improve the company's performance and cash flows. These attributes are the characteristics of what some call a "classic" LBO.

This list of characteristics is potentially useful for identifying LBO candidates. However, over time, we have seen LBO transactions spread to more and more industries, not all of which have these features. For example, in the mid- to late 1980s, LBOs were predominately observed in the manufacturing and retail industries. In the 1990s, LBO transactions spread to such industries as information technology, media, telecommunications, financial services, and health care. During this period, manufacturing and retail firms became a less important part of overall LBO activity, a fact that is discussed in Kaplan and Strömberg (2008). In the 2000s, there was an increase in companies in the services and infrastructure businesses that underwent LBO transactions. Despite the spread of LBO transactions to other industries, manufacturing businesses still represent a reasonably large percentage of LBO transactions. For example, in the sample of LBOs from 1990 to 2006 in Guo, Hotchkiss, and Song (2011), 36% of the sample came from manufacturing businesses, whereas only 28% of the sample came from service industries.

Over time, we have seen more LBO transactions undertaken in which the strategy underlying an LBO was to grow the business rather than to simply reduce costs and achieve certain efficiencies. In some cases, these more "entrepreneurial" LBO transactions involve acquisitions by the post-LBO company or by the same private equity fund and then two or more portfolio companies are combined to create a stronger company.

We do not discuss leverage recaps in detail, but it should be clear that the characteristics of companies considering leveraged recaps are not dissimilar from those considering a leveraged buyout. The ability of the company to prosper with the highly levered capital structure in place is paramount in both kinds of transactions.

Valuation Key 15.3

The candidates for a leveraged buyout are companies that are most likely to be able to handle the highly leveraged capital structure that is associated with such a transaction. LBO candidates generally have some combination of stable cash flows; excess cash or other excess assets; modest levels of debt prior to the transaction; modern plant, equipment, and infrastructure; and a strong management team.

---

[9] Acharya, V., M. Hahn, and C. Kehoe, "Corporate Governance and Value Creation: Evidence from Private Equity," NYU Stern Working Paper, 2010.

15.3 POTENTIAL MOTIVATIONS AND ECONOMIC FORCES

LO2 Decide when it is appropriate to consider an LBO transaction

In this section, we describe the potential motivations underlying an LBO transaction that might lead to value creation for LBO investors. Potential motivations associated with an LBO include:

 i. the tax advantage arising from increased interest tax shields,

 ii. a reduction in agency costs associated with the issuance of debt,

 iii. a reduction in agency costs due to management incentives,

 iv. more effective monitoring by the board of directors,

 v. information asymmetry advantages for insiders (relative to public investors), and

 vi. wealth transfers from employees and pre-buyout debtholders to equityholders.

Potential Tax Benefits from Increased Interest Tax Shields

One potential reason for an increase in the value of a company is the potential tax advantages from increasing the financial leverage of the firm. How much value the interest tax shields create depends on:

 i. the appropriate discount rate for the interest tax shields (cost of debt or unlevered cost of capital),

 ii. the firm's marginal tax rate for interest tax shields,

 iii. the effect of personal taxes on the value of interest tax shields, and

 iv. how long-lived the change in capital structure is (whether it is permanent or only in effect during the leveraged buyout).

Estimates of the proportion of the total price paid that is attributable to interest tax shields in an LBO transaction depend on assumptions made in the calculation. For example, Kaplan (1989) finds that the value of the interest tax shields can vary from 14% to 130% of the premium paid to pre-buyout shareholders, depending on the assumptions made.[10]

In acquisitions with a corporate buyer, treating the acquisition as taxable to the target can provide tax benefits to the acquirer and not impose a tax burden on the target if the target has a high basis in the assets or has NOLs. In these two situations, the target pays little to no tax and the assets are stepped up in value for income tax purposes, providing future tax write-offs for the buyer. However, since the purchaser in an LBO is often a limited partnership (a private equity fund) and not a corporation, no step-up in basis is allowed. This was not true of transactions that were closed prior to 1987, and often a step-up in basis was an additional tax benefit that was pursued in these transactions.

Potential Agency Cost Reductions from Increased Debt

The incentive effects associated with debt present another potential benefit associated with an LBO. Jensen (1986) argues that increasing leverage creates pressure on managers to not waste resources because they must meet interest and principal payments in order to avoid default, removal, or bankruptcy.[11] Jensen describes this as the "free cash flow" problem—incumbent managers in companies with weak corporate governance, large cash flows, and poor investment opportunities are more likely to waste those cash flows in negative net present value projects in order to empire build. Jensen argues that in situations such as this, if the managers of these companies were to substantially increase leverage and pay the proceeds of the debt issuance to shareholders (as a one-time dividend or share repurchase), the managers essentially commit to not wasting future cash flows. This commitment arises because they have already given the future cash flows to the shareholders in the form of a one-time dividend or share repurchase and must now rely on using future operating cash flows to service the debt. As a result, they will not have the cash to invest in negative net present value projects until the debt has been paid down—at least in part.

---

[10] See S. Kaplan, "Management Buyouts: Evidence on Taxes as a Source of Value," *Journal of Finance* vol. 44, no. 3 (1989), pp. 611–632.

[11] See M. Jensen, "Agency Costs of Free Cash Flow, Corporate Finance and Takeovers," *American Economic Review* vol. 76, no. 2 (1986), pp. 323–329.

Managers who have worked at companies that have undergone a leveraged buyout usually discuss the tremendous pressure they felt to generate cash flows in order to meet all of the required interest and principal payments. The pressure from the leverage, in conjunction with the equity incentives and the investment risk that managers bear from their personal investment in the company, provides a strong incentive to produce cash flows and not waste resources.

Potential Agency Cost Reductions from Management Ownership

Many studies examine the effects of managerial ownership on reducing the agency costs between managers and equityholders. Jensen and Meckling (1976) discuss both the agency costs associated with the separation of ownership and control and how managerial incentives to maximize firm value are diminished as the manager owns a smaller proportionate share of the company. Indeed, the interests of a CEO without any equity incentives may be more aligned with the debtholders' interests than the equityholders' interests. Managers of publicly traded companies generally own stock, options, and other forms of equity compensation in order to provide them with incentives that more closely align their interests with those of the shareholders. There is a vast literature that demonstrates how stock, options, and other forms of equity compensation can provide incentives for the managerial team (see Core, Guay, and Larcker [2003] and Armstrong, Guay, and Weber [2010] for reviews of this literature).[12]

As discussed earlier, the management team often rolls over equity into the new company in addition to making a cash investment. Given their equity incentives and personal investment, the managers' wealth is at risk, yet the managers also stand to gain a tremendous amount if the transaction succeeds. Even though it is true that equity incentives are much more commonly used in public corporations now than in the 1980s (when LBOs gained popularity), the ownership percentages in LBO transactions—and the resulting upside and downside for management—is greater than that in most public corporations.

More Effective Monitoring by the Board of Directors

Many studies have also examined the role of the board of directors in monitoring and advising management. Jensen (1993) argues that many boards of directors are ineffective, because board culture discourages conflict, the CEO determines the agenda and information provided to the board, managers and non-managers on the board have little equity ownership, boards are too large, and the CEO and board chair positions are frequently held by the same person. Crystal (1991) argues that boards of directors are ineffective in setting appropriate levels of compensation because outside directors are essentially hired and can be removed by the CEO. Core, Holthausen, and Larcker (1999) show that ineffective boards tend to pay the CEO too much relative to expected compensation (given economic determinants of pay) and that these companies perform poorly.[13]

When firms undergo an LBO, the board structure changes significantly—at least relative to the board structure of the companies when they were public. First, post-LBO boards are generally small (usually about five to seven members), and they are controlled by the private equity firm. Guo, Hotchkiss, and Song (2011) report that on average, private equity firms hold 50% of the director seats. Private equity firms represent a significant percentage of the ownership of a corporation and have a vested interest in having a positive outcome, whereas in a typical public corporation, the board holdings and associated incentives are more modest. Private equity firms actively participate in the governance of their portfolio companies. Acharya, Hahn, and Kehoe (2010) document that LBO companies usually have 12 formal director meetings every year and that representatives of the private equity firm hold numerous informal meetings with the LBO management team.[14] Acharya, Hahn, and Kehoe (2010) also find that one-third of the CEOs are replaced in the first 100 days after the date of the transaction. Thus, the active involvement of the board of directors after an LBO is quite extensive and can lead to better performance.

---

[12] Core, J., W. Guay, and D. Larcker, "Executive Equity Compensation and Incentives: A Survey," *Federal Reserve Economic Policy Review* (2003), pp. 27–50, and Armstrong, C., W. Guay, and J. Weber, "The Role of Information and Financial Reporting in Corporate Governance and Debt Contracting," *Journal of Accounting and Economics* 50 (2010), pp. 179–234.

[13] See Jensen, M., "The Modern Industrial Revolution, Exit, and the Failure of Internal Control Systems," *Journal of Finance* 48 (1993), pp. 831–880; and Core, J., R. Holthausen, and D. Larcker, "Corporate Governance, Chief Executive Officer Compensation and Firm Performance," *Journal of Financial Economics* vol. 51, no. 3 (1999), pp. 371–406.

[14] Achara, V., M. Hahn, and C. Kehoe, "Corporate Governance and Value Creation: Evidence from Private Equity," NYU Stern Working Paper, 2010.

Information Asymmetry Advantage of Insiders

Critics of LBO transactions argue that inherent conflicts of interest exist when managers are involved in the transaction because they have inside information that other shareholders do not have regarding the likely future performance of the business. These critics contend that managers share this information with financial sponsors, giving the sponsors an unfair advantage in choosing LBO companies. Kaplan (1989) examined forecasts released to the public by the management team in various SEC filings leading up to LBO transactions and found that the subsequent performance of the LBOs was slightly worse on average and certainly no better than what was forecasted.[15] In addition, there is an active market for corporate control, and many proposed LBOs wind up being taken over by other bidders, including strategic buyers. Further, in many of these transactions, there are significant equity holdings by non-participating insiders who sell their equity stakes in the transaction. If the deal price is unfair, these individuals are irrationally selling their stakes. As such, there is no compelling evidence that any value creation for the investors is due to information asymmetry between the insiders and other shareholders.

Valuation Key 15.4

There are sound economic motivations associated with LBO transactions that may lead to increases in value. These motivations have to do with incentives associated with debt and equity, tax savings, and the improved monitoring that is likely rendered by the board of directors.

Wealth Transfer from Employees and Pre-Buyout Bondholders

Some critics of LBO transactions argue that part of the wealth increase experienced by those participating in the transaction is due to wealth transfers from employees and pre-buyout lenders. Kaplan and Strömberg (2008) reviewed the evidence on layoffs from a variety of studies. All of these studies concluded that, on average, growth in employment in companies undergoing LBOs was more modest than that in other companies in the same industry, but the studies did not find evidence that LBO firms were, on average, reducing their work forces. The evidence reviewed by Kaplan and Strömberg (2008) suggested that the same general results held outside the United States. Studies on employment in LBOs in the U.K. indicated that employment growth is similar to that of non-buyout firms in the same industry but that wages increased more slowly. A study of French LBOs indicated that job and wage growth was greater for LBO firms than it was for a sample of similar non-buyout firms.

Valuation in Practice 15.2

Met Life vs. RJR Nabisco After the RJR Nabisco (RJR) LBO, Metropolitan Life sued RJR. Metropolitan Life claimed that it had held $225 million in RJR bonds that had fallen in value by $40 million because of the RJR leveraged buyout transaction—a decline of almost 20% of the value of the bonds. The bonds that Metropolitan Life owned in RJR had neither restrictions on the right of RJR to engage in a change of control nor restrictions on the amount of debt that RJR could issue. Metropolitan Life sued RJR, arguing that RJR had not acted in good faith. The court dismissed most of the suit, concluding that Metropolitan Life was a sophisticated lender with an intimate familiarity with the kinds of restrictive covenants often found in bond indentures that could have protected its investment against a transaction such as this. Further, it knew that these bonds did not contain these provisions and chose to hold the bonds anyway.

Metropolitan Life appealed the court rulings, but on January 25, 1991, before the appeals finished, RJR announced that it had settled the claim with Metropolitan Life—though the exact terms were not disclosed.

---

[15] Kaplan, S., "The Effects of Management Buyouts on Operating Performance and Value," *Journal of Financial Economics* vol. 24, no. 2 (1989) pp. 217–254.

Little empirical evidence exists on the extent to which pre-LBO debtholders experience losses from LBO transactions. We do, however, know that lenders who have bond covenants that either prohibit a change in control without approval or put limitations on the extent that debt can be raised (these are reasonably common bond covenants) do not experience losses from these transactions. The reason for this is that in order to close the transaction, the bonds have to be retired. That said, in some LBO transactions, there is clear evidence that the bondholders experienced losses. Despite the fact that in some cases pre-LBO bondholders lose value, this issue is generally not considered a significant source of value creation for buyers in LBO transactions.

15.4 THE EFFECTS ON OPERATING PERFORMANCE AND FIRM VALUE

In the previous section, we discussed the motivation, economic forces, and valuation-creation strategies underpinning LBOs. In this section, we review the extant empirical literature that examines the effects of LBOs on operating performance and value. As noted previously, LBO transactions became popular in the late 1970s, and several empirical studies have examined the effect of early LBOs on operating performance. Next, we summarize the evidence from two of these studies—Smith (1990) and Kaplan (1989).[16] Afterward, we will review studies that examined the post-LBO operating performance of more recent transactions.

The Effect of LBOs on Operating Performance—The Early Years (1970s–mid-1980s)

Examining transactions from 1977 to 1986, Smith (1990) documents a median increase in operating cash flows to assets of 4.3% (adjusted for industry performance) from the year before to the year after the transactions and a median increase of 5.9% from the year before to two years after the transactions; the average pre-transaction operating cash flows to assets was 23.9%. Thus, these increases were 18% and 25% of the pre-transaction operating cash flows to assets. Using EBITDA to assets, Kaplan (1989) shows percentage increases of 17% and 36% (that are analogous to Smith's 18% and 25%).

Part of the increase in operating cash flows documented by Smith is due to improvements in working capital. In particular, by reducing the number of days in inventory and receivables and by lengthening the number of days in payables, a firm can experience an increase in operating cash flows. Smith documents such a decrease in working capital. In particular, the median working capital operating cycle or trade cycle (days in inventory, plus days in accounts receivable, less days in accounts payable) decreased by over 11 days from the year before to the year after the transaction, and it decreased by over 13 days from the year before to two years after the transaction; the pre-transaction level was 73.8 days. Thus, these effects represent a decline in the working capital operating cycle of 15% to 18%.

Some question whether the improvements in the cash flows were a result of layoffs or from cutting back on expenditures that hurt the long-run value of the firm—expenditures for advertising, maintenance, and research and development (R&D). Kaplan finds no reduction in the absolute level of employment, but as discussed previously, the LBO firms were adding employees at a slower rate than their industry counterparts. In particular, he finds that the median increase in employees was 1% across all LBO sample firms, and for the firms that had no divestitures, the growth rate in employees was 5%. If we examine these same numbers, adjusting for changes in industry employment, the median percentage change was a negative 12% for all LBO sample companies and negative 6% for those companies having no divestitures. Smith examines the expenditures on advertising, maintenance, and R&D as a percentage of sales and finds no evidence that these are falling, suggesting that the companies are not cutting back on these activities.

Smith documents a significant decline in capital expenditures to sales from the year before to the year after the transaction, but she does not find a significant decline from the year before to two years after the transaction. Based on the median level of capital expenditures to sales of 3.4% prior to the transaction, Smith shows that the median industry-adjusted reduction to the ratio is 0.3% for the year after

---

[16] See Smith, A., "Corporate Ownership Structure and Performance," *Journal of Financial Economics* vol. 27, no. 1 (1990), pp. 143–164; and Kaplan, S., "The Effects of Management Buyouts on Operating Performance and Value," *Journal of Financial Economics* vol. 24, no. 2 (1989), pp. 217–254.

the transaction—a median percentage change of negative 9.2%, which is statistically significant. From the year before to two years after the transaction, the median industry-adjusted percentage change was only negative 3.1% and insignificant. Whether the reduction in capital expenditures is value increasing or decreasing is not known. It could be that the firms were cash constrained and, at least for some time, were unable to make the investments that should have been made. Alternatively, it could have been that the firms were overinvesting beyond what was optimal and that the incentives associated with the LBO solved the overinvestment problem.

For a subset of 25 LBO transactions in which the exit values from the LBO were estimable, Kaplan (1989) estimates the total return to all buyout investors from the date of the going-private transaction (based on the total transaction price and not just on the value of the equity) to the date of exit. The average time to exit was 2.7 years, and the median nominal total return from the going-private date to exit date was 111.3%. The total market-adjusted return (which adjusts for both the market movement and beta of the companies) was 28%. In 22 of the 25 transactions, the market-adjusted returns were positive. He also reports a nominal total return to the equityholders of 786% over the 2.7 years. This evidence suggests that value is created from these transactions, but one has to be somewhat careful in interpreting this evidence too strongly, for there is an obvious selection bias in terms of the companies for which one can find an exit value. That said, there are reasons to believe that these numbers might also underestimate the value created. For example, in the study, the debt is valued at book value at exit, and there is reason to believe that the value of the debt was greater than the book value at exit since in many cases, the leverage had been reduced. Thus, the remaining debt should have been less risky than when it was issued, and it should have had a market value that exceeded book value.

Of course, even if there is value created at the company level, this may not imply that there are excess returns for the limited partner investors in private equity funds given the fees charged by the private equity firms. We discuss this issue later in the chapter.

The Effect of LBOs on Operating Performance—More Recent Transactions

In the last few years, researchers have examined the post-LBO operating performance of more recent transactions by studying some of the operating performance metrics discussed previously. Much of the recent research examined the post-LBO performance of LBOs in the U.K., France, and Sweden. Kaplan and Strömberg (2008) summarize that evidence and conclude that the evidence is consistent with previous research on earlier transactions in the United States. In particular, the evidence suggests that LBO transactions enhance performance.

Two recent papers, however, document less of an improvement in performance subsequent to an LBO using U.S. data—Guo, Hotchkiss, and Song (2010) and Cohn, Mills, and Towery (2011).[17] Guo et al. examine LBOs completed between 1990 and 2006. They report changes in industry-adjusted EBITDA to assets of 7.1% for Year −1 to Year +1 and 2.6% for Year −1 to Year +2, but those changes are not statistically significant. The most analogous numbers from Kaplan (1989) are 16.6% and 36.1%. However, in a different analysis using the same sample and examining firms from Year −1 to the last year before exit (including exit through bankruptcy), they report a change of 10.9%, which is statistically significant. This result is not as large as the result reported by Kaplan in his earlier study, but it is still indicative of performance improvements. They also report that firms that had a loss in the year prior to their respective LBO transactions experienced a very significant positive improvement.

The paper by Cohn et al. (2011) has an advantage over the one by Guo et al. and other previous studies in that it uses U.S. tax return data. Previously, other U.S. studies relied on public information. As such, there was a potential selection bias in the sample firms of those studies, as the firms needed to have publicly traded debt and preferred stock as part of the LBO transaction or they had to exit from the transaction in such a way that revealed their financial information publicly (e.g., an IPO). Because of its use of tax data, no such selection bias exists in the Cohn et al. paper. Their sample consists of LBOs that closed between 1995 and 2007. They show a median industry-adjusted change in income before interest and federal taxes, divided by assets from Year −1 to Year +2, of 2.3%. The median ratio in the year prior to the transaction was 4.7% for their sample firms. A change of 2.3% is not large in absolute terms, but

---

[17] See Guo, S., E. Hotchkiss, and W. Song, "Do Buyouts (Still) Create Value?" *Journal of Finance* vol. 66, no. 2 (April 2011), pp. 479–517; and Cohn, J., L. Mills, and E. Towery, 2011, unpublished working paper, University of Texas at Austin.

the percentage improvement in operating performance is substantive (almost 50%). It is not clear, however, why the base is so small for this sample of firms. Kaplan (1989) used a somewhat similar measure (though his measure was before depreciation and was based on financial reporting income and not taxable income), and his median measure for the year before the transaction for his sample was 13.1%. In addition, Cohn et al. show that firms with a loss in the year prior to the LBO transaction had a significantly positive change in performance, similar to what was found by Guo et al.

Interestingly, in spite of the weaker operating performance improvement that is documented by Guo et al. (2011), they redo Kaplan's analysis of returns to post-buyout capital on their sample, and they find similar results regarding value creation. In particular, they find a median return to total post-buyout capital of 95.8% and median market- and risk-adjusted returns of 40.9%; recall that Kaplan's numbers were 111% and 28%. Thus, their results regarding value creation at the transaction level are consistent with Kaplan's earlier work. If there is little performance improvement as found in the Guo et al. sample, the value creation must be due to either an increase in the growth prospects of the portfolio companies or market timing by the private equity firms.

Valuation Key 15.5

The preponderance of evidence on the performance of LBOs suggests that, on average, the firms that undergo these transactions improve both their operating performance and working capital management. The evidence also suggests that, on average, there are no declines in the number of employees retained by LBO firms (though they do not hire as quickly as their industry counterparts). LBO firms do, however, cut back on capital expenditures—at least for some time—relative to their industry counterparts, but there is no evidence that they cut back on maintenance, advertising, or R&D.

15.5 FINANCIAL SPONSORS—WHO THEY ARE AND WHAT THEY DO

The terms financial sponsor, private equity firm, and leveraged buyout firm are often used interchangeably. There are many financial sponsors. Some of the largest are Blackstone Group; Kohlberg, Kravis, Roberts & Co. (KKR); Texas Pacific Group (TPG); Apollo Global Management; and Carlyle Group. Financial sponsors establish private equity funds, raise capital from investors, and then invest those funds in private equity deals. While a fund is invested in a company, the financial sponsor is actively engaged with the management of the company and requires representation on the board of directors. Some private equity firms do not specialize in leveraged transactions, but our discussion here is limited to those that do.

LO3 Learn about the role of financial sponsors in an LBO transaction

Private Equity Firms and Private Equity Funds

Private equity firms are generally partnerships or limited liability corporations, and they are generally private. However, between 2007 and 2012 all of the financial sponsors named in the prior paragraph, except Apollo Global Management, have gone public. Private equity firms raise money for equity investments by establishing private equity funds, which are basically commitments at some specified amount from various investors (such as endowments, pension funds, and other institutions) to provide capital when needed for investments. The private equity firm is a general partner in each of the funds launched, and the investors in the private equity fund are limited partners.

Usually, each fund has a fixed life of 10 years. Thus, given the nature of the fund's term, the expectation is that the fund will invest in and exit from these companies within 10 years. It is normally anticipated that the fund will be fully invested within five to six years before exiting over the following four or five years. Fund life can be extended for up to two or three years in many cases. Covenants usually constrain certain actions that a private equity firm can take with respect to the investments of the fund—such as restrictions on the percentage that a fund can invest in one company or in one industry and restrictions on the amount of leverage that the fund can use in aggregate across all portfolio companies.

The limited partners who invest in a fund make a commitment to invest a certain amount of capital in the fund. The commitment period usually lasts for about five to six years, which is the expected investment period. The private equity firm does not receive funds from the limited partners until it has an investment to make in a particular company. When the private equity firm (the general partner) is ready to close on a company, it sends the limited partners a **capital call**, and the limited partners are obligated to transfer capital to the fund within an agreed-upon time frame that is set forth in the contract between the limited partners and general partner; this period is often 10 days.

Successful private equity firms raise new funds every three to five years, and as such, they are constantly both trying to invest in new firms and to exit from their previous investments. How successful a private equity fund will be in raising subsequent funds depends, in part, on how their previous funds have performed. Private equity firms with successful track records can raise capital more easily than those without any record of accomplishment or those with a weak or mediocre track record.

A private equity firm receives compensation in a variety of ways. First, a private equity firm charges an annual management fee of about 2% of the capital committed for at least the first five years while the fund is being invested. The purpose of this fee is to pay for the cost of operating the fund. Many funds then drop the fee by 25 basis points per year over the following five years (1.75%, 1.5%, etc.), as it is less expensive to operate the fund after it is fully invested. Over the 10-year life of a fund, the total fee with that structure would be 16.25% of the capital committed with the remaining 83.75% being invested in portfolio companies. In addition to management fees, a private equity firm also charges various deal and monitoring fees to the portfolio companies. For example, the private equity firm often charges a fee for buying and selling the portfolio company—similar to an advisory fee that is charged by an investment bank. It is not uncommon for some of these deal and monitoring fees to be shared with the limited partners in the fund.

The last form of compensation that a private equity firm receives is a percentage of the profits of the fund—often referred to as **carried interest**. For example, a private equity firm often receives 20% of the profits of the fund. Profits are defined differently by different funds; sometimes, the profits are based on the committed capital, and sometimes the profits are based on only the capital invested in portfolio companies. If profits are based on committed capital, cash received from the sale of portfolio companies is distributed to the investors in accordance with the proportion of the capital that they had contributed to the fund. Once all of the committed capital has been returned, the private equity firm receives 20% of every dollar distributed.

Metrick and Yasuda (2010) simulate the fees and carried interest earned by using actual contracts and information on how actual funds perform. They show that the mean total revenue to private equity firms is $17.80 per $100 invested, $11.64 of which is fixed per the contract and $6.16 of which is variable and is a function of how the fund performs.[18]

What Do Private Equity Firms Do Besides Raise Funds and Buy/Sell Companies?

Private equity firms buy companies and help the companies raise other forms of capital—such as debt and preferred stock. As such, they are not only deciding which companies to buy but also arranging the financing for the companies as well, often charging a fee for doing so. As discussed earlier, the debt structures of these deals are complex, and they are tailored to particular companies within the limits of what the credit markets are willing to consider lending at the time.

Of course, at some point, the private equity fund liquidates, and so the private equity firm must exit the investments it has made. Exits most often take the form of a sale to a strategic buyer, a sale to an LBO-backed firm, an IPO, a sale to another financial sponsor, a sale to management, or bankruptcy. Thus, the private equity firm is also involved in selling the companies in which it is invested in order to liquidate the fund. If it cannot exit its transactions, it will not be able to distribute funds to its investors, and hence it will have difficulty in raising subsequent funds. Kaplan and Strömberg (2008, Table 2) report statistics regarding the type of exit and exit timing for their sample of LBOs from 1970 to 2007, which we provide in Exhibit 15.7.

These data do not reveal recent time trends. Kaplan and Strömberg (2008) document that IPOs are now a much less common form of exit than they were from the 1970s to mid-1990s, but selling the company to another financial sponsor or to a company that has already undergone an LBO is more common now than it was in the 1970s and 1980s. It is also interesting to note that despite the generally high leverage in these companies, only 6% of the known outcomes ended in bankruptcy, suggesting that such firms usually have the necessary characteristics to service the high leverage of an LBO transaction. Even if we do not consider the 11% of transactions for which the exit is unknown, the overall failure rate for almost

---

[18] Both the fee structures and carried interest calculations vary across funds and can be much more complex than the relatively simple structures described here. For a thorough analysis of many of the alternative structures that are used, see Metrick, A., and A. Yasuda, "The Economics of Private Equity Funds," *Review of Financial Studies* vol. 23, no. 6 (2010), pp. 2303–2341.

EXHIBIT 15.7	Data on Type of Exit and Time to Exit for LBO Transactions*

Type of Exit	% of Deals
Bankruptcy	6%
IPO	14%
Sold to strategic buyer	38%
Sold to financial sponsor	24%
Sold to financial sponsor-backed firm	5%
Sold to management	1%
Other/Unknown	11%

Deals Exited Within	% of Deals
24 months (2 years)	12%
60 months (5 years)	42%
72 months (6 years)	51%
84 months (7 years)	58%

* Table 2 of Kaplan, S., and P. Strömberg, "Leveraged Buyouts and Private Equity" *Journal of Economic Perspectives* vol. 22, no. 4 (2008), pp. 1–27.

Exhibit may contain small rounding errors

40 years of data is less than 7%. Time to exit is, of course, also important to a private equity firm as it tries to close out its funds in 10 to 12 years. Kaplan and Strömberg (2008) also provide data on exits. Across their entire sample, the median time to exit is six years. However, some transactions take longer to exit.

As discussed earlier, one hallmark of LBO transactions is that the management team is given significant incentives in the financial outcome of the transaction, and in most cases, the management team is asked to make a significant investment in the company so that there is downside risk for them as well. The private equity firm structures these incentives.

Another part of the work of private equity firms is monitoring and advising. We have already detailed the significant representation that private equity firms have on the board of directors and the frequency with which both formal board meetings and informal meetings take place. In addition, private equity firms (or at least the larger ones) often hire former operating executives from various industries to help advise the management teams in their portfolio companies. Indeed, many private equity firms are organized around an industry focus. These former operating executives play a significant role as they advise the private equity firm's portfolio companies and advise the private equity firm on whether to buy a particular company.

Valuation Key 15.6

Private equity firms raise capital for their private equity funds from investors so they can invest in companies through leveraged buyouts. They arrange the debt financing to purchase these companies, sit on the board of directors, monitor and provide advice to their portfolio companies, and arrange for the equity incentives of the management team. Eventually, they attempt to exit their investments through the sale of the companies to strategic buyers, to other financial buyers, or via initial public offerings.

How Do Private Equity Funds Perform?

Data on the performance of private equity funds is limited, for they are not required to publish disclosures regarding their investment performance. Three studies that have examined fund performance are Kaplan and Schoar (2005), Phalippou and Gottschalg (2009), and Harris, Jenkinson, and Kaplan (2012).[19] Kaplan and Schoar (2005) study private equity funds from 1980 to 2001. They conclude that, net of fees, a limited partner (investor) in the average private equity fund earned less than the Standard and Poor's 500 Index. Their estimates indicate that investors earned between 3% and 7% less than an equivalent investment in the S&P 500 over the life of the fund (note that this is not the annual return difference but the total return difference over the fund's life). Phalippou and Gottschalg (2009) perform a slightly different analysis and risk adjust

[19] See Kaplan, S., and A. Schoar, "Private Equity Performance: Returns, Persistence and Capital Flows," *Journal of Finance* vol. 40, no. 4 (2005), pp. 1791–1823, Phalippou, L., and O. Gottschalg, "The Performance of Private Equity Funds," *Review of Financial Studies* vol. 22, no. 4 (2009), pp. 1747–1776; and Harris, R., T. Jenkinson, and S. Kaplan, "Private Equity Performance: What Do We Know?" working paper, University of Chicago, 2012.

the returns for their sample of funds from 1980 to 2003. They find that the average fund performance, net of fees, is 3% per year below that of the S&P 500 and that adjusting for risk increases the underperformance to 6% per year. Both studies find strong evidence of persistence in fund performance—in other words, if a private equity firm's current fund performs well; it is likely that the next fund will perform well too.

A more recent study by Harris, Jenkinson, and Kaplan (2012) discusses potential biases in the reported results of the two studies just discussed that could lead to downward-biased estimates of fund performance. They use data provided by over 200 institutional investors that are limited partners in private equity funds (investors such as pension funds, endowments, etc.) that track the investors' cash investments and cash returns from each fund in which they invest. The data cover over 1,400 funds from 1984 to 2008 and represent approximately 60% of the capital committed to PE funds over this time period. The authors show that, on average, the funds in the sample earn returns in excess of the S&P 500 on a risk-adjusted basis of more than 3% annually and over 20% over the life of the fund. The median risk-adjusted return of the funds is approximately 12% over the life of the fund. Of course, this sample is subject to a selection bias in that institutional investors presumably invest in the funds of the general partners in which they have the most confidence, and thus the results may be an upward-biased estimate of the average performance of all PE funds. Nevertheless, the data suggest abnormal returns to the limited partners net of the fees paid for investors in these funds.

15.6 STEPS IN ASSESSING THE INVESTMENT VALUE OF LEVERAGED BUYOUT TRANSACTIONS

LO4 Understand the steps for analyzing and valuing an LBO transaction

LBO and MBO transactions are complicated business transactions with numerous elements that have to be managed with care. As a consequence, assessing the investment value of these transactions can be quite complex. We begin this section with a discussion of the steps involved in assessing the potential investment value of leveraged buyout transactions. As you will soon read, the methods and valuation tools used in the process to assess investment value are not new; however, the process combines these methods and valuation tools in a way that is specific to the special characteristics of these highly leveraged transactions. In the following section, we use a detailed example to illustrate this process.

Steps in Assessing the Investment Value

In Exhibit 15.8, we present an outline of the steps used in assessing the investment value of a proposed LBO transaction. These steps include two iterative processes. The first iterative process sets the price, capital structure, and terms for the securities issued such that they are consistent with both the market conditions and the buyer's risk preferences. The second iterative process sets an offer price (or range of offer prices) that meets the buyer's rate-of-return hurdle (in other words, a rate of return that is acceptable to the buyer), and it includes the first iterative process as the capital structure affects these calculations.

The first iterative process (Steps 1 through 6) begins with setting an initial offer price for the LBO target—based on, for example, premiums paid in comparable transactions. Once we set an initial price (Step 1), we can then model an initial post-LBO capital structure that includes the amount and types of securities and the financial terms of those securities (Step 2). Concurrently, we develop a financial model for the target's operations and incorporate the proposed capital structure using interest rates and other financial terms based on assumed debt ratings (Steps 3 and 4). Based on the financial model and market conditions (interest rates and other financial terms for various types of debt securities), we assess the debt rating and the ability of the company to service the debt (Step 5).

In Step 6, we then iterate Steps 1 through 5 if the debt rating we assess in Step 5 is not equal to the debt rating assumed for the interest rates or if, based on the financial model, the company cannot service the debt properly. For example, if the debt rating is lower than the debt rating implicit in the interest rate used in the financial model, we reduce the amount of debt and related terms in the capital structure, which increases the debt rating, or we raise the interest rate. If the debt rating is higher than the debt rating implicit in the interest rate used in the financial model, we can either increase the amount of debt in the capital structure or reduce the interest rate on the debt. Moreover, if the model indicates that the company cannot meet the required principal and interest payments, we reduce the amount of debt in the model or lengthen the maturity. After we complete this process, we will have an offer price, a capital structure, and a set of related financial terms that are consistent with market rates and conditions.

We now have an offer price, a capital structure, and a set of related financial terms that are consistent with market rates and conditions; however, we do not know whether the proposed LBO transaction is

EXHIBIT 15.8	Steps in Assessing the Investment Value of Leveraged and Management Buyout Transactions

1. Establish an initial purchase price for the LBO target (for example, based on recent premiums paid in comparable transactions)

2. Develop the target's initial post-LBO capital structure, including the types and terms for the securities to be issued based on market conditions and the buyer's risk preferences

3. Develop a financial model for the post-LBO operations of the target and incorporate the proposed capital structure

4. Forecast all capital structure items based on the company's capital structure (type of financing, amount of financing, and amount of interest) based on an assumed debt rating, assumed deal terms, and market conditions

5. Assess the target's debt capacity based on the target's post-LBO debt rating and ability to service the debt based on the financial model

6. Iterate steps 1 through 5 until the assumed deal terms and the debt capacity (based on the target's post-LBO debt rating and ability to service the debt) align

7. Measure the internal rate of return (IRR) for each equity investor (as well as debt with option features) based on different exit years and exit valuations

8. Set a new price and iterate steps 1 through 7 until the LBO transaction IRR meets at least the minimum IRR hurdle rate set by the investors

9. Value the firm and equity using the weighted average cost of capital method with relevant exit assumptions to measure the implied market multiples and IRRs to equity investors based on the WACC valuation

10. Use the adjusted present value method and the financial model to determine the overall NPV of the investment and the cost of equity in the transaction, and compare to the IRRs

a good investment. Using the net present value method is the preferred way to assess whether or not an investment increases value, but most investors make that assessment in an LBO analysis by comparing the internal rates of return earned by various investors from the investment to the hurdle rates required by those different investors.

Thus, the next step in the process (Step 7) measures the internal rates of return (IRR) of the proposed LBO transaction to various investors based on the investment parameters resulting from the first iterative process and from an estimate of the transaction value of the company at exit. In practice, valuing the firm at various exit dates is most often done using market multiples. The second iterative process (Step 8) adjusts the offer price and capital structure (and possibly even the operating forecasts) until the IRRs of the proposed investment meet investor hurdle rates. However, any time we change the offer price, capital structure, or operating forecasts, we must also implement the first iterative process to ensure that the new investment parameters are based on a feasible capital structure. Moreover, if we change the operating forecasts, that change must be based on realistic assumptions about the company's operations.

If the analysis in Step 7 establishes exit values at different dates based on market multiples, we recommend also evaluating exit values based on a discounted cash flow analysis (Step 9). For example, a weighted average cost of capital valuation could estimate exit values based on a standard industry capital structure, indicating what the value of the company will likely be for either a sale to a strategic buyer or a sale in an IPO transaction.

Finally, in Step 10, we measure the year-by-year values of the firm and equity by using the adjusted present value method assuming no exit from the transaction. We can then measure the implied equity betas and equity costs of capital to compare them to the minimum investor hurdle rates we used for the equity investors in the LBO analysis. We note that many in the practice community stop the process at Step 8.

If we think about these two iterative processes, we can easily imagine such an analysis being used to determine the highest price one might bid for a company given the credit market conditions and internal rates of returns demanded by different investors at the time of the valuation if the company were to undergo an LBO transaction. This is indeed how this analysis is used as a fundamental valuation tool; however, it looks at the company from a particular lens—undergoing a leveraged buyout.

Valuation Key 15.7

An assessment of the investment value of a proposed leveraged buyout transaction includes two iterative processes to ensure the assumptions underlying the proposed transaction are both consistent with market conditions and able to meet investors' required hurdle rates. We use various valuation methods and tools in this analysis, including financial modeling, tools to assess debt ratings and the ability to service debt, and tools to assess the internal rate of return to various investors.

15.7 AN ILLUSTRATIVE LEVERAGED BUYOUT TRANSACTION—JOHN EDWARDSON & COMPANY

LO5 Use an LBO model to analyze and value an LBO transaction

In this section, we use a detailed example in order to illustrate how to assess the investment value of LBOs and MBOs. To do so, we follow the 10 steps outlined in the previous section. Due to space constraints, we do not show the entire iterative process, but rather, we only show the final proposed model. We assume that the company of interest is John Edwardson & Company (Edwardson), which is a publicly traded company in the retail computer industry that sells a variety of products related to computers and computer networks. A financial sponsor is assessing the investment value of a leveraged buyout of Edwardson.

Initial Price and Capital Structure (Steps 1–2)

In Exhibit 15.9, we present a summary of the offer price for Edwardson's equity and options. The company's current stock price is $40 per share and the company has 200 million shares outstanding, which will also equal the post-transaction shares outstanding. The company has a current price-to-earnings ratio of 13.1, and its firm value to EBIT, EBITDA, and revenue multiples equal 8.3, 5.7, and 1.8, respectively. After considering the company's expected performance and alternative strategies to the LBO transaction (including alternative acquisition offers), the deal premium was set at 20%. The resulting offer price is $48 per share, with transaction multiples of 15.7 for the price-to-earnings ratio and 9.7, 6.7, and 2.1 for the firm value to EBIT, EBITDA, and revenue multiples, respectively.

EXHIBIT 15.9	Offer Price for the Equity and Options				
		Market Multiples			
		P/E	**EBIT**	**EBITDA**	**Revenue**
Current stock price....................................	$40.00	13.054	8.313	5.715	1.829
Deal premium..	20.0%				
Deal stock price.....................................	$ 48.00	15.665	9.696	6.666	2.133
Number of fully diluted shares outstanding...............	213.06	million			
Purchase price of equity.............................	$10,227.00	million			

Pre-LBO Outstanding Options as of End of Year 0 (Liquidation of Options)				
Year Issued	**Exercise Price**	**Number of Options = Shares Issued (m)**	**Buyback Shares (m)**	**Net Increase in Shares (m)**
Issued Year −6...........................	$30.00	4.00	2.50	1.50
Issued Year −5...........................	$31.00	4.50	2.91	1.59
Issued Year −4...........................	$31.50	5.00	3.28	1.72
Issued Year −3...........................	$33.00	6.00	4.13	1.88
Issued Year −2...........................	$34.00	7.00	4.96	2.04
Issued Year −1...........................	$35.50	8.00	5.92	2.08
Issued Year 0	$36.00	9.00	6.75	2.25
		43.50	30.44	13.06

Exhibit may contain small rounding errors

The total offer price for the company's equity and options is $10.2 billion, which is equal to the offer price per share, multiplied by the number of shares outstanding, plus the cost of cashing out existing stock options and any other equity-based derivative equity securities. Edwardson has no convertible debt or convertible preferred, but it does have 43.5 million options outstanding with various exercise prices. In the bottom panel of Exhibit 15.9, we calculate the cost of cashing out the stock options by using the treasury stock method, which is a common way to measure the effect of options on an offer.

To use the treasury stock method, we subtract the number of shares that can be bought back (with proceeds received from the exercise of the options) from the number of shares issued in order to measure the net increase in shares. The number of shares that can be repurchased is equal to the total proceeds received divided by the offer price. The total proceeds equal the number of options multiplied by the exercise or strike price. For example, for options issued in Year −6, the company will issue 4 million shares. The number of shares the company can repurchase is equal to the 4 million shares, multiplied by the $30 exercise price (yielding total proceeds of $120 million), divided by the $48 offer price; this equals 2.5 million shares. Thus, the net effect of these options is an additional 1.5 million shares.[20] The net increase in shares from the buyout of all of the options is 13.1 million shares, and the total offer price is $10.2 billion ($10,227 million = $48 × 213.06 million equivalent shares).

In Exhibit 15.10, we present a schedule detailing how the proposed transaction will be financed (a sources and uses schedule) along with the post-LBO capital and ownership structures. The first two columns of numbers present the sources and uses in dollars and percentages. The uses portion of the schedule delineates each of the costs of closing the transaction, which includes payments to the current equityholders and payments to redeem all other securities (such as debt and preferred stock). This schedule also details all financing fees paid and the fees paid to the sponsor, to lawyers, to accountants, to financial advisors, and to other consultants.

EXHIBIT 15.10 Sources and Uses, Capital Structure, and Deal Terms

Sources and Uses of Cash—LBO Financing ($ in millions)	Amount	%	Coupon = YTM	Maturity (Years)	Post-LBO Capital Structure	Common Shares Issued	Common Shares Issued (% Owned)	Warrants and Options Issued (% of Total Shares)	Fully Diluted Equity Allocation
Sources									
Excess cash	$117.67	1.0%							
Debt assumed	0.00	0.0%							0.00%
Revolver	100.00	0.8%	4.50%	5	0.82%				0.00%
Senior secured note (bank debt)	3,620.00	29.2%	6.00%	7	29.51%				0.00%
Subordinated note (unsecured debt)	1,810.00	14.6%	10.00%	9	14.75%				0.00%
Mezzanine debt	3,020.00	24.4%	12.00%	10	24.62%			4.00%	4.00%
Preferred stock—assumed	0.00	0.0%							0.00%
Preferred stock—new	0.00	0.0%							0.00%
Common equity									0.00%
Sponsor investment	3,380.00	27.3%			27.55%	181.86	90.93%		85.23%
Management rollover	200.00	1.6%			1.63%	10.76	5.38%	1.35%	6.39%
Management new investment	137.11	1.1%			1.12%	7.38	3.69%	0.92%	4.38%
Total sources	$12,384.78	100.0%			100.00%	200.00	100.00%	6.27%	100.00%
Uses									
Common equity Non-management shares purchased	$10,027.00	81.0%							
Management rollover	200.00	1.6%							
Preferred stock—assumed	0.00	0.0%							
Preferred stock—redeemed	725.00	5.9%							
Debt assumed	0.00	0.0%							
Debt redeemed	1,000.00	8.1%	Fee Rate	Total					
Financing fees—debt	253.50	2.0%	3.00%		Debt without revolver—amortize				
Financing fees—revolver	0.00	0.0%	0.50%	$300.0	Expense annually as incurred				
Sponsor fees	119.52	1.0%	1.00%		Based on deal value (deal cost) before fees				
Other fees and expenses	59.76	0.5%	0.50%		Based on deal value (deal cost) before fees				
Total uses	$12,384.78	100.0%							

Exhibit may contain small rounding errors

The total investment (uses) for the proposed transaction is $12.4 billion, which includes the amount paid to equityholders and option holders, $725 million to redeem outstanding preferred stock, $1 billion to redeem existing debt (see Exhibit 15.11 for the company's pre- and post-LBO balance sheet), and

---

[20] An alternative to increasing the number of shares using the treasury stock method is to measure the cost of buying out the options and adding that amount to the cost of repurchasing the shares outstanding. The cost of buying out the options is equal to the difference between the exercise price and the offer price, multiplied by the number of options. This calculation, of course, results in the same total offer price.

$433 million in various fees. The existing debt and preferred stock are redeemed at par value, which equals their respective book values. The sponsor intends to finance this transaction (the sources) by using Edwardson's $117.7 million in excess cash, issuing various debt securities equaling $8.6 billion, and investing $3.7 billion of equity (including the management's contribution to equity from rollover equity and new investment).

The $8.6 billion in debt is composed of $3.6 billion of 7-year, 6.0% senior secured bank debt; $1.8 billion of 9-year, 10% subordinated unsecured debt; and $3.0 billion of 10-year, and 12% mezzanine debt. In addition, the company is arranging a $300 million revolving line of credit that has a five-year term, a 4.5% interest rate on the amount drawn, and a 0.5% annual fee on the total line of credit. The sponsor plans to use $100.0 million from this revolver in order to help finance the transaction. The sponsor will invest $3.4 billion in common stock while current management will roll over $200 million in common stock and will invest an additional $137 million in common stock. The financing of the deal is roughly 30% secured bank debt (including the revolver), 15% unsecured subordinated debt, and 24% mezzanine debt for almost 70% debt in total, with the rest coming from 1% excess cash and 30% common equity. We assume that the terms of the debt contracts require the company to use all of its available cash flow to reduce its debt, beginning with the secured debt before retiring any unsecured debt; however, it may pay down the revolver before the secured debt at any time.

In addition, an "equity kicker" will be attached to the mezzanine debt equal to 4% of the common equity ownership on a fully diluted basis. Management will also be given additional performance-based equity equal to 2.27% of the common equity ownership on a fully diluted basis. These equity-linked securities dilute the common equity that exists as of the closing date, and the fully diluted ownership percentages are shown in the last column of Exhibit 15.10. For example, management purchased 3.69% of the shares. Those shares are diluted by the total options issued, 6.27% (see total warrants and options issued shown in the second-to-last column in Exhibit 15.10), but management received .92% of those options for their new investment; thus, management's new shares on a fully diluted basis are 3.69% × (1 − 0.0627) + 0.92% = 4.38%. In the model, the fully diluted ownership structure is used to allocate the exit proceeds. Management's proportionate ownership of the equity (including incentives) is 10.8%, which is in line with our earlier discussion regarding the amount of management equity in LBO transactions.

REVIEW EXERCISE 15.1

Sources and Uses, Capital Structure, and Deal Terms

A group of managers is going to offer to purchase the company they manage with the help of a financial sponsor. The company's current stock price is $16 per share, and the company has 100 million shares outstanding; the company has a current price-to-earnings ratio equal to 14.91 and a firm-value-to-EBITDA multiple equal to 7.05. Management owns 3 million shares of the outstanding stock. After considering the company's expected performance and alternative strategies to the LBO transaction (including alternative acquisition offers), the deal premium is set at 25%. The company has no convertible debt or convertible preferred stock, but it does have 20 million stock options outstanding—all with an exercise price equal to $11.20.

In addition to redeeming the existing stock and options, management and its financial sponsor will also redeem all outstanding debt (par value of $600 million) and preferred stock (par value of $100 million) at its par value (which is equal to its book value). Initial fees will equal $101.94 million (3% on the debt financing, 1% to the sponsor and 0.5% for other fees), but these fees do not include fees for the revolver loan. The sponsor intends to finance this transaction by using $34.61 million in excess cash held by the company, issuing various debt securities equal to $1.96 billion, investing $730 million of its own equity, and having management invest $153.33 million in equity from rollover equity and new investment. The composition of the $1.96 billion in debt is $880 million of 7-year, 5.0% senior secured bank debt; $410 million of 9-year, 9% subordinated unsecured debt; and $670 million of 10-year, 11% mezzanine debt (which has an "equity kicker" equal to 5% of the fully diluted post-LBO shares). In addition, the company is arranging for a $300 million revolving line of credit with a 5-year term, a 4.5% interest rate on the amount drawn, and a 0.5% annual fee on the total amount of the line of credit. The sponsor plans to use $100.0 million from the revolver in order to finance the transaction. Management has an "equity kicker" equal to 4.1% of the fully diluted post-LBO shares. The company will have 200 million post-transaction shares outstanding.

Calculate the purchase price of the equity and prepare a sources and uses schedule similar to the one in Exhibit 15.10.

Solution on page 655.

Financial Model, Capital Structure, and Debt Rating (Steps 3–5)

In Steps 3 through 5, we develop a financial model that incorporates the proposed capital structure, and we assess the target's debt capacity based on the target's post-LBO debt rating and ability to service the debt. We then iterate the model and capital structure until the operating performance supports the proposed capital structure.

In Exhibit 15.11, we present the closing balance sheet for the proposed transaction, which is the starting balance sheet for the financial model. The closing balance sheet begins with the pre-LBO balance sheet, which we assume is for the end of Year 0.

EXHIBIT 15.11	Closing Balance Sheet						
($ in millions)	Year –1	Year 0	Redeem Existing Securities	Fees	Issue LBO Securities—Use Excess Cash	Year 0 Post-LBO Closing
Cash balance	$ 326.4	$ 285.8			$–117.7	$ 168.1
Accounts receivable.	680.0	700.4				700.4
Inventory.	401.4	393.8				393.8
Total current assets	$1,407.8	$1,379.9				$ 1,262.3
Property, plant, and equipment	$4,640.0	$5,365.1				$ 5,365.1
Accumulated depreciation	–1,344.0	–1,904.3				–1,904.3
Property, plant, and equipment (net). . .	$3,296.0	$3,460.8				$ 3,460.8
Capitalized fees	$ 0	$ 0		$432.8		$ 432.8
Total assets.	$4,703.8	$4,840.7				$ 5,155.9
Accounts payable.	$ 291.9	$ 286.4				$ 286.4
Other current operating liabilities	108.8	112.1				112.1
Total current liabilities.	$ 400.7	$ 398.4				$ 398.4
Total debt	1,000.0	1,000.0	$–1,000.0		8,550.0	8,550.0
Total liabilities.	$1,400.7	$1,398.4				$ 8,948.4
Preferred stock.	$ 725.0	$ 725.0	–725.0			$ 0
Common stock.	1,000.0	1,000.0	–1,000.0		3,717.1	3,717.1
Retained earnings	1,578.1	1,717.3	–9,227.0			–7,509.7
Total shareholders' equity	$3,303.1	$3,442.3				$–3,792.6
Total liabilities and equities.	$4,703.8	$4,840.7				$ 5,155.9

Exhibit may contain small rounding errors

As part of the transaction, we redeem all debt, preferred, and other non-common equity securities that are not assumed in the transaction. We also eliminate the old equity, issue the new equity, and capitalize any fees. In this illustration, we use "recap accounting," which essentially treats the payment to shareholders as a return of capital up to their original investment and treats the rest of the payment to the equityholders as a reduction in retained earnings. With this method of accounting, there is no goodwill created, and there is no step-up in the book value of the assets for financial reporting purposes.[21]

In Exhibit 15.12, we present the forecast drivers (assumptions) used in our financial model. These drivers show the improvements that the sponsors and management expect to make in the operating performance of the company. We have modeled this as a "classic" LBO, which contemplates increases in margins through decreases in costs of goods sold and selling, general, and administrative expenses. In addition, we assume that improvements in working capital management will occur through a decrease in days of receivables, a decrease in days of inventory, and an increase in days of payables. We do not assume a cutback in capital expenditures in the early years of the transaction as is sometimes modeled, but we do assume a short-term increase in revenue growth.

---

[21] In this illustration, we use this method because it requires fewer assumptions to create the model without compromising the reader's understanding of how LBOs are analyzed. If the company uses acquisition accounting (purchase accounting), which is typical in LBO transactions, the company will appraise all of its assets and liabilities, write-up (or down) the assets and liabilities to their appraised value, and record any goodwill (the excess of the purchase price above the appraised value of the net assets). Goodwill can be negative if the purchase price is less than the appraised value; however, accounting rules require various adjustments before a company can record negative goodwill.

EXHIBIT 15.12 Financial Model Drivers (Assumptions, calculated using year-end and not average balances)

	Year 0	Year 1	Year 2	Year 3	Year 4	Year 5	Year 6	Year 7	Year 8	Year 9	Year 10	Year 11
Expected inflation (Year 11 is a long-run expectation)	3.00%	3.00%	3.00%	3.00%	3.00%	3.00%	3.00%	3.00%	3.00%	3.00%	3.00%	3.00%
Treasury Bonds—20-year	5.00%	5.00%	5.00%	5.00%	5.00%	5.00%	5.00%	5.00%	5.00%	5.00%	5.00%	5.00%
LIBOR—3-month	4.00%	4.00%	4.00%	4.00%	4.00%	4.00%	4.00%	4.00%	4.00%	4.00%	4.00%	4.00%
Revenue growth rate	3.00%	5.00%	8.00%	8.00%	10.00%	5.00%	3.00%	3.00%	3.00%	3.00%	3.00%	3.00%
Cost of goods sold (% revenue)	46.00%	46.00%	45.00%	44.00%	44.00%	44.00%	44.00%	44.00%	44.00%	44.00%	44.00%	44.00%
Selling, general, and administrative (% revenue)	22.00%	22.00%	21.00%	20.00%	20.00%	20.00%	20.00%	20.00%	20.00%	20.00%	20.00%	20.00%
Constant income tax rate	40.00%	40.00%	40.00%	40.00%	40.00%	40.00%	40.00%	40.00%	40.00%	40.00%	40.00%	40.00%
Required cash balance (% revenue)	3.00%	3.00%	2.00%	2.00%	2.00%	2.00%	2.00%	2.00%	2.00%	2.00%	2.00%	2.00%
Accounts receivable (days to collect)	45.6	45.6	43.1	40.6	40.6	40.6	40.6	40.6	40.6	40.6	40.6	40.6
Inventory (days to sell)	55.8	54.8	52.7	50.7	50.7	50.7	50.7	50.7	50.7	50.7	50.7	50.7
Accounts payable (days to pay)	40.7	45.4	45.5	45.5	45.1	45.3	45.4	45.4	45.4	45.4	45.4	45.4
Other current operating liabilities (% revenue)	2.0%	2.0%	2.5%	3.0%	3.0%	3.0%	3.0%	3.0%	3.0%	3.0%	3.0%	3.0%
Capital expenditures—based on revenue to net property, plant, and equipment	1.70	1.70	1.75	1.80	1.80	1.80	1.80	1.80	1.80	1.80	1.80	1.80

In Exhibits 15.13 through 15.15, we present the income statement, balance sheet, and free cash flow forecasts for the financial model; all of these are based on the company's operating strategy, the changes the sponsor and management expect to make to improve the company's operations, and the proposed capital structure. The income statement forecasts in Exhibit 15.13 reflect the expected revenue growth and any efficiency expected to be gained in the cost structure. The decrease in interest expense reflects the pay-down of debt as cash becomes available to retire some of the debt.

The balance sheet forecasts in Exhibit 15.14 also reflect the pay-down of the debt. We note that the capitalized fees are declining as they are being expensed over time. The non-financing fees are expensed in the first year, and the financing fees are amortized over the life of the respective loans with which they are associated. Notice that debt is collapsed into one line on the balance sheet and that we do not separate short-term from long-term debt. This is how we present the balance sheet here, but in Exhibit 15.16, we show a detailed debt schedule with which we keep track of each element of the debt structure.

In Exhibit 15.15, we present the free cash flow forecasts. The company's cash flows (before capital expenditures) are positive in every year, and the company generates sufficient cash flow to fund all of its anticipated capital expenditures. Given that LBO transactions typically maximize the amount of debt in the capital structure based on the current credit market conditions and that the post-LBO company is privately held, it is common for a post-LBO company to finance all of its capital expenditures from internally generated funds (or at least to do so initially). Debt covenants often require this internal funding or sometimes limit capital expenditures to a specified dollar amount even if they are funded internally.

The company also generates sufficient free cash flows to pay all of its after-tax interest costs. We can see this by looking at the "cash flow after interest and preferred stock dividends" line item. (Sometimes, this line is called the "pre-debt repayment cash flow" in investment banking models.) As a result of having sufficient free cash flows, the company is able to pay off the revolver in the first year. However, having insufficient cash to make interest payments can sometimes occur in highly leveraged transactions. If this is anticipated to occur, companies often deal with this cash flow deficit by designing some of the debt contracts so that interest is not paid in the first few years after the LBO but instead the interest is accrued as part of the debt agreement; this debt is pay-in-kind or PIK debt. In our example, Edwardson did not issue any PIK debt.

EXHIBIT 15.13 Income Statement Forecasts

($ in millions)	Year -1	Year 0	Year 1	Year 2	Year 3	Year 4	Year 5	Year 6	Year 7	Year 8	Year 9	Year 10	Year 11
Revenue	$5,440.0	$5,603.2	$5,883.4	$6,354.0	$6,862.4	$7,548.6	$7,926.0	$8,163.8	$8,408.7	$8,661.0	$8,920.8	$9,188.4	$9,464.1
Cost of goods sold	-2,627.5	-2,577.5	-2,706.3	-2,859.3	-3,019.4	-3,321.4	-3,487.4	-3,592.1	-3,699.8	-3,810.8	-3,925.2	-4,042.9	-4,164.2
Gross margin	$2,812.5	$3,025.7	$3,177.0	$3,494.7	$3,842.9	$4,227.2	$4,438.6	$4,571.7	$4,708.9	$4,850.1	$4,995.6	$5,145.5	$5,299.9
Selling, general, and administrative	-1,256.6	-1,232.7	-1,294.3	-1,334.3	-1,372.5	-1,509.7	-1,585.2	-1,632.8	-1,681.7	-1,732.2	-1,784.2	-1,837.7	-1,892.8
Other expenses			-179.3										
Depreciation expense	-544.0	-560.3	-588.3	-635.4	-686.2	-754.9	-792.6	-816.4	-840.9	-866.1	-892.1	-918.8	-946.4
Operating income	$1,011.8	$1,232.7	$1,115.1	$1,525.0	$1,784.2	$1,962.6	$2,060.8	$2,122.6	$2,186.3	$2,251.9	$2,319.4	$2,389.0	$2,460.7
Interest expense	-48.0	-60.0	-797.2	-791.2	-768.7	-744.3	-715.6	-674.2	-629.9	-566.5	-486.4	-386.5	-257.0
Income before taxes	$963.8	$1,172.7	$317.9	$733.8	$1,015.6	$1,218.3	$1,345.2	$1,448.4	$1,556.3	$1,685.3	$1,833.0	$2,002.5	$2,203.6
Income tax expense	-385.5	-469.1	-127.1	-293.5	-406.2	-487.3	-538.1	-579.4	-622.5	-674.1	-733.2	-801.0	-881.5
Net income	$578.3	$703.6	$190.7	$440.3	$609.3	$731.0	$807.1	$869.0	$933.8	$1,011.2	$1,099.8	$1,201.5	$1,322.2
Earnings Per Share													
Net income	$578.3	$703.6	$190.7	$440.3	$609.3	$731.0	$807.1	$869.0	$933.8	$1,011.2	$1,099.8	$1,201.5	$1,322.2
Preferred stock dividends	-40.6	-50.8											
Net income to common equity	$537.7	$652.9	$190.7	$440.3	$609.3	$731.0	$807.1	$869.0	$933.8	$1,011.2	$1,099.8	$1,201.5	$1,322.2
Common shares outstanding (m)	200.0	200.0	200.0	200.0	200.0	200.0	200.0	200.0	200.0	200.0	200.0	200.0	200.0
Basic earnings per share	$2.689	$3.264	$0.954	$2.201	$3.047	$3.655	$4.035	$4.345	$4.669	$5.056	$5.499	$6.007	$6.611
Effect of Dilutive Securities													
Management stock options (net shares, m)	11.1	13.1											
Common shares outstanding (m)	200.0	200.0											
Adjusted shares outstanding	211.1	213.1											
Diluted earnings per share	$2.547	$3.064											
Retained Earnings													
Beginning balance	$1,043.4	$1,578.1	$-7,509.7	$-7,019.0	$-6,070.7	$-6,209.4	$-5,538.4	$-4,731.3	$-3,862.3	$-2,928.5	$-1,917.3	$-817.5	$384.0
Net income	578.3	703.6	190.7	440.3	609.3	731.0	807.1	869.0	933.8	1,011.2	1,099.8	1,201.5	1,322.2
Preferred stock dividends	-40.6	-50.8	0.0	0.0	0.0	0.0	0.0	0.0	0.0	0.0	0.0	0.0	0.0
Common equity dividends	-3.0	-513.7	0.0	0.0	0.0	0.0	0.0	0.0	0.0	0.0	0.0	0.0	0.0
Ending balance	$1,578.1	$1,717.3	$-7,319.0	$-6,878.7	$-6,269.4	$-5,538.4	$-4,731.3	$-3,862.3	$-2,928.5	$-1,917.3	$-817.5	$384.0	$1,706.2

Exhibit may contain small rounding errors

627

EXHIBIT 15.14 Balance Sheet Forecasts

($ in millions)	Year -1	Year 0 Post-LBO Closing	Year 1	Year 2	Year 3	Year 4	Year 5	Year 6	Year 7	Year 8	Year 9	Year 10	Year 11
Cash balance	$ 326.4	$ 168.1	$ 176.5	$ 127.1	$ 137.2	$ 151.0	$ 158.5	$ 163.3	$ 168.2	$ 173.2	$ 178.4	$ 183.8	$ 189.3
Accounts receivable	680.0	700.4	735.4	750.1	762.5	838.7	880.7	907.1	934.3	962.3	991.2	1,020.9	1,051.6
Inventory	401.4	393.8	406.0	413.0	419.4	461.3	484.4	498.9	513.9	529.3	545.2	561.5	578.4
Total current assets	$1,407.8	$ 1,262.3	$ 1,317.9	$ 1,290.2	$ 1,319.1	$ 1,451.0	$ 1,523.6	$ 1,569.3	$ 1,616.3	$ 1,664.8	$ 1,714.8	$ 1,766.2	$ 1,819.2
Property, plant, and equipment	$4,640.0	$ 5,365.1	$ 6,230.3	$ 7,049.4	$ 8,008.0	$ 8,972.5	$ 9,897.2	$10,849.6	$11,830.7	$12,841.1	$13,881.9	$13,843.3	$13,803.6
Accumulated depreciation	−1,344.0	−1,904.3	−2,492.7	−3,128.1	−3,814.3	−4,569.2	−5,361.8	−6,178.1	−7,019.0	−7,885.1	−8,777.2	−8,585.5	−8,388.0
Property, plant, and equipment (net)	$3,296.0	$ 3,460.8	$ 3,737.7	$ 3,921.3	$ 4,193.7	$ 4,403.3	$ 4,535.4	$ 4,671.5	$ 4,811.7	$ 4,956.0	$ 5,104.7	$ 5,257.8	$ 5,415.6
Capitalized fees	$ 0.0	$ 432.8	$ 222.9	$ 192.3	$ 161.7	$ 131.1	$ 100.5	$ 69.9	$ 39.2	$ 24.2	$ 9.1	$ 0.0	$ 0.0
Total assets	$4,703.8	$ 5,155.9	$ 5,278.4	$ 5,403.8	$ 5,674.4	$ 5,985.4	$ 6,159.5	$ 6,310.6	$ 6,467.2	$ 6,645.0	$ 6,828.5	$ 7,024.0	$ 7,234.8
Accounts payable	$ 291.9	$ 286.4	$ 338.3	$ 357.4	$ 377.4	$ 415.2	$ 435.9	$ 449.0	$ 462.5	$ 476.4	$ 490.6	$ 505.4	$ 520.5
Other current operating liabilities	108.8	112.1	117.7	158.9	205.9	226.5	237.8	244.9	252.3	259.8	267.6	275.7	283.9
Total current liabilities	$ 400.7	$ 398.4	$ 456.0	$ 516.3	$ 583.3	$ 641.6	$ 673.7	$ 693.9	$ 714.7	$ 736.2	$ 758.3	$ 781.0	$ 804.4
Total debt	1,000.0	8,550.0	8,424.4	8,049.2	7,643.4	7,165.1	6,499.9	5,761.9	4,963.8	4,109.0	3,170.6	2,141.9	1,007.0
Total liabilities	$1,400.7	$ 8,948.4	$ 8,880.3	$ 8,565.5	$ 8,226.7	$ 7,806.7	$ 7,173.6	$ 6,455.8	$ 5,678.6	$ 4,845.1	$ 3,928.9	$ 2,922.9	$ 1,811.4
Preferred stock	$ 725.0	$ 0.0	$ 0.0	$ 0.0	$ 0.0	$ 0.0	$ 0.0	$ 0.0	$ 0.0	$ 0.0	$ 0.0	$ 0.0	$ 0.0
Common stock	1,000.0	3,717.1	3,717.1	3,717.1	3,717.1	3,717.1	3,717.1	3,717.1	3,717.1	3,717.1	3,717.1	3,717.1	3,717.1
Retained earnings	1,578.1	−7,509.7	−7,319.0	−6,878.7	−6,269.4	−5,538.4	−4,731.3	−3,862.3	−2,928.5	−1,917.3	−817.5	384.0	1,706.2
Total shareholders' equity	$3,303.1	$−3,792.6	$−3,601.9	$−3,161.6	$−2,552.3	$−1,821.3	$−1,014.2	$ −145.2	$ 788.6	$ 1,799.8	$ 2,899.7	$ 4,101.1	$ 5,423.3
Total liabilities and equities	$4,703.8	$ 5,155.9	$ 5,278.4	$ 5,674.4	$ 5,674.4	$ 5,985.4	$ 6,159.5	$ 6,310.6	$ 6,467.2	$ 6,645.0	$ 6,828.5	$ 7,024.0	$ 7,234.8

Exhibit may contain small rounding errors

EXHIBIT 15.15   Free Cash Flow Forecasts

($ in millions)	Year 1	Year 2	Year 3	Year 4	Year 5	Year 6	Year 7	Year 8	Year 9	Year 10	Year 11
Earnings before interest and taxes (EBIT)	$1,115.1	$1,525.0	$1,784.2	$1,962.6	$2,060.8	$2,122.6	$2,186.3	$2,251.9	$2,319.4	$2,389.0	$2,460.7
− Income taxes paid on EBIT	−446.0	−610.0	−713.7	−785.1	−824.3	−849.0	−874.5	−900.7	−927.8	−955.6	−984.3
Earnings before interest and after taxes	$ 669.0	$ 915.0	$1,070.5	$1,177.6	$1,236.5	$1,273.6	$1,311.8	$1,351.1	$1,391.6	$1,433.4	$1,476.4
+ Depreciation expense	588.3	635.4	686.2	754.9	792.6	816.4	840.9	866.1	892.1	918.8	946.4
− Change in accounts receivable	−35.0	−14.7	−12.4	−76.2	−41.9	−26.4	−27.2	−28.0	−28.9	−29.7	−30.6
− Change in inventory	−12.2	−7.1	−6.4	−41.9	−23.1	−14.5	−15.0	−15.4	−15.9	−16.4	−16.8
+ Change in accounts payable	51.9	19.1	20.0	37.7	20.8	13.1	13.5	13.9	14.3	14.7	15.2
+ Change in other liabilities	5.6	41.2	47.0	20.6	11.3	7.1	7.3	7.6	7.8	8.0	8.3
+ LBO fees—expensed	179.3	0.0	0.0	0.0	0.0	0.0	0.0	0.0	0.0	0.0	0.0
− Change in required cash balance	−8.4	49.4	−10.2	−13.7	−7.5	−4.8	−4.9	−5.0	−5.2	−5.4	−5.5
Cash flow before capital expenditures	$1,438.6	$1,638.3	$1,794.9	$1,858.9	$1,988.6	$2,064.4	$2,126.4	$2,190.2	$2,255.9	$2,323.5	$2,393.2
− Capital expenditures	−865.2	−819.1	−958.6	−964.5	−924.7	−952.4	−981.0	−1,010.4	−1,040.8	−1,072.0	−1,104.1
Unlevered free cash flow	$ 573.4	$ 819.3	$ 836.4	$ 894.3	$1,063.9	$1,112.0	$1,145.4	$1,179.7	$1,215.1	$1,251.6	$1,289.1
− Interest paid	−766.6	−760.6	−738.1	−713.7	−685.0	−643.6	−599.3	−551.4	−471.3	−377.5	−257.0
+ Interest tax shield	318.9	316.5	307.5	297.7	286.2	269.7	252.0	226.6	194.6	154.6	102.8
− Preferred stock dividends	0.0	0.0	0.0	0.0	0.0	0.0	0.0	0.0	0.0	0.0	0.0
Cash flow after interest and preferred stock dividends	$ 125.6	$ 375.2	$ 405.8	$ 478.3	$ 665.1	$ 738.1	$ 798.0	$ 854.9	$ 938.4	$1,028.7	$1,134.9
+ Change in debt financing	−125.6	−375.2	−405.8	−478.3	−665.1	−738.1	−798.0	−854.9	−938.4	−1,028.7	−1,134.9
+ Change in preferred stock financing	0.0	0.0	0.0	0.0	0.0	0.0	0.0	0.0	0.0	0.0	0.0
Free cash flow to common equity	$ 0.0	$ 0.0	$ 0.0	$ 0.0	$ 0.0	$ 0.0	$ 0.0	$ 0.0	$ 0.0	$ 0.0	$ 0.0
+ Change in common equity financing	0.0	0.0	0.0	0.0	0.0	0.0	0.0	0.0	0.0	0.0	0.0
− Common equity dividends paid	0.0	0.0	0.0	0.0	0.0	0.0	0.0	0.0	0.0	0.0	0.0
Change in excess cash	$ 0.0	$ 0.0	$ 0.0	$ 0.0	$ 0.0	$ 0.0	$ 0.0	$ 0.0	$ 0.0	$ 0.0	$ 0.0
+ Change in required cash balance	8.4	−49.4	10.2	13.7	7.5	4.8	4.9	5.0	5.2	5.4	5.5
Change in cash balance	$ 8.4	$ −49.4	$ 10.2	$ 13.7	$ 7.5	$ 4.8	$ 4.9	$ 5.0	$ 5.2	$ 5.4	$ 5.5

Exhibit may contain small rounding errors

EXHIBIT 15.16 Debt Schedule Forecasts

Balance at Year End

($ in millions)	Total	Year 0	Year 1	Year 2	Year 3	Year 4	Year 5	Year 6	Year 7	Year 8	Year 9	Year 10	Year 11
Revolver (total commitment in 1st column)	$300.0	$100.0	$0.0	$0.0	$0.0	$0.0	$0.0	$0.0	$0.0	$0.0	$0.0	$0.0	$0.0
Debt assumed	0.0	0.0	0.0	0.0	0.0	0.0	0.0	0.0	0.0	0.0	0.0	0.0	0.0
Senior secured note (bank debt)	3,620.0	3,620.0	3,594.4	3,219.2	2,813.4	2,335.1	1,669.9	931.9	133.8	0.0	0.0	0.0	0.0
Subordinated note (unsecured debt)	1,810.0	1,810.0	1,810.0	1,810.0	1,810.0	1,810.0	1,810.0	1,810.0	1,810.0	1,089.0	150.6	0.0	0.0
Mezzanine debt	3,020.0	3,020.0	3,020.0	3,020.0	3,020.0	3,020.0	3,020.0	3,020.0	3,020.0	3,020.0	3,020.0	2,141.9	1,007.0
All debt issued at par	$8,550.0		$8,424.4	$8,049.2	$7,643.4	$7,165.1	$6,499.9	$5,761.9	$4,963.8	$4,109.0	$3,170.6	$2,141.9	$1,007.0

Repayment at Year End

($ in millions)	Total	Year 0	Year 1	Year 2	Year 3	Year 4	Year 5	Year 6	Year 7	Year 8	Year 9	Year 10	Year 11
Total cash available for repayment	$-7,543.0		$125.6	$375.2	$405.8	$478.3	$665.1	$738.1	$798.0	$854.9	$938.4	$1,028.7	$1,134.9
Revolver	$100.0		$-100.0	$0.0	$0.0	$0.0	$0.0	$0.0	$0.0	$0.0	$0.0	$0.0	$0.0
Debt assumed	0.0		0.0	0.0	0.0	0.0	0.0	0.0	0.0	0.0	0.0	0.0	0.0
Senior secured note (bank debt)	3,620.0		-25.6	-375.2	-405.8	-478.3	-665.1	-738.1	-798.0	-133.8	0.0	0.0	0.0
Subordinated note (unsecured debt)	1,810.0		0.0	0.0	0.0	0.0	0.0	0.0	0.0	-721.0	-938.4	-150.6	0.0
Mezzanine debt	2,013.0		0.0	0.0	0.0	0.0	0.0	0.0	0.0	0.0	0.0	-878.1	-1,134.9
Total debt repaid	$7,543.0		$-125.6	$-375.2	$-405.8	$-478.3	$-665.1	$-738.1	$-798.0	$-854.9	$-938.4	$-1,028.7	$-1,134.9

Interest Expense

Interest Expense	Coupon = YTM	Revolver Fee	Year 1	Year 2	Year 3	Year 4	Year 5	Year 6	Year 7	Year 8	Year 9	Year 10	Year 11
Revolver	4.500%	0.5%	$6.0	1.5	1.5	1.5	1.5	0.0	0.0	0.0	0.0	0.0	$0.0
Debt assumed	0.000%		0.0	0.0	0.0	0.0	0.0	0.0	0.0	0.0	0.0	0.0	0.0
Senior secured note (bank debt)	6.000%		217.2	215.7	193.2	168.8	140.1	100.2	55.9	8.0	0.0	0.0	0.0
Subordinated note (unsecured debt)	10.000%		181.0	181.0	181.0	181.0	181.0	181.0	181.0	181.0	108.9	15.1	0.0
Mezzanine debt	12.000%		362.4	362.4	362.4	362.4	362.4	362.4	362.4	362.4	362.4	362.4	257.0
Amortization of fees			30.6	30.6	30.6	30.6	30.6	30.6	30.6	15.1	15.1	9.1	0.0
Amortization of discount/premium on debt			0.0	0.0	0.0	0.0	0.0	0.0	0.0	0.0	0.0	0.0	0.0
Assume interest expense = interest deductible			$797.2	$791.2	$768.7	$744.3	$715.6	$674.2	$629.9	$566.5	$486.4	$386.5	$257.0
Weighted average interest rate			8.97%	9.03%	9.17%	9.34%	9.56%	9.90%	10.40%	11.11%	11.47%	11.91%	12.00%

Amortization of Fees

Amortization of Fees	Coupon = YTM	Total Fees	Year 1	Year 2	Year 3	Year 4	Year 5	Year 6	Year 7	Year 8	Year 9	Year 10	Year 11
Debt assumed													
Senior secured note (bank debt)	3.000%	$108.6	$15.5	15.5	15.5	15.5	15.5	15.5	15.5				
Subordinated note (unsecured debt)	3.000%	54.3	6.0	6.0	6.0	6.0	6.0	6.0	6.0	$6.0	$6.0		
Mezzanine debt	3.000%	90.6	9.1	9.1	9.1	9.1	9.1	9.1	9.1	9.1	9.1	$9.1	
Amortization of fees		$253.5	$30.6	30.6	30.6	30.6	30.6	30.6	30.6	$15.1	$15.1	$9.1	$0.0

Exhibit may contain small rounding errors

Naturally, various schedules underpin the summary financial statement and free cash flow forecasts in our example. We show one set of these schedules in Exhibit 15.16, which presents the schedules related to debt—the debt balance, interest expense, and capitalized loan cost amortization schedules. The first two schedules present the debt balance and the repayments (or in the case of the revolver, the repayments and draws) of the debt. As we can see from these two schedules, the company did not need to draw additional funds from the revolver after the transaction was closed, and as we indicated, the revolver was paid down completely by the end of Year 1. Note that when we discussed the senior secured debt earlier, we indicated that it is often issued in tranches with at least one of the tranches requiring amortization of the principal amount. Here, we did not model multiple tranches of senior debt, but if we had modeled one or two tranches with required principal payments starting in the first year, we would have most likely had to borrow more from the revolver in the first few years in order to make those payments.

As can be seen from the debt schedule, the company does not quite have sufficient cash flows to pay down its senior secured debt within the first seven years—the time to maturity of the debt. The company could pay off the secured debt by the end of Year 8. The company also does not have sufficient cash flows to pay down its subordinated note (unsecured) within the first nine years. The forecasts show that the company is able to pay down its unsecured debt by the end of Year 10. Alternatively, the company could use its revolver to retire the senior secured debt and subordinated note on a timely basis. Finally, the mezzanine debt will not be paid down by its maturity (Year 10). Thus, the company may need to refinance the debt in Year 7 or use its revolver to meet the maturity dates of the senior secured debt and subordinated note. This could be an impediment to securing the debt to finance this transaction and it would be up to the various lenders as to whether the capital structure needs to be altered in some way, such as allowing slightly longer maturities.

Of course, the company's need to refinance the debt or draw on the revolver will not arise if it exits from the transaction by the end of Year 7, and if you remember, the median exit time is six years. Regardless, the company's forecasts support its ability to refinance its debt given its ability to pay down the debt and generate sufficient cash flows. It is unlikely that lenders who are comfortable with these forecasts will view this as a major problem, especially if they think an exit is likely to occur within seven years. That said, note how three years after the transaction, Edwardson still has almost 90% of the original deal debt outstanding. In his study, Kaplan (1990) shows that for his sample of leveraged buyouts completed between 1980 and 1986, 85% of the debt was still outstanding one full year after the transactions, 75% was still outstanding at the end of two years, and 71% was still outstanding at the end of three years. Thus, Edwardson's pay-down is somewhat behind the average documented in Kaplan's study. One potential avenue for the company to accelerate the pay-down of the debt is to cut down on its capital expenditures in the early years—that, of course, will necessitate greater capital expenditures in later years but that action could positively impact the company's ability to repay the various debt pieces by maturity.

We measure interest expense in the third schedule of Exhibit 15.16. Interest expense is equal to the coupon rate (recall that all debt is assumed to be issued at par), multiplied by the outstanding balance at the end of the previous year, plus the amortization of any fees (which appears in the last panel in the exhibit). For the purposes of this illustration, we do not calculate interest expense based on the weighted average debt outstanding during the year (which is commonly done in these models), but rather we base it on the year-end balance from the previous year. To the extent that principal payments are made during the year, our calculation overstates the amount of interest expense. The weighted average interest rate is equal to the interest expense for a given year (excluding fee amortization), divided by the outstanding balance at the end of the previous year. For the purposes of this model (which has to convince lenders that the company has the capacity to support this capital structure), we use the coupon rates and make no adjustment for the expected default loss we discussed in Chapter 9. We will come back to this topic in a later section when we discuss the APV valuation of the company.

The last exhibit in this series of steps is assessing the debt rating of the company. In Exhibit 15.17, we show the financial leverage and performance measures that are often used to assess a company's debt rating; these are also used in the H-Z debt-rating model discussed in Chapter 9. We use this model to assess the unsecured debt ratings of the company (recall that the H-Z debt-rating model is estimated on unsecured debt ratings) for each forecasted year even though the debt rating at the time of the transaction is generally the most relevant (the exception being when the debt rating declines over time). In this case, the company's initial debt rating is a B rating. Its debt rating increases to BB by the end of Year 5 and to BBB by the end of Year 8. It increases to A by the end of Year 11. The increase in the debt rating also strengthens the argument that the company could likely refinance itself if necessary. As an alternative to the H-Z debt rating model, we can also use the information on financial ratios from S&P or Moody's in order to determine the likely rating (Chapter 9).

EXHIBIT 15.17	Debt Rating Forecasts												
	For Unsecured Debt												
	Yield to Maturity	Cost of Debt	Year 1	Year 2	Year 3	Year 4	Year 5	Year 6	Year 7	Year 8	Year 9	Year 10	Year 11
EBIT to average total debt + shareholders' equity . . .			0.233	0.314	0.358	0.376	0.381	0.382	0.385	0.386	0.387	0.388	0.388
Interest to EBITDA			0.468	0.366	0.311	0.274	0.251	0.229	0.208	0.182	0.151	0.117	0.075
Total debt to CFO − capital expenditures			62.843	24.710	18.376	14.561	9.663	7.757	6.182	4.778	3.360	2.071	0.883
Total debt to total debt + shareholders' equity			1.747	1.647	1.501	1.341	1.185	1.026	0.863	0.695	0.522	0.343	0.157
Capital expenditures to EBITDA			0.508	0.379	0.388	0.355	0.324	0.324	0.324	0.324	0.324	0.324	0.324
Probability of Debt Rating													
CCC+ & Below.	N/A	N/A	9.3%	4.3%	2.3%	1.4%	0.9%	0.6%	0.4%	0.3%	0.2%	0.1%	0.1%
B− to B+	11.0%	8.7%	75.1%	66.2%	52.9%	41.0%	32.2%	24.5%	17.9%	12.5%	8.5%	5.5%	3.5%
BB− to BB+.	9.0%	7.6%	12.0%	21.7%	30.7%	36.0%	37.9%	37.2%	34.2%	29.2%	23.2%	17.1%	11.8%
BBB− to BBB+	8.0%	6.9%	3.0%	6.3%	11.3%	17.0%	22.3%	28.0%	33.7%	38.4%	40.7%	39.8%	35.3%
A− to A+	7.0%	6.6%	0.5%	1.2%	2.3%	3.8%	5.5%	7.9%	11.1%	15.6%	21.4%	28.3%	35.3%
AA− to AAA	6.0%	6.0%	0.1%	0.3%	0.5%	0.8%	1.2%	1.8%	2.6%	3.9%	6.0%	9.1%	14.1%
Debt Rating			B	B	B	B	BB	BB	BB	BBB	BBB	BBB	A

Note that the iterative process requires us to assess whether the unsecured debt rating from the financial model is consistent with the assumption we made about the yield on the unsecured debt issued. A rating of B has a median yield to maturity of 11% at the time of the transaction (see the yield to maturity column). In Exhibit 15.10, we assume that subordinated debt and mezzanine debt have yield to maturities of 10% and 12%, respectively; thus, our assumptions about the capital structure and of the debt yield seem to be appropriate given the results of the financial model. If the financial model suggested that the debt rating in Year 1 was CCC+ and below, we would have to either change the capital structure or change the assumption about the yields until everything was internally consistent.

Investor Internal Rate of Return (Steps 7–8)

It is common for sponsors to use an IRR approach to assess proposed LBO transactions. For example, at the time that this chapter was written, private equity sponsors were requiring a 20% to 30% expected rate of return on such investments (depending on both the risk of the business and the capital structure), and mezzanine investors were requiring around a 15% rate of return. Sponsors measure the IRR at different exit dates in order to assess the most profitable time to exit the company and to determine how sensitive the success of the deal is to the timing of the exit. These calculations are, of course, very dependent on the exit value, which private equity firms often estimate using market multiples. As discussed in Chapters 13 and 14, this approach has its pros and cons, and it is best used when combined with a discounted cash flow analysis. However, generally, sponsors do not use a DCF approach; instead, they tend to rely on a market multiple valuation to assess the value at exit. In addition, sponsors typically use the same exit multiple for all potential exit years when conducting their analysis. We know from Chapters 13 and 14 that market multiples depend on a company's long-term growth rate and are not constant over time if the company's long-term growth rate changes over time. We discuss this issue in more detail later in this section.

In many analyses, the exit multiple is set at the original deal multiple. Whether that makes sense, of course, depends on the condition of the company at the time of exit relative to its condition at the time of the LBO. If the company has cut back on capital expenditures, R&D, and maintenance during the LBO, the company is likely to experience a contraction in its multiples at the time of the exit. On the other hand, if the company is being run more efficiently and/or its growth prospects have improved, it is possible that there could be multiple expansion.

In Exhibit 15.18, we present the exit value for Edwardson for every year during the forecast period using an EBITDA multiple equal to 6.67, which is the "deal multiple." For each year of the forecast

EXHIBIT 15.18 Exit Value Forecasts and Sponsor Internal Rates of Return

($ in millions)	EBITDA Multiple	Year 1	Year 2	Year 3	Year 4	Year 5	Year 6	Year 7	Year 8	Year 9	Year 10
EBITDA		$1,703.4	$2,160.4	$2,470.4	$2,717.5	$2,853.4	$2,939.0	$3,027.1	$3,117.9	$3,211.5	$3,307.8
Debt outstanding		$8,424.4	$8,049.2	$7,643.4	$7,165.1	$6,499.9	$5,761.9	$4,963.8	$4,109.0	$3,170.6	$2,141.9
Exit value—firm (using deal multiple)	6.666	$11,354.5	$14,400.7	$16,467.6	$18,114.3	$19,020.1	$19,590.7	$20,178.4	$20,783.7	$21,407.2	$22,049.5
Exit value—debt		8,424.4	8,049.2	7,643.4	7,165.1	6,499.9	5,761.9	4,963.8	4,109.0	3,170.6	2,141.9
Exit value—equity		$2,930.2	$6,351.5	$8,824.2	$10,949.3	$12,520.1	$13,828.8	$15,214.5	$16,674.8	$18,236.7	$19,907.6

Sponsor (% fully diluted participation in exit) 85.2%
Investment .... $−3,380.0
Fees .... $ 119.5
Dividends .... None
Other payments .... None

		Year 1	Year 2	Year 3	Year 4	Year 5	Year 6	Year 7	Year 8	Year 9	Year 10
Participation in exit		$2,497.5	$5,413.5	$7,521.0	$9,332.3	$10,671.1	$11,786.5	$12,967.6	$14,212.2	$15,543.4	$16,967.6
Net cash flow	$−3,260.5	$2,497.5	$5,413.5	$7,521.0	$9,332.3	$10,671.1	$11,786.5	$12,967.6	$14,212.2	$15,543.4	$16,967.6

IRR	Exit Yr		Year 1	Year 2	Year 3	Year 4	Year 5	Year 6	Year 7	Year 8	Year 9	Year 10
−23.4%	Year 1	−3,260.5	$2,497.5									
28.9%	Year 2	−3,260.5	0.0	$5,413.5								
32.1%	Year 3	−3,260.5	0.0	0.0	$7,521.0							
30.1%	Year 4	−3,260.5	0.0	0.0	0.0	$9,332.3						
26.8%	Year 5	−3,260.5	0.0	0.0	0.0	0.0	$10,671.1					
23.9%	Year 6	−3,260.5	0.0	0.0	0.0	0.0	0.0	$11,786.5				
21.8%	Year 7	−3,260.5	0.0	0.0	0.0	0.0	0.0	0.0	$12,967.6			
20.2%	Year 8	−3,260.5	0.0	0.0	0.0	0.0	0.0	0.0	0.0	$14,212.2		
18.9%	Year 9	−3,260.5	0.0	0.0	0.0	0.0	0.0	0.0	0.0	0.0	$15,543.4	
17.9%	Year 10	−3,260.5	0.0	0.0	0.0	0.0	0.0	0.0	0.0	0.0	0.0	$16,967.6

Exhibit may contain small rounding errors

633

period, the exit value of the firm is equal to the EBITDA multiple multiplied by the EBITDA forecast. The value of the equity (including the value of the warrants and options) in any given year is equal to the value of the firm minus the value of the outstanding debt at the end of that year. The value of the equity ranges from $2.9 billion in Year 1 to $19.9 billion in Year 10. The value of the equity increases in each year for several reasons. First, based on the forecasts, EBITDA increases in each year; second, we are holding the multiple applied to the company constant; and third, the company reduces its debt in each year subsequent to the LBO.

Since the company does not distribute cash flows to the equityholders before the exit year, the IRR calculation for equityholders has two cash flows—the initial investment and the exit year cash flow. In the investment year, the sponsor invests $3.4 billion and collects fees equal to $120 million. We net the fees against the investment in order to measure the Year 0 investment. The exit year distribution is equal to the value of the equity, multiplied by the fully diluted equity ownership (which was shown in Exhibit 15.10). The internal rate of return for the sponsor, who owns 85.2% of the fully diluted equity, ranges from −23.4% in Year 1 to 32.1% in Year 3. After Year 3, the IRR decreases each year until it reaches 17.9% in Year 10. Clearly, a relatively early exit from this transaction will be important to the sponsor. We should note that these IRRs do not represent the returns that the fund investors actually receive (even if every investment in the fund achieved a return identical to this one), as these calculations do not consider the fees the fund investors have to pay the sponsors. While we do not show it here, one could separately model the IRR to the limited partners of the fund separate from the financial sponsors, but to do so, we have to adjust the limited partners' returns for both the carried interest and the typical contribution that is not invested directly in the portfolio companies. We do not show this calculation, as we have not made assumptions about the form of the contract between the financial sponsor and the limited partners. Of course, whether the IRRs shown for Edwardson are high enough depends on the specific hurdle rates that the financial sponsor sets for this transaction.

The other two groups of investors with equity claims are the managers and mezzanine investors, and the expected IRRs of these investors are presented in Exhibit 15.19. The internal rate of return for the managers, who own 10.8% of the fully diluted equity, ranges from −6.4% in Year 1 to 42.4% in Year 2. After Year 2, the IRR decreases each year until it is equal to 20.3% in Year 10. The IRRs for the sponsor and management differ for two reasons. First, the sponsor receives upfront fees, which in this case, increases the IRR of the sponsor relative to the managers because the mangers paid the same price as the sponsors for their shares but did not receive any fees. Second, and the more dominant influence, the managers receive additional equity for their performance, which increases the IRR of the managers relative to the sponsors. Equity incentives to management often increase over time as the management team meets certain financial and non-financial metrics. As such, the amount of dilution from the equity incentives can change with changes to the assumption about the exit year. We do not, however, model that complication in this example.

The mezzanine investors have both a debt and equity claim. Assuming the company makes all promised interest and principal payments on a timely basis, the lower bound of their IRR is the interest rate of 12%. The cash flows in the IRR calculation include the investments, the interest paid, the principal paid, and the mezzanine investors' share of the equity exit value. The mezzanine investors own 4% of the fully diluted equity. The internal rate of return for the mezzanine investors starts at 15.9% in Years 1 and 2. After Year 2, the IRR generally decreases each year until it is equal to 13.4% in Year 10. It is apparent from our example that the year with the highest IRR is not the same for all investors due to different investment amounts and claims on the cash flows. The mezzanine providers prefer to see an exit date of no later than Year 3 if they are to achieve their 15% required rate of return. Of course, the rate of return the mezzanine investors will receive will be much smaller than this if required interest and principal payments are not made.

Using the Weighted Average Cost of Capital Valuation Method to Measure Exit Values and Reevaluate IRRs—Step 9 (Another View of Steps 7–8)

We can also use the free cash flow forecasts to measure the IRR to different groups of investors by valuing the firm at every point in time with the weighted average cost of capital method instead of an EBITDA multiple. In this case, we generally assess the likely exit value based on the assumption that the company is sold to a strategic buyer or sold via an IPO. As a consequence of this assumption, we assume the company adopts a more typical capital structure at the time of exit—for example, a typical industry capital structure as opposed to a highly levered capital structure.

EXHIBIT 15.19 Management and Mezzanine Investor Internal Rates of Return

($ in millions)		Year 1	Year 2	Year 3	Year 4	Year 5	Year 6	Year 7	Year 8	Year 9	Year 10
Management % diluted participation in exit and exit equity value	10.8%	$2,930.2	$6,351.5	$8,824.2	$10,949.3	$12,520.1	$13,828.8	$15,214.5	$16,674.8	$18,236.7	$19,907.6
Investment	$−337.1										
Fees											
Dividends											
Other payments											
Participation in exit		$ 315.5	$ 683.9	$ 950.2	$ 1,179.0	$ 1,348.2	$ 1,489.1	$ 1,638.3	$ 1,795.6	$ 1,963.7	$ 2,143.7
Net cash flow	$−337.1	$ 315.5	$ 683.9	$ 950.2	$ 1,179.0	$ 1,348.2	$ 1,489.1	$ 1,638.3	$ 1,795.6	$ 1,963.7	$ 2,143.7

IRR	Exit Yr	Year 1	Year 2	Year 3	Year 4	Year 5	Year 6	Year 7	Year 8	Year 9	Year 10
−6.4%	Year 1	$−337.1	$ 315.5								
42.4%	Year 2	−337.1	0.0	$ 683.9							
41.3%	Year 3	−337.1	0.0	0.0	$ 950.2						
36.8%	Year 4	−337.1	0.0	0.0	0.0	$ 1,179.0					
31.9%	Year 5	−337.1	0.0	0.0	0.0	0.0	$ 1,348.2				
28.1%	Year 6	−337.1	0.0	0.0	0.0	0.0	0.0	$ 1,489.1			
25.3%	Year 7	−337.1	0.0	0.0	0.0	0.0	0.0	0.0	$ 1,638.3		
23.3%	Year 8	−337.1	0.0	0.0	0.0	0.0	0.0	0.0	0.0	$ 1,795.6	
21.6%	Year 9	−337.1	0.0	0.0	0.0	0.0	0.0	0.0	0.0	0.0	$ 1,963.7
20.3%	Year 10	−337.1	0.0	0.0	0.0	0.0	0.0	0.0	0.0	0.0	0.0	$ 2,143.7

($ in millions)		Year 1	Year 2	Year 3	Year 4	Year 5	Year 6	Year 7	Year 8	Year 9	Year 10
Mezzanine debt % diluted participation in exit and exit equity value	4.0%	$2,930.2	$6,351.5	$8,824.2	$10,949.3	$12,520.1	$13,828.8	$15,214.5	$16,674.8	$18,236.7	$19,907.6
Investment	$−3,020.0										
Fees											
Interest paid		$ 362.4	$ 362.4	$ 362.4	$ 362.4	$ 362.4	$ 362.4	$ 362.4	$ 362.4	$ 362.4	$ 362.4
Repayment of principal		3,020.0	3,020.0	3,020.0	3,020.0	3,020.0	3,020.0	3,020.0	3,020.0	3,020.0	3,020.0
Participation in exit		117.2	254.1	353.0	438.0	500.8	553.0	608.6	667.0	729.5	796.3
Net cash flow	$−3,020.0	$3,499.6	$3,636.5	$3,735.4	$3,820.4	$ 3,883.2	$ 3,935.6	$ 3,991.0	$ 4,049.4	$ 4,111.9	$ 4,178.7

IRR	Exit Yr	Year 1	Year 2	Year 3	Year 4	Year 5	Year 6	Year 7	Year 8	Year 9	Year 10
15.9%	Year 1	$−3,020.0	$3,499.6								
15.9%	Year 2	−3,020.0	362.4	$3,636.5							
15.4%	Year 3	−3,020.0	362.4	$3,735.4							
14.9%	Year 4	−3,020.0	362.4	362.4	$3,820.4						
14.5%	Year 5	−3,020.0	362.4	362.4	362.4	$ 3,883.2					
14.1%	Year 6	−3,020.0	362.4	362.4	362.4	362.4	$ 3,935.6				
13.9%	Year 7	−3,020.0	362.4	362.4	362.4	362.4	362.4	$ 3,991.0			
13.7%	Year 8	−3,020.0	362.4	362.4	362.4	362.4	362.4	362.4	$ 4,049.4		
13.5%	Year 9	−3,020.0	362.4	362.4	362.4	362.4	362.4	362.4	362.4	$ 4,111.9	
13.4%	Year 10	−3,020.0	362.4	362.4	362.4	362.4	362.4	362.4	362.4	362.4	$ 4,178.7

REVIEW EXERCISE 15.2

Measuring the Internal Rate of Return

Use the information in Review Exercise 15.1 and the following information to measure the internal rates of return (on a fully diluted equity ownership basis) to the financial sponsor, management, and mezzanine debtholders; assume an exit value based on the EBITDA deal multiple. EBITDA was $346.08 in Year 0. Management has prepared the following forecasts to be used to assess the value of the LBO transaction.

($ in millions)	Year –1	Year 0 Post–LBO Closing	Year 1	Year 2	Year 3	Year 4	Year 5	Year 6	Year 7	Year 8	Year 9	Year 10	Year 11
Cash balance	$ 89.6	$ 57.7	$ 48.0	$ 37.4	$ 26.0	$ 27.0	$ 28.1	$ 29.2	$ 30.1	$ 31.0	$ 31.9	$ 32.9	$ 33.8
Accounts receivable	186.7	192.3	186.6	180.2	173.0	179.9	187.1	194.6	200.5	206.5	212.7	219.0	225.6
Inventory	125.4	123.1	121.6	114.8	107.8	107.1	111.3	115.8	119.3	128.7	138.6	149.0	153.4
Total current assets	$ 401.7	$ 373.0	$ 356.2	$ 332.5	$ 306.8	$ 314.0	$ 326.6	$ 339.6	$ 349.8	$ 366.1	$ 383.2	$ 400.9	$ 412.9
Property, plant, and equipment	$1,124.8	$1,261.6	$1,344.4	$1,435.9	$1,491.4	$1,564.9	$1,719.3	$1,872.6	$2,116.5	$2,458.9	$2,634.3	$2,604.3	$2,573.4
Accumulated depreciation	–300.8	–404.6	–512.6	–624.9	–741.7	–863.1	–989.5	–1,120.8	–1,256.1	–1,395.5	–1,539.1	–1,476.2	–1,411.4
Property, plant, and equipment (net)	$ 824.0	$ 857.0	$ 831.8	$ 811.0	$ 749.7	$ 701.8	$ 729.8	$ 751.7	$ 860.3	$1,063.3	$1,095.2	$1,128.1	$1,161.9
Capitalized fees	$0	$ 101.9	$51.7	$ 44.5	$ 37.4	$ 30.2	$ 23.1	$ 15.9	$ 8.8	$ 5.4	$ 2.0	$ 0.0	$ 0.0
Total assets	$1,225.7	$1,331.9	$1,239.7	$1,188.0	$1,093.9	$1,046.0	$1,079.5	$1,107.3	$1,218.9	$1,434.9	$1,480.4	$1,529.0	$1,574.8
Accounts payable	$ 62.7	$ 61.5	$ 72.0	$ 79.7	$ 87.2	$ 86.6	$ 90.1	$ 93.7	$ 96.5	$ 104.1	$ 112.1	$ 120.5	$ 124.1
Other current operating liabilities	56.0	57.7	96.0	137.3	142.7	148.5	154.4	160.6	165.4	170.3	175.5	180.7	186.1
Total current liabilities	$ 118.7	$ 119.2	$ 168.0	$ 217.0	$ 230.0	$ 235.0	$ 244.4	$ 254.2	$ 261.9	$ 274.4	$ 287.5	$ 301.2	$ 310.2
Total debt	600.0	2,060.0	1,894.4	1,702.5	1,459.9	1,222.6	1,044.6	842.3	706.5	688.7	529.1	393.1	242.7
Total liabilities	$ 718.7	$2,179.2	$2,062.3	$1,919.5	$1,689.9	$1,457.6	$1,289.0	$1,096.6	$ 968.3	$ 963.1	$ 816.6	$ 694.3	$ 552.9
Preferred stock	$ 100.0	$ 0.0	$ 0.0	$ 0.0	$ 0.0	$ 0.0	$ 0.0	$ 0.0	$ 0.0	$ 0.0	$ 0.0	$ 0.0	$ 0.0
Common stock	200.0	883.3	883.3	883.3	883.3	883.3	883.3	883.3	883.3	883.3	883.3	883.3	883.3
Retained earnings	207.0	–1,730.6	–1,706.0	–1,614.8	–1,479.3	–1,295.0	–1,092.9	–872.6	–632.8	–411.5	–219.5	–48.7	138.6
Total shareholders' equity	$ 507.0	$ –847.3	$ –822.7	$ –731.5	$ –595.9	$ –411.7	$ –209.6	$ 10.7	$ 250.6	$ 471.8	$ 663.8	$ 834.7	$1,021.9
Total liabilities and equities	$1,225.7	$1,331.9	$1,239.7	$1,188.0	$1,093.9	$1,046.0	$1,079.5	$1,107.3	$1,218.9	$1,434.9	$1,480.4	$1,529.0	$1,574.8

($ in millions)	Year 1	Year 2	Year 3	Year 4	Year 5	Year 6	Year 7	Year 8	Year 9	Year 10	Year 11
Earnings before interest and taxes (EBIT)	$208.8	$311.9	$376.3	$445.4	$463.2	$481.7	$496.1	$449.1	$398.8	$345.0	$355.4
– Income taxes paid on EBIT	–83.5	–124.8	–150.5	–178.1	–185.3	–192.7	–198.5	–179.6	–159.5	–138.0	–142.1
Earnings before interest and after taxes	$125.3	$187.2	$225.8	$267.2	$277.9	$289.0	$297.7	$269.5	$239.3	$207.0	$213.2
+ Depreciation expense	108.0	112.3	116.8	121.5	126.3	131.4	135.3	139.4	143.6	147.9	152.3
– Change in accounts receivable	5.6	6.4	7.2	–6.9	–7.2	–7.5	–5.8	–6.0	–6.2	–6.4	–6.6
– Change in inventory	1.5	6.8	6.9	0.8	–4.3	–4.5	–3.5	–9.4	–9.9	–10.4	–4.5
+ Change in accounts payable	10.5	7.7	7.5	–0.6	3.5	3.6	2.8	7.6	8.0	8.4	3.6
+ Change in other liabilities	38.3	41.3	5.5	5.7	5.9	6.2	4.8	5.0	5.1	5.3	5.4
+ LBO fees – expensed	43.1	0.0	0.0	0.0	0.0	0.0	0.0	0.0	0.0	0.0	0.0
– Change in required cash balance	9.7	10.6	11.5	–1.0	–1.1	–1.1	–0.9	–0.9	–0.9	–1.0	–1.0
Cash flow before capital expenditures	$342.0	$372.2	$381.2	$386.6	$401.1	$417.1	$430.4	$405.1	$378.9	$350.8	$362.5
Capital expenditures	–82.8	–91.5	–55.5	–73.5	–154.4	–153.3	–243.9	–342.4	–175.5	–180.7	–186.1
Unlevered free cash flow	$259.1	$280.7	$325.7	$313.1	$246.7	$263.8	$186.5	$ 62.7	$203.4	$170.1	$176.4

Exhibit may contain small rounding errors

Solution on pages 656–657.

In Exhibit 15.20, we use the weighted average cost of capital method to measure the exit values and implied multiples that are based on those exit values. The weighted average cost of capital of 10.34% is based on an unlevered cost of capital of 11%, a constant debt-to-value ratio of 25% at exit (regardless of when exit occurs), a cost of debt capital of 6.6%, and a marginal tax rate of 40%. Because we assume a constant debt-to-value capital structure, we use the unlevered cost of capital to value the tax shields after exit. As such, we use the levering formula that values all interest tax shields at the unlevered cost of capital. In addition, we assume a 3% continuing value growth rate beyond Year 10.

EXHIBIT 15.20 Weighted Average Cost of Capital Valuation of Exit Values

Weighted Average Cost of Capital Valuation

r_E	r_D	V_D/V_F	T_{INT}	r_{WACC}	Continuing Value Growth Rate
12.467%	6.600%	25.000%	40.000%	10.340%	3.000%

($ in millions)	Year 0	Year 1	Year 2	Year 3	Year 4	Year 5	Year 6	Year 7	Year 8	Year 9	Year 10
Weighted average cost of capital valuation of the firm	$12,331.7	$13,033.5	$13,561.9	$14,127.8	$14,694.3	$15,149.8	$15,604.3	$16,072.4	$16,554.6	$17,051.2	$17,562.7
Value of debt	8,550.0	8,424.4	8,049.2	7,643.4	7,165.1	6,499.9	5,761.9	4,963.8	4,109.0	3,170.6	2,141.9
Weighted average cost of capital valuation of the equity	$ 3,781.7	$ 4,609.1	$ 5,512.7	$ 6,484.4	$ 7,529.2	$ 8,649.8	$ 9,842.4	$11,108.5	$12,445.6	$13,880.6	$15,420.9
EBITDA	$1,793.0	$1,703.4	$2,160.4	$2,470.4	$2,717.5	$2,853.4	$2,939.0	$3,027.1	$3,117.9	$3,211.5	$3,307.8
Implied firm value to EBITDA	6.878	7.651	6.278	5.719	5.407	5.309	5.309	5.309	5.309	5.309	5.309

Exit Value Multiple and Values Used

($ in millions)	Year 0	Year 1	Year 2	Year 3	Year 4	Year 5	Year 6	Year 7	Year 8	Year 9	Year 10
Deal multiple—firm value to EBITDA		6.666	6.666	6.666	6.666	6.666	6.666	6.666	6.666	6.666	6.666
% Difference with weighted average cost of capital valuation		−12.9%	6.2%	16.6%	23.3%	25.5%	25.5%	25.5%	25.5%	25.5%	25.5%
Exit value—equity	$2,930.2	$6,351.5	$8,824.2	$10,949.3	$12,520.1	$13,828.8	$15,214.5	$16,674.8	$18,236.7	$19,907.6	
% Difference with weighted average cost of capital valuation	−36.4%	15.2%	36.1%	45.4%	44.7%	40.5%	37.0%	34.0%	31.4%	29.1%	

Exhibit may contain small rounding errors

We use the EBITDA in the financial forecasts and the year-by-year valuations from Exhibit 15.20 in order to measure the implied market multiples for each year based on the weighted average cost of capital valuations. This exhibit shows that the market multiples decline from Year 1 to Year 10. For example, the EBITDA multiple is 7.7 in Year 1 and decreases to 5.3 by Year 5, where it then remains constant through Year 10. This decline results from a decline in the long-term growth rate over the first few years. Note that the EBITDA multiple that is based on the DCF valuation of the company is lower than the deal multiple for every year except for Years 0 and 1.

In Exhibit 15.21, we use the WACC-based valuations of the exit values in order to measure the sponsor IRRs. If we compare the IRRs in Exhibit 15.21 to those in Exhibit 15.18, we will see that the IRRs in this exhibit are, for the most part, less than those in Exhibit 15.18 (the exception being for Year 1). This is because in all years but Year 1, the value of the firm from the weighted average cost of capital valuation is below the market multiple valuation. In order to save space, we do not recalculate the IRRs to the management team and to the mezzanine investors.

REVIEW EXERCISE 15.3

WACC-Based Exit Value

Use the information in Review Exercises 15.1 and 15.2 to measure the WACC-based exit values and implied EBITDA multiples; compare the implied EBITDA multiples in each year to the deal EBITDA multiple (see Exhibit 15.20). To measure the weighted average cost of capital, assume that as of the exit date, the company will use a capital structure equal to 25% debt and 75% common equity, resulting in a 5.9% cost of debt and 10.033% cost of equity. As of Year 11, the company expects its free cash flows to grow at 3% in perpetuity. Recalculate the internal rate of return to the financial sponsor using the WACC-based exit values (see Exhibit 15.21).

Solution on page 658.

There is an important lesson to be learned here. As we have seen before, multiples are a function of growth and profitability. The use of a constant deal multiple across different years in order to assess the exit value presumes that there are no changes in future growth opportunities and profitability over time, which is almost never the case except for mature, constant-growth companies. In examining the IRRs at different points in time, it is important to assess the likely exit values based on different valuation methodologies. Based on the fundamentals that we have modeled for the company, it is unlikely that we will be able to sell Edwardson for the deal multiple beyond Year 1 unless, perhaps, we sell it to another financial sponsor in a highly levered transaction. If we want to assume that the deal multiple will hold over time, we will have to model and manage the fundamentals of the company differently than they are currently being forecasted in order to hold the implied multiples at that level.[22]

Valuation Key 15.8

Most analyses of leveraged buyout transactions model the exit value as a constant multiple of EBITDA across various exit years. We recommend that exit values also be modeled based on an appropriate discounted cash flow model.

Adjusted Present Value Method Valuation, Net Present Value of the Investment, Implied Equity Costs of Capital, and Equity Betas (Step 10)

We know that the discounted cash flow method is an appropriate method with which to evaluate a potential investment. We also know that we should use the adjusted present value discounted cash flow method in order to measure the value of the firm when the capital structure is changing. In addition, by using the

---

[22] Note that deal multiples can also increase if the company improves or if the sponsor exits when market valuations are generally higher. Evidence in Acharya, Hahn, and Kehoe (2010) indicates that for their sample of Western European LBOs from 1995 to 2005, the average EBITDA multiple increases by two relative to the increase in the industry EBITDA multiple (from the entry to the exit of the LBO). See Acharya, V., M. Hahn, and C. Kehoe, "Corporate Governance and Value Creation: Evidence from Private Equity," NYU Stern Working Paper, 2010.

($ in millions)		Year 1	Year 2	Year 3	Year 4	Year 5	Year 6	Year 7	Year 8	Year 9	Year 10
Exit value—firm (weighted average cost of capital valuation)		$13,033.5	$13,561.9	$14,127.8	$14,694.3	$15,149.8	$15,604.3	$16,072.4	$16,554.6	$17,051.2	$17,562.7
Exit value—equity		$ 4,609.1	$ 5,512.7	$ 6,484.4	$ 7,529.2	$ 8,649.8	$ 9,842.4	$11,108.5	$12,445.6	$13,880.6	$15,420.9
Sponsor (% fully diluted participation in exit)	85.2%										
Investment	$–3,380.0										
Fees	$ 119.5										
Dividends	None										
Other payments	None										
Participation in exit		$ 3,928.4	$ 4,698.6	$ 5,526.8	$ 6,417.3	$ 7,372.4	$ 8,388.9	$ 9,468.0	$10,607.6	$11,830.7	$13,143.5
Net cash flow	–$3,260.5	$ 3,928.4	$ 4,698.6	$ 5,526.8	$ 6,417.3	$ 7,372.4	$ 8,388.9	$ 9,468.0	$10,607.6	$11,830.7	$13,143.5

IRR		Exit Yr										
20.5%		Year 1	$–3,260.5	$ 3,928.4								
20.0%		Year 2	–3,260.5	0.0	$ 4,698.6							
19.2%		Year 3	–3,260.5	0.0	0.0	$ 5,526.8						
18.4%		Year 4	–3,260.5	0.0	0.0	0.0	$ 6,417.3					
17.7%		Year 5	–3,260.5	0.0	0.0	0.0	0.0	$ 7,372.4				
17.1%		Year 6	–3,260.5	0.0	0.0	0.0	0.0	0.0	$ 8,388.9			
16.5%		Year 7	–3,260.5	0.0	0.0	0.0	0.0	0.0	0.0	$ 9,468.0		
15.9%		Year 8	–3,260.5	0.0	0.0	0.0	0.0	0.0	0.0	0.0	$10,607.6	
15.4%		Year 9	–3,260.5	0.0	0.0	0.0	0.0	0.0	0.0	0.0	0.0	$11,830.7
15.0%		Year 10	–3,260.5	0.0	0.0	0.0	0.0	0.0	0.0	0.0	0.0	0.0	$13,143.5

adjusted present value method to value the company every year, we can estimate the equity cost of capital and equity betas for the company during the transaction. We can then check the equity cost of capital against the IRRs coming out of the model in order to make sure that our hurdle rate for the IRR is sufficiently high given the riskiness of the investment. Of course, private equity firms want to earn a sufficiently high return for their investors, so the returns (after fees are considered) to the limited partners in the private equity funds should be equal to or greater than these estimates of the cost of equity capital. We begin this section by using the adjusted present value method to measure the value of the post-LBO company.

The inputs we need to measure the value of the firm are the unlevered cost of capital, the discount rate for the interest tax shields, the long-term capital structure strategy, and the growth rate for the continuing value. Edwardson's unlevered cost of capital is 11%. The market risk premium is 6%, and the risk-free rate is 5%, implying an unlevered beta of 1.0. The long-term growth rate after Year 10 is equal to the inflation rate of 3%. Beyond Year 10, the company plans to maintain a 25% debt-to-value ratio with a cost of debt of 6.6%; thus, the interest tax shields will grow at the long-term growth rate after Year 10.

Recall our discussion of the discount rate for interest tax shields in Chapter 10. In general, we use either the company's cost of debt or its unlevered cost of capital. We use the cost of debt to value interest tax shields that are already contracted as of the valuation date and are managed independently of the value of the firm. Further, we use the unlevered cost of capital to value interest tax shields that are not yet contracted and thus dependent on the value of the firm. Edwardson has debt contracts in place for the interest tax shields through Year 10. Afterward, the company will need to refinance its debt. We assume the company will refinance itself at the end of Year 10. Thus, we use the debt cost of capital to discount the interest tax shields through Year 10 and the unlevered cost of capital to discount the interest tax shields from the continuing value calculation.

As we see in Exhibit 15.22, the value of the firm is $13.2 billion. Since we paid $12.3 billion (net of cash) in the assumed deal, the net present value of the investment is $958 million, which is based on both its fundamentals and the capital structure being put in place. Of course, the actual value of the deal will depend on both when we exit from the transaction and the price we will be able to sell the company for at that time. This valuation assumes that we will not exit from the transaction, that we will continue to hold the company, and that we will recapitalize the debt at the end of Year 10. If we discount all of the interest tax shields at the unlevered cost of capital (not shown in the exhibits), the value of the interest tax shields decreases from $1.96 billion to $1.79 billion (or by about $170 million), reducing the net present value of the investment by the same amount.

Certain numbers in Exhibit 15.22 related to the cost of debt and the expected interest tax shields require additional explanation. In Exhibit 15.23, we present information on the debt rating, cost of debt, debt balance (including the debt recapitalization at the end of Year 10), interest (tax-deductible interest expense and cash interest paid), weighted average cost of debt, and interest tax shields. The cost of debt for the unsecured debt takes into consideration the expected default loss as discussed in Chapter 9 (we assume no expected default losses for the secured debt). In particular, we use the methodology presented in Exhibit 9.11 to calculate the costs of debt (you will find the cost of debt in the second column of Exhibit 15.17).[23] We then calculate the expected interest payments by using the cost of debt—and not the promised yield—before adding the amortization of the loan fees to determine the expected interest expense. Multiplying this by the 40% tax rate gives us the interest tax shield. We also calculate the weighted average cost of debt for each period based on the cost of debt for each instrument. The tax shields for the first 10 years are discounted back at the weighted average cost of debt (which varies over time), and the tax shields from Year 11 and after are all discounted at the unlevered cost of capital.

This valuation makes the implicit assumption that the debt is **performance priced debt**, meaning the coupon is adjusted annually in response to any changes in the rating. While this assumption may not be applicable to many LBOs as much of the debt is unlikely to be performance priced, we make this simplifying assumption as otherwise the calculations become more difficult to follow.

We can use the APV approach from Exhibit 15.22 to measure the value of the firm for every year in the forecast period, and we show this valuation in Exhibit 15.24. We can use these valuations to understand how the capital structure ratios, cost of equity, and equity beta evolve over time. Note that in Exhibit 15.24, we separate the tax shields into those that are valued at the cost of debt and those that are valued at the unlevered cost of capital, for we will need this breakdown for subsequent calculations.

---

[23] In particular, to calculate the cost of debt, we take the yield to maturity for AA bonds of 6% and add risk spreads of 0.6%, 0.9%, 1.6%, and 2.7% in order to calculate the cost of debt for bonds rated A, BBB, BB, and B, respectively.

EXHIBIT 15.22 Adjusted Present Value Method Valuation

($ in millions)	Year 0	Year 1	Year 2	Year 3	Year 4	Year 5	Year 6	Year 7	Year 8	Year 9	Year 10	CV Year 10
Value of the Unlevered Firm												
Unlevered free cash flow for continuing value												$ 1,289.1
Discount factor for continuing value												12.500
Unlevered free cash flow and continuing value		$573.4	$819.3	$836.4	$894.3	$1,063.9	$1,112.0	$1,145.4	$1,179.7	$1,215.1	$1,251.6	$16,113.8
Discount factor		0.9009	0.8116	0.7312	0.6587	0.5935	0.5346	0.4817	0.4339	0.3909	0.3522	0.3522
Discounted value		$516.5	$664.9	$611.5	$589.1	$ 631.4	$ 594.5	$ 551.7	$ 511.9	$ 475.0	$ 440.8	$ 5,675.0
Value of the unlevered firm	$11,262.4											
Value of the Interest Tax Shields												
Interest tax shield for continuing value												$ 115.9
Discount factor for continuing value												12.500
Interest tax shield and continuing value of ITS		$269.6	$267.2	$258.2	$248.4	$ 215.7	$ 199.2	$ 181.4	$ 142.6	$ 119.4	$ 91.1	$ 1,448.9
Discount factor (r_D and r_{UA})		0.9300	0.8646	0.8032	0.7456	0.6962	0.6495	0.6051	0.5662	0.5296	0.4954	0.3522
Present value		$250.7	$231.0	$207.4	$185.3	$ 150.2	$ 129.4	$ 109.8	$ 80.7	$ 63.3	$ 45.2	$ 510.3
Value of the interest tax shields	$ 1,963.1											
Value of the firm V_F w/o excess assets	$13,225.6											

Net Present Value of Investment	Firm Value		Equity Value
Value	$13,225.6		$4,675.6
Purchase price paid (sources – excess cash)	12,267.1		3,717.1
Net present value of investment	$ 958.4	7.2%	$ 958.4	20.5%

Exhibit may contain small rounding errors

EXHIBIT 15.23 Capital Structure Information for the Adjusted Present Value Valuations

($ in millions)	Total	Year 0	Year 1	Year 2	Year 3	Year 4	Year 5	Year 6	Year 7	Year 8	Year 9	Year 10	Year 11
Debt rating			B	B	B	B	BB	BB	BB	BBB	BBB	BBB	A
Debt cost of capital for unsecured debt			8.70%	8.70%	8.70%	8.70%	7.60%	7.60%	7.60%	6.90%	6.90%	6.90%	6.60%
Balance at Year End											Debt Recapitalization		
Revolver (total commitment in 1st column)	$300.0	$ 100.0	$ 0.0	$ 0.0	$ 0.0	$ 0.0	$ 0.0	$ 0.0	$ 0.0	$ 0.0	$ 0.0	$ 0.0	
Debt assumed		0.0	0.0	0.0	0.0	0.0	0.0	0.0	0.0	0.0	0.0	0.0	
Senior secured note (bank debt)		3,620.0	3,594.4	3,219.2	2,813.4	2,335.1	1,669.9	931.9	133.8	0.0	0.0		
Subordinated note (unsecured debt)		1,810.0	1,810.0	1,810.0	1,810.0	1,810.0	1,810.0	1,810.0	1,810.0	1,089.0	150.6		
Mezzanine debt		3,020.0	3,020.0	3,020.0	3,020.0	3,020.0	3,020.0	3,020.0	3,020.0	3,020.0	3,020.0		
All debt issued at par		$8,550.0	$8,424.4	$8,049.2	$7,643.4	$7,165.1	$6,499.9	$5,761.9	$4,963.8	$4,109.0	$3,170.6	$4,390.7	$4,522.4

Interest Expense	Cost of Debt	Fee	Year 1	Year 2	Year 3	Year 4	Year 5	Year 6	Year 7	Year 8	Year 9	Year 10	Year 11
Revolver	4.500%	0.5%	$ 6.0	$ 1.5	$ 1.5	$ 1.5	$ 1.5	$ 0.0	$ 0.0	$ 0.0	$ 0.0	$ 0.0	
Debt assumed	6.000%		0.0	0.0	0.0	0.0	0.0	0.0	0.0	0.0	0.0	0.0	
Senior secured note (bank debt)	Rating-based rate		217.2	215.7	193.2	168.8	140.1	100.2	55.9	8.0	0.0	0.0	
Subordinated note (unsecured debt)	Rating-based rate		157.5	157.5	157.5	157.5	137.6	137.6	137.6	124.9	75.1	10.4	
Mezzanine debt			262.7	262.7	262.7	262.7	229.5	229.5	229.5	208.4	208.4	208.4	
Expected cash interest expense			$643.4	$637.4	$614.9	$590.5	$508.7	$467.3	$423.0	$341.3	$283.5	$218.8	$289.8
Amortization of fees			30.6	30.6	30.6	30.6	30.6	30.6	30.6	15.1	15.1	9.1	0.0
Amortization of discount/premium on debt	None												
Expected interest tax deduction			$674.0	$668.0	$645.5	$621.1	$539.3	$497.9	$453.6	$356.4	$298.6	$227.8	$289.8
Weighted average cost of debt			7.5%	7.6%	7.6%	7.7%	7.1%	7.2%	7.3%	6.9%	6.9%	6.9%	6.6%
Interest tax shield			$269.6	$267.2	$258.2	$248.4	$215.7	$199.2	$181.4	$142.6	$119.4	$ 91.1	$115.9

Exhibit may contain small rounding errors

EXHIBIT 15.24 Year-by-Year Adjusted Present Value Valuations

Beginning of Year Value ($ in millions)	Year 1	Year 2	Year 3	Year 4	Year 5	Year 6	Year 7	Year 8	Year 9	Year 10	CV Year 10
Value of the Unlevered Firm											
Unlevered free cash flow for continuing value											$ 1,289.1
Discount factor for continuing value											12.500
Unlevered free cash flow	$ 573.4	$ 819.3	$ 836.4	$ 894.3	$ 1,063.9	$ 1,112.0	$ 1,145.4	$ 1,179.7	$ 1,215.1	$ 1,251.6	
Value of the firm at end of year	11,927.9	12,420.7	12,950.7	13,480.9	13,899.9	14,316.9	14,746.4	15,188.8	15,644.5	16,113.8	
V_F + unlevered free cash flow	$12,501.3	$13,240.0	$13,787.0	$14,375.2	$14,963.8	$15,428.9	$15,891.8	$16,368.5	$16,859.6	$17,365.4	
Discount factor for one year	0.901	0.901	0.901	0.901	0.901	0.901	0.901	0.901	0.901	0.901	
Value of the firm at beginning of year	$11,262.4	$11,927.9	$12,420.7	$12,950.7	$13,480.9	$13,899.9	$14,316.9	$14,746.4	$15,188.8	$15,644.5	$16,113.8
Value of the Interest Tax Shields Discounted at the Debt Cost of Capital											
Interest tax shield	$ 269.6	$ 267.2	$ 258.2	$ 248.4	$ 215.7	$ 199.2	$ 181.4	$ 142.6	$ 119.4	$ 91.1	
Value of the interest tax shields (ITSs) at end of year	1,292.6	1,123.2	950.8	775.8	615.1	460.2	312.5	191.5	85.3	0.0	
Value of the ITSs at end of year plus ITS	$ 1,562.2	$ 1,390.4	$ 1,209.0	$ 1,024.2	$ 830.9	$ 659.4	$ 494.0	$ 334.0	$ 204.7	$ 91.1	
Discount factor for one year	0.930	0.930	0.929	0.928	0.934	0.933	0.932	0.936	0.935	0.935	
Value of the ITSs at beginning of year	$ 1,452.8	$ 1,292.6	$ 1,123.2	$ 950.8	$ 775.8	$ 615.1	$ 460.2	$ 312.5	$ 191.5	$ 85.3	$ 0.0
Value of the Interest Tax Shields Discounted at the Unlevered Cost of Capital											
Interest tax shield for continuing value											$ 115.9
Discount factor for continuing value											12.500
Value of the ITSs at end of year plus ITS	$ 566.4	$ 628.7	$ 697.9	$ 774.7	$ 859.9	$ 954.5	$ 1,059.4	$ 1,176.0	$ 1,305.3	$ 1,448.9	
Discount factor for one year	0.901	0.901	0.901	0.901	0.901	0.901	0.901	0.901	0.901	0.901	
Value of the ITSs at beginning of year	$ 510.3	$ 566.4	$ 628.7	$ 697.9	$ 774.7	$ 859.9	$ 954.5	$ 1,059.4	$ 1,176.0	$ 1,305.3	
Value of interest tax shields at beginning of year	$ 1,963.1	$ 1,859.0	$ 1,751.9	$ 1,648.7	$ 1,550.4	$ 1,475.0	$ 1,414.7	$ 1,372.0	$ 1,367.5	$ 1,390.6	$ 1,448.9
Value of the firm at beginning of year	$13,225.6	$13,786.9	$14,172.6	$14,599.3	$15,031.3	$15,374.9	$15,731.6	$16,118.4	$16,556.3	$17,035.1	$17,562.7

Exhibit may contain small rounding errors

REVIEW EXERCISE 15.4

Adjusted Present Value Valuation of the LBO Transaction

Use the information in Review Exercises 15.1 through 15.3 and the following information to measure the year-by-year APV valuation of the LBO transaction. Assume the company's unlevered cost of capital is equal to 9% and as of the end of Year 10, the company will recapitalize its capital structure to 25% debt and 75% common equity as described in Review Exercise 15.3. In addition, assume that all of its cash flows will grow at 3% in perpetuity as of the end of Year 11 and that the appropriate discount rate for interest tax shields is equal to the weighted average cost of debt for Years 1 through 10 and the unlevered cost of capital for Year 11 onward. In addition, measure the value of the interest tax shields, using the unlevered cost of capital to discount all interest tax shields. Forecasts for the company's expected debt levels and interest deductions appear below.

($ in millions)	Total	Year 0	Year 1	Year 2	Year 3	Year 4	Year 5	Year 6	Year 7	Year 8	Year 9	Year 10	Year 11
Debt rating			B	B	B	BB	BBB	BBB	BBB	BBB	BBB	BBB	BBB
Debt cost of capital for unsecured debt			7.70%	7.70%	7.70%	6.60%	5.90%	5.90%	5.90%	5.90%	5.90%	5.90%	5.90%
Balance at Year End												Debt Recapitalization	
Revolver (total commitment in 1st column)	$300.0	$ 100.0	$ 0.0	$ 0.0	$ 0.0	$ 0.0	$ 0.0	$ 0.0	$ 0.0	$ 0.0	$ 0.0		
Debt assumed		0.0	0.0	0.0	0.0	0.0	0.0	0.0	0.0	0.0	0.0		
Senior secured note (bank debt)		880.0	814.4	622.5	379.9	142.6	0.0	0.0	0.0	0.0	0.0		
Subordinated note (unsecured debt)		410.0	410.0	410.0	410.0	410.0	374.6	172.3	36.5	18.7	0.0		
Mezzanine debt		670.0	670.0	670.0	670.0	670.0	670.0	670.0	670.0	670.0	529.1		
All debt issued at par		$2,060.0	$1,894.4	$1,702.5	$1,459.9	$1,222.6	$1,044.6	$842.3	$706.5	$688.7	$529.1	$815.1	$839.5

Expected Interest Deduction (Based on r_D)	Cost of Debt	Fee	Year 1	Year 2	Year 3	Year 4	Year 5	Year 6	Year 7	Year 8	Year 9	Year 10	Year 11
Revolver	4.500%	0.5%	$ 6.0	$ 1.5	$ 1.5	$ 1.5	$ 1.5	$ 0.0	$ 0.0	$ 0.0	$ 0.0	$ 0.0	
Debt assumed			0.0	0.0	0.0	0.0	0.0	0.0	0.0	0.0	0.0	0.0	
Senior secured note (bank debt)	5.000%		44.0	40.7	31.1	19.0	7.1	0.0	0.0	0.0	0.0	0.0	
Subordinated note (unsecured debt)	Rating-based rate		31.6	31.6	31.6	27.1	24.2	22.1	10.2	2.2	1.1	0.0	
Mezzanine debt	Rating-based rate		51.6	51.6	51.6	44.2	39.5	39.5	39.5	39.5	39.5	31.2	
Expected cash interest expense			$133.2	$125.4	$115.8	$91.8	$72.3	$61.6	$49.7	$41.7	$40.6	$31.2	$48.1
Amortization of fees			7.1	7.1	7.1	7.1	7.1	7.1	7.1	3.4	3.4	2.0	0.0
Expected interest tax deduction			$140.3	$132.5	$122.9	$98.9	$79.5	$68.8	$56.8	$45.1	$44.0	$33.2	$48.1

Exhibit may contain small rounding errors

Solution on pages 659–662.

In Exhibit 15.25, we measure the equity cost of capital and equity beta for each year. We see that the equity cost of capital is 16.27% as of the beginning of Year 1 and generally declines over time to 11.91% as of the beginning of Year 10. Similarly, the equity beta is 1.9 as of the beginning of Year 1 declining to 1.2 as of the beginning of Year 10. We also show the geometric average equity cost of capital from the transaction date to each assumed exit year. For example, if the transaction were exited in the fifth year, the geometric average equity cost of capital is 14.99%. The levering formula that we use to measure the cost of equity for Years 1 through 10 is the general formula provided in Chapter 10, as we are discounting the interest tax shields at the cost of debt for the first 10 years. The levering formula for Year 11 is based on valuing the interest tax shields at the unlevered cost of capital.

This information is useful, for it indicates that the equity cost of capital does not exceed 17% and shows the geometric average equity cost of capital for each exit year. As such, IRRs above 17% result in positive net present value investments from the management's and sponsor's perspectives. Of course, sponsors understand that their investors expect their investments in the private equity fund to yield satisfactory returns net of the fees paid, so the IRRs estimated for the limited partners must take these fees into consideration. It should also be noted that since the cost of equity declines every year as the capital structure is becoming less levered, the geometric average equity cost of capital declines as well. Thus, the minimum IRR for the equity investors need not be equal to the maximum equity cost of capital in order for this investment to earn a positive risk-adjusted return for the equity investors.

EXHIBIT 15.25 Implied Equity Cost of Capital and Equity Betas for the John Edwardson & Company Leveraged Buyout Transaction

As of the Beginning of Year ($ in millions)	Year 1	Year 2	Year 3	Year 4	Year 5	Year 6	Year 7	Year 8	Year 9	Year 10	Year 11
Value of the firm (V_F)	$13,225.6	$13,786.9	$14,172.6	$14,599.3	$15,031.3	$15,374.9	$15,731.6	$16,118.4	$16,556.3	$17,035.1	$17,562.7
Value of debt (V_D)	8,550.0	8,424.4	8,049.2	7,643.4	7,165.1	6,499.9	5,761.9	4,963.8	4,109.0	3,170.6	4,390.7
Value of equity (V_E)	$ 4,675.6	$ 5,362.6	$ 6,123.4	$ 6,955.9	$ 7,866.3	$ 8,875.0	$ 9,969.7	$11,154.6	$12,447.3	$13,864.5	$13,172.1
Debt-to-equity ratio	1.829	1.571	1.314	1.099	0.911	0.732	0.578	0.445	0.330	0.229	0.333
Present value of interest tax shields discounted at r_D	$ 1,452.8	$ 1,292.6	$ 1,123.2	$ 950.8	$ 775.8	$ 615.1	$ 460.2	$ 312.5	$ 191.5	$ 85.3	$ 0.0
Value of debt – value of ITS	$ 7,097.2	$ 7,131.8	$ 6,926.0	$ 6,692.6	$ 6,389.3	$ 5,884.8	$ 5,301.7	$ 4,651.3	$ 3,917.5	$ 3,085.3	$ 4,390.7
Adjusted debt to common equity ratio	1.518	1.330	1.131	0.962	0.812	0.663	0.532	0.417	0.315	0.223	0.333

	Year 1	Year 2	Year 3	Year 4	Year 5	Year 6	Year 7	Year 8	Year 9	Year 10	Year 11
Unlevered cost of capital, r_U	11.00%	11.00%	11.00%	11.00%	11.00%	11.00%	11.00%	11.00%	11.00%	11.00%	11.00%
Debt cost of capital, r_D	7.53%	7.57%	7.64%	7.73%	7.10%	7.19%	7.34%	6.88%	6.90%	6.90%	6.60%
Adjusted debt to common equity ratio	1.518	1.330	1.131	0.962	0.812	0.663	0.532	0.417	0.315	0.223	0.333
Equity cost of capital, r_E	16.27%	15.57%	14.80%	14.15%	14.17%	13.53%	12.95%	12.72%	12.29%	11.91%	12.47%
Equity beta	1.879	1.761	1.634	1.525	1.528	1.421	1.324	1.287	1.215	1.152	1.244
Geometric average equity cost of capital to exit year	16.27%	15.92%	15.55%	15.20%	14.99%	14.74%	14.49%	14.26%	14.04%	13.83%	13.70%

Exhibit may contain small rounding errors

EXHIBIT 15.26 Implied Weighted Average Cost of Capital for the John Edwardson & Company Leveraged Buyout Transaction

	Year 1	Year 2	Year 3	Year 4	Year 5	Year 6	Year 7	Year 8	Year 9	Year 10	Year 11
Equity cost of capital, r_E	16.27%	15.57%	14.80%	14.15%	14.17%	13.53%	12.95%	12.72%	12.29%	11.91%	12.47%
Equity-to-firm value	35.35%	38.90%	43.21%	47.65%	52.33%	57.72%	63.37%	69.20%	75.18%	81.39%	75.00%
Debt cost of capital, r_D	7.53%	7.57%	7.64%	7.73%	7.10%	7.19%	7.34%	6.88%	6.90%	6.90%	6.60%
Debt to firm value	64.65%	61.10%	56.79%	52.35%	47.67%	42.28%	36.63%	30.80%	24.82%	18.61%	25.00%
Income tax rate, T_{INT}	41.90%	41.92%	41.99%	42.07%	42.41%	42.62%	42.89%	41.77%	42.13%	41.66%	40.00%
Weighted average cost of capital, r_{WACC}	8.58%	8.74%	8.91%	9.08%	9.36%	9.55%	9.74%	10.04%	10.23%	10.44%	10.34%
Present value weighted average growth rate	4.24%	2.80%	3.01%	2.96%	2.29%	2.32%	2.46%	2.72%	2.89%	3.10%	3.00%

11-year geometric average of r_{WACC} = 9.55%

Valuation Key 15.9

Most analyses of potential LBOs compare the equity IRRs from the model to benchmarks that are based on heuristics. We recommend that equity costs of capital be calculated for each year in order to ensure that the benchmarks used actually result in positive risk-adjusted returns. The IRRs for the limited partners in the funds should take into consideration the fees those investors are charged.

In Exhibit 15.26, we measure the weighted average cost of capital for each year based on the equity cost of capital. We see that the equity cost of capital is decreasing as the financial leverage decreases while the weighted average cost of capital increases as the company is becoming less levered. Note that the tax rate is not 40% in this table. The reason for this is that we have to base the tax rate in the weighted average cost of capital on both the amount of debt the company has and the weighted average cost of debt. In this case, the amortization of the loan fees is not part of the calculated interest. In order to embed the interest tax shields (from the amortization of the fees) into our valuation, we have to adjust the tax rate. For example, in Exhibit 15.23, if we take (Year 1, for example) and divide the interest tax shield of 269.6 by the interest expense (before amortization of the loan fees) of $643.4, we arrive at an adjusted tax figure of 41.9%. We do not show this, but if we take the varying weighted average cost of capital figures in Exhibit 15.26 and discount the free cash flows of the unlevered firm, we replicate the APV valuation shown in Exhibit 15.22.

REVIEW EXERCISE 15.5

Post-LBO Equity and Weighted Average Costs of Capital

Use the information in Review Exercises 15.1 through 15.4 to measure the year-by-year post-LBO equity and weighted average costs of capital.

Solution on pages 663–664.

SUMMARY AND KEY CONCEPTS

In this chapter, we discussed the topic of leveraged buyouts and management buyouts. These transactions rely extensively on the credit markets. At times, they represent a significant portion of overall M&A activity, but at other times, they are just a minor part of that activity. We have provided data on the incidence of leveraged buyouts, the characteristics of their deal structures, and the characteristics of companies that generally undergo leveraged buyouts. In addition, we have discussed potential motivations for leveraged buyouts, and we have summarized the evidence on what happens to firms that undergo a leveraged buyout, especially with respect to improvements in operating performance and value creation. We have also discussed the role of private equity firms in these transactions.

We explained in detail how to analyze LBO transactions. The tools that we use to do so draw on all of the elements that we have already discussed in the book, but they are combined in such a way that the focus is on the particular characteristics of LBO transactions. One key outcome of an LBO analysis is to confirm that the assumed capital structure is feasible. In particular, this requires that the interest rate assumed in the model is consistent with both current market yields for debt and the credit risk of the debt in the transaction; it also requires that the company be able to meet the required principal and interest payments resulting from the capital structure. The second key output of an LBO analysis is to determine the internal rates of return that will be earned by various investors as a function of different assumed exit dates.

As we have indicated, this analysis is an iterative process in which we make an assumption about an offer price; then, based on this assumption, we make an assumption about the capital structure and the yields on different debt instruments. Based on our financial model for the company, we then determine if the capital structure is consistent with both current market conditions and whether the company can service the debt. If the capital structure works, we can then determine the IRR to various investors to see if the minimum hurdle rates demanded by various investors are met or even exceeded.

ADDITIONAL READING AND REFERENCES

Core, J., R. Holthausen, and D. Larcker, "Corporate Governance, Chief Executive Officer Compensation and Firm Performance," *Journal of Financial Economics* vol. 53, no. 3 (1999), pp. 371–406.

Kaplan, S. N., and P. Strömberg, "Leveraged Buyouts and Private Equity," *Journal of Economic Perspectives* 23 (2009), pp. 121–146.

Smith, A., "Corporate Ownership Structure and Performance," *Journal of Financial Economics* vol. 27, no. 1 (1990), pp. 143–164.

EXERCISES AND PROBLEMS

P15.1   **Sources and Uses, Capital Structure, and Deal Terms—T. Burrus Company:** A group of managers are making an offer to purchase the company they manage—the T. Burrus Company. The company's current stock price is $12 per share, and the company has 250 million shares outstanding; the company has a current price-to-earnings ratio equal to 14.37 and a firm-value-to-EBITDA multiple equal to 5.25. Management owns 12.5 million shares of the outstanding stock. After considering the company's expected performance and alternative strategies to the LBO transaction (including alternative acquisition offers), the deal premium is set at 20%. The company has no convertible debt or convertible preferred stock, but it does have 50 million stock options outstanding, all with an exercise price equal to $7.20.

In addition to redeeming the existing stock and options, management and its financial sponsor will redeem all outstanding debt (par value of $300 million) and preferred stock (par value of $100 million) at their par values (all of which are equal to their book values). Initial fees will equal $161.1 million (3% for the debt financing, 1% to the sponsor, and 0.5% for other fees). These fees do not include fees for a revolver loan. The sponsor intends to finance this transaction by using $141 million in excess cash held by the company, issuing various debt securities equaling $3.19 billion, investing $750 million of its own equity, and having management invest $240.1 million in equity from rollover equity and new investment. The composition of the $3.19 billion in debt is $1.39 billion of 7-year, 7.0% senior secured bank debt; $880 million of 9-year, 11% subordinated unsecured debt; and $920 million of 10-year, 13% mezzanine debt, which has an "equity kicker" equal to 4% of the fully diluted post-LBO shares. In addition, the company is arranging a $400 million revolving line of credit that has a five-year term, a 4% interest rate on the amount drawn, and a 0.5% annual fee on the total amount of the line of credit. Management has an "equity kicker" equal to 4.3% of the fully diluted post-LBO shares. The sponsor plans to use $200.0 million from the revolver to finance the transaction. The company will have 500 million post-transaction shares outstanding.

Calculate the purchase price of the equity and prepare a sources and uses schedule similar to the one in Exhibit 15.10.

P15.2   **Measuring the Internal Rate of Return—T. Burrus Company:** Use the information in Problem 15.1 and the following information to measure the internal rates of return to the financial sponsor, management, and mezzanine debtholders; assume an exit value based on the deal EBITDA multiple. T. Burrus Company's management prepared the forecasts shown in Exhibit P15.1 (on pages 650–651) to assess the value of the LBO transaction.

P15.3   **WACC-Based Exit Value—T. Burrus Company:** Use the information in Problems 15.1 and 15.2 and Exhibits P15.1 and P15.2 (on pages 650–652) to measure the WACC-based exit values and implied EBITDA multiples; compare the implied EBITDA multiples in each year to the deal EBITDA multiple (see Exhibit 15.20). To measure the weighted average cost of capital, assume that as of the exit date, the company will use a capital structure of 20% debt and 80% common equity, which will result in a 7.5% cost of debt and a 11.875% cost of equity. As of Year 11, the company expects its free cash flows to grow at 2% in perpetuity. Recalculate the internal rate of return to the financial sponsor using the WACC-based exit values.

P15.4   **Adjusted Present Value Valuation of the LBO Transaction—T. Burrus Company:** use the information in Problems 15.1 through 15.3, Exhibits P15.1 and P15.2 and the following information to measure the year-by-year APV valuation of the LBO transaction. Assume the company's unlevered cost of capital is equal to 11%; as of the end of Year 10, the company will recapitalize its capital structure to the one described in Problem 15.3. In addition, assume that all of its cash flows will growth at 2% in perpetuity as of the end of Year 11 and that the appropriate discount rate for interest tax shields is equal to the weighted average cost of debt for Years 1 through 10 and the unlevered cost of capital for Year 11 onward. In addition, measure the value of the interest tax shields using the unlevered cost of capital to discount all interest tax shields. See the debt and interest schedules in Exhibit P15.2 (on pages 652).

P15.5   **Post-LBO Equity and Weighted Average Costs of Capital—T. Burrus Company:** Use the information in Problems 15.1 through 15.4 and Exhibits P15.1 and P15.2 to measure the year-by-year post-LBO equity and weighted average costs of capital. Use these costs of capital to measure the value of the firm (using the WACC valuation method) and the value of the equity (using the equity DCF valuation method).

P15.6   **Sources and Uses, Capital Structure, and Deal Terms—H. Stauffer Company:** A group of managers is making an offer to purchase the company they manage—the H. Stauffer Company. The company's current stock price is $8 per share, and the company has 130 million shares outstanding; the company has a current price-to-earnings ratio equal to 7.52 and a firm value to EBITDA multiple equal to 4.98. Management owns 2.6 million shares of the outstanding stock. After considering the company's expected performance and alternative strategies to the LBO transaction (including alternative acquisition offers), the deal premium is set at 20%. The company has no convertible debt or convertible preferred stock, but it does have 26 million stock options outstanding, all with an exercise price equal to $4.8.

In addition to redeeming the existing stock and options, management and its financial sponsor will redeem all outstanding debt (par value of $400 million), and preferred stock (par value of $200 million) at their par values (which are equal to their book values), which are given in Exhibit P15.3 (on page 653). Initial fees will equal $71.59 million (3% for the debt financing, 1% to the sponsor, and 0.5% for other fees). These fees do not include fees for a revolver loan. The sponsor intends to finance this transaction by using $12.36 million in excess cash held by the company, issuing various debt securities equaling $1.4 billion, investing $440 million of its own equity, and having management invest $92.03 million in equity from rollover equity and new investment. The composition of the $1.4 billion in debt is $400 million of seven-year, 7.0% senior secured bank debt; $400 million of nine-year, 11% subordinated unsecured debt; and $600 million of ten-year, 13% mezzanine debt, which has an "equity kicker" equal to 4% of the fully diluted post-LBO shares. In addition, the company is arranging a $200 million revolving line of credit that has a five-year term, a 4.5% interest rate on the amount drawn, and a 0.5% annual fee on the total amount of the line of credit. Management has an "equity kicker" equal to 3.2% of the post-LBO shares. The sponsor plans to use $100.0 million from the revolver to finance the transaction. The company will have 260 million post-transaction shares outstanding.

Calculate the purchase price of the equity and prepare a sources and uses schedule similar to one in Exhibit 15.10.

EXHIBIT P15.1 Forecasts for the T. Burrus Company

Income Statement Forecasts ($ in millions)

	Year –1	Year 0	Year 1	Year 2	Year 3	Year 4	Year 5	Year 6	Year 7	Year 8	Year 9	Year 10	Year 11
Revenue	$2,304.0	$2,350.1	$ 2,397.1	$ 2,636.8	$ 2,900.5	$ 3,190.5	$ 3,445.8	$ 3,583.6	$ 3,655.3	$ 3,728.4	$ 3,802.9	$ 3,879.0	$ 3,956.6
Cost of goods sold	–822.5	–799.0	–815.0	–896.5	–957.2	–957.2	–1,033.7	–1,075.1	–1,096.6	–1,118.5	–1,293.0	–1,318.9	–1,345.2
Gross margin	$1,481.5	$1,551.1	$ 1,582.1	$ 1,740.3	$ 1,943.3	$ 2,233.4	$ 2,412.0	$ 2,508.5	$ 2,558.7	$ 2,609.9	$ 2,509.9	$ 2,560.1	$ 2,611.3
Selling, general, and administrative	–870.9	–846.0	–862.9	–922.9	–986.2	–893.3	–964.8	–1,003.4	–1,023.5	–1,043.9	–1,331.0	–1,357.6	–1,384.8
Other expenses			–65.4										
Depreciation expense	–253.4	–258.5	–263.7	–290.0	–319.1	–351.0	–379.0	–394.2	–402.1	–410.1	–418.3	–426.7	–435.2
Operating income	$ 357.1	$ 446.5	$ 390.0	$ 527.4	$ 638.1	$ 989.1	$ 1,068.2	$ 1,110.9	$ 1,133.1	$ 1,155.8	$ 760.6	$ 775.8	$ 791.3
Interest expense	–19.0	–24.0	–335.4	–334.1	–327.2	–309.5	–280.9	–251.5	–214.2	–152.8	–139.4	–96.2	–47.8
Income before taxes	$ 338.1	$ 422.5	$ 54.7	$ 193.3	$ 311.0	$ 679.5	$ 787.3	$ 859.4	$ 919.0	$ 1,003.0	$ 621.2	$ 679.6	$ 743.5
Income tax expense	–148.8	–185.9	–24.1	–85.1	–136.8	–299.0	–346.4	–378.2	–404.3	–441.3	–273.3	–299.0	–327.1
Net income	$ 189.3	$ 236.6	$ 30.6	$ 108.3	$ 174.1	$ 380.5	$ 440.9	$ 481.3	$ 514.6	$ 561.7	$ 347.8	$ 380.6	$ 416.4

Earnings Per Share

	Year –1	Year 0	Year 1	Year 2	Year 3	Year 4	Year 5	Year 6	Year 7	Year 8	Year 9	Year 10	Year 11
Net income	$ 189.3	$ 236.6	$ 30.6	$ 108.3	$ 174.1	$ 380.5	$ 440.9	$ 481.3	$ 514.6	$ 561.7	$ 347.8	$ 380.6	$ 416.4
Preferred stock dividends	–5.6	–7.0											
Net income to common equity	$ 183.7	$ 229.6	$ 30.6	$ 108.3	$ 174.1	$ 380.5	$ 440.9	$ 481.3	$ 514.6	$ 561.7	$ 347.8	$ 380.6	$ 416.4
Common shares outstanding (m)	250.0	250.0	500.0	500.0	500.0	500.0	500.0	500.0	500.0	500.0	500.0	500.0	500.0
Basic earnings per share	$ 0.735	$ 0.918	$ 0.061	$ 0.217	$ 0.348	$ 0.761	$ 0.882	$ 0.963	$ 1.029	$ 1.123	$ 0.696	$ 0.761	$ 0.833

Effect of Dilutive Securities

	Year –1	Year 0
Management stock options (net shares, m)	21.3	25.0
Common shares outstanding (m)	250.0	250.0
Adjusted shares outstanding	271.3	275.0
Diluted earnings per share	$ 0.677	$ 0.835

Retained Earnings

	Year –1	Year 0	Year 1	Year 2	Year 3	Year 4	Year 5	Year 6	Year 7	Year 8	Year 9	Year 10	Year 11
Beginning balance	$ 331.8	$ 512.5	$–3,121.0	$–3,090.4	$–2,982.1	$–2,808.0	$–2,427.4	$–1,986.6	$–1,505.3	$–990.7	$–429.0	$ –81.2	$ 299.4
Net income	189.3	236.6	30.6	108.3	174.1	380.5	440.9	481.3	514.6	561.7	347.8	380.6	416.4
Preferred stock dividends	–5.6	–7.0											
Common equity dividends	–3.0	–203.1	0.0	0.0	0.0	0.0	0.0	0.0	0.0	0.0	0.0	0.0	–15.6
Ending balance	$ 512.5	$ 539.0	$–3,090.4	$–2,982.1	$–2,808.0	$–2,427.4	$–1,986.6	$–1,505.3	$–990.7	$–429.0	$ –81.2	$ 299.4	$ 700.2

Exhibit may contain small rounding errors

Continued next page

Continued from previous page

Balance Sheet Forecasts
($ in millions)

	Year −1	Year 0	Year 1	Year 2	Year 3	Year 4	Year 5	Year 6	Year 7	Year 8	Year 9	Year 10	Year 11
Cash balance	$ 368.6	$ 235.0	$ 239.7	$ 210.9	$ 174.0	$ 191.4	$ 206.7	$ 215.0	$ 219.3	$ 223.7	$ 228.2	$ 232.7	$ 237.4
Accounts receivable	352.0	359.0	366.2	402.8	443.1	487.4	526.4	547.5	558.4	569.6	581.0	592.6	604.5
Inventory	45.7	44.4	45.3	49.8	53.2	53.2	57.4	59.7	60.9	62.1	71.8	73.3	74.7
Total current assets	$ 766.3	$ 638.4	$ 651.2	$ 663.6	$ 670.3	$ 732.0	$ 790.6	$ 822.2	$ 838.7	$ 855.5	$ 881.0	$ 898.6	$ 916.6
Property, plant, and equipment	$1,066.2	$1,337.8	$1,668.1	$1,916.3	$2,182.8	$2,470.0	$2,872.0	$3,278.1	$3,692.4	$4,537.5	$4,976.9	$5,027.0	$5,078.1
Accumulated depreciation	−413.4	−671.9	−935.6	−1,225.7	−1,544.7	−1,895.7	−2,274.7	−2,668.9	−3,071.0	−3,481.1	−3,899.4	−3,928.0	−3,957.1
Property, plant, and equipment (net)	$ 652.8	$ 665.9	$ 732.4	$ 690.6	$ 638.1	$ 574.3	$ 597.3	$ 609.2	$ 621.4	$1,056.4	$1,077.5	$1,099.0	$1,121.0
Capitalized fees	$ 0.00	$ 161.1	$ 84.0	$ 72.4	$ 60.7	$ 49.1	$ 37.4	$ 25.8	$ 14.1	$ 8.5	$ 2.8	$ 0.0	$ 0.0
Total assets	$1,419.1	$1,465.4	$1,467.7	$1,426.6	$1,369.2	$1,355.4	$1,425.3	$1,457.2	$1,474.2	$1,920.3	$1,961.3	$1,997.7	$2,037.6
Accounts payable	$ 91.4	$ 88.8	$ 90.6	$ 99.6	$ 106.4	$ 106.4	$ 114.9	$ 119.5	$ 121.8	$ 124.3	$ 143.7	$ 146.5	$ 149.5
Other current operating liabilities	115.2	117.5	119.9	131.8	145.0	159.5	172.3	179.2	182.8	186.4	190.1	193.9	197.8
Total current liabilities	$ 206.6	$ 206.3	$ 210.4	$ 231.5	$ 251.4	$ 265.9	$ 287.1	$ 298.6	$ 304.6	$ 310.7	$ 333.8	$ 340.5	$ 347.3
Total debt	300.0	3,390.0	3,357.5	3,187.1	2,935.7	2,526.9	2,134.7	1,673.8	1,170.2	1,048.5	718.5	367.7	0.0
Total liabilities	$ 506.6	$ 3,596.3	$ 3,568.0	$ 3,418.6	$ 3,187.1	$ 2,792.8	$ 2,421.8	$ 1,972.4	$ 1,474.8	$ 1,359.2	$ 1,052.3	$ 708.2	$ 347.3
Preferred stock	$ 100.0	$ 0.0											
Common stock	300.0	990.1	990.1	990.1	990.1	990.1	990.1	990.1	990.1	990.1	990.1	990.1	990.1
Retained earnings	512.5	−3,121.0	−3,090.4	−2,982.1	−2,808.0	−2,427.4	−1,988.6	−1,505.3	−990.7	−429.0	−81.2	299.4	700.2
Total shareholders' equity	$ 912.5	$−2,130.9	$−2,100.3	$−1,992.0	$−1,817.9	$−1,437.3	$−996.5	$−515.2	$ −0.6	$ 561.1	$ 908.9	$1,289.5	$1,690.3
Total liabilities and equities	$1,419.1	$ 1,465.4	$ 1,467.7	$ 1,426.6	$ 1,369.2	$ 1,355.4	$1,425.3	$1,457.2	$1,474.2	$1,920.3	$1,961.3	$1,997.7	$2,037.6

Free Cash Flow Forecasts
($ in millions)

	Year 0	Year 1	Year 2	Year 3	Year 4	Year 5	Year 6	Year 7	Year 8	Year 9	Year 10	Year 11
Earnings before interest and taxes (EBIT)	$446.5	$390.0	$527.4	$638.1	$989.1	$1,068.2	$1,110.9	$1,133.1	$1,155.8	$760.6	$775.8	$791.3
− Income taxes paid on EBIT	−196.5	−171.6	−232.0	−280.8	−435.2	−470.0	−488.8	−498.6	−508.5	−334.7	−341.4	−348.2
Earnings before interest and after taxes	$250.0	$218.4	$295.3	$357.3	$553.9	$598.2	$622.1	$634.6	$647.2	$425.9	$434.4	$443.1
+ Depreciation expense	258.5	263.7	290.0	319.1	351.0	379.0	394.2	402.1	410.1	418.3	426.7	435.2
− Change in accounts receivable	−7.0	−7.2	−36.6	−40.3	−44.3	−39.0	−21.1	−10.9	−11.2	−11.4	−11.6	−11.9
− Change in inventory	1.3	−0.9	−4.5	−3.4	0.0	−4.3	−2.3	−1.2	−1.2	−9.7	−1.4	−1.5
+ Change in accounts payable	−2.6	1.8	9.1	6.7	0.0	8.5	4.6	2.4	2.4	19.4	2.9	2.9
+ Change in other liabilities	2.3	2.4	12.0	13.2	14.5	12.8	6.9	3.6	3.7	3.7	3.8	3.9
+ LBO fees—expensed	65.4	0.0	0.0	0.0	0.0	0.0	0.0	0.0	0.0	0.0	0.0	
− Change in required cash balance	−7.4	−4.7	28.8	36.9	−17.4	−15.3	−8.3	−4.3	−4.4	−4.5	−4.6	−4.7
Cash flow before capital expenditures	$495.1	$538.9	$594.0	$689.6	$857.6	$939.9	$996.2	$1,026.2	$1,046.7	$841.8	$850.2	$867.2
− Capital expenditures	−271.6	−330.3	−248.2	−266.6	−287.1	−402.0	−406.1	−414.3	−845.1	−439.4	−448.2	−457.2
Unlevered free cash flow	$223.6	$208.6	$345.8	$423.0	$570.5	$537.9	$590.0	$611.9	$201.6	$402.4	$402.0	$410.0

Exhibit may contain small rounding errors

EXHIBIT P15.2 Debt and Interest Schedules

($ in millions)	Total	Year 0	Year 1	Year 2	Year 3	Year 4	Year 5	Year 6	Year 7	Year 8	Year 9	Year 10	Year 11
Debt rating			B	B	B	BB	BBB	A	A	A	BBB	A	A
Debt cost of capital for unsecured debt			10.00%	10.00%	10.00%	9.00%	8.00%	7.50%	7.50%	7.50%	8.00%	7.50%	7.50%
													Debt Recapitalization
Balance at Year End:													
Revolver (total commitment in 1st column)	$400.0	$ 200.0	$ 167.5	$ 0.0	$ 0.0	$ 0.0	$ 0.0	$ 0.0	$ 0.0	$ 0.0	$ 0.0	$ 0.0	
Debt assumed		0.0	0.0	0.0	0.0	0.0	0.0	0.0	0.0	0.0	0.0	0.0	
Senior secured note (bank debt)		1,390.0	1,390.0	1,387.1	1,135.7	726.9	334.7	0.0	0.0	0.0	0.0		
Subordinated note (unsecured debt)		880.0	880.0	880.0	880.0	880.0	880.0	753.8	250.2	128.5	0.0		
Mezzanine debt		920.0	920.0	920.0	920.0	920.0	920.0	920.0	920.0	920.0	718.5		
All debt issued at par		$3,390.0	$3,357.5	$3,187.1	$2,935.7	$2,526.9	$2,134.7	$1,673.8	$1,170.2	$1,048.5	$718.5	$983.2	$1,002.9

Expected Interest Deduction (Based on r_D)	Cost of Debt	Fee	Year 1	Year 2	Year 3	Year 4	Year 5	Year 6	Year 7	Year 8	Year 9	Year 10	Year 11
Revolver	4.000%	0.5%	$ 10.0	$ 8.7	$ 2.0	$ 2.0	$ 2.0	$ 0.0	$ 0.0	$ 0.0	$ 0.0	$ 0.0	
Debt assumed	7.000%		0.0	0.0	0.0	0.0	0.0	0.0	0.0	0.0	0.0	0.0	
Senior secured note (bank debt)	7.000%	Rating-based rate	97.3	97.3	97.1	79.5	50.9	23.4	0.0	0.0	0.0	0.0	
Subordinated note (unsecured debt)		Rating-based rate	88.0	88.0	88.0	79.2	70.4	66.0	56.5	18.8	10.3	0.0	
Mezzanine debt			92.0	92.0	92.0	82.8	73.6	69.0	69.0	69.0	73.6	53.9	
Expected cash interest expense			$287.3	$286.0	$279.1	$243.5	$196.9	$158.4	$125.5	$87.8	$83.9	$53.9	$73.7
Amortization of fees			11.7	11.7	11.7	11.7	11.7	11.7	11.7	5.7	5.7	2.8	0.0
Amortization of discount/premium on debt		None											
Expected interest tax deduction			$299.0	$297.7	$290.8	$255.1	$208.5	$170.1	$137.2	$93.5	$89.6	$56.6	$73.7
Weighted average cost of debt			8.5%	8.5%	8.8%	8.3%	7.8%	7.4%	7.5%	7.5%	8.0%	7.5%	7.5%
Interest tax shield			$131.5	$131.0	$127.9	$112.3	$91.8	$74.8	$60.4	$41.1	$39.4	$24.9	$32.4

Exhibit may contain small rounding errors

P15.7   **Post-LBO Balance Sheet—H. Stauffer Company:** Use the information in Problem 15.6 and Exhibit P15.3 to prepare an opening balance sheet for the H. Stauffer Company as of the end of Year 0.

EXHIBIT P15.3	Historical Financial Statements and Free Cash Flow Schedule for the H. Stauffer Company

(in millions)	Year -1	Year 0
Income Statement		
Revenue	$1,000.0	$1,030.0
Cost of goods sold	−378.0	−370.8
Gross margin	$ 622.0	$ 659.2
Selling, general, and administrative expense	−315.0	−309.0
Depreciation expense	−40.0	−41.2
Operating income	$ 267.0	$ 309.0
Interest expense	−26.0	−32.0
Income before taxes	$ 241.0	$ 277.0
Income tax expense	−96.4	−110.8
Net income	$ 144.6	$ 166.2
Balance Sheet		
Cash balance	$ 32.0	$ 33.0
Accounts receivable	208.3	214.6
Inventory	52.5	51.5
Total current assets	$ 292.8	$ 299.0
Property, plant, and equipment	$2,060.0	$2,121.8
Accumulated depreciation	−440.0	−481.2
Property, plant, and equipment (net)	$1,620.0	$1,640.6
Capitalized fees	$ 0.0	$ 0.0
Total assets	$1,912.8	$1,939.6
Accounts payable	$ 42.0	$ 41.2
Total debt	400.0	400.0
Total liabilities	$ 442.0	$ 441.2
Preferred stock	$ 200.0	$ 200.0
Common stock	600.0	600.0
Retained earnings	670.8	698.4
Total shareholders' equity	$1,470.8	$1,498.4
Total liabilities and equities	$1,912.8	$1,939.6

(in millions)	Year 0
Free Cash Flows	
Earnings before interest and taxes (EBIT)	$309.0
− Income taxes paid on EBIT	−123.6
Earnings before interest and after taxes	$185.4
+ Depreciation expense	41.2
− Change in accounts receivable	−6.3
− Change in inventory	1.0
+ Change in accounts payable	−0.8
+ LBO fees—expensed	0.0
− Change in required cash balance	−1.0
Cash flow before capital expenditures	$219.6
− Capital expenditures	−61.8
Unlevered free cash flow	$157.8
− Interest paid	−32.0
+ Interest tax shield	12.8
− Preferred stock dividends	−14.0
Cash flow after interest and preferred stock dividends	124.6
+ Change in debt financing	0.0
+ Change in preferred stock financing	0.0
Free cash flow to common equity	**$124.6**
+ Change in common equity financing	0.0
− Common equity dividends paid	−124.6
Change in excess cash	$ 0.0
+ Change in required cash balance	1.0
Change in cash balance	$ 1.0

(in millions)	Year −1	Year 0
Retained Earnings		
Beginning balance	$540.4	$670.8
Net income	144.6	166.2
Preferred stock dividends	−11.2	−14.0
Common equity dividends	−3.0	−124.6
Ending balance	$670.8	$698.4

Exhibit may contain small rounding errors

P15.8   **Financial Statement and Free Cash Flow Forecasts—H. Stauffer Company:** Use the information in Problems 15.6 and 15.7 to create a financial model for the H. Stauffer Company. The company must use all available cash flows (after investments) to pay down debt. Assume all cash flows occur at the end of each year; thus, the company's capital expenditures in a given year are the capital expenditures necessary to support the revenues in the following year. Use the following forecast drivers for Years 1–11.

Expected inflation (Year 11 is a long-run expectation)	3.00%
Treasury Bonds—20-year	5.00%
LIBOR—3-month	3.50%
Revenue growth rate	3.00%
Cost of goods sold (% revenue)	36.00%
Selling, general and administrative (% revenue)	30.00%
Constant income tax rate on all income	40.00%
Required cash balance (% revenue)	2.00%
Accounts receivable (days to collect)	75.0
Inventory (days to sell)	50.0
Accounts payable (days to pay)	40.0
CAPEX—based on gross PPEQ to rev	2.00
Depreciation (% of beginning gross PPEQ)	2.00%

Use the EBITDA coverage ratio to estimate the company's credit rating based on the following schedule.

EBITDA for Debt Rating:	EBITDA Coverage Ratio Hurdle	For Unsecured Debt	
		Yield to Maturity	Cost of Debt
CCC+ & Below.	0.5	N/A	N/A
B− to B+	1.0	12.0%	10.0%
BB− to BB+	4.0	10.5%	9.0%
BBB− to BBB+	7.0	9.0%	8.0%
A− to A+	12.0	8.0%	7.5%
AA− to AAA	18.0	7.0%	7.0%

a. Use the above assumptions to create a financial model that produces an income statement, balance sheet, and free cash flow schedule for Years 1 through 11 assuming the LBO is consummated. These are the forecasts that management prepared before the LBO transaction. (We refer to these forecasts as the Pre-LBO Forecasts.)

b. Management believes that it can improve the company's performance after the LBO transaction; specifically, management believes that it can reduce both the cost of goods sold and the selling, general, and administrative expenses by 1% of revenue in Years 2 through 4 and that it can maintain this performance in Years 5 onward. Management also believes that it can grow revenues by 5% in Years 2 through 4 (3% in all other years). Using these revised assumptions (LBO Forecasts), create a second financial model that produces an income statement, balance sheet, and free cash flow schedule for Years 1 through 11. These are the forecasts management prepared conditional on completing the LBO transaction. (We refer to these forecasts as the Post-LBO Forecasts.)

c. Discuss the change in the company's expected performance.

P15.9 **Measuring the Internal Rate of Return—H. Stauffer Company:** Use the information in Problems 15.6 through 15.8 to measure the internal rates of return to the financial sponsor, management, and mezzanine debtholders, assuming an exit value based on the deal EBITDA multiple. Measure the internal rate of return based on the Pre-LBO Forecasts and the Post-LBO Forecasts.

P15.10 **Adjusted Present Value Valuation of the LBO Transaction—H. Stauffer Company:** use the information in Problems 15.6 through 15.8 and the following information for this question. Assume the company's unlevered cost of capital is equal to 12%; as of the end of Year 10, the company will recapitalize its capital structure to 20% debt and 80% common equity. In addition, assume that all of its cash flows will grow at 3% in perpetuity as of the end of Year 11 and that the appropriate discount rate for interest tax shields is equal to weighted average the cost of debt for Years 1 through 10 (and the unlevered cost of capital afterward for Year 11 onward).

a. Measure the year-by-year APV valuation of the LBO transaction using the Pre-LBO Forecasts.

b. Measure the year-by-year APV valuation of the LBO transaction using the Post-LBO Forecasts.

c. Measure the value of the interest tax shields using the unlevered cost of capital to discount all interest tax shields using the Post-LBO Forecasts.

P15.11 **Post-LBO Equity and Weighted Average Costs of Capital—H. Stauffer Company:** Use the information in Problems 15.6 through 15.10 to measure the year-by-year post-LBO equity and weighted average costs of capital based on the Post-LBO forecasts. Use these costs of capital to measure the value of the firm (using the WACC valuation method) and the value of the equity (using the equity DCF valuation method).

Solution for Review Exercise 15.1: Sources and Uses, Capital Structure, and Deal Terms

		Market Multiples			
		P/E	EBIT	EBITDA	Revenue
Current stock price	$16.00	14.91	10.08	7.05	2.12
Deal premium	25.0%				
Deal stock price	$20.00	18.64	11.87	8.31	2.49
Number of fully diluted shares outstanding	108.8	million			
Purchase price of equity	$2,176.0	million			

Pre-LBO Outstanding Options as of End of Year 0 (Liquidation of Options)

Year Issued	Exercise Price	Number of Options = Shares Issued (m)	Buyback Shares (m)	Net Increase in Shares (m)
Various	$11.20	20.0	11.2	8.8

Sources and Uses of Cash - LBO Financing ($ in millions)	Amount	%	Coupon = YTM	Maturity (Years)	Post-LBO Capital Structure	Common Shares Issued	Common Shares Issued (% Owned)	Warrants & Options Issued (% of Total Shares)	Fully Diluted Equity Allocation
Sources									
Excess cash	$34.61	1.2%							0.00%
Debt assumed	0.00	0.0%							0.00%
Revolver	100.00	3.4%	4.50%	5	3.40%				0.00%
Senior secured note (bank debt)	880.00	29.6%	5.00%	7	29.90%				0.00%
Subordinated note (unsecured debt)	410.00	13.8%	9.00%	9	13.93%				0.00%
Mezzanine debt	670.00	22.5%	11.00%	10	22.76%			5.00%	5.00%
Preferred stock—assumed	0.00	0.0%							0.00%
Preferred stock—new	0.00	0.0%							0.00%
Common equity									
Sponsor investment	730.00	24.5%			24.80%	165.28	82.64%		75.12%
Management rollover	60.00	2.0%			2.04%	13.58	6.79%	1.60%	7.77%
Management new investment	93.33	3.1%			3.17%	21.13	10.57%	2.50%	12.10%
Total sources	$2,977.94	100.0%			100.00%	200.00	100.00%	9.10%	100.00%
Uses									
Common equity			Fee Rate	Total					
Non-management shares purchased	$2,116.00	71.1%							
Management rollover	60.00	2.0%							
Preferred stock—assumed	0.00	0.0%							
Preferred stock— redeemed	100.00	3.4%							
Debt assumed	0.00	0.0%							
Debt redeemed	600.00	20.1%							
Financing fees—debt	58.80	2.0%	3.00%	$300.0	Debt without Revolver - Amortize				
Financing fees—revolver	0.00	0.0%	0.50%		Expense Annually as Incurred				
Sponsor fees	28.76	1.0%	1.00%		Based on deal value (deal cost) before fees				
Other fees and expenses	14.38	0.5%	0.50%		Based on deal value (deal cost) before fees				
Total uses	$2,977.94	100.0%							

Exhibit may contain small rounding errors

Solution for Review Exercise 15.2: Measuring the Internal Rates of Return

($ in millions)	EBITDA Multiple	Year 1	Year 2	Year 3	Year 4	Year 5	Year 6	Year 7	Year 8	Year 9	Year 10
EBITDA		$ 316.8	$ 424.2	$ 493.1	$ 566.8	$ 589.5	$ 613.1	$ 631.5	$ 588.5	$ 542.3	$ 492.9
Debt outstanding		$1,894.4	$1,702.5	$1,459.9	$1,222.6	$1,044.6	$ 842.3	$ 706.5	$ 688.7	$ 529.1	$ 393.1
Exit value—firm (using deal multiple)	8.310	$2,632.5	$3,525.4	$4,097.8	$4,710.3	$4,898.7	$5,094.7	$5,247.5	$4,890.2	$4,506.7	$4,095.8
Exit value—debt		1,894.4	1,702.5	1,459.9	1,222.6	1,044.6	842.3	706.5	688.7	529.1	393.1
Exit value—equity		$ 738.2	$1,822.9	$2,637.9	$3,487.7	$3,854.1	$4,252.3	$4,541.0	$4,201.5	$3,977.6	$3,702.7

Sponsor (% fully diluted participation in exit)											
Sponsor (% fully diluted participation in exit)	75.1%										
Investment	$-730.0										
Fees	$ 28.8										
Dividends	None										
Other payments	None										
Participation in exit		$ 554.5	$1,369.4	$1,981.6	$2,620.0	$2,895.3	$3,194.4	$3,411.3	$3,156.2	$2,988.0	$2,781.5
Net cash flow	$-701.2	$ 554.5	$1,369.4	$1,981.6	$2,620.0	$2,895.3	$3,194.4	$3,411.3	$3,156.2	$2,988.0	$2,781.5

IRR	Exit Yr		Year 1	Year 2	Year 3	Year 4	Year 5	Year 6	Year 7	Year 8	Year 9	Year 10
-20.9%	Year 1	$-701.2	$ 554.5									
39.7%	Year 2	-701.2	0.0	$1,369.4								
41.4%	Year 3	-701.2	0.0	0.0	$1,981.6							
39.0%	Year 4	-701.2	0.0	0.0	0.0	$2,620.0						
32.8%	Year 5	-701.2	0.0	0.0	0.0	0.0	$2,895.3					
28.8%	Year 6	-701.2	0.0	0.0	0.0	0.0	0.0	$3,194.4				
25.4%	Year 7	-701.2	0.0	0.0	0.0	0.0	0.0	0.0	$3,411.3			
20.7%	Year 8	-701.2	0.0	0.0	0.0	0.0	0.0	0.0	0.0	$3,156.2		
17.5%	Year 9	-701.2	0.0	0.0	0.0	0.0	0.0	0.0	0.0	0.0	$2,988.0	
14.8%	Year 10	-701.2	0.0	0.0	0.0	0.0	0.0	0.0	0.0	0.0	0.0	$2,781.5

Exhibit may contain small rounding errors

($ in millions)

Management

		Year 1	Year 2	Year 3	Year 4	Year 5	Year 6	Year 7	Year 8	Year 9	Year 10
Management (% fully diluted participation in exit)	19.9%										
Investment	$-153.3										
Fees	None										
Dividends	None										
Other payments	None										
Participation in exit		$146.7	$362.4	$524.4	$693.3	$766.2	$845.3	$902.7	$835.2	$790.7	$736.0
Net cash flow	$-153.3	$146.7	$362.4	$524.4	$693.3	$766.2	$845.3	$902.7	$835.2	$790.7	$736.0

IRR	Exit Yr		Year 1	Year 2	Year 3	Year 4	Year 5	Year 6	Year 7	Year 8	Year 9	Year 10
-4.3%	Year 1	$-153.3	$146.7									
53.7%	Year 2	-153.3	0.0	$362.4								
50.7%	Year 3	-153.3	0.0	0.0	$524.4							
45.8%	Year 4	-153.3	0.0	0.0	0.0	$693.3						
38.0%	Year 5	-153.3	0.0	0.0	0.0	0.0	$766.2					
32.9%	Year 6	-153.3	0.0	0.0	0.0	0.0	0.0	$845.3				
28.8%	Year 7	-153.3	0.0	0.0	0.0	0.0	0.0	0.0	$902.7			
23.6%	Year 8	-153.3	0.0	0.0	0.0	0.0	0.0	0.0	0.0	$835.2		
20.0%	Year 9	-153.3	0.0	0.0	0.0	0.0	0.0	0.0	0.0	0.0	$790.7	
17.0%	Year 10	-153.3	0.0	0.0	0.0	0.0	0.0	0.0	0.0	0.0	0.0	$736.0

($ in millions)

Mezzanine debt

		Year 1	Year 2	Year 3	Year 4	Year 5	Year 6	Year 7	Year 8	Year 9	Year 10
Mezzanine debt (% fully diluted participation in exit)	5.0%										
Investment	$-670.0										
Fees	None										
Interest paid		$ 73.7	$ 73.7	$ 73.7	$ 73.7	$ 73.7	$ 73.7	$ 73.7	$ 73.7	$ 73.7	$ 58.2
Repayment of principal		670.0	670.0	670.0	670.0	670.0	670.0	670.0	670.0	670.0	529.1
Participation in exit		36.9	91.1	131.9	174.4	192.7	212.6	227.1	210.1	198.9	185.1
Net cash flow	$-670.0	$780.6	$834.8	$875.6	$918.1	$936.4	$956.3	$970.8	$953.8	$942.6	$772.4

IRR	Exit Yr		Year 1	Year 2	Year 3	Year 4	Year 5	Year 6	Year 7	Year 8	Year 9	Year 10
16.5%	Year 1	$-670.0	$780.6									
17.3%	Year 2	-670.0	73.7	$834.8								
16.6%	Year 3	-670.0	73.7	73.7	$875.6							
16.1%	Year 4	-670.0	73.7	73.7	$73.7	$918.1						
15.2%	Year 5	-670.0	73.7	73.7	73.7	73.7	$936.4					
14.7%	Year 6	-670.0	73.7	73.7	73.7	73.7	73.7	$956.3				
14.1%	Year 7	-670.0	73.7	73.7	73.7	73.7	73.7	73.7	$970.8			
13.4%	Year 8	-670.0	73.7	73.7	73.7	73.7	73.7	73.7	73.7	$953.8		
12.9%	Year 9	-670.0	73.7	73.7	73.7	73.7	73.7	73.7	73.7	73.7	$942.6	
12.6%	Year 10	-670.0	73.7	73.7	73.7	73.7	73.7	73.7	73.7	73.7	214.6	$772.4

Solution for Review Exercise 15.4: Adjusted Present Value Valuation of the LBO Transaction

($ in millions)	Total	Year 0	Year 1	Year 2	Year 3	Year 4	Year 5	Year 6	Year 7	Year 8	Year 9	Year 10	Year 11
Debt rating			B	B	B	BB	BBB	BBB	BBB	BBB	BBB	BBB	BBB
Debt cost of capital for unsecured debt			7.70%	7.70%	7.70%	6.60%	5.90%	5.90%	5.90%	5.90%	5.90%	5.90%	5.90%
Balance at Year End												Debt Recapitalization	
Revolver (total commitment in 1st column)		$ 100.0	$ 0.0	$ 0.0	$ 0.0	$ 0.0	$ 0.0	$ 0.0	$ 0.0	$ 0.0	$ 0.0		
Debt assumed		0.0	0.0	0.0	0.0	0.0	0.0	0.0	0.0	0.0	0.0		
Senior secured note (bank debt)		880.0	814.4	622.5	379.9	142.6	0.0	0.0	0.0	0.0	0.0		
Subordinated note (unsecured debt)		410.0	410.0	410.0	410.0	410.0	374.6	172.3	36.5	18.7	0.0		
Mezzanine debt		670.0	670.0	670.0	670.0	670.0	670.0	670.0	670.0	670.0	529.1		
All debt issued at par	$2,060.0		$1,894.4	$1,702.5	$1,459.9	$1,222.6	$1,044.6	$842.3	$706.5	$688.7	$529.1	$815.1	$839.5

Expected Interest Deduction (Based on r_D)	Cost of Debt	Fee	Year 1	Year 2	Year 3	Year 4	Year 5	Year 6	Year 7	Year 8	Year 9	Year 10	Year 11
Revolver	4.500%	0.5%	$ 6.0	$ 1.5	$ 1.5	$ 1.5	$ 1.5	$ 0.0	$ 0.0	$ 0.0	$ 0.0	$ 0.0	
Debt assumed			0.0	0.0	0.0	0.0	0.0	0.0	0.0	0.0	0.0	0.0	
Senior secured note (bank debt)	5.000%		44.0	40.7	31.1	19.0	7.1	0.0	0.0	0.0	0.0	0.0	
Subordinated note (unsecured debt)	Rating-based rate		31.6	31.6	31.6	27.1	24.2	22.1	10.2	2.2	1.1	0.0	
Mezzanine debt	Rating based rate		51.6	51.6	51.6	44.2	39.5	39.5	39.5	39.5	39.5	31.2	
Expected cash interest expense			$133.2	$125.4	$115.8	$91.8	$72.3	$61.6	$49.7	$41.7	$40.6	$31.2	$48.1
Amortization of fees			7.1	7.1	7.1	7.1	7.1	7.1	7.1	3.4	3.4	2.0	0.0
Expected interest tax deduction			$140.3	$132.5	$122.9	$98.9	$79.5	$68.8	$56.8	$45.1	$44.0	$33.2	$48.1
Weighted average cost of debt			6.46%	6.62%	6.80%	6.29%	5.92%	5.90%	5.90%	5.90%	5.90%	5.90%	5.90%
Interest tax shield			$56.1	$53.0	$49.2	$39.6	$31.8	$27.5	$22.7	$18.0	$17.6	$13.3	$19.2

Exhibit may contain small rounding errors

Below the calculation of the debt recapitalization at the end of Year 10 is presented:

Continuing Value Using WACC Method ($ in millions)	CV Year 10
Unlevered free cash flow for continuing value (Year 11)	$ 176.4
Discount factor for continuing value	18.48
Continuing value of the firm	$3,260.2
Debt to value ratio for continuing value	25.0%
Amount of debt as of continuing value date	$ 815.1
Debt cost of capital and interest rate for continuing value	5.9%
Interest in Year 11.	$48.1
Income tax rate for interest	40.0%
Interest tax shield in Year 11	$ 19.2
Amount of debt as of continuing value date	$ 815.1
Debt in the forecasts at the continuing value date.	529.1
Debt issued (redeemed) at the continuing value date	$ 286.0
Continuing value of the firm	$3,260.2
Preferred stock to firm value	0%
Value of preferred stock as of continuing value date.	$ 0.0
Amount of preferred stock as of continuing value date	$ 0.0
Preferred stock in the forecasts at the continuing value date	0.0
Preferred stock issued (redeemed) at the continuing value date.	$ 0.0
Continuing value of the firm	$3,260.2
Common equity to firm value.	75%
Value of common equity as of continuing value date.	$2,445.2

Exhibit may contain small rounding errors

Interest Tax Shields discounted at r_D through Year 10 and at r_{UA} after Year 10:

Adjusted Present Value Valuation ($ in millions)	Year 0	Year 1	Year 2	Year 3	Year 4	Year 5	Year 6	Year 7	Year 8	Year 9	Year 10	CV Year 10
Value of the Unlevered Firm												
Unlevered free cash flow for continuing value												$ 176.4
Discount factor for continuing value												16.667
Unlevered free cash flow and continuing value		$259.1	$280.7	$325.7	$313.1	$246.7	$263.8	$186.5	$62.7	$203.4	$170.1	$2,939.6
Discount factor		0.917	0.842	0.772	0.708	0.650	0.596	0.547	0.502	0.460	0.422	0.422
Discounted value		$237.7	$236.3	$251.5	$221.8	$160.3	$157.3	$102.0	$31.4	$93.7	$71.8	$1,241.7
Value of the unlevered firm	$2,805.7											
Value of the Interest Tax Shields												
Interest tax shield for continuing value												$ 19.2
Discount factor for continuing value												16.667
Interest tax shield and continuing value of ITS		$ 56.1	$ 53.0	$ 49.2	$ 39.6	$ 31.8	$ 27.5	$ 22.7	$18.0	$ 17.6	$ 13.3	$ 320.6
Discount factor (r_D and r_{UA})		0.939	0.881	0.825	0.776	0.733	0.692	0.653	0.617	0.583	0.550	0.422
Present value		$ 52.7	$ 46.7	$ 40.6	$ 30.7	$ 23.3	$ 19.0	$ 14.9	$11.1	$ 10.3	$ 7.3	$ 135.4
Value of the interest tax shields	$ 392.0											
Value of the firm V_F w/o excess assets	$3,197.7											

Net Present Value of Investment	Firm Value		Equity Value	
Value	$3,197.7		$1,137.7	
Purchase price paid (sources – excess cash)	2,943.3		883.3	
Net present value of investment	$ 254.3	8.0%	$ 254.3	22.4%

Exhibit may contain small rounding errors

continued

Continued from previous page

All Interest Tax Shields discounted at r_{UA}:

Adjusted Present Value Valuation ($ in millions)	Year 0	Year 1	Year 2	Year 3	Year 4	Year 5	Year 6	Year 7	Year 8	Year 9	Year 10	CV Year 10
Value of the Unlevered Firm												
Unlevered free cash flow for continuing value												$ 176.4
Discount factor for continuing value												16.667
Unlevered free cash flow and continuing value		$259.1	$280.7	$325.7	$313.1	$246.7	$263.8	$186.5	$62.7	$203.4	$170.1	$2,939.6
Discount factor		0.917	0.842	0.772	0.708	0.650	0.596	0.547	0.502	0.460	0.422	0.422
Discounted value		$237.7	$236.3	$251.5	$221.8	$160.3	$157.3	$102.0	$31.4	$93.7	$71.8	$1,241.7
Value of the unlevered firm	$2,805.7											
Value of the Interest Tax Shields												
Interest tax shield for continuing value												$ 19.2
Discount factor for continuing value												16.667
Interest tax shield and continuing value of ITS		$ 56.1	$ 53.0	$ 49.2	$ 39.6	$ 31.8	$ 27.5	$ 22.7	$18.0	$ 17.6	$ 13.3	$ 320.6
Discount factor (r_{UA})		0.917	0.842	0.772	0.708	0.650	0.596	0.547	0.502	0.460	0.422	0.422
Present value		$ 51.5	$ 44.6	$ 38.0	$ 28.0	$ 20.7	$ 16.4	$ 12.4	$ 9.0	$ 8.1	$ 5.6	$ 135.4
Value of the interest tax shields	$ 369.8											
Value of the firm V_F w/o excess assets	$3,175.5											
Change in value of interest tax shields		$369.8	$392.0	$–22.2								

Net Present Value of Investment

	$r_{ITS} = r_{UA}$	$r_{ITS} = r_D, r_{UA}$
	Firm Value	Firm Value
Value	$3,175.5	$3,197.7
Purchase price paid (sources – excess cash)	2,943.3	2,943.3
Net present value of investment	$ 232.2	$ 254.3 $–22.2

	$r_{ITS} = r_{UA}$	$r_{ITS} = r_D, r_{UA}$
	Equity Value	Equity Value
Value	$1,115.5	$1,137.7
Purchase price paid (sources – excess cash)	883.3	883.3
Net present value of investment	$ 232.2	$ 254.3 $–22.2

Exhibit may contain small rounding errors

Solution for Review Exercise 15.5: Post-LBO Equity and Weighted Average Costs of Capital

Beginning of Year Value ($ in millions)	Year 1	Year 2	Year 3	Year 4	Year 5	Year 6	Year 7	Year 8	Year 9	Year 10	CV Year 10
Value of the Unlevered Firm											
Unlevered free cash flow for continuing value											$ 176.4
Discount factor for continuing value											16.667
Unlevered free cash flow	$ 259.1	$ 280.7	$ 325.7	$ 313.1	$ 246.7	$ 263.8	$ 186.5	$ 62.7	$ 203.4	$ 170.1	
Value of the firm at end of year	2,799.1	2,770.3	2,693.9	2,623.3	2,612.7	2,584.0	2,630.0	2,804.1	2,853.0	2,939.6	2,939.6
V_F + unlevered free cash flow	$3,058.2	$3,051.0	$3,019.6	$2,936.4	$2,859.4	$2,847.8	$2,816.6	$2,866.7	$3,056.4	$3,109.7	
Discount factor for one year	0.917	0.917	0.917	0.917	0.917	0.917	0.917	0.917	0.917	0.917	
Value of the firm at beginning of year	$2,805.7	$2,799.1	$2,770.3	$2,693.9	$2,623.3	$2,612.7	$2,584.0	$2,630.0	$2,804.1	$2,853.0	
Value of the Interest Tax Shields Discounted at the Debt Cost of Capital											
Interest tax shield	$ 56.1	$ 53.0	$ 49.2	$ 39.6	$ 31.8	$ 27.5	$ 22.7	$ 18.0	$ 17.6	$ 13.3	13.3
Value of the interest tax shields (ITSs) at end of year	217.0	178.4	141.3	110.7	85.4	62.9	43.9	28.5	12.5	0.0	0.0
Value of the ITSs at end of year plus ITS	$ 273.2	$ 231.4	$ 190.5	$ 150.2	$ 117.2	$ 90.4	$ 66.6	$ 46.5	$ 30.2	$ 13.3	
Discount factor for one year	0.939	0.938	0.936	0.941	0.944	0.944	0.944	0.944	0.944	0.944	
Value of the ITSs at beginning of year	$ 256.6	$ 217.0	$ 178.4	$ 141.3	$ 110.7	$ 85.4	$ 62.9	$ 43.9	$ 28.5	$ 12.5	$ 0.0
Value of the Interest Tax Shields Discounted at the Unlevered Cost of Capital											
Interest tax shield for continuing value											$ 19.2
Discount factor for continuing value											16.667
Value of the ITSs at end of year plus ITS	$ 147.6	$ 160.9	$ 175.4	$ 191.2	$ 208.4	$ 227.1	$ 247.6	$ 269.8	$ 294.1	$ 320.6	$ 320.6
Discount factor for one year	0.917	0.917	0.917	0.917	0.917	0.917	0.917	0.917	0.917	0.917	
Value of the ITSs at beginning of year	$ 135.4	$ 147.6	$ 160.9	$ 175.4	$ 191.2	$ 208.4	$ 227.1	$ 247.6	$ 269.8	$ 294.1	
Value of interest tax shields at beginning of year	$ 392.0	$ 364.6	$ 339.3	$ 316.7	$ 301.8	$ 293.8	$ 290.0	$ 291.5	$ 298.3	$ 306.7	$ 320.6
Value of the firm at beginning of year	$3,197.7	$3,163.7	$3,109.6	$3,010.6	$2,925.1	$2,906.5	$2,874.0	$2,921.5	$3,102.4	$3,159.6	$3,260.2

Exhibit may contain small rounding errors

continued

As of the Beginning of Year ($ in millions)	Year 1	Year 2	Year 3	Year 4	Year 5	Year 6	Year 7	Year 8	Year 9	Year 10	Year 11
Value of the firm (V_F)	$3,197.7	$3,163.7	$3,109.6	$3,010.6	$2,925.1	$2,906.5	$2,874.0	$2,921.5	$3,102.4	$3,159.6	$3,260.2
Value of debt (V_D)	2,060.0	1,894.4	1,702.5	1,459.9	1,222.6	1,044.6	842.3	706.5	688.7	529.1	815.1
Value of equity (V_E)	$1,137.7	$1,269.3	$1,407.1	$1,550.7	$1,702.5	$1,861.9	$2,031.7	$2,215.0	$2,413.7	$2,630.6	$2,445.2
Debt to equity ratio	1.811	1.492	1.210	0.941	0.718	0.561	0.415	0.319	0.285	0.201	0.333
Present value of interest tax shields discounted at r_D	$ 256.6	$ 217.0	$ 178.4	$ 141.3	$ 110.7	$ 85.4	$ 62.9	$ 43.9	$ 28.5	$ 12.5	$ 0
Value of debt—value of ITS	$1,803.4	$1,677.3	$1,524.1	$1,318.5	$1,111.9	$ 959.2	$ 779.4	$ 662.6	$ 660.2	$ 516.5	$ 815.1
Adjusted debt to common equity ratio	1.585	1.321	1.083	0.850	0.653	0.515	0.384	0.299	0.274	0.196	0.333

	Year 1	Year 2	Year 3	Year 4	Year 5	Year 6	Year 7	Year 8	Year 9	Year 10	Year 11
Unlevered cost of capital, r_U	9.00%	9.00%	9.00%	9.00%	9.00%	9.00%	9.00%	9.00%	9.00%	9.00%	9.00%
Debt cost of capital, r_D	6.46%	6.62%	6.80%	6.29%	5.92%	5.90%	5.90%	5.90%	5.90%	5.90%	5.90%
Adjusted debt to common equity ratio	1.585	1.321	1.083	0.850	0.653	0.515	0.384	0.299	0.274	0.196	0.333
Equity cost of capital, r_E	13.02%	12.15%	11.38%	11.31%	11.01%	10.60%	10.19%	9.93%	9.85%	9.61%	10.03%
Equity beta	1.503	1.358	1.230	1.218	1.169	1.100	1.032	0.988	0.975	0.935	1.006
Geometric average equity cost of capital to exit year	13.02%	12.58%	12.18%	11.96%	11.77%	11.57%	11.38%	11.19%	11.04%	10.90%	10.82%

($ in millions)	Year 1	Year 2	Year 3	Year 4	Year 5	Year 6	Year 7	Year 8	Year 9	Year 10	Year 11
Equity cost of capital, r_E	13.02%	12.15%	11.38%	11.31%	11.01%	10.60%	10.19%	9.93%	9.85%	9.61%	10.03%
Equity to firm value	35.58%	40.12%	45.25%	51.51%	58.20%	64.06%	70.69%	75.82%	77.80%	83.26%	75.00%
Debt cost of capital, r_D	6.46%	6.62%	6.80%	6.29%	5.92%	5.90%	5.90%	5.90%	5.90%	5.90%	5.90%
Debt to firm value	64.42%	59.88%	54.75%	48.49%	41.80%	35.94%	29.31%	24.18%	22.20%	16.74%	25.00%
Income tax rate, T_{INT}	42.15%	42.28%	42.47%	43.12%	43.95%	44.64%	45.75%	43.24%	43.32%	42.58%	40.00%
Weighted average cost of capital, r_{WACC}	7.04%	7.16%	7.29%	7.56%	7.80%	7.96%	8.14%	8.34%	8.40%	8.57%	8.41%
Present value weighted average growth rate	-1.06%	-1.71%	-3.18%	-2.84%	-0.64%	-1.12%	1.65%	6.19%	1.85%	3.18%	3.00%

Geometric average weighted average cost of capital, r_{WACC} = 7.88%

Exhibit may contain small rounding errors

After mastering the material in this chapter, you will be able to:

1. Understand the motivations for mergers and acquisitions and whether or not, on average, they create value (16.1–16.3)

2. Identify and value synergies (16.4)

3. Value and analyze an M&A deal (16.5–16.8, 16.10)

4. Measure a negotiation range (16.9)

Mergers and Acquisitions

16

On February 17, 2004, **Cingular Wireless LLC** announced an agreement to acquire **AT&T Wireless** for $41 billion, which was the largest merger on record as of that date.[1] At the time, Cingular Wireless LLC was not publicly traded, but rather, it was jointly owned by SBC and Bell South. As of the closing of the merger, each share of AT&T Wireless common stock outstanding was converted into the right to receive $15.00 in cash (its stock was trading in the $7 range before any rumors of the merger started). Did the market believe that this merger created value? On the days on which the company made key announcements, the market capitalization of AT&T Wireless increased by $8.8 billion; however, the combined market capitalization of SBC and BellSouth decreased by $2.7 billion, resulting in a net increase in combined value of $6.1 billion (all comparisons made on a market-adjusted basis). Clearly, the market thought that this combination made economic sense given the value created by the deal; however, it is also clear that the market felt that Cingular had paid too much for AT&T Wireless.

CINGULAR AND AT&T WIRELESS

In this chapter, we discuss mergers and acquisitions—why they take place, the evidence on value creation, and how to analyze and value an M&A deal.

---

[1] The "rumor" of this merger existed as early as November 2003, and on January 14, 2004, *Business Week* reported: "While no agreement is at hand, and talks could still fall apart over delicate issues such as price, the probability of the two companies combining is described as high—about 75%" (from BusinessWeek Online.com on January 14, 2004). See the investors section of the company's website for this and other announcements as well as various financial reports and U.S. Securities and Exchange Commission (SEC) disclosures at http://www.cingular.com/investors.

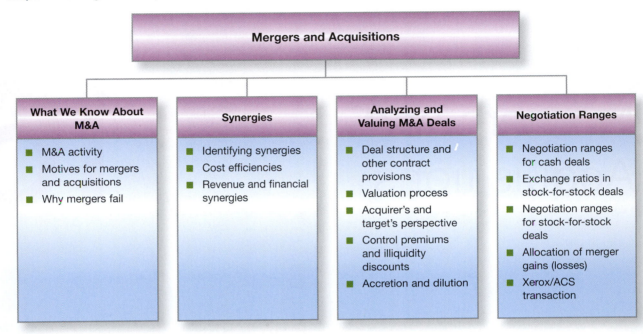

| Mergers and Acquisitions | | | |

What We Know About M&A	Synergies	Analyzing and Valuing M&A Deals	Negotiation Ranges
■ M&A activity ■ Motives for mergers and acquisitions ■ Why mergers fail	■ Identifying synergies ■ Cost efficiencies ■ Revenue and financial synergies	■ Deal structure and other contract provisions ■ Valuation process ■ Acquirer's and target's perspective ■ Control premiums and illiquidity discounts ■ Accretion and dilution	■ Negotiation ranges for cash deals ■ Exchange ratios in stock-for-stock deals ■ Negotiation ranges for stock-for-stock deals ■ Allocation of merger gains (losses) ■ Xerox/ACS transaction

INTRODUCTION

We use the term "merger and acquisition" (M&A) to describe a transaction in which a buyer or company (the **acquiring company** or **acquirer**) purchases another company (the **target company**). The acquirer can accomplish this purchase by either purchasing the target's assets directly or purchasing the target's stock from its shareholders.

An **asset acquisition** between the acquiring company and the target company typically involves the sale of a target's assets to the acquiring company. The acquirer may purchase the assets of the entire company, the assets of a subsidiary or division of the company, or only specific assets of the company. The acquirer may also assume some, or sometimes all, of the liabilities and other obligations associated with the assets acquired.

A **stock acquisition** involves the sale of stock from the shareholders of the target company to the acquiring company. In a stock acquisition, the acquirer may purchase less than 100% of the target's stock. If the acquirer purchases more than 50% of the voting interest in a company, the acquirer will own a **controlling interest**. With more than 50% of the target company's voting power, the owner of the controlling interest typically has the power to make all decisions for the company, and thus has control over the company's activities.

In this chapter, we discuss how M&A transactions can create value, the evidence on whether or not M&A transactions create value and for whom, what factors determine an M&A transaction's success or failure, various aspects of deal structure, and how to analyze an M&A transaction. Our analysis of M&A transactions includes how to value them, how to determine if a transaction is **accretive** (increases) or **dilutive** (decreases) to earnings per share and a company's price-earnings multiple, how the gains are shared in a merger, and analyzing **exchange ratios** (the number of shares of the acquirer given for every target share in a stock-for-stock transaction). We then illustrate the valuation issues related to M&A transactions with a specific example—the acquisition of Affiliated Computer Services, Inc. by Xerox Corporation.

16.1 WHAT DO WE KNOW ABOUT MERGER AND ACQUISITION TRANSACTIONS?

LO1 Understand the motivations for mergers and acquisitions and whether or not, on average, they create value

As we will soon document, the number and size of M&A transactions vary over time and across global regions. Regardless of the country, M&A transactions are more common during certain time periods than others. Various scholars document the existence of such merger waves. These studies show that merger waves depend on various industry and macroeconomic circumstances. The United States, the United Kingdom and countries that comprise the European Union have historically been the dominant countries for both the number and value of M&A transactions; however, more recently, M&A transactions have become more common in other countries. In addition, because of globalization, **cross-border M&A** transactions (where the acquirer and target are headquartered in different countries) have increased in importance as well. We discuss cross-border valuation explicitly in Chapter 17.

In the remainder of this section, we present descriptive characteristics of M&A transactions by global region. Using the merger database from FactSet,[2] we select transactions that were either completed or pending between 1996 and 2010 with a value (enterprise value) of at least $10 million, which includes both publicly traded and privately held acquirers and targets. We provide descriptive information on the number and enterprise value of transactions for 13 countries and geographic regions. These countries/regions include Africa, Australia, Canada, China, China—Hong Kong, the European Union (E.U.), Japan, Latin America, the Middle East, the United Kingdom (U.K.), the United States (U.S.), Asia—Other, and Europe—Other (the last two of which include all countries in their respective regions other than those listed separately).[3] Based on these criteria, we initially examine 44,317 completed public and private M&A transactions that resulted in either 100% ownership of the target or a majority ownership of the target.

Time-Series of Merger and Acquisition Transactions

Historically, M&A transactions were most common in the U.S., the U.K., and the countries that comprise the E.U., but were less common in other countries. In Exhibit 16.1, we present descriptive information on the time-series of the frequency and size (enterprise value) of M&A transactions for the 13 regions based on the location of the acquiring companies. This exhibit has two panels. The top panel presents the number of transactions for each region, and the bottom panel presents the sum of the enterprise values for all transactions in each region. Both the number and size of the transactions vary over time and across regions.

The number of transactions during this period peaked in 1997 (almost 5,000 transactions). In that year, the U.S. and U.K. had a large number of M&A transactions related to the "dot.com" phenomenon.[4] Even though 1997 was the peak year for the number of transactions, it was not, however, the peak year for the total value of the transactions. In 1997, the total value of the transactions was $1.7 trillion—a value that was surpassed in eight other years in this time period. The peak years in terms of the value of global transactions were 2006 and 2007 (each with a value of $2.7 trillion) followed closely by 2000 and 2008. The Internet and technology frenzy from 1997 to 2001 drove M&A activity for that period. The time period from 2004 through 2008 was an era of tremendous liquidity and low interest rates, both of which drove M&A activity for that period. Finally, if we look at the numbers for 2009, we can see evidence of the economic and financial crisis that unfolded in the fall of 2008 as M&A activity dropped significantly from 2008 to 2009. Because of such events like the ones just described, neither the number of transactions nor the size of the transactions indicates a clear upward or downward trend, which is consistent with the existence of merger waves that are dependent on various industry and macroeconomic circumstances. For example, deregulation may release backlogged acquisition demand, technological innovation may require asset reallocations, liquidity in the capital markets may make capital more accessible, and higher-than-average market valuations (and possible overvaluations) may drive companies to use stock to purchase other companies.[5]

Globally, the U.S. had the largest number and value of M&A transactions over this entire period. On average, the U.S. was responsible for 46% of the transactions and 41% of the value of the transactions. In 2010, these percentages were 36% and 28%, respectively. No other country or region had more than 30% of the number or value of M&A transactions during this time period, and the two closest countries/regions to the U.S. were the E.U. and the U.K.

---

[2] We report results from FactSet Research Systems Inc. (FactSet), which is a U.S. financial data and software company. The data we report are summary data from the FactSet Mergers database, which combines data from FactSet's Mergerstat and MergerMetrics products.

[3] To clarify, Latin American Countries are any countries in the Americas that are not the United States or Canada. Europe—Other represents all Eastern and Western European countries that are not in the European Union.

[4] See, for example, Goldfarb, B., D. Kirsch, and D. A. Miller, "Was There Too Little Entry During the Dot Com Era?" *Journal of Financial Economics* vol. 86, no. 1 (October 2007), pp. 100–144.

[5] See, for example, Shleifer, A., and R. Vishny, "Stock Market Driven Acquisitions," *Journal of Financial Economics* 70 (2003), pp. 295–311; Rhodes-Kropf, M., and S. Viswanathan, "Market Valuation and Merger Waves," *The Journal of Finance* vol. 24, no. 6 (December 2004), pp. 2685–2718; and Harford, J., "What Drives Merger Waves?" *Journal of Financial Economics* 77 (2005), pp. 529–560.

EXHIBIT 16.1 Time-Series of Number of and Value of Merger Transactions for Global Regions by Acquiring Company

Number of Transactions	1996	1997	1998	1999	2000	2001	2002	2003	2004	2005	2006	2007	2008	2009	2010	% 2010	Total	% Total
Africa	3	10	10	19	20	10	11	20	23	22	26	48	33	14	29	1%	298	1%
Asia—Other	7	18	8	21	42	27	54	104	149	182	197	220	174	118	218	8%	1,539	3%
Australia	9	22	12	15	25	60	59	75	84	113	182	227	110	77	133	5%	1,203	3%
Canada	31	84	43	57	199	131	118	104	172	205	263	278	182	142	213	8%	2,222	5%
China	0	0	0	0	4	6	4	18	38	32	68	97	93	97	151	6%	608	1%
China—Hong Kong	2	8	2	4	8	11	11	21	41	61	45	112	65	47	51	2%	489	1%
Europe—Other	21	80	48	69	81	69	85	88	71	117	140	171	119	61	96	4%	1,316	3%
European Union	138	434	291	534	656	454	360	288	294	439	567	677	463	233	284	11%	6,112	14%
Japan	7	12	6	11	30	29	64	66	127	158	159	180	126	136	121	5%	1,232	3%
Latin America	7	14	23	20	54	45	31	59	59	76	122	163	148	121	156	6%	1,066	2%
Middle East	5	8	7	7	19	5	10	6	22	36	50	52	48	25	31	1%	331	1%
United Kingdom	592	1,348	738	682	670	433	356	292	348	445	455	545	322	139	210	8%	7,575	17%
United States	1,199	2,940	1,670	1,776	1,815	1,104	905	929	1,183	1,344	1,548	1,447	924	571	971	36%	20,326	46%
Total	2,021	4,978	2,858	3,215	3,623	2,384	2,068	2,038	2,611	3,230	3,822	4,217	2,807	1,781	2,664	100%	44,317	100%

Enterprise Value ($ in billions USD)	1996	1997	1998	1999	2000	2001	2002	2003	2004	2005	2006	2007	2008	2009	2010	% 2010	Total	% Total
Africa	$ 2	$ 1	$ 2	$ 2	$ 2	$ 1	$ 5	$ 13	$ 14	$ 4	$ 15	$ 46	$ 4	$ 2	$ 8	0%	$ 122	0%
Asia—Other	0	8	2	8	8	12	10	73	46	57	101	87	43	54	382	22%	891	3%
Australia	3	15	7	12	17	24	20	24	45	67	72	153	93	8	88	5%	647	2%
Canada	5	16	20	40	64	47	29	37	42	47	101	112	49	54	70	4%	732	3%
China	0	0	0	0	0	0	0	2	4	7	29	10	95	30	33	2%	211	1%
China—Hong Kong	0	0	0	0	39	1	2	2	6	19	8	32	12	12	18	1%	151	1%
Europe—Other	7	115	27	31	95	81	21	40	29	78	76	124	158	55	150	9%	1,085	4%
European Union	53	295	261	547	715	596	696	240	649	701	909	928	472	227	208	12%	7,498	28%
Japan	3	5	2	2	45	28	19	42	165	71	115	142	109	84	83	5%	914	3%
Latin America	3	1	5	21	32	11	15	12	18	15	111	92	33	42	135	8%	546	2%
Middle East	1	2	1	1	1	1	1	4	1	19	32	34	23	7	11	1%	139	1%
United Kingdom	74	145	228	465	374	160	179	75	98	140	142	183	573	28	50	3%	2,915	11%
United States	352	1,068	1,099	1,022	1,225	656	260	363	636	769	956	747	940	443	474	28%	11,010	41%
Total	$503	$1,671	$1,654	$2,150	$2,617	$1,619	$1,258	$926	$1,754	$1,993	$2,666	$2,691	$2,604	$1,048	$1,709	100%	$26,862	100%

Acquirer Region

In Exhibit 16.2, we present a measure of regional year-by-year market share of the total value of global M&A transactions. We measure this market share metric as the value of the transactions in that country or region in a given year, divided by the total market value of the transactions in that year. If we look from the beginning to the end of this time-series, we observe that the market shares of both the U.S. and U.K. decreased over this period while the market shares of the countries and regions in much of Asia (including Australia, China, Asia—Other, and Japan) and Latin America increased. Of course, there was little (if any) M&A activity in these regions at the start of this period.

EXHIBIT 16.2	"Market Share" of Enterprise Value of Merger Transactions for Global Regions														

"Market Share"	1996	1997	1998	1999	2000	2001	2002	2003	2004	2005	2006	2007	2008	2009	2010
Africa	0%	0%	0%	0%	0%	0%	0%	1%	1%	0%	1%	2%	0%	0%	0%
Asia—Other	0%	0%	0%	0%	0%	1%	1%	8%	3%	3%	4%	3%	2%	5%	22%
Australia	1%	1%	0%	1%	1%	1%	2%	3%	3%	3%	3%	6%	4%	1%	5%
Canada	1%	1%	1%	2%	2%	3%	2%	4%	2%	2%	4%	4%	2%	5%	4%
China	0%	0%	0%	0%	0%	0%	0%	0%	0%	0%	1%	0%	4%	3%	2%
China—Hong Kong	0%	0%	0%	0%	1%	0%	0%	0%	0%	1%	0%	1%	0%	1%	1%
Europe—Other	1%	7%	2%	1%	4%	5%	2%	4%	2%	4%	3%	5%	6%	5%	9%
European Union	11%	18%	16%	25%	27%	37%	55%	26%	37%	35%	34%	34%	18%	22%	12%
Japan	1%	0%	0%	0%	2%	2%	2%	4%	9%	4%	4%	5%	4%	8%	5%
Latin America	1%	0%	0%	1%	1%	1%	1%	1%	1%	1%	4%	3%	1%	4%	8%
Middle East	0%	0%	0%	0%	0%	0%	0%	0%	0%	1%	1%	1%	1%	1%	1%
United Kingdom	15%	9%	14%	22%	14%	10%	14%	8%	6%	7%	5%	7%	22%	3%	3%
United States	70%	64%	66%	48%	47%	41%	21%	39%	36%	39%	36%	28%	36%	42%	28%
Total	100%	100%	100%	100%	100%	100%	100%	100%	100%	100%	100%	100%	100%	100%	100%

(Acquirer Region label appears vertically along the left side of the table)

Exhibit may contain small rounding errors

Cross-Border Merger and Acquisitions

One motivation for M&A transactions is global expansion (in other words, the acquirer moves its business into new regions of the world through acquisitions). An alternative global expansion strategy is to enter new countries through **organic growth** or **greenfield investments**. It turns out that acquiring companies is the dominant strategy, as approximately 80% to 90% of foreign direct investment from developing countries is in the form of acquisitions. Cross-border acquisitions, as a percentage of total global M&A activity, peaked at 44% in 2007 and were 40% in 2010. In Exhibit 16.3, we present the distribution of cross-border acquisitions based on enterprise value. In the top part of the exhibit, we anchor on acquirers, and we present cross-border acquisitions by acquirer country/region for the 1996 to 2010 time period. In the bottom part of the exhibit, we anchor on targets, and we present cross-border acquisitions by target country/region for the same time period. We will see that there are benefits to looking at both panels simultaneously. We will discuss a few countries/regions to help you understand the tables fully.

In the Middle Eastern region, the value of the targets purchased by Middle Eastern acquirers was 41% of the total value of targets acquired by Middle Eastern acquirers; the value of U.S. targets purchased by Middle Eastern acquirers in this region was 26% of the total value acquired (see top panel). While 41% of the value of the M&A targets of Middle Eastern acquirers was in the Middle East, these transactions represented 46% of the value of all of the targets acquired in the Middle East (see bottom panel). Of the non-Middle Eastern acquirers that purchased Middle Eastern companies, U.S. acquirers purchased 16% of the value of the Middle Eastern target companies, E.U. acquirers purchased 23% of the value of these targets, and acquirers in the Africa region (which is predominately South Africa) purchased 5%. In addition, 26% of the value of the acquisitions of Middle Eastern acquirers was made up of U.S. targets (top panel), but these targets represented only 0.3% of the value of all U.S. targets acquired during this time period (bottom panel).

In the U.S., 89% of the value of the targets of U.S. acquirers was attributable to U.S. targets; thus, only 11% of the value of the targets of U.S. acquirers was non-U.S. targets. European Union and U.K. targets were the next largest groups of targets acquired by U.S. acquirers, respectively representing 3.6%

and 2.6% of the value of the targets of U.S. acquirers. For U.S. targets (see the bottom panel), U.S. acquirers purchased 83% of the value of these target companies. Of the U.S. target companies purchased by non-U.S. acquirers, E.U. acquirers purchased 6% of the value of U.S. target companies, and U.K. acquirers purchased 4%.

EXHIBIT 16.3   Cross-Border Merger and Acquisition Transactions by the Global Region of the Acquirer and Target

Acquirer Region

Enterprise Value of Acquirer Transactions by Region	Africa	Asia—Other	Australia	Canada	China	China—Hong Kong	Europe—Other	European Union	Japan	Latin America	Middle East	United Kingdom	United States	Total
Africa	46.1%	2.0%	1.9%	0.7%	0.0%	0.1%	0.6%	2.0%	0.0%	0.6%	4.8%	39.5%	1.6%	100%
Asia—Other	0.2%	86.7%	2.1%	0.4%	0.6%	0.4%	1.0%	1.0%	0.3%	0.6%	0.1%	2.6%	4.0%	100%
Australia	0.2%	3.3%	54.8%	7.6%	0.0%	0.1%	0.1%	14.4%	0.1%	0.2%	0.0%	9.6%	9.6%	100%
Canada	0.3%	0.7%	3.7%	52.5%	0.1%	0.0%	1.0%	2.1%	0.0%	2.1%	0.0%	8.9%	28.7%	100%
China	0.0%	3.8%	1.3%	1.9%	51.2%	29.0%	8.0%	0.2%	0.1%	3.9%	0.0%	0.1%	0.5%	100%
China—Hong Kong	0.1%	12.3%	2.9%	0.7%	12.2%	62.3%	0.4%	1.9%	0.4%	3.4%	0.0%	0.8%	2.6%	100%
Europe—Other	0.1%	1.5%	0.5%	3.9%	0.0%	0.0%	45.4%	8.6%	1.1%	5.4%	0.2%	4.2%	29.0%	100%
European Union	0.2%	0.4%	0.1%	1.3%	0.0%	0.0%	4.7%	73.1%	0.4%	2.0%	0.4%	7.7%	9.7%	100%
Japan	0.5%	2.1%	0.8%	0.1%	0.0%	0.1%	0.1%	1.5%	82.3%	0.1%	0.1%	3.6%	8.7%	100%
Latin America	0.1%	1.6%	3.0%	3.8%	1.4%	2.1%	3.9%	3.7%	1.1%	64.2%	0.9%	3.1%	11.1%	100%
Middle East	5.9%	5.2%	0.0%	7.6%	0.0%	0.0%	6.6%	4.3%	0.0%	0.9%	41.4%	2.4%	25.6%	100%
United Kingdom	1.3%	1.3%	0.9%	0.5%	0.0%	0.1%	0.8%	15.3%	1.1%	1.0%	0.1%	59.9%	17.7%	100%
United States	0.1%	0.3%	0.4%	1.8%	0.0%	0.1%	0.5%	3.6%	0.6%	0.6%	0.2%	2.6%	89.3%	100%

Acquirer Region

Enterprise Value of Target Transactions by Region	Africa	Asia—Other	Australia	Canada	China	China—Hong Kong	Europe—Other	European Union	Japan	Latin America	Middle East	United Kingdom	United States
Africa	40.2%	0.3%	0.5%	0.1%	0.0%	0.1%	0.1%	0.0%	0.0%	0.1%	4.7%	1.7%	0.0%
Asia—Other	1.1%	78.7%	3.7%	0.4%	3.8%	2.0%	0.9%	0.1%	0.3%	0.8%	0.4%	0.8%	0.3%
Australia	1.1%	2.2%	69.1%	6.0%	0.1%	0.4%	0.1%	1.4%	0.1%	0.1%	0.1%	2.1%	0.5%
Canada	1.4%	0.5%	5.3%	46.6%	0.3%	0.2%	0.7%	0.2%	0.0%	2.2%	0.1%	2.2%	1.8%
China	0.0%	0.8%	0.6%	0.5%	72.2%	32.4%	1.7%	0.0%	0.0%	1.2%	0.0%	0.0%	0.0%
China—Hong Kong	0.1%	1.9%	0.8%	0.1%	12.3%	50.0%	0.1%	0.0%	0.1%	0.7%	0.0%	0.0%	0.0%
Europe—Other	0.9%	1.7%	1.0%	5.2%	0.0%	0.0%	49.9%	1.4%	1.3%	8.3%	1.3%	1.6%	2.7%
European Union	12.5%	2.8%	1.4%	12.0%	1.7%	1.6%	36.0%	83.4%	3.0%	21.7%	23.4%	19.8%	6.1%
Japan	3.2%	1.9%	1.5%	0.1%	0.2%	0.2%	0.1%	0.2%	83.8%	0.2%	1.0%	1.1%	0.7%
Latin America	0.3%	0.9%	3.2%	2.5%	5.0%	6.0%	2.1%	0.3%	0.7%	50.1%	4.2%	0.6%	0.5%
Middle East	5.8%	0.7%	0.0%	1.3%	0.0%	0.0%	0.9%	0.1%	0.0%	0.2%	46.3%	0.1%	0.3%
United Kingdom	26.6%	3.9%	5.2%	1.7%	0.8%	2.3%	2.2%	6.8%	3.5%	4.3%	2.8%	60.1%	4.3%
United States	6.9%	3.6%	7.7%	23.5%	3.5%	5.0%	5.2%	6.0%	7.2%	10.0%	15.7%	9.8%	82.8%
Total	100%	100%	100%	100%	100%	100%	100%	100%	100%	100%	100%	100%	100%

Exhibit may contain small rounding errors

In the U.K., 60% of the value of the targets of U.K. acquirers was U.K. targets. U.S. targets were the next largest group of targets acquired by U.K. acquirers, representing 18% of the value of the targets of U.K. acquirers; this group was followed by E.U. targets, which were 15% of the value of the targets of U.K. acquirers. For U.K. targets, U.K. acquirers purchased 60% of the value of these target companies. Of the U.K. target companies purchased by non-U.K. acquirers, E.U. acquirers purchased 20% of the value of the target companies, and U.S. acquirers purchased 10%.

Private Versus Public Targets and Acquirers

As discussed at the beginning of this section, the 44,317 M&A transactions in the sample include both privately held and publicly traded targets and acquirers. In Exhibit 16.4, we present the percentages of the number and value of the transactions for both privately held and publicly traded targets as well as privately held and publicly traded acquirers.

| **EXHIBIT 16.4** | The Number and Value of Transactions for Public Versus Private Targets and Acquirers |

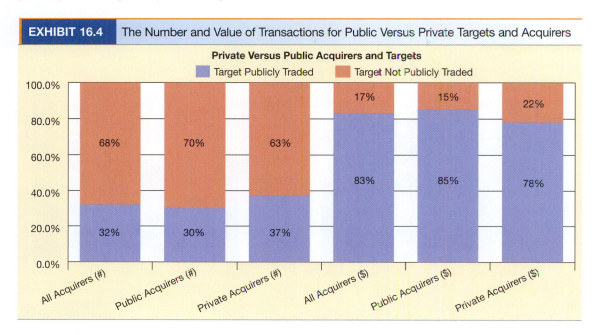

The first set of three bars reports the percentage of privately held and publicly traded targets purchased based on the number of transactions. The second set of three bars reports these percentages based on the value of the transactions. For all acquirers, 68% of targets were privately held companies. This result is qualitatively the same for publicly traded acquirers. Privately held acquirers purchased a slightly smaller proportion of privately held targets—63%. However, as expected, the privately held target transactions were smaller than the publicly traded transactions. As a result, across all acquirers, the value of the privately held targets was only 17% of the value of all targets. Again, this result is qualitatively the same for publicly traded acquirers, but privately held acquirers acquired a slightly higher percentage of the value of privately held targets—22%.

Merger Premiums and Market Multiples

In this section, we present the merger premiums paid to target shareholders and the transaction multiples implied by M&A transactions by geographic region. FactSet measures merger premiums based on changes in the publicly traded market prices of target companies; thus, we report merger premiums for the publicly traded target companies. Although transaction multiples based on enterprise value are available for both privately held and publicly traded targets, these multiples may not be the same for reasons that we discuss later in the chapter. As such, we only report transaction multiples for publicly traded target companies. Since publicly traded targets constitute 32% of all targets, the dataset we use in Exhibits 16.5 and 16.6 has about 14,000 observations, about 10,000 of which have the data required for the exhibits.

In Exhibit 16.5, we report the average five-day merger premiums.[6] As expected, the average merger premium is positive for all regions. Across all targets, the average premium is 22%, and the premiums range from 11% (Africa) to 26% (United States). The average premiums in China, the E.U., and the U.K. are 12%, 16%, and 20%, respectively. Premium differences across regions are not due to differences in the timing of mergers that result from some regions having relatively fewer transactions in the beginning

---

[6] FactSet divides the closing price of the target company—immediately after the merger announcement—by the target's closing price five days earlier. FactSet also reports a one-day and 30-day merger premium. Although the one-day premiums are, on average, smaller than the 30-day premiums which are, on average, larger than the five-day premiums, overall, the results across global regions using either the one-day or the 30-day premiums are qualitatively the same as those being reported in this exhibit. We trimmed the sample at the 5th and 95th percentiles to eliminate the effect of outliers.

of the time period analyzed. We compare the average five-day merger premiums from 1996 to 2010 to those for 2009 to 2010. The results for 2009–2010 are qualitatively the same as those for 1996–2010. Although it is beyond the scope of our discussion, economic factors that may have driven the differences in premiums across regions include regional differences in the industry composition of targets, systematic differences in the value of expected synergies, the degree of competition for targets among acquirers, and regulatory differences.

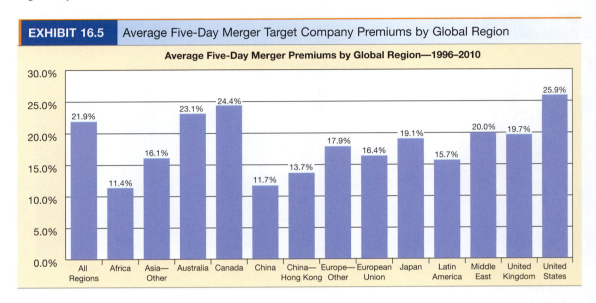

EXHIBIT 16.5 Average Five-Day Merger Target Company Premiums by Global Region

In Exhibit 16.6, we present averages for three enterprise-value-based transaction multiples for the global regions—earnings before interest and taxes (EBIT); earnings before interest, taxes, depreciation and amortization, (EBITDA); and revenue. The ranges for the EBIT, EBITDA, and revenue multiples are 8.7 to 13.7, 7.2 to 10.1, and 1.1 to 2.4, respectively. The relative magnitudes of the three multiples across regions share some similarities, but they are not the same (even though we restrict the set of transactions used in the exhibit to be the same for all three multiples). The relative magnitudes of the EBIT and EBITDA multiples across regions are more similar to each other. For example, China ranks fifth in terms of its average EBIT multiple and third highest in terms of its average EBITDA multiple, but of the 13 regions, it ranks 10th in terms of its revenue multiple; the U.S. ranks 9th and 8th for its EBIT and EBITDA multiples, respectively, but it only ranks 4th for its revenue multiple. However, not all of the EBIT and EBITDA multiples are the same. Canada, for example, has the largest EBIT multiple but the ninth largest EBITDA multiple. Differences across countries may be due to a large variety of factors, including the composition of the industries acquired in countries/regions, competition for targets, and so forth.

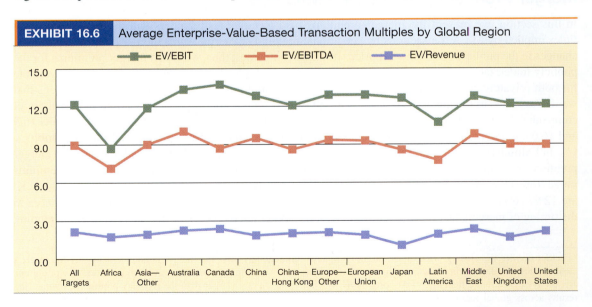

EXHIBIT 16.6 Average Enterprise-Value-Based Transaction Multiples by Global Region

16.2 WHAT MOTIVATES MERGERS AND ACQUISITIONS, AND DO THEY CREATE VALUE?

There are many plausible economic rationales for M&A transactions. Of course, the overarching motivation for acquisitions is to create value for shareholders. However, managers of acquiring companies may also be motivated to acquire companies for personal reasons, which might not create value. Academics have studied how acquisitions perform. Do they lead to economic efficiency? Do they create value for the shareholders of both the acquiring and target companies? In this section, we examine these topics.

What Motivates Merger and Acquisition Transactions?

Naturally, managers should first develop a complete strategic plan in which they identify the opportunities with which to grow the company and establish, enhance, and protect their competitive advantages in order to create value for the company's shareholders. Without a strategic plan, it is difficult to evaluate acquisition opportunities. Moreover, a strategic plan will further inform the acquisition process if it delineates the goals that are best attained organically and the goals that are best attained through acquisitions. An acquisition can help a company establish a competitive advantage, raise barriers to imitation, raise barriers to entry, raise barriers to substitution, enhance or protect power over the supply chain, provide access to foreign markets, and so on.

In general, managers are motivated to acquire other companies because they want to create value. How might an acquirer create value from an acquisition? Acquirers attempt to create value through acquisitions by taking advantage of various economic forces or regulatory frictions. Examples of how to take advantage of these economic forces and regulatory frictions include increasing scale and scope, efficiently entering new markets (especially new global markets), combining complementary resources, capturing superior or new technology and expertise, reacting to changes in regulation, reducing capacity in the industry, removing inefficient management, and capturing tax benefits that otherwise would have been lost. Some managers claim to acquire other companies for diversification purposes; however, we know that the value-creation benefits of diversification are relatively minor and may not even be positive in well-developed economies. Lastly, if a company's stock is overvalued, it may be motivated to use its stock as currency to purchase other companies.

A company can create value from increasing either its scale or its scope. Scale efficiencies may arise from spreading fixed costs over a larger scale of activities (for example, sharing fixed cost infrastructure investments or research and development activities) and from increased purchasing power. For example, a large company that performs diagnostic tests for doctors and hospitals might acquire smaller labs, and the resulting purchasing power can substantially reduce the cost structure of the smaller labs due to the purchasing power of the acquirer. Scope efficiencies may arise from increasing a company's product or service offerings by sharing costs related to these product or service offerings.

An acquisition can create value if companies combine complementary assets or if a company acquires assets needed to improve its products, reduce its costs, or increase its revenues, such as combining a company with very good products but weak distribution channels with a company that has very good distribution channels. Alternatively, a manager might use an acquisition to acquire technology, intellectual property (patents), or human capital with unusual expertise. For example, a larger pharmaceutical company might acquire a smaller biotech company in order to acquire new drugs in the early stages of their development.

Forces that drive companies to try to grow faster and enter new markets also motivate acquisitions. For example, as the global economy expands to include more products and services, global competition and opportunities require companies to, in turn, expand their products and services globally. Companies can enter foreign markets through organic growth, but sometimes, timing and excess capacity in the industry may lead companies to use acquisitions in order to enter new global markets. Changes in the regulatory environment can provide opportunities for companies to expand. For example, deregulation can make acquisitions possible where they were not previously. Regulatory changes can also affect the profitability of an acquisition, which may also motivate acquisitions. For example, over the last two decades, changes in the regulations affecting the financial services industry made acquisitions both feasible and potentially profitable.

Holding everything else constant, changes in industry capacity will change product prices. When an industry has too much capacity, reducing capacity is necessary to increase margins to allow for the survival of the remaining companies in the industry. Companies are also motivated to reduce industry capacity by eliminating competition in order to earn economic rents. Antitrust regulatory bodies around the world, however, are responsible for preventing the latter type of acquisitions if they violate antitrust laws.

Valuation in Practice 16.1

Managers Forecast Synergies to Value the Benefits from a Merger—Daimler-Benz and Chrysler Merger Naturally, when two companies merge, the managers of both companies measure the value of the merger based on the potential synergies resulting from combining the two companies. In May 1998, Daimler-Benz, AG (Daimler) and Chrysler Corporation (Chrysler) announced the merger of the two companies. The shareholders approved the merger and the companies merged in November 1998. The companies disclosed certain forecasts and the value drivers resulting from the merger. For example, Daimler's management stated,

> . . . the reasons for the business combination including, among other things, general consolidation in the automotive industry and the strong potential for synergies between the constituent companies, the company profile of Chrysler, the transaction structure, organizational issues relating to the structure and composition of the DaimlerChrysler Management Board and Supervisory Board and the prospects for enhancing the value of the combined entity in the future. . . .
>
> The opportunities for significant synergies afforded by a combination of Chrysler and Daimler-Benz—based not on plant closings or lay-offs, but on such factors as shared technologies, distribution, purchasing and know-how. Management expects benefits of $1.4 billion in the first year of merged operations, and annual benefits of $3 billion within three to five years.

The stock market also thought that this merger had significant and positive potential synergies. When the companies announced the merger, Daimler's stock price rose from $102.0625 to $111.375 (from the day before the announcement to the day after), and its market capitalization rose from $52.8 billion to $57.6 billion ($4.8 billion). Chrysler's stock price rose from $41.4375 to $53.8125, and its market capitalization rose from $26.8 billion to $34.8 billion ($8.0 billion). The combined increase in market capitalization was close to $13 billion. It turned out, however, that the synergies did not materialize, and after paying over $36 billion for Chrysler, Daimler eventually sold it for less than $1 billion.

Source: See the DaimlerChrysler AG SEC Form F-4 (Registration Statement), pp. 48 and 50. See the company's website at http://www.daimlerchrysler.com/index_e.htm for this statement as well as updated financial information.

A poorly managed company can become an acquisition target if its inefficiency has a sufficient impact on value. The management of an acquiring company may purchase a poorly managed target company in order to make changes to the target's strategy, operations, and management that will increase its value. For example, many of the acquisitions of oil companies in the 1980s were motivated by potential value creation resulting from changing the companies' operating strategies—in particular, their exploration strategies.

Sometimes, a company states that it acquired another company in order to diversify the company's products and services, even though the acquisition has no cost or revenue synergies. Historically, some companies have made acquisitions that were pure diversification plays, but no definitive evidence exists that pure diversification strategies create substantial value in well-developed economies. In fact, some studies suggest that pure diversification destroys value, because management may lose focus, and the allocation of capital within the organization might not be based on the investments that can create the most value for the company; however, other studies suggest that diversification is a more neutral activity with minimal benefits. On the other hand, it appears that diversification in countries with less-developed capital markets can function as an internal capital market and avoid the high costs of obtaining external financing in such markets.[7]

---

[7] See Berger, P., and E. Ofek "Diversification's Effect on Firm Value," *Journal of Financial Economics* 37 (1995), pp. 39–65, which suggests that diversified firms sell at a 13% to 15% discount relative to the sum of the standalone components. Also, see Villalonga, B., "Diversification Discount or Premium? New Evidence from the Business Information Tracking Series," *Journal of Finance* 59 (2004), pp. 475–502, which suggests that there is no diversification discount. Also, see Khanna, T., and K. Palepu, "Is Group Affiliation Profitable in Emerging Markets? An Analysis of Diversified Indian Business Groups," *Journal of Finance* 55 (2000), pp. 867–891, on the benefits of conglomerate groups in emerging markets.

much relative to acquisitions financed with cash. Indeed, they show that companies that failed to close their stock-for-stock transactions for exogenous reasons (such as an antitrust issue) fared worse than companies that completed their stock-for-stock transactions.[9]

Valuation Key 16.2

The evidence on whether mergers and acquisitions create value is reasonably clear from both academic and practitioner studies. Almost all of the studies conclude that, on average, mergers and acquisitions increase economic efficiency. However, most of the gains go to target shareholders. Some studies find, on average, significant negative returns to the acquirers, and some find insignificant returns to acquirers; the variance around the mean is large.

Why do some acquirers overpay? We consider an overpayment to have occurred for merger transactions where the value of the acquirer's stock decreases as a result of the merger, and note that this can happen even if the combined value of the acquirer's and target's stock increases. In such cases, regardless of the strategic benefits of an acquisition and the economic efficiencies it is able to create, the acquirer pays more than what is economically justified based on the expected benefits of the merger. Various factors might cause an acquirer to pay too much, including conflicts of interests, psychological factors, and/or errors in judgment.

A competitive auction process often leads to an increase in the premium paid relative to a situation in which the process has only one bidder. Auctions have become more common over time due to changes in case law and changes in securities laws. An acquirer may overpay if the acquirer is overly optimistic in its forecast of the synergies or future performance of the combined companies. In an auction, the winning bidder may be too optimistic about the merger even if, on average, all of the bidders have rational expectations—the so-called winner's curse. In order to avoid overbidding in an auction, bidders must conduct a thorough analysis of the benefits of the acquisition and establish a firm walk-away price that they will not violate without new and substantive positive information.

The nature of the acquisition process can sometimes create incentives and environments that lead to overbidding. For example, an acquirer's financial advisors may have a conflict of interest because they are often compensated based on "success fees;" in other words, they only receive their fees if the transaction is closed. The managers of the acquiring company might have incentives—either financial or psychological—to overbid. For example, managerial compensation may be linked to either the size or growth of the overall company without an appropriate adjustment for its risk-adjusted stock market performance. From a psychological perspective, managers of the acquiring company may become too personally invested in acquiring the target. Managers often invest many hours of their own time in addition to a sizeable amount of the company's resources; as such, they do not want to "lose" the deal—a **sunk cost** phenomenon. If a target is slipping away, a manager may resort to changing the valuation at the last minute in order to justify a higher bid.

16.3 WHY DO MERGERS SOMETIMES FAIL TO CREATE VALUE FOR ACQUIRERS?

Mergers and acquisitions are complicated business transactions with numerous elements that have to be managed with care. Even if a merger makes sense economically, it is difficult for an acquisition to be free of unforeseen events and negative surprises. The goal, of course, is to avoid having such unforeseen events and surprises derail the success of an acquisition. What are some of the reasons for an acquisition to fail to create value for the acquirer? At the most basic level, of course, the acquirer just paid too much, and that is most likely to occur because of errors in process, expectations, and execution.

Strategic Failures

One reason why an acquisition might fail is an inappropriate strategy underlying the merger. In other words, the acquisition may not fit within the company's strategy (e.g., buying a company for non-strategic reasons), or the company's strategy may be flawed. Another strategy-related failure can occur if the

---

[9] See Savor, P., and Q. Lu, "Do Stock Mergers Create Value for Acquirers?" *Journal of Finance* 64 (2009), pp. 1061–1097.

company does not fully anticipate the strategic responses of its competitors. For example, suppose that a company operates in a competitive industry and that the company completes an acquisition that reduces its costs; in turn, the company assumes this will increase its operating margins. If the company is able to achieve these higher margins, the company's competitors will likely take actions to achieve similar cost savings. If the competitors manage to do so, product prices are likely to fall and reduce margins to their previous competitive level. Thus, though the company may benefit from an improvement in operating margins for some limited amount of time, the improvement will not be permanent. If the company fails to anticipate this response, the merger may fail to create value, for the acquirer may have forecasted more persistent benefits than actually materialized and, hence, overpaid for the target.

Due Diligence Failures

Due diligence is a process that usually takes place after a non-binding letter of intent is signed. The due diligence process allows the acquirer to perform a more detailed examination of the target's records, to carefully examine the target, and to make judgments about the value of the acquisition. The due diligence process entails an examination of various accounting records and legal documents, but it is primarily an assessment of the value of the acquisition—a test of the investment thesis. In addition to the various financial aspects of the transaction, the due diligence process investigates such non-financial aspects as the quality of the executives and work force, the culture of the target, and how well or poorly the cultures of the acquirer and target fit together. The due diligence process also affords the acquirer the opportunity to begin developing an integration plan. All of these are important aspects of the due diligence process.

A recent Bain and Company survey of 250 senior managers with M&A responsibilities showed that only 30% of the managers surveyed were satisfied with their due diligence.[10] In particular, the Bain survey reported that about two-thirds of the managers ignored the integration challenges that were apparent in the due diligence and, as such, overestimated the synergies. The survey also noted that about one-half of the managers indicated that their due diligence process failed to uncover and highlight such key issues as the target being "dressed up for sale," the stuffing of a sales channel, the treatment of expenses as non-recurring or extraordinary, and cutbacks on maintenance, capital expenditures, and research and development. More than 45% of the managers indicated that due diligence failed to uncover the fact that the strategies of the target and acquirer did not mesh, and more than one-third indicated that neither the valuation nor the bid was updated for the findings of the due diligence process.

Integration Planning and Execution Failures

A successful acquisition requires that management successfully execute a well-thought-out **integration plan**. The integration of the operations of two companies is important for a merger to be successful unless the companies continue to operate on a standalone basis after the acquisition. Integration includes combining operations, eliminating redundant or unnecessary operations or personnel, and integrating cultures and compensation plans. A timetable with clear milestones is important to an integration plan—what does the acquirer need to accomplish in the first 30 days, 60 days, 90 days, and so forth? The integration plan includes detailed, well-developed plans to achieve revenue and cost synergies as well as plans to incur the one-time and ongoing costs of integrating the target.

Communication strategies for customers, employees, and investors are a key part of the integration process. Both employees and customers are at risk when two companies announce an acquisition. Key customers and employees should be identified, and retention strategies should be developed. An integration plan should also explicitly consider the cultural issues associated with the transaction. If two organizations have very different cultures, it may be best not to fully integrate the companies. Of course, whether this is feasible depends on both the nature of the two businesses and the level of integration that is required to achieve the benefits of the acquisition.

For example, the Daimler-Chrysler merger failed in spite of a strong positive stock market reaction to the merger announcement (see Valuation in Practice 16.1). Cultural differences between the two companies appear to have played an important role in the failure, as they prevented operations and management from being successfully integrated. The two companies also held very different views on compensation. As a result of these differences and the increasing control of Daimler over the merged company, performance and

---

[10] Cullinan, G., J. Le Roux, R. Weddigen, Bain and Company Brief Newsletter, April 28, 2004, http://www.bain.com /bainweb/Publications/publications_detail.asp?id=16346&menu_url=publications%2Easp.

employee satisfaction at Chrysler decreased substantially, resulting in the departures of many of Chrysler's key executives and engineers.[11]

An integration plan is multifaceted, and the team putting the plan together should continually revisit the strategic rationale for the acquisition. What is the acquisition supposed to achieve? Given the investment thesis, are we integrating the two organizations in a manner that maximizes the likelihood of achieving our goals? Constantly revisiting the strategic rationale of the acquisition will help ensure that the integration plan is focused on achieving the major goals of the acquisition. Finally, the integration team needs to react to integration issues as they arise. If the integration is not going as smoothly as planned, proactive steps should be taken, for it is highly unlikely that any such issues will fix themselves. Indeed, most integration problems become more problematic over time.

Poorly Run Acquisition Process

The entire acquisition process has to be thoughtful and well run. What are some of the traits of a well-run acquisition process? To begin, the strategic rationale for the acquisition needs to continually inform all elements of the process—such as the valuation, negotiation strategy, deal structure, due diligence, and integration planning. If the team leading the acquisition process does not keep the strategic rationale of the acquisition in constant focus, important mistakes are likely to be made. The due diligence process needs to update the valuation, integration plan, and negotiations taking place. A well-run acquisition process will actively consider whether or when to walk away from a deal. This can happen in the negotiation stage, in the due diligence process, or in response to a competing bid that exceeds the walk-away price. Developing budgets for the business after the acquisition should be based on the assumptions in the valuation model that justified the bid, and operational personnel should sign off on these budgets. The success of the acquisition should be tracked in order to ensure that the acquisition is meeting its financial and strategic goals. If these goals are not being met, proactive steps should be taken to put the acquisition back on track. After every acquisition, the M&A team should consider the lessons learned from the acquisition so that mistakes are not repeated in subsequent transactions. Over time, the organization should develop an "M&A playbook."

Cross-Border Acquisitions

Cross-border acquisitions are even more difficult to integrate successfully, and the risk of failure is higher. In a cross-border acquisition, cultural issues can be even more difficult to manage than a domestic acquisition. Moreover, cross-border acquisitions have the added complexity of accommodating two different legal and regulatory environments and two different tax jurisdictions.[12]

Mitigating Risks

A company has a limited number of ways to mitigate risks in an acquisition transaction. For example, it is possible to buy insurance for certain risks (such as environmental liabilities and the expropriation of assets by a foreign government), but these insurance products can be expensive. In addition, an acquirer can transfer some of the risk to the target by having contingent payments such as an **earn-out provision**. **Escrow accounts** are also used to mitigate risks in a transaction. Earn-outs and escrow accounts are generally used with targets that are private companies, and we discuss them later in the chapter. As we will soon show, acquiring a company with at least some stock consideration also mitigates some of the risk because if the deal winds up destroying value, the target shareholders will bear some of the resulting loss; of course, if the transaction does well, they stand to gain more, but this is how risk sharing works.

Valuation Key 16.3

There are many reasons why an acquisition may fail to meet its strategic and financial goals. However, a well-run acquisition process can mitigate the risk of failure. In addition, in certain circumstances, there may be creative ways to shift some of the risk onto the target.

---

[11] Weber, R. A., and C. F. Camerer, "Cultural Conflict and Merger Failure: An Experimental Approach," *Management Science* vol. 49, no. 4 (April 2003), pp. 400–415.

[12] See KPMG, "Unlocking the Keys to Shareholder Value," *Mergers and Acquisitions Global Research Report* (1999).

16.4 SYNERGIES

Synergies result from combining the operations of the two companies. If achieved, synergies ultimately increase the value of the post-merger company above the sum of the values of the standalone companies. In general, there are two types of synergies—increases in revenues and cost efficiencies. Revenue and cost synergies result from some of the economic forces we elaborated upon in discussing the potential motivations for M&A transactions. Synergies might also reduce required investments. It is also possible to have financial synergies, but these are not as common and are usually small in magnitude if they exist at all.

LO2 Identify and value synergies

It is relatively easy to generate ideas about the potential synergistic effects of an acquisition. However, forecasting synergies with a reasonable degree of accuracy and then capturing them after the merger is not as easy. Many cost efficiencies are more easily quantified than revenue synergies, but both can be difficult to forecast and difficult to achieve. Naturally, not all of the value creation that is expected to occur in a merger results from combining the assets of the two companies—for example, replacing bad management could increase value without any synergies. Another example of non-synergistic value creation could occur by acquiring a company, breaking it up into different pieces, and selling the pieces, never integrating it into any of the acquirer's operations. In this case, the acquisition has no synergistic value—only value from breaking the company up into more sensible component businesses. It is sometimes useful to differentiate between synergies that may be achieved because of two companies combining operations versus increases in performance that do not require combining the two companies.

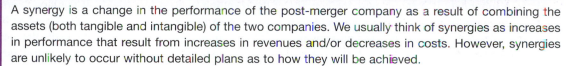

Valuation Key 16.4

A synergy is a change in the performance of the post-merger company as a result of combining the assets (both tangible and intangible) of the two companies. We usually think of synergies as increases in performance that result from increases in revenues and/or decreases in costs. However, synergies are unlikely to occur without detailed plans as to how they will be achieved.

Cost Efficiency Synergies

Cost efficiency synergies (or cost efficiencies) are cost reductions that result from combining the operations of two companies. A company can gain cost efficiencies if it can use its fixed costs to support a larger scale of operations. A company can also gain cost efficiencies if it can lower its variable costs, which typically results from economies of scale or scope. Naturally, if two companies are combined, the surviving company only needs one chief executive officer, one chief financial officer, one treasury function, one legal department, and so forth. Moreover, it only needs one board of directors and one corporate headquarters; thus, combining two companies eliminates these costs even though the company might need additional layers of management as a result of the increase in the company's scale, or the legal department might need more attorneys than the acquiring firm currently has to service the expanded corporation. The costs of being a public company include the costs of following regulatory rules and regulations, holding annual meetings, maintaining investor relations, and so forth. Some of these costs are reduced as a result of two public companies combining.

When companies combine, they have a variety of ways to share their existing infrastructures and other fixed costs in order to reduce their post-merger cost structure. Companies can share research and development functions to reduce headcount, gain other cost reductions, and share patents in order to increase patent utilization. They may also share production facilities in order to gain better capacity utilization, share distribution channels and sales forces in order to reduce headcount and increase productivity, and share infrastructures (such as software platforms, delivery systems, back office services, and marketing costs) in order to reduce headcount and other costs.

Another type of cost reduction results from more efficient procurement. To the extent that companies have negotiated different prices for the different goods and services they use (office supplies, computer equipment, travel, manufacturing components, etc.), costs can be reduced by adopting the least expensive pricing for both companies. In addition, an increase in scale may provide the company with more market power over its suppliers, leading to further cost reductions.

Companies may also be able to lower combined income taxes by using, for example, foreign income tax credits or net operating loss carryforwards that are not being utilized.

Revenue Synergies

Companies can share distribution channels and brands in order to better promote the products of the other company. It is possible for one company to have a better marketing plan or a better sales force, both of which can increase revenues after the companies are combined. Acquirers often characterize international acquisitions as a way of gaining quicker access to international markets. Sharing brands or customer lists in order to grow revenues into a new customer base—especially globally—is another common type of revenue synergy. This is often referred to as cross-selling; the acquirer sells its products to the customers of the target, and the target sells its products to the customers of the acquirer.

> ## Valuation Key 16.5
>
> Cost efficiency synergies include savings from eliminating such redundant costs as the C-suite (CEO, CFO, etc.), a board of directors, and potentially cutting back on other costs even if not fully eliminated. They also can occur from cost sharing, additional market power with suppliers, and technology sharing. Revenue synergies can come from brand sharing, as well as sharing distribution channels and customer lists. Revenue synergies are generally harder to forecast and achieve than cost synergies.

Financial Synergies

Can an acquirer increase value by the way it finances an acquisition? We know a company can create value by issuing debt if it can capture the benefits of the resulting interest tax shields. If the target company is, for some reason, underutilizing debt in its capital structure, the acquirer can increase value by financing an acquisition with debt and moving the target to its optimal capital structure. We know that part of the value creation associated with leveraged buyouts is related to the capital structures put in place (see Chapter 15). Such an increase in value is not a synergy per se, for this increase in value can be achieved independently of the acquisition, but it can still create value.

If the combination of two companies is able to reduce the combined weighted average cost of capital, this will result in a financial synergy. All else equal, we know that a company's cost of capital will decrease if it can reduce its operating leverage. If the combination allows the ratio of fixed to variable costs to decline due to economies of scale, operating leverage should fall. If the overall operating leverage declines, the company's risk will decrease, assuming everything else remains constant. Another way to reduce the cost of capital is to reduce financial distress costs. If a target company is facing high financial distress costs, combining the target company with a complementary acquiring company can reduce the target company's financial distress costs and, in turn, reduce its cost of capital.

Synergy Uncertainty

Some synergies are more quantifiable than others are, and most synergies have at least some degree of uncertainty associated with their achievement in the post-merger company. Some of the factors that play into this uncertainty are the innate achievability of the synergy, the cost of achieving the synergy, and the ability of the companies to create a feasible plan to capture the synergy. For example, eliminating the C-suite of the target company is quantifiable and definite, but the cost of closing plants may be difficult to estimate precisely. In addition, even though a reduction in headcount (from combining research and development departments) is both quantifiable and certain, quantifying the revenue synergies from new products is much more difficult and uncertain, and forecasting how much business the customers of both companies will do with each other is also difficult and uncertain.

The time needed to achieve all the synergies and how long the synergies will last are both uncertain. This is an important consideration to make in valuing a transaction—how long will it take to achieve the synergies, and how long will they last? Some cost savings can occur relatively quickly, but others may take longer to achieve. Moreover, to the extent that they are even achievable, revenue synergies usually take longer than many types of cost savings. It is also useful to consider carefully whether the synergies are expected to last in perpetuity or whether they are likely to dissipate over time. For example, if an industry is consolidating and capturing scale economies, an acquirer is likely to see margin improvements

Valuation in Practice 16.2

Synergies in the LATAM Airlines Group Merger

In 2012, LAN Airlines S.A. (LAN), a Chilean company; TAM S.A. (TAM), a Brazilian company; and their respective controlling shareholders entered into an exchange offer agreement and an implementation agreement in order to combine LAN and TAM to form LATAM Airlines Group S.A. According to both companies, the businesses of LAN and TAM were highly complementary from both a geographic and business line perspective.

The companies expected to achieve substantial synergies and cost reductions by coordinating flights at their hubs. By harmonizing the flight schedules of LAN's and TAM's complementary passenger networks, LATAM was expected to be able to offer better services to its customers in the form of more connections, more travel alternatives, new destinations, extended lounge access, and more extensive frequent flyer programs. LAN expected all of this to result in increased passenger revenues and better benefits to customers. The companies also expected the merger to create substantial opportunities for LATAM's international cargo business by optimizing the cargo network, creating efficiencies and cost savings in the cargo business through coordinated freight planning, sharing best practices, and deploying new routes with the combination of passenger and cargo revenue. LAN estimated that the combined synergies arising from the proposed combination could increase LATAM's annual operating income (before depreciation and taxes) over time by $600 million to $700 million. Of the total expected annual pre-tax synergies, between $170 million and $200 million is achievable within the first year after the transaction's completion. Approximately 40% of the total potential synergies were expected to be generated from increased revenues from the passenger business, 20% to be generated from increased revenues from the cargo business, and the remaining 40% of the potential synergies to be generated from cost savings.

Source: Offer to Exchange Each Common Share, Preferred Share and American Depository Share of TAM S.A. for 0.90 of a Common Share of LAN AIRLINES S.A. Represented by American Depository Shares or Brazilian Depository Shares dated May 10, 2012—see pp. 142–145.

if it is on the leading edge of that consolidation. However, after the industry has consolidated, and once the scale economies have been captured by competitors, it is possible that prices will decrease, reducing margins until they return to the level that just sustains the industry. Thus, the increase in profit margins associated with the cost synergies may not be sustainable. At some point in the future, competitive forces may erode the value of the synergies. On the other hand, some mergers may help create an enduring competitive advantage and result in more sustainable margins.

REVIEW EXERCISE 16.1

Valuing Synergies—LATAM Airlines Group

Use the following information (taken from the offering memorandum) to measure the value of the synergies for the LAN and TAM merger discussed in Valuation in Practice 16.2. After the completion of the proposed combination, the breakdown of the expected range of annual pre-tax synergies was estimated to be as follows (realized in full in the fourth year after the merger):

- Increased revenues—$225 million to $260 million from the combination of passenger networks and $120 million to $125 million from the combination of cargo services.
- Cost savings—$15 million to $25 million from the consolidation of frequent flyer programs; $100 million to $135 million from the coordination of airport and procurement activities; $20 million to $25 million from the coordination and improved efficiency of maintenance operations; and $120 million to $130 million from the convergence of information technology systems, the increased efficiency of combined sales and distribution processes, and the increased efficiency in corporate overhead costs.

LAN and TAM expected the one-time merger costs—including banking, consulting, and legal advisory fees—to be between $170 million and $200 million. LAN expected a reduction of approximately $150 million in working capital from not having to inventory as many engines and spare parts, which was expected to be fully realized at the end of 2013.

Use the midpoint of the synergy forecasts in the calculations. Assume that all synergies are actual cash flows, that LATAM's average income tax rate is 30%, and that fees are deductible in 2012. Further assume that 28.5% of the annual synergies will be achieved by the end of the first year after the merger (2013), that 50% of the annual synergies will be achieved by the end of the second year after the merger (2014), that 80% will be achieved by the end of the third year (2015), and 100% will be achieved by the end of the fourth year. Further, assume that the synergies will begin to erode at a rate of 10% per year, beginning in the fifth year after the merger. The weighted average cost of capital for valuing the synergies is 10%. Calculate the value of the synergies as of mid-year 2012, which we assume is the merger close date (similar to the analysis provided in Exhibit 16.15). Thus, the end-of-year 2012 cash flows are only a half-year away and so on for subsequent years. Examine the sensitivity of the value of the synergies to variation in the weighted average cost of capital between 9% and 11% and to variation in the continuing value growth rates between −20% and 0%.

Solution on pages 715–716.

16.5 DEAL STRUCTURE, INCOME TAXES, AND OTHER CONTRACT PROVISIONS

LO3 Value and analyze an M&A deal

Deal structure and other contract provisions are important to understand, as they have implications for the value and risk of a transaction. Deal structure and income taxes are complex topics that we will only touch on lightly. Deal structure can influence a number of important factors—the form of payment; the tax effects of the transaction; how, if at all, risk is shared between the acquirer and target; whether the acquirer is responsible for the target's liabilities; whether contracts and items (such as leases) are still in effect after the target is acquired; whether the shareholders of both the target and acquirer have to vote on the merger; and whether minority shareholders will exist after the transaction.

Is it important that the contracts remain in effect after the transaction? The answer depends on the situation. If the target has a large number of leases or long-term contracts with suppliers and customers that are both advantageous and would be difficult to renegotiate on the same terms, then trying to keep those contracts may be important. Of course, some contracts may have change-of-control provisions that require the contract to be renegotiated whenever a change of control occurs. The issue of whether a vote is required by the shareholders (of either the acquirer or the target) speaks to the potential risk of completing a transaction, for approval has to be sought. Whether minority shareholders will survive the transaction is important, as minority shareholders can be costly to deal with, and they can be disruptive to management.

In choosing the deal structure, we usually want to maximize the size of the "economic pie," and we will likely need to adjust the purchase price or other elements of the merger agreement for the effects of the deal structure on each party. For example, the offer price that an acquirer will be willing to pay and that a target will be willing to accept is influenced by whether the transaction is tax free to the target and its shareholders. Associated with the tax effect on the target and its shareholders is whether the acquirer can take a step-up in the tax basis of the assets, as these two issues are linked in the tax code. When we say that a transaction is tax free, we really mean that it is tax free at the time of the transaction. If a target shareholder receives shares of the acquirer's stock in a tax-free transaction, the target shareholder will recognize a gain or a loss upon the ultimate sale of the acquirer's shares. Obviously, the form of the transaction will affect both the buyer's valuation of the target and the target's valuation of the offer—for both tax and other reasons. We choose the structure that maximizes the size of the "economic pie" by considering taxes and other attributes affected by the deal structure.

We will discuss a few different deal structures and the impact of each structure on the just-discussed considerations. The first two deal structures engender immediate tax consequences for the target shareholders and, in some cases, for the target. The subsequent structures do not necessarily have immediate tax consequences for the target or target shareholders, unless consideration other than stock is received or special elections are made.

Types of Transactions

Cash Purchase of Assets.   As outlined in the introduction, companies use different types of transactions to acquire another company or another company's assets. For example, in a cash purchase of assets, the buyer pays cash for the assets of the target. In this form of transaction, the liabilities of the target are not transferred to the buyer unless it is agreed upon in the purchase agreement or if the liabilities

Valuation in Practice 16.3

Affiliated Computer Services, Inc. Super Voting Common Stock and Effective Voting Control

Affiliated Computer Services, Inc. (ACS) was founded by Mr. Darwin Deason in 1988. Mr. Deason served as ACS's chief executive officer until 1999 and as its Chairman of the Board of Directors until ACS merged with Xerox Corporation in 2010 (see the Xerox—ACS merger valuation, Section 16.10). ACS had two types of common stock outstanding—Class A and Class B. The Class A common was publicly traded on the New York Stock Exchange, and each share had one vote. The Class B common was privately held (mostly by Mr. Deason) and each share had 10 votes.

According to ACS's 2009 SEC 10-K report,

> As of August 20, 2009, 91,042,152 shares of Class A common stock and 6,599,372 shares of Class B common stock were outstanding. . . .
>
> In addition, as of August 20, 2009, Darwin Deason beneficially owns 6,599,372 shares of Class B common stock and 2,140,884 shares of the Class A common stock and controls approximately 43.6% of our total voting power (based on shares of both classes of common stock outstanding). As a result, Mr. Deason has the requisite voting power to significantly affect many of our significant decisions, including the power to block corporate actions such as an amendment to most provisions of our certificate of incorporation.

Source: See Affiliated Computer Services, Inc. 2009 SEC 10-K filing, p. 19.

are not separable from the assets. For example, under U.S. law, if a company buys a chemical plant, it cannot escape the environmental liabilities associated with the plant, even if it did nothing to contribute to the environmental issue. On the other side of the transaction, the target company pays a tax on the sale of the assets if it sells them at a gain, and target shareholders pay a tax if and when the proceeds are distributed to them. For the buyer, the taxable basis of the assets is equal to the payment made, and this has to be allocated across the assets and potentially to goodwill—the latter if the purchase price exceeds the value allocated to the inventory, other tangible assets, and intangible assets. In these transactions, the tax basis of the assets is normally stepped up for the buyer; this can be beneficial if a large portion of the purchase price can be allocated to inventory and depreciable assets (assuming the buyer has taxable income). This is particularly useful if the target has a high tax basis in the assets or has net operating loss carryforwards such that a large tax is not triggered for the target. The contracts of the target are not transferred to the buyer in an asset purchase. Thus, if the target has important leased assets that the buyer wants to use, the buyer will need to enter into new leases on all of the leased assets that it wants to continue using. Moreover, contracts with suppliers and customers will not survive. In addition, the acquirer will not have to deal with any of the target's minority shareholders after the transaction.

Purchase of Stock Using Cash and Debt. Another type of transaction is the purchase of the target's stock using cash or debt payments. In this form of transaction, the acquirer buys the target shareholders' stock directly from them. Each target shareholder pays a tax based on the difference between the consideration received and the shareholders' taxable basis in the stock. The target itself pays no tax.[13] The acquirer will be responsible for all of the target's liabilities, and all existing contracts (leased assets and agreements with suppliers and customers) will stay in force unless they have change-in-control termination clauses. No shareholder vote is needed, but of course, the target shareholders have to tender their shares, and those who do not tender will become minority shareholders.

Purchase of Stock Using Stock and Potentially Other Consideration. We will barely scratch the surface here, as there are multiple forms of these transactions. Many, but not all, of these transactions can be tax free to the target and to the target shareholders. If the transaction is tax free, there is no step-up in the tax basis of the assets for the acquirer. In order to qualify as tax free, there are certain requirements that must be met. For example, in the simplest form of a pure stock-for-stock merger, the

---

[13] The target itself pays no tax unless the parties agree to a special income tax treatment called a 338 election. The acquirer can treat this as a straight purchase of stock, or it can treat it as an asset purchase (a section 338 election). In the latter case, the target pays income taxes as if it were an asset purchase and the acquirer can also step up the basis in the assets. This is particularly useful if the target has net operating losses that can offset the gain it will recognize from the asset sale. The unused net operating losses of the target can also be used by the acquirer.

acquirer can only exchange voting common stock or voting preferred stock and must control at least 80% of the votes after the transaction. If cash or other consideration is given in a stock-for-stock transaction, there are generally restrictions on the amount of non-voting stock consideration that can be given before the entire transaction is considered taxable. If the transaction meets these restrictions and qualifies for tax-free treatment, there will be some tax levied to the extent of the cash and other consideration, but the entire transaction will not be taxable. There are many different forms of these transactions, and understanding all of these types of transactions is beyond the scope of our discussion here. Suffice it to say the exact form of the transaction will determine if the acquirer is responsible for the target's liabilities, whether minority shareholders exist after the transaction, who has to approve the transaction, and whether the target's contracts survive the transaction.

Purchase of Assets Using Stock and Potentially Other Consideration. In a stock-for-assets merger, the acquirer exchanges shares of its voting stock for the assets of the company. To qualify as a tax-free transaction, no more than 20% of the consideration may be in a form that is not voting common stock, and the acquirer must acquire at least 70% of the fair market value of the gross assets and 90% of the fair market value of the net assets. If the acquirer assumes any liabilities, they count toward meeting the 20% rule if anything other than voting common stock is used as consideration. In such a transaction, there is no step-up in the basis of the assets for the acquirer, and any liabilities that are explicitly assumed are the responsibility of the acquirer. No minority shareholders exist after the transaction, and the target does not survive; thus, contracts and leases need to be renegotiated.

Other Common Contract Provisions

As we have just seen, the form of the transaction affects the tax treatment, whether the target's liabilities are assumed by the acquirer, how risk is shared between the acquirer and target (if at all), whether existing contracts survive the acquisition, who approves the transaction, and whether minority shareholders exist after the transaction. There are other contract provisions that affect the underlying economics and who bears certain risks.

Earn-outs are payments that are made some time after the close of a transaction (usually several years) for which the payment is contingent upon the performance of the target over a specified time period. This is one way to bridge a difference in opinion on the value of the target. The size of the earn-out is usually related to the degree of this difference. For example, if the founder of a target is much more optimistic about the future of the business than the acquirer is, an earn-out can be structured such that the acquirer will pay more if certain performance goals are met. Earn-outs are most common when the target is a private company, but we occasionally observe them used with public targets. Earn-outs may also be useful in ensuring the retention of a founder or the target company's management. Earn-outs are usually based on such financial measures as earnings, revenues, and EBITDA, but sometimes, they are based on non-financial measures—for example, getting a new drug through clinical trials or getting FDA approval for it. Earn-outs can be used in both taxable and tax-free transactions.

Earn-outs, while useful, are not without issues. For example, assume a target is deeply integrated into an acquirer's business and, for the most part, does not operate on its own. If the target fails to achieve the performance goals set in the earn-out, the parties will likely disagree over why the failure occurred—specifically, those who are to receive the earn-out may believe that the acquirer interfered with the target's ability to perform. Another issue is that earn-outs may provide incentives for the target's management to act in unintended ways if they are the potential recipients of the earn-out. For example, in order to achieve the maximum earn-out, the target management might cut back on expenditures such as advertising, research and development, and maintenance. These actions can increase earnings in the short run but not be in the best long-run interests of the company.

Other forms of contingent payments are sometimes used. For example, some proportion of the consideration can be held in escrow. If the buyer identifies some problem after the acquisition, then the escrow can be used to make the buyer whole. An example of this type of issue is observing that working capital is less than what the target promised would be in place at the date of close.

In a stock-for-stock transaction, once the exchange ratio is fixed, the target's shareholders will bear the risk of the acquirer's shares potentially declining in value. For example, the market may react negatively to the announcement of the transaction, causing the acquirer's share price to decline. In order to mitigate this risk, **floors** are often put into place, meaning that the deal will not take place if the acquirer's share price falls below a certain amount or that the **exchange ratio** (the number and/or fraction of the acquirer's shares for each target share) will have to be adjusted. On the other hand, if the acquirer's share price rises substantially, the buyer may want to be protected against overpaying. In this case, a **cap** is put in that specifies a maximum price above which the deal will not take place or the exchange ratio will be adjusted. Putting in a floor and a cap creates what is known as a **collar**. If the deal simply has a fixed exchange ratio with no collar, then the consideration that will ultimately be received is linearly related to the acquirer's share price. If the deal is for a fixed value, there will be uncertainty over the ultimate number of shares that will be issued, which will move inversely with the acquirer's share price. There are many, many variations on how collars can be constructed, and the different risk scenarios for the buyer and seller are associated with the various forms. As we discuss later in the chapter, stock-for-stock transactions lead to risk sharing between the target and acquirer.

A **material adverse change clause (MAC)** allows the buyer to back out of the deal if there is a sudden change to the target's business that seriously undermines it. When a buyer uses this clause, there is often a suit brought against the buyer by the target alleging that the event did not constitute a material adverse change. A well-known case of this involved Enron in the month prior to its filing for bankruptcy. Enron was supposed to be merged into Dynegy, but a few days after the merger was announced, Enron announced a major restatement of its financial statements because of its trading business. A few weeks later, Dynegy indicated that it would not proceed with the deal and relied on the material adverse change clause to do so. Enron sued, but the case was eventually dropped.

In many acquisitions, the parties agree to **termination fees** (or **breakup fees**) in case one of the parties fails to close on the transaction (unless certain conditions are met that allow one side to cancel the deal). Termination fees are meant to compensate the other party for its costs as well as to invoke a penalty in order to make sure that both parties close. Bates and Lemmon (2003) study termination fees and find that, on average, the fee is approximately 3% of the deal value. They also find that if the contract contains a termination fee, a higher incidence of deal completion is observed. In their sample (which ended in the late 1990s), termination fees paid to the acquirer by the target were much more prevalent than termination fees paid by the acquirer to the target.[14] Interestingly, there have recently been a few cases in which the target required the acquirer to pay the full purchase price if the acquisition was blocked by antitrust authorities, effectively imposing all of the antitrust risk on the acquirer.

A **no shop clause** or a **no solicitation** or **exclusivity provision** prevents a target from pursuing offers from other potentially interested parties for a specified amount of time—usually 45 to 60 days. The rationale for a "no shop" clause is that once a letter of intent is signed, the buyer will expend considerable time and money in due diligence, arranging financing and other activities, and this gives the buyer some protection. A **go shop** clause gives the target an opportunity to continue shopping for another buyer. A "go shop" clause allows the target's board of directors to exercise its fiduciary duty to shareholders by making sure that there are no higher bidders. This is particularly important if the company has neither been shopped extensively nor been through an auction process. From the buyer's perspective, this can be seen as advantageous, for it removes the likelihood of the target being sued by its shareholders, which can be costly and lead to delays in closing the transaction. Of course, it also increases the probability that there will be a higher competing bid.

A **lock-up right** gives a buyer the right to buy shares at a specified price if another buyer acquires the company. The price is often set at the current market value (or lower) at the time the lock-up right is given. Targets often give lock-up rights to friendly buyers in an attempt to thwart a takeover by an unfriendly suitor. There are also asset lock-up rights that give a buyer the ability to buy certain assets or divisions if another buyer acquires the company. These are also used to thwart takeover attempts by unfriendly suitors.

Valuation Key 16.6

The specific form of a transaction can affect the value of the target to the bidder and the value that the target shareholders will receive. Taxes are a major consideration, and the bidder's valuation of the target and the target's valuation of the offer have to consider tax consequences. In addition, the bidder also needs to understand both the liabilities that it is assuming and the status of the target's existing contracts. Contract provisions can also affect who bears certain risks in a transaction.

---

[14] Bates, T., and M. Lemmon, "Breaking Up Is Hard to Do? An Analysis of Termination Fee Provisions and Merger Outcomes," *Journal of Financial Economics* 69 (2003), pp. 469–504.

16.6 OVERVIEW OF HOW TO VALUE MERGER AND ACQUISITION TRANSACTIONS

The value of a post-merger company after completing an M&A transaction is equal to the sum of the values of the standalone companies plus the value of the synergies and other efficiencies created, minus the costs associated with the transaction and integration and adjusted for tax and other considerations. In general, we value M&A transactions with all the same valuation methods and processes discussed in previous chapters, but now, we also need to measure the value of the synergies, efficiencies, and costs associated with the transaction and integration. We also want to take into consideration the tax effects of the transaction and other relevant elements of the deal structure. The typical valuation methods used to do this include the discounted cash flow method and the market multiples method. Market multiple valuations are based on comparable transactions or on publicly traded comparable companies adjusted for a merger premium. We briefly discuss the methods used to value an acquisition (from the acquirer's perspective) before discussing the types of techniques used by investment bankers in rendering fairness opinions; we then discuss the valuation issue from the target's perspective.

The Acquirer's Perspective on Valuation

The acquirer usually first values the target on a standalone basis as it is currently being operated. If the company is publicly traded, the acquirer can then examine whether the target is fairly valued in the marketplace. Understanding the market's valuation is useful for the acquirer, as the market price already builds in expectations of future growth and profitability prospects. It is important to understand the standalone value, as this is the bid that would leave the target shareholders no better or worse off (and hence indifferent), assuming that they did not have to pay any income taxes as a result of the transaction.

In order to answer the question of how much value the transaction can create, we must understand how the acquirer intends to utilize the target. Knowing this allows us to value the incremental cash flows from operating the target more efficiently than on a standalone basis, plus the value of the synergies from the combination of the two companies, less the value of any integration and transaction costs. The acquisition might also have an effect on how the acquirer manages itself, which must also be considered in the valuation of the acquisition. As indicated previously, the tax effects of the transaction are important as well, as they could impact the valuation.

To value the synergies, net of any costs associated with the transaction and with the integration, the acquirer needs a detailed integration plan. This plan will cover revenue, expense, and capital investment synergies, integration costs, and other forecasts. Thus, a detailed integration plan contains many of the inputs needed to measure the value of the synergies, net of any costs, using the discounted cash flow method.

To be sure, the acquirer or its financial advisors will perform market multiple valuations based on either precedent transactions or publicly traded companies (adjusted for merger premiums). These analyses, however, are more useful for understanding what price might be acceptable to the target and not for estimating the value of the combined companies to the acquirer. Thus, a market multiple valuation will help inform the negotiation process and provide input into the likelihood of a target accepting an offer at a certain price, but these analyses do not provide a clear indication of how the target company will create value for the acquirer—that perspective normally comes from a discounted cash flow (DCF) valuation. Recent premiums or valuations based on market multiples from precedent transactions can provide some, albeit limited, guidance from which a range of reasonable values for the synergies from the current deal might be gauged.

From the acquirer's perspective, the negotiating range for the transaction is between two values. The minimum value is equal to the standalone value of the target as it is currently operating (assuming the transaction is tax free to the target and its shareholders). The maximum value is equal to the target's post-acquisition value including all efficiencies and synergies net of costs associated with combining the two companies. If the acquirer's bid is equal to the maximum value, the expected net present value of the acquisition (or the value created) for the acquirer will be zero. In other words, the investment will simply earn its cost of capital. As such, in order to create value, the acquirer must submit a bid that is less than the maximum value as defined earlier.

We will discuss this in detail later, but it is necessary to value the acquirer on a post-transaction basis in a stock-for-stock transaction in order to understand the implications of a given exchange ratio. This allows us to determine how the expected gains from the merger are split between the acquirer and the target. The acquirer needs to understand what its post-transaction value will be (with the target) in order to determine the exchange ratio that appropriately reflects the amount the acquirer wants to bid for the target and how any potential value creation will be allocated between itself and the target.

The Target's Perspective on Valuation

While the parties might not agree on the value of the acquisition, the target and acquirer use standard valuations methods—the discounted cash flow method, market multiples of publicly traded companies (adjusted for merger premiums), a premium analysis, the market multiples from precedent transactions, and a leveraged buyout analysis. Naturally, the target company's management, board of directors, and shareholders want to know that the offer is reasonable; indeed, it is the fiduciary responsibility of the board and officers, and they will look extensively at other transactions involving similar companies and even at other transaction types (such as a leveraged buyout) in order to make this determination. Thus, targets often rely more heavily on market-based valuations (to the extent that they are reasonably comparable), for these valuations rely more heavily on the market prices of other transactions.

Publicly traded target companies (and often larger private companies with minority shareholders) hire financial advisors to render a fairness opinion for any offer that the target expects to accept. As discussed in Chapter 1, the practice of securing a fairness opinion has been common since the Van Gorkom case (see Valuation in Practice 1.2). The board of directors also uses other information to assess the fairness of any offer. For example, if the company is extensively shopped to potential buyers, yet no other bids emerge, the board of directors will have a better idea of the likelihood that higher bids can be obtained.

As we discussed earlier, in a stock-for-stock transaction, we must value the acquirer with the target on a post-transaction basis. Since the target shareholders are receiving stock in the acquirer, we need to value the acquirer post-transaction to understand the offer being made to the target shareholders. Without performing this valuation, we do not have any basis for even understanding if the target shareholders are being offered a premium.

In the merger of ACS and Xerox (see Section 16.10), the fairness opinions rendered by the advisors for both companies utilized various valuation methods and conducted other analyses. The analyses included analyses of the stock trading history of both companies, deal premiums, precedent transaction premiums, and valuations based on precedent transaction multiples, public company trading multiples, analysts' forecasts of future projected prices, discounted cash flow, and a leveraged buyout analysis.

> ## Valuation Key 16.7
>
> Acquirers rely most heavily on a discounted cash flow analysis to measure the value of the target to the acquirer. However, the acquirer also knows that the target and its financial advisors rely on a variety of valuation methods and merger premium analyses to assess the fairness of a deal. Hence, these techniques also help to inform the acquirer of the likely offer a target might expect to receive.

16.7 CONTROL PREMIUMS (MINORITY DISCOUNTS) AND LIQUIDITY PREMIUMS (ILLIQUIDITY DISCOUNTS)

In this section, we discuss two additional adjustments that are sometimes relevant to a valuation of an acquisition transaction—control premiums and illiquidity discounts. As we will soon explain, depending on the valuation context and valuation methods we use to value the acquisition transaction, the valuation methods may need to be adjusted for control premiums and illiquidity discounts. Minority discounts (the inverse of control premiums) may occur when a company has diffusely held ownership. Agency cost theory suggests that because of the inherent conflict between a company's management and its owners, the shares of such a company will ultimately trade at a lower price than if the manager owned 100% of the company.[15] Liquidity premiums, illiquidity discounts, or discounts for non-marketability occur when

---

[15] See, for example, Jensen, M., and W. Meckling, "Theory of the Firm: Managerial Behavior, Agency Costs, and Ownership Structure," *Journal of Financial Economics* 3 (1976), pp. 305–360. Conflicts between groups of shareholders can also exist, and another type of control premium can occur when a shareholder has a majority ownership position and control of the shares. This type of control premium is based on the assumption that control provides the ability of the controlling shareholder to engage in self-dealing, which occurs when a controlling shareholder benefits at the expense of minority shareholders.

an asset does not have a readily available liquid market in which it can be traded. A private company is an example of such an asset. Scholarly research documents that the price of an asset trading in an illiquid market is lower than what it would have been had it been traded in a liquid market. In certain settings, our valuation of an acquisition transaction may need to include an appropriate illiquidity discount.

Control Premiums (Minority Discounts)

A control premium—as it relates to mergers and acquisitions—is the increase in value that results from reducing or eliminating the agency costs that result from the inherent conflict between managers and owners. The factors underlying a control premium include the power to elect directors, appoint management, set compensation, control the company's financial strategy, and make investment decisions. If an acquirer purchases more than 50% of the voting interest in a target company, the acquirer will own a controlling interest. When an acquirer has a controlling interest, it will gain control over decision making in that company. With more than 50% of the voting power in the target company, the owner of the controlling interest has the power to make all decisions for the company and, thus, has control over the target company's activities.

Control alone, however, does not imply the elimination or even the reduction of agency costs. For example, if a publicly traded target that has diffuse ownership is acquired by a publicly traded acquirer that has diffuse ownership, the agency costs may either stay the same, increase, or decrease, depending on the relative effectiveness of the governance structures of the target and acquirer. If the target has a governance structure that controls agency costs more efficiently than the acquirer's governance structure, a purchase of the target by that acquirer may not lead to a reduction in agency costs.

A minority discount is the inverse of a control premium. For example, assume that the value of a company's stock is $10 per share when the company is optimally managed (no agency costs) and $8 per share when the company's shares are diffusely held and the company is managed suboptimally. The control premium in this example is 25% ($0.25 = \$10/\$8 - 1$), and the minority discount is 20% ($0.2 = 1 - \$8/\$10$). Thus, the control premium (CP) and the minority discount (MD) are related in the following way: $MD = CP/(CP + 1)$. In our example, the minority discount is $0.2 = 0.25/1.25$.

Should M&A valuations include a control premium, or, in other words, should M&A valuations exclude a minority discount? If so, how do we measure them? It is not at all apparent if an acquirer purchases a control position in a target company, whether the acquirer will include a control premium in its valuation. As stated earlier, whether or not an increase in value from control results from the transaction depends on the relative effectiveness of the target and acquirer to control agency costs.

If we value a target company using a discounted cash flow valuation based on free cash flow forecasts that include the effect of any change in agency costs after the acquisition, we do not adjust for a minority discount or control premium. This is because the discounted cash flow valuation already should incorporate the extent to which agency costs will persist or are eliminated after the acquisition.

Now consider a valuation of a target that is based on market multiples measured using publicly traded and diffusely owned comparable companies. Assume for a moment that the extent of any agency costs or ineffective governance structure affects the value of a firm but not any of the denominators used in the multiple valuation. Some might argue that the valuation implicitly includes a minority discount (excludes a control premium), but that depends on the effectiveness of the governance structure of the comparables used in the multiples valuation. The value of the target will exceed the multiple valuation if the governance structure of the target post-transaction is more effective than the governance structure of the comparables used in the market multiple valuation. In addition, it is important to recognize that if both the numerator and the denominator of a market multiple are impacted by a minority discount in identical proportions (for example, both value and earnings are 10% lower), it is possible that the market multiples will not be affected by minority discounts or ineffective governance at all.

Some argue that in order to assess the control premium, the valuations of publicly traded comparable companies should be increased by the typical premiums paid in mergers. It is important to note that observed merger premiums do not equal control premiums; in fact, it is possible for a bid not to include any control premium even when the merger premium is large. It is incorrect to conclude that merger premiums merely reflect control premiums. Rather, merger premiums often reflect the fact that some of the synergy gains are allocated to the target shareholders in a transaction. Indeed, if you recall our review of the studies on whether M&A activity creates value for acquirers and targets, empirical evidence suggests that, on average, all economic gains from mergers (and maybe more than 100% of the gains) are given to the target shareholders. In addition, some of the premiums can also be compensation to the target shareholders for the taxes that they will have to pay in a transaction.

The takeaway from this discussion is that we want to be careful when we "tack on" control premiums in valuations in an M&A setting. Moreover, estimating a control premium is difficult. It is misguided to think that merger premiums are synonymous with control premiums, for merger premiums also reflect the synergies that are allocated to the target shareholders in the deal price.

Valuation Key 16.8

A control premium—as it relates to mergers and acquisitions—is the increase in value of a company's equity that results from the elimination or reduction of agency costs inherent in the conflict between managers and owners. The factors underlying a control premium include the power to elect directors, appoint management, set compensation, control the company's financial strategy, and make investment decisions. A minority discount is the inverse of a control premium. Valuation specialists need to consider whether or not to include a control premium and how it is to be measured.

Liquidity Premiums (Illiquidity Discount)

Liquidity (or marketability) is a concept related to how much time it takes to sell an asset and the cost of selling it. All else equal, investors prefer to hold assets that can be sold quickly at a price that reflects their underlying value when sold without undue time pressure.[16] We cannot observe liquidity premiums (or illiquidity discounts) directly; thus, researchers attempt to estimate illiquidity discounts based on empirical analysis.

Researchers estimate illiquidity discounts using various approaches. One approach is to compare the prices of restricted stocks (stocks that cannot be sold for some time period—say, three years) to the prices of freely traded stocks for companies that have both types of stocks.[17] Another approach examines private stock issuances in private companies just prior to the company going public through an initial public offering (IPO) in order to estimate the difference between the prices paid in the private equity transaction and the IPO. Another approach compares transaction multiples for privately held company M&A transactions to publicly held company M&A transactions.[18] Unfortunately, the results from these studies do not converge to provide a straightforward way of adjusting value for illiquidity discounts, as the discounts measured in these studies vary.

Together, the results of these studies show that illiquidity discounts vary over time and across estimation methods. In general, these studies do not examine illiquidity discounts by industry, so we do not have many insights into whether these discounts vary across industries. However, the studies consistently document the existence of illiquidity discounts, which can have implications for how we value an entity. Longstaff (2001) uses an option valuation approach to measure the illiquidity discount, and he begins by examining an investor's inter-temporal portfolio choice when the investor's trading is restricted;[19] he shows that a 35% illiquidity discount is plausible. The research documents differences between public

---

[16] This concept of liquidity is discussed in Keynes, J., *A Treatise on Money*, Vol. 2, London (1930).

[17] For restricted stock studies, see Wruck, K. H., "Equity Ownership Concentration and Firm Value: Evidence from Private Equity Financings," *Journal of Financial Economics* vol. 23, no. 1 (1989), pp. 3–28; Silber, William L., "Discounts on Restricted Stock: The Impact of Illiquidity on Stock Prices," *Financial Analysts Journal* (July–August 1991), pp. 60–64; Hertzel, Michael, and Richard L. Smith, "Market Discounts and Shareholder Gains for Placing Equity Privately," *Journal of Finance* (1993), pp. 459–485; Pratt, Shannon, P., *Business Valuation Discounts and Premiums*, 2nd ed., New York, NY: John Wiley and Sons (1999); Bajaj, Mukesh, David J. Denis, Stephen P. Ferris, and Atulya Sarin, "Firm Value and Marketability Discounts," *Journal of Corporate Law* (2001); and Barclay, M. J., C. G. Holderness, and D. P. Sheehan, "Private Placements and Managerial Entrenchment," *Journal of Corporate Finance* 13 (2007), pp. 461–484.

[18] For private company sales transactions see, Koeplin, J., A. Sarin, and A. Shapiro, "The Private Company Discount," *Journal of Applied Corporate Finance* vol. 12, no. 4 (2007), pp. 94–101; Officer, M. S., "The Price of Corporate Liquidity: Acquisition Discounts for Unlisted Targets," *Journal of Financial Economics* vol. 83, no. 3 (2007), pp. 571–98; Paglia, J. K., and M. Harjoto, "The Discount for Lack of Marketability in Privately Owned Companies: A Multiples Approach," *Journal of Business Valuation and Economic Loss Analysis* vol. 5, no. 1 (2010), Article 5; and De Franco, G., I. Gavious, J. Y. Jin, and G. D. Richardson, "Do Private Company Targets that Hire Big 4 Auditors Receive Higher Proceeds?" *Contemporary Accounting Research* XX (2011), pp. 1–48.

[19] Longstaff, Francis A., "Optimal Portfolio Choice and the Valuation of Illiquid Assets," *Review of Financial Studies* 14 (2001), pp. 407–431.

company and private company transaction multiples, suggesting the potential existence of illiquidity discounts for privately held companies. On the other hand, these differences may be due to systematic differences between public and private companies.

Valuation Key 16.9

Liquidity is a concept related to how much time it takes to sell an asset as well as the cost of selling the asset. All else equal, investors prefer to hold assets that can be sold quickly at a price that reflects their underlying value when sold without undue time pressure. Empirical research documents that illiquidity discounts can be as large as 35% or even larger.

De Franco et al. (2011)[20] estimate cross-sectional regressions, controlling for growth, size, and profit margin in the estimation of private company discounts, and they show discounts between 20% and 40%. Interestingly, they show that having a Big 4 auditor mitigates this discount (or, in other words, the discount is even worse for private companies with non-Big 4 auditors). Of course, this does not mean that every company should hire a Big 4 auditor if it wants to be sold, for there are costs associated with hiring a Big 4 auditor in terms of additional audit fees, additional costs of personnel, additional internal control costs, and so forth.

As a valuation specialist, we have to consider whether, and under what circumstances, we should adjust our valuation for illiquidity. In general, the discounted cash flow and market multiple valuation methods do not include an illiquidity discount. The discounted cash flow approach does not include illiquidity discounts because it uses a cost of capital measured from publicly traded stocks. We have no asset pricing model for private and illiquid companies. As such, in order to apply an illiquidity discount, one has to calculate the "as-if" public company equity value before applying the discount to the equity value. Market multiples for public companies would also not include an illiquidity discount. Transaction multiples from private companies may include synergies and control premiums, and may or may not include illiquidity discounts. However, if the synergies and potential control premiums are the same in public company and private company transaction multiples, and if other determinants are controlled for as well (growth, profitability, etc.), the difference between the multiples may give an estimate of the private company discount, especially when the buyer is a private company as well.

The resolution of this issue is unclear. We should consider several factors when we are deciding whether to include an illiquidity discount. For example, if we are valuing a private company because it is about to issue publicly traded stock in an IPO, we do not include an illiquidity or private company discount, as it is going public. In the case in which a private company is being purchased by a public company, the public company might argue that there should be a discount for non-marketability, but the private company will likely argue that once it is acquired, it will no longer be private. Obviously, the resolution of this debate will depend on the relative negotiating power of the two parties, which will be influenced by the number of potential acquirers interested in acquiring the private company. To include an illiquidity discount, we estimate its magnitude by relying on some of the extant empirical evidence.

16.8 IS THE MERGER AND ACQUISITION TRANSACTION ACCRETIVE OR DILUTIVE?

In addition to valuing the company using the methods we discussed earlier, managers often analyze the effect of a potential transaction on earnings and other performance measures. These managers may be concerned about the effects of the transaction on the company's debt covenants, compensation agreements, and other contracts, or they may be concerned with the difficulty of explaining to analysts and investors why a merger is value increasing when the common measures of performance—such as earnings per share—are not accretive (increasing). The focus of this section is on measuring the accretive or dilutive (decreasing) effect of a transaction on short-run (one or two years) earnings per share. We can, of course, examine whether a transaction is accretive to value or to something other than earnings per share, but earnings per share is often used for analyzing accretion and dilution. Managers of public companies

---

[20] De Franco, G., I. Gavious, J. Y. Jin, and G. D. Richardson, "Do Private Company Targets that Hire Big 4 Auditors Receive Higher Proceeds?" *Contemporary Accounting Research* XX (2011), pp. 1–48.

are interested in knowing what the likely effect is on earnings per share so that they can provide investors with information on the likely earnings impact, which can be negative in the short–run even if the transaction creates value.

Accretive and Dilutive Effects of Merger and Acquisition Transactions on Earnings per Share and Other Performance Measures

To analyze a transaction's accretive and dilutive effects on an acquirer, we create a financial model and measure various performance metrics for the expected post-merger company. The financial model can be as simple as measuring the effect of the transaction on earnings or as complex as creating a complete and detailed financial model for the entire post-merger company.

Assume our focus is on the accretion or dilution of earnings per share. We begin with the financial statements of the standalone companies. We then measure any financing costs that affect earnings and the related income tax effects in order to measure the after-tax financing costs. Some of these costs might be short term (bridge financing), but some may be long term (long-term debt issued to finance the transaction). In addition, the financing might involve the use of excess cash, the after-tax proceeds from the sale of excess assets (the assets that do not fit the post-merger strategy of the company), or newly issued shares. We also adjust the financials for revenue and cost synergies, other efficiencies, integration costs, and other costs of the transaction. We then adjust the combined earnings for all the above effects of the transaction on an after-tax basis and adjust for any change in the number of shares outstanding of the acquirer.

In Exhibit 16.7, we illustrate this analysis. Assume the acquirer plans to acquire the target company's equity for $6,000, which is financed with $5,000 in excess cash and $1,000 in new debt. In Exhibit 16.7, we assume that the merger occurred on the first day of the year and that it is now the end of the first year. First, we adjust the standalone financial statements for the debt financing of the transaction, increasing the debt and excess cash on the balance sheet by $1,000. The increase in debt, which has a cost of debt and

EXHIBIT 16.7	Measuring the Accretive and Dilutive Effects of Merger and Acquisition Transactions on Earnings

	Standalone Acquirer	Standalone Target	Financing	Asset Changes	Synergies	Post-Merger Company
Income Statement						
Revenues	$ 4,200.0	$3,000.0			$ 50.0	$ 7,250.0
Operating expenses	−3,113.3	−2,166.7		$ −200.0	120.0	−5,360.0
Interest income	100.0	0.0		−100.0		0.0
Interest expense	−120.0	−60.0	$ −80.0			−260.0
Income taxes	−426.7	−309.3	32.0	120.0	−68.0	−652.0
Earnings	$ 640.0	$ 464.0	$ −48.0	$ −180.0	$102.0	$ 978.0
Shares outstanding	500.0	300.0	500.0	500.0	500.0	500.0
Earnings per share	$ 1.280	$ 1.547	$ −0.096	$ −0.360	$0.204	$ 1.956
Balance Sheet						
Excess cash	$ 5,000.0	$ 0.0	$1,000.0	$−6,000.0		$ 0.0
Operating assets	6,000.0	5,000.0		2,000.0		13,000.0
Total assets	$11,000.0	$5,000.0	$1,000.0	$−4,000.0	$ 0.0	$13,000.0
Debt	$ 2,000.0	$1,000.0	$1,000.0			$ 4,000.0
Equity	9,000.0	4,000.0		$−4,000.0		9,000.0
Liabilities and equity	$11,000.0	$5,000.0	$1,000.0	$−4,000.0	$ 0.0	$13,000.0

interest rate equal to 8%, increases interest expense by $80 ($80 = 0.08 × $1,000) and decreases income taxes by $32. In the next adjustment, we eliminate $6,000 in excess cash and the target company's $4,000 book value of equity. This difference represents a write-up of the target's assets to the price paid. This difference can reflect an increase in the market value of specific assets that were recorded on the target's balance sheet at book value, or it can reflect an amount paid over the value of the target's individual assets—goodwill. We assume that we can deduct 10% of this amount per year for income tax and financial statement purposes. The reduction in excess cash has the effect of eliminating interest income ($100).

Finally, we adjust the financial statements for synergies. We measure the revenue synergies ($50 increase, which results from price increases and has no change in expenses related to it), the expense synergies ($120 decrease), and the related income taxes (40%) in order to calculate the after-tax effect of synergies on earnings of $102. If the synergies required additional investments, these investments would be reflected on the post-merger balance sheet. The sum of these components is equal to the earnings of the post-merger company. In our example, the post-merger earnings are $978, which we measure first by adding the earnings of the acquirer ($640) to the earnings of the target ($464). We then subtract the increased after-tax financing costs ($48) and the lost interest income and additional amortization of the purchase premium after taxes ($180). Finally, we add the after-tax synergies of $102.

To measure the effect of the transaction on earnings per share, we also measure the effect of the transaction on the number of shares outstanding. In this example, we use excess cash and issued debt to finance the transaction, so the number of shares outstanding is unaffected by the transaction. Thus, the earnings per share for the post-merger company is $1.956 versus $1.280 for the acquirer before the merger, indicating that the transaction is accretive to earnings per share. Note that in this example, we did not allow for integration costs, investment banking fees, and other costs associated with the initial years of an M&A transaction. Sometimes it is these costs that make a transaction dilutive for the first few years after the transaction.

The key question, of course, is whether the transaction is accretive to value. Before we answer this, it is worth noting that how an acquirer finances a transaction results in different measures of earnings per share for the post-merger company. In addition, even though our example focuses on the accretion of earnings per share, we can use the financial modeling and financial analysis (ratio) tools from Chapters 2 and 4 to measure the accretive and dilutive effect of a transaction on many other financial statement relations, such as return on assets or return on equity.

Valuation Key 16.10

In addition to assessing the effect of an M&A transaction on value, acquiring managers often assess the accretive and dilutive effects of the transaction on performance measures such as earnings per share. To measure the accretive and dilutive effects of a transaction, we create a financial model of the post-merger company with which we then examine various performance measures. The post-merger company includes both standalone companies and the effects of the transaction on these companies (synergies, transactions costs, integration costs, etc.).

REVIEW EXERCISE 16.2

Measuring Earnings Accretion

A company (the acquirer) purchased another company (the target) for a 20% premium over the target's stock price of $25 per share; the acquirer's stock price at that time was $23 per share. The acquirer financed the transaction with $4,000 of excess cash and $2,000 of debt, the latter of which had a 6% cost of capital and interest rate. The interest tax shields from the incremental debt were valued at $400. As a result of the merger, the companies expected to be able to annually increase revenues by $30 and decrease expenses by $270 for some period; in total, these synergies were valued at $1,500. The company planned to amortize any purchase premium at an average rate of 4.5% per year, which is tax deductible, and the resulting tax shelter from this amortization was valued at $150. The reported interest income was all due to the excess cash being used in the transaction. Assume an income tax rate of 40%. Prepare a post-merger income statement and balance sheet (similar to the ones in Exhibit 16.7) and analyze the impact on earnings and earnings per share.

	Standalone Acquirer	Standalone Target		Standalone Acquirer	Standalone Target
Income Statement			**Balance Sheet**		
Revenues	$4,000.0	$2,750.0	Excess cash	$ 3,000.0	$1,000.0
Operating expenses . . .	−2,280.0	−1,790.0	Operating assets.	8,000.0	5,000.0
Interest income.	60.0	20.0	Total assets.	$11,000.0	$6,000.0
Interest expense.	−180.0	−60.0			
Income taxes	−640.0	−368.0			
Earnings	$ 960.0	$552.0	Debt	$ 3,000.0	$1,000.0
			Equity	8,000.0	5,000.0
			Liabilities and equity. . . .	$11,000.0	$6,000.0
Shares outstanding	400.0	200.0			
Earnings per share	$ 2.400	$2.760			

Solution on page 716.

Accretive and Dilutive Effects of Merger and Acquisition Transactions on Market Multiples (and Value)

Managers may also be concerned with the market multiples of the post-merger company. M&A transactions can affect earnings, value, and the number of shares outstanding—all of which can affect P/E multiples. Even if a merger has synergies, an increase in earnings per share does not necessarily mean that the merger created value for the acquirer. Even if the post-merger earnings per share increases, the value of the acquirer will decrease if an acquirer overpays for a target company. In Exhibit 16.8, we present valuation information for the example in Exhibit 16.7.

| **EXHIBIT 16.8** | Effect of Merger and Acquisition Transaction on Post-Merger Market Multiples | | | | | |

	Standalone Acquirer	Standalone Target	Financing	Asset Changes	Value of Synergies	Post-Merger Company Including Synergies
Firm value.	$12,000.00	$5,240.00	$ 320.00	$−4,200.00	$1,020.00	$14,380.00
Debt	2,000.00	1,000.00	1,000.00	0.00	0.00	4,000.00
Equity value	$10,000.00	$4,240.00	$−680.00	$−4,200.00	$1,020.00	$10,380.00
Shares outstanding	500.00	300.00			500.00	500.00
Price per share.	$ 20.00	$ 14.13			$ 2.04	$ 20.76
Earnings per share	$ 1.280	$ 1.547			$ 0.204	$ 1.956
Price-to-earnings ratio	15.6	9.1			10.0	10.6

The standalone acquirer has a firm value of $12,000, which includes $2,000 in debt and an equity value of $10,000 with a stock price of $20; the acquirer also holds $5,000 in excess cash. The target has a firm value equal to $5,240, an equity value equal to $4,240, and a stock price of $14.13. An analyst has already valued the transaction and has valuation estimates of the operating and financing synergies. Upon merging, the value of the operating synergies is estimated at $1,020, and the value of the interest tax shields from issuing $1,000 in debt is estimated to be $320. The change in the value of the firm from using its excess cash of $5,000—net of gaining the tax shelter benefit from the amortization of the purchase premium—is a $4,200 decrease. The post-merger firm value is equal to $14,380, which is the sum of the two standalone values, the value of the synergies, and the value of the incremental interest tax shields, less a reduction in excess cash net of the benefit of the purchase premium amortization ($14,380 = $12,000 + $5,240 + $320 − $4,200 + $1,020). The post-merger debt is equal to the sum of the debt of the standalone companies and the newly issued debt, $4,000 ($4,000 = $2,000 + $1,000 + $1,000). The resulting post-merger equity value is equal to the value of the firm minus the value of the debt, $10,380

expected value creation from this acquisition is $300; however, since the outcome of the merger is uncertain, we assume that the potential outcomes—the value created or destroyed—ranges from a gain of $1,200 to a loss of $600. Thus, the value of the post-merger company ranges from $2,400 to $4,200 ($2,400 = $1,000 + $2,000 − $600; $4,200 = $1,000 + $2,000 + $1,200) with an expected value of $3,300 ($3,300 = $1,000 + $2,000 + $300).

The minimum price that the target shareholders will accept is equal to its standalone equity value, $V_T = \$1,000$. This minimum value stays constant, independent of the range of potential post-merger outcomes, and the target will never accept a price that is lower than its standalone value. The maximum price that the acquirer will pay is the amount it can pay without reducing its standalone value of $2,000. This maximum is equal to the post-merger value of the company, minus the standalone value of the acquirer $(V_P - V_A)$. The maximum value is a function of the expected value of the potential outcomes. We show the minimum and maximum prices for a range of possible outcomes in Exhibit 16.9.

EXHIBIT 16.9	Negotiation Strategy Minimum and Maximum Price for a Cash Deal

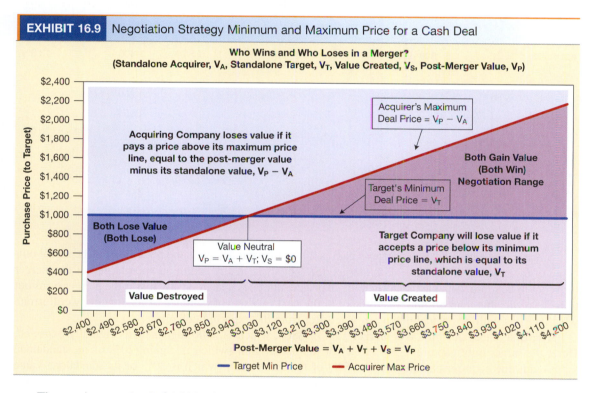

The maximum price is $1,300 when the value of the synergies is equal to its expected value of $300 ($1,300 = $3,300 − $2,000). The premium paid to the target is equal to the acquisition price, minus the target's standalone value, $V_{T, Premium} = V_{T, Paid} - V_T$. The premium paid to the target at this price is $300 ($300 = $1,300 − $1,000). However, the maximum price—and hence the maximum premium—increases as the value of the expected synergies increases. When the value of the synergies is equal to zero, the maximum and minimum price lines intersect; this is the value neutral point—the point at which the maximum and minimum prices are equal to each other. When the value of the synergies is negative, the maximum value the acquirer will be willing to pay is below the minimum value the target will accept.

In this illustration, the parties negotiate between the maximum and minimum prices shown in the exhibit as a function of value of the post-transaction company. The acquirer creates value (in expectation) from the merger as long as it negotiates a price below its maximum price, and the target gains value from the merger as long as it negotiates a price above its minimum price. In short, both parties will increase their values in expectation as long as they negotiate a price between the minimum and maximum prices; however, this can occur only if the transaction is expected to create value (to the right of the neutral value point in the exhibit). To the left of the neutral value point, one party must lose value in order for the other party to gain value, and it is possible for both parties to lose value.

In cash deals, the acquirer keeps all of the deal risk (the uncertainty of the actual outcome of the merger). The upside of keeping all of the deal risk is larger than expected returns if the actual outcome is better than expected, and the downside is lower than expected returns if the actual outcome is worse than expected. We illustrate this effect with our example. Assume that the negotiated cash price for the target is $1,200—a $200 premium. In the first column of Exhibit 16.10, we present the allocation of the gain from our merger, which is based on the expected value of the synergies of $300. The target captures 67% (0.667 = $200/$300) of the expected gain (20% of its standalone value; 0.2 = $200/$1,000), and the acquirer captures 33% (0.333 = $100/$300) of the expected gain (5% of its standalone value; 0.05 = $100/$2,000).

EXHIBIT 16.10	Allocation of Merger Gain (Loss) for the Cash Deal Example								
Cash Deal–Equity Values	**Expected Outcome Used in Deal Negotiation**			**Actual Outcome with More Value Created**			**Actual Outcome with Value Destroyed**		
	Outcome	% Split	% Gain	Outcome	% Split	% Gain	Outcome	% Split	% Gain
Standalone value of acquirer	$2,000			$2,000			$2,000		
Standalone value of target	1,000			1,000			1,000		
Combined standalone value.	$3,000			$3,000			$3,000		
Value created (merger gain (loss))	300			800			–400		
Post-merger value	$3,300			$3,800			$2,600		
Overall gain or (loss) on acquisition	$ 300		10.0%	$ 800		26.7%	$–400		–13.3%
Post-merger value to target (cash received)	$1,200	36.4%		$1,200	31.6%		$1,200	46.2%	
Standalone value of target	–1,000			–1,000			–1,000		
Gain (loss) to target—merger premium	$ 200	66.7%	20.0%	$ 200	25.0%	20.0%	$ 200	nmf	20.0%
Post-merger value to acquirer	$2,100	63.6%		$2,600	68.4%		$1,400	53.8%	
Standalone value of acquirer	–2,000			–2,000			–2,000		
Gain or (loss) to acquirer	$ 100	33.3%	5.0%	$ 600	75.0%	30.0%	$ –600	nmf	–30.0%

Since this is a cash deal, the target's gain is 20% of its standalone value regardless of the actual outcome of the merger. In a cash deal, the target does not share in any additional merger gain if the merger turns out to be more valuable than originally expected, nor does it share in any loss if the merger turns out to be less valuable than originally expected. In the next two sets of columns of the exhibit, we illustrate what happens with two actual outcomes that differ from the expected outcome.

The first actual outcome is a merger gain of $800, which is $500 higher than originally expected. Here, the target only captures $200 (25%) of the actual gain (which is, again, 20% of its standalone value), and the acquirer captures $600 (75%) of the actual gain (which is 30% of its standalone value versus the expected 5%). The second actual outcome is a merger loss of −$400, which is $700 lower than originally expected. The target's merger premium remains unchanged at $200, but now, the acquirer suffers the $400 actual merger loss in addition to the $200 premium paid to the target; thus, the acquirer suffers a 30% loss (0.30 = $−600/$2,000) instead of the 5% expected gain.

Valuation Key 16.11

The target's minimum price is equal to its standalone value, and the acquirer's maximum price is equal to the post-merger value of the company minus the acquirer's standalone value. When value is expected to be created, the negotiation range is the difference between the maximum price the acquirer is willing to pay and the minimum price the target is willing to accept. The parties negotiate within this range, and the final deal price depends on a variety of factors—bargaining power, market conditions, income taxes, and such agency problems as owner-manager conflicts of interest.

Negotiating a Price within the Negotiation Range

The point within the negotiation range at which the parties negotiate a final deal price depends on a variety of factors, such as relative bargaining power, market conditions, income taxes, and such agency problems as owner–manager conflicts of interest. For example, all else equal, the target has more negotiating power if it has the ability to create synergies with more than one acquirer. Of course, not all acquirers have the same ability to create synergies with a target. For example, if the acquisition process is competitive, the acquirer with the highest ability to create synergies will most likely win the auction if it pays an acquisition price that is equal to the maximum price of the acquirer with the second highest ability to create synergies (assuming that none of the acquirers is overly optimistic in their forecasts).

REVIEW EXERCISE 16.4

Negotiation and Allocation of Synergies—Cash Deals

The standalone equity values of the target and acquirer are $4,000 and $10,000, respectively. The acquirer has 1,000 shares outstanding, and the target has 2,000 shares outstanding. Assume that the expected value creation from this acquisition is $3,000, but since the outcome of the merger is uncertain, assume a set of potential outcomes that ranges from a merger gain of $5,000 to a merger loss of $2,500. Assuming that the acquirer pays $6,000 in cash for the target's equity, calculate the gain or loss to the acquirer and target when the actual outcome of the merger is the expected, highest, and lowest outcome (see Exhibit 16.10).

Solution on pages 717–718.

Exchange Ratios

Not all acquisitions are cash deals. Acquirers often issue other securities instead of or in addition to cash. Acquirers sometimes issue such securities as debt or convertible debt, and in some acquisitions, the acquirer exchanges its stock for the target's stock, called a **stock-for-stock merger**. In a stock-for-stock merger, the target's shareholders exchange their ownership interests for ownership interests in the post-merger company. The number of shares of the acquirer that can be exchanged for one of the target's shares is called the exchange ratio. For example, if the acquirer exchanges 1.5 shares of its stock for every share of the target's stock, the exchange ratio is 1.5.

Although the concept of an exchange ratio is straightforward, calculating it based on the economics underlying the acquisition and deciding on how the gains are to be split between the acquirer and the target can be complex. The exchange ratio along with the number of shares of the target and an estimate of the post-transaction value of the acquirer (with the target) allows us to measure the expected acquisition price paid for the target. A higher exchange ratio allocates more post-merger shares to the target, which, in turn, allocates a higher proportion of the post-merger value to the target; in other words, a higher exchange ratio results in a higher acquisition price paid to the target shareholders. Analogous to the cash deal, the acquirer will have a maximum exchange ratio that it will offer, and the target will have a minimum exchange ratio that it will accept. However, no one knows with certainty what the price of the acquirer's shares will be after the merger closes. Thus, the parties face uncertainty about the value of the shares that will be exchanged in the transaction, and the parties face uncertainty about how the benefits of the merger will be split between the shareholders of the two companies. This is why floors and caps (discussed earlier) are often used in stock-for-stock acquisitions.

Minimum and Maximum Exchange Ratios for the Negotiation Range

We begin our discussion with the case of no change in value or zero synergies. When no value is created (no synergies), the maximum and minimum prices will intersect, and thus the minimum and maximum exchange ratios will equal each other. Once we introduce value creation into the merger, the minimum and maximum prices and the minimum and maximum exchange ratios will change.

Zero Synergies (No Value Created or Destroyed).   Since the acquirer is issuing shares to the target company, the number of shares held by the acquiring shareholders remains fixed. Shares are issued only to the target shareholders. The only way that the allocation of the post-merger company to the acquirer's shareholders will equal the acquirer's standalone value is when the acquirer's post-merger price per share, P_P, equals its pre-merger price per share, P_A ($P_P = P_A$). Thus, the value of the acquirer, V_A, before the merger or standalone value is equal to the number of acquirer shares, S_A, multiplied by the pre-merger price per share of the acquirer, P_A ($V_A = P_A \times S_A$). This value must be equal to the value of the acquirer to the acquirer's shareholders after the merger—the number of acquirer shares, S_A, multiplied by the post-merger price of the acquirer, P_P, or $P_P \times S_A$.

Since the number of shares held by the acquirer's pre-merger shareholders does not change, the maximum exchange ratio that the acquirer is willing to pay is the exchange ratio that leaves the price of

Valuation in Practice 16.4

Exchange Ratio in the LATAM Airlines Group Merger Below are the factors that LAN Airlines S.A. and TAM S.A. (see Valuation in Practice 16.3) considered in determining the exchange ratio:

> To define a range of exchange ratios and implied premiums acceptable to both parties, the parties reviewed the exchange ratios and implied premiums in comparable transactions during the last five years. The comparable transactions were selected after taking into account many different criteria, of which the most important were the industry in which the companies operated, the size of the transaction, board and key management representation, whether the companies continued to operate under their own names or a new or combined name, future headquarters locations, the ultimate relative share ownership of the two groups of shareholders, the form of consideration (e.g., cash, stock or a combination thereof) and whether the synergies were shared proportionally to the new ownership or otherwise. In addition to the criteria described above, the companies were valued using several different quantitative methodologies, including an analysis of the historical relative share trading prices, an analysis of historical and projected multiples of enterprise value to earnings before interest, taxes, depreciation, amortization and rentals based on public information, discounted cash flows based on free cash flow public projections, a contribution analysis and a comparison of research analysts' target prices. Finally, the parties took into account the net present value of estimated synergies and how they should be allocated.

Source: Offer to Exchange Each Common Share, Preferred Share and American Depositary Share of TAM S.A. for 0.90 of a Common Share of LAN AIRLINES S.A. Represented by American Depositary Shares or Brazilian Depositary Shares dated May 10, 2012—see p. 140.

the acquirer unchanged (again, $P_P = P_A$). The minimum exchange ratio that the target is willing to accept is the exchange ratio that results in a post-merger value for the target's shareholders equal to the target's pre-merger or standalone value ($V_T = P_T \times S_T$). The post-merger value for the target's shareholders is equal to the number of shares held by the target's shareholders, multiplied by the exchange ratio and the post-merger price, which is also equal to the acquirer's pre-merger price ($P_P \times S_T \times ER = P_A \times S_T \times ER$). The exchange ratio that results in a post-merger value (for the target's shareholders) equal to the target's standalone value is the ratio of the target's price to the acquirer's price, P_T/P_A

$$P_T \times S_T = P_A \times S_T \times ER_{MIN=MAX,Synergies=0}$$

$$ER_{MIN=MAX,Synergies=0} = \frac{P_T \times S_T}{P_A \times S_T} = \frac{P_T}{P_A} \tag{16.1}$$

Minimum Exchange Ratio When Synergies Exist (Value Is Created).

The minimum exchange ratio that the target will accept is the exchange ratio that allocates 100% of the merger's gain or loss to the acquirer. The post-merger price, P_P, will no longer be equal to the acquirer's price. The post-merger value of the company is equal to the post-merger price, multiplied by the number of post-merger shares ($V_P = P_P \times (S_A + S_T \times ER)$). The minimum exchange ratio that the target is willing to accept is the exchange ratio that results in a post-merger value for the target's shareholders ($P_P \times S_T \times ER$) equal to its standalone value ($V_T = P_T \times S_T$). We measure the minimum exchange ratio as follows:[21]

---

[21] The derivation of this exchange ratio is

$$P_T \times S_T = P_P \times S_T \times ER_{MIN}$$

$$P_T \times S_T = \frac{V_P}{S_A + S_T \times ER_{MIN}} \times S_T \times ER_{MIN}$$

$$ER_{MIN} = \frac{\frac{P_T}{V_P}}{S_A + S_T \times ER_{MIN}}$$

$$ER_{MIN} \times \frac{V_P - P_T \times S_T}{V_P} = \frac{P_T \times S_A}{V_P}$$

$$ER_{MIN} = \frac{P_T \times S_A}{V_P - V_T}$$

$$P_T \times S_T = P_P \times S_T \times ER_{MIN}$$

$$P_T \times S_T = \frac{V_P}{S_A + S_T \times ER_{MIN}} \times S_T \times ER_{MIN}$$

$$ER_{MIN} = \frac{P_T \times S_A}{V_P - V_T} \tag{16.2}$$

We now revisit the cash deal example. Recall that the standalone values of the target and acquirer are $1,000 and $2,000, respectively. Now, assume that the acquirer has 200 shares outstanding and a price of $10 per share and that the target has 50 shares outstanding and a price of $20 per share. The expected value created from this acquisition is $300. We measure the minimum exchange ratio for this example in Exhibit 16.11, assuming that the value of the synergies is equal to the expected value of $300 and that the post-merger value of the company is $3,300. Using this information, the minimum exchange ratio is equal to 1.739.

$$ER_{MIN} = \frac{P_T \times S_A}{V_P - V_T} = \frac{\$20 \times 200}{\$3,300 - \$1,000} = 1.739$$

Multiplying the minimum exchange ratio by 50 (the number of target shares) results in 86.96 shares, which is the amount of stock issued by the acquirer in exchange for the target's stock. Thus, the acquirer has 287 post-merger shares, 200 (69.7%) of which are held by the acquirer's original shareholders and 87 (30.3%) of which are held by the target's shareholders. If we multiply the post-merger value by these ownership percentages, the value of the post-merger shares being held by the acquirer's original share-holders is $2,300, which is equal to the acquirer's standalone value, plus 100% of the expected synergies. The value allocated to the target's shareholders is $1,000, which is equal to the target's standalone value.

EXHIBIT 16.11	Minimum Exchange Ratio—All Value Created (Destroyed) to Acquirer—Target's Value Is Equal to Its Standalone Value			

ER_{MIN}		1.739		
Shares issued to target = $ER_{MIN} \times S_T$		86.96	1.739	50

Post-Merger—Check	Shares	%	Value	Price (P_P)
Acquirer shares (not changed)	200	69.7%	$2,300	$11.50
Target shares	87	30.3%	1,000	$11.50
Total shares	287	100.0%	$3,300	$11.50

Maximum Exchange Ratio When Synergies Exist. The maximum exchange ratio is the exchange ratio that allocates 100% of the merger's gain to the target. Again, since the acquirer's sharehold-ers are not issued additional shares, the value of their pre-merger shares is left unchanged as long as the post-merger price is equal to the acquirer's pre-merger price ($P_P = P_A$). Thus, the maximum exchange ratio is the exchange ratio at which the post-merger price is equal to the acquirer's pre-merger price ($P_A = P_P$). The post-merger price of the company, $P_P = P_A$, is equal to the post-merger value of the company, V_P, divided by the post-merger number of shares ($S_A + S_T \times ER$). We can measure this maximum exchange ratio as

$$P_A = \frac{V_P}{S_A + S_T \times ER_{MAX}}$$

$$ER_{MAX} = \frac{V_P - V_A}{P_A \times S_T} \tag{16.3}$$

In Exhibit 16.12, we measure the maximum exchange ratio for our example; again, we assume that the value of the synergies is equal to the expected value of $300 and that the post-merger value of the company is $3,300. The maximum exchange ratio is equal to 2.6, and the resulting post-merger price, P_P, is equal to P_A ($10).

$$ER_{MAX} = \frac{V_P - V_A}{P_A \times S_T} = \frac{\$3,300 - \$2,000}{\$10 \times 50} = 2.6$$

EXHIBIT 16.12	Maximum Exchange Ratio—All Value Created (Destroyed) to Target—Acquirer's Value Is Equal to Its Standalone Value			

ER_{MAX}		2.600		
Shares issued to target = $ER_{MAX} \times S_T$		130.00	2.600	50

Post-Merger—Check	**Shares**	**%**	**Value**	**Price (P_P)**
Acquirer shares (not changed)	200	60.6%	$2,000	$10.00
Target shares	130	39.4%	1,300	$10.00
Total shares	330	100.0%	$3,300	$10.00

Multiplying the maximum exchange ratio by 50 (the number of target shares) results in 130 shares of the acquirer's stock being issued to the target's shareholders in exchange for the target's stock. Thus, the number of post-merger shares is 330, 200 (60.6%) of which are held by the acquirer's original shareholders and 130 (39.4%) of which are held by the target's shareholders. If we multiply the post-merger value by these percentage ownerships, the value of the post-merger shares of the acquirer's original shareholders is $2,000, which is equal to the acquirer's standalone value. The value allocated to the target's shareholders is $1,300, which is equal to the target's standalone value, plus 100% of the expected synergies.

Valuation Key 16.12

In some acquisitions, the acquirer's stock is exchanged for the target's stock, called a stock-for-stock merger. The number of shares of the acquirer's stock that is exchanged per share for the target's stock is called the exchange ratio. The exchange ratio affects the acquisition price paid for the target. A higher exchange ratio allocates more post-merger shares to the target, which, in turn, allocates a higher proportion of the post-merger value to the target.

Exchange-Ratio-Based Negotiation Range. We measure the negotiation range by calculating the minimum and maximum exchange ratios at various points within the range of post-merger values. We present a chart of the minimum and maximum exchange ratios for this example in Exhibit 16.13. The maximum exchange ratio increases as the expected value of the post-merger company increases, for all of the synergies are allocated to the target in the calculation of the maximum exchange ratio. The minimum exchange ratio decreases as the value of the post-merger company increases, and this change is non-linear. It decreases, because as the post-merger value of the company increases, the number of shares that are issued to the target's shareholders to maintain the target's standalone value decreases.

The Exchange Ratio Based on a Proportional Allocation of the Post-Merger Value

We can also calculate the exchange ratio for a proportional allocation of the post-merger company to the acquirer's shareholders, C_A, and the target's shareholders, $1 - C_A$. Since no additional shares are issued to the acquirer's shareholders, the proportion of the post-merger company that is allocated to the acquirer's shareholders is equal to

$$C_A = \frac{S_A}{S_A + S_T \times ER_{C_A}} \tag{16.4}$$

Using the above relation, we can solve for the exchange ratio as follows:

$$C_A \times (S_A + S_T \times ER_{C_A}) = S_A$$

$$ER_{C_A} = \frac{S_A}{C_A \times S_T} - \frac{S_A}{S_T} \tag{16.5}$$

EXHIBIT 16.13 Negotiation Strategy Minimum and Maximum Exchange Ratio for a Stock-for-Stock Acquisition

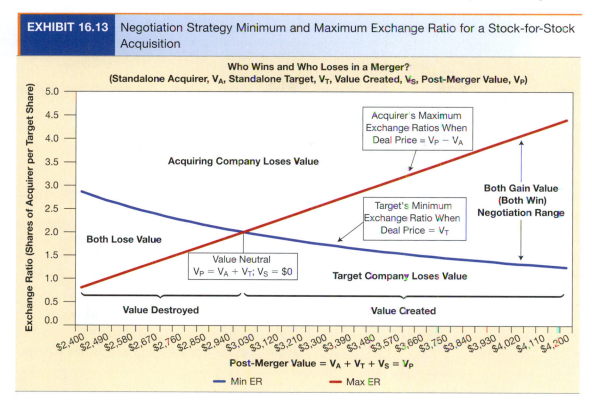

Allocating Synergies Based on the Proportion of Pre-Merger Standalone Values

Assume the companies agree to base this allocation of synergies and post-merger value on the companies' relative pre-merger standalone values. In other words, the parties agree to allocate $V_A/(V_A + V_T)$ to the acquirer's shareholders and $V_T/(V_A + V_T)$ to the target's shareholders. We can substitute these proportions (in terms of prices and shares) into the above formula for C_A in order to allocate synergies in terms of the companies' relative pre-merger standalone values:

$$ER_{C_A = \frac{V_A}{V_A + V_T}} = \frac{S_A}{\left(\frac{P_A \times S_A}{P_A \times S_A + P_T \times S_T} \right) \times S_T} - \frac{S_A}{S_T}$$

$$ER_{C_A = \frac{V_A}{V_A + V_T}} = \frac{P_T}{P_A} \tag{16.6}$$

Note that this is the same formula as the zero synergies formula; thus, as long as the parties agree to base the allocation synergies and post-merger value on their relative pre-merger standalone values, the appropriate exchange ratio is equal to the ratio of the target's pre-merger price to the acquirer's pre-merger price, P_T/P_A.

Allocation of Merger Gains and Losses in a Stock-for-Stock Merger

Recall that in the cash deal example (see Exhibit 16.10), the merger gain to the target was fixed at the deal price (using the expected value of the synergies), and all of the change in the merger gain—based on the actual (rather than the expected) outcome (post-merger valuation)—accrued to the acquirer. In a stock-for-stock merger, the two parties share in any changes in the merger gain based on the actual outcome. Recall that the standalone values of the target and acquirer are $1,000 and $2,000, respectively, and while the expected value created from this acquisition is $300, the potential outcomes—value created or destroyed—ranges from a merger gain of $1,200 to a merger loss of −$600. We show the allocation of the gain and loss for the expected outcome and two outcomes that differ from the expected in Exhibit 16.14.

EXHIBIT 16.14 Allocation of Merger Gain (Loss) for Stock-for-Stock Deal Example

Stock Deal–Equity Values	Expected Outcome Used in Deal Negotiation			Actual Outcome with More Value Created			Actual Outcome with Value Destroyed		
	Outcome	% Split	% Gain	Outcome	% Split	% Gain	Outcome	% Split	% Gain
Standalone value of acquirer	$2,000			$2,000			$2,000		
Standalone value of target	1,000			1,000			1,000		
Combined standalone value.	$3,000			$3,000			$3,000		
Value created (merger gain (loss))	300			800			–400		
Post-merger value	$3,300			$3,800			$2,600		
Overall gain or (loss) on acquisition	$ 300		10.0%	$ 800		26.7%	$ –400		–13.3%
Post-merger value to target (stock received)	$1,200	36.4%		$1,382	36.4%		$ 945	36.4%	
Standalone value of target	–1,000			–1,000			–1,000		
Gain (loss) to target—merger premium	$ 200	66.7%	20.0%	$ 382	47.7%	38.2%	$ –55	13.6%	–5.5%
Post-merger value to acquirer	$2,100	63.6%		$2,418	63.6%		$1,655	63.6%	
Standalone value of acquirer	–2,000			–2,000			–2,000		
Gain or (loss) to acquirer	$ 100	33.3%	5.0%	$ 418	52.3%	20.9%	$ –345	86.4%	–17.3%

As we calculated in the cash example in Exhibit 16.10, we assume the parties negotiate the deal based on the expected value of the synergies and that they agree to allocate $200 of the synergies to the target. This is the same outcome as the one in the cash deal; however, here, the target's shareholders end up owning 36.4% of the post-merger company, which is equal to the proportion of the value that they were assigned in the cash deal (0.364 = $1,200/$3,300). The exchange ratio that achieves this is 2.2857 [2.2857 = (200/0.63636 × 50) − 200/50]. As such, the target's shareholders share in any changes in the post-merger value that result from differences between the expected and actual outcome of the merger. In cash deals, the target shareholders are guaranteed a specific return based on the terms of the deal and the acquirer's shareholders face all of the uncertainty.

Gains and losses are shared in a stock-for-stock transaction. For example, in the first actual outcome in the exhibit for the stock-for-stock merger, the actual merger gain is $800, which is $500 higher than originally expected. In this outcome, the post-merger value of the shares issued to the target increases from $1,200 to $1,382 (or by 36.4% of the $500 increase in the value of the synergies). The value of the shares held by the acquirer's original shareholders increases from $2,100 to $2,418 (or by 63.6% of the $500 increase in the value of the synergies). When this same outcome occurred in the cash deal, the target shareholders received none of the increase in value (see Exhibit 16.10); thus, the target's share of the post-merger value decreased below 36.4% in the cash deal. The second actual outcome is an actual merger loss of −$400, which is $700 lower than originally expected. In this outcome, the post-merger value of the newly issued shares to the target's shareholders decreases from $1,200 to $945 (or by 36.4% of the $700 decrease in the value of the synergies). The value of the shares held by the acquirer's original shareholders decreases from $2,100 to $1,655 (or by 63.6% of the $700 decrease in the value of the synergies). When this outcome occurred in the cash deal, the target shareholders did not share the effects of the decrease in value. As a result, in the cash deal, the target shareholders end up with 46.2% of the value, while the acquiring shareholders only end up with 53.8% of the value (see Exhibit 16.10).

REVIEW EXERCISE 16.5

Allocation of Synergies—Stock-for-Stock Deals

Use the information in Review Exercise 16.4 to respond to the following questions regarding stock-for-stock transactions.

a. Measure the exchange ratio and resulting stock price that allocates $6,000 of the post-merger value (based on the expected outcome) to the target.

b. Measure the exchange ratio and resulting stock price that allocates the value of the synergies based on the relative standalone values of the two companies.

c. Based on a post-merger value equal to the expected outcome for the merger, calculate the target's minimum exchange ratio, the acquirer's maximum exchange ratio, and the resulting stock prices.

d. Assuming the acquirer allocates $6,000 of the post-merger value based on the expected outcome to the target in a stock-for-stock transaction, calculate the gain or loss to the acquirer and target when the actual outcome of the merger is the expected, highest, and lowest outcome (see Exhibit 16.14).

Solution on pages 718–719.

16.10 THE XEROX CORPORATION AND AFFILIATED COMPUTER SERVICES, INC. MERGER

Stock-for-stock swaps involve complex valuation issues because the post-merger stock price of the acquirer is an important component of the payment to the target shareholders. In these transactions, the target shareholders must assess the values of the acquirer, target, and the value creation from the transaction in order to value the post-merger stock price of the acquirer. Once we assess the expected post-merger stock price of the acquirer, we can determine the expected value of the transaction to the target shareholders. In this section, we use Xerox's acquisition of ACS as an example in order to illustrate these valuation issues. The companies announced the merger on September 27, 2009, and the merger closed on February 5, 2010. As we will soon describe, the terms of the acquisition involved a cash payment to the ACS shareholders as well as an exchange of ACS stock for shares of Xerox stock. Xerox's public disclosures identified a variety of potential cost and revenue synergies that it expected to occur as a result of the merger.

The common stock of both companies was publicly traded as of the date of the merger. It is possible, of course, that prior to the merger, the publicly traded stock prices did not reflect the standalone values of the companies, since management expectations were not disclosed to the market. As such, the financial advisors for both companies conducted a thorough valuation of the standalone values of Xerox and ACS as well as the expected value creation from the transaction.

The Deal

ACS and Xerox each had two financial advisors. ACS's financial advisors were Citigroup Global Markets Inc. (Citi) and Evercore Group L.L.C. (Evercore). Xerox's financial advisors were Blackstone Advisory Services L.P. (Blackstone) and J.P. Morgan Securities Inc. (JPM). Between May 2009 and June 2009, the financial advisors of ACS and Xerox discussed a potential transaction between the two companies as well as alternative structures for the deal. Over a two-month negotiation process, the Xerox board of directors held special meetings in which management discussed various aspects of the acquisition. The topics discussed included the strategic rationale for the combination, ACS's fit within Xerox's business process outsourcing strategy, the expected cost and revenue synergies, the strengths of ACS's business process outsourcing business, the challenges associated with the transaction, how ACS was to be managed, and potential integration issues.

At the same time, the financial advisors of ACS conducted an analysis of the effects of potential strategic transaction announcements on the stock price of ACS and the potential effects of the ACS announcement on Xerox's stock price.[22] The ACS board established $62 per ACS share as the lowest price it would accept, and it instructed its financial advisors to include a floor to protect the value of its shares from falling in case Xerox's stock price fell following the transaction announcement.[23] On September 27, 2009, the companies finalized and announced the merger. In a public filing, ACS described the merger as follows:

---

[22] Xerox's Amendment No. 4 to Form S-4, dated December 23, 2009, contains fairly detailed descriptions of the analyses the financial advisors conducted in order to assess the "fairness, from a financial point of view, to the holders of the Class A common stock of Affiliated Computer Services, Inc. ("ACS") of the Class A Merger Consideration.

[23] Xerox never agreed to the floor, and thus an analysis of what Xerox's stock price would be post-merger became important to ACS's evaluation of the Xerox offer. Affiliated Computer Services, Inc. Form 8-K, dated September 29, 2009, p. 1.

On September 27, 2009, Xerox Corporation ("Xerox"), Boulder Acquisition Corp. ("Merger Sub"), a wholly-owned subsidiary of Xerox, and Affiliated Computer Services, Inc. ("ACS") entered into an Agreement and Plan of Merger (the "Merger Agreement"), providing for the acquisition of ACS by Xerox. Subject to the terms and conditions of the Merger Agreement, which has been approved by the boards of directors of all parties (and recommended by a special committee of independent directors of ACS), ACS will be merged with and into Merger Sub (the "Merger").

As a result of the merger, each outstanding share of ACS's *Class A* common stock, other than shares owned by Xerox, Merger Sub, or ACS (which will be cancelled) and other than those shares with respect to which appraisal rights are properly exercised and not withdrawn (collectively, "Excluded Shares"), will be converted into the right to receive a combination of (i) 4.935 shares of common stock of Xerox ("Common Stock") and (ii) $18.60 in cash, without interest.

As a result of the merger, each outstanding share of *Class B* common stock of ACS, other than Excluded Shares, will be converted into the right to receive (i) 4.935 shares of Common Stock, (ii) $18.60 in cash, without interest and (iii) a fraction of a share of a new series of convertible preferred stock to be issued by Xerox and designated as Series A Convertible Perpetual Preferred Stock ("Convertible Preferred Stock") . . .

Source: Affiliated Computer Services, Inc., Form 8-K, dated September 29, 2009.

ACS had 91.04 million Class A shares and 6.6 million Class B shares outstanding for a total of 97.64 million shares outstanding; thus, the cash consideration for the merger was $1.8 billion ($1,816 million = $18.60 × 97.64 million).

Post-Merger Value of Xerox Corporation

To estimate the post-merger enterprise value of Xerox, we measure the value of Xerox as a standalone company and combine this value with both the standalone value of ACS and the value of the Xerox/ACS synergies, net of all transaction and integration costs. With this analysis, we must include the effects of financing on the values of the standalone companies; for example, Xerox used ACS's excess cash, refinanced some debt, repaid some debt, issued new debt, and issued new shares of stock in order to finance the transaction. Thus, we must consider all of the effects of financing on the value of the combined companies.

To measure the post-merger stock price of Xerox, we subtract post-merger debt, convertible preferred, minority interests, and any other non-common-equity claims—such as stock options—from the value of the post-merger firm in order to measure the value of the post-merger common equity. After we calculate the post-merger common equity shares outstanding, we calculate the post-merger stock price by dividing the post-merger value of common equity by the post-merger shares outstanding. Using the post-merger stock price and the cash component of the deal, we can measure the gain to ACS shareholders relative to ACS' publicly traded stock price.

Standalone Values of ACS and Xerox.
As discussed in the fairness opinions, the financial advisors used the various valuation methods we discussed in this book in order to measure the standalone values of ACS and Xerox. As we will soon discuss, we assume that both companies have excess cash before the transaction and that Xerox uses all of the excess cash of both companies to finance the transaction. Although we do not show the details of the pre-merger valuations, the standalone firm value of ACS without excess cash is estimated at $8.2 billion, and the standalone firm value of Xerox without excess cash is $16.1 billion. It should be noted that the $6.3 billion market value for ACS was well below the $8.2 billion obtained in this valuation. It could be that the market discounted the value of ACS because of its founder's controlling interest (see Valuation in Practice 16.3) or because the market did not share the expectations management had for the future of the company.

Valuation of Xerox/ACS Synergies.
Xerox discussed various types of synergies, fees, restructuring charges, and integration costs in its Form S-4 filed with the SEC. [24] Xerox expected the transaction

---

[24] Xerox Corporation Amendment No. 4 to Form S-4, dated December 23, 2009, p. C-2, which is an excerpt from Citi's fairness opinion letter.

to create $250 million in tax credits, which we assume Xerox will use in the first year of the merger. Xerox discussed both cost and revenue synergies (for example, cross selling of products and services), but it only provided forecasts for cost synergies. In addition, the financial analysts appeared to be less confident in the potential revenue synergies. For these reasons, we do not include any potential revenue synergies in our valuation.

We assume that ACS's weighted average cost of capital of 9% is appropriate for valuing the synergies. To make this assumption, we assume that the synergies were of similar risk to ACS's free cash flows and that the post-merger capital structure was similar to the pre-merger ACS capital structure. The forecasted synergies for the first five years are shown in Exhibit 16.15 along with the investment banking fees, restructuring charges, and integration costs. We assume a percentage growth rate of -5% for the synergies beginning in the year ending June 2013. For the year ending June 2010, the cash flows are discounted for one-half year as the merger closed in February 2010, and that timing is maintained across the subsequent years. As shown in the exhibit, the value of the synergies, net of transaction and integration costs, is $1.5 billion. The set of values for the synergies, using different cost of capital and growth rate assumptions, ranges from $1.1 billion (g $= -10\%$ and $r_{wacc} = 9.6\%$) to $2.3 billion (g $= 0\%$ and $r_{wacc} = 8.6\%$).

| **EXHIBIT 16.15** | Valuation of Xerox Corporation/Affiliated Computer Services, Inc. Synergies |

| Weighted average cost of capital valuation of synergies | 9.08% | g = | −5.00% |
| Tax rate = | 36.0% | | |

($ in millions)	June-10	June-11	June-12	June-13	June-14	CV June-14
Pre-tax cost synergies	$ 95.0	$300.0	$300.0	$285.0	$270.8	$ 257.2
Investment banker fees	−50.0	−183.0				
Restructuring charges and integration costs	−45.0	−30.0				
Less: taxes	0.0	−31.3	−108.0	−102.6	−97.5	−92.6
After-tax cost synergies	$ 0.0	$ 55.7	$192.0	$182.4	$173.3	$ 164.6
Income tax credits	$250.0					
Unlevered free cash flow for continuing value (CV)						$ 164.6
Discount factor for continuing value						7.104
Unlevered free cash flow and CV.	$250.0	$ 55.7	$192.0	$182.4	$173.3	$1,169.4
Discount factor.	0.957	0.878	0.805	0.738	0.676	0.676
Present value	$239.4	$ 48.9	$154.5	$134.6	$117.2	$ 791.0
Value of synergies. $1,485.6						

		Continuing Value Growth Rate				
		−10.00%	**−7.50%**	**−5.00%**	**−2.50%**	**0.00%**
	8.58%	$1,202.7	$1,344.7	$1,539.1	$1,821.2	$2,267.8
r_{WACC}	8.83%	$1,187.0	$1,324.6	$1,511.8	$1,781.8	$2,204.7
	9.08%	$1,171.7	$1,305.0	$1,485.6	$1,744.1	$2,145.1
	9.33%	$1,156.9	$1,286.0	$1,460.2	$1,708.0	$2,088.7
	9.58%	$1,142.4	$1,267.6	$1,435.7	$1,673.4	$2,035.2

Post-Merger Financing. Xerox planned to finance the transaction with excess cash and additional debt of $2.7 billion and to issue additional shares to ACS shareholders. It planned to redeem some existing ACS debt ($1.8 billion) and provide cash compensation to ACS shareholders ($1.8 billion). In Exhibit 16.16, based on Xerox's financing plan, we present sources and uses of cash for the transaction. The financing and other fees for the deal totaled $222 million (these are separate from the investment banking fees in Exhibit 16.15). The net effect of the transaction was to reduce the combined cash holdings of Xerox and ACS by $1,109 million. We assume that Xerox was using all of ACS's excess cash as well as all of its own excess cash to help finance the transaction. The post-merger Xerox was to hold no excess cash.

EXHIBIT 16.16	ACS/Xerox Merger Sources and Uses of Cash and Post-Merger Cash Balance

Sources and Uses of Cash ($ in millions)

Sources

Expected new senior unsecured notes	$ 1,950.0
Revolving credit facility.	750.0
Total sources of cash	$ 2,700.0

Uses

Repayment of ACS's debt	$ 1,771.0
Cash consideration to ACS common stock at $18.60 per share.	1,816.1
Fees and various transactions costs	222.0
Total uses	$ 3,809.1
Net effect on cash	$–1,109.1

Cash and Cash Equivalents (expected at the closing date)	Balance	Required	Excess
Xerox	$1,159.0	$558.9	$ 600.1
ACS	559.0	50.0	509.0
Net effect on cash	–1,109.1		
Pro forma combined cash balance (no excess cash)	$ 608.9	$608.9	$1,109.1

The book value of Xerox's debt as of June 30, 2009 (including its liability to a subsidiary trust issuing preferred stock) was $8.3 billion, and the market value of these securities was $8.7 billion. The market value of ACS's pre-merger debt was $2.3 billion, but Xerox planned to redeem $1.8 billion of this debt; thus, the post-merger debt attributable to ACS was $0.5 billion. In addition to the existing debt, Xerox planned to issue $2.7 billion in additional debt in order to redeem the ACS debt and pay the $1.8 billion cash consideration to the ACS shareholders. Exhibit 16.17 presents the expected market value of the post-merger debt that Xerox intended to hold, which included Xerox's pre-merger debt, the new debt issued in the transaction, and the remaining amount of ACS outstanding debt. After the merger, Xerox was expected to have $11.9 billion in debt and trust preferred stock outstanding. In addition, Xerox planned to issue $300 million in convertible preferred stock to the ACS Class B shareholders as extra compensation for the Class B shares.

EXHIBIT 16.17	Xerox Corporation—Post-Merger Debt

($ in millions)

Market value of Xerox existing debt (including trust preferred)	$ 8,686.4
Market value of additional new borrowings	2,700.0
Market value of remaining ACS debt	524.3
Total market value of post-merger combined debt	$11,910.7

REVIEW EXERCISE 16.6

Merger Sources and Uses Schedule

An acquirer makes an offer to purchase a target company. The target company's current stock price is $10 per share, and the target company has 100 million shares outstanding. Given the expected synergies from the acquisition, the deal premium is negotiated to be 25%. The target has no convertible debt or convertible preferred stock, but it does have 50 million stock options outstanding with an exercise price equal to $9. The acquirer will assume the debt and preferred stock of the target, buy out the option holders, and finance the acquisition with $200 million of its own excess cash, $100 million of the target's excess cash, and the remainder with debt. Initial fees will equal $47.3 million (3% on the debt financing and 1% for other fees). These fees do not include fees for a revolver loan. The debt issued to finance the transaction includes $400 million of seven-year, 6.0% senior secured bank debt and $700 million of nine-year, 8% subordinated unsecured debt; the remainder is financed with a revolving line of credit. The revolving line of credit of $200 million has a five-year term, a 4% interest rate on the amount drawn, and a 0.5% annual fee on the total amount of the line of credit. Calculate the purchase price of the equity and prepare a sources and uses schedule similar to the one in Exhibit 16.16.

Solution on page 720.

Post-Merger Xerox Common Shares and Stock Options Outstanding.   To measure the post-merger per share value of Xerox, we must first measure the number of post-merger common shares outstanding and the number of options outstanding, which we show in Exhibit 16.18. To calculate the number of Xerox shares issued to ACS shareholders, we multiply the number of Class A and Class B shares by the 4.935 exchange ratio. We perform a similar calculation for the number of Xerox options issued to the ACS employees for their existing options using the option exchange ratio of 7.085, as the ACS options were not cashed out at the time of the transaction, but instead were converted into Xerox options.

EXHIBIT 16.18	Xerox Corporation—Post-Merger Common Shares Outstanding

Shares and Options Outstanding	
Xerox—Number of Shares and Options Outstanding (millions)	
Common shares	869.08
Restricted stock units and performance shares	6.45
Convertible securities	1.99
Total Xerox shares outstanding	877.52
Total number of Xerox options	28.4
ACS—Number of Shares and Options Outstanding	
Class A	91.04
Class B	6.60
Total ACS shares outstanding	97.64
× ACS/Xerox exchange ratio	4.935
Total number of ACS converted shares	481.86
ACS options	14.4
Option exchange ratio	7.085
Total number of ACS converted options	102.1

Post-Merger Xerox Value.   We now have all of the inputs we need to measure the post-merger value of Xerox and the implied post-merger stock price. To calculate the post-merger value of Xerox, we add the standalone values of ACS and Xerox to the value of the synergies net of integration costs and fees. Ignoring synergies, this presumes that Xerox management will be able to manage ACS at the same level of efficiency that ACS management expected, that the transaction will not interfere with the ability of the Xerox management team to manage Xerox, that the projected synergies will be achieved, and that the value-weighted capital structure of the two companies represents the post-merger capital structure. We use the value of ACS and the value of Xerox without its excess cash, as Xerox will use all excess cash of both companies to fund the transaction.[25]

From the value of the firm, we subtract the value of Xerox's post-merger debt (Exhibit 16.17) and the value of the convertible preferred stock. Since Xerox has subsidiaries that have minority interests, we also subtract the value of the minority interests;[26] this yields the combined value of the common equity

---

[25] For simplicity, we assume that the fees and transaction costs of $222.0 million (shown in Exhibit 16.16) were not tax deductible. However, most of these fees were probably tax deductible, and fees related to arranging the debt financing would typically be amortized to interest expense over the life of the loans (see Chapter 15 for the typical treatment of these financing fees).

[26] We assume that the minority interests had not yet been subtracted out in determining Xerox's standalone value. Had Xerox's value already been adjusted for the minority interests, we would not subtract them here.

and options. The value of the equity securities includes the value of the Xerox stock options (including the ACS converted options), which we subtract in order to measure the post-merger value of Xerox's common equity. To do this, we use the iterative approach we discussed in Chapter 12 to simultaneously solve for the value per option and the equity value per share.

Recall that since the value of the outstanding stock options is a function of the per share value of the underlying equity, we calculate the value of the options when we calculate the per share value of the common equity. We solve this equality using an iterative process, changing the value of the stock price until the sum of the value of the equity and the value of the outstanding equity-based compensation contracts equals the value of the equity and the options. In this case, the calculations are slightly more complicated, for the terms of the preexisting Xerox options differ from the terms of the ACS options that were converted into Xerox options, but the approach is the same. However, before we perform this calculation, we must first decide if the valuation included the value of the tax shelter from the options. If the initial valuation excluded the value of the tax shelter (as would likely be the case in a DCF valuation), we must measure the value of the tax shelter from the options and increase our initial valuation for this value. If the valuations were based on publicly traded prices of the company's claims, then it is likely that the value includes the tax shelter from the options. We illustrate the effect of both assumptions in the following calculations.

We show the calculation of the stock price in Exhibit 16.19. Using the initial valuations, the value of the post-merger firm is $25.7 billion. From this value, we subtract the value of the post-merger debt and preferred stock of $12.2 billion and subtract the value of the Xerox minority interest of $150 million in order to measure the initial value of the common equity and options, which we find to be

---

EXHIBIT 16.19 Xerox Corporation—Post-merger Valuation

($ in millions, except per share)	Option Tax Shelter in Initial Valuation	
	Yes	**No**
Xerox firm value (after using all excess cash to close the transaction)	$16,055.0	
ACS firm value (after using all excess cash to close the transaction)	8,186.9	
Value of synergies	1,485.6	
Post-merger Xerox firm value (including ACS and synergies)	$25,727.4	
Post-merger debt and preferred stock		
Xerox and ACS pro forma combined total debt and liabilities	$11,910.7	
Convertible preferred stock	300.0	
Post-merger total debt and preferred stock	$12,210.7	
Post-merger value of common equity financing (including minority interests)	$13,516.7	
Xerox minority interests	150.0	
Post-merger value of Xerox common equity and options	$13,366.7	$13,366.7
Tax shelter from options	N/A	131.3
Post-merger value of Xerox common equity and options	$13,366.7	$13,498.0
Value of stock options		
ACS stock options assumed in exchange for Xerox equivalent option	$ 298.4	$ 306.5
Xerox stock options	56.6	58.1
Total value of stock options	$ 355.1	$ 364.6
Value of Xerox post-merger common equity	$13,011.7	$13,133.4
Post-merger Xerox shares outstanding		
Xerox shares outstanding	877.5	877.5
ACS shares outstanding × 4.935	481.9	481.9
Total post-merger shares	1,359.4	1,359.4
Value of Xerox post-merger common equity per share	$ 9.572	$ 9.661

Exhibit may contain small rounding errors

$13.4 billion. If we assume this value includes the value of the tax shelter from options, the value of the options is $355.1 million. The resulting common equity value is $13.012 billion, and after dividing this by the post-merger number of shares, the value per share is $9.572. If we assume the $13.4 billion excludes the value of the tax shelter from the options, we use our iterative approach to solve for the stock price, the option prices for the two options, and the value of the tax shelter. We add the value of the tax shelter of $131.3 million to the initial value of the equity and options. The value of the options is now $364.6 million. The resulting common equity value is $13.133 billion, and the value per share is now $9.661.

Allocation of the Gain to ACS and Xerox Shareholders

In Exhibit 16.20, given the actual merger terms and the expected post-merger value of the Xerox shares, we calculate the allocations of the gain from the merger to Xerox and ACS shareholders. Consider the valuation effects of the merger on ACS. We calculate the value of the Xerox post-merger shares by multiplying the $9.57 per share value by the number of Xerox shares that the ACS shareholders received. We then add the value of the cash received by the Class A and Class B shareholders before adding the preferred shares received by the Class B shareholders. We compare this to the pre-merger value of the Class A and Class B shares, assuming that the majority position of the Class B shareholder is worth $300 million before the transaction as well.[27] As we show in the exhibit, the percentage increase in value for the Class A and Class B shareholders of ACS is 37%. A similar calculation for Xerox indicates that the increase in value for the Xerox shareholders is 6.1%. Thus, 79% of the increase in equity value resulting from the merger was allocated to ACS shareholders and 21% to Xerox shareholders, respectively.

EXHIBIT 16.20 Xerox Corporation—Allocation of the Gain from the Merger			
($ in millions, except per share)	**ACS Total**	**Xerox Total**	**Total**
Shares issued to ACS shareholders/Xerox outstanding shares.........	481.86	877.52	1,359.38
Value of Xerox post-merger common equity per share	$ 9.572	$ 9.572	$ 9.572
Value of Xerox post-merger shares	$4,612.3	$8,399.4	$13,011.7
Plus: cash payment for ACS shares............................	1,816.1		1,816.1
Value of the merger consideration without Class B preferred shares	$6,428.4	$8,399.4	$14,827.8
Value of Class B preferred shares	300.0		300.0
Value of the merger consideration with Class B preferred shares	$6,728.4	$8,399.4	$15,127.8
Pre-merger market capitalization (1 day before announcement)........	$4,613.6	$7,915.2	$12,528.8
Value of Class B preferred shares	300.0		300.0
Pre-merger market capitalization of the merger consideration	$4,913.6	$7,915.2	$12,828.8
Increase in value over pre-merger market capitalization	$1,814.8	$ 484.2	$ 2,299.0
Percentage increase in pre-merger value.........................	36.9%	6.1%	
Allocation of total increase.....................................	78.9%	21.1%	

---

[27] Recall from Valuation in Practice 16.3 that ACS had two classes of common stock. In this analysis, we assume that all of the Class B shares are converted into Class A shares and that all of the shares are treated (valued) equally. Naturally, since the Class B shares had super voting rights (10 votes per share), and since these shares were essentially owned by one individual (providing that individual with effective voting control and the ability to prevent an acquisition from occurring), the Class B shares would be valued at a higher price than the Class A shares. We assume the premium for the Class B shares is $300 million in total, and the premium is achieved by issuing the Class B shareholder convertible preferred stock in addition to what the Class A shareholders received. Again, as stated earlier, we do not value the convertible preferred in this chapter. See Lease, R., J. McConnell, and W. Mikkelson, "The Market Value of Control in Publicly Traded Corporations," *Journal of Financial Economics* 11 (1983), pp. 439–473, who show that the average premium for stocks with superior voting rights is 5.44%.

SUMMARY AND KEY CONCEPTS

In this chapter, we discussed the topic of mergers and acquisitions. Mergers and acquisitions are an important component of corporate strategy, and worldwide M&A activity is significant. Financial advisors and valuation experts need to be well versed in the intricacies of the many aspects of M&A in order to provide advice to their clients. In this chapter, we provided some descriptive statistics on the amount of M&A activity that takes place globally, the typical premiums paid, what motivates M&A transactions, whether and for whom acquisitions create value, and why mergers may fail to create value for acquirers. We also discussed fundamental deal structure, contract provisions, and the income tax ramifications associated with various deal structures. We then discussed how to analyze and value M&A transactions, including the valuation of synergies and analyzing accretion and dilution, exchange ratios, and the allocation of expected gains from a merger between the target and acquirer.

As we illustrated, cash transactions are more straightforward to evaluate, for the consideration given to the target shareholders is easy to evaluate. When payment to the target shareholders is in the form of debt, convertible securities, or the common stock of the acquirer, the acquisitions are more difficult to evaluate, for one has to assess the value of these securities that are given as consideration. This is particularly true when the stock of the acquirer is given as consideration, for one has to estimate the post-merger value of the acquirer's stock. We discussed the conceptual negotiation range for an acquisition as well as a variety of issues related to exchange ratios (the ratio of acquirer shares given per share of the target). Finally, we illustrated the potential complexity of analyzing a stock-for-stock transaction in the context of the acquisition of Affiliated Computer Services, Inc. by Xerox Corporation—a transaction that involved both cash and stock in Xerox.

ADDITIONAL READING AND REFERENCES

Andrade, G., M. Mitchell, and E. Stafford, "New Evidence and Perspectives on Mergers," *Journal of Economic Perspectives* 15 (2001), pp. 103–120.

Savor, P., and Q. Lu, "Do Stock Mergers Create Value for Acquirers?" *Journal of Finance* 64 (2009), pp. 1061–1097.

EXERCISES AND PROBLEMS

P16.1   **Valuing Synergies—Oracle Acquisition of PeopleSoft**: Oracle Corporation acquires another business software applications vendor, PeopleSoft, Inc., for approximately $10.3 billion. Oracle expects to achieve various synergies, and its strategy is to continue to support existing versions of PeopleSoft software solutions, create Oracle software to replace all of PeopleSoft's software, and then migrate PeopleSoft customers to Oracle software. Assume that as a result of the merger, the company expects annual selling and administrative costs to decrease by $750 million, annual research and development costs to decrease by $300 million, and annual general and administrative costs to decrease by $200 million. Also, assume that Oracle will be able to migrate about 80% of PeopleSoft's customers (roughly 10,000) and $3 billion in revenue but that it will lose the remaining 20%. Assume that the company will incur $400 million in fees, expenses, and integration- and synergy-related costs in the first year after the merger and none thereafter. Assume that the appropriate discount rate for discounting synergies is 12%; that the post-merger income tax rate is 40% on all income; that revenues are expected to grow with inflation, which is expected to be 3% annually; and that variable costs are, on average, 55% of revenues.

Measure the value of the synergies, assuming that the cost synergies begin in the first year after the merger, remain constant for the following two years despite inflation, and then decline at a rate of 10% in perpetuity beginning in the fourth year after the merger. Also assume that the migration of the customers will take place immediately after the merger and impact the Year 1 cash flows.

P16.2   **Valuing Synergies—SIRIUS XM Radio Inc.:** SIRIUS Satellite Radio and XM Satellite Radio announced the completion of their merger, which will be called SIRIUS XM Radio Inc. XM shareholders will receive 4.6 shares of SIRIUS common stock for each share of XM stock. The company states that it will be able to offer consumers new packages in audio entertainment and that it will offer subscribers the option of expanding their subscriptions to include the "Best of Both" services. SIRIUS XM Radio states that it expects to begin realizing synergies immediately. The company expects to achieve synergies of approximately $400 million in 2009, net of costs. The company states that it expects synergies to grow beyond 2009. The combined revenues of the two companies equal approximately $2.2 billion. Assume the expected post-merger variable cost is 65% of revenues. Also, assume that the company will incur $200 million in fees, expenses, and integration and synergy related costs in the first year after the merger and none thereafter. Assume that the appropriate discount rate for discounting synergies is 13%; that the post-merger income tax rate is 40% on all income; that annual inflation is expected to be 3%; and that the breakdown of the expected 2009 pre-tax synergies, all of which are cash flows, is estimated as follows:

- $300 million revenue increase from an increase in the number of channels that is expected to grow with inflation.
- $105 million from a reduction in costs for the design and production of radios for automobiles provided to auto manufacturers
- $60 million from a reduction in costs for the design and production of non-auto radios
- $50 million from the reduction in costs for the production of overlapping entertainment channels
- $20 million from a reduction in marketing costs
- $20 million from the reduction in corporate overhead costs
- $40 million from a reduction in information and other technology costs from eliminating overlapping technologies

Measure the value of the synergies, assuming the cost synergies grow 50% in 2010 and then decline at a rate of 20% in perpetuity; assume revenue synergies continue in perpetuity.

P16.3 **Measuring Earnings Accretion/Dilution—Cash Deal:** A company (acquirer) purchases another company (target) for a 25% premium over the target's current stock price, which is $5 per share. The acquirer's stock price is $10 per share. The acquirer finances the transaction with all of its available excess cash, and it finances the remainder with debt, which has an 8% cost of capital and interest rate. The value of the interest tax shields from the incremental debt is $640. As a result of the merger, the companies expect to be able to increase annual revenues by $50 and decrease annual expenses by $200, which, in total, the companies value at $1,500. The company will amortize any purchase premium at an average rate of 5% per year, and the company values the tax shelter from the amortization at $400. Prepare a post-merger income statement and balance sheet (similar to the ones in Exhibit 16.7).

	Standalone Acquirer	Standalone Target		Standalone Acquirer	Standalone Target
Income Statement			**Balance Sheet**		
Revenues	$4,000.0	$2,750.0	Excess cash	$ 2,000.0	$1,000.0
Operating expenses . . .	−2,213.3	−1,826.7	Operating assets.	8,000.0	5,000.0
Interest income.	40.0	20.0	Total assets.	$10,000.0	$6,000.0
Interest expense	−320.0	−240.0			
Income taxes	−602.7	−281.3	Debt	$ 4,000.0	$3,000.0
Earnings	$ 904.0	$ 422.0	Equity	6,000.0	3,000.0
			Liabilities and equity . . .	$10,000.0	$6,000.0
Shares outstanding	1,000.0	800.0			
Earnings per share	$ 0.904	$ 0.528			

P16.4 **Measuring Value and Market Multiple Accretion/Dilution—Cash Deal:** Use the information in Problem 16.3 to measure the post-merger firm value, equity value, stock price, and P/E multiple. Compare these values to the acquirer's standalone values.

P16.5 **Measuring Earnings Accretion/Dilution—Stock-for-Stock Deal:** A company (acquirer) purchases another company (target) for a 42.5% premium over the target's then current stock price, which was $10 per share. The acquirer's stock price at that time was $11 per share. The acquirer finances the transaction by issuing common stock to the shareholders of the target company in exchange for all of the target's common stock. The exchange ratio is 1.25. As a result of the merger, the companies expect to be able to increase annual revenues by $200, and decrease annual expenses by $400, which in total, the companies value at $3,200. The company will amortize any purchase premium at an average rate of 5% per year, and the company values the tax shelter from the amortization at $1,000. Prepare a post-merger income statement and balance sheet (similar to Exhibit 16.7).

	Standalone Acquirer	Standalone Target		Standalone Acquirer	Standalone Target
Income Statement			**Balance Sheet**		
Revenues	$14,000.0	$3,600.0	Excess cash	$ 0.0	$ 0.0
Operating expenses . . .	−9,066.7	−2,160.0	Operating assets.	20,000.0	6,000.0
Interest income.	0.0	0.0	Total assets.	$20,000.0	$6,000.0
Interest expense.	−600.0	−240.0			
Income taxes	−1,733.3	−480.0	Debt	$10,000.0	$4,000.0
Earnings	$ 2,600.0	$ 720.0	Equity	10,000.0	2,000.0
			Liabilities and equity . . .	$20,000.0	$6,000.0
Shares outstanding	2,000.0	800.0			
Earnings per share	$ 1.300	$ 0.900			

P16.6 **Measuring Value and Market Multiple Accretion/Dilution—Stock-for-Stock Deal:** Use the information in Problem 16.5 to measure the post-merger firm value, equity value, stock price, and P/E multiple. Compare these values to the acquirer's standalone values.

P16.7 **Negotiation and Allocation of Merger Gains – Cash Deal –** The standalone equity values of the acquirer and target are $5,000 and $3,000, respectively. The acquirer has 500 shares outstanding, and the target has 1,500 shares outstanding. Assume that the expected value created from this acquisition is $1,000, but since the outcome of the merger is uncertain, assume a set of potential outcomes (value created or destroyed) that range from a merger gain of $2,000 to a merger loss of $1,000. Assuming the acquirer pays $3,500 for the target's shares, calculate the gain or loss to the acquirer and target when the actual outcome of the merger is the expected, highest, and lowest outcome (see Exhibit 16.10).

P16.8 **Negotiation and Allocation of Merger Gains—Stock-for-Stock Deal:** Use the information in Problem 16.7 to respond to the following questions.

    a. Measure the exchange ratio and resulting stock price that allocates $5,500 of the post-merger value (based on the expected outcome) to the acquirer.

    b. Measure the exchange ratio and resulting stock price that allocates the value of the synergies based on the relative standalone values of the two companies.

    c. Based on a post-merger value equal to the expected outcome for the merger, calculate the target's minimum exchange ratio, the acquirer's maximum exchange ratio and the resulting stock prices.

    d. Assuming the exchange ratio is 0.2121, calculate the gain or loss to the acquirer and target when the actual outcome of the merger is the expected, highest, and lowest outcome (see Exhibit 16.14).

P16.9 **Sources and Uses:** An acquirer makes an offer to purchase a target company. The target company's current stock price is $3 per share, and it has 300 million shares outstanding. Given the expected synergies from the acquisition, the deal premium is negotiated at 20%. The target has no convertible debt or convertible preferred stock, but it does have 100 million stock options outstanding, all with an exercise price equal to $3. The acquirer has to redeem the debt and preferred stock of the target for $100 million and $200 million, respectively and buy out the option holders. The acquirer plans to finance the acquisition with $100 million of its own excess cash and $20 million of the target's excess cash; it plans to finance the remainder with debt. Initial fees will equal $47.4 million (3% on the debt financing and 1% for other fees). These fees do not include fees for a revolver loan. Debt issued to finance the transaction includes $400 million of seven-year, 7.0% senior secured bank debt and $800 million of nine-year, 9% subordinated unsecured debt; the remainder is financed with a revolving line of credit. The revolving line of credit of $300 million has a five-year term, a 4% interest rate on the amount drawn, and a 0.5% annual fee on the total amount. Calculate the purchase price of the equity and prepare a sources and uses schedule similar to the sources and uses schedule in Exhibit 16.16.

P16.10 **LATAM Airline Group—Negotiation Range and Allocation of Synergies:** See Valuation in Practice 16.2, Valuation in Practice 16.4, and Review Exercise 16.1 for background information for this problem. The stock price of the acquiring company, LAN, prior to the merger announcement was approximately $18 per share, and LAN had 339.36 million shares outstanding. TAM, the target company, had a stock price of $14.60 and 156.21 million shares outstanding. Assume that the value of the synergies (merger gain) was expected to be $3 billion but range from a loss of $2 billion to a gain of $5 billion. The companies agreed to an exchange ratio of 0.9.

    a. Calculate the exchange ratio that would allocate 70% of the post-merger value to LAN shareholders.

    b. Calculate the minimum exchange ratio that TAM shareholders would be willing to accept.

    c. Calculate the maximum exchange ratio that LAN shareholders would be willing to accept.

		Continuing Value Growth Rate				
		−20.00%	**−15.00%**	**−10.00%**	**−5.00%**	**0.00%**
	9.00%	$1,734.6	$1,976.4	$2,345.4	$2,978.0	$4,313.4
	9.50%	$1,689.1	$1,918.2	$2,264.8	$2,850.4	$4,052.5
r_{WACC}	10.00%	$1,645.3	$1,862.6	$2,188.5	$2,731.7	$3,818.2
	10.50%	$1,603.1	$1,809.4	$2,116.2	$2,621.0	$3,606.6
	11.00%	$1,562.6	$1,758.5	$2,047.7	$2,517.6	$3,414.7

25th percentile $1,809.4
50th percentile $2,188.5
75th percentile $2,850.4
Mean. $2,457.1

Note: The investment synergy does not increase income taxes because it does not affect income but only the amount of investment.

Review Exercise 16.2: Measuring Earnings Accretion

	Standalone Acquirer	Standalone Target	Financing	Asset Changes	Synergies	Post-Merger Company
Income Statement						
Revenues	$ 4,000.0	$2,750.0			$ 30.0	$ 6,780.0
Operating expenses	−2,280.0	−1,790.0		$ −45.0	270.0	−3,845.0
Interest income.	60.0	20.0		−80.0		0.0
Interest expense.	−180.0	−60.0	$ −120.0			−360.0
Income taxes	−640.0	−368.0	48.0	50.0	−120.0	−1,030.0
Earnings	$ 960.0	$ 552.0	$ −72.0	$ −75.0	$180.0	$ 1,545.0
Shares outstanding	400.0	200.0	400.0	400.0	400.0	400.0
Earnings per share	$ 2.400	$ 2.760	$ −0.180	$ −0.188	$0.450	$ 3.863
Balance Sheet						
Excess cash	$ 3,000.0	$1,000.0	$2,000.0	$−6,000.0		$ 0
Operating assets	8,000.0	5,000.0		1,000.0		14,000.0
Total assets.	$11,000.0	$6,000.0	$2,000.0	$−5,000.0	$ 0	$14,000.0
Debt	$ 3,000.0	$1,000.0	$2,000.0			$ 6,000.0
Equity	8,000.0	5,000.0		$−5,000.0		8,000.0
Liabilities and equity.	$11,000.0	$6,000.0	$2,000.0	$−5,000.0	$ 0	$14,000.0

Rates of Return (excluding excess assets & using ending balances)

Return on assets	12.9%	11.5%				12.6%
Return on equity.	18.5%	13.5%				19.3%

Review Exercise 16.3: Effect of Accretion on Market Multiples

	Standalone Acquirer	Standalone Target	Financing	Excess Cash	Value of Snyergies	Post-Merger Company Including Synergies
Firm value...............	$12,200.0	$6,000.0	$ 400.0	$-3,850.0	$1,500.0	$16,250.0
Debt	3,000.0	1,000.0	2,000.0	0.0	0.0	6,000.0
Equity value	$ 9,200.0	$5,000.0	$-1,600.0	$-3,850.0	$1,500.0	$10,250.0
Shares outstanding	400.0	200.0			400.0	400.0
Price per share...........	$ 23.00	$ 25.00			$ 3.75	$ 25.63
Earnings per share........	$ 2.400	$ 2.760			$ 0.450	$ 3.863
Price-to-earnings ratio	9.6	9.1			8.3	6.6

Review Exercise 16.4: Negotiation and Allocation of Synergies—Cash Deals

	Value	Shares	Price	Symbol
Standalone Equity Values				
Standalone value of acquirer	$10,000	1000	$10.00	V_A
Standalone value of target	$ 4,000	2000	$ 2.00	V_T
Combined standalone value.................	$14,000			$V_A + V_T$
Potential Outcomes of Value Created or Destroyed (Synergies)				
Expected value of valued created	$ 3,000			$E(V_S)$
Lower bound of value created (destroyed).....	$-2,500			V_S
Upper bound of value created (destroyed).....	$ 5,000			V_S
Potential Outcomes of the Post-Merger Equity Value				
Expected value of post-merger company	$17,000			$E(V_P)$
Lower bound of post-merger company	$11,500			V_P
Upper bound of post-merger company	$19,000			V_P
Negotiated Deal				
Expected value created (merger gain (loss)) ...	$ 3,000			$E(V_S)$
Expected value of post-merger equity........	$17,000			$E(V_P)$
Premium paid to target....................	$ 2,000	66.7%	% of Synergies Allocated	$V_{T, premium}$
Standalone value of target	4,000			V_T
Amount paid for target....................	$ 6,000	50.0%	% Premium Paid for Target	$V_{T, paid}$

Cash Deal–Equity Values	Expected Outcome Used in Deal Negotiation			Actual Outcome with More Value Created			Actual Outcome with Value Destroyed		
	Outcome	% Split	% Gain	Outcome	% Split	% Gain	Outcome	% Split	% Gain
Standalone value of acquirer	$10,000			$10,000			$10,000		
Standalone value of target	4,000			4,000			4,000		
Combined standalone value................	$14,000			$14,000			$14,000		
Value created (merger gain (loss))	3,000			5,000			–2,500		
Post-merger value	$17,000			$19,000			$11,500		
Overall gain or (loss) on acquisition	$ 3,000		21.4%	$ 5,000		35.7%	$–2,500		–17.9%
Post-merger value to target (cash received) ...	$ 6,000	35.3%		$ 6,000	31.6%		$ 6,000	52.2%	
Standalone value of target	–4,000			–4,000			–4,000		
Gain (loss) to target—merger premium	$ 2,000	66.7%	50.0%	$ 2,000	40.0%	50.0%	$ 2,000	nmf	50.0%
Post-merger value to acquirer	$11,000	64.7%		$13,000	68.4%		$ 5,500	47.8%	
Standalone value of acquirer	–10,000			–10,000			–10,000		
Gain or (loss) to acquirer	$ 1,000	33.3%	10.0%	$ 3,000	60.0%	30.0%	$–4,500	nmf	–45.0%

Review Exercise 16.5: Allocation of Synergies—Stock-for-Stock Deals ($ in millions)

Exchange Ratio Based on a Percentage Allocation of Value			
	S_A/S_T	S_A	S_T
S_A/S_T..	0.50	1,000	2,000
		C_A	S_T
$C_A \times S_T$.......................................	1,294	64.7%	
ER_{CA}...	0.273		
Shares issued to target = $ER_{CA} \times S_T$..............................	545.45		2,000

Post-Merger—Check	Shares	%	Value	Price
Acquirer shares (not changed)	1,000	64.7%	$11,000	$11.00
Target shares	545	35.3%	$ 6,000	$11.00
Total shares	1,545	100.0%	$17,000	$11.00

Exchange Ratio to Allocate Synergies and Total Value by Relative Standalone Values			
	ER	P_T	P_A	S_T
ER..	0.200	$2.00	$ 10.00	
Shares issued to target = $ER \times S_T$	400.00			2000

Post-Merger—Check	Shares	%	Value	Price
Acquirer shares (not changed)	1,000	71.4%	$12,143	$12.14
Target shares	400	28.6%	$ 4,857	$12.14
Total shares	1,400	100.0%	$17,000	$12.14

Minimum Exchange Ratio—All Value Created (Destroyed) to Acquirer—Target's Value Is Equal to Its Standalone Value

	$P_T \times S_A$	P_T	S_A
$P_T \times S_A$	$2,000	$2	1,000

	V_P	V_T	S_T
$V_P - V_T$	$13,000	$17,000	$4,000
ER_{MIN}	0.154		
Shares issued to target $= ER_{MIN} \times S_T$	307.69		2,000

Post-Merger—Check	Shares	%	Value	Price
Acquirer shares (not changed)	1,000	76.5%	$13,000	$13.00
Target shares	308	23.5%	$ 4,000	$13.00
Total shares	1,308	100.0%	$17,000	$13.00

Maximum Exchange Ratio—All Value Created (Destroyed) to Target—Acquirer's Value Is Equal to Its Standalone Value

	$V_P - V_A$	V_P	V_A
$V_P - V_A$	$7,000	$17,000	$10,000

	P_A	S_T
$P_A \times S_T$	$20,000	$10	2,000
ER_{MAX}	0.350		
Shares issued to target $= ER_{MAX} \times S_T$	700.00		

Post-Merger—Check	Shares	%	Value	Price
Acquirer shares (not changed)	1,000	58.8%	$10,000	$10.00
Target shares	700	41.2%	$ 7,000	$10.00
Total shares	1,700	100.0%	$17,000	$10.00

Stock Deal–Equity Values	Expected Outcome Used in Deal Negotiation			Actual Outcome with More Value Created			Actual Outcome with Value Destroyed		
	Outcome	% Split	% Gain	Outcome	% Split	% Gain	Outcome	% Split	% Gain
Standalone value of acquirer	$10,000			$10,000			$10,000		
Standalone value of target	4,000			4,000			4,000		
Combined standalone value	$14,000			$14,000			$14,000		
Value created (merger gain (loss))	3,000			5,000			–2,500		
Post-merger value	$17,000			$19,000			$11,500		
Overall gain or (loss) on acquisition	$ 3,000		21.4%	$ 5,000		35.7%	$–2,500		–17.9%
Post-merger value to target (stock received)	$ 6,000	35.3%		$ 6,706	35.3%		$ 4,059	35.3%	
Standalone value of target	–4,000			–4,000			–4,000		
Gain (loss) to target—merger premium	$ 2,000	66.7%	50.0%	$ 2,706	54.1%	67.6%	$ 59	nmf	1.5%
Post-merger value to acquirer	$11,000	64.7%		$12,294	64.7%		$ 7,441	64.7%	
Standalone value of acquirer	–10,000			–10,000			–10,000		
Gain or (loss) to acquirer	$ 1,000	33.3%	10.0%	$ 2,294	45.9%	22.9%	$–2,559	nmf	–25.6%

Review Exercise 16.6: Merger Sources and Uses Schedule

Current stock price.	$ 10.00			
Deal premium.	25.0%			
Deal stock price	$ 12.50			
Number of fully diluted shares outstanding	114.0		100.00	14.00
Purchase price of equity.	$1,425.0			

Pre-Merger Outstanding Options as of End of Year 0 (Liquidation of Options)				
Year Issued	**Exercise Price**	**Number of Options = Shares Issued (m)**	**Buyback Shares (m)**	**Net Increase in Shares (m)**
Various	$9.00	50.0	36.0	14.0

Sources and Uses of Cash— Merger Financing ($ in millions)	Amount	%	Coupon = YTM	Maturity (Years)
Sources				
Excess cash—acquirer.	$ 200.0	13.6%		
Excess cash—target	100.0	6.8%		
Revolver	72.3	4.9%	4.00%	5
Senior secured note (bank debt)	400.0	27.2%	6.00%	7
Subordinated note (unsecured debt)	700.0	47.5%	8.00%	9
Preferred stock—new.	0.0	0.0%		
Common equity	0.0	0.0%		
Total sources	$1,472.3	100.0%		
Uses				
Common equity	$1,425.0	96.8%		
Preferred stock—redeemed.	0.0	0.0%		
Debt redeemed.	0.0	0.0%		
			Fee rate	Total
Initial fees:				
Financing fees—debt.	33.0	2.2%	3.0%	
Financing fees—revolver			0.5%	$200
Other fees and expenses	14.3	1.0%	1.0%	
Total uses	$1,472.3	100.0%		

Note: The treasury stock method (see Chapter 15) was used to calculate the number of shares issued for the target's outstanding options.

After mastering the material in this chapter, you will be able to:

1. Explain how cross-border valuations differ from within-country (domestic) valuations (17.1)

2. Use exchange rate theories to forecast exchange rates (17.2–17.3)

3. Measure income taxes for a cross-border valuation (17.4)

4. Measure discount rates and adjust free cash flows for country-specific risks (17.5–17.6)

5. Explain the limitations of using cross-border market multiples and measure exchange rate exposure (17.7–17.8)

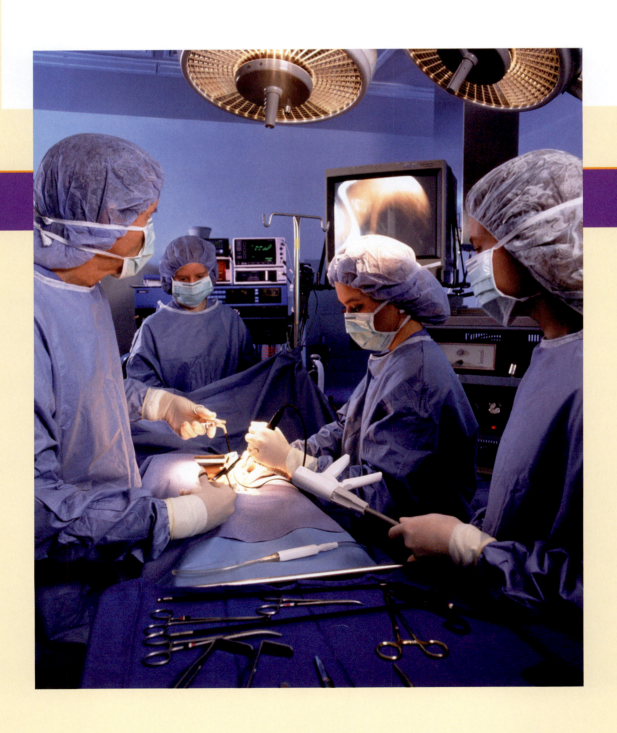

Valuing Businesses Across Borders

A common reason for cross-border acquisitions is to gain access to new markets, technology, or products. On April 27, 2011, Johnson & Johnson (J&J), a U.S. company, announced a definitive merger agreement with Synthes, Inc. (Synthes),

SYNTHES, INC.

a Swiss Company. J&J announced that it would acquire Synthes for $21.3 billion in a cash and stock purchase of Synthes' shares (a 27% premium relative to the closing stock price 30 days prior to the announcement). The companies stated the following reasons for the merger:[1]

Together, the companies will offer surgeons and patients a unique breadth and depth of technology and service worldwide to meet their orthopedic needs. . . . Synthes is widely respected for its innovative high-quality products, world-class R&D capabilities, its commitment to education, the highest standards of service, and extensive global footprint. The combination presents a significant opportunity to jointly bring our products, services and educational offerings to the next level. . . . Together, we will be a more attractive and exciting company for our employees, and a more resourceful partner for our customers. . . .

In this chapter, we explore and highlight the key differences between the valuation of a company operating in a single country and the valuation of a cross-border acquisition target or a multinational company.

---

[1] See Johnson and Johnson's Form 8-K, filed with the U.S. Securities and Exchange Commission (SEC) on August 7, 2011.

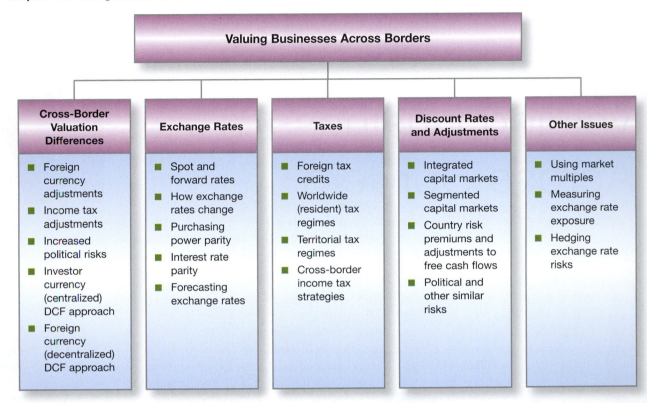

INTRODUCTION

For many years, companies throughout the world generated most of their revenues and incurred most of their expenses in the countries in which they were located. One reason cited for the focus of business activities in home or domestic markets is that business activities conducted outside of domestic markets are potentially more uncertain. This uncertainty results from different political, legal, and regulatory environments. It also results from operating in a different environment and culture, making it more difficult for a company to generate revenues and manage its operations efficiently. These uncertainties exist for all cross-border expansions, but they are generally greater when companies expand into countries with less developed economies and legal systems.

In spite of these uncertainties, we know from Chapter 16 that cross-border mergers and acquisitions have become more popular as business has become more global. Why? Companies can gain access to new markets, technology, and products by expanding globally. They can also gain access to more resources in addition to cheaper inputs in the production process (such as labor). In addition, innovations in technology are reducing the barriers to conducting business across borders. The Internet, for example, has made it easier, quicker, and less costly to communicate over long distances; it is also said to be "shrinking the globe," reducing some of the environmental and cultural differences as well as some of the uncertainties of doing business in other parts of the world.

Up until now in this book, we assumed that companies operated in the same country in which they were located and that the country in which they operated had well-established capital markets. The valuation models and frameworks discussed throughout the previous chapters are applicable to cross-border valuations; however, the implementation of these models and frameworks is more complex in a cross-border valuation. In this chapter, we now assume that our company—located and operating in one country—is investing in another company (or project) that is located in and operating in another country (or countries)—in short, a cross-border valuation.

We will discuss how to adjust the valuation models and tools discussed in the previous chapters in order to use them to value cross-border business activities. The major adjustments we make address foreign currency exchange rate issues, tax complexity issues when two (or more) countries are involved, and cost-of-capital estimation issues. In addition, we will discuss other issues that specifically arise for cross-border valuations of companies in emerging markets. Finally, since cross-border business activities create potential exposure to unexpected changes in foreign currency exchange rates (the price at which one can convert one type of currency into another type of currency), we will discuss exchange rate exposure and how it is hedged. Although the context of this chapter is the valuation of a cross-border acquisition, everything discussed is germane to valuing multinational companies or projects in a foreign country.

17.1 HOW CROSS-BORDER VALUATIONS ARE DIFFERENT

As we previously stated in this chapter, we assume that a company located and operating in one country is investing in another company located and operating in another country. We refer to the first company as the **investing company** and the second company as the **foreign** or **cross-border company**. We refer to the currency for the investing company as the **investor currency** or **home currency** and to the currency for the foreign company as the **foreign currency**. Even if we assume that a company's cross-border business activities take place in a country with well-established capital markets and legal systems, valuing cross-border activities requires us to make certain adjustments to our valuation models and frameworks.

LO1 Explain how cross-border valuations differ from within-country (domestic) valuations

We adjust the implementation of these valuation models and frameworks for issues that arise in cross-border valuations but do not exist in valuations of a company that operates purely in its home market. We typically must make even further adjustments if the cross-border valuation is of a foreign company operating in a developing economy. More specifically, we adjust key inputs in the discounted cash flow (DCF) valuation model such as the unlevered free cash flow forecasts, the continuing (or terminal) value, and the risk-adjusted discount rate.

Potential Adjustments to Free Cash Flow Forecasts

Various types of issues can arise in cross-border valuations that may require an adjustment to the free cash flows used in a DCF valuation model. These issues include:

- **Exchange Rate Forecasts:** Our goal in a cross-border valuation is to value the cross-border company in terms of the investor's currency, even though the cross-border company generates revenues and incurs expenses in a foreign currency. This requires exchange rate forecasts.

- **Taxes:** An investor (company) in a company located in another country may incur additional (or fewer) taxes simply because it is a foreigner or if the target repatriates earnings (pays dividends) to the acquirer. These taxes include income taxes (of course) and withholding taxes on dividends, as well as other types of explicit or implicit taxes, including import and export taxes or tariffs, quotas, and employment taxes.

- **Nominal or Real Forecasts and Discount Rates:** Some countries experience periods of hyperinflation. To the extent that a cross-border company operates in a hyperinflationary economy, we consider whether to value the company in nominal or real terms (nominal free cash flow forecasts with a nominal discount rate or real free cash flow forecasts with a real discount rate).

- **Timing of Cash Flows:** Regulatory limitations on the repatriation of earnings and cash flows can affect the timing of when cash is available for distribution to the investors of a company. Although not directly a timing issue, liquidity issues (the ability to sell the asset if needed or expected) are issues we might also consider.

- **Increased Political and Other Foreign-Country-Related Risks:** In addition to the potential outcomes normally considered when developing free cash flow forecasts, additional uncertainty might require additional adjustments when measuring expected free cash flows. These risks are often political in nature, such as the expropriation of assets or failure to gain regulatory approval of a project, but can also include other risks specific to a country or geographic region.

Potential Adjustments to the Risk-Adjusted Discount Rate

Similarly, various types of issues can arise in cross-border valuations that may require an adjustment to the risk-adjusted discount rate used in the DCF valuation model. These issues include:

- **Asset Pricing Model Risk Factors and Risk Premiums:** We must decide how to estimate risk factors, such as the Capital Asset Pricing Model (CAPM) beta, and whether or not to include other risk factors. As we will later discuss, we estimate costs of capital differently depending on whether we assume the world's capital markets are fully integrated or segmented. We must also decide whether to include other risk factors, such as one for currency risk.

■ **Political and Other Foreign-Country-Related Risks (Country Credit Rating):** In the previous section, we discussed the potential of making adjustments to the expected free cash flows due to country-specific risks. If these risk factors are systematic risk factors, they also affect the cost of capital. We adjust the discount rate for country-related risks if the risks are systematic in nature and not embedded in the risk factors in our asset pricing model (for example, beta in the CAPM). An example of a potential systematic risk might be a country's fiscal policies, which can result in a country-specific systematic risk factor if they affect interest rates, inflation, or other macroeconomic factors that affect the value of the firm.

■ **Capital Structure and Tax Deductibility of Interest:** Tax regulations might affect the amount and type of debt a company can issue for which interest is tax deductible. We must adjust our calculations for any constraints on capital structure and the tax deductibility of interest. Differences in bankruptcy laws may also affect financial distress costs.

Valuation Key 17.1

While the discounted cash flow valuation model and framework continue to apply in cross-border valuations, specific characteristics of these valuations require adjustments to the implementation of the DCF valuation model. We adjust our free cash flow forecasts and risk-adjusted discount rates relative to the more standard procedures previously discussed.

Investor Currency (Centralized) and Foreign Currency (Decentralized) Discounted Cash Flow Valuation Approaches

We can adjust the DCF valuation model to value cross-border companies using two approaches: the investor currency (centralized) approach or the foreign currency (decentralized) approach. The primary difference between the two approaches is the timing of when we convert the foreign currency to the investor's currency. In the centralized approach, we perform this conversion in the forecasting model, and we convert each year's forecasted foreign currency free cash flows to investor currency free cash flows using exchange rate forecasts. In the decentralized approach, we perform this conversion after valuing the company in its own currency by converting the value of the company stated in the foreign currency to the value of the company stated in the investor's currency using the spot exchange rate as of the valuation date. In Exhibit 17.1, we present an outline of the steps underpinning the two approaches.

EXHIBIT 17.1   Comparison of the Investor Currency (Centralized) and Local Currency (Decentralized) DCF Approaches

Investor Currency or Centralized Approach (Discount Investor Currency Cash Flows)	Foreign Currency or Decentralized Approach (Discount Foreign Currency Cash Flows)
1 Decide on the reinvestment/repatriation (upstream cash flows) policy	1 Same as the investor currency or centralized approach
2 Assess special tax effects resulting from ownership by a foreign company	2 Same as the investor currency or centralized approach
3 Assess specific country risks affecting expected free cash flows	3 Same as the investor currency or centralized approach
4 Develop a financial model incorporating Steps 1 through 3 and forecast free cash flows in the company's local currency	4 Same as the investor currency or centralized approach
5 Develop forecasts for the exchange rates for all periods in the forecast horizon and convert the local currency free cash flows to the investor's currency	
6 Measure the cost of capital based on the investor's currency, adjusting for any country-specific systematic risks	5 Measure the cost of capital based on the foreign currency, including any country-specific systematic risks
7 Discount the free cash flows from Step 5 using the discount rate from Step 6	6 Discount the free cash flows from Step 4 using the discount rate from Step 5
	7 Convert the value of the firm measured in the foreign currency to the value of the firm measured in the investor's currency at the exchange rate as of the valuation date

The first four steps of the DCF valuation are the same in both approaches. The first step focuses on the income tax effects of repatriating cash flows from a foreign company to an investor company. We begin by deciding on a reinvestment or repatriation policy to understand the effects of repatriating cash flows—typically income tax effects. If a company decides on a repatriation policy that prevents or delays the distribution of free cash flows to the investor company, we have to consider the effect it may have on the valuation of the free cash flows (though cash may be invested in marketable securities that earn their cost of capital). The second step focuses on other potential income tax effects resulting from cross-border ownership.

In Step 3, we assess specific country risks that might affect our free cash flow forecasts. We use this step more frequently for foreign companies located and operating in developing economies. It includes such risks as the expropriation of assets or income by the government, unclear or inconsistently interpreted regulations, the difficulty of enforcing contracts, bureaucracy, and corruption; all of these risks are more likely and more severe in developing countries than in developed countries. The fourth step develops the financial model discussed in Chapter 4, but now we include the adjustments from the first three steps in the model.

Since the two approaches differ in terms of their remaining steps, we discuss them separately and begin with the investor currency (centralized) approach. In Step 5 of the centralized approach, we convert the foreign-currency-denominated free cash flows in the financial model to the investor currency. In order to perform this conversion, we first develop exchange rate forecasts for all periods in the financial model. We use these exchange rate forecasts to convert the foreign-currency-denominated free cash flow forecasts for each year into investor-currency-denominated free cash flow forecasts. In Step 6, we measure the various costs of capital needed to measure the risk-adjusted discount rate, including the effect of any country-specific systematic risks. Since we convert free cash flow forecasts to the investor's currency, we measure the costs of capital and risk-adjusted discount rate in terms of the investor's currency. Last, in Step 7, we discount the investor-currency-denominated free cash flow forecasts at the investor currency risk-adjusted discounted rate in order to value the firm.

For the foreign currency (decentralized) approach, we do not convert the free cash flows to the investor currency. Instead, in Step 5, we measure the various costs of capital needed to measure the risk-adjusted discount rate, again including the effect of any country-specific systematic risks. Since the free cash flow forecasts are denominated in the foreign currency, we measure the costs of capital and risk-adjusted discount rate in terms of the foreign currency. In Step 6, we discount the foreign-currency-denominated free cash flow forecasts at the foreign currency risk-adjusted discount rate. Last, in Step 7, we convert the foreign-currency-denominated firm value to the investor currency with the current (or spot) exchange rate as of the valuation date. Of the two approaches, the investor currency (centralized) approach is more commonly used to value cross-border acquisitions and in valuing multinational companies. We will explain this in more detail later.

Regardless of which approach we use, we always use a consistent basis for measuring the free cash flows and discount rate. In the investor approach, we discount investor currency free cash flows at the investor currency discount rate; in the foreign currency approach, we discount the foreign currency free cash flows at the foreign currency discount rate.

Valuation Key 17.2

We can use two approaches—the investor currency (centralized) approach and the foreign currency (decentralized) approach—to adjust the DCF valuation model in order to value cross-border acquisitions or multinational companies. The primary difference between the two approaches is the timing of the conversion from the foreign currency to the investor currency. In the investor currency (centralized) approach, we perform this conversion for each forecasted free cash flow in the forecasting model, and in the foreign currency (decentralized) approach, we perform this conversion after we value the company in its own currency.

Example Illustrating the Equality of the Two Approaches

A company in the United States, Booth Investor Group, is purchasing a company in Russia, the Ananiev Group. Booth is attempting to value the Ananiev Group in U.S. dollars (USD). After repatriation, taxes, and country-related risks are taken into consideration, the free cash flow forecasts of Ananiev for the next three years, stated in Russian rubles (RUB), are 10,000 RUB, 12,340 RUB, and 12,760 RUB; also, the continuing value of the company as of the end of Year 3 is 190,000 RUB. The current exchange rate is

27.8 RUB/USD, and exchange rate forecasts for the next three years for the price of $1 in Russian Rubles (RUB/USD) are 28.91, 30.28, and 31.78. The appropriate risk-adjusted discount rate for this company's cash flows, stated in USD, is 10% and is constant in each year. For ease of discussion, we assume both Booth and Ananiev are only financed with common equity.

In the top panel of Exhibit 17.2, we present the DCF valuation of the company using the investor currency (centralized) approach. We first convert the free cash flow and continuing value forecasts from rubles to dollars, using the exchange rate forecasts. Next, we discount the expected free cash flow and continuing value (stated in USD) by the constant cost of capital of 10% in order to measure their present values. The value of the firm is equal to $5,444.1.

EXHIBIT 17.2	Example Illustrating the Equality of the Two DCF Approaches					
Investor Currency/Centralized Approach		**Year 0**	**Year 1**	**Year 2**	**Year 3**	**CV$_{\text{Firm, Yr 3}}$**
Free cash flow and continuing value (in RUB × 1,000)			10,000	12,340	12,760	190,000
Exchange rate forecast (RUB/USD)			28.913	30.279	31.784	31.784
Free cash flow and continuing value (USD)			$ 346	$ 408	$ 401	$ 5,978
Risk-adjusted discount factor for investor currency		10.0%	0.909	0.826	0.751	0.751
Present value (in USD × 1,000)			$ 314.4	$ 336.8	$ 301.6	$4,491.3
Value of the firm (in USD ×1,000)		$ 5,444.1				
Foreign Currency/Decentralized Approach		**Year 0**	**Year 1**	**Year 2**	**Year 3**	**CV$_{\text{Firm, Yr 3}}$**
Free cash flow and continuing value (in RUB × 1,000)			10,000	12,340	12,760	190,000
Risk-adjusted discount rate in r_{RUB}.			14.42%	15.20%	15.47%	15.47%
Discount factor for foreign currency.			0.874	0.759	0.657	0.657
Present value (in RUB × 1,000)			8,739.7	9,362.0	8,383.5	124,837.6
Value of the firm (in RUB × 1,000)		151,322.9				
Current or spot exchange rate (RUB/USD)		27.80				
Value of the firm (in USD × 1,000)		$ 5,444.1				

Exhibit may contain small rounding errors

In the bottom panel of the exhibit, we present the DCF valuation of the company using the foreign currency (decentralized) approach. In order to use this approach, we need to measure the appropriate risk-adjusted discount rate for the free cash flow and continuing value forecasts (both stated in rubles) in conjunction with the previously stated information. For now, assume the appropriate risk-adjusted discount rates based on the foreign currency for the next three years are 14.42%, 15.20%, and 15.47%. We will explain how to calculate these discount rates from the 10% investor discount rate and the forecasted exchange rates in the next section of the chapter. We use these discount rates to measure the present value of the free cash flow and continuing value forecasts stated in rubles. Recall that since the discount rate changes in each period, the discount factor is the product of the individual one-period discount factors; for example, the discount factor for Year 2 is $(1.1442)^{-1} \times (1.1520)^{-1}$, and the discount factor for Year 3 is the discount factor for Year 2 multiplied by $(1.1547)^{-1}$. The value of the firm, stated in rubles, is 151,322.9 RUB. We convert this value to USD using the current exchange rate of 27.8 in order to arrive at a value of $5,444.1, which is identical to the value calculated using the investor currency or centralized approach.

As we can see from this example, forecasting exchange rates is an important aspect of the investor currency (centralized) approach, for this approach uses these exchange rate forecasts directly; however, we also implicitly use exchange rate forecasts to implement the foreign currency (decentralized) approach. As we might suspect from our example, in order for the two approaches to yield the same valuation, the exchange rate forecasts must be linked to the appropriate risk-adjusted discount rates for the free cash flow and continuing value forecasts stated in rubles. We will discuss this link in a later section of this chapter when we discuss exchange rate theories and exchange rate forecasts. Again, for reasons we will discuss later, the investor currency (centralized) approach—convert cash flows and discount them at the investor currency cost of capital—is the more common approach.

Valuation Key 17.3

While the investor currency (centralized) approach uses exchange rate forecasts directly, the foreign currency (decentralized) approach also uses exchange rate forecasts to convert the discount rate from one currency to the discount rate for another currency.

REVIEW EXERCISE 17.1

Investor Currency (Centralized) and Foreign Currency (Decentralized) Discounted Cash Flow Valuation Approaches

A company in France is purchasing a company in the United States. The French company is attempting to value the U.S. company in euros. After repatriation, taxes, and country-related risks are taken into consideration, the free cash flow forecasts of the U.S. company for the next three years, stated in USD, are $1.2 million, $1.4 million, and $1.7 million, respectively; also, the continuing value of the company as of the end of Year 3 is $180 million. The current and forward exchange rates appear in Exhibit P17.1 in the problem section of the chapter. The appropriate risk-adjusted discount rate for this company's cash flows, stated in euros, is 12% and is constant in each year. The appropriate discount rates for discounting USD for the next three years are 10.978%, 11.207%, and 11.361%, respectively. Both of the companies are only financed with common equity. Measure the value of the U.S. company in euros using both the investor currency and foreign currency discounted cash flow methods.

Solution on page 770.

Other Potential Economic Forces Affecting Cross-Border Valuations[2]

Depending on the relation between the foreign company's expected free cash flows and unexpected changes in exchange rates or the exchange rate forecasts we use in the valuation, we could have one or two additional components in a cross-border valuation. The first potential additional component results from a relation between the foreign company's free cash flows and unexpected changes in exchange rates—more specifically, the covariance between the foreign company's free cash flows and the exchange rate.

This covariance could be non-zero if unexpected changes in the exchange rate cause either the foreign company's revenues (quantity or price) or its cost structure to change. If this covariance is not equal to zero, it would result in another potential impact on value, and we would include it in our valuation. Generally, however, we assume that the foreign company's free cash flows, denominated in the foreign currency, are not related to the exchange rate; that is, we typically assume that unexpected changes in the exchange rate do not cause a change in the foreign-currency-denominated free cash flows or that the covariance between them is sufficiently small to allow us to ignore it in the valuation.

The second potential additional component results from using forecasted exchange rates that differ from market-based exchange rates. If we used forecasted exchange rates that differ from market-based exchange rates, we can partition the cross-border valuation into two parts: the value based on market-based exchange rates and the change in value that results from using exchange rate forecasts that differ from the market-based exchange rates.

17.2 EXCHANGE RATE BASICS

Regardless of which form of the DCF valuation model we use, we must use exchange rate forecasts to either convert cash flows from the foreign currency to the investor's currency or, as we will explain later in the chapter, to measure the appropriate risk-adjusted discount rate in the foreign currency. Understand-

LO2 Use exchange rate theories to forecast exchange rates

---

[2] For a detailed discussion of the issues in this section, see O'Brien, Thomas J., "Foreign Exchange and Cross-Border Valuation," *Journal of Corporate Finance* (Spring/Summer 2004), pp. 147–154; O'Brien, Thomas J., "The Global CAPM and a Firm's Cost of Capital in Different Currencies," *Journal of Corporate Finance* (Fall 1999), pp. 73–79; and Butler, Kirt C., and Gwynai Utete, "A Framework for Cross-Border Investment and Currency Hedging Decisions," working paper, the Eli Broad College of Business, Michigan State University, May 2011.

ing exchange rates is also important, for they can affect the demand for a company's products or its cost structure; for example, unexpected exchange rate changes can affect demand in foreign countries or demand in the domestic country when the company is competing with foreign companies. As a result, unexpected exchange rate changes can affect pricing and marketing and production decisions, all of which can affect expected free cash flows. In addition, given the global nature of capital markets, unexpected exchange rate changes can affect the impact of financing decisions. In this section, we discuss such basic concepts as the concept of an exchange rate, forward contracts, and how to think about changes in exchange rates.

Spot and Forward Exchange Rates

We can think of an **exchange rate** as the price of one currency for a unit of another currency. The exchange rate indicates the value of a unit of currency in terms of another currency. Terms used to discuss current and future exchange rates are the spot rate and forward rate or future expected spot rate. Concepts and terms related to changes in exchange rates include exchange rate appreciation (or increases in value) and exchange rate depreciation (or decreases in value). Terms related to forward contracts include the forward rate, forward premium, and forward discounts. The **spot rate** is the current exchange rate for immediate delivery of a currency (actually, most of the time, delivery typically takes about two days for the transaction to clear).

With a few exceptions, exchange rates involving U.S. dollars are traded and quoted on trading desks as the number of units of a non-U.S. currency per one U.S. dollar (USD or $), denoted, $S_{\text{non-USD/\$}}$. Examples of exceptions include the British Pound Sterling (GBP or £) and the euro, which are traded based on the number of USD per GBP ($S_{\$/£}$) or Euro ($S_{\$/EUR}$). However, we can always invert the exchange rate to measure the price of a non-U.S. currency in USD, denoted $S_{\$/\text{non-USD}} = 1/S_{\text{non-USD/\$}}$. For example, assume a company in the United States (which uses the U.S. dollar for its currency) is buying products in the United Kingdom (which has the British Pound Sterling for its currency) and must pay for the products with £. In order to complete this transaction, the U.S. company must exchange $ for £ or purchase £. If $100 purchases £61.36, then the exchange rate is 1.63 $/£, stated as $S_{\$/£} = 1.63$ (1.63 = $100/£61.36) or $S_{£/\$} = 0.6136$, which is equal to the inverse of the $S_{\$/£}$ exchange rate (0.6136 = £61.36/$100).

Valuation in Practice 17.1

Caraco Pharmaceutical Laboratories, Ltd. (a U.S. Company) Acquired by Sun Pharmaceutical Industries Limited (an Indian Company) It is common for a company to first enter a foreign market through an agreement with a local company in that foreign market. If successful, these relationships sometimes evolve into the acquisition of the company in the foreign market, which is the case of Caraco and Sun Pharma. On February 22, 2011, Caraco Pharmaceutical Laboratories, Ltd. (Caraco), a U.S. company, announced that it had entered into a "going private" merger agreement with Sun Pharmaceutical Industries Limited ("Sun Pharma"), an Indian company.

The relationship between the companies began in March 1996, when Caraco and Sun Pharma announced an agreement to produce and market Sun Pharma's generic anti-convulsant drug in the United States. Their relationship expanded intermittently from 1996 to 1998, and from 1998 to 2002, Sun Pharma made loans to Caraco totaling approximately $12 million. In a later agreement, Sun Pharma agreed to provide Caraco with 25 mutually agreed-upon generic drugs over a five-year period. During 2004, Sun Pharma acquired 3,452,291 additional shares of common stock for $9.00 per share, and it paid $11,744,964 for options in order to purchase an additional 1,679,066 shares of common stock with exercise prices ranging from $.68 to $3.50. From 2007 onward, Caraco entered into marketing agreements with Sun Pharma for Caraco to purchase selected product formulations offered by Sun Pharma.

Source: See Caraco Pharmaceutical Laboratories, Ltd. Form 8-K (Current Report) and PRER14A (Preliminary Proxy Statement), filed with the U.S. SEC on February 22, 2011, and May 6, 2011, respectively.

A **forward contract** (or forward transaction) is a contract to exchange a specified amount of one type of currency for a specified amount of another type of currency at some specified future point in time based on a specified exchange rate, called the **forward rate**. The forward currency market is very large and liquid for currencies of countries with developed economies. Currencies of countries with developed economies generally have forward contracts that mature between the short term (one day) and long term (up to several years), while currencies of countries with early-development-stage economies generally have forward contracts with only short-term maturities. In Exhibit 17.3, we present the spot and forward exchange rates for several country-pair exchange rates on August 1, 2011.

EXHIBIT 17.3	Selected Direct and Indirect Spot and Forward Exchange Rates for Different Country-Pairs on August 1, 2011*						
		Spot Rate	1 Year	2 Year	3 Year	4 Year	5 Year
Indian Rupee / U.S. Dollar (USD)							
	Bid	44.22	45.99	47.67	49.40	50.60	51.70
	Ask	44.22	46.14	48.10	50.10	51.90	53.20
	Ask/Bid	0.0%	0.3%	0.9%	1.4%	2.6%	2.9%
U.S. Dollar (USD) / Indian Rupee							
	Bid	0.0226	0.0217	0.0208	0.0199	0.0193	0.0188
	Ask	0.0227	0.0217	0.0210	0.0202	0.0197	0.0193
	Ask/Bid	0.1%	0.0%	1.0%	1.5%	2.1%	2.7%
Indian Rupee / U.K. Pound (GBP)							
	Bid	72.04	74.63	77.00	79.47	81.26	83.14
	Ask	72.06	74.91	77.76	80.73	83.53	85.91
	Ask/Bid	0.0%	0.4%	1.0%	1.6%	2.8%	3.3%
Japanese Yen / Indian Rupee							
	Bid	1.75	1.66	1.58	1.49	1.40	1.33
	Ask	1.75	1.67	1.60	1.51	1.44	1.37
	Ask/Bid	0.0%	0.4%	1.0%	1.5%	2.8%	3.3%
U.S. Dollar (USD) / U.K. Pound (GBP)							
	Bid	1.63	1.62	1.62	1.61	1.61	1.61
	Ask	1.63	1.62	1.62	1.61	1.61	1.61
	Ask/Bid	0.0%	0.1%	0.1%	0.2%	0.2%	0.4%
U.S. Dollar (USD) / Japanese Yen							
	Bid	0.0130	0.0130	0.0131	0.0134	0.0137	0.0141
	Ask	0.0130	0.0130	0.0132	0.0134	0.0137	0.0142
	Ask/Bid	0.0%	0.1%	0.1%	0.1%	0.3%	0.4%
Russian Ruble / U.S. Dollar (USD)							
	Bid	27.78	28.90	30.20	31.69	33.17	34.46
	Ask	27.81	28.93	30.35	31.88	33.52	34.80
	Ask/Bid	0.1%	0.1%	0.5%	0.6%	1.1%	1.0%
Indonesian Rupiah / U.S. Dollar (USD)							
	Bid	8.46	8.70	9.64	10.27	10.89	11.49
	Ask	8.47	8.73	9.75	10.44	11.12	11.79
	Ask/Bid	0.1%	0.2%	1.1%	1.6%	2.1%	2.6%

* Source—Bloomberg.

Each exchange rate has a bid rate and an ask rate. The **ask rate** is the home currency price at which the market maker is willing to sell the foreign currency or the price asked by the market maker of the customer interested in buying the foreign currency. The **bid rate** is the home currency price at which the market maker is willing to buy the foreign currency or the price offered by the market maker to the customer interested in selling the foreign currency. It is typical to measure the **actual exchange rate** as the midpoint between the bid and ask rates. The spread between the bid and ask rates (as a percentage of the midpoint) indicates the liquidity in that particular foreign currency market. Exhibit 17.3 also presents this percentage spread between the ask and bid exchange rates (labeled Ask/Bid). As one might expect, the percentage spread increases as the term of the forward contract increases. In addition, the percentage spread is smaller for exchange rates between established economies.

Currency Appreciation and Depreciation, Premiums and Discounts, and Real Exchange Rates

Naturally, spot rates change over time as a function of the relative underlying macroeconomic conditions of the two countries. We measure the appreciation and depreciation of one currency based on the change in its value relative to the other currency. An increase in the value of one currency indicates that the currency **appreciated** or became **stronger** relative to the other currency. A decrease in the value of the currency indicates that the currency **depreciated** or became **weaker** relative to the other currency. For example, a spot rate $(S_{\$/£})$ of 1.6 means that the value of the £ stated in USD is 1.6. An increase in the spot rate $(S_{\$/£})$ from 1.6 to 1.8 means that the value or price of a £ in USD increased; thus, the value of the £ **appreciated** or became **stronger** relative to the USD by 12.5% $(0.125 = 1.8/1.6 - 1)$. On the other hand, if the spot rate decreases from 1.6 to 1.3, that means that the value of the £ decreased relative to the USD; thus, the value of the £ decreased and **depreciated**, or became **weaker**, relative to the USD by 18.8% $(-0.188 = 1.3/1.6 - 1)$.

An appreciation of one currency implies the depreciation of the other currency. The above example, in which the spot rate $(S_{\$/£})$ increased from 1.6 to 1.8, also implies that it now takes \$1.8 to purchase £1.0 when it previously took \$1.6 to purchase £1.0, indicating that the USD depreciated. We measure the depreciation of the USD based on the value of the USD in £ $(S_{£/\$})$, decreasing from 0.625 $(0.625 = 1/1.6)$ to 0.556 $(0.556 = 1/1.8)$ or by 11.1% $(-0.111 = 0.556/0.625 - 1)$. If the spot rate $(S_{\$/£})$ decreases from 1.6 to 1.3, it means that it takes \$1.3 to purchase £1.0 when it previously took \$1.6 to purchase £1.0, indicating that the USD appreciated relative to the £. Again, we measure the appreciation of the USD based on the value of the USD in £ $(S_{£/\$})$, increasing from 0.625 $(0.625 = 1/1.6)$ to 0.769 $(0.769 = 1/1.3)$ or by 23.1% $(0.231 = 0.769/0.625 - 1)$. The percentage appreciation of one currency is not equal to the percentage depreciation of the other currency. One last point on appreciation and depreciation: the change in one exchange rate (one county pair) does not indicate the overall strength or weakness of a currency. Instead of using the change in one exchange rate, we typically use a weighted average of the changes in a group of exchange rates, weighted by relative trade flows for each pair of countries.

Investors trade forward contracts at a premium or at a discount relative to the spot rate, called the forward rate premium (or forward rate discount). The **forward rate premium** is the percentage difference between the forward and spot exchange rates—that is, the ratio of the forward rate to the spot rate minus 1. We typically present the forward rate premium on an annualized basis by multiplying the percentage by 360 over the length of the contract in days. A contract with a forward rate premium has a forward rate that is larger than the spot rate, and it indicates that, in the future and relative to the spot rate, the foreign currency is trading at a premium relative to the home currency. Conversely, a contract with a **forward rate discount** has a spot rate that is larger than the forward rate. For example, the spot Indian rupee/USD exchange rate is 44.2, and the forward rate for a five-year forward contract is 51.7; thus, the USD is selling at a forward rate premium of 17% $(0.17 = 51.7 / 44.2 - 1)$ over the five-year period, or 3.4% annually. As we will soon explain, because interest rates in India are higher than interest rates in the United States, the USD sells at a premium in subsequent years to prevent arbitrage opportunities.

The **real exchange rate** is the spot exchange rate divided by the relative price levels of the two countries; in other words, it is a nominal exchange rate (previously discussed) adjusted for the relative expected inflations between the two countries. Changes in real exchange rates provide information about changes in the relative competitiveness of the countries. Two important issues in using real exchange rates are the selection of the base year and the use of the correct price indices. Price indices used in real exchange rates can include the consumer price index, wholesale price index, producers' price index, and gross domestic product deflator. Another approach adjusts nominal exchange rates for the relative prices of tradable and non-tradable goods. Regardless of the approach and index used, a decline in the real exchange rate—say, over the last five years—indicates a real depreciation of one currency relative to another currency.

17.3 EXCHANGE RATE THEORIES AND FORECASTING METHODS

Naturally, in order to develop exchange rate forecasts that we need for the investor currency valuation approach, we must first understand why and how exchange rates change over time. Fortunately, we have some well-established exchange rate theories to help us. These theories delineate how the relative underlying macroeconomic conditions of two countries determine the exchange rates between the two countries. All of the exchange rate theories rely on a "no arbitrage condition." For us, **arbitrage** occurs when an investor can earn a positive risk-free return with no investment by exploiting a difference in prices of the same asset in different markets—for example, by buying in the market in which the asset has a lower price and simultaneously selling that asset in the market with the higher price. A **no arbitrage condition** exists when market forces set prices so that no arbitrage opportunity exists. In the remainder of this section, we will explain how we can use exchange rate theories to forecast exchange rates in cross-border valuations.

Purchasing Power Parity (PPP) and Relative Purchasing Power Parity (RPPP)

In its most basic form, purchasing power parity assumes the **law of one price**—namely, all products and services each have one global price. Assuming all products and services each have one price, **purchasing power parity** asserts that the ratio of prices in different currencies determines exchange rates. Although the underpinning of the theory utilizes average prices across a large group of products and services, we illustrate it using one good (gold) in order to highlight the intuitive nature of this theory.

Assume that gold was selling in the United States for $1,000 per some agreed-upon unit of weight and that it was selling in the U.K. for £625 per unit. As long as gold can be easily bought and sold across borders, the USD/GBP exchange rate must be $S_{\$/£} = 1.6$ ($1.6 = \$1,000/£625$). Although purchasing power parity is one of the oldest and longest lasting exchange rate theories, it does not explain movements in exchange rates in the short run, but it appears to work well over the longer run.[3] Reasons why this theory does not explain exchange rate movements include various transactions costs (such as shipping costs) and market frictions (such as government regulations or interventions).

Relative purchasing power parity relaxes the assumption of the law of one price behind purchasing power parity, and, instead of assuming that relative prices determine exchange rates, it assumes that changes in the relative prices (relative inflation rates) in two countries determine the change in exchange rates. **Relative purchasing power parity** asserts that changes in exchange rates result from changes in the relative prices of the goods in two countries. Relative purchasing power parity asserts that the ratio of the expected future spot rate to the current spot rate is equal to the ratio of (1 plus) the expected inflation rates, i, of the two countries over that same period. While this theory is somewhat better at explaining exchange rate changes, it has less explanatory power over the short run and more over the longer run.[4] In order to use this theory to forecast an exchange rate (expected exchange rate, S^E) N periods into the future, we multiple the current spot rate by the ratio of the expected relative inflation rates over the period:

$$S^E_{HC/FC, t+N} = S_{HC/FC, t} \times \frac{(1 + i_{HC})^N}{(1 + i_{FC})^N} \tag{17.1}$$

For example, assume that the current (time t) spot exchange rate is $S_{HC/FC} = 2.0$ and that the expected annual inflation is 5% annually for the home country and 10% annually for the foreign country. Based on this information, the relative purchasing power parity theory provides a way to forecast the exchange rate using the above equation, which we show for one, two, and five years as follows:

$$S^E_{HC/FC, t+1} = 2.0 \times \frac{(1.05)}{(1.1)} = 1.91; \ S^E_{HC/FC, t+2} = 2.0 \times \frac{(1.05)^2}{(1.1)^2} = 1.82; \ S^E_{HC/FC, t+5} = 2.0 \times \frac{(1.05)^5}{(1.1)^5} = 1.58$$

The exchange rate declines and the home currency appreciates because of lower inflation in the home country.

Covered and Uncovered Interest Rate Parity (and the International Fisher Effect)

Financial assets are subject to fewer market frictions or interventions and lower transactions costs; in other words, financial assets are more easily and efficiently tradable relative to many non-financial assets.

---

[3] Lothian, James R., and Mark P. Taylor, "Real Exchange Rate Behavior: The Recent Float from the Perspective of the Past Two Centuries," *Journal of Political Economy* vol. 104, no. 3 (1996), pp. 488–509.

[4] See Lothian and Taylor (1996), cited previously.

est rates, 1.071/1.144. What might cause this difference? To answer this question, we explore the link between the two theories in the context of the Fisher Effect.

The Fisher Effect specifies the relation between the nominal interest rate and the real interest rate and inflation, $1 + r_{HC} = (1 + r_{Real\ HC}) \times (1 + i_{HC})$. The International Fisher Effect examines the ratio of interest rates of two countries and asserts that the real rate of interest is constant across countries, assuming no arbitrage. If the real interest rate is constant and the same across countries, then the ratio of (1 plus) the interest rates of two countries (a key factor in uncovered interest rate parity) is equal to the ratio of (1 plus) the inflation rates of two countries. If this condition holds, then the relative purchasing power forecasts and the uncovered interest rate parity forecasts are equal to each other:

$$\frac{(1 + r_{HC})}{(1 + r_{FC})} = \frac{(1 + r_{Real,\ HC}) \times (1 + i_{HC})}{(1 + r_{Real,\ FC}) \times (1 + i_{FC})} = \frac{(1 + i_{HC})}{(1 + i_{FC})}$$

In our previous example, we used a 2% real interest rate for the home country and a 4% real interest rate for the foreign country; thus, the change in the exchange rates resulted from both differences in the inflation rates and differences in the real interest rates between the two countries. If we had used a 2% real interest rate for both countries, the home country interest rate would have continued to be 7.1%, but the foreign country interest rate would have decreased to 12.2% ($0.122 = 1.02 \times 1.10$). Using these interest rates for the two countries results in the same exchange rate forecasts as we had calculated using relative purchasing power parity:

$$S^E_{HC/FC,\ t+1} = 2.0 \times \frac{(1.071)}{(1.122)} = 1.91; S^E_{HC/FC,\ t+2} = 2.0 \times \frac{(1.071)^2}{(1.122)^2} = 1.82; S^E_{HC/FC,\ t+5} = 2.0 \times \frac{(1.071)^5}{(1.122)^5} = 1.58$$

Are Forward Rates Unbiased and Efficient Forecasts of Future Spot Rates? (The Forward Premium Puzzle)

If forward rates were unbiased and efficient forecasts of future spot rates, we could use forward rates to forecast exchange rates. However, an unbiased forecast does not have to be the most accurate forecast. For a forecast to be unbiased, it only has to have a forecast error with an expected value of zero; thus, an unbiased forecast does not have to be the best forecast. Even if forward rates were unbiased forecasts of future spot rates, we would still need to test alternative forecasting models and compare the accuracy of these models for their relative forecast accuracy across different horizons. Relative forecast accuracy is one measure for describing an efficient forecast. An efficient forecast is one that incorporates all available information as of the forecast date; thus, if a forward rate is efficient, it is relatively more accurate than alternative forecasts.

Overall, empirical evidence provides mixed evidence on the issue of what results in the best forecast. It turns out that the forward rate premium (or discount) fails to accurately predict the direction of the change in the spot rate, especially for shorter-term maturities. The issue is mitigated over longer horizons.[7] As might be expected, this issue is similar to the issues discussed for uncovered interest rate parity and faces similar econometric issues for empirical tests. One explanation for the forward rate premium puzzle is the risk premium required by investors.[8] For longer maturities, some of the empirical evidence suggests that forward rates are sufficiently unbiased,[9] but some traders suggest that they may not be efficient.[10]

[7] See, Chinn, M. D., and Meredith, G., "Monetary Policy and Long Horizon Uncovered Interest Parity," *IMF Staff Papers* vol. 51, no. 3 (2004), pp. 409–430.

[8] See Verdelhan, A., "A Habit-Based Explanation of the Exchange Rate Risk Premium," working paper presented at the NBER Summer Institute, 2006.

[9] See, Chinn, M., and Frankel, J., "Patterns in Exchange Rate Forecasts for 25 Currencies," *Journal of Money, Credit and Banking* vol. 26, no. 24 (1994), pp. 759–770; and Chinn, M., and Frankel, J., "Survey Data on Exchange Rate Expectations: More Currencies, More Horizons, More Tests," in Dickinson, D., and W. Allen, eds., *Monetary Policy, Capital Flows and Financial Market Developments in the Era of Financial Globalization: Essays in Honour of Max Fry,* London and New York: Routledge (2002).

[10] For an example of a discussion of how traders might exploit inefficiencies in forward rates, see, Baz, Jamil, Frances Breedon, Vasant Naik, and Joel Press, "Optimal Portfolios of Foreign Currencies—Trading on the Forward Bias," *Journal of Portfolio Management* (Fall 2001), pp. 1–10.

Understanding the Discount Rates Used in the Example Illustrating the Equality of the Two DCF Approaches

Recall the example illustrating the equivalence of the two approaches for adjusting the DCF valuation model (Exhibit 17.2). In that example, the appropriate risk-adjusted discount rate for the investor currency (USD) stated free cash flows was 10% and constant for all three years. The appropriate discount rates for the foreign currency (ruble) free cash flows for the next three years were 14.4%, 15.2%, and 15.5%. We now have the tools to explain the relation between the discount rates for the investor and the exchange rate on foreign currencies. We make this adjustment by multiplying 1 plus the investor currency's discount rate by the ratio of 1 plus the foreign country's interest rate to 1 plus the investor country's interest rates. (If we first measure the foreign currency's discount rate, we convert it by multiplying 1 plus the discount rate by the relative investor and foreign currency interest rates.)

We know from the exchange rate theories that exchange rate forecasts are linked to current spot rates by either relative interest rates or relative inflation rates. However, recall that if real interest rates are constant across two countries, relative inflation rates must be equivalent to relative interest rates in order to make this adjustment. Thus, instead of using the relative interest rates or inflation rates directly, we use the relative interest rates that are implicit in the change in the exchange rate forecasts; specifically, we use the ratio of the exchange rate forecast for year t to the exchange rate forecast for year t − 1. This ratio measures the implicit interest rate embedded in these forecasts.

In our example, we use forward exchange rates for expected exchange rates. We adjust the investor currency discount rate for the annual percentage change in the forward rate, and we show this calculation in Exhibit 17.4. For Year 1, the ratio of the forward rate to the spot rate is 1.04. To measure the discount rate for the project in rubles, we multiply this ratio by 1 plus the investor discount rate for the project (1.1) to arrive at a discount rate of 14.42% ($0.1442 = 1.04 \times 1.10 - 1$). For Year 2, we measure the ratio of the forward rate in Year 2 to the forward rate in Year 1, which is 1.047 and yields a discount rate of 15.20% for the project in rubles ($0.152 = 1.047 \times 1.10 - 1$). Note that if the discount rate for the investor's currency remains constant in future years and the exchange rate between the investor's currency and the foreign currency is expected to continue to change, the discount rate in the foreign currency will continue to change as well.

EXHIBIT 17.4	Calculation of the Discount Rates Used in the Example Illustrating the Equality of the Two DCF Valuation Approaches (See Exhibit 17.2)			
Investor to Foreign Discount Rate		**Year 1**	**Year 2**	**Year 3**
Exchange rate forecast = Forward rate (RUB/USD) in period t...............		28.913	30.279	31.784
Exchange rate forecast = Forward rate (RUB/USD) in period t − 1		27.796	28.913	30.279
Ratio ≈ $(1 + r_{RUB})/(1 + r_{USD}) \approx (1 + i_{RUB})/(1 + i_{USD})$		1.040	1.047	1.050
One + risk-adjusted discount rate for USD, r_{USD}		1.100	1.100	1.100
Risk-adjusted discount rate for project in foreign currency, r_{RUB}		14.42%	15.20%	15.47%

Exhibit may contain small rounding errors

This link between exchange rates and discount rates assumes that markets are fully integrated. If they are not fully integrated, then the link is eroded or possibly broken. If markets are not fully integrated, the investor currency or centralized approach—which converts cash flows stated in terms of the investor's home currency and discounts them at the investor's home currency cost of capital—is the more appropriate approach to use to measure value.

REVIEW EXERCISE 17.2

Discount Rates for the Investor Currency (Centralized) and Foreign Currency (Decentralized) Approaches

Measure the discount rates for discounting U.S. dollars (USD) provided in Review Exercise 17.1.

Solution on page 770.

Practical Applications of Exchange Rate Theories and Other Potential Methods of Forecasting Exchange Rates

Based on our discussion up to now, we have a few ways to forecast future spot rates. First, we can use the forecasting model based on relative inflation rates as implied in the relative purchasing power parity theory. Second, we can use the forecasting model implied in the uncovered interest rate parity theory based on relative interest rates. Third, we can use forward rates, assuming they are unbiased and efficient forecasts of future spot rates; and fourth, we can develop or use another forecasting model that includes predictor variables in addition to those in the previous models. Variables in such a model can include other macroeconomic information on the countries' potential actions, events, or policies, which can affect exchange rates, yet are not embedded in relative inflation and interest rates. We call this approach fundamental analysis because it relies on fundamental predictor variables hypothesized to be linked causally to exchange rates. Another type of model is a model based on technical analysis, which is the study of trends in the exchange rates and sometimes includes information on trading volume as well.

Based on the current state of knowledge, it is common to use forward rates when available and traded in liquid markets, especially for the first few years in a forecast horizon. After the first few years, it is common to use forecasts from either the relative purchasing power parity or uncovered interest rate parity forecasting methods (or both). Relative purchasing power parity, however, implies that real exchange rates do not change; thus, it may not be a good method if we believe the current real exchange rate is not sustainable over the long run. Generally, unless we have some overriding reason, we do not recommend using models based on fundamental or technical analysis. By nature, these models assume inefficient market prices. If we have a model that does well, we could instead trade foreign currencies.

Although we will not discuss the issue in detail here, both parity models assume that market conditions and forces set exchange rates; however, we know that some countries have exchange rate policies that can interfere with market-determined exchange rates. We call market-determined exchange rates floating exchange rates, and we refer to a mostly government-determined rate as a fixed exchange rate. There also exist exchange rates that are pegged to another, more stable exchange rate. Why do governments have exchange rate policies? One reason is to reduce variability in exchange rates, which can discourage foreign investment. Fixed exchange rate policies are still subject to market forces; thus, governments have to counteract these market forces by buying or selling their own and other currencies and setting interest rates. Do these exchange rate policies affect our forecasts? Since market forces are still at work, stable exchange rate policies will probably not cause us to deviate from the steps we outlined. However, unexpected changes in government policies can cause issues when using these models.

We also know that government intervention can affect interest rates, especially in the short run, such that neither relative purchasing power parity nor uncovered interest rate parity forecasts are accurate predictors in the short run. In Exhibit 17.5, we present interest rates (yield to maturities, or YTMs) for government bonds and expected inflation rates for the countries for which we showed spot and future exchange rates in Exhibit 17.3. Recall that a global financial crisis and severe recession occurred around 2008, and many governments were attempting to keep interest rates low in order to stimulate the economy.

Valuation Key 17.4

Based on the current state of knowledge, it is common to use forward rates to forecast future expected spot rates when they are available and traded in liquid markets, especially for the first few years of the forecast horizon. After the first few years, it is common to use either the relative purchasing power parity or uncovered interest rate parity forecasts (or both). Generally, unless we have some overriding reason, we do not recommend using models based on fundamental or technical analysis.

From this exhibit, we see that interest rates are lower than expected inflation rates for the first two years for all countries and for the first five years for some countries, resulting in negative real interest rates as measured using the Fisher Effect. From this exhibit, we can also see that real interest rates vary across countries. The United States and the U.K. generally have similar real rates, especially for longer horizons, and Indonesia generally has real rates that are higher than both the U.S. and U.K. rates. It is an

EXHIBIT 17.5	Interest Rates (Government Bond Yields) and Expected Inflation Rates on August 1, 2011, for Different Countries*						
	1 Year	**2 Year**	**3 Year**	**4 Year**	**5 Year**	**10 Year**	**30 Year**
United States							
Interest rate	0.20%	0.37%	0.54%	1.32%	2.05%	2.75%	4.08%
Inflation rate	1.50%	1.90%	1.90%	2.00%	2.00%	2.10%	2.10%
Implied real rate	−1.28%	−1.50%	−1.33%	−0.66%	0.05%	0.63%	1.94%
United Kingdom (Great Britain)							
Interest rate	0.48%	0.61%	0.78%	1.18%	1.54%	2.80%	4.00%
Inflation rate	1.58%	2.00%	2.00%	2.00%	2.00%	2.00%	2.00%
Implied real rate	−1.08%	−1.36%	−1.20%	−0.80%	−0.46%	0.79%	1.96%
India							
Interest rate	6.96%	7.53%	8.11%	8.38%	8.46%	8.56%	8.72%
Inflation rate	8.00%	8.00%	7.50%	7.50%	7.50%	7.50%	7.50%
Implied real rate	−0.97%	−0.43%	0.57%	0.82%	0.89%	0.98%	1.13%
Japan							
Interest rate	0.12%	0.16%	0.20%	0.28%	0.37%	1.04%	2.23%
Inflation rate	0.30%	0.30%	0.50%	0.50%	0.50%	0.50%	0.50%
Implied real rate	−0.18%	−0.14%	−0.30%	−0.22%	−0.13%	0.54%	1.72%
Russia							
Interest rate	5.10%	5.67%	6.24%	6.81%	7.08%	7.63%	7.92%
Inflation rate	7.65%	7.65%	7.15%	7.15%	7.15%	7.15%	7.15%
Implied real rate	−2.37%	−1.84%	−0.85%	−0.32%	−0.07%	0.45%	0.72%
Indonesia							
Interest rate	4.36%	4.82%	5.82%	6.18%	6.44%	6.93%	8.50%
Inflation rate	6.32%	6.32%	5.36%	5.36%	5.36%	5.36%	5.36%
Implied real rate	−1.84%	−1.41%	0.44%	0.78%	1.03%	1.49%	2.98%
Implied real rate standard deviation	0.76%	0.67%	0.82%	0.71%	0.60%	0.38%	0.78%

* Interest rates are government bond yield-to-maturity rates quoted in Bloomberg. If a maturity was not available, but longer and shorter maturities were both available, we interpolated the rate. Expected U.S. inflation rates are from the *President's Economic Report* available in August 2011; other inflation rates are from Bloomberg or are the authors' estimates.

open issue as to whether the differences in these real rates are, in fact, real differences or the result of market frictions such as government regulations or interventions. The negative real rates are consistent with some of the effects of government intervention in response to the economic crisis that started in 2008.

In Exhibit 17.6, we use both relative purchasing power parity and uncovered interest rate parity to forecast the exchange rates in Exhibit 17.3. We compare our forecasts using the relative interest and inflation rates from the previous exhibit to the midpoint of the bid and ask rates in Exhibit 17.3. As we can see from this exhibit, relative to the spot rate, all of the forecasts move in the same direction as the forward rates over the five-year horizon (see the column titled "Year 5 to Spot Rate"). We can also see that some of the differences between the forecasts and forward rates (not shown in the exhibit) are relatively small (such as the case for USD/GBP, which is less than 1%) whereas some are larger (as for the Rupee/Pound). We show the average difference across the five years for the RPPP and UIRP forecasts. The average differences for the first four exchange rates are much larger than those for the last four exchange rates. Overall, the average (absolute value) forward rate difference is 4.7% for the relative purchasing power parity forecasts and 5.7% for the uncovered interest rate parity forecasts. However, the magnitude of the (absolute value) differences is not random.

Factors that may explain these differences include the following. First, for differences between the uncovered interest rate parity forecasts and the forward rates, the interest rates we used might not represent the rates used by the market makers issuing the forward contracts. Second, for differences between the relative purchasing power parity forecasts and the forward rates, the real rates of interest may differ, violating the assumption of constant real interest rates for this theory. Finally, frictions in the capital markets—for example, flow of capital controls or restrictions in India—may mean that other factors determine forward rates in addition to relative interest rates or relative inflation rates. For example, in this

EXHIBIT 17.6	Exchange Rate Forecasts Based on Relative Purchasing Power Parity and Uncovered Interest Rate Parity Compared to Forward Exchange Rates

		Forward Rates					Year 5 to Spot Rate	Average Forward Rate Difference
	Spot Rate	1 Year	2 Year	3 Year	4 Year	5 Year		
Indian Rupee / U.S. Dollar (USD)								
Midpoint	44.22	46.07	47.89	49.75	51.25	52.45	18.6%	
RPPP	44.22	47.05	49.86	52.60	55.44	58.43	32.1%	6.3%
UIRP	44.22	47.20	50.57	54.38	58.17	61.82	39.8%	9.7%
U.S. Dollar (USD) / Indian Rupee								
Midpoint	0.023	0.022	0.021	0.020	0.020	0.019	−15.8%	
RPPP	0.023	0.021	0.020	0.019	0.018	0.017	−24.3%	−5.7%
UIRP	0.023	0.021	0.020	0.018	0.017	0.016	−28.5%	−8.5%
Indian Rupee / U.K. Pound (GBP)								
Midpoint	72.05	74.77	77.38	80.10	82.40	84.53	17.3%	
RPPP	72.05	76.61	81.11	85.49	90.09	94.95	31.8%	7.1%
UIRP	72.05	76.69	81.97	87.94	94.20	100.62	39.6%	10.3%
Japanese Yen / Indian Rupee								
Midpoint	1.75	1.67	1.59	1.50	1.42	1.35	−22.9%	
RPPP	1.75	1.62	1.51	1.41	1.32	1.23	−29.5%	−6.1%
UIRP	1.75	1.63	1.52	1.41	1.31	1.21	−30.8%	−6.2%
U.S. Dollar (USD) / U.K. Pound (GBP)								
Midpoint	1.63	1.62	1.62	1.61	1.61	1.61	−1.1%	
RPPP	1.63	1.63	1.63	1.63	1.63	1.63	−0.3%	0.8%
UIRP	1.63	1.62	1.62	1.62	1.62	1.63	−0.1%	0.5%
U.S. Dollar (USD) / Japanese Yen								
Midpoint	0.0130	0.0130	0.0131	0.0134	0.0137	0.0142	9.3%	
RPPP	0.0130	0.0131	0.0133	0.0135	0.0137	0.0139	7.4%	0.2%
UIRP	0.0130	0.0130	0.0130	0.0130	0.0132	0.0134	3.4%	−2.7%
Russian Ruble / U.S. Dollar (USD)								
Midpoint	27.80	28.91	30.28	31.78	33.35	34.63	24.6%	
RPPP	27.80	29.48	31.14	32.75	34.40	36.14	30.0%	3.1%
UIRP	27.80	29.16	30.70	32.44	34.19	35.88	29.1%	2.1%
Indonesian Rupiah / U.S. Dollar (USD)								
Midpoint	8.46	8.71	9.70	10.36	11.00	11.64	37.6%	
RPPP	8.46	8.86	9.25	9.56	9.88	10.20	20.6%	−6.6%
UIRP	8.46	8.81	9.21	9.69	10.15	10.59	25.1%	−5.4%

exhibit, the smallest (absolute value) differences occur for countries with well-developed economies—the USD/GBP forecasts from both approaches have average differences of no more than 1%. The forecasts for countries with less developed economies tend to have larger differences. In addition, the differences increase with the horizon. The average (absolute value) difference in Year 1 is less than 2% for both forecast methods before increasing in subsequent years.

REVIEW EXERCISE 17.3

Exchange Rate Forecasts

Use the information in Exhibit 17.5 and Exhibit P17.2 to forecast the U.S. dollar/Polish zloty exchange rate for the next five years using relative purchasing power parity and uncovered interest rate parity.

Solution on page 770.

17.4 OVERVIEW OF POTENTIAL INCOME TAX AND OTHER TAX ISSUES IN A CROSS-BORDER SETTING

LO3 Measure income taxes for a cross-border valuation

As globalization continues, foreign source income is becoming a larger part of total income for many companies; for example, since 1990, the foreign income of the S&P 500 grew from 32% to 50% of total pre-tax income.[11] In a cross-border valuation, income tax issues can have unforeseen effects and be even more complex than for within-country valuations. In a cross-border valuation, we must consider the tax laws and regulations of both the investor's home country's various taxing authorities and the various taxing authorities of the foreign company's country; we must also consider treaties between the two countries and possibly even treaties between these countries and other countries. Types of direct and indirect taxes include income taxes at the national level (and other levels in the country), value-added taxes (a form of sales tax on the supply chain, abbreviated as VAT), various types of withholding taxes (such as withholding on payments for dividends, interest, royalties, payments to contractors, and rent), import duties, fringe benefits, and other payroll-related taxes.

The first type of tax issue we may face in a cross-border valuation is that, independent of any tax issues caused by cross-border ownership, the foreign company's country may have income taxes or other taxes that the investor's country does not have. An investor must include the effect of all of these taxes in any cross-border valuation. For example, the United States does not have a national sales tax (VAT), but other countries have a VAT paid on each stage of the production process. A U.S. company investing in a foreign company subject to a VAT has to be aware of the VAT and include its effect in a cross-border valuation. Countries also use various types of tax incentives to attract foreign investment, which we would include in a cross-border valuation by measuring the value of these subsidies separately, as we would for other types of subsidies. To add further complexity, each country can have additional taxes or regulations for companies with cross-border ownership; thus, the second type of tax issue we may face in a cross-border valuation is that taxes (or an equivalent) may occur because of cross-border ownership.

There are two basic types of tax regimes in the world. The United States, for example, has a **resident** or **worldwide tax regime**, which taxes the total worldwide income of its residents. Worldwide tax regime countries address double taxation issues by utilizing a foreign tax credit or a deduction system for foreign income taxes paid. Countries with a worldwide tax regime sometimes allow a company to defer paying income taxes on the earnings of a subsidiary until the subsidiary repatriates these earnings to the parent company, making this tax regime more similar to the territorial or source tax regime. Other countries do not tax—or if they do tax, it is at a low rate—income from foreign subsidiaries under what is called a **territorial** or **source tax regime**. In 2009, Japan and the U.K. moved to a tax regime that is closer to a territorial tax regime. Over 75% of the member countries of the Organization for Economic Coordination and Development (OECD) have a territorial tax regime. However, no country has a purely worldwide or territorial tax regime due to various deferrals, tax credits, tax deductions, and other regulations that make the tax regimes similar.

Valuation Key 17.5

In a cross-border valuation, we consider the tax laws and regulations of both the investor's home country and the foreign company's country, as well as treaties between the two countries and possibly even between these countries and other countries. Independent of any cross-border issues, the foreign company's country can have income taxes or other taxes that the investor's country does not have. An investor must include all of these taxes in any cross-border valuation. To add further complexity, each country can have additional taxes or regulations for a company with cross-border ownership.

In Exhibit 17.7, we present the tax regime (territorial or worldwide) and maximum 2010 statutory income tax rates of 34 countries; 26 of the 34 (76%) countries adopted a territorial tax regime, and the remaining 8 countries adopted a worldwide tax regime; keep in mind, however, that no country has a

---

[11] For a more detailed review of many of these issues—especially from a U.S. perspective—and a summary of the scholarly research, see, Blouin, Jennifer, "Taxation of Multinational Corporations," *Foundations and Trends® in Accounting* vol. 6, no. 1 (2012), pp. 1–64, http://dx.doi.org/10.1561/1400000017.

purely territorial or worldwide regime. The income tax rates vary from 12.5% to 39.5%. The income tax rate in the United States is one of the highest. The median tax rate across the 34 countries is 25.5%; for the 26 territorial tax regime countries, it is 26.4%; and for the worldwide tax regime countries, it is 24.1%.

EXHIBIT 17.7	Maximum 2010 Statutory Income Tax Rates for Organization for Economic Coordination and Development Countries*

Country	Tax Regime	2010 Max Statutory Tax Rate	Country	Tax Regime	2010 Max Statutory Tax Rate
Australia	Territorial	30.0%	Norway	Territorial	28.0%
Austria	Territorial	25.0%	Portugal	Territorial	26.5%
Belgium	Territorial	34.0%	Slovak Republic	Territorial	19.0%
Canada.	Territorial	29.5%	Slovenia	Territorial	20.0%
Czech Republic	Territorial	19.0%	Spain	Territorial	30.0%
Denmark.	Territorial	25.0%	Sweden	Territorial	26.3%
Estonia	Territorial	21.0%	Switzerland.	Territorial	21.2%
Finland	Territorial	26.0%	Turkey.	Territorial	20.0%
France	Territorial	34.4%	United Kingdom	Territorial	28.0%
Germany.	Territorial	30.2%	Chile	Worldwide	17.0%
Hungary	Territorial	19.0%	Greece	Worldwide	24.0%
Iceland	Territorial	18.0%	Ireland.	Worldwide	12.5%
Italy.	Territorial	27.5%	Israel.	Worldwide	25.0%
Japan	Territorial	39.5%	Mexico	Worldwide	30.0%
Luxembourg	Territorial	28.6%	Poland	Worldwide	19.0%
Netherlands	Territorial	25.5%	South Korea	Worldwide	24.2%
New Zealand	Territorial	30.0%	United States	Worldwide	39.1%

	Mean	Median	# of Countries	
All countries	25.6%	25.5%	34	
Non-U.S.	25.2%	25.5%	33	
All territorial	26.2%	26.4%	26	76%
All worldwide	23.9%	24.1%	8	24%
Non-U.S. worldwide.	21.7%	24.0%	7	

* Blouin, Jennifer, "Taxation of Multinational Corporations," *Foundations and Trends® in Accounting* vol. 6, no. 1 (2012), pp. 1–64, http://dx.doi.org/10.1561/1400000017.

Foreign Tax Credits and Deferral of Foreign Income for Worldwide (Resident) Tax Regimes

A foreign tax credit can eliminate or at least reduce double taxation on foreign income. Ignoring country-specific rules, generally, foreign tax credits limit the tax payment to the higher of the investor country's tax rate or the foreign country's tax rate in a worldwide tax regime. If the foreign tax rate is less than the domestic tax rate, an investor company will have an incremental tax liability (due to the home country) on foreign earnings equal to foreign earnings multiplied by the difference in the tax rates. In such situations, the investor company has an **excess limit position**. On the other hand, if the foreign tax rate is higher than the domestic tax rate, an investor company will have no tax liability to the home country on that income. In this situation, the investor has an **excess credit position**. If possible, companies prefer to offset an excess limit position from one country with an excess credit position from another country in order to minimize total income tax payments.

Naturally, there are various regulations and limitations on the use of foreign tax credits that vary across countries. In this section, we will provide a high-level overview of the general types of regulations that govern foreign tax credits. Some regulations limit foreign tax credits based on the source of income. For example, in the United States, foreign tax credits have two components: direct credits and indirect (or deemed-paid) credits. Both of these depend on the source of income on which a foreign tax is paid. In addition, in some countries, companies can pool—under various conditions and limitations—foreign income across countries to offset an excess limit position with an excess credit position in order to minimize total income tax payments. Pooled income allows companies to offset excess credits from high-tax countries with excess limits from low-tax countries. Companies can accomplish this offsetting in a variety of ways—for example, by simultaneously receiving dividend remittances from affiliates in high-tax and low-tax countries.

The deferral of taxes on foreign income is a common component of a worldwide tax regime. It is a way for a country with a worldwide tax regime to have an effective tax more similar to that of a territorial tax regime. A common way for countries to defer taxes on foreign income is by not recognizing the foreign income as taxable income until the income is distributed to the investor company. Again, countries have various regulations that govern the deferral of taxes on foreign income. For example, in the United States, income from a branch is not deferred. However, income is deferred—with certain constraints—if the income is from a foreign company that is a separate legal entity (subsidiary). Also, in the United States, a tax on income from passive investments and other types of generally passive income (e.g., a foreign subsidiary in country A earns income from selling products manufactured in country B to customers in countries B and C) cannot be deferred, even if the funds are not repatriated back to the United States. This type of income is called SubPart F income in U.S. income tax regulations. The idea is to prevent companies from avoiding taxes by accumulating income in foreign subsidiaries with low foreign tax rates.

Worldwide (Resident) and Territorial (Source) Tax Regime Example—The Holdem Company (with Two Foreign Subsidiaries, Lo-Tx Inc. and Hi-Tx Company)

We illustrate the differences between the worldwide and territorial tax regimes, including the effects of foreign tax credits and the deferral of income, with the Holdem Company (Holdem). Holdem is a holding company with no revenues or expenses other than the revenues and expenses of its foreign subsidiaries. It is located in a country that defers the recognition of foreign-sourced income as taxable income until the company declares it as a dividend. When the foreign subsidiary declares a dividend, the dividend declared and any related direct and indirect tax paid on that dividend becomes taxable income to the parent company. The country allows a foreign tax credit for all taxes paid on income to the foreign government. Holdem has an income tax rate of 40% on all taxable income before adjustments for foreign tax credits.

Holdem has two foreign subsidiaries. One of the subsidiaries, Lo-Tx Inc. (Lo-Tx), is located in a foreign country that has an income tax rate of 10% on all income and a dividend withholding tax of 10%. The other subsidiary, Hi-Tx Company (Hi-Tx), has an income tax rate of 45% on all income and no dividend withholding tax. Both companies have foreign taxable income of $1,000. In the first three columns of Exhibit 17.8, we present the tax calculations for the two subsidiaries and the holding company, assuming each company declares 100% of its after-tax earnings in dividends to Holdem.

Foreign Income Taxes.   In the top section of Exhibit 17.8, we calculate the foreign income tax liability for each subsidiary. Lo-Tx has a taxable income of $1,000 and a 10% tax rate, and thus it has a $100 foreign income tax liability. Hi-Tx also has a taxable income of $1,000, but it has a 45% tax rate, and thus it has a $450 foreign income tax liability. These are the two companies' income tax liabilities under a territorial tax regime, excluding withholding taxes on dividends. Holdem's weighted average income tax rate is equal to 27.5% under the territorial tax regime, excluding the withholding taxes on dividends.

Withholding Taxes on Dividends.   In the next section of Exhibit 17.8, we present the withholding tax on the dividends declared. Both companies declare 100% of their after-tax income as a dividend—$900 for Lo-Tx and $550 for Hi-Tx. Lo-Tx pays a 10% ($90) withholding tax on its dividends. Hi-Tx pays no withholding tax, for the country in which it is located does not have a withholding tax. Thus, Lo-Tx distributes an $810 dividend, and Hi-Tax distributes a $550 dividend. The total foreign tax liability for the two companies is equal to $190 (19%) for Lo-Tx and $450 (45%) for Hi-Tx. These are the companies' income tax liabilities under a territorial tax regime, including withholding taxes on dividends. Given these same conditions, Holdem's weighted average income tax rate is equal to 32.0%. The foreign tax rate, $T_{F-Total}$, for each country—including the foreign income tax, T_{F-In}, and withholding tax, T_{F-WH}—with full repatriation of income is equal to

$$T_{F-Total} = T_{F-In} + (1 - T_{F-In}) \times T_{F-WH} \tag{17.4}$$

$$T_{F-Total, Lo-Tx} = 0.1 + (1 - 0.1) \times 0.1 = 0.19$$

$$T_{F-Total, Hi-Tx} = 0.45 + (1 - 0.45) \times 0.0 = 0.45$$

EXHIBIT 17.8	Example of Worldwide and Territorial Tax Regimes					
		100% Dividend Payout			**Strategic Dividend Payout**	
	Lo-Tx Inc.	**Hi-Tx Co.**	**Holdem Co. (Pooled)**	**Lo-Tx Inc.**	**Hi-Tx Co.**	**Holdem Co. (Pooled)**
Foreign Income Tax						
Foreign taxable income	$1,000.0	$1,000.0	$2,000.0	$1,000.0	$1,000.0	$2,000.0
Foreign income tax rate	10.0%	45.0%		10.0%	45.0%	
Foreign income tax liability.	$ 100.0	$ 450.0	$ 550.0	$ 100.0	$ 450.0	$ 550.0
After-tax foreign income.	$ 900.0	$ 550.0	$1,450.0	$ 900.0	$ 550.0	$1,450.0
Territorial effective tax rate w/o WH tax	10.0%	45.0%	27.5%	10.0%	45.0%	27.5%
Foreign Dividend Withholding (WH) Tax						
Dividend payout ratio	100.0%	100.0%		0.0%	80.0%	
Dividend declared	$ 900.0	$ 550.0	$1,450.0	$ 0.0	$ 440.0	$ 440.0
Withholding tax rate	10.0%	0.0%		10.0%	0.0%	
Withholding tax	$90.0	$ 0.0	$ 90.0	$ 0.0	$ 0.0	$ 0.0
Dividend distributed	$ 810.0	$ 550.0	$1,360.0	$ 0.0	$440.0	$440.0
Total foreign tax liability	$ 190.0	$ 450.0	$ 640.0	$ 100.0	$ 450.0	$ 550.0
Territorial effective tax rate after WH tax	19.0%	45.0%	32.0%	10.0%	45.0%	27.5%
Investor Country Income Tax						
Foreign income tax liability.	$ 100.0	$ 450.0	$ 550.0	$ 100.0	$ 450.0	$ 550.0
Dividend payout ratio	100.0%	100.0%		0.0%	80.0%	
Allocated foreign income tax liability	$ 100.0	$ 450.0	$ 550.0	$ 0.0	$ 360.0	$ 360.0
Dividend declared	900.0	550.0	1,450.0	0.0	440.0	440.0
Investor country taxable income	$1,000.0	$1,000.0	$2,000.0	$ 0.0	$ 800.0	$ 800.0
Investor country tax rate	40.0%	40.0%	40.0%	40.0%	40.0%	40.0%
Investor country tax before credits.	$ 400.0	$ 400.0	$ 800.0	$ 0.0	$ 320.0	$ 320.0
Foreign tax credit for foreign income tax	−100.0	−450.0	−550.0	0.0	−360.0	−360.0
Foreign tax credit for foreign WH tax	−90.0	0.0	−90.0	0.0	0.0	0.0
Additional U.S. income tax.	$ 210.0	$ –	$ 160.0	$ –	$ –	$ –
Worldwide Tax (After Foreign Tax Credits)						
Total worldwide tax.	$ 400.0	$ 450.0	$ 800.0	$ 100.0	$ 450.0	$ 550.0
Total worldwide tax rate	40.0%	45.0%	40.0%	10.0%	45.0%	27.5%

Holdem's Income Taxes in a Worldwide Tax Regime. So far, we described the taxes that Holdem would pay if it were taxed in a territorial tax regime, as it would have no tax due to its home country. What would Holdem's taxes be if Holdem was taxed by a country that had a worldwide tax regime? After calculating total taxes for each of the foreign companies, we calculate the investor country's income tax based on the country's 40% tax rate and adjust for the foreign taxes paid. Taxable income is equal to the dividend declared (equal to the dividend distributed plus the withholding tax) plus a proportionate share of the foreign income tax liability (based on the percentage of after-tax earnings declared as a dividend). Since both companies declared 100% of their after-tax earnings as dividends, we add 100% of their foreign income tax liability to the dividend declared in order to measure the investor country taxable income. Since both companies have a 100% dividend payout ratio, both companies have an investor country taxable income equal to $1,000, which is also equal to their foreign taxable income.

The investor country income tax is 40% of each company's taxable income, which is $400 for each company. To measure the tax liability for the investor country we deduct the foreign tax liability (income and withholding taxes) allocated to the taxable income for the investor country, which is equal to 100% because both companies have a dividend payout ratio equal to 100%. For Lo-Tx, the foreign tax credits equal $190 ($100 income tax and $90 withholding tax), and the additional investor country income tax liability is equal to $210 ($210 = $400 − $100 − $90), which we call an excess limit. For Hi-Tx, the foreign tax credits equal $450, and it has no additional investor country income tax liability. In fact, Hi-Tx has unused tax credits or excess credits of $50 ($50 = $450 − $400).

The total worldwide tax regime tax liability, as a percentage of total income, is equal to 40% for Lo-Tx and 45% for Hi-Tx. The effective tax rate for each company is equal to the larger of the investor country tax rate (T_{HC} or 40%) and the foreign country tax rate (19% for Lo-Tx and 45% for Hi-Tx). In other words, for each foreign company, the effective tax rate, with full repatriation of dividends, is the

$$\text{Maximum} \left[T_{HC}, T_{F-In} + (1 - T_{F-In}) \times T_{F-WH} \right] \tag{17.5}$$

In our example, the weighted average of the two worldwide tax rates is equal to 42.5% [0.425 = ($400 + $450)/($1,000 + $1,000)]. However, if the investor country's tax regulations allow Holdem to apply the foreign tax credits on a pooled basis, then Holdem can use its excess credit to offset $50 of the $210 excess limit and reduce its tax liability to the investor country to $160. The United States allows such pooling, but, in recent discussions regarding proposed changes in the tax laws, it has considered no longer allowing pooling.

REVIEW EXERCISE 17.4

Worldwide (Resident) and Territorial (Source) Tax Regimes

A foreign subsidiary of a U.K. company has the equivalent of £10,000 in taxable income for both the foreign taxing authority and the U.K. taxing authority. The foreign income tax rate is 30% on all income with a 5% withholding tax on dividends; the U.K. income tax rate is 45% on all income paid out in dividends. The parent company intends to pay out all of the foreign subsidiary's after-tax income in dividends to the parent company. Calculate the income taxes payable based on both a territorial tax regime and a worldwide tax regime.

Solution on page 771.

Strategic Dividend Payout Scenario. In the last three columns of Exhibit 17.8, which we call "strategic dividend payout," we present the same set of calculations for Hi-Tx, Lo-Tx, and Holdem, but we change the dividend payout ratios. All of the data are the same as in the previous set of columns as well, but Lo-Tx does not distribute any dividends, and Hi-Tx has an 80% dividend payout ratio. The top section of the calculations—foreign income tax—is also the same as before. The withholding tax is equal to zero for both companies, for Lo-Tx does not distribute any dividends, and the country in which Hi-Tx operates does not have a withholding tax. Thus, the foreign overall tax rate (equivalent to the territorial tax regime tax rate) is equal to 10% instead of 19% for Lo-Tx and remains unchanged for Hi-Tx, reducing the overall weighted average tax rate from 32% to 27.5%.

The investor country income taxes also change. Since Lo-Tx does not distribute a dividend, Holdem has no taxable income for Lo-Tx, and since Hi-Tx has a dividend payout ratio of 80%, Holdem's taxable income for Hi-Tx is $800 instead of $1,000 [$800 = (0.8 × $450) + $440]. Thus, Holdem's income tax liability before foreign tax credits is zero for Lo-Tx (because Holdem has no taxable income to report from Lo-Tx) and $320 for Hi-Tx (because Hi-Tx has $800 of taxable income). Since Hi-Tx's dividend payout ratio is 80%, the allowable foreign tax credits are 80% of its foreign tax liability ($360 = $450 × 0.8). Hi-Tx continues to have a foreign tax in excess of its potential investor country tax liability, and thus it has no additional tax liability to the investor country. The resulting worldwide income tax rates are 10% for Lo-Tx, 45% for Hi-Tx, and 27.5% for Holdem. Because Holdem defers recognition of Lo-Tx's taxable income by not distributing Lo-Tx's after-tax income as dividends, it is able to reduce its worldwide weighted average income tax rate to the same rate that would have resulted had it been taxed under a territorial tax regime. In this scenario, Holdem has an excess foreign tax credit of $40, which it may be able to carry forward to use in a future period.

A Top-Level Discussion of Strategies to Minimize Tax Liabilities and Manage Cash

As is evident in the previous example, different tax rates, foreign tax credit regulations, and withholding taxes all have an effect on a company's total tax liability as well as on its ability to manage its cash. On the one hand, companies want to transfer cash to the part of the company that has the best use for it, but on the other hand, companies also want to minimize the present value of their tax payments. Continuing with the previous example, since Lo-Tx pays a withholding tax on any dividends distributed, it would, all else equal, prefer not to pay a dividend in order to avoid paying this withholding tax. Similarly, since Lo-Tax has a lower income tax rate than Holdem, and since Holdem pays taxes based on a worldwide tax regime, Holdem would prefer to defer—either temporarily or permanently—recognition of Lo-Tx's income on its tax return. Both of these frictions provide Holdem with incentives to find alternatives for the free cash flow generated by Lo-Tx. The issue that arises, of course, is how to use these retained funds in order to provide the maximum value to shareholders.

Valuation in Practice 17.2

Google Inc. Income Tax Strategies According to Bloomberg, Google Inc. (Google) used transfer pricing and tax treaty strategies to reduce its income tax liability and defer income recognition in the United States with an approach called the "Double Irish" and the "Dutch Sandwich":

> The method takes advantage of Irish tax law to legally shuttle profits into and out of subsidiaries there, largely escaping the country's 12.5% income tax. . . . The earnings wind up in island havens that levy no corporate income taxes at all.

As many U.S. companies have done, Google transferred certain intellectual property and certain business activities to a subsidiary in Ireland, which has a lower tax rate (12.5%) than that of the U.S. rate. It prearranged transfer prices for these activities with the U.S. government. In addition to this shift in income, it reduced its taxes in Ireland by paying royalties through a company in the Netherlands to another Irish company taxed in Bermuda, which has no income taxes. Because of certain tax agreements between Ireland and the Netherlands, Google can transfer these payments without incurring tax liabilities. Google then paid the subsidiary in Bermuda without being taxed, which is allowed by the Netherlands. While Google paid U.S. income taxes on all of its earnings that it repatriated, it deferred its taxable income in the United States by not paying the company located in the United States dividends from these foreign operations. In its 10-K for 2010, Google reported that approximately 54% of its total income was from foreign operations and that substantially all of its foreign income was earned by an Irish subsidiary. Google also disclosed that it had approximately $17.5 billion in income it had not repatriated back to the United States.

Source: See Drucker, Jesse, "Google 2.4% Rate Shows How $60 Billion Lost to Tax Loopholes," October 21, 2010, http://www.bloomberg.com/news/print/2010-10-21/google-2-4-rate-shows-how-60-billion-u-s-revenue-lost-to-tax-loopholes.html, accessed October 2011.

In one potential strategy to avoid a dividend payment, Holdem can use Lo-Tx's free cash flows for other positive net present value investments, assuming such investments fit with Holdem's strategy. Scholarly research indicates that firms facing higher repatriation tax burdens hold higher levels of cash, which they then hold abroad in affiliates that trigger high tax costs when repatriating earnings.[12] Alternatively, Holdem could invest the free cash flows in passive, low-risk, or risk-free investments and borrow against those investments, again assuming such a strategy fits with Holdem's overall financial strategy.[13] Potential political risks—for example, risk of expropriation of assets—are also taken into consideration when making these decisions. Another way to avoid withholding taxes is to pay a series of dividends based on tax treaties among a group of countries that have a zero withholding tax rate (see Valuation in Practice 17.2).

Hi-Tx has a higher income tax rate than Holdem. Foreign tax credits may allow Holdem to offset its excess credits from Hi-Tx against the excess limits of Lo-Tx, but if it cannot do this, Holden will opt to shift income from Hi-Tx to Holdem. In one potential strategy for shifting income, which can also be used in certain circumstances to avoid repatriation (withholding) taxes, Holdem can charge Hi-Tx management

---

[12] Foley, C. Fritz, J. C. Hartzell, S. Titman, and G. Twite, "Why Do Firms Hold So Much Cash? A Tax-Based Explanation," working paper, University of Texas at Austin, 2007.

[13] See Altshuler, R., and H. Grubert, "Repatriation Taxes, Repatriation Strategies, and Multinational Financial Policy," *Journal of Public Economics* 87 (2003), pp. 73–107.

fees, rents, and royalties. These payments can shift income from Hi-Tx to Holdem if they meet the various tax regulations, thus reducing the overall tax rate so it moves toward Holdem's domestic tax rate.[14]

Valuation Key 17.6

Companies use various strategies to minimize the present value of income taxes related to foreign subsidiaries. These strategies include deferring income by not repatriating earnings, shifting income from one company to another through royalties and fees, and borrowing against the passive investments resulting from the free cash flows of a foreign subsidiary.

Another way companies attempt to shift income from high-tax jurisdictions to lower-tax jurisdictions is through transfer pricing. A company may design a product in one country, produce its components in other countries, assemble the product in another country, and distribute and sell the product in yet another country. At each stage in the supply and value chain, the parent company must set a transfer price for the relevant goods used and services performed. This situation may provide a company an opportunity to shift income across taxing jurisdictions.

Taxing authorities are aware of this incentive and have various regulations and methods to prevent companies from using inappropriate transfer pricing. Using a market or an arm's length price (the price at which two unrelated parties will trade) is the preferred method (called the comparable uncontrolled pricing method), but many times, such prices do not exist. Other acceptable methods include the resale pricing method and the cost plus pricing methods (detailed discussions of which are beyond the scope of this book). Transferring intangible assets to low- or zero-tax jurisdictions is a common tactic used by companies. Such shifting is more valuable for companies subject to a territorial tax regime, for any tax reduction is permanent. For a company subject to a worldwide tax regime, the value lies in the present value of the deferral. Similarly, companies can use their financial strategy to shift tax-deductible interest to higher-tax-rate jurisdictions, but again, taxing authorities have various ways to prevent inappropriate uses of this tactic.

Interest Tax Shields in Cross-Border Transactions and Multinational Companies

The calculation of interest tax shields in a cross-border acquisition or for a multinational company can be complex. For example, the United States generally requires a company to allocate its interest expense—on debt issued by the U.S. (parent) company—to all of its non-U.S. investments. The basis of the typical allocation mechanism is relative to book value of assets.[15] The rules in the United States do not allow a company to allocate its non-U.S. debt to U.S. companies. For a non-U.S. investment, the U.S.-based taxable income will be less than the non-U.S. taxable income by the amount of the U.S. interest expense that is allocated to the non-U.S. company, for non-U.S. governments generally do not allow companies to deduct this allocated interest expense. This allocation can result in a loss of interest tax shields if the company is in a deficit foreign tax credit situation or even if the company has an excess foreign tax credit situation that is small relative to the allocated interest. We will not go through a detailed discussion of this, but figuring out the interest tax shields for a multinational company can be difficult. We need to know the tax situation the company faces in each tax jurisdiction, how much debt has been issued by the U.S. parent as well as by all of its non-U.S. subsidiaries (and where they are located), and whether income is repatriated back to the United States.

What Is the Bottom Line on Taxes in a Cross-Border Valuation?

It is apparent that this is a very complicated topic, and we have only scratched the surface. Moreover, to compute the taxes that a company pays on the income of a foreign subsidiary requires detailed knowledge of:

---

[14] See Grubert, H., "Taxes and the Division of Foreign Operating Income Among Royalties, Interest, Dividends and Retained Earnings," *Journal of Public Economics* 68 (1998), 269–290.

[15] Companies can also use gross income or the market value of the assets as long as market values can be measured on a reasonable basis.

- the implicit taxes (such as VAT taxes),

- the company's complete tax picture (the home country's tax regime, the foreign country's tax regime, the tax treaty, whether it has unused FTCs from other subsidiaries, etc.),

- how the company plans to operate the subsidiaries (whether it will transfer goods and services between subsidiaries and at what prices),

- whether it will use structures like Google did to defer taxes, and

- what its repatriation policy is going to be with respect to foreign income

It is probably obvious that an outsider would not be able to compute the taxes accurately. So, what do we suggest? As a first pass, one could compute the taxes for a worst-case scenario—when 100% of the earnings are repatriated as a dividend back to the parent company. If the parent company is taxed based on a territorial tax regime, then the maximum tax rate that it will face on income will be $T_{F-Total} = T_{F-In} + (1 - T_{F-In}) \times T_{F-WH}$. If, on the other hand, the parent company is taxed based on a worldwide tax regime, then the maximum tax rate that it will face on that income will be the maximum of T_{HC}, and $T_{F-In} + (1 - T_{F-In}) \times T_{F-WH}$.

An alternative (and likely upside case) is that no dividends are ever repatriated. If the parent company is taxed based on a territorial tax regime, then the maximum tax rate that it will face on income will be the foreign income tax rate—$T_{F-Total} = T_{F-In}$. If, on the other hand, the parent company is taxed based on a worldwide tax regime, then the maximum tax rate that it will face on income will be the maximum of the home country tax rate or the foreign income tax rate—Maximum $[T_{HC}, T_{F-In}]$.

17.5 MEASURING THE EQUITY COST OF CAPITAL

Various complications arise in cross-border valuations when estimating the equity cost of capital. This is an area in which we observe various alternatives used in practice, but differences in opinion among academics exist as well. We will first discuss some of the common assumptions made to estimate discount rates in the context of a cross-border valuation. Even though we will discuss this issue in the context of cross-border valuations, much of this discussion will be relevant for domestic valuations as well.

LO4 Measure discount rates and adjust free cash flows for country-specific risks

Many of the complications in estimating the cost of equity capital in a cross-border valuation stem from the question of whether the world has one global integrated capital market or has multiple capital markets that are segmented by country. If markets were completely integrated, then all investors would agree on one risk premium for a given investment in a given currency. It would not matter whether the investor was in the United States, India, or China—the risk premium for an investment would be the same. However, if the world's capital markets are segmented rather than integrated, then investors would not necessarily agree on the risk premium associated with a given investment. An investor in the United States might view an investment made in a company in Germany as being less risky than how a German investor might view that same investment, because the risk premium as observed by a U.S. investor might be different from that for a German investor.

In this section, we will explore how the cost of equity capital is estimated given these two different views of the world's capital markets.[16] One complicating factor is that the world is probably neither completely integrated nor completely segmented, so our two approaches will likely provide a reasonable range of discount rates. Another complicating feature is whether risk premiums are affected by foreign currency exchange rate risk and political risk and, if so, how to best estimate these effects. Estimating discount rates can also be more difficult, especially in emerging economies due to a lack of appropriate data. We will discuss emerging markets later in the chapter, but for now, we discuss approaches to estimating the cost of capital for assets that are traded in markets that are reasonably liquid.

Integrated Capital Markets

If capital markets were integrated, we would expect equity investors across the world to demand the same risk premium for a given investment measured in a given currency. One implication of this is that all investors use the same measure of risk, such as the systematic risk of an investment from the CAPM. In

---

[16] For an excellent discussion of these issues, see, Bodnar, G., B. Dumas, and R. Marston, "Cross-Border Valuation: The International Cost of Equity Capital," NBER Working Paper #w10115, November 2003.

addition, besides using the same measure of risk, investors must also use the same benchmark portfolio for measuring risk. Within the framework of the CAPM, these implications assume that investors diversify their portfolios across a broad array of securities from around the globe—investing beyond their local markets—and that the benchmark portfolio approximates a world-market portfolio that spans at least all equity securities—and possibly all assets—from around the globe on a value-weighted basis. In order to achieve full integration, we would also expect real risk-free rates to be the same across markets and prices of currencies to be in equilibrium (such that the various parity conditions discussed previously hold).

The International CAPM (ICAPM) assumes that capital markets are integrated.

$$r_{E,i}^{HC} = r_F^{HC} + \beta_{E,i}^W \times [E(R_{WorldMkt}^{HC} - R_F^{HC})] + \sum_{k=1}^{n} \gamma_{i,k} \times E\left[R_F^{FC_k} + \%\Delta S\left(\frac{HC}{FC_k}\right) - R_F^{HC}\right] \quad \textbf{(17.6)}$$

where:

$r_{E,i}^{HC}$ = expected rate of return (measured in the home currency) on an equity security "i" outside the home country

r_F^{HC} = home currency risk-free rate

$\beta_{E,i}^W$ = beta of security i measured with respect to the world-market risk premium

$E(R_{WorldMkt}^{HC} - R_F^{HC})$ = world-market risk premium measured against the return on the home country risk-free rate

$\gamma_{i,k}$ = the sensitivity of security i to returns on foreign currency k in excess of the home country risk-free asset

$R_F^{FC_k} + \%\Delta S\left(\frac{HC}{FC_k}\right) - R_F^{HC}$ = the relevant risk premium for the investment in foreign currency k

We do not discuss the last term in the ICAPM in detail because, generally, the effects of the systematic risk of currencies on an equity security are not material, and we typically estimate the ICAPM without estimating the effects of the risks of foreign currencies.

In order to estimate the ICAPM for, say, a U.S. company estimating the equity cost of capital for a U.K. firm it might acquire, we would use historical £-denominated returns of the equity for the U.K. firm for, say, the last 60 months and convert those returns into U.S.-dollar-based returns with historical exchange rates. We would also measure the world-market returns in U.S. dollars for the last 60 months. We estimate the market model using the U.K. firm's returns (denominated in dollars) on the dollar-denominated world-market index returns in order to estimate $\beta_{E,i}^W$. We multiply our estimated beta by our estimate of the dollar-denominated world-market risk premium, which is judged in relation to the appropriate U.S. risk-free security; to this, we then add the current yield of the appropriate U.S. risk-free security in order to measure the dollar-denominated required rate of return for the U.K. firm's equity. Assuming that the cost of equity is the appropriate discount rate for the cash flows we are discounting, we can use this discount rate to discount the future cash flows of the U.K. company that we converted into U.S. dollars with the relevant future expected exchange rates (the investor currency or centralized approach discussed earlier).

Are equity markets completely integrated? No, but they have been becoming more integrated over time, and we know that cross-border investment flows also continue to grow over time. For example, in Chapters 15 and 16, we noted an increase in cross-border leveraged buyout (LBO) and merger and acquisition (M&A) activity, which is a response to the increasingly global nature of business. In addition, many mutual funds allow investors to purchase securities of a foreign company with relatively low transaction costs. Moreover, the diversification benefits for investors increase when the investors hold foreign investments, which provides incentives for investors to invest abroad. Finally, the correlations between stock market indices across countries have increased over time, which is another indication that economic ups and downs tend to be shared globally. For example, the correlation between the S&P 500 index and an index of Europe, Australia, the Far East, and Canada is about 0.9 now, an increase from the 1980s to 1997 when the correlations were in the 0.3 to 0.5 range. Even the correlation between the S&P 500 with an index of emerging markets was close to 0.9 as of 2010 (though the correlation is not nearly as high when measured using individual emerging markets).

Segmented Markets

Even though there are economic forces that are integrating the world's capital markets, other economic forces and frictions have kept complete integration at bay. For example, many countries impose restrictions on foreign investment in such industries as natural resource industries. Many countries have tax policies that affect domestic investors and foreign investors differently. These tax policies usually work to limit foreign investment by taxing income on foreign investment at a higher rate (for example, the withholding tax on dividends paid to a foreign parent). In addition, the inability of foreign investors to garner the same information set as domestic investors can also limit foreign investment.

Another limitation on integration is the home bias of investors—that is, the proclivity to invest more in one's own country than in the global market even though global investment is optimal for diversification. Investors may have reasons not to hold a world portfolio in the proportions that each country's market represents (such as tax and information issues), and, as such, these investors are biased toward investing in their domestic economy. For example, in 2010, the U.S. stock market represented 42% of the value of the global stock market, but U.S. investors held about 77% of their portfolio in U.S. stocks. The home bias is even more apparent in other countries. One study examined 37 countries in 2003, when U.S. equity markets were 45% of the worldwide equity market. In 18 of the 37 countries, the holdings of U.S. equity securities (as a percentage of total equity securities held) were 1% or less; 13 countries held less than 10%; the rest held less than 20% (except the Netherlands, which held 29%).[17] The home bias is just as prevalent when calculating a country's total foreign holdings of equity to total equity held relative to the proportion of the world's equity market capitalization that comes from outside that country. Thus, the observed home bias does not just apply to U.S. investors or U.S. stocks.

If markets are fully segmented, the implication is that shareholders look to their local market to benchmark the risk of an investment. In other words, a U.S. investor would judge the risk of any investment against a portfolio of U.S. stocks while a U.K. investor would assess the risk of an asset against a portfolio of U.K. stocks. Recall that if markets were fully integrated, the benchmark to assess risk would be the world market portfolio for all investors.

To understand the implication of fully segmented markets for estimating the cost of capital, consider a U.S. company looking at acquiring a company in India. If markets are segmented, the U.S. company would evaluate the risk of the Indian company within a CAPM framework by using, say, the Indian company's last 60 monthly returns after converting them into U.S. dollars from Indian rupees with historical exchange rates. The U.S. company would then regress those returns on a U.S. stock market index such as the S&P 500. The estimate of the cost of equity capital would be equal to the appropriate U.S. risk-free rate, plus the estimated beta, multiplied by the market risk premium for the S&P 500 that is estimated relative to the U.S. risk-free rate. The expected free cash flows would equal the rupee-denominated expected free cash flows—converted to USD at the relevant expected future exchange rates between dollars and rupees.

If an Indian company were potentially interested in acquiring the same company, it would estimate the beta of the Indian company by regressing that company's returns (denominated in Indian rupees) against the returns of a broad-based Indian stock market index such as the SENSEX. The estimate of the cost of equity capital would be the appropriate Indian risk-free rate, plus the beta estimated against the SENSEX multiplied by an estimate of the market risk premium for the SENSEX that is estimated relative to the appropriate Indian risk-free rate. The expected free cash flows to be discounted would be the expected free cash flows in Indian rupees.

Most likely, the U.S. firm would assign a lower cost of capital to the Indian company than the Indian company would as long as the S&P 500 is not perfectly correlated with the SENSEX. The S&P 500 and the SENSEX have a correlation that is historically less than 0.4; thus, it is possible that the U.S. firm would estimate a lower discount rate for the Indian company and be able to outbid the potential Indian acquirer if the two bidders forecasted equivalent expected future free cash flows. Of course, the expected free cash flows for the two investors might also be different due to different taxes, different regulations, political risks, differences in perceived synergies, and the other reasons we discussed in this chapter.

Implications for Domestic Investments

It is important to point out that the issue of how to estimate the cost of capital is not just an issue specific to cross-border valuation. In Chapter 8, the discussion focused on U.S. data, which assumed the segmented markets view of the world was appropriate. If markets were completely integrated, a U.S. firm

---

[17] See Yago, G., J. Barth, T. Li, S. Malaiyandi, and T. Phumiswasana, "Home Bias in Global Capital Markets: What Is the Potential Demand for U.S. Asset-Backed Securities?" *Milken Institute Capital Studies*, 2006, available at http://www.milkeninstitute.org/pdf/demand_for_us_abs.pdf.

investing in a project in the United States or buying a United States target would use the global market portfolio as the benchmark portfolio for estimating both beta and the market risk premium.

Valuation Key 17.7

Finance theory provides a relatively clear guide on how to estimate the cost of capital if markets are either segmented or fully integrated. If they are integrated, we use a world market index as a benchmark for risk, and if they are segmented, we use a stock market index from the investor's home country as a benchmark for risk.

What if Markets Are Neither Fully Integrated nor Completely Segmented?

While finance theory provides a relatively clear guide on how to estimate the cost of capital if the world's capital markets are either fully integrated or completely segmented, finance theory does not provide a strong guide for when capital markets are in neither state but are somewhere in between. Some have proposed a hybrid model, which includes two risk factors—one for risk measured against a country benchmark and one for risk measured against a world-market benchmark. To estimate the effect of the two factors, one could estimate a multiple regression of a firm's returns against the country index and the world index. Bodnar, Dumas, and Marston (2003)[18] estimated this hybrid model for a variety of countries and companies and found that the betas estimated with respect to the country benchmark were generally large and significant and that the betas estimated with respect to the world index were often small and insignificant. The authors were careful to point out that although estimating these models is an interesting empirical analysis to see whether the country or world dominates in explanatory power, there is no theoretical foundation for this hybrid form of the CAPM. As such, these models may be estimable, but we cannot provide a rigorous justification for computing a firm's cost of capital using them.

As with the hybrid model discussed earlier, other solutions to the world's capital markets being neither integrated nor segmented have been proposed. Like the hybrid model, there is no theoretical justification for these alternatives. For example, one proposed solution is for a valuation expert to estimate the risk premium with a beta estimated with respect to the country index (with no world index in the regression) to estimate the country beta, and then multiply it by the country risk premium to estimate the risk premium. The valuation expert will then measure the risk premium with the beta estimated with respect to the world index (with no country index in the regression), and then multiply it by the world portfolio risk premium. Finally, the valuation expert will then assign weights to the two risk premiums such that the weights sum to 1; the assigned weights are based on the judgment of the valuation expert. As in the hybrid model discussed earlier, there is no theoretical justification for this model nor any conceptual rationale for how the weights would be chosen for the two risk premiums.

So, given all this, what do we recommend for estimating the cost of capital? In our view, it makes sense to calculate the cost of capital using both the integrated and segmented market approaches. In some cases, these estimates will be reasonably close, in other cases, there will be greater divergence, but it will at least provide a range of values.

Lack of a Publicly Traded Comparable Company in the Relevant Market

Sometimes, especially with less developed economies, we are unable to find a firm in the economy that is comparable to the firm we are valuing; hence, we cannot estimate the beta for that type of firm in a particular country with respect to either the country index or the world index. A potential solution to this problem is to assume that the unlevered beta of a particular business, with respect to that business' country, is the same across countries. [19]

---

[18] Bodnar, Gordon, Bernard Dumas, and Richard Marston, "Cross-Border Valuation: The International Cost of Equity Capital," 2003, fourth draft, working paper, Johns Hopkins University.

[19] See Lessard, D. R., "Incorporating Country Risk in the Valuation of Offshore Projects," *Journal of Applied Corporate Finance* (1996), pp. 52–63.

Assume that markets are segmented and that we are valuing a telephone company from Indonesia that is a private company. Further, assume that there are no publicly traded telephone companies in Indonesia. We could measure the betas of telephone companies from different countries (measured with respect to each telephone company's home country index). In other words, we assume that the beta of a telephone company with respect to a country index is the same across countries. This would then give us an estimate for an Indonesian telephone company's beta against the Indonesian stock market. If instead we want to assume that the world's capital markets are integrated, we would estimate the beta of the Indonesian telephone company with respect to the world market by taking our estimate of the beta of the Indonesian telephone company (derived from other countries as in earlier examples) multiplied by the beta of the Indonesian stock market with respect to the world market. In this approach, it is probably best to try to use countries at approximately the same level of economic development and that have similar laws and regulations for the type of business being valued.

Bodnar, Dumas, and Marston (2003) discussed the logic of this approach and tested it on various stocks from four different countries. What they found was that this approach worked reasonably well in the French, U.S., and Belgium markets but worked less well in the Polish market. While this issue has not been studied more extensively, the latter finding suggests that this approach is not as useful for companies operating in less developed economies, which is when we would most likely need to use it.

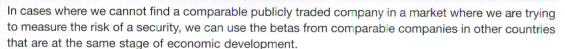

Valuation Key 17.8

In cases where we cannot find a comparable publicly traded company in a market where we are trying to measure the risk of a security, we can use the betas from comparable companies in other countries that are at the same stage of economic development.

17.6 CROSS-BORDER VALUATION IN LESS DEVELOPED OR TROUBLED ECONOMIES OR EMERGING MARKETS

In this section, we discuss additional adjustments to consider when conducting a cross-border valuation of a foreign company that is located—or has its primary business activities—in a less developed economy or an emerging market. Such cross-border valuations require special consideration, for the expected free cash flows of such companies can be affected by additional risk factors. As we discussed earlier in this chapter, these additional risk factors can be either unsystematic or systematic in nature. If they are unsystematic in nature, we adjust the expected free cash flows for the unsystematic risks, but we do not adjust the discount rate. If they are systematic in nature, we adjust the discount rate if the risks are not already embedded in the discount rate. We also adjust the expected free cash flows if the additional systematic risks affect the probabilities, magnitudes, or timing of the free cash flows.

Adjusting Expected Free Cash Flows for Country-Specific Risks

Country-specific risks can be related to various economic, political, or other types of risk. Economic-related risks include the riskiness of the country's economy, the degree of financial leverage used by the country, and the risks associated with the country's currency (exchange rate risk). Political risks are risks that affect a company's expected free cash flows that result from politically motivated decisions. They can also affect a company's operations, as is the case for risks related to promulgation, interpretation, and enforcement of regulations and laws. They can also affect ownership and the ability to transfer assets to another entity—examples include expropriation, confiscation, targeted special direct or indirect taxes to a foreign owner, reduced ability to sell assets, and reduced ability to transfer funds or assets outside the country. Finally, they can disrupt business—consider government instability, revolution, wars, strikes, or riots. To adjust our valuation for these risks, we either explicitly or implicitly

- identify the effect on free cash flows associated with each risk,
- assess the probabilities of the various outcomes,

- estimate which periods might be affected by the outcomes (for example, the potential effect of increased tax rates resulting from a political election held in three years if a certain political party is elected), and

- adjust the valuation based on the risks.

We can adjust the valuation for these additional risks in one of two ways. First, we can measure the expected effect of the risk on each unadjusted future free cash flow and deduct that amount from the unadjusted free cash flows before discounting them. Alternatively, we can measure the effect of the additional risk on the unadjusted value of the firm and deduct that amount from the unadjusted value of the firm. We use our basic DCF formula to illustrate these two approaches:

$$\text{DCF} = \sum_{t=0}^{\infty} \frac{\text{FCF}_t^{\text{Unadjusted}} - \text{E(CF Loss from Risk)}_t}{(1 + r_{\text{FCF}^{\text{U}}, \text{Loss}})^t} = \sum_{t=0}^{\infty} \frac{\text{FCF}_t^{\text{Unadjusted}}}{(1 + r_{\text{FCF}^{\text{U}}})^t} - \sum_{t=0}^{\infty} \frac{\text{E(CF Loss from Risk)}_t}{(1 + r_{\text{Loss}})^t}$$

As we discussed in Chapter 5, although it might be tempting, increasing the discount rate to account for these risks in not appropriate, as we have no basis for making this adjustment.

Valuation in Practice 17.3

Venezuela's Potential Expropriation of Oil Fields Venezuela encouraged global oil companies to invest in its oil fields with favorable terms, including a minority stake in the state oil company, Petroleos de Venezuela S.A. (PDVSA). Global oil companies such as Exxon Mobil and Chevron invested more than $16 billion in the country. In 1998, after Hugo Chavez was elected president, the country began a series of changes to the country's laws and taxes in what some interpret to be an expropriation of the oil reserves developed by these companies. In 2004, Venezuela raised royalty rates from 1% to 16.6% and reinterpreted tax rates, increasing the back taxes of foreign investors by $4 billion. In 2005, Venezuela announced that the existing agreements would have to be changed such that PDVSA would own a minimum of 51%, and it increased its royalty to 30%. Finally, in 2006, Venezuela mandated that PDVSA take operational control of the fields, and it set a deadline of May 1, 2007, for PDVSA to take operational control and a deadline of June 26, 2007, for companies to sign new agreements.

Source: See Witten, Emily A., "Arbitration of Venezuelan Oil Contracts: A Losing Strategy?" *Texas Journal of Oil, Gas, and Energy Law* vol. 4, no. 1 (2009), pp. 56–88.

Usually, we cannot observe the probabilities of these country-specific risks, but it is sometimes possible to get assessments of country-specific risks from consulting services and publications; these include Euromoney Country Risk, Economist Intelligence Unit, and International Country Risk Guide.[20] Risks assessed by these groups include such risks as the expropriation of assets, the failure to gain regulatory approval of a project, and the uncertain enforcement of laws and contracts in the legal system. These consulting companies provide assessments on such economy characteristics as credit risks, economic policies, political stability (leadership, military in politics, religion in politics, etc.), favorable or unfavorable conditions for foreign investors, government corruption, political tensions, quality of governmental systems and processes, likelihood of war (both internally and externally), expropriation or confiscation, and foreign trade collection experience.

Valuation Key 17.9

Cross-border valuations require special consideration if the expected free cash flows of the company can be affected by additional risk factors that are not already included in the forecasts or discount rate. These additional risk factors can be either unsystematic or systematic in nature. If they are unsystematic in nature, we adjust the expected free cash flows for them, but we do not adjust the discount rate; if they are systematic in nature, we adjust the discount rate and adjust the expected free cash flows if they affect the probabilities, magnitudes, or timing of the free cash flows.

---

[20] For example, regarding the International Country Risk Guide: ". . .since 1980, ICRG has produced political, economic, and financial risk ratings for countries important to international business. . . . ICRG ratings form the basis of an early warning system for opportunities and pitfalls, country-by-country." Available on October 9, 2011, at http://www.prsgroup.com/ICRG.aspx.

RiskTel's Valuation Including the Risk of the Expropriation.

We continue our RiskTel example and include political risk (which we assume to be non-systematic). Again, we assume the island-country has an annual election for control of the government. If the extremist party takes control of the government in any given year, it will expropriate all of RiskTel's assets; this election outcome only has a 1% chance of occurring in any given year. However, if this election outcome does occur, RiskTel's subsequent future cash flows will equal zero, and the government will not pay any value for the assets. How should we incorporate this risk scenario into our valuation of RiskTel? If the likelihood of a government takeover by an extremist party is independent of the economy, which may or may not be the case, this risk is unsystematic. We only have two sets (high- and low-growth scenarios) of expected free cash flows to adjust for the probability that the cash flows will equal zero if the extremist party takes control. We discussed how to perform these types of adjustments in Chapter 5, but we review them again here. If, however, this risk is systematic, we must also adjust the discount rate for a systematic risk component, assuming it is not already taken into account in the risk factors that have been included in our discount rate.

The cash flows in the top section of Exhibit 17.9 do not consider the risk of an extreme political party taking control and expropriating the company's assets. Assuming that this risk is unlikely to be systematic, we adjust the expected free cash flows, but we do not adjust the discount rate. We first examine the effect of the 1% chance of this political outcome occurring in any given year. If the political outcome occurred, it would reduce all future expected free cash flows to zero. In such a situation—that is, the possibility that all future cash flows will be reduced to zero—the adjustment we make to our calculations is straightforward. Consider the expected free cash flow in Year 1 in the high-growth case. Instead of an expected free cash flow of $120, we have a 99% chance of an expected free cash flow of $120 and a 1% chance of an expected free cash flow of $0. We present these calculations in the bottom part of Exhibit 17.9.

Thus, we can measure the high-growth expected free cash flows by multiplying the previous year's free cash flow by the growth rate factor (1.2) and then multiplying that sum by 1 minus the probability of the negative political outcome occurring (0.99 = 1.0 − 0.01). For example, the expected free cash flow in Year 1 is equal to $100 × 1.2 × 0.99, and the expected free cash flow in Year 2 is equal to the expected free cash flow in Year 1 multiplied by the product of 1.2 and 0.99—$100 × 1.2² × 0.99². Similarly, to include the effect of this risk in the continuing value perpetuity, we add the probability to the denominator, in essence treating it like a negative growth rate.[21] The perpetuity formula is equal to the Year 3 expected free cash flow multiplied by the growth rate factor (1.02), multiplied by 0.99, and divided by the discount rate (0.12) minus the long-term growth rate (0.02) plus the probability of the political outcome occurring (0.01). We show the calculation for the high-growth scenario here.

$$\$1,433.49 = \frac{\$100 \times 1.2 \times 0.99}{1.12} + \frac{\$100 \times 1.2^2 \times 0.99^2}{(1.12)^2} + \frac{\$100 \times 1.2^3 \times 0.99^3}{(1.12)^3} + \frac{\$100 \times 1.2^3 \times 1.02 \times 0.99^4}{(0.12 - 0.02 + 0.01)} \times \frac{1}{(1.12)^3}$$

The only difference between the calculations for the high- and low-growth scenarios is the growth rate factor (1.2 for the high-growth scenario versus 1.05 for the low-growth scenario). We also show the results of the calculation for the value of the low-growth scenario, which equals $993. To measure the value of RiskTel, we probability weight each of the scenario values, resulting in a value of $1,257—which is about a 10% reduction in value by including the political risk. As before, we can also measure the value of RiskTel by first measuring the expected free cash flows and then discounting them. In this case, we measure the expected free cash flows by probability weighting the high- and low-growth cash flows for each year, which we show in the line labeled "Expected cash flow valuation." Both approaches result in the same valuation of $1,257.

REVIEW EXERCISE 17.5

Country-Specific Risks—1

A company operates in a country that will have a national election at the end of each year. If the S party wins the election, the S party will expropriate the assets of the company, and the company will be paid $0 for its assets. The probability of the S party winning the election is 2% in any given year. The Year 0 free cash flow

---

[21] For a discussion of these issues, see Ruback, R. S., "Downsides and DCF: Valuing Biased Cash Flow Forecasts," *Journal of Applied Corporate Finance* vol. 23, no. 2 (2011), pp. 8–17.

for the company is $1,000. For the first three years, the company expects its cash flow to grow at 30% each year if the economy is doing well and −5% each year if the economy is doing poorly. The probability of the economy doing well is 25% in each year. For all outcomes, the economy and the company's free cash flows are expected to grow at 3% in perpetuity after Year 3. The appropriate discount rate is 15%. Measure the value of the firm under both economic scenarios (the economy doing well and the economy doing poorly), ignoring the probability of the company's assets being expropriated; then measure the value of the firm under both economic scenarios including the effects of the potential expropriation.

Solution on page 771.

RiskTel's Valuation Including the Risk of Default on Sovereign Debt.   Now, we will use an alternative and more complex country-specific risk scenario—the government defaulting on its debt. We assume the government-issued substantial debt in order to build the infrastructure necessary to support its resorts and visitor traffic. As a result, the country's credit rating is low, for it is a small emerging economy with substantial debt. The ability of Riskie Key to service its debt depends on which of the two growth scenarios the country experiences. If Riskie Key experiences the high-growth scenario, which will continue through Year 3, it will not default on its debt. If it experiences the low-growth scenario in Year 1, which will continue through Year 3, it has a 30% probability of defaulting on its debt in both Years 2 and 3. If Riskie Key defaults on its debt, the resort developers will cease to invest in the island. In that case, even RiskTel's low-growth forecasts will be optimistic in comparison to the scenario in which Riskie Key defaults on its debt, which results in a negative growth rate of −35% in the year of default through Year 3, after which growth will increase to 2% per year. If Riskie Key does not default by Year 3, it will not default subsequently, and it will grow at 2% per year.

It is clear that we need to adjust the cash flow forecasts for the effects of the government potentially defaulting on its debt. Do we also adjust the discount rate? We would only adjust the discount rate if this additional risk factor was systematic in nature and not already embedded in the other risk factors used to measure RiskTel's discount rate; for example, it may be embedded in the CAPM beta. For this example, we assume this risk does not require us to adjust the discount rate.

The adjustments we make to the expected free cash flows to account for the potential default on the sovereign debt are more complex than the ones we made to account for the risk of a political outcome occurring. These calculations quickly become quite tedious, even for this simple example, and note that we are ignoring the political risk modeled previously. Assuming the risk is unsystematic, we adjust the expected free cash flows. We present the calculation of these expected free cash flows in the top section of Exhibit 17.10 with a decision tree framework. The expected free cash flow in Year 1 is equal to the sum of the probability-weighted high- and low-growth outcomes. The probability-weighted outcome is equal to the Year 0 cash flow multiplied by the growth rate factor multiplied by the probability of the outcome. It is $42 for the low-growth scenario ($42 = $100 × 1.05 × 0.40) and $72 for the high-growth scenario ($72 = $100 × 1.2 × 0.60). The expected cash flow is the sum of the two probability-weighted outcomes ($114 = $42 + $72).

Since both the high- and low-growth scenarios are determined in Year 1 for all three years, and since no default occurs in the high-growth state, the probability-weighted expected cash flow for Year 2 in the high growth scenario is equal to the Year 1 expected cash flow multiplied by the growth factor ($86.40 = $72 × 1.2). However, the low-growth scenario has two potential outcomes in Year 2—default and no default. If the government does not default, the expected cash flow is equal to the Year 1 cash flow multiplied by the low-growth factor, 1.05, which we probability adjust to measure the probability-weighted expected cash flow ($30.87 = $42.00 × 1.05 × 0.70). If the government defaults, the expected cash flow is equal to the Year 1 cash flow multiplied by the default growth factor (0.65 = 1 + −0.35), which we again probability adjust to measure the probability-weighted expected cash flow ($8.19 = $42.00 × 0.65 × 0.30). The expected cash flow of $125.46 for Year 2 is the sum of the three probability-weighted outcomes ($125.46 = $86.40 + $30.87 + $8.19).

In Year 3, we have four different scenarios: high growth, low growth with default in Year 2, low growth with default in Year 3, and low growth with no default. For the high-growth scenario, the Year 3 probability-weighted expected free cash flow is equal to $103.68 ($103.68 = $86.40 × 1.2). For the low-growth scenario with default in Year 2, the probability-weighted expected free cash flow is equal to $5.32 [$5.32 = $8.19 × (1 − 0.35)]. We have two potential outcomes for the low-growth scenario without default in Year 2: default in Year 3 and no default in Year 3. If the government does not default in Year 3, the expected cash

EXHIBIT 17.10	RiskTel Company Free Cash Flows and Valuation Excluding and Including the Effect of the Sovereign Default Risk

Scenarios and Expected Cash Flows Including Political Costs

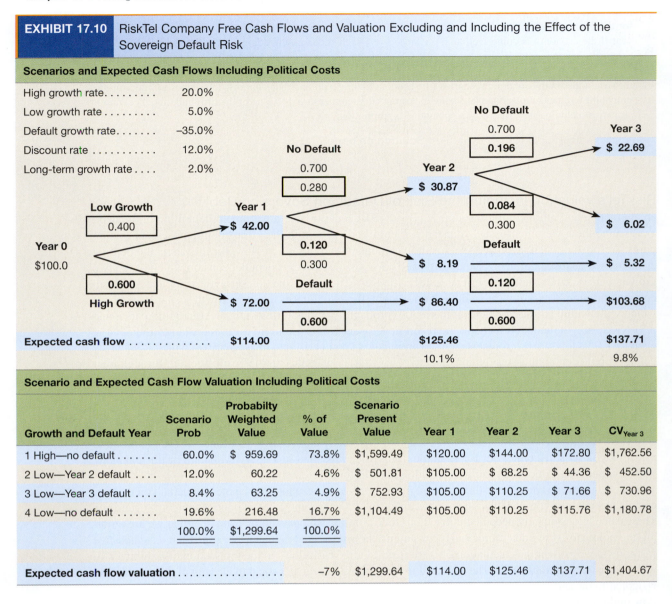

High growth rate 20.0%
Low growth rate 5.0%
Default growth rate . . . . −35.0%
Discount rate 12.0%
Long-term growth rate 2.0%

Scenario and Expected Cash Flow Valuation Including Political Costs

Growth and Default Year	Scenario Prob	Probabilty Weighted Value	% of Value	Scenario Present Value	Year 1	Year 2	Year 3	CV_Year 3
1 High—no default	60.0%	$ 959.69	73.8%	$1,599.49	$120.00	$144.00	$172.80	$1,762.56
2 Low—Year 2 default	12.0%	60.22	4.6%	$ 501.81	$105.00	$ 68.25	$ 44.36	$ 452.50
3 Low—Year 3 default	8.4%	63.25	4.9%	$ 752.93	$105.00	$110.25	$ 71.66	$ 730.96
4 Low—no default	19.6%	216.48	16.7%	$1,104.49	$105.00	$110.25	$115.76	$1,180.78
	100.0%	$1,299.64	100.0%					
Expected cash flow valuation		−7%	$1,299.64	$114.00	$125.46	$137.71	$1,404.67

flow is equal to the Year 2 cash flow multiplied by the low-growth factor (1.05), which we probability adjust to measure the probability-weighted expected cash flow ($22.69 = $30.87 × 1.05 × 0.70). If the government defaults in Year 3, the expected cash flow is equal to the Year 2 cash flow multiplied by the default growth factor (0.65 = 1 + −0.35), which we again probability adjust to measure the probability-weighted expected cash flow ($6.02 = $30.87 × 0.65 × 0.30). The expected cash flow in Year 3 of $137.71 is the sum of the four probability-weighted outcomes ($137.71 = $103.68 + $5.32 + $6.02 + $22.69).

The continuing value in Year 3 of $1,404.67, based on the expected cash flow, is simply equal to the Year 3 expected cash flow of $137.71, multiplied by the growth factor of 1.02 and divided by the discount rate of 12% minus the growth rate of 2%. We can discount both the expected free cash flows and continuing value to measure RiskTel's value of $1,300, which we show in the last line of the exhibit. There is a 7% reduction in RiskTel's value due to the sovereign default risk.

An alternative way we can measure this value is by probability weighting the values of the four scenarios—high growth, low growth with default in Year 2, low growth defaulting in Year 3, and low growth with no default. We calculate the free cash flows for the high-growth scenario by multiplying the Year 0 free cash flow ($100) by the appropriate growth factor for each of the three years—1.2, 1.2², 1.2³, respectively. The value of this cash flow stream is $1,599, which has a 60% chance of occurring.

The other three scenarios begin with the low-growth expected free cash flow in Year 1 ($105 = $100 × 1.05). For the scenario of low growth with no default, we use the same calculation used for the high-growth scenario, but we use the low growth factor of 1.05. The value of this scenario is $1,104, which has a 19.6% chance of occurring ($.196 = 0.4 \times 0.7 \times 0.7$). We calculate the free cash flows for the low-growth scenario with default in Year 2 by switching to the default growth rate in Years 2 and 3. We calculate the free cash flows for the low-growth scenario with default in Year 3 by switching to the default growth rate in Year 3. We present the probability-weighted valuations for these two scenarios in the exhibit. Of course, the probability of all four scenarios must sum to 1. The sum of all of the probability-weighted scenario valuations is again equal to $1,300.

REVIEW EXERCISE 17.6

Country-Specific Risks—2

A company operates in a country that may default on its debt if it experiences low economic growth. If the country experiences high growth in Year 1, it will continue to do so through Year 3, and it will not default on its debt; in this scenario, the company's free cash flows will grow at 15% for Years 1 through 3 and 3% thereafter. The probability of the country having high growth in Year 1 is 20%. If the country experiences low growth in Year 1, it will continue to do so through Year 3, and it will have a 40% probability of defaulting on its debt in both Years 2 and 3. If the country experiences low growth in a given year but does not default on its debt, the company's free cash flows will grow at 4%. If the country defaults on its debt, the company will have a negative growth rate of 20% in the year of the default through Year 3 and a positive growth rate of 3% thereafter. If the country does not default by Year 3, it will not default subsequently, and the country and company's free cash flows will have a positive growth rate of 3% per year. The company's discount rate is 13%, and its Year 0 free cash flow is $1,000. Measure the value of the firm, ignoring the default on country's debt and including the default on the country's debt.

Solution on page 772.

Using Insurance and Insurance Premiums as an Alternative to Adjusting for Political Risks

Various government-related organizations and private insurers offer insurance with various terms regarding both the coverage amount and time horizon in order to mitigate or limit some types of political risks. For example, the Multilateral Investment Guarantee Agency (MIGA) is a member of the World Bank Group, which promotes foreign direct investment into developing countries. It provides political risk insurance guarantees to private sector investors and lenders in order to protect investments against non-commercial risks.[22] The Political Risk Insurance Center (PRI-Center) provides free access to political risk management and insurance resources. It was established in 2006 as part of the MIGA mandate to promote direct foreign investment in developing countries. The United States has the Overseas Private Investment Corporation.[23] It is a U.S. government organization that provides investors who invest in foreign countries with financing, guarantees, political risk insurance, and support for private equity investment funds.

To the extent that insurance eliminates certain risks—that is, shifts the entire risk from the investor to the insurer—these risks do not have to be included in our cross-border valuation. It is difficult to insure against all of the risk over a long horizon when considering an investment in a foreign company, but it is often possible to insure against some of the risk for various limited horizons. For example, it is common for such insurance to be limited to the amount of invested capital or the book value of the assets; it is also common to limit the term of such insurance to no more than 20 years. It is also sometimes possible to insure a limited part of the earnings stream.

As we discussed earlier, adjusting expected free cash flows for such risks requires that we measure the expected effect of the risk on free cash flows and deduct that amount from the free cash flows. One way we measure the effect of risk on the free cash flows is to estimate the probability that a bad outcome will occur and to multiply it by the effect that the bad outcome will have on the cash flow. An insurance premium provides an estimate of that calculation plus a return (or profit) to the insurer. We can reduce either the premium or the embedded profit in order to use the insurance premiums to adjust the cash flows in the discounted cash flow model. Of course, if an acquirer is buying a company and buying the insurance, we would include the entire insurance premium when calculating the value of the insured target to the acquirer.

---

[22] See, available on October 9, 2011, http://www.miga.org/whoweare/index.cfm.

[23] See, available on October 9, 2011, http://www.opic.gov/about-us.

Estimating the Equity Cost of Capital in Emerging Markets

Issues in addition to the ones we have already discussed can arise in valuing a company in an emerging market. Assume that a U.S. company is implementing both the integrated and segmented methods to estimate the cost of capital of a company in an emerging market and that it is using the CAPM. Implementing these approaches can be more difficult for a company in an emerging market. First, in many emerging economies, the stock market is not liquid, and trading may be infrequent. How severe this problem will be depends on how infrequently the stocks trade. Regardless of whether we estimate betas against a world index, a U.S. index, or even the local country index, this issue is problematic. Thus, irrespective of whether one adopts a segmented or integrated view of the world, some adjustment for infrequent trading such as estimating betas with lead and lagged market returns—as discussed in Chapter 8—may be relevant.

Another issue in taking the segmented view is that the composition of the market (the relative values of the industry segments) can be different in emerging economies than it is in developed countries. For example, Nokia is listed on the Helsinki stock exchange in Finland and represents approximately one-third of the market capitalization of the exchange. As such, the weight of the telecommunications industry in the Finnish stock market is very different than it is in such markets as the U.S. or world market. Hence, if Nokia was contemplating the purchase of another company listed on the Helsinki exchange, it could arrive at a beta for that company (estimated against the local index) that is very different from one that is estimated against a world index. In situations like this, we have to consider whether the segmented markets approach is reasonable for estimating the cost of capital and if we thought that it was, we might have to adjust the market index.

Third, when we regress the returns for a company in a developing country on either a U.S. stock market index (like the S&P 500), a world index, or the index of another developed country, we will likely estimate betas that are very close to zero or are statistically insignificant.[24] The implication of this is that the cost of capital for the company should be very low and near or at the U.S. risk-free rate. Although, in theory, this is possible if the risk of the investment is completely diversifiable, for most practitioners and managers, this assumption seems untenable—even if cash flows are adjusted for political risks, default risk, and so forth. In light of these issues, practitioners and academics have struggled to identify ways to empirically estimate a cost of capital for companies in emerging markets with a more intuitive outcome—that is, a higher cost of capital. A variety of mostly ad hoc alternatives have been developed, and we highlight a few of them next.

Sovereign Spread Model. In this approach, a country risk premium is added to the equity cost of capital, which is first estimated using the CAPM (assuming either segregated or integrated markets). This approach is a widely adopted one. The most common method for estimating the country risk premium is to add a sovereign spread to the discount rate, such as the difference between the yield on a long-maturity bond issued by the country (denominated in U.S. dollars) and the yield on a similar maturity U.S. government bond. If the country has not issued bonds payable in U.S. dollars, we would have to adjust the yield on the country's bonds for any difference in expected inflation between the two countries.

This approach has several potential drawbacks. First, it assumes that the country risk premium is the same for all projects, for this technique makes the same adjustment to the CAPM regardless of the sector of the economy. In other words, if some sectors of the economy are impacted more by country risk factors than other sectors, this adjustment would be inappropriate. Another drawback is that this adjustment presumes that the sovereign spread represents a systematic risk, but some country risk may be diversifiable with respect to an investor in another country. If the risk, or part of the risk, is non-systematic or diversifiable, then adding this spread to determine the cost of capital is not appropriate. Finally, we have no empirical evidence to support the assumption that a country's credit risk represents purely systematic risk. In short, even though this is a common approach used in practice, it is grounded in neither theory nor empirical evidence.

Relative Volatilities Assumption. Another approach is to substitute the ratio of the volatility of the foreign stock market relative to the volatility of the U.S. stock market (assuming segmented markets)—or the volatility of the foreign stock market relative to the volatility of the world stock market

---

[24] Even the betas of an emerging economy stock market index (and not just of a particular company) with respect to the S&P 500 or a world index may have a beta that is close to zero and insignificant. An index of all emerging economies considered jointly has a correlation of about 0.9 with both the S&P 500 and the world index, but this is not true for most emerging markets when considered in isolation.

(assuming integrated markets)—for beta. Volatility is most often measured as the standard deviation of stock returns. Most emerging economies have greater volatility than either the U.S. or world markets, and hence the estimated betas—based on the relative volatilities—tend to be larger than 1 if this technique is used—and certainly higher than zero.[25] Some go a step further and even include the sovereign spread as an additional factor to this approach.[26] The drawbacks to this technique are similar to those of adding the sovereign credit spread to the CAPM estimate. Even if the sovereign credit spread is not added, the model assumes that relative volatilities measure systematic risk, and again, all companies within a country would have the same cost of capital since the relative volatilities are based on aggregate market data.

Valuation Key 17.10

There are various difficulties in estimating the cost of capital for an investment in emerging economies. The major problem is that betas of such investments—judged relative to a world index, a U.S. index, or the index of another developed country—are likely to be close to zero. Therefore, typical CAPM approaches may imply a zero risk premium. Practitioners and academics have put forth a variety of alternatives, but these are not based on any substantive theoretical underpinnings.

Summary.   Rather than discuss all of the different asset pricing model variants that have been tried, we provide our overall conclusion.[27] The integrated and segmented views of estimating the cost of capital under the CAPM have justifiable theoretical underpinnings, but the implementation of these techniques is likely to lead to the conclusion that the risk premium for investments in emerging economies is low. This is potentially justifiable if the risks within emerging economies are largely idiosyncratic with respect to an investor in a developed country. If this is the case, and if we include adjustments for such risks when measuring expected free cash flows, then the CAPM approach (as discussed earlier in the chapter) is the appropriate approach. As discussed earlier, the betas of stock market indices from emerging economies (not just of individual companies)—with respect to the world index, the S&P 500, and other developed country indices—are low, which is consistent with this view. Of course, it is important that the idiosyncratic risks be carefully analyzed and included in the cash flow forecasts as we demonstrated in this section of the chapter. Even though it seems intuitively unrealistic for the risk premium of investments in emerging economies to be low, the alternative models that attempt to increase risk premium estimates are neither firmly grounded in theory nor have strong empirical evidence that endorses their usage. Certainly, this area needs additional inquiry and study.

17.7 CHALLENGES USING MARKET AND TRANSACTIONS MULTIPLES ACROSS BORDERS

In this section, we discuss the additional challenges and limitations of using market or transaction multiples in cross-border valuations. To conduct a cross-border valuation with market or transaction multiples, we use the procedures outlined in Chapters 13 and 14. Although the models do not change for a cross-border valuation, how we implement the models does. It may or may not be appropriate to use multiples measured from comparable companies in one country in order to value a company in another country. In addition, it may or may not be appropriate to use multiples measured from comparable companies from the target's country in order to value a company being acquired by an investor in another country. As we might expect, the degree of appropriateness depends on the facts and circumstances of the particular valuation conducted. For example, the comparable domestic companies from the target's country may face a different tax structure than a foreign investor buying the target.

LO5 Explain the limitations of using cross-border market multiples and measure exchange rate exposure

---

[25] There is evidence that returns in emerging economies seem to be more highly correlated with volatility than with betas. See Harvey, C., "Drivers of Expected Returns in International Markets," *Emerging Market Quarterly* 4 (2000), pp. 32–49.

[26] See Godfrey, S., and R. Espinosa, "A Practical Approach to Calculating Costs of Equity for Investments in Emerging Markets," *Journal of Applied Corporate Finance* 9 (Fall 1996), pp. 80–89. The authors recognize that the sovereign spread and the relative volatilities may be capturing a similar risk, and therefore they multiply the estimated beta by 0.6 based on the relative volatilities. There is no strong justification for this adjustment.

[27] For a review of a variety of other alternative methods that have been proposed, see Sabal, J., "The Discount Rate in Emerging Markets: A Guide," *Journal of Applied Corporate Finance* 16 (2004), pp. 155–166.

Cross-Border Market Multiples

In Exhibit 17.11, we present some basic distributional statistics for the EBITDA multiple of 12 countries. To be included in the initial sample, a company had to be in the Compustat Global Database for fiscal year 2010 and have sufficient information to calculate at least one of the market multiples in the exhibit.[28] The initial sample consists of 16,885 companies across 87 countries. As in the database we used for U.S. market multiples that we showed in Chapters 13 and 14, we do not include a market multiple observation if its denominator is negative. In the exhibit, we only include countries having at least 200 companies with complete information.

EXHIBIT 17.11	Market Multiple Distributions for Selected Countries													
2010 Statistics	Japan	China	Taiwan	United Kingdom	Malaysia	Australia	South Korea	France	Germany	Singapore	India	Thailand	Min	Max
Earnings Before Interest, Taxes, Depreciation, and Amortization (EBITDA) Multiple														
Median	6.1	5.2	5.5	4.4	6.8	5.1	6.6	4.5	4.1	4.8	4.5	6.0	4.1	6.8
Inter-quartile range	5.6	5.5	6.9	4.6	8.0	6.9	6.2	4.1	4.0	6.3	4.0	6.6	4.0	8.0
Mean	7.7	7.2	8.1	6.1	9.7	7.6	8.8	6.1	5.9	7.5	6.2	8.0	5.9	9.7
Standard deviation	6.0	6.5	7.4	5.9	7.9	7.4	6.5	5.6	6.0	7.2	5.7	6.7	5.6	7.9
Median Market Multiples Used to Measure the Value of the Firm (Numerator Is Market Value of the Firm)														
Unlevered free cash flow	9.7	8.1	7.4	6.8	11.7	7.4	13.1	7.0	5.9	7.4	9.8	8.8	5.9	13.1
Unlevered earnings	16.4	7.6	9.3	8.1	10.8	7.9	12.2	9.5	7.9	6.9	7.3	9.1	6.9	16.4
Earnings before interest and taxes (EBIT)	10.0	6.8	7.9	6.1	8.9	6.8	10.4	6.7	6.2	6.7	5.6	8.8	5.6	10.4
Revenue or sales	0.5	0.7	0.6	0.6	0.9	1.3	0.6	0.5	0.4	0.6	0.7	0.7	0.4	1.3
Total assets	0.5	0.5	0.6	0.5	0.7	0.6	0.6	0.5	0.5	0.5	0.7	0.7	0.5	0.7

We show the minimum and maximum statistics across the 12 countries in the last two columns of the exhibit. For the EBITDA multiple, the median ranges from 4.1 to 6.8, and the mean ranges from 5.9 to 9.7. These results document the variation across the 12 countries. Both of the maximum values are more than 60% larger than their respective minimum values. We also measure within-country variation using both the inter-quartile range (difference in value between the 25th and 75th percentiles) and the standard deviation. These results also document differences across countries in their within-country variation of the EBITDA multiple. For example, the U.K. has an inter-quartile range of 4.6 and a standard deviation of 5.9, while Malaysia has an inter-quartile range of 8.0 and a standard deviation of 7.9. In this exhibit, we also present the median for other market multiples—unlevered free cash flow, unlevered earnings, EBIT, revenue, and total assets. The medians of these multiples show sizeable variation across countries.

Naturally, understanding the causes of cross-country variation in market multiples is important in deciding whether to use cross-country multiples in a particular valuation. For example, we know that market multiples differ across industries; thus, some of the cross-country variation can be due to industry differences across countries. Using appropriate comparable companies would mitigate this issue. We also know that since many of the denominators of the market multiples are numbers from financial statements, cross-country differences in accounting principles can also cause cross-country differences in market multiples. It may be possible to adjust the accounting information for these differences. Further, even for companies in the same industry, the expected growth and profitability of industry counterparts for two different countries can be very different. In addition, to the extent that capital markets are not integrated,

---

[28] According to Compustat (http://www.compustat.com/compustat_data_sets/?gclid=CKq3vPqW1KsCFd505QodHizsSQ), "Compustat Global Data is normalized according to country accounting principles, disclosure methods and specific data item definitions. This database provides financial and market data covering publicly traded companies. Hundreds of data items, ratios and concepts are included. In addition, Compustat Global offers data models specific to industrial companies and financial services sectors including: banks, insurance companies, real estate investment trusts and brokers/security dealers."

the valuations for ostensibly the same company in different countries could be different and a difference in the valuations across countries would cause cross-country differences in the market multiples.

Using Within-Country Market Multiples in a Cross-Border Valuation

Of course, using market multiples measured from companies within the same country helps us to avoid some of these issues. However, other potential issues can arise if the investor is not in the same country, making our valuation a cross-border valuation. For example, within-country market multiples do not consider valuation differences that result from segmented capital markets. In addition, they may not consider the income tax differences, other tax differences, and increased political or other foreign country risks that occur in specific cross-border valuations (but are not reflected to the same degree in the market values of the local companies).

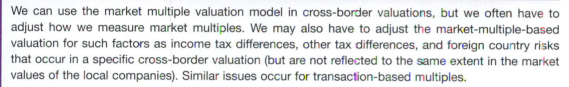

Valuation Key 17.11

We can use the market multiple valuation model in cross-border valuations, but we often have to adjust how we measure market multiples. We may also have to adjust the market-multiple-based valuation for such factors as income tax differences, other tax differences, and foreign country risks that occur in a specific cross-border valuation (but are not reflected to the same extent in the market values of the local companies). Similar issues occur for transaction-based multiples.

Using Transaction Multiples in a Cross-Border Valuation

We can face the same overarching issues when we use transaction multiples in the same way we use market multiples in a cross-border context. The one exception, of course, is when we can identify comparable cross-border transactions (where the acquirers and targets are from the same two countries we face in our valuation). If we are able to identify comparable cross-border transactions, we may then be able to use transaction multiples in the ways discussed in Chapter 16 on mergers and acquisitions. In Exhibit 16.6, we showed the variation in EBIT, EBITDA and revenue multiples across 13 different regions/countries of the world. Thus, the variation documented for market multiples based on publicly traded comparables across countries presented in this chapter is similar to the variation in transaction multiples reported in Chapter 16. Within-country transaction multiples face the same challenges that we described for within-country market multiples.

17.8 EXCHANGE RATE EXPOSURE AND HEDGING BASICS

Exchange rate exposure exists when the value of an asset or liability changes because of unexpected changes in the exchange rate. Naturally, cross-border ownership usually results in exchange rate exposure, for unexpected changes in the exchange rates can affect the acquirer's valuation of the firm. Hence, the potential hedging of exchange rate exposure is an issue that naturally arises in the context of cross-border ownership. **Exchange rate exposure** is a measure of the sensitivity of an asset's value—or in the case of a cross-border valuation, a firm's value—to unexpected or real changes in exchange rates. As it turns out, and we explain later, purely domestic companies can also face exchange rate exposure.

We classify economic exchange rate exposure into three types: operating exposure, transaction exposure, and financing exposure. Operating exposure results from a company's operations, and the other two types are related to specific transactions and financing instruments that a company may use (all stated in terms of a foreign currency). Another type of exchange rate exposure is translation exposure. Translation exposure is not an economic exposure, but it represents the effect of exchange rate changes on a company's financial statements, which may or may not be associated, in part, with some form of economic exposure. Exchange rate exposure creates uncertainty that, depending on the economic context, managers may or may not want to hedge. In this section, we will discuss exchange rate exposure and its hedging.

Operating Exchange Rate Exposure

Operating exchange rate exposure is the risk associated with changes in the value of one or more of a company's operating cash flow streams because of unexpected changes in exchange rates. It is clear from our cross-border DCF valuation model that cross-border ownership creates exchange rate exposure, for the value of the firm (to the owner) is a function of the exchange rate. Unexpected changes in exchange rates can affect the demand for a company's products, the revenue a company generates from these products, and the cost of producing these products. These effects subsequently affect the company's decisions concerning such issues as pricing, investment, marketing, and production—all of which can affect expected free cash flows. We can use our cross-border DCF valuation model to measure both the company's exchange rate exposure and the total value that is exposed to exchange rate risk for particular currencies. Alternatively, if we do not have a sufficiently detailed financial model, companies can use more top-level models to measure exposure. These models use a percentage of the revenues and profit margins from each of a company's foreign operations to measure exposure.[29] Other models estimate the exchange rate risk of a company with a regression model of prices or returns explained by changes in various exchange rates and other fundamental variables.[30]

Cross-border ownership results in operating exchange rate exposure because the company operates in a different currency than the investor's currency. However, operating exchange rate exposure is, of course, a much broader issue and occurs in economic contexts other than cross-border ownership. Consider a company that produces its products domestically but sells its products in foreign countries. This company has exchange rate exposure because unexpected changes in the exchange rates between the home and foreign countries in which it sells its products will affect the prices at which the company can sell its products, the quantity of the products sold, and the profits the company earns on its foreign sales.

Consider another company that produces and sells all of its products within the country in which it is located but purchases inputs for the production of its products from foreign vendors with transactions that are denominated in other currencies. This company has exchange rate exposure because changes in exchange rates between the home and foreign countries from which it purchases its inputs will affect the prices at which the company can sell its products, the quantity of the products sold, and the profits the company earns on its domestic sales. Even a company that purchases all of its inputs and sells all of its products domestically can face exchange rate exposure if it competes with foreign companies. Such a company faces exchange rate exposure because unexpected appreciation or depreciation of the foreign companies' currency can affect the prices at which the foreign companies compete in the domestic market.

For an acquirer, the entire free cash flow stream from a target has exchange rate exposure if the target operates completely within its country while the acquirer operates in another country. On the other hand, for a company that produces and sells its products completely within its domestic country but purchases inputs for its products in other countries, in transactions denominated in foreign currencies, it only faces exchange rate exposure for the cost of the inputs it purchases in foreign countries with transactions denominated in foreign currencies. Similarly, a company that produces it products completely within its domestic country but sells its products in other countries faces exchange rate exposure to its revenue stream. If these three companies are identical in all respects but for the cash flow stream that is affected by exchange rate exposure, which company has the largest exchange rate exposure? The answer depends on the relative sizes of the cash flow streams. The larger the cash flow stream that is denominated in foreign currency, the larger the exchange rate exposure. If all of a company's products are produced domestically and sold in foreign countries, then it is likely that this company will have the largest exposure because revenue is generally greater than expenses and free cash flows.

We can use the DCF valuation model to measure exposure if the model includes the effect of exchange rates on the free cash flows. We illustrate this approach in Exhibit 17.12 for a company located in the U.K. (U.K. Sub) and owned by a company in the United States (U.S. Parent). U.K. Sub purchases its products from U.S. parent in transactions denominated in USD. The Year 1 expected cash revenue for U.K. Sub is £1,200. The total cost of its products is $1,600 and it has no other expenses. U.K. Sub has no capital expenditure requirements and is only financed with common equity. For simplicity, we also

---

[29] See Bodnar, G., Dumas, B., and Marston, R., "Pass-Through and Exposure," *Journal of Finance* 57 (2002), pp. 199–231; and Bartram, S., G. Brown, and B. Minton, "Resolving the Exposure Puzzle: The Many Facets of Exchange Rate Exposure," *Journal of Financial Economics* 95 (2010), pp. 148–173.

[30] See, for example, Pantzalis, Christos, Betty J. Simkins, and Paul A. Laux, "Operational Hedges and the Foreign Exchange Exposure of U.S. Multinational Corporations," *Journal of International Business Studies* vol. 32, no. 4 (2001), pp. 793–812.

assume that no taxes are levied on the income of U.K. Sub. Assume that the USD discount rate for the free cash flows is 10%, that the U.K. Sub has a zero expected future growth rate, and that the current and expected future exchange rate is 2 $/£. As we show in the second column of the top panel of the exhibit, U.K. Sub has revenue of $2,400, expenses equaling $1,600, and a free cash flow of $800. With a 10% discount rate and zero growth rate, its value in USD is $8,000 ($8,000 = $800/0.10).

EXHIBIT 17.12 Example of Exchange Rate Exposure for Two Scenarios

Only Revenues in £	Year 0	Exchange Rates $/£ 2.000	2.100	1.900
Revenue (cash in £)	£ 1,200.0	$ 2,400.0	$ 2,520.0	$ 2,280.0
Expenses (cash in USD).	$−1,600.0	−1,600.0	−1,600.0	−1,600.0
Unlevered free cash flow		$ 800.0	$ 920.0	$ 680.0
Discount rate (in USD, no growth)		10.0%	10.0%	10.0%
Value of U.K. Sub in USD.		$ 8,000.0	$ 9,200.0	$ 6,800.0
Percentage change in value.			15.0%	−15.0%
Change in value			$ 1,200.0	$−1,200.0
Percentage change in exchange rate.			5.0%	−5.0%
Total amount of exposure in USD.			$24,000.0	$24,000.0
Present value of revenue stream		$24,000.0		

All Cash Flows in £	Year 0	Exchange Rates $/£ 2.000	2.100	1.900
Revenue (cash in £)	£1,200.0	$2,400.0	$2,520.0	$2,280.0
Expenses (cash in £).	£ −800.0	−1,600.0	−1,680.0	−1,520.0
Unlevered free cash flow	£ 400.0	$ 800.0	$ 840.0	$ 760.0
Discount rate (in USD, no growth)		10.0%	10.0%	10.0%
Value of the U.K. Sub in USD.		$8,000.0	$8,400.0	$7,600.0
Percentage change in value.			5.0%	−5.0%
Change in value			$ 400.0	$ −400.0
Percentage change in exchange rate.			5.0%	−5.0%
Total amount of exposure in USD.			$8,000.0	$8,000.0

If the expected future exchange rates were to unexpectedly increase by 5% to 2.1 $/£ (while U.K. Sub's expected revenues and the USD discount rate remain unchanged), the USD value of the U.K. company increases to $9,200 (or by $1,200 or 15%). The value increases because the value of the £ increased, or appreciated, relative to the USD; thus, the £-denominated free cash flows are more valuable and are thus higher when converted to USD-denominated free cash flows. If the expected future exchange rate was to unexpectedly decrease by 5% to 1.9 $/£, the USD value of the U.K. Sub decreases to $6,800 or, again, by $1,200 or 15%.

We measure exchange rate exposure as the sensitivity of the value of the U.S. company's investment in the U.K. company to unexpected changes in the $/£ exchange rate. In our example, we observe that a 5% unexpected change in the exchange rate results in a 15% change in the value of the U.K. firm; thus, the sensitivity of the value of the U.S. company's investment in the U.K. company to the $/£ exchange rate is 3 (3 = 0.15 change in value/0.05 change in exchange rate). In other words, based on our DCF valuations, an x% change in the exchange rate results in a 3x% change in the value of the firm.

In the bottom panel of Exhibit 17.12, we present an alternative scenario in which the U.K. company produces its products in the U.K. with U.K. inputs and sells all of its products domestically; thus, the company's entire free cash flow stream is exposed to $/£ exchange rate risk. Again, we can use the DCF valuation model to measure exposure to unexpected changes in the $/£ exchange rate. U.K. Sub's Year 1 expected cash revenues and cash expenses are, respectively, £1,200 and £800; thus, the company's free cash flow is £400. Using the $/£ exchange rate of 2.0, the converted USD free cash flow is equal to $800. Assuming that the USD discount rate for the free cash flows is again 10% and that the company has a zero growth rate, the value of the firm in USD is $8,000 ($8,000 = $800/0.10). Although this is the same value as previously, the two companies have different $/£ exchange rate exposures because they have different cash flow streams exposed to the $/£ exchange rate risk.

If the expected future exchange rate unexpectedly increases by 5% to 2.1 $/£, the USD value of the U.K. company increases to $8,400 (or by $400 or 5%). If the expected future exchange rate unexpectedly decreases by 5% to 1.9 $/£, the USD value of the U.K. Sub decreases to $7,600 (or by $400 or 5%). A 5% unexpected change in the exchange rate results in a 5% change in the value of the firm; thus, the sensitivity of the value of the U.S. company's investment in the U.K. company to changes in the $/£ exchange rate is 1 (1 = 0.05 change in value/0.05 change in exchange rate). The first company has an exchange rate exposure of 3x because its entire revenue stream is exposed to the $/£ exchange rate risk, but the second company offsets some of the revenue exchange rate exposure by also incurring its expenses in the same currency (£).

What is the amount or value exposed to the exchange rate risk? We can measure the exposure by multiplying the value of the investment by the sensitivity of the value of the investment to changes in the exchange rate. In the first scenario, the value of the investment is $8,000 and the sensitivity is 3, so the exposure is $24,000 ($24,000 = $8,000 × 3). In the second scenario, the value of the investment is also $8,000, but the sensitivity is 1, so the exposure is $8,000 ($8,000 = $8,000 × 1).

This calculation is equivalent to the calculation shown in the exhibit that divides the change in value by the percentage change in the exchange rate. In the first scenario, the change in the value of the investment is $1,200 and the percentage change in the exchange rate is 5%, so the exposure is $24,000 ($24,000 = $8,000/0.05). In the second scenario, the change in value of the investment is $400 and the percentage change in the exchange rate is 5%, so the exposure is $8,000 ($8,000 = $400/0.05).

In the first example, in which the U.K. company's revenues are exposed to $/£ exchange rate fluctuations, the total exchange rate exposure is equal to the present value of the revenue stream of $24,000. The implication of this exposure is that the U.S. company will have to enter into a hedging strategy that has a present value of $24,000. In the second example, the company incurs its expenses in the U.K, which reduces the amount of its exposure to the present value of the free cash flows of $8,000. The hedge would be the opposite stream of £-denominated cash flows as those in the U.K. Sub—in this case, the U.S. Parent would need £-denominated expenses or a £-denominated liability to offset the cash flows in the U.K. Sub. Naturally, measuring exchange rate exposure is more difficult when measuring more complex relationships—for example, direct and indirect effects of changes in the exchange rates on a company and its competitors.

Valuation Key 17.12

Exchange rate exposure exists when the value of an asset or liability changes because of unexpected exchange rate changes. Cross-border ownership of a company usually results in exchange rate exposure, for, by their nature, unexpected changes in exchange rates affect the value of the firm. We classify economic exchange rate exposure into three types—operating exposure, transaction exposure, and financing exposure. Another type of exchange rate exposure is translation exposure, but this is not an economic exposure.

REVIEW EXERCISE 17.7

Measuring Exchange Rate Exposure

A company is located in France (French Sub) and owned by a company in the U.K. (U.K. Parent). French Sub purchases its products from U.K. Parent in transactions denominated in £. The Year 1 expected cash revenue for France Sub is €1.85 million. The total cost of its products is £0.99 million, and it has no other expenses. French Sub has no capital expenditure requirements and is financed with only common equity. For simplicity, we also assume that no taxes will be levied on the income of French Sub. Assume that the £ discount rate for the free cash flows is 12%, that the French Sub has a zero expected growth rate in perpetuity, and that the current and expected future exchange rate is 0.9 £/€. Measure the value of the French Sub in £. Measure the value of the firm assuming the £/€ exchange rate unexpectedly changes to 0.990; do this again assuming that the exchange rate unexpectedly changes to 0.810. Measure the U.K. Parent's exposure to the euro, and measure the change in the U.K. company's exposure to the euro if its French Sub were to purchase its products with transactions denominated in euros at a total cost of €1.10 million.

Solution on page 773.

Transaction and Financial Exchange Rate Exposure

Transaction exposure and financing exposure are conceptually the same economic construct as operating exposure, but they apply to a subset of the cash flow streams of the company and are usually finite in their term. Transaction exchange rate exposure applies to net foreign-currency-denominated transactions that have fixed monetary values in a foreign currency and are fixed (or agreed upon) at a time prior to the date the transaction settles (is paid). Examples include fixed price sales, purchase contracts, receivables, and payables stated in terms of a foreign currency. Financial exchange rate exposure applies to the net foreign-currency-denominated financing instruments issued by the company. The common example of such exposure is a company issuing a debt instrument with payments that are denominated in a foreign currency. The common reason a company issues such a debt instrument is to hedge against either transaction or operating exchange rate exposure. Companies operating in countries with less stable exchange rates sometimes issue debt securities denominated in the currency of a country that has more stable exchange rates.

Translation Exposure

Companies that consolidate their foreign subsidiaries' financial statements must translate the foreign-currency-denominated financial statements into the parent company's currency. Accounting regulatory bodies throughout the world have rules that companies must follow when they translate the financial statements of their foreign subsidiaries to their own currency. These rules have the company translate the foreign-currency-denominated income statement and balance sheet, which often creates a translation gain or loss that is shown in either the income statement or the retained earnings section of the balance sheet. Thus, in addition to economic exchange rate exposure, companies also have translation exchange rate exposure. These translation gains and losses, however, do not generally represent a change in the value of the firm. Thus, translation exposure may relate more to the uncertainty of a company's accounting-based earnings and balance sheet due to the effects of foreign currency translation.

Should Managers Hedge?

What is a hedge? A **hedge** is the creation of a position in an asset or liability that has the opposite risk of the risk the investor or company is attempting to eliminate. If the asset or liability is completely hedged, the value of the company will no longer be affected by that risk. For example, assume that a U.S. company enters into a contract to purchase inventory with a payment of £100 due in three months and that the company wants to hedge its exposure to unexpected $/£ exchange rate fluctuations. If the company does not hedge its contracted £100 payment due in three months, it is subject to exchange rate risk or fluctuations in the value of a USD relative to a £. In summary, the company has a £100 liability position that has $/£ exchange rate exposure. The company can hedge this exposure if it creates an asset position with the same $/£ exchange rate exposure. For example, the company can convert USD today and invest them in a £-denominated money market account such that at the end of three months the value of the money market account will be £100.

The goal of hedging is not to change the expected value of the asset or liability; rather, the goal of hedging is to eliminate or at least reduce the uncertainty about an expected value. As we saw from the two examples in Exhibit 17.12, both companies have the same firm value of $8,000; however, the second company, which hedged part of its exchange rate exposure from revenues with expenses, had less exposure to unexpected $/£ fluctuations as a result of this hedge. This is a common hedging method used in such circumstances. For example, Toyota, one of the world's largest producers of automobiles, produces most of the cars sold in the United States within the United States.[31]

---

[31] See, Fantz, Ashley, "What Makes a Car American?" CNN, December 12, 2008, http://articles.cnn.com/2008-12-12/us/american.cars_1_foreign-brands-dutch-mandel-american-car?_s=PM:US, accessed October 22, 2011.

Valuation Key 17.13

A hedge is the creation of a position in an asset or liability that has the opposite risk of the risk the investor or company is attempting to eliminate in order for the investor or company to be unaffected by that risk. The goal of hedging is not to change the expected value of the asset or liability, but rather, it is to eliminate or at least reduce the uncertainty about the expected value that an investor or company faces.

Before we discuss hedging methods in more detail, we must first consider whether a company should hedge against exchange rate exposure. Recall that hedging does not change the value of the hedged asset or liability in its own right. At best, it is a zero net present value activity; thus, it may not be in the company's interest—or the shareholders' interest—to hedge its exchange rate exposures unless it can create value through some other means or its shareholders do not want to bear a risk that they are unable to effectively hedge. The primary argument against hedging is that shareholders can hedge such risk themselves in their own investment portfolios. An investor can hold a portfolio that naturally diversifies this risk. As such, any hedging the company does is unnecessary.

It may be possible, however, for hedging to have a positive effect on the value of the firm.[32] For example, if hedging reduces the probability of financial distress, it can reduce expected financial distress costs, other agency costs, or the cost of capital. Hedging might also allow the company to have better strategic planning and to better execute its strategic plan. Further, if additional volatility due to exchange rate fluctuations creates noise in the public information about a company that its management cannot credibly disentangle for investors, then hedging may provide better information to investors. Finally, if management has a comparative information advantage that allows it to hedge more effectively than shareholders are able, and if shareholders want to hedge that risk, then hedging can potentially create value.[33]

Valuation Key 17.14

Since hedging does not increase value in its own right, it may not be in the shareholders' interest for a company to hedge. The primary argument against hedging is that shareholders can hedge such risk themselves via investment strategy. Hedging can have a positive effect on the value of the firm if hedging reduces the probability of financial distress, thereby reducing expected financial distress costs, other agency costs, or the cost of capital. Hedging might also allow the company to have better strategic planning, better execute its strategic plan, and increase informational transparency for its investors.

What Methods Can a Company Use to Hedge Its Exchange Rate Exposure?

It is easier for a company to hedge against transaction and financing exposure as opposed to operating exposure. To perfectly hedge exposure, we must identify a matching asset or liability that has an expected cash flow stream with the opposite exposure and that perfectly matches—in timing (and thus term) and in magnitude—the cash flow stream we are hedging. In other words, we match both the value and the duration of the asset or liability position we are hedging. Since the timing (duration) and magnitude of transactions and financing instruments are typically contractually set, it is easier to identify an appropriate hedging instrument for these risks. However, a company does not want to hedge all of its contracts that are denominated in foreign currency, for it will likely incur more hedging costs than necessary. A company should examine its net exchange rate exposure across all of its transactions and hedge only the net exposure.

Financial hedges are the most direct way to hedge transaction or financing exchange rate exposure. Examples of such hedging instruments include forward exchange rate contracts, exchange rate futures contracts, and **currency swaps** (two companies agree to swap a specified amount of currency at a specified

---

[32] See Smithson, C., and B. J. Simkins, "Does Risk Management Add Value? A Survey of the Evidence," *Journal of Applied Corporate Finance* 17 (2005), pp. 8–17, for a review of the literature on this issue.

[33] See DeMarzo, P. M., and D. Duffie, "Corporate Financial Hedging with Proprietary Information," *Journal of Economic Theory* 53 (1991), pp. 261–286; and DeMarzo, P. M., and D. Duffie, "Corporate Incentives for Hedging and Hedge Accounting," *Review of Financial Studies* 8 (1995), pp. 743–771.

rate). To hedge liability positions, we can convert the appropriate amount of home currency into foreign currency and invest the foreign currency in money market investments. Conversely, for asset positions, we can borrow the appropriate amount of foreign currency, convert it into home currency, and invest it domestically. A characteristic that financial hedges tend to share is that the amount and duration of the foreign currency hedged is set contractually. That is why they can be useful methods for hedging transaction or financial exposure, but they are not as useful for hedging operational exchange rate exposure.

The more efficient way for a company to hedge its operating exposure is by using an operating hedge or real hedge from another part of its operations. In the first scenario shown at the top of Exhibit 17.12, the U.S. company is exposed to $/£ risk because the U.K. company's revenues are in £. Thus, the entire revenue stream is exposed to unexpected changes in the $/£ exchange rate. In the second example, the company used a partial operating hedge by incurring the costs of the U.K. company in £. An alternative way the U.S. company could have hedged this exposure was to purchase inputs for its U.S. production from suppliers in the U.K. Assuming the U.S. company could purchase £1,200 in inputs annually that is equal to the £1,200 of revenue from the U.K. subsidiary and that changes in the cash flow from purchases were perfectly correlated with the changes in the U.K. company's revenues, the U.S. company would have a perfect hedge. Any change in the USD value of the U.K. company resulting from an unexpected change in the exchange rate would be completely offset by a change in the present value of the cost of future inputs purchased in the U.K. Naturally, such hedges have to make financial sense in their own right; for example, the U.S. company would not begin purchasing inputs in the U.K. if the cost was higher than purchasing them in the United States; but, if the costs were the same, the U.S. company could use its purchases in the U.K. as a real hedge. More broadly, companies can use outsourcing, procurement of various inputs, the location of their production facilities, and sales and marketing management strategies to manage exchange rate risks.

SUMMARY AND KEY CONCEPTS

In this chapter, we discussed how to adjust our valuation methods for a cross-border acquisition. The major changes to our normal valuation methodology include forecasting exchange rates to measure the expected cash flows; estimating the cost of capital for a cross-border acquisition using alternative views of the capital markets (particularly the segmented and integrated views); incorporating the complexities of two (and potentially more) tax regimes in our valuation; and adjusting for political and country risk. While this chapter has primarily discussed these issues in the context of a cross-border acquisition, everything discussed is also relevant for the valuation of a multinational firm or a project in a foreign country. In addition, we discussed the topic of exposure to foreign currency exchange rate risk and how firms might hedge that risk.

Suffice it to say that valuing cross-border acquisitions and multinational companies is more time consuming and more complex than valuing a company whose activities are all within the confines of a single country.

ADDITIONAL READING AND REFERENCES

Brunera, R. F., R. M. Conroya, J. Estradab, M. Kritzmanc, and W. Lia, "Introduction to Valuation in Emerging Markets," *Emerging Markets Review* 3 (2002), pp. 310–324.

Stulz, René M., "Globalization of Capital Markets and the Cost of Capital: The Case of Nestlé," *Journal of Applied Corporate Finance* (Fall 1995), pp. 30–38.

EXERCISES AND PROBLEMS

P17.1 **Investor Currency (Centralized) and Foreign Currency (Decentralized) DCF Approaches—Spain/Russia:** A company in Spain is acquiring a company in Russia, and the Spanish company is attempting to value the Russian company in euros. After repatriation, taxes, and country-related risks are taken into consideration, the free cash flow forecasts of the Russian company for the next three years, stated in rubles, are 322.2 RUB million, 365.4 RUB million, and 430.7 RUB million, respectively; also, the continuing value of the company as of the end of Year 3 is 4,290.2 RUB million. The appropriate risk-adjusted discount rate for this company's cash flows, stated in euros, is 11% and is constant in each year. Both companies are only financed with common equity. Use the information in Exhibit P17.1 to measure the value of the Russian company in euros under both the investor currency and foreign currency discounted cash flow methods.

EXHIBIT P17.1	Selected Euro Exchange Rates						
				Forward Rates			
		Spot Rate	**1 Year**	**2 Year**	**3 Year**	**4 Year**	**5 Year**
U.S. Dollar (USD)/Euro							
Exchange rate		1.425	1.412	1.402	1.394	1.390	1.393
U.K. Pound (GBP)/Euro							
Exchange rate		0.874	0.870	0.867	0.866	0.864	0.864
Russian Ruble/Euro							
Exchange rate		39.613	40.841	42.462	44.297	46.348	48.231

P17.2 **Investor Currency (Centralized) and Foreign Currency (Decentralized) DCF Approaches—U.K./ France:** A company in the U.K. is acquiring a company in France, and the U.K. company is attempting to value the French company in GBP. After repatriation, taxes, and country-related risks are taken into consideration, the free cash flow forecasts of the French company for the next three years, stated in Euros, are €22.2 million, €25.4 million, and €30.7 million, respectively; also, the continuing value of the company as of the end of Year 3 is €290.5 million. The appropriate risk-adjusted discount rate for this company's cash flows, stated in GBP, is 14% and is constant in each year. Both companies are only financed with common equity. Use the information in Exhibit P17.1 to measure the value of the French company in GBP under both the investor currency and foreign currency discounted cash flow methods.

P17.3 **Exchange Rates:** Use the information in Exhibit P17.1 to calculate the following exchange rates: U.S. Dollar (USD) / U.K. Pound (GBP), Russian Ruble / U.S. Dollar (USD), and Russian Ruble / U.K. Pound (GBP).

P17.4 **Exchange Rate Forecasts—U.K. Pound (GBP) / Polish Zloty:** Use the information in Exhibits 17.5 and P17.2 to forecast the U.K. Pound (GBP) / Polish Zloty exchange rate for the next five years using relative purchasing power parity and uncovered interest rate parity, and compare these forecasts to the forward rates.

EXHIBIT P17.2	Poland Exchange Rates, Inflation Rates, and Interest Rates						
				Forward Rates			
		Spot Rate	**1 Year**	**2 Year**	**3 Year**	**4 Year**	**5 Year**
U.S. Dollar (USD)/Polish Zloty							
Exchange rate		0.357	0.345	0.336	0.320	0.306	0.300
U.K. Pound (GBP)/Polish Zloty							
Exchange rate		0.219	0.213	0.208	0.199	0.190	0.186
Russian Ruble/Polish Zloty							
Exchange rate		9.911	9.985	10.167	10.160	10.201	10.373
Poland							
Interest rate.			4.10%	4.50%	5.40%	6.00%	6.20%
Inflation rate			5.50%	5.00%	4.80%	4.80%	4.80%
Implied real rate			−1.33%	−0.48%	0.57%	1.15%	1.34%

P17.5 **Exchange Rate Forecasts—Russian Ruble / Polish Zloty:** Use the information in Exhibits 17.5 and P17.2 to forecast the Russian Ruble / Polish Zloty exchange rate for the next five years using relative purchasing power parity and uncovered interest rate parity, and compare these forecasts to the forward rates.

P17.6 **Worldwide (Resident) and Territorial (Source) Tax Regimes:** A foreign subsidiary of a French company has the equivalent of €100,000 in taxable income. The foreign income tax rate is 25% on all income with a 10% withholding tax on dividends; the French income tax rate is 50%.

a. Calculate the income taxes payable based on both a territorial tax regime and a worldwide tax regime, assuming the parent company pays out all of the foreign subsidiary's after-tax income in dividends to the parent company.

b. Calculate the income taxes payable based on both a territorial tax regime and a worldwide tax regime, assuming the parent company pays out none of the foreign subsidiary's after-tax income in dividends.

P17.7 **Country-Specific Risks—1:** A company operates in a country that has undergone a revolution and now has a new military controlled government. It is unclear whether the new government will expropriate the assets of the company. If the new government expropriates the assets of the company, the company will be paid $0 for its assets. The probability of expropriation is equal to 60% in Year 1; if no expropriation takes place in Year 1, the probability of expropriation in Year 2 is 30%; and if no expropriation takes place in Year 1 or Year 2, the probability of expropriation in Year 3 is 10%; and 0% thereafter if expropriation does not occur in the first three years. The Year 0 free cash flow for the company is $10,000. The company expects its cash flow to grow at -10% in Years 1 through 3 if the economy is doing well and -20% in each of those years if the economy is doing poorly. The probability of the economy doing well is 20% for Years 1 through 3. After Year 3, the economy and the company's free cash flows are expected to grow at 3% in perpetuity for all outcomes. The company's discount rate is equal to 18%.

a. Measure the value of the firm for both economic scenarios (economy doing well and economy doing poorly), ignoring the potential expropriation of the company's assets; then measure the value of the firm under both economic scenarios while including the effects of the potential expropriation.

b. Measure the value of the firm for both economic scenarios while including the effects of the potential expropriation of the company's assets and assuming the probability of expropriation is 1% per year instead of 0% in Year 4 onward.

P17.8 **Country-Specific Risks—2:** A company operates in a country that is in political turmoil, and there is a possibility that it will experience a revolution in which the military will depose the current president. If the country experiences high growth in Year 1, which will continue through Year 3, the country's president will remain in power, and the company's free cash flows will grow at 25% in Years 1 through 3 and 5% thereafter. The probability of the country having high growth in Year 1 is 10%. If the country experiences low growth in Year 1, which will continue through Year 3, the country has an 80% probability of having a revolution in either Year 2 or Year 3. If the country experiences low growth in a given year but the president remains in power, the company's free cash flows will grow at 1% through Year 3 and 5% thereafter. If the president is deposed, the company will have a negative growth rate of 35% in the year he/she is deposed through Year 3, and it will have a growth rate of 5% thereafter. If the president is not deposed by Year 3, the president will not be deposed subsequently, and the country's and company's free cash flows will grow at 5% per year. The company's discount rate is 18%, and its Year 0 free cash flow is $800. Measure the value of the firm, but ignore the possibility of the president being deposed; do this again, but this time, factor in the possibility of the president being deposed.

P17.9 **Exchange Rate Exposure:** A company is located in the U.S. (U.S. Sub) and owned by a company in the U.K. (U.K. Parent). U.S. Sub purchases its products from U.K. Parent in transactions denominated in £. The Year 1 expected cash revenue for U.S. Sub is $22.5 million. The total cost of its products is £9.1 million, and it has no other expenses. U.S. Sub has no capital expenditure requirements and is financed with only common equity. For simplicity, assume that no taxes will be levied on the income of U.S. Sub. Assume that the £ discount rate for the £-denominated free cash flows is 14%, that the U.S. Sub has a zero expected growth rate in perpetuity, and that the current and expected future exchange rate is 0.5 £/$. Measure the value of the U.S. Sub in £.

a. Measure the value of the firm assuming the £/$ exchange rate unexpectedly changed to 0.6.

b. Measure the value of the firm assuming the £/$ exchange rate unexpectedly changed to 0.4.

c. Measure the U.K. Company's exposure to the USD.

d. Measure the change in U.K. company's exposure to the USD if its U.S. Sub purchased its products with transactions denominated in $ at a total cost of $18.2 million rather than from the U.K. Parent.

SOLUTIONS FOR REVIEW EXERCISES

Review Exercise 17.1: Investor Currency (Centralized) and Foreign Currency (Decentralized) Discounted Cash Flow Valuation Approaches

Investor Currency/Centralized Approach	Year 0	Year 1	Year 2	Year 3	CV$_{\text{Firm, Yr 3}}$
Free cash flow and continuing value (in USD × 1,000)..............................		$1,200.0	$1,400.0	$1,700.0	$180,000.0
Exchange rate forecast (USD/Euro)		1.412	1.402	1.394	1.394
Free cash flow and continuing value (Euro)		€ 849.9	€ 998.6	€1,219.5	€129,124.8
Risk-adjusted discount factor for Euro	12.0%	0.893	0.797	0.712	0.712
Present value		€ 758.80	€ 796.06	€ 868.02	€91,908.50
Value of the firm (in Euro × 1,000)	€94,331.38				

Foreign Currency/Decentralized Approach	Year 0	Year 1	Year 2	Year 3	CV$_{\text{Firm, Yr 3}}$
Free cash flow and continuing value (in USD × 1,000).............................		$ 1,200.0	$ 1,400.0	$ 1,700.0	$180,000.0
Risk-adjusted discount rate for USD r$_\$$		10.978%	11.207%	11.361%	11.361%
Discount factor for foreign currency (USD)		0.901	0.810	0.728	0.728
Present value in foreign currency...................		$ 1,081.3	$ 1,134.4	$ 1,236.9	$130,969.6
Value of the firm	$134,422.2				
Current or spot exchange rate (USD/Euro)	1.425				
Value of the firm	€ 94,331.4				

Review Exercise 17.2: Discount Rates for the Investor Currency (Centralized) and Foreign Currency (Decentralized) Approaches

Investor to Foreign Discount Rate	Year 1	Year 2	Year 3
Exchange rate forecast = Forward rate (USD/Euro) in period t....................	1.412	1.402	1.394
Exchange rate forecast = Forward rate (USD/Euro) in period t-1	1.425	1.412	1.402
Ratio ≈ (1 + r$_\$$)/(1 + r$_€$) ≈ (1 + i$_\$$)/(1 + i$_€$)	0.991	0.993	0.994
One + Risk-adjusted discount rate for Euros, r$_€$.....................................	1.120	1.120	1.120
Risk-adjusted discount rate in foreign currency, r$_\$$	10.978%	11.207%	11.361%

Exhibit may contain small rounding errors

Review Exercise 17.3: Exchange Rate Forecasts

	Spot Rate	Forward Rates and Forecasts				
		1 Year	2 Year	3 Year	4 Year	5 Year
U.S. Dollar (USD)/Polish Zloty						
Actual	0.357	0.345	0.336	0.320	0.306	0.300
RPPP		0.343	0.333	0.324	0.315	0.307
		−0.4%	−0.8%	1.3%	3.1%	2.3%
UIRP		0.344	0.330	0.315	0.301	0.289
		−0.4%	−1.8%	−1.6%	−1.7%	−3.6%

Review Exercise 17.4: Worldwide (Resident) and Territorial (Source) Tax Regimes

Foreign Income Tax

Foreign taxable income	£10,000.0
Foreign income tax rate	30.0%
Foreign income tax liability.	£ 3,000.0
After-tax foreign income.	£ 7,000.0
Territorial effective tax rate w/o WH tax	30.0%

Foreign Dividend Withholding (WH) Tax

Dividend payout ratio	100.0%
Dividend declared	£ 7,000.0
Withholding tax rate	5.0%
Withholding tax	£ 350.0
Dividend distributed	£ 6,650.0
Total foreign tax liability	£ 3,350.0
Territorial effective tax rate after WH tax	33.5%

Investor Country Income Tax

Foreign income tax liability.	£ 3,000.0
Dividend payout ratio	100.0%
Allocated foreign income tax liability	£ 3,000.0
Dividend declared	7,000.0
Investor country taxable income	£10,000.0
Investor country tax rate	45.0%
Investor country tax before credits.	£ 4,500.0
Foreign tax credit for foreign income tax	−3,000.0
Foreign tax credit for foreign WH tax	−350.0
Additional U.K. income tax.	£ 1,150.0

Worldwide Tax (After Foreign Tax Credits)

Total worldwide tax.	£ 4,500.0
Total worldwide tax rate	45.0%

Review Exercise 17.5: Country-Specific Risks—1

Scenario and Expected Cash Flow Valuation Excluding Effect of the Political Risk

Economy Doing	Scenario Prob	Probabilty Weighted Value	% of Value	Scenario Present Value	Year 1	Year 2	Year 3	$CV_{Year\ 3}$
Well	0.250	$4,063.01	43.9%	$16,252.05	$1,300.00	$1,690.00	$2,197.00	$18,857.58
Poorly	0.750	$5,183.25	56.1%	$ 6,911.00	$ 950.00	$ 902.50	$ 857.38	$ 7,359.14
	1.000	$9,246.26						
Expected cash flow valuation				$ 9,246.26	$1,037.50	$1,099.38	$1,192.28	$10,233.75

Scenario and Expected Cash Flow Valuation Including Effect of the Political Risk

Economy Doing	Scenario Prob	Probabilty Weighted Value	% of Value	Scenario Present Value	Year 1	Year 2	Year 3	$CV_{Year\ 3}$
Well	0.250	$3,374.38	43.6%	$13,497.51	$1,274.00	$1,623.08	$2,067.80	$14,908.83
Poorly	0.750	$4,365.80	56.4%	$ 5,821.07	$ 931.00	$ 866.76	$ 806.95	$ 5,818.14
	1.000	$7,740.18						
Expected cash flow valuation		−16%		$ 7,740.18	$1,016.75	$1,055.84	$1,122.17	$ 8,090.81

Solution for Review Exercise 15.3: Weighted Average Cost of Capital-Based Exit Values

Weighted average cost of capital valuation

	r_E	r_D	V_D/V_F	T_{INT}	r_{WACC}	Continuing Value Growth Rate
	10.033%	5.900%	25.000%	40.000%	8.410%	3.000%

($ in millions)	Year 0	Year 1	Year 2	Year 3	Year 4	Year 5	Year 6	Year 7	Year 8	Year 9	Year 10
Weighted average cost of capital valuation of the firm	$3,054.4	$3,052.2	$3,028.2	$2,957.2	$2,892.8	$2,889.4	$2,868.5	$2,923.2	$3,106.4	$3,164.2	$3,260.2
Value of debt	2,060.0	1,894.4	1,702.5	1,459.9	1,222.6	1,044.6	842.3	706.5	688.7	529.1	393.1
Weighted average cost of capital valuation of the equity	$ 994.4	$1,157.8	$1,325.7	$1,497.3	$1,670.2	$1,844.8	$2,026.2	$2,216.8	$2,417.8	$2,635.1	$2,867.1
EBITDA	$ 346.1	$ 316.8	$ 424.2	$ 493.1	$ 566.8	$ 589.5	$ 613.1	$ 631.5	$ 588.5	$ 542.3	$ 492.9
Implied firm value to EBITDA	8.826	9.635	7.138	5.997	5.104	4.902	4.679	4.629	5.279	5.835	6.615

Exit Value Multiple and Values Used

	Year 0	Year 1	Year 2	Year 3	Year 4	Year 5	Year 6	Year 7	Year 8	Year 9	Year 10
Deal multiple—firm value to EBITDA		8.310	8.310	8.310	8.310	8.310	8.310	8.310	8.310	8.310	8.310
% difference with weighted average cost of capital valuation		-13.7%	16.4%	38.6%	62.8%	69.5%	77.6%	79.5%	57.4%	42.4%	25.6%
Exit value—equity		$ 738.2	$1,822.9	$2,637.9	$3,487.7	$3,854.1	$4,252.3	$4,541.0	$4,201.5	$3,977.6	$3,702.7
% difference with weighted average cost of capital valuation		-36.2%	37.5%	76.2%	108.8%	108.9%	109.9%	104.9%	73.8%	50.9%	29.1%

($ in millions)		Year 0	Year 1	Year 2	Year 3	Year 4	Year 5	Year 6	Year 7	Year 8	Year 9	Year 10
Exit value—firm (weighted average cost of capital valuation)			$3,052.2	$3,028.2	$2,957.2	$2,892.8	$2,889.4	$2,868.5	$2,923.2	$3,106.4	$3,164.2	$3,260.2
Exit value—equity			$1,157.8	$1,325.7	$1,497.3	$1,670.2	$1,844.8	$2,026.2	$2,216.8	$2,417.8	$2,635.1	$2,867.1
Sponsor (% fully diluted participation in exit)		75.1%										
Investment		$ -730.0										
Fees		$28.8										
Dividends	None											
Other payments	None											
Participation in exit			$ 869.8	$ 995.9	$1,124.8	$1,254.7	$1,385.8	$1,522.1	$1,665.3	$1,816.3	$1,979.6	$2,153.8
Net cash flow		$ -701.2	$ 869.8	$ 995.9	$1,124.8	$1,254.7	$1,385.8	$1,522.1	$1,665.3	$1,816.3	$1,979.6	$2,153.8

IRR	Exit Yr	Year 0	Year 1	Year 2	Year 3	Year 4	Year 5	Year 6	Year 7	Year 8	Year 9	Year 10
24.0%	Year 1	$ -701.2	$ 869.8									
19.2%	Year 2	-701.2	0.0	$ 995.9								
17.1%	Year 3	-701.2	0.0	0.0	$1,124.8							
15.7%	Year 4	-701.2	0.0	0.0	0.0	$1,254.7						
14.6%	Year 5	-701.2	0.0	0.0	0.0	0.0	$1,385.8					
13.8%	Year 6	-701.2	0.0	0.0	0.0	0.0	0.0	$1,522.1				
13.2%	Year 7	-701.2	0.0	0.0	0.0	0.0	0.0	0.0	$1,665.3			
12.6%	Year 8	-701.2	0.0	0.0	0.0	0.0	0.0	0.0	0.0	$1,816.3		
12.2%	Year 9	-701.2	0.0	0.0	0.0	0.0	0.0	0.0	0.0	0.0	$1,979.6	
11.9%	Year 10	-701.2	0.0	0.0	0.0	0.0	0.0	0.0	0.0	0.0	0.0	$2,153.8

Exhibt may contain small rounding errors

Valuation Key 16.1

Economic forces drive mergers and acquisitions. The reasons for mergers in industries vary over time with the life cycle of the industry and other economic factors. Whatever the motivation for an acquisition, it should be tied to the company's strategy and serve to either establish, enhance, and/or protect the company's competitive advantage.

Do Merger and Acquisition Transactions Create Value, and If They Do, for Whom?

A large number of studies from both academics and consulting firms have addressed this issue in various ways. The most common way to assess value creation is to examine the short-run stock market performances of the acquirer and target around the time the acquisition is announced and between the time of announcement and the close of the transaction. Other studies examine long-run stock market performance or long-run operating performance (normally one to three years after the acquisition). Using stock market performance to draw conclusions about gains in economic efficiency and value creation assumes that market participants understand the implications of acquisitions—either at the time of announcement or subsequent to the acquisition—as they observe post-merger performance and price the stocks accordingly. Since these studies do not examine individual acquisitions but instead examine a large sample of acquisitions, it might be possible that the market does not understand the ramifications of one particular acquisition, but it is much harder to argue that it does not understand (at least on average) the implications across a large sample of acquisitions.

This evidence suggests that mergers and acquisitions are generally good for economic efficiency; in other words, if we look at the combined returns to the acquirer and the target (weighted by their respective market values), they are, on average, positive when adjusted for overall stock market performance in that period. Thus, acquisitions improve economic efficiency. However, who captures the value creation from the increases in economic efficiency? The evidence indicates that, on average, the preponderance of the gains (if not all of the gains) go to the target shareholders. Risk-adjusted stock returns to target shareholders are significant and positive whereas most studies show modest negative returns to acquirers, indicating that, on average, the target companies capture all of the wealth creation and maybe even more. In some studies, these negative returns are statistically significant, and in other studies, they are not. What is clear from the literature is that many acquisitions turn out to be either zero net present value projects or negative net present value projects for the acquirer. Analyzing the three years subsequent to the merger, Mitchell and Stafford (2000) show that, on average, acquirers lose 5% and that these returns are significantly negative.[8] However, there is large variation around the average, and some transactions create substantial value whereas others destroy substantial value.

Some studies attempt to discern the factors that are associated with better or worse performance for the acquirer. The evidence strongly indicates that mergers financed with stock, as opposed to no stock, are more likely to experience negative returns. Mitchell and Stafford (2000) show that acquisitions financed with stock lost, on average, 9% over the three years following an acquisition, whereas those financed with no stock lost only 1.4%. A potential explanation for this result is that managers are more likely to use stock to finance an acquisition if they believe that their stock is overvalued, leading them to buy some hard assets before the market discovers that the stock is overvalued. As such, using stock may be a signal to the market that it has overvalued the acquiring company. An alternative reason companies use stock to acquire other companies is insufficient cash and debt capacity for the acquisition; to help secure a particular tax treatment and deal structure; and to share the risk of the transaction with the target.

Unfortunately, even though all of these studies attempt to control for the overall market or industry performance of the non-acquirers, it is difficult to ascertain what would have happened to an acquirer's stock price if an acquisition were not financed with stock. A recent paper by Savor and Qu (2009) suggests that most of the negative stock performance associated with acquisitions financed with stock is due to the overvaluation of the stock and not due to managers using their paper currency too loosely or paying too

---

[8] There are hundreds of studies that have examined the stock price and accounting performance associated with mergers and acquisitions. Two studies that examine a sample over many years are M. Mitchell and E. Stafford, "Managerial Decisions and Long-Term Stock Price Performance," *Journal of Business* 73 (2000), pp. 287–329 and G. Andrade, M. Mitchell and E. Stafford, "New Evidence and Perspectives on Mergers," *Journal of Economic Perspectives* 15 (2001), pp. 103–120.

($10,380 = $14,380 − $4,000). The stock price is equal to the equity value divided by the number of shares outstanding, $20.76 ($20.76 = $10,380/500)—about 4% higher than the acquirer's pre-merger stock price. Why does the stock price increase (i.e., why is the merger accretive to value)?

The pre-merger value of the target's equity is $4,240. We can add this value to the value of the synergies and the value resulting from the incremental interest tax shields, $6,380 ($6,380 = $4,240 + $320 + $800 + $1,020), and compare it to the price paid, $6,000. Based on this comparison, we see that the target is paid $380 less than the total value created by the merger. The remaining amount increases the acquirer's stock price by $0.76 per share ($0.76 = $380/500). Since earnings per share increases by more than 50% ($1.956/$1.280) while the stock price only increases by 4%, the P/E ratio decreases from 15.6 to 10.6.

As we stated earlier, even though we can expect synergies to increase the value of the firm, we cannot assume that this will increase the post-merger market multiple. Recall that a company's price-to-earnings multiple is a function of both its risk-adjusted return and long-term growth rate. Since the long-term growth rate for the synergies may be smaller than the long-term growth rates for the combining companies, the multiple for the synergies may be smaller than the multiple of either of the two companies as well. We illustrate a similar situation in our example, and in the last two columns of Exhibit 16.8, we add the value of the synergies to our analysis and see that the synergies have a P/E multiple of 10, which is smaller than the acquirer's P/E multiple of 15.6.

REVIEW EXERCISE 16.3

Effect of Accretion on Market Multiples

Use the information in Review Exercise 16.2 to measure the post-merger firm value, equity value, stock price, and P/E multiple. Compare these values to the acquirer's standalone values. (An analysis similar to that presented in Exhibit 16.8.)

Solution on page 717.

In closing, even if an acquisition has no synergies, an acquirer's earnings per share can increase from an acquisition if the target is profitable. For example, assuming that the companies maintain their pre-merger valuations after merging and that the transaction has no synergies, an acquirer with a high P/E ratio will increase its earnings per share when it acquires a profitable target with a lower P/E ratio. Since the transaction has no synergies, the post-merger P/E ratio must be adjusted downward to offset the upward effect on earnings per share; otherwise, the post-merger valuation of the company will be too high. Of course, companies can also destroy value from an acquisition and their earnings per share can still rise from the transaction.

16.9 NEGOTIATION RANGES AND EXCHANGE RATIOS

LO4 Measure a negotiation range

Naturally, the financial terms of the acquisition are negotiated based on the value of the acquisition, which includes the values of the equity of the standalone companies and the value created by the acquisition, net of all transaction and integration costs. We assume the acquirer and target will not agree to a price that will decrease their pre-merger standalone equity values. In other words, the maximum price that the acquirer will pay is the price at which its equity value is unchanged and the minimum price that the target will accept is the minimum price at which the target's shareholders are not made worse off. Given the post-merger equity value of the company, these constraints set the price range within which the acquirer and target will negotiate. For the purpose of our discussion, we ignore deal-related income taxes and other transaction costs the target would have to bear. For example, if the transaction is taxable to the target's shareholders, it is unlikely that they will agree to a transaction that takes place at the target's current standalone value, because after taxes the target shareholders will be worse off after the transaction. In this section, terms such as standalone value of the acquirer or target, price, post-merger value, and so forth, refer to equity values and not firm values.

Cash Deal

We begin our discussion of negotiation ranges with an example of a cash deal with the following equity values. The standalone values of the target and acquirer are $1,000 and $2,000, respectively. Assume that the

d. Calculate the exchange ratio that would allocate the merger gain based on the relative standalone equity values of the two companies.

e. Based on the actual exchange ratio of 0.9, calculate the post-merger value and the allocation of the merger gain for the shareholders of each company when the actual outcome of the merger is the expected, highest and lowest outcome.

P16.11 **XM Sirius Radio Merger—Negotiation Range and Allocation of Synergies:** See Problem 16.2 for background information for this problem. The stock price of the acquiring company, Sirius, prior to the merger announcement was approximately $3.7 per share, and Sirius had 1,460 million shares outstanding. XM, the target company, had a stock price around $14 and 314 million shares outstanding. Assume the value of the synergies (merger gain) was expected to be $1 billion but ranged from a loss of $2 billion to a gain of $3 billion. The companies agreed to an exchange ratio of 4.6.

a. Calculate the exchange ratio that would allocate 70% of the post-merger value to Sirius shareholders.
b. Calculate the minimum exchange ratio that XM shareholders would be willing to accept.
c. Calculate the maximum exchange ratio that Sirius shareholders would be willing to accept.
d. Calculate the exchange ratio that would allocate the merger gain based on the relative standalone equity values of the two companies.
e. Based on the actual exchange ratio of 4.6, calculate the post-merger value and the allocation of the merger gain for the shareholders of each company when the actual outcome of the merger is the expected, highest and lowest outcome.

SOLUTIONS FOR REVIEW EXERCISES

Review Exercise 16.1: Valuing Synergies—LATAM Airlines Group

| Weighted Average Cost of Capital Valuation of Synergies: | 10.00% | | g= | −10.00% |
| Tax rate = | 30.0% | | | |

($ in millions)	Low	High	Midpoint			
Passenger revenue.	$225	$260	$243			
Cargo revenue	120	125	123			
	$345	$385	$365			
Frequent flyer program consolidation	$ 15	$ 25	$ 20			
Airport/procurement.	100	135	118			
Maintenance.	20	25	23			
Information technology and other	120	130	125			
	$255	$315	$285			
	$600	$700	$650			
Reduced investment in working capital	$150	$150	$150			
Integration costs and fees	$170	$200	$185			
First year synergies	$171	$200	$185	28.5%		

($ in millions)	2012	2013	2014	2015	2016	CV 2016
Cumulative percentage of synergies achieved		28.5%	50.0%	80.0%	100.0%	
Pre-tax revenue synergies		$103.9	$182.5	$292.0	$365.0	$ 328.5
Pre-tax cost synergies		81.1	142.5	228.0	285.0	256.5
Integration costs and fees	$−185.0					
Less: taxes on synergies and costs.	55.5	−55.5	−97.5	−156.0	−195.0	−175.5
Reduced investment in working capital savings		150.0				
After-tax costs, fees, synergies and other	$−129.5	$279.5	$227.5	$364.0	$455.0	$ 409.5
Discount factor for continuing value						5.000
Unlevered free cash flow and CV.	$−129.5	$279.5	$227.5	$364.0	$455.0	$2,047.5
Discount factor.	0.953	0.867	0.788	0.716	0.651	0.651
Present value	$−123.5	$242.3	$179.3	$260.8	$296.3	$1,333.4
Value of synergies.	$2,188.5					

Exhibit may contain small rounding errors

In addition, as we discussed earlier, investors can purchase forward contracts for many currencies and horizons. Assuming no arbitrage and free movement of capital such that an investor can freely invest across borders (no market frictions or transactions costs), we can relate forward contract exchange rates to current spot rates using relative interest rates across countries.

Based on these assumptions, an investor can either invest in the home country and earn the home country's interest rate, r_{HC} for a specified period of time (which we assume to be one year) or invest abroad and buy a forward contract to later convert the foreign deposit with foreign interest back to the home currency. If the investor invests abroad, the investor will earn the foreign country's interest rate, r_{FC}, for that certain period, adjusted for the forward rate premium. We call this condition **covered interest rate parity**, because an investor is covered by the forward contract, and the investor is not taking any risk in the transaction (assuming no deposit risk and the forward contract settles up as written). If the costs of investing locally and of investing in a foreign country are identical, then investors will invest in the country that provides the highest return. Given the liquidity and low transaction costs in most of these markets, market forces prevent such arbitrage opportunities from occurring systematically. We observe that covered interest rate parity generally holds for shorter horizons after accounting for transactions costs, income tax effects, and the bid-ask spread. For longer horizons, we not only have higher transactions costs (including larger bid-ask spreads), but we also have an increase in the probability of government intervention—for example, restricting foreign deposits and the ability to move funds out of the country. The empirical evidence on longer horizons is more limited.[5]

Uncovered interest rate parity establishes the relation we would expect if such investors did not use forward contracts to establish a known return but instead made an uncovered investment in another country's bonds (an investment not covered by a forward contract).[6] If the forward rate were an unbiased estimate of the expected future spot rate, the expected returns on a covered and uncovered investment would be the same. However, the covered investment's return is known, and the uncovered investment's return is uncertain. If forward rates are unbiased predictors of expected future spot rates, we can use uncovered interest rate parity for forecasting expected future spot rates. The expected future spot rate is a function of the current spot rate and the relative interest rates in the two countries over the period.

$$S^E_{HC/FC, t+N} = S_{HC/FC, t} \times \frac{(1 + r_{HC})^N}{(1 + r_{FC})^N} \tag{17.2}$$

If interest rates are not constant over time, Equation 17.2 becomes

$$S^E_{HC/FC, t+N} = S_{HC/FC, t} \times \frac{1 + r_{HC, t+1}}{1 + r_{FC, t+1}} \times \frac{1 + r_{HC, t+2}}{1 + r_{FC, t+2}} \times \frac{1 + r_{HC, t+3}}{1 + r_{FC, t+3}} \times \cdots \times \frac{1 + r_{HC, t+N}}{1 + r_{FC, t+N}} \tag{17.3}$$

Continuing our previous example, assume that the current spot exchange rate today (time t) is $S_{HC/FC}$ = 2.0, that the home country's expected annual inflation is 5% annually, and that the foreign country's is 10% annually. In addition to these assumptions, we assume that the interest rate in the home country is 7.1% and that the interest rate in the foreign country is 14.4%. These assumptions assume that the real interest rate is 2% in the home country ($0.02 = 1.071/1.05 - 1$) and 4% in the foreign country ($0.04 = 1.144/1.10 - 1$). Based on this information, uncovered interest rate parity provides a way to forecast the exchange rate using the above equation, which we show for Years 1, 2 and 5 as follows:

$$S^E_{HC/FC, t+1} = 2.0 \times \frac{(1.071)}{(1.144)} = 1.87; \quad S^E_{HC/FC, t+2} = 2.0 \times \frac{(1.071)^2}{(1.144)^2} = 1.75; \quad S^E_{HC/FC, t+5} = 2.0 \times \frac{(1.071)^5}{(1.144)^5} = 1.44$$

The empirical evidence on uncovered interest rate parity is mixed. To the extent it works, it generally works better for longer-horizon forecasts.

The expected exchange rates we calculated based on relative purchasing power parity are all larger than the expected exchange rates we calculated based on uncovered interest rate parity. Why? To answer, the relative difference in the inflation rates, $(1.05)/(1.1)$, is not as large as the relative difference in inter-

---

[5] See, for example, Popper, H., "Long-Term Covered Interest Parity—Evidence from Currency Swaps," *Journal of International Money and Finance* vol. 12, no. 4 (1993), pp. 439–48.

[6] For a review of uncovered interest rate parity and some more recent empirical work, see, Chinn, Menzie D., "The (Partial) Rehabilitation of Interest Rate Parity: Longer Horizons, Alternative Expectations and Emerging Markets," *Journal of International Money and Finance* vol. 25, no. 1 (February 2006), pp. 7–21.

RiskTel's Valuation

Let us consider an example in which we value a telephone company, RiskTel Company, that operates the only mobile and landline telephone service on a remote country-island in the Pacific Ocean. This country-island, Riskie Key, is a fast growing resort island. RiskTel's management developed a financial model with two sets of forecasts based on an assumption about Riskie Key's economic growth—a high-growth and a low-growth scenario. We first value RiskTel without considering economic or political risk. RiskTel has both a high-growth and low-growth scenario. If Riskie Key experiences low growth, RiskTel will have an annual growth of 5% in its free cash flows; if Riskie Key experiences high growth, RiskTel will have an annual growth of 20% in its free cash flows for the first few years. Experts expect Riskie Key's growth scenario—either high growth or low growth—to resolve itself in Year 1 and the growth rates to continue for Years 2 and 3. After Year 3, management expects the company's free cash flows to grow at the inflation rate of 2%, regardless of the growth scenario that occurs in the earlier years. Experts assess a 60% chance of the high-growth scenario occurring and a 40% chance of the low-growth scenario occurring. The Year 0 free cash flow is equal to $100, the discount rate is equal to 12%, and we are valuing RiskTel as of the end of Year 0.

RiskTel's Initial Valuation. We begin by measuring and valuing both the free cash flows for the high- and low-growth scenarios and the expected free cash flows for the management forecasts. We present this analysis in the top section of Exhibit 17.9. The free cash flows for the high-growth scenario are equal to the $100 Year 0 (the base year) free cash flow, multiplied by the appropriate growth rate factor (1.2 in Year 1, 1.2^2 in Year 2, and 1.2^3 in Year 3). Similarly, we measure the free cash flows for the low-growth scenario using a growth rate of 5%.

EXHIBIT 17.9	RiskTel Company Free Cash Flows and Valuation Excluding and Including the Effect of the Extremist Political Party Expropriating Assets

Scenario and Expected Cash Flow Valuation Excluding the Effect of the Political Risk

	Scenario Prob	Probabilty Weighted Value	% of Value	Scenario Present Value	Year 1	Year 2	Year 3	CV$_{Year 3}$
High growth	60%	$ 959.69	68.5%	$1,599.49	$120.00	$144.00	$172.80	$1,762.56
Low growth.	40%	$ 441.80	31.5%	$1,104.49	$105.00	$110.25	$115.76	$1,180.78
	100%	$1,401.49						
Expected Cash Flow Valuation.				$1,401.49	$114.00	$130.50	$149.99	$1,529.85

Scenario and Expected Cash Flow Valuation Including the Effect of the Political Risk

	Scenario Prob	Probabilty Weighted Value	% of Value	Scenario Present Value	Year 1	Year 2	Year 3	CV$_{Year 3}$
High growth	60%	$ 860.09	68.4%	$1,433.49	$118.80	$141.13	$167.67	$1,539.19
Low growth.	40%	$ 397.14	31.6%	$ 992.85	$103.95	$108.06	$112.32	$1,031.14
	100%	$1,257.23						
Expected cash flow valuation.				$1,257.23	$112.86	$127.90	$145.53	$1,335.97

The continuing value is equal to the Year 3 free cash flow, multiplied by the long-term growth rate factor (1.02), and divided by the discount rate (12%) minus the long-term growth rate (2%). The column titled "Scenario Present Value" measures the present value of the discounted free cash flows and the continuing value as of the end of Year 0. The value of the high-growth scenario is $1,599, and the value of the low-growth scenario is $1,104. To measure the value of RiskTel, we weight each of the scenario values by their respective probability; after taking a sum of these weighted values, we arrive at a firm value of $1,401. Alternatively, we can measure the value of RiskTel by first measuring the expected free cash flows and then discounting them. In this case, we measure the expected free cash flows by probability weighting the high- and low-growth cash flows in each year, which we show in the line labeled "Expected cash flow valuation." Both approaches result in the same valuation of $1,401.

Review Exercise 17.6: Country-Specific Risks—2

Scenario and Expected Cash Flow Valuation Excluding Country Default

	Scenario Prob	Probabilty Weighted Value	% of Value	Scenario Present Value	Year 1	Year 2	Year 3	CV$_{Year 3}$
High growth	20.0%	$ 2,792.82	24.8%	$13,964.09	$1,150.00	$1,322.50	$1,520.88	$10,856.64
Low growth.	80.0%	$ 8,461.39	75.2%	$10,576.74	$1,040.00	$1,081.60	$1,124.86	$ 8,029.75
	100.0%	$11,254.21	100.0%					
Expected cash flow valuation				$11,254.21	$1,062.00	$1,129.78	$1,204.07	$ 8,595.13

Scenarios and Expected Cash Flows Including Country Default

High growth rate.	15.0%
Low growth rate	4.0%
Default growth rate.	−20.0%
Discount rate	13.0%
Long-term growth rate	3.0%

	Low Growth		Year 1		No Default		Year 2		No Default		Year 3

Expected cash flow $1,062.00 $1,049.91 $1,007.26
−1.1%   −4.1%

Scenario and Expected Cash Flow Valuation Including Country Default

Growth and Default Year	Scenario Prob	Probabilty Weighted Value	% of Value	Scenario Present Value	Year 1	Year 2	Year 3	CV$_{Year 3}$
1 High—no default	20.0%	$2,792.82	28.9%	$13,964.09	$1,150.00	$1,322.50	$1,520.88	$15,665.01
2 Low—Year 2 default	32.0%	2,171.06	22.5%	$ 6,784.56	$1,040.00	$ 832.00	$ 665.60	$ 6,855.68
3 Low—Year 3 default	19.2%	1,640.41	17.0%	$ 8,543.82	$1,040.00	$1,081.60	$ 865.28	$ 8,912.38
4 Low—no default	28.8%	3,046.10	31.6%	$10,576.74	$1,040.00	$1,081.60	$1,124.86	$11,586.10
	100.0%	$9,650.39	100.0%					
Expected cash flow valuation				$ 9,650.39	$1,062.00	$1,049.91	$1,007.26	$10,374.79

Review Exercise 17.7: Measuring Exchange Rate Exposure

Only Revenues in € × millions	Year 0	Exchange Rates £/€ 0.900	0.990	0.810
Revenue (cash in €)	€ 1.850	£ 1.665	£ 1.832	£ 1.499
Expenses (cash in £).	£–0.990	£–0.990	£–0.990	£–0.990
Unlevered free cash flow		£ 0.675	£ 0.842	£ 0.509
Discount rate (in £, no growth)		12.0%	12.0%	12.0%
Value of French sub. in £		£ 5.625	£ 7.013	£ 4.238
Percentage change in value.			24.7%	–24.7%
Change in value			£ 1.388	£–1.388
Percentage change in exchange rate.			10.0%	–10.0%
Total exposure			£13.875	£13.875
Present value of revenue stream		£13.875		

All Cash Flows in € × millions	Year 0	Exchange Rates £/€ 0.900	0.990	0.810
Revenue (cash in €)	€ 1.850	£ 1.665	£ 1.832	£ 1.499
Expenses (cash in €)	€–1.100	£–0.990	£–1.089	£–0.891
Unlevered free cash flow	€ 0.750	£ 0.675	£ 0.743	£ 0.608
Discount rate (in £, no growth)		12.0%	12.0%	12.0%
Value of the French sub. in £		£ 5.625	£ 6.188	£ 5.063
Percentage change in value.			10.0%	–10.0%
Change in value			£ 0.563	£–0.562
Percentage change in exchange rate.			10.0%	–10.0%
Total exposure			£ 5.625	£ 5.625

INDEX

Note: The letter e indicates an exhibit on that page. The letter n indicates footnote.

Note: The letter e indicates an exhibit on that page. The letter n indicates footnote.

Note: The letter e indicates an exhibit on that page. The letter n indicates footnote.

Note: The letter e indicates an exhibit on that page. The letter n indicates footnote.

Note: The letter e indicates an exhibit on that page. The letter n indicates footnote.

Note: The letter e indicates an exhibit on that page. The letter n indicates footnote.

Note: The letter e indicates an exhibit on that page. The letter n indicates footnote.

Note: The letter e indicates an exhibit on that page. The letter n indicates footnote.

Note: The letter e indicates an exhibit on that page. The letter n indicates footnote.

Note: The letter e indicates an exhibit on that page. The letter n indicates footnote.

Note: The letter e indicates an exhibit on that page. The letter n indicates footnote.

Note: The letter e indicates an exhibit on that page. The letter n indicates footnote.

Note: The letter e indicates an exhibit on that page. The letter n indicates footnote.

Note: The letter e indicates an exhibit on that page. The letter n indicates footnote.

Note: The letter e indicates an exhibit on that page. The letter n indicates footnote.

Note: The letter e indicates an exhibit on that page. The letter n indicates footnote.

Note: The letter e indicates an exhibit on that page. The letter n indicates footnote.

Note: The letter e indicates an exhibit on that page. The letter n indicates footnote.

Note: The letter e indicates an exhibit on that page. The letter n indicates footnote.

Note: The letter e indicates an exhibit on that page. The letter n indicates footnote.

Note: The letter e indicates an exhibit on that page. The letter n indicates footnote.

Note: The letter e indicates an exhibit on that page. The letter n indicates footnote.

Note: The letter e indicates an exhibit on that page. The letter n indicates footnote.

Note: The letter e indicates an exhibit on that page. The letter n indicates footnote.